COMMERCIAL AND CONSUMER TRANSACTIONS
Cases, Text and Materials

by

JACOB S. ZIEGEL
Professor of Law
University of Toronto

BENJAMIN GEVA
Associate Professor of Law
Osgoode Hall Law School
York University

1981
EMOND-MONTGOMERY LIMITED
TORONTO, CANADA

Canadian Cataloguing in Publication Data

Ziegel, Jacob S.
   Commercial and consumer transactions

Includes index.
ISBN 0-920722-04-0

1. Commercial law — Canada. 2. Commercial law —
Canada — Cases. 3. Consumer protection — Law and
legislation   —   Canada. I.   Geva,   Benjamin,
1946-   . II. Title.

KE919.Z53   346.71'07   C81-094668-8

To
Adrienne and Esther

PREFACE

This casebook is a much revised version of the earlier casebook on Commercial and Consumer Transactions prepared by us and made available in mimeographed form by the Osgoode Hall Law School. The revision has embraced every chapter of the previous edition but is particularly pronounced in the chapters on negotiable instruments (chapters 14 to 17) and the law of chattel security (chapters 20 to 24), all of which are considerably more detailed and contain many more notes than do their predecessors. The result is a casebook that covers substantially more ground, and in substantially greater detail, than the traditional materials on sales and sales financing. Indeed, in an effort to allow adequate room for non-sales developments we have regrettably had to omit the materials on class actions and other forms of consumer redress that appeared in the mimeographed edition, and materials on commercial arbitration that we should have liked to include.

The materials have been prepared bearing in mind the needs of a four-hour single semester course or its equivalent. We hasten to add, however, that we entertain no illusions about the feasibility of covering the whole casebook in this number of hours, nor would we encourage such an ambitious undertaking. We know that law teachers have widely varying views about what should be included in a basic commercial and consumer law course. We have sought to accommodate this diversity by allowing the instructor to make his or her own selection from among the three principal parts in the casebook (Sales, Negotiable Instruments, and Financing of Commercial and Consumer Transactions) without impairing the integrity of his or her preferences. Each of the three parts could also provide the foundation for a seminar or a two-hour single semester course.

One cannot fail but be impressed by the rapid changes to which these branches of the law are subject and the profusion of new materials. We have tried to keep abreast of new developments and to give the student the same sense of dynamic change. However, we cannot claim complete success. For reasons of space, we have had to omit some very recent and, at the time of this writing still unreported, Ontario and Manitoba decisions on the personal property security Acts of these provinces. Mr. Stanley Goldstein's important study for the federal government on *Changing Times: Banking in the Electronic Age* (Ottawa 1979), despite the official date of its publication, only came to our attention earlier this year and therefore too late for us to do it adequate justice. The same is true of the Saskatchewan Law Reform Commission's *Tentative Proposals for a Consumer Credit Act* (Parts I, II and III), dated August 1980 and May 1981, which only reached us when we were already well into the galley stage.

In compiling the sales materials we were confronted with a dilemma of a different order. Leaving aside its property aspects, sales law is only a particularized application of contract law. Ideally, therefore, the instructor should be entitled to assume that his students have a firm grasp of contract principles, and be able to focus on those rules that are special to sales law. Experience has taught us that the assumption cannot safely be made and that the student's knowledge will only be as good as the amount of time devoted to contract law in first year. And this varies widely among law schools. So, at the risk of appearing to be repetitive, we have included a number of cases (e.g., *Esso Petroleum Co.* v. *Mardon, Leaf* v. *International Galleries, The Heron II*) that also appear in many contract casebooks. We confess moreover to some eclecticism in determining what needed to be repeated and what could safely be assumed to be well nailed down.

The reader should be aware of certain stylistic rules that have been adopted in the casebook. With few exceptions, footnotes have been omitted throughout and case citations are given in the text even where they appear in footnotes in the original. Where less than a paragraph has been omitted in the body of a quoted text or judgment, this is indicated by means of ellipses, whereas the omission of one or more paragraphs is indicated by means of bullets. Omissions that occur at the beginning or end of a judgment have not been ellipsized.

We have not reproduced statutes that the student may be expected to acquire separately because of their pervasive importance throughout the course or a substantial part thereof. This covers, notably, the Sale of Goods Act, the Bills of Exchange Act, the Ontario Personal Property Security Act, the Consumer Protection Act, the Business Practices Act, and Articles 2 and 9 of the Uniform Commercial Code. We have however included in the appendix to the casebook a number of sale and, in particular, chattel security agreements to illustrate current contractual and financing practices in these areas. Other precedents and forms of a more restricted scope will be found in the chapters to which they belong. (See particularly chapters 14, 16, and 19). Unless otherwise indicated, all the Ontario statutory references are to the revised statutes of 1970. Regrettably the 1980 revised statutes were not available to us during the preparation of the casebook and, we understand, are only just now becoming available for general distribution.

In the course of the preparation of this casebook we have accumulated many debts. We cannot hope to identify all our benefactors by name, but some rendered too significant a service to be glossed over in a veil of anonymity. Our good friends, Paul Emond and Ann Montgomery of Emond-Montgomery Limited, were foolish enough to encourage us to put the casebook into print. They have borne with much fortitude the period of gestation between that fateful day and the present time. Patricia Bilbao did a Herculean job of editing the manuscript and, in conjunction with Gail Stewart and Ruth Peckover (all members of Copy Right Editorial Services), of proofreading the galleys and page proofs under very trying circumstances. Shirley Hinterauer displayed great virtuosity in checking citations. Renée de Jong, then an Osgoode Hall Law School student, served as Professor Geva's research assistant during the summers of 1980 and 1981; Terry Burgoyne and Donald Crawshaw, two University of Toronto law school students, rendered the same admirable services in consecutive order for Professor Ziegel during the same period. To our patient and resourceful secretaries — Joyce Flow at the University of Toronto, Sharon Levesque at the Osgoode Hall Law School, and Linda Payne at the University of Illinois Law School — we offer warm and appreciative thanks, an acknowledgement that equally belongs to Dean S.M. Beck of the Osgoode Hall Law School, Dean Peter Hay of the University of Illinois College of Law, and Dean Frank Iacobucci of the University of Toronto Law School for financial support in the preparation of the casebook. We are no less indebted to the many persons whose names appear on the following pages for readily granting us permission to use excerpts from articles and texts, and to the sources indicated in the appendix for permission to reproduce the forms of agreement that appear there. Special thanks also belong to the Toronto-Dominion Bank and the Canadian Imperial Bank of Commerce for supplying us with the many forms and documents that appear in the second half of the casebook.

Our list of acknowledgements would be incomplete were it not to include the Bell Telephone Companies of Illinois and Ontario. Professor Geva taught at the University of Illinois during the 1980-81 academic year. The companies made it possible for us to maintain efficient contact with each other when other means proved inadequate. We are comforted in the thought that, at least in their case, there was a generous *quid pro quo.*

Finally but certainly not least, there are our many colleagues at various law schools who have given generously of their advice. Needless to say, we alone are responsible for any errors that remain and for any shortcomings from which the casebook may be found to suffer.

JSZ
BG

Toronto,
July 1, 1981

ACKNOWLEDGEMENTS

A book of this nature borrows heavily from other published material. We have attempted to request permission from and acknowledge in the text all sources of such material. We wish to make specific reference here to the many authors, publishers, journals and institutions that have been generous in giving permission to reproduce in this text works already in print. If we have inadvertently overlooked any acknowledgement, we offer our sincere apologies and undertake to rectify the omission in the second edition.

Alberta Law Review	Recent Legislative and Judicial Trends in Consumer Credit in Canada	Ziegel
Bobbs-Merrill Co. Inc. (Permission to reprint from copyright 1951, by the Bobbs-Merrill Co. Inc. All Rights Reserved.)	Cases on Security (1951)	Durfee
Boston College Industrial and Commercial Law Review (reprinted with the permission of Boston College Law School)	Some Ruminations about Remedies in Consumer Credit Transactions	Felsenfeld
British Institute of International and Comparative Law	Hire-Purchase and Conditional Sale (1965)	Goode and Ziegel
Business Law Journal	Financial Assistance Through Commercial and Sales Finance Companies, Factoring and Field Warehousing	Kripke
Business Lawyer	Contract Impracticability: Courts Begin to Shape Section 2-615	Duesenberg
Butterworth and Co. Ltd.	Consumer Credit Law, in Studies in Canadian Business Law (Fridman, ed.)	Cuming
Canada Law Book	Banking and Bills of Exchange (7th Edition, 1969)	Falconbridge
	Proceedings of the 7th Annual Workshop on Commercial and Consumer Law (1979, ed. Ziegel)	Belobaba Waters
Canadian Bar Journal	Bulk Sales in Ontario	Catzman
Canadian Bar Review	Comments: Unconscionable Contracts — Some Recent Cases 'UTRA'	Davis
	Bill C-44: Repeal of the Small Loans Act and Enactment of a New Usury Law	Ziegel
	The Draft Ontario Personal Property Security Act	Ziegel

	The Future of Canadian Consumerism	Ziegel
	Range v. Corporation de Finance Belvedere — Consumer Notes	Ziegel
Canadian Business Law Journal	A Framework for the Assessment of Business Damages for Breach of Contract	Biger and Rosen
	The Position of Retail and Wholesale Financers as Secured Creditors Under The Proposed Bankruptcy Act	Colburn
	A Practitioner's Notes Upon the Ontario PPSA	Crawford
	Credit Transfers of Funds in Canada: The Current Law	Crawford
	Close Business Relationship Between a Purchase-Money Lender and a Seller of Goods — Bank of Montreal v. Kon	Geva
	Equities as to Liability on Bills and Notes — Rights of a Holder in Due Course	Geva
	The Unconscionability Business — A Comment on Tilden Rent-a-Car v. Clendenning	Hasson
	Inaccurate or Ambiguous Countermand and Payment Over Countermand	Rodgers Magnet
Canadian Consumer	The Food and Drugs Act and Other [Constitutional] Horrors	Ziegel
Canadian Manufacturers Association	Reactions to OLRC Warranties Report	
Canadian Taxation	Regulating the Income Tax Discounter	Belobaba
Carswell Co. Ltd.	Personal Property Security Law in Ontario (1976)	Catzman et al.
	Sale of Goods in Canada (2nd ed., 1979)	Fridman
Columbia Law Review	Negotiability — Who Needs It?	Rosenthal
Consumer Research Council of Canada	The Billing Practices Study (1975)	
Corporation Law Review	Bonded Construction Contracts: What are a Surety's Rights to Withhold Funds?	Geva

Department of National Revenue	Interpretation Bulletin IT-233 (1975)	
Export Development Corporation	Circulars 80-1 and 80-2	
Falconbridge Estate	The Law of Negotiable Instruments in Canada (McGraw-Hill Ryerson Limited, 1967)	Falconbridge
Government of Ontario	Hansard, 31st Parliament, 3rd Session, June 7, 1979	
Harvard International Law Journal	The Law of International Commercial Transactions	Berman and Kaufman
Harvard Law Review	Direct Loan Financing of Consumer Purchases	
	The New UCC Article 9	Coogan
International Business Lawyer	Uses of Letters of Credit and Bank Guarantees in the Insurance Industry	Ellinger
Israel Law Review	The Requirement of Consideration for Bills and Notes in Israel	Barak
Law Reform Commission of Canada	The Cheque: Some Modernizations (Report 11, 1979)	
McGill Law Journal	The Presentment and Collection of Cheques in Canada	Thomas and Orchard
Mercer Law Review	Magnuson-Moss Warranty Act: An Overview and Comparison with UCC Coverage, Disclaimer, and Remedies in Consumer Warranties	Strasser
Michigan Law Review	Consumer Protection in the Credit Card Industry: Federal Legislative Controls	Weistart
Ministry of the Attorney General, Ontario	Ontario Law Reform Commission: Report on Consumer Warranties and Guarantees in the Sale of Goods (1972), and Report on Sale of Goods (1979)	
Missouri Law Review	Mortgages to Secure Future Advances	Blackburn
New Zealand Law Review	Electronic Funds Transfer in New Zealand	Tyree
Protect Yourself (1978)	The Rust Code: What Exactly Is It?	Tardiff

Oregon Law Review	Contractual Defenses as Claims to the Instrument: The Right to Block Payment on a Banker's Instrument	Geva
Ottawa Law Review	Consumer Credit Reform: The Case for a Renewed Federal Initiative	Pitch
Saskatchewan Law Reform Commission	Proposals for a Saskatchewan PPSA (1977)	
Sijthoff & Noordhoff	Canadian Chattel Security Law: Past Experience and Current Developments, in Sauveplanne (ed.), Security over Corporeal Moveables (1974)	Ziegel
	Consumer Credit in Selected Countries: Canada	Cuming
Stanford Law Review	Profit on Default	Shuchman
Stevens and Sons Ltd.	Chalmers on Bills of Exchange (1964)	
Sweet and Maxwell	The Making of Business Contracts (1972)	Boulton
	Principles of the Law of Damages (1962)	Street
Uniform Commercial Code Law Journal	Electronic Funds Transfers and the Financial-Institution/Consumer Relationship	Greguras
University of Toronto Law Journal	Market Considerations in the Formulation of Consumer Protection Policy	Cayne and Trebilcock
	The Modernization of Canadian Personal Property Security Law	Ziegel and Cuming

We also wish to thank the following for allowing us to include copies of forms and documents in these materials:

American Express Canada Inc.
Canadian Imperial Bank of Commerce
Ford Motor Company of Canada Ltd.
John Deere Ltd.
Toronto-Dominion Bank
Westinghouse Canada Inc.

SHORT TABLE OF CONTENTS

PART I   SALES TRANSACTIONS

PART II   PAYMENT MECHANISMS

PART III   FINANCING COMMERCIAL AND CONSUMER TRANSACTIONS

TABLE OF CONTENTS

PART I
SALES TRANSACTIONS

CHAPTER 1   **EVOLUTION OF MODERN SALES AND CONSUMER LAW**

CHAPTER 2   **CONCEPT OF SALE**

CHAPTER 9   RISK OF LOSS AND FRUSTRATION OF THE CONTRACT OF SALE

PART II
PAYMENT MECHANISMS

CHAPTER 14 NEGOTIABLE INSTRUMENTS LAW: INTRODUCTION

PART III
FINANCING COMMERCIAL AND CONSUMER TRANSACTIONS

CHAPTER 20 SECURITY DEVICES AND THE PERSONAL PROPERTY SECURITY ACT

TABLE OF CASES*

---

* Includes only cases reproduced in whole or in part, or cited at some length in the textual material. [Eds.]

TABLE OF ABBREVIATIONS

A. Reference Texts and Frequently Cited Treatises, Reports, and Other Materials

ANDERSON	R.A. Anderson, Anderson on the Uniform Commercial Code, 2nd ed. (1970)
ATIYAH	P.S. Atiyah, The Sale of Goods, 5th ed. (1975)
B.C. PPSA REPORT	Law Reform Commission of British Columbia, Report on Debtor-Creditor Relationships (Project No. 2), Part V — Personal Property Security, LRC 23 (1975)
BENJAMIN	Benjamin's Sale of Goods, 1st ed., 1974 (A.G. Guest ed.)
BYLES	Byles on Bills of Exchange (24th ed., 1979)
CATZMAN	F.M. Catzman et al., Personal Property Security Law in Ontario (1976)
CHALMERS	Chalmers on Bills of Exchange (13th ed., 1964)
CCH CANADIAN	Canadian Commercial Law Guide (loose leaf, 2 vols.)
CCH (U.S.)	Instalment Credit Guide (loose leaf, 2 vols.)
FALCONBRIDGE	(1) Falconbridge on Banking & Bills of Exchange, 7th ed. (1969)
	(2) Falconbridge, The Laws of Negotiable Instruments in Canada (1967)
FRIDMAN	G.H.L. Fridman, Sale of Goods in Canada, 2nd ed. (1979)
GILMORE	G. Gilmore, Security Interests in Personal Property (1965, 2 vols.)
GOODE	R.M. Goode, Hire-Purchase Law and Practice, 2nd ed. (1970)
GOODE & ZIEGEL	R.M. Goode and J.S. Ziegel, Hire-Purchase Law and Conditional Sale: A Comparative Study (1965)
McLAREN	R.M. McLaren, Secured Transactions in Personal Property in Canada (1979) (loose leaf, 2 vols.)
NSW WORKING PAPER	Law Reform Commission, New South Wales, Working Paper on the Sale of Goods (1975)
OLRC SALES REPORT	Ontario Law Reform Commission, Report on Sale of Goods (1979, 3 vols.)
OLRC WARRANTIES REPORT	Ontario Law Reform Commission, Report on Warranties and Guarantees (August 1972)

SASK. PPSA REPORT	Law Reform Commission of Saskatchewan, Proposals for a Saskatchewan Personal Property Security Act (July 1977)
SUTTON	K.C.T. Sutton, The Law of Sale of Goods in Australia and New Zealand, 2nd ed. (1974)
ULA	Uniform Laws Annotated, 2nd ed. (1971), Uniform Commercial Code, Master Edition, and Annual Supp.
UN INTERNATIONAL SALES CONVENTION	United Nations Convention on Contracts for the International Sale of Goods, Vienna, 10 April 1980, UN Doc. A/Conf. 97/18
WHITE & SUMMERS	J.J. White and R.S. Summers, Handbook of the Law under the Uniform Commercial Code, 2nd ed. (1980)
WILLISTON	Williston on Sales (Revised ed., 4 vols.)

B.   Frequently Cited Statutes

Bank Act	Banks and Banking Law Revision Act, SC 1980, c. C-40, s. 2.
BPA	Business Practices Act 1974, SO 1974, c. 131.
BEA	Bills of Exchange Act, RSC 1970, c. B-5, as am.
BILL 110	Consumer Products Warranties Act, 1976 (Ont.) (not enacted)
CIA	Combines Investigation Act, RSC 1970, c. C-23, as am.
CPA	Consumer Protection Act, RSO 1970, c. 82, as am.
MUPPSA	(Revised) Model Uniform Personal Property Security Act (Canadian Bar Association, 1981)*
PPSA	Personal Property Security Act, RSO 1970, c. 344, as am.
SGA	Sale of Goods Act, RSO 1970, c. 421
SGA (U.K., 1893)	Sale of Goods Act 1893, 56 & 57 Vict., c. 71
SGA (U.K., 1979)	Sale of Goods Act 1979, c. 54**
SPPSA	Saskatchewan Personal Property Security Act, SS 1979-80, c. 42
UCC	Uniform Commercial Code (1972 Official Text)
UCCC	Uniform Consumer Credit Code (U.S.)

---

*   The original Model Act was adopted by the CBA in 1970; the revised version is expected to be submitted for approval in September 1981.

**   This is a consolidating Act, and incorporates the amendments made to the 1893 Act.

Concordance of the U.K. Sale of Goods Act 1893*
and the Ontario Sale of Goods Act**

U.K.		ONTARIO	
Section		*Section*	
1	Definition of sale	2	
2	Capacity	3	
3	Formation of contract	4	
4	Stat. of Frauds Provision — repealed in 1954	5	($40 substituted for £10)
5-21		6-22	
22	Sales in market overt	23	(excludes English rule)
23	Voidable title	24	
24	Revesting of property in stolen goods	Omitted	
25	Seller or buyer in possession	25	
26	Effect of writs of execution	Omitted	
27-39		26-38	
40	Attachment by seller in Scotland	Omitted	
41-58		39-56	
59	Scottish law	Omitted	
60	Repeals	Omitted	
61(1)	Bankruptcy rules	Omitted	
62	Definitions	1	

---

*   Subsequent changes in the U.K. Act, particularly those introduced by the Misrepresentation Act 1967, the Supply of Goods (Implied Terms) Act 1973, the Unfair Contract Terms Act 1977, and the Sale of Goods Act 1979 (a consolidating Act), are not included.

**   RSO 1970, c. 421.

PART I

SALES TRANSACTIONS

Chapter 1
Evolution of Modern Sales and Consumer Law

A. SALES LAW

ONTARIO LAW REFORM COMMISSION
Report on Sale of Goods*
(1979) pp. 7-22

1. THE ANGLO-CANADIAN POSITION

The principles of sales law that we know today evolved very slowly and are mainly a product of late 18th century and particularly 19th century developments. The Saxon and Norman periods apparently contributed very little to this branch of the law. Indeed, in their nature, they were perhaps ill-suited to the development of a law of sales, given the simple and feudal state of the economy, the relative unimportance of personal chattels, and the undeveloped law of contracts. Moreover, severe restrictions were imposed by the actions in debt and detinue, and by the archaic procedures to which these actions were subject. Much more flexible procedures and rules, it would seem, were applied in the local courts in which the law merchant had its medieval origins. But whatever contribution might have been made by these courts towards the accelerated development of a body of sales law was lost when the common law courts assumed exclusive jurisdiction over disputes previously tried in the local courts. The introduction of the action in assumpsit, while laying the theoretical foundations for the modern law, seemingly made little initial impact. Here, as elsewhere, economic and social conditions were the ultimate determinants of the pace of legal development, and the pressure for a detailed body of rules governing the law of sales did not really manifest itself until the arrival of the industrial revolution.

---

*   Hereafter referred to as the OLRC Sales Report. [Eds.]

Events moved quickly during the 19th century and, by 1888, it was felt that the rules were sufficiently settled to warrant their being reduced to statutory form. This was the year when MacKenzie D. Chalmers, the author of the highly successful Bills of Exchange Act, 1882, was encouraged to draft a similar bill embracing the sales area. As Chalmers himself recorded, Lord Herschell's advice to him was to endeavour "to reproduce as exactly as possible" the existing law, leaving any amendments that might seem desirable to be introduced in committee on the authority of the legislature. After detailed consideration by both Houses of Parliament, his draft bill was enacted into law in 1894 with one major and a number of minor changes. Thus was born the Sale of Goods Act, 1893.

2. POST-1893 DEVELOPMENTS

The Imperial Act was quickly copied by most Commonwealth jurisdictions that followed the common law tradition. All of the common law provinces in Canada have enacted like legislation, albeit with a number of minor changes. Manitoba was the first enacting province; for some unknown reason Ontario delayed its enactment until 1920.

In the intervening years, the U.K. Parliament, has, on the whole, made few changes to the 1893 Act that are of interest to Canadian lawyers. It should, however, be noted that, as is true in Canada's case, the sales rules codified in the 1893 Act have been affected by important developments in the public law and related private law areas. The most important direct changes are those effected by the following statutes:

(1) The Law Reform (Enforcement of Contracts) Act 1954. This Act repealed Section 4, the Statute of Frauds provision, in the parent Act of 1893;

(2) The Misrepresentation Act 1967. This Act amended the law of misrepresentation in important respects and also amended sections 11(1)(c) and 35 of the Sale of Goods Act;

(3) The Supply of Goods (Implied Terms) Act 1973. This Act amended sections 12-14 of the Sale of Goods Act and, until superseded by the Unfair Contract Terms Act 1977, restricted or excluded the use of exception clauses in consumer sales and other sales transactions, including hire-purchase and conditional sale agreements;

(4) The Unfair Contract Terms Act 1977. This Act, which came into force on February 1, 1978, introduced a comprehensive regime, not restricted to sales transactions, for the restriction or avoidance of exception clauses in consumer and non-consumer agreements.

In 1967 the U.K. Parliament also adopted the Uniform Laws on International Sales Act 1967. This Act gives municipal effect to the two Hague Conventions on the Uniform Law on the International Sale of Goods and the Uniform Law on the Formation of Contracts for the International Sale of Goods. However, the Act is of minor importance since it only applies to international sales, as defined in the Conventions, and then only if the parties have expressly adopted the Uniform Law on Sales as the law of their contract.

This description of the British position would be seriously incomplete if it did not also include a reference to the recommendations contained in a number of important reports and working papers published by the English Law Commission and Law Reform Committee. While these recommendations have not yet been implemented, the reports and working papers have been very helpful to us in our own deliberations. It should also be noted that, since the enactment of the Sale of Goods Act, 1893, the basic law of contract and tort has undergone substantial judicial development, and that this judicial development has had an impact on the law of sales. Whether the judicial creativity has been sufficient to offset the deficiencies in the Act will be discussed in later parts of this Report.

Legislative activity in Commonwealth countries, other than Canada, does not appear to have been more pronounced. Ghana adopted a slightly revised version of the U.K. Act in 1962. The New South Wales Law Reform Commission published a Working Paper in 1975 recommending substantial changes to the New South Wales Sale of Goods Act. We have derived great benefit from this Working Paper, but it does not purport to cover all aspects of the existing law or even all important aspects.

The U.K. statutory changes so far have had a limited impact in Canada. Only British Columbia has copied the 1954 amendment, and only one province, Saskatchewan, has adopted any of the 1973 amendments, and then only to a very limited extent. However, disclaimer provisions, comparable to those in the 1973 Act, were anticipated in the Consumer Protection Acts of Ontario, Manitoba and British Columbia. The Misrepresentation Act 1967 has attracted no followers and the prospect of the Unfair Contract Terms Act 1977 being copied verbatim seems equally doubtful, in view of the trade practices legislation that already covers a substantial part of the same ground in Ontario and elsewhere.

This is not to suggest that the legislative scene in Canada has remained static; it has not. A large number of federal and provincial Acts have a direct and very important bearing on the parties' rights and obligations in the sale sector, and their number has rapidly increased in the post-war period. Without attempting an exhaustive enumeration, several statutes are worthy of mention. At the federal level there are the following Acts: namely, the Bank Act; the Bills of Lading Act; the Combines Investigation Act; the Consumer Packaging and Labelling Act; the Food and Drugs Act; the Hazardous Products Act; the Motor Vehicle Safety Act; the Textile Labelling Act; and, The Weights and Measures Act. At the provincial level, legislation of Ontario includes the following enactments: The Bills of Sale Act; The Business Practices Act; The Consumer Protection Act; The Factors Act; The Mercantile Law Amendment Act; The Motor Vehicle Dealers Act; The Personal Property Security Act; and, The Warehouse Receipts Act. Much of the post-war legislation is consumer oriented, but its impact frequently extends well beyond the law of consumer sales.

The role of the Uniform Law Conference of Canada should also be noted. Since its establishment in 1918 the Conference has been active in drafting uniform or model acts in the commercial law area and urging their adoption by the provinces. The Conference's efforts now embrace bills of sale and chattel mortgages, conditional sales and personal property security legislation, as well as uniform acts on Warehouse Receipts and Warehousemen's Liens. The Conference's well-established role is of considerable importance in view of the recommendation made later in this Report with respect to the desirability of securing the uniform adoption of a revised Sale of Goods Act.

3. THE QUEBEC POSITION

As a civil law jurisdiction, Quebec has never adopted the Sale of Goods Act. Its law of sales is enshrined in the Quebec Civil Code and owes its origin primarily to the corresponding provisions in the Napoleonic Civil Code. There are numerous differences between the sales law of Quebec and that of the common law provinces. It may be useful to note briefly some of the more important points of departure.

The rules governing the formation of a contract of sale are not the same. Among other differences, written evidence is not required in the case of commercial matters, and in other transactions involving $500 or less. Further, the doctrine of *causa* is much more liberal than the common law doctrine of consideration. Thus, even though there is no separate consideration, a "firm" offer cannot, where a period of duration is specified, be revoked during such period. Moreover, a mailed acceptance is not usually effective until it is received by the offeree. Contracts for the benefit of third parties are enforceable by the beneficiaries.

The implied warranties also differ in important respects. The legal warranty against latent defects is the civil law analogue to the common law condition of merchantable quality; but it is not as potent. In the case of a sale of specific goods, the civil law warranty does not extend to discoverable defects and the buyer is expected, for his own protection, to examine the goods before purchase and, it would seem, in at least some circumstances, to retain technical assistance to enable him to conduct a proper examination. While the warranty against latent defects, unlike the condition of merchantability in the common law, applies to private as well as to commercial sales, the consequences of a breach of the warranty are not the same. In general, the buyer's remedies are limited to rescission of the agreement or a reduction in the purchase price, and consequential damages are only allowed if the buyer can show that the seller knew or ought to have known of the defect.

There are other differences, some of which may be mentioned briefly. The effectiveness of disclaimer clauses varies, though it may be that the practical result is not very different from that obtaining in the common law provinces. The unpaid seller's *in rem* remedies differ in one important respect insofar as the seller can dissolve the sale and reclaim the goods, even after delivery, so long as they remain in the buyer's possession. Finally, the *nemo dat* doctrine plays a much less important role in Quebec law. The Civil Code protects the good faith purchaser who purchases goods in a fair or market or at a public sale or from a trader dealing in similar articles or "in commercial matters generally", unless the goods have been lost or stolen. Even in the latter cases the owner is only entitled to recover the goods if he reimburses the purchaser the amount paid by him for the goods.

The number and extent of the differences between Quebec law and the common law rules might suggest serious impediments to the flow of interprovincial trade between Quebec and its important trading partners. The answers to the C.M.A. Questionnaire belie this assumption. Nevertheless, it must remain a matter of regret that the laws of Quebec and Ontario differ so materially in such an important branch of commercial law. The Quebec Civil Code Revision Office has recently completed a comprehensive review of the Civil Code, including the parts relating to sales and obligations, and has submitted proposals for a new Code. This development, coupled with Ontario's own desire to modernize its sales law, could provide the two provinces with a valuable opportunity to explore the possibility of securing greater uniformity between their respective laws. We return to this question in a later part of this Report.

4. AMERICAN SALES LAW

(a) THE PRE-CODE POSITION

Nineteenth century American sales law largely followed English principles, but the laws of the individual states differed from each other and from the English rules on many points of detail and sometimes on points of substance. An important objective, therefore, of the Uniform Sales Act drafted by Professor Samuel Williston of the Harvard Law School, and adopted by the National Conference of Commissioners on Uniform State Laws (NCCUSL) in 1906, was to reconcile the conflicting state rules and to introduce a uniform body of law. Williston admired Chalmers' Act and followed it closely. Nevertheless a substantial number of differences survived between the Uniform Sales Act and the U.K. Sale of Goods Act. The more important differences included the following: namely, the wide definition of warranty in the American Act, which was based on a reliance theory of liability and not restricted to contractual promises; the unitary classification of contractual terms as contrasted with the dichotomous classification of terms in the U.K. Act into warranties and conditions; a significantly different regime of buyer's remedies; and, the separate treatment of documents of title.

(b) THE ORIGINS OF THE UNIFORM COMMERCIAL CODE

At the time it was superseded by the Uniform Commercial Code, the Uniform Sales Act had only been adopted by thirty-six states. Williston's work has been called a "scholarly reconstruction of nineteenth century law". In any event, merchants of the Eastern seaboard felt that it no longer catered adequately to their needs and there was equal concern about the continuing lack of uniformity among the states. In 1936 the Merchants' Association of New York established a committee to prepare a federal Sales Act. In its subsequent Report the committee recommended extensive changes in the Uniform Act. A bill was drafted and introduced in the Congress in 1940.

The step was strongly opposed at the state level and the sponsors of the bill agreed to defer further action until the NCCUSL could consider revising the Uniform Sales Act. Work on the project was begun. Since the National Conference had also sponsored over the years a large number of other commercial law acts, which appeared equally in need of revision, the thought commended itself to the Commissioners that all the uniform acts in this area should be reviewed and integrated as part of a much more ambitious project. Thus was born the concept of a Uniform Commercial Code. In 1942 the prestigious American

Law Institute agreed to co-sponsor the Code project and work was begun. The first "Official Draft" of the Code was published in 1952 and approved with minor changes by the sponsoring organizations. Pennsylvania was the first state to enact the Code and, since then, one or other version of the Code has been adopted by all the common law states and by the District of Columbia. Louisiana has adopted Articles 1, 3, 4 and 5 of the Code, but not Article 2, the Sales Article. The Code has been officially revised on a number of occasions, the most recent text being the 1972 Official Text. In an effort to avoid unauthorized changes and to maintain a watchful eye over developments, the sponsoring organizations established in 1961 a Permanent Editorial Committee. The Committee has issued a series of reports and was also responsible for the production of the 1972 Official Text. It has not, however, been entirely successful in its mission since, prior to the 1972 Official Text, a large number of unauthorized amendments had been made by individual states.

(c)   THE STRUCTURE OF THE UNIFORM COMMERCIAL CODE AND SOME GENERAL CONSIDERATIONS

The 1972 Official Text is divided into eleven major parts, or Articles as they are called. Each Article deals with a separate area of substantive law, with the exceptions of Article 1, which deals with General Provisions, and Articles 10 and 11, which are concerned respectively with Effective Date and Transitional Provisions. The intervening Articles are devoted to the following topics:

Article 2: Sales
Article 3: Commercial Paper
Article 4: Bank Deposits and Collections
Article 5: Letters of Credit
Article 6: Bulk Transfers
Article 7: Warehouse Receipts, Bills of Lading and other Documents of Title
Article 8: Investment Securities
Article 9: Secured Transactions, and Sale of Accounts and Chattel Paper

It will be seen, therefore, that despite its ambitious title the Code is not exhaustive: it does not include such important branches of commercial law as insurance law or agency, and it omits an equally extensive list of subjects falling within the jurisdiction of the American federal government. The unifying thread, it has been stated, which binds together Articles 2 through 9 is the different phases in the movement of goods. Even this claim is not free of difficulty. Nevertheless, one can readily subscribe to the view that the Code is the most ambitious commercial law project ever undertaken in the Anglo-American legal world. Equally impressive, from a Canadian point of view, is its universal acceptance among the common law states of the Union.

A question of some interest is whether the Uniform Commercial Code is a true code in the continental sense. Some observers have made this claim, but it is rejected by other scholars who were closely associated with the Code project. The claim is inconsistent with the Code's own provisions and the subsequent course of judicial developments. Admittedly, the Code has a substantial number of the characteristics usually associated with a code in the civilian sense: it is systematic, comprehensive, and authoritative. But the Uniform Commercial Code is not self-sufficient. On the contrary, like the U.K. Sale of Goods Act, 1893 and Bills of Exchange Act, 1882, and other codifying statutes of British origin, it relies on the general principles of law and equity to supplement its specific provisions and to fill its numerous gaps. There is equally little evidence, if indeed any, that the Code was intended to operate as an "undefiled" source of new law, uncontaminated by what had preceded it, and serving as the exclusive repository of the solution to all future problems. Rather, the sign-posts point to a continuingly active role for judicial creativity in which the traditional techniques of lawmaking would be fully deployed within the bounds of a flexible system of *stare decisis*. The Code thus represents a higher plateau in the development of American commercial law, but many of the familiar features of the old landscape are still very much in evidence.

(d) ARTICLE 2

These remarks also apply to the sales article of the Code. As a learned scholar has observed, while it was the pressure for a revised uniform sales act that launched the Code project, in the end it was Article 9 on Secured Transactions, and its innovative solutions to the chaotic state laws governing chattel security, that ultimately commended the adoption of the Code to many of the state legislatures.

This is not to suggest that Article 2 is merely a moderately amended version of the Uniform Sales Act. In style and organization it differs fundamentally from its predecessor, but the overall result is not a revolutionary blue-print for a new sales law. Rather, it meets two of the Code's own explicit objectives, "to simplify, clarify and modernize the law governing commercial transactions" and "to permit the continued expansion of commercial practices through custom, usage and agreement of the parties". The more important changes to the Uniform Sales Act effected by the Article are the following:

(1) Article 2 is more extensive in its coverage. It contains a substantial number of sections affecting the formation and construction of the contract of sale which have no counterpart in the Uniform Sales Act and which were designed to clarify or relieve the rigidities of the prior law. Article 2 also contains six sections defining the meaning of shipping terms in use in domestic and international trade and also covering related matters.

(2) The parties' freedom to shape the terms of their contract as they see fit remains a cardinal tenet, but is qualified by important behavioural baselines in Articles 1 and 2 which cannot be excluded and which are designed to prevent overreaching and to ensure fairness and standards of decency in commercial dealings. Particularly noteworthy are the following: namely, the definition of "good faith" as applied to merchants in section 2-103; the court's power to police unconscionable terms or bargains incorporated in section 2-302; and, the restrictions on or avoidance of disclaimer clauses affecting products liability claims found in sections 2-318 and 2-719.

(3) The Code's basic framework of the seller's warranty obligations remains the same, but their scope is no longer restricted by traditional doctrines of

privity. As a result of the alternative versions of section 2-318, a seller's express or implied warranties extend to any person who may reasonably be expected to use, consume or be affected by the goods and who is injured by breach of the warranty.

(4) The concept of title and its location, which played such a critical role in the Uniform Sales Act (as it still does in the U.K. and Ontario Acts) in furnishing the answer to widely disparate problems, has been dethroned. It has been replaced by an issue oriented approach, which answers sale questions without regard to the locus of title.

(5) The exceptions to the *nemo dat* rule have been enlarged, old and troublesome distinctions between void and voidable transactions have been eliminated, and the protection of third parties dealing in good faith with a merchant to whom the goods have been entrusted has been placed on a more rational footing.

(6) The importance of a merchant's status has also been enhanced in other directions by imposing upon him, in his capacity as buyer or seller, a higher regime of obligations than is applied to non-merchants. However, this dichotomy between merchants and non-merchants is not nearly as significant as the more far-reaching distinctions between commercial and non-commercial sales known to many continental legal systems.

(7) Article 2 places greater emphasis on the enforcement of bargains and discourages the rejection of goods based on trivial breaches or contrived excuses. Particularly noteworthy are the provisions on uncertainty (sections 2-204, 2-306), the right to cure an imperfect tender (section 2-508), and the substitutional methods of performance permitted in section 2-614 in the case of unforeseen difficulties.

(8) At the remedial level, important changes have been introduced with respect to the scope and enforcement of the rights of both parties. Save in exceptional circumstances, the seller can no longer sue for the price before the buyer has accepted the goods. On the other hand, the seller's right of stoppage *in transitu* is extended and he may, at his option, where the buyer is in breach, resell the goods and recover any actual deficiency without being bound by the traditional market price test. The unpaid seller is also given a limited right to recover his goods from an insolvent buyer. The buyer, for his part, enjoys more extended powers to seek an order for specific performance, and his right to "cover" in the event of the seller's failure to perform is the counterpart of the seller's right of resale. The conscious attempt to parallel the parties' rights is also seen in the retention of the Uniform Sales Act provision giving the buyer a lien on rejected goods in his possession and in his severely circumscribed right to recover goods identified to the contract where the seller has become insolvent after receiving all or part of the purchase price. Finally, attention should be drawn to the important right conferred on both parties to seek adequate assurance of performance (section 2-609) where reasonable grounds for insecurity arise with respect to the other party's performance.

Most commentators welcomed these changes at the time they were first introduced and saw them as marked improvements over the prior law. Williston strongly dissented. He regretted the iconoclastic approach to the Uniform Sales Act and was critical of some of the major changes. He did not feel that any advantages Article 2 might possess would offset the breach in the substantial uniformity in the sales law in most of the common law jurisdictions, both in and outside the U.S., that would result from its adoption. Many of Williston's misgivings have been proved unfounded by subsequent events. On the whole, Article 2 has worked well. Although it has proved least successful in directing the growth of products liability law arising out of defectively manufactured goods, Article 2 appears to have spawned a relatively small number of important lawsuits, and only one major amendment has been found necessary since the adoption of the 1958 Official Text. Williston's prediction was, however, accurate in one respect: Article 2 *has* broken the uniformity of basic sales law in the common law jurisdictions. However, non-American commentators only see the breach as a reflection of the dated character of many of the provisions in the U.K. Act. Whether the breach can be healed and uniformity restored is a question that will be considered in a later section of this Report.

(e) UNIFORM LAND TRANSACTIONS ACT

In August, 1975, the National Conference of Commissioners on Uniform State Laws approved the Uniform Land Transactions Act and recommended it for enactment by the states. The Uniform Act deals with contractual transfers of real estate, including transfers for security and transfers of limited interests, and purports to do for transactions in land what Articles 2 and 9 of the Uniform Commercial Code do in the realm of personal property. What is significant in the present context is the fact that the ULTA follows closely the structure and concepts of the corresponding provisions in the Code. This seems to indicate both the adaptability of the Code and a pervasive feeling that it is operating well and has not lost its essential relevance.

5. INTERNATIONAL DEVELOPMENTS

This survey of the evolution of modern sales law would be incomplete without some reference to developments at the international level. The need for uniformity in the law and practices governing international trading transactions has long been obvious. Since the war, increasing efforts have been mobilized at both the governmental and non-governmental levels to advance this objective. As one of the world's major exporters and importers, Canada has an important stake in these developments. The legislative and other efforts to achieve international uiformity may also provide useful sources for national reforms and for uniformity within federal states, like Canada, where more than one legal system of private law obtains. The following organizational and legislative initiatives are of particular significance in the sales area.

(a) THE HAGUE CONVENTIONS OF 1964

Formal efforts to draft a uniform law on international sales began in 1930 when the International Institute for the Unification of Private Law (UNIDROIT) appointed a committee for this purpose. In 1939 two reports accompanied by draft uniform laws were presented by the committee to the League of Nations. Work on the project was suspended until 1951 when, following a conference on the eve of the 7th Hague Conference of Private International Law, a Special Committee of Experts was appointed to resume the work of drafting. The committee presented its revised draft in 1956. At the same time a Committee of the Rome Institute was engaged in drafting a Uniform Law on the Formation of Contracts for International Sales. The two drafts formed the basis of an intensive conference at The Hague in 1964 and resulted in the adoption of two conventions, one on a Uniform Law on the International Sale of Goods [ULIS] and the other on a Uniform Law on the Formation of Contracts for the International Sale of Goods [ULFC]. To date the conventions have only been ratified or acceded to by nine, mainly smaller, countries. Canada and the U.S. are not among them. In view of the substantial criticism to which the Uniform Law on Sales has been exposed, and the revisionary work recently completed under the auspices of the United Nations Commission on International Trade Law (UNCITRAL), it seems unlikely that many more adoptions will materialize in the foreseeable future.

The Uniform Law on Formation is by far the shorter of the two Laws and comprises thirteen articles which, needless to say, do not exhaust the subject. Articles of particular interest include the following: namely, the dispensation with writing requirements (art. 3); the binding character of an irrevocable offer (art. 5); the time and form of acceptance (arts. 6, 8); the effect of additions, limitations or other modifications in the acceptance (art. 7); the effect of a late acceptance (art. 9); and, the validity of a revoked acceptance (art. 10). Some of these provisions may have been influenced by Article 2 of the Uniform Commercial Code.

The Uniform Law on Sales is much longer and runs to 101 articles. These are divided into six chapters which deal, respectively, with the Sphere of Application of the Law (ch. I), General Provisions (ch. II), Obligations of the Seller (ch. III), Obligations of the Buyer (ch. IV), Provisions Common to the Obligations of the Seller and the Buyer (ch. V), and Passing of the Risk (ch. VI). Despite its considerable length, the Uniform Law on Sales fails to deal with some important topics. It is not concerned with the substantive validity of the contract of sale or, with minor exceptions, with its property effects or the rights of third parties acquiring the goods from the party in possession. Questions of products liability not involving the buyer are also excluded. The parties' right to exclude or vary the provisions of the Uniform Law on Sales are recognized in article 3; however, unlike Article 2 of the Uniform Commercial Code, the Uniform Law provides no behavioural baselines to discourage unconscionable terms and to ensure reasonable standards of fair dealing. These omissions are no doubt due to the much more limited objectives of the Uniform Law.

In style and methodology the Uniform Law on Sales is more abstract and succinct than Article 2 and follows the civilian style of drafting rather than the common law tradition. Nevertheless, as in the case of the Uniform Law on Formation, some important resemblances to Article 2 can be detected in a number of provisions, examples of which are as follows: namely, the right to cure an imperfect tender (arts. 37 and 44); the right to suspend performance on grounds of insecurity (art. 73); and, the buyer's right to cover and the seller's right of resale and right to recover a deficiency (art. 85). Close similarities between the solutions adopted in the Uniform Law on Sales and those obtaining in the U.K. Sale of Goods Act, 1893 are evident in other areas. In many other respects the Uniform Law on Sales differs materially both from Article 2 and Anglo-Canadian sales law. Differences that have attracted unfavourable attention include the difficult definition of fundamental breach in article 10, the complex system of notices, and the concept of *ipso facto* avoidance.

(b) UNCITRAL

The United Nations Commission on International Trade Law was established by the General Assembly in 1966 with the object of promoting the progressive harmonization and unification of the law of international trade. The Commission consists of 29 elected members of the United Nations who are drawn from the various geographical regions and principal economic and legal systems of the world.

The Commission meets annually, but the detailed work on individual projects is frequently delegated to small working groups. Since its creation the Commission has focused its activities on four major areas of international trade law: namely, international sale of goods; international payments; international commercial arbitration; and, international shipping legislation. Its principal project in the sale of goods area has been to review the Uniform Law on the International Sale of Goods. The purpose of this review has been to prepare a revised text that might render the Uniform Law more acceptable to countries of different legal, social and economic systems than the 1964 version. A working group was established in 1969 and completed its work in 1976. The draft Convention on the International Sale of Goods prepared by the Working Group was approved at a plenary session of the Commission in June, 1977. The Working Group has also subjected the Uniform Law on Formation to a similar review and completed this phase of its work in 1977. At its Eleventh Session, held from May 30 to June 14, 1978; the Commission decided to integrate the draft Convention on Formation with the draft Convention on the International Sale of Goods, and adopted a single draft Convention on Contracts for the International Sale of Goods. It is anticipated that the integrated draft Convention will be submitted for approval in the near future at a diplomatic conference to be convened for this purpose.*

The draft Convention on Sale follows the same structure as the Uniform Law, but it is substantially shorter and, in several respects, simpler. The greater economy of the draft Convention is largely achieved by substituting for repetitive provisions in the Uniform Law, an integrated regime of buyer's and seller's

---

* The Convention was adopted in Vienna on 11 April, 1980. See UN Doc. A/CONF. 97/18, 10 April 1980. An unofficial commentary on the draft convention prepared by the UNCITRAL secretariat appears in UN Doc. A/CONF./97/5, 14 March 1979. A collection of articles on the draft convention will be found in (1979) 27 Am. J. Comp. Law 201 *et seq.* [Eds.]

remedies for breach. Other significant differences are the adoption of a considerably simplified definition of fundamental breach and the elimination of the concept of *ipso facto* avoidance.

(c) UNIDROIT

The role of the International Institute for the Unification of Private Law in Rome, in initiating and promoting the drafting of the Uniform Laws, has already been noted. The Institute has also been active in cognate areas of commercial law that have an important bearing on international sales law. Work in progress or completed includes draft uniform laws on the Conditions of Validity of the Contract of Sale and on Agency of an International Character in the Sale and Purchase of Goods. Of particular interest is the draft Uniform Law on the Protection of the Bona Fide Purchaser of Corporeal Moveables, which was first published by the Institute in 1968 and subsequently revised in June, 1974.

(d) THE INTERNATIONAL CHAMBER OF COMMERCE

The Chamber, which enjoys consultative status under the charter of the United Nations, has long been active in promoting uniformity and greater harmonization in international trade terms and practices. In this regard, the Chamber has compiled interpretative and definitional manuals and standard conditions, which parties to international contracts are free to incorporate by reference in their agreements. Among the Chamber's better known publications are the *International Rules for the Interpretation of Trade Terms* (commonly referred to as INCOTERMS 1953) and the *Uniform Customs and Practice for Documentary Credits* (1974). Both documents are widely used in international trading transactions.

(e) UNITED NATIONS ECONOMIC COMMISSION FOR EUROPE

Under the auspices of the Economic Commission for Europe, a wide variety of general conditions of sale and standard forms of contracts have been drafted by working parties for use in contracts for the supply of plant and machinery for export and import. The Commission has also sponsored model contracts for the sale of cereals, citrus fruit, sawn softwood, solid fuel, potatoes, and steel products.

Note on Codification and Sources of Sales Law:

There have been intermittent debates among common law academic lawyers about the virtues and vices of codification and some of the issues were resurrected (albeit in low key and without much fervour) during the Code's gestative period. See R.B. Schlesinger, "The Uniform Commercial Code in the Light of Comparative Law" (1959) 1 Inter-Am. Law Rev. 11. Its opponents argue that codification is incompatible with the "free" spirit of the common law and that it freezes its growth and responsiveness to changing conditions — qualities that are particularly important in the commercial law area. On the other hand, the supporters of codification urge that certainty and predictability are as important as flexibility and that a busy practitioner should not be required to plough his way through many pages of frequently conflicting decisions to ascertain the law on a given point. Moreover, it is argued, in a federal system and at the international plane, meaningful uniformity can only be obtained by means of uniform legislation.

Whatever the merits of the criticism, they do not appear to have inhibited the movement towards codification of substantial areas of common law. But codification in this context does not have the same meaning as it has to the civilian. The Bills of Exchange Act (BEA), the Sale of Goods Act (SGA) and, now, the Uniform Commercial Code (UCC), preserve the common law rules except insofar as they are inconsistent with the express provisions of the statute, including in particular the general rules of contract. See e.g., SGA s. 57(1). Moreover, the SGA rules are generally so open-textured and broadly worded that there is ample scope for adaptation to changing circumstances in the hands of a creative judge.

Karl Llewellyn, the Chief Reporter of the Code, was particularly anxious to maintain this characteristic of commercial law and he inserted several key provisions which were designed to achieve this objective, viz., UCC 1-102 (purposes and policies of the Code and rules of construction); 1-203, 2-103 (obligations of good faith); and 1-205 and 2-208 (course of dealing, course of performance, and usage of trade as normative and evidentiary sources to give meaning and to supplement or qualify terms of an agreement). Good faith and flexibility are important values in governing the consensual relationships of contracting parties, but of necessity they must yield to the higher value of certainty when conflicts with the claims of third parties are involved. Hence, Article 9 of the Code, which is concerned with secured transactions (i.e., the law of chattel security), is more tightly drafted than Article 2 and unlike Article 2 has required some substantial amendments since it was first introduced.

Lord Herschell's judgment in *Bank of England* v. *Vagliano Bros.* [1891] AC 107 at 144-5, touches on a minor issue of exegesis, viz., the admissibility of prior case law to interpret the provisions of a codifying Act (in this case the BEA). Lord Herschell was of the view that the prior law is irrelevant. Rather, "the proper course is in the first instance to examine the language of the statute and to ask what is its natural meaning, uninfluenced by any considerations derived from the previous state of the law, and not to start with inquiring how the law previously stood, and then, assuming that it was probably intended to leave it unaltered, to see if the words of the enactment will bear an interpretation in conformity with this view." Do you share Lord Herschell's concern or is this a storm in a teacup? As many of the cases in this volume illustrate, Lord Herschell's stricture is more honoured in the breach than by its observance. Recent examples may be seen in *Ashington Piggeries Ltd.* v. *Christopher Hill Ltd.* (*infra*, chapter 6(B)(1)), *Hardwick Game Farm* v. *S.A.P.P.A.* (*infra*, chapter 6(B)(2)), and *Cehave N.V.* v. *Bremer Handelgesellschaft mbH* (*infra*, chapter 5(1)(A)). Do the courts use pre- or extra-code law to interpret the Act, to fill gaps, or to allow them to reflect changes in commercial practices or judicial ideology?

The SGA provisions are only presumptive and they may be "negatived or varied by express agreement or by the course of dealing between the parties, or by usage, if the usage is such as to bind both parties to the contract": SGA s. 53. The Act therefore makes it clear that course of dealing and usage of the trade are important sources in determining and explaining the parties' agreement. *Cf.* the Code's definition of "agreement" in UCC 1-201(3). "Course of dealing" and "usage" are not defined in the SGA but are carefully and comprehensively defined in UCC 1-205. A controversial feature of

English law is the non-admissibility of course of performance of an agreement to assist in determining the meaning of the agreement. *L. Schuler A.G.* v. *Wickman Machine Tool Sales Ltd.* [1974] AC 235 (HL). There is, however, contrary Canadian authority. The Code, in UCC 2-208, expressly recognizes the relevance of such evidence and this more liberal approach won the support of the OLRC. See OLRC Sales Report (1979), pp. 117-19.

B.   THE DEVELOPMENT OF CANADIAN CONSUMER LAW

JACOB S. ZIEGEL
"The Future of Canadian Consumerism"
(1973) 51 Can. Bar Rev. 191, 191-98

I.   INTRODUCTION

Fifty years ago the word consumerism had not been coined and the suggestion that consumer law should be taught as a separate intellectual discipline would have been regarded as fanciful. Today the one has become a household word and the other an accomplished fact.

Much has happened in the intervening period to justify this transformation. Concern about abuses in the marketplace is as old as the recorded history of civilized man, but the tempo of change in the character of the marketplace and the types of goods and services offered in it has been greater in this century than during any comparable period in Canadian history. From a predominantly agrarian society we have moved into a predominantly urbanized society. The simple wants of yesteryear have been replaced by the modern supermarket with its more than 7,500 items. The products of the agrarian society were for the most part uncomplicated, produced or manufactured locally, and buyer and seller dealt with each other on a basis of relative equality.

All this too has changed. Modern technology has placed at the disposal of the Canadian consumer a bewildering variety of highly complex products, consumable and non-consumable, many of which were unknown before the war. The notion of the consumer bargaining from a position of equal strength has become a fiction in any but the most attenuated sense. The contract of adhesion has replaced the hand-shake and a multi-billion-dollar credit industry is threatening to make the cash transaction a museum curiosity. The merchant himself has largely become a conduit pipe for goods manufactured and prepackaged often thousands of miles from the place of sale. The "medium is the message" accurately describes the modern salesman as a sophisticated advertising industry first creates the mass consumption markets and then sustains them by claims and images often far removed from reality.

The consumer's legitimate ignorance and his almost total dependence on the fairness and competence of those who supply his daily needs have made him a ready target for exploitation. The rapidly escalating number and variety of the complaints and enquiries received by Box 99, the federal consumer listening post, the provincial consumer protection bureaux, and the popular newspaper "action" columns attest to the consumer's concerns and vulnerability. It is not simply a matter of protecting him against outright frauds, although fraudulent transactions of all types still abound. The much greater challenge is to redress the serious imbalance in all aspects of the modern marketplace — a marketplace that encompasses the public sector no less than the private sector and the supply of services no less than the supply of goods — and this requires a magnitude of government involvement far transcending the modest levels experienced in earlier periods of Canadian history.

Despite these easily documentable facts, there are still many who question the vitality and the authenticity of the consumer movement. To some it is an ephemeral phenomenon — like the craving for striptease or the attraction of miniskirts — or, as a Canadian senator once claimed, an outlet for the energies of frustrated women unable to keep their husbands under control. These exotic views may be left to the judgment of history. Others see the consumer movement as a left wing political plot in which consumer grievances are used as a Trojan horse to undermine the free market system. This view too will not bear the test of serious analysis. The leading consumer advocates on both sides of the border are drawn from all parts of the political spectrum or have no known political affiliations of any kind. Consumer concerns are as acute, perhaps more so, in communist countries as in countries enjoying a mixed type of economy. Consumerism is no more a political ideology than is labour law or poverty law although solutions to particular problems may be influenced by one's conceptions of the role of the modern marketplace.

A more challenging criticism comes from those who deny that there is a functional or intellectual unity to the proliferating variety of causes that are espoused by consumerists. In their view they are often only old problems represented under new labels such as the problems of landlord and tenant relations, warranty problems in the sale of goods and services, and the issue of safety, first, in the realm of food and drugs and, now, with respect to motor vehicles and hazardous household products. There is some substance to this argument but not enough to tilt the balance. Some overlapping occurs between many disciplines and it is no more harmful here than it is there.

Functionally, the thread that binds all consumer problems together is the perception that they affect the individual as a purchaser of goods and services for his personal use or consumption. Analytically, I believe it will be found that every consumer problem exhibits one or more of the following characteristics. First, a disparity of bargaining power between the supplier of goods or services and the consumer to whom they are being offered; secondly, a growing and frequently total disparity of knowledge concerning the characteristics and technical components of the goods or services; and, thirdly, a no less striking disparity of resources between the two sides, whether that disparity reflects itself in a consumer's difficulty to obtain redress unaided for a legitimate grievance or in a supplier's ability to absorb the cost of a defective product as part of his general overhead as compared to the consumer to whom its malfunctioning may represent the loss of a considerable capital investment.

Two other attacks on consumerism may be briefly noted. One is the self-serving argument that "we are all consumers". If this means no more than that consumerists have no monopoly of interest or concern, it is a legitimate point. But usually the protestation is offered by the suppliers of goods or services or their spokesmen, the inference being that their dual role as suppliers and consumers ensures automatic fair play when they appear as suppliers. This is palpably fallacious. The dominant interest of a supplier is to promote his business interests as he sees them; if he has any consumer concerns (which are in any event unlikely to coincide with his professional interests) they will quickly be suppressed in favour of those considerations that provide his profit or his livelihood.

The same fallacy underlies the other line of contention. It is in the interest of business, it is argued, to keep the consumer happy because only satisfied consumers make good customers. Thus, the argument proceeds, this self-regulating rule of the marketplace protects the consumer and ensures an automatic type of equilibrium. That there may be, and in the long run often is, a common identity of interest may be readily conceded. The same no doubt could be said of other areas in which daily conflicts are common, such as labour relations or the confrontation between political parties.

But the self-operating character of the identity principle is far from self-evident. The evidence indeed points very much in the opposite direction. Almost every important piece of post-war consumer legislation has been opposed by some segment of the business community. However much that opposition may have been disguised in rhetoric about Big Brotherism and unjustifiable interference with the mechanism of the marketplace, the truth is that on those occasions the affected industries did not see regulation as being in *their* own best interests, whatever may have been the position from the consumer's point of view. There is nothing reprehensible about this pursuit of group interests. We take it for granted in all other spheres in our pluralistic society. What is surprising is that it should be thought that consumer-supplier relations are somehow exempt from this basic axiom of political and economic life.

Note: Overview of Post-War Canadian Consumer Protection Legislation:*

Canadian consumerism is not a new phenomenon and consumer protection legislation can be traced to the early days of legislative activity of Upper and Lower Canada. The federal Food and Drugs Act is almost as old as Confederation and the Interest Act has an even longer history. The federal and provincial moneylending and pawnbroking legislation is at least seventy years old.

What is true however is that, as in the U.S. and other Western industrialized nations, the post-war period spawned an enormous increase of interest in consumer problems and in the volume of remedial legislation at both the provincial and federal levels. The reasons for this phenomenon have been canvassed in the preceding article by Professor Ziegel. For a useful collection of articles on the various aspects of Canadian consumerism, see Neilson (ed.), *Consumer and the Law in Canada* (1970); Law Society of Upper Canada, *Papers and Proceedings at Consumer Protection Conference*, Toronto,

---

*   The citations of the statutes referred to in this note will be found in the table immediately following the note. [Eds.]

Feb. 1973; and C.S. Akworthy, "Recent Developments in Consumer Law in Canada" (1980) 29 ICLQ 346.

So far as Ontario is concerned, the most important phase of post-war activity dates from 1965 when the Select Committee of the Ontario Legislature on Consumer Credit presented its *Final Report on Consumer Credit*. The Committee's recommendations led to the enactment of the Consumer Protection Act (1966) and the Consumer Protection Bureau Act (1966). Originally the CPA only dealt with three major issues: the licensing of itinerant sellers and the right of cancellation of door-to-door sales (see now Pt. II and s. 33); writing requirements for "executory contracts" (Pt. III); and "truth in lending" disclosure requirements (Pt. III). Since then the scope of the Act has been substantially enlarged and it now includes the following provisions: s. 42a (avoidance of cut-off clauses in credit agreements); s. 44a (avoidance of disclaimer clauses in consumer sales); s. 46 (regulation of unsolicited goods and credit cards); and s. 46a (prohibition of referral sales). Nevertheless, the CPA still falls short of a comprehensive consumer protection code even with respect to sales and credit transactions and, in general, its draftsmanship and enforcement leave much to be desired.

Apart from the CPA and CPBA, the province has also adopted other important consumer protection legislation. In particular the student will need to familiarize himself with the following measures: the Motor Vehicle Dealers Act (primarily a licensing statute), the Unconscionable Transactions Relief Act (an old Act which empowers the courts to grant relief from usurious loan transactions), the Wages Act (this contains important provisions concerning wage assignments and the garnishment of earnings) and, more recently, the Consumer Reporting Act. The Business Practices Act, 1974, a very important enactment, widens the scope of consumer rights by proscribing unfair as well as deceptive consumer "representations" and providing new methods of policing them.

With the introduction of the Personal Property Security Act, 1967, proclaimed in force as of April 1, 1976, Ontario became the first Canadian jurisdiction to adopt a modern law of secured transactions. Similar Article 9 type legislation has been adopted in Manitoba and Saskatchewan and (most recently) in the Yukon Territory and is likely to be adopted in other provinces in the foreseeable future. With few exceptions, the PPSA is not consumer oriented but it has an important bearing on consumer as well as commercial transactions in which a security interest in personal property is involved.

In 1972 the Ontario Law Reform Commission published an important report on *Consumer Warranties and Guarantees in the Sale of Goods* which recommended extensive and basic changes in this branch of the law. Bill 110, The Consumer Product Warranties Act, 1976, gave effect to some of the recommendations but the bill was allowed to die on the order paper. Paradoxically, many of the Commission's recommendations were implemented in the Saskatchewan Consumer Products Warranties Act, 1977. The construction and sale of new homes raise similar problems to the sale of movable durable products, and their treatment has fared better in Ontario as a result of the adoption of the Ontario New Home Warranties Plan Act, 1976.

The result of the foregoing enumeration leads to the inevitable conclusion that the modern Ontario commercial and consumer lawyer has to grapple with a formidable array of statutory provisions. The table following this note supplies a brief roadmap through the statutory jungle, federal as well as provincial.

Federal intervention in the marketplace goes back to the earliest days of Confederation and, like the provincial legislation, has been increasing rapidly.

The Small Loans Act was first adopted in 1939. It has recently been amended and is likely shortly to be repealed altogether. It was designed, like its American counterpart, to encourage legitimate lenders to make loans to lower income borrowers and to combat usurious interest rates in small loans. The Act (which never applied to banks) imposed licensing requirements and set maximum interest rates for loans up to $1,500. In cases not governed by the Act, the Interest Act (a much older statute) allowed the parties to set their own rates subject to compliance with interest disclosure requirements relating to mortgages and other types of loan. Section 202 of the new (1980) Bank Act and the regulations thereunder (historically a product of the 1967 decennial revision of the Bank Act) serve a similar purpose with respect to consumer loans made by the banks. These were designed to complement the parallel provincial truth-in-lending requirements adopted in the late 60s.

The federal credit and interest legislation is badly dated and in 1976 the federal government introduced a comprehensive Borrowers and Depositors Protection Act (Bill C-16) with a view to consolidating and updating its provisions. The bill was bitterly opposed by many segments of the business community and also attracted substantial opposition from the provinces on constitutional grounds. As a result, after extensive committee hearings, the bill was abandoned by the Liberal government. Its place is likely to be taken by a series of fragmented amendments and revisions of the existing Acts. For further information see J.S. Ziegel (ed.), *Seventh Annual Workshop on Commercial and Consumer Law* (1979), Part V. The new game plan has already been partially implemented. Bill C-44, which received the royal assent on 17 December 1980, repeals, inter alia, the licensing and graduated ceiling provisions in the Small Loans Act and adds a new s. 305.1 to the Criminal Code introducing a "criminal rate" of interest (i.e., an effective annual rate of interest exceeding 60 per cent of the credit advanced) for all types of credit, consumer and otherwise. For further details see *infra*, chapter 25. The new Bank Act strengthens the earlier disclosure requirements and supplements them with rights of prepayment.

Part X of the Bankruptcy Act, the force of which in any province depends on proclamation by the Governor General in Council, is designed to relieve the plight of overcommitted consumer debtors, and provides that the debtor may apply to the court to consolidate his debts into an orderly payment schedule. These provisions are likely to reappear in modified form, together with new provisions on consumer bankruptcies, in the revised Bankruptcy Act which has been drafted for several years and unsuccessfully introduced on at least two occasions. (For the most recent version, see Bill C-12; 16 April 1980). Part V of the Bills of Exchange Act, added in 1970, allows consumers to assert against holders of negotiable instruments made or drawn by the consumer any defence the consumer would have been entitled to assert against the seller of the goods to which the instrument relates.

The Consumer Packaging and Labelling Act, enacted in 1971, prohibits deceptive packaging and labelling practices and imposes important disclosure requirements. The Food and Drugs Act and the Hazardous Products Act severally regulate or prohibit the manufacture and/or sale of an enormously wide range of consumer products. Also, with respect to safety, the Motor Vehicle Safety Act requires vehicles sold in Canada to have prescribed safety equipment, or to be safe in design to specifications. The inaptly named Combines Investigation Act was amended in 1975 and now applies, inter alia, to a substantially enlarged range of false or deceptive representations and some types of unfair practices such as pyramidic sales, referral sales, and prize schemes. The then federal government also announced its intention to proceed with a "Stage Two" program which would include a comprehensive federal Trade Practices Act to supersede the existing consumer protection provisions in the Combines Act. The bill never materialized. However, in November 1977, the Liberal government introduced Bill C-13, an Act to amend the Combines Act, which, apart from its regulatory provisions on mergers, also introduced a federal consumer class action procedure for violations of the Act's Part V provisions. Both features of the bill were strongly opposed by the business community and were not proceeded with. Mr. André Ouellet has however recently announced the government's intention to introduce new amending legislation in 1981.

With modest exceptions, it seems safe to predict that consumer legislation has reached its peak and that the 1980s will be a period of consolidation if not active retrenchment. See W.A.W. Neilson, "The Future of Canadian Consumerism: A Retrospective and Prospective View", paper delivered at the 10th Annual Workshop on Commercial and Consumer Law, Toronto, Oct. 18, 1980. The negative trend is already very evident in the U.S. as witness the determined, and partially successful, attempts by Congress to clip severely the wings of the Federal Trade Commission. See further, "The F.T.C. Starts a New Life", *Consumer Reports,* Aug. 1980, p. 504, and The Federal Trade Commission Improvements Act of 1980, PL 96-252, 94 Stat. 374, approved May 28, 1980. The Act's legislative history appears in *U.S. Code & Admin. News,* July 1980, pp. 2239 *et seq.*

SELECTED TABLE OF ONTARIO AND FEDERAL SALES, CHATTEL SECURITY AND CONSUMER PROTECTION LEGISLATION

I.   FEDERAL LEGISLATION

Banks and Banking Revision Act, Part I (Bank Act), SC 1980, c. 40, esp. ss. 178-179 and Regulations

Bankruptcy Act, RSC 1970, c. B-3 as am., Pt. X

Bills of Exchange Act, RSC 1970, c. B-5 as am., esp. Pt. V

Combines Investigation Act, SC 1974-75-76, c. 76, esp. ss. 36 et seq.

Consumer Packaging and Labelling Act, SC 1970-71-72, c. 41

Department of Consumer and Corporate Affairs Act, RSC 1970, c. C-27

Food and Drugs Act, RSC 1970, c. F-27 (as am.)

Hazardous Products Act, RSC 1970, c. H-3

Interest Act, RSC 1970, c. I-18, as am. by SC 1980, c. 43, s. 9.

Motor Vehicle Safety Act, RSC 1970 c. 26 (1st supp.), as am.

Small Loans Act, RSC 1970 c. S-11 as am. by SC 1980, c. 43

II. ONTARIO LEGISLATION

SALES LEGISLATION

Bulk Sales Act, RSO 1970, c. 52.

Factors Act, RSO 1970, c. 156.

Mercantile Law Amendment Act, RSO 1970, c. 272.

Sale of Goods Act, RSO 1970, c. 421, as am.

Warehouse Receipts Act, RSO 1970, c. 489.

CONSUMER LEGISLATION

Business Practices Act, SO 1974, c. 131.

Consumer Protection Act, RSO 1970, c. 82 as am.

Consumer Protection Bureau Act, RSO 1970, c. 83 as am.

Consumer Reporting Act, SO 1973, c. 97.

Ministry of Consumer & Commercial Relations Act, RSO 1970, c. 113 as am.

Motor Vehicle Dealers Act, RSO 1970, c. 475 as am.

Ontario New Home Warranties Plan Act, 1976, SO 1976, c. 52.

Unconscionable Transactions Relief Act, RSO 1970, c. 472.

Wages Act, RSO 1970, c. 486 as am.

_____

Bill 110, The Ontario Consumer Products Warranties Act, 1976 (not enacted).

CHATTEL SECURITY LEGISLATION

Bills of Sale Act, RSO 1970, c. 44 as am.

Corporation Securities Registration Act, RSO 1970, c. 88 as am.

Personal Property Security Act, RSO 1970, c. 344 as am.

_____

Acts repealed by the Personal Property Security Act:

Assignment of Book Debts Act, RSO 1970, c. 33 as am.

Bills of Sale and Chattel Mortgages Act, RSO 1970, c. 45 as am.

Conditional Sales Act, RSO 1970, c. 76 as am.

Chapter 2
Concept of Sale

Introductory Note:

Section 2 of the SGA defines the meaning of sale. Every word of the definition is important and should be carefully studied in the light of the cases reproduced in this chapter. The obvious reason is that if a transaction does not satisfy the statutory definition then prima facie it is not governed by the Act (or any other Act which employs the same definition).

This does not mean that the sales rule should not be applied by analogy and it is always a relevant question whether there is any functional difference between a sale and the particular transaction in question and whether the rationale of the sales rule applies equally to both types of transaction.

The distinctions canvassed in the ensuing case material are between a sale and (1) a hire-purchase agreement or equipment lease; (2) a contract for labour and materials; and (3) selling agencies and consignment agreements. Omitted have been cases dealing with the definition of goods, as to which see OLRC Sales Report, ch. 4.4. Note that, in general, the SGA draws no distinction between commercial and consumer transactions, the character of the parties, or the purpose for which the goods are intended. An important exception occurs in the case of the implied conditions of fitness and merchantability [s. 15(1) and (2)]. The condition of merchantability only applies to "a seller who deals in goods of that description", that of fitness to "goods of a description that it is in the course of the seller's business to supply". These phrases are not defined. Consider the broad definition of "merchant" in UCC 2-104(1) and see if it assists the exegesis of the SGA. Note too that Article 2 uses the merchant/non-merchant distinction much more extensively than does the SGA.

The scope of the SGA should be compared with the scope of the CPA, including the amplifying regulations under the latter Act. What are the important differences and what are their rationales? Can you suggest better definitions than those which appear in the CPA? Which of the following transactions are governed by the CPA or any part of it:

a) The repair of an automobile;

b) The rental of a colour TV set;

c)   Subscription to a book club;

d)   The rental of a cottage for the summer;

e)   The purchase of a car by a lawyer who intends to use it partly in his business and partly for pleasure;

f)   The purchase of wall-to-wall carpeting which is to be paid for within 90 days. The contract discloses no separate credit charge;

g)   The purchase of a cigarette vending machine which the purchaser intends to use to supplement his regular income?

The definitions in the CPA do not apply uniformly throughout the Act. For instance, s. 30 limits the application of Part II to executory contracts of sale. Part III applies to all consumer transactions involving the extension of credit.

Credit is defined differently in s. 46 and in s. 1(e). Why? Section 46a defines buyer and seller more broadly than s. 1. Considering the many types of consumer transactions, should the definitions in s. 46a be adopted generally for the CPA? For the SGA?

Further Questions:

1   Is the credit transaction of one who borrows money in order to purchase goods for use in his business protected by the CPA?

2   Does a professional carry on business?

3   A doctor buys a car and uses it both for house calls and for pleasure driving. Does the CPA apply?

4   Do the definitions in s. 2(1) of the Regulations apply to transactions regulated in s. 46 of the Act? Is the recipient of unsolicited goods or credit cards a "buyer", a "borrower", or both?

5   Is the making of an appointment with a dentist an executory contract protected by Part II? What rights does the individual have if, when he leaves the dentist's chair, he is presented with an unexpectedly high bill?

Note on Barter or Exchange Transactions:

OLRC Sales Report, p. 65:

Section 2 of The Sale of Goods Act stipulates that the price must be payable in money. An exchange or barter of goods will not satisfy the statutory test. This bland statement, however, requires some important qualifications. It is clear, for example, that a price which is to be satisfied by the sale from the buyer to the seller of goods of equivalent or greater value, will meet the prescribed test. It is equally well settled that the price may be paid partly in cash and partly by means of a trade-in or other exchange, at any rate where the value of the trade-in is monetized. What remains excluded, therefore, is a pure barter agreement that is not tainted by any mention of a monetary figure.

It is difficult to justify the insistence on a monetary consideration. UCC 2-304 does not do so. It provides as follows:

(1) The price can be made payable in money or otherwise. If it is payable in whole or in part in goods each party is a seller of the goods which he is to transfer.

(2) Even though all or part of the price is payable in an interest in realty the transfer of the goods and the seller's obligations with reference to them are subject to this Article, but not the transfer of the interest in realty or the transferor's obligations in connection therewith.

It may be argued that, where a simple exchange or other non-monetary form of consideration is involved, it will be difficult to assess damages if either party breaches his contract. But this will be true however the contract is characterized. The real question, in our opinion, is whether sales rules should be applied by analogy to a contract involving non-monetary consideration, or whether it would be simpler to absorb such transactions into sales law by expanding the definition of price. While acknowledging that the problem is not of the first magnitude, we prefer the latter solution. We therefore recommend the adoption of the Code section, and our Draft Bill contains a provision to this effect.

What lends force to the OLRC recommendation is the fact that the rules governing the barter agreements are uncertain and surprisingly undeveloped. It was settled in the last century that they are not subject to s. 17 or the Statute of Frauds (now reproduced in Ontario's SGA s. 5); there is also ''reasonable agreement among the authorities that it is not open to a disappointed party, who has parted with his goods without receiving the expected return, to sue for the value of the goods delivered as a price; his remedy is to claim unliquidated damages for non-delivery of the goods promised in exchange or possibly to sue the other party in fact on the basis that the property in such goods has passed to him'': *Benjamin's Sale of Goods,* p. 25, and cf. *Messenger* v. *Greene* [1937] 2 DLR 26 (NS CA). (How would these questions be decided under the Code?) Beyond these points, and perhaps a few others, there is much uncertainty as to the applicable law.

The uncertainty would not matter if one could safely assume that barter agreements are an historical curiosity and out of place in a modern industrialized society. The assumption cannot be made. In fact there is evidence of a remarkable resurgence of popularity in barter transactions of one description or another, both nationally and internationally.

At the national level part of the popularity is explained by the emergence of a ''subterranean'' economy where tax avoidance may be an added incentive for barter transactions (for example, a farmer exchanging produce for an electrician's services), but it is clear that organized barter schemes, part of the ''visible'' economy, are also growing in importance. In 1978 they are said to have accounted for an estimated $200 million worth of business in North America.

Organized barter schemes are facilitated by barter exchanges, of which apparently there are three in Toronto and an estimated 200–300 in the U.S.

The exchanges act for both private and corporate clients — basically anyone with a business and with goods or services to offer. Clients generally pay a membership fee and service charges, calculated on a percentage basis for all transactions. In return, the exchange provides a referral service, linking those with goods and services to those who want them, as well as carrying out a record-keeping function.

Most exchanges operate on a ''trade credit'' or ''futures'' system, whereby credits are added to a business's account in return for goods and services supplied to another member. These credits can then be used to ''purchase'' other goods or services at a later date — hence the term ''futures''.

While some exchanges issue credits for 100 per cent of the value of goods or services bartered, others, recognizing the need of many clients to cover operating expenses, operate on a part cash, part "futures" basis. In the latter system, the "purchaser" gives the "seller" an amount of cash equivalent to the cost of the bartered product and transfers the remainder of the "price" (representing profit to the "seller") from his account in the form of trade credits.

For more on the growth of barter organizations in Canada see *Canadian Consumer*, August 1979, p. 46.

A. LEASE OR SALE: THE FORM AND SUBSTANCE PROBLEM

HELBY v. MATTHEWS
[1895-99] All ER Rep. 821, [1895] AC 471 (HL)

LORD HERSCHELL L.C.: The appellant was the owner of a piano, of which he had given possession to one Charles Brewster, under an agreement in writing of Dec. 23, 1892, to the terms of which I shall have occasion to refer immediately. On July 21, 1893, Brewster, improperly and without the consent of the appellant, pledged the piano with the respondents, who are pawnbrokers, as security for an advance. The appellant, upon discovering this, demanded the piano from the respondents, and, on their refusing to deliver it, brought an action of trover. The defence set up by the respondents was that they had received the piano from Brewster in good faith and without notice of any claim on the part of the appellant, and that Brewster having "bought or agreed to buy" it from him, they were protected by s. 9 of the Factors Act, 1889. The county court judge held that the defence was not proved, and his judgment was upheld by the Divisional Court of the Queen's Bench. The Court of Appeal, however, came to the conclusion that the defence had been established, and reversed the judgment of the Divisional Court.

The only question is whether the respondents have made out that Brewster had bought or agreed to buy the piano. This depends upon the true effect of the agreement under which he obtained it. By that agreement Brewster, called therein the hirer, agreed to pay the "owner" on Dec. 23, 1892, a rent or hire instalment of 10s. 6d., and 10s. 6d. on the 23rd of each succeeding month, and to keep the instrument in the hirer's own custody at the address named in the agreement, and not to remove the same without the owner's previous consent in writing. He further agreed that if the hiring should be terminated by him under a subsequent clause of the agreement, and the instrument returned to the owner, the hirer should remain liable to the owner for arrears of hire up to the date of the return, and should not be entitled to any allowance, credit, return, or set-off for payments previously made. The owner, on the other hand, agreed that the hirer might terminate the hiring by delivering up the instrument to the owner, and, further, that if the hirer should punctually pay the full sum of eighteen guineas, by 10s. 6d. at the date of signing and by thirty-five monthly instalments of 10s. 6d. in advance as aforesaid, the instrument should become the sole and absolute property of the hirer. It was also agreed that unless and until the full sum of eighteen guineas was paid the instrument should be and continue the sole property of the owner.

It is said that the substance of the transaction evidenced by the agreement must be looked at, and not its mere words. I quite agree. But the substance must, of course, be ascertained by a consideration of the rights and obligations of the parties, to be derived from a consideration of the whole of the agreement. If Brewster agreed to buy the piano the parties cannot, by calling it a hiring, or by any mere juggling with words, escape from the consequences of the contract into which they entered. What then, was the real nature of the transaction? The answer to this question is not, I think, involved in any difficulty. Brewster was to obtain possession of the piano and to be entitled to its use so long as he paid the plaintiff the stipulated sum of 10s. 6d. a month, and he was bound to make these monthly payments so long as he retained possession of the piano. If he continued to make them at the appointed times for the period of three years the piano was to become his property, but he might at any time return it, and, upon doing so, would no longer be liable to make any further payment beyond the monthly sum then due.

I cannot, with all respect, concur in the view of the Court of Appeal that, upon the true construction of the agreement, Brewster had "agreed to buy" the piano. An agreement to buy imports a legal obligation to buy. If there was no such legal obligation there cannot, in my opinion, properly be said to have been an agreement to buy. Where is any such legal obligation to be found? Brewster might buy or not just as he pleased. He did not agree to make thirty-six or any number of monthly payments. All that he undertook was to make the monthly payment of 10s. 6d. so long as he kept the piano. He had an option, no doubt, to buy it by continuing the stipulated payments for a sufficient length of time. If he had exercised that option he would have become the purchaser. I cannot see, under these circumstances, how he can be said either to have bought or agreed to buy the piano. The terms of the contract did not, upon its execution, bind him to buy, but left him free to do so or not as he pleased, and nothing happened after the contract was made to impose that obligation. The Master of the Rolls said:

> It is a contract by the seller to sell, and a contract by the purchaser, if he does not change his mind, to buy; and, if this agreement goes on to its end, it ends in a purchase. Therefore, it seems to me that the true and proper construction of this instrument, after all, is this — it is an agreement by the one to sell, and an agreement by the other to buy, but with an option on the part of the buyer if he changes his mind to put an end to the contract.

I cannot think that an agreement to buy, "if he does not change his mind," is any agreement to buy at all in the eye of the law. If it rests with me to do or not to do a certain thing at a future time, according to the then state of my mind, I cannot be said to have contracted to do it.

It appears to me that the contract in question was in reality a contract of hiring, and not in name or pretence only. But for the provision that if the hirer punctually paid the 10s. 6d. a month for thirty-six months, the piano should be his property, it could not be doubted that it was a mere agreement for its hire, and I cannot see how the fact that this provision was added made it any the less a contract of hiring until that condition had been fulfilled. I think it very likely that both parties thought it would probably end in a purchase, but this is far from showing that it was an agreement to buy. The monthly payments were no doubt somewhat higher than they would have been if the agreement had contained no such provision. One can well conceive cases, however, in which a person who had not made up his mind to continue the payment for three years, would nevertheless enter into such an agreement. It might be worth his while to make somewhat larger monthly payments for the use of the piano in order that he might enjoy that option if he chose to exercise it. In such a case how could it be said that he had agreed to buy when he had not only come under no obligation to buy, but had not even made up his mind to do so? The agreement is, in its terms, just as applicable to such a case as to one where the hirer had resolved to continue the payments for the three years, and it must be construed upon a consideration of the obligations which its terms create, and not upon a mere speculation as to what was contemplated, or what would probably be done under it.

It was said in the Court of Appeal that there was an agreement by the appellant to sell, and that an agreement to sell connotes an agreement to buy. This is undoubtedly true if the words "agreement to sell" be used in their strict legal sense; but when a person has, for valuable consideration, bound himself to sell to another on certain terms, if the other chooses to avail himself of the binding offer, he may, in popular language, be said to have agreed to sell, though an agreement to sell in this sense which is in truth merely an offer which cannot be withdrawn, certainly does not connote an agreement to buy, and it is only in this sense that there can be said to have been an agreement to sell in the present case.

It was argued for the respondents that the case came within the mischief intended to be provided against by s. 9 of the Factors Act, 1889,* and that the enactment ought, therefore, to be so construed as to cover it. I can see no reason for thus straining the language of the enactment. A person who is in possession of a piano under such an agreement as that which existed in the present case is no more its apparent owner than if he had merely hired it, and in the latter case any one taking it as security would have no claim to hold it as against the owner. Reliance was placed on the decision in *Lee* v. *Butler* [1893] 2 Q.B. 318 and it was said that the present case was not, in principle, distinguishable from it. There seems to me to be the broadest distinction between the two cases. There was there an agreement to buy. The purchase money was to be paid in two instalments; but as soon as the agreement was entered into, there was an absolute obligation to pay both of them, which might have been enforced by action. The person who obtained the goods could not insist upon returning them and so absolve himself from any obligation to make further payment. Unless there was a breach of contract by the party who engaged to make the payments the transaction necessarily resulted in a sale. That there was in that case an agreement to buy appears to me, as it did to the Court of Appeal, to be beyond question. It was further urged

---

* Section 9 of the British Factors Act, 1889, does not appear in the Ontario Factors Act, RSO 1970, c. 156, but is reproduced almost verbatim in s. 25(2) of the Ont. SGA. [Eds.]

for the respondents that when Brewster pledged the piano with them it became impossible for him to return it to the appellant, and he became, therefore from that time bound to make the stipulated payment and to become the purchaser. I cannot accede to this argument. In my opinion, it is impossible to hold that Brewster, having only a right under the contract to buy, provided he complied with the prescribed conditions, could convert himself into a purchaser as against the owner by violating the conditions of the contract. I think the judgment appealed from must be reversed.

Appeal allowed.

[The other members of the House delivered concurring judgments.]

RE SPEEDRACK LIMITED
(1980) 33 CBR (NS) 209 (Ont. SC)

HENRY J. (orally): Commercial Credit Corporation Limited is a financing institution carrying on business as such throughout Canada. It is the owner of certain manufacturing equipment that might generally be described as tools and dies that it has leased to the bankrupt, Speedrack Limited, under a lease, assigned to it by Canadian Leasing Consultants, a division of Casselman Leasing Consultants Inc., that contains an option to purchase by the lessee, Speedrack, at the end of 60 months. Speedrack, then being in possession of the equipment under the lease, made an assignment in bankruptcy on 25th May 1979, before the date upon which the option could be exercised by it. The trustee in bankruptcy took possession of the leased equipment. Commercial Credit Corporation has filed a claim under s. 59 of the Bankruptcy Act, RSC 1970, c. B-3, claiming title to and return of the equipment. The trustee disallowed this claim for the reason that:

> The lease agreement, referred to in your proof of claim contains a clause providing Speedrack Limited an option to purchase the leased equipment. The lease agreement is therefore a security agreement to which The Personal Property Security Act [RSO 1970, c. 344] of Ontario applies. The agreement has not been registered pursuant to the provisions of that Act and your security had therefore not been perfected at the date of bankruptcy.

From this decision of the trustee Commercial Credit Corporation appeals to this court. The issue is that raised in the trustee's reasons.

It is the position of the appellant, Commercial Credit Corporation, that the lease agreement is a simple lease of the equipment to Speedrack not by way of security. The trustee's position is that it creates a security interest analogous to a conditional sale contract that, to be effective as against the trustee, must be registered under the Personal Property Security Act, which it is not.

Section 2 of the Personal Property Security Act provides in part:

> (2) Subject to subsection 1 of section 3, this Act applies,
>> (a) to to every transaction without regard to its form and without regard to the person who has title to the collateral that in substance creates a security interest, including, without limiting the foregoing, . . .

(ii) an assignment, lease of consignment intended as security; . . .

Section 1(y) provides by way of definition in this Act:

(y) "security interest" means an interest in goods, other than building materials that have been affixed to the realty, fixtures, documents of title, instruments,
securities, chattel papers or intangibles that secures payment or performance of an
obligation, and includes an interest arising from an assignment of book debts.

The matter was argued before me on the basis of the formal instruments and
other documents filed, together with affidavits filed and cross-examination
thereon. The facts are not in dispute, and counsel were clear that no viva voce
evidence would be required.

Speedrack manufactures a steel modular shelving system. The tooling and
dies are owned by a related company, Shelfrack Limited, and are operated by
Speedrack employees on premises occupied by both companies in common. The
shareholders and directors are common to both companies. At the material time,
the general manager of Speedrack, Mr. Doherty, was also treasurer of Shelfrack
and responsible for the financial affairs of both. Speedrack manufactured the
product and transferred it to Shelfrack as distributor to sell and to collect the
accounts from customers.

In January 1978 Speedrack was in financial difficulties and required financing. The equipment with which we are concerned was already in use and was not
new. It had a book value of $210,000 representing its cost to Shelfrack. Mr.
Doherty on behalf of both companies approached Canadian Leasing Consultants, a division of Casselman Leasing Consultants Inc., an Ontario company, to
arrange financing. The four Speedrack shareholders were to put up a total of
$150,000 by way of shareholders' advances prior to 6th February 1978 (which
apparently was not done). Canadian Leasing Consultants advanced $140,000 and
took title to the equipment, which by lease agreement dated 13th January 1978 it
leased to Speedrack for a term of 65 months at a monthly rental of $3,136. Under
the terms of the lease agreement, among other terms, the lessor gave no warranties, the lessee having selected the equipment and the supplier; orders, delivery
and installation to be at the risk of the lessee; if the lessee rejects the equipment
the lessee is to indemnify the lessor against claims of suppliers as if the lessee and
not the lessor had bought the equipment. The lease is a net lease, payments of
rent to be unaffected by failure of the equipment to perform or by damage,
destruction or theft of the equipment; the lessee to be responsible for repair.
Upon default by the lessee (including any act of bankruptcy) it is provided that:
"All monies secured hereby and payable hereunder either at or after the date of
such default and then unpaid shall forthwith become due and payable". Upon
default by the lessee the lessor may, inter alia, sue for arrears and repossess the
equipment. The lessee is to furnish audited financial statements annually. These
terms are included in a printed form. Then appears the option clause referred to,
which is typed in as follows:

Purchase Option: Lessee shall, when not in default under the lease, have the
option to purchase all, but not part of, the said chattels for the sum of $14,000.00 in

cash after the 60th month of this agreement, but before the 61st month of this agreement. The aforementioned $14,000.00 is the estimated fair market value of the said chattels after the 60th month, but before the 61st month of this agreement, based on information available on the date this schedule was entered into.

Meanwhile Canadian Leasing Consultants by bill of sale dated 13th February 1978 sold the equipment to Commercial Credit Corporation, the appellant herein, for a price of $150,850 and by assignment dated the same day assigned all its interest in the lease to Commercial Credit Corporation for the same amount, which was described as being a 65-month discount; the assignment was effective as of 6th February 1978. It is as assignee of the original lease that Commercial Credit Corporation now claims in the bankruptcy.

The nature of the transaction may be apparent on the face of the instruments, but if it is not, the court must determine its nature for purposes of s. 2 of the Personal Property Security Act from the surrounding circumstances. It is not merely a question of construing the agreement between the parties, which may be quite clear. It is a question of determining the intention of the parties, notwithstanding the form used in setting up the transaction. For this, extrinsic evidence may be relevant and admissible, and it is so in this case. The court's task is to determine the essence of the transaction in spite of its form, as prescribed in s. 2. It must determine, on the balance of probabilities, and on a practical and common-sense view of the evidence, whether the parties negotiated a loan or advance on security, or a standard lease of property, not by way of security, from the lessor to the bankrupt.

The course of argument placed considerable emphasis upon the tests laid down by the federal Department of National Revenue (Taxation) in its interpretation bulletin IT-233 of 14th July 1975. This document is designed to determine with regard to leasing agreements whether payments in respect of those agreements are in substance payments of rent or payments on account of the purchase price of property; or, in the case of sale-leaseback agreements, repayments of a loan.

The bulletin refers to the department's interest in lease-option agreements as being to see that significant sums paid for the purchase of property are not being charged against income as rent, of which no recapture can be made from a lessee who exercises his option and sells the property at a price which reimburses him for all or part of the rent; the department looks to see whether or not the object of the transaction at its inception is to transfer the equity in the property to the lessee.

The department's interest in sale-leaseback agreements is in ensuring that repayments of what are in substance borrowed funds are not being charged against income as rent; where it is apparent that the true intent of the parties is that the lessee borrow money on the security of property, the agreement is in substance a loan arrangement.

The objective of the department's tests or guidelines is to provide guidance as to the treatment of the rental payments for tax purposes by both the lessor and the lessee. I do not consider that the department's criteria for such a purpose are necessarily relevant in determining the issue before me, which is whether the transaction as a whole creates a security interest by way of a lease intended as security. I therefore do not set out the departmental criteria, as I do not wish to be taken to endorse them or reject them as valid criteria for the purpose of this issue.

Rather I proceed by considering three factors — the role of the parties, the intent of the parties, and the effect of the transaction.

Apart from the documents, the evidence is that contained in the affidavits and cross-examination on them of Mr. Milligan, the controller of Commercial Credit Corporation, and Mr. Doherty, who was at the material time responsible for the financial affairs of both Speedrack and Shelfrack. Mr. Milligan's evidence is that Commercial Credit Corporation is a financing institution with a variety of types of business, among which it leases equipment to lessees; it also finances equipment to companies or firms and carries on the loaning of money on second mortgage and other types of mortgage loans. Mr. Milligan was asked:

> Q. 8 Do you have an inventory of equipment or things of that nature which you would lease out to people? Or is it just a feed-through or financing type of leasing? A. It is a feed-through financing type of leasing.

As to the business of Canadian Leasing Consultants, he agreed that it is fair to say that it is a firm which arranges leases with various customers and it in turn will sell these leases "to finance companies such as ours". He thought it fair to say that they are finders and that they then sell their paper to organizations like Commercial Credit.

Speedrack and Shelfrack were acting in concert. Shelfrack owned the equipment, which was not new; it had been in use in the operation by Speedrack employees for varying periods of time, and 75 per cent of it had a life expectancy of 10 to 20 years. It was valued by Mr. Doherty at approximately $210,000 on the books of the company. It was sold by Shelfrack to Canadian Leasing Consultants as broker, who advanced $140,000 to Shelfrack with another $70,000 to come if Speedrack's current loss position for the fiscal years ending June 1976 and June 1977 was reversed.

This did not occur, and the $140,000 was the only advance. Canadian Leasing Consultants thus purchased the equipment and leased it back to Speedrack on the terms that I have outlined. The paper created was discounted to Commercial Credit Corporation and the equipment transferred to it, as I have indicated, Commercial Credit's recourse being, as Mr. Milligan said, not against Canadian Leasing Consultants but against Speedrack. I am unable to find that either Canadian Leasing Consultants or Commercial Credit Corporation Limited had any interest in the equipment as inventory, i.e., for general leasing to others. Indeed, the dies were of use only to Speedrack and Shelfrack, as they are used for a particular design of product called "Shelfrack" covered by a United States patent, which is pending in Canada; other items of the equipment could be put to other non-patented uses.

The only direct evidence of the intent of the parties is that of Mr. Doherty; Mr. Milligan did not take part in the negotiations, which were between Doherty and Canadian Leasing Consultants, and he had no personal knowledge of them.

On the evidence I find that Mr. Doherty set out to get cash financing on behalf of both Speedrack and Shelfrack. Canadian Leasing Consultants acted as broker, paid the initial $140,000 (which was not further supplemented), for which it took title to the equipment and leased it back to Speedrack and thereafter assigned the lease and equipment to Commercial Credit Corporation.

The lease is, in my opinion, what is commonly called a "financing lease". The purpose of the transaction is reflected in correspondence that ensued after Commercial Leasing Consultants discovered that the principals of the companies had not made certain agreed advances.

[Henry J. considered the correspondence between the parties and then concluded:]

On all the evidence I find that the whole transaction was one of financing whereby the creditors, Canadian Leasing Consultants and Commercial Credit Corporation, advanced $140,000 to Speedrack and Shelfrack acting in concert by way of a loan repayable at interest secured by the lease and the equipment. The arrangement therefore creates a security interest under s. 2(a)(ii) of the Personal Property Security Act, and registration is required to perfect it. As registration was not effected, Commercial Credit Corporation's interest is subordinated by s. 22 of the Personal Property Security Act to that of the trustee, and the trustee correctly disallowed the claim of Commercial Credit Corporation made under s. 59 of the Bankruptcy Act.

Appeal dismissed.

Interpretation Bulletin IT-233, Dept. of National Revenue (14 July 1975)

1. It is necessary to determine, with regard to leasing agreements, whether payments in respect of those agreements are in substance payments of rent or payments on account of the purchase price of property or, in the case of sale — leaseback agreements, repayments of a loan. As there is no special provision in the Income Tax Act dealing with such agreements, this determination must be made on consideration of both the written terms of the agreement (if any) and the factual circumstances relevant to both the making and execution of that agreement.

2. Individual cases will be treated in accordance with the general statements of Departmental policy that follow:

Lease-Option Agreements
3. The Department's principal interest in lease-option agreements is to see that significant sums paid for the purchase of property are not being charged against income as rent, of which no recapture can be made from a lessee who exercises his option and sells the property at a price which reimburses him for all or part of the "rent". Therefore it is necessary to determine whether or not the object of the transaction at its inception is to transfer the equity in the property to the lessee. Under conditions similar to those that follow a transaction is considered to be a sale rather than a lease:

    (a) the lessee automatically acquires title to the property after payment of a specified amount in the form of rentals,

(b) the lessee is required to buy the property from the lessor during or at the termination of the lease or is required to guarantee that the lessor will receive the full option price from the lessee or a third party (except where such guarantee is given only in respect of excessive wear and tear inflicted by the lessee),

(c) the lessee has the right during or at the expiration of the lease to acquire the property at a price which at the inception of the lease is substantially less than the probable fair market value of the property at the time or times of permitted acquisition by the lessee. An option to purchase of this nature might arise where it is exercisable within a period which is materially less than the useful life of the property with the rental payments in that period amounting to a substantial portion of the fair market value of the property at the date of inception of the lease, or

(d) the lessee has the right during or at the expiration of the lease to acquire the property at a price or under terms or conditions which at the inception of the lease is/are such that no reasonable person would fail to exercise the said option.

4. The option to purchase may be part of or separate from the lease agreement itself or may be a verbal agreement or undertaking. Where, although not specified in the agreement, it becomes apparent, for example, as a result of previous similar transactions undertaken by the parties involved, that it is the intention that the lessee be allowed to acquire the property at the termination of the lease for an amount that is less than its probable fair market value, the transaction is considered to be a sale.

5. The Department is aware that many lease contracts are in the nature of "financial leases" in which the lessor is providing a financial service only. As a result certain costs or obligations that are usually considered incidental to ownership, such as taxes, insurance, maintenance and other obligations become the responsibility of the lessee. In the Department's view the assumption of these obligations by the lessee or any other conditions of the lease that may be indicative of a sale, are not, in and by themselves, conclusive in determining whether the transaction is in substance a sale. Such conditions only add corroborative support where a transaction can be considered to be a sale under the circumstances stated in paragraph 3 above.

6. In relation to the above factors the registration of the transaction as a conditional sales contract is also not a decisive factor.

7. Where an agreement is a lease, the annual payments are made as rentals, and for income tax purposes a subsequent exercise of the option to purchase does not change their character to that of payments on account of the sale price of the property, even if the agreement provides that some part of them will be so applied should the option be exercised. Where a part of the rentals are to be so applied, for the purpose of determining whether a specified option price approximates fair market value at the time the option can be exercised, the option price is reduced by the amount of the rentals that would be applied.

8. When an agreement is, in substance, an agreement for sale, the payments made thereunder are payments on account of capital which are not deductible, as rent or otherwise, in computing income; and the purchaser's capital cost is ordinarily equal to the sum of the payments he is required to pay to the vendor.

Sale-Leaseback Agreements

10. A sale-leaseback agreement involves two separate transactions; the sale of the property to the prospective lessor and the subsequent lease of the property to the original owner. In respect of such an agreement, the Department's principal interest is in ensuring that repayments of what are in substance borrowed funds are not being charged against income as rent. Where it is apparent that the true intent of the parties is that the lessee borrow money on the security of property, the agreement is in substance a loan arrangement. Such an intent is strongly indicated where the sale price of the property is substantially different from its fair market value especially where, as would ordinarily be the case the subsequent lease of the property provides for its reacquisition by the lessee under conditions similar to those outlined in paragraph 3 above.

Note: On Hire-Purchase Agreements and Equipment Leases:*

The English conception of the hire-purchase agreement as a genuine lease with an option to purchase has created numerous difficulties, both on the contractual side and with respect to the status of the agreement as a form of chattel security. (The chattel security aspects are discussed further *infra*, chapter 20.) For a discussion of the English problems, see R.M. Goode and J.S. Ziegel, *Hire-Purchase and Conditional Sale: A Comparative Study* (1965), ch. 14. A leading textbook on the English law is that by Professor R.M. Goode, *Hire-Purchase Law and Practice* (2nd ed., 1970). Nevertheless the English hire-purchase agreement has shown remarkable powers of survival (primarily for reasons associated with s. 9 of the Factors Act, 1889 and s. 25(2) of the British Sale of Goods Act) and until recently it constituted the principal method for financing the acquisition of durable goods for business as well as consumer purposes.

This was never true in Canada. Nevertheless, until the recent statutory changes, Canadian courts generally followed the English characterization and treated such agreements as true chattel leases unless they came within the *Lee* v. *Butler* type of exception discussed in *Helby* v. *Matthews*. See, for example, *Commercial Acceptance Corp. Ltd.* v. *Regent Park Butcher Shop Ltd, infra,* chapter 24(8). English precedents were applied even though many of the provincial conditional sales acts (including Ontario's former Conditional Sales Act) defined a conditional sale** as including a bailment with an option to purchase. The Crowther Committee in England recommended in 1971 the abolition

---

* "Hire-purchase agreement" is the accepted English term for a chattel lease with an option to purchase; "equipment lease" is standard terminology in North America whether or not there is an option to purchase. Neither term is a term of art and they are not used in any technical sense in the present notes.

** Students are often perplexed by the term "conditional sale" and believe it to be some kind of contingent agreement. This is not correct. The agreement is firm and satisfies all the prerequisites of a contract of sale in SGA s. 2(1). The only contingent element is the transfer of title, which is postponed until payment of the price or performance of any other obligation by the buyer. It is this property feature therefore that makes the *sale* conditional.

of the hire-purchase agreement as a separate security device and its assimilation to other chattel security devices in a new Lending and Security Act, but this recommendation has not so far been implemented.

From an early date the Americans followed not the legal obligation test adopted in *Helby* v. *Matthews, supra*, but the intention or substantial purpose test, and this is the test adopted in UCC 1-201(37). It is also the test adopted in ss. 2 and 1(*y*) of the OPPSA, and in Interpretation Bulletin IT-233 (July 4, 1975), *supra*, under the Canadian Income Tax Act. By virtue of these provisions the test is not whether the lessee under a hire-purchase agreement or equipment lease is obliged to pay the full purchase price and whether he becomes the owner of the goods at the end of the payments, but the substantial effect of the total agreement. The test therefore is a relative one and not as easy to apply as the obligation test:

> The difference between a true lease and a security transaction lies in whether the lessee acquires an equity of ownership through his rent payments. If the lessee can never become the owner it may be argued persuasively that the transaction is certainly a true lease. But who is the owner under a finance lease? While the lessee does not acquire title, the lessor has no equity because presumably the goods will be worn out or obsolete before they revert to him. His reversion rights, in short, are meaningless. At the same time the lessee has all the benefits of ownership. [W.D. Hawkland, "The Impact of the Uniform Commercial Code on Equipment Leasing" [1972] U. of Ill. Law Forum 446 at 450.]

See further J.R. Peden, "The Treatment of Equipment Leases as Security Agreements under the Uniform Commercial Code" (1971) 13 Wm. & Mary L. Rev. 110 and Goode and Ziegel, *op. cit.* ch. 14.

The difference between the two tests is illustrated by the following examples:

(a)   The "rental" payments are equal to the cash price of the goods and at the end of the lease period the lessee is entitled to purchase the goods on paying a token sum which does not represent their estimated depreciated value: *Borromée Marcotte* v. *M.N.R.* (1960) 25 Tax ABC 129; *Chibougamau Lumber Ltee* v. *M.N.R.* (1973) 73 DTC 134.

(b)   The facts are the same as in (a) save that at the end of the leasing period the lessee has the right to renew the lease at a nominal rent: *Darngavil Coal Co., Ltd.* v. *Inland Revenue* (1913) 7 Tax Cas. 1, [1913] SC 602 (Scot.).

(c)   The facts are the same as in (a) and (b) save that the option to purchase or the renewal rentals are for a substantial amount with approximate commercial market values: *Beckwith Machinery Co.* v. *Matthews* (1948) 175 ALR 1360 (Md. CA).

(d)   The facts are the same as in (a) but there is no option to purchase and no right to renew. However, the equipment has little or no foreseeable commercial value at the end of the leasing period.

Equipment leases of all types have grown greatly in value and popularity during the past decade — primarily for tax reasons but sometimes also for other reasons. Characterization of these agreements is of pervasive importance and affects inter alia the following questions: (a) the capital cost write-off of the lessor, and the tax deductibility of the lease payments as current operating expenditures to the lessee; (b) the applicability of the SGA and the scope and liability of the lessor for breach of the implied warranties of quality; (c) the applicability of the OPPSA; and (d) the rights and remedies of the lessor in case of lessee's default.

To resolve some of the problems attendant on equipment leases, the Saskatchewan and British Columbia Law Reform Commissions have made similar recommendations that leases of goods with a term of one year or more be included in the definition of "security interest" in the proposed Personal Property Security Act of their respective jurisdictions, whether or not the lease is intended as security, and be governed by all the provisions of the Act with one exception. The exception is that Part V of the Act (which deals with enforcement of the security interest) is not to apply to leases not intended as security. See Law Reform Commission of British Columbia, *Report on Debtor-Creditor Relations, Part 5 — Personal Property Security* (1975) pp. 29-32, and Law Reform Commission of Saskatchewan, *Proposals for a Saskatchewan Personal Property Security Act* (1977) pp. 7-8. The Saskatchewan recommendations have been implemented in the Saskatchewn Personal Property Security Act, SS 1979-80, c. 42. By virtue of s. 3(*b*) the Act applies, inter alia, to "a lease for a term of more than one year, notwithstanding that [it] may not secure payment or performance of an obligation." "Lease for a term of more than one year" is extensively defined in s. 2(*y*).

B. CONTRACTS FOR WORK AND MATERIALS

ROBINSON v. GRAVES
[1935] 1 KB 579, [1935] All ER Rep. 935 (CA)

The plaintiff, a portrait painter, sued to recover from the defendant the agreed fee of £262.10s for a portrait commission given him by the defendant, or damages for breach of contract.

The plaintiff relied on a verbal contract made on July 27, 1932, pursuant to which the defendant commissioned him to paint a three-quarter length portrait of a lady who subsequently became the defendant's wife. One half of the fee was to be paid in advance, and the work was to commence forthwith as the defendant was getting married in September. The lady came to the studio for a sitting and the plaintiff made rough crayon studies for the portrait and purchased canvas and other materials. The plaintiff alleged that, despite reminders, the defendant failed to pay the advance and that the defendant had subsequently wholly repudiated the contract.

The defendant in his defence denied any contract between him and the plaintiff and he also relied on the provisions of s. 4 of the Sale of Goods Act, 1893 [s. 5 of the Ontario Act].

At the trial before him Acton J. found in the facts that a verbal contract had been concluded. He also held, applying Blackburn J's judgment in *Lee* v. *Griffin* (1861) 30 LJ (QB) 252, that the contract was one for the sale of goods of the value of £10 or more, and therefore unenforceable.

The plaintiff appealed.

GREER L.J.: This appeal raises a very interesting question, which has been well argued and is not free from difficulty, having regard to the fact that there has not yet been any actual decision on the point involved in this case, though there have been in some of the cases dicta tending in one direction and in others dicta tending in the other direction. The question to be decided is this: Whether when a person goes to an artist to have a portrait painted, it may be his own portrait or the portrait of some friend (as for instance his wife), and the commission is accepted by the artist, they are making a bargain for the manufacture of future goods to be delivered when those goods come into existence in circumstances which make it a sale of goods within the meaning of s. 4 of the Sale of Goods Act, 1893, which has now taken the place of s. 17 of the Statute of Frauds relating to the sale of goods.

I propose to look at the question first without dealing with the authorities, because after all we are dealing with the meaning of the English language in the statute and its application to particular facts. I can imagine that nothing would be more surprising to a client going to a portrait painter to have his portrait painted and to the artist who was accepting the commission than to be told that they were making a bargain about the sale of goods. It is, of course, possible that a picture may be ordered in such circumstances as will make it an order for goods to be supplied in the future, but it does not follow that that is the inference to be drawn in every case as between the client and the artist. Looking at the propositions involved from the point of view of interpreting the words in the English language it seems to me that the painting of a portrait in these circumstances would not, in the ordinary use of the English language, be deemed to be the purchase and sale of that which is produced by the artist. It would, on the contrary, be held to be an undertaking by the artist to exercise such skill as he was possessed of in order to produce for reward a thing which would ultimately have to be accepted by the client. If that is so, the contract in this case was not a contract for the sale of goods within the meaning of s. 4 of the Sale of Goods Act, 1893.

There are only two cases to which I think it is necessary to refer. The first case is *Clay* v. *Yates* (1856), 1 H & N 73. That case was concerned with the question whether a contract with a printer to print and deliver a book to a customer who desired to have it printed was or was not a sale of goods. In the course of the argument Martin B. said this (at 76): "Suppose an artist paints a portrait for 300 guineas, and supplies the canvas for it, which is worth 10s., surely he might recover under a count for work and labour." I regard that as an expression of opinion by a high authority on all questions of the common law that in those circumstances there would not be any sale of goods, but there would be a contract for work and labour; and in the judgments which follow the learned judges seem to me to agree with that view, because Pollock C.B. uses these words (at 78): "My impression is, that in the case of a work of art, whether in gold, silver, marble or plaster, where the application of skill and labour is of the highest description, and the material is of no importance as compared with the labour, the price may be recovered as work, labour and materials." Alderson B. agreed with that judgment and did not find it necessary to add anything, and then Martin B. says (at 79): "I am of the same opinion. There are three matters of charge well known to the law, viz., for labour simply, for labour and materials, and for goods sold and delivered. Now every case must be judged of by itself, and what is the present case?" Then he deals with that case and agrees with the judgment that had been delivered by the Chief Baron. Bramwell B. says (at 80): "I did not hear the whole of the argument, and will not therefore give a decided opinion, but I am inclined to think the plaintiff is entitled to recover, even assuming Mr. Quain's argument to be right. The contract is to print a treatise and a dedication, the latter to be thereafter furnished. That imposed on the defendant the obligation of furnishing a dedication, such as the plaintiff could by law print." A contract to make a portrait or produce a portrait involves the fact that the person whose portrait is to be painted should contribute something, that is to say he should contribute the sittings which are necessary for the purpose of enabling the portrait to be painted.

Now it is said that that case is inconsistent with the subsequent case of *Lee* v. *Griffin* (1861) 30 LJ (QB) 252. So far as the facts of that case are concerned it affords no help to the decision of the present case, because it was concerned with the question whether, when a dentist undertakes to make a plate of false teeth — more frequently called a denture — that is or is not a sale of goods. In that case the principal part of that which the parties are dealing with is the chattel which will come into existence when such skill as may be necessary to produce it has been applied by the dentist and those who work for him; but in the course of delivering the judgments in that case Crompton J. and Hill J. said nothing whatever which would throw any doubt upon the views expressed in the earlier case of *Clay* v. *Yates*. Crompton J. says (at 253): "However, on the point which was made at the trial, whether the plaintiff could not succeed on the count for work, labour, and materials, I am also clearly of opinion against the plaintiff. Whether the cause of action be work and labour, or goods sold and delivered, depends on the particular nature of each individual contract"; and then he refers to the case of *Clay* v. *Yates* as turning upon the peculiar circumstances of the case, and concludes with these words: "I do not agree with the proposition, that whenever skill is to be exercised in carrying out the contract, that fact makes it a contract for work and labour, and not for the sale of a chattel; it may be the cause of action is for work and labour, when the materials supplied are merely ancillary, as in the case put of an attorney or printer. But in the present case the goods to be furnished, viz., the teeth, are the principal subject-matter; and the case is nearer that of a tailor, who measures for a garment and afterwards supplies the article fitted." In giving judgment Hill J. says this (at 253): "The proposition of Bayley J., that where a person has bestowed work and labour on his own materials he cannot maintain an action for work and labour, is certainly not universally true; and Tindal C.J., as well as the other members of the Court, in *Grafton* v. *Armitage*, repudiated that doctrine, and explained that Bayley J. must be regarded as speaking with reference to the particular circumstances of the case then before this Court; and the same view was taken by the Court of Exchequer in *Clay* v. *Yates*", the case to which I have already referred. It is quite true that in giving judgment Blackburn J. (to whose views on any question of contract or of common law the greatest weight is to be attached) uses these words (at 254): "The other question is, whether the present was a contract for the sale of goods, or for work and labour. In order to ascertain this you must of course, in each case, look at the contract itself. If the contract be such that it will result in the sale of a chattel, the proper form of action, if the employer refuses to accept the article when made, would be for not accepting." Lower down in his judgment he says: "An attorney employed to draw a deed is a familiar instance of the latter proposition" — that is to say where the action is for work and labour — "and it would be an abuse of language to say that the paper or parchment of the deed were goods sold and delivered." Then he quotes Tindal C.J. in *Grafton* v. *Armitage* (1845) 2 CB 336, observing of *Atkinson* v. *Bell* (1828) 8 B & C 227: "The substance of the contract was, goods to be sold and delivered by the one party to the other." I treat that judgment as indicating that in the view of Blackburn J. one has to look to the substance of the contract. If you find, as they did in *Lee* v. *Griffin*, that the substance of the contract was the production of something to be sold by the dentist to the dentist's customer, then that is a sale of goods. But if the substance of the contract, on the other hand, is that skill and labour have to be exercised for the production of the article and that it is only ancillary to that that there will pass from the artist to his client or customer some materials in addition to the skill involved in the production of the portrait, that does not make any difference to the result, because the substance of the contract is the skill and experience of the artist in producing the picture.

For these reasons I am of opinion that in this case the substance of the matter was an agreement for the exercise of skill and it was only incidental that some materials would have to pass from the artist to the gentleman who commissioned the portrait. For these reasons I think that this was not a contract for the sale of goods within the meaning of s. 4 of the Sale of Goods Act, 1893, but it was a contract for work and labour and materials.

That disposes of the subject-matter of this appeal with this exception, that it does not follow that the plaintiff is entitled, as damages, to the full amount that he would have recovered if he had been allowed to complete the contract, because there would have to be some expenditure by the artist upon the cost of the canvas and the coats of paint to be put upon the canvas, and that ought to be deducted for that as well as for release of the artist's time for other work. As no such question was raised or discussed at the trial we think that in the circumstances it is open to this Court to say that something ought to be deducted, and the damages, therefore, should be, not the 250*l.* claimed, but, say, 200*l.* We have to make a guess, and this is rather on the generous side towards the artist; but the only alternative would be to send the case back for a new trial, a course which, as I understand the argument, neither party is desirous should be taken.

For these reasons I think there ought to be judgment for the plaintiff for 200*l.* damages.

Judgment for plaintiff.

[Slesser and Roche L.JJ. delivered concurring judgments.]

Notes on Contracts for Work and Materials:

1   **OLRC Report.** The OLRC Sales Report distinguishes between two types of contract for work and materials (at pp. 45-46):

In the first case, the labour and skill are incorporated in the production of the finished chattel. In the second, however, labour or services are provided *in addition* to materials, although they constitute part of the same contract; the concept of incorporation is absent. In both types of case the question is one of characterization of the contract.

The first type of case is illustrated by a contract to have a suit made to order, the tailor providing both skill and materials which "become" the final product. In this situation, the OLRC approves of the "property" test applied by Blackburn J. in *Lee* v. *Griffith* (1861) 1 B & S 272, 30 LJQB 252, and reflected in the definition of contract of sale in SGA s. 2. The Commission disapproved of the "relative value" or "essential character" test adopted by the English Court of Appeal in *Robinson* v. *Graves, supra*, as, in their opinion (at p. 46), it

> draws an arbitrary and untenable distinction between a contract for the purchase of finished goods and a contract for an article that is to be made to the buyer's order. The essential character test, insofar as it differs from the relative value test, is equally open to criticism because it overlooks the fact that "what passes to the client is not the materials but the finished [product], of which both the work and materials are components".

The OLRC dismissed the concern that products such as portraits are different in nature from manufactured goods on the ground that the Sale of Goods Act is concerned with the transfer of title to all types of goods and not just commercial products.

The second type of "work and materials" contract is illustrated by a contract to perform work on a building, under which both materials and labour are to be supplied. In *Young & Marten Ltd.* v. *McManus Childs Ltd.* [1968] 3 WLR 630, [1969] 1 AC 454 (HL), a sub-contractor agreed to supply and install a particular brand of roof tile. The tile used by the sub-contractor (which he had purchased from a supplier) had a latent defect which caused the tiles to break in cold temperatures. The builder brought an action against the sub-contractor for breach of an implied warranty of fitness with respect to the suitability of the tiles. The House of Lords, as a matter of principle (there being a dearth of authority on the question), agreed that the sub-contractor was deemed to have given a warranty of quality. However, this warranty, by analogy to the implied conditions of merchantability and fitness in the SGA, was limited to the materials themselves. The law lords reasoned that since there was no privity between the primary contractor and the manufacturer of the tiles the plaintiff would be remediless unless he could sue the sub-contractor who had installed the tiles. The sub-contractor in turn would have his remedy over against the manufacturer. In this way the claim of liability would run without interruption from the ultimate buyer of the home to the manufacturer of the defective goods. With regard to the labour component of the contract, the sub-contractor was only held to the standard of "proper skill and care", rather than the strict liability imposed for defects in materials. See also, *Dodd and Dodd* v. *Wilson and McWilliams* [1946] 2 All ER 691 (KB) for a similar conclusion with respect to the liability of veterinarians for the injection of a contaminated serum.

The OLRC recommended that the implied warranties under the SGA be applied to goods supplied under contracts for work and materials, while the labour component in such contracts be left to judicial development. See the Draft Bill, s. 5.15(2) and Sales Report, p. 48. See also S. Waddams, "Strict Liability, Warranties, and the Sale of Goods" (1969) 19 Univ. Tor. LJ 157 for an excellent discussion of the anomalous consequences which follow when different warranty and tortious liability standards are applied in essentially similar transactions.

2   **American Approach.** The American courts have approached the issue of characterization from a functional point of view. See, for example, *Temple* v. *Keeler* (1924) 144 NE 635 (NY CA), in which it was held that when a customer "enters a restaurant, receives, eats, and pays for food, delivered to him on his order", the transaction is a sale of goods. The court reasoned that, even if services are performed, there is still a qualified sale of what is actually eaten. On the other hand, in *Perlmutter* v. *Beth David Hospital* (1954) 123 NE 2d 792 (NY CA), the same court held that a blood transfusion for which a charge was itemized on the patient's bill was not a sales transaction, since the main object sought and contracted for was the care and treatment of the patient. The supplying of blood was held to be entirely subordinate to this. Both cases involved claims for damages for breach of the implied warranty of fitness.

In *Newmark* v. *Gimbel's Inc.* (1969) 258 A 2d 697 (NJ SC) the court held that the application by a beauty parlour of a permanent wave solution, which allegedly injured the plaintiff, was a hybrid transaction involving incidents of a sale and a service. Therefore, it was reasoned, an implied warranty of fitness of the products used existed with as much force as in the case of a simple sale. The court remarked that the overall price charged took into account the value of the product, and that the no-separate-charge argument of the defendant would, if adopted, place form over substance. As this case illustrates, since the adoption of Article 2 the American courts have shown a ready disposition to assimilate near-sales to sales transactions for the purpose of applying the warranty provisions in the Code. For another familiar example, see *Hertz* v. *Transportation Credit Clearing* (1969) 298 NYS 2d 392, and *cf.* E.A. Farnsworth, "Implied Warranties of Quality in Non-Sales Cases" (1957) 57 Col. L. Rev. 653.

What functional criteria have influenced the courts in these cases? Consider the trend towards strict liability for defective products and the possible reluctance to impose strict liability on a charitable institution (such as a hospital). Are the functional criteria applied by the courts always articulated? Should they be?

3   The Retail Sales Tax Act, RSO 1970, c. 45, s. 1(13), as amended, sets out a very broad definition of "sale" encompassing, inter alia:

[any contract] whereby at a price or other consideration a person delivers to another person tangible personal property or renders to another person a taxable service [para. a];

the furnishing, preparation or service for a consideration of food, meals, or drinks [para. d];

a transfer for a consideration of the title to or possession of tangible personal property that has been produced, fabricated, printed or imprinted to the order of the purchaser [para. f].

Should the SGA adopt a similar broad definition? Consider the different purposes of the two Acts. What concerns are addressed by the SGA that lie beyond the scope of consideration of the Retail Sales Tax Act, and vice versa?

C. CONSIGNMENT AGREEMENTS, CONTRACTS OF "SALE OR RETURN", AND SALES "ON APPROVAL"

WEINER v. HARRIS
[1910] 1 KB 285, [1909] All ER Rep. 405 (CA)

The plaintiff was a manufacturing jeweller carrying on business in Hatton Garden, London. The defendant was a money-lender and pawnbroker and carried on business in Cardiff. The plaintiff brought the action to recover certain articles of jewellery pledged with the defendant by one Fisher as security for a loan.

Fisher travelled about the country selling jewellery. The articles in question had been entrusted to him by the plaintiff pursuant to the terms of a letter dated July 31, 1905, the relevant parts of which read as follows:

> I acknowledge that I have from you on sale or return the goods entered up to this date in the book labelled "Goods sent to Mr. Fisher," which is in your possession, and which I have examined, and I admit that I have to account to you for such goods. The goods referred to in the book mentioned, and all further goods you may hereafter send to me, I admit are your property, and to remain so until sold or paid for, they being only left with me for the purposes of sale or return, and not to be kept as my own stock. The goods I receive from you are to be entered at cost price, and my remuneration for selling them is agreed at one-half of the profit — i.e., I retain one-half of the difference between the price at which I sell each article and the cost price of it, and immediately I receive the price of any article sold I am to remit to you the cost price and one-half of the profit as above. It is clearly understood you have no interest in my business, and I have none in yours, and that no partnership of any kind is existing or to exist between us, and that any goods I may at any time have from you are to be returned on demand.

On the trial of the action Pickford J. held, on the construction of this letter, that there was no partnership between Fisher and the plaintiff, that title in the jewellery had never passed to Fisher and that he merely held it on a contract of sale or return, that he was not a mercantile agent entrusted with the plaintiff's goods and that accordingly the defendant was not entitled to rely on the provisions of the Factors Act, 1889. Pickford J. therefore gave judgment for the plaintiff. The defendant appealed.

COZENS-HARDY M.R.: This appeal raises a question which is undoubtedly one of some difficulty, because the document upon which everything depends has been construed by two learned judges, for whom I have the most profound respect, in a manner which I am unable to adopt. [The Master of the Rolls stated the facts, and continued:—] The only point which arises for consideration before us is what is the meaning and legal effect of a letter of July 31, 1905, upon the faith of which the business relations between the parties were carried on? That involves, before I read the letter, this important consideration: Was the transaction the ordinary well-known transaction of goods taken on sale or return, or was it a transaction under which Fisher was constituted agent for sale, with authority to sell, and bound to account to his principal for the proceeds of such sale? If it was the former, it is quite plain that the property never has passed from the plaintiff Weiner, and that Weiner is entitled to recover it; the Factors Act is altogether out of the question and does not require any consideration from us. If it was the latter, the Sale of Goods Act is equally out of the question, and we have only to consider what is the true meaning and effect of one or two sections of the Factors Act as between the plaintiff and the defendant. In my opinion this is not a transaction in which goods are sent on sale or return. It is quite plain that by the mere use of a well-known legal phrase you cannot constitute a transaction that which you attempt to describe by that phrase. Perhaps the commonest instance of all, which has come before the Courts in many phases, is this: Two parties enter into a transaction and say "It is hereby declared there is no partnership between us." The Court pays no regard to that. The Court looks at the transaction and says "Is this, in point of law, really a partnership? It is not in the least conclusive that the parties have used a term or language intended to indicate that the transaction is not that which in law it is." So here the mere fact that goods are said to be taken on sale or return is not in any way conclusive of the real nature of the contract. You must look at the thing as a whole and see whether that is the real meaning and effect of it. [The Master of the Rolls read the letter of July 31, 1905, and continued:—] In my opinion it is impossible to say, on the fair construction of that letter, that the parties ever contemplated or intended that Fisher should be the purchaser of the goods, because on the very terms of it the price could not be ascertained until after he resold them, and he was not to put them in his stock. In the ordinary transaction of purchase and sale, directly one party to the contract says "I will not return, I will elect to take the goods," he becomes the buyer. This is plainly, as it seems to me, a transaction in which Fisher had no right to buy. Fisher only had a duty towards Weiner to sell, and he was to be remunerated for his services in selling the goods by half the excess of the cost price; no more. It is all the more extraordinary because he was not even accountable to Weiner for the so-called purchase price, that is to say, the cost price plus half the sale price, until he actually received the money from the buyer. I ought not to say "the ultimate buyer," because I do not consider that Fisher was a buyer at all. Take another instance: you never hear in an ordinary transaction of sale and return that the goods are only left with the man for the purposes of sale or return and not to be kept in his own stock. Then there was the phrase, although I do not attach too much importance to it, of accounting for the goods used in a simple transaction of sale and return. I have come unhesitatingly to the conclusion that this was a transaction in which Fisher was not and could not become the buyer of the goods, but a transaction in which Fisher was employed solely as agent, and as agent was to be remunerated by a certain percentage; and the very fact that he was to be remunerated for his services is alone, I think, almost sufficient to shew that he could not be a buyer, because it is quite plain that no person who is an agent, or is to be remunerated as agent, can be allowed to buy that which he is instructed and authorized to sell.

Appeal allowed.

[Fletcher Moulton and Farwell L.JJ. delivered concurring reasons.]

RE STEPHANIAN'S PERSIAN CARPETS LIMITED
(1979) 34 CBR (NS) 35 (Ont. SC in Bkcy)

SAUNDERS J.: The dispute giving rise to these applications [to Ferron, Registrar, 31 CBR (NS) 196, now being appealed in this court] is a contest between the trustee in bankruptcy of Stephanian's Persian Carpets Limited and Anglo-Oriental Rugs Ltd. ("Anglo") with respect to 14 oriental rugs in the possession of the bankrupt at the time of its assignment. The trustee asks for a declaration that the "Consignment Agreement, or arrangement" between the bankrupt and Anglo is subordinate to the interests of the trustee by reason of it being an unperfected security interest within the meaning of the Personal Property Security Act, RSO 1970, c. 344 (the "PPSA"). Anglo counters for a declaration that it is entitled to all rights, title and interest in the rugs notwithstanding its failure to perfect "its security interest" within the meaning of the statute.

Prior to the assignment, the bankrupt carried on the business of selling oriental rugs on a retail basis. Anglo carried on the business of selling such rugs on a wholesale basis and, in the course of conducting such business, supplied rugs to the bankrupt for sale by it to third parties or for purchase on its own account. It is not disputed that the terms on which the rugs were supplied are set out in the form of a memorandum attached to the affidavit of Vahe Edouard Oundjian, the president of Anglo. Such memorandum provides as follows:

AGREEMENT
The merchandise described below is entrusted to the Consignee above mentioned upon the following terms namely: From the time of delivery thereof at Toronto until the same severally is returned to the Consignor at its place of business in Toronto or to such other address as it may require, in as good condition as when entrusted, all charges prepaid by the Consignee, or until such time as it may be sold by the Consignee as hereinafter provided, the said merchandise shall remain the property of the Consignor, and the Consignee is an absolute insurer to the Consignor of the merchandise for and against any and all hazards or risks of whatever nature and liable to the Consignor for the wholesale price thereof as indicated below. The Consignee shall pay all cartage, shipping and storage charges necessary to deliver the merchandise to him and to maintain it or to reship or reconsign the same to the Consignor; the Consignor shall have the right at any time to enter upon the premises where the merchandise may be found for the purpose of inspection and/or for the purpose of removal thereof; the Consignee may sell the merchandise in the ordinary course of his business as agent of the Consignor only at prices in excess of the wholesale prices marked below opposite each item and may retain as his commission on the sale thereof the amount realized over and above the said wholesale prices; the Consignee shall also be entitled at any time upon cash payment to the Consignor of the wholesale price of the merchandise to become the purchaser thereof himself; all monies received or collected by the Consignee for or on behalf of the Consignor shall be securely held by the Consignee as a fiduciary trust and shall not be used by the Consignee for any purpose whatsoever but shall be forthwith paid over to the Consignor; the Consignee agrees to accept responsibility for refinishing and cleaning costs on any merchandise returned in a soiled or shop-

worn condition; the Consignee agrees to render immediate reports of all sales of the merchandise and to return and deliver any part or the whole of any unsold merchandise to the Consignor at its place of business in Toronto on demand.

Upon the bankruptcy, there were 14 rugs supplied by Anglo in the possession of the bankrupt, and such rugs are now in the possession of the trustee. Anglo has not registered its interest in the rugs under the PPSA.

There are two issues on these applications:

(1) Were the fourteen rugs sold or consigned to the bankrupt? If they were sold, that is the end of the matter. The rugs are the property of the bankrupt and are properly in the possession of the trustee for liquidation and distribution to the creditors; and

(2) If the rugs were consigned by Anglo to the bankrupt and not sold, was such consignment a consignment "intended as security" within the meaning of s. 2(a)(ii) of the PPSA? If the consignment was so intended, then, as there was no registration, the trustee has priority over Anglo by reason of s. 22(1)(a)(iii) and is entitled to retain the rugs. If the consignment was not so intended, the trustee should return the rugs to Anglo.

In its simplest terms, a consignment is the sending of goods to another. An arrangement whereby an owner sends goods to another on the understanding that such other will sell the goods to a third party and remit the proceeds to the owner after deducting his compensation for effecting the sale is an example of a consignment agreement. The evidence of Mr. Oundjian is that it is "usual and customary in this business trade [the sale of oriental rugs] throughout the world" for a wholesaler to deliver rugs to a retailer for the purpose of retail sale by the retailer to consumers or purchase by the retailer for his own account with the unrestricted right to return such goods at any time prior to the sale or purchase. The evidence of Mr. Oundjian also is that approximately 50 per cent of Anglo's goods are supplied on consignment, and in para. 4 of his affidavit he states as follows:

> 4. Since the year 1971 Anglo-Oriental Rugs Ltd., has periodically consigned rugs to the Bankrupt, Stephanian's Persian Carpets Limited, on the basis that if a retail sale is consummated a predetermined price set by Anglo-Oriental Rugs Ltd., is paid to Anglo-Oriental Rugs Ltd., and if no such sale is consummated the rugs may be retained by the consignee if accounted for by it, and must be returned if demand is made by the consignor. Until such time as the goods are sold or demanded to be returned or are accounted for by the consignee, the consignee has no liability to pay for the goods.

Mr. Stephen Y. Stephanian, the president of the bankrupt, in his affidavit says at para. 5:

> 5. Oriental rugs individually are very expensive items, and most retailers would be unable to maintain very much of an inventory without some form of financing. The customary form of financing in the Oriental rugs retail trade is by way of consignment of rugs from wholesalers.

The difficulty in situations of this kind is that suppliers of goods to customers who become bankrupt are tempted to say that the goods were supplied on consignment so that they may be returned to them to the prejudice of the creditors of the bankrupt. For this reason, the arrangement between the supplier and the receiver of the goods must be carefully looked at to make sure that the arrangement does not constitute a sale. In addition to any written understanding, the actual conduct of the parties in carrying out their dealings should be considered in determining the nature of the agreement.

Under the arrangement between Anglo and the bankrupt, the bankrupt was responsible for all charges for cartage, shipping and storage and was to insure the rugs while in its possession. It was obliged to retain them "in as good condition as when entrusted". Anglo had the right to enter the premises of the bankrupt for inspection or removal of the rugs and the right to demand their return. There is no right expressed permitting the bankrupt to return the rugs to Anglo but, in my opinion, such a right may be implied from the language of the memorandum. Furthermore, it is the uncontradicted evidence of Mr. Oundjian that unsold goods were to be periodically returned or accounted for. The evidence does not disclose any obligation on the bankrupt to pay for the rugs unless he either exercised his right to purchase them or sold them to a third party. The memorandum provides that all moneys received or collected by the bankrupt for or on behalf of Anglo shall be securely held by the bankrupt as a fiduciary trust and shall not be used by the bankrupt for any purpose whatsoever but shall forthwith be paid over to Anglo. In para. 7 of this affidavit, Mr. Stephanian says:

> 7. In the course of dealings with Anglo-Oriental Rugs Ltd., Stephanian's Persian Carpets Limited would make more or less regular payments to Anglo-Oriental Rugs Ltd. on account of monies outstanding on the inventory owing to Anglo-Oriental Rugs Ltd. At no time did Anglo-Oriental Rugs Ltd. demand an accounting for the sale of individual rugs, nor was such an accounting rendered.

The bankrupt was obliged to sell at prices "in excess of the wholesale prices" of Anglo and was entitled to retain as commission the amount realized over and above such wholesale price. Such an arrangement does not of itself mean that the transaction is one of sale: see *Re Smith; Ex parte Bright* (1879) 10 Ch. D. 566 (CA).

On the basis that there was no obligation on the bankrupt to pay Anglo for the rugs until it either purchased them or sold them to a third party, and that the bankrupt had the right to return unsold rugs, I conclude that there was no sale of the rugs to the bankrupt notwithstanding that the accounting arrangements may not have been carried out in the manner contemplated by the memorandum.

The issue then to be determined is whether the arrangement is a consignment intended as security. Section 2 of the PPSA provides as follows:

• • •

Counsel for the trustee did not strenuously dispute that the arrangement, in form at least, was a consignment but drew a distinction between what he called a "true" consignment and a consignment intended as security. He argued that a true consignment was where the consignee acted as a selling agent for the consignor and was paid a commission for so doing. The purpose of such an arrangement might be to control the ultimate selling price or to maximize the return to the consignor. In the case at bar, there could be no such purpose, as the return to Anglo was fixed at the wholesale price, no matter what the retail customer paid for the rugs. In contrast, a consignment arrangement whose purpose is to alleviate a cash flow problem of the consignee (sometimes referred to as a "floor plan financing") and to provide protection to the consignor from claims of creditors of the consignee was submitted to be a consignment intended as security.

There can be many different forms of consignment arrangements, but it would appear that in the United States the courts have drawn the distinction suggested by counsel for the trustee between "true" consignments and consignments "intended as security". Such cases have arisen in the context of the American personal property law which, while similar in some respects, is not identical to the law of Ontario. It seems to me that this issue should be approached by first considering the phrase "consignment intended as security" in s. 2 of the PPSA. Three preliminary conclusions may be made:

(1) The legislature did not intend to cover all consignments but only those "intended as security";

(2) It is a common feature of all consignment arrangements that the consignor retains title to the goods. As the legislature did not intend the PPSA to apply to all consignment arrangements, it would follow that the title retention feature alone cannot render a consignment subject to the statute; and

(3) The word "security" is not defined in the PPSA, but the words "security interest" are defined in s. 1(y) as follows:

> 1. In this Act, . . .
> (y) "security interest" means an interest in goods, other than building materials that have been affixed to the realty, fixtures, documents of title, instruments, securities, chattel papers or intangibles that secures payment or performance of an obligation, and includes an interest arising from an assignment of book debts.

In order for a consignment arrangement to come within the PPSA, it must create a security interest within the meaning of s. 1(y), and, in my view, in the context of the statute, such an agreement must be intended to secure the payment or performance of an obligation on the part of the consignee.

The intention of the parties may be inferred from the language of the agreement and the conduct of their dealings. Mr. Stephanian deposes that it is his opinion that the consignment agreement was a device to provide security to Anglo for the payment of moneys outstanding for rugs provided to the bankrupt. As he states, oriental rugs are expensive, and most retailers cannot maintain an inventory without some form of financing, and the customary form of financing is by consignment. Counsel for the trustee stressed the aspect of the arrangement whereby Anglo would receive no more than its wholesale price no matter what the price at which the bankrupt was able to sell. He submitted that there could be no other purpose or function of the consignment arrangement other than to provide security to Anglo. I am not sure that it can be said that he is correct in this. In order for the rugs to be marketed, they had to be available for inspection by potential retail customers. There would appear to be a mutual advantage in the arrangement that was arrived at. Anglo was able to market its wares through the bankrupt, and the bankrupt was not required to pay unless and until there was a sale or purchase. The result of the arrangement was that Anglo was able to expose its goods for sale and the bankrupt's risk was minimized and its cash flow problem solved.

Both Mr. Stephanian and the trustee deposed that the agreement provided security to Anglo for payment for rugs supplied to the bankrupt, but I fail to see how this is so. There is no evidence that the bankrupt ever exercised its right to purchase on its own account and could only do so "upon cash payment". Accordingly, the only moneys that would be owing to Anglo from time to time would be for rugs sold and presumably delivered and hence out of the bankrupt's possession. While the accounting and payments may have been carried out at variance with the provisions of the memorandum, there is no suggestion that any payments were made or were to be made by the bankrupt except for rugs sold or purchased. I cannot see how the unsold rugs remaining in inventory provide any security to Anglo for the obligations of the bankrupt. If they were to be repossessed, Anglo would be in the same position with respect to them as when they were delivered, and presumably the payments owing for the rugs that had been sold would remain unsecured.

It is true that under the arrangement Anglo is protected from the claims of the creditors of the bankrupt, but that, in my view, is not the kind of security contemplated in the phrase "intended as security". If such were the case, all consignment agreements would be agreements intended as security, and the legislature did not intend that. It may be that, if the arrangement served no function other than to protect the consignor against creditors, it might be considered to be within the statute, but that is not the case here. The arrangement with Stephanian's provided a means for Anglo to have its products marketed, which could not be accomplished by means of a sale to Stephanian's because of cash flow problems. I conclude that the arrangement was not a consignment intended as security within the meaning of s. 2 of the PPSA and that, therefore, no registration or other compliance with that statute was required on the part of Anglo.

I recognize that I may have taken a narrow view of the ambit of the phrase "intended as security" and that, as a result, there may rarely be consignment arrangements to which the PPSA will apply. Some examples do come to mind, such as where the consignee enters into lease option arrangements with his customers remitting rental payments to the consignor. There could also be cases where the consignee was a secured party creating a situation in reverse of that contemplated by the Bills of Sale Act, RSO 1970, c. 44. As the PPSA creates rights and priorities in personal property "without regard to the person who has title to the collateral", it seems to me that a narrow construction is justified in the circumstances.

The trustee submitted that the purpose of the PPSA was to provide notice to third parties dealing with the party in possession of collateral as to the rights of others. In this case, the bankrupt appeared to the world to be the ostensible owner of the rugs. It came as a surprise to its creditors to learn that title belonged to Anglo. In the United States Commercial Code, there are provisions requiring a "true" consignor to take steps which have the effect of providing notice of his title to creditors and other third parties dealing with the consignee. It may be that the legislature will see fit to enact provisions of this nature, if thought desirable, as was done in the case of the situation described in the Bills of Sale Act.

In the result, there will be a declaration that, as against the trustee, Anglo is entitled to the 14 unsold rugs.

Appeal dismissed.

[For another decision by Saunders J. to the same effect see *Re Toyerama Ltd.* (1980) 34 CBR (NS) 153 (Ont. SC in Bkcy).]

Note on Consignment Agreements, Contracts of "Sale or Return", and Sales "on Approval":

The congeries of agreement denominated under the above titles have a common feature but also differ from each other in important respects. The common feature is that goods are delivered by their owner to a consignee for his prospective use or for sale or resale but that title is not to pass until some future event prescribed in the agreement between the parties. The differences reside in the character of the relationship established between the parties, the purpose of the agreement, and the rights of third parties dealing with the consignee. These questions cannot be answered by looking at the title which the parties themselves have attached to the agreement. Rather, as *Weiner* v. *Harris, supra,* and *Re Stephanian's Persian Carpets Ltd., supra,* make clear, the answer depends on the substance of the agreement and the fair construction of its provisions.

More particularly,

(a) the agreement is an *agency contract for sale* if the consignee of the goods undertakes to sell them as a disclosed or undisclosed agent for the owner;

(b) the agreement is a *contract of "sale or return"* if the consignee will become the buyer of the goods on a prescribed event (usually the resale of the goods by him);

(c) the agreement is a *security agreement* if, on an analysis of its terms, the consignee has agreed to buy the goods and pay their price, and title in the meantime merely remains in the consignor by way of security; and

(d) the agreement is a *sale "on approval"* if the goods are delivered for the consignee's use or consumption but he wishes to examine them or try them out before deciding whether to retain them. If he decides to retain them, or is deemed by his conduct to have so decided, the agreement ripens into a normal contract of sale.

In North American parlance the first three types of agreement are frequently referred to as "consignment agreements". It will be obvious however from the above analysis that the term is not a term of art and that it provides little guidance as to the true relationship between the parties. *Cf.* OLRC Sales Report, pp. 48-49. Nor do the existing statutory provisions. The Ontario Factors Act (RSO 1970, c. 156), which is based on the British Factors Act of 1889, determines when a "mercantile agent" can make an effective disposition of the goods in favour of a third person. SGA s. 19, r. 4 provides a presumptive rule as to when the property in the goods passes to the buyer under a contract of sale or return or sale on approval, and s. 25(2) of the Act determines his powers of disposition before the property has passed. These provisions are quite different in concept and application from the provisions of the Factors Act. Again, OPPSA, s. 2(a)(ii) provides that the Act applies to a consignment "intended as security" but provides no guidance as to how that intention is to be determined. Once again important rights and duties turn on the answer to that question.

The OLRC Sales Report, p. 49, felt that the rights of third parties dealing with the consignee should not depend on difficult questions of construction of the consignment agreement if the external appearances are the same, and ch. 12 of the Report offered some solutions. The MUPPSA Committee and the Saskatchewan Law Reform Commission reached a similar conclusion with respect to the distinction between genuine consignment agreements and consignment agreements intended as security. Accordingly SPPSA s. 3(b) now provides that the Act applies to a consignment "notwithstanding that [the consignment agreement] may not secure payment or performance of an obligation". "Consignment" is defined in s. 1(g) as follows:

> (g) "consignment" means an agreement under which goods are delivered to a person, who in the ordinary course of his business deals in goods of that description, for sale, resale or lease, by a person who:
> (i) in the ordinary course of his business deals in goods of that description; and
> (ii) reserves a proprietary interest in the goods after they have been delivered;
> but does not include an agreement under which goods are delivered to a person for sale or lease if the person is generally known in the area in which he carries on business to be selling or leasing goods of others;

The effect of these provisions is that the consignor must comply with the perfection rules in the Act and is subject to its priority rules. Part V of the Act (remedies on default) will not apply, however. Similar provisions appear in the Model Act.

For further discussion of the above issues see J.B. Colburn, "Consignment Sales and the Personal Property Security Act" (in course of publication in the Can. Bus. LJ); J.C. Macfarlane, "Sale of Goods on Consignment" (1937) 22 Proc. Can. Bar Assoc. 175; and B. Geva (1979) 25 McGill LJ 32, esp. at 53.

Chapter 3
Formation of the Contract

Introductory Note:

With modest exceptions, the SGA does not attempt to codify the rules governing the formational elements of contracts of sale. The exceptions cover the contractual capacity of infants and others (s. 3), the form of the contract (s. 4), writing requirements (s. 5), contracts concluded under a mistaken assumption that the goods exist (s. 7), and determination of the price (ss. 8-10). In other cases, the general principles of contract continue to apply. See s. 57. True to its reform spirit the Uniform Commercial Code contains a substantially larger number of formational rules. See in particular UCC 2-201 through -210; and 2-302 through -305; and 2-613.

For many years the Statute of Frauds requirement (Ont., s. 5) loomed large in the sales syllabuses of law schools and in the standard texts. In the post-war period the opinion of the legal profession has swung heavily against the utility of the requirement and, in England, s. 4 of the Sale of Goods Act (which corresponds to Ontario's s. 5) was repealed by the Law Reform (Enforcement of Contracts) Act 1954. While only British Columbia has so far followed the British precedent, there has been a marked decline in the number of reported Canadian cases in which the defence has been raised. Can you suggest why? In Ontario the OLRC has now recommended the repeal of s. 5. See Sales Report, p. 110. The Americans still have a surprisingly strong attachment to the Statute of Frauds and its sales component survived, albeit in a much modified form, the drafting of the Code. See UCC 2-201. Examine the section and consider whether it has resolved all the cases of hardship arising out of all the old section. Which of the two modern approaches do you prefer, the English or the American?

While the movement in commercial transactions has been *away* from formal requirements, the trend in consumer transactions has been strongly *towards* them. This is shown by a flock of post-war statutes, of which the Ontario Consumer Protection Act and its equivalent in the other provinces are the best known. Can you explain this paradox and, whatever the reason for the revival of interest in formal requirements in this area, do you think they accomplish their purpose? See the table following this note for a comparison of the formal requirements of the UCC, SGA, and CPA.

Interest in the contract-making process in consumer transactions is by no means confined to the evidentiary aspects and increasingly it embraces all aspects of the phenomenon. It is not difficult to see why. Nineteenth century contract law, strongly influenced by utilitarian concepts of the economy, idealized the process of private decision-making and felt that the parties to a contract were the best judges of what was in their best interests. Twentieth century developments made the assumption increasingly suspect as highly urbanized life styles, complex products and mass-produced goods replaced the personal relationships and simpler products of an earlier and still predominantly agrarian age. The problem was compounded because, paradoxically, greater influence gave the average consumer greater discretionary income and therefore made him more vulnerable to abuses in the modern marketplace.

As illustrated by the materials in this chapter, the courts and the legislatures have been challenged to fashion appropriate responses to two distinct types of problems. The first arises when a seller of goods or services takes advantage of the gullibility, weakness or ignorance of a consumer to strike a manifestly unfair bargain, or uses high-pressure sales techniques or other unethical selling practices to overcome the consumer's resistance. *W.W. Distributors & Co. Ltd.* v. *Thorsteinsen; Gaertner* v. *Fiesta Dance Studios Ltd.;* and *Trans Canada Credit Corp. Ltd.* v. *Zaluski,* reproduced in this chapter, illustrate these forms of procedural unconscionability. Many other examples will be found in chapter 5(B) under the heading of public law aspects of false advertising.

The second type of problem raises issues of substantive unconscionability. No unfair pressure has been brought to bear on the consumer to induce him to sign the contract. Nevertheless, the contract may still be objectionable because of its one-sided character and the overwhelmingly greater bargaining strength of the other party. Contracts of adhesion are the classical illustration of this type of problem.

As will be seen, the judicial reaction to both types of problem has been diverse and unpredictable as the courts have been torn between traditional respect for *pacta sunt servanda* principles and a desire to protect abused consumers. The legislative response has been much clearer. In Ontario's case, for example, the Ontario CPA addresses itself specifically to problems engendered by door-to-door sales, unsolicited goods and credit cards, "cut-off" clauses in consumer credit agreements, and disclaimers of warranty obligations in contracts of sale. Similar provisions will be found in many of the other provincial consumer protection acts.

A much more innovative approach was introduced in 1974 with the adoption of the British Columbia Trade Practices Act and the Ontario Business Practices Act. While the two Acts differ widely on points of detail they agree in seeking to substitute a generic approach to unfair or deceptive trade practices for the specifically oriented CPA provisions. In this respect they mirror comparable developments in the general contracts area as represented by such well known landmarks as UCC 2-302 and the more recent British Unfair Contract Terms Act 1977. Needless to say, the theoretical soundness of these approaches has been much debated in Canada and the U.S. For a recent exchange of Canadian views see the "Symposium on Unconscionability in Contract Law" in (1979-80) 4 Can. Bus. LJ 383 and *cf.* Michael J. Trebilcock, "An Economic Approach of Unconscionability", Study 11 in *Studies in Contract Law* (B. Reiter and J. Swan, eds., 1980), p. 379.

The present chapter concludes with discussion of an old problem accompanying the conclusion of written contracts, viz. the buyer's allegation that the nature of the document was misrepresented to him, or that there were blank spaces in the document (e.g., involving finance charges and other expenses) that were completed afterwards by the seller without the buyer's authority. What distinguishes this type of case from other abuses discussed earlier in the chapter is the fact that the consumer seeks to raise the defence in an action brought by a third party in whose favour the document has been signed or with whom the agreement may have been discounted. *Gallie* v. *Lee* (*infra*, section (D)) is not a consumer's case but it deserved to be included because it is the most recent and most comprehensive exposition of the *non est factum* doctrine. The student should examine the Ontario Consumer Protection Act to determine to what extent it has solved these and kindred problems.

A. WRITING REQUIREMENTS

COMPARISON OF STATUTORY PROVISIONS

Contents of Provision	UCC 2-201	SGA, s. 5	CPA, s. 31
1. Minimum monetary amount	$500	$40	$50
2. Extent of writing required	Some writing sufficient to indicate that a contract for sale has been made between the parties	Note or memorandum	"Executory contract" must be "in writing" and contain prescribed particulars
3. Notice of confirmation sufficient between merchants	Yes	No	Not applicable
4. Exception for specially manufactured goods	Yes	No	No
5. Alternatives to writing requirement	Yes	Yes	No
6. Disclosure of cost of credit	No	No	Yes
7. Itemization of price required	No	No	Yes

J. SCHOFIELD MANUEL LTD. v. ROSE
(1975) 9 OR (2d) 404 (Ont. Co. Ct.)

CORNISH Co. Ct. J.: The defendants, on the advice of friends, decided to retain the services of the plaintiff company, a firm of interior decorators, in furnishing their new home at 47 Rondeau Drive. After some discussion and visits by Mr.

Manuel, president of the plaintiff company, and Mrs. Christie Hansen, one of the firm's employees, Mr. Manuel supplied the Roses with three estimates of costs in duplicate.

The plaintiffs' total bills amounted to $11,758.05, particulars of which will be found in exs. 4, 5 and 6 — dated June 7, 1972, June 9, 1972, and July 31, 1972, which estimates are signed by the defendant, Douglas Rose, but not by anyone on behalf of the plaintiff company. The balance of the charges appear to be in statements found in ex. 7 and dated August 29, 1972. Payments amounted to a total of $7,902.48. The plaintiff asks for judgment for the balance owing of $3,855.57 and interest at the rate of two per cent (2%) per month on this amount and the costs of this action.

The defence of the defendants to the plaintiff's claim for this balance rests on s. 31 of the Consumer Protection Act, RSO 1970, c. 82, so I will now quote it in full except for s. 31(3) which deals with trade in situations and is irrelevant to this case:

> **31** (1) Every executory contract, other than an executory contract under an agreement for variable credit, shall be in writing and shall contain,
> (a)   the name and address of the seller and the buyer;
> (b)   a description of the goods or services sufficient to identify them with certainty;
> (c)   the itemized price of the goods or services and a detailed statement of the terms of payment;
> (d)   where credit is extended, a statement of any security for payment under the contract, including the particulars of any negotiable instrument, conditional sale agreement, chattel mortgage or any other security;
> (e)   where credit is extended, the statement required to be furnished by section 36;
> (f)   any warranty or guarantee applying to the goods or services and, where there is no warranty or guarantee, a statement to this effect; and
> (g)   any other matter required by the regulations.
>
> (2) An executory contract is not binding on the buyer unless the contract is made in accordance with this Part and the regulations and is signed by the parties, and a duplicate original copy thereof is in the possession of each of the parties thereto.

Douglas Rose signed each of these [estimates?] and returned one copy to the plaintiff and kept one copy for the use of his wife and himself.

It is to be noted that none of these documents were signed in the usual way by the plaintiff, nor do they contain a warranty or a statement that no warranty is being given, as required by s. 31(1)(f). It is open to argument prior to the work commencing that these documents are merely approved estimates and not contracts. I am of the opinion that, once the work commenced with the consent of the defendants, there can be no doubt that a contract has arisen between the parties unless such is prevented by s. 31 of the Consumer Protection Act.

In any event, the goods were delivered and the services completed by the end of August, 1972, and various payments on account were made. While the Roses expressed dissatisfaction with some of the plaintiff's work, I am of the opinion that it was only to be expected in a $10,000 contract that everything would not be completely pleasing to the customer. I find that their objections were minor and that the plaintiff did attempt to remedy these complaints. I am confirmed in this view by the fact that two months after these contracts were completed the defendants asked the plaintiff to give them an estimate on the furnishing of the den in this house.

The plaintiff made various attempts through his firm and through their lawyers (see exs. 1 and 2) to collect the balance owing, to which there was no reply, and then issued the writ in this action.

The statement of defence alleges that the defendants are not obliged to pay the balance owing on two grounds:

I.   The contract is an executory contract as defined in s. 1(*h*) of the Consumer Protection Act and since the plaintiff must comply with all the terms of s. 31 of the Act and it has not done so. The defendant does not ask for a refund of the moneys paid but merely declines to pay the balance, and thus apparently recognizes the contract as being valid and subsisting up to the amount paid but invalid as to the balance claimed as owing.

II. The prices charged by the plaintiff for goods delivered and services rendered were grossly excessive.

Let us now consider defence I: There is no doubt in my mind that the contract, if it is an executory contract as defined in s. 1(*h*), does not comply with s. 31(1)(*f*) above mentioned. This makes it unecessary for me to spend much time on the question of whether it also offends s. 31(2) in that it did not bear the signature of the plaintiff, other than to say that Mr. Kohm presented an ingenious argument which impressed me that it should be considered as having been signed by the plaintiff because it was on the letterhead of the plaintiff and signed by the defendants and adopted by the plaintiff by carrying out its terms. In support of this proposition, he cited *Cohen* v. *Roche* [1927] 1 KB 169, and other English cases quoted in the 8th edition of Cheshire and Fifoot, *The Law of Contracts* (1972), at p. 176.

Now let us consider whether this contract should be treated as an executory contract as defined in s. 1.

It is quite obvious that a contract which, at the time of signing, is an executory contract, can with the passage of time become a partly executed contract or a discharged contract or an executed contract.

In order to give this section of the Act any intelligent meaning, one must conclude that while the contract is in its executory stage the seller must comply with s. 31 and that, if he does not do so, the purchaser can consider the contract as void but that, once the contract becomes partly executed, the requirements of s. 31 are waived. If one does not adopt this interpretation, the only way one can avoid the statute producing a ridiculous result in such situations as we have here is by turning to the doctrine of *quantum meruit*.

If the framers of the statute wanted sellers to resort to *quantum meruit* to get redress in certain seller-buyer situations under the Act, they should have said so and they did not do so.

I find support for my view that this is not an "executory contract" governed by s. 31(1) by a perusal of s. 35 of the Act. This section provides that, where two-thirds of the purchase price has been paid on an executory contract, any provisions of that contract whereby the seller may retake possession of the goods upon default in payment is not enforceable except by leave of a Judge. This indicates to me that a contract must exist at the time two-thirds of the purchase price has been paid. If there was no contract at that time, title in the goods could not have passed to the purchaser and he could have no right to possession of the goods.

I have therefore come to the conclusion that the three contracts here in question are not governed by the requirements of s. 31 and are in fact binding contracts on the parties hereto.

• • •

There was a reference in argument to the proposition that the plaintiff, by reason of the failure to fully comply with s. 31, was — by s. 48 — made guilty of an offence punishable on summary conviction and hence the contract was illegal. However, s-s. (4) of s. 48 provides that: ". . . an error or omission in any form prescribed . . . by this Act or the regulations shall not be deemed to be in contravention of this Act . . .", where it is proved that "the error or omission is a *bona fide* accidental or clerical error or omission. . . ." I am satisfied that the plaintiff qualifies for this exception to the rule.

Judgment for plaintiff.

Notes and Questions:

1   Do you agree with the court's reasoning? With the result? Could the result have been reached without doing violence to the meaning of "executory contract"? Should courts have a dispensing power to waive technical breaches of the Consumer Protection Act? If so, what type of test would you recommend? Should CPA s. 48, discussed *supra*, be applied to civil as well as criminal sanctions?

2   *Disclosure Requirements.* While the purpose of the original Statute of Frauds writing requirement was primarily evidentiary (to avoid misunderstanding about the terms of the agreement and to prevent false allegations that an agreement had been concluded), modern writing requirements in consumer legislation are also intended to serve important cautionary and informational functions. The requirements in CPA s. 31, discussed in *J. Schofield Manuel Ltd.* v. *Rose, supra*, are one example. The "truth in lending" disclosure requirements in CPA, s. 36 are another. Important disclosure requirements, not necessarily of a contractual character, will be found in the regulations adopted under such federal Acts as the Food and Drugs Act, the Consumer Packaging and Labelling Act, the Textile Labelling Act, and in such provincial legislation as the Ontario New Home Warranty Plan Act 1976 and the "additional written warranties" provisions in Saskatchewan's Consumer Products Warranties Act, 1977, s. 17. Such legislation is designed, inter alia, to assist the consumer to make more informed shopping decisions, to compare products and prices, and to appreciate better what he is buying and the financial commitments that he is being asked to make.

While the notion of legislating disclosure of information from sellers and other suppliers to consumers has gained widespread acceptance, the difficulties involved in this area should not be underestimated. For a comprehensive analysis of the problem as viewed from an American perspective, see W.C. Whitford, "The Functions of Disclosure Regulations in Consumer Transactions" [1973] Wisc. L. Rev. 400. Whitford notes, for example, that almost all of the legislation in the area is aimed at the written contract, but that most consumers view the signing of the contract as little more than a formality, much like a handshake, and usually feel already morally bound to sign the contract once a verbal agreement has been reached. Whitford also observes that few consumers read the contract prior to signing and that, of those who do, many find the document incomprehensible even when the wording is specified by legislation. (See the note on "plain language" legislation, *infra*, section (C)(1)).

There are many other problems. For example, how does one aid lower-income consumers through disclosure requirements when almost all of the literature suggests that middle-class consumers are the only beneficiaries of such legislation? Given the limited physical mobility of the poor, is greater disclosure going to be of any benefit to this group if it merely reveals that better prices are available in middle-class areas which are some distance from the poorer neighbourhoods?

A significant body of consumer literature now exists with respect to the importance of information in transactional analyses. See inter alia Mackaay, "The Costliness of Information and its Effect on the Analysis of Law" in Ziegel (ed.) *Proceedings of the Seventh Annual Workshop on Commercial and Consumer Law* (1979) p. 121, and Stigler, "The Economics of Information" (1961), 69 J. Pol. Econ. 213.

B. CONSUMER PROTECTION AND THE CONTRACT MAKING PROCESS: SPECIFIC RESPONSES

W.W. DISTRIBUTORS & CO. LTD. v. THORSTEINSON
(1960) 26 DLR (2d) 365, 33 WWR 669 (Man. CA)

FREEDMAN J.A. (for the court): Although this appeal raised two or three points of law — the exploration of which doubtless have been of some interest — I feel that this case can and should be disposed of on the basis of its particular facts.

Those facts show that the plaintiff (the appellant) brought to Court a contract that was tainted with misrepresentation; that the sale thereunder was effected by a combined process of pressure and deception; and that the signatures of the defendants thereto were procured by deliberate non-disclosure of certain very pertinent facts.

The plaintiff is a corporation engaged in the sale of cooking utensils. The defendants are mother and daughter — the latter having been an infant on July 22, 1959, when the contract was entered into, but being now of full age. On the date mentioned she was employed as a clerk and receptionist in a Winnipeg department store. She was engaged to be married to a young man whose wife she has since become.

While at work on July 22nd the infant defendant received a telephone call from a man who was a stranger to her. He told her that he had an engagement gift which he wished to present to her. She replied that she was busy at the time but suggested that he get in touch with her at her home in the evening. The caller was a salesman employed by the plaintiff company. The evidence does not show how he came to know of the infant defendant, but it was indicated to us by counsel in argument that the newspaper announcement of the young lady's engagement was the source of his information. Here we have a clue to the pattern of operation of the plaintiff company. This was the method of securing for its salesmen an "approach" to a member of the public who might be induced to become a purchaser.

One may perhaps disapprove of such a method, but it would be wrong to say that a contract arising therefrom would necessarily be invalid. In a free enterprise economy a reasonable latitude should be allowed for the play of individual initiative and originality. Hence I do not stress too strongly the somewhat covert method by which the plaintiff succeeded in getting into communication with the defendants. It is rather to what followed thereafter that we must look if we are to determine whether the plaintiff secured a contract which should be given the support and sanction of the Court.

The plaintiff's salesman and manager arrived at the home of the defendant on July 22, 1959, about 7 p.m. When they left two hours later they had succeeded in procuring the signatures of the infant and her mother to a contract for the purchase of three items of kitchen utensils, namely, a set of Queen Anne cookware, a set of Spring Tulip flatware, and an electric skillet. At the trial of this action a thoroughly qualified expert put the aggregate value of these three items at a maximum of $145.95. On July 23, 1959 — that is to say, the day following the transaction in question — the plaintiff sued the defendants for payment under the contract. The amount claimed was $342.99. Such a claim in the circumstances becomes at once suspect. Close examination of the transaction shows that the contract cannot be maintained.

An exorbitant price is not in itself a ground for setting aside a contract of sale. But where the defence of misrepresentation has been raised, and where the evidence (p. 52) indicates a specific warranty by the salesman that the defendants "were getting good value in exchange for their money", the Court must examine the circumstances of the transaction to determine whether what occurred was mere puffery by a salesman or whether it constituted a deliberate act of deception which could vitiate the contract. If, as was assuredly the case here, the representation was part of an entire pattern of improper conduct — consisting of material misstatements on the one hand and of wilful non-disclosure on the other — the Court is more easily led to a conclusion against the validity of the contract.

The actual sale price of the three items in the contract came to $239.50. How then did the plaintiff come to sue the next day for $342.99? The answer is to be found in a number of special provisions in the contract, some of them unusual in their nature and oppressive and onerous in their effect. There was, first of all, a service charge of $22.35 which, if it stood alone, could not be regarded as particularly objectionable as the contract called for a cash payment of $50 and then monthly payments of $20 extending over a period of 10 or 11 months. But then there was a recording fee of $2, which was simply for recording the contract in the office of the plaintiff. Another provision called for 10% interest after maturity. Finally it was provided that if the contract were placed in the hands of a solicitor the defendants should pay an additional 20% as solicitor's fees. The evidence of the infant and her mother makes it plain that these special provisions were not brought to their notice in any way. It is clear, too, from the judgment of Philp, Sr. Co. Ct. J., that he accepted the testimony of the defendants. It is true, of course, that as a general rule a person who signs a contract will be bound by its terms. But the rule is not inflexible. It may be departed from in appropriate cases, of which in my view this is one. Here it is clear that the representatives of the plaintiff not only did not provide an opportunity to the defendants to read and understand the contract, but by their tactics of pressure and speed deliberately sought to deny and succeeded in denying such opportunity to them. In such circumstances the Court may grant protection on grounds of equity, the more so where one of the victims is an infant.

What occurred at the home on the evening in question emerges from the evidence. The salesman, assisted by the manager, proceeded to give the infant plaintiff a demonstration of the cookware. Attempts on her part to ask pertinent questions were blocked by speedy interruptions on the part either of the salesman or of the manager. The infant plaintiff stated that she entered into the contract only as a result of the high-pressure tactics of the two men. The evidence reveals the picture of such tactics. As for the mother, the evidence indicates how her signature was procured. She had given a cheque for $50 for the cash payment merely by way of loan to her daughter. This was openly stated at the time, and indeed at the trial was admitted by the salesman and the manager. She was not a purchaser or intending to become a purchaser, yet they asked her to sign the contract. When she demurred the salesman said, "It is not important. It doesn't really mean anything except we would like to have your name on it with your daughter's." Clearly the salesman knew better. He was fully aware that if the mother signed the contract it would mean something. His statement was a deliberate act of deception designed to procure the mother's signature to the document.

Within minutes after the two men left, the infant and her mother sought to repudiate the contract but were unable to locate any representative of the plaintiff. The next morning payment on the cheque was stopped. When the salesman, after failing in his attempt to certify the cheque, called at the defendants' home he was at once informed of the repudiation of the contract. The defendants asked him to take the goods back. This he refused to do, saying that he had no such authority. The goods, still unused, are now exhibits in Court, available for return to the plaintiff.

Misrepresentation was raised as a defence, and the evidence amply confirms it. I think it would be unjust and inequitable to hold these ladies to a contract procured in the manner in which this one was. The learned trial Judge dismissed the plaintiff's action. I would dismiss the appeal, with costs.

Appeal dismissed.

Notes on Cooling Off Legislation and Unsolicited Goods:

Cooling Off Legislation

1   *Thorsteinson* was decided before Manitoba adopted its cooling off legislation in the Manitoba Consumer Protection Act. All the provinces and many of the American jurisdictions now have such provisions. For the Ontario provisions, see CPA Pt. I, and s. 33. For a general discussion of the Canadian legislation, see R.C.C. Cuming, (1967) 32 Sask. L. Rev. 113 and *cf.* Byron Sher, (1968) 15 UCLA L Rev. 717. See also *Stubbe* v. *P.F. Collier & Son Ltd.* (1977) 74 DLR (3d) 605 (BC SC) and *Stubbe* v. *P.F. Collier & Son Ltd. (No. 2)* (1978) 85 DLR (3d) 77 (BC SC), decided under the B.C. Trade Practices Act, for a detailed description of practices held to be unfair in the door to door sale of the defendant's encyclopedias.

2   In the context of the Ontario provisions, consider the following questions:

a)   What types of sale are caught by them? Are the definitional provisions in Pt. I and s. 33 consistent with one another? What is the meaning of "solicits, negotiates or arranges for the signing by a buyer . . . at a place other than the seller's permanent place of business" in s. 33? Does "signing by a buyer" qualify "solicits, negotiates" as well as "arranges"? In what circumstances would a newspaper advertisement be deemed a solicitation?

b)   Would it be practicable to extend the concept of a cooling off period to sales concluded at trade premises? If not, what alternative means can you suggest to protect a consumer against ill-considered and impetuous decisions?

c)   What is the legal effect of a contract negotiated by an unlicensed itinerant seller? Does it make the contract totally illegal or only unenforceable against the consumer?

d)   Consider the following situations and determine to what extent the statutory provisions apply to them:
   (1)   purchase through a mail-order catalogue;
   (2)   purchase through an application form in a newspaper advertisement;
   (3)   solicitation by telephone;
   (4)   solicitation begun at consumer's home but contract completed at merchant's premises;
   (5)   contract signed at consumer's home after he has visited the merchant's premises;
   (6)   contract signed at home by consumer who took contract away for further study.

3   Consider also these problems related to the buyer's right to rescind:

a)   Where the vendor has not complied with section 31, is the right to rescind still limited to two days?

b)   How does the buyer learn of his right to rescind? *Cf. Zaluski's* case, *infra*, this chapter.

c) With respect to the two day limit, what is the position where the sale is concluded on a Friday or before a long weekend? How can the buyer notify the seller in time of his decision to rescind? What if the seller's address is not shown on the contract?

d) The right to rescind only applies if the contract is for more than $50. Is this figure too high? Too low?

e) With respect to the provision ''after the duplicate original copy of the contract first comes into the possession of the buyer'' (s. 33(1)), how does this affect mail order sales, book club subscriptions, and similar transactions?

Unsolicited Goods

A fertile source of consumer complaints over the years has been the practice of some suppliers of delivering goods such as books or periodicals that have not been requested and that are accompanied or followed by a demand for payment. Understandably, consumers were unsure of their rights and responsibilities in such circumstances. Section 46 of the Ontario CPA was enacted to give consumers some (additional) protection against claims involving unsolicited goods. Many of the other provinces have similar legislation.

What does s. 46 add to the common law position? Note the exclusions in s. 46(1)(*b*). How is the consumer to know of his or her rights under the section (or, for that matter, at common law)? If the ''contract in writing'' (s. 46(1)(*b*)(ii)) is for a consideration of more than $50, then presumably s. 31 will also apply. If it is for a lesser amount, what action by the consumer will be sufficient to show his acceptance of the goods?

GAERTNER v. FIESTA DANCE STUDIOS LTD.
(1972) 32 DLR (3d) 639 (BC SC)

MCKAY J. (orally): The plaintiff is 31 years of age, unmarried and a registered nurse. She is claiming the return of $6,506 paid by her to the defendant, Fiesta Dance Studios Limited which carries on business under several names including Fred Astaire Dance Studios. This is one of several such claims now pending in this Court against the same defendant. This case has shown the incredible gullibility of some people and the readiness of others to take advantage of that gullibility. On October 24, 1969, the plaintiff entered into a contract with Fiesta for 32 hours of dancing lessons for a fee of $126 with $21 down and $21 a month. On October 31, 1969, one week later, the plaintiff entered into a second contract. This contract superseded the original one. It provided for 37 hours of private lessons and 37 hours of group lessons. The fee was $962 with the deposit from the first contract in the amount of $21 to be applied on the fee. On November 19, 1969, three weeks later, the plaintiff entered into yet another contract with Fiesta. This one provided for a further 65 hours of private lessons and 135 hours of group lessons for a fee of $2,340. This contract was not in substitution for the contract of October 31, 1969, but was in addition to that contract. Three weeks later on December 10, 1969, there was yet another contract. This one provided for a further 75 hours of private lessons and 150 hours of group lessons for a fee of $2,573. Again, this was in addition to the earlier contracts. On February 6, 1970, seven weeks later, the plaintiff entered into a contract to take a further 20 hours of private lessons for a fee of $685. On May 27, 1970, the plaintiff entered into a contract to take a further 25 hours of private lessons and 25 hours of group lessons for a fee of $650. Again, these latter two contracts were in addition to the earlier ones.

The plaintiff took lessons two or three times a week until February 13, 1971. At that time she had unused and due to her 118 hours of private lessons and 281 hours of group lessons. Thankfully, during the signing of the later contracts one of the clauses was deleted. It was a clause to the effect that all of the lessons had to be used up within a year. This poor lady would have been dancing night and day if that clause had not been deleted. Remarkable as it may seem, she was also taking dancing lessons on the side from a teacher who had departed from Fiesta and was conducting dancing lessons on his own. The reason given by the plaintiff for ceasing to take lessons was that she was not satisfied with the calibre of instruction she was receiving. In April, 1971, however, she wrote to the defendant enclosing a doctor's certificate to the effect that she had a bad knee and requested a refund for lessons not taken. There was no mention made as to the alleged inadequacies of her dancing instructors.

The evidence disclosed that there are various standards of dancing taught in chain studios of the defendant type. A student may progress, providing his or her ability, enthusiasm and finances permit (and it seems that the latter two are the most important) from the bronze standard to the silver standard to the gold standard and thence on to several other higher and exotic categories. The contract of October 31, 1969, was to cover the bronze standard but once embarked upon this she was encouraged by her instructors and the management to incorporate some of the silver standard steps with her bronze programme under a scheme called the silver amalgamation. This was the contract of November 19, 1969. The contract of December 10, 1969, relates to membership in the Gold Key Club to which I will later refer. The contract of February 2, 1970, was to prepare the plaintiff for a dance competition in Seattle referred to as the "Seattle Dance Olympics" which competition the plaintiff later attended. The final contract of May 27, 1970, purportedly covered supplemental lessons on styling.

Evidence was given by former instructors, both male and female, as to the various techniques used to induce some of the students to sign up for more and more lessons. This evidence satisfied me that the officers and employees of the defendant company are a thoroughly unscrupulous lot preying on lonely and foolish people. However, the evidence with respect to the techniques used on this plaintiff is not such as to permit me on the authorities to order rescission of the contracts except only the contract relating to the Gold Key Club.

Leaving that contract aside for the moment, the plaintiff's complaints are, first, the inadequacy of some of the instructors and, secondly, that the instructors talked in glowing terms of her dancing ability and by this means induced her to sign up for more and more lessons. In the case of *Miller et al.* v. *Lavoie et al.* (1966) 60 DLR (2d) 495, 63 WWR 359, the present Chief Justice of this Court was dealing with a case in which the provisions of the Contracts Relief Act had been invoked. That is not the case here, but his words are in my view appropriate and I quote [at p. 501]:

> This Court exists for many purposes and one of these purposes is the protection of unsophisticated and defenceless persons against the exactions of conscienceless persons who seek to take advantage of them. This legislation provides one method of exercising that benevolent authority. But the Courts are not empowered to relieve a man of the burden of a contract he has made under no pressure and with his eyes open, merely because his contract is an act of folly.

The situation with respect to the Gold Key Club is, however, in a different category. It was a demeaning, cruel and fraudulent device used to induce certain students, including the plaintiff, to sign up for more lessons. Her instructor, Barnard, now the dance supervisor of the defendant organization, told her that because of her great ability and certain other qualities he was prepared to propose her as a member of the Gold Key Club. She was told that this was a great honour; that it was a special project of Fred Astaire's; that certain benefits would flow from membership including outings with male members of the staff; that she would, in effect, be an honorary member of the staff with certain special duties relating to new students and so on and so on. She was told she would have to dance before a three-member board of dance instructors and that the whole proceeding would have to be filmed with a movie camera and that the film would have to be sent to New York to obtain final approval of membership. She agreed to this great "honour". Arrangements were made. She appeared before a panel and danced with her partner. The movie camera was operated by the then manager of the organization. At the conclusion of this performance the staff members who had been present rushed up and congratulated her; champagne was opened; a cake was produced; still photographs were taken and then she was led off to the office of the manager at which time she was told that she had to sign up for more lessons — $2,573 worth of lessons. This, said the manager, was to bring her up to the standards required of a Gold Key Member. The plaintiff objected but finally signed. The "queen for a day" routine made it difficult for her to back out. Unknown to the plaintiff, the whole performance was carried out without film in the camera. The procedure was a standing joke among the staff members. As I said before, it was a demeaning, cruel and fraudulent hoax perpetrated on this plaintiff and the contract cannot stand.

Counsel for the plaintiff took the position that the defendant was in breach of its contract in that it failed to supply the plaintiff with competent and qualified instructors. A clause in the contract reads as follows:

> Student hereby acknowledges that studio herein obligates itself to furnish student at all times herein set forth with a competent and qualified instructor but that studio is under no obligation whatsoever and is not agreed to provide a specific or designated instructor selected by student.

This strange wording indicates either sloppiness or deviousness in draftsmanship. Assuming, but without deciding, that the clause creates an obligation to supply competent and qualified instructors, I am of the view that the staff was reasonably competent to teach at the level required and was qualified within the staff qualification structure of the defendant company.

This submission is, in my view, without merit. There will be judgment for the plaintiff in the amount of $2,573 and costs.

Judgment for plaintiff.

Note On Long-Term Contracts and Rights of Cancellation:

Gaertner's case is illustrative of a much larger number of service contracts in which consumers are persuaded, not always by reputable methods, to enter into long-term contracts involving substantial sums of money. If fraud can be shown, the consumer of course has well established common law and equitable remedies, but what if this element is missing?

The New York City Department of Consumer Affairs has produced an interesting solution. Consumer Protection Law Reg. 16 provides that consumers who cancel future service contracts may not be charged more than 5% of the total cash price of the contract up to a maximum of $50 plus a pro-rated fee for lessons or services already used. The regulation covers such service contracts as dancing lessons, reducing salons, vocational training, correspondence courses, and other contracts which have been the subject of frequent complaints. Is the regulation too Draconian? Will it discourage reputable businessmen from engaging in capital intensive forms of consumer enterprises? What criteria would you adopt to determine the type of contracts that should be subject to a right of cancellation?

The B.C. Consumer Protection Act, SBC 1977, c. 8, ss. 9 and 13, contains a modified version of the N.Y. provisions, but these were not proclaimed in force as of April 2, 1981. The new Quebec Consumer Protection Act, Stat. Que. 1978, c. 9, ss. 194-195, generally follows the N.Y. model. Sections 194-195 were proclaimed in force effective April 30, 1980.

TRANS CANADA CREDIT CORP. LTD. v. ZALUSKI
(1969) 5 DLR (3d) 702, [1969] 2 OR 496 (Ont. Co. Ct.)

LEACH Co. Ct. J.: The plaintiff claims, as a holder in due course, against the defendants, as makers of a promissory note. The defendants allege that the execution of the note was obtained by the fraudulent misrepresentation of the agent of the third party and claim over against the third party for the amount of the plaintiff's claim.

The first concern of the Court was to determine if this action was a proper one for a claim for relief over against a third party under Rule 167 [rep. & sub. O. Reg. 180/64, s. 3] of the Rules of Practice. The Court is satisfied that the third party claim is proper as the same issue was raised in *Imperial Bank of Canada* v. *Wenige* (1924) 26 OWN 327. In that case the late Rose, J., held it was proper for the defendant as maker of the note to claim over against the third party whose fraud it was alleged brought about its execution.

The plaintiff company is what is commonly known as a "finance company", and carries on business in St. Catharines and other parts of Ontario. The defendant, Peter Zaluski, is a garage mechanic, who was unemployed at the time of execution of the note. The defendants impressed the Court as being decent, simple people. The third party carries on the business of selling vacuum cleaners from door to door in the Niagara Peninsula and other parts of Canada.

On February 8, 1968, one Green, a salesman for the third party, attended at the defendant's home and Mrs. Zaluski answered the door. Green said he had something he would like to show her. Mrs. Zaluski told him if he was selling vacuum cleaners she was not interested as she had just purchased one, and furthermore her husband was out of work. Green denied he was selling vacuum cleaners, but wanted to show her a book of pictures which demonstrated the inventions of his company to ease the labour of the housewife. The ruse worked and he gained entrance to the house. Once inside he showed the booklet to Mr. and Mrs. Zaluski and their son Alan. It was apparently impressive. It showed pictures of motors, rockets and other advanced machinery. He then advised the Zaluski family he had a surprise for them, which was outside in the car. He was told not to bring it in if it was a vacuum cleaner. He then reappeared with a large box and asked them to guess what was inside it. Mr. and Mrs. Zaluski offered no guesses but Alan said he thought it was a vacuum cleaner. Green did not reply. He then opened a box and pulled out a vacuum cleaner. Mr. and Mrs. Zaluski reiterated the fact they did not want a vacuum cleaner as they had bought one a month previously. Green insisted on demonstrating it. Mr. Zaluski left for the basement in frustration, with Alan. Upon completion of the demonstration Green advised Mrs. Zaluski that he was not selling vacuum cleaners but was going to give her an opportunity to earn some money. Mrs. Zaluski, no doubt, was anxious to do so, as her husband was out of work. She allowed Green to continue with his proposal. He advised her that if she would write letters to her friends, his company would contact them and she would receive $25 for each sale of a vacuum cleaner. Green suggested thirty names and advised her if only nine persons bought, the vacuum cleaner would be hers to keep, free of charge. He further advised her he would pay the $19.90 deposit on the cleaner he would leave with her. Green then produced a conditional sales agreement (ex. 1) and a promissory note (ex. 2) which Mrs. Zaluski signed without reading. Mr. Zaluski was then called from the basement and requested to sign. Green advised him this was a chance to make some money. Upon this representation and some urging by his wife he signed the agreement and the note. He too did not read the documents. Green then prepared to leave and the defendants asked him to take the vacuum cleaner but he refused alleging he could not sell it as it was now used. The cleaner was then placed in the carton, where it remained unused to this date.

Green, before leaving, left with Mrs. Zaluski the form letter she was to write out to be sent to her friends. This letter (ex. 4) read as follows:

Dear Mary:
I know that you will be surprised to hear from me. John and I have recently been given the opportunity to see a most interesting exhibition plus a pleasant surprise and a chance to earn some extra money. I have arranged for you to have the same chance.

Mary you are under no obligation and, we feel, knowing you as we do, that you will be as impressed as we were. I have asked these people to come and see you both, and at the same time explain the contest to you.

I hope Bill will be able to arrange to see this exhibition as I am sure he would enjoy it.

Sincerely,
Joyce Smith

Mrs. Zaluski wrote out in her own handwriting 30 copies of this letter and forwarded them to the third party together with addressed envelopes. The third party then stamped the envelopes and mailed them out.

The third party on February 8, 1968, assigned the conditional sales contract and promissory note to the plaintiff who gave valuable consideration for the same.

On March 25, 1968, the defendants received a cheque for $25 from the third party representing their commission on a sale of a vacuum cleaner to one of the persons solicited by the defendant's letters. The defendants have not cashed the cheque. Shortly thereafter the defendants were contacted by the plaintiff for the payment of the first instalment on the note. This was the first notice the defendants received from the plaintiff since the transaction was carried out on February 8. The defendants have refused to pay the plaintiff and as a result this action was brought.

I shall deal firstly with the plaintiff's claim. I am satisfied on the evidence that the plaintiff is a holder in due course for valuable consideration without notice of the alleged fraudulent misrepresentation. The evidence further indicates there is no relationship between the plaintiff and the third party so as to effect the plaintiff with the inequities, as was held in *Federal Discount Corp. Ltd.* v. *St. Pierre* [1962] OR 310, 32 DLR (2d) 86.

There will therefore be judgment for the plaintiff against the defendants for $252.72 and costs and counsel fee of $25.

Turning now to the defendant's claim over against the third party. Before dealing with the alleged fraudulent aspects of this transaction, I wish to give my reason for a ruling on evidence made during the course of the trial. Counsel for the third party submitted the Court should not admit any extrinsic evidence concerning the sale as this would offend against the parol evidence rule. This was so, he submitted the conditional sales agreement provided in fine print on the reverse side in para. 13:

> There are no representations, collateral agreements, conditions or warranties, express or implied by statute or otherwise on the part of Vendor or Trans Canada Credit with respect to the property or this contract or affecting the rights of the parties other than as specifically contained herein.

It is well-established law and the general rule that where the parties have embodied the terms of their contract in a written document then extrinsic evidence is not admissible to add to, vary, subtract from or contradict the terms of the written instrument: *Phipson on Evidence*, 9th ed., p. 599.

There are, however, a number of situations in which the written instrument is not conclusive evidence of the contract alleged to be embodied in it. These situations may be recorded either as exceptions to the general rule or simply as cases falling outside the general rule: *Cross on Evidence* (1958), p. 476.

Extrinsic evidence will always be admitted to defeat a deed or written contract on the grounds of fraud or misrepresentation: *Chitty on Contracts*, p. 635, para. 633.

For the reasons given, *infra*, I am satisfied that the third party was guilty of fraudulent misrepresentation, and that the Court was correct in admitting extrinsic evidence to establish this fact.

The Court is satisfied on the evidence that the agent of the third party throughout misrepresented the transaction to the defendants. It was a clever, subtle and misleading scheme to sell a vacuum cleaner to persons who did not want one and could not afford it. From the time that Green appeared at the door until he left he stated he was not selling a vacuum cleaner but was giving the defendants an opportunity to earn money and receive a free vacuum cleaner as a bonus. The sample letter (ex. 4) verifies the subtlety of the scheme. In paragraph one it provides:

> John and I have recently been given the opportunity to see a most interesting exhibition plus a pleasant surprise and a chance to earn some extra money.

The agent Green paid the deposit which further indicates misrepresentation that the defendants would not be called on to pay.

The defendants were unwise in signing the promissory note and conditional sales agreement without reading them, but the Court is satisfied that any reasonable person subjected to such a deceptive, cunning sales scheme may have done the same.

Fraud is proved when it is shown that a false representation has been made, (1) knowingly, or (2) without belief in its truth or (3) recklessly, careless whether it be true or false. *Derry* v. *Peek* (1889) 14 App. Cas. 337. The Court is satisfied the agent Green fulfilled all these requirements amply. The third party as principal is responsible for the fraud committed by its agent within the scope of the agency: *Wilson* v. *Hotchkiss* (1901) 2 OLR 261.

The defendants will therefore have judgment against the third party for the amount of the judgment of the plaintiff against them, together with costs and a counsel fee of $25. Upon payment of the same, the defendants shall return the vacuum cleaner to the third party.

Judgment for plaintiff in action and
defendants in third party proceedings.

Note on Referral and Pyramidic Sales:

1   *Referral Sales.* The referral sales plan described in *Zaluski, supra*, is fairly typical of the genre. For other descriptions of such plans and American legislative reactions, see W.G. Magnuson and J. Carper, *The Dark Side of the Marketplace* (1968), pp. 13-16 and 73-75. (The holder-in-due-course problems arising out of such agreements are discussed *infra*, chapter 16.)

Ontario's reaction to referral sales has been divided. *The Report of the Minister's Committee on Franchising* (July 1971) recommended a regime of strict controls but not the prohibition of the practice. The government apparently thought this too cumbersome and preferred instead to follow the abolition path now adopted by most of the other provinces. See CPA, s. 46a. Section 36.4 of the Combines Investigation Act (CIA), as amended in 1975, now prohibits referral sales schemes except in respect of a scheme that is licensed or otherwise permitted by or pursuant to provincial legislation.

2   *Pyramidic Sales.* Pyramidic selling schemes are a sophisticated version of referral selling and have spawned an even greater number of abuses. As a result a substantial number of jurisdictions have adopted remedial legislation which subjects such schemes to strict licensing or prospectus clearance requirements coupled with rights of cancellation, or outlaws them altogether. In several provinces and American states the promoters have been successfully prosecuted for running an illegal lottery. For further details see Ontario, *Report of the Minister's Committee on Franchising* (July 1971).

The Committee's recommendations were implemented in the Pyramidic Sales Act, 1972 (SO 1972, c. 57). The Act was introduced because the Criminal Code had proved inadequate in controlling the proliferation of pyramidic schemes. The Pyramidic Sales Act attempted to regulate pyramidic selling by establishing, inter alia, a filing requirement and an escrow fund. The Act attracted very few filings and the decline in the popularity of pyramidic schemes — attributed to government regulation — and the desire to eliminate schemes which benefit from ''the public's inability to understand the transaction'' prompted the introduction and passage of the Pyramidic Sales Repeal Act, 1978 (SO 1978, c. 105). The Act's complicated repeal provisions freeze the escrow fund and place it under the registrar's direction, and provide for the appointment of an administrator to give notice to investors, to advise, and to set up dispute resolution procedures. The Act presumably will make the federal prohibitory legislation (CIA amendments, 1975, adding ss. 36.3-36.4) operative in Ontario with respect to future pyramidic schemes.

C. CONTRACT POLICING: A GENERALIZED DOCTRINE OF UNCONSCIONABILITY

1. JUDICIAL DEVELOPMENTS

LLOYDS BANK LTD. v. BUNDY
[1974] 3 WLR 501, [1975] QB 326 (CA)

LORD DENNING M.R.: Broadchalke is one of the most pleasing villages in England. Old Herbert Bundy, the defendant, was a farmer there. His home was at Yew Tree Farm. It went back for 300 years. His family had been there for generations. It was his only asset. But he did a very foolish thing. He mortgaged it to the bank. Up to the very hilt. Not to borrow money for himself, but for the sake of his son. Now the bank have come down on him. They have foreclosed. They want to get him out of Yew Tree Farm and to sell it. They have brought this action against him for possession. Going out means ruin for him. He was granted legal aid. His lawyers put in a defence. They said that, when he executed the charge to the bank he did not know what he was doing: or at any rate that the circumstances were such that he ought not to be bound by it. At the trial his plight was plain. The judge was sorry for him. He said he was a "poor old gentleman." He was so obviously incapacitated that the judge admitted his proof in evidence. He had a heart attack in the witness-box. Yet the judge felt he could do nothing for him. There is nothing, he said, "which takes this out of the vast range of commercial transactions." He ordered Herbert Bundy to give up possession of Yew Tree Farm to the bank. Now there is an appeal to this court. The ground is that the circumstances were so exceptional that Herbert Bundy should not be held bound.

The events before December 1969

Herbert Bundy had only one son, Michael Bundy. He had great faith in him. They were both customers of Lloyds Bank Ltd., the plaintiff, at the Salisbury branch. They had been customers for many years. The son formed a company called M.J.B. Plant Hire Ltd. It hired out earth-moving machinery and so forth. The company banked at Lloyds too at the same branch.

In 1961 the son's company was in difficulties. The father on September 19, 1966, guaranteed the company's overdraft for £1,500 and charged Yew Tree Farm to the bank to secure the £1,500. Afterwards the son's company got further into difficulties. The overdraft ran into thousands. In May 1969 the assistant bank manager, Mr. Bennett, told the son the bank must have further security. The son said his father would give it. So Mr. Bennett and the son went together to see the father. Mr. Bennett produced the papers. He suggested that the father should sign a further guarantee for £5,000 and to execute a further charge for £6,000. The father said that he would help his son as far as he possibly could. Mr. Bennett did not ask the father to sign the papers there and then. He left them with the father so that he could consider them overnight and take advice on them. The father showed them to his solicitor, Mr. Trethowan, who lived in the same village. The solicitor told the father that £5,000 was the utmost that he could sink in his son's affairs. The house was worth about £10,000 and this was half his assets. On that advice the father on May 27, 1969, did execute the further guarantee and the charge, and Mr. Bennett witnessed it. So at the end of May 1969 the father had charged the house to secure £7,500.

The events of December 1969

During the next six months the affairs of the son and his company went from bad to worse. The bank had granted the son's company an overdraft up to a limit of £10,000, but this was not enough to meet the outgoings. The son's company drew cheques which the bank returned unpaid. The bank were anxious. By this time Mr. Bennett had left to go to another branch. He was succeeded by a new assistant manager, Mr. Head. In November 1969 Mr. Head saw the son and told him that the account was unsatisfactory and that he considered that the company might have to cease operations. The son suggested that the difficulty was only temporary and that his father would be prepared to provide further money if necessary.

On December 17, 1969, there came the occasion which, in the judge's words, was "important and disastrous" for the father. The son took Mr. Head to see his father. Mr. Head had never met the father before. This was his first visit. He went prepared. He took with him a form of guarantee and a form of charge filled in with the father's name ready for signature. There was a family gathering. The father and mother were there. The son and the son's wife. Mr. Head said that the bank had given serious thought as to whether they could continue to support the son's company. But that the bank were prepared to do so in this way; (i) the bank would continue to allow the company to draw money on overdraft up to the existing level of £10,000, but the bank would require the company to pay 10 per cent of its incomings into a separate account. So that 10 per cent would not go to reduce the overdraft. Mr. Head said that this would have the effect "of reducing the level of borrowing." In other words, the bank was cutting down the overdraft. (ii) The bank would require the father to give a guarantee of the company's account in a sum of £11,000 and to give the bank a further charge on the house of £3,500, so as to bring the total charge to £11,000. The house was only worth about £10,000, so this charge for £11,000 would sweep up all that the father had.

On hearing the proposal, the father said that Michael was his only son and that he was 100 per cent behind him. Mr. Head produced the forms that had already been filled in. The father signed them and Mr. Head witnessed them there and then. On this occasion, Mr. Head, unlike Mr. Bennett, did not leave the forms with the father: nor did the father have any independent advice.

It is important to notice the state of mind of Mr. Head and of the father. Mr. Head said in evidence:

> Defendant asked me what in my opinion the company was doing wrong and company's position. I told him. I did not explain the company's affairs very fully as I had only just taken over the account. . . . Michael said that company had a number of bad debts. I was not entirely satisfied with this. I thought the trouble was more deep seated. . . . It did not occur to me that there was any conflict of interest. I thought there was no conflict of interest. I would think the defendant relied on me implicitly to advise him about the transaction as bank manager. . . . I knew he had no other assets except Yew Tree Cottage.

The father said in evidence:

> I always thought Head was genuine. I have always trusted him. . . . No discussion how business was doing that I can remember. I simply sat back and did what they said.

The solicitor, Mr. Trethowan, said of the father: "He is straightforward. Agrees with anyone. . . . I doubt if he understood all that Head explained to him."

So the father signed the papers. Mr. Head witnessed them and took them away. The father had charged the whole of his remaining asset, leaving himself with nothing. The son and his company gained a respite. But only for a short time. Five months later, in May 1970, a receiving order was made against the son.

Thereupon the bank stopped all overdraft facilities for the company. It ceased to trade. The father's solicitor, Mr. Trethowan, at once went to see Mr. Head. He said he was concerned that the father had signed the guarantee.

In due course the bank insisted on the sale of the house. In December 1971 they agreed to sell it for £9,500 with vacant possession. The family were very disappointed with this figure. It was, they said, worth much more. Estate agents were called to say so. But the judge held it was a valid sale and that the bank could take all the proceeds. The sale has not been completed because Herbert Bundy is still in possession. The bank have brought these proceedings to evict Herbert Bundy.

The general rule

Now let me say at once that in the vast majority of cases a customer who signs a bank guarantee or a charge cannot get out of it. No bargain will be upset which is the result of the ordinary interplay of forces. There are many hard cases which are caught by this rule. Take the case of a poor man who is homeless. He agrees to pay a high rent to a landlord just to get a roof over his head. The common law will not interfere. It is left to Parliament. Next take the case of a borrower in urgent need of money. He borrows it from the bank at high interest and it is guaranteed by a friend. The guarantor gives his bond and gets nothing in return. The common law will not interfere. Parliament has intervened to prevent moneylenders charging excessive interest. But it has never interfered with banks.

Yet there are exceptions to this general rule. There are cases in our books in which the courts will set aside a contract, or a transfer of property, when the parties have not met on equal terms — when the one is so strong in bargaining power and the other so weak — that, as a matter of common fairness, it is not right that the strong should be allowed to push the weak to the wall. Hitherto those exceptional cases have been treated each as a separate category in itself. But I think the time has come when we should seek to find a principle to unite them. I put on one side contracts or transactions which are voidable for fraud or misrepresentation or mistake. All those are governed by settled principles. I go only to those where there has been inequality of bargaining power, such as to merit the intervention of the court.

The categories

The first category is that of "duress of goods." A typical case is when a man is in a strong bargaining position by being in possession of the goods of another by virtue of a legal right, such as by way of pawn or pledge or taken in distress. The owner is in a weak position because he is in urgent need of the goods. The stronger demands of the weaker more than is justly due: and he pays it in order to get the goods. Such a transaction is voidable. He can recover the excess: see *Astley* v. *Reynolds* (1731) 2 Stra. 915 and *Green* v. *Duckett* (1883) 11 QBD 275. To which may be added the cases of "colore officii," where a man is in a strong bargaining position by virtue of his official position or public profession. He relies upon it so as to gain from the weaker — who is urgently in need — more than is justly due: see *Pigott's* case cited by Lord Kenyon C.J. in *Cartwright* v. *Rowley* (1799) 2 Esp. 723,

723-724; *Parker* v. *Bristol & Exeter Railway Co.* (1851) 6 Exch. 702 and *Steele* v. *Williams* (1853) 8 Exch. 625. In such cases the stronger may make his claim in good faith honestly believing that he is entitled to make his demand. He may not be guilty of any fraud or misrepresentation. The inequality of bargaining power — the strength of the one versus the urgent need of the other — renders the transaction voidable and the money paid to be recovered back: see *Maskell* v. *Horner* [1915] 3 KB 106.

The second category is that of the "unconscionable transaction." A man is so placed as to be in need of special care and protection and yet his weakness is exploited by another far stronger than himself so as to get his property at a gross undervalue. The typical case is that of the "expectant heir." But it applies to all cases where a man comes into property, or is expected to come into it — and then being in urgent need — another gives him ready cash for it, greatly below its true worth, and so gets the property transferred to him: see *Evans* v. *Llewellyn* (1787) 1 Cox 333. Even though there be no evidence of fraud or misrepresentation, nevertheless the transaction will be set aside: see *Fry* v. *Lane* (1888) 40 Ch. D. 312, 322 where Kay J. said:

> The result of the decisions is that where a purchase is made from a poor and ignorant man at a considerable undervalue, *the vendor having no independent advice*, a court of equity will set aside the transaction.

This second category is said to extend to all cases where an unfair advantage has been gained by an unconscientious use of power by a stronger party against a weaker: see the cases cited in *Halsbury's Laws of England*, 3rd ed., vol. 17 (1956), p. 682 and, in Canada, *Morrison* v. *Coast Finance Ltd.* (1966) 55 DLR (2d) 710 and *Knupp* v. *Bell* (1968) 67 DLR (2d) 256. The third category is that of "undue influence" usually so called. These are divided into two classes as stated by Cotton L.J. in *Allcard* v. *Skinner* (1887) 36 Ch. D. 145, 171. The first are those where the stronger has been guilty of some fraud or wrongful act — expressly so as to gain some gift or advantage from the weaker. The second are those where the stronger has not been guilty of any wrongful act, but has, through the relationship which existed between him and the weaker, gained some gift or advantage for himself. Sometimes the relationship is such as to raise a presumption of undue influence, such as parent over child, solicitor over client, doctor over patient, spiritual adviser over follower. At other times a relationship of confidence must be proved to exist. But to all of them the general principle obtains which was stated by Lord Chelmsford L.C. in *Tate* v. *Williamson* (1866) 2 Ch. App. 55, 61:

> Wherever two persons stand in such a relation that, while it continues, confidence is necessarily reposed by one, and the influence which naturally grows out of that confidence is possessed by the other, and this confidence is abused, or the influence is exerted to obtain an advantage at the expense of the confiding party, the person so availing himself of his position will not be permitted to retain the advantage, although the transaction could not have been impeached if no such confidential relation had existed.

Such a case was *Tufton* v. *Sperni* [1952] 2 TLR 516.

The fourth category is that of "undue pressure." The most apposite of that is *Williams* v. *Bayley* (1866) LR 1 HL 200, where a son forged his father's name to a promissory note, and by means of it, raised money from the bank of which they were both customers. The bank said to the father, in effect: "Take your choice — give us security for your son's debt. If you do take that on yourself, then it will all go smoothly: if you do not, we shall be bound to exercise pressure." Thereupon the father charged his property to the bank with payment of the note. The House of Lords held that the charge was invalid because of undue pressure exerted by the bank. Lord Westbury said, at pp. 218-219:

> A contract to give security for the debt of another, which is a contract without consideration, is above all things, a contract that should be based upon the free and voluntary agency of the individual who enters into it.

Other instances of undue pressure are where one party stipulates for an unfair advantage to which the other has no option but to submit. As where an employer — the stronger party — has employed a builder — the weaker party — to do work for him. When the builder asked for payment of sums properly due (so as to pay his workmen) the employer refused to pay unless he was given some added advantage. Stuart V.-C. said: "Where an agreement, hard and inequitable in itself, has been exacted under circumstances of pressure on the part of the person who exacts it, this court will set it aside"; see *Ormes* v. *Beadel* (1860) 2 Giff. 166, 174 (reversed on another ground, 2 De GF & J 333) and *D. & C. Builders Ltd.* v. *Rees* [1966] 2 QB 617, 625.

The fifth category is that of salvage agreements. When a vessel is in danger of sinking and seeks help, the rescuer is in a strong bargaining position. The vessel in distress is in urgent need. The parties cannot be truly said to be on equal terms. The Court of Admiralty have always recognised that fact. The "fundamental rule" is

> if the parties have made an agreement, the court will enforce it, unless it be manifestly unfair and unjust; but if it be manifestly unfair and unjust, the court will disregard it and decree what is fair and just.

See *Akerblom* v. *Price* (1881) 7 QBD 129, 133, *per* Brett L.J., applied in a striking case *The Port Caledonia and The Anna* [1903] P. 184, when the rescuer refused to help with a rope unless he was paid £1,000.

The general principles

Gathering all together, I would suggest that through all these instances there runs a single thread. They rest on "inequality of bargaining power." By virtue of it, the English law gives relief to one who, without independent advice, enters into a contract upon terms which are very unfair or transfers property for a consideration which is grossly inadequate, when his bargaining power is grievously impaired by reason of his own needs or desires, or by his own ignorance or infirmity, coupled with undue influences or pressures brought to bear on him by or for the benefit of the other. When I use the word "undue" I do not mean to suggest that the principle depends on proof of any wrongdoing. The one who stipulates for an unfair advantage may be moved solely by his own self-interest, unconscious of the distress he is bringing to the other. I have also avoided any reference to the will of the one being "dominated" or "overcome" by the other. One who is in extreme need may knowingly consent to a most improvident bargain, solely to relieve the straits in which he finds himself. Again, I do not mean to suggest that every transaction is saved by independent advice. But the absence of it may be fatal. With these explanations, I hope this principle will be found to reconcile the cases. Applying it to the present case, I would notice these points:

(1) The consideration moving from the bank was grossly inadequate. The son's company was in serious difficulty. The overdraft was at its limit of £10,000. The bank considered that its existing security was insufficient. In order to get further security, it asked the father to charge the house — his sole asset — to the uttermost. It was worth £10,000. The charge was for £11,000. That was for the benefit of the bank. But not at all for the benefit of the father, or indeed for the company. The bank did not promise to continue the overdraft or to increase it. On the contrary, it required the overdraft to be reduced. All that the company gained was a short respite from impending doom.

(2) The relationship between the bank and the father was one of trust and confidence. The bank knew that the father relied on it implicitly to advise him about the transaction. The father trusted the bank. This gave the bank much influence on the father. Yet the bank failed in that trust. It allowed the father to charge the house to his ruin.

(3) The relationship between the father and the son was one where the father's natural affection had much influence on him. He would naturally desire to accede to his son's request. He trusted his son.

(4) There was a conflict of interest between the bank and the father. Yet the bank did not realise it. Nor did it suggest that the father should get independent advice. If the father had gone to his solicitor — or to any man of business — there is no doubt that any one of them would say: "You must not enter into this transaction. You are giving up your house, your sole remaining asset, for no benefit to you. The company is in such a parlous state that you must not do it."

These considerations seem to me to bring this case within the principles I have stated. But, in case the principle is wrong, I would also say that the case falls within the category of undue influence of the second class stated by Cotton L.J. in *Allcard* v. *Skinner*, 36 Ch. D. 145, 171. I have no doubt that the assistant bank manager acted in the utmost good faith and was straightforward and genuine. Indeed the father said so. But beyond doubt he was acting in the interests of the bank — to get further security for a bad debt. There was such a relationship of trust and confidence between them that the bank ought not to have swept up his sole remaining asset into its hands — for nothing — without his having independent advice. I would therefore allow this appeal.

Appeal allowed.

[Sir Eric Sachs, in whose judgment Cairns L.J. concurred, wrote a concurring judgment resting his decision on the special relationship between the bank and Mr. Bundy.]

Notes:

1   As will be noted from Lord Denning's judgment, *supra*, a series of post-war Canadian decisions had previously embraced the concept of unconscionable bargains where the parties were not bargaining at arm's length and advantage had clearly been taken of the weakness or ignorance of one of the contracting parties to conclude a contract that was greatly to his disadvantage. See e.g., *Morrison* v. *Coast Finance Ltd.* (1966) 55 DLR (2d) 710 (BC CA); *Knupp* v. *Bell* (1968) 67 DLR (2d) 256 (Sask. CA); *Black* v. *Wilcox* (1976) 70 DLR (3d) 192 (Ont. CA); and the influential comment by B. Crawford in (1966) 44 Can. Bar Rev. 142. That being the case, what does Lord Denning's judgment add to the prior Canadian position?

2   Lord Denning's felicitous statement of the applicable principle has been generally well received by Canadian courts and it has been adopted in such cases as *McKenzie* v. *Bank of Montreal* (1975) 55 DLR (3d) 641 (OHC); aff'd 70 DLR (3d) 113 (CA); *Royal Bank* v. *Hinds* (1978) 20 OR (2d) 613 (HCJ); *Buchanan* v. *Canadian Imperial Bank of Commerce* (1979) 100 DLR (3d) 624 (BC SC), and *Harry* v. *Kreutziger* (1978) 9 BCLR 166, 95 DLR (3d) 231 (CA). On the other hand, *Bundy* was distinguished on the facts in *Royal Bank* v. *Girgulus* [1977] 6 WWR 439 (Sask. QB); rev'd on other grounds, [1979] 3 WWR 451 (CA); *Thermo-flo Corp. Ltd.* v. *Kuryluk* (1978) 84 DLR (3d) 529 (NS SC) and *Ronald Elwyn Lister Ltd.* v. *Dunlop Canada Ltd.* (1978) 19 OR (2d) 380 (HCJ).

3   An interesting approach to the generalized doctrine of unconscionability was taken by Lambert J.A. in *Harry* v. *Kreutziger, supra*. He held that the principle of unconscionability adopted in the earlier cases was "only of the most general guidance", and that the decisions in *Bundy* and *Morrison* v. *Coast Finance Ltd.* (1965) 55 DLR (2d) 710 (BC CA) were really aspects of a single question:

> whether the transaction, seen as a whole, is sufficiently divergent from community standards of commercial morality that it should be rescinded . . . [p. 177].

This question, he added, must be answered by examining fact patterns in decided cases. Cases closest in time and jurisdiction will be the most relevant in this regard. It was also appropriate to seek guidance as to community standards of commercial morality from contemporary provincial legislation and Lambert J.A. said he had taken into consideration the provisions of the B.C. Consumer Protection Act and Trade Practices Act. As a result he found the bargain before the court to be a "marked departure" from such standards and agreed that it should be rescinded.

   What, if anything, does this approach add to the doctrine of *Lloyds Bank Ltd.* v. *Bundy*?

4   There has been much discussion — and considerable confusion — with respect to whether a doctrine of unconscionability has any place in contracts between businessmen. UCC 2-302 and other post-war legislation (such as the British Unfair Contract Terms Act 1977, the provisions in the proposed revised Quebec Civil Code, and the German Standard Form Contracts Act 1976) conferring a general reviewing power on the courts, do not exclude commercial transactions. The OLRC Sales Report thought this was the correct approach and recommended that

no distinction should be drawn, either, between commercial and consumer transactions in the 2-302 version of the proposed revised Ontario Sale of Goods Act. See Report, p. 156. Do you agree?

TILDEN RENT-A-CAR CO. v. CLENDENNING
(1978) 83 DLR (3d) 400, 18 OR (2d) 601 (Ont. CA)

DUBIN J.A.: Upon his arrival at Vancouver airport, Mr. Clendenning, a resident of Woodstock, Ontario, attended upon the office of Tilden Rent-A-Car Company for the purpose of renting a car while he was in Vancouver. He was an experienced traveller and had used Tilden Rent-A-Car Company on many prior occasions. He provided the clerk employed at the airport office of Tilden Rent-A-Car Company with the minimum information which was asked of him, and produced his American Express credit card. He was asked by the clerk whether he desired additional coverage, and, as was his practice, he said "yes". A contract was submitted to him for his signature, which he signed in the presence of the clerk, and he returned the contract to her. She placed his copy of it in an envelope and gave him the keys to the car. He then placed the contract in the glove compartment of the vehicle. He did not read the terms of the contract before signing it, as was readily apparent to the clerk, and in fact he did not read the contract until this litigation was commenced, nor had he read a copy of a similar contract on any prior occasion.

The issue on the appeal is whether the defendant is liable for the damage caused to the automobile while being driven by him by reason of the exclusionary provisions which appear in the contract.

On the front of the contract are two relevant clauses set forth in box form. They are as follows:

15 Collision Damage Waiver By Customers Initials "J.C."

In consideration of the payment of 2.00 per day customers liability for damage to rented vehicle including windshield is limited to NIL. But notwithstanding payment of said fee, customer shall be fully liable for all collision damage if vehicle is used, operated or driven in violation of any of the provisions of this rental agreement or off highways serviced by federal, provincial, or municipal governments, and for all damages to vehicle by striking overhead objects.

16 I, the undersigned have read and received a copy of above and reverse side of this contract

Signature of customer or employee of customer "John T. Clendenning"

(Emphasis added.)

On the back of the contract in particularly small type and so faint in the customer's copy as to be hardly legible, there are a series of conditions, the relevant ones being as follows:

6. The customer agrees not to use the vehicle in violation of any law, ordinance, rule or regulation of any public authority.

7. The customer agrees that the vehicle will not be operated:

(a) By any person who has drunk or consumed any intoxicating liquor, whatever be the quantity, or who is under the influence of drugs or narcotics;

The rented vehicle was damaged while being driven by Mr. Clendenning in Vancouver. His evidence at trial, which was accepted by the trial Judge, was to the effect that in endeavouring to avoid a collision with another vehicle and acting out of a sudden emergency, he drove the car into a pole. He stated that although he had pleaded guilty to a charge of driving while impaired in Vancouver, he did so on the advice of counsel, and at the time of the impact he was capable of the proper control of the motor vehicle. This evidence was also accepted by the trial Judge.

Mr. Clendenning testified that on earlier occasions when he had inquired as to what added coverage he would receive for the payment of $2 per day, he had been advised that "such payment provided full non-deductible coverage". It is to be observed that the portion of the contract reproduced above does provide that "In consideration of the payment of $2.00 per day customers liability for damage to rented vehicle including windshield is limited to NIL".

A witness called on behalf of the plaintiff gave evidence as to the instructions given to its employees as to what was to be said by them to their customers about the conditions in the contract. He stated that unless inquiries were made, nothing was to be said by its clerks to the customer with respect to the exclusionary conditions. He went on to state that if inquiries were made, the clerks were instructed to advise the customer that by the payment of the $2 additional fee the customer had complete coverage "unless he were intoxicated, or unless he committed an offence under the *Criminal Code* such as intoxication".

Mr. Clendenning acknowledged that he had assumed, either by what had been told to him in the past or otherwise, that he would not be responsible for any damage to the vehicle on payment of the extra premium unless such damage was caused by reason of his being so intoxicated as to be incapable of the proper control of the vehicle, a provision with which he was familiar as being a statutory provision in his own insurance contract.

The provisions fastening liability for damage to the vehicle on the hirer, as contained in the clauses hereinbefore referred to, are completely inconsistent with the express terms which purport to provide complete coverage for damage to the vehicle in exchange for the additional premium. It is to be noted, for example, that if the driver of the vehicle exceeded the speed-limit even by one mile per hour, or parked the vehicle in a no-parking area, or even had one glass of wine or one bottle of beer, the contract purports to make the hirer completely responsible for all damage to the vehicle. Indeed, if the vehicle at the time of any damage to it was being driven off a federal, provincial or municipal highway, such as a shopping plaza for instance, the hirer purportedly would be responsible for all damage to the vehicle.

Mr. Clendenning stated that if he had known of the full terms of the written instrument, he would not have entered into such a contract. Having regard to the findings made by the trial Judge, it is apparent that Mr. Clendenning had not in fact acquiesced to such terms.

It was urged that the rights of the parties were governed by what has come to be known as "the rule in *L'Estrange* v. *F. Graucob, Ltd.*", [1934] 2 KB 394. . . .

* * *

Consensus ad idem is as much a part of the law of written contracts as it is of oral contracts. The signature to a contract is only one way of manifesting assent to contractual terms. However, in the case of *L'Estrange* v. *F. Graucob, Ltd.*, there was in fact no *consensus ad idem*. Miss L'Estrange was a proprietor of a cafe. Two salesmen of the defendant company persuaded her to order a cigarette machine to be sold to her by their employer. They produced an order form which Miss L'Estrange signed without reading all of its terms. Amongst the many clauses in the document signed by her, there was included a paragraph, with respect to which she was completely unaware, which stated "any express or implied condition, statement, or warranty, statutory or otherwise not stated herein is hereby excluded". In her action against the company she alleged that the article sold to her was unfit for the purposes for which it was sold and contrary to the *Sale of Goods Act*. The company successfully defended on the basis of that exemption clause.

Although the subject of critical analysis by learned authors (see, for example, J. R. Spencer, "Signature, Consent, and the Rule in *L'Estrange* v. *Graucob*", [1973] CLJ 104), the case has survived, and it is now said that it applies to all contracts irrespective of the circumstances under which they are entered into, if they are signed by the party who seeks to escape their provisions.

Thus, it was submitted that the ticket cases, which in the circumstances of this case would afford a ready defence for the hirer of the automobile, are not applicable.

As is pointed out in Waddams, *The Law of Contracts*, at p. 191:

> From the 19th century until recent times an extraordinary status has been accorded to the signed document that will be seen in retrospect, it is suggested, to have been excessive.

The justification for the rule in *L'Estrange* v. *F. Graucob, Ltd.*, appears to have been founded upon the objective theory of contracts, by which means parties are bound to a contract in writing by measuring their conduct by outward appearance rather than what the parties inwardly meant to decide. This, in turn, stems from the classic statement of Blackburn, J., in *Smith* v. *Hughes* (1871), LR 6 QB 597 at p. 607:

> I apprehend that if one of the parties intends to make a contract on one set of terms, and the other intends to make a contract on another set of terms, or, as it is sometimes expressed, if the parties are not *ad idem*, there is no contract, unless the circumstances are such as to preclude one of the parties from denying that he has agreed to the terms of the other. The rule of law is that stated in *Freeman* v. *Cooke* (1848), 2 Ex. 654, 154 ER 652. *If, whatever a man's real intention may be, he so conducts himself that a reasonable man would believe that he was assenting to the terms proposed by the other party, and that other party upon that belief enters into the contract with him, the man thus conducting himself would be equally bound as if he had intended to agree to the other party's terms.*

(Emphasis added.)

Even accepting the objective theory to determine whether Mr. Clendenning had entered into a contract which included all the terms of the written instrument, it is to be observed that an essential part of that test is whether the other party entered into the contract in the belief that Mr. Clendenning was assenting to all such terms. In the instant case, it was apparent to the employee of Tilden-Rent-A-Car that Mr. Clendenning had not in fact read the document in its entirety before he signed it. It follows under such circumstances that Tilden-Rent-A-Car cannot rely on provisions of the contract which it had no reason to believe were being assented to by the other contracting party.

As stated in Waddams, *The Law of Contracts,* p. 191:

> One who signs a written document cannot complain if the other party reasonably relies on the signature as a manifestation of assent to the contents, or ascribes to words he uses their reasonable meaning. But the other side of the same coin is that only a reasonable expectation will be protected. If the party seeking to enforce the document knew or had reason to know the other's mistake the document should not be enforced.

In ordinary commercial practice where there is frequently a sense of formality in the transaction, and where there is a full opportunity for the parties to consider the terms of the proposed contract submitted for signature, it might well be safe to assume that the party who attaches his signature to the contract intends by so doing to acknowledge his acquiescence to its terms, and that the other party entered into the contract upon that belief. This can hardly be said, however, where the contract is entered into in circumstances such as were present in this case.

A transaction, such as this one, is invariably carried out in a hurried, informal manner. The speed with which the transaction is completed is said to be one of the attractive features of the services provided.

The clauses relied on in this case, as I have already stated, are inconsistent with the over-all purpose for which the contract is entered into by the hirer. Under such circumstances, something more should be done by the party submitting the contract for signature than merely handing it over to be signed.

[Dubin J.A. quoted from Lord Devlin's judgment in *McCutcheon* v. *David MacBrayne Ltd.* [1964] 1 WLR 125, at 132-4, reaffirming the general rule that "a signature to a contract is conclusive" and continued]:

An analysis of the Canadian cases, however, indicates that the approach in this country has not been so rigid. In the case of *Colonial Investment Co. of Winnipeg, Man.* v. *Borland* [1911] 1 WWR 171 at p. 189, 19 WLR 588, 5 Alta. LR at p. 72 [affirmed 6 DLR 21, 2 WWR 960, 22 WLR 145, 5 Alta. LR 71], Beck, J., set forth the following propositions:

> *Consensus ad idem* is essential to the creation of a contract, whether oral, in writing or under seal, subject to this, that as between the immediate parties (and merely voluntary assigns) apparent — as distinguished from real — consent will on the ground of estoppel effect a binding obligation unless the party denying the obligation proves:

(1) That the other party knew at the time of the making of the alleged contract that the mind of the denying party did not accompany the expression of his consent; or

(2) Such facts and circumstances as show that it was not reasonable and natural for the other party to suppose that the denying party was giving his real consent and he did not in fact give it;

In commenting on the *Colonial Investment Co. of Winnipeg* v. *Borland* case, Spencer, in the article above cited, observes at p. 121:

It is instructive to compare a Canadian approach to the problem of confusing documents which are signed but not fully understood.

And at p. 122 the author concludes his article with the following analysis:

Policy considerations, but of different kinds, no doubt lay behind both the Canadian and the English approaches to this problem. The Canadian court was impressed by the abuses which would result — and, in England, *have* resulted — from enabling companies to hold ignorant signatories to the letter of sweeping exemption clauses contained in contracts in standard form. The English courts, however, were much more impressed with the danger of furnishing an easy line of defence by which liars could evade contractual liabilities freely assumed. It would be very dangerous to allow a man over the age of legal infancy to escape from the legal effect of a document he has, after reading it, signed, in the absence of any express misrepresentation by the other party of that legal effect. Forty years later, most lawyers would admit that the English courts made a bad choice between two evils.

• • •

In modern commercial practice, many standard form printed documents are signed without being read or understood. In many cases the parties seeking to rely on the terms of the contract know or ought to know that the signature of a party to the contract does not represent the true intention of the signer, and that the party signing is unaware of the stringent and onerous provisions which the standard form contains. Under such circumstances, I am of the opinion that the party seeking to rely on such terms should not be able to do so in the absence of first having taken reasonable measures to draw such terms to the attention of the other party, and, in the absence of such reasonable measures, it is not necessary for the party denying knowledge of such terms to prove either fraud, misrepresentation or *non est factum*.

In the case at bar, Tilden Rent-A-Car took no steps to alert Mr. Clendenning to the onerous provisions in the standard form of contract presented by it. The clerk could not help but have known that Mr. Clendenning had not in fact read the contract before signing it. Indeed the form of the contract itself with the important provisions on the reverse side and in very small type would discourage even the most cautious customer from endeavouring to read and understand it. Mr. Clendenning was in fact unaware of the exempting provisions. Under such circumstances, it was not open to Tilden Rent-A-Car to rely on those clauses, and it was not incumbent on Mr. Clendenning to establish fraud, misrepresentation or *non est factum*. Having paid the premium, he was not liable for any damage to the vehicle while being driven by him.

As Lord Denning stated in *Neuchatel Asphalte Co. Ltd.* v. *Barnett* [1957] 1 WLR 356 at p. 360: "We do not allow printed forms to be made a trap for the unwary."

In this case the trial Judge held that "the rule in *L'Estrange* v. *Graucob*" governed. He dismissed the action, however, on the ground that Tilden Rent-A-Car had by their prior oral representations misrepresented the terms of the contract. He imputed into the contract the assumption of Mr. Clendenning that by the payment of the premium he was "provided full non-deductible coverage unless at the time of the damage he was operating the automobile while under the influence of intoxicating liquor to such an extent as to be for the time incapable of the proper control of the automobile". Having found that Mr. Clendenning had not breached such a provision, the action was dismissed.

For the reasons already expressed, I do not think that in the circumstances of this case "the rule in *L'Estrange* v. *Graucob*" governed, and it was not incumbent upon Mr. Clendenning to prove misrepresentation.

In any event, if "the rule in *L'Estrange* v. *Graucob*" were applicable, it was in error, in my respectful opinion, to impute into the contract a provision which Tilden Rent-A-Car had not in fact represented as being a term of the contract.

As was stated in *Canadian Indemnity Co.* v. *Okanagan Mainline Real Estate Board et al.*, [1971] SCR 493 at p. 500, 16 DLR (3d) 715 at p. 720, [1971] 1 WWR 289:

> A party who misrepresents, albeit innocently, the contents or effect of a clause inserted by him into a contract cannot rely on the clause in the face of his misrepresentation:

Under such circumstances, absent the exclusionary provisions of the contract, the defendant was entitled to the benefit of the contract in the manner provided without the exclusionary provisions, and the action, therefore, had to fail.

In the result, therefore, I would dismiss the appeal with costs.

LACOURCIERE J.A. (dissenting): I have had the advantage of reading the reasons for judgment prepared for release by my brother Dubin, which relieves me of the obligation of setting out the facts in this appeal, which are not really in dispute, or the relevant clauses of the contract. In my view the printing is not difficult to read, and the presence of conditions on the reverse side of the signed contract is brought to the signatory's attention in a very clear way.

It is not in dispute that the respondent violated two conditions of the contract: he drove the company's vehicle into a post, after drinking an unrecalled quantity of alcohol between 11.30 p.m. and 2 a.m. He was given a breathalyzer test, indicating a police officer's belief, on reasonable and probable grounds, that he had committed an offence of driving a motor vehicle while his ability to drive was impaired by alcohol or after having consumed alcohol in such quantity that the proportion of alcohol in his blood exceeded the penal limit. On the advice of counsel he pleaded guilty to a charge of impaired driving. I have set this out only to show that the respondent's violation of the contractual conditions was not a mere technical breach of an admittedly strict clause.

In the wisdom of the common law there has been a traditional distinction with respect to standard form contracts between the position of a person who signed the contract and the one who did not do so. In the absence of duress, fraud or misrepresentation — and subject to the defence of *non est factum* — the former was bound by the printed conditions, even if he or she did not read them: *L'Estrange* v. *F. Graucob, Ltd.,* [1934] 2 KB 394. The non-signatory was also bound if that person knew of the existence of the conditions; in the absence of knowledge, the question of the notice given by the other party became important. The distinction rests clearly on that essential prerequisite of a contract, *consensus ad idem*. The signatory is legally bound by the plain meaning of the words to which he has given assent, whereas the non-signatory should not be deemed to have assented to unknown printed conditions, unless he was given notice of their existence: see H. B. Sales, "Standard Form Contracts", 16 Mod. LR 318 (1953).

The respondent, a frequent user of rented vehicles, could not recall what was said at the Tilden counter before he signed the agreement and initialled the collision damage waiver clause. He was aware that the contract contained writing on the back, but he claims that his attention was never drawn to the printed conditions until the action was brought against him.

After careful examination of the evidence, I am unable to agree with the learned trial Judge's conclusion that Tilden's counter-clerk misrepresented the contract. The evidence of all witnesses concerning the common practice at a car rental counter had minimal probative value, and was probably inadmissible by reason of the parol evidence rule, in addition to being, at best, secondary evidence of what passed between the parties before the signing of the written contract.

I am, therefore, in agreement with Dubin J.A., that the learned trial Judge was in error when he imported into the contract an assumption made by the respondent concerning the extent and import of the exemption clause relating to alcohol, on the basis of tenuous and doubtful evidence. Once the respondent, not claiming fraud or duress, admitted having signed the contract, the onus was on him to prove by a preponderance of acceptable evidence that the conditions were misrepresented to him. In my view, this onus was not met by the respondent. The appellant has accordingly shown reversible error in the trial below.

Although the above would be sufficient to dispose of the appeal, I feel bound to express my view on the submission made on behalf of the respondent that the contract contained such unusual and onerous exculpatory terms that the respondent is not bound by them unless the appellant proves that reasonable measures were taken to draw them to his attention. The words "onerous and unusual", used by Beck, J.A., in *Can. Bk. Commerce* v. *Foreman* [1927] 2 DLR 530 at p. 537, [1927] 1 WWR 783, 22 Alta. LR 443, correspond to the words "unreasonable or oppressive" used by Lord Denning in *Jaques* v. *Lloyd D. George & Partners Ltd.* [1968] 1 WLR 625 at p. 630. The principle developed in these cases relied upon by the appellant for the above submission, was there applied to signed documents.

I note, first, that these decisions, however persuasive they may be, have no binding effect on this Court, and that in the *Jaques* case Edmund Davies, L.J., and Cairns, J., agreed in the result, but for different reasons (misrepresentation and uncertainty) and they did not refer to Lord Denning's dicta on unreasonableness and oppression. Even Lord Denning found the clause there in question to be not merely "wholly unreasonable", but also "totally uncertain", at p. 630. He went on to find misrepresentation on the facts. In *Can. Bk. Commerce* v. *Foreman* the question of whether the defendant there understood the effect of certain exemption clauses did not arise. Beck, J.A., at p. 537, was of the opinion that the clause relied on by the plaintiff bank was not of an "onerous or special character". He did not expand on what was meant by those words.

• • •

I set out here for convenience the impugned clauses in this case:

6. The customer agrees not to use the vehicle in violation of any law, ordinance, rule or regulation of any public authority.

7. The customer agrees that the vehicle will not be operated:
   (a) By any person who has drunk or consumed any intoxicating liquor, whatever be the quantity, or who is under the influence of drugs or narcotics;
   (b) By any person who is for the time being not authorized by law or qualified to drive or operate the vehicle or under the age of 18 years in any event;
   (c) In any race, speed test or contest;
   (d) To propel or tow any vehicle;
   (e) To carry explosives or to carry radioactive material;
   (f) Outside the scope of the employment of the driver, when the driver is the employee of the customer;
   (g) At an illegal, reckless or otherwise abusive speed;
   (h) For the transportation of passengers or goods for a consideration expressed or implied;
   (i) For any illicit or prohibited trade or transportation.

These clauses are certainly not irrelevant or foreign to the contract in the sense of the *Gibaud* case. . . . They do not, for example, purport to exempt Tilden from any implied undertaking as to the roadworthy fitness of the vehicle. They are not exemptions from common law liability or statutory liability, as was the impugned clause in *Gillespie Brothers.* . . .

In this contract of bailment of a vehicle for a fixed remuneration, the customer is normally bound to take reasonable care of the vehicle, and is liable for damages caused by his negligence. This is subject to collision insurance: the customer is responsible for the deductible amount, $100 or $200, depending on location. By the payment of an additional premium, this liability of the customer is eliminated with this proviso:

. . . notwithstanding payment of said fee, customer shall be fully liable for all collision damage if vehicle is used, operated or driven in violation of any of the provisions of this rental agreement or off highways serviced by federal, provincial, or municipal governments, and for all damages to vehicle by striking overhead objects.

The clause is undoubtedly a strict one. It is not for a court to nullify its effect by branding it unfair, unreasonable and oppressive. It may be perfectly sound and reasonable from an insurance risk viewpoint, and may indeed be necessary in the competitive business of car rentals, where rates are calculated on the basis of the whole contract. On this point, see the majority judgment delivered by Lord Wilberforce in *New Zealand Shipping Co. Ltd.* v. *A.M. Satterthwaite & Co. Ltd.* [1975] AC 154 at p. 169, where it was held that the Court must give effect to the clear intent of a commercial document.

I am of the view that, even if the respondent's signature is not conclusive, the terms of the contract are not unusual, oppressive or unreasonable and are binding on the respondent. I would, therefore, allow the appeal with costs, set aside the judgment below and in lieu thereof substitute a judgment for the amount of the agreed damages and costs.

Appeal dismissed.

[Zuber J.A. concurred with Dubin J.A.]

REUBEN HASSON
"The Unconscionability Business —
A Comment on Tilden Rent-A-Car v. Clendenning"
(1979-80) 3 CBLJ 193-98

The sad fact is that, just as consideration performs an indifferent job in deciding which promises should be enforced, so does unconscionability serve as a poor device for regulating unfair provisions in standard form contracts.

It is the purpose of this brief comment to suggest that we should regulate standard form contracts which are commonly used by consumers by adopting mandatory statutory terms and conditions. These conditions would serve to protect the legitimate interests of the seller (or provider of services) as well as providing minimum protection for the buyer.

• • •

One senses that the result in the present case would have been different if the trial judge had found that the defendant was unable to control the vehicle because of intoxication. The question that then arises is why the court did not state this. The answer, of course, is that the common law tradition works by indirection and by "case-to-case sniping". The majority, rightly, felt it did not have the mandate to formulate a legislative rule. The question of what protection (if any) we want to give to people who damage cars as a result of drunken or reckless driving is a political one and it is one that should therefore be made by politicians. That point has been grasped in the area of tax discounting, an area in which there was at least one unconscionability precedent. I am not suggesting statutory standard form contracts for every single contractual transaction; there is no need, for example, to have a statutory contract dealing with alcoholics selling their property at gross undervalue, although that has been the subject of at least one reported case. I am also not opposed to using unconscionability as a means of striking out unfair provisions in standard form contracts, provided this device is recognized as being the poor second best that it is.

A Statutory Car Rental Contract

I shall resist the temptation of drafting a statutory car rental contract. I will do this because, like the judiciary, I know very little about the car rental business. Instead, I will set out the procedure that I think should be followed in drawing one up and an outline of what should be included in the contract. To deal with the procedure first: the Minister of Corporate and Consumer Affairs should consult with the car rental companies, insurance companies, Superintendent of Insurance and consumer organizations with a view to devising a statutory standard form contract. The contract should state *all* the disqualifying conditions with as much precision as possible; thus, if drunkenness is to be an excluded risk, drunkenness should be defined as precisely as possible. A disqualification which depended on the proportion of alcohol in a driver's blood would be better than one that depended on the trial judge's finding of whether the hirer was sufficiently impaired or not. Similarly, if a disqualification is to be made for driving at "an illegal, reckless or otherwise abusive speed", that speed should be quantified. If there is to be a deductible provision, the size of the deductible should be regulated.

Two arguments can be made against a statutory contract. In the first place, it might be argued that the resulting statutory contract will be an unhappy compromise between the interests of the car rental companies and consumers. This is likely to be true, but it is also true of every piece of legislation on the statute books. A statutory rental contract makes private legislation that previously was invisible and uncertain, visible and less uncertain.

The second fear that might be expressed is that a statutory standard form contract would merely restate the present horrific contract already used by car rental companies. This is a possibility but an exceedingly remote one. For one thing, it is difficult to believe that the executives of car rental companies will fight desperately to retain some of the clauses that presently appear in car rental contracts. Second, it would be a foolhardy Minister of Consumer and Corporate Affairs who would merely rubber-stamp the present car rental contracts. Experience with administrative control over insurance contracts shows that while it is difficult to counter "the significant role of industry representatives in drafting standard policies", some obnoxious clauses are removed. Further, those who are afraid of codifying contract terms, fail to take into account that we already have unfair contract terms. It is true that some of these unfair clauses can be successfully challenged but the consumer does not know which clauses will be held to be unfair and few will have the resources and tenacity of a Mr. Clendenning to pursue a challenge to the fairness of a particular clause up to the highest court in the land.

Conclusion

It is very seldom that the interests of sellers (and providers of services) and consumers coincide. It is my belief that both would benefit from having a statutory form contract. Sellers would be assured that their legitimate interests were protected and consumers would be assured of a minimum level of protection at very low cost. Judges would also benefit from a movement to statutory contracts. They would be relieved of the thankless task of having to make difficult policy judgments in situations where the relevant evidence necessary to make an informed judgment is unavailable. Practising lawyers would lose very little by the adoption of statutory form contracts, since there are more lucrative fields of law than consumer litigation. Academic commentators might well be the principal losers if we moved from the present system of "catch-as-catch-can" to a more rational system of controlling private economic power. But this seems a small price to pay. Anyway, it is not much fun criticizing judges for failing to achieve impossible goals.

Note: Professor Hasson's views about the unsuitability of the judicial mechanisms for handling any but the simplest and most obvious cases of contract unconscionability are vigorously pursued by him in "Unconscionability in Contract Law and in the New Sales Act — Confessions of a Doubting Thomas" (1979-80) 4 Can. Bus. LJ 383. For an equally spirited reply see Prof. Barry Reiter's contribution in the same symposium, "Unconscionability: Is there a Choice?", *ibid.*, 403.

Notes on Clendenning and "Plain English" Legislation:

1   In your view, does *Clendenning* really come to grips with the problem of standard form agreements containing unfair provisions? Suppose that in *Clendenning*'s case, the onerous clauses had been printed in bold type. Would this have helped Clendenning? Could he have rented a car elsewhere and, assuming he had had the time to shop around, would he have found the other rental agreements significantly different?

2   *Clendenning* is not discussed in the recent decision of the Supreme Court of Canada in *Bauer* v. *Bank of Montreal* (1980) 110 DLR (3d) 424, but the judgment of the court, written by McIntyre J., strongly suggests that he had it in mind in the following passage (at 429-30):

> To the argument that the clause was onerous and unreasonable and that the bank could not rely upon it, various arguments were advanced. It was stressed that the guarantee was on a standard bank form, that it was drawn by a party seeking to rely upon the clause, that there was inequality between the parties, and that the clause was unusual in nature. I can find no merit in this position. While it is, of course, true that the guarantee was on the bank's standard form, it is difficult to say that the clause was unusual. It was the one the bank always used and the guarantor, an experienced businessman, admitted that he had signed three previous guarantees to the bank on the same form and that he knew the general scope and purpose of the guarantee and what it would require of him. The guarantor was a customer of the bank; he had been for some years. While I suppose it could be said that there is always a degree of inequality between borrower and lender, banker and guarantor, there was no such inequality here that would void the arrangements. Nor, in my opinion, can it be said that there was any unreasonableness in the arrangement. This contract concluded between the bank and the guarantor was an ordinary commercial transaction carried out between the bank and an experienced businessman in the same manner and upon the same terms as are employed daily in such matters. The contract created no unusual or onerous burden in ordinary commercial terms. I can find no merit in this argument.

Bauer involved an action by the bank to enforce a guarantee given by Mr. Bauer. The guarantee empowered the bank to abstain from taking securities or from perfecting any security given to the bank by the debtor. Security was given but, owing to an error, it was registered in the wrong office, with the result that Mr. Bauer lost the benefit of it. The Supreme Court, affirming the decision of the Ontario Court of Appeal (85 DLR (3d) 752), upheld the validity of the exoneration clause. Do these facts suggest that *Clendenning* will be carefully circumscribed in future cases?

3   *"Plain English" legislation.* One approach to the standard form conundrum in the consumer context, recently pioneered in the U.S., is to require such contracts to be written in simple and plain terms so that the average layperson can understand them. New York State, Maine and Connecticut have so far adopted such legislation. A substantial number of other states are considering similar legislation.

The New York statute (McKinney's N.Y. 1977 Regular Session c. 747, as amended by ch. 199 in 1978, in force November 1, 1978) provides that all written consumer contracts (including residential leases) must be written "in a clear and coherent manner using words with common and every day meaning" and "appropriately divided and captioned by its various sections". Agreements involving amounts greater than $50,000 are excluded. Violation of the statute does not make the agreement void or voidable or provide a defence to an action on the agreement. However, failure to comply provides a basis for a consumer action for damages resulting from the violation plus a $50 penalty. The state attorney general is also empowered to bring an action to prohibit further violations. For further details see C. Felsenfeld and A. Siegel, *Simplified Consumer Credit Forms* (1979, with Cum. Ann. Suppl.).

For a discussion of the New York legislation as well as "plain English" legislation in general, see W.J. O'Connor, "Plain English" (1979) 34 Bus. Law. 1453 and Felsenfeld and Siegel, *op. cit.* Mr. O'Connor expresses various concerns about this new approach. He points out, inter alia, that when technical terms are fully explained in an agreement, the result is often longer than the technical version. His general conclusion is that "plain English is not only a subject whose time has arrived, but also one involving complex legal issues on which there is as yet little, if any, consensus" (at 1458). Felsenfeld and Siegel appear to be more optimistic.

The plain language movement in the U.S. seems to have originated with the efforts of some American corporations to improve customer relations and efficiency by using simplified forms. A similar trend is discernible in Canada, as several large banks and insurance companies have revised their standard form contracts using simpler language than before.

In your opinion, to what extent does plain language legislation meet the dilemma of standard form contracts? Would a more clearly written agreement, with more conspicuous warnings, have met the objections to the insurance terms in the Tilden Rent-A-Car agreement?

2. LEGISLATIVE DEVELOPMENTS: CONSUMER SALES PRACTICES LEGISLATION

The preceding pages have illustrated a broad variety of unconscionable consumer contracts and selling techniques. The list could be substantially extended as indicated in Magnuson & Carper, *The Dark Side of the Market Place* (c.u. 1968) and F.H.R. Rowell, *An Examination of Deceptive and Unethical Selling Practices in Canada* (Can. Consumer Council, 1970). Many of the contracts are objectionable because of the methods employed by the vendor (procedural unconscionability), while others attract hostility because of their one-sided and harsh terms (substantive unconscionability). Frequently both elements are present.

Until recently Canadian legislation adopted a piecemeal approach to these abuses and dealt with them largely on an individual footing. And, as we have seen, with modest exceptions Canadian courts have shown themselves reluctant to abandon traditional contract concepts, preferring instead to invoke such orthodox recipes as rescission for fraud or gross overreaching.

Ontario's Business Practices Act (SO 1974, c. 131) and the B.C. Trade Practices Act (SBC 1974, c. 96) mark a decisive shift in legislative philosophy and legal techniques. In the context of these measures consider the following issues:

(a)   Do they vest too much power in consumer protection agencies and/or the courts?

(b)   Is unconscionability or unfairness a defensible concept or does it merely sanction a new form of arbitrariness?

(c)   How helpful is the shopping list in the Ontario Business Practices Act, s. 2(2)? What is the difference between an "excessively one-sided" transaction (clause v) and "inequitable" terms and conditions (clause vi)? Could the shopping list be invoked to attack the following types of clause:
   (i)   A car rental agreement which holds the hirer responsible for any form of damage to the vehicle, whether caused through his negligence or not?
   (ii)   "Cut-off" clauses and disclaimer clauses in consumer sales contracts discounted with a finance company?
   (iii)   Acceleration clauses in consumer credit agreements?
   (iv)   A holiday "package" tour which entitles the organizer to switch airlines or hotel accommodation without giving the consumer the option to cancel his reservation?
   (v)   A subscription to a book club which obliges the member to accept and pay for the monthly selection unless he has previously notified the club that he does not wish the item?

(d)   To what extent does Ont. s. 2(2) distinguish between procedural and substantive unfairness?

(e)   What differences are there with respect to the types of transactions caught in the Ontario and B.C. Acts respectively? Does the Ontario Act embrace acts or practices not linked to a subsisting or prospective agreement, e.g., unfair collection practices by a collection agency or unfair billing practices by a department store?

(f)   What is the difference between the public and private remedies provided in the two measures?

(g)   Can the consumer under Ont. s. 4 avoid a transaction tainted with an unfair representation even though, in the case of a false advertisement, he has not seen or relied on the representation? Can he always sue for damages or is the remedy only available where the transaction has been avoided by him?

(h) Is a decision by the Commercial Registration Appeal Tribunal (CRAT) under Ont. s. 6 refusing a cease and desist order *res judicata*, thus precluding the remedy under s. 4 even though the consumer has not been a party to the proceedings before the Tribunal?

Consider also the various approaches to trade practices regulation reviewed in two studies commissioned by the federal Dept. of Corporate and Consumer Affairs: Trebilcock *et al.*, *A Study on Consumer Misleading and Unfair Trade Practices* (1976); and R.I. Cohen and J.S. Ziegel, *A Proposal for Consumer Misleading and Unfair Trade Practices Legislation for Canada* (1976), both published by the Department.

Apart from British Columbia and Ontario, five other provinces — Alberta, Manitoba, Newfoundland, Prince Edward Island and Quebec — have now adopted some type of unfair trade practices legislation. For the details see CCH, *Canadian Commercial Law Guide*, para. 15-450 *et seq.* The measures differ widely in content and even in their titles. Quebec's provisions are found in title II of the Consumer Protection Act. Manitoba's Trade Practices Inquiry Act is unusual since, as its name indicates, it does little more than authorize official inquiries into alleged marketplace abuses.

The legislation has so far generated only a modest volume of reported litigation. This is presumably because much of the action is of an administrative character — assurances of voluntary compliance, cease and desist orders, etc. — that does not involve the courts. The inaptly named Ontario Commercial Registration Appeal Tribunal has not been inundated with appeals from proposed orders by the director, and its decisions are not reported by CCH. The Ontario Business Practices Act was ruled constitutional in *R. v. F.A.D.S. of Ottawa Ltd. and Kester* (1979) 49 CCC (2d) 441 (rev'd on other grounds, (1981) 32 OR (2d) 231 (Div. Ct.) and in *Re Aamco Automatic Transmission Inc. and Simpson* (1980) 29 OR (2d) 565 (Div. Ct.). The administration of the Ontario Act is reviewed in W.A.W. Neilson, "Administrative Remedies: the Canadian Experience with Assurances of Voluntary Compliance", Lewtas Annual Lecture, Osgoode Hall Law School, Feb. 1981 (in course of publication). The degree of particularity required in the director's notice of a proposed cease and desist order were also considered in *Re Aamco, supra.*

E.P. BELOBABA
"Some Features of a Model Consumer Trade Practices Act"
in J.S. Ziegel (ed.), *Proceedings of the 7th Annual Workshop on Commercial and Consumer Law* (1979) pp. 1-9

Three provinces have now enacted what can be described as omnibus consumer unfair trade practices legislation. The British Columbia Trade Practices Act, proclaimed in force on July 5, 1974, was quickly followed by the Ontario Business Practices Act, and the Alberta Unfair Trade Practices Act. Saskatchewan is on the verge of enacting a similar trade practices statute and there are indications that other provinces are close behind.

I do not propose to embark upon an extensive comparative analysis and evaluation of these recent provincial legislative efforts. The history of the legislation, the influence of the Uniform Consumer Sales Practices Act, the extent of conceptual and structural uniformity, the general commitment to common law reform, the integrated framework of private and public enforcement vehicles, the analytical exegesis of specific statutory provisions, each of these matters has already been explored in some detail elsewhere. Some of you may already have read my article. Let me reassure you that my task today is not to retill plowed ground, but to build upon my earlier work and consider what lessons, if any, one might have learned over the last several years in the drafting and enforcement of a consumer Trade Practices Act.

Although the provincial experience to date has been understandably limited, an interim evaluation and re-appraisal is possible and worthwhile. In particular, provincial draftsmen should now be in a position to incorporate the best features of the legislation that has been enacted to date and, by doing so, come very close to a "model" trade practices statute.

I offer for your consideration my own proposal of this Model Consumer Trade Practices Act, or at least what I would consider to be the six most important features of such an Act. In a sense this is an attempt to draw together the very best of the B.C., Ontario and Alberta statutes. The Saskatchewan Trade Practices Act, although not yet enacted, was also evaluated for this statutory composite.

SIX ESSENTIAL FEATURES

(1) *A Full Scope of Scrutiny.* The Act must have a realistic focus. Its scope cannot be limited to "representations" as is currently the case in Ontario. The definitional focus should be the entire consumer transaction. Any representation or conduct, including non-disclosure, that has the capacity to deceive or mislead the consumer purchaser, should be subject to action under the Act. And this should be the case whether the representation or conduct takes place before, during or after the consumer transaction. The scope of the B.C. Act is in this respect the most sensible. The Alberta and Ontario statutes, by limiting actionability to those abusive practices that occur prior to actual agreement, are deficient in two respects: post-contractual collection practices escape regulation, and the confusion of the *Nunes Diamonds* decision regarding the availability of a tort remedy for intra-contractual misrepresentations is perpetuated.

The scope of the Ontario and Alberta statutes is deficient in two further respects. The first relates to the explicit statutory exclusion of money-lending transactions. Only the B.C. Act has sought to apply the deceptive and unconscionable trade practices protections to consumer money-lending contracts. Given the limited protection provided by the federal Small Loans Act and by provincial unconscionable transactions statutes, it is my submission that money-lending transactions should fall within the ambit of a comprehensive trade practices act. The potential for deception and unconscionability is no less significant in the lender-credit field than in the area of vendor-credit. Why limit the scope of the trade practices statute to the latter?

The second deficiency in the Ontario, Alberta and Saskatchewan legislation is the unrealistically and unjustifiably restrictive definition of "services". Again, only the B.C. Act has unequivocally included all services within its definition of "consumer transaction". The other provincial statutes, however, have limited coverage to repair, self-improvement and educational services. But what about professional services? Why shouldn't a consumer trade practices statute apply to cases of deception or unfairness in the delivery of professional services? This gap in the Ontario, Alberta and Saskatchewan statutes was obviously the inevitable consequence of deliberate and influential lobbying. And until this loop-hole is plugged, these statutes might just as well have said "no person shall engage in an unfair trade practice unless he is a member of a profession."

(2) *A Comprehensive Itemization of Prohibited Practices.* All of the provincial trade practices statutes to date have adopted the structure of the Uniform Consumer Sales Practices Act — a general prohibition of all deceptive and unconscionable practices followed by a non-exhaustive "shopping list" of specific proscriptions. Our Model Act could easily adopt any of the three statutory "shopping lists". The Alberta Act has twenty-four itemizations; both the B.C. and Ontario Acts have twenty-two. In general terms the proscribed practices are more or less uniform with a sensible range. The only questionable aspect of this second general feature of our Model Act is the extent to which the itemization of unfair trade practices should go beyond mere "procedural unconscionability" and specifically list instances of "substantive unconscionability". The Ontario Act has included three important examples of the latter and has deemed the following practices to be unfair: where the seller ought to have known that (1) there was no reasonable probability of full payment of the price, or (2) the consumer would not receive a substantial benefit from the subject-matter of the consumer transaction, or (3) the price grossly exceeded the price at which similar goods were readily obtainable by like consumers elsewhere. These three itemizations make it quite clear that the trade practices "shopping lists" are intended not only as vehicles for the clarification of the common law but also as guidelines for its extension. The question here is whether we will be able to rely upon judicial interpretation of such highly open-textured guidelines as "substantial benefit", "excessively one-sided", "grossly over-priced", or will we require the implementation of a rule-making facility to give suppliers and consumers the necessary definitional specificity. I will return to this point.

My only immediate concern here is the extent to which our Model Act should allow additions to, or exemptions from, the shopping list proscriptions. Clearly, there ought to be a mechanism that would allow the government to respond quickly to innovative market-place abuses. The B.C. Act has dealt with this need sensibly. It permits the provincial Cabinet to add to both the deceptive and unconscionable practices shopping lists by regulation. The Ontario Act is more limited in this respect; the power to add by regulation applies only to the deceptive practices listing. The Alberta and Saskatchewan statutes make no provision for adding to the itemizations of prohibited practices. These are serious deficiencies.

One final pitfall that should be avoided appears in all four statutes. The Lieutenant-Governor-in-Council has been given the power to exempt by regulation certain suppliers or types of consumer transactions from the operation and application of the legislation. The potential dangers are self-evident. Even if one could hypothesize a situation where the public interest would tolerate business practices that were otherwise deceptive or unconscionable, why should exemption be available simply by executive action? The sensible and politically more accountable approach would place any exempting power with the full Legislature; otherwise the inevitable lobbies and special interest pressures could render even a Model Act useless in no time at all.

(3) *A Full Range of Private Remedies.* This may be the single most important feature of any trade practices statute. The need to legislatively encourage and facilitate consumer redress initiatives is becoming increasingly important. A trade practices statute that fails to provide a full range of civil remedies for the individually motivated consumer, fails fundamentally. In this respect, the Ontario Act is glaringly deficient. Whatever provincial draftsmen may do with their private remedies provisions, they should at all costs avoid the legislative horror show that is section 4(1) of the Ontario Business Practices Act. One will search in vain for a provision in a Canadian consumer protection statute that is more restrictive or more obscure than Ontario's section 4(1). The less said about it the better. Fortunately, the B.C. and Alberta Acts have provided a more sensible range of private remedies, including injunctive and declaratory relief, rescission, damages and a flexibly worded direction empowering the court to make such other orders or judgments as may be necessary to achieve a just result. Both the B.C. and Alberta statutes also permit awards of punitive damages. All of these features would be essential elements of a model private remedies provision.

Of course, to make private redress meaningful, the financial disincentives that currently frustrate or impede consumer initiative would have to be eliminated or at least minimized. Minimum recovery provisions, treble damages, consumer class actions, each of these incentives has been advocated and in some cases implemented south of the border. To what extent will their adoption remove the existing barriers to private redress? The American experience has been mixed but one thing is indisputably clear: we can no longer draft civil remedy provisions in a statutory vacuum that refuses to recognize the real world of financial barriers. Either we take private initiative seriously and provide the necessary incentives or we should statutorily concede the impotence of consumer initiative.

(4) *Effective Administrative Remedies.* The importance of comprehensive administrative or government-initiated remedies cannot be overstated. Because it is unrealistic to rely soley upon private policing of the market-place, our Model Act must give a structural pre-eminence to a government enforcing authority armed with a broad range of powers. There are three administrative mechanisms that in my view deserve special emphasis: (1) a cease and desist power, (2) an AVC mechanism, and (3) a substituted action procedure.

The public enforcing authority should be able to issue cease and desist orders that require immediate compliance. The Ontario Act provides for such a director-initiated cease and desist procedure. The difficulty with the B.C. and Alberta version which requires an application to a court of law is twofold: first, even an *ex parte* application for an interim injunction cannot be as immediate or as convenient as the cease and desist route; secondly, as the B.C. experience suggests, judges may be reluctant to discard common law trappings and enforce the legislation as written. A director-initiated cease and desist procedure requiring immediate compliance is preferable.

Another valuable administrative mechanism is the assurance of voluntary compliance or AVC. A voluntary compliance procedure would spare the government enforcing authority the costs of a protracted injunction or cease and desist proceeding and, at the same time, provide an expeditious vehicle for consumer restitution. Care, however, should be taken in drafting the guidelines as to the terms upon which an AVC can be concluded. I would have thought that the guidelines in the B.C. Act were sufficiently explicit. As it turns out, B.C. is beginning to question the efficacy of the voluntary compliance mechanism. There is a growing concern that the AVC has a very limited exemplary effect, but an unlimited potential for actual or perceived abuse in the hands of a government authority that might use the AVC to "blackmail" suppliers into half-hearted compliance. The answer may lie in greater legislative specificity as to the terms and conditions upon which an AVC can issue. Or, it may well be the case that the AVC is due for an extensive re-examination. Either way, legislative draftsmen should proceed with caution.

The third administrative feature, the substituted action, is a non-controversial essential. The director of trade practices must be empowered to act in a representative capacity on behalf of any aggrieved consumer litigant. I have argued elsewhere that the substituted action provision is "the single most important administrative measure to ensure that worthwhile consumer-initiated litigational efforts are not abandoned." The widest and most sensible approach to the substituted action is found in the B.C. Act and can serve as a model for uniform provincial adoption. Ontario's refusal to provide a substitute action procedure is simply indefensible.

(5) *A Workable Criminal Sanction.* I am persuaded by the many commentators and law reform commission studies that the criminal sanction is a clumsy regulatory device and, in the context of a Trade Practices Act, should be relegated to a tertiary level. None the less, even as a remedy of last resort, the criminal sanction could still prove worthwhile. In my view it should be retained to be utilized whenever the supplier has engaged in a deceptive or unconscionable trade practice and can be shown to have done so knowingly or without having taken all reasonable precautions to avoid the commission of the violation. The important point here is that the criminal offence provision be drafted to permit a "due diligence" defence. This would mean that a supplier would not be criminally liable where he could show that all reasonable precautions were taken and that he exercised due diligence to avoid the commission of the offence. Both the B.C. and Saskatchewan legislation have the "due diligence" feature. The generally unsatisfactory aspects of strict liability were canvassed by the Federal Law Reform Commission in a recent study. Their recommendation that criminal liability

should not attach to conduct in violation of a regulatory statute unless negligence can be shown is, in my view, eminently sensible. Ontario, unfortunately, has gone too far in the opposite direction. Although the scope of the criminal offence provision is as broad as that of the B.C. or Saskatchewan statutes, the Ontario Act requires a finding that the defendant "knowingly" contravened the legislation. This full *mens rea* requirement unavoidably excludes the reckless or negligent supplier whose unfair trade practices could be deterred by the imposition of criminal liability. Ontario and others should adopt the "due diligence" approach discussed above.

(6) *Rule-Making Powers.* The final feature of my Model Trade Practices Act is one that I put forward with some hesitation. Whenever a rule-making facility is proposed, someone will invariably extrapolate from this proposal a picture of a sprawling, bureaucratic, provincial FTC. Let me be absolutely clear. Although I have suggested elsewhere that we ought to rethink our traditional court-oriented approaches to trade practices regulation and consider the possible advantages of a non-curial regulatory model, that is not the point that I am making here. My concern today is simply to endorse the benefits of a rule-making power — benefits of greater specificity, more predictability and, consequently, more fairness. Where would this rule-making power reside? I would urge all provincial draftsmen to examine the possibility of giving rule-making powers to the Minister responsible for the enforcement of the trade practices legislation. One model that can be used is the U.K. Fair Trading Act, which contains a comprehensive rule-making procedure involving a three-stage screening process: the Director submits his proposals for desirable trade regulation rules to a Consumer Protection Advisory Committee consisting of representatives from industry, consumer groups, and government; the Advisory Committee studies the requests and determines which are sufficiently justifiable for recommendation to the Secretary of State; the Secretary of State receives the Committee's report and has the sole authority to promulgate rules through orders made by statutory instrument reviewable by Parliament. This triple-screening procedure has at least two advantages over the normal regulation-making power of the provincial Cabinet: director-initiative and procedural fairness.

I have attempted to present what in my view would be the highlights of a Model Trade Practices Act. In many respects, of course, this is a foray into a world of legislative science fiction. I say this not because model legislation is never enacted. In fact, oftentimes it is. But once enacted, there is a very high probability that the legislation will not be enforced. Increasingly, consumers are recognizing the "name-only" quality of much of the legislation that is supposedly enacted in their best interests. Inadequate funding, understaffing, a general lack of governmental commitment to legislative enforcement: these factors will combine to ensure a quiet death for even a Model Trade Practices Act. Thus the science fiction aspect to much of what I have said today. But that is another matter. On the assumption that sooner or later governments will begin to take their consumer protection legislation seriously, I offer these proposals for your consideration.

D. THIRD PARTIES AND THE BALANCING OF COMPETING EQUITIES: THE *NON EST FACTUM* PROBLEM

GALLIE v. LEE

[1969] 2 Ch. 17, [1969] 1 All ER 1062 (CA)

LORD DENNING M.R.: Mrs. Gallie is now an old lady of 84 years of age. She is a widow who lost her husband many years ago. She has no children of her own. She has a nephew, Walter Parkin, who is 46. She has made a will leaving everything to him and she relies very much on his advice.

Over 30 years ago Mrs. Gallie bought a house — No. 12 Dunkeld Road, Goodmayes, Essex. It was leasehold with over 900 years to go, at a small ground rent. She has lived in it herself ever since and has carried on there the business of a boarding-house. For the last eight or nine years she has been helped greatly by her nephew, Walter Parkin. She has given him the money to pay the bills for repairs, the insurance, and so forth. Some years ago she raised some money on mortgage from a building society but this was paid off by the end of 1961 and she got the deeds back. On getting the deeds, she handed them over to her nephew. She did it, because, in her own words: "I had made my will already and everything I possessed belonged to him." She knew that he wanted to raise money on it: and she was quite content for him to do so, so long as she could stay in the house during her life. When she handed him the deeds, she said to him: "Here you are, so as I can continue to live here." She was asked: "The whole purpose of giving the house to your nephew in your lifetime was so that he could get money on it, was it not?" She answered: "Yes."

Now Walter Parkin had a friend called William Lee. He told Lee that his aunt had a house — No. 12 Dunkeld Road — and she had left it to him in her will. Lee was heavily in debt and wanted money to pay off his creditors. There were conversations between them to see how money could be raised on No. 12 Dunkeld Road. Lee went to his solicitors, Lincoln and Lincoln, where he saw a managing clerk — Mr. Bertram Hall. Mr. Hall was unlike most managing clerks. He was dishonest, and has since been sent to prison. He advised Lee that documents should be drawn up by which Mrs. Gallie would sell the house to Lee, for £3000, but that sum would not be paid, and then Lee would mortgage it for £1,500. He wrote a letter on May 19, 1962, in these terms:

> Mr. Lee, c/o Mr. M. M. Parkin:
> The simplest way of dealing with the matter would be for you to purchase the property for £3,000. No stamp duty would be payable and it would not affect Mrs. Gallie from a tax angle. We could then arrange a mortgage without any difficulty for, say, £1,500. Lincoln and Lincoln.

Lee adopted this suggestion. The solicitors drew up a document ready for signature, whereby Mrs. Gallie was to sell the house to Lee. It contained the recital:

> The vendor has agreed with the purchaser for the sale to him of the premises comprised in and demised by the lease for the sum of £3,000.

and the habendum:

> In pursuance of the said agreement and in consideration of the sum of £3,000 now paid by the purchaser to the vendor (the receipt whereof the vendor hereby acknowledges) the vendor as beneficial owner hereby assigns unto the purchaser all the premises comprised and demised by the lease TO HOLD the same unto the purchaser for all the residue of the term granted therein.

On receiving that document from the solicitors on June 15, 1962, Lee took it round to Mrs. Gallie and got her to sign it. Mr. Parkin witnessed her signature, so presumably he was there at the time. The old lady did not read the document as she had broken her glasses. She said to Mr. Lee: "What is it for?" He said: "It is a deed of gift for Wally for the house." So she signed it thinking it was a deed of gift for her nephew Walter. She thought that her nephew was going to borrow money on the deeds through Mr. Lee. She said:

> I done it to help my nephew with his business. I thought I was signing it over to Wally. . . . I would not have made it over to Mr. Lee. . . . You wouldn't do that for a man you hardly knew.

She understood that she was still going to live in the house herself rent free. She said to her nephew: "I don't mind what I do, Wally, to help you along."

According to the document, Mr. Lee was to pay her £3,000 for the property, but he paid her nothing. As soon as Lee got the document signed, he let the solicitors have it. They put it before the Northampton Building Society and obtained a loan of £2,000 for Mr. Lee. Walter Parkin gave a reference for Mr. Lee, saying that he was completely reliable, and adding a good deal more of false information about Lee. The £2,000 was paid to the solicitors who paid their own costs out of it and paid the rest into Lee's bank, where it was used up to pay his creditors. Afterwards Lee raised more money on the property by a second charge: and later on he defaulted in the instalments on both mortgages. The building society sought to recover possession. Whereupon Mrs. Gallie and Mr. Parkin saw solicitors. She got legal aid to bring proceedings claiming that she was not bound by the assignment to Lee. It was, she said, not her deed. In Latin — non est factum. With the result that the building society could not gain any rights through or under it, as it was not her deed.

Stamp J. made these findings of fact:

> I find as a fact that Mrs. Gallie did not read the document, that Lee represented it to her as a deed of gift to Parkin and that Mrs. Gallie executed it in the belief that that was what it was. I also find as a fact that Mrs. Gallie had no idea that the document took the form of a conveyance on sale from her to Lee and that a sale or gift to him was something which she did not and would not for one moment have contemplated.

On these facts the judge found that the assignment was not her deed: and that she was entitled to the property free of any mortgage or charge. I must say at once that, as the case then stood, this would lead to a most unjust result. The one person to benefit would be Mr. Parkin. He would get the house under his aunt's will, free of any mortgage or charge, on the footing that the deed of assignment *was not her deed*: yet he was the very person who witnessed her signature to the assignment and thus vouched that it *was* her deed.

The case thus raises the important question: What is the effect in law when a man signs a deed, or a contract, or other legal document without reading it; and afterwards it turns out to be an entirely different transaction from what he thought it was? He says that he was induced to sign the documeent by the fraud of another, or, at any rate, that he was under a fundamental mistake about it. So he comes to the court and claims that he is not bound by it.

In such a case, the legal effect is one of two: *Either* the deed is not his deed at all (*non est factum*): or it is his deed, but it was induced by fraud or mistake (*fraud or mistake*). There is a great difference between the two. If the deed was not his deed at all (non est factum), he is not bound by his signature any more than he is bound by a forgery. The document is a nullity just as if a rogue had forged his signature. No one can claim title under it, not even an innocent purchaser who bought on the faith of it nor an innocent lender who lent his money on the faith of it. No matter that this innocent person acted in the utmost good faith, without notice of anything wrong, yet he takes nothing by the document. On the other hand, if the deed was his deed, but his signature was obtained from him by fraud or under the influence of mistake (fraud or mistake), the document is not a nullity at all. It is not void ab initio it is only voidable: and in order to avoid it, the person who signed the document must avoid it before innocent persons have acquired title under it. If a person pays out money or lends money on the faith of it, not knowing of the fraud or mistake, he can rely on the document and enforce it against the maker. It avails the maker nothing, as against him, to say it was induced by fraud or mistake.

Such being the difference in consequences between non est factum on the one hand and fraud or mistake on the other hand, the question is: How can we tell which is which? In each case the man signs the document without reading it. In each case his signature is obtained by fraud or induced by mistake. In each case his error is fundamental. Wherein, then, lies the difference between one and the other?

1. *The distinction between class and contents*

The most favoured distinction is this: If the man was mistaken as to the *class and character* to which the transaction belonged, that is to say, as to the essential nature of the transaction, it is not his document and he can rely on non est factum. If he was aware of its essential nature, but only mistaken as to the *contents* of the document, it *is* his document and he can only rely on fraud or mistake. Thus in *Anson on Contracts*, 22nd ed. (1964), p. 282, it is said that

> In order for the defence [of non est factum] to succeed the party executing the document must show that he was mistaken not merely as regards the contents, but as to the essential nature of the contract.

And in *Cheshire and Fifoot on Contracts*, 6th ed. (1964), p. 220, it is said that

> He must be able to prove that he intended to sign a document or enter into a

transaction fundamentally different in character and class from that which he actually signed. If he fully appreciated the class of contract that he was making, he cannot deny that the contract is his, merely because he was mistaken as to its details or its contents or its legal effect.

I cannot myself accept this distinction as valid. In the first place, it is not a sensible distinction. A mistake as to contents may be just as fundamental as a mistake as to class and character. Take an instance of each: (1) A mistake as to contents. Suppose a man signs a paper without reading it. He is told it is a bill of exchange for £100: whereas it is in truth a bill of exchange for a much larger sum of £10,000. It afterwards comes into the hands of an innocent holder for value. The maker there made a fundamental mistake but it was only a mistake as to the *contents* of the document, and not as to its class and character: for it was, in any case, a bill of exchange. It is agreed on all hands that in that case he *cannot* plead that it was not his document. He is liable on it to the innocent holder for the whole £10,000. (2) A mistake as to class and character. Suppose a man is told that a paper is a guarantee for £1,000. In truth it is the back of a bill of exchange for the self-same sum of £1,000. It afterwards comes into the hands of an innocent holder for value. The maker there made a mistake, but not so fundamental a mistake as in the first instance: but it was a mistake as to the class and character of the document — a bill of exchange instead of a simple guarantee. On that account he can, it is said, plead that it is not his document, and avoid liability to the innocent holder: see *Foster* v. *Mackinnon* (1869) LR 4 CP 704. I see no rhyme or reason for distinguishing those two cases. The man who does not take trouble to read the document should be liable in each case to the innocent holder. His remedy is against the man who deceived him.

In the second place the distinction is not really a distinction at all. A document takes its class and character from its contents: and a mistake as to the one is often also a mistake as to the other. Take again two instances: (1) Suppose a bare trustee is asked by his solicitor to sign a transfer of the trust property to the beneficiary who is of full age. He is told it is a simple transfer. He signs it without reading it. It turns out to be a mortgage by which the trustee commits himself to pay £10,000 to the mortgagee although the trustee never received a penny of it. I should myself have said that a *mortgage* was in an entirely different class from a simple *transfer*. But several distinguished judges would put them in the same class, and on that ground hold the trustee liable: see *Howatson* v. *Webb* [1907] 1 Ch. 537; [1908] 1 Ch. 1. (2) Suppose next that the owner of a house, who is going away, is asked by his solicitor to give a *power of attorney* to enable him to sell it. He signs the deed without reading it. It turns out to be a *conveyance* of the house to the solicitor himself. The solicitor afterwards sells it to an innocent purchaser and goes off with the money. In this case in contrast to the first, there are other judges, equally distinguished, who would have said that the maker had been deceived as to the nature and class of the document — a power of attorney is in a different class from a conveyance — so that it was not his document; and he could recover the property from the innocent purchaser: see *Muskham Finance Ltd.* v. *Howard* [1963] 1 QB 904, *per* Donovan L.J. at p. 913. I see no justification for distinguishing those two cases. The man who signs a document without reading it, relying on the advice of his solicitor, ought not to be allowed to repudiate it as against an innocent purchaser. His remedy is against his solicitor.

In the third place, the cases, as they were *actually decided*, do not warrant any such distinction. There are many in which a man has been under a mistake as to the essential nature of the document — a mistake as to its class and character which is completely fundamental — and yet he has been held bound by it as against innocent third persons. In *Hunter* v. *Walters* (1871) LR 7 Ch. App. 75, Hunter thought he was signing a mere form, and it turned out to be an out-and-out conveyance of his property. In *National Provincial Bank of England* v. *Jackson* (1886) 33 Ch. D. 1, the two sisters thought they were clearing off a mortgage and it turned out to be an absolute conveyance to their solicitor brother. In *King* v. *Smith* [1900] 2 Ch. 425, and *Howatson* v. *Webb* [1907] 1 Ch. 537; [1908] 1 Ch. 1, the makers thought they were signing innocuous conveyances, whereas they were mortgages making themselves liable in large sums. Yet none of those mistakes — fundamental as they were — enabled them to throw over the documents as against innocent purchasers. I reject, therefore, the supposed distinction between mistake as to contents and mistake as to class and character.

2. *The Distinction concerning Mistake as to the Person*

Another suggested distinction is this: If a man was mistaken as to the *person* in whose favour the deed was made, it is not his document and he can rely on non est factum. That is one of the grounds relied on by the judge in this case. And it is supported by a passage in *Halsbury's Laws of England*, 3rd ed. vol. 11 (1955) p. 360 note (o), which says that the plea of non est factum is available when a deed is executed under a mistake as to "the person in whose favour the deed is made, as where property is conveyed to John in the belief that it is being assured to William". The cases cited for that proposition are the contract cases such as *Cundy* v. *Lindsay* (1878) 3 App. Cas. 459, where a mistake as to the identity of the other contracting party has been said to make the contract void ab initio and not merely voidable. But Professor Winfield in his edition of *Pollock on Contracts*, 13th ed. (1950) at p. 387 suggests that that doctrine of mistake as to the person does not apply to non est factum.

I have long had doubts about the theory that, in the law of contract, mistake as to the identity of the person renders the contract a nullity and void. *Cundy* v. *Lindsay* can be explained on the ground that the offer was made to one person (Blenkiron & Co.) and accepted by another person (Alfred Blenkarn) and for that reason there was no contract at all. But, whatever be the merits of the rule in contract, I am quite clear that it has no application to the plea of non est factum. That is shown by *Howatson* v. *Webb* [1907] 1 Ch. 537; [1908] 1 Ch. 1. Webb signed the deeds under the mistaken impression (induced by fraud) that they were simple deeds of transfer to his principal Hooper, whereas in truth they were deeds of mortgage to a stranger, Whitaker. He pleaded non est factum, but the plea did not succeed.

Sowler v. *Potter* [1940] 1 KB 271, would appear at first sight to give some support to this distinction. Sowler's agent let a room to a woman under the impression that she was an innocent *Mrs. Potter,* whereas in truth she was the convicted *Mrs. Robinson.* That was not a case of non est factum. The lease was not void ab initio. It was only voidable and the decision should have been put on that ground.

In my opinion a man cannot plead non est factum simply because he has made a mistake as to the person in whose favour the document is made.

3. *The Distinction concerning Negotiable Instruments*

Next, it has been suggested that there is a distinction between a negotiable instrument and other written contracts. In *Carlisle and Cumberland Banking Co.* v. *Bragg* [1911] 1 KB 489, it was said in this court that a man who negligently signed a negotiable instrument, such as a bill of exchange, could not rely on non est factum: but that a man who negligently signed some other written contract, such as a guarantee, could rely on non est factum. This distinction is not warranted by the earlier cases. It is contrary to all good sense. Ex hypothesi the man has no knowledge of what he is signing. He signs without troubling to read it. It may be a guarantee or a bill of exchange or a receipt for money. He cannot be sure which it is. He may be able to get out of it for fraud or mistake: but he cannot say it was never his document. He made it his document by signing it carelessly without reading it.

4. *The Point of Estoppel*

Finally there is the point of estoppel. It is said that if a man signs a document without troubling to read it, and it comes into the hands of an innocent third person who acts on the faith of it, he is bound by the document. He cannot plead non est factum so as to defeat by his conduct the innocent third person, though he may plead fraud or mistake as against the immediate party.

Nearly all the cases support the existence of such an estoppel. Take *Thoroughgood's Case* in 1582, Co. Rep. 9b., which is the foundation of all the learning on the subject. Thoroughgood could not read or write. He was, says Lord Coke, "a layman, not lettered". He let some land to William Chicken, who was in arrear with his rent. A deed was put before Thoroughgood for him to affix his seal. John Ward, who was present, told him: "Goodman Thoroughgood, the effect of it is this, that you do release to William Chicken all the arrearages of rent that he doth owe you, and no otherwise, and then you shall have your land again." Thoroughgood said: "If it be no otherwise, I am content" and then and there sealed the said writing of release and delivered it to William Chicken. It was in truth a deed by which Thoroughgood released the land itself to William Chicken. Afterwards William Chicken sold the land to an innocent purchaser. The Court of Common Pleas held that the land still belonged to Thoroughgood and that he could eject the purchaser. The deed of release was not Thoroughgood's deed.

Note that there was nothing whatever to estop Thoroughgood from denying that it was his deed. He could not read or write and had perforce to rely on it being read to him or its effect declared unto him. But Lord Coke, at 9b, says it would have been different if he had not wanted it read or its effect declared.

> If the party who should deliver the deed, doth not require it (to be read to him or the effect of it declared to him) he shall be bound by the deed, although it be penned against his meaning.

In other words, his conduct in not troubling to have it read to him would estop him from saying it was not his deed.

The self-same point is made in all the authoritative works of that time. Thus in *Sheppard's Touchstone*, 7th ed. (1820) Vol. 1, at p. 56, it is said:

> So if the party that is to seal the deed, can read himself and doth not, or being an illiterate or a blind man, doth not require to hear the deed read, or the contents thereof declared, in those cases albeit the deed be contrary to his mind, yet it is good and unavoidable at law. But equity may correct mistakes, frauds, etc.

Again in *Comyn's Digest Fait* (B2) 5th ed. (1822) Vol. 4 it is said:

> So it is not necessary that the deed be read before sealing and delivery: for if the party executes it without hearing, or desiring that it may be read, yet it binds him.

Now leap over 250 years and you will find a similar estoppel emerging. In *Foster* v. *Mackinnon* (1869) LR 4 CP 704, Mackinnon was an old man who could hardly see. The secretary of a company put a paper before him, telling him it was a guarantee for the company, just as he had signed before. It was in truth the back of a bill of exchange. It came into the hands of Foster who was an innocent holder for value. The Court of Common Pleas held that if Mackinnon was negligent he was liable to the innocent holder. In other words, he would be estopped by his conduct. They sent the case back for a new trial on the issue of negligence.

Skipping over cases at first instance, I come to the vexed case of *Carlisle and Cumberland Banking Co.* v. *Bragg* [1911] 1 KB 489. Bragg sat drinking with Rigg. Rigg produced a paper for him to sign, and said: "You know the paper you signed a few days ago for me about insurance. It got wet and blurred in the rain. So would you sign this instead?" Bragg signed it without reading it. He was negligent in so doing and the jury so found. It was in truth a guarantee of Rigg's banking account: and the bank innocently lent Rigg money on the faith of it. This court held that the bank could not recover from Bragg. I think that case was wrongly decided. Bragg was plainly estopped by his negligence from denying his signature. I will mention it again later.

In *Muskham Finance* v. *Howard* [1963] 1 QB 904, Kennesson had a car on hire purchase which he sold to Howard. He signed a form thinking it was a note releasing all his interest in the car. In truth it was an indemnity whereby he promised the finance company that he would pay the instalments on the car in case Howard did not do so. This court held that he was not bound by the document: and that he was not liable to the finance company. But the court drew special attention to the fact that the finance company did not take the point that he was estopped by his negligence. If that point had been raised, the decision might have been different.

5. *The Question Posed by Mellish L.J.*

On this question of estoppel, I would now gather together some important pronouncements which go to show that when a man negligently signs a document without reading it, he may be estopped by his negligence from saying that it is not his document. In *Hunter* v. *Walters* (1871) LR 7 Ch. App. 75, James L.J. said at p. 84:

> Many a trustee has endeavoured in vain in this court to escape from the consequences of his acts by saying, "I signed a deed, and I signed a receipt for money as a matter of conformity"; which is another mode for saying, "I executed it as a matter of form." But those trustees have been made most painfully to learn that the instrument they have so signed will, with the consequences, follow them, and cause them to suffer *for their negligence*.

And Mellish L.J. said, at p. 87:

> Now, in my opinion, it is still a doubtful question at law, on which I do not wish to give any decisive opinion, whether, if there be a false representation respecting the contents of a deed, a person who is an educated person, and who might, by very simple means, have satisfied himself as to what the contents of the deed really were, may not, *by executing it negligently be estopped* as between himself and a person who innocently acts upon the faith of the deed being valid, and who accepts an estate under it.

Next is *Howatson* v. *Webb* [1908] 1 Ch. 1, 4, where Farwell L.J. echoed that sentiment of Mellish L.J., adding that it is a question

> whether at the present time an educated person, who is not blind, is not *estopped* from availing himself of the plea of non est factum against a person who innocently acts upon the faith of the deed being valid.

And Cozens-Hardy, M.R., said at p. 4, "I quite assent."

Those sayings were quoted to this court in *Carlisle and Cumberland Banking Co.* v. *Bragg* [1911] 1 KB 489, but were put on one side because it was said that Bragg did not owe any duty to the bank. That was, I think, a mistake. When Bragg put his signature to the document, he owed a duty to the general public of which the bank was one (to use Blackburn J.'s words in *Swan* v. *North British Australasian Co.* (1863) 2 H & C 175, 182) just as in *Howatson* v. *Webb*, Webb owed a duty to the general public of whom Miss Howatson was one. To my mind the finding of negligence against Bragg was of cardinal importance. He should have been held to be estopped by his negligence from denying that it was his document. Just as the presence of negligence would have rendered Mackinnon liable in *Foster* v. *Mackinnon*, so its presence should have landed Bragg in liability. *Carlisle and Cumberland Banking Co.* v. *Bragg* was condemned by Sir William Anson. It has been shown by Professor Cheshire to be erroneous, and it has been exposed by Professor Guest. It went clean contrary to a long line of authority and should not be followed.

But I desire to say that estoppel by negligence is not quite the right expression. It should be estoppel by conduct. The estoppel arises because the conduct of the defendant has been such as to lead the plaintiff to believe that the document was the defendant's document: this is so whether the conduct can rightly be labelled negligence or not, though it usually can. Even if he was not negligent, nevertheless, his conduct in signing without reading will work an estoppel in the present day just as it did in the sixteenth century.

Conclusion

After all this long discussion, I would endeavour to state the principle. It seems to me to be this: whenever a man of full age and understanding, who can read and write, signs a legal document which is put before him for signature — by which I mean a document which, it is apparent on the face of it, is intended to have legal consequences — then, if he does not take the trouble to read it but signs it as it is, relying on the word of another as to its character or contents or effect, he cannot be heard to say that it is not his document. By his conduct in signing it he has represented, to all those into whose hands it may come, that it is his document; and once they act upon it as being his document, he cannot go back on it and say it was a nullity from the beginning. If his signature was obtained by fraud, or under the influence of mistake, or something of the kind, he may be able to avoid it up to a point — but not when it has come into the hands of one who has in all innocence advanced money on the faith of it being his document or otherwise has relied upon it as being his document.

Appeal dismissed.

[Russell and Salmon L.JJ. delivered concurring judgments.]

Notes:

1   The House of Lords [1971] AC 1004, (*sub nom. Saunders* v. *Anglia Building Society*) unanimously affirmed the Court of Appeal's decision and overruled *Carlisle and Cumberland Banking Co.* v. *Bragg* [1911] 1 KB 489. The judgments of the law lords show a broad consensus on the following points:

    a)   While the doctrine of *non est factum* is not confined to the blind or illiterate and also applies to persons under other forms of temporary or permanent mental or physical disability, it is doubtful whether the defence will ever avail a person of ordinary education and competence who chooses to sign a document without informing himself of its purport and effect. (Lord Wilberforce was more categorical on the point and, like Lord Denning, thought that the defence would not be available.)

    b)   In any event, even in those cases to which the doctrine applies, (i) there must be a radical or fundamental difference between the document signed by the person raising the plea and the document he intended to sign, and (ii) the signor must exercise reasonable care before adding his signature, "negligence" here not being used in any technical sense or connoting breach of a duty of care owed to a third party.

    c)   The burden of showing that the doctrine applies rests on the party raising the defence.

2   *Gallie* v. *Lee* was extended in England by *United Dominions Trust* v. *Western* [1976]

2 WLR 64 (CA). In *Western* the defendant, W, agreed to buy a used car from a dealer, R, who was understood by W to be in a position to arrange financing. W put up a deposit and signed partially in blank UDT's standard form loan agreement. W intended, and thought, that R would fill in the form with the agreed figures. In fact, substantially different figures were inserted. When W received from UDT a copy of the form he took no steps to complain. The car proved to be defective and was stolen several months later. During this period the car became involved in an accident and because of the accident became a total write-off. As W had paid no installments, UDT sued. Megaw L.J., in upholding the trial judge's decision in favour of UDT, held (1) that there was no reason to suppose that UDT was aware, or that anything existed which might reasonably have brought to UDT's notice, that the document was anything other than what it purported to be; (2) that in light of *Gallie* v. *Lee*, W could not claim that there was no contract because the document did not represent his true intention (''the doctrine of estoppel by negligence does not apply only to negotiable instruments''); (3) that it would offend common sense for the court to distinguish, as W argued, between the careless signing of a complete document and the careless signing of a document in blank; and (4) that W failed to show, as was his onus, that he acted carefully in permitting R to fill in the document. Scarman and Bridge L.JJ. delivered concurring judgments.

3   Early Canadian jurisprudence followed the contents-character analysis rejected by Lord Denning and the House of Lords. In view of *Gallie* v. *Lee* will the Canadian courts now adopt a more functional analysis? The trend is not clear: see *Commercial Credit Corp. Ltd.* v. *Carroll Bros. Ltd.* (1970) 16 DLR (3d) 201 (Man. QB), aff'd 20 DLR (3d) 504*n* (CA). The Saskatchewan Court of Appeal continued to apply the old analysis in *Bank of Montreal* v. *Fetcher* [1975] WWD 138. On the other hand, in *Canadian Imperial Bank of Commerce* v. *Kanadian Kiddee Photo Ltd.* [1979] 3 WWR 256 the B.C. Supreme Court applied the test in *Saunders* v. *Anglia*. The functional approach has also been adopted in Nova Scotia: *Van de Sande* v. *Kirk* (1976) 22 NSR (2d) 339, 31 APR 339 (SC) and *Dwinell* v. *Custom Motors Ltd.* (1975) 61 DLR (3d) 342 (NS CA).

4   *Relationship of the Doctrine to Assignment of Choses in Action.* The *non est factum* rule originally developed at common law to allow illiterates to argue fraud in the procurement of their signatures: see *Thoroughgood's Case* (1582) 2 Co. Rep. 9a. By the 19th century the grounds for the defence extended beyond illiteracy to a general lack of intention to sign: *Foster* v. *Mackinnon* (1869) LR 4 CP 704, at 711.

Choses in action were not assignable at common law, except those assigned to or by the Crown and, later, those evidenced by bills of exchange and promissory notes. Equity, in contrast, eventually recognized and enforced such assignments but the assignee in equity took ''subject to all equities'' between the immediate parties to the transaction giving rise to the chose. The defence was retained when the British and Canadian legislatures subsequently created a statutory form of assignment. See e.g., the Conveyancing and Law of Property Act, RSO 1970, c. 85, s. 54. For a valuable discussion of the development of this area of the law, see *Di Guilo* v. *Boland* (1958) 13 DLR (2d) 510 (Ont. CA); aff'd [1961] SCR *vii*. See also *Crossley Vaines' Personal Property*, 5th ed. (1973), pp. 264 *et seq.*

The relationship between the common law doctrine of *non est factum* and the much broader equitable defence in cases involving assignments of choses awaits clarification. As an example of the problem, assume that a debtor has carelessly signed an agreement creating a debt believing it to be some other document. His creditor assigns the agreement to a third party. Under the *non est factum* doctrine, as restricted by *Gallie* v. *Lee*, the debtor would have no defence in an action by the third party, as he has acted carelessly. However, under CLPA s. 54 the assignee takes subject to defences between the original parties to the chose in action. How can the two doctrines be reconciled in this case? Should the equitable defence prevail because choses in action were not assignable at common law and therefore not subject to the *non est factum* doctrine in the first place?

The point actually arose in *Commercial Credit Corp. Ltd.* v. *Carroll Bros.* (1970) 16 DLR (3d) 201 (Man. QB); aff'd 20 DLR (3d) 504*n* (CA), but the conflict was not resolved. In that case Tritschler C.J.Q.B. affirmed both the *non est factum* defence and the preservation of defences against assignees under s. 32(2) of the Manitoba Law of Property Act (equivalent to CLPA, s. 54) as available to the defendants who had been fraudulently induced to sign a lien note agreement in blank that was subsequently completed by the dealer and discounted by him with the finance company.

5 There are indications that some Canadian courts have misunderstood the *non est factum* doctrine in a fundamental respect. In *Canadian Imperial Bank of Commerce* v. *Dura Wood Preservers Ltd.* (1979) 102 DLR (3d) 78 (BC SC) the defendant company was indebted to the plaintiff bank for nearly $90,000. R., an employee of the defendant company, was asked to sign a guarantee of indebtedness. At the time the bank was considering making an additional secured loan of $15,000 to Dura Wood. R. signed the guarantee without reading it or having it explained to him. McEachern C.J.B.C. found that R. was innocently misled into believing that the guarantee only covered the $15,000 secured loan, when it in fact covered the entire indebtedness of the defendant company. However, on the basis of *Saunders* v. *Anglia*, McEachern C.J.B.C. held that the plea of *non est factum* was not available to R. and that he was therefore liable for the full amount of the guarantee.

Given the development of the *non est factum* doctrine as a method of balancing the interests of third parties with those of innocent signers, was the decision correct? McEachern C.J.B.C. seemed to find (at p. 81 DLR) that the guarantee had been innocently misrepresented. Why was equitable relief then not granted as between the bank and R., both immediate parties to the guarantee agreement?

Other courts seem to be similarly confused over the role of the *non est factum* defence in applying it to situations involving no third party interests. See *Bank of Nova Scotia* v. *Battiste* (1979) 22 N & PEIR 192 (Nfld. SC); *Hurlburt* v. *Hunter* [1975] 2 WWR 230 (Alta. SC); *Dwinell* v. *Custom Motors Ltd., supra;* and *Canadian Imperial Bank of Commerce* v. *Kanadian Kiddee Photo Ltd.* [1979] 3 WWR 256 (BC SC).

What explanations can be offered for this confusion? Do you agree with Professor S. Waddam's statement that "[t]he 'negligence' if any, of the signer should surely not be relevant as against the very party who was responsible for his deception'' (*The Law of Contracts*, p. 205, n. 64)? Is there a danger of this happening should the confusion continue?

6   In the consumer setting the *non est factum* defence is sometimes raised, in conjunction with other defences, in actions on chattel paper brought by finance companies and other financial intermediaries with whom the paper has been discounted by the merchant. The statutory thrust is now clearly in favour of the consumer as evidenced by such legislation as CPA s. 42a and Part V of the Bills of Exchange Act. See further *infra* chapter 14. Does this suggest that the courts and the legislatures are pursuing conflicting policies?

The *non est factum* rule covers only one type of situation (and not necessarily the most common one at that) where the consumer complains that some aspect of the transaction has been misrepresented. The following table indicates some of the possible permutations and the consequent legal position:

Variations on the Non Est Factum Theme in the Consumer Context

Abbreviations

A = Position between consumer and other party to the transaction.

B = Position between consumer and third party.

SITUATION	LEGAL RESULT*	
	A	B
1 Character of document basically misrepresented.	Document is either complete nullity or, if only voidable, consumer should be entitled to have it set aside.	(a) Governed by the n.e.f. rules as explained by the HL in *Saunders* v. *Anglia*.
		(b) *Quaere:* the position where the document creates a debt that has been assigned to a third party. See preceding note. See also CLPA s. 54 and *C.C.C.* v. *Carroll Bros, supra.*
2 Contents of document partially misrepresented.	(a) Depending on the nature and quality of the misrepresentation, and the underlying circumstances, a remedy may be available as in 1.	(a) Whether the *non est factum* rule applies will depend upon the extent of the misrepresentation and whether the court will abandon

---

* The answers, where given, are only suggestive and should not be treated as definitive.

| SITUATION | LEGAL RESULT | |
	A	B
	(b) In any event, the representor may be precluded from relying on the misrepresented terms: *Mendelssohn* v. *Normand Ltd.* [1970] 1 QB 177 (CA); *Curtis* v. *Chemical Cleaning & Dyeing Co.* [1951] 1 KB 805; but *cf. Hawrish* v. *Bank of Montreal* [1969] SCR 515.	the old contents/character distinction in favour of the *Saunders* v. *Anglia* functional test. The law in Canada is uncertain: see note 3, *supra*. (b) Buyer may be able to set up equities (*cf.* CLPA, s. 54) unless otherwise precluded from doing so.
3 No misrepresentation, but undertaking not to release the document and not to complete blank spaces until agreed event.	Contract with suspensive condition.	(a) If document negotiable instrument, arguably no "delivery" within ss. 31-2, of the Bills of Exchange Act: *cf. C.A.C.* v. *Paris* (1964) 45 DLR (2d) 493 (Ont. Dist. Ct.). (b) Other documents: presumably similar result as in (a) subject to rules relating to holding out and estoppel.
4 Documents signed wholly or partially in blank:		
i) where other party authorized to complete and authority not exceeded.	Binding contract (but note CPA s. 31(2)).	Same.
ii) where other party authorized to complete but authority exceeded.	Insertion not binding: *cf. Campbell Discount Co. Ltd.* v. *Gall*, [1961] 1 QB 431 (CCA), not foll'd on other grounds in *U.D.T.* v. *Western, supra.*	See *Mercantile Credit Co. Ltd.* v. *Hamblin, supra*, and *U.D.T.* v. *Western*, noted *supra.*
iii) where third party notifies consumer of assignment; consumer does not object.	——————	Consumer may be estopped: *Ostrikoff* v. *Vancouver Finance Co.* (1955) 1 DLR (2d) 179 (BC CA).

	SITUATION	LEGAL RESULT	
		A	*B*

5 Special situations governed by statutory provisions:

	SITUATION	A	B
i)	CPA s. 31: non-compliance as to contents.	Contract not binding. *Quaere*: whether supplier can recover value of goods or services actually supplied: see *Schofield Manuel* v. *Rose, supra*.	Same?
ii)	cut-off clauses.		
iii)	consumer notes.		Nullified by CPA, s. 42a. Holder with notice of character of note takes subject to equities: BEA Part V, s. 191. See further, *infra* chapter 16(C).

Chapter 4
Uncertainty of Price and Other Terms

Introductory Note:

Traditionally the basic problem in this area has been to determine the price when the contract is silent with respect to it or the parties have agreed that the price shall be fixed in the future. The first question is treated in the SGA as giving rise to an implied term; the second has provoked much litigation and differences of judicial opinion in England and Canada. The student may already have encountered the problem in the basic contract course. Extracts from some of the leading cases are reproduced in the following pages both to refresh the student's recollection and to put the problem in its sales setting.

In the consumer setting price problems assume additional, and sometimes novel, dimensions. Here is a brief listing:

1. To enable the consumer to shop intelligently and comparatively, should the price of prepackaged products on supermarket shelves be shown in unit as well as absolute terms? In an age of computerized check-outs, should the supermarket be obliged to retain individualized product price labelling at all?

2. Disclosure problems also arise in the context of the cost of consumer credit. A long enduring controversy throughout much of the 60s (the so-called "truth in lending" debate) was whether the cost of credit should be shown as an annual percentage rate as well as in dollars and cents. A much older problem, the usury problem, going back to biblical days, is whether ceilings should be imposed on the cost of credit so as to protect necessitous or improvident borrowers.

3. Finally, many questions are raised by the use of false or deceptive price representations and similar selling techniques ranging from "switch and bait" methods to claims about low prices that are not supported by the facts.

Some materials on item 1 appear at the end of the present chapter. The questions in item 2 are dealt with in the chapter on consumer credit (chapter 25), and problems of false price advertising are examined in chapter 5(B) as part of the broader theme of the public law policing of false or deceptive representations.

MAY AND BUTCHER LTD. v. THE KING
[1934] 2 KB 17n (HL)

LORD BUCKMASTER: My Lords, consequent upon the War there remained at the disposal of the Government a considerable quantity of goods which had formerly been required for the prosecution of the War. In order that these goods might be effectively disposed of, a Disposals Board was set up into whose charge the various Departments handed over such of the surplus stock as they from time to time possessed. The Disposals Board then proceeded to deal with those goods by sale to various people. The present appellants were among the purchasers of that class of goods that related to the construction and equipment of tents and which was called by a word, which has convenience if it has not euphony in its favour, tentage. The first arrangement made between the Disposals Board and the appellants was in April, 1920. The transactions between them all appear to have taken a similar form. There was an agreement for the sale of the goods; there was an agreement that the price for the goods should be subsequently fixed between the parties; and there were provisions with regard to arbitration in the event of dispute. A dispute then arose out of the bargain dated January 7, 1922. At or about that time the control of the Disposals Board was changed; Major Lethaby formerly had charge of it, and Sir Maurice Levy took charge from him. It has been suggested that this caused a difference of relationship between the parties which led to the dispute. Such a suggestion certainly is in no way material to the matter we have to decide, and I am quite unable to find anything throughout these proceedings to justify the suggestion that Sir Maurice Levy did otherwise than what was his duty to do — namely, take the steps he thought most effective to secure the largest price for the goods.

The earlier course of business appears to have been this: the Disposals Board received from the various Departments something in the nature of specifications of the goods that were to be handed over, and these specifications were in turn handed over to the would-be purchaser, who could check them if he liked for himself, or, if not, accept them as they were offered. Sir Maurice Levy discontinued this practice. He said that he did not think it was unreasonable on the part of the appellants to ask for the specifications, but he did not deliver them, and I think it is not difficult to understand why, because if he proceeded to sell by specification instead of selling after inspection, which was always open to the purchaser, he would be bound by the statements in the specification, many of which contained references to the quality and character of the goods which he himself had no opportunity of checking. As a business arrangement it was much better he should let the would-be purchaser have the fullest opportunity of inspecting the goods he was going to buy; he could then make his offer; and that was the course in fact pursued. The proposals made by the appellants for purchase were not acceptable to Sir Maurice Levy; the parties were unable to come to an agreement; and the Disposals Board said that they considered themselves no longer bound by the contract. Negotiations failed and the Board declined to deliver any more goods under the attempted bargain. It is that which has given rise to these proceedings.

The points that arise for determination are these: Whether or not the terms of the contract were sufficiently defined to constitute a legal binding contract between the parties. The Crown says that the price was never agreed. The suppliants say first, that if it was not agreed, it would be a reasonable price. Secondly, they say that even if the price was not agreed, the arbitration clause in the contract was intended to cover this very question of price, and that consequently the reasonableness of the price was referred to arbitration under the contract. Thirdly, they say that even if they are wrong on their first two contentions the fact that the whole of the bargain was ended in 1922 was doing them a wrong, because in any event they were entitled to have the opportunity of entering into a further agreement for future parcels of the goods which were referred to in the terms of the contract.

My Lords, those being the contentions, it is obvious that the whole matter depends upon the construction of the actual words of the bargain itself. The contract is contained in the form of a letter. It is written by Major Lethaby, the then Controller of the Disposals Board, to the appellants. It was a letter based upon the payment by the appellants of 1000*l.* as a consideration for the bargain, and it opens in these words: "In consideration of your agreeing to allow the sum of 1000*l.* (one thousand pounds) now held by the Commission to remain on deposit as a security for the due performance of this extended contract, the Commission hereby confirm the sale to you of the whole of the tentage which may become available in the United Kingdom for disposal up to and including March 31, 1923," upon the terms of the earlier contracts. The provision as to price is in these words: "The prices to be agreed upon between the Commission and the purchasers in accordance with the terms of clause 3 of the said earlier contract shall include delivery free"; and it is provided that the actual price that has to be paid is to be the subject of further agreement between the parties. That is the result of the terms of one of the earlier bargains incorporated by the reference I have read. There is then a provision that the Commission may "at any time in their uncontrolled discretion and before it has been despatched to or collected by or resold by the purchasers, certify that any portion of the said tentage is required by the British Government and the Commission shall be at liberty to withhold delivery of such portion"; while finally there is an agreement as to arbitration, which again is contained in one of the earlier contracts. The arbitration clause may be important; it is in these words: "It is understood that all disputes with reference to or arising out of this agreement will be submitted to arbitration in accordance with the provisions of the Arbitration Act, 1889."

What resulted was this: it was impossible to agree [on] the prices, and unless the appellants are in a position to establish either that this failure to agree resulted out of a definite agreement to buy at a reasonable price, or that the price had become subject to arbitration, it is plain on the first two points which have been mentioned that this appeal must fail.

In my opinion there never was a concluded contract between the parties. It has long been a well recognized principle of contract law that an agreement between two parties to enter into an agreement in which some critical part of the contract matter is left undetermined is no contract at all. It is of course perfectly possible for two people to contract that they will sign a document which contains all the relevant terms, but it is not open to them to agree that they will in the future agree upon a matter which is vital to the arrangement between them and has not yet been determined. It has been argued that as the fixing of the price has broken down, a reasonable price must be assumed. That depends in part upon the terms of the Sale of Goods Act, which no doubt reproduces, and is known to have reproduced, the old law upon the matter. That provides in s. 8 that "the price in a contract of sale may be fixed by the contract, or may be left to be fixed in manner thereby agreed, or may be determined by the course of dealing between the parties. Where the price is not determined in accordance with the foregoing provisions the buyer must pay a reasonable price"; while, if the agreement is to sell goods on the terms that the price is to be fixed by the valuation of a third party, and such third party cannot or does not make such valuation, s. 9 says that the agreement is avoided. I find myself quite unable to understand the distinction between an agreement to permit the price to be fixed by a third party and an agreement to permit the price to be fixed in the future by the two parties to the contract themselves. In principle it appears to me that they are one and the same thing. This principle is not without one or two important authorities. I think that Parker J.'s decision in *Von Hatzfeldt Wildenburg* v. *Alexander* [1912] 1 Ch. 284 really covers the whole of this dispute, although I agree that the comment upon it by Sargant L.J. in *Chillingworth* v. *Esche* [1924] 1 Ch. 97, 113 more fully and accurately expresses the whole position; but the principle that you cannot agree to agree remains entirely unchanged. *Loftus* v. *Roberts* [1902] 18 TLR 532 is to the same effect. The only way the appellants seek to escape from those authorities is by saying that all related to another subject-matter. If it could be shown that the different subject-matter was the cause of different principles of contract being applied, that would be an effective and relevant argument, but apart from the fact that a contract, one, for example, for the sale of land, requires the consideration of a large number of special details that are wholly unnecessary in relation to a contract for the sale of goods, and apart also from the way in which either of these contracts may be regulated by the Statute of Frauds on the one hand, or by the Sale of Goods Act on the other hand, the general underlying principles of contract are the same in each and there is no reason why those principles should be in any way varied because of the subject-matter with which they deal. I therefore find myself quite unable to accede to the argument that the authorities to which I have referred are weakened in their application to the present case because it happens that their subject-matter is not the same.

The next question is about the arbitration clause, and there I entirely agree with the majority of the Court of Appeal and also with Rowlatt J. The clause refers "disputes with reference to or arising out of this agreement" to arbitration, but until the price has been fixed, the agreement is not there. The arbitration clause relates to the settlement of whatever may happen when the agreement has been completed and the parties are regularly bound. There is nothing in the arbitration clause to enable a contract to be made which in fact the original bargain has left quite open.

Finally, I cannot take the view that the parties are entitled to an offer for the further parcels, because in my opinion this agreement is not a binding agreement at all, and the suggestion that the payment of the deposit entitled the appellants as of right to these offers, and constituted a valid and binding option, is not to my mind the true construction of what that deposit was for. The deposit was really for the purpose of securing the carrying out of the terms of the bargain when it had been made complete, and for the reasons I have already stated such completion never took place; there never was a complete bargain between the parties, and in my opinion the appellants fail.

Appeal dismissed.

[Concurring judgments were delivered by Viscount Dunedin and Lord Warrington.]

W.N. HILLAS & CO. LTD. v. ARCOS LTD.
(1932) 38 Com. Cas. 23, [1932] All ER Rep. 494 (HL)

On May 21, 1930, Hillas & Co. agreed to buy from Arcos Ltd. "22,000 standards of softwood goods of fair specification over the season 1930". Clause 9 of the contract provided that "buyers shall also have the option of entering into a contract with the sellers for the purchase of 100,000 standards for delivery during 1931. Such contract to stipulate that whatever the conditions are the buyers shall obtain the goods on conditions and at price which show to them a reduction of 5% on the f.o.b. value of the official price list at any time ruling during 1931. Such option to be declared before 1st January 1931." On December 22, 1930, Hillas purported to exercise the option. Arcos had entered into other agreements making the sale to Hillas of 1931 timber impossible. Arcos contended that the May 1930 agreement had previously been cancelled by agreement of the parties and that in any event the option clause was unenforceable for uncertainty.

On the initial hearing before Roche J. the jury rejected the first defence and at the renewed hearing before MacKinnon J. he held that cl. 9 was not void for uncertainty. The Court of Appeal reversed this finding and Hillas appealed.

LORD WRIGHT: The document of May 21, 1930, cannot be regarded as other than inartistic, and may appear repellent to the trained sense of an equity draftsman. But it is clear that the parties both intended to make a contract and thought they had done so. Business men often record the most important agreements in crude and summary fashion: modes of expression sufficient and clear to them in the course of their business may appear to those unfamiliar with the business far from complete or precise. It is accordingly the duty of the Court to construe such documents fairly and broadly, without being too astute or subtle in finding defects; but, on the contrary, the Court should seek to apply the old maxim of English law, *Verba ita sunt intelligenda ut res magis valeat quam pereat.* That maxim, however, does not mean that the Court is to make a contract for the parties, or to go outside the words they have used, except in so far as there are appropriate implications of law, as for instance, the implication of what is just and reasonable to be ascertained by the Court as matter of machinery where the contractual intention is clear but the contract is silent on some detail. Thus in contracts for future performance over a period, the parties may neither be able nor desire to specify many matters of detail, but leave them to be adjusted in the working out of the contract. Save for the legal implication I have mentioned, such contracts might well be incomplete or uncertain: with that implication in reserve they are neither incomplete nor uncertain. As obvious illustrations I may refer to such matters as prices or times of delivery in contracts for the sale of goods, or times for loading or discharging in a contract of sea carriage. Furthermore, even if the construction of the words used may be difficult, that is not a reason for holding them too ambiguous or uncertain to be enforced if the fair meaning of the parties can be extracted.

• • •

[Clause 9, the option,] must not be construed as if it stood by itself; it is an integral part of the whole agreement: the option under it is given as one of the conditions under which the appellants agree to buy the 22,000 standards, and is part of the consideration for their agreeing to do so. It is accordingly a binding offer, which the appellants are entitled, by accepting before January 1, 1931, to turn into a contract if other objections do not prevail. Some confusion has been imported, as I think, into the question by dwelling on the exact words — "the option of entering into a contract," and it is said that this is merely a contract to enter into a contract, whereas in law there cannot be a contract to enter into a contract. The phrase is epigrammatic, but may be either meaningless or misleading. A contract *de praesenti* to enter into what, in law, is an enforceable contract, is simply that enforceable contract, and no more and no less; and if what may not very accurately be called the second contract is not to take effect till some future date but is otherwise an enforceable contract, the position is as in the preceding illustration, save that the operation of the contract is postponed. But in each case there is *eo instanti* a complete obligation. If, however, what is meant is that the parties agree to negotiate in the hope of effecting a valid contract, the position is different. There is then no bargain except to negotiate, and negotiations may be fruitless and end without any contract ensuing; yet even then, in strict theory, there is a contract (if there is good consideration) to negotiate, though in the event of repudiation by one party the damages may be nominal, unless a jury think that the opportunity to negotiate was of some appreciable value to the injured party. However, I think the words of clause 9 in this case simply mean that the appellants had the option of accepting an offer in the terms of clause 9, so that when it was exercised a contract at once came into existence, unless indeed the terms of the option embodied in the clause were not sufficiently certain and complete: before considering this matter I ought to deal with a further contention based on a construction of the second paragraph of clause 9, which is in these terms: "such contract to stipulate that, whatever the conditions are, buyers shall obtain the goods on conditions and at prices which show to them a reduction of 5 per cent on the f.o.b. value of the official price list at any time ruling during 1931." It is argued that these words read with the preceding paragraph confirm the view that the option was merely for the preparation and agreeing of a formal contract, because the words "whatever the conditions are" mean "whatever the conditions of the contract are." Such an argument involves adding the words "of the contract," which are not expressed, and on other grounds I do not think that it is correct. I think the word "conditions" refers to conditions affecting other people in the trade, primarily as regards price, and such analogous advantages as are dealt with in clause 8 in connexion with the 1930 season. What the appellants are stipulating is that they are to have, throughout the year 1931, such conditions of this character and such prices as will secure to them in any event a clear 5 per cent advantage over other buyers who might compete. On a fair reading of the words, I think the contract is clear and complete in its stipulations as to price. It was contended that no official price list might be issued in 1931, so that the contract price was in that way uncertain and contingent. But in past years in the conduct of this business it had been an invariable practice of the respondents to issue such a list: the evidence and finding in the present case are that an official price list was issued in 1931: indeed it is difficult to see how the respondents could carry on the business unless it was issued. I think that as regards the definition of the machinery for fixing the price there is sufficient certainty here for a business transaction; the issue in 1931 of the official price list is not a mere contingency but a practical certainty: it is unnecessary to consider what would have been the legal position if the respondents had ceased to carry on business or had been dis-possessed by war or revolution. Such considerations are not relevant to deter-mining whether there is a good contract or not, but relate to such questions as frustration or breach of the contract.

The description of the goods offered to be sold in 1931, in clause 9, is also in my judgment sufficient in law. I so hold simply as a matter of construction, having regard to the context: "100,000 standards," divorced from the rest of the agreement, no doubt would be too uncertain: abstractly they might be incapable of any definite meaning. But the definition comes from the context: the agree-ment is headed as being for the purchase of Russian goods which to this extent must define the 100,000 standards; the words 50,000 standards in clause 7 have clearly to be read as embodying the same description as in the first paragraph of the agreement, that is, standards of softwood goods of fair specification; and, in my judgment, the same description must apply to the 100,000 standards in clause 9, not as a matter of implication but of construction. Hence the 100,000 standards are to be of Russian softwood goods of fair specification. In practice, under such a description, the parties will work out the necessary adjustments by a process of give and take in order to arrive at an equitable or reasonable apportionment on the basis of the respondents' actual available output, according to kinds, qualities, sizes and scantlings; but, if they fail to do so, the law can be invoked to determine what is reasonable in the way of specification, and thus the machinery is always available to give the necessary certainty. As a matter of strict procedure, the sellers would make a tender as being of fair specification, the buyers would reject it, and the Court or an arbitrator decide whether it was or was not a good tender. It is, however, said that in the present case the contract quantity is too large, and the range of variety in descriptions, qualities, and sizes is too compli-cated to admit of this being done. But I see no reason in principle to think that such an operation is beyond the powers of an expert tribunal, or of a judge of fact assisted by expert witnesses. I cannot find in the Record any evidence to justify this contention of the respondents, even if such evidence be at all competent. On the contrary, it seems that a prospective specification for the 500,000 or 600,000 standards which formed the subject of the contract of November 20, 1930, between the respondents and the Central Softwood Corporation, Limited, was agreed between these parties at Moscow in a few days, which appears to confirm that the ascertainment of a fair specification of Russian softwood goods, even for a very large quantity and over a whole season, is not of insuperable difficulty to experts. Accordingly I see no reason to think that, as regards the quality and description of the goods, the contract is either uncertain or incomplete. Nor can it justly be objected that the ascertainment of a reasonable specification is impossible. The law, in determining what is reasonable, is not concerned with ideal truth, but with something much less ambitious, though more practical.

There still remains the question of shipping dates or times or ports of delivery. I think here again, as matter of construction, clause 9 is to be read as embodying clause 6, which therefore I think applies equally to the 100,000 standards as to the 22,000 standards. I have explained my view of the operation and effect of that clause. If I were wrong in that, I should still regard the matter as sufficiently dealt with by the term which the law would imply in such a case — viz., that the deliveries are to be at reasonable times: section 29(2) of the Sale of Goods Act, 1893, applies, I think, to a contract such as this, where delivery is to be by instalments, equally with a contract under which there is only to be a single delivery, and imports the standard of reasonable time, which, by section 56 of the same Act, is a question of fact, no doubt to be determined in view of all the relevant circumstances, however complicated. In my judgment, the contract is neither uncertain nor incomplete as regards times of delivery or shipment.

In the result I arrive at the same conclusion as MacKinnon J. — viz., that the contract is valid and enforceable and that the appellants are entitled to recover damages from the respondents for its repudiation. The judgment of the Court of Appeal was otherwise. Apart from their conclusion that clause 9 was no more than an arrangement to negotiate in the future terms of a new contract for 1931, they held that in any view clause 9 was uncertain and incomplete. . . .

When the learned Lord Justice [Scrutton L.J.] speaks of essential terms not being precisely determined, *i.e.* — by express terms of the contract — he is, I venture with respect to think, wrong in deducing as a matter of law that they must therefore be determined by a subsequent contract; he is ignoring, as it seems to me, the legal implication in contracts of what is reasonable, which runs throughout the whole of modern English law in relation to business contracts. To take only one instance, in *Hoadly* v. *M'Laine* [1834] 10 Bing 482, Tindal C.J. (after quoting older authority) said: "What is implied by law is as strong to bind the parties as if it were under their hand. This is a contract in which the parties are silent as to price and therefore leave it to the law to ascertain what the commodity contracted for is reasonably worth." It is unnecessary, in my judgment, to multiply illustrations of this principle, which goes far beyond matters of price. After all, the parties being business men ought to be left to decide what degree of precision it is essential to express in their contracts, if no legal principle is violated. The learned Lords Justices (for Romer L.J. took the same view) relied, I think, mainly in regard to this aspect of the case on an unreported decision of this House in the appeal of *May and Butcher, Limited* v. *The King* [1934] 2 KB 17n, which Scrutton L.J. thought compelled him to decide as he did. There was there a contract for the sale of certain goods, somewhat inelegantly called "tentage," with an option to buy further quantities at prices to be agreed upon between the parties when the material was ready for sale. Scrutton L.J. had taken the view in the Court of Appeal that there was an effective intention to contract to sell and buy, on the terms that if the parties did not agree [on] the price it was by implication to be a reasonable price; but he was in a minority in the Court of Appeal, and this House held that there was no binding contract there till prices had been agreed. A somewhat similar decision on another contract was given in the Court of Appeal in the case of *Loftus* v. *Roberts* [1902] 18 TLR 532, where the rule was summed up as being "Promissory expressions reserving an option as to performance do not create a contract." No one would dispute such a rule, and its application to the instrument before the House in *May and Butcher, Limited* v. *The King* has been finally determined in that case; but, in my judgment, the Court of Appeal were not justified in thinking that this House intended to lay down universal principles of construction or to negative the rule that it must be in each case a question of the true construction of the particular instrument. In my judgment, the parties here did intend to enter into, and did enter into, a complete and binding agreement, not dependent on any future agreement for its validity. But in any event the cases cited by the Court of Appeal do not, in my judgment, apply here, because this contract contains no such terms as were considered in those cases; it is not stipulated in the contract now in question that such matters as prices or times or quantities were to be agreed. I should certainly share the regret of the Lords Justices if I were compelled to think such important forward contracts as the present could have no legal effect and were mere "gentlemen's agreements" or honourable obligations. But for the reasons given I feel constrained to dissent from their conclusions — I have only with great diffidence arrived at this conclusion — but I am supported by reflecting that I am in agreement with a learned Judge very experienced in these questions.

Appeal allowed.

[Lord Tomlin and Lord Thankerton delivered concurring judgments.]

FOLEY v. CLASSIQUE COACHES LTD.
[1934] 2 KB 1, [1934] All ER 88 (C.A.)

The plaintiff was a retail dealer in petrol (gasoline). The defendants were the owners of motor coaches and carried on business on premises adjoining those of the plaintiff. Part of the plaintiff's land was vacant and the defendants were interested in acquiring it for their business. The plaintiff was willing to sell the land on condition that the defendants would agree to buy from him thereafter all their requirements of petrol.

Two agreements in writing embodying these terms were signed by the parties on April 11, 1930. The first agreement dealt with the sale of the land, the second contained the defendants' undertaking to buy their requirements of petrol from the plaintiff. Clause 1 of the latter agreement read:

> 1. The vendor shall sell to the company and the company shall purchase from the vendor all petrol which shall be required by the company for the running of their said business at a price to be agreed by the parties in writing and from time to time.

Cl. 8 provided for the resolution by arbitration of any differences between the parties with respect to the subject matter or construction of the agreement.

The land was duly conveyed to the defendants and from April 26, 1930, to October 7, 1933, the defendants bought their petrol from the plaintiff at prices apparently fixed by the plaintiff. Disputes then arose between the parties as to the price and quality of the petrol and the defendants' solicitor subsequently wrote a letter to the plaintiff repudiating the second document of April 11, 1930, on the ground that it did not consitute a binding agreement and notifying the plaintiff that the defendants would buy their petrol elsewhere as from October 8, 1933.

The plaintiff commenced action alleging breach of agreement and subsequently obtained an injunction from the Lord Chief Justice (Lord Hewart) restraining the defendants from buying their requirements of petrol elsewhere in breach of the agreement. The defendants appealed.

SCRUTTON L.J. summarized the facts and continued: It is quite clear that the parties intended to make an agreement, and for the space of three years no doubt entered the mind of the appellants that they had a business agreement, for they acted on it during that time. The petrol supplied by the respondent was non-combine petrol, but he had also combine petrol pumps. The non-combine petrol was supplied to the appellants at a price lower than that paid by the public, and an account was rendered periodically in writing and paid. In the third year some one acting for the appellants thought he could get better petrol elsewhere, and on September 29, 1933, their solicitor, thinking he saw a way out of the agreement, wrote on behalf of the appellants the letter of September 29, 1933, repudiating the agreement. Possibly the solicitor had heard something about the decision of the House of Lords in *May & Butcher* v. *The King* [1934] 2 KB 17n but probably had not heard of *Braithwaite* v. *Foreign Hardwood Co.* [1905] 2 KB 543, in which the Court of Appeal decided that the wrongful repudiation of a contract by one party relieves the other party from the performance of any conditions precedent. If the solicitor had known of that decision he would not have written the letter in the terms he did. Thereafter the respondent brought his action claiming damages for breach of the agreement, a declaration that the agreement is binding, and an injunction to restrain the appellants from purchasing petrol from any other person. The Lord Chief Justice decided that the respondent was entitled to judgment, as there was a binding agreement by which the appellants got the land on condition that they should buy their petrol from the respondent. I observe that the appellants' solicitor in his letter made no suggestion that the land would be returned, and I suppose the appellants would have been extremely annoyed if they had been asked to return it when they repudiated the condition.

A good deal of the case turns upon the effect of two decisions of the House of Lords which are not easy to fit in with each other. The first of these cases is *May & Butcher* v. *The King*, which related to a claim in respect of a purchase of surplus stores from a Government department. In the Court of Appeal two members of the Court took the view that inasmuch as there was a provision that the price of the stores which were to be offered from time to time was to be agreed there was no binding contract because an agreement to make an agreement does not constitute a contract, and that the language of clause 10 that any dispute as to the construction of the agreement was to be submitted to arbitration was irrelevant, because there was not an agreement, although the parties thought there was. In the second case, *Hillas & Co.* v. *Arcos* (1932) 147 LT 503, there was an agreement between Hillas & Co. and the Russian authorities under which Hillas & Co. were to take in one year 22,000 standards of Russian timber, and in the same agreement they had an option to take in the next year 100,000 standards, with no particulars as to the kind of timber or as to the terms of shipment or any of the other matters one expects to find dealt with on a sale of a large quantity of Russian timber over a period. The Court of Appeal, which included Greer L.J. and myself, both having a very large experience in these timber cases, came to the conclusion that as the House of Lords in *May & Butcher* v. *The King* considered that where a detail had to be agreed upon there was no agreement until that detail was agreed, we were bound to follow the decision in *May & Butcher* v. *The King* and hold that there was no effective agreement in respect of the option, because the terms had not been agreed. It was, however, held by the House of Lords in *Hillas & Co.* v. *Arcos* that we were wrong in so deciding and that we had misunderstood the decision in *May & Butcher* v. *The King*. The House took this line: it is quite true that there seems to be considerable vagueness about the agreement but the parties contrived to get through it on the contract for 22,000 standards, and so the House thought there was an agreement as to the option which the parties would be able to get through also despite the absence of details. It is true that in the first year the parties got through quite satisfactorily; that was because during that year the great bulk of English buyers were boycotting the Russian sellers. In the second year the position was different. The English buyers had changed their view and were buying large quantities of Russian timber, so that different conditions were then prevailing. In *Hillas & Co.* v. *Arcos* the House of Lords said that they had not laid down universal principles of construction in *May & Butcher* v. *The King* and that each case must be decided on the construction of the particular document, while in *Hillas & Co.* v. *Arcos* they found that the parties believed they had a contract. In the present case the parties obviously believed they had a contract and they acted for three years as if they had; they had an arbitration clause which relates to the subject-matter of the agreement as to the supply of petrol, and it seems to me that this arbitration clause applies to any failure to agree as to the price. By analogy to the case of a tied house there is to be implied in this contract a term that the petrol shall be supplied at a reasonable price and shall be of reasonable quality. For these reasons I think the Lord Chief Justice was right in holding that there was an effective and enforceable contract, although as to the future no definite price had been agreed with regard to the petrol.

Appeal dismissed.

[Greer and Maugham L.JJ. delivered concurring judgments.]

G. SCAMMELL & NEPHEW LTD. v. OUSTON
[1941] AC 251, [1941] 1 All ER 14 (HL)

The following statement of facts is taken from the judgment of L. Russell of Killowen:

> The respondents wished to acquire a new motor van, giving in part exchange a Bedford van which they owned. On November 23, 1937, an interview took place between a partner in the respondents' firm, one John Ouston, and a Mr. Cook, who represented the appellants, at which Mr. Cook recommended a Commer 15-cwt. van as suitable for the respondents' requirements, and suggested 80*l.* as the figure at which the Bedford van should be taken in part exchange, a figure, however, which Mr. Ouston considered too low. On the following day the appellants (by Mr. Cook) wrote to the respondents a letter giving a quotation for the proposed Commer van at 268*l.*, and stating that they were prepared to allow the sum of 100*l.* for the Bedford van. On December 6, 1937, an interview took place at which John Ouston, his father and co-partner Harry Ouston, and Mr. Cook were present. At that interview the offer contained in the letter of November 24, 1937, was accepted by the respondents. On December 7, 1937, the appellants (by Mr. Cook) wrote to Mr. Ouston thanking him for the order placed with Mr. Cook, on the previous evening, and asking him to let them have the official order in order to complete their records. This request was complied with by a letter from Mr. Harry Ouston dated December 8, 1937, in the following terms: "We beg to acknowledge receipt of your acceptance of our order for: One Commer 15-cwt. chassis complete with body as per your specification sent us on 25th November, Number 5263. This order is given on the understanding that the balance of purchase price can be had on hire-purchase terms over a period of two years."

The defendants subsequently refused to proceed any further and no hire-purchase agreement was ever signed or its provisions agreed upon, whether between the parties themselves or between them and any third party. The plaintiffs brought action against the defendants for breach of contract to supply the vehicle. The defendants took the position that no binding contract was intended to be created until the terms of the hire-purchase agreement had been agreed upon or, in the alternative, that the alleged contract was void for uncertainty.

The trial judge, Tucker J., was of the opinion that there was a binding contract between the parties, and that the concluding sentence of the letter of December 8, 1937, was a condition precedent to the contract becoming an effective contract on which the defendants were not entitled to rely since they had repudiated the contract on wrong grounds. The members of the Court of Appeal treated the sentence in question as a term of the contract and not as a condition precedent, but differed among themselves as to the construction of the contract. They agreed however that the sentence was not void for uncertainty and affirmed Tucker J.'s judgment in favour of the plaintiffs. The defendants appealed further.

LORD WRIGHT: [I]n my opinion the correct view is that put forward by Mr. Miller on behalf of the appellants, namely, that there never was a concluded contract between the parties. It is true that when the appellants broke off the affair they gave reasons for doing so which they could not justify. But when they were sued for breach of contract they were entitled to resist the claim on any good ground that was available, regardless of reasons which they had previously given. As Lord Sumner pointed out in *British & Benningtons, Ld.* v. *N. W. Cachar Tea Co.* [1923] AC 48, 71, if a party repudiated a contract giving no reasons at all, all reasons and all defences in the action, partial or complete, would be open to him. Equally would this be so, I think, if he gave reasons which he could not substantiate. If there never was a contract, they could not be made liable for breach of contract. There are in my opinion two grounds on which the court ought to hold that there was never a contract. The first is that the language used was so obscure and so incapable of any definite or precise meaning that the court is unable to attribute to the parties any particular contractual intention. The object of the court is to do justice between the parties, and the court will do its best, if satisfied that there was an ascertainable and determinate intention to contract, to give effect to that intention, looking at substance and not mere form. It will not be deterred by mere difficulties of interpretation. Difficulty is not synonymous with ambiguity so long as any definite meaning can be extracted. But the test of intention is to be found in the words used. If these words, considered however broadly and untechnically and with due regard to all the just implications, fail to evince any definite meaning on which the court can safely act, the court has no choice but to say that there is no contract. Such a position is not often found. But I think that it is found in this case. My reason for so thinking is not only based on the actual vagueness and unintelligibility of the words used, but is confirmed by the startling diversity of explanations, tendered by those who think there was a bargain, of what the bargain was. I do not think it would be right to hold the appellants to any particular version. It was all left too vague. There are many cases in the books of what are called illusory contracts, that is, where the parties may have thought they were making a contract but failed to arrive at a definite bargain. It is a necessary requirement that an agreement in order to be binding must be sufficiently definite to enable the court to give it a practical meaning. Its terms must be so definite, or capable of being made definite without further agreement of the parties, that the promises and performances to be rendered by each party are reasonably certain. In my opinion that requirement was not satisfied in this case.

But I think the other reason, which is that the parties never in intention nor even in appearance reached an agreement, is a still sounder reason against enforcing the claim. In truth, in my opinion, their agreement was inchoate and never got beyond negotiations. They did, indeed, accept the position that there should be some form of hire-purchase agreement, but they never went on to complete their agreement by settling between them what the terms of the hire-purchase agreement were to be. The furthest point they reached was an understanding or agreement to agree upon hire-purchase terms.

Appeal allowed.

[Concurring judgments were delivered by Viscount Simon L.C., Viscount Maugham, and Lord Russell of Killowen.]

Notes on Uncertainty of Price and Other Terms:

1   Are the British cases on uncertainty reconcilable, or do they proceed from two different theories about the extent to which the courts should be willing to enforce imperfect contracts? Which approach is preferable, and why?

2   *Canadian Position.* The conflict between the principle that commercial contracts should be upheld whenever possible and the reluctance of courts to repair imperfect agreements is also reflected in the Canadian cases. See, for example, *Murphy v. McSorley* [1929] SCR 542, and *Jackson v. Macaulay, Nicholls, Maitland & Co.* [1942] 2 DLR 609 (BC CA), and contrast with *De Laval Co. v. Bloomfield* [1938] 3 DLR 405 (Ont. CA) and *Marquest Industries Ltd. v. Willows Poultry Farms Ltd.* (1968) 1 DLR (3d) 513 (BC CA). The case law is reviewed in G.H.L. Fridman, *The Law of Contract in Canada* (1976), pp. 39 *et seq.*

3   Note the distinction between a contract silent as to price and one where the price has been expressly reserved for agreement in the future. In the former case, SGA s. 9(2) provides that a reasonable price will be implied. In the latter case, the House of Lords in *May and Butcher* (*supra*), held that s. 9(2) cannot be invoked. The courts seem to be less willing to imply a reasonable price where the parties have expressed an intention to agree on the term in the future. Is this anomalous? For an argument supporting the distinction, see S. Waddams, *The Law of Contracts* (1977), p. 26.

4   UCC 2-204(3) provides that a contract does not fail for indefiniteness even though one or more terms have been left open "if the parties have intended to make a contract and there is a reasonably certain basis for giving an appropriate remedy". UCC 2-305 spells out the implications of UCC 2-204(3) with respect to the specific case of price. The Code has therefore firmly placed its support in favour of the enforceability of contracts of sale with open terms if (and it is an important if) it conforms with the parties' intentions. The Ontario Law Reform Commission has recommended the adoption of similar provisions: see OLRC Sales Report, pp. 177-81. For further analysis of the Code provisions see J.J. White and R.S. Summers, *Uniform Commercial Code*, (2nd ed., 1980) pp. 115-21.

5   *Inflation and Price Indexing.* The adherence of the common law to the principle of nominalism (the value of money is presumed to be constant for the purpose of discharging legal obligations) means that inflation can have a marked effect on payment obligations under a contract. In the absence of a contrary provision, the rule is that a price stipulation in an agreement is in terms of current dollars. If price levels have risen unexpectedly since the agreement was reached the buyer gains at the seller's expense, all other things being equal, since he will be required to pay the same number of cheaper units of currency to discharge his obligation.

    Several alternatives are open to contracting parties to avoid this result when price levels are expected to rise before performance is completed. Simply avoiding fixed-price contracts and agreeing to set a price in the future is not a recommended solution since, in the absence of an arbitration clause, it may leave the agreement open to attack on the grounds of uncertainty (see *May and Butcher, supra*). If there is a regular market for the goods, a better alternative is to provide for payment at the market price (or the seller's catalogue price) at the time of delivery. The parties may also estimate the inflation rate over the contract period and build this factor into their price agreement. Another approach is to link the contract price to a broadly based price index ("index clauses") or to specific commodity prices. Payment in strong currencies or precious metals ("gold clauses") can also help eliminate the problem. For an overview of these and other methods see R.S. Rosenn, "Protecting Contracts from Inflation" (1977-78) 33 Bus. Law 729. For an excellent discussion of "gold clauses", once a popular stabilization method, see F.A. Mann, *The Legal Aspect of Money* (3rd ed., 1971) Ch. IV.

It should be noted that "index" clauses are not immune from traditional contract difficulties. In the recent case of *Re Collins Cartage & Storage Co. Ltd. and McDonald* (1979) 103 DLR (3d) 534 (Ont. HCJ) Lerner J. held that a clause in a lease of commercial premises purporting to adjust the rental payments by reference to "the cost of living index" was too uncertain to be enforceable. He found that no specific price index was referred to and that there was insufficient evidence to conclude that the parties intended the Consumer Price Index (Statistics Canada) to be used. This would indicate that great care must be taken when drafting clauses to protect contract benefits from inflation.

Notes on Standardized Sizes, Unit Pricing and Price Scanning:

1   *Standardized Sizes and Unit Pricing.* In response to public discontent with packaging and labelling practices of manufacturers and retailers, especially in the food industry, the Consumer Packaging and Labelling Act (CPLA) was enacted by the federal government in 1971 and proclaimed in force in 1974. The all important regulations under the Act are being introduced incrementally. Among other provisions, s. 11 of the Act permits the Governor in Council to issue regulations requiring any pre-packaged product to be sold only in certain sizes. The object is to allow for easier price comparison between brands; e.g., it is far more simple for the consumer to compare 100 ml. at $.50 to 100 ml. at $.52 than to wrack his brain trying to decide between 95 ml. at $.50 and 105 ml. at $.53. (In the past, some products, e.g., toothpaste, cereals, detergents, have been sold in a dozen or more sizes.) So far, the power has been used sparingly and as of Dec. 1980, the Regulations only applied to 14 products. See CPLA Regs., s. 36, and CCH, Canadian Commercial Law Guide, para. 26-935.

Moreover, the Act as it now stands remedies only half the problem. Having determined that the 7½ oz. can of brand A tuna fish is cheaper than the 7¾ oz. can of brand B, the consumer still has to decide whether to buy the 7½, 9½, or 15 ounce container of brand A. Without a calculator or unit pricing labels telling the consumer how much each package costs per ounce, shopping becomes a guessing game. The Act does not impose or otherwise provide for unit pricing. As a result the consumer is still handicapped in making informed purchasing decisions. A substantial number of American and Canadian supermarket chains have introduced unit pricing voluntarily, e.g., Loblaws and Dominion stores in Canada. A few American jurisdictions have also made it mandatory, though not for all stores or all products. For further details see "Progress Report on Unit Pricing", *Consumer Reports*, Feb. 1971, p. 84.

Unit Pricing, Cons. Res. Report No. 3, Dept. of Consumer & Corp. Affairs, Ottawa, May/72, p. 9, argues: "Legislation in this area is not appropriate at the federal level, but, in any case, legislation for mandatory unit pricing would be difficult both to draft [and] administer." Why is such legislation not appropriate at the federal level and would it be more difficult to administer than the detailed regulations under the Food and Drugs Act? Would the costs of such legislation exceed any possible benefits? Is consumer indifference a more important factor?

2   *Price Scanning and Automatic Checkouts.* A lively controversy has been raging for some time concerning supermarkets' desire to do away altogether with individual price labelling of products in order to capture the full benefits of modern computer technology. The reasoning goes this way. Supermarket computers are able to maintain an up-to-date electronic inventory of all prices on packaged products offered for sale in the store. When the consumer presents his products at the checkout counter a fixed or hand-held optical scanner operated by the cashier reads a machine readable symbol affixed to the item and identifying it. This information is linked to the price stored in the computer's memory and details of the item are tabulated in and printed by the electronic terminal.

It is claimed that such automatic checkouts (also referred to as electronic check-stands, automatic front ends or point-of-sale systems) will greatly speed up checkouts, ensure great accuracy in cash register tabulations, facilitate the mainte-nance of up-to-date inventory and product movement information, and, not least, effect substantial cost savings if stores can dispense with price markings on indi-vidual products. Product prices would however continue to be shown on the shelves themselves. So far, consumer organizations in Canada and the U.S. have successfully opposed the elimination of individual price markings on the ground that the consumer has no assurance, other than the stores' own word, that the prices stored in the computer's memory will always coincide with the shelf prices. There the controversy rests at the moment, with the supermarkets, in Ontario at any rate, having agreed to wait for a more favourable consumer climate before abandoning individual price marking.

For further information on this topic, see M.S. Moyer and B.L. Seitz, "The Marketing Implications of Automated Store Checkouts" (1975) 40 Bus. Quar. 68 and Ontario, Ministry of Consumer and Commercial Relations, *Interim Report on Computerized Checkout Systems in Food Supermarkets in Ontario,* June 1980.

Chapter 5
Scope of the Contract

The present chapter deals with a variety of issues, some old and some new, but all equally important. The first question is: how does the law distinguish between "mere" representations and those representations which are deemed to have become a term of the contract when the agreement has not been reduced to writing? Under existing law the distinction is fundamental because of the different remedies provided by the law in each of the two situations. A non-contractual misrepresentation only gives rise to equitable and sometimes tortious remedies whereas a contractual misrepresentation provides the aggrieved party with a much more powerful range of remedies. So it is very much in the representor's interest to argue for a contractual characterization of the representation.

Assuming the first hurdle has been successfully overcome, there often arises a second: how is the contractual term itself to be characterized, for this too carries profoundly important remedial implications. As will be seen, such a seemingly simple question arouses strong emotions and equally varied responses depending on whether one prefers certainty over flexibility and predictability over good faith conduct in the individual situation.

The third question is very much a product of 20th century merchandising and distributive techniques, for it is concerned with the legal effect of a representation or promise made to the ultimate buyer by a manufacturer or other person in the distributive chain who is not in direct privity with the buyer. Analytically and functionally, the question is part of the broader issue of the manufacturer's responsibility for defective goods resulting only in economic loss. Anglo-Canadian law has been slow however to recognize the unity and it seems appropriate to approach the issues in two stages. The first, the manufacturer's responsibility for express representations and promises, is dealt with here; the second stage, the manufacturer's liability for breach of implied warranties, is dealt with in chapter 7.

In the modern context a purely private law treatment of the above questions is quite inadequate. The pervasiveness of advertising requires a response commensurate with its importance; hence the role of public law in policing the honesty and integrity of commercial advertisements in the modern marketplace. This is the concern of Part B of this chapter.

A. PRIVATE LAW ASPECTS

1. GENERAL CHARACTERIZATION ISSUES

A. H. BOULTON
The Making of Business Contracts
2nd ed. (1972) pp. 15-18

(i) *Definition of the contract*

As a general principle it will be universally agreed that the more precisely one can define the provisions of a contract the better, and it is desirable to be able to limit with certainty the documents which are to be examined in order to establish those provisions. This is not to say, however, that in any given contractual situation the parties will agree where the limit is to be drawn.

The Act [SGA (UK) 1893] does not give a great deal of assistance, and one is led back to the general law of contract, and to the necessity of defining a point at which it is possible to construe the documentation as constituting an offer and an acceptance of that offer. If, as often happens, the actual contract of sale comes at the end of a long period of negotiation in which a number of representations have been made regarding the goods, sometimes in an express and specific form, and sometimes by means of general statements in advertising media, it tends to be to the advantage of the buyer to regard all these representations as being germane to the contract, whereas it is to the advantage of the seller to set a clear limit to the number of documents that are to be relied upon. It is clearly established that unless the immediate terms of the contract expressly provide to the contrary a representation regarding the goods made by the seller before the sale, and designed to influence the buyer towards entering into the contract, is a condition of the contract. This doctrine has been recently extended by the courts, so that a buyer may be able to sue a manufacturer on a representation made by him regarding the goods sold by a distributor notwithstanding that the contract of sale was not made with the manufacturer but with the distributor.

The law has for a long time recognised that a distinction exists between a mere commendation of goods for the purpose of advertisement and a representation made in order to induce a buyer. Under the contemptuous expression "a mere puff" much of the output of the contemporary art of advertising may be dismissed. No action would lie at the instance of an aggrieved buyer who complained that a detergent advertised as washing "whiter than white" did no more than wash white, if only because it would be difficult to give any meaning to the phrase. But it is far from easy to determine exactly at what point a statement ceases to be a mere advertising commendation and becomes a representation to be imported into the contract.

The matter becomes more complicated when the goods of sale are technical products. The typical selling transaction today, outside the range of the retail market, takes place between the sales representative of manufacturing industry and the commercial buyer. In the case of technical products the commercial buyer may have to refer to specialists on his own side whose expertise is involved, and on the seller's side the transaction may move from the sales representative to the technologist. Not infrequently the final state is the evolution of a specification by negotiation between the parties. Over the course of the negotiations the seller may be represented at different times by different persons whose authority to make representations on his behalf may not be very clearly defined — and in this respect it is the representative's apparent authority that matters more than his real authority — so that it is possible for a number of assertions to be made as to the quality of the goods and in the case of machinery as to its anticipated performance. There may also be a wealth of published material in the shape of catalogues, specifications, and the like, all of which may be regarded as having influenced the buyer.

In view of this it is in the interest of the seller to make sure that, at the point of time at which the contract is entered into, all irrelevant and casual statements regarding the goods are clearly excluded from the scope of the contract proper. Thus in the typical B.E.A.M.A. "A" conditions:

> All specifications, drawings and particulars of weights and dimensions submitted with our tender are approximate only, and the descriptions and illustrations contained in our catalogues, price lists and other advertisement matter are intended merely to present a general idea of the goods described therein, and none of these shall form part of the contract. After acceptance of our tender a set of certified outline drawings will be supplied free of charge on request.

This clause is skilfully drawn. It will be noted that it excludes from the scope of the contract particulars "submitted with" the tender, and contained in the more general sales literature, but does not exclude particulars that may be *contained in* the tender, to do which would be unreasonable. In the interpretation of a contract governed by a clause of this kind it may therefore be important to determine whether a specification or drawing is "submitted with" the tender or is an integral part of the tender, a distinction which can be easily overlooked. There are practical reasons why, especially to a manufacturer of technical products which are in the course of constant development and refinement, such a safeguard is necessary. It is not practicable, every time some technical change of a minor type is made, for a complete scrutiny of all extant sales literature to be made and alterations effected in order to bring the literature into line with practice. However, the question must sometimes arise how far the protection which such a clause purports to give is reasonable. The wise buyer of a technical product will seek some assurance and guarantee of its specification and performance in a form that will bring it within the substantive contract, and will take steps to ensure that everything he has been told about the goods he is buying will will no be arbitrarily excluded from the contract by such a clause.

It is not usual to find any clause matching this in conditions which buyers seek to impose. Naturally the interests of the buyer are best served by leaving the matter open so that any of the seller's negotiating representations can be relied upon. Buyers' conditions naturally tend to throw the emphasis upon the order as the ruling document without, however, expressly excluding other documents.

Thus the Purchasing Officers Association conditions provide:

> . . . the goods shall
> (i) conform, as to quantity, quality and description with the particulars stated in the order,
> (ii) be of sound materials and workmanship,
> (iii) be equal in all respects to the samples, patterns or specifications provided or given by either party.

The conditions put forward by a United Kingdom nationalised industry are of interest in this connection.

> The Articles shall be of the qualities and sorts described and equal in all respects to the Specifications, Patterns, Drawings and Samples which form part of the Contract Documents *or are otherwise relevant for the purposes of the Contract.* . . .

The words italicised can open the door to a great deal of argument, and would seem to be wide enough to include practically any express statement regarding the goods.

LEAF v. INTERNATIONAL GALLERIES
[1950] 2 KB 86, [1950] 1 All ER 693 (CA)

In March 1944 the plaintiff bought from the defendants an oil painting of Salisbury Cathedral for £85. During the negotiations for the purchase the sellers represented that it was a painting by Constable. The trial judge found that that representation had been incorporated as one of the terms of the contract. Nearly five years later the buyer tried to sell the picture and then discovered that it was not a Constable. He asked the defendants to take back the picture and to return the purchase price. The defendants refused and adhered to their view that the painting was by Constable. As a result the plaintiff brought this action for rescission of the agreement. He did not seek damages.

The county court judge found that the defendants had made an innocent misrepresentation and that the picture was not by Constable. Nevertheless, he denied relief on the ground that the equitable remedy was not available in the case of an executed contract. The plaintiff appealed.

DENNING L.J.: The question is whether the plaintiff is entitled to rescind the contract on the ground that the picture in question was not painted by Constable. I emphasize that it is a claim to rescind only: there is no claim in this action for damages for breach of condition or breach of warranty. The claim is simply one for rescission. At a very late stage before the county court judge counsel did ask for leave to amend by claiming damages for breach of warranty, but it was not allowed. No claim for damages is before us at all. The only question is whether the plaintiff is entitled to rescind.

The way in which the case is put by Mr. Weitzman, on behalf of the plaintiff, is this: he says that this was an innocent misrepresentation and that in equity he is, or should be, entitled to claim rescission even of an executed contract of sale on that account. He points out that the judge has found that it is quite possible to restore the parties to their original position. It can be done by simply handing back the picture to the defendants.

In my opinion, this case is to be decided according to the well known principles applicable to the sale of goods. This was a contract for the sale of goods. There was a mistake about the quality of the subject-matter, because both parties believed the picture to be a Constable; and that mistake was in one sense essential or fundamental. But such a mistake does not avoid the contract: there was no mistake at all about the subject-matter of the sale. It was a specific picture, "Salisbury Cathedral". The parties were agreed in the same terms on the same subject-matter, and that is sufficient to make a contract: see *Solle* v. *Butcher* [1950] 1 KB 671.

There was a term in the contract as to the quality of the subject-matter: namely, as to the person by whom the picture was painted — that it was by Constable. That term of the contract was, according to our terminology, either a condition or a warranty. If it was a condition, the buyer could reject the picture for breach of the condition at any time before he accepted it, or is deemed to have accepted it; whereas, if it was only a warranty, he could not reject it at all but was confined to a claim for damages.

I think it right to assume in the buyer's favour that this term was a condition, and that, if he had come in proper time he could have rejected the picture; but the right to reject for breach of condition has always been limited by the rule that, once the buyer has accepted, or is deemed to have accepted, the goods in performance of the contract, then he cannot thereafter reject, but is relegated to his claim for damages: see s. II, sub-s. I(c), of the Sale of Goods Act, 1893, and *Wallis, Son & Wells* v. *Pratt & Haynes* [1910] 2 KB 1003.

The circumstances in which a buyer is deemed to have accepted goods in performance of the contract are set out in s. 35 of the Act, which says that the buyer is deemed to have accepted the goods, amongst other things, "when, after the lapse of a reasonable time, he retains the goods without intimating to the seller that he has rejected them." In this case the buyer took the picture into his house and, apparently, hung it there, and five years passed before he intimated any rejection at all. That, I need hardly say, is much more than a reasonable time. It is far too late for him at the end of five years to reject this picture for breach of any condition. His remedy after that length of time is for damages only, a claim which he has not brought before the court.

Is it to be said that the buyer is in any better position by relying on the representation, not as a condition, but as an innocent misrepresentation? I agree that on a contract for the sale of goods an innocent material misrepresentation may, in a proper case, be a ground for rescission even after the contract has been executed. The observations of Joyce J. in *Seddon* v. *North Eastern Salt Co. Ld.* [1905] 1 Ch. 326, are, in my opinion, not good law. Many judges have treated it as plain that an executed contract of sale may be rescinded for innocent misrepresentation: see, for instance, *per* Warrington L.J. and Scrutton L.J. in *T. & J. Harrison* v. *Knowles and Foster* [1918] 1 KB 608, 609, 610; *per* Lord Atkin in *Bell* v. *Lever Bros. Ld.* [1932] AC 161, 224; and *per* Scrutton L.J. and Maugham L.J. in *L'Estrange* v. *F. Graucob Ld.* [1934] 2 KB 394, 400, 405.

Apart from that, there is now the decision of the majority of this court in *Solle* v. *Butcher* [1950] 1 KB 671, which overrules the first ground of decision in *Angel* v. *Jay* [1911] 1 KB 666. But it is unnecessary to explore these matters now.

Although rescission may in some cases be a proper remedy, it is to be remembered that an innocent misrepresentation is much less potent than a breach of condition; and a claim to rescission for innocent misrepresentation must at any rate be barred when a right to reject for breach of condition is barred. A condition is a term of the contract of a most material character, and if a claim to reject on that account is barred, it seems to me a fortiori that a claim to rescission on the ground of innocent misrepresentation is also barred.

So, assuming that a contract for the sale of goods may be rescinded in a proper case for innocent misrepresentation, the claim is barred in this case for the self-same reason as a right to reject is barred. The buyer has accepted the picture. He had ample opportunity for examination in the first few days after he had bought it. Then was the time to see if the condition or representation was fulfilled. Yet he has kept it all this time. Five years have elapsed without any notice of rejection. In my judgment he cannot now claim to rescind. His only claim, if any, as the county court judge said, was one for damages, which he has not made in this action. In my judgment, therefore, the appeal should be dismissed.

Appeal dismissed.

[Jenkins L.J. and Evershed M.R. delivered concurring judgments.]

Notes:

1   The judgments in *Leaf* seem to favour a merger of the remedies of rescission where the representation gives rise both to an equitable action for misrepresentation and an action for breach of condition. Is there any justification for retaining the equitable remedy at all where the representation amounts to a term of the contract? *Riddiford* v. *Warren* (1901) 20 NZLR 572 (CA), foll'd in *Watt* v. *Westhoven* [1933] VLR 458, held that the equitable remedies have not survived the SGA because s. 57(1), in preserving the general principles of law, only refers to "the rules of the common law". This rather subtle distinction has not so far been adopted in any reported Anglo-Canadian case and it did not appeal to the OLRC (Sales Report, p. 142) which recommended against formal abolition of the equitable remedy. The same position, albeit in a broader setting, has been adopted in s. 1 of the British Misrepresentation Act 1967.

2   In *Leaf*'s case the plaintiff does not appear to have pleaded common mistake. What would have been the effect of his doing so?

ESSO PETROLEUM CO. LTD. v. MARDON
[1976] 2 WLR 583, [1976] 2 All ER 5 (CA)

LORD DENNING M.R.: "This is," said the judge, "a tragic story of wasted endeavour and financial disaster." It is a long story starting as long ago as 1961, and finishing in 1967. Since then eight years have been spent in litigation.

In 1961 Esso Petroleum wanted an outlet for their petrol in Southport. They found a vacant site which was very suitable. It was on Eastbank Street, one of the busiest streets of the town. It had already got outline planning permission for a filling station. Esso thought of putting in a bid for the site. But before doing so, they made calculations to see if it would be a paying proposition. They made a careful forecast of the "estimated annual consumption" of petrol. This was the yardstick by which they measured the worth of a filling station. They called it the "e.a.c." In this case they estimated that the throughput of petrol would reach 200,000 gallons a year by the second year after development. This would accrue to their benefit by sales of petrol. In addition, they would get a substantial rental from a tenant. On May 25, 1961, the Esso local representatives recommended the go ahead. They gave the figures, and said: "We feel most strongly that this does genuinely represent a first-class opportunity of gaining representation in the centre of Southport." On that recommendation Esso bought the site and proceeded to erect a service station.

But then something happened which falsified all their calculations. Esso had thought that they could have the forecourt and pumps fronting on to the busy main street. But the Southport Corporation, who were the planning authority, refused to allow this. They insisted that the station should be built "back to front." So that only the showroom fronted on to the main street. The forecourt and pumps were at the back of the site and only accessible by side streets. They could not be seen from the main street. Esso had no choice but to comply with these planning requirements. They built the station "back to front." It was finished early in 1963.

Now at this point Esso made an error which the judge described as a "fatal error." They did not revise their original estimate which they had made in 1961. They still assessed the e.a.c. (estimated annual consumption) of petrol at 200,000 gallons. Whereas they should have made a reappraisal in the light of the building being now "back to front." This adversely affected the site's potential: because passing traffic could not see the station. It would reduce the throughput greatly. The judge found that this "fatal error" was due to want of care on the part of Esso. There can be no doubt about it.

It was under the influence of this "fatal error" that Esso sought to find a tenant for the service station. They found an excellent man, Mr. Philip Lionel Mardon. He was seen by Esso's local manager, Mr. Leitch. Now Mr. Leitch had had 40 years' experience in the petrol trade. It was on his calculations and recommendations that Esso had bought this site and developed it. At the decisive interview Mr. Leitch was accompanied by the new area manager, Mr. Allen. I will give what took place in the words of the judge:

> Mr. Mardon was told that Esso estimated that the throughput of the Eastbank Street site, in its third year of operation, would amount to 200,000 gallons a year. I also find that Mr. Mardon then indicated that he thought 100,000 to 150,000 gallons would be a more realistic estimate, but he was convinced by the far greater expertise of, particularly, Mr. Leitch. Mr. Allen is a far younger man and, although on his appointment as manager for the area I am satisfied he made his own observations as to the potentiality of the Eastbank Street site, in the result he accepted Mr. Leitch's estimate. Mr. Mardon, having indicated that he thought that a lower figure would be

a more realistic estimate, had his doubts quelled by the experience and the estimate furnished by Mr. Leitch; and it was for that reason, I am satisfied, because of what he was told about the estimated throughput in the third year, that he then proceeded to negotiate for and obtain the grant of a three-year tenancy at a rent of £2,500 a year for the first two years, rising to £3,000 yearly in the last year.

• • •

All the dealings were based on that estimate of a throughput of 200,000 gallons. It was on that estimate that Esso developed the site at a cost of £40,000: and that the tenant agreed to pay a rent of £2,500, rising to £3,000. . . .

Having induced Mr. Mardon to accept, Mr. Leitch and Mr. Allen sent this telegram to their head office:

> We have interviewed a Mr. Philip Lionel Mardon for tenancy and find him excellent in all respects. We recommend strongly that he be granted tenancy.

So a tenancy was granted to Mr. Mardon. It was dated April 10, 1963, and was for three years at a rent of £2,500 for the first two years, and £3,000 for the third year. It required him to keep open all day every day of the week, including Sunday. It forbade him to assign or underlet.

On the next day Mr. Mardon went into occupation of the service station and did everything that could be desired of him. He was an extremely good tenant and he tried every method to increase the sales and profitability of the service station. Esso freely acknowledge this.

But the throughput was most disappointing. It never got anywhere near the 200,000 gallons. Mr. Mardon put all his available capital into it. It was over £6,000. He raised an overdraft with the bank and used it in the business. He put all his work and endeavour into it. No one could have done more to make it a success. Yet when the accounts were taken for the first 15 months, the throughput was only 78,000 gallons. After paying all outgoings, such as rent, wages and so forth, there was a net loss of £5,800. The position was so serious that Mr. Mardon felt he could not continue. On July 17, 1964, he wrote to Mr. Allen: "I reluctantly give notice to quit forthwith. This is an endeavour to salvage as much as I can in lieu of inevitable bankruptcy." Mr. Allen did not reply in writing, but saw Mr. Mardon. As a result he put in a written report to his superiors recommending that Mr. Mardon's rent should be reduced to £1,000 a year, plus a surcharge according to the amount of petrol sold. Mr. Allen telexed to his superiors on several occasions pressing for a decision. . . .

On September 1, 1964, a new tenancy agreement was made in writing. It granted Mr. Mardon a tenancy for one year certain and thereafter determinable on three months' notice. The rent was reduced to £1,000 a year, and a surcharge of 1d. to 2d. a gallon, according to the amount sold.

Again Mr. Mardon tried hard to make a success of the service station: but again he failed. It was not his fault. The site was simply not good enough to have a throughput of more than 60,000 or 70,000 gallons. He lost more and more money over it. In order to help him, Esso tried to get another site for him — a "cream" site — so that he could run the two sites in conjunction to offset his losses. But they never found him one. Eventually on January 1, 1966, he wrote to Esso appealing to them to find a solution. He consulted solicitors who wrote on his behalf. But Esso did nothing to help. Quite the contrary. They insisted on the petrol being paid for every day on delivery. On August 28, 1966 (by some mistake or misunderstanding while Mr. Mardon was away), they came and drained his tanks of petrol and cut off his supplies. That put him out of business as a petrol station. He carried on as best he could with odd jobs for customers, like washing cars. Esso had no pity for him. On December 1, 1966, they issued a writ against him claiming possession and £1,133 13s. 9d. for petrol supplied. This defeated him. On March 7, 1967, he gave up the site. He had tried for four years to make a success of it. It was all wasted endeavour. He had lost all his capital and had incurred a large overdraft. It was a financial disaster.

Such being the facts, I turn to consider the law. It is founded on the representation that the estimated throughput of the service station was 200,000 gallons. No claim can be brought under the Misrepresentation Act 1967, because that Act did not come into force until April 22, 1967: whereas this representation was made in April 1963. So the claim is put in two ways. First, that the representation was a collateral warranty. Second, that it was a negligent misrepresentation. I will take them in order.

Collateral warranty

Ever since *Heilbut, Symons & Co.* v. *Buckleton* [1913] AC 30, we have had to contend with the law as laid down by the House of Lords that an innocent misrepresentation gives no right to damages. In order to escape from that rule, the pleader used to allege — I often did it myself — that the misrepresentation was fraudulent, or alternatively a collateral warranty. At the trial we nearly always succeeded on collateral warranty. We had to reckon, of course, with the dictum of Lord Moulton, at p. 47, that "such collateral contracts must from their very nature be rare." But more often than not the court elevated the innocent misrepresentation into a collateral warranty: and thereby did justice — in advance of the Misrepresentation Act 1967. I remember scores of cases of that kind, especially on the sale of a business. A representation as to the profits that had been made in the past was invariably held to be a warranty. Besides that experience, there have been many cases since I have sat in this court where we have readily held a representation — which induces a person to enter into a contract — to be a warranty sounding in damages. I summarised them in *Dick Bentley Productions Ltd.* v. *Harold Smith (Motors) Ltd.* [1965] 1 WLR 623, 627, when I said:

> Looking at the cases once more, as we have done so often, it seems to me that if a representation is made in the course of dealings for a contract for the very purpose of inducing the other party to act upon it, and actually inducing him to act upon it, by entering into the contract, that is prima facie ground for inferring that it was intended as a warranty. It is not necessary to speak of it as being collateral. Suffice it that it was intended to be acted upon and was in fact acted on.

Mr. Ross-Munro retaliated, however, by citing *Bisset* v. *Wilkinson* [1927] AC 177, where the Privy Council said that a statement by a New Zealand farmer that an area of land "would carry 2,000 sheep" was only an expression of opinion. He submitted that the forecast here of 200,000 gallons was an expression of opinion and not a statement of fact: and that it could not be interpreted as a warranty or promise.

Now I would quite agree with Mr. Ross-Munro that it was not a warranty — in this sense — that it did not *guarantee* that the throughput *would be* 200,000 gallons. But, nevertheless, it was a forecast made by a party — Esso — who had special knowledge and skill. It was the yardstick (the e.a.c.) by which they measured the worth of a filling station. They knew the facts. They knew the traffic in the town. They knew the throughput of comparable stations. They had much experience and expertise at their disposal. They were in a much better position than Mr. Mardon to make a forecast. It seems to me that if such a person makes a forecast, intending that the other should act upon it — and he does act upon it, it can well be interpreted as a warranty that the forecast is sound and reliable in the sense that they made it with reasonable care and skill. It is just as if Esso said to Mr. Mardon: "Our forecast of throughput is 200,000 gallons. You can rely upon it as being a sound forecast of what the service station should do. The rent is calculated on that footing." If the forecast turned out to be an unsound forecast such as no person of skill or experience should have made, there is a breach of warranty. Just as there is a breach of warranty when a forecast is made — "expected to load" by a certain date — if the maker has no reasonable grounds for it: see *Samuel Sanday and Co.* v. *Keighley, Maxted and Co.* (1922) 27 Com. Cas. 296; or bunkers "expected 600/700 tons": see *Efploia Shipping Corporation Ltd.* v. *Canadian Transport Co. Ltd.* (*The Pantanassa*) [1958] 2 Lloyd's Rep. 449, 455-457 by Diplock J. It is very different from the New Zealand case where the land had never been used as a sheep farm and both parties were equally able to form an opinion as to its carrying capacity: see particularly *Bisset* v. *Wilkinson* [1927] AC 177, 183-184.

In the present case it seems to me that there was a warranty that the forecast was sound, that is, Esso made it with reasonable care and skill. That warranty was broken. Most negligently Esso made a "fatal error" in the forecast they stated to Mr. Mardon, and on which he took the tenancy. For this they are liable in damages. The judge, however, declined to find a warranty. So I must go further.

Negligent misrepresentation

Assuming that there was no warranty, the question arises whether Esso are liable for negligent misstatement under the doctrine of *Hedley Byrne & Co. Ltd.* v. *Heller & Partners Ltd.* [1964] AC 465. It has been suggested that *Hedley Byrne* cannot be used so as to impose liability for negligent pre-contractual statements: and that, in a pre-contract situation, the remedy (at any rate before the Act of 1967) was only in warranty or nothing. Thus in *Hedley Byrne* itself Lord Reid said, at p. 483: "Where there is a contract there is no difficulty as regards the contracting parties: the question is whether there is a warranty." And in *Oleificio Zucchi S.P.A.* v. *Northern Sales Ltd.* [1965] 2 Lloyd's Rep. 496, 519, McNair J. said:

> . . . as at present advised, I consider the submission advanced by the buyers, that the ruling in [*Hedley Byrne* [1964] AC 465] applies as between contracting parties, is without foundation.

As against these, I took a different view in *McInerny* v. *Lloyds Bank Ltd.* [1974] 1 Lloyd's Rep. 246, 253 when I said:

> . . . if one person, by a negligent misstatement, induces another to enter into a contract — with himself or with a third person — he may be liable in damages.

In arguing this point, Mr. Ross-Munro took his stand in this way. He submitted that when the negotiations between two parties resulted in a contract between them, their rights and duties were governed by the law of contract and not by the law of tort. There was, therefore, no place in their relationship for *Hedley Byrne* [1964] AC 465, which was solely on liability in tort. He relied particularly on *Clark* v. *Kirby-Smith* [1964] Ch. 506 where Plowman J. held that the liability of a solicitor for negligence was a liability in contract and not in tort, following the observations of Sir Wilfrid Greene M.R. in *Groom* v. *Crocker* [1939] 1 KB 194, 206. Mr. Ross-Munro might also have cited *Bagot* v. *Stevens Scanlan & Co. Ltd.* [1966] 1 QB 197, about an architect; and other cases too. But I venture to suggest that those cases are in conflict with other decisions of high authority which were not cited in them. These decisions show that, in the case of a professional man, the duty to use reasonable care arises not only in contract, but is also imposed by the law apart from contract, and is therefore actionable in tort. It is comparable to the duty of reasonable care which is owed by a master to his servant, or vice versa. It can be put either in contract or in tort: see *Lister* v. *Romford Ice and Cold Storage Co. Ltd.* [1957] AC 555, 587 by Lord Radcliffe and *Matthews* v. *Kuwait Bechtel Corporation* [1959] 2 QB 57. The position was stated by Tindal C.J., delivering the judgment of the Court of Exchequer Chamber in *Boorman* v. *Brown* (1842) 3 QB 511, 525-526:

> That there is a large class of cases in which the foundation of the action springs out of privity of contract between the parties, but in which, nevertheless, the remedy for the breach, or non-performance, is indifferently either assumpsit or case upon tort, is not disputed. Such are actions against attorneys, surgeons, and other professional men, for want of competent skill or proper care in the service they undertake to render: . . . The principle in all these cases would seem to be that the contract creates a duty, and the neglect to perform that duty, or the nonfeasance, is a ground of action upon a tort.

That decision was affirmed in the House of Lords in (1844) 11 Cl. & Fin. 1, when Lord Campbell, giving the one speech, said, at p. 44:

> . . . wherever there is a contract, and something to be done in the course of the employment which is the subject of that contract, if there is a breach of a duty in the course of that employment, the plaintiff may either recover in tort or in contract.

To this there is to be added the high authority of Viscount Haldane L.C., in *Nocton* v. *Lord Ashburton* [1914] AC 932, 956:

> . . . the solicitor contracts with his client to be skilful and careful. For failure to perform his obligation he may be made liable at law in contract or even in tort, for negligence in breach of a duty imposed on him.

That seems to me right. A professional man may give advice under a contract for reward; or without a contract, in pursuance of a voluntary assumption of responsibility, gratuitously without reward. In either case he is under one and the same duty to use reasonable care: see *Cassidy* v. *Ministry of Health* [1951] 2 KB 343, 359-360. In the one case it is by reason of a term implied by law. In the other, it is by reason of a duty imposed by law. For a breach of that duty he is liable in damages: and those damages should be, and are, the same, whether he is sued in contract or in tort.

It follows that I cannot accept Mr. Ross-Munro's proposition. It seems to me that *Hedley Byrne & Co. Ltd.* v. *Heller & Partners Ltd.* [1964] AC 465, properly understood, covers this particular proposition: if a man, who has or professes to have special knowledge or skill, makes a representation by virtue thereof to another — be it advice, information or opinion — with the intention of inducing him to enter into a contract with him, he is under a duty to use reasonable care to see that the representation is correct, and that the advice, information or opinion is reliable. If he negligently gives unsound advice or misleading information or expresses an erroneous opinion, and thereby induces the other side to enter into a contract with him, he is liable in damages. This proposition is in line with what I said in *Candler* v. *Crane, Christmas & Co.* [1951] 2 KB 164, 179-180, which was approved by the majority of the Privy Council in *Mutual Life and Citizens' Assurance Co. Ltd.* v. *Evatt* [1971] AC 793. And the judges of the Commonwealth have shown themselves quite ready to apply *Hedley Byrne* [1964] AC 465, between contracting parties; see in *Sealand of the Pacific Ltd.* v. *Ocean Cement Ltd.* (1973) 33 DLR (3d) 625; and New Zealand *Capital Motors Ltd.* v. *Beecham* [1975] 1 NZLR 576.

Applying this principle, it is plain that Esso professed to have — and did in fact have — special knowledge or skill in estimating the throughput of a filling station. They made the representation — they forecast a throughput of 200,000 gallons — intending to induce Mr. Mardon to enter into a tenancy on the faith of it. They made it negligently. It was a "fatal error." And thereby induced Mr. Mardon to enter into a contract of tenancy that was disastrous to him. For this misrepresentation they are liable in damages.

Defendant's appeal allowed;
plaintiff's cross-appeal dismissed.

[Ormrod and Shaw L.JJ. delivered concurring judgments.]

Notes: Two major issues are dealt with in *Esso* v. *Mardon* and will also be addressed separately here: the test for a collateral warranty, and the relationship between the *Hedley Byrne* doctrine and contractual warranties.

1   *The test for collateral warranty.* As Lord Denning points out in *Mardon*, the English courts have never experienced much difficulty in satisfying the theoretical requirement of an "intention" to contract, at least where the representation was made by a merchant and the buyer has acted reasonably in relying on the representation. The same no doubt is true of the Canadian decisions although one must be careful not to be dogmatic. *How* the courts divine the parties' intention remains a judicial secret and is the principal weakness of the intention or promissory test. It may be

argued however that the intention test also provides the courts with a suitable excuse where the judge deems it inappropriate to apply contractual remedies to a false representation. This argument would carry greater persuasiveness if the equitable and tortious remedies for misrepresentation were adequate, but it is clear that often they are not. In the eyes of various observers, the defectively drafted British Misrepresentations Act 1967 has merely complicated the picture and added a new layer of artificial distinctions.

Many observers prefer the simpler reliance test first formally adopted in American law in s. 12 of the American Uniform Sales Act (1906) on the initiative of its draftsman, Prof. Williston. Williston's historical research convinced him that the claim for breach of warranty originally was an action on the case for deceit (i.e., a tortious claim) and that only in the second half of the 18th century did such claims sound in contract. Williston thought that *Heilbut, Symons & Co.* v. *Buckleton* [1913] AC 30 (HL) was wrongly decided. See his "Representation and Warranty in Sales — *Heilbut* v. *Buckleton*" (1913) 27 Harv. L. Rev. 1 as well as his earlier "What Constitutes an Express Warranty in the Law of Sales?" (1908) 21 Harv. L. Rev. 555.

The reliance test was endorsed by the Ontario Law Reform Commission in both its Report on Warranties and Guarantees (pp. 28-29) and its Report on Sale of Goods (pp. 135 *et seq.*). A generous reliance test was also adopted in the definition of express warranty in the (Ontario) Consumer Products Warranties Act (Bill 110, 1976), s. 1(c), and appears in the Saskatchewan Consumer Products Warranties Act, 1977, SS 1976-77, c. 15, s. 8. Paradoxically, the Uniform Commercial Code has abandoned a simple reliance test since the test of express warranty adopted in UCC 2-313(a) is whether the representation or promise has become "part of the basis of the bargain" — a test that in its own way appears as difficult and elusive as the English test.

A novel solution to the definitional problem appears in the New Zealand Contractual Remedies Act (1979, No. 11). Section 6 provides that if a party to a contract has been induced to enter into it by a misrepresentation, innocent or fraudulent, made to him by or on behalf of another party to the contract, "he shall be entitled to damages from that other party in the same manner and to the same extent as if the representation were a term of the contract that has been broken." Section 7(3) applies a similar approach with respect to the representee's right to cancel the contract.

It will be seen therefore that the modern draftsman has a rich smorgasbord of precedents to draw upon in formulating his solution to the problem — unless he decides to do nothing and to leave it in the hands of the courts. But if he is an activist and opts for a legislative solution he must also take into account the following issues:

a) *Representations by private sellers.* Should they be governed by the same test as representations by merchant sellers? Cases such as *Oscar Chess Ltd.* v. *Williams* [1957] 1 WLR 370 (CA) show the reluctance of courts to imply a contractual intention as readily in the first case as in the second, no doubt because it was felt that the merchant buyer was quite capable of protecting his own interests and could better bear the loss than the (innocent) seller representor. Would we feel equally confident about the answer if the buyer is also a non-merchant, or would it depend on the remedy sought by him? *Cf. Beale* v. *Taylor* [1967] 1 WLR 1193 where the English Court of Appeal had no hesitation in granting relief to the consumer buyer although the actual issue before the court was a different one, viz. whether the seller had committed a breach of the implied condition of description.

b)   *Relevance of negligence.* Lord Denning has referred to this on several occasions as a relevant factor, especially in claims against a non-merchant seller, but it has been treated coolly by commentators on the grounds that it confuses tortious and contractual claims. The assumption appears to be that once the contract or the collateral warranty is proven, then negligence in the making of the contractual representation is irrelevant. The criticism may have some formal validity but closer analysis shows it to be weak in substance, as is shown by *Mardon* itself. There the Court of Appeal treated the collateral warranty as meaning that Esso's officers had exercised *reasonable care* in their estimate of the likely sales at the service station. They did not warrant it absolutely. This should be contrasted with the well established sales rule that the implied conditions of title, description, merchantability, fitness for purpose and conformity to sample (SGA ss. 13-16) impose strict obligations and do not turn on the presence or absence of negligence on the seller's part. Indeed, negligence is quite irrelevant. Whether a warranty — or any other contractual obligation for that matter — is construed as strict or only as imposing a duty of reasonable care and skill is a matter of policy and should not turn on *a priori* characterization of the duty. (The same reasoning of course also applies to tortious duties.) The fact that in *Mardon's* case the warranty was restricted to a representation that reasonable care had been exercised shows the confluence of contractual and tortious theories in this branch of the law and supports the American reasoning about the hybrid character of warranty claims.

c)   *Types of damage claims.* Underlying the characterization debate is a very legitimate concern that the representor should not unfairly be burdened with heavy damage claims, the often unstated assumption being that once the representation is characterized as a warranty, and is found to be inaccurate, the warrantor is liable for all the heads of damages — restitutionary, reliance and expectancy — appropriate to breach of a contractual term. In equity damages are generally not recoverable for innocent misrepresentation and, under the *Hedley Byrne* doctrine, the damages are limited to reliance damages. The question then is whether, as a matter of policy, every breach of a warranty should give rise to a claim for expectancy damages. There is no reason why this should be so and it is significant that the reported cases (including *Mardon's* case) in which the courts have found a collateral warranty have not involved such types of claim. Nevertheless, it is surprising that there has been so little explicit discussion of the problem. It is not clear for example how a New Zealand court would answer the question under the New Zealand Contractual Remedies Act.

2   *The Hedley Byrne Doctrine and Warranty Law.* But for the Supreme Court of

Canada's decision in *J. Nunes Diamonds Ltd.* v. *Dominion Electric Protection Co.* [1972] SCR 769 one would anticipate little difficulty about Canadian courts following *Mardon's* case on the availability of the tortious claim in addition to any claim for breach of contract regardless of when the negligent representation was made.

The reasoning, if not the actual decision, in *Nunes'* case has been widely criticized by commentators and subsequent Canadian courts have shown a ready willingness to distinguish it and to follow *Mardon*. *Mardon* was followed by the Ontario Court of Appeal in *Sodd Corp.* v. *Tessis* (1977) 79 DLR (3d) 632, where Lacourciere J.A., speaking for the court, held the defendant, a chartered accountant and licensed trustee in bankruptcy, liable for a negligent misrepresentation respecting the value of a bankrupt's inventory offered for sale. *Nunes* was distinguished as not involving an independent tort, whereas the case at bar, like *Mardon*, was concerned with a pre-contractual representation which induced the formation of the contract. See also *Ronald Elwyn Lister Ltd.* v. *Dunlop Canada Ltd.* (1978) 85 DLR (3d) 321 (OHC), where Rutherford J. found that *Nunes* presented no bar to recovery in tort for pre-contractual negligent misrepresentations, and *Sealand of the Pacific Ltd.* v. *Robert C. McHaffie Ltd.* (1974) 51 DLR (3d) 702 (BC CA) where a similar distinction was drawn. Can or should a distinction be drawn between pre-contractual and intra-contractual representations in terms of the *Hedley Byrne* doctrine?

For further discussion of the above issues see B. Reiter, ``Contracts, Torts, Relations and Reliance'', Study 8 in B. Reiter and J. Swan (eds.) *Studies in Contract Law* (1980) p. 235; and S. Schwartz, ``Annual Survey of Canadian Law: Part 3: Contracts'' (1976) 8 Ott. LR 588 at 618-26.

3   *The Parol evidence rule.* No discussion of modern warranty law would be complete without a reference to the parol evidence rule. In practice sellers and other persons faced with a collateral warranty claim make the rule their first line of defence since its successful invocation solves so many other problems as well. Merchant sellers however do not simply rely on the rule and well drafted sales agreements invariably contain ``merger'' clauses precluding the admissibility of extrinsic evidence to prove representations or terms not contained in the document itself.

It is easy to understand the merchant seller's concern, especially the merchant with a large sales staff, to prevent unauthorized promises and representations by subordinates and perhaps unverifiable verbal claims by the buyer. Both equally destroy the predictability and efficiency of the standard form contract prepared by the seller's legal advisors. It is equally obvious however that, from the buyer's point of view, an indiscriminate application of the parol evidence rule — with or without the support of a merger clause — can be as oppressive as the rule that he is bound by the terms of a contract of adhesion, however Draconian in content.

It is clear that the sympathies of the English courts have swung in favour of the customer, as is shown by such cases as *Curtis* v. *Chemical Cleaning & Dyeing Co. Ltd.* [1951] 1 KB 805; *Mendelssohn* v. *Normand Ltd.* [1970] 1 QB 177 (CA) and *J. Evans & Son (Portsmouth) Ltd.* v. *Andrea Merzario Ltd.* [1976] 1 WLR 1078 (CA). As a result it is widely believed that the parol evidence rule is largely dead in England, at least in standard form type transactions. No such easy assumption can be made of the Canadian position, especially since the Supreme Court of Canada continues to refuse to admit extrinsic evidence, in support of an alleged collateral warranty, that contradicts the written terms of an agreement. See *Hawrish* v. *Bank of Montreal* [1969] SCR 515, recently reaffirmed by the Supreme Court in *Bauer* v. *Bank of Montreal* (1980) 110 DLR (3d) 424.

It looks then as if any decisive changes in the parol evidence rule will have to come from the legislatures. Section 4(7) of the Ontario Business Practices Act in effect abolishes the rule in the consumer context and a similar provision is found in the B.C. Trade Practices Act. The English Law Commission, in a 1976 Working Paper, took the much bolder step of recommending the abolition of the rule for *all* purposes. See English Law Commission, Working Paper No. 70, *Law of Contracts, The Parol Evidence Rule*. The recommendation was endorsed by the OLRC with respect to contracts for the sale of goods (see OLRC Sales Report, pp. 110-16) and more recently, but *semble* for all contractual purposes, by the Law Reform Commission of British Columbia in its Report No. 44 on *The Parol Evidence Rule* (1979). None of the three recommendations has so far been implemented. It is nevertheless significant that three very experienced commissions entertained so little hesitation in recommending the abrogation of a rule for which the Supreme Court of Canada still shows considerable affection.

Abrogation of the rule does not mean of course that the extrinsic evidence must be believed; it merely means that the court is free to review all the relevant evidence with a view to determining the true agreement between the parties. Nevertheless, businessmen may wonder how, without the benefit of the parol evidence rule, they would be able to protect themselves against unauthorized representations or invest any confidence in the conclusiveness and finality of their standard form agreements. What answer would you give? Do you see an intermediate solution between abrogation of the parol evidence rule and maintenance of the status quo?

CEHAVE N.V. v. BREMER HANDELSGESELLSCHAFT m.b.H.
[1976] 1 QB 44 (CA)

LORD DENNING M.R.: In 1970, the sellers, a German company, agreed to sell to the buyers, a Dutch company, 12,000 metric tons of U.S. citrus pulp pellets. Those pellets are a by-product of oranges. The juice is extracted and tinned. The orange rinds are dried and made into pellets. The pellets are used as an ingredient in making cattle food.

In September 1970, there were two contracts of sale, each for 6,000 metric tons, delivery in bulk [to] be made by six instalments of 1,000 tons each over the first six months of 1971. Under the first contract of September 24, the price was $73.50 per metric ton. Under the second contract of September 28, the price was $73.75. In each case c.i.f. Rotterdam. Each contract incorporated the terms issued by the Cattle Food Trade Association, form 100, for shipment of feeding stuffs in bulk "Talequale c.i.f. terms." That form contained two sentences material to this dispute in clause no. 7: "Shipment to be made in good condition . . . each shipment shall be considered a separate contract."

The first three or four shipments were quite satisfactory. This case is concerned with a shipment made early in May 1971. It was by the German vessel the *Hansa Nord*. She took on about 3,400 metric tons of citrus pulp pellets at Port Manatee in Florida. Four bills of lading were issued. They were appropriated by the sellers as follows: two were for 1,000 tons each on the second contract. One for 1,000 tons and one for 419.856 tons on the first contract. But there was no physical appropriation of the cargo as between the two contracts.

On May 14 the buyers paid the price and got the shipping documents. The *Hansa Nord* arrived in Rotterdam on Friday, May 21, and started unloading on Saturday, May 22. It was finished by May 25. The cargo was discharged into lighters. The out-turn weights were:

Ex-hold no. 1 . . . 1,260 metric tons
Ex-hold no. 2 . . . 2,053 metric tons.

It is to be noticed that by this time the market price had fallen greatly. The contract price for these 3,400 tons was (when converted into sterling) about £100,000. But the market price on May 24 in Rotterdam was, for sound goods, only £86,000. This may give an explanation of subsequent happenings.

The cargo ex no. 2 hold (2,053 tons) was in good condition. But some of the cargo ex no. 1 hold (1,260 tons) was found to be damaged. On May 24 the buyers rejected the whole cargo (both no. 2 and no. 1 holds) on the ground that it was not shipped in good condition and they claimed repayment of the purchase price of £100,000. On the next day the sellers refused, saying that the goods were shipped in good condition: and that the damage must have occurred at sea and that the buyers ought to lodge their claim with the insurers.

So there it was. The goods were in the lighters with both sellers and buyers disclaiming ownership. Now comes an astonishing sequence of events. There was a Mr. Baas in Rotterdam who was an importer of feeding products (including citrus pulp pellets). On May 29, 1971, if not before, he inspected the cargo in the lighters. On June 1, 1971, the lighter owners applied ex parte to the Rotterdam County Court, the Commercial Court I expect, asking it to authorize a sale of the goods. They applied by their lawyer, a Mr. Driessen. The sellers were not told of this application. But the buyers were. They were represented by the same lawyer as the lighter owners, Mr. Driessen. On the same day this court granted the application and authorised the sale. It appointed agents to make the sale. The agents approached Mr. Baas. They did not approach any other possible bidders. They sold the whole cargo to Mr. Baas (out of both no. 2 and no. 1 holds) for a sum equivalent to £33,720. The expenses of sale were deducted, leaving the net proceeds at £29,903. These were paid into a Dutch bank "to the order of whom it may concern". On the self-same day, Mr. Baas sold the whole cargo to the buyers (i.e., the original buyers under the two contracts) at the same price and upon the same terms as he had himself bought them from the agents of the court. The board of appeal found:

> as a fair inference from the evidence . . . that the buyers and Mr. Baas intended that

he (Baas) should acquire the cargo for their (the buyers') benefit, or on their behalf.
. . .

Having bought the whole cargo from Mr. Baas, the buyers transported it in the same way as they would have done if it had never suffered any damage. They took the lighters by canal to their plant at Veghel, a journey of some 60 miles. The buyers then used the entire cargo to manufacture cattle food at their processing plant at Veghel. They used it in the self-same way as they would sound goods except that they used "smaller percentages in their compound feeds than would be normal with sound goods". This difference in manufacture did not cause them any loss. At any rate, there is no finding that it did. And it was surely for them to prove it.

The upshot of it all was, therefore, that the buyers took the whole cargo and used all of it for their business just as if they had never rejected it save for the smaller percentages. So the ubiquitous Mr. Baas had helped them greatly. They paid only £33,720 for it instead of the contract price of £100,000. The board of appeal of the trade association felt it necessary to make this comment:

> We wish to record that we are not satisfied that we have been presented with a full account of how the goods were disposed of in Rotterdam after rejection by the buyers. The witnesses produced by the buyers gave contradictory evidence on this question, as well as on other less vital issues.

That is a devastating comment. The buyers must have known the truth. But they did not tell it to the board of appeal. At any rate, not the whole truth.

Nevertheless, despite that devastating comment, the board of appeal made their award in favour of the buyers. They ordered the sellers to repay to the buyers the £100,000 with interest, and directed the proceeds of sale (£29,903) to be repaid to the sellers. So the buyers have got the entire cargo and used it for their cattle food, but instead of paying £100,000 for it, they have only paid them £30,000. The judge has upheld this award [1974] 2 Lloyd's Rep. 216, 227. The sellers appeal to this court. They recognise that they may have to pay something by way of damages for the damaged goods, but they deny that the buyers had any right to reject the whole cargo.

The board of appeal found a breach of the express clause "Shipped in good condition". They said:

> . . . on the balance of probability, not all the goods in hold no. 1 were shipped in good condition as required by the contract, nor on balance of probability were they reasonably fit to be carried on the contemplated voyage.

The board of appeal also found a breach of the implied condition as to merchantability contained in section 14(2) of the Sale of Goods Act 1893. They said:

> The goods in hold 1 were "merchantable" on arrival in Rotterdam in a commercial sense, though at a lower price than would be paid for sound goods: we find and hold, however, that they were not "of merchantable quality" within the meaning of the phrase when used in the Sale of Goods Act 1893.

The board of appeal did not find a breach of the implied condition of fitness contained in section 14(1) of the Act. They found all the elements about reliance and so forth, but they did not find that the goods were unfit. They could hardly have found them unfit, seeing that they were in fact used for that purpose.

"Shipped in good condition"

The judge held that, in contracts for the sale of goods, a stipulation must either be a "condition" or a "warranty" and that there could be no tertium quid. Accepting that distinction, he held that this stipulation "shipped in good condition" was a "condition" and not a "warranty" [1974] 2 Lloyd's Rep. 216, 225; so that, for any breach of it by the seller, the buyer was entitled to treat the contract as repudiated.

Those decisions by the judge are so important that they deserve careful consideration.

The general law apart from the sale of goods

For the last 300 or 400 years the courts have had to grapple with this problem: in what circumstances can a party, who is in breach himself of a stipulation of the contract, call upon the other side to perform his part or sue him for non-performance? At one time the solution was thought to depend on the nature of the stipulation itself, and not on the extent of the breach or its consequences. Under the old forms of pleading, a plaintiff had to aver and prove that he had performed all conditions precedent or that he was ready and willing to perform them. The question, therefore, was whether the stipulation (which he had broken) was a condition precedent or not: or, in the terminology of the 18th century, whether it was an *independent* covenant (the breach of which did not debar him from suing the other side), or a *dependent* covenant (the breach of which did debar the plaintiff because the performance by the other was *dependent* on the plaintiff performing his). This distinction was well stated by Serjeant Williams in his notes to *Pordage* v. *Cole* (1669) 1 Wms. Saund. 319, 320b:

> ... where there are several covenants, promises or agreements, which are *independent* of each other, one party may bring an action against the other for a breach of his covenants, etc. without averring a performance of the covenants, etc. on his, the plaintiff's part; and it is no excuse for the defendant to allege in his plea a breach of the covenants, etc. on the part of the plaintiff; ... But where the covenants, etc. are *dependent*, it is necessary for the plaintiff to aver and prove a performance of the covenants, etc. on his part, to entitle himself to an action for the breach of the covenants on the part of the defendant; ...

Although that division was treated as exhaustive, nevertheless, when the courts came to apply it, they had regard to the extent of the breach. This was done by Lord Mansfield in 1777 in the great case of *Boone* v. *Eyre* (*Note*) (1777) 1 Hy. Bl. 273, of which there was no satisfactory record until Lord Kenyon in 1796 produced a manuscript note of it: see *Campbell* v. *Jones* (1796) 6 Term Rep. 570, 573 and *Glazebrook* v. *Woodrow* (1799) 8 Term Rep. 366, 373. It is summarised in the notes to *Cutter* v. *Powell* (1795) 6 Term Rep. 320 (*Smith's Leading Cases*, 13th ed. (1929), vol. 2, pp. 16-17). The plaintiff conveyed to the defendant a plantation in the West Indies, together with the stock of negroes on it, in consideration of £500 down and an annuity of £100 a year, and covenanted that he had a good title to the plantation and was lawfully possessed of the negroes. Some time later the defendant discovered that the plaintiff had no title to the negroes and stopped paying the annuity. The court held that the defendant was liable to pay the annuity. He could not escape simply because the plaintiff had not "a title to a few negroes." His remedy was to bring a cross-action for damages. It would be different "if the plaintiff had no title at all to the plantation itself" (see 8 Term Rep. 366, 374): for then the plaintiff could not have recovered the annuity. In the language of those times, if the breach went to the whole consideration, the covenant was considered to be a condition precedent and the defendant could plead the breach in bar of the action: but if the breach went

> only to a part, where a breach may be paid for in damages, there the defendant has a remedy on his covenant, and shall not plead it as a condition precedent (1 Hy. Bl. 273n.).

In short, if the breach went to the root of the matter, the stipulation was to be considered a condition precedent: but if the breach did not go to the root, the stipulation was considered to be an independent covenant which could be compensated for in damages: see *Davidson* v. *Gwynne* (1810) 12 East 381, 389, *per* Lord Ellenborough C.J.; *Ellen* v. *Topp* (1851) 6 Exch. 424, 441; and *Graves* v. *Legg* (1854) 9 Exch. 709, 716.

Apart from those cases of "breach going to the root," the courts at the same time were developing the doctrine of "anticipatory breach." When one party, before the day when he is obliged to perform his part, declares in advance that he will not perform it when the day comes, or by his conduct evinces an intention not to perform it, the other may elect to treat his declaration or conduct as a breach going to the root of the matter and to treat himself as discharged from further performance: see *Hochster* v. *De la Tour* (1853) 2 E & B 678. By his prior declaration or conduct, the guilty party is said to repudiate the contract. The word "repudiation" should be confined to those cases of an *anticipatory* breach, but it is also used in connection with cases of an *actual* breach going to the root of the contract: see *Heyman* v. *Darwins Ltd.* [1942] AC 356, 378-379 by Lord Wright. All of them were gathered together by Lord Blackburn in his famous speech in *Mersey Steel and Iron Co. Ltd.* v. *Naylor, Benzon & Co.* (1884) 9 App. Cas. 434, 443-444:

> The rule of law, as I always understood it, is that where there is a contract in which there are two parties, each side having to do something (it is so laid down in the notes to *Pordage* v. *Cole*, 1 Wms. Saund. 319, 320) if you see that the failure to perform one part of it goes to the root of the contract, goes to the foundation of the whole, it is a good defence to say, "I am not going on to perform my part of it when that which is the root of the whole and the substantial consideration for my performance is defeated by your misconduct." . . . I repeatedly asked Mr. Cohen whether or not he could find any authority which justified him in saying that every breach of a contract . . . must be considered to go to the root of the contract, and he produced no such authority. There are many cases in which the breach may do so; it depends upon the construction of the contract.

Those last words are clearly a reference to a "condition" strictly so called, in which any breach entitled the other to be discharged from further performance. But the earlier words are quite general. They refer to all terms other than conditions strictly so called.

The Sale of Goods Act

Such was the state of the law when the Sale of Goods Act 1893 was passed on February 20, 1894. I have studied the then current edition of *Benjamin, Sale of Personal Property*, 4th ed. (1888), and the little books which Judge Chalmers wrote before (1890) and after the Act (*Chalmers' Sale of Goods Act*, 1893, 1st ed. (1894)), and the proceedings in Parliament. These show that until the year 1893 there was much confusion in the use of the words "condition" and "warranty." But that confusion was removed by the Act itself and by the judgment of Bowen L.J. in *Bentsen v. Taylor, Sons & Co.* [1893] 2 QB 274, 280. Thenceforward those words were used by lawyers as terms of art. The difference between them was that if the promisor broke a *condition* in any respect, however slight, it gave the other party a right to be quit of his obligations and to sue for damages: unless he by his conduct waived the condition, in which case he was bound to perform his future obligations but could sue for the damage he had suffered. If the promisor broke a *warranty* in any respect however serious, the other party was not quit of his future obligations. He had to perform them. His only remedy was to sue for damages: see *The Mihalis Angelos* [1971] 1 QB 164, 193 and *Wickman Machine Tool Sales Ltd. v. L. Schuler A.G.* [1972] 1 WLR 840, 851.

Now that division was not exhaustive. It left out of account the vast majority of stipulations which were neither "conditions" nor "warranties" strictly so called: but were intermediate stipulations, the effect of which depended on the breach. The cases about these stipulations were legion. They stretched continuously from *Boone v. Eyre (Note)*, 1 Hy. Bl. 273, in 1777 to *Mersey Steel and Iron Co. Ltd. v. Naylor, Benzon & Co.* (1884) 9 App. Cas. 434. I cannot believe that Parliament in 1893 intended to give the go-by to all these cases: or to say that they did not apply to the sale of goods. Those cases expressed the rules of the common law. They were preserved by section 61(2) of the Act of 1893, which said:

> The rules of the common law, including the law merchant, save in so far as they are inconsistent with the express provisions of this Act . . . shall continue to apply to contracts for the sale of goods.

There was nothing in the Act inconsistent with those cases. So they continued to apply.

In 1962 in the *Hong Kong Fir Shipping Co. Ltd. v. Kawasaki Kisen Kaisha Ltd.* [1962] 2 QB 26, the Court of Appeal drew attention to this vast body of case law. They showed that, besides conditions and warranties, strictly so called, there are many stipulations of which the effect depends on this: if the breach goes to the root of the contract, the other party is entitled to treat himself as discharged: but if it does not go to the root, he is not. In my opinion, the principle embodied in these cases applies to contracts for the sale of goods just as to all other contracts.

The task of the court can be stated simply in the way in which Upjohn L.J. stated it at p. 64. First, see whether the stipulation, on its true construction, is a condition strictly so called, that is, a stipulation such that, for any breach of it, the other party is entitled to treat himself as discharged. Second, if it is not such a condition, then look to the extent of the actual breach which has taken place. If it is such as to go to the root of the contract, the other party is entitled to treat himself as discharged: but, otherwise, not. To this may be added an anticipatory breach. If the one party, before the day on which he is due to perform his part, shows by his words or conduct that he will not perform it in a vital respect when the day comes, the other party is entitled to treat himself as discharged.

"Shipped in good condition"

This brings me back to the particular stipulation in this case: "Shipped in good condition". Was this a condition strictly so called, so that *any* breach of it entitled the buyer to reject the goods? Or was it an intermediate stipulation, so that the buyer cannot reject unless the breach is so serious as to go to the root of the contract?

If there was any previous authority holding it to be a *condition* strictly so called, we should abide by it, just as we did with the clause "expected ready to load": see *Finnish Government (Ministry of Food)* v. *H. Ford & Co. Ltd.* (1921) 6 Ll. L. Rep. 188; *The Mihalis Angelos* [1971] 1 QB 164. But, there is no such authority with the clause "shipped in good condition". I regard this clause as comparable to a clause as to quality, such as "fair average quality". If a small portion of the goods sold was a little below that standard, it would be met by commercial men by an allowance off the price. The buyer would have no right to reject the whole lot unless the divergence was serious and substantial: see *Biggin & Co. Ltd.* v. *Permanite Ltd.* [1951] 1 KB 422, 439, *per* Devlin J. and *Christopher Hill Ltd.* v. *Ashington Piggeries Ltd.* [1972] AC 441, 511, *per* Lord Diplock. That is shown in this very case by clause 5 in form no. 100 which contains percentages of contamination, below which there is a price allowance, and above which there is a right in the buyer to reject. Likewise with the clause "shipped in good condition". If a small portion of the whole cargo was not in good condition and arrived a little unsound, it should be met by a price allowance. The buyers should not have a right to reject the whole cargo unless it was serious and substantial. This is borne out by the difficulty which often arises (as in this case) on a c.i.f. contract as to whether the damage was done before shipment or took place after shipment: for in the latter case the buyer would have no claim against the seller but would be left to his claim against the insurers. So, as matter of good sense, the buyer should be bound to accept the goods and not reject them unless there is a serious and substantial breach, fairly attributable to the seller.

In my opinion, therefore, the term "shipped in good condition" was not a condition strictly so called: nor was it a warranty strictly so called. It was one of those intermediate stipulations which gives no right to reject unless the breach goes to the root of the contract.

On the facts stated by the board of appeal, I do not think the buyer was entitled to reject these instalments of the contract. The board only said that "not all the goods in hold no. 1 were shipped in good condition." That does not say how many were bad. In any case, their condition cannot have been very bad, seeing that all of them were in fact used for the intended purpose. The breach did not go to the root of the contract. The buyer is entitled to damages, but not to rejection.

Appeal dismissed.

[Roskill and Ormrod L.JJ. delivered concurring judgments.]

Note: The concept of an intermediate stipulation adopted by Lord Denning in the above case was also applied in *Tradax International S.A.* v. *Goldschmidt S.A.* [1977] 2 Ll. L. Rep. 604 (QB). What virtues do you see in Lord Denning's approach? What difficulties? If even a minor breach of a condition entitled the aggrieved party to cancel the agreement and, where the buyer is the aggrieved party, to reject the goods, is it consistent with such an a priori scheme of classification to introduce an innominate stipulation whose effect depends on the severity of the breach?

OLRC Sales Report
pp. 145-47

A distinctive feature of the present Sale of Goods Act is its division of contractual obligations into conditions and warranties. "Condition", a notoriously ambiguous term, is used in several senses in the Act, but is not defined anywhere. "Warranty", which is also a term with multiple meanings, is defined in section 1(1)(*n*) as "an agreement with reference to goods that are the subject of a contract of sale but collateral to the main purpose of the contract, the breach of which gives rise to a claim for damages but not to a right to reject the goods and treat the contract as repudiated". The distinction, then, between a warranty and a condition is that breach of a warranty only gives rise to a claim in damages, whereas breach of a condition, as emerges from section 12(2) and other parts of the Act, entitles the aggrieved party to rescind the contract and to claim damages, or to do either.

This dichotomous classification of obligations into warranties and conditions appears to have its origins in the attempts by Lord Mansfield in the late 18th century to mitigate the rigours of the law of covenants. In this evolution, the right of an aggrieved party to treat the contract as at an end was restricted to circumstances where the breach by the other involved a "dependent" covenant and the breach was fundamental in nature. These developments merely mirrored a problem with which all legal systems must come to grips: namely, the remedies to be afforded for different breaches of contract. There was, however, a peculiarity about English sales law, as it developed during the 19th century. Having once categorized a term as amounting to a condition or warranty for the purposes of one contract, the classification was then adopted as binding in later cases involving other contracts of sale and without regard to the severity of the breach in the individual case. This was particularly true of the great terms of title, description, merchantability and fitness, imported in the buyer's favour, and later reproduced in sections 12 to 15 of the U.K. Act.

While there may be some terms whose breach will so seriously prejudice the other party's position that they may fairly be treated as essential terms, this is more likely to be the exception than the rule. As Lord Justice Diplock pointed out in a leading case (*Hong Kong Fir Shipping Co. Ltd.* v. *Kawasaki Kisen Kaisha Ltd.* [1962] 2 QB 26 (CA)):

> There are, however, many contractual undertakings of a more complex character which cannot be categorised as being "conditions" or "warranties", if the late nineteenth-century meaning adopted in the Sale of Goods Act, 1893 . . . be given to those terms. Of such undertakings all that can be predicated is that some breaches will and others will not give rise to an event which will deprive the party not in default of substantially the whole benefit which it was intended that he should obtain from the contract; and the legal consequences of a breach of such an undertaking, unless provided for expressly in the contract, depend upon the nature of the event to which the breach gives rise and do not follow automatically from a prior classification of the undertaking as a "condition" or a "warranty".

The case did not involve a contract for the sale of goods, but these observations seem just as relevant in a sales context.

The *a priori* classification of contractual terms in The Sale of Goods Act has come under increasing criticism. The reason for this criticism is the arbitrary results to which such a classification may give rise, and the encouragement it provides for contrived excuses by a contracting party who wants to relieve himself of a bargain that he no longer finds profitable. It has meant, for example, that a buyer may reject an expensive machine because of a broken glass dial costing only a few cents to replace, or that he may refuse a large shipment of staves because of minor and inconsequential deviations from the contractual description. The distinction is not generally or consistently adopted in other branches of contract law and it was not adopted in the Uniform Sales Act, nor, subsequently, by the draftsmen of the Uniform Commercial Code. Nor does it appear in the Hague Uniform Law on Sales or the draft sales Convention prepared by UNCITRAL. Recent English decisions also indicate a judicial willingness to erode what had been regarded previously as an impregnable scheme of classification. In *Cehave N.V.* v. *Bremer Handelsgesellschaft m.b.H.*, the English Court of Appeal held that the Sale of Goods Act did not require the *a priori* classification of express terms of a contract of sale. In a later decision, *Reardon Smith Line Ltd.* v. *Hansen-Tangen ("The Diana Prosperity")*, Lord Wilberforce, whose judgment was concurred in by Lord Simon of Glaisdale and Lord Kilbrandon, expressed his dissatisfaction with earlier cases involving the construction of the implied condition of description.

Even before these trends had emerged, we recommended, in our *Report on Consumer Warranties and Guarantees*, the abolition of the distinction between warranties and conditions in consumer sales and the substitution of a single term "warranty" to describe the seller's obligations with respect to the attributes of the goods. We also recommended the adoption of a new regime of remedies for breach of warranty obligations that would turn on the gravity of the breach and not on an *a priori* classification of the term breached. The New South Wales

Working Paper has, since then, adopted a similar set of recommendations with respect to both non-consumer and consumer sales.

We have again reviewed the position and we are satisfied that our earlier recommendations are as appropriate for general contracts of sale as they are for consumer sales. However, since our earlier recommendations were restricted to consumer warranties, they need to be adapted to meet the broader requirements of the revised Act. We therefore make two recommendations, which are incorporated in our Draft Bill. First, we recommend the elimination of the distinction between warranties and conditions in the revised Act and the substitution of the single term, "warranty", to describe express or implied terms relating to goods. Secondly, we recommend the adoption of a unitary concept of substantial breach to determine the remedies available for breach of contract by the buyer or seller and, in particular, to determine when an aggrieved party may cancel the contract because of breach by the other. We discuss in chapter 18 our recommended definition of substantial breach.

These recommendations will have their primary impact on the buyer's remedies, because the present Act only adopts a system of *a priori* classification with respect to the seller's implied obligations as to title, description, merchantability, fitness, and conformity to sample in cases of sale by sample. So far as their effect on express obligations is concerned, our recommendations have already been foreshadowed by the recent English decisions mentioned above, certainly with respect to the seller's obligations and probably also with respect to the buyer's obligations.

2. SELLER'S ADOPTION OF MANUFACTURER'S REPRESENTATIONS

COCHRAN v. McDONALD
(1945) 161 P 2d 305 (Wash. Sup. Ct.)

GRADY, Justice: This action was originally brought by O.K. Cochran against Winterine Manufacturing Company, a corporation, to recover damages for breach of warranty. In an amended complaint H. D. McDonald, doing business as McDonald & Company, was joined as a defendant. The plaintiff was unable to secure legal service of process upon Winterine Manufacturing Company, and the case proceeded to trial against McDonald & Company as the sole defendant. At the close of the evidence submitted by the plaintiff its sufficiency was challenged by the defendant, which challenge was sustained by the court and a judgment was entered dismissing the action. The motion of the plaintiff for a new trial was denied and this appeal followed.

The factual situation as disclosed by the record is as follows: Winterine Manufacturing Company manufactured a product known as Antarctic Antifreeze to be used in motor vehicles to prevent freezing in cold weather. The company assigned to respondent the western part of Washington for the distribution of its product and he purchased from it a large quantity of the antifreeze. The antifreeze was put up in sealed gallon jugs and to each jug the manufacturer affixed a label upon which was printed the following:

> Antarctic Antifreeze. The Manufacturer's Guarantee on Antarctic Antifreeze is Insured by an Old Line Casualty Company. Manufactured by Winterine Manufacturing Company, Denver, Colorado.
>
> Guarantee. The Manufacturer of this Antifreeze Guarantees: 1. If used according to directions, in a normal cooling system, Antarctic Antifreeze will protect the cooling system from freezing for a full winter season. 2. It will not cause rust or deteriorate the hose, radiator or engine of your car. 3. It will not cause damage to the finish of your car. 4. It will not evaporate. 5. It will not leak out of a cooling system tight enough to hold water.
>
> Directions for Use. Do not mix with any other antifreeze. Drain cooling system, make certain it is clean and leakproof. Put in proper amount of Antarctic to afford the required freezing protection. (See your dealer's "Protective Chart.") Add water. Fill to within about 2 inches of top of radiator.

The respondent sold a quantity of the antifreeze to Huletz Auto Electric Co. and it resold to a Texaco service station. The appellant purchased a gallon jug of the antifreeze from the service station. Before making the purchase appellant read what was on the label. He testified that this induced him to buy the antifreeze and that he relied upon the representations printed thereon. Appellant put the antifreeze in the radiator of his automobile. Damage was done to the radiator and motor of appellant's automobile. An analysis of the antifreeze showed that it contained highly corrosive elements and was unfit for the purpose designed. The inherently dangerous character of the article was not known to respondent and there was nothing about it as handled by him indicating anything out of the ordinary. It was only upon use of the antifreeze that its character became known.

The appellant presents three grounds of liability of respondent to him:

(1) Upon the express warranty printed upon the label affixed to the article by the manufacturer.

(2) Upon an implied warranty of fitness for the purpose intended when the article resold is noxious and dangerous to property.

(3) Upon an implied warranty of fitness for the purpose intended under the Uniform Sales Act.

We shall discuss the foregoing in the order set forth.

(1) The question presented is whether a wholesaler, who purchases goods from the manufacturer of them who has affixed a written warranty of quality or fitness for the purpose intended by reselling the goods to a vendee, is liable upon the warranty to an ultimate purchaser who relies upon the warranty in making his purchase, puts the goods to use and suffers damage to his property by reason of a breach of the warranty.

In our discussion of this branch of the case we shall refer only to express warranties as the subject of implied warranty is treated later in this opinion.

[1] We have not found in our research many cases dealing with the precise question we are now considering, but the courts passing upon the question, and the text writers, seem to agree that the applicable principle of law is that a dealer

is not liable upon an express warranty of a manufacturer which is put out with or attached to the goods manufactured unless he, in some way, adopts the warranty and makes it his own when selling the goods to others, and that by merely selling the goods he does not adopt the warranty of the manufacturer as his own. *Pemberton* v. *Dean*, 88 Minn. 60, 92 NW 478, 60 LRA 311, 97 Am. St. Rep. 503; *Cool* v. *Fighter*, 239 Mich. 42, 214 NE 162; *Wallace et al.* v. *McCampbell*, 178 Tenn. 224, 156 SW 2d 442, 55 CJ Sales, 684, §687.

In 55 CJ, *supra*, the author states:

> A purchaser of personal property with warranty, who in reselling it to another adopts, by his conduct at the resale, the warranty of his seller, thereby assumes a warranty of the same character as that which was expressly accorded to him. The fact of resale does not of itself constitute an adoption of prior warranties so as to render the seller liable for failure of the goods to comply with such warranties; and this is true even though the words of warranty are physically affixed to the goods.

Judgment affirmed.

Notes:

1   See also *Courtesy Ford Sales, Inc.* v. *Farrior* (1974) 298 So. 2d 26 (Ala. CA) and *Bill McDavid Oldsmobile, Inc.* v. *Mulcahy* (1976) 533 SW 2d 160 (Tex. CA), in both of which the courts held that an automobile dealer was not a party to the manufacturer's warranty delivered by him to the buyer at the time of sale. In *Farrior* the court said (at 31):

> The question then arises as to whether the dealer can be held liable for the guarantees of the manufacturer. We have been cited to no cases, nor have we found any, so holding. It has been decided, however, that unless a dealer specifically adopts the warranty of the manufacturer then he is not bound thereby. *Cool* v. *Fighter*, 239 Mich. 42, 214 NW 162; *Pemberton* v. *Dean*, 88 Minn. 60, 92 NW 478; *Wallace* v. *McCampbell*, 178 Tenn. 224, 156 SW 2d 442; *Cochran* v. *McDonald*, 23 Wash. 2d 348, 161 P. 2d 305. There is no evidence that Courtesy Ford adopted the warranty sued on. Appellee argues that Courtesy Ford is bound by the warranty issued by Ford Motor Company and cites *General Motors Corp.* v. *Earnest*, 279 Ala. 299, 184 So. 2d 811 as authority. In the *Earnest* case, the dealer admitted that he was liable under the manufacturer's warranty, but in the instant case, the dealer has steadfastly maintained that it was not liable under the manufacturer's warranty. Therefore, we do not perceive how *Earnest* could be apt authority for the contention that Courtesy Ford is bound by Ford Motor's warranty.

Can one fairly draw a distinction between adoption of a manufacturer's labelling on a package (e.g., identifying the goods, their weight, or the purpose for which they are to be used) and adoption of a manufacturer's performance warranty? If there is no distinction, and there is no presumption of adoption in either case, how does one determine what the merchant has agreed to sell and what his responsibilities are under the implied conditions of description and merchantability in SGA ss. 14 and 15? Despite its obvious importance, there does not appear to be a reported English or Canadian case in which the merchant seller's deemed adoption of the manufacturer's description of the goods or a warranty relating to the goods has squarely arisen for decision.

2   UCC 2-314(2) provides that, to be of merchantable quality, goods must conform to promises or statements of fact appearing on the label or container. Compare this approach with Ontario's Bill 110, s. 7(2), which would hold a retailer jointly liable with the manufacturer for express warranties made in writing or published or broadcast by the manufacturer. Contrast CIA, s. 36(2), which deems a representation of the types described (including a representation expressed on an article offered or displayed for sale, its wrapper or container) to be made to the public by, and only by, the person to be so expressed, made or contained.

3   In its Sales Report, the OLRC recommended (at p. 204) that:

> the general proposition should be that a description of the goods given by a third person is binding on the seller only if by his words or conduct he has adopted the description as his own.

See also Draft Bill, s. 5.11(2).

This general recommendation was qualified in two respects. First, in its Report on Consumer Warranties and Guarantees the OLRC had recommended that, in a consumer sale, promises or affirmations on or accompanying goods should be deemed to be an express warranty by the seller, whether or not the seller had actually caused the promise or statement to be made. Secondly, with respect to all sales by merchants, the Sales Report recommended a slightly enlarged version of UCC 2-314(2)(f) as one of the requirements of the warranty of merchantability. The Commission reasoned that this imposed no greater hardship on the merchant than holding him responsible for the merchantability and fitness of goods produced by someone else and that the merchant, if sued, would be entitled to claim indemnity from the party actually responsible for the labelling. See OLRC Warranties Report, pp. 34-35, and OLRC Sales Report, pp. 204-06.

3.   THE PRIVITY ISSUE: MANUFACTURER'S LIABILITY FOR EXPRESS REPRESENTATIONS

MURRAY v. SPERRY RAND CORP.
(1979) 5 BLR 284, 96 DLR (3d) 113 (OHC)

REID J.: This action concerns the purchase by the plaintiff of a forage harvester. At the relevant times:

(a) Plaintiff was a farmer.

(b) Sperry Rand Corporation was the American manufacturer of the forage harvester.

(c) Sperry Rand Canada Limited was the Canadian distributor of the machine.

(d) Farm Supplies and Services was a business carried on by the late Charles Church in Barrie, Ontario. It was the New Holland dealer. For convenience I refer to this company, and the late Charles Church, as "Church".

(e) The forage harvester was the New Holland S.P. 818. "S.P." stood for "self-propelled".

A forage harvester simultaneously cuts and chops hay and grass crops. Plaintiff had been thinking for some time about purchasing a new forage harvester. He owned one and had used it for some time. It was not a self-propelled type. That is, it had to be pulled by a tractor. He was particularly interested in a self-propelled type because he had a back problem. He hoped to avoid having to twist in his seat on the tractor, a necessary part of pulling a harvester.

He had seen the S.P. 818 in action at a ploughing match and, on a later occasion, displayed at a stand operated by Church at the 1967 Barrie Fall Fair. He discussed the machine with Church's salesman Hogarth, who was at the stand. Hogarth gave him a sales brochure describing the machine. Plaintiff took the brochure home and read it for several nights. It described the machine's features and performance. He was particularly interested in the "fineness of the cut", that is to say, the size to which the machine would chop the crops it harvested. The quality of silage rose as the fineness increased. He was also interested in the productive capacity of the machine for he was planning to expand his operations. On these points the brochure said:

> You'll fine-chop forage to ³/₁₆ of an inch . . . season after season!

> You'll harvest over 45 tons per hour with ease, . . .

> Under test conditions, the big New Holland harvesters have harvested well over 60 tons per hour.

> And Micro-Shear cutting action gives you a choice of crop fineness — from ³/₁₆ of an inch to 2¹/₄".

In consequence of his interest, Church and Hogarth visited plaintiff's farm. So did William Hutchinson, a representative of Sperry Rand Canada. In the course of the conversations that occurred on these visits, plaintiff explained his type of farming and the operation for which he intended the machine. He received assurances that the harvester would perform as described in the brochure, that it was ideally suited to plaintiff's type of farming, and that it would do a better job than his existing machine.

In the result, plaintiff placed an order for the harvester. It was dated September 26, 1967, addressed to Farm Supplies and Services and signed by plaintiff as purchaser. It was accepted by Hogarth on behalf of Church as vendor. The order was written out on the date it bears by Hutchinson at plaintiff's farm. This was on the occasion of a meeting between plaintiff and Hutchinson at plaintiff's farm when the S.P. 818 was discussed at length.

The price was $12,600.

The harvester was delivered to plaintiff. He began to use it. This litigation arose out of his repeated but unsuccessful attempts to operate the harvester at anything like the promise of the brochure.

During the long course of these attempts plaintiff complained to Church and to both Sperry Rand Companies. These complaints were responded to with interest and reasonable alacrity. The machine suffered from the problem, described by the experts who testified, of "wrappage". That is to say, the crop being cut fouled the cutting apparatus. This caused frequent stops to free it. The result was repeated delays. Defendants sent machines and technicians to the farm. They inspected and adjusted, replaced and modified parts over several years.

There is absolutely no question, however, that despite all their efforts Church and the Sperry Rand Companies were unable to achieve the level of performance set forth in the brochure, or get reasonably near it. After their best efforts the manufacturer's representatives were able to achieve a rate of only 16 tons per hour while operating it themselves at plaintiff's farm. This corresponds with plaintiff's calculations in July 1970. This was a far cry from the 46-60 tons per hour advertised in the sales brochure.

The abject failure of the machine seriously delayed plaintiff's harvest. This had a number of unfortunate consequences. Part of the crop was lost entirely. Much of what was harvested was over-ripe. This reduced the value of the silage made from it. Plaintiff's plans to raise and board cattle were frustrated. Ultimately he sold the harvester and gave up farming.

• • •

On the evidence I make the following findings:

(1) Plaintiff was induced to purchase the harvester through oral representations made by the personnel of Church and Sperry Rand Canada and through the sales brochure prepared and published by Sperry Rand Corporation.

(2) The performance of the machine fell seriously short of that represented in the sales brochure.

In relation to liability, the real questions in this litigation are not questions of fact. There is no doubt about the failure of the machine. It was confirmed very clearly by the evidence of both defendants. Defendants' attempts, particularly those of Sperry Rand Corporation, to blame the failure of the machine upon plaintiff were unsuccessful. There is no question in my mind that the machine failed because of an inherent defect or because the machine was not suitable for plaintiff's farming conditions, or both. Defendant manufacturer denied that the machine suffered from an inherent defect. Yet it was not able to explain why in the hands of its own people the machine would not perform properly.

(3) I find also that the consequence of the machine's failure was damage suffered by plaintiff.

[Reid J. found that (1) Church was liable as a signatory to the contract and as a party to the representations; (2) the representations made to the plaintiff were collateral warranties because they were made with the intention of inducing contractual relations; (3) the plaintiff was entitled to the benefit of the implied conditions of fitness for purpose and merchantable quality in SGA, s. 15; (4) the contract's disclaimer clause was ineffective in its attempt to exclude the implied conditions or the collateral warranties. Reid J. continued:]

The Liability of the Manufacturer

Sperry Rand Corporation was not a party to the written contract between plaintiff and Church. It had manufactured the harvester. It had also published the sales brochure.

I refer to it as a sales brochure notwithstanding evidence from an official of Sperry Rand Corporation that it was not intended to persuade people to buy the machines it describes. That view is, in my opinion, contradicted by the brochure itself. Its tone is strongly promotional. It goes far beyond any simple intention to furnish specifications. It was, in my opinion, a sales tool. It was intended to be one and was used in this case as one.

The representations contained in it, so far as they related to this litigation have already been set out. In the circumstances of this case those representations amounted to collateral warranties given by the manufacturer.

It is, in my opinion, the law that a person may be liable for breach of a warranty notwithstanding that he has no contractual relationship with the person to whom the warranty is given: *Shanklin Pier Ltd.* v. *Detel Products Ltd.*, [1951] 2 KB 854, [1951] 2 All ER 471, [1951] 2 Lloyd's Rep. 187; *Traders Finance Corpn.* v. *Haley; Haley* v. *Ford Motor Co.* (1966), 57 DLR (2d) 15 at 18, affirmed 62 DLR (2d) 329 (SCC); *Andrews* v. *Hopkinson*, [1957] 1 QB 229, [1956] 3 All ER 422. See also K.W. Wedderburn, *Collateral Contracts* (1959), Cambridge LJ 48 at 68 and Cheshire and Fifoot, *The Law of Contract* (7th ed.), at pp. 54-56.

It has been stressed that the intention behind the affirmations govern. I can see no difference whether the affirmations are made orally or in writing.

I have given my opinion that the brochure was put out to entice sales. I can see no other purpose for it. It contained a number of warranties that were proven to be inaccurate. The breach of these creates liability upon the dealer. I can see no legal basis for differentiating between dealer and manufacturer in relation to collateral warranties. The manufacturer initiated the affirmations; it was the manufacturer who apparently prepared and certainly published the brochure. The dealer would perforce have to rely on the manufacturer.

The dealer induced a sale through the use of the brochure and thus acquired liability. Should the manufacturer who published the brochure in an obvious attempt to induce sales be shielded from liability because it had no direct contact with plaintiff?

In *Shanklin Pier Ltd., supra,* McNair J. was dealing with a case in which a paint manufacturer made representations concerning the qualities of its paint to pier owners. Owners caused the paint to be specified in a contract for painting the pier. The painting contractors therefore purchased the paint and applied it to the pier. The paint failed. The owners sued the manufacturers: a mirror image of this case.

McNair J. held that the representations were warranties given by manufacturers to owners. The defence submitted that "in law a warranty could give rise to no enforceable cause of action except between the same parties as the parties to the main contract in relation to which the warranty was given."

McNair J. said [at p. 856]:

> In principle this submission seems to me to be unsound. If, as is elementary, the consideration for the warranty in the usual case is the entering into of the main contract in relation to which the warranty is given, I see no reason why there may not be an enforceable warranty between A and B supported by the consideration that B should cause C to enter into a contract with A or that B should do some other act for the benefit of A.

In other words, manufacturers would have been liable if they had supplied the paint directly to the owners and were equally liable in supplying the paint indirectly.

I see no significant difference between the oral warranties given by the paint manufacturer in that case and the written warranties given by the harvester manufacturer in this. The intention was the same in both cases, viz., to induce the recipient of such representations to purchase the product described. I see no real difference either in the way in which the representations were placed before the prospective purchasers. Dissemination of a sale brochure through dealers is a well-known and normal method of distribution for manufacturers whose products are not sold directly to the public. Through the brochure, the manufacturer presents his case to the potential customer just as directly as he would if they were sitting down together to discuss the matter.

Plaintiff's purchase from the dealer in this case seems clearly to be "some other act for the benefit of the manufacturer" contemplated by McNair J.

Traders Finance Corpn. v. *Haley, supra,* involved somewhat different circumstances. There, a sale of trucks had been arranged between a prospective purchaser and the manufacturer, Ford. It was held that statements made by a Ford officer to purchaser amounted to warranties. Hall J. said in the appeal to the Supreme Court of Canada (*Ford Motor Co.* v. *Haley,* 62 DLR (2d) 329):

> To conform with the appellant's agency arrangements, the deal was put through in the name of Universal Garage as vendor although Universal Garage had no actual part or interest in the transaction.

The sale was financed by Traders Finance.

The case differs from this one in that Ford was held to be the seller within The Sale of Goods Act. Nevertheless, it was recognized that the warranties had been given by a person who was a third party to the agreement. The words of Johnson J.A. in the Court of Appeal are therefore apposite. He said, at p. 18 of the report (57 DLR (2d)):

> The learned trial Judge has found, and the evidence amply bears him out, that a warranty was given by the respondent (Ford). Such warranty, although given by a person not a party to the agreement, is nonetheless binding upon him.

In *Shanklin Pier Ltd.,* McNair J. referred to the case of *Brown* v. *Sheen & Richmond Car Sales Ltd.,* [1950] 1 All ER 1102. There judgment was given against a motor car dealer on an express oral warranty given in relation to the purchaser of a car, notwithstanding that the transaction had been "carried through with the assistance of a finance company" and there was not "in any legal sense any agreement to sell between the [purchaser] plaintiff and the defendants [dealer]" [p. 857].

In *Andrews* v. *Hopkinson, supra,* another decision of McNair J. the basic situation in *Brown* v. *Sheen, supra,* was repeated. It led to the same result.

I cannot see any significant difference in the situation of the paint manufacturer in *Shanklin,* the car manufacturer in *Haley* (apart from the question who was "seller") and the harvester manufacturer in this case.

The Liability of the Distributor

It could hardly be argued that Sperry Rand Canada Ltd. was not the agent of Sperry Rand Corporation. Its liability could rest on that ground. It seems to me, however, to be a fair inference from the evidence that this defendant is directly liable as a warrantor in the same way in which I have held the manufacturer liable.

Again, the evidence is not overwhelming. Plaintiff's recollection was less than precise on the point. Yet the evidence given on behalf of this defendant tended to support the impression that warranties of the same type that were given by Church and the manufacturer were also given by this defendant.

Mr. William Hutchinson said that he had visited the farm before the sale. He called on plaintiff on September 26, 1967 in response to a retail inquiry. He met plaintiff. The meeting lasted from two to three hours. Plaintiff described his interest and the crops he proposed to cut. He was interested in the length of cut. They discussed a self-propelled forage harvester. They went through the New Holland product book. He was there with another person, other than plaintiff.

This resulted in his writing up the order and plaintiff's signing it.

I think it is a fair inference from this and plaintiff's evidence that the product book was the sales brochure and that Hutchinson gave plaintiff the same type of assurances given by Church.

While I recognize difficulties with this evidence, I am satisfied that this has been established on the balance of probabilities.

This defendant is therefore liable to plaintiff directly for breach of warranty.

Judgment for the plaintiff.

Notes:

1   When *Sperry Rand* was first reported in the media it was described as a revolutionary decision. Do you agree? To what extent does it expand the doctrine in *Shanklin Pier?* Although the precedent is frequently overlooked, one of the earliest examples of the courts constructing a collateral contract between a manufacturer and a consumer is *Carlill* v. *Carbolic Smoke Ball Co.* [1893] 1 QB 256 (CA).

2   In light of *Esso Petroleum* v. *Mardon* could the plaintiff in *Sperry Rand* also have brought a successful action under the *Hedley Byrne* doctrine? Would it have been to his advantage to have done so in view of the fact that he was also claiming damages for lost profits?

3   The doctrine of collateral contract as a method for avoiding privity problems with respect to manufacturers' representations does not surmount all the difficulties. For example, can the doctrine be invoked by a buyer who did not himself see the representation but relied on the information of a friend who had seen or heard about it? Should it also be necessary for the buyer to prove he relied on the representation, or should it be sufficient to show that the representation was generally calculated to induce reliance by members of the public and would normally do so in whole or in part? (*Cf. Naken* v. *General Motors of Canada Ltd.*

(1979) 21 OR (2d) 780 (CA) and *Lambert* v. *Lewis, infra,* note 4.) Many representations by manufacturers are contained inside the product's packaging (e.g., the
warranty card for an electric toaster) and would normally not be seen by a
purchaser until the sale has been completed. Could reliance sufficient to satisfy the
doctrine be shown under such circumstances? These problems are briefly discussed in the OLRC Sales Report, pp. 138-39, and at least partially answered in s.
5.10 of the draft bill.

4   *Lambert* v. *Lewis.* The decisions and approaches in *Esso Petroleum* v. *Mardon,
supra,* and *Murray* v. *Sperry Rand, supra,* should be compared with the recent
decision of the English Court of Appeal in *Lambert* v. *Lewis* [1980] 2 WLR 299 (CA);
rev'd on other grounds, *The Times,* April 8, 1981 (HL). The owner of a Land Rover
purchased a towing hitch from a firm of retailers who operated a garage. The
towing hitch was manufactured by a reputable company which had widely advertised the towing hitch, by means of brochures and otherwise, as being foolproof
and requiring no maintenance. The retailers had bought the towing hitch from one
of the wholesalers with whom they dealt. However, they were unable to identify
the particular wholesaler from whom they bought this towing hitch.

The owner used the article to attach a trailer to his Land Rover. The towing
hitch suffered from a serious design defect. As a result, while an employee was
driving the Land Rover, the trailer became detached and careened across the road
into the path of an oncoming car killing the driver of the car and his son and injuring
his wife and daughter.

The wife and daughter brought an action for damages against the driver of the
Land Rover, its owner, the retailers, and the manufacturers of the towing hitch
based on the alleged negligence of each of them. The owner brought third-party
proceedings against the retailers claiming an indemnity in contract for any damages
for which he might be held liable to the plaintiffs on the ground that the retailers had
breached the implied conditions of fitness and merchantability under s. 14 of the
British Sale of Goods Act 1893. The retailers in turn claimed an indemnity or
contribution in tort or contract from the manufacturers. The trial judge found the
driver, the owner, and the manufacturers liable in negligence and assessed the
driver's and owner's liability at 25 per cent and that of the manufacturers at 75 per
cent. He dismissed the plaintiffs' claim against the retailers and the third-party
proceedings against the retailers by the owner. He did not therefore have to
adjudicate the retailers' claim over against the manufacturers but stated that had it
been necessary for him to decide the question he would have dismissed the claim
over.

On appeal the Court of Appeal reversed the trial judge's dismissal of the
owner's claim against the retailers and allowed the owner's claim in full.* It
therefore became necessary for the Court of Appeal to consider the merits of the
retailers' claim for an indemnity or contribution from the manufacturers. The
retailers based their claim on three grounds: (a) breach of collateral warranty; (b)
negligent misrepresentation; and (c) negligent manufacture of the towing hitch. The

---

*   This aspect of the Court of Appeal's judgment is considered below in ch. 12(B).

Court of Appeal unanimously rejected all three grounds. The present note is only concerned with the first two grounds. (The third ground is considered below in chapter 7(A)).

a) *Collateral warranty.* Speaking for the court, Stephenson L.J. said (at 326-27):

> We accept Mr. Turner's submission that not much is needed to conclude that when a warranty of suitability for a particular purpose is expressed or implied in a contract of sale that warranty has been relied on by the purchaser: *Hardwick Game Farm* v. *Suffolk Agricultural Poultry Producers Association* [1969] 2 AC 31, *per* Lord Reid at p. 84 and *per* Lord Pearce at p. 115; *Christopher Hill Ltd.* v. *Ashington Piggeries Ltd.* [1972] AC 441, 495, *per* Lord Wilberforce. But the difficulty is to show that what the manufacturers stated in the literature advertising and accompanying their products as to their safety and suitability was intended to be a contractual warranty or binding promise. It is one thing to express or imply it in a contract of sale, another to treat it as expressed or implied as a contract, or a term of a contract, collateral to a contract of sale. There may be cases where the purchase from an intermediate seller may be regarded as fortuitous and the original supplier or seller can properly be held liable for breaches of warranty given by the intermediate seller as well as for those given by him: *Wells (Merstham) Ltd.* v. *Buckland Sand and Silica Ltd.* [1965] 2 QB 170. But that is not, in our judgment, this case.

He distinguished *Carlill* v. *Carbolic Smoke Ball Co., supra,* on the ground that the manufacturer's promise there was made directly to the plaintiff, and was meant to be binding, and that the case was no authority for holding that the manufacturers were saying to the retailers: "if you acquire our product we promise it is safe and merchantable and if it is not we will pay you such damages as the law requires". Stephenson L.J. accepted the interpretation of *Shanklin Pier Ltd.* v. *Detel Products Ltd.* adopted by the trial judge in the present case, viz that "consideration for the representation was the procurement by the plaintiffs of a contract of sale by their contractors with the defendants". The trial judge had also found that the retailers had not purchased the towing hitch in reliance on the alleged warranty, although apparently there was ample evidence that the retailers' employees had seen and accepted at face value the manufacturers' sales literature. Stephenson L.J. did not find it necessary to rest his rejection of the collateral warranty claim on this ground.

b) *Negligent misrepresentation — the Hedley Byrne doctrine.* The trial judge dismissed the claim based on the *Hedley Byrne* doctrine on the ground apparently that there was no enquiry from the retailers to the manufacturers that prompted the manufacturers to make the claims about their product — they did it voluntarily. Counsel argued that a request for the information was not an essential ingredient in an action for negligent misrepresentation if the statement was made seriously, intended to be acted upon, and in fact acted upon. Stephenson L.J. replied as follows (at 328-29):

> This may sometimes be so. A doctor who goes to the help of an unconscious patient will be liable to him if he injures him by negligent treatment. But we cannot regard the manufacturer and supplier of an article as putting

himself into a special relationship with every distributor who obtains his product and reads what he says or prints about it and so owing him a duty to take reasonable care to give him true information or good advice. Bearing in mind what for instance Lord Reid said in the *Hedley Byrne* case [1964] AC 465, 482 and what Lord Pearce said at p. 539, we consider that cases of liability for statements volunteered negligently must be rare and that statements made in such circumstances as these are not actionable at the suit of those who have not asked for them. To make such statements with the serious intention that others will or may rely on them — and here parol evidence of intent may be admissible — is not, in our opinion, enough to establish a special relationship with those others or a duty to them.

Stephenson L.J. neither referred to nor discussed the Court of Appeal's judgment in *Esso Petroleum* v. *Mardon, supra*, although one would have thought it relevant both on the definition of collateral warranty and on the scope of the *Hedley Byrne* doctrine. Do you see any incompatibility between the ethos of the two judgments? Why should the Court of Appeal in *Lambert* v. *Lewis* have been so anxious to protect the manufacturers from the retailers' claim? The student will find it instructive to compare the Court of Appeal's conservative position with the judgment of the New York Court of Appeals in *Randy Knitwear Inc.* v. *American Cyanamid Co.* which follows.

RANDY KNITWEAR INC. v. AMERICAN CYANAMID CO.
(1962) 181 NE 2d 399 (NY CA)

FULD Judge: "The assault upon the citadel of privity", Chief Judge Cardozo wrote in 1931, "is proceeding in these days apace." (*Ultramares Corp.* v. *Touche*, 255 NY 170, 180, 174 NE 441, 445, 74 ALR 1139.) In these days, too, for the present appeal, here by leave of the Appellate Division on a certified question, calls upon us to decide whether, under the facts disclosed, privity of contract is essential to maintenance of an action against a manufacturer for breach of express warranty.

American Cyanamid Company is the manufacturer of chemical resins, marketed under the registered trade-mark "Cyana", which are used by textile manufacturers and finishers to process fabrics in order to prevent them from shrinking. Apex Knitted Fabrics and Fairtex Mills are manufacturers of fabrics who were licensed or otherwise authorized by Cyanamid to treat their goods with "Cyana" and to sell such goods under the "Cyana" label and, with the guaranty that they were "Cyana" finished. Randy Knitwear, a manufacturer of children's knitted sportswear and play clothes, purchased large quantities of these "Cyana" treated fabrics from Apex and Fairtex. After most of such fabrics had been made up into garments and sold by Randy to customers, it was claimed that ordinary washing caused them to shrink and to lose their shape. This action for breach of express warranty followed, each of the 3 parties being made the subject of a separate count. After serving its answer, Cyanamid, urging lack of privity of contract, moved for summary judgment dismissing the cause of action asserted against it, and it is solely with this cause of action that we are concerned.

Insofar as relevant, the complaint alleges that Cyanamid "represented" and "warranted" that the "Cyana" finished fabrics sold by Fairtex and Apex to the plaintiff would not shrink or lose their shape when washed and that the plaintiff purchased the fabrics and agreed to pay the additional charge for the cost involved in rendering them shrink-proof "in reliance upon" Cyanamid's representations. However, the complaint continues, the fabrics were not as represented since, when manufactured into garments and subjected to ordinary washing, they shrank and failed to hold their shape. The damages suffered are alleged to be over $208,000.

According to the complaint and the affidavits submitted in opposition to Cyanamid's motion, the representations relied upon by the plaintiff took the form of written statements expressed not only in numerous advertisements appearing in trade journals and in direct mail pieces to clothing manufacturers, but also in labels or garment tags furnished by Cyanamid. These labels bore the legend

A

CYANA

FINISH

This Fabric Treated for

SHRINKAGE

CONTROL

Will Not Shrink or

Stretch Out of Fit

CYANAMID

and were issued to fabric manufacturers using the "Cyana Finish" only after Cyanamid had tested samples of the fabrics and approved them. Cyanamid delivered a large number of these labels to Fairtex and Apex and they, with Cyanamid's knowledge and approval, passed them on to garment manufacturers, including the plaintiff, so that they might attach them to the clothing which they manufactured from the fabrics purchased.

As noted, Cyanamid moved for summary judgment dismissing the complaint against it on the ground that there was no privity of contract to support the plaintiff's action. The court at Special Term denied the motion and the Appellate Division unanimously affirmed the resulting order.

Thirty-nine years ago, in *Chysky* v. *Drake Bros. Co.*, 235 NY 468, 139 NE 576, 27 ALR 1533, this court decided that an action for breach of implied warranty could not succeed, absent privity between plaintiff and defendant and, some time later, in *Turner* v. *Edison Storage Battery Co.*, 248 NY 73, 161 NE 423, we reached a similar conclusion with respect to express warranties, writing, "There can be no warranty where there is no privity of contract" (p. 74, 161 NE p. 424). This traditional privity limitation on a seller's liability for damage resulting from breach of warranty has not, however, been adhered to with perfect logical consistency (see e.g., *Ryan* v. *Progressive Grocery Stores*, 255 NY 388, 175 NE 105, 74 ALR 339; *Bowman* v. *Great A. & P. Tea Co.*, 308 NY 780, 125 NE 2d 165; *Mouren* v. *Great A. & P. Tea Co.*, 1 NY 2d 884, 154 NY 2d 642, 136 NE 2d 715) and, just a year ago, in *Greenberg* v. *Lorenz*, 9 NY 2d 195, 213 NYS 2d 39, 173 NE 2d 773, we noted the definite shift away from the technical privity requirement and recognized that it should be dispensed with in a proper case in the interest of justice and reason. More specifically, we held in Greenberg that, in cases involving foodstuffs and other household goods, the implied warranties of fitness and merchantability run from the retailer to the members of the purchaser's household, regardless of privity of contract. We are now confronted with the further but related question whether the traditional privity limitation shall also be dispensed with in an action for breach of express warranty by a remote purchaser against a manufacturer who induced the purchase by representing the quality of the goods in public advertising and on labels which accompanied the goods.

It was in this precise type of case, where express representations were made by a manufacturer to induce reliance by remote purchasers, that "the citadel of privity" was successfully breached in the State of Washington in 1932. (See *Baxter v. Ford Motor Co.*, 168 Wash. 456, 12 P. 2d 409, 15 P. 2d 1118, 88 ALR 521; same case after new trial, 179 Wash. 123, 35 P. 2d 1090.) It was the holding in the Baxter case that the manufacturer was liable for breach of express warranty to one who purchased an automobile from a retailer since such purchaser had a right to rely on representations made by the manufacturer in its sales literature, even though there was no privity of contract between them. And in the 30 years which have passed since that decision, not only have the courts throughout the country shown a marked, and almost uniform, tendency to discard the privity limitation and hold the manufacturer strictly accountable for the truthfulness of representations made to the public and relied upon by the plaintiff in making his purchase, but the vast majority of the authoritative commentators have applauded the trend and approved the result.

The rationale underlying the decisions rejecting the privity requirement is easily understood in the light of present-day commercial practices. It may once have been true that the warranty which really induced the sale was normally an actual term of the contract of sale. Today, however, the significant warranty, the one which effectively induces the purchase, is frequently that given by the manufacturer through mass advertising and labeling to ultimate business users or to consumers with whom he has no direct contractual relationship.

The world of merchandising is, in brief, no longer a world of direct contract; it is, rather, a world of advertising and, when representations expressed and disseminated in the mass communications media and on labels (attached to the goods themselves) prove false and the user or consumer is damaged by reason of his reliance on those representations, it is difficult to justify the manufacturer's denial of liability on the sole ground of the absence of technical privity. Manufacturers make extensive use of newspapers, periodicals and other media to call attention, in glowing terms, to the qualities and virtues of their products, and this advertising is directed at the ultimate consumer or at some manufacturer or supplier who is not in privity with them. Equally sanguine representations on packages and labels frequently accompany the article throughout its journey to the ultimate consumer and, as intended, are relied upon by remote purchasers. Under these circumstances, it is highly unrealistic to limit a purchaser's protection to warranties made directly to him by his immediate seller. The protection he really needs is against the manufacturer whose published representations caused him to make the purchase.

The policy of protecting the public from injury, physical or pecuniary, resulting from misrepresentations outweighs allegiance to an old and out-moded technical rule of law which, if observed, might be productive of great injustice. The manufacturer places his product upon the market and, by advertising and labeling it, represents its quality to the public in such a way as to induce reliance upon his representations. He unquestionably intends and expects that the product will be purchased and used in reliance upon his express assurance of its quality and, in fact, it is so purchased and used. Having invited and solicited the use, the manufacturer should not be permitted to avoid responsibility, when the expected use leads to injury and loss, by claiming that he made no contract directly with the user.

It is true that in many cases the manufacturer will ultimately be held accountable for the falsity of his representations, but only after an unduly wasteful process of litigation. Thus, if the consumer or ultimate business user sues and recovers, for breach of warranty, from his immediate seller and if the latter in turn, sues and recovers against his supplier in recoupment of his damages and costs, eventually, after several separate actions by those in the chain of distribution, the manufacturer may finally be obliged "to shoulder the responsibility which should have been his in the first instance." (*Hamon* v. *Digliani*, 148 Conn. 710, 717, 174 A. 2d 294, 297; see *Kasler & Cohen* v. *Slavouski* [1928], 1 KB 78, where there was a series of 5 recoveries, the manufacturer ultimately paying the consumer's damages, plus a much larger sum covering the costs of the entire litigation.) As is manifest, and as Dean Prosser observes this circuity of action is "an expensive, time-consuming and wasteful process, and it may be interrupted by insolvency, lack of jurisdiction, disclaimers, or the statute of limitations". (Prosser, "The Assault upon the Citadel" [Strict Liability to the Consumer], 69 Yale LJ 1099, 1124.)

Indeed, and it points up the injustice of the rule, insistence upon the privity requirement may well leave the aggrieved party, whether he be ultimate business user or consumer, without a remedy in a number of situations. For instance, he would be remediless either where his immediate seller's representations as to quality were less extravagant or enthusiastic than those of the manufacturer or where — as is asserted by Fairtex in this very case (7 NY 2d 791, 194 NYS 2d 530, 163 NE 2d 349; see, also, *supra*, 11 NY 2d p. 9, n. 1, 226 NYS 2d 365, 181 NE 2d 400) — there has been an effective disclaimer of any and all warranties by the plaintiff's immediate seller. Turning to the case before us, even if the representations respecting "Cyana" treated fabric were false, the plaintiff would be foreclosed of all remedy against Fairtex, if it were to succeed on its defense of disclaimer, and against Cyanamid because of a lack of privity. (*Cf. Baxter* v. *Ford Motor Co.*, 168 Wash. 456, 12 P. 2d 409, 15 P. 2d 1118, 88 ALR 521; same case, 179 Wash. 123, 35 P. 2d 1090, *supra*.)

Although we believe that it has already been made clear, it is to be particularly remarked that in the present case the plaintiff's reliance is not on newspaper advertisements alone. It places heavy emphasis on the fact that the defendant not only made representations (as to the nonshrinkable character of "Cyana Finish" fabrics) in newspapers and periodicals, but also repeated them on its own labels and tags which accompanied the fabrics purchased by the plaintiff from Fairtex and Apex. There is little in reason or logic to support Cyanamid's submission that it should not be held liable to the plaintiff even though the representations prove false in fact and it is ultimately found that the plaintiff relied to its harm upon such representations in making its purchases.

We perceive no warrant for holding — as the appellant urges — that strict liability should not here be imposed because the defect involved, fabric shrinkage, is not likely to cause personal harm or injury. Although there is language in some of the opinions which appears to support Cyanamid's contention (see *Worley* v. *Proctor & Gamble Mfg. Co.*, 241 Mo. App. 1114, 1121, 253 SW 2d 532; *Dimoff* v. *Ernie Majer, Inc.*, 55 Wash. 2d 385, 347 P. 2d 1056; see, also, *Laclede Steel Co.* v. *Silas Mason Co.*, D.C., 67 F. Supp. 751), most of the courts which have dispensed with the requirement of privity in this sort of case have not limited their decisions in this manner. (See, e.g., *Burr* v. *Sherwin Williams Co.*, 42 Cal. 2d 682, 696-697, 268 P. 2d 1041 [insecticide; damage to crops]; *State Farm Mut. Auto Ins. Co.* v. *Anderson-Weber, Inc.*, 110 NW 2d 449 [Iowa], [automobile; property damage]; *Graham* v. *John R. Watts & Son*, 238 Ky. 96, 36 SW 2d 859 [mislabeled seed; wrong crop]; *Silberman* v. *Samuel Mallinger Co.*, 375 Pa. 422, 428-129, 100 A. 2d 715 [glass jars; commercial loss]; *United States Pipe & Foundry Co.* v. *City of Waco*, 130 Tex. 126, 108 SW 2d 432, cert. den. 302 U.S. 749, 58 S. Ct. 266, 82 L.Ed. 579 [cast iron pipes; property damage].) And this makes sense. Since the basis of liability turns not upon the character of the product but upon the representation, there is no justification for a distinction on the basis of the type of injury suffered or the type of article or goods involved.

We are also agreed that the present case may not be distinguished, and liability denied, on the ground that the article sold by the appellant, *resin*, is different from that purchased by the plaintiff, *fabric*. To be sure, as Cyanamid urges, the failure to render the fabric shrink-proof may rest with Fairtex and Apex, but the short and simple answer is that Cyanamid actually and expressly represented that fabrics accompanied by the labels which it supplied were "Cyana Finish" and would not shrink or lose their shape. Since it made such representations, Cyanamid may not disclaim responsibility for them. If the ultimate fault for the plaintiff's loss is actually that of Fairtex and Apex, Cyanamid's appropriate recourse is against them.

Nor may it be urged that section 93 of the Personal Property Law renders privity of contract necessary. The Legislature has there defined a warranty as "affirmation" (or "promise") made by a seller, but the section nowhere states that liability for breach of express warranty extends only to the warranting seller's immediate buyer and cannot extend to a later buyer who made the purchase from an intermediate seller but in foreseeable and natural reliance on the original seller's affirmations. Indeed, we made the matter clear in *Greenberg* v. *Lorenz* when, after observing that the rule requiring a direct contractual relationship between the plaintiff and the defendant is of "judicial making", we went on to say, "our statutes say nothing at all about privity" (9 NY 2d 195, 200, 213 NYS 2d 39, 42, 173 NE 2d 773, 775).

In concluding that the old court-made rule should be modified to dispense with the requirement of privity, we are doing nothing more or less than carrying out an historic and necessary function of the court to bring the law into harmony "with modern-day needs and with concepts of justice and fair dealing." (*Bing* v. *Thunig*, 2 NY 2d 656, 667, 163 NYS 2d 3, 11, 143 NE 2d 3, 9; see *Greenberg* v. *Lorenz*, 9 NY 2d 195, 200, 213 NYS 2d 39, 42, 173 NE 2d 773, 775, *supra*; *Woods* v. *Lancet*, 303 NY 349, 355, 102 NE 2d 691, 694, 27 ALR 2d 1250.)

The order appealed from should be affirmed, with costs, and the question certified answered in the negative.

Notes and Questions:

1   What is the practical difference between the Anglo-Canadian approach and the American approach to a manufacturer's liability for false representations concerning his goods made to the public? Does the non-contractual approach adopted in *Randy Knitwear* mean that neither party would be able to rely on the provisions of the sales article of the Code, or does the case create a hybrid cause of action, combining elements of both tort and contract? Chief Justice Traynor's judgment in *Seely* v. *White Motor Co.* (1965) 403 P. 2d 145 (Cal. SC), quoted in *Morrow* v. *New Moon Homes Inc. (infra,* chapter 7(A)), clearly assumed the Code provisions would apply to false representations resulting only in economic loss. This willingness to blur traditional contract-tort boundaries, although not unknown in Anglo-Canadian law, is a much more distinctive feature of the realist approach in modern American law and won the support of the OLRC Sales Report. The recommended definition of express warranty in s. 5.10 of the draft bill applies to representations or promises made by the "seller, manufacturer or distributor of the goods" and regardless of whether "there is privity of contract between the person making the representation or promise and the buyer" or whether "it was made with a contractual intention".

2   Suppose Mrs. M purchased a garment to which there was attached the "Cyana" label. Would she have a remedy against Cyanamid on the ground that the garment was not shrink-proof? Against Randy Knitwear? Would it make any difference if she did not notice the label until she unwrapped the package at home?

Suppose she had given the garment to her daughter as a birthday present, what would be her daughter's position? On these problems, see OLRC Warranties Report, ch. 5, and OLRC Sales Report, ch. 10 and Draft Bill s. 5.10. See also chapter 7, *infra*.

4. LIABILITY OF TESTING OR SPONSORING ORGANIZATIONS

Problem: H. purchased a new pair of shoes. Because of the design and construction of the soles they were allegedly slippery and unsafe on vinyl covered floors. Unaware of this defect, H. wore the shoes and, on the same day she purchased them, slipped and injured herself on the vinyl floor of her kitchen. The shoes had been advertised in Good Housekeeping magazine and, with the consent of the magazine's publisher, bore the "Good Housekeeping's Consumers' Guaranty Seal" both in advertisements and in labels affixed to the container of the shoes. With respect to the seal, the magazine stated: "We satisfy ourselves that products advertised in Good Housekeeping are good ones and that the advertising claims made for them in our magazine are truthful." The seal itself contained the promise, "If the product or performance is defective, Good Housekeeping guarantees replacement or refund to consumer."

H. brings an action for damages against the publishers of Good Housekeeping magazine. Should she recover and, if so, on what theory of liability (express warranty, *Donoghue* v. *Stevenson*, *Hedley Byrne*)? Is a claim for damages excluded by the terms of the seal? See *Hanberry* v. *Hearst Corp.* (1969) 276 Cal. App. 2d 680, 81 Cal. Rptr 519, and *Hempstead* v. *General Fire Extinguisher Corp.* (1967) 269 F. Supp. 109 (U.S. Dist. Ct. Del.) and contrast *Benco Plastics, Inc.* v. *Westinghouse Electric Corp.* (1974) 387 F. Supp. 772, esp. at 786 (U.S. Dist. Ct. Tenn.). See also M.P. Diepenbrock, "Annotation — Liability of Product Indorser or Certifier for Product Caused Injury" (1971) 39 ALR 3d 181 and Comments in (1970) 74 Dick. L. Rev. 792, (1970) 4 Ga. L. Rev. 260, and (1970) 5 U. San Francisco L. Rev. 137.

B. PUBLIC LAW ASPECTS OF FALSE ADVERTISING

1. INTRODUCTION

The Victorians had a lax attitude towards false and wildly exaggerated advertising claims, as may be seen by studying turn of the century newspapers and catalogues and, outside the public health area, they made few attempts to restrain them through public law sanctions. This indulgence may be ascribed to a variety of factors: the relative novelty of the "penny" press and the undeveloped state of mass communication techniques, the limited purchasing power of most consumers, a still heavily agrarian society, and no doubt a stronger belief than we would entertain today in the capacity of the average reader or listener to separate the wheat from the chaff. See further E.S. Turner, *The Shocking History of Advertising* (1965).

Changes in public attitudes only came slowly, with the Americans apparently taking the first initiatives. The Federal Trade Commission Act (38 Stat. 717) adopted by the Congress on September 26, 1914, declared unlawful "unfair methods of competition" and conferred broad powers on the newly created Federal Trade Commission to enjoin such practices by means of "cease and desist" orders. Section 5 of the Act was broad enough to include false or deceptive advertising claims but only, as the U.S. Supreme Court subsequently held in *F.T.C.* v. *Raladam Co.* (1931) 283 US 643, if the advertisements injured or tended to injure competition. The thrust of the original Act, in other words, was to encourage honest competition and not consumer protection per se. The Act was amended in 1938 (52 Stat. 111) and the Commission's powers were extended to the policing of "unfair or deceptive acts or practices" in interstate commerce, without regard to their effect on competition. The Act has been amended again since then (and most recently in 1980: see the Federal Trade Commission Improvements Act of 1980, PL

96-252, 94 Stat. 374), but section 5 remains an anchor section in the overall scheme of the Act. For the current provisions see 15 USC §§45 *et seq.*

The FTC Act has been copied at the state level in the form of ''little FTC'' acts and the National Conference on Uniform State Legislation has also adopted a Uniform Consumer Sales Practices Act. Nevertheless, the FTC has retained its preeminent position in the U.S. as the senior and generally most active watchdog of unfair market practices. Even then its level of performance attracted much criticism in the 60s. See, for example, the lively account by Edward Cox, Robert Felmeth and John Schultz, *The Consumer and the Federal Trade Commission*, also reprinted in 115 Cong. Rec. (daily ed.) Jan. 22, 1969, and compare *Report of the ABA Commission to Study the Federal Trade Commission* (Sept. 15, 1969).

General public law legislation dealing with false representations did not materialize in the U.K. until the adoption of the Trade Descriptions Act 1968. The Act is exclusively criminal in character and, unlike the FTC Act, spells out the proscribed types of representation with considerable specificity. Another distinctive feature of the Act is that its enforcement is entrusted primarily to local inspectors of weights and measures. The provisions of the 1968 Act were supplemented by the Fair Trading Act 1973 (U.K. Statutes 1973, c. 41). This established the Office of Fair Trading and a Director General of Fair Trading. Under Part II of the Act the director may refer to a newly created body, the Consumer Protection Advisory Committee, the question whether a misleading or confusing consumer trade practice adversely affects the economic interests of U.K. consumers (s. 14(1)), and he can make proposals for the creation of new criminal offences by statutory orders (ss. 13-26). Part III of the Act provides novel powers to cope with rogue traders who have persistently broken the law to the detriment of consumers. In such cases the director must use his ''best endeavours'' to obtain a satisfactory written assurance from the trader that he will refrain from continuing to break the law and, if the trader refuses to give the assurance, the director may seek a court injunction. These provisions appear to have been influenced by American precedents and, as has been seen previously (*supra*, chapter 3(C)(2)), have their counterparts in the provincial trade practices Acts. See further, Gordon Borrie, ''The Office of Fair Trading'' in Ziegel (ed.) *Proc. 7th Ann. Workshop on Comm. & Consumer Law* (1979) p. 49.

The Canadian public law response to false representations has its own distinctive history and characteristics. A section dealing with false advertising claims was added to the Criminal Code as early as 1914 (4-5 Geo. V, SC 1914, c. 24, adding s. 406A, subsequently renumbered with amendments, as section 306) but between this date and the transfer of the section to the Combines Investigation Act in 1969 there was only one reported prosecution under it. Obviously the provinces did not attach much importance to this species of white collar crime.

A new, much more activist, era was ushered in with the addition of 33C to the Combines Investigation Act dealing with misrepresentations as to the ordinary price of goods (SC 1960, c. 45, s. 13). This was followed, in 1969, by the transfer to the Act of s. 306 of the Criminal Code in the form of a new s. 33D (SC 1968-69, c. 38, s. 116; ss. 33C and 33D were renumbered respectively ss. 36 and 37 in the 1970 RSC revision). In the same year the Economic Council of Canada published its *Interim Report on Competition Policy* (Ottawa, July 1969) and this event, coupled with the need to remove some obvious technical differences between ss. 33C and 33D, led to the introduction of a series of abortive government bills to amend the Combines Investigation Act (Bill C-256, 1971, Bill C-227, 1973, Bill C-7, 1973), culminating in Bill C-2, which was adopted in 1975 and came into effect on January 1, 1976 (SC 1974-75-76, c. 76).

The new advertising and related provisions appear in ss. 36 to 37.3 of the current Act. The following are some of the most significant differences between the old provisions and the new:

(1) The old distinction between price advertising and other types of misleading advertising has been abolished. New s. 36 applies generally to "a representation to the public that is false or misleading in a material respect" (s. 36(1)(a)).

(2) New s. 36 applies to representations for the purpose of promoting "the supply or use" of a product whereas the former section was restricted to the "sale or use" of an "article".

(3) "Product" is defined in s. 2 of the current Act as including an article "and a service" whereas old s. 36's "article" was confined to "an article or commodity that may be the subject of trade or commerce".

(4) "Due diligence" was no defence in a prosecution under the old provisions except in the case of bona fide publishers and printers [s. 37(3)]; it is a recognized defence in new s. 37.3.

(5) The new provisions deal with specific types of proscribed market practices relating to: "double ticketting" (s. 36.2); pyramid selling schemes (s. 36.3); referral sales (s. 36.4); switch and bait-selling (s. 37); sales above advertised price (s. 37.1); and promotional contests (s. 37.2). Finally,

(6) new s. 31.1 permits the recovery of civil damages by any person who has suffered loss or damage as a result of conduct contrary to the misleading advertising and other provisions of Part V of the Act, or the failure of any person to comply with an order of the Commission or a court under the Act.

These differences must be borne in mind when reading the pre-1976 decisions. For further discussions of the new provisions, see R.I. Cohen (1974) 13 CPR (2d) 197, and J.S. Ziegel (1975) 17 CPR (2d) 182.

Even before the introduction, from 1974 onwards, of the trade practices legislation the provincial statutes contained scattered provisions (such as CPA (Ont.), s. 47) dealing with various types of false representations. However, as with s. 306 of the Criminal Code, they have been largely conspicuous by their non-enforcement. Experience to date suggests a much better track record for enforcement of the Trade Practices Act provisions, due in part to the superior enforcement mechanisms provided in the Acts and in part to a better level of funding.

Nevertheless, federal prosecutions under the Combines Act have acquired a significantly higher profile, both because of their longer history and because of their predominantly curial, non-administrative character. The enforcement activities are reviewed in the *Annual Report of the Director of Investigation and Research* under the Combines Investigation Act and in the *Misleading Advertising Bulletin* (a quarterly publication) published by the Department of Consumer and Corporate Affairs. In 1978, for example, the Department laid 216 charges against 124 offenders resulting in fines of $212,914.50. The earlier case law is analyzed by Ronald Cohen in (1969) 15 McGill LJ 622. Some of the judgments are only reported in the Canadian Patent Reporter (CPR).

The above description of legislative developments in Canada and other countries discloses a wide diversity of regulatory philosophies and means used to restrain false advertisements. Here is a short list of some of the numerous issues that call for consideration:

1. *How important is the phenomenon of false advertisements?* Are advertising agencies right in claiming that the worst offenders are small enterprises and that the national advertisers exercise stringent internal control?

2. *In Canada, who should have principal responsibility for policing advertisements,* the federal government or the provinces? Assuming they both have constitutional policing powers, how should they allocate responsibility between themselves? And regardless of where the jurisdiction lies, should the actual enforcement of the laws be entrusted to local Crown prosecutors or consumer protection officials, or should it be centralized (as it largely is at the present time)? Do we have something to learn in this respect from the British experience?

3. *The types of advertisements proscribed:* should they be limited to false or misleading advertisements or should they include, *pace* s. 5 of the FTC Act, "unfair" claims? *Cf.* BPA s. 2(*b*) and 2(*c*). Should the offending types of representation be spelled out in detail, as is done in the British Act, or is it better to use general prohibitory language? Should there be regulation making power, as in CPLA, s. 18(1)(*g*) and BPA, s. 16(1)(*c*), allowing government officials to define what is deemed to be false or deceptive or is such power incompatible with the rule of law?

4. *Should the offences be absolute in character?* If not, what defences should be permitted? *Cf. R.* v. *City of Sault Ste. Marie* [1978] 2 SCR 1299, noted *infra*, with CIA, s. 37.3.

5. *What should be the responsibility of advertising agencies* with respect to false advertisements and that of the media for publishing them? For the present position, see CIA ss. 36(2) and 37.3, applied in *R.* v. *Consumers Distributing Co.* (1981) 57 CCC (2d) 317 (Ont. CA).

6. *The burden of proof: on whom should it rest, the advertiser or the Crown?* Cf. CIA, ss. 36(1)(*b*) and 36.1. Is a reverse onus provision appropriate in a criminal context?

7. *How should the legislation be enforced?* By use of criminal sanctions (CIA), by administrative cease and desist powers (a familiar and favoured American device), or both? What role should the individual play, as common informer, prosecutor, or plaintiff suing for double or treble damages? Can the class action play a useful policing role? In what circumstances can corrective advertising expunge the harm that has been done and to what extent should the Canadian Radio and Television Commission recognize a "right of reply" or "counter-advertising" by public interest groups? Finally, how far can the advertising industry police itself? *Cf.* the operations of the Canadian Advertising Standards Council. Are pre-clearance mechanisms such as those operated by the CBC and the Food and Drug Directorate of the Department of Health and Welfare good prophylactic devices or again do they offend our sense of administrative justice?

For useful Canadian materials on many of these questions, see Canadian Consumer Council, *Symposium on Misleading Advertising* (December 1970); R.I. Cohen and J.S.

Ziegel, *A Proposal for Consumer and Misleading Trade Practices Legislation for Canada* (1976); Trebilcock *et al.*, *A Study on Consumer Misleading and Unfair Trade Practices*, DCCA, 1976; M.S. Moyer and J.C. Banks, "Industry Self-Regulation: Some Lessons from the Canadian Advertising Industry", in D. Thompson (ed.) *Problems in Canadian Marketing* (1977) ch. 8.

8. *Should the statute spell out the private law remedies* for a violation of its standards or should this be left to the common law? See CIA, s. 31.1 and *cf.* Ont. BPA, s. 4. What are the substantive differences between them?

Constitutional Position. As in other areas of commercial and consumer law, the rational and efficient resolution of the above issues is bedevilled by an increasingly complex and conflicting overlay of jurisprudence affecting the distribution of constitutional powers between the federal and provincial governments. In *Proprietary Articles Trade Assn.* v. *A.-G. Can.* [1931] AC 310, the Privy Council upheld the anti-conspiracy provisions of the then Combines Act as a legitimate exercise of the criminal law power. While the criminal law characterization may also safely be assumed to apply to the misleading advertising provisions, it is not clear whether the federal government can prosecute them without provincial concurrence.

The difficulty arises because the administration of justice in each province is a provincial responsibility and because s. 91(27) of the BNA Act restricts the federal power to the enactment of criminal laws, "including the Procedure in Criminal Matters". In *R.* v. *Hauser* [1979] 1 SCR 984, which involved a prosecution under the federal Narcotics Control Act, the intervening provinces argued vigorously that the provinces alone have the power to enforce the criminal law because of the provisions of BNA 92(14). The majority of the Supreme Court of Canada side-stepped the issue by validating the Act as an exercise of the federal government's peace, order and good government power. Mr. Justice Dickson delivered a scholarly and powerful dissent. The question was raised again, *inter alia*, before Linden J. in *R.* v. *Hoffman-Laroche Limited* (1980) 14 CR (3d) 289 (Ont. HCJ), which involved a prosecution under s. 34 of the CIA, and he read 91(27) broadly to include the determination of prosecutorial powers. On the other hand, Wetmore C.C.J. in *R.* v. *Kripps Pharmacy Ltd.* (1980) 114 DLR (3d) 457 (BC Co. Ct.); mandamus refused [1981] 1 WWR 753 (BC SC), preferred Dickson J.'s dissenting judgment to Linden J.'s view. The issue will no doubt reach the Supreme Court again soon.

There are other constitutional problems. The lower courts are sharply divided with respect to the validity of CIA s. 31.1 empowering the recovery of civil damages. See *Rocois Construction Inc.* v. *Quebec Ready Mix Inc.* (1979) 105 DLR (3d) 15; *Henuset Bros. Ltd.* v. *Syncrude Canada Ltd.* (1980) 114 DLR (3d) 300, (Alta. QB); *Seiko Time Canada Ltd.* v. *Consumers Distributing Co. Ltd.* (1980) 112 DLR (3d) 500 (Ont. HCJ); and *cf. R.* v. *Zelensky* [1978] 2 SCR 940 and *MacDonald* v. *Vapor Canada* [1977] 2 SCR 940. Further difficulties arise because recent decisions of the Supreme Court of Canada in the agricultural products and food and drugs act areas (viz. *Dominion Stores* v. *The Queen* (1979) 106 DLR (3d) 581, and *Labatt Breweries of Canada Ltd.* v. *A.-G. Can.* (1979) 30 NR 496) have construed the federal government's trade and commerce power very narrowly and this may have a spillover effect on those substantive provisions in the Combines Investigation Act, including the misleading advertising and trade practices area, that cannot clearly be justified as an exercise of the criminal law power. In contrast, in *A.-G. Que.* v. *Kellogg's Co. of Canada* [1978] 2 SCR 211 the Supreme Court upheld the Quebec children's advertising provisions even when they appeared to conflict with the federal government's radio and telecommunications jurisdiction.

For further discussion of the above issues, see P.W. Hogg and W. Grover, "The Constitutionality of the Competition Bill" (1975-76) 1 Can. Bus. LJ 197; James C. MacPherson, "Economic Regulation and the British North America Act: Labatt Breweries and other Constitutional Imbroglios" (1981) 5 Can. Bus. LJ 172; and *infra*, chapter 6(5).

2. THE CREDULOUS MAN TEST

REGINA v. IMPERIAL TOBACCO PRODUCTS LTD.
(1971) 64 CPR 3, 16 DLR (3d) 470 (Alta. SC); aff'd 3 CPR (2d) 178, 22 DLR (3d) 51 (CA)

[The following statement of facts is taken from the judgment of KANE J.A. in the Appellate Division:]

This is an appeal from a judgment convicting the appellant on the following counts in an indictment:

> that it did, at the City of Edmonton, in the Province of Alberta, on or about the 26th day of November, 1969, to promote the sale of property, namely Casino cigarettes unlawfully cause to be published, by means of a sign on premises occupied by United Cigar Stores Limited at the Northgate Shopping Center in the City of Edmonton, aforesaid, an advertisement containing a statement, to wit: "$5 in Every Pack of New Casino" which statement purported to be a statement in fact, but which statement was untrue, and did thereby commit an indictable offence contrary to the provisions of Section 33D(1) of the Combines Investigation Act, RSC 1952, Chapter 314, as amended.

> that it did, at the City of Edmonton, in the Province of Alberta, on or about the 20th day of September, A.D. 1969, to promote the sale of property, namely Casino cigarettes, unlawfully cause to be published, by means of a sign on premises occupied by Sandy Lane Food Market M. & M. Stores at 15618-95 Avenue, in the City of Edmonton, aforesaid, an advertisement containing a statement, to wit: '$5 in Every Pack of New Casino' which statement purported to be a statement of fact, but which statement was untrue, and did thereby commit an indictable offence contrary to the provisions of Section 33D(1) of the Combines Investigation Act, RSC 1952, Chapter 314, as amended.

On the first conviction a fine of $2,500 was imposed and on the second a fine of $500 was imposed.

In addition, the Crown asked for and obtained a prohibition order prohibiting the continuation or repetition of the offences by the appellant, appellant's directors, officers, servants or agents, and without limiting its generality, further specifically prohibiting the appellant, its directors, officers, servants or agents from publishing or causing to be published any advertisement to promote the sale of cigarettes that contained a statement that purported to be a statement of fact but that was untrue.

From the sentences and order of prohibition the appellant also appeals.

Certain facts were agreed on and *viva voce* and documentary evidence was presented at the trial. I will set out what I understand are the material facts. The appellant introduced into Alberta on September 12, 1969, a new brand of cigarettes called "Casino". Marketing of this brand was restricted to Alberta and marketing of the brand ceased on December 12, 1969.

William John Harris, the marketing development manager of the appellant, described Casino cigarettes as "an incentive brand or contest brand". An extensive advertising program was carried on to introduce these cigarettes.

As part of the promotion of the sale of this brand of cigarettes a large display card in colour being part of the point of purchase advertising, was placed by an employee of the appellant at the premises of Sandy Lane Food Market M. & M. Stores at 15619-95 Ave., Edmonton, where it remained on display until about September 20, 1969.

That display card I reproduce herein in black and white:

Another display card was placed by the employees of the appellant in the United Cigar Store in Northgate Shopping Centre, Edmonton. This was smaller than the one at the Sandy Lane Food Market but arranged in similar manner so that the words "$5 in every pack of new Casino" received the most prominence. This sign also showed a corner of the casino card in the cigarette package in the same manner as the other.

None of the Casino brand cigarette packages contained any currency nor did the appellant intend to place any money in any of the packages.

Each package did contain what was referred to in the evidence as a "contest card" or "casino card".

With respect to the casino card contained in each pack of cigarettes, the following is reproduced from the agreed statement of facts as it appears in the Appeal Book:

> The Casino cards have imprinted on one side two concentric squares. In the interior square four numbers or letters are printed. In the area between the two concentric squares another series of numbers or letters is printed. All figures are covered by an opaque substance which can be scraped away to reveal the figure beneath. There is a set of rules printed on the reverse side of each card and each has the potential, if the "player" . . . uncover the figures in the sequence provided for in the rules, to "win" for the player $5 and some have the additional potential to "win" the player $100.

TRIAL JUDGMENT OF SINCLAIR J.:

I shall deal first with counts 1 and 3. The essence of the charges in these counts is that the words "$5 in Every Pack of New Casino" published in advertisements amounted to a statement of fact that was untrue.

Literally taken, these words amount to a statement of fact that was untrue. There was not $5 in currency in each pack, nor was there a coupon or anything else that could simply be exchanged for $5 or its equivalent. What there was in each pack was a game that could be played by the purchaser. He had one chance in 400 to select the winning combination, and thus to gain $5 after answering a "skill-testing" question.

It is true that the possibility existed in each pack to win $5 if the purchaser played the game and was lucky enough to uncover the winning combination present in the pack. I am referring to the average purchaser — the person for whom the programme was undoubtedly intended — and not to those who are able, as it turned out, by the purchase of many packages to "break" the contest, and to win large sums of money. This unforeseen twist to the campaign is irrelevant to the charges I am considering.

The company says the entire Casino advertising programme showed there was a game to be played before any money could be won. It says the average person — the "reasonable man" if you will — would not have been so incredulous as to believe that Imperial Tobacco was going to give $5 in cash in exchange for the purchase price of the package.

In my view, that is not the test to be applied. Section 33D makes no reference to standards such as those. It seems to me the protection afforded by the section is for "the public — that vast multitude which includes the ignorant, the unthinking and the credulous", to use an expression that appears in Federal Trade Commission Prosecution cases in the United States, and of which *Charles of the Ritz Distributors Corp.* v. *Federal Trade Com'n* (1944) 143 F. 2d 676 is an example.

The plain fact of the matter is that the accused, to promote the sale of the Casino cigarettes, caused to be published an advertisement containing a statement purporting to be a statement of fact but which statement was untrue.

Is *"mens rea"* an essential ingredient of an offence under the section as regards causing to be published an untrue statement of fact? In my opinion the answer is "No," except for the protection afforded by s-s. 3 to a person, such as a newspaper, who publishes an advertisement that he accepts in good faith for publication in the ordinary course of his business. It seems to me that the reasons given by Jessup, J.A., in *R.* v. *Allied Towers Merchants Ltd.*, 46 CPR 239 [1965] 2 OR 628, [1966] 1 CCC 220 in holding that *mens rea* is not an essential ingredient of an offence under s. 33c of the Act are equally applicable to s. 33D. . . .

JUDGMENTS ON APPEAL:

KANE J.A.: In respect of the appeal from conviction, counsel for the appellant contended that the learned trial Judge [2 CCC (2d) 533, 16 DLR (3d) 470, 64 CPR 3] erred in reading the statement "$5 in every pack of new Casino" out of context and thereby concluding that those words amounted to a statement of fact that was untrue. It was also argued that even if an advertisement contained a statement which by itself purported to be one of fact, but might be untrue, explanations elsewhere in the advertisement might clarify what was said so that it could not be regarded as untrue; and that the statement above referred to must be read in the context of the entire advertising campaign.

Counsel further submitted that the advertisement did not convey to a reader the impression that there is in it what purports to be a statement of fact that is untrue; that a Court cannot convict on the "necessary imperfection and incompleteness of one statement where, taken with other statements and pictures in the body of the advertisement, the material facts are presented truthfully and candidly to the public". Accordingly it was argued that the statement that there was $5 in every pack of the brand, read in context, could not convey to the reader the impression that there was $5 in currency or its equivalent in every pack of cigarettes.

In my opinion, however, the offence under s. 33D(1) is complete if the published statement is untrue, unless *mens rea* is an essential requirement.

The appellant is not assisted by a consideration of the other words and pictures in the advertisement. The lead statement promises $5 in every pack. Then it goes on to tell that in many packs there is $100. This is also a false statement. If the whole of the advertisement is looked at then, in my opinion, what is promised to a purchaser is that on buying a pack the buyer will find in that pack $5 and will have the opportunity to win $100.

In considering whether in an offence under s. 33D(1) *mens rea* is an essential requirement, it is necessary in the first place to consider the wording of s. 33D of the Combines Investigation Act. As was pointed out by Locke, J., delivering the judgment of the majority of the Court in *Smallman* v. *Moore* [1948] 3 DLR 657 at p. 666, [1948] SCR 295:

> In the *Sussex Peerage Case* (1844), 11 Cl. & Fin. 85 at p. 143, 8 ER 1034, Tindal C.J. said:
>
> > The only rule for the construction of Acts of Parliament is, that they should be construed according to the intent of the Parliament which passed the Act. If the words of the statute are in themselves precise and unambiguous, then no more can be necessary than to expound these words in their natural and ordinary sense. The words themselves alone do, in such case, best declare the intention of the lawgiver.

Section 33D(1) refers to two different kinds of statement: one that in itself is untrue, deceptive or misleading, and one intentionally so worded or arranged as to be deceptive or misleading. It seems clear that as to the second kind of statement, intention to deceive or mislead would be a requisite to conviction. But on the precise and unambiguous wording of the first portion of the section, and having in mind the expressed necessity of there being intention as to the second portion as well as having also in mind the provisions of s-s. (3) of s. 33D, I am of opinion that *mens rea* or intention to do an act forbidden by statute, is not, in such a case as that before us, an essential ingredient of the offence.

In *R.* v. *Allied Towers Merchants Ltd.* [1966] 1 CCC 220, 46 CPR 239, [1965] 2 OR 628, s. 33C [enacted 1960, c. 45, s. 13 (now s. 36)] of the Combines Investigation Act was under consideration. That section provided:

> 33C(1) Every one who, for the purpose of promoting the sale or use of an article, makes any materially misleading representation to the public, by any means whatever, concerning the price at which such or like articles have been, are, or will be, ordinarily sold, is guilty of an offence punishable on summary conviction.
>
> (2) Subsection (1) does not apply to a person who publishes an advertisement that he accepts in good faith for publication in the ordinary course of his business.

Jessup, J., held that the offence under the section was one of strict liability not requiring *mens rea*. It was the learned Judge's opinion that it was the intention of this legislation that the maker of a materially misleading representation should take the risk, that the public should be protected irrespective of the guilt or innocence of the maker, subject to the exceptions provided by s-s. (2).

Jessup, J., expressed the view that while nothing in the express language of s. 33C(1) disclosed any intention that *mens rea* was not an essential ingredient of the offence, that intention was derived from s-s. (2) because if it is necessary to the offence that the accused know the representation he makes is materially misleading, the publisher who accepts an advertisement in good faith for publication in the ordinary course of business would not require the special defence provided by s-s. (2).

The learned Judge gave as an additional reason for reaching his conclusion that the class of acts legislated about in s. 33C(1) are not criminal in any real sense but are acts prohibited under a penalty.

It will be noted that the offence under s. 33C is punishable on summary conviction by a fine not exceeding $500 or imprisonment for six months or both.

In *Beaver* v. *The Queen*, 118 CCC 129 at p. 141, [1957] SCR 531, 26 CR 193, Cartwright, J., for the majority of the Court said that although it would, of course, be in the power of Parliament to enact that a person without having knowledge must on conviction of an offence be sentenced to a term of imprisonment, he would refuse to impute such an intention to Parliament unless the words of the statute were clear and admitted of no other interpretation.

In the *R.* v. *Allied Towers* case, Jessup, J., expressed the view that since imprisonment under s. 33C(1) is not a necessary penalty, the case before him was distinguishable from the *Beaver* case. With respect, I agree (see also *R.* v. *Pierce Fisheries Ltd.* [1970] 5 CCC 193 at p. 203 *et seq.*, 12 DLR (3d) 591 at p. 602, [1971] SCR 5).

At the time of the decision in the *Allied Towers* case the *Criminal Code*, 1953-54 (Can.), c. 51 [now RSC 1970, c. C-34] contained as s. 306 a section in words identical with the present wording of s. 33D of the Combines Investigation Act. By amendment to the Criminal Code (1968-69, c. 38, s. 21) that section was repealed and the Combines Investigation Act was amended by adding as s. 33D, the section now under consideration, in the same wording in which it had appeared in the Criminal Code.

Commenting on s. 306 of the Criminal Code, Jessup, J., said (at pp. 224-5 CCC, pp. 243-4 CPR):

> In this regard I have been given pause however by the consideration of s. 306 of the Cr. Code which deals with false advertisements and of which s. 33C(1) appears to be an extension. Subsection (3) of s. 306 is in substantially identical terms to s-s. (2) of s. 33C and I find nothing in the language of s. 306 that would prevent its s-s. (3) having the same necessary implication in the construction of s. 306(1) as I have found is the necessary implication from s-s. (2), when construing s. 33C(1). However, s. 306(1) is an indictable offence providing liability to imprisonment for 5 years so that the words adopted by Cartwright, J., and just mentioned, appear to become very apposite. Their relevance however is diminished by s. 622 [am. 1959, c. 41, s. 27] of the Cr. Code which provides that on conviction of an indictable offence punishable by imprisonment of 5 years or less a fine may be imposed in lieu of other punishment. I have therefore found any doubts raised by a consideration of s. 306 resolved by the words of Kennedy, L.J., in *Hobbs* v. *Winchester Corp.* [1910] 2 KB 471 also quoted by Cartwright, J., in *Beaver* v. *The Queen* at pp. 140-1:
>
>> Great stress is laid on the character of the punishment that may be inflicted under s. 117. I protest for myself that we are not to assume that where a judicial discretion is granted by the Legislature the tribunal, whatever its rank may be, exercising that discretion will exercise it otherwise than in a judicial manner. Because there may be a case, as there obviously may be, in which a man unknowingly exposes for sale food which is dangerous to health, and because the offence created by the statute is punishable by imprisonment in the first instance, that to my mind is not a ground for holding that a mens rea must be shewn in every case. If it is shewn that the man had no guilty knowledge the Magistrate would probably inflict a merely nominal fine.

I agree with the views expressed by Jessup, J. Accordingly, in my opinion, the published advertisement in the case before us having contained a statement that was untrue, *mens rea* was not an essential element of the offence.

The appellant further contended that the proper standard to apply to s.

33D(1) is whether a reasonable man would be misled or fooled by the advertisement. I do not agree. In my opinion once the statement is shown to be untrue that is sufficient.

Nor do I agree that it was incumbent upon the Crown to show that some person was misled. The case against the appellant, in my opinion, was complete, as I have indicated above, upon proof of the publication of the advertisement containing the untrue statement. I would therefore dismiss the appeal from convictions. . . .

CLEMENT J.A.: Turning now to the final question whether the impugned advertisement evidences an offence, the first point is whether the one sentence in large type "$5 in every pack of new Casino" on which the Crown rests its case, can be considered completely divorced from its context in determining whether the advertisement contains "a statement that purports to be a statement of fact but that is untrue". I am of opinion that it would be contrary to accepted tenets of common law to attribute to a phrase a meaning which it bears standing alone, when in the context in which it is used it bears a different meaning. Whether a statement purports to be one of fact can only be determined by reference to the circumstances and context in which it was made. I do not gather from the reasons for judgment of the learned trial Judge that he necessarily held a different view on this point.

Nevertheless, the determination should not be coerced one way or the other, either by narrow or by vague parameters. The issue is whether in the context of the whole advertisement, the statement purports to be true, and the question is the standard to be used in the determination. The learned trial Judge adopted as his, a phrase appearing in *Aronberg et al.* v. *F.T.C.* (1943), 132 F. 2d 165 at p. 167. The paragraph in which that phrase occurs is in these terms:

> The law is not made for experts but to protect the public, — that vast multitude which includes the ignorant, the unthinking and the credulous, who, in making purchases, do not stop to analyze but too often are governed by appearances and general impressions. Advertisements must be considered in their entirety, and as they would be read by those to whom they appeal.

On this point, the following passage appears in *F.T.C.* v. *Sterling Drug, Inc., supra,* [at p. 674]:

> It is therefore necessary in these cases to consider the advertisement in its entirety and not to engage in disputatious dissection. The entire mosaic should be viewed rather than each tile separately. "The buying public does not ordinarily carefully study or weigh each word in an advertisement. The ultimate impression upon the mind of the reader arises from the sum total of not only what is said but also of all that is reasonably implied."

And, in *Charles of the Ritz Distributors Corp.* v. *F.T.C.* (1944), 143 F. 2d 676, specifically referred to by the learned trial Judge, it was said [at p. 679]:

> . . . and the "fact that a false statement may be obviously false to those who are trained and experienced does not change its character, nor take away its power to deceive others less experienced."

As I have noted above, an offence in respect of advertising under the Federal Trade Commission Act, has somewhat different characteristics from the offence with which we are here concerned, but nevertheless it appears to me that the foregoing observations afford some sensible guidance. The law does not recognize a particular class of the public as ignorant, unthinking and credulous; nor should it measure these matters by the standards of the skeptical who have learned by bitter experience to beware of commercial advertisements. What is the immediate impression that the advertisement makes? Does the impugned statement stand out so that in fact it does not appear to be modified by the context in which it appears unless the whole is examined with care? Having these considerations in mind, I am not prepared to disagree with the conclusion reached by the learned trial Judge.

I concur in the disposition made by my brother Kane of the appeal against penalty, and of the order made under s. 31.

Appeal as to conviction dismissed.

[Johnson J.A.'s dissenting judgment on the question of *mens rea* has been omitted.]

CHARLES OF THE RITZ DISTRIBUTORS CORP. v. F.T.C.
(1944) 143 F. 2d 676 (2nd Cir. CA)

Petition to review and set aside a cease and desist order issued by the Federal Trade Commission. The petitioner, a New York corporation engaged in the sale and distribution of various cosmetics, had carried on an extensive advertising campaign for its cosmetic preparation "Charles of the Ritz Rejuvenescence Cream". The advertisements alleged, inter alia, that the cream contained "a vital organic ingredient" and certain "essences and compounds", and brought to the "skin quickly the clear radiance . . . the petal-like quality and texture of youth", restoring "natural moisture necessary for a live, healthy skin".

After finding that there were in fact no rejuvenating qualities in the petitioner's cream, and rejecting the argument that "rejuvenescence" is a nondescriptive "boastful and fanciful word", the court continued:

CLARK Circuit Judge: There is no merit to petitioner's argument that, since no straight-thinking person could believe that its cream would actually rejuvenate, there could be no deception. Such a view results from a grave misconception of the purposes of the Federal Trade Commission Act. That law was not "made for the protection of experts, but for the public — that vast multitude which includes the ignorant, the unthinking and the credulous," *Florence Mfg. Co.* v. *J. C. Dowd & Co.*, 2 Cir., 178 F. 73, 75; and the "fact that a false statement may be obviously false to those who are trained and experienced does not change its character, nor take away its power to deceive others less experienced." *Federal Trade Commission* v. *Standard Education Soc.*, 302 U.S. 112, 116, 58 S. Ct. 113, 115, 82 L. Ed. 141. See, also, *Stanley Laboratories, Inc.*, v. *Federal Trade Commission*, 9 Cir., 138 F. 2d 388, 392, 393; *Aronberg* v. *Federal Trade Commission*, 7 Cir., 132 F. 2d 165, 167; *D. D. D. Corp.* v. *Federal Trade Commission*, 7 Cir., 125 F. 2d 679, 682. The important criterion is the net impression which the advertisement is likely to make upon the general populace. *Stanley Laboratories, Inc.,* v. *Federal Trade Commission, supra; Aronberg* v. *Federal Trade Commission, supra; Federal Trade Commission* v. *Standard Education Soc., supra; Ford Motor Co.* v. *Federal Trade Commission,* 6 Cir., 120 F. 2d 175, 182, *certiorari* denied 314 U.S. 668, 62 S. Ct. 130, 86 L. Ed. 535; *Newton Tea & Spice Co.* v. *United States,* 6 Cir., 288 F. 475, 479. And, while the wise and the worldly may well realize the falsity of any representations that the present product can roll back the years, there remains "that vast multitude" of others who, like Ponce de Leon, still seek a perpetual fountain of youth. As the Commission's expert further testified, the average woman, conditioned by talk in magazines and over the radio of "vitamins, hormones, and God knows what," might take "rejuvenescence" to mean that this "is one of the modern miracles" and is "something which would actually cause her youth to be restored." It is for this reason that the Commission may "insist upon the most literal truthfulness" in advertisements, *Moretrench Corp.* v. *Federal Trade Commission,* 2 Cir., 127 F. 2d 792, 795, and should have the discretion, undisturbed by the courts, to insist if it chooses "upon a form of advertising clear enough so that, in the words of the prophet Isaiah, 'wayfaring men, though fools, shall not err therein.' " *General Motors Corp.* v. *Federal Trade Commission,* 2 Cir., 114 F. 2d 33, 36, certiorari denied 312 U.S. 682, 61 S. Ct. 550, 85 L. Ed. 1120.

Notes on the Credulous Man Test:

1 At the time of his decision the advertising profession expressed great dismay at Sinclair J.'s adoption of this test. Was the apprehension warranted? Was it necessary to decide the issue for the purposes of the *Imperial Tobacco* case?

2 Since *Imperial Tobacco* Canadian cases have been decided on both sides of the issue. In *R.* v. *Kraft Foods Ltd.* (1972) 36 DLR (3d) 376 (Que. QB); *R.* v. *Colgate-Palmolive Ltd.* (1972) 9 CPR (2d) 62 (Ont. Co. Ct.); *R.* v. *Broadway Clothiers Ltd.* (1974) 20 CCC (2d) 35 (BC Prov. Ct.); and *R.* v. *Whitehall Dev. Corp. Ltd.* (1977) 43 CPR (2d) 64 (Ont. Co. Ct.) the test was approved. On the other hand, in *R.* v. *Golden* (1973) 19 CPR (2d) 118 (Man. Prov. Ct.); *R.* v. *City Tire Services Ltd.* (1974) 21 CCC (2d) 244 (NB Co. Ct.); *R.* v. *T. Eaton Co. Ltd.* (1975) 26 CPR (2d) 118 (Alta. SC); and *R.* v. *Bristol-Myers of Canada Ltd.,* (1979) 48 CCC (2d) 384 (Ont. Co. Ct.), the courts appear to have applied a reasonableness test and not a literal meaning test. Generally, the Canadian cases are not as clear as might be wished and lack a sound theoretical base.

3 Does the CIA, as amended in 1975, make any reference to the standards to be applied? Consider CIA ss. 36(4), s. 37(1)(*b*). Should the courts protect those who will believe anything or is there a minimum threshold of intelligence? Or does it depend on the nature of the advertisement and the types of persons to whom it is directed? See F.A. Miniter, "Misleading Advertising: The Standard of Deceptiveness" (1975-76) 1 Can. Bus. LJ 435 and compare Note, "Developments in the Law: Deceptive Advertising" (1966-67) 80 Harv. L. Rev. 1005 at 1040 *et seq.*

3. PROMISES OR STATEMENTS OF FACT?

REGINA v. STEINBERG'S LTD.
(1977) 31 CCC (2d) 30, 13 OR (2d) 293 (Ont. CA)

ARNUP J.A. (for the court): The primary issue in this appeal is whether the false advertising provisions of the Combines Investigation Act, RSC 1970, c. C-23, s. 37(1)(a) [rep. & sub. 1974-75, c. 76, s. 18(1)], are infringed by the operator of a supermarket when it advertises "specials" at reduced prices but the prices on the "specials" on its shelves are not changed to conform with the advertised prices, with the result that some items are sold at the old prices.

A secondary issue is whether there is a breach of the same provisions of the Act when the store runs out of an item advertised as a "special", so that a customer seeking to purchase it is unable to do so.

In the fall of 1973 Steinberg's Limited operated 58 stores in the Toronto area under the name Miracle Mart Food Stores. At that time the central management had a merchandising practice of advertising some items every Wednesday at reduced prices. These items were called "a Miracle extra". They were selected by central management, including the grocery buying department. Their buyers seek special prices from suppliers. The expectation is that the volume of sales of special items will be several times normal, and purchase orders are placed accordingly. While the complete procedure was fully brought out at the trial, it is not necessary to set it out here.

Advertisements were placed in the Toronto Star every Wednesday for goods to be sold in 28 of Steinberg's Toronto stores; the advertised prices were in effect from 9:00 a.m. Wednesday until 6:00 p.m. Saturday, but frequently the item would continue to be advertised and sold at the special price for a period of three weeks. The advertisements covered many items not classified as "Miracle extras"; some of these were coupled with the words "Everyday Low Prices".

On the Saturday previous to the Wednesday publication of the advertisement, each store received a "price change notice", which included instructions that after the close of business on the following Tuesday night, the retail prices in the store were to be changed from the current price to the advertised price. Each store has a crew whose job it is to make the changes. Some changes are made by stamping a new price on the item, some by affixing a new price sticker.

On the Wednesday morning the grocery manager of the store and the store manager or his designate were supposed to take the price change notice and check to see if the prices had been changed overnight in accordance with the notice. The first edition of the newspaper comes out about 11:30 a.m. Two of the advertisements were displayed in the store at 600 Sheppard Ave. West (the only store involved in this prosecution), in locations where a customer could see them.

One further background fact is that Steinberg's had three merchandising policies relevant to this case. If an item presented at the check-out counter had two prices on it, the cashier was instructed to charge the lower. If the cashier's attention was called to the fact that the price on an item was higher than an advertised price, she was to charge the advertised price. If the store was out of an item that was advertised, the customer on request could get an "honour card", and by presenting the honour card at a later time, within 15 days, the customer could buy the item at the advertised price.

Mr. William Howe, an investigator with the federal Department of Consumer and Corporate Affairs, was instructed to investigate the Steinberg's store at 600 Sheppard Ave. West, which is one of the 28 stores for which advertisements were placed in the Toronto Star. An advertisement had been "run" on Wednesday, October 31, 1973. Howe went to the store on Thursday, November 1st. There is no doubt he was checking to see if prices of "specials" on the shelves conformed to those in the advertisement. When an item did not conform, he bought it, saying nothing to the cashier or anybody else about the discrepancy. There is no doubt that in all the instances where the price of the special, on the shelf, was higher than the advertised price, Howe could have bought the item at the advertised price by drawing this to the attention of the cashier. (He had the advertisement with him, and two were on display.)

He examined 42 items referred to in the advertisement and selected nine for purchase. Three were bought at the unchanged former price, the discrepancies being:

Item	Advertised price	Price paid
Nescafe Instant Coffee, 10 oz.	$1.79	$1.99
Steinberg Light Bulbs (6)	$ .88	$ .98
Welch's Grape Jam	$ .35	$ .40

On Wednesday, November 7, 1973, another advertisement was published in the Star. Howe again visited the store on the Thursday (November 8th). He purchased seven advertised specials and one other item. Prices on three specials had not been changed. In addition, the store was out of stock on four advertised items, although on three of them much larger quantities than usual had been ordered and received, and the central warehouse had ample stock to replenish the store. (The records concerning the fourth out of stock item could not be located at the time of trial).

Eventually 12 charges were laid against the appellant, by indictment, and the appellant was tried by a County Court Judge at Toronto. (No objection was made that one charge respecting each advertisement would have been sufficient.) The appellant was convicted on 10 charges, embracing the three infractions found on November 1st, three more on November 8th, and four charges in respect of the out of stock specials on November 8th. Two charges were dismissed (one item had an obviously defective price stamp, and another had two prices, on opposite ends of a box, being the old and the advertised prices).

The trial Judge, quite properly, grouped the charges when imposing sentence. For the three instances of November 1st, he imposed a fine of $10,000 plus two suspended sentences. For the three instances of unchanged prices on November 8th, he imposed a fine of $10,000 and two suspended sentences. On the four charges respecting "out of stock" items he imposed a fine of $500 and three suspended sentences. The appellant appeals from both the convictions and the sentences.

Section 37(1)(a) of the Combines Investigation Act reads:

> **37.**(1) Every one who publishes or causes to be published an advertisement containing a statement that purports to be a statement of fact but that is untrue, deceptive or misleading or is intentionally so worded or arranged that it is deceptive or misleading, is guilty of an indictable offence and is liable to imprisonment for five years, if the advertisement is published.
>
> (a)   to promote, directly or indirectly, the sale or disposal of property or any interest therein, . . .

It is obvious that the advertisement was published to promote the sale of merchandise. The Crown relies on the first part of the description of a proscribed advertisement, *i.e.*, "containing a statement that purports to be a statement of fact but that is untrue, deceptive or misleading".

The first question therefore is: What is the "statement of fact" in these advertisements? One illustration is typical. The entire text of the advertisement relating to the first charge is:

The Crown submits that it does not matter what the seller intended to convey by the advertisement; what matters is the impression which the words of the advertisement, in context, make upon the mind of the reader. Counsel also submits that an advertisement may be true when published but become untrue as a result of subsequent events in the store (for example, when a clerk fails to change the price when replenishing the stock on the shelf, or puts on a wrong price). In substance, the Crown says the statement of fact is: "With respect to the goods advertised, those items on the shelves of all our stores are marked and for sale at the advertised price".

The appellant submits that the advertisement is a notice to the public that the articles advertised will be sold at the advertised prices. It is, therefore, not a statement of fact but a reference to a future event. If it *is* a statement of fact, it was true when the advertisement was published, which is the only relevant time. Alternatively, the evidence demonstrated that the appellant *would* sell at the advertised prices, if errors in affixing prices to items had been brought to its notice, and therefore the advertisement remained true, even if through error sales were made at higher prices.

The appellant submits that counsel for the Crown at the trial, and the trial Judge, treated the offence as being one of having prices on shelf items different from those advertised, or as one of selling items at prices other than those advertised — neither of which, he submits, is an offence under s. 37(1)(*a*).

• • •

The distinction between words creating a promise of future action or the happening of future events, on the one hand, and words constituting a statement as to existing fact, on the other, has long been made in cases of fraud or deceit. It has recently become relevant in relation to legislation such as the Canadian misleading or false advertising provisions. The House of Lords recently considered it in *British Airways Board* v. *Taylor* [1976] 1 WLR 13, a case under the Trade Descriptions Act, 1968, which contains, among other things, a section making it an offence for a person in the course of trade or business to make a statement which he knows to be false (thereby differing from s. 37(1)). Lord Wilberforce said at p. 17:

> My Lords, the distinction in law between a promise as to future action, which may be broken or kept, and a statement as to existing fact, which may be true or false, is clear enough. There may be inherent in a promise an implied statement as to a fact, and where this is really the case, the court can attach appropriate consequences to any falsity in, or recklessness in the making of, that statement. Everyone is familiar with the proposition that a statement of intention may itself be a statement of fact and so capable of being true or false. But this proposition should not be used as a general solvent to transform the one type of assurance with another: the distinction is a real one and requires to be respected, particularly where the effect of treating an assurance as a statement is to attract criminal consequences, as in the present case. As Lord Widgery C.J. said in *Beckett* v. *Cohen* [1972] 1 WLR 1593, 1596, it was never intended that the Act of 1968 should be used so as to make a criminal statement out of what is really a breach of warranty.

There has been very little law developed in this country as to the legal characterization of what happens in a supermarket. Who makes the "offer" and when? Who accepts it and where, and when? Is an advertisement an offer to sell? Is the offer subject to automatic expiry when the supply is exhausted? These questions are raised and discussed in Treitel, *Law of Contract*, 4th ed. (1975), at pp. 9-11 and in more general terms in Cheshire and Fifoot, *Law of Contract*, 8th ed. (1972), at pp. 26-8: see also 9 Hals., 4th ed., "Contracts", para. 229, p. 101, notes 14, 15. I think it is clear that the sale takes place at the check-out counter and (leaving aside questions of mistakes by the cashier) at the moment when the cashier has rung up the price and moved the article along the conveyor belt from the "unchecked" side to the "checked side".

I think it is also clear (as Treitel says it is in England) that there is no "offer to treat" involved in this operation, and that sales take place at the seller's price.

Against this background, is there a "statement of fact" in this advertisement? In my view, there is. It is partly implied from the customs of the trade as outlined above. In its shortest form the advertisement states: "Our selling price for the items listed is the price stated in this advertisement". But from the point of view of the cashier, who is the employee who makes the sale, the selling price of an item is the price marked on it, unless in some way she becomes aware that the selling price is supposed to be something different.

In my view it follows that if in a particular store there are on the shelves *at the time the advertisement is published* items marked with prices different from those in the advertisement, the statement of fact in the advertisement is untrue. The advertisement may be published more than once in one day, as the advertisements in question undoubtedly were. Statements of fact must be true at the time of each publication. Here Mr. Howe made his investigation on the *following* day; there is no evidence that what he found on Thursday was any different on Wednesday, so far as the marking of prices was concerned, and the appellant does not argue that it was different.

I do not accept the Crown's submission that the statements in an advertisement can be true when published but can become untrue by subsequent events. I termed this, during the argument, "wandering in and out of a cloud of untruth". If Parliament wants to pass a law that when a seller of goods has published an advertisement stating the price of them, all of the items of that kind on the shelves for selection by the customer must bear that price, or must be sold at that price, or both, it will have to enact something different from the present s. 37(1)(*a*), which is not aimed directly at an operation taking place in the store, but at the advertisement. On this issue I agree with the appellant.

On the other hand, I do not accept the appellant's submission as to the advertisement being a representation of a future event, or alternatively, a statement of present intention that it "would sell" at the listed prices.

Turning to the specific charges, it follows from what I have said that, in my view, the appellant was rightly convicted on the eight charges where the prices had not been changed and the sales were made at the higher unchanged price. The appellant should have been acquitted on the four charges where the advertised item was out of stock. There is no evidence that at the time of the publication of the advertisement, the store did not have all of these items, with prices correctly marked. There is, of course, no suggestion whatever that the advertising of these items at the prices listed was a sham.

I would therefore allow the appeals from conviction on charges 9, 10, 11 and 12, quash the convictions, and direct that verdicts of acquittal be entered on those charges. I would dismiss the appeal from conviction on charges 1, 2, 3, 6, 7 and 8.

On the appeals from sentence, it is quite clear from the evidence that what happened in this store was completely contrary to company policy. If the directions from headquarters had been followed, the prices would all have been changed and if any had been missed on Tuesday night, it would have been caught on the check directed to be made on Wednesday morning, before the advertisement had even been published. Furthermore, if Mr. Howe — or any other customer who had read the advertisement — had drawn to the cashier's attention that the price marked on the advertised item was wrong, the cashier would have checked the price, and sold the item at the advertised price. The very cashier who served Mr. Howe on November 1st testified to that effect. Mr. Howe agreed that this would likely have happened. I do not suggest that he was under any obligation to speak up. He was doing his job, which was to find the facts and report them.

Nevertheless, the case is quite different from those where the breach of the statute has been occasioned by deliberate company policy (as in *R. v. Browning Arms* (1974) 18 CCC (2d) 298, 15 CPR (2d) 298; *R. v. Dominion Stores Ltd.*, unreported (Provincial Court, November 22, 1973) [since reported 20 CCC (2d) 378, 15 CPR (2d) 35] and *R. v. Family Tire Centres Ltd.* (Ont. CA, December 4, 1975) [since reported 25 CPR (2d) 219, 28 CCC (2d) 473]).

Furthermore we are really dealing with only two advertisements, as the trial Judge recognized in his grouping of the charges, already referred to. The two were published on successive weeks.

I recognize the relationship of $10,000 to the volume of sales by a supermarket chain such as the appellant, but when the company is being punished not for deliberately breaking the law, but for failure to ensure that its employees observed it, I think $10,000 per advertisement is too large a fine.

I would allow the appeals as to sentence with respect to charges 1 and 6 and reduce each of the fines on those charges to $5,000. The appeals from the four suspended sentences on charges 2, 3, 7 and 8 should of course be dismissed.

Order accordingly.

Note: *Steinberg's* was followed in *R. v. John Jaworski Boats and Motors* (1977) 45 CPR (2d) 223 (Ont. Prov. Ct.). Do you agree with the court's reasoning in *Steinberg's*? As a matter of statutory policy, should a distinction be drawn between affirmations of fact and performance of promises?

The old CIA provision, s. 37(1), made it an offence to publish an advertisement containing a statement "that purports to be a statement of fact but that is untrue, deceptive or misleading". Compare this with the amended CIA s. 36(1)(*a*), which makes it an offence to "make a representation to the public that is false or misleading in a material respect". Would *Steinberg's* be decided similarly under the new CIA? For a discussion of this important issue, see J.S. Ziegel, "Comment — Misleading Advertising and the Fact-Promise dichotomy: *R. v. Steinberg's Limited*" (1977-78) 2 Can. Bus. LJ 114.

4. CORPORATE CRIMINAL LIABILITY

TESCO SUPERMARKETS LTD. v. NATTRASS
[1972] AC 153, [1971] 2 All ER 127 (HL)

LORD REID: My Lords, the appellants own a large number of supermarkets in which they sell a wide variety of goods. The goods are put out for sale on shelves or stands, each article being marked with the price at which it is offered for sale. The customer selects the articles he wants, takes them to the cashier, and pays the price. From time to time the appellants, apparently by way of advertisement, sell "flash packs" at prices lower than the normal price. In September 1969 they were selling Radiant washing powder in this way. The normal price was 3s. 11d. but these packs were marked and sold at 2s. 11d. Posters were displayed in the shops drawing attention to this reduction in price.

These prices were displayed in the appellants' shop at Northwich on September 26. Mr. Coane, an old age pensioner, saw this and went to buy a pack. He could only find packs marked 3s. 11d. He took one to the cashier who told him that there were none in stock for sale at 2s. 11d. He paid 3s. 11d. and complained to an inspector of weights and measures. This resulted in a prosecution under the Trade Descriptions Act 1968 and the appellants were fined £25 and costs.

Section 11(2) provides:

> If any person offering to supply any goods gives, by whatever means, any indication likely to be taken as an indication that the goods are being offered at a price less than that at which they are in fact being offered he shall, subject to the provisions of this Act, be guilty of an offence.

It is not disputed that that section applies to this case. The appellants relied on section 24(1) which provides:

> In any proceedings for an offence under this Act it shall, subject to subsection (2) of this section, be a defence for the person charged to prove — (a) that the commission of the offence was due to a mistake or to reliance on information supplied to him or to the act or default of another person, an accident or some other cause beyond his control; and (b) that he took all reasonable precautions and exercised all due diligence to avoid the commission of such an offence by himself or any person under his control.

The relevant facts as found by the magistrates were that on the previous evening a shop assistant, Miss Rogers, whose duty it was to put out fresh stock found that there were no more of the specially marked packs in stock. There were a number of packs marked with the ordinary price so she put them out. She ought to have told the shop manager, Mr. Clement, about this, but she failed to do so. Mr. Clement was responsible for seeing that the proper packs were on sale, but he failed to see to this although he marked his daily return "all special offers O.K." The magistrates found that if he had known about this he would either have removed the poster advertising the reduced price or given instructions that only 2s. 11d. was to be charged for the packs marked 3s. 11d.

Section 24(2) requires notice to be given to the prosecutor if the accused is blaming another person and such notice was duly given naming Mr. Clement.

In order to avoid conviction the appellants had to prove facts sufficient to satisfy both parts of section 24(1) of the Act of 1968. The magistrates held that they

> had exercised all due diligence in devising a proper system for the operation of the said store and by securing so far as was reasonably practicable that it was fully implemented and thus had fulfilled the requirements of section 24(1)(b).

But they convicted the appellants because in their view the requirements of section 24(1)(a) had not been fulfilled: they held that Clement was not "another person" within the meaning of that provision.

The Divisional Court held that the magistrates were wrong in holding that Clement was not "another person." The respondent did not challenge this finding of the Divisional Court so I need say no more about it than that I think that on this matter the Divisional Court was plainly right. But that court sustained the conviction on the ground that the magistrates had applied the wrong test in deciding that the requirements of section 24(1)(b) had been fulfilled. In effect that court held that the words "he took all reasonable precautions . . ." do not mean what they say: "he" does not mean the accused, it means the accused and all his servants who were acting in a managerial or supervisory capacity. I think that earlier authorities virtually compelled the Divisional Court to reach this strange construction. So the real question in this appeal is whether these earlier authorities were rightly decided.

But before examining those earlier cases I think it necessary to make some general observations.

Over a century ago the courts invented the idea of an absolute offence. The accepted doctrines of the common law put them in a difficulty. There was a presumption that when Parliament makes the commission of certain acts an offence it intends that mens rea shall be a constituent of that offence whether or not there is any reference to the knowledge or state of mind of the accused. And it was and is held to be an invariable rule that where mens rea is a constituent of any offence the burden of proving mens rea is on the prosecution. Some day this House may have to re-examine that rule, but that is another matter. For the protection of purchasers or consumers Parliament in many cases made it an offence for a trader to do certain things. Normally those things were done on his behalf by his servants and cases arose where the doing of the forbidden thing was solely the fault of a servant, the master having done all he could to prevent it and being entirely ignorant of its having been done. The just course would have been to hold that, once the facts constituting the offence had been proved, mens rea would be presumed unless the accused proved that he was blameless. The courts could not, or thought they could not, take that course. But they could and did hold in many such cases on a construction of the statutory provision that Parliament must be deemed to have intended to depart from the general rule and to make the offence absolute in the sense that mens rea was not to be a constituent of the offence.

This has led to great difficulties. If the offence is not held to be absolute the requirement that the prosecutor must prove mens rea makes it impossible to enforce the enactment in very many cases. If the offence is held to be absolute that leads to the conviction of persons who are entirely blameless: an injustice which brings the law into disrepute. So Parliament has found it necessary to devise a method of avoiding this difficulty. But instead of passing a general enactment that it shall always be a defence for the accused to prove that he was no party to the offence and had done all he could to prevent it, Parliament has chosen to deal with the problem piecemeal, and has in an increasing number of cases enacted in various forms with regard to particular offences that it shall be a defence to prove various exculpatory circumstances.

In my judgment the main object of these provisions must have been to distinguish between those who are in some degree blameworthy and those who are not, and to enable the latter to escape from conviction if they can show that they were in no way to blame. I find it almost impossible to suppose that Parliament or any reasonable body of men would as a matter of policy think it right to make employers criminally liable for the acts of some of their servants but not for those of others and I find it incredible that a draftsman, aware of that intention, would fail to insert any words to express it. But in several cases the courts, for reasons which it is not easy to discover, have given a restricted meaning to such provisions. It has been held that such provisions afford a defence if the master proves that the servant at fault was the person who himself did the prohibited act, but that they afford no defence if the servant at fault was one who failed in his duty of supervision to see that his subordinates did not commit the prohibited act. Why Parliament should be thought to have intended this distinction or how as a matter of construction these provisions can reasonably be held to have that meaning is not apparent.

In some of these cases the employer charged with the offence was a limited company. But in others the employer was an individual and still it was held that he, though personally entirely blameless, could not rely on these provisions if the fault which led to the commission of the offence was the fault of a servant in failing to carry out his duty to instruct or supervise his subordinates.

Where a limited company is the employer difficult questions do arise in a wide variety of circumstances in deciding which of its officers or servants is to be identified with the company so that his guilt is the guilt of the company.

I must start by considering the nature of the personality which by a fiction the law attributes to a corporation. A living person has a mind which can have knowledge or intention or be negligent and he has hands to carry out his intentions. A corporation has none of these: it must act through living persons, though not always one or the same person. Then the person who acts is not speaking or acting for the company. He is acting as the company and his mind which directs his acts is the mind of the company. There is no question of the company being vicariously liable. He is not acting as a servant, representative, agent or delegate. He is an embodiment of the company or, one could say, he hears and speaks through the persona of the company within his appropriate sphere, and his mind is the mind of the company. If it is a guilty mind then that guilt is the guilt of the company. It must be a question of law whether, once the facts have been ascertained, a person in doing particular things is to be regarded as the company or merely as the company's servant or agent. In that case any liability of the company can only be a statutory or vicarious liability.

In *Lennard's Carrying Co. Ltd.* v. *Asiatic Petroleum Co. Ltd.* [1915] AC 705 the question was whether damage had occurred without the "actual fault or privity" of the owner of a ship. The owners were a company. The fault was that of the registered managing owner who managed the ship on behalf of the owners and it was held that the company could not dissociate itself from him so as to say that there was no actual fault or privity on the part of the company. Viscount Haldane L.C. said, at pp. 713, 714:

> For if Mr. Lennard was the directing mind of the company, then his action must, unless a corporation is not to be liable at all, have been an action which was the action of the company itself within the meaning of section 502 . . . It must be upon the true construction of that section in such a case as the present one that the fault or privity is the fault or privity of somebody who is not merely a servant or agent for whom the company is liable upon the footing respondeat superior, but somebody for whom the company is liable because his action is the very action of the company itself.

Reference is frequently made to the judgment of Denning L.J. in *H. L. Bolton (Engineering) Co. Ltd.* v. *T. J. Graham & Sons Ltd.* [1957] 1 QB 159. He said, at p. 172:

> A company may in many ways be likened to a human body. It has a brain and nerve centre which controls what it does. It also has hands which hold the tools and act in accordance with directions from the centre. Some of the people in the company are mere servants and agents who are nothing more than hands to do the work and cannot be said to represent the mind or will. Others are directors and managers who represent the directing mind and will of the company, and control what it does. The state of mind of these managers is the state of mind of the company and is treated by the law as such.

In that case the directors of the company only met once a year: they left the management of the business to others, and it was the intention of those managers which was imputed to the company. I think that was right. There have been attempts to apply Lord Denning's words to all servants of a company whose work is brain work, or who exercise some managerial discretion under the direction of superior officers of the company. I do not think that Lord Denning intended to refer to them. He only referred to those who "represent the directing mind and will of the company, and control what it does."

I think that is right for this reason. Normally the board of directors, the managing director and perhaps other superior officers of a company carry out the functions of management and speak and act as the company. Their subordinates do not. They carry out orders from above and it can make no difference that they are given some measure of discretion. But the board of directors may delegate some part of their functions of management giving to their delegate full discretion to act independently of instructions from them. I see no difficulty in holding that they have thereby put such a delegate in their place so that within the scope of the delegation he can act as the company. It may not always be easy to draw the line but there are cases in which the line must be drawn. *Lennard's* case [1915] AC 705 was one of them.

[Lord Reid proceeded to discuss earlier lower court decisions on the meaning of delegation and due diligence, and concluded:]

I have already said that the phrase alter ego is misleading. In my judgment this case was wrongly decided and should be overruled. When the second statute introduced a defence if the accused proved that "he used all due diligence" I think that it meant what it said. As a matter of construction I can see no ground for reading in "he and all persons to whom he has delegated responsibility." And if I look to the purpose and apparent intention of Parliament in enacting this defence I think that it was plainly intended to make a just and reasonable distinction between the employer who is wholly blameless and ought to be acquitted and the employer who was in some way at fault, leaving it to the employer to prove that he was in no way to blame.

What good purpose could be served by making an employer criminally responsible for the misdeeds of some of his servants but not for those of others? It is sometimes argued — it was argued in the present case — that making an employer criminally responsible, even when he has done all that he could to prevent an offence, affords some additional protection to the public because this will induce him to do more. But if he has done all he can how can he do more? I think that what lies behind this argument is a suspicion that magistrates too readily accept evidence that an employer has done all he can to prevent offences. But if magistrates were to accept as sufficient a paper scheme and perfunctory efforts to enforce it they would not be doing their duty — that would not be "due diligence" on the part of the employer.

Then it is said that this would involve discrimination in favour of a large employer like the appellants against a small shopkeeper. But that is not so. Mr. Clement was the "opposite number" of the small shopkeeper and he was liable to prosecution in this case. The purpose of this Act must have been to penalise those at fault, not those who were in no way to blame.

The Divisional Court decided this case on a theory of delegation. In that they were following some earlier authorities. But they gave far too wide a meaning to delegation. I have said that a board of directors can delegate part of their functions of management so as to make their delegate an embodiment of the company within the sphere of the delegation. But here the board never delegated any part of their functions. They set up a chain of command through regional and district supervisors, but they remained in control. The shop managers had to obey their general directions and also take orders from their superiors. The acts or omissions of shop managers were not acts of the company itself.

In my judgment the appellants established the statutory defence. I would therefore allow this appeal.

Appeal allowed.

Notes:

1   Lords Diplock, Pearson and Morris of Borth-y-Gest and Viscount Dilhorne gave concurring opinions. Viscount Dilhorne posed the following question (at p. 184):

> If the chain of supermarkets owned and run by the appellants, some eight hundred we were told, were owned and run by an individual or partnership, then it could not be disputed that Mr. Clement was another person within the meaning of the subsection. Does he cease to be "another person" because the stores are owned by a limited company?

2   The decision in *Tesco* has been described as a "blow against enterprise liability": Note (1971) 34 Mod. L. Rev. 676. Do you agree? What public policies are served by holding large corporations strictly liable for violation of consumer protection legislation without the benefit of a due diligence defence? Is a magistrate in a good position to assess the validity of a defence under a provision like s. 24(1) of the British Trade Descriptions Act 1968?

3   The test of corporate criminal liability approved by the House of Lords in *Tesco* also applies in Canada, as is shown by Schroeder J.A.'s comprehensive judgment in *R. v. St. Lawrence Corp. Ltd.* [1969] 2 OR 305 (CA). A less stringent test was however applied in a leading American case, *Commonwealth of Massachusetts* v. *Beneficial Finance Co.* (1971) 275 NE 2d 33 (Supp. Jud. Ct. Mass.) which expressed the view that the previously accepted American equivalent of the organic liability test was out of touch with modern organizational realities.

5.   STRICT LIABILITY AND DUE DILIGENCE DEFENCE

REGINA v. CITY OF SAULT STE. MARIE
(1978) 85 DLR (3d) 161, [1978] 2 SCR 1299

The City of Sault Ste. Marie was charged under the Ontario Water Resources Act for discharging or permitting to be discharged into two waterways materials that might impair the quality of water. The City had entered into an agreement with a disposal firm to furnish a site for and to dispose of all refuse originating in the City. The site's resulting high mound of garbage sloped toward one of the waterways which consequently became polluted. The disposal firm was convicted under the same section of the Act under which the City had been charged. The issue before the Supreme Court of Canada was whether the offence was one of absolute liability and, if it was, whether due diligence by the accused to comply with the statute was a defence at common law.

The Court, speaking through Mr. Justice Dickson, in a decision of far reaching importance, discussed at length the academic arguments and case law on the issue and concluded (DLR, at 181-82): ·

DICKSON J.: [T]here are compelling grounds for the recognition of three categories of offences rather than the traditional two:

1.   Offences in which *mens rea*, consisting of some positive state of mind such as intent, knowledge, or recklessness, must be proved by the prosecution either as an inference from the nature of the act committed, or by additional evidence.

2.   Offences in which there is no necessity for the prosecution to prove the existence of *mens rea*; the doing of the prohibited act *prima facie* imports the offence, leaving it open to the accused to avoid liability by proving that he took all reasonable care. This involves consideration of what a reasonable man would have done in the circumstances. The defence will be available if the accused reasonably believed in a mistaken set of facts which, if true, would render the act or omission innocent, or if he took all reasonable steps

to avoid the particular event. These offences may properly be called offences of strict liability. Mr. Justice Estey so referred to them in *Hickey's* case.

3. Offences of absolute liability where it is not open to the accused to exculpate himself by showing that he was free of fault.

Offences which are criminal in the true sense fall in the first category. Public welfare offences would, *prima facie,* be in the second category. They are not subject to the presumption of full *mens rea.* An offence of this type would fall in the first category only if such words as "wilfully", "with intent", "knowingly", or "intentionally" are contained in the statutory provision creating the offence. On the other hand, the principle that punishment should in general not be inflicted on those without fault applies. Offences of absolute liability would be those in respect of which the Legislature had made it clear that guilt would follow proof merely of the proscribed act. The over-all regulatory pattern adopted by the Legislature, the subject-matter of the legislation, the importance of the penalty, and the precision of the language used will be primary considerations in determining whether the offence falls into the third category.

Notes on Vicarious Liability, Strict Liability and the Defence of Due Diligence

1   *Vicarious Liability.* There is no express provision in the Combines Investigation Act dealing with vicarious liability, but the Canadian cases to date have always proceeded on the assumption that the principle applies: *R.* v. *Steinberg's Ltd., supra; R.* v. *G. Tamblyn Ltd.* (1972) 6 CCC (2d) 471 (Ont. CA); and many others. The assumption seems to be made that since the Ontario High Court in *R.* v. *Allied Towers Merchants Ltd.* [1965] 2 OR 628 construed the Act as imposing strict liability, that this must also lead to vicarious liability. Strict liability and vicarious liability are not, however, coextensive concepts, and the explanation must be sought elsewhere. Glanville Williams, *Textbook of Criminal Law* (1978), p. 944, sums up the applicable principle as follows:

> Where the statute forbids an act, the defendant will be regarded as having done it through his employee or partner if the statute expressly says so, or if the verb is capable of this extended meaning, and if the offence, being of a regulatory character, does not require *mens rea.* (The fact that the offence carries strict liability does not mean that it carries vicarious liability unless the language permits of this.)

Rees v. *Munday* [1974] 1 WLR 1284 is an illustration of the application of this approach to a charge against an employer under s. 1 of the U.K. Trade Descriptions Act 1968.

In the case of the CIA, however, the above observations are subject to the important qualification in s. 36(2)(*d*) relating to representations "made in the course of in-store, door-to-door or telephone selling to a person as ultimate user". In *R.* v. *Yukon Automobile Brokers Ltd.* (1978) 50 CPR (2d) 85 (Y.T. Mag. Ct.) the accused was charged with falsely representing that a pick-up truck offered for sale was a "demonstrator". In fact the truck had previously been involved in an accident. The evidence showed that the representation was made, without authorization, by the accused's salesman. What result? Is CIA s. 36(2)(*d*) necessary in view of the defence of due diligence under s. 37.3(2)? Does s. 36(2)(*d*) significantly weaken the enforceability of the false representations provisions?

2   *Due Diligence*. Until the 1975 amendments the Combines Act did not admit a due diligence defence. (A complete exemption from old s. 36(1) was however granted in s. 36(2) to a person who published an advertisement that he accepted in good faith for publication in the ordinary course of his business. The provision is reproduced in amended form in present s. 37.3(1).) New s. 37.3(2) now recognizes the defence subject to the exclusions in s. 37.3(3). Examine the subsection carefully and consider the following questions: (a) how does it differ from the common law defence embraced in *Sault Ste. Marie*; (b) how does it differ from s. 24(1) of the U.K. Trade Descriptions Act 1968 considered in *Tesco*; and (c) how would *Tesco* be decided under s. 37.3(2)?

3   The relationship between CIA s. 37.3(2) and the common law defence of due diligence was considered in *R. v. Consumers Distributing Co. Ltd.* (1981) 57 CCC (2d) 317 (Ont. CA). The accused was charged with making a false or misleading representation with respect to the fuel savings to be achieved from a "GT Mini Fueljector" which the company was offering for sale. The product was also being sold by other reputable stores in Canada and had apparently received favourable review in several technical reports. The accused bought the product from its Canadian distributor and had no reason to suspect the accuracy of the claims being made for it until it was advised on November 9, 1977, that the National Research Council had tested the product and found the claims unsubstantiated. Consumers immediately withdrew the product from sale but failed to publish any retraction of their representations (as required by s. 37.3(2)(*c*)) because it wished first to see a copy of the NRC's report. It was not successful in its quest.

Speaking for the court, Blair J.A. held that if the common law test of due diligence was the applicable one, Consumers had discharged the burden in the present case. However, he concluded that "Parliament, by providing an explicit defence to the charge of false and misleading advertising several years before the common law defence was established by the Supreme Court of Canada, intended that it should be the only defence available to the charge." The statutory defence was not satisfied even though it was the Crown's own conduct in refusing to release a copy of the NRC's report that made it "extremely difficult" for Consumers to comply with the requirements of s. 37.3(2)(*c*) and (*d*). On the issue of the primacy of s. 36.3(2) the court followed its earlier decision in *R. v. Grottoli* (1978) 43 CCC (2d) 158. In the light of the decision in the present case, what recommendations would you make with respect to the revision of s. 37.3(2)?

6.   FALSE ADVERTISING RELATING TO PRICE: A SPECIFIC CONCERN

REGINA v. COLGATE-PALMOLIVE LTD.
(1969) 3 DLR (3d) 707, [1969]1 OR 731 (Ont. Co. Ct.)

MATHESON CO. CT. J.: This is an appeal against an acquittal by C. Edward Carter, Magistrate, now Prov. Ct. J., at Ottawa, on a charge of contravention of s.

33C(1) of the Combines Investigation Act, RSC 1952, c. 314, as enacted by 1960, c. 45, s. 13. The case was heard by Magistrate Carter on April 8, 1968. His reasons for judgment are dated April 15, 1968.

With the oral consent of counsel, the appeal was heard on the evidence taken before the learned Magistrate as set out in a transcript of that evidence.

Colgate-Palmolive Limited were charged that they did on October 25, 1967, at the City of Ottawa, in said County of Carleton, unlawfully for the purpose of promoting the sale of Halo Economy Size Shampoo for Dry Hair in the 13^1/$_8$ ounce bottle, by means of a label bearing the representation "Special $1.49", make a materially misleading representation to the public at the I.G.A. Capital Foodliner Store, 245 Rideau St., in the City of Ottawa, in the County of Carleton, concerning the price at which said Halo Economy Size Shampoo for Dry Hair in the 13^1/$_8$ ounce bottle has been or is ordinarily sold, contrary to s. 33C(1) of the Combines Investigation Act, and amendments thereto.

Section 33C(1) of the Combines Investigation Act reads as follows:

> 33C(1) Every one who, for the purpose of promoting the sale or use of an article, makes any materially misleading representation to the public, by any means whatever, concerning the price at which such or like articles have been, are, or will be, ordinarily sold, is guilty of an offence punishable on summary conviction.

The facts in this matter are simply that between the month of March, 1965, and the month of October, 1967, Colgate-Palmolive Ltd. manufactured a product known as Halo Shampoo for Dry Hair which was green in colour and contained 13^1/$_8$ fluid ounces. The label had printed across the left top corner on a diagonal red band the words and numbers "Special $1.49". Nothing else was printed on this portion of the label. The rest of the label contained the following words: "Halo Shampoo — for dry hair, pour cheveux secs — ECONOMY SIZE." There was also printed matter on the reverse side of the label which could be read by looking through the back of the bottle and through the liquid contained in the bottle. The fluid content of the bottle, 13^1/$_8$ fluid ounces, was printed on this latter portion of the label.

It was also established in evidence that this economy size bottle of Halo Shampoo was rarely, if ever, placed alone on retail store shelves. It was invariably beside three other smaller green bottles of Halo Shampoo, the prices and fluid ounce content of which were less than this bottle with the "Special $1.49" label.

Colgate-Palmolive Ltd. was the manufacturer of the product in question and by various distribution methods, the product reached the shelves of retail outlets. The labels were placed on the bottles by Colgate-Palmolive prior to their reaching their retail outlets.

LARGE SIZE	— 1^1/$_2$ fluid ounces, (selling at 45¢ or 30¢ per ounce)
GIANT SIZE	— 3^5/$_8$ fluid ounces, (selling at 75¢ or 20.7¢ per ounce)
FAMILY SIZE	— 8^5/$_{16}$ fluid ounces, (selling at 99¢ or 12¢ per ounce)

ECONOMY SIZE   —   13¹/₈ fluid ounces,
(selling at $1.49 or 11.2¢ per
ounce)

The question before me is whether or not the label on the economy size
bottle bearing the diagonal red band with the words and numbers "Special $1.49"
constitutes a misrepresentation as to ordinary price.

The scope and purpose of s. 33C(1) is clear. It is designed to provide consumer protection by establishing as an offence in relation to trade any misrepresentation as to the regular price of an article. It has been established by Jessup, J.,
in the Supreme Court of Ontario (in Chambers) on March 19, 1965, in *R.* v. *Allied
Towers Merchants Ltd.*, [1965] 2 OR 628, [1966] 1 CCC 220, 46 CPR 239, that s. 33C(1)
is an offence of strict liability in the sense that *mens rea* is not an ingredient of the
offence. This legislation is the expression of a social purpose, namely the establishment of more ethical trade practices calculated to afford greater protection to
the consuming public. It represents the will of the people of Canada that the old
maxim *caveat emptor*, let the purchaser beware, yield somewhat to the more
enlightened view *caveat venditor* — let the seller beware.

The importance of this case is that heretofore there has been so little enforcement of this provision that its full meaning is not yet determined. General
principles or standards adopted by Parliament must, by experience in the Courts,
be focused on concrete fact situations where the social implications of the
principle can be thrown into dramatic relief. The Court must demonstrate the
compatibility of a principled adherence to legal values with a continuing re-
evaluation of social needs. The problem remains to fix bounds, in the language of
Cardozo, "There is an endless 'becoming'." Thus, as it was stated by Edmond
Cahn, "Justice is the active process of the preventing or repairing of injustice."

I believe the test in this case should be simple:

(a) Would a reasonable shopper draw the conclusion from the diagonal red
band with the words and numbers "Special $1.49", that he was being offered
Economy Size Halo Shampoo at a price below which that size bottle is
ordinarily sold?

(b) If the answer is "yes", would such a representation be true?

The transcript of evidence at the trial indicates that Ronald Joseph Kinsley,
an investigator with the Combines Investigation Branch, conducted an investigation of this particular matter, namely the merchandizing of Halo Shampoo,
size 13¹/₈ fluid ounces for dry hair, commencing on July 27, 1966. His initial
survey consisted of visiting outlets of Loblaw's, Dominion Stores, Steinberg's
Stores and I.G.A. Stores throughout the Ottawa area twelve times, returning to
each store every other week. With respect to the aforesaid shampoo product
marked "Special $1.49", he found the price varied from a minimum of 99¢ to a
maximum of $1.49. Nowhere, during the initial survey, nor upon subsequent
surveys which were conducted on August 31, 1967, and on October 25, 1967,
covering several dozens of well-known retail outlets, was Halo Shampoo for Dry
Hair, 13¹/₈ fluid ounces, found to be displayed for sale at a price greater than $1.49.

On a number of occasions, the sale price was substantially lower. The economy size bottle of Halo Shampoo, which is the subject of this prosecution, was purchased at I.G.A. Capital Foodliner, 245 Rideau St., Ottawa, by Mr. Kinsley on October 25, 1967. This bottle, filed as ex. 1, bears the representation "Special $1.49".

I feel that to accede to the argument of defence counsel that ex. 1 should not be examined in isolation, but rather that a shopper must be assumed to interpret this economy size label "Special $1.49" only after examination of the three smaller bottles in the Halo series would diminish very considerably the independent meaning to be accorded the labelling of a product offered for sale. The effect of such a conclusion would impose, surely, upon the purchaser a burden to compare not contemplated within the wording of s. 33C(1).

Upon a review of all of the evidence before me, I have no difficulty in answering the two questions already posed. My answers are:

(a) A reasonable shopper upon reading the words and numbers "Special $1.49" upon the diagonal red band might very well conclude that he was being offered Economy Size Halo Shampoo at a price below which it is ordinarily sold.

(b) Such a representation would not be true.

I must accordingly allow the appeal and convict the respondent of the offence charged.

I have already alluded to the fact that s. 33C(1) represents largely untested legislation in terms of the limits to be applied. In form and substance this statute is criminal law. Parliament has embodied the principles that it has sought to establish in a series of prohibitions. Bearing in mind the fact that s. 33C(1), being an offence of strict liability, does not afford the defence of *mens rea*. I find myself with a large sympathy for the respondent corporation. There is no evidence before me of intention to mislead. The Court has the solemn duty to collaborate with the Legislature in reworking the legal *status quo*. In seeking to enunciate higher standards, we should strive not to do so at the expense of a respected corporation selling a good product at good value.

Colgate-Palmolive Ltd. produced the label in question, "Special $1.49", in the month of March, 1965. Prior to that time there was another label which was "Special, Economy Size $1.39". I am informed that on September 20, 1967, there was a written order for a change of label, and the exact specifications therein are dated October 6, 1967. This new label for Economy Size Halo Shampoo provides, in place of the offensive "Special $1.49", the following:

Prix Suggéré
$1.49
Suggested Retail Price

Noting that the information herein of Alexander Synnett, a member of the RCMP, is dated December 21, 1967, and taking into account the obvious effort of the respondent corporation to co-operate with the Director of Investigation and Research under the Combines Investigation Act after this complaint was brought to the attention of the company, I feel in the circumstances that no more than a recorded conviction is indicated.

Appeal allowed.

Note on Price Misrepresentation: The bulk of the prosecutions under the old CIA and the present Act have dealt with misleading and false representations as to price.

The following is a summary indicating some of the complex questions raised in this branch of advertising law. The student should note carefully that many of the cases cited deal with the pre-1976 version of the CIA and differences in the drafting of the new provisions should always be kept in mind when dealing with these issues.

Questions:

1   What is the meaning of "sale"? See *R. v. T. Eaton Co. Ltd.* (1972) 4 CPR (2d) 226 (Ont. Prov. Ct.); rev'd 10 CPR (2d) 36 (Co. Ct.). When does a "sale" cease to be a "sale"? See *R. v. T. Eaton Co. Ltd., supra,* and *R. v. Broadway Clothiers Ltd.* (1974) 20 CCC (2d) 35 (BC Prov. Ct.). What is the meaning of "fire sale"? "Bargain"? "Discount price"? See *R. v. S.S. Kresge Co. Ltd.* (1972) 5 CPR (2d) 133 (Alta. SC). Must the price quoted be the only or highest price available at all times during the period offered? See *R. v. Suntours Ltd. and Algonquin Travel Services Ltd.* (1974) 21 CCC (2d) 239 (Ont. Prov. Ct.).

2   Under what circumstances is it false or misleading for an advertiser to offer or purport to offer two articles for the price of one? See *R. v. G. Tamblyn Ltd.* (1972) 6 CCC (2d) 471, 6 CPR (2d) 27 (Ont. CA), and *R. v. City Tire Services Ltd.* (1974) 21 CCC (2d) 244 (NB Co. Ct.).

3   If a person purports to offer an item at a discount from a "regular" price, does this refer to (1) his own normal price as well as those of competitors or (2) the price charged by other retail outlets generally? See
     (a) *R. v. McKay's Television & Appliances Ltd.* (1970), 65 CPR 126 (Ont. Co. Ct.); *R. v. Simpsons-Sears Ltd.* [1972] 3 OR 186, 6 CPR (2d) 179 (CA); *R. v. N.R. Motors Ltd.* [1979] 2 WWR 614 (BC Co. Ct.).
     (b) *R. v. J. Pascal Hardware Co. Ltd.* (1972) 8 CPR (2d) 155 (Ont. Co. Ct.); *R. v. Allied Towers Merchants Ltd. (1)* (Ont. Co. Ct.), March 17, 1965 (unreported, but see (1969) 15 McGill LJ 654); *R. v. R. & A. Cohen Ltd.* (Ont. Mag. Ct.) (unreported, but see (1969) 15 McGill LJ 659).

4   What is the geographical area encompassed in such a test? See *R. v. Cunningham Drug Stores Ltd.* (1973) 12 CCC (2d) 4 (BC SC); aff'd 17 CCC (2d) 279 (BC CA); *R. v. Zeller's (Western) Ltd.* (1972) 5 CPR (2d) 3 (Man. Mag. Ct.); *R. v. F. W. Woolworth Co. Ltd.* (1969) 58 CPR 223 (Sask. Mag. Ct.); *R. v. T. Eaton Co. Ltd.* (1974) 15 CPR (2d) 25 (Man. CA); *R. v. Simpsons-Sears Ltd.* [1972] 3 OR 186 (CA); *R. v. N. R. Motors Ltd.* [1979] 2 WWR 614 (BC Co. Ct.).

5   In cases of mail order catalogues distributed throughout the country or throughout a region of the country, how should the "marketing area" be construed? See *R. v.*

Simpsons-Sears Ltd. (1969) 58 CPR 56 (Ont. Prov. Ct.); rev'd 65 CPR 92 (Co. Ct.), and on further appeal [1972] 3 OR 186, 6 CPR (2d) 179 (Ont. CA).

6   The ABC Co. issued membership cards entitling those receiving them to a catalogue of the company's products and admission to their large retail warehouse outlet. Both the catalogue and tags found on a number of the goods in the warehouse included a manufacturer's suggested retail price which was, in fact, incorrect. Has the company violated the provisions of CIA s. 36? See *Alberta Giftwares Ltd.* v. *The Queen* [1974] SCR 584. On the question whether, in the designated market area, the goods have to sell at the manufacturer's suggested price, see *R.* v. *Gagnon* (1975) 27 CPR (2d) 133 (Que. Prov. Ct.).

7   A sign in the window of the XYZ Drug Mart advertised the sale of shaving cream. The sign read as follows: "Save 49¢. With each purchase of a can of shaving cream you receive ABSOLUTELY FREE, a package of our new and improved double-edged blades." The two products come packaged together and similar words are found on the package itself. The can of shaving cream sold for $1.19, but there was evidence which showed that prior to this "introductory offer" the can had sold for only 98¢. Has the XYZ Drug Mart committed an offence under the CIA misleading advertising provisions? For cases dealing with the meaning of the word "free", see *R.* v. *Bowell McLean Motor Co. Ltd.* (1972) 6 CPR (2d) 201 (BC Prov. Ct.); *R.* v. *Centennial Pharmacy Ltd.* (1970) 64 CPR 87 (BC Prov. Ct.); *R.* v. *G. Tamblyn Ltd.* (1972) 4 CPR (2d) 68 (Ont. Co. Ct.) on appeal [1972] 2 OR 704 (CA); *R.* v. *Colgate-Palmolive Ltd.* (1972) 9 CPR (2d) 62 (Ont. Co. Ct.); *R.* v. *Whitehouse* (1972) 8 CPR (2d) 96 (Alta. Dist. Ct.).

Would it make any difference if there were no sign in the window and the "introductory offer" appeared only on the package? See *Paramount Industries Inc.* v. *The Queen* (1973) 10 CPR (2d) 216 (Que. CA); *R.* v. *Colgate-Palmolive Ltd.* (1972) 9 CPR (2d) 62 (Ont. Co. Ct.). *Cf. R.* v. *Lepage's Ltd.* (1973) 9 CPR (2d) 16 (Ont. Prov. Ct.); *R.* v. *General Foods Ltd.* (1971) 8 CCC (2d) 371 (Ont. Prov. Ct.). Compare also the provisions of the current CIA with the provision of the pre-1976 version of the Act.

Chapter 6
Seller's Implied Warranty Obligations

OLRC Report on Consumer Warranties and Guarantees
(1972) p. 31-2

In practice the buyer with defective goods on his hands is more likely to complain of breach of one of the implied quality obligations in The Sale of Goods Act than of a breach by the seller of an express warranty. How is he likely to fare? The answer is, on the whole, very well, assuming the absence of an effective disclaimer clause or other debilitating circumstance.

The Research Team for this project reported finding that among laymen, including many government officials, there is still a surprising lack of knowledge about the seller's implied obligations at law, and an extremely strong belief that the only obligations binding on a seller are those expressly assumed by him. The source of this misunderstanding appears to be the idea of "let the buyer beware" — expressed in the legal maxim *"caveat emptor"* — and the assumption that this maxim is the foundation of the common law of sales.

Historically this is an inaccurate description of the law.[18] The maxim apparently is not of Roman origin. It was well established in the classical period of Roman law that a buyer who had been sold goods with a latent defect was entitled to bring an action *in quanti minoris* for a reduction of the purchase price, or a redhibitory action for rescission of the sale. The maxim equally did not reflect the state of early English law, and a learned writer has shown that medieval society imposed sanctions of one kind or another on a seller who was guilty of sharp practices or unfair dealing. The maxim is first cited by Fitzherbert in the 16th century (without authority to support it) but did not make its appearance in the scant and not always relevant case law until the 17th century.

Its life as an accurate reflection of the law was relatively short-lived. Erosions of the rule that a seller did not vouch his title began as early as the middle of the

---

[18] See generally Hamilton, *The Ancient Maxim Caveat Emptor* (1933), 40 Yale LJ 1133.

18th century and the implied condition of merchantability in the case of manufacturers and non-specific goods was established by 1815. The implied condition of fitness followed in 1829, and in 1877 it was authoritatively settled that a seller was strictly liable for latent defects even though they could not have been avoided by the exercise of reasonable care and skill on his part. By the time Chalmers began to draft his Sale of Goods Act, the contours of the modern sales rules had been substantially settled. The only areas in which the maxim still has any vitality (ignoring again for this purpose the impact of disclaimer clauses) is with respect to private sales and sales of specific goods where the buyer has inspected the goods and is deemed to have bought them subject to such defects as his examination ought to have revealed.

A. TITLE, QUIET POSSESSION, AND FREEDOM FROM ENCUMBRANCES

NIBLETT LTD. v. CONFECTIONERS' MATERIALS CO. LTD.
[1921] 3 KB 387, [1921] All ER Rep. 459 (CA)

BANKES L.J.: In this case the buyers seek to recover damages from the sellers on the ground that the goods delivered were not in accordance with the contract of sale. The case as presented to us rests on one or another of three enactments. It is said that the buyers had a right of action under s. 12 or under s. 14 of the Sale of Goods Act, 1893, or under s. 17 of the Merchandise Marks Act, 1887. Upon this last alternative I need say nothing. No reference was made to it at the trial. If it had been insisted on it would have required evidence which the respondents had no opportunity of giving in the Court below, and the appellants ought not to be allowed to make that point now. I therefore confine myself to the claims under s. 12 and s. 14 of the Sale of Goods Act, 1893, though it does not appear that s. 14 was much relied on by counsel or considered by the judge at the trial.

In August, 1919, the parties entered into a contract for the sale of 3000 cases of condensed milk. The contract was originally made at an interview, but it was subsequently confirmed by writing in the form of a sold note dated August 18 sent by the respondents to the appellants with a request that they would sign a counterpart, that is to say, a bought note, in the same terms, which the appellants did. The contract appears to be wholly embodied in the writing. Notwithstanding this both parties seem to have treated the contract as partly oral and partly in writing, and to have adduced parol evidence as to its terms, and counsel for the respondents have contended that it was agreed that one or more of three brands of condensed milk, including the "Nissly" brand, might be delivered in fulfilment of the contract, and Bailhache J. appears to have dealt with the case on that footing. Two thousand cases were delivered, and give rise to no question. One thousand arrived bearing labels with the word "Nissly" upon them. It came to the knowledge of the Nestlé and Anglo-Swiss Co. that parcels of condensed milk were being imported with this label upon them, and they took up the position that these 1000 cases infringed their registered trade mark. They objected to these goods being dealt with in any way. The justice of their objection was admitted by the respondents, who gave an undertaking not to sell, offer for sale, or dispose of any condensed milk under the title of "Nissly." The appellants did their best to sell, exchange, or export the goods, but found that the only possible way of dealing with them was to strip them of their labels and sell them without marks or labels.

Bailhache J. came to the clear conclusion that if s. 12 of the Sale of Goods Act, 1893, is to be construed literally the respondents had no right to sell the goods as they were, and that the appellants were not enjoying and never had enjoyed quiet possession of the goods; that they could never get them from the Commissioners of Customs, and that if they had got them they were never in a position to deal with them, because of the Nestlé Co.'s threat. But he felt himself bound by the judgment of Lord Russell C.J. in *Monforts* v. *Marsden* (1895) 12 RPC 266 to give to s. 12 a meaning and effect which he would not have attributed to it but for that case. With the greatest respect to Lord Russell C.J. I think the doubts cast by Bailhache J. upon that decision are justified. The case was heard and decided by Lord Russell C.J. on circuit. He took the view that s. 12 was to be read with qualifications like those which limit the implied covenant for quiet enjoyment in a conveyance of real property by a grantor who conveys as beneficial owner under s. 7 of the Conveyancing Act, 1881, and he imposed upon the implied obligations in s. 12 of the Sale of Goods Act, 1893, a restriction limiting their operation to acts and omissions of the vendor and those acting by his authority. I cannot agree with the view thus expressed by Lord Russell. I think s. 12 has a much wider effect, and that the language does not warrant the limitation imposed by Lord Russell. I express no opinion as to what "circumstances" of a contract are "such as to show a different intention," to use the earlier words of s. 12. Mr. Spence contended that these circumstances are not confined to matters relating to the making of the contract, but would include the fact that at the time of making a written contract for the sale of goods it was understood that the goods would be of one or another brand. He argued that this was a circumstance which would show an intention to exclude the warranties otherwise implied. But assuming that goods of one or more of three brands might be delivered under the contract, that circumstance does not show any intention that if two of those brands are free from objection, and the third is an infringement of trade mark rights, the vendor may tender goods of the third brand in fulfilment of his contract. The goods tendered must still be goods which the vendor has a right to sell. Therefore in my opinion the appellants have established a right of action under s. 12, sub-s. 1, of the Act.

Appeal allowed.

ROWLAND v. DIVALL
[1923] 2 KB 500, [1923] All ER Rep. 270 (CA)

BANKES L.J.: Whatever doubt there may have been in former times as to the legal rights of a purchaser in the position of the present plaintiff was settled by the Sale of Goods Act, 1893, by s. 12 of which it was provided that: "In a contract of sale, unless the circumstances of the contract are such as to show a different intention, there is (1.) An implied condition on the part of the seller that . . . he has a right to sell the goods." The facts are shortly these. The plaintiff bought a motor car at Brighton from the defendant in May, 1922. He took possession of it at once, drove it to his place of business at Blandford, where he exhibited it for sale in his shop, and ultimately sold it to a purchaser. It was not discovered that the car was a stolen car until September, when possession was taken of it by the police. The plaintiff and his purchaser between them had possession of it for about four months. The plaintiff now brings his action to recover back the price that he paid to the defendant upon the ground of total failure of consideration. As I have said, it cannot now be disputed that there was an implied condition on the part of the defendant that he had a right to sell the car, and unless something happened to change that condition into a warranty the plaintiff is entitled to rescind the contract and recover back the money. The Sale of Goods Act itself indicates in s. 53 [Ont. s. 51] the circumstances in which a condition may be changed into a warranty: "Where the buyer elects, or is compelled, to treat any breach of a condition on the part of the seller as a breach of warranty" the buyer is not entitled to reject the goods, but his remedy is in damages. Mr. Doughty contends that this is a case in which the buyer is compelled to treat the condition as a warranty within the meaning of that section, because, having had the use of the car for four months, he cannot put the seller in statu quo and therefore cannot now rescind, and he has referred to several authorities in support of that contention. But when those authorities are looked at I think it will be found that in all of them the buyer got some part of what he contracted for. In *Taylor* v. *Hare* (1805) 1 B & P (NR) 260, 262 the question was as to the right of the plaintiff to recover back money which he had paid for the use of a patent which turned out to be void. But there the Court treated the parties, who had made a common mistake about the validity of the patent, as being in the nature of joint adventurers in the benefit of the patent; and Chambre J. expressly pointed out that "The plaintiff has had the enjoyment of what he stipulated for." The language there used by Heath J., though it may have been correct as applied to the facts of that case, is much too wide to be applied to such a case as the present. In *Hunt* v. *Silk* (1804) 5 East 449, 452 Lord Ellenborough went upon the ground that the plaintiff had received part of what he bargained for. He said: "Where a contract is to be rescinded at all, it must be rescinded in toto, and the parties put in statu quo. But here was an intermediate occupation, a part execution of the agreement, which was incapable of being rescinded." And *Lawes* v. *Purser* (1856) 6 E & B 930 proceeded on the same ground, that the defendant had derived benefit from the execution of the contract. But in the present case it cannot possibly be said that the plaintiff received any portion of what he had agreed to buy. It is true that a motor car was delivered to him, but the person who sold it to him had no right to sell it, and therefore he did not get what he paid for — namely, a car to which he would have title; and under those circumstances the user of the car by the purchaser seems to me quite immaterial for the purpose of considering whether the condition had been converted into a warranty. In my opinion the plaintiff was entitled to recover the whole of the purchase money, and was not limited to his remedy in damages as the judge below held.

SCRUTTON L.J.: [B]efore the passing of the Sale of Goods Act there was a good deal of confusion in the authorities as to the exact nature of the vendor's contract with respect to his title to sell. It was originally said that a vendor did not warrant his title. But gradually a number of exceptions crept in, till at last the exceptions became the rule, the rule being that the vendor warranted that he had title to what he purported to sell, except in certain special cases, such as that of a sale by a sheriff, who does not so warrant. Then came the Sale of Goods Act, which re-enacted that rule, but did so with this alteration: it re-enacted it as a condition, not as a warranty. Sect. 12 [Ont. s. 13] says in express terms that there shall be "An implied condition on the part of the seller that . . . he has a right to sell the goods." It being now a condition, wherever that condition is broken the contract can be rescinded, and with the rescission the buyer can demand a return of the purchase money, unless he has, with knowledge of the facts, held on to the bargain so as to waive the condition. But Mr. Doughty argues that there can never be a rescission where a restitutio in integrum is impossible, and that here the plaintiff cannot rescind because he cannot return the car. To that the buyer's answer is that the reason of his inability to return it — namely, the fact that the defendant had no title to it — is the very thing of which he is complaining, and that it does not lie in the defendant's mouth to set up as a defence to the action his own breach of the implied condition that he had a right to sell. In my opinion that answer is well founded, and it would, I think, be absurd to apply the rule as to restitutio in integrum to such a state of facts. No doubt the general rule is that a buyer cannot rescind a contract of sale and get back the purchase money unless he can restore the subject matter. There are a large number of cases on the subject, some of which are not very easy to reconcile with others. Some of them make it highly probable that a certain degree of deterioration of the goods is not sufficient to take away the right to recover the purchase money. However I do not think it necessary to refer to them. It certainly seems to me that, in a case of rescission for the breach of the condition that the seller had a right to sell the goods, it cannot be that the buyer is deprived of his right to get back the purchase money because he cannot restore the goods which, from the nature of the transaction, are not the goods of the seller at all, and which the seller therefore has no right to under any circumstances. For these reasons I think that the plaintiff is entitled to recover the whole of the purchase money as for a total failure of consideration, and that the appeal must be allowed.

ATKIN L.J.: I agree. It seems to me that in this case there has been a total failure of consideration, that is to say that the buyer has not got any part of that for which he paid the purchase money. He paid the money in order that he might get the property, and he has not got it. It is true that the seller delivered to him the de facto possession, but the seller had not got the right to possession and consequently could not give it to the buyer. Therefore the buyer, during the time that he had the car in his actual possession had no right to it, and was at all times liable to the true owner for its conversion. Now there is no doubt that what the buyer had a right to get was the property in the car, for the Sale of Goods Act expressly provides that in every contract of sale there is an implied condition that the seller has a right to sell; and the only difficulty that I have felt in this case arises out of the wording of s. 11, sub-s. 1(c) [Ont. s. 12(3)], which says that: "Where a contract of sale is not severable, and the buyer has accepted the goods . . . the breach of any condition to be fulfilled by the seller can only be treated as a breach of warranty, and not as a ground for rejecting the goods and treating the contract as repudiated, unless there be a term of the contract, express or implied, to that effect." It is said that this case falls within that provision, for the contract of sale was not severable and the buyer had accepted the car. But I think that the answer is that there can be no sale at all of goods which the seller has no right to sell. The whole object of a sale is to transfer property from one person to another. And I think that in every contract of sale of goods there is an implied term to the effect that a breach of the condition that the seller has a right to sell the goods may be treated as a ground for rejecting the goods and repudiating the contract notwithstanding the acceptance, within the meaning of the concluding words of sub-s. (c); or in other words that the sub-section has no application to a breach of that particular condition. It seems to me that in this case there must be a right to reject, and also a right to sue for the price paid as money had and received on failure of the consideration, and further that there is no obligation on the part of the buyer to return the car, for ex hypothesi the seller had no right to receive it. Under those circumstances can it make any difference that the buyer has used the car before he found out that there was a breach of the condition? To my mind it makes no difference at all. The buyer accepted the car on the representation of the seller that he had a right to sell it, and inasmuch as the seller had no such right he is not entitled to say that the buyer has enjoyed a benefit under the contract. In fact the buyer has not received any part of that which he contracted to receive — namely, the property and right to possession — and, that being so, there has been a total failure of consideration. The plaintiff is entitled to recover the 334*l.* which he paid.

Appeal allowed.

BUTTERWORTH v. KINGSWAY MOTORS LTD.
[1954] 1 WLR 1286, [1954] 2 All ER 694 (QB)

PEARSON J.: The subject-matter of this litigation is a Jowett Javelin motor-car which was first registered in November, 1949. We have no evidence as to what happened to it between November, 1949, and about the end of 1950, but Miss Rudolph, the fifth party, became interested in it late in the year 1950. On January 3, 1951, she took it from Messrs. Bowmaker Ld. on a hire-purchase agreement containing not unfamiliar provisions.

• • •

Miss Rudolph paid some of the monthly payments due under the hire-purchase agreement, but she had not paid all of them nor, of course, had she exercised the option to purchase by August 1, 1951, when she purported to sell this Jowett Javelin car to a motor dealer named Leonard Kennedy, the fourth party. The price was £1,000 and that was paid by him by means of a cash payment of £350 and the delivery of an A.C. shooting brake, which was valued for the purpose of that transaction at £650. That sale was wrongful because the car still belonged to Bowmaker Ld., and Miss Rudolph had no right to sell it. There was, therefore, a clear breach of the implied condition under section 12(1) of the Sale of Goods Act, 1893. It may well be that Miss Rudolph did not then realize that she was acting in an unlawful manner, but it is quite clear that she was.

On or about August 11, the fourth party, Mr. Kennedy, purported to sell this car for a little more than he had given for it — namely, £1,015 — to Hayton, the third party. Hayton was a produce merchant and, so far as Kennedy knew, Hayton required the car for his own use and not for re-sale. This second transaction was again a completely wrongful sale as the car still belonged to Bowmaker Ld., so that, again, there was a breach of the same implied condition, but I find that he acted in good faith in believing he had a right to sell the car.

On the same day, August 11, Hayton, the third party, purported to sell the car for £1,030, to the defendants, Kingsway Motors, who are motor dealers, and Hayton knew that they were buying the car for re-sale. Here again, the sale was wrongful as the car still belonged to Bowmaker Ld., so that there was a breach of the same implied condition. Hayton also acted in good faith in believing that he had a right to sell the car.

After certain negotiations from about August 15 onwards, the defendants, on or about August 30, 1951, purported to sell the car to the plaintiff for £1,275, which was paid by means of certain cash payments amounting to £550 and the delivery of a Standard car which for this purpose was considered to be worth £725. Here, again, there was a wrongful sale as the car still belonged to Bowmaker Ld. and the defendants had no right to sell it, so there was a breach of the same implied condition. Here, also, the defendants acted in good faith, believing that they had a right to sell.

It appears from the registration book that the plaintiff was registered as owner on January 15, 1952. From the time of its acquisition on about August 30, 1951, until some time in July, 1952, he made full use of the car, fully believing that it was his car and that he had every right to use it. Miss Rudolph continued to make some monthly payments to Bowmaker Ld., under the hire-purchase agreement. In the end, however, she learned that she ought not to have sold the car as she had done and she informed Bowmaker Ld. of the actual position. Her conduct in those two respects, of course, affords strong evidence that she was acting in good faith and not with any intention of deceit, but it was a wrongful sale.

On July 15, 1952, Bowmaker Ld. wrote to the plaintiff in these terms:

Re: Jowett Javelin — Regd. No. HGA 4. We have reason to believe that the vehicle described above is at present in your possession and we wish to advise you that it is our property the subject of a hiring agreement into which we entered with a Miss G. Rudolph. Assuming our information to be correct, we have to ask you to be good enough to arrange at once for the vehicle to be returned into the possession of our Liverpool office, and we shall be obliged if you will confirm that you have given

effect to our requirements. It occurs to us that you might perhaps like the opportunity to acquire title in the vehicle and quite without prejudice, we would be
prepared to allow you to do so in consideration of an immediate payment of £175 14s.
2d.

If the plaintiff had been willing to enter into some arrangement on the lines
suggested by Bowmaker Ld., a great deal of trouble would have been saved
because no doubt it would have been possible to arrange what ultimately happened in fact, that Miss Rudolph herself would repay the outstanding balance to
Bowmaker Ld. The plaintiff would then have had what he had originally bargained for at the price he originally agreed to pay, and did pay, and it would have
saved a great deal of expense to everybody. On the other hand, he would have
lost the chance he had in 1952 of reclaiming the full 1951 price in return for giving
up this motor-car in July, 1952, by which time it had substantially depreciated in
its realizable value by reason of a general fall in the market price of second-hand
cars, but I do not think those considerations ultimately affect the legal issue here.
I only mention them to show that I have not left out of consideration possible
arguments on the grounds of hardship. In my view, the plaintiff's position is
somewhat lacking in merits.

On July 17, 1952, acting very promptly in the matter, the plaintiff's solicitors
wrote to the defendants:

> We have been consulted by Mr. H. Butterworth of 44, Dee Lane, West Kirby, who
> informed us that he purchased a Jowett Javelin car for £1,275 on August 30 last. We
> are instructed that this motor-car was not yours to sell, and in the circumstances our
> client will expect the return of the money paid.

That shows that the plaintiff is claiming the repayment of the money and not
wishing to retain the car. That second point becomes even more clear in later
letters. On July 18 there is a reply from the defendants' solicitors to the plaintiff's
solicitors:

> . . . The allegation that the Jowett Javelin car was not the property of our clients to
> sell has come as a complete surprise. Our clients purchased the car from a motor
> dealer. . . .

On July 23 Bowmaker Ld. write to the plaintiff's solicitors:

> *Re: Miss G. Rudolph, Agreement No.* _____: . . . Since we wrote to Mr. Butterworth,
> we have received from our hirer a post-dated cheque which, if met, will be sufficient
> to discharge our interests and to enable us to release the vehicle to Mr. Butterworth.
> The cheque in question is dated [July 25], so we propose to write you again during
> the course of a day or two.

It is understood and accepted by all counsel that in fact that cheque was made
out by Miss Rudolph and made payable to Bowmaker Ld. for the outstanding
amount of the hire-purchase payments and, I suppose, for the 10s. necessary to
complete the purchase; and that cheque was met on or about July 25, 1952. The
effect of that is that Miss Rudolph must be deemed to have exercised her option to
purchase, and it follows that as between her and Bowmaker Ld. the ownership
passed from Bowmaker Ld. to her. That is only as between those two parties.

Bowmaker Ld. were willing to take that cheque, as they pointed out in their letter, in discharge of their interests and as enabling them to release the vehicle. They say in their letter "to release the vehicle to Mr. Butterworth."

On August 9 there is a further letter from the plaintiff's solicitors to the defendants' solicitors, which reads: ". . . We are now instructed to apply for the return of the purchase price, namely, £1,275, and we should be obliged by your letting us have your instructions with regard to the return of the motor-car." On August 14 Bowmaker Ld. wrote to the plaintiff's solicitors: ". . . We are pleased to say that the cheque to which we referred in our last communication has been duly met so that our interests in this case and in the Jowett Javelin HGA 4 is completed."

On August 22 the plaintiff's solicitors write to the defendants' solicitors again asking for the return of the purchase price and again asking for instructions regarding the return of the motor-car. On October 11, 1952, the plaintiff's solicitors write again asking for some instructions as to the disposal of the car. The plaintiff did not use the car after July 16, 1952, but the car has remained on his premises ever since that date and, most unfortunately, no arrangement was made for that car to be disposed of in July or August or later in 1952, while its price was still comparatively high.

The proceedings began with a specially indorsed writ issued on September 12. The claim was

> for money received by the defendants to the use of the plaintiff and payable by the defendants to the plaintiff on a consideration which has wholly failed. The said money, namely, £1,275, was paid by the plaintiff to the defendants on August 30, 1951, or thereabouts, as the consideration for the delivery by the defendants to the plaintiff of a Jowett Javelin motor-car, registration number HGA 4, and the consideration wholly failed by reason of the fact that the defendants were not the owners of the said motor-car, and had no title to the said motor-car. And the plaintiff claims the said sum of £1,275.

* * *

There was a third party notice served by the defendants against the third party claiming to be indemnified against the plaintiff's claim and costs of the action on the ground that there was an implied condition that the third party had a good title to the motor-car. There is a statement of claim in those proceedings and the defence. It is sufficient to say that, in substance, the defendants' claim against the third party is now, at any rate, for damages for breach of the implied condition that the third party had a good title. The claim is for damages because any alleged breach of the alleged condition has been reduced to a breach of warranty, either by the events which have happened or by the election of the defendants to deal with the matter on that basis. The main plea in the defence is that the title was perfected afterwards. There is a similar fourth party notice dated November 26, 1952, by the third party against the fourth party and a somewhat similar statement of claim and defence. Then there is a similar fifth party notice dated January 6, 1953, by the fourth party against Miss Rudolph.

On those facts, the first question is the relation between the plaintiff and the defendants, and a very important question is whether the plaintiff, by his letter of July 17, 1952, duly and effectually rescinded the contract of sale between him and the defendants. I hold, first, that that letter of July 17, as a matter of construction, constituted a rescission of that contract of sale. When I say "a rescission of the contract of sale," I am using the wording which was used in the Court of Appeal in *Rowland* v. *Divall* [1923] 2 KB 500, and without prejudice to the question whether it could also be put in rather a different way: that there was a fundamental breach by the defendants and the plaintiff elected to treat that breach as a repudiation of that contract of sale. I do not think that it makes any difference which way one looks at it in the end. Secondly, I hold that, on the authority of *Rowland* v. *Divall*, the plaintiff was on that date entitled to rescind that contract of sale. The possible contention for the defendants that such rescission was precluded by the plaintiff's use of the car for a substantial period and the deterioration in its condition and/or depreciation in its market value during that period is answered by the reasoning of Bankes L.J. (at 503) in that case. Another possible contention that such rescission was precluded by the plaintiff's acceptance of the motor-car when it was delivered or after delivery is answered by the reasoning of Atkin L.J. (at 506).

The contention mainly relied upon by Mr. Atkinson for the defendants as against the plaintiff was that there was not a total failure of the consideration. That question he said was to be determined as at the date of the issue of the writ, and that, as at that date, the plaintiff was still in undisturbed possession of the car; there was no outstanding adverse claim against him because Miss Rudolph had paid the outstanding instalments and the hire-purchase money, and Bowmaker Ld. were willing to accept such payment in full discharge of their interest in the car and to release the vehicle to the plaintiff. The answer to that contention is that on July 17 the plaintiff was entitled to, and did, rescind the contract of sale and thereby he established, and in a sense crystallized, his right to receive repayment of the purchase price as money paid in consideration for the sale of the motor-car. He could not consistently with that claim for repayment of the purchase price also claim to retain possession of the car, but at all times it was sufficiently clear that he was not adopting any attitude of seeking to retain possession of the car. He was holding the car at the disposal of the defendants. I further hold that after he had written that letter the plaintiff was entitled to, and did, maintain his position of having no claim to possession of the car, but having a right to repayment of the purchase price. Having regard to that, whatever the general merits of his position may be, I hold that the plaintiff is in law entitled to recover, and there will be judgment for £1,275 against the defendants.

The next question is as to the present ownership of the car. The various purported sales all took place at times when Bowmaker Ld. were still the owners of the car, so that all the purported sellers in this rather long chain had no title to it at the times when the sales, or purported sales, were made; but on or about July 25, 1952, Miss Rudolph acquired a good title from Bowmaker Ld. or, at any rate, made a payment to Bowmaker Ld. which extinguished their title and induced them to relinquish any claim they had to the car. I think the right view is that Miss Rudolph did acquire the title as between her and Bowmaker Ld., but I further hold on authority that the title so acquired went to feed the previously defective titles of the subsequent buyers and enured to their benefit. It is a rather curious position but I so hold mainly on the authority of the Court of Appeal decision in *Whitehorn Brothers* v. *Davison* [1911] 1 KB 463.

• • •

The next set of questions is concerned with the rights of the defendants against Hayton, and Hayton against Kennedy, and Kennedy against Miss Rudolph. The defendants are entitled to claim damages against Hayton for breach of the condition as to good title to the car, but that breach of the condition is now reduced to a breach of warranty and damages can be claimed on that basis. In consequence of that breach, the defendants lost the purchase price of £1,275 but, on the other hand, they eventually acquired ownership of the car. For the value of that car which they so acquired, they must give credit in reduction of the prima facie sum of £1,275.

The next question is: At what date is the value of that car to be assessed? One possible argument for the third party would be that it was the duty of the defendants to mitigate the damage by taking all reasonable steps to dispose of the car and it would have been reasonable for the defendants at once, in July or August or thereabouts in 1952, to take the car and dispose of it at the price it would then fetch in order to avoid further depreciation. It may be that there was a duty to mitigate the damage in that way, but the argument to the contrary is formidable: namely, that the defendants at that time were faced with a difficult legal position, and they were entitled to maintain their attitude against the plaintiff that the car belonged to him and it did not belong to them and they were not liable. I think there is a possibility of a good deal of argument as to what the "reasonable" steps to mitigate the damage would be, but I think this problem can be solved much more simply.

What the defendants gained was the ownership and right to possession of that car and, when one comes to assess the value of what they gained, one should take it at the date when it was gained. That is the position here. Then one has to arrive as best one can at the proper value of that car in or about July, 1952. [His Lordship referred to the evidence and continued:] The present value of this car is something like £450 and, making the best assessment I can, I assess its value in July, 1952, at £800. Therefore, the net claim of the defendants against the third party, all questions of the parties' costs being left over, is £475; that is to say, the difference between the full claim of £1,275 and the £800 deducted for the value of the car, leaving a difference of £475, and the decision is that the defendants are entitled to recover that sum from the third party.

The next step in the chain is the claim of Hayton, the third party, against Kennedy, the fourth party. This is possibly complicated by the fact that so far as the fourth party knew at the time of the contract of sale, Hayton was buying for his own use and not for re-sale; but Hayton paid £1,015 for the ownership of the car and he received initially no ownership at all so there was at that time a clear breach of contract. Prima facie his claim would be for the whole sum of £1,015 because he paid £1,015 and received nothing in exchange. In fact, subsequent events have reduced his claim. He has not suffered as much damage as that, but I think the fair view is that the subsequent events have to be taken as a whole and the effect is that his net claim against the fourth party is for £475, always leaving aside any question as to the parties' costs in this matter.

Similarly, I think the same result can be arrived at between Kennedy and Miss Rudolph. The previously mentioned complication does not exist here because Miss Rudolph knew that Kennedy was a motor dealer and was buying for re-sale. I do not think that that ultimately alters the result. Mr. Kennedy's claim against Miss Rudolph is £475, leaving aside the question of costs.

Judgment for the plaintiff.

Notes on Title: Plaintiff purchased electrical lamps from the defendant for resale. Upon taking delivery of the initial shipment it was discovered that the lamps had not been approved by the Canadian Standards Association as required by British Columbia law. Plaintiff sued for breach of s. 18 of the British Columbia SGA (Ont. SGA s. 13), arguing that since the lamps could not lawfully be sold where the purchaser wanted to resell them, there was no right in the defendant to sell the goods. What result? See *J. Barry Winsor & Associates Ltd.* v. *Belgo Canadian Manufacturing Co. Ltd.* (1975) 61 DLR (3d) 352 (BC SC); aff'd 76 DLR (3d) 685 (CA).

It will be observed that SGA 13(1) deems the seller to warrant his title at the time he purports to transfer it to the buyer. Literally interpreted, this means that in a conditional sale agreement in which the seller retains title until completion of the buyer's payments the seller would not be deemed to warrant his title until the buyer has finished his payments — a manifestly unsatisfactory result. A similar result would follow in hire-purchase agreements and other types of lease with an option to purchase. Happily, the courts have navigated their course around this obstacle. See *Karflex Ltd.* v. *Poole* [1933] 2 KB 251, extended in *Warman* v. *Southern Counties Car Finance Corp. Ltd.* [1949] 2 KB 576, and *cf. Sloan* v. *Empire Motors Ltd. and Vancouver Finance Co.* (1956) 3 DLR (2d) 53, (BC CA) and OLRC Sales Report, pp. 195-96, and pp. 223-26.

As *Rowland* v. *Divall, supra,* and *Butterworth* v. *Kingsway Motors, supra,* show, where the seller has breached his condition of title the buyer is entitled to recover the price without any allowance being made for the use of the goods. Various commentators have argued that the result is unjust. The issue is dealt with in the OLRC Sales Report in the extract that follows.

OLRC Sales Report
pp. 506-09

In *Rowland* v. *Divall* [1923] 2 KB 500 (CA), the plaintiff-buyer had, in good faith, purchased a motor vehicle from the defendant-seller. It transpired that the motor vehicle had been stolen and that the defendant did not have a good title. The car was taken by the police and the buyer brought an action to recover the purchase price he had paid on the ground of total failure of consideration. All members of the Court were agreed that the buyer had derived no benefits under the contract of sale that would defeat his restitutionary claim. He obviously had not received the title and, equally obviously, he had not obtained lawful possession. It was true that he had had the use of the car for several months but, as the judgments observed, it was not a lawful use. It is, therefore, difficult to see how the decision could have been different unless it is argued that the lawfulness or unlawfulness of the derived benefits is immaterial for the purpose of adjusting restitutionary claims. An example has been given of a buyer who purchases a crate of whisky that turns out to be stolen. In the meantime the buyer has consumed the liquor. It has been argued that it would be unjust that the buyer should be able to avoid paying the price, or be entitled to recover the price if it has already been paid; but, as has been pointed out, much will depend on what the true owner decides to do. If he elects to sue the seller in conversion and the seller pays him, the buyer's position looks weak. If it is the buyer who has been sued, or is being threatened with suit by the true owner, it is difficult to see why he should not be entitled to be fully indemnified by the seller; although, presumably, he cannot claim both an indemnity *and* the refund of the payments made by him. The difficulties will be most acute where the true owner has not yet determined whom he will sue, or where the identity of the true owner is unknown. However, there is much to be said for the argument accepted by Finnemore, J., in *Warman* v. *Southern Counties Car Finance Corp. Ltd.* [1949] 2 KB 576 that the buyer should not have to wait to be sued before being entitled to exercise his rescissionary remedy. Alternatively, he should at least be entitled to demand that the seller cure the defect in his title.

Leaving aside these difficulties, and assuming that the buyer has received some benefit from the use of the goods, there is still the difficult question of valuing the benefit. In the *Warman* case, Finnemore, J., rejected the contention that the hirer who had agreed "to rent" a car under a hire-purchase agreement should be subject to a set-off in respect of the rental value of the car while it was in his possession. Finnemore, J., observed that if the hirer had simply wanted to rent a car he would have done so. Similar difficulties arise if other criteria are adopted such as depreciation or profits made through the use of the goods.

These problems have been the subject of study and recommendations both in the New South Wales Working Paper and in a Working Paper on *Pecuniary Restitution on Breach of Contract* published by the English Law Commission in 1975. The New South Wales Working Paper made two recommendations: first, that the seller should be given a reasonable time to perfect his title before the buyer can rescind for breach of warranty of title; and, secondly, that if the seller fails to perfect his title within a reasonable time, the buyer should be entitled to claim a refund of the purchase price. However, it would be a condition of the buyer's right to recovery that he join the true owner as a party to the action, and that he offer to pay the true owner reasonable compensation for his use and enjoyment of the goods. The buyer should also have the alternative remedy of damages. The English Working Paper offered the following provisional recommendations:

(a) If he has conferred a valuable benefit on the buyer by the delivery of possession of the goods, the seller should be entitled to be paid (or as the case may [sic], to retain) the value of the benefit so conferred.

(b) The seller should be regarded as having conferred a valuable benefit on the buyer for the purposes of (a) where — but only where — a suitable replacement for the goods delivered may reasonably be obtained by the buyer at less than the original contract price, in which event the value of the benefit should be the difference between the original contract price and the price of the replacement *or* the amount by which the market price of the goods in question has fallen during the period of the buyer's possession, whichever may be the less.

(c) The seller's entitlement under (a) should be conditional upon the satisfaction of the true owner's claims against the buyer.

(d) Proposal (a) should not apply where the seller has sold stolen goods knowing or believing them to be stolen.

We do not find either set of recommendations completely satisfactory. We support the New South Wales recommendation that the seller should have an opportunity to cure the defect in title because it is consistent with the seller's general right to cure that we have recommended for adoption earlier in this chapter. However, in our opinion there is no justification for imposing on the buyer, if he seeks to recover the purchase price from the seller, the onus of joining the owner as a third party. We find two difficulties with the English proposals for measuring the value of the benefits conferred on the buyer: first, they are too rigid and, secondly, for obvious reasons, they do not concern themselves with the valuation of benefits where the buyer revokes his acceptance. In all cases we would prefer to leave the assessment of benefits to the discretion of the court, and not to draw a distinction between different types of restitutionary claim.

In our opinion, restitutionary claims for defects in title should be put on the same footing as claims arising out of other defects that entitle the buyer to claim the return of the price. We have previously recommended that where the buyer has received the goods any claim by a buyer to recover so much of the price as has been paid should be subject to such a reduction on account of any benefits derived by him from the use or possession of the goods as is just in the circumstances. In our view this recommendation should also apply to a buyer's claim to recover the purchase price where there is a defect in the seller's title and we so recommend. In addition, following our earlier recommendations the seller will have an opportunity to cure the defect in title if he satisfies the requirements generally applicable to a seller's right to cure a non-conforming tender or delivery.

We would anticipate that, to the extent that the seller is given an opportunity to cure the defect in his title, and exercises it, the need for the court to exercise its discretion in quantifying the benefits conferred upon the buyer will be greatly diminished in practice. To a lesser extent this will also be true in other cases where the seller has a right to cure other forms of defective performance. On the other hand, where the court is called upon to exercise its discretion in quantifying the benefits conferred, there is no reason why it may not take into consideration the good faith of each of the parties. It should, however, be clearly understood that the buyer is not obliged to pursue his restitutionary remedy and that, as under existing law, he should continue to have the option of suing for damages. . . .

MICROBEADS A.C. v. VINHURST ROAD MARKINGS LTD.
[1975] 1 All ER 529, [1975] 1 WLR 218 (CA)

LORD DENNING M.R.: This case raises a new and interesting point on the sale of goods. The defendants, an English company ("Vinhurst"), bought some special machinery from the plaintiffs, a Swiss company. They used the machines for making white lines on roads. Two or three years later another English company, who owned a patent, came along and said that these machines infringed their patent. They sought an injunction to prevent the use of the machines. Have the English company, who bought the machines, a cause of action against the Swiss company who sold them?

The dates are important. I will start with the owners of the patent. They are an English company, Prismo Universal Ltd. ("Prismo"), who carry on business near Crawley in Sussex. They hold a patent for an apparatus for applying markings on roads. It is done by the machine which carries a spray gun and a quantity of thermoplastic material. This gun sprays the material on to the roads so as to make a white and yellow line.

For some time the invention was kept secret. The application for a patent was filed on 28th December 1966. The complete specification was filed on 28 December 1967. The Patent Office made their various examinations. Eventually, on the 11th November 1970, the complete specification was published. It was on that date that it became open to the world to learn about it. It was only after that date that the patentee had any right or privileges in respect of it: see ss. 13(4) and 22 of the Patents Act 1949. On 12th January 1972 letters patent were granted to Prismo in respect of the invention. It was only then the patentee was entitled to institute proceedings for infringement: see s. 13(4) of the 1949 Act.

Now, before that invention was made public, Vinhurst bought some road marking machines and accessories from the Swiss company. These machines were sold and delivered to Vinhurst between January and April 1970, that is some months before the Prismo specification was published in November 1970. The price of the machines and accessories was nearly £15,000 of which Vinhurst paid £5,000, leaving the £10,000 balance to be paid. The buyers, Vinhurst, did not know anything about the patent. They had no idea that the machines might be infringing machines. They took them in good faith and used them. But they found the machines very unsatisfactory. They were dissatisfied. They did not pay the balance of the price.

On 30th November 1970 the sellers, the Swiss company, sued Vinhurst for the balance of £10,000 owing for the machines. At first Vinhurst put in a defence saying that the machines were not reasonably fit for the purpose of marking roads.

But then in 1972 Prismo came down on Vinhurst and said these machines (supplied by the Swiss company) infringed their patent. Thereupon Vinhurst amended their defence so as to set up the infringement as a defence and counterclaim. The point was set down as a preliminary issue. The judge found that the sellers, the Swiss company, were not guilty of a breach of contract in this respect. The buyers appeal to this court.

The preliminary issue was directed on these assumptions: (1) that the letters patent were valid; (2) that the machines sold by the Swiss company to Vinhurst were such as to fall within the scope of the claims in the specification; (3) that the property in each of the machines was to pass prior to November 1970. On those assumptions the point of law was whether there was any breach of contract on the part of the Swiss company under s. 12(1) or s. 12(2) of the Sale of Goods Act 1893 having regard to the dates of filing and publication of the specification and of the grant of the patent.

Before the judge most of the discussion was on s. 12(1). It says that there is an "implied condition on the part of the seller that . . . he has a right to sell the goods . . ." That means that he has, *at the time of the sale*, a right to sell the goods. The words "a right to sell the goods" mean not only a right to pass the property in the machines to the buyer, but also a right to confer on the buyer the undisturbed possession of the goods: see *Niblett Ltd* v. *Confectioners' Materials Co Ltd* [1921] 3 KB 387 at 402, by Atkin L.J. Now, at the time of the sale in January 1970 the Swiss company were able to confer those rights. They had made the machines out of their own materials and they could undoubtedly pass the property in them to the buyers. Moreover there was no one at that time entitled to disturb their possession. There was then no subsisting patent. The specification had not been published. No one could sue for infringement. The buyers could, *at that time*, use the machines undisturbed. So I agree with the judge that there was no breach of s. 12(1).

Now I turn to s. 12(2). It says that there is an "implied warranty that the buyer shall have and enjoy quiet possession of the goods". Taking those words in their ordinary meaning, they seem to cover this case. The words "shall have and enjoy" apply not only to the time of the sale but also to the future; "shall enjoy" means in the future. If a patentee comes two or three years later and gets an injunction to restrain the use of the goods, there would seem to be a breach of the warranty. But it is said that there are limitations on the ordinary meaning such limitations being derived from the civil law (as suggested by Benjamin on Sale) or from conveyancing cases.

One such limitation is said to follow from the words of Lord Ellenborough C.J. in *Howell* v. *Richards* (1809) 11 East 633 at 642 when he said:

> The covenant for title is an assurance to the purchaser, that the grantor has the very estate in quantity and quality which he purports to convey, viz, in this case an indefeasible estate in fee simple. The covenant for quiet enjoyment is an assurance against the consequences of a defective title, and of any disturbances thereupon.

Counsel for the Swiss company said that Lord Ellenborough C.J. there meant a defective title existing at the time of the sale. The covenant, he said, did not apply to a defective title which only appeared some time after the sale. The defect here appeared after the sale; it [appeared] in November 1970 when the complete specification was published.

The other limitation, derived from the conveyancing cases, was that the covenant for quiet enjoyment protected the purchaser or tenant only from the acts or operations of the vendor or lessor and those claiming under him, but not against the acts or operations of those claiming by title paramount: see *Jones* v. *Lavington* [1903] 1 KB 253. Counsel for the Swiss company submitted that that conveyancing rule applied to s. 12(2) also. Here the claim by the patentee was by title paramount.

There is one case which supports this contention. It is a decision of Lord Russell of Killowen C.J. in 1895 when he was on the Northern Circuit. It is *Monforts* v. *Marsden* (1895) 12 RPC 266. But that case was disapproved by this court in *Niblett Ltd* v. *Confectioners' Materials Co Ltd.* and must be taken to be overruled. Afterwards in *Mason* v. *Burningham* [1949] 2 KB 545 at 563 Lord Greene M.R. made it clear that the conveyancing cases should not be applied to s. 12 of the Sale of Goods Act 1893. He said:

> It is to be observed that in the language used in the Sale of Goods Act, 1893, s. 12(2), there is no exception for any disturbance by title paramount. The words are as I have quoted them, "that the buyer shall have and enjoy quiet possession of the goods." I invited counsel for the defendant to refer us to any authority that would justify the insertion into that statutory phrase of an exception in the case of disturbance by title paramount, but he was unable to do so, and, in the absence of any authority, I can only express my opinion that the statute means what it says and is not to have any such gloss put on it.

I would follow the guidance of Lord Greene M.R. Even if the disturbance is by title paramount — such as by the patentee coming in and claiming an injunction to restrain the use of the machine — there is a breach of the implied warranty under s. 12(2).

But the main point of counsel for the Swiss company before us — a point which the judge accepted — was that the defects of title must be present *at the time of the sale*. That is why so much turned on the date of publication, 11th November 1970. After that date the Swiss company, could by taking reasonable steps, have known that their machines were infringing machines and that they could not have a right to use them. So, if they had sold after 11th November 1970, they would be in breach of s. 12(2) and of s. 12(1) also. But counsel for the Swiss company says that before that date the Swiss company may have been perfectly innocent. Nothing had been published about this patent. The machines were sold in January and April 1970. There was no defect in title existing at the time of the sale. Accordingly counsel submitted there was no breach of s. 12(2).

Appeal allowed.

Notes:

1   Do you think the construction placed in *Microbeads* on the implied warranty of quiet possession is too harsh from the seller's point of view? Would the court have

reached the same conclusion if the sale had not been in the ordinary course of the seller's business? *Cf.* OLRC Sales Report, pp. 196-97.

2   It will be noted that *Microbeads* really involved the seller's liability for innocent patent infringement. The UCC, unlike the SGA, contains a separate provision under this head and only holds a *merchant seller* liable for such infringements [UCC 2-312(3)]. Why should a private seller be held strictly responsible for the defects in his title and not be held responsible for defects arising out of patent or trade mark infringements? Happily, patent and trademark owners do not generally appear to be concerned with private infringements — at least judging by the absence of reported Canadian cases. See further, OLRC Sales Report, pp. 198-99.

B. THE SELLER'S OBLIGATIONS WITH RESPECT TO DESCRIPTION, QUALITY AND SAMPLE

1. THE IMPLIED CONDITION OF DESCRIPTION

Introductory Note:

SGA s. 14 imposes on the seller the fundamental obligation to supply goods that conform to the contract description. The meaning of "description" is not self-evident and the materials in the present section illustrate the various contexts in which the courts and other agencies have had to grapple with the question. What gives particular punch to s. 14 is the fact that it applies to all sellers and that the obligation is characterized as a condition with the important remedial consequences that this entails.

The term "description" is also used in several other places in the Act, viz. ss. 15.1, 15.2, 19, rule 5(1), and 29.3. Initially there was a tendency to interpret the term uniformly, without regard to this particular context, but this liberal approach appears to have been arrested by the agreement of the law lords in the *Ashington Piggeries* case (*infra*, this chapter) that description in s. 15 does not have the same meaning as in s. 14. On this terminological point see further OLRC Sales Report, pp. 205-06, 208.

The determination of the meaning of "description" in its various settings in the SGA has been complicated by the blurring of lines between a sale "by description" and a sale of specific goods. A sale of specific goods carried great significance before the adoption of the SGA, and much of this significance has been retained in the Act: see e.g., SGA ss. 7-8, 12(3), 19, rule 1, and 50. In the 19th century too the implied conditions of quality (and quality in an extended sense included the implied condition of description: see the judgment of Mellor J. in *Jones* v. *Just* (1868) LR 3 QB 197, 202-203) did not apply to a sale of specific goods when the goods were available for inspection and traces of this rule may be found in the requirement of SGA 15(2), dealing with the condition of merchantability, that the goods must be bought "by description". See further *Benjamin's Sale of Goods*, para. 765; S.J. Stoljar (1952) 15 Mod. L. Rev. 425, (1953) 16 Mod. L. Rev. 174. As will be seen, however, from the cases in this section, so far as the obligation to deliver goods of the right description and merchantable quality are concerned, any lingering distinction between a sale of specific goods and non-specific goods has been more or less abandoned in the post-1893 jurisprudence.

ANDREWS BROTHERS (BOURNEMOUTH) LTD. v. SINGER & CO. LTD.
[1934] 1 KB 17, [1933] All ER Rep. 479 (CA)

SCRUTTON L.J.: This is an appeal from a judgment of Goddard J. in an action by the plaintiffs, a company carrying on business at Bournemouth, who in the agreement between them and the defendants out of which the dispute has arisen are called agents for manufacturers, which is quite a misleading term inasmuch as they are really purchasers of motor cars which they intend to sell. They brought their action against Singer & Co. alleging that the latter delivered a car which did not comply with the terms of the contract.

The facts which are fully set out in the careful judgment of Goddard J. may be shortly summarised: the description of the kind of car the plaintiffs wanted could have been satisfied by delivery to them of a new car; but the particular car which Singer & Co. tendered to them was in this position. Another agent, who thought he had in view a purchaser for the car, had it sent to Darlington and thence it was driven some distance further to show to the prospective customer, but as that person did not like it the agent returned it to Singer & Co., the result being that it had run a very considerable mileage with the consequence no doubt that certain changes had taken place in it. When the car was tendered to the plaintiffs' representative he noticed or suspected that it had run a considerable distance, but he took it, doing nothing, however, so far as I can see, to abandon any claim for damages on the ground that it was not a new car.

At the trial two points arose: First, the plaintiffs said that the car was not a new car as that term was understood in the trade. The defendants on the other hand said it was. Goddard J. came to the conclusion that it was not a new car, and in this Court his decision on that point has not been questioned and I therefore proceed on the assumption that the defendants, who were bound to supply a new car, tendered a car which was not a new one. The defendants contended secondly that they are exempted from liability by reason of clause 5 of the agreement entered into. That clause reads as follows: "All cars sold by the company are subject to the terms of the warranty set out in Schedule No. 3 of this agreement and all conditions, warranties and liabilities implied by statute, common law or otherwise are excluded." The defendants say that their obligation to supply a car complying with the description in the contract is a condition implied by statute, and as the plaintiffs accepted the car under the agreement containing clause 5 they cannot bring an action in respect of the supplying of a car which was not a new one. Clause 5 is, I take it, a sequel to *Wallis, Son & Wells* v. *Pratt & Haynes* [1910] 2 KB 1003. In that case the subject matter of the sale was "common English sainfoin," and the contract contained this clause: "Sellers give no warranty express or implied as to growth, description or any other matters." What in fact was sold under the contract was not "common English sainfoin" but something quite different, namely, "giant sainfoin." On discovering this the purchasers sued for damages, to which claim the sellers replied that they gave no warranty express or implied as to description. The Court of Appeal (Moulton L.J. dissenting) took the view that the clause excluded any liability even though the seed supplied was not of the description contracted to be supplied. The House of Lords adopted Moulton L.J.'s judgment and said that the goods tendered should comply with the description in the contract, which description was not a warranty but a condition, and as the clause relied on did not include "condition" it did not operate to protect the sellers. Those advising the present defendants in preparing this agreement appear to have thought that by the inclusion of the word "conditions" in the relevant clause liability would be excluded, although what was supplied did not comply with the description. The question therefore is whether the defendants have succeeded in excluding liability in this case — whether they can tender under the contract goods not complying with the description in the contract and say that the plaintiffs having accepted the car cannot now sue for breach of contract.

In my opinion this was a contract for the sale of a new Singer car. The contract continually uses the phrase "new Singer cars." At the end of the agreement I find this: "In the event of the dealer having purchased from the Company during the period of this agreement 250 new cars of current season's models"; and in the very beginning of the agreement I find this: "The Company hereby appoint the dealer their sole dealer for the sale of new Singer cars." The same phrase also occurs in other parts of the agreement, and the subject-matter is therefore expressly stated to be "new Singer cars." The judge has found, and his view is not now contested, that the car tendered in this case was not a new Singer car. Does then clause 5 prevent the vendors being liable in damages for having tendered and supplied a car which is not within the express terms of the contract? Clause 5 says this: "All conditions, warranties and liabilities implied by statute, common law or otherwise are excluded." There are well-known obligations in various classes of contracts which are not expressly mentioned but are implied. During the argument Greer, L.J. mentioned an apt illustration, namely, where an agent contracts on behalf of A he warrants that he has authority to make the contract on behalf of A although no such warranty is expressed in the contract. Mr. Pritt relied on s. 13 of the Sale of Goods Act, 1893, which provides that "where there is a contract for the sale of goods by description, there is an implied condition that the goods shall correspond with the description . . .," and from that he says it follows that this particular condition comes within the words employed by the section. That, I think, is putting a very strained meaning on the word "implied" in the section. Where goods are expressly described in the contract and do not comply with that description, it is quite inaccurate to say that there is an implied term; the term is expressed in the contract. Suppose the contract is for the supply of a car of 1932 manufacture, and a car is supplied which is of 1930 manufacture, there has not been a breach of an implied term; there has been a breach of an express term of the contract. It leads to a very startling result if it can be said that clause 5 allows a vendor to supply to a purchaser an article which does not comply with the express description of the article in the contract, and then, though the purchaser did not know of the matter which prevented the article supplied from complying with the express terms of the contract, to say, "We are under no liability to you because this is a condition implied by statute and we have excluded such liability."

In my view there has been in this case a breach of an express term of the contract. If a vendor desires to protect himself from liability in such a case he must do so by much clearer language than this, which, in my opinion, does not exempt the defendants from liability where they have failed to comply with the express term of the contract. For these reasons I think Goddard J. came to a correct conclusion, and this appeal therefore fails.

Appeal dismissed.

[Greer L.J. and Eve J. delivered concurring judgments.]

Notes:

1   Scrutton L.J. is no doubt correct in his assertion that, analytically, words of description are an express part of the contract in which they appear. It is equally clear however that Chalmers, following 19th century usage, treated the descriptive language as giving rise to an *implied* obligation on the seller to deliver goods conforming to the description. See e.g., *Chalmer's Sale of Goods Act,* 13th ed. (1957), p. 50, and cases cited in note (h). That being the case, should Scrutton L.J. not have respected the SGA's characterization of the obligation?

2   UCC 2-313(1)(*b*) now provides that "any description of the goods which is made part of the basis of the bargain creates an express warranty that the goods shall conform to the description." The OLRC Sales Report, pp. 202-03, favoured a similar treatment of the obligation in the revised Sale of Goods Act. The English and Scottish Law Commissions, in their *First Report on Exemption Clauses in Contracts* (1969), para. 22, admitted the anomalous characterization in the U.K. Act but felt it was harmless and served the useful purpose of making it clear that the term amounts to a condition of the contract, and not a mere warranty. Do you agree?

VARLEY v. WHIPP
[1900] 1 QB 513, 69 LJQB 333 (Div. Ct.)

In June 1899 the plaintiff and the defendant met in Huddersfield, at which time the plaintiff offered to sell to the defendant for £21 a second-hand self-binder reaping machine, which the plaintiff said was then at Upton, and he also said that it had been new the previous year, and had only been used to cut fifty or sixty acres. The defendant had not then seen the machine but he agreed to buy it. The machine was not then the plaintiff's property, but he bought it immediately afterwards for £18. On June 28 the plaintiff put the machine on the railway to send to Beverley.

On July 2 the defendant wrote the plaintiff as follows: "I have had a look at the 'self binder' you sent me but it is not what I expected; it is a very old one and has been mended and you told me that it had only cut about 50 acres, and was practically new. I think you must never have seen it. It will be no use to me as I don't care about old things, and especially machinery, but I shall be at Huddersfield this week . . . where I shall be pleased to see you." After some further correspondence the defendant returned the machine on August 14, and the plaintiff brought this action to recover the price. The county court judge held that the contract was a sale by description, and that the defendant could only treat the misdescription as a breach of warranty but not as a ground for rejecting the machine. He therefore gave judgment for the plaintiff for the amount claimed. The defendant appealed.

CHANNELL J.: I am of opinion that this appeal ought to be allowed. The case turns on a fine point, namely, whether the words used by the seller with regard to the machine were part of the description, or merely amounted to a collateral warranty. If the property in the machine passed prior to July 2, nothing that the buyer could do afterwards would divest it. The question is, did the property pass? The machine which was to be sold had never been seen by the buyer, and it was not the property of the seller at the time. It was described as being at Upton, as being a self-binder, as being nearly new, and as having been used to cut only about fifty or sixty acres. All these statements were made with regard to the machine, and we have to consider how much of these statements was identification of the machine, and how much was mere collateral warranty. If a man says that he will sell the black horse in the last stall in his stable, and the stall is empty, or there is no horse in it, but only a cow, no property could pass. Again, if he says he will sell a four-year old horse in the last stall, and there is a horse in the stall, but it is not a four-year old, the property would not pass. But if he says he will sell a four-year old horse, and there is a four-year old horse in the stall, and he says that the horse is sound, this last statement would only be a collateral warranty. The term "sale of goods by description" must apply to all cases where the purchaser has not seen the goods, but is relying on the description alone. It applies in a case like the present, where the buyer has never seen the article sold, but has bought by the description. In that case, by the Sale of Goods Act, 1893, s. 13, there is an implied condition that the goods shall correspond with the description, which is a different thing from a warranty. The most usual application of that section no doubt is to the case of unascertained goods, but I think it must also be applied to cases such as this where there is no identification otherwise than by description. Then the sale being a sale by description, when did the property pass, if it did not pass when the bargain was made? The section of the Sale of Goods Act dealing with the passing of the property is s. 17, by which "(1.) where there is a contract for the sale of specific or ascertained goods, the property in them is transferred to the buyer at such time as the parties to the contract intend it to be transferred. (2.) For the purpose of ascertaining the intention of the parties regard shall be had to the terms of the contract, the conduct of the parties, and the circumstances of the case." It is impossible to imagine a clause more vague than this, but I think it correctly represents the state of the authorities when the Act was passed. Sect. 18 does not apply; the only clause in that section which could possibly apply would be rule 1, but I do not think that this was "an unconditional contract for the sale of specific goods." Then when did the property pass? Not when the machine was put on the railway for the vendor could not make the property pass by putting on the railway that which did not fulfil the implied condition. The earliest date therefore at which the property could be said to pass would be when the machine was accepted by the purchaser. But it never was accepted. I am doubtful whether the letter of July 2 could be treated as amounting to a rejection, but the purchaser certainly did not accept the machine by that letter, and therefore the property never had passed. The result is that the defendant is entitled to judgment, and the appeal must be allowed.

BUCKNILL J.: I am of the same opinion. The county court judge has found that there was a sale by description, and I think that finding is right. The machine was sold as a self-binder, which was then at Upton, was nearly new, and had only been used to cut fifty or sixty acres. Was that a collateral warranty, or was it the description of the article intended to be sold? I am of opinion that it was the description, and that there was a contract for sale by description, within the meaning of s. 13 of the Sale of Goods Act. The machine was put on the railway, and got to the defendant's place of business. He could then accept or reject it. He wrote the letter of July 2, by which, though possibly he did not reject the machine, certainly he did not accept it. I am of opinion that the appeal must be allowed, and judgment given for the defendant.

Appeal allowed.

Notes:

1   *Varley* v. *Whipp* cannot be properly understood without recalling the anomalous rule in what was then s. 11(1)(*c*) of the U.K. Act [Ont., s. 12(3)] that where the contract is for the sale of specific goods, the property in which has passed to the buyer, the breach of any condition to be fulfilled by the seller can only be treated as a warranty and not as a ground for rejecting the goods. See *infra,* chapter 12(A). Thus the Divisional Court had to consider two separate issues: (1) had the seller committed a breach of the implied condition of description; and (2) if he had, did this prevent the presumptive transfer of title as envisaged in s. 18, rule 1 [Ont., s. 19, r. 1] of the Act? The writers have generally concentrated on the latter question and less on the court's analysis of the meaning of description in s. 13 of the U.K. Act. See inter alia P. Atiyah, *The Sale of Goods* (5th ed. 1975) pp. 146-47, and G.H.L. Fridman, *The Sale of Goods in Canada* (2nd ed. 1979) pp. 89-90.

2   *Williston on Sales,* rev. ed., pp. 224-25, is critical of the broad meaning given to "description" in *Varley* v. *Whipp* and other post-1893 English cases and argues that the term should be confined to cases where the identification of the goods which are the subject-matter of the bargain depends upon the description. He points out that the English courts have been forced to give an extended meaning to the term in order to provide the disappointed buyer with an effective right of rejection, and that the difficulty does not arise under the American Uniform Sales Act since that Act generally allows rescission for breach of warranty whether or not the implied term of description, strictly construed, has been breached. Williston's strictures derive some support from several of the law lords' judgments in the *Ashington Piggeries* case (*infra,* Chapter 6(A)(1)), and from Lord Wilberforce's judgment in the *Reardon Smith Line* case (*infra,* this chapter) but for a different reason, viz. that a right of rejection should not be recognized for inconsequential breaches that can be adequately compensated for in damages.

3   Section 11(1)(c) of the U.K. Act was amended by the Misrepresentation Act 1967, s. 4(1), which omitted the words "or where the contract is for specific goods, the property in which has passed to the buyer." None of the Canadian provincial acts has so far copied the amendment.

BEALE v. TAYLOR
[1967] 3 All ER 253, [1967] 1 WLR 1193 (CA)

SELLERS L.J.: I have come to the conclusion that this appeal should be allowed. It is an unfortunate case which I would have hoped might have been disposed of satisfactorily within the confines of the county court, either by the learned judge in the first instance or on an application to him to hear the matter again if, as it is suggested here, there was some misunderstanding as to the contentions on behalf of the plaintiff. However, it has now come on appeal and this court has to decide it. It is an unusual case, and for both parties — who, as the judge said, are both innocent in the matter — an unfortunate one.

The defendant seller, Mr. Taylor, had a car which he believed to be a Herald convertible, 1961, 1200 twin-carburetter car. He apparently had driven it for some time and done a considerable mileage with it and wished to dispose of it. I think that it had been in an accident, and certainly it was not in very good condition. The seller inserted an advertisement in about April, 1966, in a well-known paper for the sale of secondhand cars. That was in these terms: "Herald convertible, white, 1961, twin carbs., £190. Telephone Welwyn Garden", and it gives a telephone number, "after 6.0 p.m." The plaintiff buyer, who was born in 1946 and has been driving cars for some little time, or his mother, or both, saw the advertisement, got in touch with the seller, and went along to his home to see the car. They saw it and had a run in it. The buyer did not drive because there was no insurance for him. I do not know whether his mother went in the car too. After that run and some discussion the buyer made an offer, or his mother made an offer to buy the car for £160, which the seller accepted. There was a little delay while the balance of the purchase price was paid, and then the buyer drove it away. From the outset apparently the buyer found that the steering was pulling to the left-hand side, so much so that he said that, in his journey from Welwyn Garden City to St. Albans, his arms ached; and he eventually after a short time put it in a garage to be checked over. Then it was found by the garage people that, instead of being a car of that description — that being a 1961 1200 Triumph Herald convertible — it was in fact a car which was made up of two cars. The back portion apparently was of that description but the front portion, which had been welded on about half-way, somewhere under the driver's seat, and which contained the engine, was an older, earlier model, the 948 c.c. model, and these two parts had been made into this one structure. Having regard to the nature of the welding of the two chassis together, as described by the expert who was called, it is not surprising that the car was not running properly. It had also apparently had an accident, as I have said, and it was condemned as being unsafe to take on the road.

The question then arose what was to happen with regard to the purchase price which the buyer had paid to the seller. Instead of the matter being settled amicably, which might have been the wisest thing to do in order to save the money which has been involved in costs, the matter went to court. The buyer relied on the fact that there had been a description of this vehicle as a Triumph Herald 1200 motor car with the registration number 400 RDH and that the vehicle which was delivered did not correspond with that description. The seller, who conducted his own defence and apparently put in his written defence as well, denied that it was a sale by description and said that, on the contrary, it was

> the sale of a particular car as seen, tried and approved, the [buyer] having an abundant opportunity to inspect and test the car.

He denied that the buyer had in the circumstances suffered any loss or damage. Of course a person may purchase a commodity relying entirely on his own judgment in the matter, and there may be no representation at all. Perhaps one hundred years ago more credence might have been given to the seller's defence than is given now, but, since the Sale of Goods Act, 1893, the rule caveat emptor has been very much modified. Section 13 of the Sale of Goods Act, 1893, provides that

> Where there is a contract for the sale of goods by description, there is an implied condition that the goods shall correspond with that description; . . .

and certainly there is good authority for saying that, if the buyer has not seen the goods, then in the ordinary way the contract would be one where the buyer relied on the description alone. Sale of goods by description may, however, apply where the buyer has seen the goods if the deviation of the goods from the description is not apparent; but even then (and I am quoting now from a well-known text book, *Chalmers' Sale of Goods* (15th Edn.)), when the parties are really agreed on the thing sold a misdescription of it in the contract may be immaterial.

The question in this case is whether this was a sale by description or whether, as the seller contends, this was a sale of a particular thing seen by the buyer and bought by him purely on his own assessment of the value of the thing to him. We were referred to a passage in the speech of Lord Wright in *Grant* v. *Australian Knitting Mills, Ltd.* [1936] AC 85 at 100, which I think is apt as far as this case is concerned. Lord Wright said:

> It may also be pointed out that there is a sale by description even though the buyer is buying something displayed before him on the counter; a thing is sold by description, though it is specific, so long as it is sold not merely as the specific thing but as a thing corresponding to a description, e.g., woollen under-garments, a hot water bottle, a secondhand reaping machine, to select a few obvious illustrations

and, I might add, a secondhand motor car. I think that, on the facts of this case, the buyer, when he came along to see this car, was coming along to see a car as advertised, that is, a car described as a "Herald convertible, white, 1961". When he came along he saw what ostensibly was a Herald convertible, white, 1961, because the evidence shows that the "1200" which was exhibited on the rear of this motor car is the first model of the "1200" which came out in 1961; it was on that basis that he was making the offer and in the belief that the seller was advancing his car as that which his advertisement indicated. Apart from that, the selling of a car of that make, I would on the face of it rather agree with the submission of the seller that he was making no warranties at all and making no contractual terms; but fundamentally he was selling a car of that description. The facts as revealed very shortly afterwards show that that description was false. It was unfortunately not false to the knowledge of the owner who was selling nor of the buyer, because no one could see from looking at the car in the ordinary sort of examination which would be made that it was anything other than that which it purported to be. It was only afterwards that, on examination, it was found to be in two parts. I think that that is a sufficient ground on which to decide this case in favour of the buyer.

Appeal allowed.

Question: Under a contract to supply "ethanol-ethylene glycol antifreeze", the seller delivered a fluid containing only 4.01% ethylene glycol. Antifreeze then on the market and sold to the general motoring public contained approximately 95% ethylene glycol. Would the buyer be entitled to reject on the basis of a breach of the implied/express condition of description? See *Bakker* v. *Bowness Auto Parts Co. Ltd.* (1976) 68 DLR (3d) 173 (Alta. AD).

ONTARIO HANSARD
(31st Parl., 3rd Sess.) June 7, 1979

GM SETTLEMENTS

Mr. Rotenberg: Mr. Speaker, I have a question for the Minister of Consumer and Commercial Relations. I would like to question the minister about the problem of the Chevrolet engines in Oldsmobile cars. In view of the fact two other provinces have settled with the owners on the basis of $200 compensation plus extended warranties, is the ministry and is the minister prepared to recommend this type of settlement? What will be happening to the consumers in Ontario?

Hon. Mr. Drea: In conjunction with the Attorney General of this province (Mr. McMurtry), who must be consulted before such an arrangement could be consummated, we are not going to file the mandatory consents General Motors wants.

The history of this particular problem, Mr. Speaker, you will recall, was that people in good faith bought Buicks — the Century, the Regal or the Skylark models — with LM1 or LG3 engines; the Delta 88 model with an LM1 or an L65 engine, or a Pontiac Ventura or Ventura SJ equipped with an LG3 engine. They thought they were buying either a Buick, an Oldsmobile or a Pontiac engine. They weren't. General Motors deceived them. It stuck a Chevrolet engine in there.

General Motors now wants to make things good. They're not just offering $200. It also includes a 36-month special mechanical performance certificate and reimbursement for some actual expenses. However, in return for that, General Motors wants the Attorney General of this province to sign a modified release form. The Attorney General of this province, and up until a few days ago the Attorneys General of the other nine provinces, refused to do this, because it would be giving General Motors a special consideration not available to anybody else.

For reasons best known to themselves, three provinces — Quebec, British Columbia and Prince Edward Island — signed that form. In any negotiations this ministry has had with General Motors we have consulted with the Attorney General of this province and we have been advised he will not sign that release form for General Motors, so General Motors, before it gets settled in the province of Ontario, is going to have to come up with something better. After all, it deceived the public.

Mr. Rotenberg: Mr. Minister, that's all very well, but in the meantime people in three other provinces have received a settlement and people in Ontario have not. Can you indicate to this House when the people of Ontario can expect to get some settlement and some resolution of this matter?

Hon. Mr. Drea: As the Minister of Consumer Relations in this province, I am not going to sell the consumer down the river for the sake of expediency. The matter will be settled, it will be settled very equitably. General Motors notwithstanding its worldwide reputation or its immensity, is not going to dictate to the province of Ontario how it is going to settle up with people it deliberately deceived.

Mr. Breithaupt: Can the minister tell us approximately how many of these particular vehicles are in this circumstance of the wrong engine?

Hon. Mr. Drea: I can't. I can get the information for the honourable member. The reason I indulged the members' generosity to read the engine numbers is we have a feeling a number of people have not yet submitted claims because they are still not aware of the fact they were peddled a Chevrolet engine when they bought an Oldsmobile or a Buick.

Mr. Swart: Are we to assume from what the minister said that he is going to insist that in fact they replace the motors with the type of motors that were supposed to be in the car the first time?

Hon. Mr. Drea: No, Mr. Speaker, we are not putting terms and conditions on this. General Motors has made an offer to the people for whom we have been negotiating. We — and I emphasize we, because the Attorney General is involved — do not feel it is an offer we will endorse by the Attorney General's signing that release form. What General Motors does to persuade the Attorney General of this province to give me consent I know not, but it is going to have to sweeten the offer.

Mr. Makarchuk: They'll make you an offer you can't refuse.

Hon. Mr. Drea: Mr. Speaker, it won't be an offer I can't refuse. I will just draw one more point to the attention of the honourable members. None of the negotiations that my ministry and the Attorney General are carrying on affect the right of the owners of these cars to take direct action in court, if they so choose.

OLRC Sales Report
(1979) pp. 203-04

(b) *SALES IN SELF-SERVICE STORES*

The second question that arises in connection with the implied condition of description concerns sales in self-service stores. As noted, there may still be some doubt as to whether such a sale is a sale "by description". The English and Scottish Law Commissions recommended that this problem should be resolved by adding a new subsection to section 13 of the U.K. Sale of Goods Act, the provision equivalent to section 14 of the Ontario Act. This has now been done. The new clause provides as follows:

> 13.(2) A sale of goods shall not be prevented from being a sale by description by reason only that, being exposed for sale or hire, they are selected by the buyer.

A similar, but enlarged, recommendation appears in the New South Wales Working Paper. The problem to which the U.K. amendment is addressed arises because of earlier doubts as to whether the seller in a self-service store warrants the merchantable quality of his goods. These doubts were raised in part because section 15.2 of the existing Act only applies where goods are bought "by description". Later in this chapter, we recommend deletion of this phrase in section 15.2, with the result that this particular problem will cease to exist. It is also probable that a court today would have little hesitation in holding that a sale, at least of labelled goods, in a self-service store is a sale by description; as an earlier American court remarked about such a sale (*Corvan N. Sarris* v. *Ezy-Way Foodliner Co.* (1961) 170 A 2d 160 (Me. Sup. Ct.), "the printed word [is] the silent salesman". Nevertheless, to resolve any lingering doubts, we recommend the adoption of a provision comparable to section 13(2) of the U.K. Act in the revised Ontario Act.

ARCOS, LIMITED v. E.A. RONAASEN AND SON
[1933] AC 470, [1933] All ER Rep. 646 (HL)

LORD ATKIN: My Lords, the question between the parties arises on an award stated in the form of a special case by an umpire appointed under a submission contained in two contracts for the sale of timber. The contracts were in the White Sea 1928 C.I.F. form and were between the appellants, Arcos, Ld., sellers, and the respondents, E.A. Ronaasen & Son, buyers.

It is unnecessary to set them out at length. The substance was that the sellers agreed to sell to the buyers "the wood goods hereinafter specified" subject to a variation of 20 per cent. in sellers' option on any item, to be shipped from Archangel "during the summer 1930." The first contract specified "Redwood and whitewood staves bundled:

90 standards $^1/_2$ inch by 28 inches by 2 inches to 5 inches.
10 standards $^1/_2$ inch by 17 inches by $2^1/_2$ inches to 5 inches.

Messrs. Arcos, Ld., promise to do their best to induce the shippers not to cut any 2 inches in the $^1/_2$ inch by 17 inches headings, but should a few 2 inches width fall buyers agree to take same at a reduction in price of 40s. per standard." There were further conditions on the back of the contract which it is unnecessary at present to consider.

The second contract was in identical terms save as to quantities of standards and provided for 135/180 and 27 standards of 28 inches length, and 15/20 and 3 standards of 17 inches length.

The staves were required by the buyers for making cement barrels, and this was made known to the sellers in circumstances that implied a condition that they should be fit for that purpose. The goods in question were shipped under the contracts in October. When the shipping documents were tendered the buyers refused them on the ground that there had not been a summer shipment. There was an arbitration to determine this dispute, and the umpire held that the shipment was a summer shipment.

The buyers thereupon examined the goods which had been landed and claimed to reject them on the ground that they were not of contract description. This dispute went to arbitration and the umpire made his award in the form of a special case in which, after stating the facts, he awarded subject to the opinion of the Court that the buyers were not entitled to reject. On the hearing of the special case Wright J., and on appeal the Court of Appeal, differed from the umpire and held that the buyers were entitled to reject. The simple question is whether the goods when shipped complied with the implied condition (see the Sale of Goods Act, 1893, s. 13) that they should correspond with the description.

When the umpire inspected them on July 9, 1931, some nine months after landing and exposure to rain, he found the actual measurements to be as follows:

28-inch staves.
>   None less than $^1/_2$ inch.
>   4.3 per cent. were $^1/_2$ inch.
>   85.3 per cent. between $^1/_2$ inch and $^9/_{16}$ inch.
>   9.4 per cent. between $^9/_{16}$ inch and $^5/_8$ inch.
>   1 per cent. between $^5/_8$ and $^3/_4$ inch.
>   None over $^3/_4$ inch.

17-inch staves.
>   None less than $^1/_2$ inch.
>   6.4 per cent. were $^1/_2$ inch.
>   75.3 per cent. between $^1/_2$ inch and $^9/_{16}$ inch.
>   18.3 per cent. between $^9/_{16}$ inch and $^5/_8$ inch.
>   None over $^5/_8$ inch.

He found that they were all fit for use in the manufacture of cement barrels. He was unable with accuracy to say what was their thickness when shipped, but, he stated, "their thickness was closer to $^1/_2$ inch than it is now and I am satisfied that the staves when shipped were commercially within and merchantable under the contract specification."

The decisions of the learned judge and of the Court of Appeal appear to me to have been unquestionably right. On the facts as stated by the umpire as of the time of inspection only about 5 per cent. of the goods corresponded with the description: and the umpire finds it impossible to say what proportion conformed at the time of shipment.

It was contended that in all commercial contracts the question was whether there was a "substantial" compliance with the contract: there always must be some margin: and it is for the tribunal of fact to determine whether the margin is exceeded or not. I cannot agree. If the written contract specifies conditions of weight, measurement and the like, those conditions must be complied with. A ton does not mean about a ton, or a yard about a yard. Still less when you descend to minute measurements does $\frac{1}{2}$ inch mean about $\frac{1}{2}$ inch. If the seller wants a margin he must and in my experience does stipulate for it. Of course by recognized trade usage particular figures may be given a different meaning, as in a baker's dozen; or there may be even incorporated a definite margin more or less: but there is no evidence or finding of such a usage in the present case.

No doubt there may be microscopic deviations which business men and therefore lawyers will ignore. And in this respect it is necessary to remember that description and quantity are not necessarily the same: and that the legal rights in respect of them are regulated by different sections of the code, description by s. 13, quantity by s. 30. It will be found that most of the cases that admit any deviation from the contract are cases where there has been an excess or deficiency in quantity which the Court has considered negligible. But apart from this consideration the right view is that the conditions of the contract must be strictly performed. If a condition is not performed the buyer has a right to reject. I do not myself think that there is any difference between business men and lawyers on this matter. No doubt, in business, men often find it unnecessary or inexpedient to insist on their strict legal rights. In a normal market if they get something substantially like the specified goods they may take them with or without grumbling and a claim for an allowance. But in a falling market I find that buyers are often as eager to insist on their legal rights as courts of law are ready to maintain them. No doubt at all times sellers are prepared to take a liberal view as to the rigidity of their own obligations, and possibly buyers who in turn are sellers may also dislike too much precision. But buyers are not, as far as my experience goes, inclined to think that the rights defined in the code are in excess of business needs.

It may be desirable to add that the result in this case is in no way affected by the umpire's finding that the goods were fit for the particular purpose for which they were required. The implied condition under s. 14, sub-s. 1, unless of course the contract provides otherwise, is additional to the condition under s. 13. A man may require goods for a particular purpose and make it known to the seller so as to secure the implied condition of fitness for that purpose: but there is no reason why he should not abandon that purpose if he pleases, and apply the goods to any purpose for which the description makes them suitable. If they do not correspond with the description there seems no business or legal reason why he should not reject them if he finds it convenient so to do.

Agreeing as I do with the reasoning of the judgments below, I find it unnecessary to say more than that I agree that the appeal should be dismissed with costs.

Appeal dismissed.

[Concurring judgments were delivered by Lord Buckmaster and Lord Warrington.]

Notes:

1   Do you agree with Lord Atkin's reasoning or, in your opinion, is the "perfect tender" rule, viz. the rule that the goods tendered must conform in every respect with the contract description, too harsh? Should the law draw a distinction between major and minor breaches of the descriptive terms and limit the buyer to a claim for damages in a breach of the latter type? Does the Sale of Goods Act, ss. 29, 33, draw any distinction with respect to the severity of breach and the buyer's right of rejection? Would the case be decided differently today in light of *Cehave, supra,* ch. 5, and *Reardon Smith Line Ltd.* v. *Hansen-Tangen, infra*? Sharp market price fluctuations are a frequent cause of commodity buyers' seeking to reject goods on minor grounds. See Eno, "Price Movement and Unstated Objections to the Defective Performance of Sales Contracts" (1935) 44 Yale LJ 782.

2   A very modest exception to the perfect tender rule is found in the judicially evolved gloss that "a deficiency or excess in quantity which is microscopic and which is not capable of influencing the mind of the buyer will not entitle him to reject the goods, for *de minimis non curat lex*" (*Benjamin's Sale of Goods*, p. 281). Benjamin continues:

> Some slight elasticity in carrying out a commercial contract for the supply of goods in bulk is unavoidable, and the courts will not allow the buyer to take advantage of a merely trivial difference in quantity if the delivery is substantially of the quantity named. Thus, in *Shipton Anderson and Co.* v. *Weil Brothers & Co.* (1912) 1 KB 524 an excess of 55 lb. of wheat over and above an agreed limit of 4,950 tons was held to fall within the rule. It seems, however, that the seller cannot invoke the rule except as a defence to an allegation that he has not substantially performed his obligation under the contract of sale and the burden of proving that the deficiency or excess falls within the rule rests upon him. The *de minimis* rule does not apply to documentary credits.

ASHINGTON PIGGERIES LTD. v. CHRISTOPHER HILL LTD.; CHRISTOPHER HILL LTD. v. NORSILDMEL
(Conjoined Appeals)
[1972] AC 441 (HL) [1971] 1 All ER 847

The following statement of facts is taken from the judgment of Lord Hodson:

In July 1961 the first case was noticed of a new and hitherto unknown disease afflicting mink which are bred in a large number of farms in this country. A male kit was found with a grossly enlarged abdomen and died within a few days. Similar cases were reported from that time onwards in various parts of the country. The common factor was that all the afflicted mink had been fed a fortified cereal mink food marketed under the brand name "King Size" and made up according to a formula. This formula emanated from a Mr. Udall who, since the early nineteen-fifties, had been concerned with the breeding of mink in the Wimborne area and was recognised as an expert on mink farming. The company, Ashington Piggeries Ltd., the defendants in the action, was controlled by Mr. Udall. In 1960 he approached a Mr. Granger, who was the personal assistant to the managing director of the plaintiff company (Christopher Hill Ltd.) with a view to the latter company compounding for him a mink food to be called "King Size" in accordance with a formula prepared by himself. This last-named company is an old-established and well-known animal feeding stuff compounder carrying on business at Poole. At this time the company was compounding 167 varieties of feeding stuffs principally for poultry, pheasants, calves and pigs but, until the events giving rise to this case, had had no experience or knowledge of mink.

To put the matter shortly, the ingredients were to be supplied by the plaintiffs and were to be of the best quality available. These were commodities which the plaintiffs were in the habit of handling in the course of their business and the manufacture of compounds for animal feeding to customers' formula was something which the trial judge found the plaintiffs habitually undertook. The contract of sale was entered into in May 1960 and deliveries of "King Size" commenced immediately either to the defendants or to their customers. Between May 1960 and the end of March 1961 "King Size" had been supplied to about 100 farms, but no real trouble arose until the end of July 1961. Mr. Udall's herd of mink was affected and he began to suffer increasing losses. "King Size" came under suspicion as being the cause of the outbreak of the severe liver disease from which the animals were suffering.

These proceedings were started by the plaintiffs claiming the price of goods sold and delivered, namely, the "King Size." To this the defendants answered that the goods were worthless and relied in the first instance on a change made in the formula of the goods without their consent, making their attack on the use of an anti-oxidant called Santoquin No. 6 as being the cause of the liver disease in the mink. After several days this attack was abandoned and in its place the attack was directed against Norwegian herring meal claimed to have been included in "King Size" and to have been the cause of the toxin which killed the mink. It was said that the meal was manufactured from herring preserved with sodium nitrite in circumstances which rendered the meal toxic to animals and in particular mink. The substance said to be toxic was dimethylnitrasomine (DMNA) which was not a constituent of the formula. There was at the trial a conflict as to causation which no longer subsists. The findings of fact made at the trial and no longer disputed are that the cause of the liver disease in the mink was "King Size" and that the toxic element was DMNA which was in the herring meal because of the use of sodium nitrite for preservation purposes.

[The following extract from L. Wilberforce's judgment deals with the appellants' argument that the respondents had committed a breach of the condition of description.

(Other extracts from the decision dealing with the implied condition of fitness are reproduced in section (3), *infra*.)]

LORD WILBERFORCE:

1. *Section 13 of the Act*: The question is whether the compound mink food sold by the respondents (under the name "King Size") corresponded with the description. The appellants' case was that the food was to be made up according to a formula which identified generically the ingredients and specifically the chemical additives, quantifying precisely the proportions of each ingredient. One of these ingredients was herring meal. The food delivered in certain relevant months, it was claimed, did not correspond with the description because it contained a significant quantity of DMNA. The proposition is that "King Size" made partly of herring meal which contains DMNA does not correspond with the description "King Size." This can be reduced to the proposition that the herring meal ingredient did not correspond with the description because it contained DMNA. The analogy was invoked, inevitably, by the appellants of copra cake with castor seed; the respondents invoked that of oxidised iron. The learned judge accepted the former, the Court of Appeal the latter.

Whether in a given case a substance in or upon which there has been produced by chemical interaction some additional substance can properly be described or, if one prefers the word, identified, as the original substance qualified by the addition of a past participle such as contaminated or oxidised, or as the original substance plus, or intermixed with, an additional substance, may, if pressed to analysis, be a question of an Aristotelian character. Where does a substance with a quality pass into an aggregate of substance? I do not think that it can be solved by asking whether the chemical interaction came about by some natural or normal process, e.g., preservation by the addition of salt (sodium chloride), or by some alien intrusion by the production of DMNA from sodium nitrite through a heating effect. I cannot see any distinction in principle in this difference. Further I do not believe that the Sale of Goods Act was designed to provoke metaphysical discussions as to the nature of what is delivered, in comparison with what is sold. The test of description, at least where commodities are concerned, is intended to be a broader, more common sense, test of a mercantile character. The question whether that is what the buyer bargained for has to be answered according to such tests as men in the market would apply, leaving more delicate questions of condition, or quality, to be determined under other clauses of the contract or sections of the Act. Perhaps this is to admit an element of impression into the decision, but I think it is more than impression which leads me to prefer the answer, if not all of the reasoning, of the Court of Appeal that the defect in the meal was a matter of quality or condition rather than of description. I think that buyers and sellers and arbitrators in the market, asked what this was, could only have said that the relevant ingredient was herring meal and, therefore, that there was no failure to correspond with description. In my opinion, the appellants do not succeed under section 13.

[The other law lords, Lord Dilhorne dissenting, agreed with Lord Wilberforce's interpretation on the meaning of description in U.K. SGA s. 13 (Ont. s. 14).]

REARDON SMITH LINE LTD. v. HANSEN-TANGEN
(THE "DIANA PROSPERITY")
[1976] 2 Lloyd's Rep. 621, [1976] 3 All ER 570 (HL)

This case involved a charter-party and a sub-charter-party, both relating to a new oil tanker to be built in Japan. By the time the tanker was ready for delivery the market had collapsed because of the 1974 oil crisis. It was therefore in the interests of the charterers to try to escape from their obligations by rejecting the ship. They sought to do so on the ground that the tanker tendered did not correspond with the contractual description.

For the purposes of the appeals it was assumed that the vessel complied in all respects with the detailed particulars contained in a form incorporated in the agreements. However, the appellants seized upon a provision in the sub-charter (referred to in the judgment of Lord Wilberforce as the "box") which made reference to ". . . (the good) Japanese flag (subject to Clause 41) Newbuilding motor tank vessel called Hull No. 354 at Osaka Zosen", as well as apparently a clause in an addendum to the intermediate charter which read, in part, "the vessel to perform this Charter is to be built by Osaka Shipbuilding Co. Ltd. . . ." In fact, because the vessel was too large to be built at the Osaka yards, Osaka entered into a joint venture for production of the ship at another yard 300 miles away.

The following extract from Lord Wilberforce's judgment reflects his view of the changing character of "description" in the law of sales and the characterization generally of sales terms:

LORD WILBERFORCE: The appellants sought, necessarily, to give to the "box" and the corresponding provision in the intermediate charter contractual effect. They argued that these words formed part of the "description" of the future goods contracted to be provided, that, by analogy with contracts for the sale of goods, any departure from the description entitled the other party to reject, that there were departures in that the vessel was not built by Osaka Shipbuilding Co. Ltd., and was not hull no. 354. I shall attempt to deal with each of these contentions.

In the first place, I am not prepared to accept that authorities as to "description" in Sale of Goods cases are to be extended, or applied, to such a contract as we have here. Some of these cases either in themselves, e.g. *Moore* v. *Landauer*, [1921] 2 KB 519, or as they have been interpreted, e.g. *Behn* v. *Burness* (1863) 3 B & S 751, I find to be excessively technical and due for fresh examination in this House. Even if a strict and technical view must be taken as regards the description of unascertained future goods (e.g. commodities) as to which each detail of the description must be assumed to be vital, it may be, and in my opinion is, right to treat other contracts of sale of goods in a similar manner to other contracts generally so as to ask whether a particular item in a description constitutes a substantial ingredient of the "identity" of the thing sold, and only if it does to treat it as a condition, see *Couchman* v. *Hill*, [1947] 1 KB 554, 559, *per* Lord Justice Scott. I would respectfully endorse what was recently said by Lord Justice Roskill in *Cehave N.V.* v. *Bremer Handelgesellschaft m.b.H.* (*The Hansa Nord*), [1975] 2 Lloyd's Rep. 445 at p. 458; [1976] 1 QB 44 at p. 71:

> In principle it is not easy to see why the law relating to contracts for the sale of goods should be different from the law relating to the performance of other contractual obligations, whether charter-parties or other types of contract. Sale of goods law is but one branch of the general law of contract. It is desirable that the same legal principles should apply to the law of contract as a whole and that different legal principles should not apply to different branches of that law.

and similarly by Mr. Justice Devlin in *Cargo Ships "El-Yam" Ltd.* v. *Invoer-En Transport Onderneming "Invotra"*, [1958] 1 Lloyd's Rep. 39 at p. 52. The general law of contract has developed, along much more rational lines e.g., *Hong Kong Fir Shipping Co. Ltd.* v. *Kawasaki Kisen Kaisha Ltd.*, [1961] 2 Lloyd's Rep. 478; [1962] 2 QB 28, in attending to the nature and gravity of a breach or departure rather than in accepting rigid categories which do or do not automatically give a right to rescind, and if the choice were between extending cases under the Sale of Goods Act, 1893, into other fields, or allowing more modern doctrine to infect those cases, my preference would be clear. The importance of this line of argument, is that Mr. Justice Mocatta and Lord Denning, M.R., used it in the present case so as to reject the appellants' argument on "description" and I agree with them. But in case it does not appeal to this House, I am also satisfied that the appellants fail to bring the present case within the strictest rules as to "description".

2 The Implied Warranty of Merchantable Quality

Introductory Note:

Both the expression ''merchantable quality'' and the implied condition by that name are frequently ascribed to an early 19th century decision, *Gardiner* v. *Gray* (1815) 171 ER 46, which involved a contract for the sale of 12 bags of waste silk. The sale note said nothing about the quality of the silk. On their arrival the buyer found the silk much inferior in quality to the sample that had previously been supplied to his agent, and of a quality not saleable under the denomination of ''waste silk''. The buyer pleaded the seller's promise to be that the silk should be waste silk of a good and merchantable quality. In allowing the buyer's claim Lord Ellenborough said, ''the intention of both parties must be taken to be, that it shall be saleable in the market under the denomination mentioned in the contract between them. The purchaser cannot be supposed to buy goods to lay them on a dunghill.'' As will be noted, Lord Ellenborough's test of merchantable quality is a relative one — what is acceptable in the marketplace. Not surprisingly this allows much room for differences of opinion and much of the jurisprudence has been concerned to give some content to the term in the widely varying circumstances in which the problem arises for decision.

Two preliminary points deserve to be made about the structure of SGA s. 15. First, the preamble to the section suggests that caveat emptor is the dominant rule and the implied conditions of merchantability and fitness the exceptions to it. The OLRC Sales Report (p. 207) thought this anomalous since the great majority of sellers are professionals to whom one or the other of the two terms, and frequently both, will apply unless they have been successfully excluded. The Commission therefore recommended the deletion of the preamble, a change that has already been implemented in UCC 2-314 and 2-315.

The second point arises out of the fact that s. 15 places the implied condition of fitness before the implied condition of merchantability. To modern eyes this seems curious since merchantable quality is broader in scope than fitness for purposes, although frequently the two overlap. The explanation is historical and is given in *Benjamin's Sale of Goods* p. [352]. Since the circumstances have changed in the meantime, the English and Scottish Law Commissions recommended the reversal of the two subsections and this recommendation was implemented in the Supply of Goods (Implied Terms) Act, 1973. See now U.K. SGA 1979, s. 14. The implied warranty of merchantability also appears in the Code before the implied warranty of fitness. See UCC 2-314, -315. In view of these considerations, in the present chapter the materials on merchantability also precede those on fitness.

a) Sale "by Description", Character of Seller, and Sale by an Agent

(i) *Sale "by description"*. See Lord Wright's judgment in *Grant* v. *Australian Knitting Mills Ltd.* [1936] AC 85, 100, cited in *Beale* v. *Taylor* (*supra*, chapter 6(b)(1)).

(ii) *Character of seller*. See the extract from Lord Wilberforce's judgment in *Ashington Piggeries Ltd.* v. *Christopher Hill Ltd.*, section (3), *infra*, and note the following observations in the OLRC Sales Report, p. 209, on the amendment to the implied conditions of merchantability and fitness now appearing in s. 14(2) and (3) of the U.K. Sale of Goods Act 1979:

> Section 15.2 of the Ontario Act not only requires a sale "by description", but also requires that the goods be purchased from a seller "who deals in goods of that description". In the amended U.K. Act, it need only be shown that the seller sold the goods "in the course of *a* business" [emphasis in original]. In our view, undesirable results could flow from imposing a condition of merchantability on a business seller, regardless of whether he deals, or has ever purported to deal, in goods of the kind offered for sale. As commentators have noted a literal reading of the U.K. language would lead, as the Law Commissioners apparently intended it to lead, to liability attaching to a seller who was disposing of a piece of capital equipment that had become surplus to his requirements; for example, disposition of a truck by a fuel supplier.
>
> If the only result of the British approach were to entitle the buyer to a reduction in the price if the truck turned out to be in poorer condition than the buyer had a right to assume, we could accept it with equanimity. Indeed, a persuasive argument could be made for permitting such an action *in quanti minoris* against any seller.[58] It

---

58 The *actio redhibitoria* and action *in quanti minoris* were permitted in classical Roman law for rescission of the sale or a reduction in the price if the goods suffered from a latent vice unknown to the buyer and which he could not have discovered by reasonable examination before the purchase. The seller's knowledge of the defects was equally immaterial. Apparently the remedies were not restricted to suits against commercial sellers. See Buckland, *A Text-Book of Roman Law from Augustus*

seems reasonable to assume, however, that, under the U.K. approach, the seller's liability would encompass the full measure of damages recoverable under the rule in *Hadley* v. *Baxendale*, including any consequential damages suffered by the buyer. We do not think this desirable. Accordingly, we recommend that the warranty of merchantability should be restricted in the revised Act to a seller who deals in goods of the kind supplied under the contract of sale. We note that this is the same test as is used in UCC 2-314(1), although the Code employs slightly different language.

(iii)   *Sales by an Agent* (OLRC Sales Report, p. 210):

The English and Scottish Law Commissions recommended that, where a sale by a private seller is effected through an agent acting in the course of business, the conditions of merchantable quality and fitness for purpose should be implied, unless reasonable steps have been taken to inform the buyer before the contract is made that the sale is on behalf of a private seller, or unless the buyer was otherwise aware of the fact. This recommendation, too, has been implemented in the Supply of Goods (Implied Terms) Act 1973,[61] which added a new section 14(5) to the U.K. Sale of Goods Act. After careful consideration, a majority of the Commission has decided not to follow this recommendation. It appears to us that the equities are fairly evenly divided as between the private seller and the buyer, and that an insufficient case has been made out for changing the existing law. Let us suppose, for example, that a dealer who holds goods on consignment from a non-merchant seller fails to disclose his agency capacity to the buyer. Although, under existing law, the buyer would appear to be unable to sue the undisclosed principal for breach of the warranties of merchantability or fitness, he would still have his remedy against the agent. It would seem less obvious that the principal would have a right of indemnity against the agent for failure to disclose his agency capacity, if the U.K. amendment were adopted, unless a provision to this effect were also added. Again, it would not occur to the average principal that he must instruct his agent to be sure to disclose not only his status as agent, but also the fact that he is acting for a private seller. Moreover, if he did give such instructions, it is not clear whether they would satisfy the requirements of section 14(5) of the U.K. Act that "reasonable steps" must be taken to bring the facts to the notice of the buyer before the contract is made. In the result, the U.K. amendment raises as many difficulties as it purports to resolve. So far as we have been able to ascertain, the existing law has not caused serious practical problems and, in the absence of persuasive evidence to the contrary, we see no sufficient justification for change. Accordingly, we recommend that the revised Act should not contain a provision similar to section 14(5) of the U.K. Sale of Goods Act, as amended.

---

to *Justinian* (3rd ed., 1966), pp. 491 *et seq*. These grounds of relief, seemingly rooted in concepts of unjust enrichment and fair dealing, survive in modern civil law systems. See, for example, Quebec C. Civ., arts. 1522 *et seq.;* and compare, Treitel, "Remedies for Breach of Contract", in *International Encyclopedia of Comparative Law*, Vol. VII, pp. 16-57 to 16-60.

61 1973, c. 13 (U.K.), s. 3. [See now the Sale of Goods Act 1979, s. 14(5)].

b) The Meaning of Merchantable Quality

HARDWICK GAME FARM v. SUFFOLK AGRICULTURAL AND POULTRY PRODUCERS ASSOCIATION*
[1969] 2 AC 31, [1968] 2 All ER 444 (HL)

LORD REID: My Lords, in the summer of 1960 very large numbers of young turkeys died in what appeared to be an epidemic of an unknown disease. But the outbreaks were curiously patchy and the trouble was soon traced to feeding stuffs. Such birds are generally fed on mixtures of various ingredients. It was common to include up to about ten per cent. of groundnut extractions, and it was found that in the mixture fed to these birds there had been a proportion of groundnut extractions imported from Brazil. Then it was found that much of this Brazilian food was contaminated by a poison, aflatoxin, to amounts up to five parts per million. Then it appeared that, owing to climatic conditions in Brazil, spores of a fungus, aspergillus flavus, had caused a mould to grow on the groundnuts and secrete this poison. Groundnut extractions had for many years been imported from India. It has now been found that the Indian product sometimes contains some of this poison, though generally in smaller amounts, but in 1960 there was no reason to suspect that any groundnut extractions might contain this poison.

The plaintiffs, Hardwick Game Farm, had about 2,000 breeding pheasants. The eggs were collected and hatched and the young pheasants reared in much the same way as chickens and turkeys. A large number of them died in 1960 from this poison and it is not disputed that it was contained in compound feeding stuffs supplied by a local compounder referred to in this case as SAPPA. They sued SAPPA and SAPPA agreed to pay £3,000 damages. That settlement is admitted to have been reasonable and proper. But SAPPA brought in their suppliers, Grimsdale and Lillico and they in turn brought in their suppliers, Kendall and Holland Colombo. It has been held that Grimsdale and Lillico are liable to SAPPA and that Kendall and Holland Colombo are liable to Grimsdale and Lillico. In the first appeal Kendall and Holland Colombo maintain that they are not liable. Lillico do not appeal. But Grimsdale in effect maintain in the second appeal that, if they cannot recover from Kendall and Holland Colombo, then SAPPA cannot recover from them. I need make no further mention of Lillico and Holland Colombo and it will be clearer simply to have in mind the chain, Kendall to Grimsdale to SAPPA to the game farm.

Kendall and Grimsdale are both members of the London Cattle Food Traders' Association. Brazilian groundnuts had not been imported until 1959 but early in 1960 there were large shipments. Kendall had acquired a large quantity and while the goods were afloat Kendall sold a considerable quantity in the London Market to Grimsdale. Then Grimsdale sold a part of this to SAPPA at the

---

*   The case is also reported and cited under the name of *Henry Kendall & Sons* v. *William Lillico & Sons Ltd.,* two of the parties involved in this multipartite litigation. We have adopted the above style of cause for reasons of consistency with the judgments in the *Ashington Piggeries* case, *infra,* section (3) of this chapter. [Eds.]

market at Bury St. Edmunds; SAPPA took delivery shortly after the arrival of the goods in London.

The case raises a number of points and I shall first consider the position under the Sale of Goods Act, 1893, section 14. The relevant subsections are [see Ont. SGA s. 15] . . . .

Conflicting arguments have been submitted about the meaning of almost every part of these subsections. If one puts aside for the moment the encrustations of authority their meaning appears to me to be reasonably clear. But, if a whole chapter of the law is compressed into one section of a code, one cannot expect its words to apply to unusual cases without expansion or adaptation. That is the task of the court: but it is not in my view legitimate to substitute for the words of the code some general words used by an eminent judge in a particular case and treat them as a test of universal application. Where that has been done in other chapters of the law it has led to trouble, and there has been a tendency to do that here.

I take first subsection (2) because it is of more general application. It applies to all sales by description where the seller deals in such goods. There may be a question whether the sale of a particular article is not really a sale by description but that does not arise here: these are clearly sales by description. Then it is a condition (unless excluded by the contract) that the goods must be of merchantable quality. Merchantable can only mean commercially saleable. If the description is a familiar one it may be that in practice only one quality of goods answers that description — then that quality and only that quality is merchantable quality. Or it may be that various qualities of goods are commonly sold under that description — then it is not disputed that the lowest quality commonly so sold is what is meant by merchantable quality: it is commercially saleable under that description. I need not consider here what expansion or adaptation of the statutory words is required where there is a sale of a particular article or a sale under a novel description. Here the description groundnut extractions had been in common use.

The novel feature of this case is that whereas in 1960 there appears to have been thought to be only one quality of this product, subject to minor variations, it has now been discovered that particular parcels though apparently of the usual quality may really be of a very different quality because they are contaminated by minute quantities of a powerful poison. So the question at once arises — do you judge merchantable quality in light of what was known at the time of the sale or in light of later knowledge?

It is quite clear that some later knowledge must be brought in for otherwise it would never be possible to hold that goods were unmerchantable by reason of a latent defect. By definition a latent defect is something that could not have been discovered at the time by any examination which in light of then existing knowledge it was reasonable to make. But there is a question as to how much later knowledge ought to be brought in. In the present case it had become well known before the date of the trial that the defect was that these Brazilian groundnut extractions were contaminated by poison: but it had also become well known that, while this poison made the goods unsuitable for inclusion in food for poultry, it was generally regarded as proper to include such extractions in cattle food, provided that the proportion included did not exceed 5 per cent. of the whole. The question is whether this latter fact should be taken into account in deciding whether these goods were of merchantable quality in 1960.

I think it would be very artificial to bring in some part of the later knowledge and exclude other parts. In this case it is quite true that there was a period, after the nature and effect of this contamination had been discovered but before it had become accepted that small quantities of contaminated goods could safely be included in cattle foods, during which contaminated groundnut extractions were virtually unsaleable. But suppose that in this case it had been discovered at an early stage that these goods could be used for cattle food, so that there never was a period during which they were unsaleable. In that case I would not think it possible to take into account the nature of the defect but to exclude from consideration the effect which knowledge of the defect had on the market.

There is clear evidence that before the date of the trial Indian groundnut extractions so contaminated were sold under the ordinary description and were not rejected by the buyers when the contamination was discovered; a director of British Oil and Cake Mills who are by far the largest compounders in this country said that they bought these goods untested and then tested them. If they were found to be very highly contaminated they were destroyed: but otherwise they were included in feeding stuffs for cattle. This company apparently did not claim any relief on the ground that such goods were of defective quality or were of no use if highly contaminated. And it appears that other buyers who found poison in the goods which they bought did not try to reject the goods but merely asked for rebates on the price: they never got any rebates and the evidence is that they did not press their claims. So I think that it sufficiently appears that groundnut extractions contaminated to an extent not said to be different from the contamination of the Brazilian product were regarded as of merchantable quality under the ordinary description at the date of the trial.

I do not think I am precluded from taking this view of the meaning of subsection (2) by any of the authorities.

A statement with regard to the meaning of section 14(2) which has been commonly accepted is that of Lord Wright in *Cammell Laird & Co.* v. *The Manganese Bronze and Brass Co.* [1934] AC 402. In that case the respondents contracted to supply two specially designed ship's propellers. They first supplied propellers which were unsatisfactory and it was only at a third attempt that they supplied propellers which were satisfactory. Cammell Laird sued for damages caused by the delay. They succeeded on the terms of the contract and under section 14(1). But Lord Wright went on to consider the application of section 14(2). Apart from a short general statement at the end of the speech of Lord Tomlin, at p. 413, none of the other noble and learned lords said anything about section 14(2) or Lord Wright's gloss on it. Lord Wright said, at p. 430:

> In earlier times, the rule of caveat emptor applied, save only where an action could be sustained in deceit on the ground that the seller knew of the defect, or for breach of express warranty (warrantizando vendidit). But with the growing complexity of trade, dealings increased in what are now called "unascertained or future goods,"

and more generally "goods sold by description." As early as 1815 in *Gardiner* v. *Gray* (1815) 4 Camp. 144, Lord Ellenborough stated the rule. Goods had been sold as waste silk; a breach was held to have been committed on the ground that the goods were unfit for the purpose of waste silk and of such a quality that they could not be sold under that denomination. What subsection (2) now means by "merchantable quality" is that the goods in the form in which they were tendered were of no use for any purpose for which such goods would normally be used and hence were not saleable under that description.

I feel sure that Lord Wright did not really mean this to be a test of universal application in the form in which he stated it. If he did I disagree for reasons which I shall state. In the *Cammell Laird* case, if the propellers were of no use for the ship for which they had been designed it was true to say that they were of no use for any other ship and therefore unsaleable as propellers. But there are many cases in which different qualities of a particular kind of goods are commonly sold under different descriptions. Suppose goods are sold under the description commonly used to denote a high quality and the goods delivered are not of that high quality but are of a lower quality which is commonly sold under a different description, then it could not possibly be said that the goods in the form in which they were tendered were of no use for any purpose for which those goods would normally be used. They would be readily saleable under the appropriate description for the lower quality. But surely Lord Wright did not mean to say that therefore they were merchantable under the description which was appropriate for the higher quality. They plainly were not. Lord Wright said, [1934] AC 402, 430, "no use for any purpose for which *such goods* would normally be used." Grammatically "such goods" refers back to "the goods in the form in which they were tendered." But what he must have meant by "such goods" were goods which complied with the description in the contract under which they were sold. Otherwise the last part of the sentence "and hence were not saleable under that description" involves a non sequitur. If I now set out what I am sure he meant to say I think it would be accurate for a great many cases though it would be dangerous to say that it must be universally accurate. The amended version would be:

> "What subsection (2) now means by 'merchantable quality' is that the goods in the form in which they were tendered were of no use for any purpose for which goods which complied with the description under which these goods were sold would normally be used, and hence were not saleable under that description." This is an objective test: "were of no use for any purpose . . ." must mean "would not have been used by a reasonable man for any purpose. . . ."

That would produce a sensible result. If the description in the contract was so limited that goods sold under it would normally be used for only one purpose, then the goods would be unmerchantable under that description if they were of no use for that purpose. But if the description was so general that goods sold under it are normally used for several purposes, then goods are merchantable under that description if they are fit for any one of these purposes: if the buyer wanted the goods for one of those several purposes for which the goods delivered did not happen to be suitable, though they were suitable for other purposes for which goods bought under that description are normally bought, then he cannot complain. He ought either to have taken the necessary steps to bring subsection (1) into operation or to have insisted that a more specific description must be inserted in the contract.

That would be in line with the judgment of Mellor J. in *Jones* v. *Just* (1868) LR 3 QB 197 which has always been regarded as high authority. He said, at p. 205:

> It appears to us that, in every contract to supply goods of a specified description which the buyer has no opportunity to inspect, the goods must not only in fact answer the specific description, but must also be saleable or merchantable under that description.

The buyer bought manilla hemp: on arrival the goods were found to be damaged to such an extent as not to be saleable under that description and the buyer resold under the description "Manilla hemp with all faults" and received about 75 per cent. of what merchantable manilla hemp would have fetched. So it certainly could not be said that the goods were of no use. But the buyer recovered, as damages for breach of the implied warranty, the difference between what the hemp would have been worth if merchantable as manilla hemp and what he was able to get for it when sold "with all faults."

It would also be in line with what Lord Wright said in *Canada Atlantic Grain Export Co.* v. *Eilers* (1929) 35 Ll.L.Rep. 206, 213:

> . . . if goods are sold under a description which they fulfil, and if goods under that description are reasonably capable in ordinary use of several purposes, they are of merchantable quality within section 14(2) of the Act if they are reasonably capable of being used for any one or more of such purposes, even if unfit for use for that one of those purposes which the particular buyer intended.

There is another statement by Lord Wright regarding section 14(2) in *Grant* v. *Australian Knitting Mills Ltd.* [1936] AC 85, 99:

> The second exception (i.e., section 14(2)) in a case like this in truth overlaps in its application the first exception (i.e., section 14(1)); whatever else merchantable may mean, it does mean that the article sold, if only meant for one particular use in ordinary course, is fit for that use; merchantable does not mean that the thing is saleable in the market simply because it looks all right.

That too appears to me to be in line with my amended version of what he said in the *Cammell Laird* case [1934] AC 402, 413.

Another explanation of the phrase "merchantable quality" which has frequently been quoted is that of Farwell L.J. in *Bristol Tramways, etc., Carriage Co. Ltd.* v. *Fiat Motors Ltd.* [1910] 2 KB 831, 841, CA:

> The phrase in section 14(2) is, in my opinion, used as meaning that the article is of such quality and in such condition that a reasonable man acting reasonably would after a full examination accept it under the circumstances of the case in performance of his offer to buy that article whether he buys for his own use or to sell again.

I do not find this entirely satisfactory. I think what is meant is that a reasonable man in the shoes of the actual buyer would accept the goods as fulfilling the contract which was in fact made. But if the description was so wide that goods required for different purposes were commonly bought under it and if these goods were suitable for some of those purposes but not for the purpose for which the buyer bought them, it would have to be a very reasonable buyer indeed who admitted that the goods were merchantable, and that it was his own fault for not realising that goods might be merchantable under that description although unsuitable for his particular purpose.

There was also another explanation brought to our attention. In *Australian Knitting Mills Ltd.* v. *Grant* (1933) 50 CLR 387, 413, Dixon J. said:

> The condition that goods are of merchantable quality requires that they should be in such an actual state that a buyer fully acquainted with the facts and, therefore, knowing what hidden defects exist and not being limited to their apparent condition would buy them without abatement of the price obtainable for such goods if in reasonable sound order and condition and without special terms.

I would only qualify this by substituting "some buyers" for "a buyer." "A buyer" might mean any buyer: but for the purposes for which some buyers wanted the goods the defects might make the goods useless, whereas for the purposes for which other buyers wanted them the existence of the defects would make little or no difference. That is in fact the position in the present case. I think that it must be inferred from the evidence that buyers who include groundnut extractions in their cattle foods are prepared to pay a full price for goods which may be contaminated. But buyers who only compound poultry foods would obviously not be prepared to buy contaminated goods at any price. Nevertheless contaminated groundnut extractions are merchantable under the general description of groundnut extractions because, rather surprisingly, some buyers appear to be ready to buy them under that description and to pay the ordinary market price for them.

LORD PEARCE (dissenting): In my opinion, the definition of Farwell L.J. [1910] 2 KB 831, 840 as amplified by Dixon J., 50 CLR 387, 418, is to be preferred to that of Lord Wright [1934] AC 402, 430, which has, I think, the following weakness. The suggestion, without more, that goods are merchantable unless they are no use for any purpose for which they would normally be used and hence would be unsaleable under that description may be misleading, if it contains no reference to price. One could not say that a new carpet which happens to have a hole in it or a car with its wings buckled are of no use for their normal purposes and hence would be unsaleable under that description. They would no doubt, if their price was reduced, find a ready market. In return for a substantial abatement of price a purchaser is ready to put up with serious defects, or use part of the price reduction in having the defects remedied. In several classes of goods there is a regular retail market for "seconds," that is, goods which are not good enough in the manufacturer's or retailer's view to fulfil an order and are therefore sold off at a cheaper price. It would be wrong to say that "seconds" are necessarily merchantable.

Sir Owen Dixon was clearly right in saying (above) that in order to judge merchantability one must assume a knowledge of hidden defects, although these do not manifest themselves or are not discovered until some date later than the date of delivery which is the time as at which one must estimate merchantability (see also Atkin L.J. in *Niblett Ltd.* v. *Confectioners Materials Co. Ltd.* [1921] 3 KB 387, 404: "No one who knew the facts would buy them in that state or condition; in other words they were unsaleable and unmerchantable.") But what additional after-acquired knowledge must one assume? Logic might seem to indicate that the court should bring to the task all the after-acquired knowledge which it possesses at the date of trial. But I do not think that this is always so. For one is trying to find what market the goods would have had if their subsequently ascertained condition had been known. As it is a hypothetical exercise, one must create a hypothetical market. Nevertheless the hypothetical market should be one that could have existed, not one which could *not* have existed at the date of delivery. Suppose goods contained a hidden deadly poison to which there was discovered by scientists two years after delivery a simple, easy, inexpensive antidote which could render the goods harmless. They would be unmarketable at the date of delivery if the existence of the poison was brought to light, since no purchaser could then have known the antidote to the poison. Hypothesis is no reason for complete departure from possibility. One must keep the hypothesis in touch with the facts as far as possible. But I do not think that the point is important on the present facts.

Appeals dismissed.

Note: Lord Morris concurred with Lord Reid on the issue of merchantability, preferring the view of Lord Wright in *Cammell Laird* to that of Farwell L.J. in *Bristol Tramways*. Lord Guest felt that the test under s. 14(2) must be "whether the article is saleable in the ordinary market for such goods under that description" (at p. 108). He held that Lord Wright's test was but one factor in the determination of merchantability, and could not be determinative since it omits all reference to price. Lord Guest preferred the test formulated by Dixon J. in *Grant* v. *Australian Knitting Mills*. Lord Wilberforce expressed no opinion on the application of s. 14(2) to the facts, but agreed with Lord Pearce on the interpretation of the subsection.

The law lords' position on the applicability of the implied condition of fitness to the facts at bar is dealt with *infra* in Section (3).

For a classic article on the meaning of merchantability, see W.L. Prosser, "The Implied Warranty of Merchantable Quality" (1943) 21 Can. Bar Rev. 446.

B.S. BROWN & SON LTD. v. CRAIKS LTD.
[1970] 1 WLR 752, [1970] 1 All ER 823 (HL)

LORD REID: My Lords, this case arises out of two orders given by the appellants, who are textile merchants, to the respondents, who are cloth manufacturers.

Those orders were for the manufacture of considerable quantities of rayon cloth to a detailed specification. There was a misunderstanding as to the purpose for which the buyers wanted the cloth. They wanted it to fulfil contracts for cloth for making dresses. The sellers thought it was for industrial use. The Lord Ordinary found that they were "astounded" when they first heard, some months after deliveries had commenced, that it was to be used for dresses, and they would not have accepted the order if they had known that. When the contract was determined both parties were left with considerable quantities on their hands.

The buyers sue for damages. Admittedly this was a sale by description within the meaning of the Sale of Goods Act, 1893, and the cloth delivered complied with the description. But the buyers alleged breach of the conditions implied by section 14(1) and (2) of the Sale of Goods Act, 1893. The Lord Ordinary held there was no breach and assoilzied the defenders. The buyers accepted this decision as regards section 14(1) but reclaimed as regards section 14(2). They accept all the Lord Ordinary's findings of fact. The First Division adhered to the Lord Ordinary's interlocutor. The only question now before your Lordships is whether the goods were of merchantable quality within the meaning of section 14(2) which is as follows:

> Where goods are bought by description from a seller who deals in goods of that description (whether he be the manufacturer or not), there is an implied condition that the goods shall be of merchantable quality; provided that if the buyer has examined the goods, there shall be no implied condition as regards defects which such examination ought to have revealed.

It is common ground that the cloth, though complying with the contract description, was not suitable for making dresses — apparently because of irregular weaving. But it was suitable for a number of industrial uses, such as making bags. Was it therefore of merchantable quality?

The Lord Ordinary found (1969 SLT 107, 108) that the contract price was a low price for cloth of that description for making dresses but

> higher than would have been normal for it as an industrial fabric, but not unreasonably high for the sellers constructing it for such a purpose.

There is no doubt that cloth of this or very similar description was in common use for making dresses. There was no evidence that cloth of this precise description had been used for industrial purposes, but there is a finding that the respondents "had made rayon material of a very similar construction for industrial use before." The Lord Ordinary appears to have accepted the evidence of an expert who said that he had never seen this particular construction of cloth before because the material was viscose, not cotton.

It is evident that at the proof the appellants put most weight on their case under section 14(1), so it is not surprising that the findings of fact with regard to their case under section 14(2) are not as detailed as one might have desired. Certainly this kind of cloth of the quality delivered was suitable for industrial use, but we do not know why it was not more frequently used for industrial purposes. There is no suggestion in the findings that the manufacturers, as dealers in goods of that description, ought to have known, or even suspected, that these goods were not intended for industrial use.

All the well-known authorities were cited on the proper interpretation of "merchantable quality." Some importance was attached to what I said in *Hardwick Game Farm* v. *Suffolk Agricultural Poultry Producers Association* [1969] 2 AC 31, 75:

> If the description is a familiar one it may be that in practice only one quality of goods answers that description — then that quality and only that quality is merchantable quality. Or it may be that various qualities of goods are commonly sold under that description — then it is not disputed that the lowest quality commonly so sold is what is meant by merchantable quality: it is commercially saleable under that description.

I see no reason to alter what I said, but judicial observations can never be regarded as complete definitions: they must be read in light of the facts and issues raised in the particular case. I do not think it is possible to frame, except in the vaguest terms, a definition of "merchantable quality" which can apply to every kind of case. In the *Hardwick* case no question as to price arose because the evidence showed that, even when all the facts were known, the market price was the same for tainted and untainted goods. But suppose that the market price for the better quality is substantially higher than that for the lower quality. Then it could not be right that, if the contract price is appropriate for the better quality, the seller should be entitled to tender the lower quality and say that, because the lower quality is commercially saleable under the contract description, he had fulfilled his contract by delivering goods of the lower quality. But I think that the evidence in this case with regard to prices is much too indefinite to support a case on that basis.

The appellants mainly relied on the contention that, whereas cloth of this description had been commonly used for making dresses, there was no evidence that such cloth had ever been put to any industrial use. There is, I think, some ambiguity in saying that goods are of the same description where the contract description is a precise and detailed specification for their manufacture. One may mean of the same precise and detailed description, and that may be novel: or one may mean of the same general description, and that may be common. In most of the authorities the latter meaning seems to have been adopted. Here, as I read the findings of fact, it is not clear whether cloth had commonly been made to this precise specification: but it is clear that cloth of this general description had commonly been used for making dresses and had sometimes been put to an industrial purpose.

Of the various general statements of the law I think that the most applicable to the present case is that of Lord Wright in *Cammell Laird & Co. Ltd.* v. *Manganese Bronze & Brass Co. Ltd.* [1934] AC 402, 430. In the *Hardwick* case [1969] 2 AC 31, 77 I suggested that a slight alteration was necessary and that this statement should read:

> What subsection (2) now means by "merchantable quality" is that the goods in the form in which they were tendered were of no use for any purpose for which goods

which complied with the description under which these goods were sold would normally be used, and hence were not saleable under that description.

The question, then, is whether this cloth "would normally be used" for industrial purposes. It was suitable for such use. Moreover, the manufacturers assumed it was for such use and their good faith is not disputed: there is no finding that other skilled and knowledgeable manufacturers would have thought differently. So I cannot find any ground for holding that the cloth delivered would not normally be used for any industrial purpose. And if one is entitled to look at the facts and the statutory condition apart from authority, I would not hold that it had been proved that the cloth delivered was not of merchantable quality. I would, therefore, dismiss this appeal.

LORD GUEST: Passing now to the question of price, this does not seem to have bulked very largely in the arguments before the courts below. In my view, this case must be approached on the basis that the goods were not one-purpose-only goods but goods which were reasonably capable of being used for more than one purpose, as the Lord Ordinary has found. In the case of such dual purpose goods it is not, in my opinion, legitimate for the purpose of deciding whether the goods are of merchantable quality to compare the contract price too closely with the price at which the goods were sold for the secondary purpose. There will always be a discrepancy in cases of breach of contract; otherwise there could be no claim of damages. The assumption is that the goods are merchantable for a secondary purpose and unless the price is what has been described as a "throw away price" the discrepancy sheds little or no light on the question of merchantable quality. "Commercially saleable" suggests that the price must be unreasonably low. The Lord Ordinary has disposed of the question of price upon the footing that it only arises where there is a case of latent defect, which was the case in *Hardwick Game Farm* v. *Suffolk Agricultural Poultry Producers Association* [1969] 2 AC 31. I am not satisfied that this is a sound distinction. I cannot, for my part, see that the question of latent defect makes any difference. I would hold to the view I expressed in *Hardwick* [1969] 2 AC 31, 108 that price cannot be omitted entirely but, on mature reconsideration, I think that the test of Dixon J. in *Australian Knitting Mills Ltd.* v. *Grant* (1933) 50 CLR 387, 418 which I approved was expressed too broadly. The expression he used: "without abatement of the price obtainable," cannot be construed strictly. It cannot be a necessary requirement of merchantability that there should be no abatement of price. If the difference in price is substantial so as to indicate that the goods would only be sold at a "throw away price," then that may indicate that the goods were not of merchantable quality. In the present case the difference in price of 6.25d. on 30.25d. is not, in my view, so material as to justify any such inference. The Lord Ordinary finds, 1969 SLT 107, 108:

> The price of 36.25d. per yard was higher than would have been normal for it as an industrial fabric, but not unreasonably high for the defenders constructing it for such a purpose. On the other hand, this price of 36.25d. per yard was low for a dress

fabric, and the defenders' price for constructing it as a dress fabric would have been higher.

Appeal dismissed.

[Lords Wilberforce and Hodson concurred with Lord Guest. Viscount Dilhorne concurred for separate reasons.]

INTERNATIONAL BUSINESS MACHINES CO. LTD. v. SHCHERBAN
[1925] 1 DLR 864, [1925] 1 WWR 405 (Sask. CA)

HAULTAIN, C.J.S. (dissenting): The defendants refused to accept a counting device or computing scale, valued at $294, because a piece of glass which covered the dial, and which could be replaced for 25 or 30¢, was broken.

The only ground upon which the defendants can be justified in refusing to accept the scale is, that it is not of merchantable quality as required by s. 16(2) of the Sale of Goods Act, RSS 1920, c. 197.

With deference and a great deal of diffidence, I cannot agree with the other members of the Court that such a trivial defect justified the rejection of the scale. In *Bristol Tramways etc. Co.* v. *Fiat Motors Ltd.*, [1910] 2 KB 831, 79 LJKB 1107, Farwell, C.J., at p. 1111, defines "merchantable quality" as, "meaning that the article is of such quality and in such condition that a reasonable man acting reasonably would after a full examination accept it under the circumstances of the case in performance of his offer to buy that article and whether he buys it for his own use or to sell again so as to make the term 'saleable' apply".

The article in question in this case was bought for the defendants' own use. I should gather from its description that it is rather a complicated bit of machinery. So far as we know it was in perfect working order, and the absence of a piece of glass worth 30¢ in no way affected the efficiency of the machine. Under all the circumstances, the case seems to come within the maxim *"de minimis non curat lex "*, and I cannot agree that the defendants in rejecting the machine were "reasonable men acting reasonably".

The facts in *Jackson* v. *Rotax Motor & Cycle Co.*, [1910] 2 KB 937, distinguish it from the present case. In that case 364 out of 609 motor horns delivered under contract were defective, and it would have cost at least £35 to put them in proper condition. The Court of Appeal held that the horns were not merchantable. Cozens-Hardy, M.R., at p. 945, said:

> It is true that a large proportion of the goods were merchantable, but that does not justify an action by the vendor for the price of the goods unless he can prove that he was ready and willing to deliver and had delivered or had tendered all the goods in a merchantable condition and of the quality required, subject, of course, to the qualification, if it be necessary to mention it, that the law does not regard as an exception that to which the rule of de minimis can apply; but, subject only to that qualification, it is for the vendor in a case like this to prove that he has delivered or has tendered delivery of goods which were in accordance with the contract.

Farwell, L.J., in the same case, at p. 945, says:

Of the tubes in question more than half were defective and of the horns also a very considerable number were defective, so that a very large number of the aggregate were in fact unmerchantable. It may well be that in the case of a single horn out of hundreds or a tube or two out of hundreds the rule de minimis would apply, and it would be open to the jury, or to the official referee, to find that, notwithstanding the fact that one or two items were unmerchantable, the consignment as a whole, treating the contract as for a consignment, was merchantable.

While the decision in that case was in favour of the purchaser, the passages I have quoted from the judgments seem to support the conclusion I have arrived at on the question of merchantable quality.

As the other members of the Court are for allowing the appeal, it will be unnecessary for me to say any more with regard to the judgment appealed from, except that, in my opinion the trial Judge proceeded on a wrong principle in awarding damages. If the defendants were not justified in rejecting the scale, the plaintiff was only entitled to damages as provided for in s. 48 of the Sale of Goods Act.

LAMONT J.A.: Whatever the terms of the agreement between the parties as to payment may have been, one thing is clear, and that is, that the scale was to be delivered at Hafford. The first scale was so delivered. Then the plaintiffs agree to ship a new scale and take back the first one shipped. This was done. Whether we look upon this as merely a substitution of one scale for another under an original verbal contract, or as delivery of a machine under a new contract, as contended by counsel for the defendants, is, in my opinion, immaterial; for the second scale when it arrived at Hafford was not in a deliverable condition, and this was recognized by the plaintiffs when, in their letter of December 8 they asked the defendants to have the repairs made and they would pay for them. The scale delivered, therefore, was not of merchantable quality, as required by s. 16(2) of the Sale of Goods Act, which reads as follows: —

> 2.   Where goods are bought by description from a seller who deals in goods of that description (whether he be the manufacturer or not) there is an implied condition that the goods shall be of merchantable quality:

The "quality" of goods includes their state or condition (s. 2(10)).

In *Bristol Tramways, etc. Co.* v. *Fiat Motors Ltd.*, [1910] 2 KB 831, Farwell L.J., at p. 841, said:

> The phrase in s. 14, sub-s. 2 [Sale of Goods Act 1893 (Imp.), c. 71, our s. 16 (2)] is, in my opinion, used as meaning that the article is of such quality and in such condition that a reasonable man acting reasonably would after a full examination accept it under the circumstances of the case in performance of his offer to buy that article whether he buys for his own use or to sell again.

Applying the test there laid down, we have to ask ourselves here if a reasonable man, buying the scale in question to resell it to a customer, would accept it with the glass of the dial broken. In my opinion, he would not. The glass must have been intended to fill some useful purpose, or it would not have been put over the dial. The object of having it there was presumably to protect the dial, and to keep the dust out of the delicate machinery. Without that protection, it is improbable that the machine would work efficiently for the same length of time as with it. The defendants were, therefore, in my opinion, within their strict legal rights in refusing to accept the scale until it was put into a merchantable shape.

For the plaintiffs it was contended that, as the cost of a new glass was trifling — some 30¢ — the Court could apply the maxim *de minimis non curat lex*. This maxim is frequently applied where trifling irregularities or infractions of the strict letter of the law are brought to the notice of the Court. (*Broom's Legal Maxims*, 9th ed., p. 102) I am of opinion, however, that the present is not a case for the application of the maxim. . . .

[After quoting from the judgments in *Jackson* v. *Rotax Motors,* Lamont J.A. continued:]

A fortiori, where the consignment contains but a single article which is unmerchantable, the maxim has no application. To be immediately saleable or merchantable, the scale required the glass over the dial. It was the plaintiffs' duty to put it on. A vendor who contracts to sell a new scale complete, cannot compel the acceptance of one with a broken part when the defect is objected to by the purchaser. He must, before he is entitled to damages for non-acceptance, put the scale in deliverable shape, that is, he must tender in fulfilment of his contract a machine which is of "merchantable quality". This the plaintiffs did not do. That they were most anxious to meet the demands of the defendants in every way they could, and were exceedingly generous in varying the terms of payment to suit their convenience, does not, in my opinion, affect the question; for the defendants clearly set up that the scale tendered was a damaged machine.

Appeal allowed, judgment for defendants.

Notes:

1   Could the court in *Shcherban* have distinguished *Jackson* v. *Rotax Motors* and, if so, how? *Shcherban's* case was referred to and followed in *Winsley Brothers* v. *Woodfield Importing Company* [1929] NZLR 480, which involved the sale of a "thicknessing machine". The machine had been delivered with a broken shield which could be replaced for £1. The New Zealand Supreme Court, reversing the lower court, held that because of this defect the machine was not merchantable and the buyer was entitled to reject it. The trial judge had held the defect was *de minimis* and had allowed the seller recovery of the price of the machine less a £1 deduction on account of the defect. See also Trueman J.A.'s judgment in *Scott* v. *Rogers Fruit Co.* [1928] 1 DLR 201, at 206-08 (Man. CA).

2   *Shcherban* and *Jackson* v. *Rotax Motors, supra,* show that in order to be merchantable the goods must be saleable in their then condition as well as being fit for their general use or, to put it slightly differently, merchantability implies *use value* and *exchange value*. See further Prosser, "The Implied Warranty of Merchantable Quality" (1943) 21 Can. Bar Rev. 446, 450 *et seq*. Unfit goods obviously are not saleable at the same price as fit goods but it does not follow that the goods are

merchantable because they are fit to be used. A serious cosmetic or other nonfunctional defect (such as a tear in a coat or a significant blemish in the body of a new automobile) may make the goods equally unappealing.

The distinction is of importance because of the definition of "merchantable quality" which now appears in s. 14(*b*) of the U.K. Sale of Goods Act 1979. The definition was first introduced in the Supply of Goods (Implied Terms) Act 1973 on the recommendations of the English and Scottish Law Commissions. The definition reads:

> Goods of any kind are of merchantable quality within the meaning of subsection (2) above if they are as fit for the purpose or purposes for which goods of that kind are commonly bought as it is reasonable to expect having regard to any description applied to them, the price (if relevant) and all the other relevant circumstances [1979, c. 54, s. 14(6)].

Some U.K. observers apparently feel that this definition is too narrow and that the reference to fitness for "the purpose or purposes" for which goods of that kind are commonly bought excludes cosmetic and other defects which, although reducing their resale value or acceptability, do not affect the functional or use value of the goods.

The Ontario Law Reform Commission has sought to avoid this "unjustifiably narrow" construction of the meaning of "fitness" and to resolve the doubt created by the above phrase by recommending the following definition:

> In this section "merchantable quality" means
>   (*a*)   that the goods, whether new or used, are as fit for the one or more purposes for which goods of that kind are commonly bought *and are of such quality and in such condition* as it is reasonable to expect having regard to any description applied to them, the price, and all other relevant circumstances. . . . [italics added].

See, Draft Bill, s. 5.13(1)(*a*). The italicized words were added to make it clear that merchantable quality is not limited to the use value of the goods. See OLRC Sales Report, p. 212, and generally, pp. 210-15.

Two other features of the OLRC definition should be noted. First, it applies to used as well as new goods. This aspect of the concept of merchantability is dealt with in section (*c*)(ii) of this chapter. Secondly, the definition rejects the narrow construction of merchantability adopted by the majority of the law lords in the *Hardwick Game Farm* case by requiring the goods to be "as fit for the purposes *or purposes* for which goods of that kind are commonly bought" etc. The Commission reasoned that the test adopted in the *Hardwick Game Farm* case leads to arbitrary results and that it is inconsistent with the broad test of the implied condition of fitness also adopted in the *Hardwick Game Farm* case. See Report, p. 212, and extract from the *Hardwick Game Farm* case, section (3) *infra*.

c) Merchantability and Motor Vehicles

As will be obvious from earlier materials in this chapter, motor vehicles have contributed more than their share to this branch of sales law and indeed to all aspects of sales law. In the present subsection materials are presented on two facets of the concept of merchantability, viz. the problems of rust and a dealer's obligations in the sale of a used vehicle, that have attracted particular attention in recent years.

THAUBERGER v. SIMON FRASER SALES LTD., MAZDA MOTORS OF CANADA LTD. AND TOYO KOGYO CO. LTD.
(1977) 3 BCLR 193 (Prov. Ct.)

O'DONNELL Prov. J.: On 29th June 1974 the plaintiff took delivery of a 1974 Mazda RX 4 which he had purchased from the defendant, Simon Fraser Sales Ltd.

The vehicle was manufactured in Japan by Toyo Kogyo Co. Ltd.

The transaction of sale and purchase is set out in Ex. 1, the retail buyers agreement. There is an exclusion of warranties set out in para. (d) of the conditions of sale on the reverse of the form. The relevant parts read:

> There are no warranties, expressed or implied, made by the seller herein, or the manufacturer, on the vehicle or chassis described on the face hereof except in the case of a new vehicle or chassis, the manufacturer's new vehicle warranty delivered to purchaser with such vehicle or chassis and hereby made a part hereof as though fully set out herein. The new vehicle warranty is the only warranty applicable to such new vehicle or chassis and is expressly in lieu of all other warranties, expressed or implied, including any implied warranty of merchantability or fitness for a particular purpose.

The defendant, Toyo Kogyo Co. Ltd., gave the warranties set out in the warranty booklet, being Ex. 3.

In summary, the vehicle is warranted to be free, under normal use and maintenance, of any defects in material and workmanship for a period of 12 months, or until the vehicle had been driven 12,000 miles, subject to various specific conditions set out.

From the evidence I find the plaintiff used his vehicle in a normal manner for a resident of the province of British Columbia, and had the normal maintenance work performed at the appropriate times.

In or about April 1976 various small blisters appeared on the paint work.

The paint work has continued to deteriorate since that time. The blisters contain rust particles.

I find, from the evidence, the blistering condition of the paint work is due to the excessive permeability of the paint film on the vehicle. I find, on the balance of probabilities, this excessive permeability is due to a defect in manufacture, and not to external factors occurring since the vehicle was delivered to the plaintiff.

From the evidence I find the vehicle was purchased from the seller by description. He did not choose the particular vehicle, but rather a 1974 Mazda RX 4 of a jewel green colour. As such, I find there was an implied warranty under s. 20(b) of The Sale of Goods Act, RSBC 1960, c. 344, that the vehicle would be of merchantable quality. Despite the terms of para. (d) of the retail buyers agreement, I find pursuant to s. 21A [en. 1971, c. 52, s. 1; am. 1973, c. 84, s. 5(b)] of The Sale of Goods Act that such a warranty cannot be excluded by the wording of the retail buyers agreement.

I respectfully adopt the explanation of the warranty of merchantable quality given by Dixon J., in *Grant* v. *Australian Knitting Mills* (1933) 50 CLR 387 at 418, where he said:

> The condition that goods are of merchantable quality requires that they should be in such an actual state that a buyer fully acquainted with the facts, and, therefore, knowing what hidden defects exist and not being limited to their apparent condition would buy them without abatement of the price obtainable for such goods if in reasonably sound order and condition and without special terms.

In my judgment, if a reasonable man had been aware of the manufacturing defects, which would involve random, widespread and continuing rusting becoming evident within 21 months from the date of delivery, he would have been entitled to an abatement of the purchase price.

I find the seller, therefore, liable in damages for breach of the implied warranty of merchantable quality.

I find the defendant, Toyo Kogyo Co. Ltd., as manufacturer, granted an express warranty in the warranty booklet: Ex. 3.

I find this was one of the inducements which led the plaintiff to purchase his vehicle.

I respectfully adopt the considerations which underlie the judgment of the Court of Appeal in Alberta in *Traders' Finance Corpn. Ltd.* v. *Haley* (1966) 57 DLR (2d) 15, and find there was a collateral contract of sale between the plaintiff and Toyo Kogyo Co. Ltd. I find the last-named defendant is therefore also liable for breach of the warranty of merchantable quality under s. 20(*d*) of The Sale of Goods Act.

An alternative claim for damages for negligence has been put forward by the plaintiff. But other than this condition I find the only injury suffered by the plaintiff is in the condition of the vehicle which is the subject matter of this action. I consider myself bound by the decision of the majority of the Supreme Court of Canada in the appeal from the British Columbia Court of Appeal in *Rivtow Marine Ltd.* v. *Washington Iron Works* [1973] 6 WWR 692, 40 DLR (3d) 530, reversing [1972] 3 WWR 735, 26 DLR (3d) 559, and that no cause of action in negligence arises in this case. I find the fact that the case at bar is a consumer transaction within the meaning of The Trade Practices Act, 1974 (BC), c. 96, does not distinguish it from the *Rivtow* decision.

From the evidence I find the plaintiff has proved it will cost him $792.75 to strip the paint work from his vehicle to bare metal, and repaint.

Even then the result will not be guaranteed.

I find this estimated loss directly and naturally results in the ordinary course of events from the breach of warranty of merchantable quality, and furthermore that it may be deemed to be the abatement of price which would have occurred had the latent defect in the paint film been known at the time of the purchase of the vehicle.

I find the breach of warranty occurred at the date of delivery of the vehicle to the plaintiff.

Judgment for the plaintiff.

[As will be noted, *Thauberger* involved a claim against the manufacturer as well as a claim against the dealer. The problems of suing the manufacturer where no direct privity exists between the parties is further explored below in chapter 7.]

MONIQUE B. TARDIFF
"The Rust Code: What Exactly Is It?"
Protect Yourself*, April 1978, p. 8

Will January 19, 1978 be a memorable date for the Canadian car owner? That was the day that the federal Consumer and Corporate Affairs minister, Warren Allmand, declared that his department and those of the different provinces had agreed on fixing certain rust resistance norms for automobiles manufactured in Canada or imported into the country as of production year 1978.

You will remember that a preliminary code had already been the subject of headlines a little more than six months ago, but that the bill had to be submitted to a federal-provincial committee and receive approval from the provincial ministers concerned.

The code itself in its final version is only one of three steps described by the minister which, according to his statements, will do battle against premature rusting affecting the Canadian automobile fleet. The two other steps in the process are a maintenance guide aimed at owners and the setting up of an evaluation method which would allow consumer groups to follow the progress of automobiles in relation to the rust code norms. We will confine ourselves here to the code and the maintenance guide.

THE CODE

It's very important to remember that the application of the code is entirely voluntary and consequently contains no coercive or punitive measures against companies who refuse to submit to it or who wish to interpret it in their own way. As such, it is absolutely not a guarantee against rusting as long as the manufacturers and importers do not formally commit themselves to applying the rust code either in a contractual warranty extended to the buyer or in their advertising. It is for this reason that Mr. Allmand said he was counting on the good will of manufacturers who participated in the development of the code. For the moment then, the only coercive measure is the good or bad publicity that manufacturers will get from publicly accepting or refusing to cooperate with the program. We must also hope that our courts will react favourably to the code and use it from now on in determining the outcome of cases which are presented to them.

Before we examine the diagram showing the minimum durability standards established by the code, here are some brief definitions which will help the reader better understand what it's all about.

It goes without saying that the code itself is the document that should be referred to in order to grasp all the subtleties.

1. body: the entire vehicle except for the drive, steering, shock, brake and exhaust systems.

---

*   This magazine is published by L'Office de la Protection du Consommateur, Montreal. [Eds.]

2. surface rusting: the surface is all easily visible parts of the body, except the underside of the automobile.

3. structural damage: when a part of the body is so rusted it can no longer fulfill its function.

4. normal conditions of use: this implies that the owner should follow the recommendations and conditions of the manufacturer's guarantee, at least with respect to general rust protection; that he must have all accident damage repaired by body experts; and that he conform to compulsory inspections and the owner care guidelines (see further on).

Type of damage (for all passenger transport vehicles under 10 000 pounds)	1978-79-80	1981 and on
Surface rusting due to defective design, manufacture or materials	1 year or 40 000 km	1¹/₂ years on 60 000 km
Perforations in the body under normal conditions of use	3 years or 120 000 km	5 years or 200 000 km
Structural damage under normal conditions of use	6 years	or 240 000 km

THE CONDITIONS

It is also important to note that the application of the code involves maintenance conditions which must be fulfilled by the owner himself; if he fails to, the norms become null and void. For example, every 12 months from the date the vehicle comes into use, the owner must have it inspected for rust. These inspections must be done free by any dealer or agent duly authorized by the manufacturer. A written report giving an account of the inspection and the necessary repairs will then be given to the owner who must have these repairs carried out by skilled labour within a reasonable period. If this condition is not fulfilled, the area of the body for which the repairs were required will no longer be protected by the code.

WHO WILL HAVE TO PAY FOR THESE REPAIRS?

The answer to this question depends entirely on the type of rust which has been detected: if it is only surface rust caused by paint damage, the owner of the car will foot the bill. On the other hand, if the repairs were brought about by a defect in the anti-rust protection or by its deterioration within the period mentioned in the table above, the manufacturer or the importer must take care of the repairs without charge to the owner. In both cases you must not forget to keep the repair bills as proof.

BARTLETT v. SIDNEY MARCUS LTD.
[1965] 1 WLR 1013, [1965] 2 All ER 753 (CA)

LORD DENNING M.R.: This case raises the question on the sale of a secondhand car: What is the effect of the statutory conditions implied therein?

The defendants are very reputable dealers in secondhand cars. The plaintiff was minded in January, 1964, to buy a secondhand Jaguar motor car. He bought it from the defendants for the sum of £950. They took his Ford Zodiac in exchange for £400, so he paid on balance £550. This is what happened: Walker, the salesman for the dealers, took the car down from Sloane Street to Romford to show to the plaintiff. On his way through the City he noticed that there was something wrong with the clutch and with the oil pressure gauge. He thought himself that *either* the clutch needed bleeding, that is, to get the air out, *or* there was a leak between the principal and the slave cylinders. Neither of those would be very serious matters. When Walker took the car out to the plaintiff, he told him about those defects. He mentioned the clutch and the oil pressure. He suggested two alternative reasons: either it needed bleeding or there was a leak between the cylinders. Then they discussed the price. He asked £600. The plaintiff said only £500. Then there was a question about repairs to the clutch. Then Walker said: "I will take it back and have it attended to and you pay £575, or you can have it done yourself and have it at £550." That is what they agreed, that the plaintiff should take the car and repair the clutch himself. So he had it for £550.

A written contract was drawn up in which it was said, after noting the price: "Oil pressure and filter circuit to be checked. Clutch to be bled, At client's expense." There were printed terms and conditions, none of which apply here. The plaintiff took the car and drove it for at least a fortnight. He thought it was in good condition and it seemed to be running smoothly. He noticed the oil consumption was considerable and something was wrong with the clutch, but he was not unduly alarmed about it because he had been told of it. He drove it for another fortnight and then he took it in to the garage to be repaired. At the garage it was found there were a number of things wrong with it and a lot of things worn. Most serious of all was this: the clutch thrust was found to be worn away. This was a far more serious defect to the clutch than either Walker or the plaintiff had imagined. The work was done. The engine had to be taken down, and whilst it was taken down, they repaired other things. Because the clutch thrust was so worn out the cost of putting it right came to some £45. The plaintiff claimed that sum as damages from the defendants. He alleged that there was an express term that the car was in perfect condition except that the clutch needed bleeding. The judge held there was no such express term and there is no appeal from that finding. The plaintiff alleged also that the defendants were in breach of the conditions in section 14 of the Sale of Goods Act.

I think there was an implied condition under section 14 (1). The plaintiff did make known to the dealer the purpose for which he wanted the goods, so as to show that he relied on his skill and judgment. There was therefore an implied condition that the goods were reasonably fit for the purpose, that is, as a motor car to drive along the road. I think also there was an implied condition under section

14(2). These goods were bought by description from a seller who dealt in goods of that description. There was therefore an implied condition that they should be of merchantable quality. The judge has found that both these conditions were broken and has awarded damages of £45. The defendants now appeal.

Sir John Hobson, for the plaintiff, said that in this case the two implied conditions came very much to the same thing. But he seemed to rely most on the implied condition as to merchantability under section 14 (2). I have always understood that the condition under section 14 (2) is less stringent than the condition under section 14 (1). But nevertheless I agree with Sir John that they do in this case overlap. I will approach this case, as he did, on section 14 (2). I take the tests as to merchantability stated by Lord Wright in *Cammell Laird & Co.* v. *Manganese Bronze and Brass Co. Ltd* [1934] AC 402, 430 and *Grant* v. *Australian Knitting Mills Ltd.* [1936] AC 85, 99. In the *Cammell Laird* case, Lord Wright said the goods were unmerchantable if they were "of no use" for any purpose for which such goods would normally be used. In the *Grant* case (at p. 100 AC) he said that merchantable meant that the article, if only meant for one particular use in the ordinary course, is "fit for that use." It seems to me that those two tests do not cover the whole ground. There is a considerable territory where on the one hand you cannot say that the article is "of no use" at all, and on the other hand cannot say that it is entirely "fit for use." The article may be of some use though not entirely efficient use for the purpose. It may not be in perfect condition but yet it is in a usable condition. It is then, I think, merchantable. The propeller in the *Cammell Laird* case was in a usable condition: whereas the underpants in the *Grant* case were not. I prefer this test to the more complicated test stated by Farwell L.J. in *Bristol Tramways &c. Co. Ltd.* v. *Fiat Motors Ltd.* [1910] 2 KB 831, 841. It means that on a sale of a secondhand car, it is merchantable if it is in usable condition, even though not perfect. This is very similar to the position under section 14(1). A secondhand car is "reasonably fit for the purpose" if it is in a roadworthy condition, fit to be driven along the road in safety, even though not as perfect as a new car.

Applying those tests here, the car was far from perfect. It required a good deal of work to be done on it. But so do many secondhand cars. A buyer should realise that when he buys a secondhand car defects may appear sooner or later; and, in the absence of an express warranty, he has no redress. Even when he buys from a dealer the most he can require is that it should be reasonably fit for the purpose of being driven along the road. This car came up to that requirement. The plaintiff drove the car away himself. It seemed to be running smoothly. He drove it for four weeks before he put it into the garage to have the clutch repaired. Then more work was necessary than he anticipated. But that does not mean that, at the time of the sale, it was not fit for use as a car. I do not think that, on the judge's findings, there was any evidence of a breach of the implied conditions.

On the whole I would find that this car was reasonably fit for use as a car on the road and in those circumstances there was no breach of either section 14 (1) or (2) and I would allow the appeal accordingly.

Appeal allowed.

[Danckwerts and Salmon L.JJ. delivered concurring judgments.]

CROWTHER v. SHANNON MOTOR CO.
[1975] 1 WLR 30, [1975] 1 All ER 139 (CA)

LORD DENNING M.R.: Mr. Crowther is a young man interested in art. In 1972 he bought a secondhand motor car from reputable dealers in Southampton. It was a 1964 Jaguar. He bought it on July 17, 1972, for the sum of £390. The dealers commended it. They said that "it would be difficult to find a 1964 Jaguar of this quality inside and out." They added that for a Jaguar "it is hardly run in." Mr. Crowther looked carefully at it. He took it for a trial run. The next day it was tested by the Ministry of Transport officials. The report of the test was satisfactory. So Mr. Crowther bought the Jaguar. He did not take the words of puff seriously. But he relied on the sellers' skill and judgment. There was clearly an implied condition under section 14(1) of the Sale of Goods Act 1893 that the car was reasonably fit for the purpose for which he required it and which he made known to the seller.

That was July 17, 1972. The mileage as stated on the mileometer at that time was 82,165 miles. Mr. Crowther took the car. He drove it on some long journeys. He went up to the North of England and back. He went round Hampshire. He went over 2,000 miles in it. He found that it used a great deal of oil. But he managed to drive it for three weeks. Then on August 8, 1972, when he was driving up the M3 motorway, it came to a full stop. The engine seized up. The car was towed into a garage. The engine was found to be in an extremely bad condition. So much so that it had to be scrapped and replaced by a reconditioned engine. The car was out of use for a couple of months or so.

Mr. Crowther brought an action in the county court for damages from the dealers. He called as a witness a previous owner of the car, a Mr. Hall. He gave evidence that he had bought it from these selfsame dealers about eight months before. He had paid them about £400 for it. He had used it for those eight months and then sold it back in July 1972 to these very dealers. When he resold it to them he knew the engine was in a very bad state, but he did not disclose it to them. He left them to find out for themselves. He was himself an engineer. He gave a trenchant description of the engine:

> At the time of resale I thought the engine was clapped out. I do not think this engine was fit to be used on a road, not really, it needed a rebore.

The judge accepted the evidence of Mr. Hall. He held that there was a breach of section 14(1) of the Act. He awarded Mr. Crowther damages in the sum of £460.37 with costs. Now there is an appeal to this court by the dealers. They say there was no justification for the finding that this car was not reasonably fit for the purpose. The mileage when they sold it was 82,165 miles. The mileage when it clapped out was 84,519 miles. So that in the three weeks it had gone 2,354 miles.

Mr. Rudd, who put the case very cogently before us, submitted that a car which had covered 2,354 miles must have been reasonably fit for the purpose of driving along the road. He drew attention to a case some years ago in this court of

Bartlett v. *Sydney Marcus Ltd.* [1965] 1 WLR 1013. We emphasised then that a buyer, when he buys a secondhand car, should realise that defects may appear sooner or later. In that particular case a defect did appear in the clutch. It was more expensive to repair than had been anticipated. It was held by this court that the fact that the defect was more expensive than had been anticipated did not mean that there had been any breach of the implied condition. But that case seems to me to be entirely distinguishable from the present case. In that case it was a minor repair costing £45 after 300 miles. Here we have a very different case. On the dealers' own evidence, a buyer could reasonably expect to get 100,000 miles life out of a Jaguar engine. Here the Jaguar had only done 80,000 miles. Yet it was in such a bad condition that it was "clapped out" and after some 2,300 miles it failed altogether. That is very different from a minor repair. The dealers themselves said that if they had known that the engine would blow up after 2,000 miles, they would not have sold it. The reason obviously was because it would not have been reasonably fit for the purpose.

Some criticism was made of a phrase used by the judge. He said "What does 'fit for the purpose' mean?" He answered: "To go as a car for reasonable time." I am not quite sure that that is entirely accurate. The relevant time is the time of sale. But there is no doubt what the judge meant. If the car does not go for a reasonable time but the engine breaks up within a short time, that is evidence which goes to show it was not reasonably fit for the purpose at the time it was sold. On the evidence in this case, the engine was liable to go at any time. It was "nearing the point of failure," said the expert, Mr. Wise. The time interval was merely "staving off the inevitable." That shows that at the time of the sale it was not reasonably fit for the purpose of being driven on the road. I think the judge on the evidence was quite entitled to find there was a breach of section 14(1) of the Sale of Goods Act 1893 and I would therefore dismiss the appeal.

Appeal dismissed.

[Orr and Browne L.JJ. delivered short concurring judgments.]

Questions:

1   Do you find Lord Denning's explanation of the distinction between *Crowther* and *Bartlett* v. *Sidney Marcus Ltd.* persuasive? How would you reconcile the two decisions? What is the economic effect of holding a used-car dealer responsible for defects of which he could not reasonably have been aware at the time of sale? Does CPA s.58 allow him to exclude or limit his warranty liabilities under SGA s.15?

2   A car dealer knew that a 1968 Firebird in his inventory had been used extensively for drag racing. He sold the car to G in 1972 for $2,895, the price of such a car in good condition, without disclosing the car's unusual history. G bought it as an ordinary used car for normal driving purposes. But the car was not suitable for highway driving and its engine exploded two days after the sale was completed. G sues for the return of his money. What result? See *Green* v. *Holiday Chevrolet-Oldsmobile Ltd.* (1975) 55 DLR (3d) 637 (Man. CA).

Notes on Used-Vehicle Warranty and Disclosure Legislation:

Used vehicles have been a more fertile source of complaints and litigation than any other group of used goods, and for this reason there has been a growing tendency for the provinces to legislate separately in this area. The legislation takes two forms. The first is a licensing requirement for motor vehicle dealers and their salesmen. We have encountered this type of control mechanism before and will encounter it again. The advantages of this type of approach — an *ex ante* screening mechanism coupled with powerful *post factum* sanctions for violations — are offset by the reluctance of licensing agencies to deprive a licensee of his livelihood even when persistent misconduct is involved. In Ontario appeals from a refusal by the Registrar of Motor Vehicle Dealers and Salesmen to grant or renew a licence, or a proposal by him to suspend or cancel a licence, are heard by the Commercial Registration Appeals Tribunal (CRAT). The judgments of the Tribunal are published in mimeographed form and a summary of decisions is published by it periodically.

The second type of legislation is represented by section 58 of the Ontario Highway Traffic Act, reproduced below, which has its counterpart in some of the other provinces. The section has had an interesting evolution. Originally a dealer was merely enjoined not to sell a vehicle that was unroadworthy. This standard was found to be too vague and was therefore supplemented by specific regulations. This too was found insufficient since the dealer was not required to certify anything in writing. Hence the addition of a Certificate of Mechanical Fitness. However, difficulties continue to subsist. Some of them are related in the OLRC Warranties Report, ch. 9, pp. 141 *et seq.* Particularly important are or were the following:

(a) There was a ready traffic in false and even forged certificates. Motor vehicle mechanics were not subject to the jurisdiction of the Registrar of Motor Vehicle Dealers, and the Apprenticeship and Tradesmen's Qualifications Act did not, it was claimed, permit the cancellation of a mechanic's licence on grounds of moral turpitude.

(b) The title of the certificate was misleading since most of the checks performed for the purposes of the certificate were (and are) directed to the roadworthiness of the vehicle and not to its mechanical condition.

(c) Dealers frequently take the position that they are not civilly responsible for the consequences of a false certificate. Section 58 does not address itself to this question and the jurisprudence, though favourable to the buyer, cannot be regarded as conclusively settling the point.

(d) Likewise it is not clear how s. 58 dovetails with the dealer's warranty obligations under the SGA. Does an accurate certificate discharge his warranty obligations under s. 15(2) or are the two obligations quite separate?

The first two difficulties were largely taken care of in the 1973 amendments to the Highway Traffic Act (SO 1973, c. 167); the other two remain at large.

The typical used-car agreement used to exclude the statutory implied warranties and substitute a 30 day or (less frequently) 60 day 50-50 warranty. See the warranty given in *Presley* v. *MacDonald, infra.* A new type of agreement has been adopted by the Ontario Automobile Dealers Association for new and used vehicles and is reproduced in the Appendix of this casebook. It is not clear to what extent the new agreement is intended to supersede the old 50-50, 30 day warranty.

A different approach to protecting the buyer civilly from undisclosed mechanical defects has been adopted in New Zealand and many of the Australian states. Under the terms of this type of legislation, the dealer is deemed to warrant the vehicle's mechanical fitness for a stipulated time and number of miles depending on the price unless he has disclosed the defects and given a reasonably accurate estimate of the cost of repair. If the vehicle does suffer from undisclosed defects, the dealer is responsible for the cost of repair. He is likewise responsible for any substantial inaccuracy in his estimate of the cost of repairing disclosed defects. Do you support this type of approach to the problem of used cars? According to earlier reports, the Australian schemes appeared to be working well, although some observers claim that they are economically inefficient and help to inflate the price of used cars. Why should this be and, assuming the legislation does lead to increased prices, is this fatal to its soundness?

Quebec is so far the only Canadian jurisdiction to have followed the Australian precedents. See the Quebec Consumer Protection Act 1978, Division IV, also reproduced below.

Highway Traffic Act, RSO 1970, c. 202, as am.

58. In this section and sections 58a to 58m,

(a) "Director" means the Director of Vehicle Inspection Standards appointed under section 58a;

(b) "licensee" means a person who is the holder of a motor vehicle inspection station licence issued under section 58d;

(c) "motor vehicle inspection mechanic" means a person who certifies by means of a safety standards certificate that a motor vehicle complies with the equipment and performance standards prescribed by the regulations;

(d) "motor vehicle inspection station" means any premises maintained or operated for the inspection of motor vehicles and the issuance of safety standards certificates in respect of such motor vehicles;

(e) "registrant" means a person who is registered as a motor vehicle inspection station mechanic under section 58e.

(f) "vehicle inspection record" means a form required to be completed in accordance with regulations prior to the issue of a vehicle inspection sticker; [SO 1975 (2nd sess.), c. 6, s. 2].

(g) "vehicle inspection sticker" means the device issued as evidence that the inspection requirements and performance standards referred to in section 57a have been complied with. [SO 1975 (2nd sess.), c. 6, s. 2.]

58a. The Minister shall appoint an officer of the Ministry to be the Director of Vehicle Inspection Standards for the purposes of sections 58 to 58m.

58b.—(1) No person shall sell a used motor vehicle unless,

(a) on the delivery of the vehicle to the purchaser, the seller gives to the purchaser a safety standards certificate that was issued upon an inspection that was completed in respect of the motor vehicle not more than thirty days before the date of the delivery of the used motor vehicle to the purchaser; or

(b) the seller forwards to the Ministry the notice required under subsection 2 of section 9 together with the current number plates and permit issued with respect to the motor vehicle.

(2) A person who applies to transfer the permit issued in respect of a used motor vehicle shall,

(a) deliver to the Ministry a safety standards certificate that was issued in respect of the vehicle not more than thirty-six days before the date of the application; or

(b) forward to the Ministry notice of transfer of the vehicle in the form referred to in subsection 2 of section 9 together with the current number plates and permit issued with respect to the motor vehicle.

(3) The Ministry shall not issue a permit or number plates to any person upon an application to transfer the permit issued in respect of a motor vehicle or upon an application to register a used motor vehicle that is registered in another jurisdiction unless there is delivered to the Ministry a safety standards certificate issued upon an inspection that was completed in respect of the motor vehicle not more than thirty-six days before the date of the application. . . .

58c.—(1) No person other than a licensee or a person authorized in writing by the licensee shall issue a safety standards certificate.

(1a) No person other than a licensee, a motor vehicle inspection mechanic or a person authorized in writing by the licensee shall affix a vehicle inspection sticker to a vehicle. [SO 1975 (2nd sess.), c. 6, s. 4.]

(2) A safety standards certificate in respect of a motor vehicle shall not be issued or a vehicle inspection sticker affixed to a vehicle unless,

(a) the vehicle has been inspected by a motor vehicle inspection mechanic in the motor vehicle inspection station and the vehicle is found to comply with the inspection requirements and performance standards prescribed by the regulations; and [SO 1976, c. 37, s. 7]

(b) the safety standards certificate or a vehicle inspection record,

(i) is made by the motor vehicle inspection mechanic who inspected the vehicle, and

(ii) is countersigned by the licensee or a person authorized in writing by the licensee. [SO 1975 (2nd sess.), c. 6, s. 4.]

58*d*.—(1) No person shall establish, operate or maintain a motor vehicle inspection station except under the authority of a licence issued by the Director under this Act and the Director may issue a licence for a motor vehicle inspection station subject to such conditions as the Director may specify in the licence.

(2) Subject to subsection 3 any person who applies in accordance with this Act and the regulations for a licence to establish, operate or maintain a motor vehicle inspection station and who meets the requirements of this Act and the regulations and who pays the prescribed fee is entitled to be issued the licence. . . .

58*e*.—(1) No person shall certify in a safety standards certificate that a motor vehicle complies with the standards of equipment and performance prescribed by the regulations unless he is registered by the Director as a motor vehicle inspection mechanic in a motor vehicle inspection station and the Director may so register any person for whom application is made pursuant to subsection 2. . . .

Safety Standards Certificate

Ministry of
Transportation and
Communications
Ontario

Form 2

SAFETY STANDARDS CERTIFICATE

ISSUED PURSUANT TO THE HIGHWAY TRAFFIC ACT AND REGULATIONS

NOTE: PLEASE PRINT

7156724

MINISTRY USE ONLY

AGENT NO.   DATE RECEIVED

LICENCE PLATE NO.

MAKE OF VEHICLE   19

TYPE OF BODY

INDICATE MANUFACTURER'S GROSS VEHICLE WEIGHT RATING   ☐ 4600 kg OR UNDER   ☐ OVER 4600 kg

V.I.N./SERIAL NO.

ODOMETER READING (ON DATE OF INSPECTION)

MOTOR VEHICLE INSPECTION STATION LICENCE NO.

INSPECTION STATION NAME

CITY, TOWN OR VILLAGE

NAME OF INSPECTING MECHANIC AND TRADE CODE AND CERTIFICATE NUMBER

DATE OF INSPECTION   DAY   MO.   YR.

WE HEREBY CERTIFY THAT THE ABOVE DESCRIBED MOTOR VEHICLE HAS BEEN INSPECTED IN ACCORDANCE WITH THE PROVISIONS OF SECTIONS 58 TO 58m OF THE HIGHWAY TRAFFIC ACT AND REGULATIONS ISSUED THERETO, AND THAT THE ITEMS INSPECTED MET THE PRESCRIBED STANDARDS ON THE DATE OF INSPECTION.

SIGNATURE OF INSPECTING MECHANIC

SIGNATURE OF LICENSEE/AGENT

NOTICE: THE MINISTRY CANNOT TRANSFER A PERMIT ON THE BASIS OF A CERTIFICATE THAT WAS MADE MORE THAN 36 DAYS BEFORE THE DATE OF APPLICATION.

NV-27 80-10

M.T.C. COPY

THIS COPY TO BE SURRENDERED WITH APPLICATION FOR TRANSFER OF OWNERSHIP, ON REGISTRATION OF AN OUT OF PROVINCE VEHICLE, OR A VEHICLE WHICH WAS PREVIOUSLY UNFIT.

RECEIPT OF A TRUE COPY HEREOF IS ACKNOWLEDGED.

DATE _ _ _ _ _ _ _ _ 19 _

SIGNATURE OF PURCHASER

Reverse side

DEFECTS NOTED DURING THE INSPECTION AND CORRECTED PRIOR TO
THE ISSUANCE OF THIS CERTIFICATE ARE SHOWN THUS: [X]

WORK ORDER NO.

CHECK HERE IF NO DEFECTS FOUND ☐

☐ 01. Bodywork-underbody	☐ 21. Brakes - service brake performance, adjustment
☐ 02. Bodywork-hinges and latches	☐ 22. Brakes - emergency brake performance
☐ 03. Bodywork-sheet metal and bumpers	☐ 23. Brakes - dual system warning
☐ 04. Seat and Seat Belt Assemblies	☐ 24. Horn
☐ 05. Chassis frame components	☐ 25. Accelerator linkage
☐ 06. Mirrors	☐ 26. Steering - column and box
☐ 07. Glazing materials	☐ 27. Steering - linkage
☐ 08. Windshield Wiper, Washer and Defroster	☐ 28. Steering - power assist
☐ 09. Speedometer	☐ 29. Suspension - ball joints
☐ 10. Lamps and Reflectors	☐ 30. Suspension - springs
☐ 11. Headlamp aim	☐ 31. Suspension - other items
☐ 12. Fuel system components	☐ 32. Neutral starting switch
☐ 13. Exhaust system components	☐ 33. Tires
☐ 14. Brakes - drums and discs	☐ 34. Wheels, rims and fasteners
☐ 15. Brakes - friction materials	☐ 35. Trailer Hitches
☐ 16. Brakes - hydraulic system components	☐ 36. Fifth wheel (truck-tractor)
☐ 17. Brakes - mechanical components	ADDITIONAL FOR MOTORCYCLES
☐ 18. Brakes - air system components	☐ 37. Wiring
☐ 19. Brakes - vacuum system components	☐ 38. Footrests
☐ 20. Brakes - parking brake performance, adjustment	☐ 39. Steering head bearings
	☐ 40. Handlebars

Quebec Consumer Protection Act, SQ 1978, c. 9

[Division IV]

§2.-*Contracts of sale of used automobiles and used motorcycles*

155. The merchant must affix a label on every used automobile that he offers for sale.

The label must be so affixed that it may be read entirely from outside the automobile.

156. The label must disclose:

(a) the price at which the used automobile is offered;

(b) the number of miles or kilometres registered on the odometer, and the number of miles or kilometres actually travelled by the automobile, if different from that indicated on the odometer;

(c) the model year ascribed by the manufacturer, the serial number, the make, the model and the cubic capacity of the engine;

(d) if such is the case, the fact that the automobile has been used as a taxi-cab, a drivers' school automobile, a police car, an ambulance, a leased automobile, an automobile for customers or as a demonstrator and the identity of every business or of every public agency that owned the automobile or rented it on a long term basis;

(e) if such is the case, every repair done on the used automobile since it has been in the possession of the merchant;

(f) the class provided for in section 160;

(g) the characteristics of the warranty offered by the merchant;

(h) that a certificate of inspection of the vehicle issued in conformity with subsection 4 of section 23 of the Highway Code (Revised Statutes, 1964, chapter 231) will be given to the purchaser upon the signing of the contract; and

(i) that the merchant must, at the request of the consumer, provide him with the name and telephone number of the last owner other than the merchant.

For the application of paragraphs b and d of this section, the merchant may base himself on a written declaration of the last owner unless he has reasonable grounds to believe that it is false.

157. The label must be appended to the contract.

All that is disclosed on the label forms an integral part of the contract, except the price at which the automobile is offered and the specifications of the warranty, which may be changed.

158. The contract must be evidenced in writing and indicate:

(a) the number of the licence issued to the merchant under section 23 of the Highway Code (Revised Statutes, 1964, chapter 231);

(b) the place and date of the contract;

(c) the name and address of the consumer and of the merchant;

(d) the price of the automobile; and

(e) the specifications of the warranty.

159. The sale of a used automobile carries with it a warranty that the automobile will remain in good working order

(a) for a period of six months or 10 000 kilometres, whichever occurs first, in the case of a class A automobile;

(b) for a period of three months or 5 000 kilometres, whichever comes first, in the case of a class B automobile;

(c) for a period of one month or 1 700 kilometres, whichever occurs first, in the case of a class C automobile.

160. For the application of section 159, used automobiles are divided into the following classes:

(a) class A automobiles, namely, where not more than two years have elapsed between the date the manufacturer put his automobiles of the same model and of the same model year on the market and the date of the sale contemplated in the said section, provided that the automobile has not covered more than 40 000 kilometres;

(b)   class B automobiles, namely, where they are not contemplated in paragraph *a* and not more than three years have elapsed between the date the manufacturer put his automobiles of the same model and of the same model year on the market and the date of the sale contemplated in the said section, provided that the automobile has not covered more than 60 000 kilometres;

(c)   class C automobiles, namely, where they are not contemplated in paragraph *a* or *b* and not more than five years have elapsed between the date the manufacturer put his automobiles of the same model and of the same model year on the market and the date of the sale contemplated in the said section, provided that the automobile has not covered more than 80 000 kilometres;

(d)   class D automobiles, namely automobiles not contemplated in any of paragraphs *a*, *b* and *c*.

161. The warranty provided for by section 159 does not cover;

(a)   normal maintenance service and the replacement of parts resulting from it;

(b)   interior upholstery or exterior decorative items;

(c)   damage resulting from abuse by the consumer after delivery of the automobile and

(d)   any accessory provided for by regulation.

162. Where the merchant offers a class A, B or C automobile for sale, he may indicate on the label all the defects which exist in the automobile, with an estimate of the cost of repair thereof. The merchant is bound by the estimate and he guarantees that the repair may be carried out for the price mentioned in the estimate.

In that case, the merchant is not subject to the obligation of warranty for the defects mentioned on the label.

163. The warranty takes effect upon the delivery of the used automobile.

164. Sections 155 to 158 and 161 to 163 apply, *mutatis mutandis*, to the sale of a used motorcycle adapted for transportation on public highways.

The sale of a used motorcycle adapted for transportation on public highways carries with it a warranty that the motorcycle and its accessories will remain in good working order.

(a)   for a period of two months, in the case of a class A motorcycle;

(b)   for a period of one month, in the case of a class B motorcycle.

Used motorcycles adapted for transportation on public highways are divided into the following classes;

(a)   class A motorcycles, namely, where not more than two years have elapsed between the date the manufacturer put his motorcycles of the same model and of the same model year on the market and the date of the sale contemplated in this section;

(*b*) class B motorcycles, namely, where more than two years but not more than three years have elapsed between the date the manufacturer put his motorcycles of the same model and of the same model year on the market and the date of the sale contemplated in this section;

(*c*) class C motorcycles, namely, motorcycles not contemplated in either of paragraphs *a* and *b*.

165. A person who, for valuable consideration, acts as an intermediary between consumers in the sale of used automobiles or used motorcycles adapted for transportation on public highways is subject to the obligations imposed on the merchant under this division.

166. Section 155 to 165 do not apply to a new automobile which has been the object of a contract of lease comprising an option to purchase of which the lessee decides to avail himself.

PRESLEY v. MacDONALD
(1963) 38 DLR (2d) 237, [1963] 1 OR 619 (Ont. Co. Ct.)

KENNEDY Co. Ct. J.: About July 3, 1961, the plaintiff Presley, who was then 20 years old, went to see the defendant MacDonald in Cornwall, where the latter carried on business under the name of Uptown Motor Sales, and looked at a 1956 Oldsmobile sedan and went for a ride in it. He asked the defendant MacDonald what kind of warranty he would get with the car, whereupon the defendant MacDonald said he would give him a "30 day 50-50 mechanical warranty". The plaintiff Presley thereupon purchased the car for $1,095 and a purchase order dated July 3, 1961, was executed by the plaintiff Presley and by Uptown Motor Sales.

The purchase order (ex. 1) has the following words in brackets written on the face of it:

(30 day 50-50)
(mechanical)
(warranty)

Also on the front of the purchase order appear the following words: "The front and back of this order comprise the entire agreement affecting this purchase and no other agreement or understanding of any nature concerning same has been made or entered into, or will be recognized."

Notwithstanding the wording of the purchase order a "certificate of mechanical fitness" dated July 3, 1961, (ex. 2) was executed by Uptown Motor Sales and delivered to the plaintiff Presley who signed his name thereon acknowledging the receipt thereof, which (after stating that certain parts of the car, which have nothing to do with the accident, had been checked), states as follows: "We hereby certify that the above described motor vehicle is in a safe condition to be operated on a highway." This certificate of mechanical fitness was not properly pleaded in the statement of claim but was produced by the plaintiff Presley while he was being cross-examined by counsel for the defendant MacDonald and was marked as ex. 2 without objection.

A day or two after the plaintiff Presley signed the purchase order and was given the certificate of mechanical fitness he took delivery of the car and drove it from Cornwall to Lindsay. Later on July 8, 1961, he drove the car from Lindsay to Oshawa and on the return journey while driving from Oshawa to Lindsay there was a "bang", the car started to "shake", the rear wheels seized, the car skidded sideways, went into a ditch and rolled over with the result that the car was wrecked and the plaintiff Presley and one of his passengers were injured.

The police officer who investigated the accident found on the road oil and pieces of metal and tire marks indicating that as the car travelled over a small knoll it started to travel sideways along the road and the shoulder thereof for some 160 ft. until it went into a ditch and turned over. On examining the car after the accident he found that the transmission of the car was broken and that the pieces of metal he had picked up on the road matched the metal of the transmission of the car.

The special and general damages claimed by the plaintiff have been agreed upon by the parties at the sum of $950 which I presume includes an allowance for the sale price of the wrecked car.

I think it is well-established law, that if a prospective purchaser chooses an article such as a second-hand car from a second-hand car dealer, and in the exercise of his own judgment buys the car without any warranty or misrepresentation by the seller, the purchaser in such case would have no cause of action against the seller for any defect in the car.

In this case, however, in my opinion, there were two warranties consisting, firstly of the certificate of mechanical fitness (ex. 2), and secondly of the "30 day 50-50 mechanical warranty" (ex. 1). I must therefore endeavour to reach a conclusion as to what were the terms of each warranty.

The Sale of Goods Act, RSO 1960, c. 358, s. 1 (*n*) defines a warranty as follows: . . .

And s. 51(1), leaving out the words which are not applicable, provides the following remedy for a breach of warranty: . . .

I will deal first of all with the warranty contained in the certificate of mechanical fitness (ex. 2).

Section 49 of the Highway Traffic Act, RSO 1960, c. 172, provides as follows:

> **49** (1) When a used motor vehicle is sold by a dealer in used motor vehicles, the dealer shall deliver to the purchaser at the time of the sale a certificate of mechanical fitness signed by the dealer stating that the motor vehicle is, or is not, in a safe condition to be operated on a highway, and such certificate shall be on a separate form from any bill of sale or other document.
>
> (2) Every dealer who contravenes any of the provisions of subsection 1 or who makes a false statement in any such certificate is liable to a fine of not less than $50 and not more than $300.

Pursuant to such section the defendant MacDonald gave to the plaintiff Presley the certificate of mechanical fitness (ex. 2) executed by Uptown Motor Sales which (after stating that certain parts of the car, which had nothing to do with the accident, had been checked) states as follows: "We hereby certify that the above described motor vehicle is in a safe condition to be operated on a highway." Since the Highway Traffic Act by s. 49 creates a duty and provides a penalty for the breach thereof, it seems to me that I should record the reasons why, in my opinion, the rights of the plaintiff Presley are not affected by the general rule applicable to the interpretation of such statutory provision.

The cases indicate that the general rule of interpretation applicable to a statute which creates a duty and imposes a penalty for a breach thereof is that

(a) when a statute creates a duty and does not provide any remedy for the breach of the duty, an individual is entitled to bring an action for damages for any special damages he may have suffered by reason of the breach,

(b) but when a statute creates a duty and provides a special remedy for the breach of it, there is a presumption that the statute intended to exclude any other remedy.

If the plaintiff Presley was suing the defendant MacDonald for damages for a breach of the duty imposed on the defendant MacDonald by s. 49 to "deliver to the purchaser at the time of the sale a certificate of mechanical fitness . . ." the rule of interpretation mentioned in para. (b) above might be applicable. But in the instant case the defendant MacDonald did in fact deliver to the plaintiff Presley at the time of the sale a certificate of mechanical fitness as required by s. 49, and the plaintiff Presley is not suing the defendant MacDonald for damages for breach of any statutory duty but is suing the defendant MacDonald for damages for the breach of a warranty which the defendant MacDonald gave with the car when he sold it to the plaintiff Presley. In such circumstances, in my opinion, the rule of interpretation mentioned in para. (b) is not applicable and the plaintiff Presley has a right to maintain an action against the defendant MacDonald for damages for a breach of the warranty given to him by the defendant MacDonald.

. . .

In my opinion, when the defendant MacDonald gave to the plaintiff Presley a certificate of mechanical fitness (ex. 2) which states "We hereby certify that the above described motor vehicle is in a safe condition to be operated on a highway", such certificate constitutes a warranty or an agreement within the meaning of s. 1 (n) of the Sale of Goods Act that the motor vehicle sold by the defendant MacDonald to the plaintiff Presley was "in a safe condition to be operated on a highway", and that when the transmission broke causing the rear wheels to lock and the motor vehicle to go into the ditch and be wrecked, there was a breach of such warranty which entitled the plaintiff Presley to "maintain an action against the seller for damages for the breach of warranty, . . . the measure of damages for breach of warranty [being] the estimated loss directly and naturally resulting in the ordinary course of events from the breach of warranty".

It seems to me that the general and special damages suffered by the plaintiff Presley which have been agreed at $950 represent "loss directly and naturally resulting in the ordinary course of events from the breach of the warranty" and that, if it were not for the "30 day 50-50 mechanical warranty" the plaintiff Presley would be entitled to judgment against the defendant MacDonald for $950 and costs. (It will be noted that the defendant MacDonald did not introduce any evidence as to what if any tests were made to see that the car was "in a safe condition to be operated on a highway".)

I will now deal with the purchase order (ex. 1) which in my opinion contains a further warranty. The plaintiff Presley at the trial testified to the effect that when he was negotiating for the purchase of the car with the defendant MacDonald he asked him what kind of warranty he would get with the car and the defendant MacDonald agreed to give him a "30 day 50-50 mechanical warranty", and these words were then written on the face of the purchase order. The plaintiff Presley impressed me as being a truthful witness, and I have no doubt that he understood the words to mean as he said several times with slight variations when he was being examined, "I figure if anything mechanical went wrong with the car any damage caused by it would be paid one-half by the garage". It seems to me that a reasonable interpretation of the words, "30 day 50-50 mechanical warranty" and of the evidence of the plaintiff Presley is that if within 30 days of the sale, any of the parts of the car became defective the defendant MacDonald would repair or replace them and would pay one-half of the cost thereof and that if the car was damaged by reason of a mechanical defect the defendant MacDonald would pay one-half of the cost of repairing the damage, and since in the instant case the car was by reason of a mechanical defect damaged beyond repair, it seems to me it follows as a logical sequence that the defendant MacDonald is liable to pay one-half the damages suffered by the plaintiff Presley. Since the defendant MacDonald did not testify or call any evidence, it seems to me that the uncontradicted evidence given by the plaintiff Presley in this connection which is against his own interest and the above reasonable interpretation of the words in question should be accepted.

Counsel for the defendant if I understand his argument correctly, has argued that the "30 day 50-50 mechanical warranty" only meant that if within 30 days of the sale any of the parts of the car became defective the defendant MacDonald would repair or replace them and would pay one-half the cost thereof. This argument, if carried to its conclusion, would mean in this case, that when the transmission broke and as a consequence the car went off the road and was wrecked, all that the defendant MacDonald would have to do would be to pay one-half of the cost of a new transmission. If the argument of counsel for the defendant MacDonald is to prevail, then in such circumstances it seems to me that the plaintiff Presley as previously stated would be entitled under the warranty contained in the certificate of mechanical fitness (ex. 2) to the full sum of $950. But, unfortunately for the plaintiff Presley, he has in my opinion, through an abundance of precaution by insisting on the "30 day 50-50 mechanical warranty" reduced the liability of the defendant MacDonald to 50% of the damage he has suffered. In such circumstances there will be judgment for the plaintiff Presley for $475 and costs.

Judgment for plaintiff.

Questions and Notes:

1   Do you agree with the decision in *Presley*? Had there been a breach of the certificate of mechanical fitness? If there had, could its civil consequences be reduced by a disclaimer clause? What would have been the position if the plaintiff or a passenger in the vehicle had been injured as a result of the accident? Are the answers to the foregoing questions affected by a dealer's or mechanic's negligence in carrying out the certified inspection? See *Hawke* v. *Waterloo-Wellington Flying Club Ltd.* (1972) 22 DLR (3d) 266 (Ont. Co. Ct.); *L.G. Wilson Motors Ltd.* v. *Woods* (1970) 2 NBR (2d) 581 (SC); and *Henzel* v. *Brussels Motors Ltd.* [1973] 1 OR 339, 31 DLR (3d) 131 (Co. Ct.).

2   Plaintiff purchased from defendant for cash a used truck, taking delivery on October 8. A certificate of mechanical fitness was supplied at the same time. On November 17, he began to use the vehicle in his franchise business. On December 23, the brakes gave way and as a result plaintiff collided with a third party. Plaintiff sues inter alia for damages for the repair of the truck and for the cost of replacing the brake system. Evidence was given that if the brakes had been in acceptable condition at the time of the sale, they could not have worn to the condition they were in at the time of the accident, 2,000 miles later. What result? See *Henzel v. Brussels Motors Ltd., supra.*

d) Perishable Goods and Durability

MASH & MURRELL LTD. v. JOSEPH I. EMANUEL LTD.
[1961] 1 WLR 862 [1961] 1 All ER 485 (QB)

The plaintiffs carried on business in the United Kingdom as dealers in potatoes fit for human consumption. The defendants were also dealers in and importers of potatoes. On July 8, 1957, the defendant's agents agreed to sell the plaintiffs 2,000 half-bags of Cyprus potatoes, then afloat the s.s. *Ionian*, at 16s. per half-bag, c. & f. Liverpool, plus commission.

The potatoes had been loaded on the *Ionian* on June 29, 1957, at Limassol on the south coast of Cyprus for shipment to Liverpool and, after several intervening port calls, reached Liverpool on July 18. On their arrival there the potatoes were found to be rotten and were condemned by the port authorities as unfit for human consumption.

The plaintiffs brought this action for damages alleging breach of several implied warranties as described in Diplock J.'s judgment below. The defendants denied liability.

DIPLOCK J.: The plaintiffs claim that they are entitled to recover damages from the defendants arising out of the state of the goods on arrival at Liverpool. They rely on the rotten state of the potatoes on arrival and ask me to infer that the potatoes shipped cannot have been fit to travel at the time of shipment. By "fit to travel" I mean fit to be carried to Liverpool so as to arrive in a condition fit for the purpose for which they would normally be used.

There is no doubt at all that on arrival the potatoes were rotten and were wholly unfit for human consumption. As this is the purpose for which Cyprus spring crop potatoes would normally be used, I do not think it is seriously contended that they were then merchantable. I find that on arrival at Liverpool they were unmerchantable.

• • •

On those findings of fact a question of law, which has been hotly debated, arises. I have so far travelled through my legal life under the impression, shared by a number of other judges who have sat in this court, that when goods are sold under a contract such as a c.i.f. contract, or f.o.b. contract, which involves transit before use, there is an implied warranty not merely that they shall be merchantable at the time they are put on the vessel, but that they shall be in such a state that they can endure the normal journey and be in a merchantable condition upon arrival. But it has been strenuously argued by Mr. Roskill for the defendants that that impression under which I have been for so long is quite erroneous and, like a similar impression of Lord Atkin when he was Atkin J., is founded on a misreading of the famous old case about rabbits, *Beer* v. *Walker* (1877) 46 LJQB 677. It is, therefore, necessary to analyse the way in which the plaintiffs put their case.

They have put their case in three different ways. First, founding themselves on section 14 (1) of the Sale of Goods Act, 1893, they say that here was a case where the buyer by implication made known to the seller the particular purpose for which the goods were required so as to show that they relied on his skill and judgment, and that, accordingly, they rely on the implied condition that the goods were fit for that purpose, namely, the purpose of being carried by the *Ionian* on her voyage to Liverpool, and for the purpose of being carried to Liverpool for sale for use for human consumption after arrival.

Alternatively, they put their case on section 14 (2), namely, the warranty as to merchantable quality, and they say the merchantable quality as regards these potatoes is that at the time of shipment they should be merchantable as potatoes sold for carrying and delivery to Liverpool by the *Ionian*.

The third way they put it is that there is an implied warranty in a c.i.f. or c. & f. contract, as this was, that the goods should be fit to stand the voyage from Cyprus to Liverpool on which the *Ionian* was about to embark, a normal voyage from Cyprus to Liverpool, and should arrive sound and fit for sale for human consumption after arrival.

For those propositions, Mr. Roche relies primarily on *Beer* v. *Walker*, *Ollett* v. *Jordan* [1918] 2 KB 41 (DC), and, for the last proposition, on a decision of McCardie J. in *Evangelinos* v. *Leslie & Anderson* (1920) 4 Ll. LR 17. I shall have to examine those cases a little more carefully.

It does not seem to me that there is really any very great distinction between the three alternative ways in which the plaintiffs put their case. Had the case been tried before the Sale of Goods Act, 1893, it would have been unnecessary to put it in the first two ways, and it seems to me, in a case of this kind, that subsections (1) and (2) of section 14 of the Act are really two sides of the same coin. If a buyer makes known a particular purpose — those, of course, are the words of the subsection — to the seller so as to show that he relies on the seller's skill and judgment, then the suitability for that particular purpose is a warranty and implied condition of the contract. If he does not make known any particular purpose, then, the assumption being that he requires them for the ordinary purposes for which such goods are intended to be used, the implied condition is one that they are fit for those ordinary purposes, that is to say, that they are merchantable, and I venture to think there is no other distiction between subsection (1) and subsection (2).

If it were possible for the coin to have three sides, I should have said the implied term on which Mr. Roche relies as a third ground, applicable to c.i.f., c. & f. and f.o.b. contracts, was a third side of the same coin. I think it really comes to no more than this, that merchantability in the case of goods sold c.i.f. or c. & f. means that the goods must remain merchantable for a reasonable time, and that, in the case of such contracts, a reasonable time means time for arrival and disposal upon arrival.

However, I think it is necessary, in the way this case has been argued, that I should deal with the three alternatives. So far as section 14 (1) is concerned, the evidence which I have already alluded to shows, first, that the defendants' agents knew the nature of the plaintiffs' business; they knew it as the result of having had dealings with them for many years; indeed, there was produced by Mr. Mash a letter from them of 1951 which refers particularly to their hotel and ships' stores trade in which they say they know him to be well established.

It is also plain from the evidence that Mash made it clear to the defendants' agents that he wanted the potatoes for use in his trade in this country. Mr. Roche, in those circumstances, relies on the well-known case of *Manchester Liners Ltd.* v. *Rea Ltd.*, [1922] 2 AC 74, (HL), which he says, I think rightly, establishes the proposition that if the particular purpose is made known by the buyer to the seller, then, unless there is something in effect to rebut the presumption, that in itself is sufficient to raise the presumption that he relies upon the skill and judgment of the seller; and Mr. Roche relies particularly on a passage in Lord Atkinson's speech. . . .

If that is so — and Mr. Roskill, of course, contests it — I do not think he contests that the decision of the Divisional Court in *Beer v. Walker* 46 LJQB 677 does get the plaintiffs home. I think it is right, however, that I should deal with the second way in which the plaintiffs put it, namely, "merchantability," because I think the result is the same. So far as merchantability is concerned, it is, I think, convenient for me to take, as the definition of "merchantable quality" — to follow the words of section 14 — a statement again in Lord Wright's speech in the *Cammell Laird* case, where he says [1934] AC 402, 430:

> What subsection (2) now means by "merchantable quality" is that the goods in the form in which they were tendered were of no use for any purpose for which such goods would normally be used and hence were not saleable under that description.

I do not think it is seriously contended, as I have said, that these goods were fit for any purpose for which Cyprus spring potatoes in bags would be normally used, which is human consumption, at the time of their arrival.

The question, therefore, is whether merchantability in a contract of this kind does require that they should remain, from the time of delivery, which is, of course, in a c.i.f. contract, the time of shipment, in a merchantable condition until arrival at destination and for a reasonable time for disposal. The authority for the affirmative proposition relied on by Mr. Roche is *Beer* v. *Walker* 46 LJQB 677. What Atkin J. thought the effect of *Beer* v. *Walker* to be is to be found in *Ollett* v. *Jordan* [1918] 2 KB 41 where he said (at p. 47):

> I think that the effect of the decision in *Beer* v. *Walker* is that the condition that the goods must be merchantable means that they must be in that condition when appropriated to the contract and that they will continue so for a reasonable time. That does not necessarily mean that goods shall be merchantable on delivery if the vendee directs them to be sent by a long and unusual transit. It is, however, not necessary to decide that.

Mr. Roskill contends that in so summarising the effect of *Beer* v. *Walker* Atkin J. was doing what he seldom did — nodding — and that *Beer* v. *Walker* was, or would have been, had it been tried after the Sale of Goods Act, 1893, a section 14(1) case and not a section 14(2) case, because it had got nothing to do with merchantable quality but only with fitness for a particular purpose.

I must therefore turn to *Beer* v. *Walker*. That was a case of rabbits being sent from London to Brighton. The rabbits were of merchantable quality, that is to say, fit for human consumption, when they were sent from London, but when they were delivered to the defendants in Brighton they were putrid and valueless. The case came before the Divisional Court on appeal from the county court. I think it is necessary to read a little of the judgment from which the appeal came. The deputy county court judge said:

> When the rabbits were sent from London they were in good order and condition, but when they were delivered to the defendant they were putrid and valueless. The question in the case is, upon whom is the loss to fall? There is no doubt that in such a case there was an implied warranty that the rabbits would be merchantable, but I am of opinion that that condition was satisfied if they were delivered in good order and condition to the railway in London: see *Dawes* v. *Peck* (1799) 8 Term Rep. 330 and *Dutton* v. *Solomonson* (1803) 3 Bos. & P. 582. There is, therefore, no breach of warranty, and the plaintiff is entitled to be paid the contract price for the rabbits. There will, therefore, be judgment for the plaintiff with costs.

The report goes on:

> From this judgment the defendant appealed. The questions for the opinion of the court were: (1) Whether there was, under the said circumstances, such an implied warranty. (2) Whether such implied warranty (if any) was satisfied by the delivery of the said rabbits to the railway company in the order, condition and state so warranted,

the implied warranty referred to being an implied warranty that the rabbits would be merchantable. I think that statement of the questions for the opinion of the court is probably the statement by the editor of the report.

I think I must read the judgment in full. Grove J. said (at p. 678):

> The case finds that what took place was in the ordinary course of business, so that there was nothing in the mode of sending the rabbits which was out of the usual course, and therefore the rabbits which were unfit for human food had become so in the ordinary course of transit. Then, that being so, the question is, was there an implied warranty that they should be fit for food? It cannot, I think, be contended that when a person undertakes to supply another with goods which are not specific goods, there is not an implied warranty that the goods shall be fit for the purpose for which they ordinarily would be intended to be used, and that with regard to animals used for human food that they are fit to be so used.

I emphasise those words, because they are an exact definition of what is meant by "merchantable quality," almost the *ipsissima verba* of Lord Wright in the *Cammell Laird* case. The judgment goes on:

> Then the second, and in fact the only question, which is really arguable in this case is, whether such a warranty was satisfied by the delivery to the railway company at their station in London, or whether the warranty was not such that if nothing happened out of the ordinary course, the rabbits should reach the person for whom they were destined in good order and fit for human food. Now I am of opinion that the implied warranty extended to the time at which, in the ordinary course of transit, the rabbits should reach the defendant, and not only to that time, but that it continued until the defendant should have a reasonable opportunity of dealing with them in the ordinary course of business. Our judgment, therefore, will be for the appellant.

Remembering that *Beer* v. *Walker* was decided before the Sale of Goods Act, 1893 (so there was no particular magic in fitness for a purpose of merchantable quality), it seems to me to be clear that the court in that case was dealing with a warranty which today would be called a "warranty of merchantable quality," and I respectfully agree with Atkin J.'s analysis of what the decision in *Beer* v. *Walker* really meant.

Judgment for plaintiff.

Notes: Diplock J.'s decision was reversed on appeal [1962] 1 WLR 16 on questions of fact. The Court of Appeal did not adopt any position with respect to the implied warranties. For a later Canadian decision supporting the same view of the law as Diplock J.'s see *Georgetown Seafoods Ltd.* v. *Usen Fisheries Ltd.* (1977) 78 DLR (3d) 542 (PEI SC) and *cf.* the following statement by Laidlaw J.A. in *Tregunno* v. *Aldershot* [1944] 1 DLR 102 (Ont. CA) at 107-08, in dealing with a shipment of peaches:

> The contract to be considered is between the grower as plaintiff and the wholesale dealer as defendant. Importing into that contract the implied condition that the goods shall be of merchantable quality and applying the proper principle of law, I think the condition is satisfied after the defendant had a reasonable opportunity of dealing with the goods in the ordinary course of business at the place where delivery of them in that condition was made to it by the plaintiff.

See also Fridman, *Sale of Goods in Canada*, 2nd ed., pp. 218, 230-31.

To what extent is Diplock J.'s reasoning applicable to non-perishable goods? How can his decision be reconciled with SGA s. 32? See *Georgetown Seafoods Ltd., supra,* at pp. 548-49. Is there an implied condition of durability which extends beyond the time of arrival of the goods? How would you determine the expectable period of durability in a particular case, e.g., with respect to an automobile? What would you do in the case of a product with many components? Is it feasible to set standards of durability by legislation? For a brief discussion of some of these questions, see OLRC Warranties Report, pp. 37-38, reproduced below.

OLRC Warranties Report, pp. 37-8

(i) *Durability.* It is often said that it is no part of the condition of merchantability that the goods or, in the case of mechanical products, the particular components making up the article, shall last for any particular period of time. As a matter of common sense this proposition cannot be correct and it appears to conflict with both the concept of fitness, general or particular, and the relevance of price as an indication of the quality of goods which the buyer is entitled to expect. Nevertheless, there is a surprising dearth of authority on the question. The reported cases appear to be confined to perishable goods and to deal with the issue whether the seller impliedly warrants that the goods will reach their destination in a merchantable condition.

The Commission recommends that the position be clarified, and that the condition of merchantability be expanded to include a requirement that the goods shall be durable for a reasonable length of time, having regard to the price and the other surrounding circumstances. This recommendation is not particularly novel. The farm implements legislation of several of the Western provinces has long contained provisions governing this aspect of a seller's obligations.

It is a common practice for many manufacturers to undertake to replace some or all parts of a product sold by them which turns out to be defective within a prescribed period. The question that arises is whether, in the same vein, a seller should be entitled to limit his obligation to supply goods that remain fit for their purpose by reference to a time period, or whether the statutory test should always be paramount. As will be shown in a later chapter, manufacturers' and sellers' warranties vary widely with respect even to the same type of product and, in the case of new cars, fluctuate from year to year. Some warranties are of very limited value or even worthless.

In the opinion of the Commission, it is no more consistent with public policy to allow sellers to limit the duration of their warranties unilaterally than it is to allow them to exclude their implied obligations of quality altogether. It is therefore recommended, subject to what we say hereafter, that the statutory test of reasonable durability should remain the paramount test and that a buyer should not be precluded from challenging the adequacy of an express warranty of durability. In reaching this conclusion, the Commission has considered, but does not agree with the policy expressed in the Alberta and Prince Edward Island Farm Implements Acts. These Acts provide that a manufacturer's express warranty of durability shall supersede the statutory warranty of reasonable durability. The proposed legislation should not, of course, preclude or discourage the giving of express warranties of durability by manufacturers, since they may wish, for competitive reasons, to assume by contract a higher duty than required by the statute. Where an express warranty of durability is given by a manufacturer, it should be operative unless it is inconsistent with the minimum terms and conditions of the statutory warranty of reasonable durability.

Note: An implied warranty of durability was adopted in s. 4(a) of Ontario's Bill 110 and now also appears in s. 11.7 of the Saskatchewan Consumer Products Warranties Act 1977. In the latter case the retail seller is deemed to have given the following warranty:

> 11.7. that the product and all its components shall be durable for a reasonable period of time, having regard to all the relevant circumstances of the sale, including the description and nature of the product, the purchase price, the express warranties of the retail seller or manufacturer, the necessary maintenance the product normally requires and the manner in which it has been used. . . .

CANADIAN MANUFACTURERS' ASSOCIATION REACTIONS TO OLRC WARRANTIES REPORT

Comments on Durability (1973)

We recognize that a product when purchased is deemed by the consumer to be essentially capable of fulfilling the function for which it was purchased. We agree that it should when purchased and for some time thereafter "work". If it does not, then the vendor and/or manufacturer should be responsible for the defective product. Hitherto, this result has been met by the legal concept of an implied warranty of merchantability and the implied warranty of fitness for special purpose. If it is merchantable it should be saleable in the market place as goods of the kind described, free from defects and reasonably fit for normal use. The concept of merchantability is closely allied to honesty in the market place. If a product does not "work" the law concludes that the purchaser has been deceived and has purchased a non-merchantable product. The Report, however, expresses a concern for the length of time a product will remain merchantable. This concern with the life of a product, or its durability is one that we feel has very serious failings as a concept.

1. The warranty of durability means that every product should have a reasonable life expectancy. But this reasonableness can only be decided by reference to the criteria of price, quality, use and maintenance. Price is the product of complex inter-related market factors such as product cost, competition and the laws of supply and demand. Because the retail price of a Canadian made toaster is twice the price of an imported toaster will it mean that a court will presume its durability or life expectancy to be proportionately higher than that of the imported model? The Canadian price may relate primarily to costs and not in any way create an accurate presumption as to durability. The result is that if a court is

attempting to accurately determine "reasonableness" it is going to be faced with a virtually impossible task involving detailed research of all factors determining price. If the retail selling price is treated as the price criterion then the Canadian company in our example above will be arbitrarily penalized.

2. The concept of durability is not simply an extension of the concept of merchantability which rested on the premise that commercial dealings should be fair and honest. It is a concept which assumes that society, using law as its instrument, should prescribe not just minimum standards related to fair dealing but life expectancy standards or in effect product quality standards. Under this concept the element of market choice would continue only in so far as the manufacturer is prepared to meet or exceed the unpredictable norm of "reasonable durability". This conceptual difference involves interference with the natural forces of the market place and reflects an undesirable socio-economic philosophy. However desirable it may be that product standards be upgraded we submit that it is not desirable that an implied standard of life expectancy be imposed by regulation to determine what goods may enter the consumer market.

3. Because a product is sold at a distress price presumably it will not mean that its durability will thereby be reduced to a correspondingly low level that might, relative to other products, approach a zero level. We would assume that at a certain low level of life expectancy the criteria for determining a product's reasonable durability must return to the concept of merchantability. In other words, a court will have to say it must "work" for some minimum period of time and therefore ignore the "super bargain" or distress price factor. It will be insufficient to say that a $2 toaster should only be durable for say, seven days (relating it to the durability of higher priced toasters). It will have to meet a basic merchantability test. At this point the criteria for determining reasonable durability ceases to apply and the court switches to the merchantability standard. A court then will be looking at two standards — merchantability for the bottom end of the price spectrum and durability for the part above. At some arbitrary point between the two a court will move from the one fundamentally different concept to the other. Surely this is an illogical basis for a law designed to get away from the admitted "imprecise meaning" of merchantability. Durability would appear to illogically compound the confusion.

4. Moving from the conceptual to the practical we view the following as some of the practical problems that a warranty of durability presents:

(a) The manufacturer will be faced with an "unknown" to be determined only by the court's interpretation of "reasonable". This unknown will remain largely unknown due to the myriad of consumer products. To ensure compliance with the warranty of durability, many manufacturers will increase their manufacturing standards beyond what would now be considered necessary to provide for the products normal use. However desirable this may be as a socio-economic goal we do not believe law is the appropriate instrument to achieve it. Furthermore, insurance will no doubt be a significant cost factor as manufacturers attempt to meet a durability standard.

Manufacturers will no doubt be building safety factors into these standards. Whatever way you look at it, durability must increase the cost to the consumer.

(b) It is questionable whether manufacturers will care to provide express warranties exceeding a warranty of durability when the ambit of the latter will be largely unknown. Express warranties will probably rarely be used as a competitive part of a sale transaction. The incentive to improve quality as a selling tool will be replaced by a legal requirement to meet a durability standard. This would not appear to be in the long run best interest of the consumer.

(c) Often a consumer opts for a low price product knowing that its durability will be less but feeling that it meets his particular requirement and circumstances. Manufacturers faced with the unknowns of "reasonable durability" and the risk inherent in the bottom of a line product will we suggest, assuming the product is merchantable, either upgrade their product into a higher price area, insure that risk at the consumer's expense, or discontinue selling products where the threat of meeting an undetermined standard is uneconomic. The end result is that the low priced end of the price spectrum might have fewer products. This may not always be in the consumer's best interest.

(d) We foresee considerable practical difficulty in a court determining durability in a particular instance without relating the product to other competitive products on the market. The difficulty in determining the reasonable durability of fountain pen X would seem to involve relating it to most of the other perhaps twenty-five competitive products on the market. The task would appear to be totally unrealistic both for a court of law, considering the time at its disposal and for the parties to the action, considering their ability to amass the evidence.

We believe the well tested legal concept of merchantability is essentially sound and sufficient — namely that a product should "work" when purchased and for some time thereafter. We believe, however, that the concept can be modified to meet today's market place requirements. We propose that "merchantability" be modified so that as a standard it will survive for a prescribed minimum period of time after sale. We suggest that this period of time be called the "minimum statutory warranty period". The duration of this time period would be determined by regulation for each product grouping having similar characteristics and functions. The buyer, seller and manufacturer will then know exactly how long a product must remain merchantable after the date of sale. The buyer of a defective product will have straightforward, simple and absolute remedies against the appropriate party or parties during this period. Merchantability will not be left to imprecise determination by the courts but will be prescribed in advance by regulation. This minimum statutory warranty period, however, will in no way relate to the "life expectancy" or "durability" of the product. It will simply be a minimum period after sale during which the implied warranties of merchantability and fitness for purpose will rest wholly and absolutely in favour of the consumer. Most inherent defects in a product will reveal themselves during the minimum statutory warranty period and this should meet the vast majority of consumer complaints. The manufacturer will be free to continue using express warranties that exceed the minimum statutory warranty and in fact will be encouraged to do so as a competitive tool.

In resumé we believe that a minimum statutory warranty adds precision to the essentially sound legal concept of merchantability. As a minimum period it will constitute basic protection for the consumer in most cases, yet leave the question of life expectancy or durability to be settled by consumer demand in the market place.

OLRC RESPONSE

OLRC Sales Report
pp. 215-16

We sympathize with the manufacturers' apprehensions, but we do not believe that their objections come to grips with the basic problem. As our *Warranties Report* points out, the concept of durability is not new; it is inherent in the concept of merchantability, and there is respectable authority to support the concept. The purpose of our recommendation in the *Warranties Report* was not to innovate, but to clarify. Moreover, it may, indeed, be questioned whether the concept of durability is more uncertain than the concept of merchantability. A concept of minimum durability is helpful in the consumer context, where regulations are a feasible device to provide certainty; but this solution is not likely to be available in a general sales act, which must of necessity encompass an infinite range of goods. For this reason, a concept of minimum durability can do little to dispel uncertainty in the general sales area.

Having regard to these considerations, we believe it is as desirable for this revised Sale of Goods Act to clarify the status of durability, as it is in an act dealing with consumer warranties. The Saskatchewan Consumer Products Warranties Act, 1977 imports a statutory warranty of reasonable durability, as did Ontario Bill 110. It would be anomalous, in our view, if a retailer's basic warranty rights against a manufacturer, who supplies him with a defective product, were to be treated less favourably than the consumer's rights against the retailer when the product is resold to the consumer. We would, however, modify our earlier recommendation in one respect: we would treat reasonable durability as one of the requirements of the warranty of merchantable quality, and not as a wholly separate warranty. This meets the comments of friendly British critics, who have argued that a separate warranty is not required because the concept of merchantable quality is sufficiently flexible to embrace a requirement of reasonable durability. Accordingly, the Commission recommends that the definition of merchantable quality in the revised Act should require that the goods will remain fit or perform satisfactorily, as the case may be, for a reasonable length of time having regard to all the circumstances. Finally, we would stress that, as with any other implied warranty, it will be open to sellers under the revised Act to modify the warranty of merchantable quality and to specify their own periods of minimum durability. To the extent that such provisions are not regarded as unconscionable, sellers should thus be able to avoid the uncertainty to which they object in an undefined statutory term.

Note: The OLRC's recommendation is given effect to in s. 5.13(1)(*b*)(vi) of the draft bill.

e) Compliance with Public Law of Buyer's Jurisdiction

SUMNER, PERMAIN & CO. v. WEBB & CO.
[1922] 1 KB 55, [1921] All ER Rep. 680 (CA)

SCRUTTON L.J.: The defendants sold f.o.b. in England to the plaintiffs a large quantity of "Webb's Indian Tonic" of which the defendants were the manufacturers, and which they knew was intended to be sent out to the Argentine where the plaintiffs carry on business. Unknown to the plaintiffs, the defendants' tonic contained a small proportion of salicylic acid, a fact which by reason of a certain law of the Argentine rendered it legally unsaleable in that country. The plaintiffs now contend that the impossibility of legally selling it in the market for which it was intended constitutes a breach of the implied condition that the goods should be of merchantable quality. In *Niblett* v. *Confectioners' Materials Co.* [1921] 3 KB 381, 398, which has been referred to, I agreed with my brothers' view under s. 12, sub-s. 1, that the sellers had broken the implied condition that they would have a right to sell the goods, but as Bankes L.J. has pointed out, I did not discuss s. 14, sub-s. 2, further than to say this: "I have not been able to trace the origin or history of the condition that goods shall be of merchantable quality. If I had to express my present opinion it is that the condition does not touch the title to the goods or the right to sell them." I have looked a little further into the matter and can now finally express my opinion that "merchantable quality" does not cover legal title to goods or the legal right to sell. In my view "merchantable quality" means that the goods comply with the description in the contract, so that to a purchaser buying goods of that description the goods would be good tender. It does not mean that there shall in fact be persons ready to buy the goods. For instance take the case that I put during the argument; if you sell "vestings" of a particular fancy pattern for sale in China, you do not warrant that the Chinese buyer will like that pattern and will buy it when it goes out there; if the goods are vestings of the pattern contracted for, they are merchantable though nobody likes the pattern or is willing to buy. Similarly I do not think "merchantable quality" means that there can legally be buyers of that article. If the goods are of the contract description the possibility of legally making a sale of them does not in my view come within the expression "merchantable quality." I am still not quite clear when that expression first began to be used. I see that in *Randall* v. *Newson* 2 QBD 102 at 109 Lord Esher (or Brett J.A. as he then was) appears to have thought that it was first used in *Gardiner* v *Gray* (1815) 4 Camp. 144 at 145. There was in that case a count "that the silk should be waste silk of a good and merchantable quality," and it was in reference to that count that Lord Ellen-borough used the language which has repeatedly been quoted in other cases. "The intention of both parties must be taken to be that it shall be saleable in the market under the denomination mentioned in the contract between them. The purchaser cannot be supposed to buy goods to lay them on a dunghill"; and that particularly picturesque passage has been cited by judge after judge in cases on this point ever since. Now when Lord Ellenborough there uses the word "salea-ble" I do not think he means "legally saleable." As explained by Lord Esher himself in *Randall* v. *Newson*, the fundamental thing is that "the article offered or delivered shall answer the description of it contained in the contract." And in a passage a little later on he adds: "If that subject matter be merely the commercial article or commodity, the undertaking is, that the thing offered or delivered shall answer that description, that is to say, shall be that article or commodity, saleable or merchantable," or in other words shall be a good tender under a contract for a sale of goods of that description. I am quite unable to find that any case since has ever dealt with the possibility of legally selling the goods in the particular market and has treated that possibility as included in the definition of "merchan-table." For these reasons I disagree with the view taken by Bailhache J.

Appeal allowed.

[Concurring judgments were delivered by Bankes and Atkin L.JJ.]

Notes:

1   Do you agree with Scrutton L.J.'s reasoning? It is consistent with the test of merchantability adopted in *Hardwick Game Farm*? With the decision in *Niblett* v. *Confectioners' Materials Co.*, *supra*, chapter 6(A)? Would the court in *Sumner, Permain* have reached the same conclusion if the tonic water had failed to comply with the requirements of the British food and drug legislation, or is such compliance better left as an aspect of the implied condition of fitness? In discussing whether a revised Ontario Sale of Goods Act should address itself to the problem of the merchantability of goods not in compliance with the law of the buyer's jurisdiction, the OLRC Sales Report remarks (p. 218):

> It would not be right, as a general proposition, to oblige a seller to familiarize himself with the requirements of every jurisdiction to which his goods may be exported. If the foreign buyer seeks compliance with his own law, he should bring this home to the seller. In our view, the implied warranty of fitness is sufficiently flexible to cope with this problem.

Do you agree? For the modern scope of the implied condition of fitness see *infra*, chapter 5(B)(3).

2   In *Sumner, Permain* the buyer also claimed relief under the implied condition of fitness. The court held that the condition had not been breached because the buyers were unable to show that they relied on the sellers' skill and judgment to supply tonic water that complied with the law of the Argentine. The lord justices were influenced in this conclusion by the fact that the plaintiffs had for years sold

this tonic water in the Argentine without objection. For a similar conclusion on the facts see *Teheran-Europe Co. Ltd.* v. *S.T. Belton (Tractors) Ltd.* [1968] 2 QB 545 (CA). Diplock L.J. said (*ibid.*, at 560-61):

> Where a foreign merchant buys by description goods, not for his own use, but for resale in his own country of which he has no reason to suppose the English seller has any special knowledge, it flies in the face of common sense to suppose that he relies on anything but his own knowledge of the market in his own country and his own commercial judgment as to what is saleable there. To hold the contrary would mean that whenever anyone known by the seller to be a foreign merchant bought from a seller in England goods for sale in his own country there would arise automatically an undertaking on the part of the seller, unless he expressly disclaimed it, that the goods would be suitable for sale in the market of which the foreign buyer knew everything and he, the seller, knew nothing. With great respect, that would be nonsense.

3 An important constitutional question is whether the buyer's province can oblige a seller to comply with its sales legislation where the seller has his place of business in another jurisdiction and the "proper law of the contract" (in the conflict of law sense) is not the law of the buyer's province. In *R.* v. *Thomas Equipment Ltd.* (1979) 96 DLR (3d) 1, the Supreme Court of Canada, distinguishing its earlier decision in *Interprovincial Co-operatives Ltd.* v. *The Queen* [1976] 1 SCR 477, upheld Alberta's constitutional power to enforce its Farm Implement Act, RSA 1970, c. 136, against a New Brunswick manufacturer which had terminated the selling agency of an Alberta dealer. The decision has important implications for the general reach of provincial consumer and business protection laws. See further Robert K. Paterson, "Do Unto Others: the Extraterritorial Reach of Regulatory Legislation in Canada" (1980-81) 5 Can. Bus. LJ 114.

(f) Examination under s. 15.2

THORNETT & FEHR v. BEERS & SON
[1919] 1 KB 486, 24 Com. Cas. 133

The plaintiffs, merchants in vegetable glues, sued the defendants for £363.1s, being the balance of the price of certain barrels of vegetable glue sold by them to the defendants. The defendants pleaded that the sale was a sale by sample, that this term has been mistakenly omitted from the sold note, and that the glue was not equal to sample. In the alternative, they claimed that the glue was not merchantable, and they also counterclaimed for the return of £3,000 which they had paid, and for damages, on the ground that the glue was valueless.

Bray J. found on the facts that the sale was not a sale by sample, and the balance of his judgment (reproduced below) is concerned with the applicability of the proviso to s. 14(2) [Ont. s. 15(2)].

The evidence on this point was that the parties had agreed that they should meet at Nottingham where the glue, in barrels, was lying in a warehouse, so that the defendants could see it. On September 18, 1918, the defendants wrote to the plaintiffs: "We are arranging for our representative who is at present in Birmingham to visit Nottingham to-morrow morning in order to inspect the thirty-five tons adhesive in question." Mr. Anholt, the plaintiffs' representative, went down to Nottingham, and attended at the warehouse on the following morning. He remained there till 12, but the defendants did not materialize. He had other business to do, so he left word where he could be found, and that he would return if called. He also told the foreman at the warehouse to give the defendants' representative every facility for inspection. The defendants' representatives, a Mr. Halfhide and a Mr. Beers, called between 12 and 1:30 but when Mr. Anholt returned at 1:30 they had left. Mr Halfhide stated in evidence that they did not have any of the casks opened and only looked at the outside, but he admitted they had been offered every facility and had received Mr. Anholt's message that he would come. However they had no time as they had another appointment. Mr. Anholt stated that the foreman told him that the defendants had seen two or three casks which had been opened. The foreman was not called by either side. The next day the defendants told Mr. Tobias, another representative of the plaintiffs, that they had inspected the parcel and offered him £90 a ton for it. A deal was ultimately struck at £95 a ton.

BRAY J.: The next question is whether under s. 14, sub-s. 2, of the Sale of Goods Act, 1893, there was an implied condition that the goods should be merchantable. This raises a somewhat difficult question. The sub-section is as follows: "Where goods are bought by description from a seller who deals in goods of that description ... there is an implied condition that the goods shall be of merchantable quality; provided that if the buyer has examined the goods, there shall be no implied condition as regards defects which such examination ought to have revealed." First, were the goods bought by description? In *Varley* v. *Whipp* [1900] 1 QB 513 the headnote, which I think accurately states the actual decision, reads thus: "The expression 'contract for the sale of goods by description,' in the Sale of Goods Act, 1893, s. 13, applies to all cases where the buyer has not seen the goods, but relies solely on the description given by the seller." I do not think it can be said here that the buyers relied solely on the description. They had seen the goods, and certainly relied partly on what they had seen. I infer this from what they stated on September 20 when Mr. Halfhide began by saying, "I have inspected the goods." I do not think, however, that it is necessary for the decision to lay down so broad a proposition that there could not be a sale by description where the buyer had seen the goods, and relied only partly on the description. I desire to leave that question open and not to decide that there was no implied condition that the goods were merchantable on the ground that it was not a sale by description.

Proceeding with the section, it is not disputed that the plaintiffs were sellers who dealt in vegetable glue. I now come to the proviso. Before the passing of the Act I think the law stood as laid down in *Jones* v. *Just* (1868) LR 3 QB 197, 202, where it is said that "where goods are in esse, and may be inspected by the buyer, and there is no fraud on the part of the seller, the maxim caveat emptor applies." The sub-section, however does not use the words "where the goods may be inspected by the buyer," but "if the buyer has examined the goods." In other words, it is not sufficient that the buyer should have had the opportunity of inspecting the goods, he must have examined them. I think the change of language must have been intentional, and I must see whether the buyers examined the goods. I do not think the statute requires a full examination, because the words that follow show that the proviso deals with the case where the buyer has not made a full examination. Was there an examination? I find that on September 18 both parties intended a full examination. The facts that both parties were to be present, that the foreman was told by the plaintiffs to offer the defendants every facility, and the defendants' letter of September 18 go to show this. I think I must take it that the defendants did not in fact have any barrels opened, but I think that the reason was that they had no time; they were satisfied with their inspection of the barrels, and they were willing to take the risk, the price being so low, and Mr. Halfhide himself, as I have found, told the plaintiffs at the beginning of the interview when the bargain was made that he had inspected the parcel. It may be a question whether, after this statement, the defendants could be heard to say that they had not examined the glue, but however that may be, I think they examined the goods within the meaning of the sub-section. There can be no doubt that revealed the defects complained of. The defects complained of were apparent the moment the casks were opened. The examination agreed to on September 18, which they had full opportunity of making on September 19, would involve the opening of a sufficient number of casks to ascertain the condition of the glue. I hold that this case falls within the proviso, and consequently there was no implied condition. Having found that it was not a sale by sample, and that there was no implied condition that the glue was merchantable, the defence fails, and the plaintiffs are entitled to judgment.

Judgment for plaintiffs.

OLRC Sales Report
pp. 218-19

Section 15.2 of the Ontario Sale of Goods Act provides that, if the buyer has examined the goods, the condition of merchantable quality does not apply as regards defects that "*such* examination ought to have revealed". This test has been criticized as being too favourable to the buyer. First, it is said, it encourages the buyer not to examine the goods. Secondly, even if he does examine the goods, the buyer is only deemed to have notice of defects that "such" (that is, his actual) examination ought to have revealed. On a literal reading of this proviso, the buyer is under no obligation to conduct a reasonably careful examination. It will be observed, however, that the test is not wholly subjective, since the buyer will be deemed to be aware of defects which his examination "ought to have revealed". A further criticism is that section 15.2 is not consistent with the buyer's position in the case of a sale by sample, dealt with in section 16(2)(c) of the existing Act, since, in this instance, the seller's warranty only extends to freedom from defects that would not be apparent on "reasonable examination of the sample". The test here is wholly objective.

As to the latter criticism, it is our view that the inconsistency between sections 15.2 and 16(2)(c) is more apparent than real, since the purpose of a sample is to enable the buyer to determine for himself the quality of the goods offered. The first criticism was examined by the English and Scottish Law Commissions. The Commissions concluded that it would not be desirable to return to the pre-1893 position, which deemed the buyer to have notice of any defects discoverable on examination whether or not he had examined the goods. We agree with this conclusion. We are somewhat more troubled by the criticism that the buyer who conducts a perfunctory examination of the goods may be better off than the diligent buyer, especially since the code has avoided this anomaly. On balance, however, we have decided to recommend no change. The problem does not appear to be of great practical importance, and we believe there is sufficient elasticity in the language of the provisio, coupled with the general requirement of good faith, to enable a court to avoid its unfair operation against either party. Accordingly, our Draft Bill provides that the implied warranty of merchantability does not apply, if the buyer examined the goods before the contract was made, "with respect to any defect that such an examination ought to have revealed".

The Law Commissions did not, however, consider the present statutory provision to be entirely satisfactory. The Commissions recommended extending the proviso in one direction by excluding the condition of merchantability with respect to defects in the goods specifically drawn by the seller to the buyer's attention. We support this change and recommend that a similar provision be incorporated in the revised Act.

3. THE IMPLIED CONDITION OF FITNESS

As will have been noted from the cases on merchantability, there is a good deal of overlap between the implied conditions of merchantability and fitness and frequently the two conditions may be successfully invoked in the same case. This conclusion would not be obvious from a literal reading of SGA s. 15.1, and at first sight its requirements would appear to impose formidable burdens on a buyer seeking to hold the seller liable for breach of the implied condition of fitness. As will be seen however from the cases that follow, recent judgments have so successfully eroded the requirements that s. 15.1 can no longer be regarded as an accurate reflection of the modern position.

a) The Scope of s. 15.1

HARDWICK GAME FARM v. SUFFOLK AGRICULTURAL AND POULTRY PRODUCERS ASSOCIATION
[1971] 2 AC 31, [1968] 2 All ER 444 (HL)

For the facts of this case, see *supra*, chapter 6(B)(2). The following extract deals with the general scope of the implied condition of fitness and its application to the facts at bar.

LORD PEARCE: The judge and the Court of Appeal held that the purpose of Grimsdale was "a particular purpose" within section 14(1). It was argued that such a purpose was too wide and had not enough particularity to constitute a particular purpose. I do not accept this contention. Almost every purpose is capable of some sub-division, some further and better particulars. But a particular purpose means a given purpose, known or communicated. It is not necessarily a narrow or closely particularised purpose (see *Benjamin on Sale* (1950), 8th ed., p. 630: "A particular purpose is not some purpose necessarily distinct from a general purpose"). A purpose may be put in wide terms or it may be circumscribed or narrowed. An example of the former is to be found in *Bartlett* v. *Sydney Marcus Ltd.* [1965] 1 WLR 1013, where the purpose was that of a car to drive on the road. See also *Baldry* v. *Marshall* [1925] 1 KB 260 ["a comfortable car suitable for touring purposes"]. A somewhat narrower purpose was to be found in *Bristol Tramways, etc., Carriage Co. Ltd.* v. *Fiat Motors Ltd.* [1910] 2 KB 831 ["an omnibus for heavy traffic in a hilly district"]. The less circumscribed the purpose, the less circumscribed will be, as a rule, the range of goods which are reasonably fit for such purpose. The purpose of a car to drive on the road will be satisfied by almost any car so long as it will function reasonably; but the narrower purpose of an omnibus suitable to the crowed streets of a city can only be achieved by a narrower range of vehicles. This, however, is a question of fact and degree. Lord Herschell said in *Drummond* v. *Van Ingen*, 12 App. Cas. 284, 293:

> Where the article may be used as one of the elements in a variety of other manufacturers, I think it may be too much to impute to the maker of this common article a knowledge of the details of every manufacture into which it may enter in combination with other materials.

In general it would be wrong to say, as was suggested in argument, that a wide purpose is unfair to the seller because it purports to require fitness for every conceivable subdivision of purpose within the main purpose.

I would expect a tribunal of fact to decide that a car sold in this country was reasonably fit for touring even though it was not well adapted for conditions in a heat wave; but not, if it could not cope adequately with rain. If, however, it developed some lethal or dangerous trick in very hot weather, I would expect it to be found unfit. In deciding the question of fact the rarity of the unsuitability would be weighed against the gravity of its consequences. Again, if food was merely unpalatable or useless on rare occasions, it might well be reasonably suitable for food. But I should certainly not expect it to be held reasonably suitable if even on very rare occasions it killed the consumer. The question for the tribunal of fact is simply "were these goods reasonably fit for the specified purpose?"

"To resell in smaller quantities to be compounded into food for cattle and poultry" was therefore, a particular purpose within section 14(1). If a particular purpose is made known, that is sufficient to raise the inference that the buyer relies on the seller's skill and judgment unless there is something to displace the inference. There is no need for a buyer formally to "make known" that which is already known. See *Manchester Liners Ltd.* v. *Rea Ltd.* [1922] 2 AC 74, 92; *Cammell Laird & Co.* v. *The Manganese Bronze & Brass Co.* [1934] AC 402; *Mash and Murrell Ltd.* v. *Joseph I. Emanuel Ltd.* [1961] 1 WLR 862, 867 (a sale from one merchant to another). The reliance need not be exclusive. Partial reliance will suffice.

The judge considered that the inference that the buyer relied on the seller's skill and judgment was displaced by the fact that Grimsdale and Kendall were members of the same Association, the London Cattle Food Traders Association. I do not, with respect, accept this view. The whole trend of authority has inclined towards an assumption of reliance wherever the seller knows the particular purpose. And where there are several subsales and the purpose is obvious, the liability is frequently passed up the line. To cut the chain of liability at one particular point is not fair unless there is some cogent reason for doing so. In the present case I see no ground for holding that Kendall were in any relevantly different position from Grimsdale. The fellow-membership of the C.T.F.A. was irrelevant. One member may rely on another member just as much as he relies on an outside trader. The fellow-membership may even increase his reliance.

Reliance is not excluded by the fact that the seller may not himself have seen the goods he sells. In *Bigge* v. *Parkinson* (1862) 7 H & N 955, 959 where it was implied that stores for troops in India must be fit for their purpose, Cockburn C.J. said:

> Where a person undertakes to supply provisions, and they are supplied in cases hermetically sealed, but turn out to be putrid, it is no answer to say that he has been deceived by the person from whom he got them.

The seller, not the buyer, is aware of the provenance of the goods and has chosen to acquire them for disposal. It would, therefore, be not unreasonable that the buyer should rely on the seller's "knowledge and trade wisdom" to use a phrase quoted in *Australian Knitting Mills Ltd.* v. *Grant*, 50 CLR 387, 446 by Evatt J. from *Ward* v. *Great Atlantic & Pacific Tea Co.* (1918) 231 Mass. 90, 93, 94. And Walton J. in *Preist* v. *Last* (1903) 89 LT 33, 35, refers to the buyer's reliance that the seller will not sell him "mere rubbish." This expression is echoed in the evidence in the present case where Mr. Brown of Lillico said that they relied on Kendall "not to sell what they knew was rubbish" (Appendix 2, p. 208).

It is argued that the width of the purpose should prevent one from inferring that there was reliance. I do not think so. The compounders of food for cattle and poultry need healthy ingredients, as the sellers knew. The parties were not considering what admixture of healthy groundnut meal would be good for particular animals or birds, but whether assuming a certain quantity of groundnut meal would be a fit ingredient, the goods delivered would be healthy or harmful groundnut meal. It was reasonable that the buyer should rely on the seller to deliver groundnut meal which would, as groundnut meal, be a healthy and not a harmful ingredient in a compound.

In my opinion, there was on the circumstances of this case sufficient to establish reliance by Grimsdale on Kendall and a resulting condition.

The condition did not mean that the food was fit, however strange or unsuitable the proportions of the compound might prove to be. It meant that the food was fit if compounded reasonably and competently according to current standards. Goods are not fit if they have hidden limitations requiring special precautions unknown to the buyer or seller. The groundnut meal delivered was plainly not fit for the purpose of reselling in small lots to compounders of food for cattle and poultry. It was highly toxic. It is beside the point that Kendalls were unaware of the proportions in which it was to be compounded. It was unfit for use in the normal range of proportions. The evidence shows that 10 per cent was included in the feeding stuff for pheasants. This was not abnormal. When the toxicity had been discovered and investigated the recommendation of a reputable working party was that not more than 5 per cent of meal with a high toxicity should be included even in cattle rations and none should be included in rations for birds. Moreover, while its toxicity was unknown, the meal was thereby far more harmful and dangerous. Even had the buyer known of its toxic qualities, it was not fit for compounding for poultry. For a compounder's business is to mix healthy foods in suitable compounds. It is quite unsuitable that he should get toxic meal which can be only used by inserting it in quantities so abnormally small that the dilution of other compounds removes its lethal effect. All the courts below have held rightly without any dissent that this meal was not reasonably fit for the purpose for which it was supplied by Kendall to Grimsdale.

ASHINGTON PIGGERIES LTD. v. CHRISTOPHER HILL LTD.;
CHRISTOPHER HILL LTD. v. NORSILDMEL
[Conjoined Appeals]
[1972] AC 441, [1971] 1 All ER 874 (HL)

For the facts of this case, see *supra*, chapter 6(B)(1). The following extract from Lord Wilberforce's judgment deals with the application of SGA s. 14(1) [Ont. s. 15.1] to the facts at bar.

LORD WILBERFORCE:

2. *Section 14(1) of the Act*: I do not think it is disputed, or in any case disputable, that a particular purpose was made known by the buyers so as to show that they relied on the sellers' skill and judgment. The particular purpose for which "King Size" was required was as food for mink.

Equally I think it is clear (as both courts have found) that there was reliance on the respondents' skill and judgment. Although the Act makes no references to partial reliance, it was settled, well before the *Cammell Laird* case [1934] AC 402 was decided in this House, that there may be cases where the buyer relies on his own skill or judgment for some purposes and on that of the seller for others. This House gave to that principle emphatic endorsement.

The present is certainly such a case. In the words of Milmo J. [1968] 1 Lloyd's Rep. 457, 480:

> On the one hand Mr. Udall was relying on his own judgment as to what his formula should contain and the levels at which the various ingredients in it should be included. On the other, he was relying, and had no alternative but to rely, upon the [respondents] to obtain the ingredients, to see they were of good quality and not to use ingredients which, as a result of contamination, were toxic.

The word "toxic" will require some examination but, subject to this, I consider that this passage correctly states the position as regards reliance.

The field thus left to the sellers can be described in terms of their responsibility as merchants, to obtain and deliver ingredients, and relevantly herring meal, not unfit by reason of contamination, to be fed to animals, including mink. The field reserved to the buyers, on the other hand, was that of particular or specific suitability for mink. There was no doubt that herring meal, as such, was suitable for mink; on the other hand, the particular consignments supplied in 1961 were unsuitable because of the presence of DMNA. What, then, was the nature of this unsuitability?

If mink possessed an idiosyncrasy, which made the food as supplied unsuitable for them though it was perfectly suitable for other animals, this would be the buyers' responsibility, unless, as is not the case here, they had made this idiosyncrasy known to the sellers so as to show reliance on them to provide for it. But any general unsuitability would be the sellers' responsibility. Although the evidence was not very complete, it is sufficiently shown, in my opinion, that mink are more sensitive to DMNA than most other animals to whom compound foods would be sold. Chicken and pigs are among the least sensitive, next cattle and then sheep, with mink at the top of the scale. So the question arises, what does the buyer, alleging unfitness, have to prove? If the fact were that the herring meal supplied, while damaging to mink, was perfectly harmless to all other animals to whom it might be fed, it would be unjust to hold the sellers liable. If, on the other hand, the herring meal was not only lethal to mink but also deleterious, though not lethal, to other animals, the sellers' responsibility could be fairly engaged. A man can hardly claim that the product he sells is suitable, especially if that is a foodstuff, merely because it fails to kill more than one species to which it is fed.

In this case, because of the difficulty of tracing the lethal element, the evidence as to its presence, its strength and its effect was not scientifically complete. It was not until 1964 the DMNA was identified. By that time all the infected herring meal had been disposed of, and all other animals to which it had been fed had died. The critical question in this part of the appeal is whether the buyers proved enough to show that their mink died because of some general, that is, non-specific, unsuitability of the herring meal through contamination. The burden was upon the buyers to show that this was so.

• • •

In my opinion, the appellants made good their case: they proved the cause of their losses to lie in the inclusion of a generally (viz. non-specific as regards mink) toxic ingredient in the food. It was not for them to show that this same food killed, or poisoned, other species. So to require would place far too high a burden on a buyer. The buyer may have no means of ascertaining what the effect on other species may be. The whole of the contaminated consignment may have been fed to the buyer's animals: is the buyer to fail because he cannot show that this particular consignment killed, or at least injured, other animals? He must, I think, carry his proof to the point of showing that the guilty ingredient has some generally (as opposed to specifically) toxic quality. But once he has done this, has he not shown, at least with strong prima facie force, that a feeding stuff which contained it was unsuitable? Is he not entitled to throw on to the seller the burden of showing, if he can, that the damage to the buyer's animals was due to some factor within the field of responsibility reserved to the buyer? I would answer yes to these questions. In the end, it is for the judge to decide whether, on the evidence, the buyers have proved their case. Milmo J.'s conclusions are expressed in three passages, one in the main action, the others in the third party proceedings (the whole case was heard together):

> Herring meal does not normally contain a poison. The herring meal which killed the English mink contained DMNA which is a poison, and it contained it at a level sufficiently high to be lethal to mink, which are animals to which herring meal can properly be fed. All animals are sensitive to DMNA poisoning, though mink are more sensitive than most. ([1968] 1 Lloyd's Rep. 457, 481.)

> I find that the meal which poisoned the English mink was not reasonably fit for use as an ingredient in animal foodstuffs because of the fact that it contained in substantial and significant quantities DMNA which is a toxic substance to which all animals are sensitive. (p. 487.)

> While I accept that there was no evidence that the meal *had a deleterious effect* upon any animal or other type of livestock other than mink, I do not consider that it was proved affirmatively that the meal which killed the mink *could have been fed with impunity* to all other types of livestock. (p. 486 — emphasis supplied.)

This is precisely the position: coupled with the general finding as to toxicity (something to which all animals are sensitive, i.e., liable to suffer liver damage) it amounts to a rejection of the only line of defence open to the respondents — namely, that the relevant consignment was fit to be fed to all normal animals and only unfit to be fed to mink.

In my opinion, these findings were justified and correct.

So much for the facts, but there remains one legal argument on this part of the case. Section 14(1) contains the words "and the goods are of a description which it is in the course of the seller's business to supply." The respondents relied on these words and persuaded the Court of Appeal to decide that the requirement was not satisfied because, briefly, the respondents were not dealers in mink food. A similar argument was put forward on the words in section 14(2) "where goods are bought by description from a seller who deals in goods of that description." The Court of Appeal decided this point too, in the respondents' favour. The respondents, they held, did not deal in mink food, or "King Size," before Mr. Udall placed with them the orders which produced the defective goods. I have some doubt whether this argument is even correct on the facts, because Mr. Udall had been ordering "King Size" for several months before he ordered the fatal consignment. But we must deal with the legal argument because it is clearly of general importance. It appears never previously to have been accepted and it substantially narrows the scope of both subsections. It rests, in the first place, upon a linguistic comparison of the meaning of the word "description" in the three places where it appears and on the argument that it must mean the same in each place.

I do not accept that, taken in its most linguistic strictness, either subsection bears the meaning contended for. I would hold that (as to subsection (1)) it is in the course of the seller's business to supply goods if he agrees, either generally, or in a particular case, to supply the goods when ordered, and (as to subsection (2)) that a seller deals in goods of that description if his business is such that he is willing to accept orders for them. I cannot comprehend the rationale of holding that the subsections do not apply if the seller is dealing in the particular goods for the first time or the sense of distinguishing between the first and the second order for the goods or for goods of the description. The Court of Appeal offered the analogy of a doctor sending a novel prescription to a pharmacist, which turns out to be deleterious. But as often happens to arguments of this kind, the analogy is faulty: if the prescription is wrong, of course the doctor is responsible. The fitness of the prescription is within his field of responsibility. The relevant question is whether the pharmacist is responsible for the purity of his ingredients and one does not see why not.

But, moreover, consideration of the preceding common law shows that what the Act had in mind was something quite simple and rational: to limit the implied conditions of fitness or quality to persons in the way of business, as distinct from private persons. Whether this should be the law was a problem which had emerged, and been resolved, well before 1893. The first indication of the point arose in *Jones* v. *Bright* (1829) 15 Bing. 533 (copper sheathing). Two of the judges regarded it as an essential allegation that the defendant should have been the manufacturer of the defective copper. Park J. in fact, at p. 546, used the words "distinguishing, as I do, between the manufacturer of an article and the mere seller." In *Brown* v. *Edgington* (1841) 2 Man. & G. 279, 291 (the crane rope) we find a description of the defendant by Bosanquet J. as "a dealer in articles of that description," clearly a reason for holding him liable though he was not the manufacturer. The distinction between the dealer and the private seller is clearly brought out in *Burnaby* v. *Bollet* (1847) 16 M & W 644, where a man bought a carcase in the market but later sold it to another farmer. His exemption from liability for defects in the carcase was explicitly based on his private character; he was "not clothed with any character of general dealer in provisions" (p. 649), he was "not dealing in the way of a common trade" (p. 655). And finally in the forerunner case of *Jones* v. *Just* (1868) LR 3 QB 197 we find Mellor J. in his fourth and fifth categories, which anticipate respectively section 14(1) and 14(2) of the Sale of Goods Act 1893, referring to a manufacturer or dealer contracting to supply an article which he manufactures or produces, or in which he deals, and to a manufacturer undertaking to supply foods manufactured by himself or in which he deals, so clearly following and adopting the prior accepted division between sales by way of trade and private sales.

One asks, therefore, what difference the insertion in the Sale of Goods Act of the word "description" made to these well-accepted rules. It seems at least clear that the words now appearing in section 14(1) "and the goods are of a description which it is the seller's business to supply" cannot mean more than "the goods are of a kind...." "Description" here cannot be used in the sense in which the word is used when the Act speaks of "sales by description," for section 14(1) is not dealing with sales by description at all. If this is so, I find no obstacle against reading "goods of that description" in a similar way in section 14(2). In both cases the word means "goods of that kind" and nothing more. Moreover, even if this is wrong, and "description" is to be understood in a technical sense, I would have no difficulty in holding that a seller deals in goods "of that description" if he accepts orders to supply them in the way of business; and this whether or not he has previously accepted orders for goods of that description.

So, all other elements being present as I have tried to show, I would hold that section 14(1) applies to the present case. I would agree with the judge that section 14(2) equally applies and disagree with the reasons (based on the "description" argument) which led the Court of Appeal to a contrary opinion.

That the goods were unmerchantable was conceded in both courts — in my opinion, rightly so. Goods may quite well be unmerchantable even if "purpose built." Lord Wright made this quite clear in the *Cammell Laird* case [1934] AC 402; so equally with "King Size" mink food.

I would therefore allow the appeal.

The appeal of Christopher Hill Ltd. (the respondents) against Norsildmel ("the third parties") raises different, and, in one respect at least, more difficult issues. The goods supplied were in this case Norwegian herring meal and they were supplied under the terms of a commodity market contract in writing. A number of points arise under it. On the following I express my concurrence with others of your Lordships, and do not think it necessary to add reasons of my own.

1. The respondents were not in breach of a term in the contract implied by virtue of section 13 of the Sale of Goods Act 1893. The goods supplied were, in my opinion, Norwegian herring meal. The words "fair average quality of the season" were not in this contract part of the description. I do not find it necessary to consider whether, if they were, there was a breach of any implied condition that the goods should correspond with this description. They were not relied upon as themselves importing a warranty; but, if the contention is open, I am in agreement with my noble and learned friend, Lord Diplock, for the reasons which he gives, that they do not cover the particular defect which existed.

2. The exemption clause contained in general condition 3 does not exclude a claim for breach of any warranty implied under section 14(1) of the Act.

This leaves the substantial question whether a term as to reasonable fitness ought to be implied under section 14(1) of the Act. There was also raised a question as to remoteness of damage but, in the view which I take, this depends on the same considerations as those necessary for determination of liability under section 14(1). I now consider this question.

In so doing I should make it clear that, although I refer to Norsildmel as the third parties, the actual contract for sale was made with a committee called Sildemelutvalget to whom Norsildmel succeeded in 1964, but no distinction has been made between these organisations. What is necessary to determine is whether any particular purpose for which the goods were required was made known by the buyers to the sellers so as to show that the buyers relied on the sellers' skill and judgment: what the particular purpose was: finally, whether the particular purpose included feeding to mink. The particular purpose relied upon by the respondents was that the meal was required for inclusion in animal feeding stuffs to be compounded by them. They do not contend that feeding to mink was explicitly stated as a purpose; but they say that feeding to mink was known to both parties as a normal user for herring meal, and that it was sold without any reservation or restriction as to the use to which it might be put. The sale was negotiated through an agent in England — C.T. Bowring & Co. Ltd. on behalf of Sildmelutvalget, but no point has been taken as to any limitation upon their knowledge as compared with that of their principals.

The scope and application of section 14(1) of the Sale of Goods Act 1893 was fully considered by this House in *Hardwick Game Farm* v. *Suffolk Agricultural Poultry Producers Association Ltd.* [1969] 2 AC 31. The opinion expressed in that case endorsed a tendency which other cases (such as *Manchester Liners Ltd.* v. *Rea Ltd.* [1922] 2 AC 74) had shown, to expand the scope of section 14(1) so as to cover territory which might otherwise, on a first reading, have been thought to belong to section 14(2). I think that this tendency essentially reflects a reversion to the more general approach to questions of the seller's liability under implied warranty adopted by the common law, as contrasted with the compartmentalisation into separate, but inevitably overlapping, provisions adopted by the Sale of Goods Act. *Naturam expellas furca* is a maxim which tends to apply to codifications. At any rate it is clear that this House in the *Hardwick* case [1969] 2 AC 31 accepted that the "making known" so as to show reliance which the section requires is easily deduced from the nature and circumstances of the sale, and that the word "particular" means little more than "stated" or "defined." As Lord Pearce said in *Hardwick*, at p. 115: "There is no need for a buyer formally to 'make known' that which is already known": and here there is no doubt that the third parties, through their selling agents C.T. Bowring & Co. Ltd., and also directly, knew what the herring meal was required for, namely, for inclusion in animal feeding stuffs to be compounded by the buyers, and no special purpose in relation to mink was relied on. The third parties were, moreover, a committee, or co-operative, of manufacturers of herring meal: in this case, whether one speaks of implication or presumption, the conclusion can hardly be otherwise than that of reliance by the buyers to produce a product reasonably fit for the purpose. I observe, indeed, that my noble and learned friend, Lord Guest, who felt difficulty in *Hardwick* as to the application of section 14(1) against persons who were dealers in the market, said that he could well understand, where the sale is by a manufacturer to a customer, that the inference (sc. of reliance) can easily be drawn (p. 106). I agree with Milmo J. that it ought to be drawn in this case.

Then was the purpose, to be used for inclusion in animal feeding stuffs to be compounded by the buyers, a particular purpose? In my opinion, certainly yes. It is true that the purpose was wide, wider even than the purpose accepted as particular in *Hardwick* (for compounding into food for cattle and poultry), and, if one leaves aside a possible alternative use as fertiliser, on which there was some indefinite evidence, the purpose so made known covers a large part of the area which would be within section 14(2). But I do not think, as the law has developed, that this can be regarded as an objection or that in accepting a purpose so defined, as a "particular purpose," the court is crossing any forbidden line. There remains a distinction between a statement (express or implied) of a particular purpose, though a wide one, with the implied condition (or warranty) which this attracts, and a purchase by description with no purpose stated and the different condition (or warranty) which that attracts. Moreover, width of the purpose is compensated, from the seller's point of view, by the dilution of his responsibility: and to hold him liable under an implied warranty of fitness for the purpose of which he has been made aware, wide though this may be, appears as fair as to leave him exposed to the vaguer and less defined standard of merchantability. After all, the seller's liability is, if I may borrow the expression of my noble and learned friend, Lord Morris of Borth-y-Gest, no more than to meet the requirement of a buyer who is saying to him "that is what I want it for, but I only want to buy if you sell me something that will do." I think that well expresses the situation here.

[Lord Wilberforce went on to find that feeding to mink was a normal user in 1961 and known as such to the third party, that the respondents were entitled to rely on the third party to supply herring meal suitable for their purposes, and that the consignment was in fact unsuitable so that a breach of the implied condition under s. 14(1) had been proved].

Appeals allowed.

Notes:

1   Lord Hodson, Lord Guest, Viscount Dilhorne and Lord Diplock concurred with Lord Wilberforce on the interpretation of s. 14(1) and its application to the contracts between the appellants and the respondents and between the respondents and the third party. With respect to the phrase in s. 14(1), "goods are of a description which it is . . . the seller's business to supply", Lord Hodson and Viscount Dilhorne found that the respondents' business was to make compounds for animal feeding. In producing the mink food they were only using raw materials which it was in the course of their business to supply. Lords Guest and Diplock agreed with Lord Wilberforce that "description" was not here used in the same sense as in "sale by description", but rather in a wider sense to mean goods "of that kind". Lord Guest further agreed with Lord Wilberforce that it was in the course of a seller's business to supply goods if he agreed, either generally or in a specific case, to supply them in the way of business, regardless of whether he had entered into a similar agreement before.

2   Lord Diplock, in a long and thoughtful judgment, dissented from the majority both on the proper interpretation of s. 14(1) and its relationship to s. 14(2) and on whether there had been sufficient disclosure by the respondents to the third party of the intended purpose of the herring meal so as to trigger the operation of s. 14(1). The following extracts illustrate Lord Diplock's position:

a)   *The interpretation of s. 14(1) and its relationship to s. 14(2)* (*ibid.,* 506-07):

   The key to both subsections is reliance — the reasonable reliance of the buyer upon the seller's ability to make or select goods which are reasonably fit for the buyer's purpose coupled with the seller's acceptance of responsibility to do so. The seller has a choice whether or not to accept that responsibility. To enable him to exercise it he must be supplied by the buyer with sufficient information to acquaint him with what he is being relied upon to do and to enable him to appreciate what exercise of skill or judgment is called for in order to make or select goods which will be fit for the purpose for which the buyer requires them.

This consideration, in my view, throws light upon two matters arising under section 14. The first is the meaning of "particular purpose" in subsection (1). The second is the application of the doctrine of "partial reliance" under both subsection (1) and subsection (2).

To attract the condition to be implied by subsection (1) the buyer must make known the purpose for which he requires the goods with sufficient particularity to enable a reasonable seller, engaged in the business of supplying goods of the kind ordered, to identify the characteristics which the goods need to possess to fit them for that purpose. If all that the buyer does make known to the seller is a range of purposes which do not all call for goods possessing identical characteristics and he does not identify the particular purpose or purposes within that range for which he in fact requires the goods, he does not give the seller sufficient information to enable him to make or to select goods possessing a characteristic which is needed to make them fit for any one of those purposes in particular, if the same characteristic either is not needed to make them fit, or makes them unfit, for other purposes within the range.

A "range of purposes" case thus poses a stark question of legal policy as to whether the seller's responsibility ought to be to supply goods which are fit for at least one of the purposes within the range or to supply goods which are fit for all of those purposes unless he expressly disclaims responsibility for their fitness for any one or more of them. The answer to this question of policy has, in my view, been pre-empted by subsection (2) of section 14 of the Sale of Goods Act 1893.

The commonest way in which a buyer makes known to the seller a range of purposes for which the goods are required is by the description by which he buys them and by nothing more. This is the case that is contemplated by subsection (2). This, as it has been authoritatively construed by the courts, provides that the only condition to be implied as to the responsibility of the seller is that the goods should be reasonably fit for one of the purposes within the range.

To supplement the description by which the goods are bought, or to replace it if they are not bought by description, the buyer may identify with greater precision the purpose for which the goods are required, by making it known to the seller in some other way. This is the case contemplated by subsection (1). He may do this expressly or by implication. At any rate, if he does so expressly he can make it known to the seller that he relies upon the seller to supply goods that are fit for more than one purpose or, indeed, for all possible purposes which lie within a range. But the mere fact that the seller knows that the buyer is engaged in a business in which goods of the description by which they are bought *may* be needed for any one of a number of purposes within the range of those for which goods of that description are normally used, adds nothing to what he might reasonably infer from the fact that the buyer ordered the goods by a description which covers goods fit for a range of purposes, without particularising which of those purposes he requires goods for. It might be otherwise if the seller knew that the buyer was engaged in a business in which goods of the description by which they were bought were needed for one or more only of the purposes within the whole range.

It would, in my view, conflict with the principle of reliance which underlies section 14(1) and (2) and would be a misuse of a statutory code of this kind, to treat a range of purposes for any one of which the buyer *may* require the goods, on the one hand, as constituting "the particular purpose for which the goods are required" and so giving rise to an implied condition under subsection (1) that they shall be reasonably fit for all purposes within the range, if the seller's knowledge of the *range* is derived in whole or in part from some circumstance other than the description by which the goods are ordered; and, on the other hand, as giving rise to an implied condition under subsection (2) that the goods need only be fit for one of the purposes within the range, if the seller's knowledge of the *range* is derived solely from the description by which the goods are ordered. So to construe the code would for practical purposes deprive subsection (2) of any effect.

b) *Adequacy of disclosure of purpose to third party* (*ibid., 512*):

> I turn next to section 14(1) upon which Hill also relies. The most that Hill made known to the Norwegians about the purposes for which the herring meal was required was what I have previously termed a "range of purposes." The extent of that range was limited to what their agent in London had learnt from Hill in the course of previous dealings as to the nature of Hill's business. The range so made known included use as an ingredient in feeding-stuffs for many kinds of domestic animals and poultry. What it did not include was use as an ingredient in feeding-stuffs for mink. This seems to me to be conclusive that even if the Norwegians knew that Norwegian herring meal was a commodity which might be used as an ingredient in the diet of mink, use for that purpose can neither be nor form any part of the particular purpose for which the goods were required which was *made known by the buyer to the seller*, so as to give rise to the implied condition under section 14(1) that they should be reasonably fit for feeding mink.
>
> My Lords, it will already be apparent that, for the reasons which I have already advanced in discussing "range of purposes," the decision of this House in *Hardwick Game Farm* v. *Suffolk Agricultural Poultry Producers Association* [1969] 2 AC 31 that the fourth parties were liable to the third parties for breach of the condition implied under section 14(1) in my view goes to the utmost limit of what can be held to be a "particular purpose" within the meaning of that section without amending the Act itself. However desirable it may be to make such an amendment, to do so lies beyond the competence of this House of Parliament acting alone — even in its judicial capacity. I myself would distinguish that part of the decision in the *Hardwick Game Farm* case whenever I can. I do not think that it is open to your Lordships to extend it.

3   In the light of the broad scope given by the majority of the law lords in the *Hardwick Game Farm* and *Ashington Piggeries* cases to the implied condition of fitness, and the ready implication of reliance on the seller's skill and knowledge even in dealings between merchants, what significant differences remain between the condition of merchantability and the condition of fitness? Was Lord Diplock (in *Ashington Piggeries*) right in complaining that the scales had been tipped too generously in the buyer's favour? To what extent were the law lords in both cases influenced by the lethal nature of the defect in the goods? Would it be better to treat the cases as examples of the American inspired movement to hold manufacturers, producers and distributors strictly liable in tort for the supply of defective goods causing injury to person or other property? (On this aspect of the modern law of sales see further *infra*, chapter 7.)

4   In the light of the ready implication of reliance, the English and Scottish Law Commissions recommended modifying s. 14(1) of the U.K. Act to give effect to the

judicial interpretation. The recommendation was adopted in the Supply of Goods (Implied Terms) Act 1973. Section 14(3) of the U.K. Sale of Goods Act 1979 now reads as follows:

> (3) Where the seller sells goods in the course of a business and the buyer, expressly or by implication, makes known —
>
> (*a*)   to the seller, or
>
> (*b*)   where the purchase price or part of it is payable by instalments and the goods were previously sold by a credit-broker to the seller, to that credit-broker,
>
> any particular purpose for which the goods are being bought, there is an implied condition that the goods supplied under the contract are reasonably fit for that purpose, whether or not that is a purpose for which such goods are commonly supplied, except where the circumstances show that the buyer does not rely, or that it is unreasonable for him to rely, on the skill or judgment of the seller or credit-broker.

Does s. 14(3) put to rest the proper meaning of "any particular purpose"? The OLRC Sales Report (p. 221) supported the British changes, with the exception of the reference in the opening line of s. 14(3) to a sale by the seller "in the course of a business". On this point the Commission explained its position as follows (*ibid.*):

> The exception to which we refer relates to the opening line of section 14(3) of the U.K. Act, which makes the implied warranty of fitness applicable to all sales by a seller "in the course of a business". Here, consistently with the position adopted by us with respect to the condition of merchantable quality, we recommend that the new warranty of fitness continue to be restricted to sales by a seller who deals in goods of the kind supplied under the contract of sale. We realize that, where the seller does not deal in goods of the kind supplied under the contract, there will be no warranty of fitness. This should not, however, preclude a buyer from being able to show that, even though the seller was not a merchant with respect to the goods sold to the buyer, there was communicated reliance on his skill and judgment, and that the seller had expressly warranted the fitness of the goods for the indicated purpose. In such circumstances, we think it better that the burden should rest on the buyer to make out such a case; the seller should not have to show, as apparently he would have to show under the U.K. amendment, that the buyer did not rely, or that it was unreasonable for him to rely, on the seller's skill and judgment.

b)   Allergies

INGHAM v. EMES
[1955] 2 All ER 740, [1955] 2 QB 366 (CA)

DENNING, L.J.: Mrs. Ingham, the second plaintiff, is the wife of the licensee of the Sun Hotel, Dunsfold. In March, 1954, she had her hair dyed by a ladies' hairdresser called Maison Emes in Godalming. The preparation which was used was called Inecto Rapid. As a result of it she suffered acute dermatitis and she brings this action against the hairdresser for damages.

The story starts, however, seven years before, in 1947, when the second plaintiff was attending another hairdresser. She then had her hair dyed with Inecto and after about two days her eyes became puffy. She consulted a doctor and he suspected that it might be the Inecto which caused the trouble. After that experience she did not have Inecto for a long time because she knew it might have a bad effect on her. In September, 1951, she started going to Maison Emes in Godalming where she was attended by an assistant named Mrs. Hughes. Thenceforward for two and a half years the second plaintiff regularly had her hair tinted by Mrs. Hughes with henna and they were on excellent terms with one another. During one of these visits the second plaintiff may well have told Mrs. Hughes about her previous Inecto experience, but rather in a gossipy manner, not in such a way as to make any impression on Mrs. Hughes' mind. In March, 1954, the second plaintiff had a coming engagement, when she was going with her husband to see the brewers and she wanted to look her best. She was getting tired of the henna shampoos, as they needed to be done so often and were expensive. Thereupon, the assistant, Mrs. Hughes, suggested that the second plaintiff should try Inecto, and went on to say that, if she tried Inecto, she must have a test first, because it was dangerous. There was a conflict between the two ladies whether the second plaintiff on that occasion reminded Mrs. Hughes of her previous experience with Inecto. The second plaintiff says that she reminded Mrs. Hughes of it. Mrs. Hughes says that she did not. The judge found that Mrs. Hughes was right about this, because he did not think that Mrs. Hughes would have been so rash as to go on with Inecto if she had known of previous trouble. On Mar. 9, 1954, the second plaintiff went to have the test to see if she was likely to be harmed by Inecto. Mrs. Hughes opened a package of Inecto and put the instructions on the table. The second plaintiff read them. The instructions said:

> The manufacturers . . . draw attention below to a simple and easy test, which in the opinion of eminent skin specialists will disclose any predisposition to skin trouble from the use of the dye. The test must, as a matter of routine, be employed on each occasion prior to using the dye, regardless of the fact that it has been used with success on the same person on a previous occasion.

Then follows in large letters "It may be dangerous to use Inecto Rapid without this test". The test is then described of applying a little Inecto behind the ear, painting a film of collodion over it and leaving it for forty-eight hours. The instructions then say:

> If no irritation has been experienced and there is no redness or inflammation then the skin is free from predisposition and the colouring may be used.

On Mar. 9 Mrs. Hughes applied the test in exact accordance with the instructions. On Mar. 11 the second plaintiff returned. Mrs. Hughes examined the patch and said her skin was perfectly clear. She told the second plaintiff that she was not a reactor and that she was a safe person to have Inecto. The second plaintiff thereupon made an appointment to have her hair dyed with Inecto on Mar. 16. It was done on that day, and within a few days the second plaintiff was suffering from acute dermatitis. There is no doubt that it was due to the Inecto.

It appears from the evidence that the test is not infallible. Dr. Hassan, the expert called by the defendant, described Inecto as "an extremely dangerous substance". In very rare cases, even when the test is negative, the subject herself may be sensitive to it. For instance, she may be negative when the test is done, but sensitive a few days later when the dye is applied. Or she may not react to the small test but may react to the full dose. The judge came to the conclusion that the second plaintiff was "of the rare type to whom the ordinary test will not apply but who is allergic to a large dose", and he found that there was "no fault of either party". He dismissed the claim, therefore, founded on negligence, but he found in favour of the second plaintiff on the ground of breach of warranty. He found that there was a warranty by the hairdresser that the Inecto was suitable for this particular person, the second plaintiff, and that the defendant was liable when it turned out not to be suitable. If the second plaintiff had not had any previous trouble with Inecto, then I think the judge would have been right. She was apparently a perfectly normal person, and Mrs. Hughes said, or as good as said, to her: "If you pass the test you may safely have Inecto". There would be, I think, in those circumstances, an implied term that Inecto was reasonably fit for the purpose of dyeing the hair of this particular person, the second plaintiff, if she passed the test. But the second plaintiff to her own knowledge was not in this regard a perfectly normal person. She had experienced Inecto before and she knew that it might have a bad effect on her. In the modern phrase she knew that she was allergic to it. She ought clearly to have made that known to Mrs. Hughes; and she knew that she ought to have done so. That is shown by the fact that she herself insisted at the trial that she had told Mrs. Hughes about it on the very day that Inecto was suggested; but, unfortunately for her, the judge did not accept her evidence on this point. If she had made it known, Mrs. Hughes would never have gone on with the Inecto. It is rather like the case which I put in the course of the argument: if a doctor suggests penicillin, and the patient knows by experience that he is allergic to penicillin, he ought to tell the doctor so. I appreciate that cases of medical treatment are very different from the present, but there is in each case a duty to use reasonable care to disclose known peculiarities. The second plaintiff ought to have brought home to Mrs. Hughes that she was allergic to Inecto.

The difficulty that I have felt is that this looks to me like a plea of contributory negligence, or a plea that the second plaintiff was the author of her own misfortune; and that has never been pleaded or found. But I think the same result is reached by saying that the implied term as to fitness is dependent on proper disclosure by the customer of any relevant peculiarities known to her, and in particular of the fact that she knew by experience that Inecto might have a bad effect on her. The way this result is reached in law is this: in a contract for work and materials (such as the present), there is an implied term that the materials are reasonably fit for the purpose for which they are required: see *G.H. Myers & Co.* v. *Brent Cross Service Co.* [1934] 1 KB 46. This term is analogous to the corresponding term in the sale of goods: see *Stewart v. Reavell's Garage* [1952] 1 All ER 1191. In order for the implied term to arise, however, the customer must make known to the contractor expressly or by implication the "particular purpose" for which the materials are required, so as to show that he relies on the contractor's skill or judgment. The particular purpose in this case was to dye the hair, not of a normal person, but of a person known to be allergic to Inecto. The second plaintiff did not make that particular purpose known to Mrs. Hughes. She cannot therefore recover on the implied term.

I ought perhaps to say that I do not think this case is governed by the Harris tweed case, *Griffiths* v. *Peter Conway, Ltd.* [1939] 1 All ER 685. In that case a lady suffered from dermatitis owing to wearing a Harris tweed coat, which was specially made for her, and she failed to recover. Harris tweed is not a dangerous thing and it is reasonably fit for any normal person, test or no test: whereas Inecto is a dangerous thing which is not reasonably fit for anyone unless she passes a test. The manufacturers in their instructions represent in effect that, if a person passes the test, Inecto is safe. The hairdresser passed on that representation to her customer on her own account. That brings an implied term into operation in favour of all persons who pass the test except those, such as the second plaintiff, who know that they are allergic and do not disclose it. I would therefore allow the appeal and give judgment for the defendant.

Appeal allowed.

[Birkett and Romer L.JJ. delivered concurring judgments.]

Notes:

1　See also *Griffiths* v. *Peter Conway, Ltd.* [1939] 1 All ER 685 (CA); *Mayne* v. *Silvermere Cleaners Ltd.* [1939] 1 All ER 693, and cf. Note, (1961) 46 Corn. LQ 465.

2　For the American position, see C.C.H., *Products Liability Reporter,* Vol. 1, para. 3100. The following extract from this publication (at p. 3077) gives a brief overview of American developments in this area:

> Injuries traceable to allergy and unusual susceptibility on the part of users of cosmetics and similar products are ordinarily not compensable. The reason advanced for the rule is that the manufacturer or seller is entitled to assume that a cosmetics product will be put to a normal use by a normal buyer and that a reasonable manufacturer or seller is not expected to foresee an allergy and to anticipate harmful consequence therefrom. However, the trend of the recent decisions has been that allergy is not a defense where a particular product has a tendency to affect injuriously an appreciable number of persons, although they cannot be designated as within the class of so-called normal persons. Therefore, where a manufacturer knows or has reason to believe that a substantial number of persons will develop an allergy or sensitivity to his product, he is obligated to warn of the possibility of harm.
>
> There is support for the view that where a cosmetics manufacturer makes claims amounting to assurances of safety and gentleness in advertisements or through labels on its products, the manufacturer cannot avoid liability on the ground that the injured user had an allergy or a peculiar sensitivity to the product. This view seems to have support in only those cases alleging breach of express warranty.

3　The rule that the implied condition of fitness only applies to a normal user of the goods (unless of course he has disclosed his particular condition at the time of purchase) also applies to the *manner* in which the goods are used. Thus it has been held that a buyer of infected pork chops cannot complain if proper cooking would have eliminated the problem and he (or she) failed to follow the normal procedure. See *Yachetti* v. *John Duff & Sons Ltd.* [1943] 1 DLR 194, foll'd in *Heil* v. *Hedges* [1951] 1 TLR 512. In cases of this nature is it open to the court to apportion liability between the buyer and seller on a basis analogous to contributory negligence? See the discussion of *Lambert* v. *Lewis* [1980] 2 WLR 299 (CA), *infra*, chapter 12(B)(5).

c) Patent or Trade Name Exception

BALDRY v. MARSHALL
[1925] 1 KB 260, [1924] All ER Rep. 155 (CA)

BANKES L.J.: This is an appeal from a judgment of Greer J., and upon the facts as found by the learned judge his conclusion was in my opinion quite right. It appears that the plaintiff wrote to the defendants, "Can you tell me if the Bugatti eight cylinder is likely to be on the market this year, if so will you send particulars?" indicating that according to his impression this was a new type of car that was going to be put on the market. In their reply the defendants said: "As no doubt you are already aware, we specialize in the sale of these cars, and are in a position to supply you with all information necessary," thereby intimating that the plaintiff might regard them as persons upon whose skill and judgment he could safely rely. Those letters were followed by an interview at which the plaintiff made plain to the defendants the purpose for which he required the car. Then came the contract, which was on a printed form. It was in the form of a request by the plaintiff to the defendants to supply him with "one eight cylinder Bugatti car fully equipped and finished to standard specification as per the car inspected." On the back of the contract there was printed "The company reserves the right to withdraw any model or alter specifications or prices without notice. Illustrations and specifications must be taken as a general guide and not as binding in detail," and under the heading "Guarantee" the words, "The same as received by us from the manufacturers." The guarantee which they had so received from the manufacturers was expressed to be "against any breakage of parts due to faulty material," and contained the following clause: "Cars are sold on condition that the foregoing guarantee is accepted instead of and expressly excludes any other guarantee or warranty, statutory or otherwise." It is said that by the use of that language the defendants meant to exclude conditions as well as warranties; but they have not done so, and if there is one thing more clearly established than another it is the distinction which the law recognizes between a condition and a warranty. In *Wallis* v. *Pratt* [1911] AC 394 the sellers by a clause stating that "Sellers give no warranty express or implied" endeavoured to exclude the condition implied under s. 13 of the Sale of Goods Act, that the goods sold should correspond with the description, but the House of Lords held that they had not used apt words to effect that purpose. So here the defendants have not used the necessary language to exclude the implied condition which arises under s. 14 as to fitness for the particular purpose of which the plaintiff had given them notice. But then it is said that even if the implication of that condition is not excluded by the terms of the contract it is excluded by the proviso to sub-s. 1 on the ground that the car was sold under its trade name. It is however clear to my mind upon the evidence that it was not in fact sold under a trade name within the meaning of the proviso. The mere fact that an article sold is described in the contract by its trade name does not necessarily make the sale a sale under a trade name. Whether it is so or not depends upon the circumstances. I may illustrate my meaning by reference to three different cases. First, where a buyer asks a seller for an article which will fulfil some particular purpose, and in answer to that request the seller sells him an article by a well-known trade name, there I think it is clear that the proviso does not apply. Secondly, where the buyer says to the seller, "I have been recommended such and such an article" — mentioning it by its trade name — "will it suit my particular purpose?" naming the purpose, and thereupon the seller sells it without more, there again I think the proviso has no application. But there is a third case where the buyer says to a seller, "I have been recommended so and so" — giving its trade name — "as suitable for the particular purpose for which I want it. Please sell it to me." In that case I think it is equally clear that the proviso would apply and that the implied condition of the thing's fitness for the purpose named would not arise. In my opinion the test of an article having been sold under its trade name within the meaning of the proviso is: Did the buyer specify it under its trade name in such a way as to indicate that he is satisfied, rightly or wrongly, that it will answer his purpose, and that he is not relying on the skill or judgment of the seller, however great that skill or judgment may be? Here there is nothing to show that the plaintiff when describing the car in the contract as an "eight cylinder Bugatti car," after he had communicated to the defendants the purpose for which he wanted it, meant to intimate that he was not relying on their skill and judgment. The evidence seems to be all the other way. In my opinion the appeal must be dismissed.

Appeal dismissed.

[The concurring judgments of Atkin and Sargant L.JJ. are omitted.]

G. H. L. FRIDMAN
Sale of Goods in Canada
2nd ed. (1979), pp. 218-20

It is provided in section 15(1) of the Ontario Act that "in the case of a contract for the sale of a specified article under its patent or other trade name, there is no implied condition as to its fitness for any particular purpose." The meaning and application of this proviso have caused some difficulty. The proviso assumes the absence of any express assurance by the seller and deals only with cases of express or implied information by the buyer of the purpose for which he requires the article, so framed as to show that the buyer relies on the seller's skill or judgment. The idea behind the proviso is that by ordering an article under its patent or trade name the buyer is explicitly not relying on the seller's skill or judgment as to the fitness of the article for its intended purpose. Hence to make a sale, one under a trade or other patent name, the buyer must "specify it under its trade name in such a way as to indicate that he is satisfied, rightly or wrongly, that it will answer his purposes and that he is not relying on the skill or judgment of the seller." As *Baldry* v. *Marshall* shows, there may be a sale under a trade name but not within the proviso, by the reintroduction of the concept of reliance: a point that was reiterated by Masten J.A., in *Advance-Rumely Thresher Co.* v. *Lister* [1927] 4 DLR 51. In the case of *Bristol Tramways & Carriage Co. Ltd.* v. *Fiat Motors Ltd.* [1910] 2 KB 831 a sale of a 24/40 h.p. Fiat omnibus and six 24/40 h.p. motor chassis was not a sale under a patent or trade name and the condition implied by the subsection applied. This was because "Fiat" had not become a trade or patent name, and the proviso was held to be confined to articles which in fact had a patent or trade name under which they could be ordered. Such a name is acquired by user, and whether or not it has been so acquired is a question of fact in each case. In *Baldry* v. *Marshall*, it was said that although a "Bugatti" car was ordered, the proviso might not apply to an article like a motor car which was sold under a very elaborate and specific description. A sale of "Coalite," however, was held to be a sale under a trade or patent name in *Wilson* v. *Rickett Cockerell & Co. Ltd.* [1954] 1 QB 598 thereby excluding the operation of the implied condition as to fitness for purpose where explosive material was mixed with the "Coalite" and caused damage to the room of the purchaser. Similarly in *O'Fallon* v. *Inecto Rapid (Can.) Ltd.*[1940] 2 WWR 714 a sale of a specific hair dye was held to be outside the protection of the implied condition as to fitness because the dye was bought under a trade name. Though the manufacturer and wholesale distributor could be liable (for negligently failing to warn of the possible damages to inexperienced users) the retailer, who was not negligent, could not. And in *Simon* v. *Imperial Oil Ltd.* a sale of a drum of "Esso stove oil" came within the proviso, and was a sale under a trade name excluding liability except on the basis of negligence. However, in *Fillmore's Valley Nurseries Ltd* v. *North Amer. Cyanamid Ltd.*, (1958) 14 DLR (2d) 297 the sale of a chemical "amino triazole", a herbicide used to control weeds in the growing of pansy plants, was held not to be a sale of a specified article under its trade name. Nor was the sale of the insecticide and herbicide in *Willis* v. *F.M.C. Machinery & Chemicals Ltd.* (1976) 68 DLR (3d) 127. In these cases, therefore, the implied condition was not excluded.

The proviso may be excluded, as seen above, by the circumstances, from which it may be deduced that the sale was not in actuality one under a trade or patent name. The possibility of this occurring seems to make the utility of the proviso questionable. Moreover, where the operation of the proviso renders the condition implied as to fitness inapplicable, it may well be that the implied condition as to merchantability can still operate for the benefit of the buyer. This, as will be seen has been the effect of the judicial interpretation of the language of the two subsections now contained in s. 15(1)(2) of the Ontario Act. Consequently, and justifiably it may be admitted, as is shown by the redrafting of the law on this subject in the U.S.A. by the Uniform Commercial Code, it has been argued that the differentiation between the conditions implied in the two subsections is outmoded, and indeed has been outflanked by the decisions of the court.

Note: Saskatchewan never adopted the trade name proviso. The proviso was eliminated in the British Supply of Goods (Implied Terms) Act 1973, s. 3. See now U.K. Sale of Goods Act 1979, s. 14(3). The OLRC has also recommended the abolition of the proviso. See Sales Report, pp. 220-21, and draft bill, s. 5.14.

4. THE IMPLIED CONDITIONS IN A SALE BY SAMPLE

STEELS & BUSKS LTD. v. BLEECKER BIK & CO. LTD.
[1956] 1 Lloyd's Rep. 228 (QB)

Steels & Busks Ltd. required rubber for use in the manufacture of suspenders on corsets. In May of 1949 a representative of the company first approached the sellers. The sellers were informed that Steels & Busks required crepe rubber for manufacturing suspenders and that a light colour for the rubber was important because of the delicate colour of the suspender ends. A discussion ensued, chiefly involving the relative merits and prices of "water white crepe" and "first grade pale crepe". On May 5, 1949, the representative of Steels & Busks placed an order referring to a particular sample ("Ref. 601"). Subsequently, all orders by the buyers with the sellers were made "as previously delivered" or in like terms.

In September of 1951 the buyers began to receive complaints from their customers. An expert hired by the buyers determined that a chemical, "PNP", in the rubber supplied by the sellers had caused discoloration and stains on the manufactured corsets. In March of 1953 the buyers brought an action against the sellers claiming, inter alia, that the rubber did not conform in quality with the sample or that supplied under previous contracts.

SELLERS J.: The question of law for the decision of the Court is whether on the facts as found the goods delivered were or were not in accordance with the contractual terms.

• • •

The buyers wanted the pale crepe rubber for the manufacture of the ends of suspenders for use on corsets. The earlier deliveries had proved suitable for this purpose after whatever processing took place. The final delivery, while apparently suitable in the course of processing and manufacture, proved as to part of the delivery unsuitable because the garments became stained in the boxes in which they were packed and in the shops, due to the presence of a chemical conveniently described as "PNP." These defects were traced to 21 bales which alone are the subject of complaint in these proceedings.

At the time of the sale neither of the parties was aware that "PNP" was used in the treatment of rubber or that it might be detrimental, as it proved to be in this case. Indeed, no thought was given to the matter at all. By reason of the presence of "PNP" in the 21 bales, the buyers' loss, as alleged, has been heavy.

• • •

If the buyers are to succeed in their claim, it must, I think, only be on the ground that the 21 bales did not comply with the sample, that is, the first delivery.

In one respect the bales complained of did not so comply. They contained "PNP," whereas the sample did not, and it was submitted that Sect. 15 (2) (*a*) of the Sale of Goods Act [Ont., s. 16(2)(*a*)] had not been complied with as the bulk did not correspond with the sample in quality. Sect. 15 (2) of the Act is as follows:

> In the case of a contract for sale by sample —
>
> (*a*)   There is an implied condition that the bulk shall correspond with the sample in quality;
>
> (*b*)   There is an implied condition that the buyer shall have a reasonable opportunity of comparing the bulk with the sample;
>
> (*c*)   There is an implied condition that the goods shall be free from any defect, rendering them unmerchantable, which would not be apparent on reasonable examination of the sample.

Sect. 15 (2) is not inconsistent with the view that where there is (as here) a defect not apparent on reasonable examination of the sample, the buyers' rights arise, if at all, under sub-s. (2) (*c*) and not under sub-s. (2) (*a*), but it is not, I think, conclusive as a matter of construction.

The law arising on Sect. 15 has recently been considered by Mr. Justice Devlin in *F.E. Hookway & Co., Ltd.* v. *Alfred Isaacs & Sons and Others* [1954] 1 Lloyd's Rep. 491. It was submitted by Mr. Mocatta that this case was wrongly decided and I was asked to take a different view. In that long and somewhat complicated case it appears that the parties traded in a commodity called shellac, a substance used in the manufacture of gramophone records. In the case of the delivery contract, business was done upon the basis of a "standard sample" kept in the offices of the Association and which was selected from time to time with great care to represent a standard in each of the qualities of shellac in which the market deals. There was no official analysis of the sample; comparisons were always made visually by those skilled in the trade. Any member could obtain a part of the sample for his own use, so that it diminished in size and had to be renewed. Any member might have what he got analysed. Quality under the delivery was judged entirely visually except with regard to the presence of resin, which called for an analysis. I take a considerable extract from the judgment, commencing at p. 511:

> . . . the clause "Quality equal to London standard" has the effect of making this contract analogous to the contract for sale by sample which is dealt with in the Sale of Goods Act, 1893, Sect. 15. Instead of a specific sample being given in each case to the seller, there is one standard sample with which the bulk must correspond in quality. But the word "quality," in my judgment, is in its place in this contract confined — as it would be in the case of the ordinary sale by sample — to such qualities as are apparent on an ordinary examination of the sample as usually done in the trade.
>
> *James Drummond & Sons* v. *E.H. Van Ingen & Co.* (1887) 12 App. Cas. 284, is the case upon which Sect. 15 is largely based. In that case, the cloth sold had a latent defect which was not apparent on a reasonable examination of the sample, which had the same latent defect. The House of Lords held that it was not sufficient that the goods should correspond with the sample; they must also be merchantable and fit for the purpose for which they were required. The seller was therefore responsible for the

latent defect. In a famous passage, Lord Macnaghten, at p. 297, describes the function of the sample:

> After all [he says], the office of a sample is to present to the eye the real meaning and intention of the parties with regard to the subject-matter of the contract which, owing to the imperfection of language, it may be difficult or impossible to express in words. The sample speaks for itself. But it cannot be treated as saying more than such a sample would tell a merchant of the class to which the buyer belongs, using due care and diligence, and appealing to it in the ordinary way and with the knowledge possessed by merchants of that class at the time. No doubt the sample might be made to say a great deal more. Pulled to pieces and examined by unusual tests which curiosity or suspicion might suggest, it would doubtless reveal every secret of its construction. But that is not the way in which business is done in this country.

In that case [that is, the *Drummond* case], the contract expressly provided that quality and weight should be equal to certain numbered samples; and the Earl of Selborne, L.C., at p. 288, said this about its construction:

> I think that the word "quality" as used in the contracts, ought to be restricted to those qualities which were patent or discoverable from such examination and inspection of the samples as, under the circumstances, the respondents might reasonably be expected to make.

In *James Drummond & Sons* v. *E.H. Van Ingen & Co.*, the House of Lords was able, by giving the sample clause a restricted meaning, to hold that its terms did not exclude an implied warranty covering latent defects. It is of the essence of this reasoning that a clause of this sort does not cover latent qualities or defects at all. In that case it was the seller's argument that was defeated by this construction. But, by the same token, it is not open to a buyer to submit a sample to an analysis unusual in the trade so as to reveal in it certain attributes or qualities hitherto unsuspected, and then to require, by virtue of the sample clause alone, that the bulk should contain the same qualities. If, for example, a buyer, to use the words of Lord Macnaghten, pulls a sample of cloth to pieces and discovers by means of analysis that the dye contains a certain proportion of a certain chemical, he cannot by virtue of the same clause require that the dye in the bulk shall contain the same proportion of the same chemical. He may, of course, complain that if it does not contain that proportion it would be unmerchantable or would fail to satisfy some other express or implied condition as to quality; but he cannot say that it breaks the condition that the bulk shall correspond with the sample in quality, for that condition is dealing only with apparent quality. There is abundant evidence in this case that in the shellac trade, as in most other trades, the method of examination usual in the trade is the visual method. As flow is not a quality detectable by the visual method, it follows that a defective flow cannot be a breach of the sample clause.

I am in complete agreement with that construction of Sect. 15(2)(*a*), and I am grateful for that passage, which I adopt and apply here. *James Drummond & Sons* v. *E.H. Van Ingen & Co., sup.*, as Mr. Justice Devlin indicates, is the forerunner very largely of Sect. 15. Although it is before the Act and therefore perhaps not technically an authority, I should not feel emboldened to disregard it even if I wished to do so.

The extent to which a sample may be held to "speak" must depend on the contract and what is contemplated by the parties in regard to it. A sample may be analysed, X-rayed — tested to destruction. In the present case the parties were content, in accordance with the normal practice of the trade, to rely on a visual examination. Neither "PNP" nor, I think, any other chemical in general use for coagulation and preservation or either is detectable by visual examination, and therefore the presence or absence of the chemical cannot in itself be a breach of the sample clause. It is like the "flow" in the shellac case.

The buyers had in fact used the first delivery and found it satisfactory and that no doubt resulted in the repeat orders. The crude rubber had received treatment and processing by them and revealed no defect. Such circumstances would not enlarge the liability of the sellers, as the contract remained, as far as the compliance with a sample was concerned, a contract which called for compliance in those matters revealed by visual examination and those matters only.

In my judgment, the Appeal Committee (and also, indeed, the original arbitrators) were entitled to come to the decision that the goods delivered under the last contract were in accordance with the contractual terms, and I answer the question raised accordingly.

Award upheld.

5. PUBLIC CONTROL OF FOOD, DRUGS, AND HAZARDOUS PRODUCTS

a) Food and Drugs

Note on the History of Food and Drug Legislation in Canada.*

The need for strict food and drug laws and their enforcement has become painfully apparent in the post-war period in the light of the thalidomide tragedy and the discovery or apprehension of carcinogenic properties in food additives, artificial sweeteners, synthetic growth hormones and other products of the modern laboratory. The need for watchfulness has been accentuated by the rapid strides of food technology and the pharmacological sciences and by the proliferation of items on the typical supermarket and drugstore shelves.

It must therefore come as a surprise to discover that until a hundred years ago no such protective legislation existed in Canada at all. In England it took a number of scandals, such as the case of the adulteration of lozenges with arsenic instead of the usual plaster of Paris, resulting in more than fifteen deaths and affecting more than 400 people, to prod the British Parliament into action. The first British Act to deal with this danger to public health was adopted in 1860. What might be considered as the first real food and drug legislation in Canada was passed in 1874 (SC 1874, c. 8), more than twenty-five years before similar legislation was enacted by the U.S. Congress. These first efforts were mainly directed at the sale of adulterated liquor; protection of the public was of secondary importance. The main objectives of the Canadian Act were the imposition of licensing fees on the compounders of spirits and the imposition of various

---

* The editors of this casebook are particularly indebted to Eric Gertner and Terry Burgoyne, two former students, for researching and, to a substantial extent, preparing this note. [Eds.]

duties on these same individuals. Significantly, the legislation was adopted as an amendment to the Internal Revenue Act.

In 1884 (SC 1884, c. 34) the legislation was removed from the Internal Revenue Act and put into a separate Act, best known as the Adulteration Act. That Act, for the first time, provided an extensive definition of the term "adulterated". What has turned out to be one of the most important provisions of what is now known as the Food and Drugs Act was introduced in 1890 (SC 1890, c. 26) — the provisions authorizing the government to prescribe standards for foodstuffs. The first such standards were promulgated in 1910 and today they govern, inter alia, such matters as food enrichment, food additives and vitamins, and cover many hundreds of items.

Amendments in 1920 (SC 1920, c. 27) provided for an even more detailed definition of the terms "adulterated food" and "adulterated drugs". Still more important was the provision dealing with "misbranding", i.e., the mislabelling of products. This provision is still extremely important today. The Act was again amended in 1934 (SC 1934, c. 54) to prohibit the sale of products labelled or advertised as remedies for a wide variety of illnesses (set out in Schedule A). In 1939 (SC 1939, c. 3), this power of prohibition was extended to therapeutic devices and cosmetics.

In the post-war period there have been several major amendments. An amendment in 1961 (SC 1960-61, c. 37) permitted the authorities to deal with the possession of and trafficking in certain drugs, known as "controlled drugs" (now set out in Schedule G), which may be considered to be dangerous. Similar legislation was enacted a few years later with respect to "restricted drugs" (set out in Schedule H). In 1969 (SC 1968-69, c. 41), Parliament also empowered the government to regulate or prohibit the importation of any drug manufactured outside Canada and the distribution, sale and possession for sale of any such drugs.

Besides the substantive provisions outlined above, the present Act (RSC 1970, c. F-27) provides for administration and enforcement of the provisions of the Act by inspectors appointed by the government. An inspector is given substantial powers by s. 22 of the Act, including the right to "enter any place where on reasonable grounds he believes any article to which this Act or its regulations apply is manufactured, prepared, preserved, packaged or stored" (s. 22(1)(a)). In addition, the Act makes it an offence to obstruct an inspector in the carrying out of his duties (s. 22(5)) or knowingly to make any false or misleading statement (s. 22(6)).

By far the most important section of the Act is s. 25, which sets out the regulatory powers of the government. This allows the government to give flesh to the skeletal bones of the Act, including the power to declare any food or drug adulterated (s. 25(1)(a)), the power to act with respect to labelling and packaging to prevent the consumer or purchaser from being deceived or misled as to its quantity, character, value, composition, merit or safety, or to prevent injury to the health of the consumer or purchaser (s. 25(1)(b)) and the power to prescribe standards of composition, strength, potency, purity, quality or other property of any article, drug, cosmetic or device (s. 25(1)(c)). Anyone found to be in contravention of the Act or its regulations is guilty of an offence and liable to a fine or imprisonment or both (s. 26).

An example of the exercise of the regulatory power for the protection and safety of the public are those regulations dealing with the introduction of new drugs. Before new drugs may be sold or even advertised for sale, the manufacturer must provide the

Minister with a "new drug submission", which must include details of the tests to be applied to control the potency, purity, stability and safety of the new drug, detailed reports of the tests made to establish the safety of the new drug for the purpose and under the conditions of use recommended, and substantial evidence of its clinical effectiveness. If satisfied that the submission meets the requirements of Reg. C.08.002(2) the Minister will issue a notice of compliance. However, the notice may be suspended where the Minister believes it is necessary to do so in the interests of public health because, for instance, new evidence reveals that the drug is not safe for the use represented, or because upon the basis of new information there is lack of substantial evidence that the drug will have the effect represented or because it has been found that the labelling of the drug is false, misleading or incomplete. The extensive regulations under the Act can be found at CRC 1978, c. 869-871.

Before the Second World War the constitutionality of the Food and Drugs Act was affirmed on two occasions as a proper exercise of the criminal law power, s. 91(27) of the BNA Act, of the federal government. See *Standard Sausage Co.* v. *Lee* [1934] 1 DLR 706 (BC CA) and *R. v. Goldsmid* (1932) 45 BCR 435. The position has now changed significantly as a result of the Supreme Court of Canada's decision in the *Labatt Breweries* case and the other developments related in the article in *The Canadian Consumer* following these notes.

For other federal legislation in this area, see the Patent Act, RSC 1970, c. P-4, and the Proprietary or Patent Medicine Act, RSC 1970, c. P-25. The former requires the Commissioner of Patents to grant to any person applying for it a license for the use of any patented invention intended for, or capable of being used for, the preparation or production of food or intended or capable of being used for medicine or for the preparation or production of medicine (ss. 41(3), (4)). The granting of a license is compulsory unless the Commissioner sees good reason to the contrary. In settling the terms of the licence and fixing the amount of royalty or other consideration, the Commissioner must have regard to the desirability of making the food or medicine available to the public at the lowest possible price consistent with giving the patentee due reward for the research leading to the invention.

The Proprietary or Patent Medicine Act requires manufacturers of proprietary medicines (i.e., artificial remedies or prescriptions for the internal or external use of man not listed in any one of a number of books of pharmacopoeia) to obtain a certificate of registration for any medicine containing any of the drugs listed in the schedule. Manufacturers are also required to supply the Department of National Health and Welfare with a sworn statement of the quantity of such drug or drugs. Annual licences to sell such medicines must also be obtained.

In addition, the Act prohibits certain acts such as the sale, manufacture or importation of medicines containing opium intended for internal use, the manufacture, importation, exposing or offering for sale in Canada of any medicines containing an excessive amount of alcohol or an excessive amount of any of the drugs listed in the schedule. Moreover, manufacturers are required to list the name and dosage of any of the scheduled drugs conspicuously on the label of every proprietary or patent medicine. If any such medicine is represented as a cure for any disease or any false, misleading or exaggerated claim appears or is made in any advertisement it shall not be manufactured, imported, exposed, offered for sale or sold in Canada.

There is provincial legislation in this area as well. In Ontario the former Pharmacy Act, RSO 1970, c. 348 as amended, now superseded by the Health Disciplines Act 1974, SO 1974, c. 74, sets out the requirements for those wishing to be pharmaceutical chemists, prohibits persons other than pharmaceutical chemists from selling drugs or poisons and generally regulates the pharmaceutical trade in the province. In 1972 the Pharmacy Amendment Act 1972, SO 1972, c. 99, empowered pharmacists to select a lower priced drug within the same category as the one prescribed (popularly referred to as the "Parcost program"). These provisions have been substantially retained in the Health Disciplines Act, *supra*. The present provisions read as follows:

116.(1)(i) "Parcost C.D.I." means the Parcost Comparative Drug Index prescribed by the regulations;

· · ·

158.—(1) Every person who dispenses a prescription may, unless otherwise directed by the prescriber, select and dispense an interchangeable pharmaceutical product other than the one prescribed, if the interchangeable pharmaceutical product dispensed is listed as interchangeable in the Parcost C.D.I., and is lower in cost than the drug prescribed.

(2) Where a drug prescribed is listed in the Parcost C.D.I. and the identity of the manufacturer is not specified by the prescriber every person who dispenses a prescription shall select and dispense an interchangeable pharmaceutical product listed in the Parcost C.D.I.

(3) No person shall knowingly supply an interchangeable product under subsection 1 or 2 at a price in excess of the cost of the lowest priced interchangeable pharmaceutical product in his inventory and the maximum dispensing fee as set out in the Parcost C.D.I.

(4) No action or other proceeding lies or shall be instituted against a prescriber or pharmacist on the grounds that an interchangeable pharmaceutical product other than the one prescribed was dispensed in accordance with this section.

In its earlier phase, at any rate, the *Parcost* program is said not to have been entirely successful because of the lack of cooperation on the part of some drug manufacturers, doctors and particularly pharmacists, who felt that the dispensing fees were too low. The legislation and the *Parcost* dispensing fee agreements have, however, resulted in some savings to consumers. For further particulars, see James Shenkman, "The Pharmacist, the Consumer and the Price of Prescriptions in Ontario", Consumer Law Seminar Paper, spring 1974 (on deposit in the OHLS library). For an American viewpoint, see P.G. Rozof, "Improving Michigan's Generic Drug Law" (1976) 9 U. Mich. JL Ref. 394.

Selected Bibliography:

D.N.J. Bennett, "The Liability of the Manufacturers of Thalidomide to the Affected Children" (1965) 39 Aust. LJ 256.
R. Cranston, *Consumers and the Law* (1978), ch. 10.
R.E. Curran, *Canada's Food and Drug Laws* (1953).
Kallett and Schink, *One Hundred Million Guinea Pigs* (1932, New York).
K.I. Macduff, "*Thalidomide — The Aftermath*" (1968-71) 1 Auckland UL Rev. 53 (No. 3).
Turner, *The Chemical Feast* (1970, New York).

Periodicals and Reports:
Food, Drug and Cosmetic Law Journal (U.S.).
Rx Bulletin (Food and Drug Directorate of the Department of National Health and Welfare, Ottawa).
Annual Report, Department of National Health and Welfare, Ottawa.

Food and Drugs Act, RSC 1970, c. F-27, as am.

Food

4. No person shall sell an article of food that

(*a*)   has in or upon it any poisonous or harmful substance;

(*b*)   is unfit for human consumption;

(*c*)   consists in whole or in part of any filthy, putrid, disgusting, rotten, decomposed or diseased animal or vegetable substance;

(*d*)   is adulterated; or

(*e*)   was manufactured, prepared, preserved, packaged or stored under unsanitary conditions. 1952-53, c. 38, s. 4.

6. Where a standard has been prescribed for a food, no person shall laabel, package, sell or advertise any article in such a manner that it is likely to be mistaken for such food, unless the article complies with the prescribed standard. 1952-53, c. 38, s. 6.

Drugs

8. No person shall sell any drug that

(*a*)   was manufactured, prepared, preserved, packed or stored under unsanitary conditions; or

(*b*)   is adulterated. 1952-53, c. 38, s. 8.

Cosmetics

16. No person shall sell any cosmetic that

(*a*)   has in or upon it any substance that may cause injury to the health of the user when the cosmetic is used,

(*i*)   according to the directions on the label or accompanying such cosmetic, or

(*ii*)   for such purposes and by such methods of use as are customary or usual therefor;

(*b*)   consists in whole or in part of any filthy or decomposed substance or of any foreign matter; or

(*c*)   was manufactured, prepared, preserved, packed or stored under unsanitary conditions. 1952-53, c. 38, s. 15.

Devices

19. No person shall sell any device that, when used according to directions or under such conditions as are customary or usual, may cause injury to the health of the purchaser or user thereof. 1952-53, c. 38, s. 18.

Regulations

25. (1) The Governor in Council may make regulations for carrying the purposes and provisions of this Act into effect, and, in particular, but not so as to restrict the generality of the foregoing, may make regulations.

(*a*)   declaring that any food or drug or class of food or drugs is adulterated if any prescribed substance or class of substances is present therein or has been added thereto or extracted or omitted therefrom;

(*b*)   respecting

    (*i*)   the labelling and packaging and the offering, exposing and advertising for sale of food, drugs, cosmetics and devices,

    (*ii*)   the size, dimensions, fill and other specifications of packages of food, drugs, cosmetics and devices,

    (*iii*)   the sale or the condition of sale of any food, drug, cosmetic or device, and

    (*iv*)   the use of any substance as an ingredient in any food, drug, cosmetic or device,

to prevent the consumer or purchaser thereof from being deceived or misled as to its design, construction, performance, intended use, quantity, character, value, composition, merit or safety, or to prevent injury to the health of the consumer or purchaser;

(*c*)   prescribing standards of composition, strength, potency, purity, quality or other property of any article of food, drug, cosmetic or device;

(*d*)   respecting the importation of foods, drugs, cosmetics and devices in order to ensure compliance with this Act and the regulations;

(*e*)   respecting the method of preparation, manufacture, preserving, packing, storing and testing of any food, drug, cosmetic or device in the interest of, or for the prevention of injury to, the health of the consumer or purchaser;

(*f*)   requiring persons who sell food, drugs, cosmetics or devices to maintain such books and records as the Governor in Council considers necessary for the proper enforcement and administration of this Act and the regulations;

(*g*)   respecting the form and manner of the Minister's indication under section 12, including the fees payable therefor, and prescribing what premises or what processes or conditions of manufacture, including qualifications of technical staff, shall or shall not be deemed to be suitable for the purposes of that section;

(*h*)   requiring manufacturers of any drugs described in Schedule E to submit test portions of any batch of such drugs and respecting the form and manner of the Minister's indication under section 13, including the fees payable therefor;

(*i*)   not inconsistent with this Act, respecting the powers and duties of inspectors and analysts and the taking of samples and the seizure, detention, forfeiture and disposition of articles;

(*j*)   exempting any food, drug, cosmetic or device from all or any of the provisions of this Act and prescribing the conditions of such exemption;

(*k*)   prescribing forms for the purposes of this Act and the regulations;

(*l*)   providing for the analysis of food, drugs or cosmetics other than for the purposes of this Act and prescribing a tariff of fees to be paid for such analysis;

(*m*)   adding anything to any of the schedules, in the interest of, or for the prevention of injury to, the health of the consumer or purchaser, or deleting anything therefrom;

(*n*)   respecting the distribution or the conditions of distribution of samples of any drug;

(*o*)   respecting

(*i*)   the method of preparation, manufacture, preserving, packing, labelling, storing and testing of any new drug, and

(*ii*)   the sale or the conditions of sale of any new drug,

and defining for the purposes of this Act the expression "new drug"; and

(*p*)   authorizing the advertising to the general public of contraceptive devices and drugs manufactured, sold or represented for use in the prevention of conception and prescribing the circumstances and conditions under which and the persons by whom such contraceptive devices and drugs may be so advertised.

(2) Without limiting or restricting the authority conferred by any other provisions of this Act or any Part thereof for carrying into effect the purposes and provisions of this Act or any Part thereof, the Governor in Council may make such regulations governing, regulating or prohibiting

(*a*)   the importation into Canada of any drug or class of drugs manufactured outside Canada, or

(*b*)   the distribution or sale in Canada, or the offering, exposing or having in possession for sale in Canada, of any drug or class of drugs manufactured outside Canada,

as the Governor in Council deems necessary for the protection of the public in relation to the safety and quality of any such drug or class of drugs.

(3) The Governor in Council may designate as an analyst any person on the staff of the Department for such time as that person is employed in the Department or for such time during the period of such employment as he may direct.

(4) The Governor in Council may designate as an inspector any person on the staff of the Department or the Department of Consumer and Corporate Affairs for such time as that person is employed in either the Department or the Department of Consumer and Corporate Affairs or for such time during the period of such employment as he may direct. 1952-53, c. 38, s. 24; 1962-63, c. 15, s. 3; 1968-69, c. 28, s. 105; 1968-69, c. 41, s. 3; 1968-69, c. 49, s. 5.

Penalties

26. Every person who violates any of the provisions of this Act or the regulations is guilty of an offence and is liable

(*a*)   on summary conviction for a first offence to a fine not exceeding five hundred dollars or to imprisonment for a term not exceeding three months, or to both, and for a subsequent offence to a fine not exceeding one thousand dollars or to imprisonment for a term not exceeding six months, or to both; and

(*b*)   on conviction upon indictment to a fine not exceeding five thousand dollars or to imprisonment for a term not exceeding three years, or to both. 1952-53, c. 38, s. 25.

The Food and Drugs Act and Other Constitutional Horrors*
A CAC Report . . ., *The Canadian Consumer*, Oct. 1980, p. 15.

If Canadian consumers had been asked a year ago whether they thought there was a possibility that the federal Food and Drugs Act might be in constitutional jeopardy, they would have treated the question as a cruel joke. No single Act, federal or provincial, has rightly been regarded as more basic to the consumer's welfare than the Food and Drugs Act. Yet the seemingly impossible has happened. An important part of the Act has been ruled unconstitutional by the Supreme Court of Canada in its decision of December 1979 in the *Labatt Breweries*** case.

No less important, in a decision rendered in March of this year†, County Court Judge Wetmore held in Vancouver that federal authorities cannot prosecute violations of other parts of the Act, though admittedly valid, without the consent of the appropriate provincial Attorney General.

These two decisions merely represent the tip of an iceberg. Not only is the federal government's right to enact and administer the Food and Drugs Act being questioned; equally in doubt is the constitutionality of such other post-war consumer legislation as the Consumer Packaging and Labelling Act and the Textile Labelling Act. The inaptly named Combines Investigation Act, the linch pin of Canada's competition policy containing important provisions on misleading advertising and unfair marketing practices, is also under attack. In December 1979 a Federal Court judge ruled unconstitutional section 31.1 of the Act. This section empowers a person who has been injured as a result of the violation of the substantive provisions of the Act to bring a civil damage action. And again, as in the Vancouver case, the ability of the federal authorities to prosecute under the Combines Act without provincial concurrence is being questioned in other cases before the courts.

It is no exaggeration then to say that we face a major constitutional crisis. Unless it is successfully resolved, it will seriously cripple the capacity of the federal government to discharge responsibilities that in any other Western state would be regarded naturally as those of a national government. They are responsibilities that cannot adequately be met by the provincial governments.

The crisis was triggered by the interpretation of several key provisions in sections 91 and 92 of the British North America Act (which contains Canada's constitution) and a dispute as old as Confederation itself. The dispute involves the allocation of powers between the federal and provincial governments. Section 92(13) of the BNA Act entrusts the provinces with the power to regulate property and civil rights within each province. Section 92(14) does the same with respect to the administration of justice. On the other hand, section 91(2) of the Act confers on the federal government the paramount power to enact legislation dealing with trade and commerce. And section 91(27) makes the federal government responsible for the enactment of criminal laws, including laws governing

---

* An error in the original title has been corrected by the editors of this casebook. [Eds.]

** *Labatt Breweries of Canada Ltd.* v. *A.-G. Can.* (1979) 106 DLR (3d) 594 (SCC). [Eds.]

† *R.* v. *Kripps Pharmacy Ltd.* (1980) 14 CR (3d) 355 (BC Co. Ct.). [Eds.]

criminal procedure. Finally, the federal government also enjoys a catch-all power to make laws for the "peace, order and good government" of the country.

A lay person might be forgiven for thinking that these federal powers were more than adequate to justify the provisions in the Food and Drugs Act and (more arguably) to prosecute any violations of the Act. No doubt the federal government's legal advisors thought the same. The courts have now held otherwise.

Section 25(1)(c) of the Food and Drugs Act empowers the Minister of National Health and Welfare to prescribe compositional standards for foods. Section 6 makes it an offence to label, package, sell or advertise an article that fails to comply with a prescribed standard. The federal government has used these powers to prescribe compositional standards for many types of food, including beer. In the *Labatt Breweries* case the issue was whether Labatt's *Special Lite Beer* violated the prescribed standard for light beer since it contained 4 per cent alcohol instead of the maximum permissible level of 2.5 per cent. A majority of the judges of the Supreme Court of Canada agreed that the standard had been violated. But they also held that the federal government had no constitutional power to adopt the standard in the first place.

Briefly, their reasons for the constitutional decision were as follows. First, the majority reasoned that the compositional standards for beer are regulatory in character. They cannot be justified as an exercise of the federal government's criminal-law power. The second reason was that the standards could not be justified as an exercise of the trade and commerce power. A long line of decisions have held that section 91(2) of the BNA Act does not entitle the federal government to regulate particular trades or commercial activities *within* a province as distinct from regulating trade *between* the provinces. The compositional standards regulations in the Food and Drugs Act do not distinguish between intra-provincial and inter-provincial sales of products.

Finally the court held that the peace, order and good government power was likewise foreclosed. The precedents have established that the power can only be used to cope with national emergencies and serious national problems, not existing at the time of Confederation, that are not otherwise dealt with in the BNA Act. In the view of the judges the compositional standards fell far short of these requirements.

Some observers are of the view that the Supreme Court was mistaken with respect to at least the first two grounds of its decision and that the majority judges seriously misunderstood the function of compositional standards. The fact remains that the Supreme Court is the final arbiter of what the constitution means and how it applies in a particular context. What is important is that the Supreme Court's reasoning may equally invalidate dozens of other compositional standards adopted under the Food and Drugs Act, removing one of the basic pillars of all modern food and drugs legislation. And what is true of compositional standards may also be true of the disclosure requirements in the Consumer Packaging and Labelling Act and the Textile Labelling Act. They are vulnerable to the same types of constitutional criticisms as were used in the *Labatt Breweries* case.

The implications of the *Labatt Breweries* case are serious enough. But those arising out of Judge Wetmore's decision strike still more deeply at the federal government's capacity to function effectively across a broad spectrum of activities extending well beyond the consumer sphere. In *The Queen* v. *Kripps Pharmacy* the accused were charged with violations of the Food and Drugs Act arising out of the sale of a new drug, *Amygdaline*. The indictment alleged that the accused had failed to file with the Minister of National Health and Welfare a new drug submission as required by the regulations. They were also charged with violations of sections 8 and 9 of the Act, which deal with the preparation of drugs in unsanitary conditions and false or misleading labelling or other practices in relation to drugs.

The County Court judge agreed with counsel for the accused that the charges were unconstitutional on a number of grounds. So far as the first count was concerned, he held (following the decision in the *Labatt Breweries* case) that the new-drug submission requirements are regulatory and not criminal in character. They are therefore open to the same objections as the compositional standards regulations considered in the Supreme Court decision. So far as the charges under sections 8 and 9 of the Act were concerned, he held that assuming these provisions fell within the criminal-law competence of the federal government, nevertheless the *enforcement* of the criminal law was a provincial prerogative (because of section 92(14) of the BNA Act). The federal government could not prosecute even federal criminal offences without provincial concurrence. On the latter point Judge Wetmore, in the face of much conflicting provincial jurisprudence, followed the views of Mr. Justice Dickson in another Supreme Court of Canada decision, *The Queen* v. *Hauser* [1979] 8 CR (3d) 89, which was also decided in 1979.

Judge Wetmore's decision is being appealed to the British Columbia Court of Appeal and may well be appealed further to the Supreme Court of Canada. It is anyone's guess how, in the strained constitutional environment of the 1980s, the Supreme Court will decide the question. It raises very sensitive political issues as well as purely legal ones and the answer is far from being a foregone conclusion.

The Executive of CAC was so concerned about these developments that in May CAC's then President Yvonne Miles wrote a detailed letter about them to Prime Minister Trudeau. She drew attention to the chilling effect that the decisions referred to earlier have had on federal enforcement activities under the Food and Drugs Act and made the following recommendations:

> First, that the cases currently before the courts be expedited and consolidated wherever possible and that consideration be given to making one or more References to the Supreme Court of Canada to determine the constitutional validity of the whole of the Food and Drugs Act and the regulations made under it, as well as the competence of the federal government to prosecute offences enacted pursuant to BNA 91(27).

> Second, the convening of a federal-provincial conference to seek mutually acceptable solutions to the problems presented by the decision in the *Labatt Breweries* case.

> Third, that the important questions raised by the decisions to which we have referred be included in any agenda for future constitutional reform.

Two of these recommendations deserve some elaboration. It is not clear whether the Supreme Court of Canada fully appreciated the implications of its decision in the *Labatt Breweries* case. It may not have intended to sweep aside the great complex of compositional standards which have been laboriously built up over many years to protect Canadian manufacturers as well as consumers against deceptive marketing practices and unfair competition. There is wisdom therefore in asking the Supreme Court to review the Act as an entirety without waiting for the haphazard progression of single cases involving discrete provisions in the Act.

The other point concerns the scope of federal-provincial co-operation in this area. Certainly there are many other areas (the agricultural marketing boards are a notable example) in which, because of constitutional difficulties, the federal and provincial governments have co-operated to find a common solution. But food and drugs present special features. Historically, the provinces have evinced little interest in this area. Since *Labatt*, they have shown little enthusiasm for being dragged into it. (Only one province participated in the hearings in *Labatt*.) The area is much more complex than even marketing legislation and requires expensive and elaborate technical facilities that few of the provinces possess or can afford. Again, the market for most processed foods and most drugs is overwhelmingly a national market. Some manufacturers have already expressed alarm at the prospect of being subjected to 11 sets of regulatory food standards (10 provinces plus the federal government) and 11 sets of enforcement agencies. Consumers will be legitimately concerned that they may not be effectively protected by either level of government if *Labatt* leads to a jurisdictional free-for-all. . . .

Note: For a detailed critique of the *Labatt Breweries* case, see the symposium on "Economic Regulation and the British North America Act: Labatt Breweries and other Constitutional Imbroglios" (1980-81) 5 CBLJ 172. Judge Wetmore's decision on the constitutional issues in *Kripps Pharmacy* was affirmed on a mandamus application before Mr. Justice Berger. See [1981] 1 WWR 753 (BC SC).

b) Hazardous Products

Hazardous Products Act, RSC 1970, c. H-3

Short Title

1. This Act may be cited as the Hazardous Products Act, 1968-69, c. 42, s. 1.

Interpretation

2. In this Act

"advertise" includes any representation by any means whatever for the purpose of promoting directly or indirectly the sale or other disposition of a hazardous product;

"analyst" means a person designated as an analyst under the food and Drugs Act or by the Minister pursuant to section 4;

"hazardous product" means any product or substance included in Part 1 or Part II of the schedule;

"inspector" means any person designated as a hazardous products inspector pursuant to section 4;

"Minister" means the Minister of Consumer and Corporate Affairs and in sections 9 and 10 includes the Minister of National Health and Welfare;

"sell" includes sell, offer for sale, expose for sale, and distribute. 1968-69, c. 42, s. 2.

Offence

3. (1) No person shall advertise, sell or import into Canada a hazardous product included in Part I of the schedule.

(2) No person shall advertise, sell or import into Canada a hazardous product included in Part II of the schedule except as authorized by the regulations.

(3) Every person who violates subsection (1) or (2) is guilty of

(a) an offence and liable on summary conviction to a fine of one thousand dollars or to imprisonment for six months, or to both; or

(b) an indictable offence and liable to imprisonment for two years.

(4) A prosecution under paragraph (3)(a) may be instituted at any time within twelve months after the time when the subject-matter of the prosecution arose. 1968-69, c. 42, s. 3.

Inspectors and Analysts

4. (1) The Minister may designate as a hazardous products inspector for the purposes of this Act any person who, in his opinion, is qualified to be so designated.

(2) An inspector shall be furnished with a certificate of his designation as an inspector and on entering any place pursuant to subsection 5(1) shall, if so required, produce the certificate to the person in charge thereof.

(3) The Minister may designate as an analyst for the purposes of this Act any person employed in the public service of Canada who, in his opinion, is qualified to be so designated. 1968-69, c. 42, s. 4.

Search, Seizure and Forfeiture

5. (1) An inspector may at any reasonable time enter any place where on reasonable grounds he believes any hazardous product is manufactured, prepared, preserved, packaged, sold or stored for sale and

(a) examine any product or substance that he reasonably believes is a hazardous product and take samples thereof, and examine any other thing that he reasonably believes is used or is capable of being used for the manufacture, preparation, preservation, packaging, sale or storage of a hazardous product;

(b) open and examine any receptacle or package that on reasonable grounds he believes contains any hazardous product;

(c) examine any books, records or other documents that on reasonable grounds he believes contain any information relevant to the enforcement of this Act and make copies thereof or extracts therefrom; and (*d*) seize any product or substance, or any labelling, advertising material or other thing, by means of or in relation to which he reasonably believes any provision of this Act or the regulations has been violated.

Regulations

7. The Governor in Council may make regulations

(*a*) authorizing the advertising, sale or importation into Canada of any hazardous product included in Part II of the schedule and prescribing the circumstances and conditions under which and the persons by whom such hazardous product may be sold, advertised or imported into Canada;

(*b*) respecting the powers and duties of inspectors and analysts and the taking of samples and the seizure, detention, forfeiture and disposition of products, substances and other things;

(*c*) prescribing the procedures to be followed by a Hazardous Products Board of Review established pursuant to section 9 in conducting an inquiry; and

(*d*) generally, for carrying out the purposes and provisions of this Act. 1968-69, c. 42, s. 7.

Schedule

8. (1) The Governor in Council may by order amend Part 1 or Part II of the schedule by adding thereto

(*a*) any product or substance that is or contains a poisonous, toxic, inflammable, explosive or corrosive product or substance or other product or substance of a similar nature that he is satisfied is or is likely to be a danger to the health or safety of the public, or

(*b*) any product designed for household, garden or personal use, for use in sports or recreational activities, as life-saving equipment or as a toy, plaything or equipment for use by children that he is satisfied is or is likely to be a danger to the health or safety of the public because of its design, construction or contents,

or by deleting therefrom any product or substance the inclusion of which therein he is satisfied is no longer necessary.

(2) An order amending Part I of the schedule may be made by the Governor in Council on the recommendation of the Minister or the Minister of National Health and Welfare.

(3) Every order adding a product or substance to Part I or Part II of the schedule shall be laid before the Senate and the House of Commons not later than fifteen days after it is made or, if Parliament is not then sitting, on any of the first fifteen days next thereafter that Parliament is sitting.

(4) If both Houses of Parliament resolve that an order or any part thereof should be revoked, the order or that part thereof is thereupon revoked. 1968-69, c. 42, s. 8.

Board of Review

9. (1) Where a product or substance is added to Part I or Part II of the schedule by order of the Governor in Council, any manufacturer or distributor of that product or substance or any person having that product or substance in his possession for sale may, within sixty days from the date of the making of the order, request the Minister that the order be referred to a Hazardous Products Board of Review.

(2) Upon receipt of a request described in subsection (1), the Minister shall establish a Hazardous Products Board of Review (hereinafter referred to as the "Board"), consisting of not more than three persons and shall refer the order in respect of which the request was made to the Board.

(3) The Board shall inquire into the nature and characteristics of any product or substance to which an order referred to it under subsection (2) applies and shall give the person making the request and any other person affected by the order a reasonable opportunity of appearing before the Board, presenting evidence and making representations to it.

(4)The Board has all the powers that are or may be conferred by or under sections 4, 5, and 11 of the Inquiries Act on commissioners appointed under Part I of that Act.

(5) The Board, as soon as possible after the conclusion of its inquiry, shall submit a report with its recommendations to the Minister, together with all evidence and other material that was before the Board.

(6) Any report of the Board shall, within thirty days after its receipt by the Minister, be made public by him, unless the Board states in writing to the Minister that it believes the public interest would be better served by withholding publication, in which case the Minister may decide whether the report, either in whole or in part, shall be made public.

(7) The Minister may publish and supply copies of a report referred to in subsection (5) in such manner and upon such terms as he deems proper. 1968-69, c. 42, s. 9.

Disclosure

10. (1) Where the Minister has reason to believe that a product or substance is a product or substance that may be added to Part I or Part II of the schedule by an order made pursuant to section 8, he may send a written notice to the manufacturer of the product or substance requesting him to disclose to the Minister the formula, composition or chemical ingredients of the product or substance and such other information in the possession of the manufacturer as the Minister deems necessary for the purpose of determining whether the product or substance is or is likely to be a danger to the health or safety of the public.

(2) Every manufacturer to whom a written notice referred to in subsection (1) is sent shall disclose to the Minister, within the time specified by the Minister in the notice, any information described in subsection (1) that is requested in the notice.

(3) Information received by the Minister from a manufacturer pursuant to subsection (1) is privileged and shall not be disclosed to any other person except as may be necessary for the administration or enforcement of this section or for the purposes of section 8. 1968-69, c. 42, s. 10.

Application of Act

15. This Act does not apply to any product or substance that is

(*a*) an explosive within the meaning of the Explosives Act;

(*b*) a cosmetic, device, drug or food within the meaning of the Food and Drugs Act;

(*c*) a control product within the meaning of the Pest Control Products Act; or

(*d*) a prescribed substance within the meaning of the Atomic Energy Control Act. 1968-69, c. 42, s. 15.

Notes: Since the introduction of the original Act a large number of products have been added to the Schedule by regulation. Parts I and II now each contain well in excess of thirty classes of products and substances. For a current listing of these classes, see *Canadian Product Safety Guide*, CCH, Vol. 1, paragraphs 31-190 to 31-251. As well, as of April 1980, regulations have been promulgated under the Act governing seventeen classes of products and substances. See CRC 1978, c. 921-934 as amended, and SOR 79-605, 79-732, 79-843.

The Canadian Act raises a substantial number of legal and practical problems which have assumed increasing importance in the light of well publicized incidents such as lead soldering in electric kettles and large pop bottles which explode upon impact. Some of the more important questions are the following:

a)   What is the criterion for determining whether a product is hazardous? Should cost-benefit analysis play a role in such a determination?

b)   Should there be a more systematic effort to determine the safety of the major household items in current use?

c)   Should manufacturers be under statutory obligation to notify the Department of any dangers associated with their product which come to their attention, or are there sufficient private law incentives on manufacturers to dispense with such a regulatory requirement?

d)   When a product is put on the prohibited list, prohibiting the further sale of the product, what is the position of distributors, retailers and consumers who have previously purchased the item and still have it in their possession? Should the manufacturer be obliged to accept the goods back and make an appropriate refund of all or part of the purchase price? Should there be any deduction for use? (*Cf.* the U.S. Consumer Product Safety Act, ss. 12 and 15, which makes provisions for such civil remedies.) Does existing sales law already take care of the problem and, if so, how?

e)   Should a consumer be entitled to petition for the placing of a product on the restricted list and be entitled to appeal hearing?

GENERAL REFERENCES (Canadian and U.S.): *Canadian Product Safety Guide*, CCH Canadian Ltd., 2 vols.; Kimble, *Federal Consumer Product Safety Act* (West, 1975).

Chapter 7

Manufacturer's Liability for Defective Goods: The Privity Problem

Introductory Note:

Since the Sale of Goods Act is based on contractual relationships it is only concerned with the warranty claims of a buyer against the person from whom he bought the goods. The Act has nothing to say about his rights against prior parties in the distribution chain and in particular it is silent about the buyer's rights against the manufacturer of the goods when the manufacturer is not the seller.

We have previously encountered the problem in chapter 5(3) in the context of a manufacturer's liability for express warranties and have seen how the courts in England, Canada and the U.S. have surmounted the privity problem by relying on theories of collateral contracts (Anglo-Canadian courts) or on the hybrid origins of the action for breach of warranty (U.S. courts). A much more difficult question, both conceptually and in terms of public policy, is whether the walls of privity should also be breached to hold the manufacturer liable in damages to the ultimate buyer for breach of the implied statutory warranties resulting only in economic loss.

As will be seen, with the notable exception of the Supreme Court of Canada's decision in the *Kravitz* case, a civil law decision (see *infra*), the wall is still firm in Canada but somewhat less so in the U.S. In both countries some important inroads, at least for consumer goods and agricultural machinery, have been made by legislation and more will be made if, in Canada's case, the examples of New Brunswick, Quebec and Saskatchewan are generally followed. In reading the materials in the present chapter the student is urged to bear in mind the important distinctions between consumer and non-consumer goods, and between defective goods causing injury to person or other property, and defective goods only resulting in economic loss to the buyer.

OLRC Report on Consumer Warranties
(1972) pp. 65-8

It has often been remarked that in the modern marketing milieu it is the manufacturer who plays the dominant role. It is he who is responsible for putting the goods into the stream of commerce and, in most cases, of creating the consumer demand for them by continuous advertising. The retailer is little more than a way station. It is the manufacturer who endows the goods with their characteristics and it is he who determines the type of materials and components that shall be used and who establishes the quality control mechanism. It is also he who determines what express guarantees shall be given to the consumer and who is responsible for the availability of spare parts and the adequacy of servicing facilities. Almost all the consumer's knowledge about the goods is derived from the labels or markings attached to the goods on the sales literature that accompanies them — and these too originate from the manufacturer.

These are not the only factors that strongly militate in favour of holding the manufacturer responsible for breach of any express warranties and the warranties implied under The Sale of Goods Act. The present Anglo-Canadian law involves circuity of actions and an unnecessary multiplication of costs and proceedings. Typically the buyer sues the retailer who then joins the wholesale distributor or importer, and they in turn will bring in the manufacturer. If the retailer is insolvent or has otherwise closed his business for any reason, the consumer may not even be able to initiate an action. If the consumer has moved a substantial distance from the original place of purchase or to another province, he will be faced with new procedural hurdles. If the cause of the breakdown of the goods is disputed, the buyer will not have the right to obtain discovery of documents from the manufacturer or to examine his officers, although the manufacturer rather than the retailer is likely to be in possession of all the pertinent facts.

The retailer's lot is also an unhappy one. Ontario law has no procedural rule comparable to the American device of "vouching over" and the retailer is forced to go to the expense and trouble of formally joining the person next in the distributive link as a third party. If the consumer for some reason has delayed his action against the retailer, the retailer may find that the prescriptive period has lapsed, and that it is too late for him to issue a third party notice.

Despite these weighty reasons, Anglo-Canadian law has made little progress in permitting the consumer to proceed directly against the manufacturer. The doctrine of privity still remains a most formidable barrier. For practical purposes there appear to be very few exceptions to the rule. The rule in *Donaghue* v. *Stevenson* [1932] AC 562 does not apply to actions in negligence for pure economic losses. It is conceivable that the consumer may have an action against the manufacturer for negligent misstatements of fact under the *Hedley, Byrne* doctrine, but such an action would place a very heavy onus on the plaintiff. A more promising avenue would be via the concept of "collateral warranties" or "collateral contract". It is now well established that a manufacturer may be liable for breach of an express warranty if the warranty is intended to induce the buyer to order the manufacturer's product from another person. The English courts have applied the doctrine in a wide variety of situations but we have not been able to find a reported case in which the Anglo-Canadian courts have applied it to a consumer transaction.

In principle, however, there appears to be no reason why it should not apply and, in particular, why it should not apply to a manufacturer's express guarantee. But even allowing for this possibility, the consumer still faces several major difficulties. In the first place, the doctrine only applies to express representations. Second, the consumer must show that the representation was intended to have contractual force and, third, that he saw or knew of the representation *before* making his purchase and relied on it — that is, intended to accept the offer implicit in the representation. It is apparent that the doctrine of collateral waranty is not the full answer to the practical problems faced by the consumer.

In the light of the foregoing considerations the Commission recommends that the proposed Act contain a clearly stated statutory rule holding a manufacturer liable for breach of any express representations, and also deeming him to have given the same implied warranties as are attributed to the immediate seller under our sales law. For the purposes of this rule, the doctrine of privity of contract should be abolished in warranty claims by a buyer against the manufacturer of the goods.

b. CANADIAN PRECEDENTS

The change which we propose in Ontario law is not novel in Canada. At the turn of the century much new farming machinery was being introduced in the prairie provinces. The machinery did not always work satisfactorily and there was also widespread concern about the use of disclaimer clauses. To meet these difficulties, remedial legislation was adopted in Alberta as early as 1913[9] and was copied during the next six years by Saskatchewan and Manitoba. Similar legislation was adopted in Prince Edward Island at a much later date. Today, all of these acts imply various warranties in favour of the retail buyer of the equipment and all of them provide, in slightly varying language, that the manufacturer or provincial distributor as well as the dealer "are liable to the purchaser to observe, keep and perform the warranties" and that the purchaser "may maintain an action against any such manufacturer or general provincial distributor, as well as against the vendor, or against any one or more of them, for any breach of any of these warranties".[11] So far as we have been able to ascertain, these provisions, which clearly breach the walls of privity, have not created any particular difficulties.

c. AMERICAN DEVELOPMENTS

American developments provide another and still more important source of precedents. In discussing the developments it is important to distinguish between two separate problems, first, the liability of a manufacturer for defective goods that cause personal injuries or physical damage to the property of the buyer or some other person and, second, the liability of the manufacturer for defective goods that only cause economic losses. We are primarily concerned with the second problem, though, for reasons stated later in this chapter, the two problems interact closely.

---

[9]   The Farm Implements Act, Stat. Alta 1913, c. 15.
[11] The Agricultural Implements Act, 1968, Stat. Sask. 1968, c. 1, as am., s. 24.

As early as 1933 the Supreme Court of Washington held the Ford Motor Company liable for breach of an express warranty that the windshield on its passenger cars was shatter-proof.[13] This precedent was followed in another landmark decision, *Randy Knitwear Inc.* v. *American Cyanamid Co.,*[14] in which the New York Court of Appeals held a manufacturer of chemical resins liable for a false representation that fabrics treated with the resin were shrink-proof. In both these and other cases technical requirements of privity were ignored and liability was based on some other ground. One of the grounds was the hybrid nature of the action for breach of warranty, which was said to sound both in contract and in tort. The courts did not rely on the English doctrine of collateral contracts.

An important turning point in the development of this branch of American law occurred in *Henningsen* v. *Bloomfield Motors* (1960) 161 A 2d 69. In this historic decision the New Jersey Supreme Court held the Chrysler Corporation strictly responsible for a defect in one of its cars which caused a serious accident resulting in injuries to the buyer's wife and the total loss of the vehicle. Liability was predicated upon a theory of implied warranties running with the vehicle from the manufacturer to the ultimate buyer or user, and again any requirement of privity of contract was expressly rejected. In *Greenman* v. *Yuba Power Products, Inc.*(1963) 377 P 2d 897, the California Supreme Court abandoned the rationale of implied warranties as fictitious and held that the manufacturer's liability was imposed as a rule of public policy and was tortious in character. Many other courts have since followed this characterization.

This issue which still remains unresolved is whether the theory of strict tortious liability also applies to defects causing only economic loss. In *Santor* v. *A. & M. Karaghensian Inc.* (1965) 207 A 2d 305, another New Jersey decision, the court held that it did, but in *Seely* v. *White Motor Co.*(1965)P 2d 145, the California Supreme Court rejected the merger and held that sales law principles (including particularly Article 2 of the Uniform Commercial Code) continued to govern claims for economic losses. Subsequent courts have been divided in their approach, as have the authors of numerous law review articles. We shall return to this conflict.

There have also been some developments at the legislative level. Article 2-318 of the 1962 official text of the Uniform Commercial Code provided that:

> A seller's warranty whether express or implied extends to any natural person who is in the family or household of his buyer or who is a guest in his home if it is reasonable to expect that such person may use, consume or be affected by the goods and who is injured in person by breach of the warranty. A seller may not exclude or limit the operation of this section.

It was widely felt that this version was too restrictive and that it was out of step with the developing case law. The disapproval was reflected in unauthorized versions of the section adopted by a substantial number of Code states. With a view to discouraging the further proliferation of non-uniform versions the

---

[13]   *Baxter* v. *Ford Motor Co.*(1933), 12 P.2d 409, 15 P.2d 1188, 88 ALR 521.

[14]   (1962), 181 NE 2d 399 (NYCA). This was said to be based on the history of the action for breach of warranty. Later American decisions base their reasoning squarely on grounds of public policy.

sponsors of the Code promulgated a revised Article 2-318 in 1966. This contains three alternatives, Alternatives A, B and C. Alternative A corresponds to the previous version of the section. Alternatives B and C read as follows.

ALTERNATIVE B

A seller's warranty whether express or implied extends to any natural person who may reasonably be expected to use, consume or be affected by the goods and who is injured in person by breach of the warranty. A seller may not exclude or limit the operation of this section.

ALTERNATIVE C

A seller's warranty whether express or implied extends to any person who may reasonably be expected to use, consume or be affected by the goods and who is injured by breach of the warranty. A seller may not exclude or limit the operation of this section with respect to injury to the person of an individual to whom the warranty extends.

These alternatives go considerably beyond Alternative A. Alternative B extends the seller's express or implied warranties to *any* natural person who may reasonably be expected to use, consume or be affected by the goods. Unlike his counterpart in Alternative A, the beneficiary is not restricted to a member of the *buyer's* family or household or to a guest — a restriction that in most cases would make Alternative A inapplicable against the manufacturer. On the other hand, Alternative B is still limited to claims arising out of personal injuries. A critical difference between Alternatives B and C is that Alternative C applies, it seems, to any injury. However, it is not clear whether a claim solely for economic losses is deemed to an "injury".

It seems clear that the seller contemplated in Alternatives B and C includes the manufacturer of the goods if the other conditions of the provisions are satisfied. A number of Congressional bills on product warranties that have been introduced in recent years would have imposed liability on a manufacturer towards a consumer buyer for breach of the implied warranties. So far none of them has been enacted. More progress has been made at the state level, and several state acts now impose such liability. One of them is the Song-Beverley Consumer Warranty Act, which was adopted in California in 1970.

A. RECENT CANADIAN AND U.S. JUDICIAL AND LEGISLATIVE DEVELOPMENTS

1. CANADIAN JUDICIAL DEVELOPMENTS

RIVTOW MARINE LTD. v. WASHINGTON IRON WORKS
(1973) 40 DLR (3d) 530, [1974] SCR 1189

The plaintiff, Rivtow, operated a barge fitted with a crane designed and manufactured by the respondent, Washington, for which the respondent, Walkem, was the sole British Columbia representative and distributor. The crane had serious structural defects owing to design errors, but although both defendants by January 1966 were aware of the defects neither took steps to warn Rivtow. In September 1966 a crane which was identical to Rivtow's and which had been designed, manufactured, and installed on a barge by Washington collapsed, killing its operator. When Rivtow's crane was investigated after the incident its structural defects were discovered and it was withdrawn from service for repairs during one of the year's busiest seasons. Rivtow sued for the cost of repairs and for profits lost while its barge was out of service.

The Supreme Court of Canada speaking through Mr. Justice Ritchie, held:

(1) that both Washington and Walkem knew that Rivtow relied on them concerning the operation of the crane, and that a duty lay upon them both as soon as they became aware of the defects to warn Rivtow that repairs were necessary;

(2) that liability for the damage sustained through the inactivity of Rivtow's barge flowed from the failure to warn (on the part of both defendants) rather than from negligent design;

(3) that Rivtow's economic loss was attributable solely to the interruption of business, which was the immediate consequence of the breach of the duty to warn;

(4) that owing to "the proximity of relationship giving rise to a duty to warn", Rivtow's economic losses "were recoverable as compensation for the direct and demonstrably foreseeable result of the breach of that duty";

(5) that the cost of repairs could not be recovered from the manufacturer, Washington, because to do so would in effect be to allow recovery for breach of an implied warranty of fitness.

Laskin J. dissented on the last point and the following extract from his judgment provides his reasoning:

LASKIN J.: This is the first occasion upon which this Court has been called upon to determine whether recovery may be had in a negligence action for economic loss which stands alone and is not consequent upon physical injury. The trial Judge awarded damages for loss of earnings suffered by the appellant for a certain down period required for repairs to the pintle crane, but he denied recovery for the cost of repairs to make the faultily-designed and manufactured crane fit for service. In this view he is sustained in the reasons of my brother Ritchie which I have had an opportunity to read. I agree with the award of damages so far as it goes, but I would enlarge it to include as well the cost of repairs.

I would do this because I do not agree that the liability of the respondents should be rested on the one basis of a failure to warn of the probability of injury by reason of the defective design of the crane. The failure to warn is, of course, the only basis upon which, on the facts herein, liability could be imposed upon Walkem. However, Washington, as the designer and manufacturer of the crane, was under an anterior duty to prevent injury which foreseeably would result from its negligence in the design and manufacture of this piece of equipment. If physical harm had resulted, whether personal injury or damage to property (other than to the crane itself), Washington's liability to the person affected, under its anterior duty as a designer and manufacturer of a negligently produced crane, would not be open to question. Should it then be any less liable for the direct economic loss to the appellant resulting from the faulty crane merely because the likelihood of physical harm, either by way of personal injury to a third person or property damage to the appellant, was averted by the withdrawal of the crane from service so that it could be repaired?

Two new points are involved in this question. The first is whether Washington's liability for negligence should embrace economic loss when there has been no physical harm in fact, and the second is whether the appellant is a proper plaintiff to recover for economic loss and as well the cost of repairing the defective crane.

. . .

In brief, given the case of a manufacturer who is under a duty not to expose consumers or users of its products to an unreasonable risk of harm (and I would place builders of houses under the same duty), what are the limits on the kind or range of harm for which liability will be imposed if there is a breach of duty? One type of answer has been to invoke the notion of remoteness which may relate to physical harm no less than to economic loss: *cf. Seaway Hotels Ltd.* v. *Cragg (Canada) Ltd. and Consumers Gas Co.* (1960), 21 DLR (2d) 264, [1959] OR 581, and *Spartan Steel Alloys Ltd.* v. *Martin & Co. (Contractors) Ltd.,* [1972] 3 WLR 502. Another, and more usual answer since *MacPherson* v. *Buick Motor Co.* (1916), 217 NY 382, and *M'Alister (or Donoghue)* v. *Stevenson,* [1932] AC 562, has been to deny manufacturers' liability unless physical harm has resulted from the breach of duty. Put another way, liability has been denied on the ground that there is no duty to a consumer or user in respect of economic loss alone. It seems to me that this restriction on liability has in it more of a concern to avoid limitless claims for economic loss from any kind of negligence than a concern for the particular basis upon which manufacturers' liability for negligence rests. That liability rests upon a conviction that manufacturers should bear the risk of injury to consumers or users of their products when such products are carelessly manufactured because the manufacturers create the risk in the carrying on of their enterprises, and they will be more likely to safeguard the members of the public to whom their products are marketed if they must stand behind them as safe products to consume or to use. They are better able to insure against such risks, and the cost of insurance, as a business expense, can be spread with less pain among the buying public than would be the case if an injured consumer or user was saddled with the entire loss that befalls him.

This rationale embraces, in my opinion, threatened physical harm from a negligently-designed and manufactured product resulting in economic loss. I need not decide whether it extends to claims for economic loss where there is no threat of physical harm or to claims for damage, without more, to the defective product.

It is foreseeable injury to person or to property which supports recovery for economic loss suffered by a consumer or user who is fortunate enough to avert such injury. If recovery for economic loss is allowed when such injury is suffered, I see no reason to deny it when the threatened injury is forestalled. Washington can be no better off in the latter case than in the former. On the admitted facts, a crane on another person's barge, of similar design to that installed on the appellant's barge, had collapsed, killing its operator. It was when this fact came to its notice that the appellant took its crane out of service. Its crane had the same cracks in it that were found in the collapsed crane, and they were due to the same faulty design in both cases. Here then was a piece of equipment whose use was fraught with danger to person and property because of negligence in its design and manufacture; one death had already resulted from the use of a similar piece of equipment that had been marketed by Washington. I see nothing untoward in holding Washington liable in such circumstances for economic loss resulting from the down time necessary to effect repairs to the crane. The case is not one where a manufactured product proves to be merely defective (in short, where it has not met promised expectations), but rather one where by reason of the defect there is a foreseeable risk of physical harm from its use and where the alert avoidance of such harm gives rise to economic loss. Prevention of threatened harm resulting directly in economic loss should not be treated differently from post-injury cure.

Liability of Washington to make good the appellant's loss of profits being established, it remains to consider its liability for the cost of repairs. It is unnecessary in this case to see this cost as necessarily a foreseeable consequence of the breach of anterior duty resting upon Washington. It can stand on another footing. A plaintiff injured by another's negligence is required to act reasonably to mitigate his damages. If his damages are economic damages only, mitigation may involve him in repairing the defect which brought them about. It may not be open to him to do that because the tortfeasor is in control of the matter that invites repair or correction, as in the *Cragg* and *Spartan Steel* cases already cited. But where the defective product which threatened injury has been in use by the plaintiff, it may be reasonable for him, upon learning of the threat of likely injury from its continued use, to expend money for its repair to make it fit for service. Such an expenditure then becomes part of the economic loss for which Washington must respond. No question was raised in this case about the reasonableness of the appellant's conduct in suspending use of the crane nor about the reasonableness of having it repaired nor of the reasonableness of the cost of repair.

Note: In *Lambert* v. *Lewis* [1980] 2 WLR 299 (CA), the facts of which have been previously given (*supra*, chapter 5(A)(1)), the retailers argued that they were entitled to rely on the doctrine of *Donaghue* v. *Stevenson* [1932] AC 562 (HL) to recover damages from the manufacturers of the towing hitch coextensive with their liability to the owner even though the defect had only caused the retailers economic loss. Counsel for the retailers distinguished *S.C.M. (U.K.) Ltd.* v. *W.J. Whittal & Son Ltd.* [1971] 1 QB 337 and *Spartan Steel & Alloys Ltd.* v. *Martin & Co. (Contractors) Ltd.* [1973] 1 QB 27 on the ground that in the present case there were a limited number of contractors buying and selling, stocking and distributing the manufacturers' article and that the manufacturers could expect any and all of these couplings which they manufactured to go through the chain of such contractors to the ultimate consumer with some such result of its use as happened in this case of physical damage and consequent legal liability.

Speaking for the court, Stephenson L.J. rejected the argument on the following grounds (*ibid.*, at 331):

> The answer seems to us to be found in principle and on authority, in particular the authority of those two recent decisions of this court, not in a detailed examination of the cases nor in a logical analysis of the distinction between physical damage to the owner's trailer and physical injury to the first plaintiff and her family, or between loss of profits and financial loss incurred by legal liability to pay damages, but in applying common sense to draw a line between circumstances where the financial loss can and cannot be held to be recoverable for a breach of duty owed the party who incurs the loss. Whether we follow the first thoughts of Lord Denning M.R. in *S.C.M. (United Kingdom) Ltd.* v. *W.J. Whittall & Son Ltd.* [1971] 1 QB 337 with which Winn L.J. agreed, and consider remoteness, or his second thoughts in *Spartan Steel & Alloys Ltd.* v. *Martin & Co. (Contractors) Ltd.* [1973] QB 27 with which Lawton L.J. agreed, and discard everything but policy in setting bounds to duty and damage, we reach the conclusion that the loss which the retailers incurred by their liability to indemnify the owner against his legal liability to compensate the plaintiffs cannot be recovered from the manufacturers.

Stephenson L.J. also observed (at 331):

> There comes a point where the logical extension of the boundaries of duty and damage is halted by the barrier of commercial sense and practical convenience. In our judgment, the facts of this case do not enable the retailers to push that barrier back as far as to include themselves and their damage within the range of the manufacturers and the towing hitch which they put into the market, or to surmount the barrier where we think common sense would place it.

Are you persuaded by this reasoning? In the House of Lords ([1981] 1 All ER 1185, at 1192), Lord Diplock expressly left open the question for future decisions.

ITAL-CANADIAN INVESTMENTS LTD. v. NORTH SHORE PLUMBING AND HEATING
[1978] 4 WWR 289 (BC SC)

ANDERSON J.: This is a motion to dispose of the following points of law prior to trial, as follows:

> (i) That the Statement of Claim herein discloses no cause of action against the Defendant W. H. Olsen Manufacturing Co. Ltd., as the law does not permit recovery of damages for economic loss in a negligence action where there has been no damage to person or property;
> (ii) Whether the Plaintiff's claim against the Defendant W. H. Olsen Manufacturing Co. Ltd. is barred by the Limitations Act, SBC 1975, chapter 37.

The plaintiff has applied to amend its statement of claim, and without determining whether the amendment should be permitted I have approached the above issues on the footing that the statement of claim has been amended in accordance with the plaintiff's motion.

The "amended" statement of claim reads, in part, as follows:

4. On or about the months of June, July, October, November and December of 1970, the Plaintiff contracted with the Defendant North Shore Plumbing & Heating Co. Ltd., both verbally and in writing to supply and install the heating system to a premises situate at 1370 Main Street, in the Municipality of North Vancouver, in the Province of British Columbia.

5. The Plaintiff paid to the Defendant, North Shore Plumbing & Heating Co. Ltd., for the above-mentioned contract the sum of Seventeen Thousand and Eighty-seven ($17,087.00) Dollars.

6. The said heating system was to consist, at least in part, of oil-fired heaters, manufactured by the Defendant, W. H. Olsen Manufacturing Co. Ltd.

7. *The Plaintiff relied on the advice and selection of the Defendant, North Shore Plumbing & Heating Co. Ltd. in determining what unit heaters were to be provided and installed.*

8. The said heating system and the said unit heaters were selected, supplied and installed in a negligent manner by the Defendant, North Shore Plumbing & Heating Co. Ltd.

9. The said unit heaters were negligently manufactured by the Defendant, W. H. Olsen Manufacturing Co. Ltd.

10. In or about the month of December, 1970, the Plaintiff encountered a number of difficulties with the said heating system and in particular, encountered difficulties with the gas-fired heaters in that there were continual break-downs.

11. In or about the month of November, 1976, the said heating system had become inoperational and had caused such financial and other damage to the Plaintiff that it became necessary to remove the entire heating system and reinstall another at great cost to the Plaintiff herein.

12. *The Plaintiff was not aware of the fundamental breach of contract or the breach of the warranty of fitness and the negligence until February 1977 when an engineer's study was completed.*

13. The said difficulties and damage caused by the problems with the heating system and gas-fired heaters was [sic] so great that there was a fundamental breach of the said contract.

14. *The Plaintiff claims damages for breach of an implied warranty of fitness.*

15. *The Plaintiff pleads the provisions of the Sale of Goods Act, RSBC 1960, Chapter 344.*

• • •

Counsel for the plaintiff agrees that the only claim for damages is in respect of the heating system and the gas-fired heaters. There is no claim for loss of profits or for damages to persons or property.

As to the first point, the plaintiff cannot succeed against the defendant W.H. Olsen Manufacturing Co. Ltd. (hereinafter called the "manufacturer") on the basis of the facts outlined in the pleadings. There is no contractual relationship, express or implied, between the plaintiff and the manufacturer so the plaintiff cannot succeed on this basis. The plaintiff cannot succeed against the defendant for recovery of damages for economic loss in a negligence action where there has been no damage to persons or property. The judgment of Ritchie J. in *Rivtow Marine Ltd.* v. *Washington Iron Works Ltd.* [1973] 6 WWR 692, 40 DLR (3d) 530 at 541 (Can.), reads as follows:

As I have indicated, the judgment of the Court of Appeal in this case [1972] 3

WWR 735, 26 DLR (3d) 559] appears to me to proceed on the assumption that Walkem and Washington owed a duty of care to the appellant as being a person ". . . so closely and directly affected" by the faulty design of the cranes that they ought reasonably to have had it in contemplation as being so affected in directing their mind to the known defects which are here called in question.

Proceeding on this assumption, I take it that the Court of Appeal would have treated the respondents as being liable for damages attributable to personal injury or damage to property resulting from defects in the cranes, but Mr. Justice Tysoe, in concluding his reasons for judgment at p. 579 said:

> In my opinion the law of British Columbia as it exists today is that neither a manufacturer of a potentially dangerous or defective article nor other person who is within the proximity of relationship contemplated in *M'Alister (Donoghue)* v. *Stevenson* [1932] AC 562 (HL), is liable in tort, as distinct from contract, to an ultimate consumer or user for damage arising in the article itself, or for economic loss resulting from the defect in the article, but only for personal injury and damage to other property caused by the article or its use. It is my view that to give effect to the claims of Rivtow it would be necessary to extend the rule of liability laid down in *Donoghue's* case beyond what it now is. I do not feel this Court would be justified in extending it so that it covers the character of damage suffered by Rivtow. I think that, if that is to be done, it must be left to a higher Court to do it.

Mr. Justice Tysoe's conclusion was based in large measure on a series of American cases, and particularly *Trans World Airlines Inc.* v. *Curtiss-Wright Corpn.* (1955) 148 NYS 2d 284, where it is pointed out that the liability for the cost of repairing damage to the defective article itself and for the economic loss flowing directly from the negligence, is akin to liability under the terms of an express or implied warranty of fitness and as it is contractual in origin cannot be enforced against the manufacturer by a stranger to the contract. It was, I think, on this basis that the learned trial Judge disallowed the appellant's claim for repairs and for such economic loss as it would, in any event, have sustained even if the proper warning had been given. I agree with this conclusion for the same reasons; but while this finding excludes recovery for damage to the article and economic loss directly flowing from Washington's negligence and faulty design, it does not exclude the additional damage occasioned by breach of the duty to warn of the danger.

While the judgment of Ritchie J. has been subject to much discussion and criticism, it is not for me to depart from what appears to me to be a clear statement of the law relating to claims for damages in respect of alleged negligent manufacture of products (in this case the gas-fired heaters).

For a contrary opinion see the judgment of Lord Wilberforce in *Anns* v. *London Borough of Merton* [1977] 2 All ER 492 at 505 (HL), as follows:

> *Nature of the damages recoverable and arising out of the cause of action.* There are many questions here which do not directly arise at this stage and which may never arise if the actions are tried. But some conclusions are necessary if we are to deal with the issue as to limitation. The damages recoverable include all those which foreseeably arise from the breach of the duty of care which, as regards the council, I have held to be a duty to take reasonable care to secure compliance with the byelaws. Subject always to adequate proof of causation, these damages may include damages for personal injury and damage to property. In my opinion they may also include damage to the dwelling-house itself; for the whole purpose of the byelaws in requiring foundations to be of certain standard is to prevent damage arising from

weakness of the foundations which is certain to endanger the health or safety of occupants.

To allow recovery for such damage to the house follows, in my opinion, from normal principle. If classification is required, the relevant damage is in my opinion material, physical damage, and what is recoverable is the amount of expenditure necessary to restore the dwelling to a condition in which it is no longer a danger to the health or safety of persons occupying and possibly (depending on the circumstances) expenses arising from necessary displacement. On the question of damages generally I have derived much assistance from the judgment (dissenting on this point, but of strong persuasive force) of Laskin C.J. in the Canadian Supreme Court case of *Rivtow Marine Ltd.* v. *Washington Iron Works* [*supra*] and from the judgments of the New Zealand Court of Appeal (furnished by courtesy of that court) in *Bowen* v. *Paramount Bldrs. (Hamilton) Ltd.*, 22nd December 1976 (not yet reported).

In the result, I hold that the statement of claim discloses no cause of action against the manufacturer.

Motion allowed.

[Anderson J. also held that the negligence claim fell within s. 3(4) of the Limitations Act, 1975 (BC) and was statute-barred.]

FULLER v. FORD MOTOR COMPANY OF CANADA LTD.
(1978) 22 OR (2d) 764, 94 DLR (3d) 127 (Ont. Co. Ct.)

HOUSTON Co. Ct. J.: The plaintiff purchased a motor vehicle from the defendant Lange & Fetter Motors Limited on October 16, 1974. It was agreed that the defendant Ford Motor Company of Canada Limited manufactures cars in the Province of Ontario. The motor vehicle purchased by the plaintiff was manufactured by the Ford Motor Company Limited. The vehicle was a 1974 Econoline 8-cylinder half-ton panel truck. The vehicle was a new vehicle. The contract entered into between Lange & Fetter Motors Limited was entitled Retail Buyer's Car Order And Agreement — ex. 1. The plaintiff operated the vehicle in connection with his electrical business in the Village of Campbellford, near the town of Trenton where the vehicle was purchased. The vehicle was taken in to the defendant Lange & Fetter Motors Limited for minor repairs from time to time.

On February 28, 1975, the plaintiff accompanied by his wife was returning from a shopping trip to Campbellford on the Campbellford Road travelling from Stirling, Ontario. The plaintiff testified that he was travelling on an asphalt surface at a speed of 20 to 25 m.p.h. The speed limit on the highway was 50 m.p.h., so far as the plaintiff was aware. There had been some snow and the surface of the roads was partly icy. The plaintiff was executing a turn which he says was about a 90-degree turn, and a long one. He entered the turn without difficulty but when he applied the brakes nothing happened. The vehicle continued to the left and eventually went into the ditch where the front wheels struck a culvert and the vehicle stopped.

I accept the evidence of the plaintiff and I find as a fact that when he got out of the vehicle he found on the pavement the tire, the rear hub cap and part of the axle, all of which was in one piece. The portion had become detached from the right rear of the vehicle. I believe the plaintiff when he says that the tire was not flat when he went back and that he picked it up and bounced it on the pavement. Mr. Burkholder, an independent appraiser from Belleville, Ontario, testified on behalf of the plaintiff. He was obviously a person experienced in the appraisal business and an impressive witness. I find as a fact that the vehicle had not been in a previous accident and I reject the evidence that the damage was caused by the vehicle striking the culvert after it left the travelled portion of the highway.

• • •

The plaintiff claims against both defendants in contract. He relies on the breach of warranty which was given to the plaintiff at the time he purchased the vehicle. The Warranty Facts Booklet, ex. 4, says:

> All Ford and the Selling Dealer require is that you properly operate, maintain and care for your vehicle, and that you return for warranty service to your Selling Dealer's place of business or to any authorized Ford or Lincoln-Mercury dealer if you are traveling, have moved a long distance or need emergency repairs. Warranty repairs will be made with Ford Authorized Service or Remanufactured Parts.

In an apparent attempt to limit liability, the booklet states:

> To the extent allowed by law, THIS WARRANTY IS IN PLACE of all other warranties, express or implied, including ANY IMPLIED WARRANTY OF MERCHANTABILITY OR FITNESS. Under this warranty, repair or replacement of parts is the only remedy.

The plaintiff also relies on s. 15 of the Sale of Goods Act, RSO 1970, c. 421 . . .

Claim in contract

The vehicle was defective as I have found. The evidence revealed that it is possible that mistakes are made on the assembly line. It is not possible to say in many cases of manufacturers' liability what was the precise cause of the failure of the product or a component part of the product, *i.e.*, the axle, in this lawsuit. I find as a fact that there was a latent defect in the axle of this vehicle

Mr. Justice R. E. Holland in *Bradshaw et al. v. Boothe's Marine Ltd. et al.; Snelling, Third Party; Superior Propane Ltd., Fourth Party* [1973] 2 OR 646 at p. 653, 35 DLR (3d) 43 at p. 50, considers s. 15, para. 1 of the Sale of Goods Act and refers to *Marleau v. People's Gas Supply Co. Ltd.* [1940] SCR 708, [1940] 4 DLR 433.

Mr. Justice Lerner in *McMorran v. Dominion Stores Ltd. et al.* (1977) 14 OR (2d) 559, 74 DLR (3d) 186, considered a claim which was founded both on breach of warranty in the sale and negligence in the manufacture of a bottle of carbonated soda-water. I have adopted Mr. Justice Lerner's reasoning. There was a defect in the factory materials or workmanship. The vehicle had had only normal use. Accordingly I find that both defendants are liable to the plaintiff for a breach of the warranty given to the plaintiff. I find it is unnecessary to consider s. 15 of the Sale of Goods Act which the plaintiff relied upon.

• • •

The claim in negligence

Professor Linden (as he then was) has a chapter in his admirable work, *Canadian Tort Law*, on "Products Liability" — c. 15. At p. 489 the learned author (now Mr. Justice Linden) says:

> In demanding proof that the product was in the same condition when it left the manufacturer's plant as it was when it did the damage complained of, the courts are merely reiterating the sensible view that a producer will not be held liable for damages he did not cause. Earlier the courts had flirted with a requirement that the product be in a sealed container, but this was soon abandoned. Nevertheless, some courts have gone overboard in the strength of the evidence of causation they require.

The plaintiff in this case had no opportunity to inspect and detect the latent defect. I have already said that I find there was no other intervening cause for the failure in this axle.

For some obscure reason it has been the policy of the law in Canada, but not in the U.S.A., to limit economic losses in cases where negligence is the basis of the claim and property damage has been caused rather than physical injury. Laskin, J. (as he then was), in *Rivtow Marine Ltd.* v. *Washington Iron Works et al.* [1974] SCR 1189, 40 DLR (3d) 530, [1973] 6 WWR 692, commented on this. . . .

[Houston J. quoted several passages from the judgment of Laskin J., reproduced *supra*, and continued:]

It is trite to say as stated on more than one occasion by Chief Justice Cartwright that each case must be decided on its own facts. In this case a corporation produced a motor vehicle knowing that it would be eventually bought by someone who would operate it on a highway. The manufacturer owed a duty to that person to use reasonable care in the manufacturing process. The car was defective and the burden of proof is to prove negligence on a balance of probabilities. The reasoning of Mr. Justice Laskin (as he then was) I have applied to the facts in the case at bar and I find that defendant Ford Motor Company Limited is liable to the plaintiff in negligence. Mr. Justice Laskin's judgment was a dissenting one, in part.

Counsel for the defendant Ford Motor Company Limited referred me to *J. Nunes Diamonds Ltd.* v. *Dominion Electric Protection Co.* [1972] SCR 769, 26 DLR (3d) 699; *Phillips et al.* v. *Ford Motor Co. of Canada Ltd. et al.* [1971] 2 OR 637, 18 DLR (3d) 641, and *Phillips* v. *Chrysler Corp. of Canada Ltd. and Roxburgh Motors Ltd.* [1962] OR 375, 32 DLR (2d) 347. In the *J. Nunes Diamonds* decision, liability was held to be governed by the contract entered into between the parties. The *Phillips* decision in our Court of Appeal was based on the particular facts in that lawsuit. In *Phillips* v. *Chrysler Corp. of Canada Ltd.* the trial Judge did not find any defect in the motor vehicle.

Counsel agreed at the outset that the damages for repair to the vehicle was $715.85. At the commencement of the trial, I did not allow an amendment by the defendant Lange & Fetter Motors Limited to add a third party claim over against the defendant Ford Motor Company of Canada Limited. In the result the plaintiff will have judgment against both defendants jointly and severally for the sum of $715.85 and costs.

Judgment for plaintiff.

Notes:

1   Did Houston J. correctly apply the *majority* judgment in *Rivtow* to the facts at bar? What would be the practical consequence of holding a manufacturer liable in negligence for a dangerous defect causing property damage to the product itself? In the case of motor vehicles and similar products can one always draw a meaningful distinction between dangerous and non-dangerous defects? Should it be possible for a manufacturer to limit his exposure to damage claims where no accident has yet occurred and, if so, how should he go about it where there is no privity between him and potential claimants?

For a review of the recent Canadian jurisprudence in this area, see S. Schwartz, "Jurisprudential Developments in Manufacturers' Liability for Defective Products Where the Only Damage is Economic Loss (1979-80) 4 CBLJ 164.

2   In *General Motors Products of Canada Ltd.* v. *Kravitz* [1979] 1 SCR 790, the Supreme Court of Canada considered a claim by a buyer that an automobile manufacturer is liable under the Quebec Civil Code for latent defects in a new vehicle purchased by the buyer from one of the manufacturer's authorized dealers, quite apart from the dealer's liability and notwithstanding the absence of privity between the parties. Kravitz brought an action against GM and the dealer claiming: (1) that his tender of the automobile to GM be declared valid; (2) that the sale of the automobile to him by the dealer be cancelled; and (3) that GM and the dealer be compelled jointly and severally to pay back the purchase price of the automobile and to pay certain damages. The Quebec Court of Appeal upheld the Superior Court judgment which found that the presence of serious latent defects in the automobile justified cancellation of the sale and that GM and the dealer were liable for the defects. Only GM appealed.

A unanimous Supreme Court of Canada, speaking through Pratte J., upheld the Court of Appeal's decision. The Court found that the "no-warranty" provision in the contract of sale between the dealer and Kravitz was null and void on the principle adopted by the French courts and consistent with the Civil Code that a manufacturer or professional seller cannot "contract out of the [Code's (Article 1522)] legal warranty against latent defects or limit the liability resulting from such warranty". The GM standard new car warranty given to Kravitz when he bought the automobile was also no bar to Kravitz's claim because to accept its limitation would be in effect "to relieve GM from its liability under the legal warranty for latent defects . . .". On the important question of whether Kravitz could exercise a direct remedy against GM the Court found that the legal warranty against latent defects given by GM in its sale to the dealer was effective not only between the parties to the immediate contract but also enured for the benefit of a subsequent purchaser:

> A claim in warranty against latent defects is not one that is personal to the purchaser in the sense that he is entitled to it *intuitu personae*; the purchaser is entitled to it as the owner of the thing. As we have seen, it is a claim that is tied to the thing to which it relates. It is therefore transferred to the successors by particular title at the same time as the thing itself, in that the initial seller is liable on it to any purchaser of the thing sold. This solution is in keeping with the relevant articles of the *Civil Code* and with the principles on which they are based. [p. 496-7, DLR].

The court found that as Kravitz "became the creditor of G.M.'s warranty against latent defects" he could bring an action for cancellation and damages against GM.

As will be seen from the above extract, the court's reasoning is strikingly reminiscent of the theory of liability adopted by the court in *Henningsen's* case except that there the plaintiffs were suing to recover for personal injuries as well as other heads of damages. In *Kravitz's* case, on the other hand, the car had not been involved in an accident and the plaintiff was not basing his claim on any delictual liability of GM. *Kravitz* therefore stands for the important proposition that, under Quebec law, a manufacturer is liable to the ultimate buyer for breach of the implied (legal) warranty that his goods are free from inherent defects. This goes much further than any comparable jurisprudence on the common law side though *Kravitz* may well have a spill-over effect. What remains unclear is whether *Kravitz* will be extended to non-consumer cases and cases where the manufacturer's product is processed, transformed or otherwise changed before it reaches the ultimate buyer's hands. All the earlier Quebec cases referred to in Pratte J.'s judgment involved consumer products — usually motor vehicles.

See the special issue of the McGill Law Journal on the *Kravitz* decision: (1980) 25 McGill LJ 296 *et seq*. See also Schwartz, "The Manufacturer's Liability to the Purchaser of a 'Lemon': A Review of the Situation in Canada After *General Motors Products of Canada Ltd.* v. *Kravitz*" (1979) 11 Ottawa L. Rev. 583, and Wm. E. Tetley, Q.C., in J. Ziegel (ed.), *Papers and Comments, Ninth Annual Workshop on Commercial and Consumer Law* (1981) pp. 244 *et seq*.

2. CANADIAN LEGISLATIVE DEVELOPMENTS

Note: The extract from the OLRC Warranties Report, *supra*, pp. 367 *et seq*., shows that as early as 1913 remedial legislation in Alberta breached the walls of privity in order to protect retail buyers of new farm machinery. The Ontario Law Reform Commission, building upon this precedent and grounding manufacturers' liability in sales law rather than in tort, recommended that the doctrine of privity be abolished in warranty claims by a consumer buyer against the manufacturer of the goods. They recommended that a manufacturer be held civilly liable for breach of any express warranties and that the manufacturer be deemed to have given to the consumer buyer (whether or not the goods were purchased directly from the manufacturer) implied warranties comparable to those that run from retailer to buyer.

The Commission's recommendations were incorporated into Bill 110, the Consumer Products Warranties Act, 1976, which received first reading on June 16, 1979. The Bill did not proceed beyond its introduction and has not been reintroduced since then. Apparently, industry opposition and the government's hope that agreement would be reached among the provinces on a substantially uniform bill account for the lack of progress. Examine the provisions of the Bill, especially ss. 1(a) to (e), 3(2), 4, 5, 8(1), 9, 10(3), and determine to what extent it implements the OLRC recommendations. Bill 110 generally contains, inter alia, four implied warranties deemed to be given by the manufacturer and retailer jointly to a consumer buyer: (1) that the product corresponds to its description where the sale is "by description made by a person other than the retail seller"; (2) that the product will perform for a reasonable length of time; (3) that the product is in such condition that a consumer buyer fully aware of the product's defects would buy without price abatement; and (4) that "spare parts and reasonable repair facilities will be available for a reasonable period of time."

The Saskatchewan Consumer Products Warranties Act, 1977 (RSS 1978, c. C-30) adopted the OLRC's recommendation to abolish the doctrine of privity for consumer warranty claims (see s. 14(1) and L. J. Romero, "The Consumer Products Warranties Act" (1978-79) 43 Sask. L. Rev. 81 at 187-89). The Saskatchewan Act also provides statutory warranties similar to those found in Bill 110. Examine ss. 13(2), 13(3) and 11 of the Saskatchewan Act. To what extent do they differ significantly from the implied warranties in Bill 110? See Romero, *op cit.*, at 156-57.

New Brunswick has also enacted similar legislation in its Consumer Product Warranty and Liability Act (SNB 1978, c. C-18.1; proclaimed in force effective January 1, 1980, with the exception of the provision dealing with warranties for repairs). Sections 23 and 27(1) provide as follows:

> **23.** Where the seller is in breach of a warranty provided by this Act, any person who is not a party to the contract but who suffers a consumer loss because of the breach may recover damages against the seller for the loss if it was reasonably foreseeable at the time of the contract as liable to result from the breach.

> **27.** (1) A supplier of a consumer product that is unreasonably dangerous to person or property because of a defect in design, materials or workmanship is liable to any person who suffers a consumer loss in the Province because of the defect, if the loss was reasonably foreseeable at the time of his supply as liable to result from the defect and

> (a) he has supplied the consumer product in the Province;
>
> (b) he has supplied the consumer product outside the Province but has done something in the Province that contributes to the consumer loss suffered in the Province; or
>
> (c) he has supplied the consumer product outside the Province but the defect arose in whole or in part because of his failure to comply with any mandatory federal standards in relation to health or safety, or the defect caused the consumer product to fail to comply with any such standards.

"Consumer loss" is broadly defined in s. 1(1) to include all non-business losses. What is the relationship between s. 23 and s. 27(1)? How do they differ conceptually and in practical effect from the implied warranty provisions in Bill 110 and the Saskatchewan Act? Would the New Brunswick Act entitle the buyer of a defective vehicle to bring a direct claim against its manufacturer to recover the purchase price paid by the buyer to the motor vehicle dealer from whom he bought it?

Three other developments also require attention. The first involves the Quebec Consumer Protection Act 1978, which became effective April 30, 1980, with the exception of section 6(c) and (d). Title I, Chapter II, Division I of the Act deals with warranties, and s. 54 in effect deems the manufacturer to have given warranties similar to those imposed upon the retail seller. These provisions appear to have been influenced by the corresponding developments in the common law provinces described above. For an analysis of these provisions see Applebaum, "The Law of Warranty in the Province of Quebec", *Meredith Memorial Lectures 1979*, p. 71.

Secondly, in its Report on Products Liability (1979), the OLRC made the following recommendations (p. 129):

1. Ontario should enact a principle of strict liability in accordance with recommendations 2 and 3 below.
2. A person who supplies a defective product that causes injury should be strictly liable in tort for damages.
3. A person who supplies a product and who makes a false statement concerning the product, reliance upon which causes injury, should be strictly liable in tort for damages, whether or not the reliance is that of the person injured.
4. Subject to recommendation 5, the principle of strict liability proposed in recommendations 2 and 3 should cover personal injury and damage to property, together with economic loss directly consequent thereon.
5. The principle of strict liability proposed in recommendations 2 and 3 should not extend to damage to property used in the course of carrying on a business.
6. The principle of strict liability proposed in recommendations 2 and 3 should not extend to pure economic loss.

This last recommendation merits special attention. Does it mean that *Rivtow Marine* and its progeny would retain their relevance, assuming the Commission's recommendations are implemented in due course? So far the Ontario government has not shown its hand.

The third development concerns the OLRC's approach to the problem in its Sales Report in the context of claims for pure economic losses. As will be seen from the extract below, the Commission chose not to take a firm position but preferred to put forward some tentative recommendations for discussion purposes.

OLRC Sales Report
pp. 247-48

The Commission supports in principle the desirability of extending the express and implied warranties of a seller in favour of a subsequent buyer. After careful deliberation, however, we have decided not to take a firm position on the issue at this time, but to postpone a final decision until interested parties have had an opportunity to express their views. We adopt this position primarily because of the novelty and importance of the issue in Ontario, and because of the absence of hard data on the probable impact of such an extension of warranty liability. The only precedent in Canada appears to be the farm implement and agricultural machinery legislation in the Prairie Provinces and Prince Edward

Island. These are useful guides if one is considering an incremental approach, but they provide little assistance in seeking to assess the impact of a general change in warranty law.

There appears to be an equal paucity of precedents in other common law jurisdictions. American law is still in a state of flux. We noted in our *Warranties Report*, the decision of the New Jersey Supreme Court in *Santor* v. *A. & M. Karagheusian, Inc.* (1965) 207 A 2d 305 (NJ Sup. Ct.). In that case, the Court extended the concept of tortious liability for personal injury and physical damage caused by a defective product to purely economic losses in the case of consumer goods. This extension was disapproved in the majority judgment of the Supreme Court of California in *Seeley* v. *White Motor Co.*, (1965) 403 P. 2d 145 (Cal. Sup. Ct.) and has been rejected by the majority of other courts. American courts have been equally divided with respect to whether the remote seller can be sued on a theory of implied warranty running with the goods. On the strength of the recent decision of the Supreme Court of Alaska in *Morrow* v. *New Moon Homes, Inc.*, (1976) 548 P. 2d 279 (Ala. Sup. Ct.) there appears, however, to be a trend in favour of allowing consumer claims, subject to the usual defences available to a seller under the Uniform Commercial Code. The question of the manufacturer's liability to the ultimate buyer in non-consumer transactions remains at large.

Finally, reference should be made to the important recommendations in the New South Wales *Working Paper on the Sale of Goods*. This Working Paper, basing itself in part on our *Warranties Report*, recommended extending the warranty of merchantable quality in favour of a remote buyer, but without confining it to consumer goods. The remote buyer's claim would, however, generally be subject to any defence that would have been available to the remote seller in an action for breach of warranty by the immediate buyer. We consider other aspects of the New South Wales recommendations more fully below.

The Commission's exposure draft statutory provision will be found in s. 5.18. (In considering the Commission's hesitancy bear in mind that the Sales Report is concerned with all types of sale of goods and not only with consumer goods.)

3. U.S. JUDICIAL DEVELOPMENTS

MORROW v. NEW MOON HOMES, INC.
(1976) 548 P. 2d 279 (SC of Alaska)

RABINOWITZ CHIEF JUSTICE: This appeal raises questions concerning personal jurisdiction over, and the liability of, a nonresident manufacturer of a defective mobile home that was purchased in Alaska from a resident seller.

In October of 1969, Joseph R. and Nikki Morrow bought a mobile home from Golden Heart Mobile Homes, a Fairbanks retailer of mobile homes. A plaque on the side of the mobile home disclosed that the home had been manufactured in Oregon by New Moon Homes, Inc. The Morrows made a down payment of $1,800, taking out a loan for the balance of the purchase price from the First National Bank of Fairbanks. The loan amount of $10,546.49, plus interest of 9 percent per year, was to be repaid by the Morrows in 72 monthly installments of $190.13 each.

At the time of the purchase, the Morrows inspected the mobile home and noticed that the carpeting had not been laid and that several windows were broken. Roy Miller, Golden Heart's salesman, assured them that these problems would be corrected and later made good his assurances. Miller also told the Morrows that the mobile home was a "good trailer", ". . . as warm as . . . any other trailer." After the sale, Miller moved the Morrows' mobile home to Lakeview Terrace, set it up on the space the Morrows had rented, and made sure the utilities were connected. Then the troubles started.

On the first night that the mobile home's furnace was in use, the motor went out and had to be replaced. The electric furnace installed by the manufacturer had been removed by someone who had replaced the original with an oil furnace. The furnace vent did not fit, and consequently the "stove pipe" vibrated when the furnace was running. Subsequent events showed the furnace malfunction was not the primary problem with the mobile home.

About four days after the mobile home had been set up, the Morrows noticed that the doors did not close all the way and that the windows were cracked. The bathtub leaked water into the middle bedroom. In March of 1970 when the snow on the roof began to melt, the roof leaked. Water came through gaps between the ceiling and the wall panels, as well as along the bottom of the wallboard. A short circuit developed in the electrical system; the lights flickered at various times. When it rained, water came out of the light fixture in the hallway. Other problems with the mobile home included the following: the interior walls did not fit together at the corners; the paneling came off the walls; the windows and doors were out of square; the door frames on the bedroom doors fell off and the closet doors would not slide properly; the curtains had glue on them; and the finish came off the kitchen cabinet doors.

Despite all these problems, the Morrows continued to live in the mobile home and make the loan payments. Golden Heart Mobile Homes was notified many times of the difficulties the Morrows were having with their mobile home. Roy Miller, the Golden Heart salesman with whom the Morrows had dealt, did put some caulking around the bathtub, but otherwise he was of little assistance. Finally, sometime before April 1, 1970, Nikki Morrow informed Miller that if Golden Heart did not fix the mobile home the Morrows wanted to return it. Miller said the Morrows would "[h]ave to take it up with the bank." Subsequently, Golden Heart went out of business.

The First National Bank of Fairbanks was more sensitive to the Morrows' plight. Upon being informed by the Morrows that they intended to make no further payments on the mobile home, bank personnel went out and inspected the home several times. In addition, on May 27, 1970, the bank wrote to New Moon Homes, Inc. in Silverton, Oregon. Its letter informed New Moon of the problems the Morrows were having with their New Moon mobile home and asked whether New Moon expected to send a representative to Fairbanks since Golden Heart, the dealer, was no longer in business. Apparently, New Moon did not respond to the bank's letter.

A short time later the Morrows' counsel wrote a letter to New Moon Homes notifying New Moon that the Morrows intended to hold the company liable for damages for breach of implied warranties. About a month later the Morrows separated, with Nikki Morrow continuing to live in the mobile home. She continued to make payments to First National because she "couldn't afford Alaskan rents." Nikki Morrow eventually moved out of the mobile home but made no effort to sell or rent it because she considered it "not fit to live in." In October of 1971 the Morrows filed this action against both New Moon Homes and Golden Heart Mobile Homes, alleging that defendants had breached implied warranties of merchantability and fitness for particular purpose in manufacturing and selling an improperly constructed mobile home. . . .

The heart of this appeal concerns the remedies which are available to a remote purchaser against the manufacturer of defective goods for direct economic loss. The superior court held that the Morrows had no legal claim against New Moon because they were not in privity of contract with New Moon. The first argument advanced here by the Morrows amounts to an end run around the requirement of privity. The Morrows contend that their complaint asserted a theory of strict liability in tort. They further argue that they should have prevailed irrespective of any lack of privity of contract between New Moon and themselves, because lack of privity of contract is not a defense to a strict tort liability claim. it is true that in *Bachner* v. *Pearson*, 479 P. 2d 319 (Alaska 1970), we held:

> that implied warranty and strict products liability are sufficiently similar to require that a complaint worded in terms of the former theory should be deemed to raise a claim under the latter theory.

Thus, although the Morrows' complaint sounded in breach of implied warranties, it also raised a strict liability claim if such a claim is legally cognizable against New Moon.

In *Clary* v. *Fifth Avenue Chrysler Center, Inc.*, 454 P 2d 244 (Alaska 1969), Alaska adopted the *Greenman* v. *Yuba Power Products, Inc.*, 377 P. 2d 897 (Cal. 1962), rule of strict products liability, which provides that

> [a] manufacturer is strictly liable in tort when an article he places on the market, knowing that it is to be used without inspection for defects, proves to have a defect that causes injury to a human being.

By its terms the *Greenman* formulation applies only when the defective product causes personal injury. Since the Morrows did not sustain any personal injuries which were caused by the defects in their mobile home, strict liability is seemingly unavailable to them in the instant case. However, the Morrows argue that strict liability should nonetheless apply in the situation where a consumer sues a manufacturer solely for economic loss attributable to the manufacturer's defective product. This precise contention presents a question of first impression in Alaska.

The issue whether strict liability in tort should extend to economic loss has prompted no small amount of discussion in legal journals.[6] The two leading

---

6 Among the better articles are: Speidel, *Products Liability, Economic Loss and the UCC*, 40 Tenn. L. Rev. 309 (1973); Prosser, *The Fall of the Citadel (Strict Liability to the Consumer)*, 50 Minn. L. Rev. 791 (1966);

judicial opinions are probably *Santor v. A. and M. Karaghesian, Inc.* 44 NJ 52, 297 A. 2d 305 (1965), and *Seely v. White Motor Co.,* 63 Cal. 2d 9, 45 Cal. Rptr. 17, 403 P. 2d 145 (1965). In the former case, Santor purchased from a retailer certain carpeting manufactured and advertised by Karagheusian. Almost immediately after the carpet was laid, Santor noticed an unusual line in it. As the pile wore down, the line became worse and two additional lines appeared. Since the retailer had gone out of business, Santor sued the manufacturer for damages for breach of the implied warranty of merchantability. In a unanimous decision, the Supreme Court of New Jersey held that the plaintiff, as the ultimate purchaser of defective carpeting, could maintain an action against the manufacturer on either of two theories, breach of implied warranty of reasonable fitness or strict liability in tort. Privity of contract was not necessary in order to pursue either theory, although damages were limited to loss of value of the carpeting. Although the opinion emphasized the widespread advertising carried on by Karagheusian, the *Santor* court made clear that "strict liability in tort is not conditioned upon advertising to promote sales."

> [W]hen the manufacturer presents his goods to the public for sale he accompanies them with a representation that they are suitable and safe for the intended use. . . . [S]uch a representation must be regarded as implicit in their presence on the market. . . . The obligation of the manufacturer thus becomes what in justice it ought to be — an enterprise liability and one which should not depend on the intricacies of the law of sales. The purpose of such liability is to insure that the cost of injuries or damage, either to the goods sold or to other property, resulting from defective products, is borne by the makers of the products who put them in the channels of trade, rather than by the injured or damaged persons who ordinarily are powerless to protect themselves.

Barely four months after *Santor* came down, its strict liability holding was rejected by the Supreme Court of California in *Seely v. White Motor Co., supra.* Seely purchased a truck manufactured by White Motor Co. for use in his heavy duty hauling business. Upon taking possession of the truck, Seely found that it bounced violently. This "galloping" continued for 11 months until the truck's brakes failed and the truck overturned, sustaining in excess of $5,000 in damages. Seely was not injured in the incident.

Seely sued White Motor Co. seeking damages for the cost of repairing the truck and for both the money paid on the purchase price and the profits lost in his business because he was unable to make normal use of the truck. The Supreme Court of California affirmed the trial court's award of damages in the amount of

---

Comment, *The Vexing Problem of Purely Economic Loss in Products Liability: An Injury in Search of a Remedy,* 4 Seton Hall L. Rev. 145 (1972); Note, *Economic Loss in Products Liability Jurisprudence,* 66 Colum. L. Rev. 917 (1966); Comment, *Manufacturers' Liability to Remote Purchasers for Economic Loss Damages — Tort or Contract?,* 114 U. Pa. L. Rev. 539 (1966).

Other articles on the subject include: Note, *Products Liability in Oregon: Present and Future,* 8 Willamette LJ 410 (1972); Comment, 7 Creighton L. Rev. 396 (1974); Note, *Economic Loss from Defective Products,* 4 Willamette LJ 402 (1967); Note, *The Demise of Vertical Privity: Economic Loss Under the Uniform Commercial Code,* 2 Hofstra L. Rev. 749 (1974). *See also* W. Prosser, Law of Torts 664-67 (4th ed. 1971).

the payments made plus lost profits, on the grounds that White Motor Co. had breached an express warranty to Seely, the ultimate purchaser. The majority opinion, written by Chief Justice Traynor, condemned in broad dicta Santor's application of strict liability principles to a case involving only economic loss:

> The distinction that the law has drawn between tort recovery for physical injuries and warranty recovery for economic loss is not arbitrary and does not rest on the "luck" of one plaintiff in having an accident causing physical injury. The distinction rests, rather, on an understanding of the nature of the responsibility a manufacturer must undertake in distributing his products. He can appropriately be held liable for physical injuries caused by defects by requiring his goods to match a standard of safety defined in terms of conditions that create unreasonable risks of harm. He cannot be held for the level of performance of his products in the consumer's business unless he agrees that the product was designed to meet the consumer's demands. A consumer should not be charged at the will of manufacturer with bearing the risk of physical injury when he buys a product on the market. He can, however, be fairly charged with the risk that the product will not match his economic expectations unless the manufacturer agrees that it will.

Seely appears to enjoy the support of the vast majority of the other courts which have considered the question whether strict liability in tort should extend to instances of economic loss. We also prefer the result in *Seely*, although our reasoning differs slightly in emphasis from that of the *Seely* court. Under the Uniform Commercial Code the manufacturer is given the right to avail himself of certain affirmative defenses which can minimize his liability for a purely economic loss. Specifically, the manufacturer has the opportunity, pursuant to AS 45.05.100, to disclaim liability and under AS 45.05.230 to limit the consumer's remedies, although the Code further provides that such disclaimers and limitations cannot be so oppressive as to be unconscionable and thus violate AS 45.05.072. In addition, the manufacturer is entitled to reasonably prompt notice from the consumer of the claimed breach of warranties, pursuant to AS 45.05.174 (c)(1).

In our view, recognition of a doctrine of strict liability in tort for economic loss would seriously jeopardize the continued viability of these rights. The economically injured consumer would have a theory of redress not envisioned by our legislature when it enacted the UCC, since this strict liability remedy would be completely unrestrained by disclaimer, liability limitation and notice provisions. Further, manufacturers could no longer look to the Uniform Commercial Code provisions to provide a predictable definition of potential liability for direct economic loss. In short, adoption of the doctrine of strict liability for economic loss would be contrary to the legislature's intent when it authorized the aforementioned remedy limitations and risk allocation provisions of Article II of the Code. To extend strict tort liability to reach the Morrow's case would in effect be an assumption of legislative prerogative on our part and would vitiate clearly articulated statutory rights. This we decline to do. Thus, we hold that the theory of strict liability in tort which we recognized in *Clary* does not extend to the consumer who suffers only economic loss because of defective goods.

The principal theory of liability advocated by the Morrows at trial was that

New Moon had breached statutory warranties which arose by operation of law with the manufacture and distribution of this mobile home. Specifically, the Morrows rely upon AS 45.05.096 and AS 45.05.098 of the Uniform Commercial Code as enacted in Alaska. The former section provides for an implied warranty of "merchantability" in the sale of goods governed by the Code; the latter establishes an implied warranty that the goods are fit for the particular purpose for which they were purchased. The superior court was of the view that these Code warranties operated only for the benefit of those purchasing directly from a manufacturer or seller. Since the Morrows were not in privity of contract with New Moon, the superior court concluded that a warranty theory based on AS 45.05.096 and AS 45.05.098 could not serve as a basis for liability.

There is little question that the Code applies to the distribution of mobile homes. New Moon qualifies as a "merchant" within the meaning of the relevant section, AS 45.05.042, and mobile homes, being highly movable, are "goods" as defined in AS 45.05.044. Further, in *George* v. *Willman*, 379 P 2d 103 (Alaska 1963), we held that the implied warranty of merchantable quality established by the Code's predecessor, the Uniform Sales Act, was fully applicable to the sale of mobile homes. The result is no different under AS 45.05.096 and AS 45.05.098 of the Code.

It is equally clear that in this jurisdiction the Morrows, as immediate purchasers, can recover against their seller for breach of the Code's implied warranties. Indeed, this was the theory upon which the default judgment against Golden Heart Mobile Homes was predicated. The critical question in this case is whether the Morrows, as remote purchasers, can invoke the warranties attributable to the manufacturer which arose when New Moon passed title of the mobile home to the next party in the chain of distribution. In other words, do the implied warranties of merchantability and fitness run from a manufacturer only to those with whom the manufacturer is in privity of contract?

Although sometimes criticized, the distinction between horizontal and vertical privity is significant in this case. The issue of horizontal privity raises the question whether persons other than the buyer of defective goods can recover from the buyer's immediate seller on a warranty theory. The question of vertical privity is whether parties in the distributive chain prior to the immediate seller can be held liable to the ultimate purchaser for loss caused by the defective product. The Code addresses the matter of horizontal privity in AS 45.05.104, extending the claim for relief in warranty to any ". . . person who is in the family or household of his buyer or who is a guest in his home if it is reasonable to expect that the person may use, consume, or be affected by the goods . . . ." With regard to vertical privity, the Code is totally silent and strictly neutral, as Official Comment 3 to AS 45.05.104 makes eminently clear. The Code leaves to the courts the question of the extent to which vertical privity of contract will or will not be required.

This court has never previously confronted the question whether a requirement of privity of contract will preclude a purchaser from recovering against the original manufacturer on a theory of implied warranties. As mentioned previously, we expressly held in *Clary* v. *Fifth Avenue Chrysler Center, Inc.*, 454 P 2d

244 (Alaska 1969), that a manufacturer is strictly liable in tort for personal injuries attributable to his defective goods. In approving a theory based on strict liability in tort, we stressed the efficacy, simplicity, and comprehensiveness of that theory. Appellees in *Clary* had urged this court to limit the consumer's source of redress to possible application of the statutory provisions governing sales warranties, particularly AS 45.05.096. This we declined to do. As we have noted, under the statutory scheme an injured consumer is required to give notice of the defect to the warrantor within a relatively short period of time, and potential liability may be circumscribed by express disclaimers from the manufacturer. The *Clary* court was concerned that such provisions might operate as a trap for the unwary, and it expressed a preference for a tort theory more solicitous of the needs of the consumer in the modern, prepackaged, mass merchandised market place. However, this preference was never intended to imply that reliance on the statutory warranty provisions was not available as an alternative vehicle for relief. There is nothing incompatible in affording parallel consumer remedies sounding in tort and in contract, and several jurisdictions which have adopted strict liability in tort also make available an implied warranty theory without regard to privity of contract.

The dispute here is whether the requirement of vertical privity of contract should be abolished in Alaska. This battle has already been waged in many jurisdictions, and the results are well known; the citadel of privity has largely toppled. The course of this modern development is familiar history and we need not recount it at length here. Contrived "exceptions" which paid deference to the hoary doctrine of privity while obviating its unjust results have given way in more recent years to an open frontal assault. The initial attack came in *Spence* v. *Three Rivers Builders & Masonry Supply, Inc.*, 353 Mich. 120, 90 NW 2d 873 (1958), but the leading case probably remains *Henningsen* v. *Bloomfield Motors. Inc.*, 32 NJ 358, 161 A. 2d 69 (1960), in which the New Jersey Supreme Court held liable for personal injuries and property damages both the manufacturer of an automobile and the dealer who sold the vehicle. The rationale for the widespread abolition of the requirement of privity stems from the structure and operation of the free market economy in contemporary society; it was succinctly summed up not long ago by the Supreme Court of Pennsylvania (*Kassab* v. *Central Soya*, 246 A. 2d 853 (1968)):

> Courts and scholars alike have recognized that the typical consumer does not deal at arms length with the party whose product he buys. Rather, he buys from a retail merchant who is usually little more than a economic conduit. It is not the merchant who has defectively manufactured the product. Nor is it usually the merchant who advertises the product on such a large scale as to attract consumers. We have in our society literally scores of large, financially responsible manufacturers who place their wares in the stream of commerce not only with the realization, but with the avowed purpose, that these goods will find their way into the hands of the consumer. Only the consumer will use these products; and only the consumer will be injured by them should they prove defective.

The policy considerations which dictate the abolition of privity are largely those which also warranted imposing strict tort liability on the manufacturer: the consumer's inability to protect himself adequately from defectively manufactured goods, the implied assurance of the maker when he puts his goods on the market that they are safe, and the superior risk bearing ability of the manufacturer. In addition, limiting a consumer under the Code to an implied warranty action against his immediate seller in those instances when the product defect is attributable to the manufacturer would effectively promote circularity of litigation and waste of judicial resources. Therefore, we decide that a manufacturer may be held liable for a breach of the implied warranties of AS 45.05.096 and AS 45.05.098 without regard to privity of contract between the manufacturer and the consumer.

The more difficult question before this court is whether we should extend this abolition of privity to embrace not only warranty actions for personal injuries and property damage but also those for economic loss. Contemporary courts have been more reticent to discard the privity requirement and to permit recovery in warranty by a remote consumer for purely economic losses. In considering this issue we note that economic loss may be categorized into direct economic loss and consequential economic loss, a distinction maintained in the Code's structure of damage remedies. One commentator has summarized the distinction:

> Direct economic loss may be said to encompass damage based on insufficient product value; thus, direct economic loss may be "out of pocket" — the difference in value between what is given and received — or "loss of bargain" — the difference between the value of what is received and its value as represented. Direct economic loss also may be measured by costs of replacement and repair. Consequential economic loss includes all indirect loss, such as loss of profits resulting from inability to make use of the defective product.[35]

The claim of the Morrows in this case is one for direct economic loss.

A number of courts recently confronting this issue have declined to overturn the privity requirement in warranty actions for economic loss.[36] One principal factor seems to be that these courts simply do not find the social and economic reasons which justify extending enterprise liability to the victims of personal injury or property damage equally compelling in the case of a disappointed buyer suffering "only" economic loss. There is an apparent fear that economic losses may be of a far greater magnitude in value than personal injuries, and being somehow less foreseeable these losses would be less insurable, undermining the risk spreading theory of enterprise liability.

Several of the courts which have recently considered this aspect of the

---

35 Note *Economic Loss in Products Liability Jurisprudence*, 66 Colum. L. Rev. 917, 918 (1966).

36 *Koellmer* v. *Chrysler Motors Corp.*, 6 Conn. Cir. 478, 276 A. 2d 807 (1970); *General Motors Corp.* v. *Halco Instruments, Inc.*, 124 Ga. App. 630, 185 SE 2d 619 (1971); *Necktas* v. *General Motors Corp.*, 357 Mass. 546, 259 NE 2d 234 (1970); *Hupp Corp.* v. *Metered Washer Service*, 256 Or. 245, 472 P. 2d 816 (1970); *State ex rel. Western Seed Prod. Corp.* v. *Campbell*, 250 Or. 262, 442 P. 2d 215 (1968); *Price* v. *Gatlin*, 241 Or. 315, 405 P. 2d 502 (1965); *Henry* v. *John W. Eshelman & Sons*, 99 RI 518, 209 A. 2d 46 (1965); *Dimoff* v. *Ernie Majer, Inc.*, 55 Wash. 2d 385, 347 P. 2d 1056 (1960).

privity issue have found those arguments unpersuasive.[39] We are in agreement and hold that there is no satisfactory justification for a remedial scheme which extends the warranty action to a consumer suffering personal injury or property damage but denies similar relief to the consumer "fortunate" enough to suffer only direct economic loss. Justice Peter's separate opinion in *Seely* v. *White Motor Co.*, 63 Cal. 2d 9, 45 Cal. Rptr. 17, 24, 403 P 2d 145, 152 (1965), persuasively establishes that the cleavage between economic loss and other types of harm is a false one, that each species of harm can constitute the "overwhelming misfortune" in one's life which warrants judicial redress. The Supreme Court of New Jersey is also in complete agreement with this view:

> From the standpoint of principle, we perceive no sound reason why the implication of reasonable fitness should be attached to the transaction and be actionable against the manufacturer where the defectively made product has caused personal injury and not actionable when inadequate manufacture has put a worthless article in the hands of an innocent purchaser who has paid the required price for it. In such situations considerations of justice require a court to interest itself in originating causes and to apply the principle of implied warranty on that basis, rather than to test its application by whether personal injury or simply loss of bargain resulted in the breach of the warranty. True, the rule of implied warranty had its gestative stirrings because of the greater appeal of the personal injury claim. But, once in existence, the field of operation of the remedy should not be fenced in by such a factor.[40]

The fear that if the implied warranty action is extended to direct economic loss, manufacturers will be subjected to liability for damages of unknown and unlimited scope would seem unfounded. The manufacturer may possibly delimit the scope of his potential liability by use of a disclaimer in compliance with AS 45.05.100 or by resort to the limitations authorized in AS 45.05.230. These statutory rights not only preclude extending the theory of strict liability in tort, *supra*, but also make highly appropriate this extension of the theory of implied warranties. Further, by expanding warranty rights to redress this form of harm, we preserve ". . . the well developed notion that the law of contract should control actions for purely economic losses and that the law of tort should control actions

---

39 *Lynn Carol Fashions, Inc.* v. *Cranston Print Works Co.*, 453 F. 2d 1177 (3d Cir. 1972) (stating Pennsylvania law); *Gherna* v. *Ford Motor Co.*, 246 Cal. App. 2d 639, 55 Cal. Rptr. 94 (1966); *Manheim* v. *Ford Motor Co.*, 201 So. 2d 440 (Fla. 1967); *Hoskins* v. *Jackson Grain Co.*, 63 So. 2d 514 (Fla. 1953); *Smith* v. *Platt Motors, Inc.*, 137 So. 2d 239 (Fla. App. 1962); *Continental Copper & Steel Industries, Inc.* v. *E. C. "Red" Cornelius, Inc.*, 104 So. 2d 40 (Fla. App. 1958); *Rhodes Pharmacal Co.* v. *Continental Can Co.*, 72 Ill. App. 2d 362, 219 NE 2d 726 (1966); *State Farm Mat. Auto. Ins. Co.* v. *Anderson-Weber, Inc.*, 252 Iowa 1289, 110 NW 2d 449 (1961); *Spence* v. *Three Rivers Builders & Masonry Supply, Inc.*, 353 Mich. 120, 90 NW 2d 873 (1958); *Cova* v. *Harley Davidson Motor Co.*, 26 Mich. App. 602, 182 NW 2d 800 (1970); *Beck* v. *Spindler*, 256 Minn. 543, 99 NW 2d 670 (1959); *Santor* v. *A. & M. Karagheusian, Inc.*, 44 NJ 52, 207 A. 2d 305 (1965); *Lang* v. *General Motors Corp.*, 136 NW 2d 805 (ND 1965); *Kassab* v. *Central Soya*, 432 Pa. 217, 246 A. 2d 848 (1968); *Ford Motor Co.* v. *Grimes*, 408 SW 2d 313 (Tex. Civ. App. 1966).

40 *Santor* v. *A. & M. Karagheusian, Inc.*, 44 NJ 52, CO, 207 A 2d 305, 309 (1965). *See also Lang* v. *General Motors Corp.*, 136 NW 2d 805 (ND 1965); Note, *Economic Loss in Products Liability Jurisprudence*, 66 Colum. L. Rev. 917, 964 (1966).

for personal injuries." We therefore hold that a manufacturer can be held liable for direct economic loss attributable to a breach of his implied warranties, without regard to privity of contract between the manufacturer and the ultimate purchaser.[42] It was therefore error for the trial court to dismiss the Morrows' action against New Moon for want of privity.

Our decision today preserves the statutory rights of the manufacturer to define his potential liability to the ultimate consumer, by means of express disclaimers and limitations, while protecting the legitimate expectation of the consumer that goods distributed on a wide scale by the use of conduit retailers are fit for their intended use. The manufacturer's rights are not, of course, unfettered. Disclaimers and limitations must comport with the relevant statutory prerequisites and cannot be so oppressive as to be unconscionable within the meaning of AS 45.05.072. On the other hand, under the Code the consumer has a number of responsibilities if he is to enjoy the right of action we recognize today, not the least of which is that he must give notice of the breach of warranty to the manufacturer pursuant to AS 45.05.174(c)(1). The warranty action brought under the Code must be brought within the statute of limitations period prescribed in AS 45.05.242. If the action is for breach of the implied warranty of fitness for particular purpose, created by AS 45.05.098, the consumer must establish that the warrantor had reason to know the particular purpose for which the goods were required and that the consumer relied on the seller's skill or judgment to select or furnish suitable goods. In the case of litigation against a remote manufacturer, it would appear that often it will be quite difficult to establish this element of actual or constructive knowledge essential to this particular warranty.

In the case at bar the trial judge failed to enter written findings of fact, as are required by Alaska Rule of Civil Procedure 52. We cannot determine from the record whether the Morrows would have prevailed on a theory of breach of implied warranties had the trial court not erred in raising the barrier of privity. Trial was had over two years ago. We are therefore of the opinion that, if the dismissal for want of jurisdiction was also erroneous, a new trial is warranted at which the Morrows will have the opportunity to assert their warranty theories free from the confines of privity.

Appeal allowed.

---

42 We recognize that the arguments against the abolition of privity are more compelling when the injury alleged is damages of a consequential nature many times the value of the manufacturer's product. *See, e.g.,* Note, *Economic Loss in Products Liability Jurisprudence,* 66 Colum. L. Rev. 917, 965-66 (1965). We do not speak today to the issue of consequential economic loss, other than to note that AS 45.05.222 governs the recovery of such damages and requires, among other things, that said damages must have been foreseeable by the manufacturer. *Adams* v. *J. I. Case Co.,* 125 Ill. App. 2d 388, 261 NE 2d 1 (1970).

B. THE PROBLEM OF HORIZONTAL PRIVITY AND THE POSITION OF SUBSEQUENT TRANSFEREES

OLRC Report on Consumer Warranties
(1972), pp. 74-6

It frequently happens that goods are bought by a consumer not for his own use or enjoyment but for the use of the members of his family or to be given as a gift to a friend. Or again, the consumer may be moving to another city or another province and may not wish to take all his household goods with him. Another common situation arises where appliances are installed in a new home and the builder sells the home to a consumer or the home is sold by one consumer to another. In all these cases, if the goods turn out to be defective the person who received or purchased the goods directly or indirectly from the original buyer would have no contractual rights of recovery against the retailer or manufacturer because of the absence or privity of contract between him and them. If he is prescient, he might have obtained an assignment to him of the original buyer's rights, but even this measure of foresight may not help him much, since it is doubtful whether such an assignment is valid at common law. To compound the third party's difficulties, he will usually have no right of recourse against his immediate seller (assuming he bought the goods and did not receive them as a gift) because neither the quality warranties appearing in The Sale of Goods Act nor the warranties recommended by us for inclusion in the proposed Consumer Products Warranties Act will apply to private sellers. In the case of passenger cars a second purchaser may be able to invoke the manufacturer's express warranty since such warranties usually apply, with or without qualifications, to the first and second owner. In the case of other durable goods, the warranty is usually silent on the question of its assignability or the warranty is expressly restricted to the first buyer.

We see no reason however why the right of a consumer with a derivative title to enforce the express or implied warranties which accompanied the first retail sale of the goods should depend on the largesse of the manufacturer or retailer, or on the consumer's somewhat tenuous ability to prove some kind of a collateral contract between him and the retailer or manufacturer. It seems to us that the reasoning which militates in favour of allowing the retail buyer to sue the manufacturer directly without a showing of privity applies at least as strongly in the present circumstances. Indeed, it can be argued that the consumer with a derivative title has a stronger case. The retailer buyer at least has a right of recourse against the dealer whereas the later consumer at present is left remediless. It may also be remarked that the current legal position provides an undeserved windfall for the retailer, since in many instances it may not be practicable for the original buyer to lay a complaint. Even if he could be persuaded to do so, his damages would not necessarily coincide with the damages suffered by his successor in title.

Accordingly, the Commission recommends that the rights of the successor in title be expressly recognized by statute. The change can probably be effected most easily by defining "consumer buyer" to include any person deriving his interest in the goods from or through the original purchaser, whether by purchase, gift, operation of law or otherwise. Such a definition will also make it clear that the rights of the successor in title are derivative and are no greater than those of the original buyer.

This recommendation is not a novel one. By invoking a doctrine of implied warranties running with the goods, the Supreme Court of New Jersey in the *Henningsen* case discussed above extended protection both to the buyer and his wife (albeit only for the purposes of a personal injury claim) and, as has been seen, section 2-318 of the Uniform Commercial Code and its revised versions contemplate warranties running directly to third parties, at least where injury to person or to property is involved. In the opinion of the Commission, for the purpose of applying express or implied warranties, it would be illogical to distinguish between physical injury or damage and pure economic losses, assuming both were reasonably foreseeable. It is not anticipated that the relaxation of the horizontal rules of privity will lead to a flood of unwarranted claims. The successor in title will still have to show that the malfunction in the article was due to a defect in the manufacturing process and not to some intervening cause and, in the absence of long term express warranties, most of the claims are likely to be brought within a short period following the original purchase.

Note: Examine Bill 110 and the Saskatchewan Act and determine to what extent they have implemented the above recommendations. Do you agree with the Commission that, for the purpose of applying express or implied warranties, it would be illogical to distinguish between physical injury or damage and pure economic losses?

C. MANUFACTURER'S EXPRESS PERFORMANCE WARRANTIES

HENNINGSEN v. BLOOMFIELD MOTORS INC.
(1960) 161 A 2d 69 (NJ Sup. Ct.)

Mr. Henningsen purchased a Plymouth automobile from the defendant dealer for his wife as a Mother's Day gift. The purchase order was a printed form of one page, the reverse side of which contained the manufacturer's warranty. The warranty by its terms expressly limited the manufacturer's obligation to make good at its factory any part or parts that were returned within ninety days after delivery of the vehicle to the original purchaser or before the vehicle had been driven 4,000 miles, whichever event occurred first. The warranty further stated that it was given expressly in lieu of all other warranties expressed or implied, and all other obligations or liabilities on the part of the manufacturer.

Mrs. Henningsen was driving the car when she lost control and crashed into a highway sign and a brick wall. The vehicle was a total loss and the collision insurance carrier, after inspection, advanced the opinion that something definitely went "wrong from the steering wheel down to the front wheels" and that the untoward happening must have been due to mechanical defect or failure.

The trial court felt that the proof was not sufficient to make out a *prima facie* case as to the negligence of either the manufacturer or the dealer, but plaintiffs succeeded against both on the ground of breach of warranty.

The extract which follows contains the court's observations on Chrysler's express performance warranty.

FRANCIS J. (for the court): The terms of the warranty are a sad commentary upon the automobile manufacturers' marketing practices. Warranties developed in the law in the interest of and to protect the ordinary consumer who cannot be expected to have the knowledge or capacity or even the opportunity to make adequate inspection of mechanical instrumentalities, like automobiles, and to decide for himself whether they are reasonably fit for the designed purpose. *Greenland Develop. Corp.* v. *Allied Heat. Prod. Co.,* 184 Va. 588, 35 SE 2d 801, 164 ALR 1312 (Sup. Ct. App. 1945); 1 Williston, *supra,* pp. 625, 626. But the ingenuity of the Automobile Manufacturers Association, by means of its standardized form, has metamorphosed the warranty into a device to limit the maker's liability. To call it an "equivocal" agreement, as the Minnesota Supreme Court did, is the least that can be said in criticism of it. *Federal Motor Truck Sales Corporation* v. *Shamus,* 190 Minn. 5, 250 NW 713, 714 (Sup. Ct. 1933).

The manufacturer agrees to replace defective parts for 90 days after the sale or until the car has been driven 4,000 miles, whichever is first to occur, *if the part is sent to the factory, transportation charges prepaid, and if examination discloses to its satisfaction that the part is defective.* It is difficult to imagine a greater burden on the consumer, or less satisfactory remedy.

Aside from imposing on the buyer the trouble of removing and shipping the part, the maker has sought to retain the uncontrolled discretion to decide the issue of defectiveness. Some courts have removed much of the force of that reservation by declaring that the purchaser is not bound by the manufacturer's decision. *Mills* v. *Maxwell Motor Sales Corporation,* 105 Neb. 465, 181 NW 152, 22 ALR 130 (Sup. Ct. 1920); *Cannon* v. *Pulliam Motor Company,* 230 SC 131, 94 SE 2d 397 (Sup. Ct. 1956). In the *Mills* case, the court said:

> It would nevertheless be repugnant to every conception of justice to hold that, if the parts thus returned for examination were, in point of fact, so defective as to constitute a breach of warranty, the appellee's right of action could be defeated by the appellant's arbitrary refusal to recognize that fact. Such an interpretation would substitute the appellant for the courts in passing upon the question of fact, and would be unreasonable. Supra, 181 NW at page 154.

Also suppose, as in this case, a defective part or parts caused an accident and that the car was so damaged as to render it impossible to discover the precise part or parts responsible, although the circumstances clearly pointed to such fact as the cause of the mishap. Can it be said that the impossibility of performance deprived the buyer of the benefit of the warranty?

Moreover, the guaranty is against defective workmanship. That condition may arise from good parts improperly assembled. There being no defective parts to return to the maker, is all remedy to be denied? One court met that type of problem by holding that where the purchaser does not know the precise cause of inoperability, calling a car a "vibrator" would be sufficient to state a claim for relief. It said that such a car is not an uncommon one in the industry. The general cause of the vibration is not known. Some part or parts have been either defectively manufactured or improperly assembled in the construction and manufacture of the automobile. In the operation of the car, these parts give rise to vibrations. The difficulty lies in locating the precise spot and cause. *Allen* v. *Brown*, 181 Kan. 301, 310 P 2d 23 (Sup. Ct. 1957). But the warranty does not specify what the purchaser must do to obtain relief in such case, if a remedy is intended to be provided. Must the purchaser return the car, transportation charges prepaid, over a great distance to the factory? It may be said that in the usual case the dealer also gives the same warranty and that as a matter of expediency the purchaser should turn to him. But under the law the buyer is entitled to proceed against the manufacturer. Further, dealers' franchises are precarious (see, *Automobile Franchise Agreements*, Hewitt (1956)). For example, Bloomfield Motors' franchise may be cancelled by Chrysler on 90 days' notice. And obviously dealers' facilities and capacity, financial and otherwise are not as sufficient as those of the primarily responsible manufacturer in his distant factory.

The matters referred to represent only a small part of the illusory character of the security presented by the warranty. Thus far the analysis has dealt only with the remedy provided in the case of a defective part. What relief is provided when the breach of the warranty results in personal injury to the buyer? (Injury to third persons using the car in the purchaser's right will be treated hereafter.) As we have said above, the law is clear that such damages are recoverable under an ordinary warranty. The right exists whether the warranty sued on is express or implied. . . . And, of course, it has long since been settled that where the buyer or a member of his family driving with his permission suffers injuries because of negligent manufacture or construction of the vehicle, the manufacturer's liability exists. Prosser, *supra*, §§ 83, 84. But in this instance, after reciting that defective parts will be replaced at the factory, the alleged agreement relied upon by Chrysler provides that the manufacturer's "obligation under this warranty" is limited to that undertaking; further, that such remedy is "in lieu of all other warranties, express or implied, and all other obligations or liabilities on its part." The contention has been raised that such language bars any claim for personal injuries which may emanate from a breach of the warranty. Although not urged in this case, it has been successfully maintained that the exclusion "of all other obligations and liabilities on its part" precludes a cause of action for injuries based on negligence. *Shafer* v. *Reo Motors*, 205 F 2d 685 (3 Cir. 1953). Another Federal Circuit Court of Appeals holds to the contrary. *Doughnut Mach. Corporation* v. *Bibbey*, 65 F 2d 634 (1 Cir. 1933). There can be little doubt that justice is served only by the latter ruling.

Note: Since *Henningsen's* case, automobile manufacturers' warranties have changed significantly and generally for the better. See for example the 1981 Ford of Canada *New Vehicle Warranties for 1981 New Cars and Trucks*, reproduced below. What changes do you observe? What problems, if any?

FORD OF CANADA*
NEW VEHICLE WARRANTIES

1981 NEW CARS AND LIGHT TRUCKS

BASIC WARRANTY — 12 MONTHS OR 20,000 KILOMETRES

FORD NEW VEHICLE WARRANTY

Ford Motor Company of Canada, Limited warrants that the Selling Dealer will repair, replace or adjust any defective parts, except tires, on 1981 Ford of Canada cars and light trucks covered by this warranty.

NO CHARGE REPAIRS

Your Ford of Canada dealer will perform warranty repairs (parts and labour) at no charge, using Ford or Motorcraft Service Parts or Ford Authorized Remanufactured Parts.

WARRANTY BEGINS

This warranty begins on the earlier of the date the vehicle is first delivered to a retail customer or put in use as a demonstrator or otherwise. We require that you properly operate and maintain your vehicle as specified in the Owner's Guide.

WARRANTY ENDS

This warranty is for 12 months or 20,000 kilometres, whichever occurs first, except where otherwise specified.

IMPORTANT — PLEASE RETAIN THIS WARRANTY BOOKLET IN YOUR VEHICLE.

 *FORD MOTOR COMPANY OF CANADA, LIMITED, THE CANADIAN ROAD, OAKVILLE, ONTARIO L6J 5E4

CAN-7972-C181   LITHO IN CANADA

TRAVEL OR EMERGENCY

Under normal circumstances warranty service will be performed by your selling Ford of Canada Dealer but if you are travelling, have moved a long distance or need emergency repairs, any Ford or Mercury dealer will make the repairs or adjustments.

WARRANTY APPLIES

This warranty applies only to Ford of Canada cars and light trucks registered and normally operated in Canada or the U.S.A. When a vehicle is registered in another country, the time and distance travelled limits of the warranty will be those of the warranty offered by the Ford Motor Company affiliate in that country.

EMISSIONS SYSTEMS

The emissions control system of the 1981 vehicle is also included in this warranty but for a period of 5 years or 80,000 kilometres whichever occurs first from the earlier of the date the vehicle is first delivered to a retail customer or put in use as a demonstrator or otherwise.

OPTIONAL EQUIPMENT

The new Ford radio or tape player system components, antennae and clocks installed prior to delivery, are covered for 12 months (unlimited distance).

The sealed refrigerant portion of the factory installed air conditioning system, heater, engine block heater, window defogger or deicer, or heated outside rear view mirror are covered for 12 months (unlimited distance).

BATTERY

The original battery is fully covered for 12 months or 20,000 kilometres, whichever occurs first, and thereafter to 36 months (unlimited distance) on a pro rata basis. The pro rata adjustment price of the new Motorcraft battery will be its current suggested retail price less 1/36th of that price for each month remaining in the 36 month period. This pro rata warranty applies only to batteries installed in vehicles used in normal service. For batteries installed in police cars and taxi cabs, the dealer can advise of the adjustment period applicable to the battery in the particular vehicle.

CORROSION PERFORATION WARRANTY — 1981 MODEL CARS AND LIGHT TRUCKS — 36 MONTHS (UNLIMITED DISTANCE)

Ford Motor Company of Canada, Limited warrants for its 1981 model cars and light trucks, that the Selling Dealer will repair or replace free of charge, any part, except exhaust system components, found under normal use in Canada or the U.S.A. to have developed perforation from corrosion within 36 months (unlimited distance) from the earlier of the date the vehicle is first delivered to a retail customer or put in use as a demonstrator or otherwise.

All we require is that you maintain your vehicle as specified in the Owner's Guide and other written instructions supplied with your new 1981 model car or light truck.

This warranty applies only to perforation of parts caused by corrosion. Corrosion other than perforation, which is due to defective factory materials or workmanship is covered for 12 months or 20,000 kilometres, whichever occurs first. Corrosion due to accident or damage is not covered by the Basic Warranty or by the Corrosion Perforation Warranty.

Prior to repair or replacement, we require that you take your vehicle to your selling dealer for examination and approval by Ford of Canada.

NEW VEHICLE WARRANTIES LIMITATIONS

THE FOREGOING BASIC AND CORROSION PERFORATION WARRANTIES ARE THE ONLY EXPRESS WARRANTIES ON THE PART OF FORD OF CANADA AND THE SELLING DEALER. YOU MAY HAVE OTHER RIGHTS WHICH MAY VARY BY PROVINCE.

THE FOREGOING EXPRESS WARRANTIES ARE IN SUBSTITUTION FOR AND EXCLUDE ALL OTHER LIABILITIES OF ANY KIND WHETHER ARISING UNDER STATUTE, IN TORT, BY IMPLICATION OF LAW OR OTHERWISE, INCLUDING, TO THE FULL EXTENT AS MAY BE ALLOWED BY LAW, LIABILITY FOR ANY OTHER REPRESENTATIONS RESPECTING THE VEHICLE, STATUTORY WARRANTIES OR IMPLIED WARRANTIES OR CONDITIONS AS TO ITS MERCHANTABILITY OR FITNESS.

ANY IMPLIED WARRANTY OR CONDITION AS TO MERCHANTABILITY OR FITNESS IS LIMITED TO THE APPLICABLE WARRANTY DURATION PERIOD AS SPECIFIED HEREIN.

IN NO EVENT SHALL FORD OF CANADA OR THE SELLING DEALER BE LIABLE FOR THE LOSS OF OR DAMAGE TO THE VEHICLE OR ITS PARTS, LOSS OF USE OF THE VEHICLE, LOSS OF TIME, INCONVENIENCE, COMMERCIAL LOSS, OR SPECIAL, CONSEQUENTIAL OR OTHER DAMAGES OR ON ANY OTHER CLAIMS RELATING TO OR ARISING FROM ANY DEFECT IN FACTORY MATERIALS OR WORKMANSHIP WHENEVER FOUND EXCEPT AS PROVIDED FOR HEREIN.

THE ABOVE PROVISIONS DO NOT PRECLUDE THE OPERATION OF ANY APPLICABLE PROVINCIAL STATUTE WHICH IN CERTAIN CIRCUMSTANCES MAY NOT ALLOW SOME OF THE LIMITATIONS AND EXCLUSION DESCRIBED IN THESE WARRANTIES.

IN THE PROVINCE OF SASKATCHEWAN THE DURATION OF THE APPLICABLE STATUTORY WARRANTIES OF THAT PROVINCE SHALL BE CONCURRENT WITH AND NOT CONSECUTIVE TO THE DURATION OF THE FOREGONG FORD OF CANADA WARRANTIES.

ITEMS NOT COVERED BY NEW VEHICLE WARRANTIES

TIRES

Tires are NOT warranted by Ford of Canada but are warranted by the tire manufacturer under a separate warranty included with the owner literature supplied with your vehicle. Any Ford of Canada dealer will assist you in the requesting an adjustment from the tire manufacturer if this becomes necessary.

MAINTENANCE

Cleaning and polishing, lubrication and filters, engine tune-up and replacing worn windshield wiper blades, are some of the normal maintenance services all vehicles require. See Owner's Guide for full details.

EXTRA EXPENSES

The warranty does NOT cover payment for loss of the use of the vehicle during warranty repairs nor other payments such as lodging bills, vehicle rentals, other travel costs or loss of pay.

DAMAGE DUE TO LACK OF MAINTENANCE

Lack of compliance with maintenance procedures as described in the Owner's Guide. We require that you use Ford or Motorcraft parts or Ford Authorized Remanufactured Parts or parts of equivalent quality to repair or maintain your vehicle.

OTHER DAMAGE

The owner is responsible for repairs due to: *FIRE, ACCIDENTS* or *DAMAGE* from objects striking the vehicle, *MISUSE* of the vehicle such as driving over curbs, *OVERLOADING* or *RACING* of the vehicle, (proper use is described in the Owner's Guide), *ALTERATIONS* (changing or adding to the vehicle), *AIRBORN FALLOUT* (chemicals, tree sap, etc.), *CORROSION* due to bare metal exposed by accident, collision, damage or similar causes which remove paint and protective coatings, *ROAD ABRASION* (such as salt, sand or stone chips), *HAIL, WINDSTORM, LIGHTNING* or *ROAD HAZARDS.*

QUESTIONS YOU MAY HAVE ABOUT THE NEW VEHICLE WARRANTIES

1. WHAT SHOULD I DO TO OBTAIN WARRANTY SERVICE?

The Dealer where you purchased your vehicle has the responsibility for performing warranty repairs; therefore, take your vehicle to that Dealer. If the Ownercard that you received with your vehicle when it was delivered is presented to the Dealer, it can result in faster warranty service.

2. ARE THESE WARRANTIES LIMITED TO THE ORIGINAL PURCHASER ONLY?

No. Your New Vehicle Warranties apply to the original and subsequent owners of the vehicle if a defect is found within the applicable warranty duration period as specified.

3. ARE SCHEDULED INSPECTIONS REQUIRED TO MAINTAIN THESE WARRANTIES?

No. Scheduled inspections are not required to validate these warranties. However, you are required to take your vehicle to the Selling Dealer as soon as possible when corrosion perforation is apparent.

4. WHAT CAN I DO TO HELP PREVENT CORROSION?

It is the responsibility of the owner to wash the vehicle including the under body often using cold, clean, fresh water. If tree sap, insects, sprays, ocean or road salt, snow or dust control materials, atmospheric fallout, tar or anything similar is on the vehicle, wash it as soon as possible. These deposits often contain chemicals that may cause damage if allowed to remain. It is also important that drain holes in the bottom of the doors and tailgates be kept clear.

Nicks or scratches in the paint should be covered immediately with paint "touch up" to prevent further damage.

5. WOULD IT BE DESIRABLE TO HAVE A "RUST INHIBITOR" APPLIED TO MY VEHICLE AFTER PURCHASE?

Application after purchase of a "rust inhibitor" is left to the discretion of the owner; it is not a necessary requirement to the applicablity of the Ford of Canada 36 month corrosion perforation warranty.

THINGS YOU SHOULD KNOW ABOUT THE NEW VEHICLE WARRANTIES

PAINT, SHEET METAL AND OTHER APPEARANCE ITEMS

Defects or damage to paint, sheet metal or other appearance items may occur during assembly or when the vehicle is in transit to the dealer. Normally, these defects are noted and corrected at the factory or by your dealer during new vehicle inspection. Paint, sheet metal or appearance defects present at the time your car is delivered to you are covered by these warranties. For your protection, we suggest that if you do find any such defects, you advise your dealer without delay, as normal deterioration due to use and exposure is not covered by these warranties.

REPAIRS AND ADJUSTMENTS

The Basic Warranty covers any repairs and needed adjustments to correct defects in material and workmanship made or supplied by Ford. The term "adjust" refers to minor repairs not usually associated with the replacement of parts.

FRICTIONAL MATERIALS

Frictional materials are subject to wear through normal usage. The life expectancy can vary due to individual driving habits, therefore, the replacement of frictional materials (e.g. brake lining, pads, clutch lining, etc.) after 10,500 kilometres because of wear is considered normal maintenance.

GENERAL

Please note the distinction between "defects" and "damage" as used in the warranty. Defects are covered because we, the manufacturer, are responsible. This includes defects in Ford-Supplied parts used in making warranty repairs as well as in the original parts of the vehicle. On the other hand, we have no control over damage caused by such things as collision, misuse and lack of maintenance. Therefore, damage for any reason is not covered under these warranties.

Maintenance services also are excluded from these warranties because it is the owner's responsibility to maintain the vehicle in accordance with the Owner's Guide.

WARRANTY SERVICE — CANADA AND U.S.

Warranty service will be performed by the Ford of Canada dealer who sold you your vehicle (selling dealer) because of his continued and personal interest in you. However, if you are touring or move, warranty service will be performed by any Ford or Mercury dealer in Canada or the U.S.A.

WARRANTY SERVICE — FOREIGN COUNTRIES

Where Ford or Mercury dealer service is not available in the country in which you are touring and warranty repairs are needed, obtain paid receipts covering the work from the service station that performed it. Upon your return home, a statement of the circumstances relative to the work performed along with the paid receipts, should be given to your dealer for reimbursement consideration.

Notes:

1   *Henningsen's* case, *supra,* expresses judicial dissatisfaction with the state of automobile warranties in the past. A number of American and Canadian studies have
documented the same dissatisfaction at the non-judicial level and with respect to a
broader range of goods. See e.g. Federal Trade Commission, *Staff Report on
Automobile Warranties* (1968); Federal Trade Commission, *Report on Automobile
Warranties* (1970); and OLRC Warranties Report, ch. 7.

This dissatisfaction led to the adoption of remedial legislation in the U.S. and
Canada. The best known, and most important, of the American initiatives is the
Magnuson-Moss Warranty — Federal Trade Commission Improvement Act (1975),
15 USC § 2301-2312, the contents of which are summarized below in the extract
from Professor Strasser's article.

Canadian reactions to some extent antedate American post-war developments. The various Prairie farm implement Acts have to a varying degree regulated
the form and content of express and implied warranties in the sale of such products
since before the Second World War. For details, see OLRC Warranties Report,
Table 10, pp. 98-99. The Prairie legislation was of course very restricted in its scope
but it served as a precedent for the OLRC recommendation that the proposed
Consumer Products Warranties Act contain basic guidelines with respect to the
form and content of written (performance) warranties for consumer products. See
the Warranties Report, pp. 101-02. Once again Saskatchewan has been more
persuaded by the Commission's reasoning than Ontario itself: see the
Saskatchewan Consumer Products Warranties Act 1976, and L.J. Romero, "The
Consumer Products Warranties Act" (1978-79) 43 Sask. L Rev. 81.

2   If a consumer is entitled to the benefit of non-excludeable implied warranties (as is
true in Ontario as a result of CPA s. 44a), why is it necessary to regulate express
performance warranties as well? Should one or the other suffice?

K. A. STRASSER
**"Magnuson-Moss Warranty Act: An Overview and Comparison with UCC Coverage,
Disclaimer, and Remedies in Consumer Warranties"**
(1976) 27 Mercer L. Rev. 1111, 1113-14

The Act was passed in response to the specific consumer problems discussed
above and to the generalized feeling of consumer helplessness in the face of
warrantors' practice of using existing state law to effectively deny the consumer
redress under consumer warranties. The Act was passed to make warranties more
understandable to the consumer and to insure that obligations arising under
either express or implied warranties are enforceable. As stated in the House
Committee Report, the Act is designed to solve consumer warranties problems
by:

1. [R]equiring that the terms and conditions of written warranties on
consumer products be clearly and conspicuously stated in simple and readily understood language,

2. [P]rohibiting the proliferation of classes of warranties on consumer products and requiring that such warranties be either a full or limited warranty with the requirements of a full warranty clearly stated,

3. [S]afeguards against the disclaimer or modification of the implied warranties of merchantability and fitness on consumer products where a written warranty is given with respect thereto, and

4. [P]roviding consumers with access to reasonable and effective remedies where there is a breach of a warranty on consumer products.

The Senate consideration of the matter added consumer need for greater product reliability. This need would be met, it was thought, by making it economically rewarding for a manufacturer to build in better quality. Under the present system, to achieve a competitive price, a manufacturer must make products as cheaply as possible and then must disclaim all warranties possible. The Act rewards those manufacturers who make the more reliable products by giving them the competitive sales advantage of a "full" warranty. By making warranties more understandable, the Act will permit the consumer to make an informed choice between products on the basis of their warranties and will make consumer warranties a more important factor in the competition for sales. Thus, the legislation is an attempt to change the "rules of the warranty game:"

> Only when the rules of the warranty game are clarified so that the consumer can look to the warranty duration of the guaranteed product as an indicator of product reliability (because all costs of breakdown have been internalized) will consumers be able to differentiate on the basis of price between more reliable and less reliable products. This ability to differentiate should produce economic rewards from increased sales and reduce service costs to the producer of more reliable products. . . .

> Only a warrantor giving this type of "full" warranty is in a position to increase his profit, by making product reliability or service capability improvements. Furthermore, to the extent that consumer choice in the market place is guided by the desire for product reliability measured by the duration of the warranty, there will be an incentive for suppliers of consumer products to offer full warranties of relatively long duration. Therefore, there is a need to identify for the consumer which products are fully warranted and to create standards for "full" warranties.

The Act is also designed to help the consumer by strengthening the enforcement powers of the Federal Trade Commission which is the consumer's primary protector in the market place. This aspect of the Act is dealt with in Title Two and is beyond the scope of this discussion.

SELECTED BIBLIOGRAPHY ON THE MAGNUSON-MOSS WARRANTIES ACT

D.G. Adams and M.F. Schwartz, "Consumer Protection — The Magnuson-Moss Act" [1976] Ann. Survey Am. L. 257.

M.T. Hymson, "The Magnuson-Moss Warranty-Federal Trade Commission Impovement Act: Should the Consumer Rejoice?" (1976-77) 15 J. Family L. 77.

W.R. Kutner, "Consumer Product Warranties Under the Magnuson-Moss Warranty Act and the Uniform Commercial Code" (1977) 62 Corn. L. Rev. 738.

P.D. Rothschild, "The Magnuson-Moss Warranty Act: Does It Balance Warrantor and Consumer Interests?" (1976) 44 Geo. Wash. L. Rev. 335.

M.J. Wisdom, "An Empirical Study of the Magnuson-Moss Warranty Act" (1979) 31 Stan. L. Rev. 1117.

Chapter 8
Seller's Delivery Obligations

A. MEANING OF DELIVERY

OLRC Sales Report
pp. 331-33

A number of preliminary observations are in order. First, by virtue of sections 26 and 27 of the Ontario Sale of Goods Act, the seller's basic obligation to deliver the goods conditions his *prima facie* right to payment and acceptance by the buyer. However, delivery also has other important consequences, both under existing Anglo-Canadian law and even more so under Article 2 of the Uniform Commercial Code. Under The Sale of Goods Act, delivery affects the seller's lien rights and the rights of third parties who deal in good faith with a buyer who has been entrusted with goods or with the documents of title thereto. Further, in the case of a sale of future or unascertained goods, delivery usually coincides with the transfer of title, and therefore determines the time for the transfer of risk.

These important consequences have not been diminished by the Code. Indeed, Article 2 has increased their number. It may, therefore, fairly be said that, while the role of title has been demoted under the Code, that of delivery has been enhanced. This is not surprising, since most buyers are more conscious of the need to obtain possession of the goods, than they are to ascertain the status of an abstraction; the seller's right to sell is usually taken for granted. All this leads to the conclusion that there is no difference in doctrinal approach with respect to problems of delivery between The Sale of Goods Act and Article 2. The difference lies in matters of detail, and in the greater particularization of rules and situations adopted in Article 2. There is a further point. The Article 2 rules differ from the Ontario provisions in that they are closely integrated with the other Articles of the Code on Documents of Title (Article 7) and Secured Transactions (Article 9). The Ontario seller, on the other hand, is confronted with a large variety of statutes, federal as well as provincial, which are not necessarily consistent with one another or with the provisions of The Sale of Goods Act, and which need to be consulted for a full statement of his delivery obligations.

Delivery, as defined in The Sale of Goods Act, does not coincide with the layman's understanding of the term. It means the transfer of possession of goods from the seller to the buyer. The concept does not require the physical movement of goods. Regrettably, neither the Code nor the Act is consistent in the use of the term. Delivery is sometimes used in its broad generic sense, and sometimes to describe the manner in which a transfer of possession may be effected: for example, by shipment or dispatch. Further terminological confusion may be engendered by the failure to distinguish adequately between a *tender of delivery* and *delivery*. The two concepts are distinct, and trigger different results and different obligations. Article 2 has made some progress in sorting out the terminological muddle. The process is not, however, complete, and a further effort seems worthwhile, particularly in the light of the precedents afforded by the Hague Uniform Law on the International Sale of Goods and the draft UNCITRAL Convention. So far, the terminological confusion seems to have caused the courts little difficulty. While we do not wish to exaggerate the importance of the problem, we nevertheless recommend that the revised Act should strive for greater clarity in the use of the term "delivery" and its various derivatives, and that it should also distinguish more clearly between "tender of delivery" and "delivery".

B. TIME OF DELIVERY

HARTLEY v. HYMANS
[1920] 3 KB 475, [1920] All ER Rep. 328

McCARDIE J.: In the first place I think that time was here of the essence of the contract. This, indeed, was not really disputed by the plaintiff. It is curious that s. 10 of the Sale of Goods Act, 1893, deals so ambiguously with this point. That section provides: "(1.) Unless a different intention appears from the terms of the contract, stipulations as to time of payment are not deemed to be of the essence of a contract of sale. Whether any other stipulation as to time is of the essence of the contract or not depends on the terms of the contract." This section gives a very slender notion of the existing law, and it is well to remember s. 61 which provides (inter alia): "(2.) the rules of the common law, including the law merchant, save in so far as they are inconsistent with the express provisions of this Act . . . shall continue to apply to contracts for the sale of goods." Now the common law and the law merchant did not make the question whether time was of the essence depend on the terms of the contract, unless indeed those terms were express on the point. It looked rather to the nature of the contract and the character of the goods dealt with. In ordinary commercial contracts for the sale of goods the rule clearly is that time is prima facie of the essence with respect to delivery: see per Lord Carins L.C. in *Bowes* v. *Shand* (1877) 2 AC 455, 463, 464 (the sale of rice); per Cotton L.J. in *Reuter* v. *Sala* (1879) 4 CPD 239, 249 (sale of pepper); and per Lord Esher M.R. in *Sharp* v. *Christmas* (1892) 8 TLR 687 (the sale of potatoes). In *Paton & Sons* v. *Payne & Co.* (1897) 35 SLR 112, however, it was held by the House of Lords that in a contract for the sale and delivery of a printing machine time was not of the essence. This point is not fully dealt with in *Benjamin on Sale*, 5th ed., pp. 588 *et seq.*, and no general rule appears to be stated in that treatise. But in *Blackburn on Sale*, 3rd ed., pp. 244 *et seq.*, the matter is more clearly treated and it is laid down that " In mercantile contracts, stipulations as to time (except as regards time of payment) are usually of the essence of the contract." I may add that the relevant decisions on the point are excellently summarized in *Halsbury's Laws of England*, vol. xxv., p. 152, in the section on *Sale of Goods* written by Sir Mackenzie Chalmers and Mr. W. C. A. Ker. With the above text-books may be contrasted the passage in *Addison on Contracts*, 11th ed., p. 543.

Now, if time for delivery be of the essence of the contract, as in the present case, it follows that a vendor who has failed to deliver within the stipulated period cannot prima facie call upon the buyer to accept delivery after that period has expired. He has himself failed to fulfil the bargain and the buyer can plead the seller's default and assert that he was not ready and willing to carry out his contract. That this is so seems clear. It is, I take it, the essential juristic result, when time is of the essence of the contract. This is cogently shown by the judgment in *Plevins* v. *Downing* 1 CPD 220 where the plaintiff vendors agreed to deliver iron in the month of July; as Brett J. put it (at p. 226) when delivering the opinion of the Court: "The day after the end of July they could not have insisted on an acceptance of iron then offered to the defendant": see also per Martin B. in *Coddington* v. *Paleologo* (1867) LR 2 Ex. 193, 196, 197; and upon an analogous point see *Pearl Mill Co.* v. *Ivy Tannery Co.* [1919] 1 KB 78, 83.

Notes and Questions:

1   For a general discussion of the treatment of time as a contractual term, see S. J. Stoljar, "Untimely Performance in the Law of Contract" (1955) 71 LQR 527.

2   Why should the common law distinguish between the importance of time for purposes of delivery and the importance of time for the purposes of payment by the buyer?

3   SGA s. 27 provides that, unless otherwise agreed, delivery and payment are concurrent conditions. Does this import a qualification to SGA s. 11, and mean that in cash transactions the buyer is in breach of a condition unless he is able and willing to pay for the goods at the time of delivery? See OLRC Sales Report, pp. 147-48, 350, and 391, and *infra*, chapter 9.

ALLEN v. DANFORTH MOTORS LTD.
(1957) 12 DLR (2d) 572 (Ont. CA)

SCHROEDER J.A. (for the court): The defendant appeals from the judgment of Smily J. pronounced on June 10, 1957, whereby it was adjudged that the plaintiff do recover from the defendant the sum of $2,477 and costs.

The plaintiff, a married woman, entered into a contract with the defendant, a motor car dealer, to purchase a Regent Sedan motor car from the defendant, an enfranchised dealer in Dodge Motor products. The contract was in writing and was executed on April 9, 1957. The price of the car was stated to be $2,877 less a discount of $400, so that the net price was $2,477. Although the price was payable "cash on delivery of car", the plaintiff gave the defendant a cheque for the full purchase-price on the date of the contract.

After some discussion it was agreed that the defendant would provide a motor vehicle of a "heron grey colour with grey trim". No delivery date was specified in the written contract which contained the following terms: "The undersigned hereby purchases from you for delivery on or about . . ."

This is followed by a description of the motor car and particulars of the price. The contract also contains the following terms:

> I clearly understand that delivery of this car is contingent upon strikes, fires and other causes beyond your control, and hereby agree to extend delivery date (as may be reasonably required accordingly).

and —

> It is mutually agreed that there are no warranties or representations except as stated herein and made in writing.

The plaintiff was permitted to give evidence of a discussion which took place between her and the defendant's general manager as to the time of delivery. She stated: "It didn't seem there was any question of delivery on the colour. It would be a matter of three days or twenty-four hours. He would let me know if he could get it." Apparently, however, the manager found that he would have some difficulty in finding a car of the colour specified and informed the plaintiff of his difficulty two or three days later. The plaintiff stated that she informed the defendant's representative that she required the vehicle on Saturday, April 14th, as she had planned to take a trip to Buffalo with some friends during that weekend. She herself was not a licenced driver but only a learner and it had been arranged that a friend would drive the motor vehicle for her. When he was unsuccessful in obtaining a car of the desired colour from other dealers in Toronto, the defendant's manager offered her a blue car which she declined to accept. In order that she might have her contemplated trip to Buffalo, he offered to let her have the use of a new motor car of the same make and model as the one which she had ordered but she did not take advantage of this offer.

The plaintiff further testified that the defendant's manager telephoned her on Monday, April 16th, or Tuesday, April 17th, to state that he had been obliged to put in a special order with the manufacturer and that she then repudiated the contract and cancelled the order "because I couldn't wait as I wanted it to practice on for lessons." Her evidence as to the discussions relating to the time of delivery was substantially corroborated by Mr. George Cartwright who had been instrumental in bringing the parties together.

There was a conflict between the evidence of the plaintiff and the defendant's general manager as to the delivery date. Mr. Stratton, the manager, testified that no delivery date had been specified. He alleged that he had told the plaintiff that the normal delivery period was within two or three weeks but admitted that he had agreed "to get in touch with Mrs. Allen within two or three days and advise her what had taken place".

On the conflicting evidence the learned trial Judge made the following finding: "I think I must find on this evidence that the defendant agreed to deliver the car which the plaintiff agreed to purchase, within a few days, two or three or at least by the end of the week as the plaintiff has said." Mr. Stratton stated that as a result of the rush order which he had submitted to the manufacturer, a motor car answering the description of the motor car described in the written contract was available for delivery to the plaintiff on April 19th, ten days after the date of the contract; that he advised the plaintiff to this effect but she refused to accept delivery.

In this action the plaintiff sought to recover the sum of $2,477 paid by her as the purchase-price of the automobile.

The contract being one for the sale of goods of the value of more than $40, it is one required by the statute to be in writing; s. 5(1) Sale of Goods Act, RSO 1950, c. 345.

It is provided by s. 26 of the Act that the seller is under a duty to deliver the goods and the buyer to accept and pay for them in accordance with the terms of the contract of sale. I refer also to s. 28(1) and (2) relating to the rules as to delivery under a contract for the sale of goods. Under the Act, as under the common law, where no time for delivery of the goods is fixed, they are to be delivered within a reasonable time.

If extrinsic evidence were admissible, the finding of the learned trial Judge as to the date fixed for delivery must be treated as having established the governing date, but in the present case not only have the parties reduced the transaction to writing, but the contract is one which is required by law to be in writing. Extrinsic evidence is, therefore, inadmissible to contradict, vary, add to or subtract from the terms of the document. Where a contract, not required by law to be in writing, purports to be contained in an instrument which the Court infers was not intended to express the whole agreement between the parties, proof may be given of any omitted or supplemental oral term expressly agreed upon before or at the time of executing a document but only if it is not inconsistent with the documentary terms. We are concerned here, however, with a formal contract in writing and one which is required by law to be in writing.

One of the incidents of a contract for the sale of goods where no date of delivery is specified is that the goods must be delivered within a reasonable time. The incidents which are impliedly contained in a written contract, whether by construction of its terms or by implication of law, are as much within the general rule as if expressed in written terms in the instrument, and it cannot be varied or contradicted by extrinsic evidence: *Heyworth* v. *Knight* (1864) 17 CB NS 298, 144 ER 120; *Burges* v. *Wickham* (1863) 3 B & S 669, 122 ER 251.

It has been held that a written contract for the sale of goods expressing no time for payment and delivery and therefore importing by construction of law a sale for ready money, does not admit of evidence of credit given except under a general usage of the trade: *Ford* v. *Yates* (1841) 2 Man. & G. 549, 133 ER 866. In that case the contract of sale was silent as to the time of payment but was construed by the Court to be a sale for cash on delivery, and evidence of a course of dealing by which the purchaser was allowed 6 months' credit was held inadmissible.

I refer also to *Greaves* v. *Ashlin* (1813) 3 Camp 426, 170 ER 1433. There the vendor had agreed in writing, sufficient under the Statute of Frauds, to sell certain goods, the contract being silent as to the time of delivery. Since this imported a reasonable time for the removal of goods by the buyer, oral evidence that he was to take them away immediately was held to be inadmissible.

It has been well settled that if the real contract of the parties is reduced into writing, whether it be a contract required by the Statute of Frauds to be in writing or not, verbal evidence is not allowed to be given of what passed between the parties either before the written instrument was made or during the time that it was in a state of preparation so as to add to or subtract from or in any manner vary or qualify the written contract: *Hickman* v. *Haynes* (1875) LR 10 CP 598; *Goss* v. *Lord Nugent* (1833) 5 B & Ad. 58, 110 ER 713; *Evans* v. *Roe* (1872) LR 7 CP 138. In *Inglis* v. *Buttery & Co.* (1878) 3 App. Cas. 552, it was held that even deleted words could not be looked at. The same point arose for determination in *King's Old Country Ltd.* v. *Liquid Carbonic Can. Corp.* [1943] 1 DLR 538, 50 Man. R. 359. There the contract in writing for the sale of goods called for delivery "as soon as possible" and it was held that those words could not be qualified or altered by a prior oral agreement by which the seller gave an unconditional promise to deliver before a fixed date; that there was no way by which the parol undertaking by the defendant to deliver the subject matter of the sale on or before May 15th could qualify the written agreement or resolve it into an operative prior and collateral agreement.

It is provided by s. 54 of the Sale of Goods Act that where in the Act any reference is made to "reasonable time", the question of what is a reasonable time is a question of fact. The uncontradicted evidence adduced by the defendant on this point is that if a car were specially ordered from the manufacturer, as was done in this case, it was impossible to secure delivery in less than 2 weeks. In the present case the car was available for delivery within 10 days of the date of the contract.

Even if the plaintiff were entitled to prove by extrinsic evidence that Saturday, April 14, was the date stipulated for delivery to be made, there is no term or provision of the contract nor is there anything in the surrounding circumstances from which it can be inferred that the time so stipulated was of the essence of the contract. Nor is there any finding upon that issue. Section 11 of the statute provides that unless a different intention appears from the terms of the contract, stipulations as to time of payment are not deemed to be of the essence of a contract of sale and whether any other stipulation as to time is of the essence or not depends on the terms of the contract. Assuming that April 14th had been established as the date of delivery, I am not convinced that it would be a stipulation constituting aa condition, performance of which went to the whole consideration of the purchaser, for a breach of which she was entitled to reject the motor car in question and treat the contract as repudiated. It is unnecessary, however, to decide this point.

The crucial question to be determined in this case arises from the construction of the contract and, in my view, it is unquestionably a contract which required performance by the defendant within a reasonable time. The defendant offered to make delivery of the motor vehicle within a reasonable time and the plaintiff was not, in my opinion, entitled to refuse acceptance.

I would, therefore, allow the appeal with costs and dismiss the action with costs.

Appeal allowed.

Questions:

1 In cases such as the above, should the plaintiff forfeit his whole payment? What was the defendant's measure of damages? See *Charter* v. *Sullivan (infra*, chapter 11). *Cf. Dies* v. *British and International Mining and Finance Corp. Ltd.* [1939] 1 KB 724, and *Stockloser* v. *Johnson (infra*, chapter 11).

2 S ordered a steel building from I at a price of $11,485, delivery to be made in the first week of June. S paid a deposit of $2,485. I failed to deliver on time and S agreed to wait until the end of June. By the end of July delivery had not been made, so S ordered another building from a different supplier without informing I. In late August, I notified S that it could then deliver. S refused delivery, informing I that it now had a substitute, and sued for the return of its deposit. What result? See *Sunstrum Ranching Co. Ltd.* v. *International Building Systems Ltd.* [1975] 4 WWR 86 (Sask. Dist. Ct.).

CHAS. RICKARDS LTD. v. OPPENHEIM
[1950] 1 KB 616, [1950] 1 All ER 420 (CA)

The defendant ordered from the plaintiff a Rolls-Royce chassis, which was delivered on July 30, 1947. At the request of the defendant, who wanted a body built on the chassis, the plaintiffs contacted various coachbuilders, one of which said it would be able to complete the work "within six or, at the most, seven months". On that footing the defendant gave the work order to the plaintiffs, who subcontracted with the coachbuilders. On August 20, 1947, the specifications for the body were finally agreed upon, placing the time for delivery, at the latest, at March 20, 1948.

The work was not completed by that date. Evidence indicated that the subcontractors were plagued by labour and materials problems. The defendant continued to press for delivery, choosing not to cancel the contract. He requested delivery in time for Ascot, 1948, but received no compliance. On June 29, 1948, the defendant wrote to the coachbuilders, referring to their latest promise of delivery of two weeks, as follows:

> I regret that I shall be unable, unless my plans change, to accept delivery of the Rolls you are making for me after July 25. For six months I have had a reservation to take a car abroad on August 3 for my holiday and it would appear to me to be impossible to alter this date. I shall, therefore, have to buy another car.

On July 8, 1948, the defendant was informed that the car would not be ready by July 25, whereupon he purchased another car and claimed from the plaintiffs £2,041, the amount he had paid for the chassis. The car was completed and tendered on October 18, 1948, but the defendant refused to accept delivery.

In this action the plaintiffs claimed £4,530 from the defendant, representing the balance of the price of the car under the agreement, or a similar amount for work and materials with respect to the body. The defendant counterclaimed for the chassis or, alternatively, its value. Finnemore J. held that as the work on the car had not been completed by July 25 the defendant was entitled to cancel the contracts and gave judgment in his favour on both the claim and the counterclaim. The plaintiffs appealed.

DENNING L.J.: It is clear on the finding of the trial judge that there was an initial stipulation making time of the essence of the contract between the plaintiffs and the defendant: the body of the car was to be completed "within six, or, at the most seven months." Mr Sachs (for the plaintiffs) did not seek to disturb that finding; indeed, he could not successfully have done so. But what he did say was that that stipulated time was waived. His argument was that, the stipulated time having been waived, the time became at large, and that thereupon the only obligation of the plaintiffs was to deliver within a reasonable time. He said that "a reasonable time" meant, in accordance with well-known authorities, a reasonable time in the circumstances as they actually existed, that is, that the plaintiffs would not exceed a reasonable time if they were prevented from delivering by causes outside their control, such as strikes or the impossibility of getting parts, and events of that kind; and that on the evidence in this case it could not be said that a reasonable time was in that sense exceeded. He cited the well-known words of Lord Watson in *Hick* v. *Raymond and Reid* [1893] AC 22, 32, 33, that where the law implies that a contract shall be performed within a reasonable time, it had "invariably been held to mean that the party upon whom it is incumbent duly fulfils his obligation, notwithstanding protracted delay, so long as such delay is attributable to causes beyond his control and he has neither acted negligently nor unreasonably." These words, he said, supported the view that in this case, on the evidence, a reasonable time had not been exceeded.

If this had been originally a contract without any stipulation as to time and, therefore, with only the implication of reasonable time, it may be that the plaintiffs could have said that they had fulfilled the contract; but in my opinion the case is very different when there was an initial contract, making time of the essence of the contract: "within six or at the most, seven months." I agree that that initial time was waived by reason of the requests that the defendant made after March, 1948, for delivery; and that, if delivery had been tendered in compliance with those requests, the defendant could not have refused to accept the coach-body. Suppose, for instance, that delivery had been tendered in April, May, or June, 1948: the defendant would have had no answer. It would be true that the plaintiffs could not aver and prove they were ready and willing to deliver in accordance with the original contract. They would have had, in effect, to rely on the waiver almost as a cause of action. At one time there would have been theoretical difficulties about their doing that. It would have been said that there was no consideration; or, if the contract was for the sale of goods, that there was nothing in writing to support the variation. There is the well-known case of *Plevins* v. *Downing* (1876) 1 CPD 220, coupled with what was said in *Bessler, Waechter, Glover & Co.* v. *South Derwent Coal Co. Ld.* [1938] 1 KB 408, which gave rise to a good deal of difficulty on that score; but all those difficulties are swept away now. If the defendant, as he did, led the plaintiffs to believe that he would not insist on the stipulation as to time, and that, if they carried out the work, he would accept it, and they did it, he could not afterwards set up the stipulation as to the time against them. Whether it be called waiver or forbearance on his part, or an agreed variation or substituted performance, does not matter. It is a kind of estoppel. By his conduct he evinced an intention to affect their legal relations. He made, in effect, a promise not to insist on his strict legal rights. That promise was intended to be acted on, and was in fact acted on. He cannot afterwards go back on it. I think not only that that follows from *Panoutsos* v. *Raymond Hadley Corporation of New York* [1917] 2 KB 473, a decision of this court, but that it was also anticipated in *Bruner* v. *Moore* [1904] 1 Ch. 305. It is a particular application of the principle which I endeavoured to state in *Central London Property Trust Ld.* v. *High Trees House Ld.* [1947] KB 130.

So, if the matter had stopped there, the plaintiffs could have said, notwithstanding that more than seven months had elapsed, that the defendant was bound to accept; but the matter did not stop there, because delivery was not given in compliance with the requests of the defendant. Time and time again the defendant pressed for delivery, time and time again he was assured he would have early delivery; but he never got satisfaction; and eventually at the end of June he gave notice saying that, unless the car were delivered by July 25, 1948, he would not accept it.

The question thus arises whether he was entitled to give such a notice, making time of the essence, and that is the question that Mr. Sachs has argued before us. He agrees that, if this were a contract for the sale of goods, the defendant could give such a notice. He accepted the statement of McCardie J., in *Hartley* v. *Hymans* [1920] 3 KB 474, 494-95, as accurately stating the law in regard to the sale of goods, but he said that that did not apply to contracts for work and labour. He said that no notice making time of the essence could be given in regard to contracts for work and labour. The judge thought that it was a contract for the sale of goods. But in my view it is unnecessary to determine whether it was a contract for the sale of goods or a contract for work and labour, because, whatever it was, the defendant was entitled to give a notice bringing the matter to a head. It would be most unreasonable if the defendant, having been lenient and waived the initial expressed time, should, by so doing, have prevented himself from ever thereafter insisting on reasonably quick delivery. In my judgment he was entitled to give a reasonable notice making time of the essence of the matter. Adequate protection to the suppliers is given by the requirement that the notice should be reasonable.

So the next question is: was this a reasonable notice? Mr. Sachs argued that it was not. He said that a reasonable notice must give sufficient time for the work, then outstanding, to be completed. He says that, on the evidence in this case, four weeks was not a reasonable time because it would, and did in fact, require three and a half months to complete it. In my opinion, however, the words of Lord Parker in *Stickney* v. *Keeble* [1915] AC 386, 419 apply to such a case as the present just as much as they do to a contract for the sale of land. He said that

> in considering whether the time so limited is a reasonable time the court will consider all the circumstances of the case. No doubt what remains to be done at the

date of the notice is of importance, but it is by no means the only relevant fact. The fact that the purchaser has continually been pressing for completion, or has before given similar notices which he has waived, or that it is specially important to him to obtain early completion, are equally relevant facts

— to which I would add, in the present case, the fact that the original contract made time of the essence of the contract. In this particular case, not only did the defendant press continually for delivery, not only was he given promises of speedy delivery, but on the very day before he gave this notice he was told by the works manager in charge of the work that it would be ready within two weeks. Then he gave a four weeks' notice. The judge found that it was a reasonable notice, and, in my judgment, there is no ground on which this court could in any way differ from that finding. The reasonableness of the time fixed by the notice must, of course, be judged at the time at which it is given. It cannot be held to be a bad notice because, after it is given, the suppliers find themselves in unanticipated difficulties in making delivery.

Appeal dismissed.

[Singleton L.J. delivered a reasoned concurring judgment. Bucknil L.J. concurred without separate reasons.]

Notes and Questions:

1   Compare *Oppenheim* with *McNeill* v. *Associated Car Markets Ltd.* (1962) 35 DLR (2d) 581 (BC CA). For the Code provisions on modification of contractual terms and waiver, see UCC 2-209.

2   Why did the plaintiff sue in this case? Was it because it had completed the work and a benefit had been conferred on the defendant (because the body had been built on the chassis) even though the plaintiff was in breach of the time of delivery? Was the plaintiff's only alternative to dismantle the body and simply return the chassis to the defendant, or would this have amounted to an act of conversion? Could theories of unjust enrichment be invoked here to prevent unjust results and if so how would you formulate them for this purpose?

A. H. BOULTON
The Making of Business Contracts
(2nd ed., 1972) pp. 27-31

There is little doubt that the most intractable problem in the attempt to create completely fair and workable conditions to operate between the buyer and seller of goods is this one of the sanction to be applied in the event of late delivery, and consequently the means available to the buyer to ensure that he obtains his goods at the time he needs them. It has been seen that the typical conditions extant fall into three groups. Sellers' conditions seek to avoid liability, buyers' to fix full responsibility, including consequential damages, and more moderate conditions provide for liquidated damages. In modern industry the problem of late dispatch is a serious one, and in the opinion of many observers failure to keep quoted dispatch times is the prime sin of modern industry. There are both reasons and excuses for lateness, however, and the problem is not as easy in practice as it appears to the lawyers in the uncomplicated atmosphere of a court. It may therefore be of value to stand back from this problem and, forgetting the wording of rival conditions, attempt to see it whole and objectively. Upon almost every other point in the cleavage of interest between buyer and seller a compromise can readily be found by negotiation. Upon this, however, the difference of approach between the two parties is so fundamental that the unsatisfactory compromise of "liquidated damages" is very frequently adopted simply because it is difficult to find a better.

It is unsatisfactory for a number of reasons. The very fact that the adverse consequences to the seller of defaulting in the matter of time can be measured with accuracy may constitute a temptation to allow in his costing for a measure of "penalty" to be applied, and then to hope for the best. If pressures develop which give rise to a general deterioration in the delivery position the manufacturer will naturally balance penalty against penalty and bias his production plans so as to operate to his least disadvantage in this respect, rather than consider the extent to which his customers will in fact be damaged by his default. The reduction in price which the application of "liquidated damages" affords to the buyer seldom matches the damage actually suffered. Sometimes the buyer who is kept waiting for his goods loses nothing thereby, but if he suffers at all his loss is likely to exceed anything he may receive as liquidated damages. Thus the device fails in its ostensible purpose, in that it is seldom a genuine pre-estimate of the damage that will be suffered by the buyer. It is normally qualified by a provision under which the seller is entitled to call for an extension of time if delay is due to circumstances over which he has no control, and it is so easy for the seller to make such a claim with his full knowledge of the circumstances and to find plausible excuses, and so difficult for the buyer to refute it, that in practice it is found that to invoke the liquidated damages clause is to invite vexatious argument and to generate ill-will.

In this book the attempt throughout is to concentrate upon typical situations, and the typical situation in which the maintenance of delivery promises is of vital importance is that in which the goods to be supplied are made specially for the customer, and are such that their manufacture is a relatively lengthy process. In other situations the problem is not acute. If the goods of like kind can be readily purchased elsewhere the buyer can help himself out of the difficulty by buying in the market, and the seller who is left with goods on his hands can similarly sell them on the market. The damage which either suffers if there is a breach of contract is easily measurable as the difference in price, and the situation is adequately dealt with in the Sale of Goods Act, which, as has already been observed, grew out of the decisions of the courts made over a period when the contract of sale was mostly a matter for merchants dealing with commodities. When, however, an order is placed for goods which are specially made, the buyer has placed himself in the hands of the seller in a quite different way. Probably only those concerned in manufacturing industry can have a proper sense of the problems that arise when default occurs, or properly assess the difficulties that may be the cause of default. It is by no means unusual for the construction of a complicated machine, or, indeed, for a relatively standard article, if it is large and made only to order, to occupy a year of factory time. It is easy for the law to apply principles, valid enough in their proper place, granting the aggrieved buyer the right to repudiate the contract breached by the defaulting seller and to buy the goods elsewhere, but in practice that is the last thing he is likely to do, because to do it is to sacrifice such progress as has been made in the factory, and to recommence, with a new manufacturer, the long waiting period required for design and the organisation of manufacture. If he does cancel the contract the true reason may be that he has changed his plans and is using the opportunity thus gratuitously offered to escape from his commitments. Looking at the same situation from the point of view of the seller, it is equally easy for the law to say that he has defaulted and has failed to deliver the goods at the proper time so that the buyer is released from the contract and that he, as the seller, has only himself to blame. But to be left with a nearly completed machine for which there is no immediate prospect of sale and which represents the investment of many thousands of pounds in production costs is a major catastrophe which he cannot contemplate with any equanimity. Thus, once an order for this type of article is placed, the two parties are deeply committed to each other by the practical realities of the situation.

From the point of view of the buyer, however, the availability of the goods at the time contracted for may be absolutely vital. He may himself have entered into commitments upon the strength of the seller's undertakings. When the goods are themselves to be used for production purposes as earning assets, delay may involve him in trading losses and in breach of his own undertakings. Of what value to him is a liquidated damages clause yielding a maximum of £1,000, if, as a result of the delay he loses profits worth ten times as much, involves himself in lawsuits from the breach of his own contracts, and suffers a loss of reputation which cannot be appraised? For him, the best position is to be able to recognise time as of the essence of the contract, and to rest upon the common law principle expressed in the Sale of Goods Act, "The measure of damages is the estimated loss directly and naturally resulting in the ordinary course of events from the seller's breach of contract." As has been seen, the damages recoverable at common law by the application of this principle can be very heavy and can include loss of profits.

But the seller also has his point of view. When he quotes a time for the supply of the goods he is looking into the future, which is always a risky business. It is not merely a matter of fire, flood, act of God, industrial dispute, embargo, riot, or any other hair-raising possibilities which legal draftsmen love to write into their escape clauses. His chief designer may fall sick, or find another job, or a flaw may be found in a major casting, so that it has to be replaced from the foundry, or he may be kept waiting for components he has ordered from other suppliers. He may find it difficult to work to required tolerances without seeking new standards of material. It may simply happen that a job takes longer than he had expected, or that a sub-assembly has to be redesigned because of teething troubles. Just how far can he expect to stretch an escape clause based upon the magical words "circumstances beyond his reasonable control"? The two things he dare not expose himself to are to have his custom built machine left on his hands and to be held liable to damages when he has genuinely done his best to fulfil his promises.

Now practical men can see these two points of view. Buyers are not, as human beings, unreasonable, nor are sellers. There is, none the less, real importance in the principle that promises are made to be kept, and that the seller who breaks his promises should be held responsible. The truth is that the practice which buyers wish to be armed against is the tendency of sellers to quote delivery times frivolously or recklessly or fraudulently. This last is a strong word to use, but one that is sometimes justified. It is very frequently the case that the time quoted for delivery is of more significance in the award of a competitive tender than is the price quoted. If the earning power of a production machine is £2,000 per month it is better to buy it for £10,000 and have it in six months than to pay £8,000 and to wait for a year. It is plainly fraudulent for a manufacturer in order to obtain business against honest competitors who have quoted realistically, to add ten per cent to his proper price and state a delivery date which he well knows is impossible of achievement, offering a liquidated damages clause which at the maximum will absorb the loading he has injected into his price. It is fraudulent, but that is not to say that it has never been done.

What are the possible sanctions for non-delivery at the promised time, and when, in fairness, ought they to be applied? It is suggested that the reasonable answers are as follows:

(a) The right of the buyer to cancel the contract and to buy elsewhere. This, as has been shown, is often impracticable, and operates unjustly against the seller who has made a reasonable effort to fulfil his obligations, but has met with unexpected difficulties, even though those difficulties do not come within the usually accepted meaning of *force majeure*. It is, however, a sanction which should be available as a last resort to relieve the buyer from a contract in the event of complete incompetence on the part of the seller.

(b) The right on the part of the buyer to claim damages at large, which can include loss of profits provided they are reasonably foreseeable. This operates excessively harshly against an honest seller who has met with unexpected difficulties, but is fully justifiable against a seller who has quoted recklessly or fraudulently in the matter of delivery time.

(c) Liquidated damages, usually subject to an escape clause dealing with the more obvious kinds of *force majeure*. This is unlikely to recompense the aggrieved buyer adequately, but provides an incentive to a seller to do his utmost to minimise delays which occur in respect of promises made in good faith, but arise in the course of manufacture when there has been some lack of alertness on the part of the manufacturer.

Note: In view of the difficulties to which Boulton alludes, what type of clause dealing with the time of delivery and the buyer's remedies for breach therefor would fairly balance both parties' interests? Is Boulton right in characterizing as fraudulent a seller's promise to deliver by a given date when he knows he cannot meet the deadline? What remedies does the law give the buyer in such circumstances? It is often said that the common law recognizes no doctrine of good faith in bargaining or in the performance of contracts. Does this example (among others) prove the need for such a doctrine, a doctrine that is familiar in many civilian systems?

See generally OLRC Sales Report, *supra*, chapter 7 (B).

C. USE AND INTERPRETATION OF MERCANTILE SHIPPING TERMS

OLRC Sales Report
pp. 346-50

4. THE USE OF MERCANTILE TERMS

For over 150 years, the custom of merchants dealing in international trade has been to describe their mutual obligations of performance in a symbolic shorthand of initials and words. The commonest of these are "f.o.b." and "c.i.f.", which signify "free on board" and "cost, insurance and freight" respectively. In North America, these terms have not been restricted to use in export transactions, or to shipment by sea. Their earliest use in Canada was in connection with the internal or domestic Great Lakes grain trade, but they were soon extended to carriage by rail, and are now also used in truck shipments. The different types of shipping terms, and the frequency of their use among the respondents to the CMA Questionnaire, are shown in Table 2, set out below.

TABLE 2
SHIPPING TERMS

		Always or often %	Mid %	Rarely or never %
(a)	Ex works (factory, warehouse, etc.)	42.1	22.3	35.5
(b)	F.O.R. — F.O.T. (free on rail — truck) named departure point	8.0	14.4	77.6
(c)	F.A.S. (free along ship) named port of shipment	2.6	9.0	88.5
(d)	F.O.B. (free on board) named port of shipment	36.6	22.6	40.7
(e)	C. & F. (cost and freight) named port of destination	4.1	10.8	85.1
(f)	C.I.F. (cost, insurance, freight) named port of destination	6.9	15.7	77.5

(g)	Freight or carriage paid to named point of destination (inland)	20.5	30.8	48.7
(h)	Ex ship — named port of destination	1.2	3.7	95.7
(i)	Ex quay — named port of destination	0.8	2.3	96.5
(j)	Other	7.7	3.7	88.5

It will be noted that, while shipment "ex works" is the single most common term, "f.o.b. named port of shipment" comes a close second, and that, when combined, the various other forms of shipment terms substantially exceed in frequency sales made "ex works". However, frequency of use is not coterminous with agreement as to the meaning of the terms used, or variations thereof. To what extent, therefore, should the revised Ontario Act follow the lead of Article 2 in providing an authoritative catalogue of definitions? The preliminary, but far from exhaustive, inquiries made on our behalf indicate considerable sympathy for such an enterprise. The Canadian decisions interpreting the meaning of shipping terms are modest in number, and the courts have generally resorted to British precedents. We were advised that, even among shipping managers, the terms are not always fully understood, and that their statutory codification might help to dispel some of the uncertainty.

It goes without saying that no final decision should be taken without further and comprehensive consultation with the interested parties. Assuming the reaction remains positive, two further questions arise: (a) which model should be adopted; and, (b) what provision should be made with respect to the impact of containerization?

(a) WHICH MODEL?

There are only two approaches that seriously commend themselves as precedents: namely, the provisions in sections 2-319 to 2-323 of the Uniform Commercial Code, and the *Incoterms* adopted by the International Chamber of Commerce. The two sets of terms have been compared for us, and the overall conclusion appears to be that the differences between them are modest. Nevertheless, there is little doubt in our minds that the Code terms make a more logical choice. We say this for two reasons. In the first place, the United States is our closest trading partner, and it is obviously desirable that Canadian and American businessmen should attach the same meaning to each other's trade terms. Secondly, the Article 2 definitions are better geared to North American practices and traditions since, unlike the *Incoterms*, they are not restricted to foreign trade contracts. Accordingly, we recommend that the revised Act incorporate a definition of common trade terms. The definitions contained in UCC 2-319 to 2-323 should be adopted in preference to the *Incoterms* promulgated by the International Chamber of Commerce.

(b) IMPACT OF CONTAINERIZATION

Containerization is a mode of shipment in which large numbers of packages or units are stored in sealed metal crates. The primary advantages of containerization are simplicity of handling and increased security. The container revolution, which began in the middle 1960's, has had its most significant impact so far on the overseas shipping trade. To a lesser extent, it has influenced domestic shipping, with most container carriage going to those carriers, known as "combined transport operators", who containerize the shipper's goods in anticipation of their shipment by sea. In the future, intermodal domestic containerization may be expected to grow as regulatory difficulties are solved and shipper awareness of its advantages is increased.

The containerization process differs from traditional breakbulk carriage in many ways. First, it eliminates the individual handling of packages by carriers and forwarding agents, thus making traditional bills of lading inappropriate for such carriage. Secondly, it complicates the process of determining which carrier is liable for damage to the goods, because the container is sealed by the first carrier and not opened until the destination is reached. This may result in the initial carrier, usually the combined transport operator, bearing a greater burden of liability than in the past; it further points out the incongruous limitations on liability to which the various modes of carriage are now subject. Thirdly, it raises new problems of passage of title and risk of loss as between buyer and seller, especially where the contract is f.o.b. or c.i.f. and the seller is obliged to obtain a bill of lading. The reason, as some commentators have pointed out, is that a clean bill of lading for "shipped" not "received" goods may not be obtainable. Fourthly, questions of what constitutes a package for purposes of liability limitations have only begun to be litigated, and no uniform principles have yet emerged.

As now constituted, the usual requirements of a bill of lading (that is, that it be issued by a shipowner, not a forwarding agent, that the goods be "on board" or "shipped" and not "received", that it be "clean", and that it should confirm storage under deck) cannot ordinarily be satisfied by container carriage. This fact indicates that the traditional rules will have to be adapted in time to conform to this new, and vastly more efficient, means of transportation. It may be that the terms f.o.b. and c.i.f. will have to be redefined to encompass container transport. Or, it may be that commerce will develop a new term or terms to signify the rights and duties of the parties where goods are shipped in this manner.

Many problems have yet to be litigated, and commercial handling of these transactions is still evolving. We therefore conclude that any attempt to codify the law regarding the rights and obligations of sellers and buyers under a container transport of goods at this time would be premature, and might stunt the development of containerization.

Note on Containerization:

As the OLRC Report indicates, the introduction of containerization has numerous legal implications, many of which have still to be worked out. For a sampling of some of the voluminous literature in this area, see D.M. Sassoon, "Trade Terms and the Container Revolution" (1969-70) 1 J. Mar. L. & Comm. 73; S. Simon, "Container Law: A Recent Reappraisal" (1976-77) 8 J. Mar. L. & Comm. 489; and *Benjamin's Sale of Goods*, §1834-51.

BEAVER SPECIALTY LTD. v. DONALD H. BAIN LTD.
(1973) 39 DLR (3d) 574, [1974] SCR 903

RITCHIE J. (for the Court): This is an appeal by Beaver Specialty Limited (hereinafter referred to as "Beaver") from a judgment of the Court of Appeal for Ontario varying the judgment rendered by King, J., at trial and directing that the respondent, Donald H. Bain Limited (hereinafter referred to as "Bain") recover the sum of $31,616.48, together with interest from February 7, 1963, from Beaver in respect of the purchase price of 2,000 cases of Chinese walnuts which had become unmerchantable in the course of transit between Vancouver from whence they had been shipped by Bain and Toronto where Beaver had refused to accept delivery of the cargo.

There was also an appeal by Pacific Inland Express Limited (hereinafter referred to as "PIX") the truckers responsible for the carriage of the cargo, against the finding of the Court of Appeal that Beaver was entitled to recover $19,269.75 from that company in respect of the loss of value of the walnuts through damage in transit and also for storage charges.

This litigation arises out of a contract for purchase and delivery of the 2,000 cases of walnuts entered into by Beaver in Toronto through the Toronto office of Bain which was engaged in the business of wholesale commission merchants and brokers having its head office in Winnipeg and branch offices at both Toronto and Vancouver.

The original order was for 4,000 cases of these walnuts and it was passed on in this form by Bain (Toronto) to its Vancouver office by telephone on January 16, 1963, and by confirmatory letter of the same day, whereupon Bain's Vancouver office appears to have at once prepared a contract note addressed to Beaver in the following terms:

Order 508

Vancouver, B.C. January 16, 1963
Canada

Messrs. Beaver Specialty Company, Ltd.
Toronto, Ontario.

We have this day booked for you as per your order to —

Donald H. Bain Limited,
159 Bay St., Toronto, Ont.

4,000 cases CHINESE 1961 crop Light Dry Cracked
    walnut meats PIECES, packed in veneer
    cases, parchment paper lined of 55
    net shipping weight each   @ per lb.
    Can. $.59

"Seller to supply original Chinese Quality Certificates"
Prices as above f.o.b. Toronto, Ont.
Terms NET CASH

Shipment 2,000 cases to be invoiced and
transferred to buyer's account in ware-

house January 31, 1963. Balance of
2,000 cases to be invoiced and transferred to buyer's account in warehouse
February 28, 1963.
        This contract is made subject to terms
        printed on the reverse side of this form.

Yours truly,
DONALD H. BAIN LTD.
Agents

The 2,000 cases first referred to in this note were not transferred to the buyer's (*i.e.*, Beaver's) account in the warehouse but by agreement between the parties were delivered to PIX for shipment to Beaver in Toronto. The agreement between the parties in this regard is evidenced by the further contract note of the same date which contains the following and was marked ex. 7 at the trial:

Prices   .... all charges paid Toronto in truckload quantities, ...

Terms   ..... Net Cash, ...

Shipment   .. To be taken by Beaver Specialty Co., Toronto — ....

2,000 cases by January 31/63 — 2,000 cases by February 28/63. ....

and is further corroborated by the terms of a letter dated January 18, 1968, from Bain Toronto to Bain Vancouver, which contains the following paragraph:

> Our buyer, Beaver Specialty Company, Toronto, has asked that 2,000 cases of their contract be shipped January 31st, 1963 to them, by Pacific Inland Express trucks. They do not want these goods before that time, but want them shipped on the date they are to come out. Please invoice them also, at the same time.

PIX undertook to transport these walnuts from Vancouver to Toronto under protective service at temperatures between 45° and 50°. These shipments arrived at the Federal Cold Storage in Toronto on February 5, 6, and 7, 1963, and there is no dispute, at least between Bain and Beaver that the walnuts arrived in Toronto in seriously damaged condition apparently occasioned by freezing.

The question at issue between Beaver and Bain is as to which company had title to the walnuts while they were in transit and the difference arising between the trial Judge and the Court of Appeal is that the trial Judge proceeded on the basis that the goods remained the property of Bain until delivery "f.o.b. Toronto" to Beaver, whereas the Court of Appeal interpreted the evidence as disclosing that the 2,000 cases were transferred to Beaver's account when they were delivered to PIX for transportation. The question is a very narrow one and turns on the interpretation of the contract note, and upon a consideration of the provisions of the Sale of Goods Act. There appears to be no doubt that the contract was for sale by description rather than by sample, and the respondent accordingly invokes the provisions of s. 19, Rule 5 of the Sale of Goods Act, RSO 1960, c. 356 [now RSO 1970, c. 421]. This section reads: . . .

The appellant on the other hand invokes the provisions of s. 33 of the same Act which read as follows: . . .

The appellant contends, as the trial Judge found, that the intention of the parties is made manifest by the contract note to which I have referred and by the documents which accompanied its execution and that that intention was that the goods were to be shipped "f.o.b. Toronto, Ont." and that it was never intended that title should pass to Beaver until its acceptance of delivery in Toronto.

The respondent Bain contends, in conformity with the reasons for judgment of the Court of Appeal, that the words "f.o.b. Toronto, Ont." as they occur in the contract note have reference entirely to the price of the goods and this is because, as I have indicated, they are found in one line of the contract which reads: "Prices as above f.o.b. Toronto, Ont." The absence of any punctuation after the word "above" in this line cannot, in my opinion, be treated as meaning that the words and letters "f.o.b. Toronto, Ont." were referable only to the price. "Prices as above" is a clear reference to the fact that the prices had been designated in the earlier part of the contract note.

In the course of the reasons for judgment rendered orally by Mr. Justice Kelly on behalf of the Court of Appeal [11 DLR (3d) 432, [1970] 2 OR 555], he expressed the view that the contract [at pp. 435-6]

> . . . contemplated that Bain should fulfil it by transferring, in the Vancouver ware-house, to Beaver's order, successively two lots of 2,000 cases each and that upon each such transfer Bain would be entitled to the payment for the purchase price of such 2,000 cases; that the revised instructions substituted for the first transfer in the warehouse, the physical delivery of the 2,000 cases to the carrier; that when such delivery was made, the contract in respect of that 2,000 cases was fully performed by Bain and Bain was entitled to payment, the cases thereafter being at the risk of Beaver.

With the greatest respect for this view, it appears to me to ignore the circumstances which surrounded the preparation of the contract note. When Beaver gave its original instructions to Bain (Toronto) Mr. Carter of that firm took a handwritten note regarding the order which was preserved and became ex. 5 at trial. This memorandum reads as follows:

16 Beaver Spec. Co. Toronto
4000 cs Chinese LDC walnuts
      Pe's 55 # — 59¢
      Dev'd Toronto in
      truck loads.
2000 by Jan. 31/63 from Vancouver
2000 by Feb. 28/63 from Vancouver
Invoiced by D.H.B. Ltd. Vancouver.

At the hearing before us the abbreviations in this note were explained by appellant's counsel and were not questioned on behalf of other counsel and are as follows:

In the first line "16" refers to January 16, 1963.

In the 2nd line L.D.C. means "Light Dry Cracked"

In the 3rd line Pe's indicates the price 55 lbs. at 59¢ per lb.

In the 4th line "Dev'd" means "delivered"

In the last line "D.H.B. Ltd." refers to "Donald H. Bain Limited."

•   •   •

It thus appears to me to have been established that when issuing the contract note to Beaver, Bain was carrying out the intention of the parties made manifest by the telephone call from Beaver to Bain (Toronto) and the pencil note made at the time. I am therefore of opinion that the entry "f.o.b. Toronto, Ont." occurring on the contract note is to be read in conjunction with the pencilled memorandum of the order given by Beaver and accepted by Bain which provided for "delivery Toronto in truck loads", which in my view means that Beaver was to take delivery in Toronto. This is confirmed by the letter of January 18th and by ex. 7, to both of which I have made reference.

In this regard, the case of *Winnipeg Fish Co.* v. *Whitman Fish Co.* (1909), 41 SCR 453, appears to me to be highly relevant. There a contract was made in Winnipeg between the agents of the shippers (Whitman Fish Co.) and the purchasers (Winnipeg Fish Co.) for the shipment of a car load of fish from Canso, N.S., where the shippers' plant was located to Winnipeg. The sale was by sample and the written order as conveyed by the shippers' agent in Winnipeg to his company in Canso contained the words "On condition you ship them the same quality haddies as sample."

Under the terms of the contract the goods were to be shipped "f.o.b. Winnipeg" and in the course of the reasons for judgment rendered by Mr. Justice Davies and concurred in by Mr. Justice Duff, it was said at page 460:

> I agree with the holding of the Court of Appeal that the contract in the case must in the circumstances under which it was made he held to have "required delivery of the fish in Winnipeg and that the property in the fish did not pass until such delivery." Such a determination does not necessarily follow from the use of the letters and words "f.o.b. Winnipeg" in the contract made. There is room for much contention as to their real effect and the language may be said to be ambiguous. But when we consider the circumstances surrounding the making of the contract, that the agent of the plaintiffs and of the defendants were both in Winnipeg, when they made it and that the fish were to be shipped from Canso, Nova Scotia, thousands of miles from Winnipeg and delivered "f.o.b. Winnipeg," that they were to be in accordance with a sample then and there produced and that the plaintiffs in suing upon the contract in expressly setting forth another claim that their goods were to be delivered in Winnipeg, I agree that the contention [*sic*] of the parties must fairly be determined to have been that the property in the fish should not pass until they were in Winnipeg ready for delivery to the defendants.

In the course of his reasons for judgment in the Court of Appeal in the present case, Mr. Justice Kelly found himself able to distinguish the *Winnipeg Fish Co.* case on the ground that in that case the plaintiffs included in their statement of claim a paragraph alleging that the fish were "to be delivered at Winnipeg".

I appreciate that this was an added factor favouring the purchasers' contention in that case, but in the present case the circumstances surrounding the making of the contract were that the agents of Beaver and Bain were both in Toronto when they made it; that the walnuts were to be shipped from Vancouver thousands of miles from Toronto and delivered "f.o.b. Toronto"; and I find that the pencilled note taken by Mr. Carter of Bain when the Beaver order was given and specifying that the goods were to be "delivered Toronto in truck loads" is sufficient to resolve any ambiguity to which the letters and words "f.o.b. Toronto" might give rise in favour of the primary meaning attributed to this phrase by leading authorities on the sale of goods.

In this regard I have reference to what is said in Mr. Williston's work on *The Law Governing Sales of Goods*, rev. ed. (1948), s. 280(b), where it is said:

> As it is a necessary implication in f.o.b. contracts that the buyer is put at all expense in regard to the goods after the time when they are delivered f.o.b., the presumption follows that the property passes to the buyer at that time and not before, . . . *and the further presumption follows that the place where the goods are to be delivered f.o.b. is the place of delivery to the buyer.*

(The italics are my own.) Further authority to the same effect is to be found in Vold on *The Law of Sales*, 2nd ed., s. 33, where it is said:

> Under shipment "f.o.b. destination" the presumption is that the property interest was not meant to pass until the goods reached destination.

In the case of *Steel Co. of Canada Ltd.* v. *The Queen* [1955] 2 DLR 593, [1955] SCR 161, [1955] CTC 21, certain manufactured goods had been shipped by the appellant in Montreal and delivered by it to Canada Steamship Lines Limited for shipment to various companies beyond the head of the Lakes and the contract contained a printed heading: "f.o.b." under which was typed "Hd. of Lakes". The vendors, like Bain in this case, relied on the provisions of s. 20 of the Manitoba Sale of Goods Act and particularly Rule 5 thereof. (This section is the almost exact equivalent of s. 19, Rule 5 of the Ontario Sale of Goods Act hereinbefore referred to.) In the course of his reasons for judgment which he delivered on behalf of himself and Mr. Justice Fauteux, Kerwin, C.J.C., had occasion to say, at pp. 595-6:

> I agree with the contention on behalf of the appellant that, while it might have been argued that the goods were unconditionally appropriated to the contracts by the marks, or tags, and by the delivery of them to the carrier, if "F.O.B. HD. OF LAKES" had not appeared in the invoices, the presence of these words brings the case within the opening part of s. 20 of the Manitoba Sale of Goods Act "Unless a different intention appears". The authorities justify the statement in *Benjamin on Sale*, 8th ed., p. 691: "The meaning of these words [f.o.b.] is that the seller is to put the goods on board at his own expense on account of the person for whom they are shipped; delivery is made, and the goods are at the risk, of the buyer, from the time when they are so put on board." This does not mean that in all F.O.B. cases the property in the goods contracted to be sold passes only when the goods are so put on board, but the circumstances in the present instance do not take it out of the general rule. The duty of the appellant to pay the freight to the Head of the Lakes is one that would usually accompany the obligation to put the goods Free on Board.

Having regard to all the above, it will be seen that I take the view that the circumstances surrounding and immediately preceding the issuance of the contract note are such as to support the contention of the appellant that this note evidenced the intention of the parties that the walnuts were to be delivered to Beaver in Toronto and this being the case the provisions of s. 33(1) of the Sale of Goods Act to which I have already referred, apply and Beaver which had had no reasonable previous opportunity of examining the goods must be deemed not to have accepted them and was therefore fully justified in its refusal of the cargo.

Appeal allowed.

Questions: What is the ratio of this decision — that in a f.o.b. destination contract, title, and therefore risk, does not pass to the buyer until the goods are delivered at destination? Suppose the parties *do* intend that title shall pass to the buyer before the goods are delivered to him (as will typically be true in a documentary sale where the buyer receives the bill of lading and pays for the goods before the goods have reached their destination), does this mean that risk passes to the buyer at the earlier date? On the relationship between risk and the transfer of title, see further, *infra*, chapter 9, and *cf.* UCC 2-319.

D. DELIVERY AND DOCUMENTS OF TITLE

1. NATURE OF DOCUMENT OF TITLE

OLRC Sales Report
pp. 319-22

A document of title, as commonly understood in the sales context, is a writing, generally issued by a person in the business of warehousing or transporting goods, purporting to cover goods in his possession, and entitling the holder of the writing to deal with the goods. There are two kinds of documents of title: (1) a bill of lading, being an acknowledgment by a carrier that the goods have been received for carriage; and (2) a warehouse receipt, being an acknowledgment by a bailee that goods have been received for storage. Documents of title are comparable to bills of exchange, notes and cheques in that, in the ordinary course of commerce, the rights represented by the document can be transferred by transferring possession of the document itself, with any necessary endorsement. They are also similar in that a bill, note or cheque represents the right to receive payment, while a document of title represents the right to receive possession of goods. However, the comparison is not exact. The incidents attached to bills, notes and cheques are clearly established as a result of comprehensive federal legislation, while the incidents attached to documents of title are less clear. Moreover, both at common law and under the relevant statutes, there are important differences in these incidents.

We have not undertaken an exhaustive examination of the law relating to documents of title, but their role cannot be ignored. They are mentioned in several sections of the existing Sale of Goods Act and affect some basic issues of sales law. These issues include the effect of documents of title on the following: (1) the passing of title and risk between seller and buyer; (2) the seller's delivery obligations; (3) the seller's remedies; and, (4) the operation of the *nemo dat* rule and the statutory protection given to innocent third parties. In examining these issues we have encountered two basic difficulties with the existing law. The first difficulty is the lack of codification of the law relating to documents of title in Ontario. The second difficulty concerns the nature of the legislative changes that have been made to the common law.

As to the first difficulty, there is, as stated, no modern comprehensive codification of the law relating to documents of title in Ontario. Nor are documents of title governed by a clear body of common law. We are told by Falconbridge that, by the late nineteenth century, bills of lading were instruments well known to commerce and that, by the custom of merchants, peculiar incidents were attached to them. Peculiar incidents were not, on the other hand, attached by custom to warehouse receipts. There are few modern Canadian cases dealing with the law relating to documents of title, and some of the older cases are inconsistent with the assumptions underlying modern usage of these documents.

This point can be illustrated by examining a distinction commonly made in modern commercial practice. Borrowing ideas and nomenclature from other branches of negotiable instrument law, and perhaps relying upon American precedents, it is common in practice to distinguish between negotiable and non-negotiable documents of title. This distinction may center, according to trade usage, on one or more of a number of things. First, it may go to the issue of whether the document is transferable at all. Secondly, the distinction may relate to the form of the transfer; that is, whether the bailee must acknowledge or attorn to the transferee before the transferee has any right under the document. Thirdly, the distinction between negotiable and non-negotiable documents of title may determine whether the document is intended to be assignable free from the equities existing between the original parties; that is, whether the bailee can raise any claim or defense that he had against the original holder against a subsequent holder of the document. Fourthly, the distinction may be relevant in determining whether a transferee of an apparently regular document, who takes in good faith for value and without notice of a defect in the title of his transferor, or of the want of title of his transferor, takes free from that defect or want of title.

In contexts other than documents of title, it is primarily the fourth meaning that is the essence of negotiability. Yet at common law, according to Falconbridge,

> A bill of lading, and *a fortiori* any other document of title to goods, is not negotiable in the same sense as a bill of exchange may be negotiable, and therefore the mere honest *possession* of a bill of lading endorsed in blank, or in which the goods are made deliverable to the bearer, is not such a title to the goods as the like possession of a bill of exchange would be to the money promised to be paid by the acceptor. The endorsement of a bill of lading gives no better right to the goods than the endorser himself had . . . .

By The Warehouse Receipts Act, negotiable warehouse receipts are given incidents of negotiability similar to those attached to bills and notes. However, there
is no federal or provincial legislation that does the same for bills of lading.

Since the documents themselves seldom set out what is meant by "negotiable" or "non-negotiable", the parties are left, in the event of a dispute, to
establish the meaning of these terms by trade usage. This they must do against a
background of common law rules, which have developed little since the last
century and which seem flatly to contradict the parties' assumptions.

The second basic difficulty with the existing law governing documents of
title is the nature of the legislative changes that have been made to the common
law. There are references to documents of title scattered throughout several
Ontario statutes, including The Sale of Goods Act, The Factors Act, The Personal
Property Security Act, The Mercantile Law Amendment Act and The Warehouse
Receipts Act. In addition, there is federal legislation covering some aspects of
bills of lading, such as the Bills of Lading Act and the regulations made pursuant
to the Railway Act. The provincial legislation is marked by significant inconsistencies, much duplication and numerous gaps. The inconsistencies include such
a basic matter as the lack of a uniform definition of documents of title. Further,
these inconsistencies extend to the radically different treatment accorded to
warehouse receipts and bills of lading: the former are covered by fairly comprehensive legislation, while the latter are governed by the common law. The
duplication in provincial legislation centers on the overlapping protection given
to innocent holders of documents of title. They are protected by provisions in
four acts: namely, The Sale of Goods Act, The Factors Act, The Mercantile Law
Amendment Act and The Warehouse Receipts Act. These acts do not, however,
adopt any consistent theory as to the circumstances in which innocent holders
should be protected from defects of title. The gaps in provincial legislation relate
primarily to bills of lading, rather than to warehouse receipts. They include such
basic matters as the formal requirements of a document of title, the obligations of
a bailee who holds goods under a document of title, the extent of the bailee's lien,
and the form and effect of negotiation or transfer of these instruments.

2. DOCUMENTS OF TITLE AND THE SELLER'S DELIVERY OBLIGATIONS

OLRC Sales Report
pp. 326-27

The existing Sale of Goods Act says little about the effect of the issuance of a
document of title on the seller's obligation to deliver the goods. Two provisions
of the Act merit reference. Cases in which a document of title has been issued are
specifically excluded from the operation of section 28(3), which controls the time
of delivery where goods are held by a bailee that are not to be shipped. Section
31(1) of The Sale of Goods Act, which deals with the effect of delivery to a carrier
where the seller is authorized or required to send the goods to the buyer, does not
specifically exclude from its operation cases where documents of title have been
issued. The courts have, however, arrived at this result by emphasizing that

section 31 is only a *prima facie* rule. We turn now to consider the situations contemplated by these provisions.

(i) *Goods Held by a Bailee That Are Not to be Shipped*

As noted, cases in which a document of title has been issued are expressly excluded from the operation of section 28(3) of The Sale of Goods Act. As a result, what constitutes an effective tender of delivery where goods are covered by a document of title is left to be resolved by the common law and other statutes. In Ontario, sections 21 and 22 of The Warehouse Receipts Act provide that a transferee of a warehouse receipt receives "the benefit of the obligation of the warehouseman to hold possession of the goods for him ...". A similar, but more elaborate, rule is found in UCC 2-503(4). This provision contains additional qualifications that clarify the circumstances in which failure by the bailee to honour a document of title will defeat the seller's tender. We think that the provisions of UCC 2-503(4) as they relate to documents of title would be useful additions to our revised Act, and recommend their adoption in lieu of the provisions of section 28(3) of the existing Act. Our Draft Bill contains a provision giving effect to this recommendation.

(ii) *Goods Authorized or Required to be Shipped*

The *prima facie* rule found in section 31(1) of the Ontario Sale of Goods Act, that delivery to the carrier is delivery to the buyer, may be displaced where the seller reserves a right of disposal in the goods. Section 20(2) provides that, where the goods are shipped and by the bill of lading the goods are deliverable to the order of the seller or his agent, the seller is *prima facie* deemed to reserve the right of disposal. In this way a bill of lading may determine whether there has been delivery of the goods and, arguably, locate the place of the buyer's right of inspection, since delivery and the right of inspection are usually treated as coterminous events. In contrast, the Code has specific provisions for inspection in section 2-513, which are functionally oriented and divorced from questions of delivery. In addition, as indicated, section 2-505 has recognized that the reservation of a right of disposal has the limited purpose of giving the seller a security interest, and has no bearing on other issues. Finally, sections 2-503(2) and (3) and 2-504 set out more fully the seller's general duty of tender and delivery in shipment and destination contracts, including those involving documents of title. These provisions are examined in greater detail in chapter 14. We also explain elsewhere, in a more general context, the advantages of the Code's separate provisions for inspection, and its limitation of the seller's right of disposal to a security interest. The rationale that supports these provisions is equally applicable where documents of title are involved. Accordingly, we recommend that the revised Act should incorporate provisions similar to UCC 2-503 (2) and (3) and UCC 2-504 with respect to the role of documents of title affecting the seller's delivery obligations in shipment and destination contracts. As under the Uniform Commercial Code, the revised Act should incorporate separate rules, unconnected with questions of delivery, with respect to the effect of the reservation of a right of disposal and the place of inspection of goods after delivery.

Chapter 9
Risk of Loss and Frustration of the Contract of Sale

A. RISK OF LOSS

1. INTRODUCTION

OLRC Sales Report
pp. 265-266

Multiple hazards can accompany goods between the time of their identification to the contract and the time of their actual receipt by the buyer. This possibility has led to the adoption of rules governing the location of the risk of loss that go back at least to Roman times.

Risk rules and rules of frustration intersect; but they are not the same. Unless otherwise provided, a frustrating event discharges both parties from further obligations under the contract. This result does not, however, necessarily follow from loss of, or damage to, the goods. If risk of loss at the material time lies with the buyer, he remains liable for the price; obviously, the contract is not discharged so far as he is concerned. Conversely, if the risk is with the seller, the buyer will be excused from further obligations, but whether the seller will also be relieved will turn on other factors. In this Report, therefore, it will be convenient to postpone discussion of frustration problems to a later chapter.

Four basic tests have been adopted by different legal systems to determine the time when risk of loss passes from the seller to the buyer. According to these tests, risk passes as follows: (a) when the contract is concluded; (b) when title in the goods is transferred; (c) when the seller has delivered the goods, actually or constructively; and, (d) when the buyer has actually received the goods. Roman law was the source of the first test. It is a test that survives in a substantial number of civil law jurisdictions, including Switzerland, the Netherlands, Japan and members of the Latin American legal system. The title or property test has been adopted in France, among other jurisdictions. This test was also part of the common law, and was codified in the UK Sale of Goods Act, 1893. It is reproduced in section 21 of the Ontario Act. The "delivery" test is in force in the Scandinavian countries and, as will be seen, has been substantially adopted in the Uniform Commercial Code. The fourth test, the one that turns on transfer of possession, obtains under German and Austrian law, and under the laws of various Eastern European countries. An important aspect of it also appears in the Code.

If one groups together, as others have done, the first two and the last two tests, it will be seen that there are only two basic tests: namely, those that turn upon identification and appropriation of the goods to the contract, and those that apply a delivery or control test.

2. ILLUSTRATIONS OF THE OPERATION OF THE CURRENT RULES

JEROME v. CLEMENTS MOTOR SALES LTD.
(1958) 15 DLR (2d) 689, [1958] OR 738 (CA)

SCHROEDER J.A.: This action arose out of the following circumstances: The plaintiff had entered into negotiations with the appellant for the purchase of a used 1955 Nash sedan in the month of July, 1957. The bargain was reduced to a formal contract in writing bearing date July 8, 1957. Under the terms of the agreement the total purchase-price of the 1955 Nash sedan was $2,395. The appellant agreed to accept in trade a used Ford car owned by the plaintiff's daughter for which it made an allowance of $1,000 and a 1951 Nash motor car owned by the plaintiff for which it agreed to allow the sum of $495, the balance of $900 to be paid in cash. On the same date, the plaintiff gave the appellant her cheque for $902 to cover the balance of the purchase-price and to provide for the transfer fee of the motor-vehicle permit for the 1955 Nash motor car. At the same time the plaintiff delivered to the appellant the motor-vehicle permits in respect of the two cars which were being accepted in trade, the transfer form on which were signed by the plaintiff's daughter and the plaintiff respectively. It was arranged between the parties that the plaintiff should retain possession and enjoy the use of the 1951 Nash car until she obtained delivery of the 1955 Nash automobile. The agreement also contained the following clause: "No warranties or representations whatever are made upon any secondhand car or used car ordered (unless specified hereon in writing), said car being purchased in its present condition and having been examined and accepted by me, and subject to any repairs above provided for." The agreement provided for the installation of a new tail pipe, checking of an oil leak on the rear wheel and the changing of the battery. This involved the removal of the comparatively new battery in the 1951 Nash motor car to the 1955 Nash motor car, an operation which was to be effected at the time that delivery of the motor car was taken by the plaintiff. The appellant agreed to effect the repairs which were specifically mentioned in the agreement and certain other minor repairs not set forth in the document without cost to the plaintiff.

It was stated in evidence that all the repairs to the 1955 Nash, with the exception of the installation of the battery, were effected on Thursday July 11th, on which date the motor car was removed from the repair shop and placed in the defendant's showroom. A fire of undetermined origin occurred on these premises at 3 o'clock in the morning on Friday July 12, 1957, in the course of which the repair shop and the showroom were laid waste and the motor car in question was seriously damaged and greatly deteriorated in value. As the appellant was unable to make delivery of the motor car, the plaintiff instituted action to recover the $900 paid by her in addition to the value of the two motor cars which the appellant had agreed to accept in trade on the terms hereinbefore stated.

[Schroeder J.A. referred to the plaintiff's alternative claim against the respondent insurance company, and continued]:

The question of substance in this action is whether at the time of the fire the motor vehicle in question was at the seller's risk or at the buyer's risk. Section 21 of the Sale of Goods Act, RSO 1950, c. 345 provides as follows: . . .

The rules governing the transfer of property from a seller to a buyer are set forth in ss. 18 and 19 of the Sale of Goods Act, and I shall refer to those portions thereof which are relevant: . . .

The learned trial Judge came to the conclusion that there was nothing in the terms of the contract or the conduct of the parties or the circumstances of the case on which he could base a finding as to the time at which the parties to the contract intended the property in the motor vehicle to be transferred to the buyer and that it was therefore necessary to resort to the provisions of the Rules contained in s. 19 of the Act to ascertain their intention. He held that under the contract the appellant, as the seller, was bound to do something to the motor vehicle for the purpose of putting it into a deliverable state and that although the repairs, except the installation of the battery, were said to have been completed on Thursday July 11th, the buyer did not have notice of that fact, and accordingly the property in the vehicle had not passed to the purchaser at the time of the fire.

The fact that the things which were required to be done to the vehicle to put it into a deliverable state were trivial in nature does not affect the question. In *Wilde* v. *Fedirko* (1920) 13 SLR 190, the plaintiff had undertaken to place certain fire bricks in the engine of a threshing machine to enable straw to be burned and it was held that the placing of the bricks in position was a condition precedent to the passing of the property. In *McDill* v. *Hilson* (1920) 53 DLR 228, 30 Man. R. 454, a decision of the Manitoba Court of Appeal, it was held that the undertaking to polish furniture and remedy the chipped condition thereof not having been carried out by the vendor, the goods were not in a deliverable state, and that this prevented the property therein from passing to the purchaser.

It is not seriously contended that R. 2 of s. 19 is not applicable to this contract, having regard to those things which under the contract the vendor was bound to do for the purpose of putting the vehicle into a deliverable state but it is argued that it can be inferred from the terms of the contract, the conduct of the parties and the surrounding circumstances, that the parties intended that the property in the motor vehicle was to be transferred to the purchaser on July 8, 1957, the date of the contract, so that "a different intention appears". The burden of showing that "a different intention appears" within the meaning of R. 2 of s. 19, lies upon the appellant who so alleges.

In his work on Sales, Lord Blackburn pointed out that where the vendor has undertaken to perform certain things to the subject-matter of the sale, it is important to ascertain whether the performance thereof is meant to precede the vesting of the property or not. This, he states, is a question of the construction of the agreement; that it may often happen that the parties have expressed their intention in a manner that leaves no room for doubt. When, however, they have not done so in express terms, their intention must be collected from the whole agreement. He then refers to Rules, such as are now found in s. 19 of the Sale of Goods Act, which were adopted in the English Courts since the beginning of the Nineteenth Century as rules of construction "which are perhaps some of them a little artificial". In the opinion of Lord Blackburn, the Rule as set forth in *R. 2* of s. 19, seems to be founded in reason. He states that in general it is for the benefit of the vendor that the property should pass. The risk of loss is thereby transferred to the purchaser, and as the vendor may still retain possession of the goods, so as to retain a security for payment of the price, the transference of the property is to the vendor pure gain. It is therefore reasonable that where, by the agreement, the vendor is to do something before he can call on the purchaser to accept the goods as corresponding to the agreement, the intention of the parties should be taken to be that the vendor was to do this before he obtained the benefit of the transfer of the property. He adds: "'The presumption does not arise if the things might be done after the vendor had put the goods in the state in which he had the right to call upon the purchaser to accept them, and would be unreasonable where the acts were to be done by the buyer who would thus be rewarded for his own default.'" This passage was quoted in the judgment of King J., in *McLellan* v. *Nor. British & Mercantile Ins. Co.* (1891) 30 NBR 363 at p. 376; affd (1892) 21 SCR 288.

There is no doubt but that the operation of *R. 2*, s. 19 is subordinated to the real intention of the parties as to when the property in the subject-matter of the sale should pass to the purchaser if that intention has been manifested in some other manner.

It is contended on behalf of the appellant that the work to be done to the 1955 Nash motor car was completed on Thursday July 11th, and that the plaintiff must be taken to have notice thereof because the appellant had agreed to make delivery to the plaintiff on Thursday July 11th. Under the Sale of Goods Act, one of the incidents of a contract for the sale of goods where no date of delivery is specified in the written contract (as in this case), is that the goods must be delivered within a reasonable time and what is a reasonable time is a question of fact: see s. 28(2) and s. 54. In *Allen* v. *Danforth Motors Ltd.* (1958) 12 DLR (2d) 572, this Court held that where a contract for the sale of an automobile, whether it be one required by law to be in writing or one which purported to express the whole agreement between the parties, contained no specification of the date of delivery, the implication arose under the statute that delivery would be made within a reasonable time; that the incidents which were impliedly contained in a written contract, whether by construction of its terms or by the implication of law, were as much within the general rule as if expressed in written terms in the instrument and could not be varied or contradicted by extrinsic evidence. It cannot be said, therefore, that this contract provided for delivery of the motor car to the purchaser on Thursday July 11th, if the appellant relies upon an oral agreement fixing that date as the date of delivery, since that would be a term clearly at variance with the terms and provisions of the written document. I am therefore unable to give effect to this argument advanced by the appellant. There is, however, this further fallacy in that argument, namely, that the time at which the buyer has notice of the performance of the things required to be done by the seller under the terms of the contract referred to in *R. 2* relates to a period of time at, or after, which the work is completed. That burden can not be discharged in advance by inserting an express stipulation in the contract that the workk is to be performed by a specified date. The crucial question is — did the buyer actually have notice or knowledge of the performance of these things at the time of the destruction of the motor vehicle by fire on Friday July 12, 1957? The final words "and the buyer has notice thereof" were not found in the common law rule but, as was pointed out by Chalmers in his work on the *Sale of Goods,* 11th ed., p. 66, these words were added in Committee on a suggestion from Scotland that it was unfair that the risk should be transferred to the buyer without notice. The rule is expressed negatively and under it the property *does not pass* until the things required to be done by the vendor are done *and the buyer has notice thereof.*

Counsel for the appellant contends that the fact of payment of the purchase-price in advance, the transfer of the two motor-vehicle permits for the motor cars which were being traded in by the purchaser, and the payment by her of the transfer fee in respect of the 1955 Nash motor car indicated a contrary intention within the meaning of s. 19. *McDill* v. *Hilson* and *Wilde* v. *Fedirko, supra,* –and the cases therein cited are authority for the proposition that payment of the purchase-price could not be indicative of such a contrary intention. No more can it be said, in my opinion, that the transfer of the two motor-vehicle licences previously mentioned justify drawing the inference of a contrary intention. The manager of the appellant company stated in evidence that a motor-vehicle permit for the 1955 Nash automobile, made out in the name of the plaintiff, was in his possession on July 9th and had been placed in the motor car to be delivered to the plaintiff when she was given possession of the vehicle. At the time of the fire this permit was still in the possession of the vendor and I would not regard the issuance of the new permit as having any significant bearing upon the question of the intention of the parties as to the passing of the property in the vehicle.

It was further contended that the condition of the contract providing for the reservation of the title and right of possession in the motor car to the vendor until the full purchase-price was paid in money, was a term of vital significance. The sum of $900, the monetary consideration required to be paid by the purchaser, having been paid on July 8th, the appellant maintained that the title and right to possession which theretofore had been vested in the vendor, *ipso facto* became vested in the purchaser. This, it was argued, was a clear manifestation of a different intention. The provision of the agreement upon which this contention is based reads as follows:

"The title to and right of possession in said motor car shall remain with you until conveyed or until the full purchase price is paid in money." In the view which I have formed this provision of the contract has no bearing on the issue whatsoever. It is important to ascertain the reason for the inclusion of this term in the contract. Under s. 38 of the Sale of Goods Act, it is provided that notwithstanding that the property in goods may have passed to a buyer, the unpaid seller has by implication of law a lien on the goods or right to retain them for the price while he is in possession of them. Under the provisions of s. 41, however, he loses his lien or right of retention thereon when he delivers the goods to a carrier or other bailee for the purpose of transmission to the buyer without reserving the right of disposal of the goods or when the buyer or his agent lawfully obtains possession of the goods. It is plainly evident that the real purpose of inserting this particular term or provision in the contract, was to protect the seller against loss of its lien if the subject-matter of the sale came into the possession of the purchaser before the payment of the full purchase-price. In any event, the word "property" as used in ss. 18 and 19 of the Act, is used in a distinct and specific sense and must be given the particular meaning assigned to it under the provisions of s. 1(*i*) where the word "property" is defined as meaning "general property in goods and not merely a special property". The essence of sale, as pointed out in *Burdick* v. *Sewell* (1884) 13 QBD 159 at p. 175; 10 App. Cas 74 at p. 93, is the transfer of the ownership or general property in goods from seller to buyer for a price. The definite article "the" preceding the word "property" indicates the general property as distinguished from "a" property, that is merely a special property. The general property in certain goods may be in one person while a special property in them is in another person, as in the case of a pledge where the pledgee has only a special property or interest, the general property remaining in the pledgor: *Halliday* v. *Holgate* (1868) LR 3 Ex. 299. So, therefore, the general property in goods may be transferred to one person, subject to a special property or interest in another: *Franklin* v. *Neate* (1844) 13 M & W 481, 153 ER 200. A person therefore to whom the general property in a material object is transferred becomes the owner thereof who owns a right to the aggregate of its uses. The person upon whom the ownership of a thing devolves has the general property therein whereas he who has merely a special interest in it is not an owner of the thing but merely an encumbrancer of it.

Where the general property in a material object is vested in A, although it may be subject to lien or some other kind of encumbrance held by B, A is nevertheless still entitled to the residue of its uses, and whatever right over the object is not vested in B is vested in A. That residuary use may be of lesser dimensions or less valuable than the rights of B, but the ownership is in A and not in B. When B's right is determined in some manner, A's right, relieved from the encumbrance weighing it down, will immediately assume its full stature and will once more have its full effect. That which is a right of ownership when there are no encumbrances, remains a right of ownership notwithstanding any number of them.

The appellant's argument is predicated on the premise that on July 8th the purchaser had paid the full purchase of the motor car, hence the title and right to possession thereof could not be said to remain with the vendor and since it had to vest somewhere it must be deemed to have vested in the purchaser. Even if this argument were otherwise sound, the words "full purchase price as paid in money" must, of necessity, where part of the consideration was paid by the trading in of two other motor cars, be given a broader interpretation and the word "money" should be construed as including "money's worth". In that aspect of the matter, since the plaintiff still had possession of the 1951 Nash car for which an allowance of $495 was to be made, the full purchase-price could not be said to have been paid to the appellant on July 8th. It would therefore be open to the plaintiff to argue that if any significance were to be attached to this provision as bearing upon the question of the transfer of the general property in the 1955 Nash car the title thereto and the right of possession thereof were still vested in the vendor on the date of the fire. As stated, however, I am unable to hold that the reservation of this special property in the motor car to the vendor could prevent the passing of the general property therein to the purchaser within the meaning of ss. 18 and 19 of the statute, once the intention of the parties is established.

In my opinion, the learned trial Judge has rightly determined that at the time of the fire on the appellant's premises, the property in the 1955 Nash motor car had not passed from the seller to the purchaser and that it was therefore at the appellant's risk. Accordingly the appeal should be dismissed as against the plaintiff with costs. The plaintiff still has the 1951 Nash motor car in her possession and evidently intends to retain it. The judgment should, therefore, be varied by reducing the amount of the recovery to $1,900.

Appeal dismissed.

[McGillivray J.A. delivered a concurring judgment; Laidlaw J.A. dissented.]

Questions:

1   Suppose the vehicle had been in a deliverable condition at the time of the contract of sale and the defendant had not agreed to make repairs but the plaintiff had said that he needed several days to raise the purchase price and requested a delay in delivery until then, would the result have been different? Should it have been?

2   Suppose the dealer had gone bankrupt before the vehicle had been delivered to the buyer; would it then have been in the buyer's interest to argue that the title had passed to him and that he was entitled to claim release of the vehicle? *Cf. Carlos Federspiel & Co. S.A.* v. *Chas. Twigg & Co. Ltd., infra,* chapter 10(A)(2). Does this demonstrate the undesirability of linking risk rules to title questions?

3. CRITIQUE OF THE CURRENT RULE; OTHER APPROACHES

OLRC Sales Report
pp. 266-69

The title test adopted by the common law is difficult to justify functionally. It may seem reasonable to argue that the party in whom ownership is vested at the material time should also assume the risks incident to ownership. However, as

398 CH. 9 RISK OF LOSS AND FRUSTRATION OF SALE CONTRACT

has also been observed of the Roman test, it shows little concern for practical considerations. The title test ignores insurance factors; it disregards the fact that the party in possession of the goods is best able to ensure their safekeeping and to determine the cause of an accident; and, it overlooks the fact that until the seller has delivered the goods, he has not completed his contractual obligations. A strict application of the title test leads to anomalous results that run counter to the expectations of practical persons. It would greatly surprise a consumer buyer, and no doubt his seller, to be told that, by selecting a particular item on the seller's floor for subsequent delivery to his home, he could be deemed to have assumed the risk forthwith. Conversely, a seller would find it difficult to understand why, following delivery, the risk of loss should remain with him simply because he retained title until payment of the price. These difficulties have not gone unobserved. In overseas shipment contracts, the business community long ago rejected the title test by the adoption of trade terms, such as "f.o.b." and "c.i.f.". These terms transfer the risk of loss to the buyer when the goods are delivered to the carrier, regardless of the locus of title. The courts, too, carved out an important exception in the case of the sale of a part of a larger bulk of goods in storage that is accompanied by the transfer of a delivery warrant. Technically, there is no transfer of title in such a case, since no particular part of the bulk has been appropriated to the contract; nevertheless, in the interests of mercantile convenience, the courts found an implied intention that risk was to pass upon delivery of the warrant.

These exceptions demonstrate the fundamental weakness of the title test and the superiority of the delivery test. As has been observed, the "passing of risk upon actual delivery is the modern solution. It conforms with commercial views and practices; it has been adopted by the more recent national and international codifications". The Uniform Commercial Code, too, has adopted the "modern" solution.

This solution is contained in section 2-509, which reads as follows:

> **2-509.** (1) Where the contract requires or authorizes the seller to ship the goods by carrier
>
>   (a)   if it does not require him to deliver them at a particular destination, the risk of loss passes to the buyer when the goods are duly delivered to the carrier even though the shipment is under reservation (Section 2-505); but
>
>   (b)   if it does require him to deliver them at a particular destination and the goods are there duly tendered while in the possession of the carrier, the risk of loss passes to the buyer when the goods are there duly so tendered as to enable the buyer to take delivery.
>
> (2) Where the goods are held by a bailee to be delivered without being moved, the risk of loss passes to the buyer
>
>   (a)   on his receipt of a negotiable document of title covering the goods; or
>
>   (b)   on acknowledgment by the bailee of the buyer's right to possession of the goods; or
>
>   (c)   after his receipt of a non-negotiable document of title or other written direction to deliver, as provided in subsection (4)(b) of Section 2-503.

(3) In any case not within subsection (1) or (2), the risk of loss passes to the buyer on his receipt of the goods if the seller is a merchant; otherwise the risk passes to the buyer on tender of delivery.

(4) The provisions of this section are subject to contrary agreement of the parties and to the provisions of this Article on sale on approval (Section 2-327) and on effect of breach on risk of loss (Section 2-510).

The first three subsections of section 2-509 distinguish between three types of situation. The first involves contracts that require or authorize the seller to ship the goods by independent carrier ("shipment contracts"). Here, the risk passes to the buyer when the goods are delivered to the carrier, unless the seller is required to deliver them at a particular destination ("destination contracts"). In the latter event, risk passes when the goods are there duly tendered while in the hands of the carrier. The second type of situation concerns goods in the hands of a bailee that are to be delivered without being moved. Here, risk of loss passes upon the buyer's receipt of a document of title or acknowledgment by the bailee of the buyer's right to possession. Finally, in cases not falling within the preceding rules, risk of loss passes to the buyer upon his receipt of the goods, if the seller is a merchant, and, if he is not, upon tender of delivery. It should be noted that, by virtue of section 2-509(4), the provisions of subsections (1), (2) and (3) are subject, *inter alia*, to contrary agreement of the parties.

It will be observed that a common thread runs throughout these rules: that is, the transfer of possession of the goods from the seller to the buyer, or a tender thereof. The *situs* of title plays no role whatever. It has been said that section 2-509 has been very successful in its objectives and that, unlike pre-Code law, it has generated very little litigation. We support the general philosophy of section 2-509 and recommend the adoption of a comparable provision in the revised Act.

Note: The OLRC also recommended a number of changes and some clarification in the prospective Ontario version of UCC 2-509, two of which merit special mention:

(i) *Application of 2-509(1)(a) to sales where the buyer is a non-merchant*:

Assume A, a non-merchant in Vancouver, orders a newly published book from a firm of publishers in Toronto. Assume, also, that the book is lost in transit. Who should bear the risk of loss? If the agreement contains no provision to the contrary, the contract may be deemed a "shipment" contract and the risk will lie with the non-merchant buyer, assuming the seller has made a proper contract of carriage with the seller. It is doubtful that the buyer would appreciate this result, and even more doubtful that he would carry insurance against such risks. The problem does not appear to be discussed in the standard Anglo-Canadian or American textbooks. Our inquiries have shown that some large retail stores and other merchants with a mail order practice will not hold buyers responsible for risk of loss in transit. This policy, however, is based on the commendable grounds of fairness and good public relations, and not on the obligations implied by sales law. In any event, we have no reason to believe that this practice is universally followed by retail sellers. We deem it desirable, therefore, to deal directly with the matter. We recommend that a provision be added to the revised Act to make it clear that, where the seller is a merchant and the buyer is not, risk passes when the goods are tendered to the buyer at their destination. In other words, in such a case, the presumptive rule applicable to shipment contracts will not apply. It will, of course, be open to the parties to adopt a different rule; but we think it better that the burden of shifting the risk of loss should be upon the merchant than upon the buyer. [OLRC Sales Report, p. 270]

(ii) *Section 2-509(3) and distinction between merchant seller and non-merchant seller:*

[T]he rationale of the distinction appears to be that a merchant seller may be expected to insure the goods, whereas no such assumption can be made in the case of a non-merchant seller. This reasoning overlooks the fact that the seller still has control over the goods, and that it is more likely that he will be insured than a non-merchant buyer. It may be that the problem does not admit of a simple answer, and that a new rule should be devised that would take into consideration the parties' insurance coverage. Until such time, we are of the view that no distinction should be drawn in this context between merchant and non-merchant sellers. Accordingly, we recommend that the provision comparable to UCC 2-509(3) adopted in the revised Act should provide that, whether or not the seller is a merchant, risk of loss shall pass to the buyer upon receipt of the goods. It should be emphasized that this does not mean that the non-merchant seller will remain at risk indefinitely. Like the merchant seller he will have the benefit of UCC 2-510(3); hence, once the buyer is in default, the risk of loss will lie with the buyer for a reasonable period, to the extent of any deficiency in the seller's insurance. [OLRC Sales Report, pp. 271-72]

UN Convention on Contracts for the International Sale of Goods

Reproduced below are the risk provisions in the Convention. How do they differ from the Code provisions?

Article 66

Loss of or damage to the goods after the risk has passed to the buyer does not discharge him from his obligation to pay the price, unless the loss or damage is due to an act or omission of the seller.

Article 67

(1) If the contract of sale involves carriage of the goods and the seller is not bound to hand them over at a particular place, the risk passes to the buyer when the goods are handed over to the first carrier for transmission to the buyer in accordance with the contract of sale. If the seller is bound to hand the goods over to a carrier at a particular place, the risk does not pass to the buyer until the goods are handed over to the carrier at that place. The fact that the seller is authorized to retain documents controlling the disposition of the goods does not affect the passage of the risk.

(2) Nevertheless, the risk does not pass to the buyer until the goods are clearly identified to the contract, whether by markings on the goods, by shipping documents, by notice given to the buyer or otherwise.

Article 68

The risk in respect of goods sold in transit passes to the buyer from the time of the conclusion of the contract. However, if the circumstances so indicate, the risk is assumed by the buyer from the time the goods were handed over to the carrier who issued the documents embodying the contract of carriage. Nevertheless, if at the time of the conclusion of the contract of sale the seller knew or ought to have known that the goods had been lost or damaged and did not disclose this to the buyer, the loss or damage is at the risk of the seller.

Article 69

(1) In cases not within articles 67 and 68, the risk passes to the buyer when he takes over the goods or, if he does not do so in due time, from the time when the goods are placed at his disposal and he commits a breach of contract by failing to take delivery.

(2) However, if the buyer is bound to take over the goods at a place other than a place of business of the seller, the risk passes when delivery is due and the buyer is aware of the fact that the goods are placed at his disposal at that place.

(3) If the contract relates to goods not then identified, the goods are considered not to be placed at the disposal of the buyer until they are clearly identified to the contract.

Article 70

If the seller has committed a fundamental breach of contract, articles 67, 68 and 69 do not impair the remedies available to the buyer on account of the breach.

4. Risk of Loss and the Effect of a Party's Breach

A difficult question is whether and to what extent normal rules for transfer of risk of loss should be modified when one or the other party is in breach of his contractual obligations at the time of loss. The only express provision in the SGA which deals with this situation is s. 21(a), which provides that

> where delivery has been delayed through the fault of either the buyer or seller, the goods are at the risk of the party in fault as regards any loss that might not have occurred but for such fault . . .

The comparable Code rules appear in UCC 2-510 and are much more detailed than s. 21(a):

> **2-510.** (1) Where a tender or delivery of goods so fails to conform to the contract as to give a right of rejection the risk of their loss remains on the seller until cure or acceptance.
>
> (2) Where the buyer rightfully revokes acceptance he may to the extent of any deficiency in his effective insurance coverage treat the risk of loss as having rested on the seller from the beginning.
>
> (3) Where the buyer as to conforming goods already identified to the contract for sale repudiates or is otherwise in breach before risk of their loss has passed to him, the seller may to the extent of any deficiency in his effective insurance coverage treat the risk of loss as resting on the buyer for a commercially reasonable time.

J.J. White and R.S. Summers, *Uniform Commercial Code,* 2nd ed. 1980, p. 187, criticize 2-510 on the ground that "the draftsmen never clearly articulated why the party in breach should bear the risk of loss in certain circumstances when he would not bear that risk were he not in breach." They admit however that the section has given rise to little appellate litigation, an observation that in Canada applies to risk of loss cases generally. (Can you suggest why?)

At first blush s. 21(a) appears to differ fundamentally from 2-510. Section 21(a) presents however a very incomplete statement of existing Anglo-Canadian law on the effect of breach and, taking this into consideration, the OLRC came to the conclusion that the Code provision was substantially consistent with existing law and supported its adoption with some modifications (Sales Report, pp. 273-75). Note however the influence of insurance coverage and the non-subrogation effect of UCC 2-510(2) and (3).

Problem: A ordered a new vehicle from dealer X, the vehicle to be delivered "on or about December 1". On December 2, X telephoned A and said the vehicle was ready for delivery. A replied that he needed a few extra days to complete his financing arrangements and asked for a three-day delay in delivery. X agreed. On December 4 a fire occurred on X's premises and the vehicle was badly damaged. As between A and X, who bears the risk of loss, assuming (a) the SGA applies and (b) that UCC 2-509 and 2-510 apply?

B.   FRUSTRATION OF CONTRACT OF SALE

1.   FRUSTRATION THROUGH CASUALTY TO THE GOODS

OLRC Sales Report
pp. 365-68

1. INTRODUCTION

Like the law of mistake, the rules governing the frustration of agreements belong to one of the most difficult branches of contract law. The relatively small number of Canadian sales cases involving frustration issues and the infrequency with which the parties themselves may encounter the problem in periods of national and international stability mask the legal difficulties. In an environment of intense inflation and rapidly changing economic and political conditions, the parties are often faced with contingencies not foreseen at the time of contracting or which undermine their common assumptions. *Force majeure* clauses are a regular feature in well drafted contracts, and the parties may seek to protect themselves against future imponderables by the insertion of other appropriate clauses in their contracts. These drafting devices may diminish the need for clear rules; they do not replace them.

With the exception of section 8, The Sale of Goods Act does not purport to codify the law of frustration in its relation to contracts of sale. Cases falling outside the provisions of section 8 continue to be governed by common law principles. The common law position, though much litigated in this century in the United Kingdom, is far from clear, and both the theory of frustration and its scope as a defence remain unsettled. There is, therefore, much to be said for an attempt to clarify the present law. As will be seen, the Uniform Commercial Code contains a substantial number of provisions which, while disclaiming any pretence at a comprehensive statement, do clarify and improve the existing position in important respects in so far as contracts of sale are concerned. For a number of reasons, we support a similar approach in the revised Act to that adopted in the Code. The desirability of a general restatement of frustration principles should, we believe, be left for future consideration as part of our proposed Law of Contract Amendment Project.

2. THE SALE OF GOODS ACT, SECTION 8

Section 8 of The Sale of Goods Act deals with one aspect of the law of frustration in relation to a contract of sale; that is, the loss of specific goods. The section provides as follows:

> **8.** Where there is an agreement to sell specific goods and subsequently the goods without any fault of the seller or buyer perish before the risk passes to the buyer, the agreement is thereby avoided.

The effect of section 8 is to discharge the seller's obligation to deliver and the buyer's obligation to pay the price. The section should be read in conjunction with its companion provision, section 7, which applies similar principles to determine the effect on the contract of the parties' mistaken assumption with respect to the existence of the goods. As was noted in an earlier chapter, section 7 raises problems of construction. This is also the case with section 8. The section is, moreover, seriously incomplete. We turn now to consider the deficiencies of section 8.

First, section 8 deals only with the loss of "specific" goods. It is not clear whether the term "specific" is to be interpreted as referring solely to goods in existence at the time of making the contract. The Act defines "specific goods" in section 1(1)(*m*) as "goods identified and agreed upon at the time the contract of sale is made". In *Howell* v. *Coupland* (1876) 1 QBD 258 (CA), however, a seller was excused from a contract of sale of potatoes to be grown on his land when the crop failed. This case, decided before the enactment of the Sale of Goods Act, 1893, and other similar decisions, have raised the possibility of the application of section 8 to "quasi-specific goods". The law has not, however, developed.

Secondly, it will be noted that section 8 of The Sale of Goods Act only applies where the goods "perish". In chapter 5 of this Report, in the context of mistake, we considered the question when goods have "perished" within the meaning of section 7 of the Act. The term "perish" raises similar problems of interpretation in the context of section 8. For example, it is difficult to determine what degree of deterioration of the subject matter will bring the section into operation. There is some authority, disputed though it is, that the concept of perishment includes deterioration that alters, but does not destroy, the goods. Similarly, the concept of perishment causes difficulty in indivisible contracts where part of the subject matter of the contract is destroyed. There is authority that partial destruction will result in frustration of an indivisible contract, with the result that, even though the buyer is willing to take the remaining goods, he cannot force the seller to deliver.

Thirdly, it is not clear to what extent "fault" includes loss due to negligence. Section 1(1)(*f*) of The Sale of Goods Act defines "fault" to mean "a wrongful act or default". This definition is wide enough to embrace negligent conduct, and such a reading would be consistent with the rule applied in the case of self-induced frustration. Still, a small amendment to the definition would put the point beyond doubt.

Fourthly, difficulties are created by the restriction of section 8 to an "agreement to sell". By virtue of section 2(3) of The Sale of Goods Act, there is an agreement to sell where there has been no transfer of property in the goods to the buyer, but where such transfer is to take place at a future time or subject to some condition to be fulfilled thereafter. It seems clear, therefore, that section 8 has no application to contracts of sale where property or title has passed to the buyer. Yet, where title has passed, risk may nevertheless remain with the seller by agreement, or control of the goods may not have passed to the buyer. In the latter case, it is true that the line between frustration concepts and the seller's obligation to deliver the goods blurs. Nevertheless, it may well be argued that the doctrine of frustration should apply in the situations discussed above, notwithstanding that title may have passed to the buyer.

Fifthly, similar difficulties arise because section 8 is restricted to cases where goods perish "before the risk passes to the buyer". The section will not apply, therefore, where risk of loss has been assumed by the buyer, even though property in and possession of the goods remain with the seller. Indeed, there might be a difficulty in applying the concept of frustration to this situation: to discharge the seller from his obligation to deliver, on the ground of frustration, would also discharge the buyer from his obligation to pay the price, and this would conflict with the term of the contract placing the risk of loss on the buyer. Professor Glanville Williams would resolve this dilemma by applying frustration only to the obligation of the seller to deliver and not to the contract as a whole.

Sixthly, section 8 contains no reference to the relevance of foreseeability. A literal application of the section would lead to the conclusion, contrary at least to one line of frustration theory, that the seller is excused from non-performance, even though he could reasonably foresee a substantial risk of loss of or damage to the goods.

Apart from these constructional points, section 8 is open to the further objection of serious incompleteness. The section fails to deal with accepted forms of frustration, other than those where specific goods have perished. For example, it omits any reference to impossibility with reference to the designated means of delivery, illegality, or frustration of purpose. Such cases are left to the common law for resolution. Again, there would appear to be no justification for the distinction drawn by the section between specific and unascertained goods, if one accepts, as we do, that frustration doctrines can apply just as readily to agreed or assumed sources of supply as to goods identified at the time of the formation of the contract. The courts have applied common law frustration concepts where the contractual source of supply fails, but have not extended this analysis to the area of so-called "economic frustration"; that is, situations where alternative sources of supply, or performance generally, have become prohibitively expensive or otherwise burdensome.

HOWELL v. COUPLAND
[1874-80] All ER Rep. 878, 1 QBD 258 (CA)

LORD COLERIDGE C.J.: I am of opinion that the judgment of the Court of Queen's Bench should be affirmed. The contract here is a contract between the plaintiff and the defendant, that the defendant shall sell and the plaintiff shall buy 200 tons of Regent potatoes, grown on land belonging to the defendant in Whaplode, at a certain rate per ton. From the facts found in the case, it appears that at the time of making the contract the defendant had sixty-eight acres ready for potatoes, twenty-five acres had been already sown, the other forty-three acres were afterwards sown, an amount which by ordinary calculation would be enough to raise the stipulated quantity of potatoes. Before the time for delivery it is found that the potato disease had appeared — a disease which it is expressly found no amount of skill, care, or diligence on the part of the defendant could prevent. The crop is attacked by this disease, and by it reduced so low as to make it impossible for the defendant to deliver the requisite quantity of potatoes; and it is also found that at the time the disease was discovered to have made its appearance, the defendant had no other land suitable for the purpose of sowing other potatoes so as to supply, if possible, the deficiency in the quantity contracted to be delivered. Under these circumstances the Court of Queen's Bench have held that the principle of *Taylor* v. *Caldwell* (1863) 32 LJQB 164 and *Appleby* v. *Myers* (1867) LR 2 CP 651 applies, and the defendant is excused from the performance of his contract.

It appears to me that the true ground of construction on which this contract should be interpreted, and I believe the ground on which the Court of Queen's Bench have decided, is that by the clear and simple construction of the contract both parties agreed there should be a condition that the potatoes should be or have been in existence at the time named for the performance of the contract. They had been in existence, and had been destroyed by causes over which the defendant had no control, and, therefore, it became impossible for him to perform his contract, and according to the law in such case, as applicable to the condition both parties agreed to be bound by, he is excused. It was not an absolute contract to deliver under all circumstances, but it was a contract to deliver a certain quantity of potatoes of a specific crop, and if at the time of delivery such quantity is not forthcoming through reasons over which the defendant has no control, such condition will exempt the defendant from performance of the contract.

Judgment of the Court of Queen's Bench affirmed.

[Concurring judgments were delivered by James and Mellish L.JJ., Baggallay J.A., and Cleasby B.]

OLRC Sales Report
pp. 370-73

It will be recalled that we have already discussed UCC 2-613 in chapter 5 of this Report, in the context of section 7 of The Sale of Goods Act. In chapter 5, we recommended that the revised Act should adopt, in place of section 7 of the existing Act, a provision comparable to UCC 2-613 with respect to the effect on the contract of the parties' mistaken assumption as to the existence of the goods. In the context of our discussion of frustration, it will be convenient to set out, once again, the provisions of UCC 2-613, which read as follows:

> **2-613.** Where the contract requires for its performance goods identified when the contract is made, and the goods suffer casualty without fault of either party before the risk of loss passes to the buyer, or in a proper case under a 'no arrival, no sale' term (Section 2-324) then
>
> (a)   if the loss is total the contract is avoided; and
>
> (b)   if the loss is partial or the goods have so deteriorated as no longer to conform to the contract the buyer may nevertheless demand inspection and at his option either treat the contract as avoided or accept the goods with due allowance from the contract price for the deterioration or the deficiency in quantity but without further right against the seller.

This section felicitously fuses the old provisions in sections 7 and 8 of the Uniform Sales Act. As has been previously noted, it improves on them, and *a fortiori* on the provisions of section 8 of the Ontario Act, insofar as it confers an option on the buyer to obtain the surviving or deteriorated goods with an abatement in the price. Further, in our view, the term "casualty" is more meaningful to express the applicability of the Code section to all forms of loss or damage affecting the goods, without regard to the extent or value of the loss or damage, and overcomes the difficulties inherent in the use of the word "perish" in our Sale of Goods Act. But the section also has its weaknesses and, in our view, could be improved or clarified in a number of respects. We therefore recommend adoption in the revised Act of a provision similar to UCC 2-613 with respect to casualty to identified goods, but subject to the following amendments.

First, the section should not be confined to "goods identified when the contract is made". This phraseology continues the present requirement of specific goods, with its attendant problems. There appears to be no sufficient reason why the rule should not also apply where goods are subsequently identified to the contract with the consent of both parties. Accordingly, we recommend that the provision in the revised Act comparable to UCC 2-613 should apply to "goods identified when the contract is made or goods that have been subsequently identified to the contract with the consent of the buyer and the seller".

Secondly, the application of the section should not be confined, as under section 8 of The Sale of Goods Act, to cases in which goods suffer casualty "before the risk" passes to the buyer. As Glanville Williams first suggested, this linking of discharge of the seller to the location of risk is misconceived. Earlier in this chapter, we discussed the difficulties that can arise where risk has passed to the buyer, but property in and possession of the goods remains with the seller. These difficulties may occur equally under UCC 2-613. The function of the rules governing passage of risk, which in Ontario are contained in section 21 of The Sale of Goods Act, is to determine which party to a contract bears the risk of loss of, or damage to, the goods. Section 21 does not, of itself, answer the question whether, where the goods have suffered casualty, the seller is discharged from his obligation to perform. That function is served by the doctrine of frustration. In our opinion, the question whether a seller should be discharged from his obligations should be wholly severed from the question of who bears the risk of loss at the time of casualty. Furthermore, the seller's right to be discharged, in whole or in part, from the performance of his obligations should not affect the buyer's obligation to pay the price if he has assumed the risk of loss. Accordingly, we recommend that the application of the provision in the revised Act comparable to UCC 2-613 should not be restricted to cases where goods suffer casualty before risk of loss has passed to the buyer. This recommendation is subject to the qualification that the buyer should retain the right to compel partial perform- ance, with due allowance, in the case of partial loss or destruction of the goods, where the risk of such casualty has not passed to him. Where the risk of casualty is with the buyer, he should also have the right to claim the remaining goods, but without an abatement in the price. It follows from what we have said that the section in the revised Act comparable to UCC 2-613 should expressly provide that, in the case of casualty to goods, the seller's obligation is discharged, but the buyer is discharged from the obligation to pay the price only if the risk of such loss has not passed to the buyer.

Thirdly, like its predecessors, section 2-613 appears to operate absolutely, without regard to the foreseeability of the casualty, or to any undertaking on the seller's part to assume liability for delivery in any event. To cover this con- tingency, it has been suggested to us that the operation of the section be excluded where the promisor has special knowledge leading him to "anticipate" the casualty which he does not communicate to the buyer, even though he has reason to believe that the buyer does not possess the knowledge. A further suggestion is that the section should not apply where the seller assumes responsibility for the continued and unblemished existence of the goods. We think that both these factors can be accommodated by making it clear that the section applies "unless the circumstances indicate that either party has assumed a greater obligation". We therefore recommend that these words be added to the provision in the revised Act corresponding to UCC 2-613. Any remaining *lacunae* will be picked up by the existing requirement in UCC 2-613 that both parties must be "without fault", and by the general requirement of good faith applicable throughout the revised Act.

Earlier in this chapter, we indicated that it is unclear whether "fault", as used in section 8 of The Sale of Goods Act, includes loss due to negligence. Comment 1 to UCC 2-613 states that " 'fault' is intended to include negligence and not merely wilful wrong". We are of the view that "fault" as used in the revised Act should include loss due to negligence, and accordingly recommend that the revised Act adopt the Code definition of "fault".

While we do not favour retaining even an improved version of section 8 of the Ontario Act as an isolated provision governing one aspect of the rules of frustration, we support a provision comparable to UCC 2-613 in the context of a larger group of frustration provisions. We appreciate that it may be contended that UCC 2-613 deals with but one instance of the application of the broader rule codified in UCC 2-615, and that no good purpose would be served by including such a provision in the revised Act. We are not, however, persuaded by this line of reasoning, and favour a specific provision along the lines of UCC 2-613 on two grounds. First, it would set forth expressly the buyer's rights in the event of the seller's discharge, whereas such a provision is lacking at present in section 2-615. Secondly, it would make it clear that casualty to identified goods is unarguably a frustrating event.

Note: A friendly critic (Professor Michael Bridge) has suggested that the OLRC erred in recommending the expansion of UCC 2-613 to include goods subsequently identified to the contract and that the Commission would have been better advised to have omitted UCC 2-613 altogether and to allow all claims of frustration to be governed by a general frustration provision such as UCC 2-615. Apparently he feels that there is no self-evident reason why a contract for the sale of specific goods should be deemed automatically frustrated because something has happened to the goods, and particularly so if there is nothing unique about the goods and the seller is in a position to supply other goods identical in all essential respects to the goods that have suffered casualty.

Do you agree with this reasoning? What implications would its adoption have for general sales law? Would it lead to too much uncertainty? If the reasoning is sound should it be restricted to questions of frustration? Could it lead for example to a seller always being able to substitute other goods for those identified to the contract provided the essential qualities of the substitutional goods are the same?

2. COMMERCIAL FRUSTRATION

OCEAN TRAMP TANKERS CORP. v. V/O SOVFRACHT (The "Eugenia")
[1964] 1 All ER 161, [1964] 2 QB 226 (CA)

The present case was one of a series of cases arising out of the closure of the Suez Canal in 1956. The parties had entered on September 8, 1956, into a charterparty for the leasing of the Eugenia ``for a trip out to India via Black Sea''. The vessel entered the Suez Canal on October 31 but was unable to leave the canal because the canal was blocked. On January 4, 1957, the charterers claimed that the contract had been frustrated by the blocking of the canal. The owners denied that there had been a frustration and treated the conduct of the charterers as a repudiation.

Lord Denning's judgment is reproduced here for his interpretation of current frustration theory in English law.

LORD DENNING M.R.: The second question is whether the charterparty was frustrated by what took place. The arbitrator has held that it was not. The judge has held that it was. Which is right? One thing that is obvious is that the charterers cannot rely on the fact that the Eugenia was trapped in the canal; for that was their own fault. They were in breach of the war clause in entering it. They cannot rely on a self-induced frustration; see *Maritime National Fish, Ltd.* v. *Ocean Trawlers, Ltd.* [1935] AC 524. But they seek to rely on the fact that the canal itself was blocked. They assert that, even if the Eugenia had never gone into the canal but had stayed outside (in which case she would not have been in breach of the war clause), nevertheless she would still have had to go round by the Cape; and that, they say, brings about a frustration, for it makes the venture fundamentally different from what they contracted for. The judge has accepted this view. He has held that, on Nov. 16, 1956, the charterparty was frustrated. The reason for his taking Nov. 16, 1956, was this: Prior to Nov. 16, 1956, mercantile men (even if she had stayed outside) would not have formed any conclusion whether the obstructions in the canal were other than temporary. There was insufficient information available to form a judgment. On Nov. 16, 1956, mercantile men would conclude that the blockage of the southern end would last till March or April, 1975; so that, by that time, it would be clear that the only thing to do (if the ship had never entered the canal) would be to go round the Cape. The judge said:

> I hold that the adventure, involving a voyage round the Cape, is basically or fundamentally different from the adventure involving a voyage via the Suez Canal.

So he held that the contract was frustrated. He was comforted to find that, in *Société Franco Tunisienne D'Armement* v. *Sidermar S.P.A.* [1961] 2 QB 278 at 307, Pearson, J., came to a similar conclusion. I must confess that I find it difficult to apply the doctrine of frustration to a hypothetical situation, that is, to treat this vessel as if she had never entered the canal and then ask whether the charter was frustrated. The doctrine should be applied to the facts as they really are. But I will swallow this difficulty and ask myself what would be the position if the vessel had never entered the canal but stayed at Port Said. Would the contract be frustrated? This means that, once again, we have had to consider the authorities on this vexed topic of frustration. But I think that the position is now reasonably clear. It is simply this: If it should happen, in the course of carrying out a contract, that a fundamentally different situation arises for which the parties made no provision — so much so that it would not be just in the new situation to hold them bound to its terms — then the contract is at an end.

It was originally said that the doctrine of frustration was based on an implied term. In short, that the parties, if they had foreseen the new situation, would have said to one another: "If that happens, of course, it is all over between us". But the theory of an implied term has now been discarded by everyone, or nearly everyone, for the simple reason that it does not represent the truth. The parties would not have said: "It is all over between us". They would have differed about what was to happen. Each would have sought to insert reservations or qualifications of one kind or another. Take this very case. The parties realised that the canal might become impassable. They tried to agree on a clause to provide for the contingency. But they failed to agree. So there is no room for an implied term.

It has frequently been said that the doctrine of frustration only applies when the new situation is "unforeseen" or "unexpected" or "uncontemplated", as if that were an essential feature. But it is not so. It is not so much that it is "unexpected", but rather that the parties have made no provision for it in their contract. The point about it, however, is this: If the parties did not foresee anything of the kind happening, you can readily infer that they have made no provision for it. Whereas, if they did foresee it, you would expect them to make provision for it. But cases have occurred where the parties have foreseen the danger ahead, and yet made no provision for it in the contract. Such was the case in the Spanish Civil War when a ship was let on charter to the Republican Government. The purpose was to evacuate refugees. The parties foresaw that she might be seized by the Nationalists. But they made no provision for it in their contract. Yet, when she was seized, the contract was frustrated: see *W.J. Tatem, Ltd.* v. *Gamboa* [1939] 1 KB 132. So, here, the parties foresaw that the canal might become impassable. It was the very thing that they feared. But they made no provision for it. So the doctrine may still apply, if it be a proper case for it.

We are thus left with the simple test that a situation must arise which renders performance of the contract "a thing radically different from that which was undertaken by the contract": see *Davis Contractors, Ltd.* v. *Fareham U.D.C.* [1956] AC 696 at 729, *per* Lord Radcliffe. To see if the doctrine applies, you have first to construe the contract and see whether the parties have themselves provided the situation that has arisen. If they have provided for it, the contract must govern. There is no frustration. If they have not provided for it, then you have to compare the new situation with the old situation for which they did provide. Then you must see how different it is. The fact that it has become more onerous or more expensive for one party than he thought is not sufficient to bring about a frustration. It must be more than merely more onerous or more expensive. It must be positively unjust to hold the parties bound. It is often difficult to draw the line. But it must be done, and it is for the courts to do it as a matter of law: see *Tsakiroglou & Co., Ltd.* v. *Noblee & Thorl G.m.b.H.* [1962] AC 93 at 116, 119, *per* Viscount Simonds and *per* Lord Reid.

Appeal allowed.

[Donovan and Danckwerts L.JJ. concurred.]

OLRC Sales Report
pp. 374-77

Section 2-615 of the Uniform Commercial Code provides as follows:

2-615. Except so far as a seller may have assumed a greater obligation and subject to the preceding section on substituted performance:

    (a) Delay in delivery or non-delivery in whole or in part by a seller who complies with paragraphs (b) and (c) is not a breach of his duty under a contract for sale if performance as agreed has been made impracticable by the occurance of a contingency the non-occurence of which was a basic assumption on which the contract was made or by compliance in good faith with any applicable foreign or domestic governmental regulation or order whether or not it later proves to be invalid.

    (b) Where the causes mentioned in paragraph (a) affect only a part of the seller's capacity to perform, he must allocate production and deliveries among his customers but may at his option include regular customers not then under contract as well as his own requirements for further manufacture. He may so allocate in any manner which is fair and reasonable.

    (c) The seller must notify the buyer seasonally that there will be delay or non-delivery and, when allocation is required under paragraph (b), of the estimated quota thus made available for the buyer.

This section has three principal components. Paragraph (a) states the circumstances in which a "delay in delivery or non-delivery in whole or in part" will be excused on grounds of frustration. Paragraph (b) introduces the principle of apportionment where, following the frustrating event, the seller is not left with sufficient supplies to meet all legitimate demands. Paragraph (c) imposes a notice requirement on the seller and follows logically from the duty to allocate and the right of election conferred on the buyer under section 2-616. It will be convenient to postpone discussion of paragraph (c) until we consider the provisions of UCC 2-616.

Paragraph (a) of UCC 2-615 raises the question of the basic purposes and applications of the doctrine of frustration. Various theories of the true "basis" of the frustration doctrine have been judicially asserted. One theory was stated by Lord Blackburn in *Taylor* v. *Caldwell* (1863) 3 B & S 824, 122 ER 309 (QB), and holds that, from the nature of the contract, the courts find an implied term to the effect that, on the occurrence of certain events, performance will be excused. A second theory, which has its origins in the dissenting opinion of Viscount Haldane in *F.A. Tamplin Steamship Co. Ltd.* v. *Anglo-Mexican Petroleum Products Co. Ltd.,* [1916] 2 AC 397 (HL), would view the contract as vanishing with the disappearance of the foundations of the contract. A third theory sees frustration as a device by which courts may reach the result that justice demands. The first theory has come under attack lately in England and in Canada, and the third theory has gained in popularity. By contrast, UCC 2-615 follows the middle path; that is, the theory that the contract vanishes with the disappearance of its foundations.

Apart from the possible theoretical basis of the doctrine of frustration, there is the question of the situations to which the doctrine applies. Since *Taylor* v. *Caldwell*, no one has questioned the application of a doctrine of frustration, however it is rationalized, to situations where performance has become impossible. The case of *Krell* v. *Henry* [1903] 2 KB 740 (CA) expanded the application of the doctrine to instances where literal performance remained possible, but the underlying purpose of the contract seemed defeated. This extension, by means of a frustration of purpose test, met with mixed criticism; and its status was uncertain in Ontario, at least until recently, and still remains so in England. A third possible situation to which the frustration doctrine might be applied is the case where performance is possible, but would impose severe hardship upon the promisor. This extension has received little judicial encouragement. It is to the second situation, that is, to frustration of the underlying purposes of the contract, that UCC 2-615 appears to address itself by applying a test of commercial impracticality, or commercial frustration. The question that needs consideration is whether this test should now be formally adopted in the revised Sale of Goods Act. Such a step would not be radical, and, we believe, can be justified on two grounds.

First, the existing law is not simply a test of literal impossibility. The frustration of purpose test has been present, though little used, in Anglo-Canadian law since at least *Krell* v. *Henry*, in which Vaughan Williams, L.J., stated a test of frustration, extending *Taylor* v. *Caldwell* in terms not dissimilar to those adopted by the draftsmen of UCC 2-615. While, as noted, the courts have been divided in their reaction to *Krell* v. *Henry*, the Ontario Court of Appeal, in *Capital Quality Homes Ltd.* v. *Colwyn Construction Ltd.* (1975) 61 DLR (3d) 385*, recently gave new life to the principle expressed in that decision. The Court of Appeal held that a contract for the sale of land was frustrated by the enactment of certain provisions of The Planning Act that prevented subdivision of the land. The Court stated as follows with respect to the "supervening event" that gives rise to frustration:

> The supervening event must be something beyond the control of the parties and must result in a significant change in the obligation assumed by them.

This language clearly supports a frustration of purpose test, and is consistent with the Code's test of commercial impracticability or frustration. The Court also emphasized that, in its view, the theory of the implied term "has been replaced by the more realistic view that the Court imposes upon the parties the just and reasonable solution that the new situation demands". Since the buyer's known purpose to subdivide the land could not be realized, the contract was frustrated.

The second reason for believing the change is not radical lies in the draftsmen's own interpretation of the scope of section 2-615(a), and in the cautious attitude toward this provision displayed by American courts. Official Comment 4 to section 2-615 makes it clear that "increased cost alone does not excuse performance unless the rise in cost is due to some unforeseen contingency which alters the essential nature of performance". Something more substantial is required. The American courts have moved hesitantly in granting a non-performing party the shelter of UCC 2-615(a). A good example is the recent case of *Eastern Airlines Inc.* v. *Gulf Oil Corp.* (1975) 19 UCC Rep. 721 (SD Fla.). This case involved a contract for the supply of oil by Gulf Oil to Eastern Airlines. The contract rate was frozen because it had been pegged to a certain index for Texas oil that was itself artificially frozen by the U.S. Government. World prices, which Gulf had to pay, had, on the other hand, risen 400%. Gulf argued that it was a basic assumption of the contract that the index for Texas oil would continue to reflect world prices. On the basis of the available evidence and all the surrounding circumstances, the Court refused to make such a finding, and accordingly held that the contract had not been frustrated. The same reluctance has been shown by other American courts confronted with a defence under UCC 2-615, and one must look hard to find a case where frustration was permitted on grounds other than impossibility.

There is little danger, therefore, that the adoption in Ontario of a provision similar to paragraph (a) of section 2-615 would result in ready acquiescence by the courts to attempts by dissatisfied buyers and sellers to seek relief from contracts that have lost their initial attraction. Further, we feel that the provision has positive merit, in that it leads to a more direct canvassing by the courts of the factors underlying the parties' common assumptions, and the important role played by economic considerations in shaping those assumptions.

---

* Subsequently distinguished however in *Victoria Wood Devpt. Corp.* v. *Ondrey* (1978) 22 OR (2d) 1, 92 DLR (3d) 229 (CA).

We accept the test of commercial impracticability or frustration contained in UCC 2-615(a). Subject to the following consequential issues, we recommend that a provision comparable to UCC 2-615(a) be incorporated in the revised Ontario Act.

R. W. DUESENBERG
"Contract Impracticability: Courts Begin to Shape Section 2-615"
(1977) 32 Bus. Law. 1089, 1093-1101 (footnotes edited)

THE SECTION IN COURT

For a long time, only a smattering of cases called on the defense of impracticability. Following the 1973 oil embargo, however, things changed. Not only was petroleum hard to get, but the price spirals set off by the Arab action precipitated many situations sending sellers in search of ways out of their contractual commitments. Section 2-615 emerged from its quiescent past. But, while many cases soon paid lip service to the proposition that "impracticability" replaces "impossibility" in order to liberalize the common law rule, none has yet given conclusive aid to any seller. The incantations of the Code's abandoning the older strict rule for the newer liberal one are iterated as if a holy ritual vital to decision-making, but then when the ceremonies are over with, few benefits have blessed sellers.

The problem is that not only is what is impracticable hard to define or identify, but it is rarely found alone. Other circumstances, such as foreseeability, facts evidencing greater risk assumption or even self-infliction of the cause rendering performance substantially more burdensom than originally contemplated, often taint the plea for shelter. Few circumstances display the black and white distinction between "I can" and "I cannot," and even when they do, the presence of factors which mitigate [sic] against excusing a party from performance of his consensually assumed obligations prompts a denial of refuge through impracticability. This was true of pre-Code cases, and it is continuing true under the Code.

Of all decisions to date, probably the sternest language of any defining impracticability is found in *Eastern Air Lines, Inc.* v. *Gulf Oil Corporation.*[11] Gulf had a long term contract to supply Eastern with fuel. It turned out to be a burdensome arrangement, not only because of a nearly 400 percent rise in the price of foreign crude, but because of the institution of a two tiered pricing structure in the United States that helped send skyward the price Gulf paid for certain domestic crude. Gulf claimed that its cost of oil was in the neighborhood of $10 a barrel, though its long-standing customer was paying only about $6 under the contract. The record developed at trial revealed that Gulf's alleged cost of $10 included "in-house" transfer prices, which in turn resulted in profits to its supplying arms. Gulf testified that there was no way it could determine its actual cost for the oil destined for Eastern. Too bad, the court said, but unless Gulf isolated these costs, there was a failure of a fundamental issue for demonstrating impracticability.

---

[11]   415 F. Supp. 429 (S.D. Fla. 1975).

The court ventured that "under no theory of law can it be held that Gulf is guaranteed preservation of its intra-company profits, moving from the left-hand to the right-hand. . . ." Even though it was fairly well demonstrated that the contract had lost much of its lustre because of increased crude costs, the court denied the defense of impracticability, noting that during the time when deliveries of higher priced fuel continued, Gulf enjoyed record profits.

This segment of the decision comes close to supporting the proposition that a corporation whose profit picture is healthy and improving will be hard pressed to establish impracticability in the performance of a contract which increased costs alone have turned burdensome and economically unattractive.

Such a thesis has intriguing ramifications. What is impracticable for one seller might not be for another. The difference could be attributable to size, profitability, management capabilities, competence of engineers, scientists, and almost any other of the many qualities which distinguish individual from individual and organization from organization. It is, therefore, a predication which would make the rule of impracticability highly subjective, which maybe it should be. But in the surge of cases spawned by recent inflationary conditions, most of the opinions seem to search for a magical mathematical line past which an increase in costs would support an impracticability defense. That yearning is implicit when relief is denied because of the absence of any precedence for granting it where the cost increase is "something less than 100%. . . ."[12] A one hundred percent cost increase to some sellers might be disastrous; to others, the profit and loss charts might not even register a minor blip. To the extent that the Official Comments to section 2-615 bless an increase in costs as an excusing event, they do so in terms of their altering "the essential nature of performance."[13] This is sufficiently vague to accomodate a view which either looks only to the specific contract in issue or beyond it to the peculiar qualities and capabilities of the party seeking relief. *Eastern Air Lines* v. *Gulf Oil* has portentous qualities in that it appears to opt in the latter direction.

The *Eastern* v. *Gulf* court had yet another string to its bow, and that was the one dealing with foreseeability. Even had Gulf established great hardship, the court said it could not prevail "because the events associated with the so-called energy crises were reasonably foreseeable at the time the contract was executed. If a contingency is foreseeable, it and its consequences are taken outside the scope of UCC §2-615, because the party disadvantaged by fruition of the contingency might have protected himself in his contract. . . ."[14]

---

[12] *Publicker Industries Inc.* v. *Union Carbide Corp.*, F. Supp. (E.D. Pa. 1975). *See also, Maple Farms, Inc.* v. *City School District of the City of Elmira*, 352 NYS 2d 784 (NYS Ct. 1974).

[13] Official Comment 4: "Increased cost alone does not excuse performance unless the rise in cost is due to some unforeseen contingency which alters the essential nature of the performance. Neither is a rise nor a collapse in the market in itself a justification, for that is exactly the type of business risk which business contracts made at fixed prices are intended to cover. But a severe shortage of raw materials or of supplies due to a contingency such as war, embargo, local crop failure, unforeseen shutdown or major sources of supply or the like, which either causes a marked increase in cost or altogether prevents the seller from securing supplies necessary to his performance, is within the contemplation of the section."

[14] 415 F Supp., at 441.

Foreseeability has been central to impossibility cases for as long as they have been around. It is proving no less important under section 2-615, even though the word nowhere appears in its lines. The theory is that the non-occurrence of a contingency cannot fairly be said to be a basic assumption of the agreement, if its occurrence is reasonably foreseeable. By their silence, the parties are deemed to allocate the risk to the promisor. Massachusetts' highest court expressed it well in a case debating whether impracticability could be predicated on the occurrence of a labor dispute. "Much must depend," it said, "on the facts known to the parties at the time of contracting with respect to the history of and prospects for labor difficulties during the period of performance of the contract, as well as the likely severity of the effect of such disputes on the ability to perform. From these facts it is possible to draw an inference as to whether or not the parties intended performance to be carried out even in the face of labor difficulty. Where the probability of a labor dispute appears to be practically nil, and where the occurrence of such a dispute provides unusual difficulty, the excuse of impracticability might well be applicable."[15] Espousing the same theme is an oft-cited case coming out of the Suez closing, and although not involving a sale of goods, it did discuss foreseeability under Section 2-615, and said in denying relief: "the parties were aware, as were most commercial men with interests affected by the Suez situation . . . that the Canal might become a dangerous area, . . . and it is arguable that the risk of closure became part of the dickered terms."[16]

Many, if not most, of the Code impracticability cases have been ones involving cost increases, and just about all of them have been disposed of on the basis of foreseeability. Inflation has regrettably become such a badge of contemporary society that even substantial increases in cost do not escape being classed as foreseeable. A 23 percent year-to-year increase in the cost of raw milk did not excuse a seller, who was charged with knowledge of steady increases in the years preceding its contract. The court observed that the very purpose of a long term contract from the buyer's perspective is to protect against such changes.[17] A similar attitude is relevant in the growing line of cases holding farmers to contracts for the sale of crops which they failed to deliver because their own were destroyed and the price of substitutes turned out too unattractive by the time for

---

[15] *Mishara Construction Co., Inc.* v. *Transit-Mixed Concrete Corp.,* 310 NE 2d 363, 368 (Mass. 1974). The court also said: "It is implicit in the doctrine of impossibility (and the companion rule of 'frustration of purpose') that certain risks are so unusual and have such severe consequences that they must have been beyond the scope of the assignment of risks inherent in the contract, that is, beyond the agreement made by the parties." In relation to the travail being experienced by Westinghouse Electric, this comment is very significant.

[16] *Transatlantic Financing Corp.* v. *United States,* 363 F 2d 312 (DC Cir. 1966). The court also said that "Foreseeability or even recognition of a risk does not necessarily prove its allocation. . . . Parties to a contract are not always able to provide for all the possibilities of which they are aware, sometimes because they cannot agree, often simply because they are too busy. Moreover, that some abnormal risk was contemplated is probative but does not necessarily establish an allocation of the risk of the contingency which actually occurs." As applied to the case at hand, however, the court said that the carrier knew enough so that the test of impracticability should be judged by an indicated willingness to assume the risk of a canal closing.

[17] *Maple Farms Inc.* v. *City School District of the City of Elmira,* 352 NYS 2d 784 (NYS Ct. 1974) . . .

performance.[18] These are relatively easy applications of foreseeability. When the rule is applied to the sinking of ships to close a canal,[19] to a multinational embargo on oil,[20] to the "jawboning" of government bureaucrats to force delays on civilian contracts in favor of military procurement,[21] or even possibly to illegal conspiracies to restrain production and force up prices,[22] something of the severity with which it can operate is perceived. Even in a world grown accustomed to international political tensions, these are not exactly events which are predictable from day to day, month to month, or year to year. Since the rule is not tested by one's actual knowledge, but by what should be reasonably anticipated, its application imposes an enormous burden for possessing broad market intelligence. As an issue in litigation, it can be fun and games for researchers, consultants, economists and an army of lawyers swarming over files and records to find the tidbits which will evoke the cry "Eureka!" in one of the protracted orgies we call lawsuits.

Aside from foreseeability, two other routes to impeding successful advocacy of impracticability are the specific assumption of liability for the risk at issue, or causing one's own inability to perform. The Code expressly allows for assuming a greater obligation, and the common law always visited upon one the consequences of his own iniquities.[23] Under the Code, the same is happening. A seller of potash who shifted its source of supply from Utah to a Canadian mine ruefully learned this in *Neal-Cooper Grain Co.* v. *Texas Gulf Sulphur Co.*,[24] when it pleaded impracticability because an intervening Canadian regulation prohibited deliveries at prices lower than a level which was higher than the price at which it had contracted to sell. In denying relief, the court wrote that "the present case is one in which performance may have become burdensome but was not excused," and the reasons it gave were twofold: first, there was no showing that deliveries could not be made from the original Utah mine, and second, nothing was introduced to establish that an exchange arrangement might not have been possible to avoid the consequences of the Canadian proscription. The predicament in which the seller found himself after commencing performance resulted from its own ac-

---

[18] The traditional common law view was that if the farmer did not contract for the sale of crops grown on specific land, then the destruction of his own crops did not relieve him of liability. This view continues under the Code. E.g., *Bunge Corp.* v. *Recker*, 519 F. 2d 449 (8th Cir. 1975) . . . *Bunge Corp.* v. *Miller*, 381 F. Supp. 176 (WD Tenn. 1974); *Ralston Purina Co.* v. *McNabb*, 381 F. Supp. 181 (WD Tenn. 1974), . . . *Semo Grain Co.* v. *Oliver Farms, Inc.*, 530 S.W. 2d 256 (Mo. App. 1975); *Paymaster Oil Mill Co.* v. *Mitchell*, 319 So. 2d 652 (Miss. 1975) (holding section 2-615 applicable where the crop destroyed was that which was contracted to be delivered; section 2-614 would have been more appropriate.); *Low's Ezy-Fry Potato Co.* v. *J. A. Wood Co.*, 26 AD 583 (USDA 1967).

[19] *Transatlantic Financing Corporation* v. *United States*, 363 F. 2d 312 (DC Cir. 1966).

[20] *Eastern Air Lines, Inc.* v. *Gulf Oil Corporation*, 415 F. Supp. 429 (SD Fla. 1975) . . . *Cf. Gay* v. *Seafarer Fiberglass Yachts, Inc.*, 14 UCC Rep. Serv. 1335 (NYS Ct. 1974), where cost increases precipitated by the oil embargo were said at least to be a triable issue under the doctrine of impracticability.

[21] *Eastern Air Lines, Inc.* v. *McDonnell Douglas Corp.*, 532 F. 2d 957 (5th Cir. 1976).

[22] *See, Westinghouse Charges 29 Firms in Uranium Suit*, Wall St. J., Oct. 18, 1976, at Page 2, Col. 2-3 and Page 22, Col. 5.

[23] Section 2-615 begins: "Except so far as a seller may have assumed a greater obligation. . . ." *See also Duff* v. *Trenton Beverage Co.*, 4 NJ 595, 73 A. 2d 578 (1950), stating the common law position.

[24] 508 F. 2d 283 (7th Cir. 1974).

tion, and not from the conduct of the Canadian government. The same would hold true as to a seller who failed to take reasonable efforts to acquire or produce the goods it had contracted to sell,[25] or who, crippled by a *force majeure* event, agreed to a postponed date for performance.[26]

Overselling a product, too, is a no-no that can invoke the self-caused rule and thwart the use of impracticability. By contracting for a certain quantity with knowledge that capacity will not permit its production, a seller incurs liability for a later inability to perform.[27] Excessive confidence in one's technical capabilities tempts the same consequence. In *United States* v. *Wegematic Corp.*,[28] the seller was denied refuge under impracticability though it was incapable of developing the product it had agreed to deliver. Its sin was to have promoted its computer hardware system as a revolutionary breakthrough. The court said that the risk of the revolution's triumph should fall not on the buyer, but on the seller. The "reasonable supposition is," it wrote, "that it has already occurred or, at least, that the manufacturer is assuring the purchaser that it will be found to have when the machine is assembled." To rule otherwise would have meant that though a buyer makes his choice on the basis of his seller's representations, the latter would be free to espouse its aspirations and then gamble on its competence to perform. Impracticability is not a concept designed to encourage rolling dice on the ability to produce what is promised.

Other Code decisions dealing with section 2-615's greater risk assumption rule bear witness to the care which must be exercised in contract drafting. Lawyers occasionally outdo themselves in draftsmanship, and an unwitting reduction of protection afforded by section 2-615 is clearly suggested by some cases. For example, price escalators with ceilings beyond which adjustments cannot be made have operated to foreclose a seller from relief, even where cost increases threatened a multi-million dollar loss.[29] Foreseeability of cost increases is witnessed by the escalator, and a price ceiling, the somewhat unpersuasive reasoning goes, evidences the intent to place all major risk on the seller.

Lawyers all know that on a seller's default, the buyer has a right to cover, and to recoup as damages the difference between its cost and the agreed price.[30]

---

[25] *Center Garment Co., Inc.* v. *United Refrigerator Co.*, 341 NE 2d 669 (Mass. 1976). In this case, the defendant had agreed either to supply directly or find a source for the buyer, and its failure to use reasonable efforts in this regard were said to be the cause of its inability to perform, and not the termination of an existing source.

[26] *SCA International Inc.* v. *Garfield & Rosen, Inc.*, 337 F. Supp. 246 (D. Mass. 1971), in which the seller, unable to deliver because of a flood, agreed to a later delivery date, and then failed to perform even though the effect of the disaster had ended.

[27] *Deardorff-Jackson Co.* v. *National Produce Distributors, Inc.*, 26 AD 1309 (Dept. Agr. 1967), *remanded* 447 F. 2d 676 (7th Cir. 1971) (contract to sell 50 carloads of potatoes with knowledge that the grower would only be able to harvest 27 carloads).

[28] 360 F. 2d 674 (2nd Cir. 1966).

[29] *Publicker Industries Inc.* v. *Union Carbide Corp.*, F. Supp. (ED Pa. 1975). The court said that the escalator evidenced that the contract contemplated cost increases, and "the existence of a specific provision which put a ceiling on contract price increases resulting from a rise in the cost of Ethylene impels the conclusion that the parties intended that the risk of a substantial and unforeseen rise in cost would be borne by the seller. . . ."

[30] Sections 2-711, 2-712.

Contractual embellishment of these remedies by agreeing in any event to pay damages on failure to make shipment when due may inspire the contention that the seller has relinquished its right to assert impracticability. This actually happened in a case where the recitation appeared in conjunction with a listing of *force majeure* events.[31] A similar lesson could be experienced under a typical excuse clause which reads that for it to apply, "all" of a delay must be due to causes beyond the seller's control. Does such language allow for application of the Code's impracticability standard, or does it revert to the allegedly stricter common law test of absolute impossibility? At least one court has said this is a triable issue.[32]

The most consequential case in this area, however, is one in which a near $25,000,000 dollar judgment in favor of the buyer got turned around for, among other reasons, the error of the trial court in construing an "excusable delay" clause.[33] The proviso read that the seller would not be "deemed to be in default on account of delays in performance due to causes beyond Seller's control and not occasioned by its fault or negligence, including but not being limited to any act of government, . . . or failure of vendors, . . . provided such cause is beyond Seller's control." The jury was instructed that any event relied upon as excusing performance would have to be of the same class as those listed. Not so, the appeals court said. What other purpose was intended by the phrase, "not being limited to," than to make certain that the causes invoking it could be broader than those enumerated? Lesson number one taught by the opinion is always to include such language, and even to strengthen it.[34]

Lesson two centers on the seller's protest that the trial court erred in ruling that excusable delay would be limited only to those events which were not "reasonably foreseeable" at the time of contracting, as distinguished from encompassing any occurrence beyond the seller's control, whether or not foreseeable. This was important, because the event relied upon was pressure from the government to delay civilian contracts in favor of military procurement, this being the time of the Vietnam war build up. Undergirding the buyer's stand was that while section 2-615 allows for the assumption of a greater obligation, silence as to a reduction of those obligations implies that this is not permitted. Correctly, the court rejected this proposition, saying that section 2-615 should not be construed to prevent a consensual constriction of duties. But it added that while the contested excusable delay clause should be interpreted as incorporating the Code's commercial impracticability doctrine, it should not necessarily be con-

---

[31] *Swift Textiles, Inc.* v. *Lawson*, 219 SE 2d 167 (Ga. App. 1975) (in which the contract contained a clause excusing the seller from liability if certain events occurred, and which continued: "If for any reasons except those mentioned above the seller fails to make shipment or delivery within the time specified in the contract, the buyer may cancel the contract for the portion within default, or may buy in open market cotton equal that contracted for, in either case the market difference to be adjusted between the buyer and seller. . . .").

[32] *Tennessee Valley Authority* v. *Westinghouse Electric Corp.*, 69 FRD 5 (ED Tenn. 1975) (relief sought because of substantial cost increases).

[33] *Eastern Air Lines, Inc.* v. *McDonnell Douglas Corp.*, 532 F 2d 957 (5th Cir. 1976).

[34] After delineating events, a phrase might be added reading to the effect ". . . or any other event, whether or not of the class or kind enumerated herein, beyond the reasonable control . . .", etc.

strued as requiring, for those events specifically listed in the clause, foreseeability at the time of contracting. The court reasoned that underlying the doctrine of impracticability is the presumption that in the absence of evidence to the contrary, the promisor intends to bear any loss occasioned by an event which was foreseeable at the time of contracting. This, in turn, is based on the presumption that a promisor can protect himself against foreseeable events by means of an express provision. "Therefore," the court concluded, "when the promisor has anticipated a particular event by specifically providing for it in a contract, he should be relieved of liability for the occurrence of such event regardless of whether it was foreseeable." Any lawyer entertaining doubt of the wisdom of a detailed force majeure or excusable delay provision in a long term contract, now that impracticability is codified in the law, need only study this Fifth Circuit exposition to cure that doubt.

FINAL COMMENT

The foregoing review demonstrates that, short of physical or scientific incapability, identifying what is impracticable is proving no less difficult than it has always been. Notwithstanding the Code's announced purpose to loosen up on the tight restraints imposed by the common law, there is little sign of any judicial appetite to use section 2-615 to jeopardize the certainty of contractual duties on which parties have a right to rely. Additionally, the consequences of foreseeability, risk assumption and causation of one's own misfortune are as severe and relevant as they were prior to when excuse of performance took its place in the Code as a codified contract principle.

Expanding the scope of events which will qualify for section 2-615 protection is not something which should be recklessly pursued. Section 2-615 touches at the very nerve center of contract law. Along with other principles and provisions of the Code, it points a way for avoiding a promise, rather than applying a sanction to its performance. This continued ability jealously to protect the certainty of contractual commitments from assaults under section 2-615 is directly attributable to its pliant terms and the influence on them of a centuries-old tradition that has been niggardly in yielding to broader bounds for impossibility. If the disposition to restrict contract impracticability prevails, it can be accomplished without doing violence to the text of the Code prescription. But doing so will compromise the objective sought when the term "impossibility" was jettisoned for "impracticability." While it will always remain that no precise line may ever be drawn to separate those facts meriting relief from those deficient in cause, that such line was meant to be drawn with greater liberality cannot be challenged. As stated in Official Comment 3, "impracticability" is used "to call attention to the commercial character of the criterion," rather than focusing on scientific capability.

Irrespective of this avowed purpose, few cases have aided burdened sellers. More precisely, it can be said that not one has, although operation of the section has been implicitly accepted in one or two decisions. These have been instances disputing the merits of an allocation program and it might be argued that ruling on the propriety of a seller's allocation scheme concedes an impracticability defense.[35] An equally relevant explanation of such cases can be that the challenger simply declined to argue impracticability, choosing out of carelessness or design to launch an attack on grounds perceived to be more easily overtaken. The point is that, whether the cause be an increase in costs, shortages or other extraordinary event, section 2-615 is not a ready exit from contract liability. As has often been observed, the law is a jealous mistress, and she isn't yielding gracefully to the new Code term.

---

[35]   *See e.g., Mansfield Propane Gas Co., Inc.* v. *Folger Gas Co.,* 204 SE 2d 625 (1974); *G.W.S. Service Stations, Inc.* v. *Amoco Oil Co.,* 346 NYS 2d 132 (NYS Ct. 1973).

Chapter 10
Property (Title) Aspects of the Contract of Sale

A. TRANSFER OF TITLE BETWEEN BUYER AND SELLER

OLRC Sales Report
pp. 259-62

The focal role occupied by property concepts in traditional sales law is hardly surprising, since the overriding purpose of a contract of sale is to transfer the general property in goods from the seller to the buyer. Its importance, moreover, is greatly enhanced in existing Anglo-Canadian law in two respects. First, there are the rules in the Act dealing with the following matters: namely, the transfer of risk; the right to payment of the price; the right to reject specific goods; and, the seller's rights of resale and the measurement of damages. These rules are presumptively linked to, or affected by, the locus of title. Secondly, there is the much broader range of non-sales rules whose operative effect turns on the same question. Examples are as follows: namely, the existence of an insurable interest; the right to replevy or to claim goods in bankruptcy; the right to sue third parties in conversion and for injury to the goods; exigibility of goods by execution; exposure to various forms of taxation; liability as "owner" under motor vehicle acts; and, criminal liability under a variety of penal or regulatory statutes. A sales act cannot be expected to regulate all the non-sales incidents of transfer of title, but it may well be asked, as it has been asked, what features the questions of risk, price, rejection, and rights of resale have in common that cause them to be governed by the same metaphysical abstraction.

The picture is further complicated. The rules adopted by the Ontario Sale of Goods Act to determine the time of transfer of title are so complex, and frequently turn on such highly subjective factors, that accurate prediction of the outcome of a litigated issue is well nigh impossible, and incongruous results may well occur. The existing Sale of Goods Act proceeds from two basic principles, and then elaborates a series of presumptive rules to assist the court in discharging its task. The overriding principles are contained in sections 17 and 18 of the existing Act, and may be stated in this way. First, title cannot pass before the goods have been ascertained. Secondly, where there is a contract for the sale of specific or ascertained goods, the parties' own intentions govern as to the time of transfer.

If a different intention has not been manifested (and many contracts are silent on the question) then the presumptive rules in section 19 of the Act, relating to the intention of the parties as to the time at which the property in the goods is to pass, come into play. These rules are notoriously difficult to apply and, not surprisingly, different courts have often reached different results on substantially similar facts. The difficulties are particularly acute in the case of a contract involving the sale of future or unascertained goods. In such a case, in one set of circumstances, the presumptive rule in section 19, Rule 5(i) of the Act requires the court to inquire not only whether goods of the correct "description" and in a "deliverable state" were "unconditionally" appropriated to the contract, but also whether the buyer gave his "assent" to the appropriation and whether the assent was "express" or "implied". The resulting confusion was aptly described by Lord Cresswell in a judgment written more than a century ago [*Gilmour* v. *Supple* (1858) 14 ER 803, 809 (PC)]. This description remains very relevant today. Lord Cresswell stated:

> It is impossible to examine the decisions on this subject without being struck by the ingenuity with which sellers have contended that the property in goods contracted for had, or had not, become vested in the buyers, according as it suited their interests; and buyers, or their representatives, have, with equal ingenuity, endeavoured to show that they had, or had not, acquired the property in that for which they contracted; and Judges have not unnaturally appeared anxious to find reasons for giving a judgment which seemed to them most consistent with natural justice. Under such circumstances, it cannot occasion much surprise if some of the numerous reported decisions have been made to depend upon very nice and subtle distinctions, and if some of them should not appear altogether reconcilable with each other.

If the courts manipulate the rules to achieve equitable results, would it not be simpler, it may well be asked, to achieve the same results by providing issue oriented rules that are not geared to an elusive "title"?

A further group of difficulties arises from the failure of the Act to distinguish between a reservation of title by the seller before the goods have been delivered to the buyer, and those situations in which the seller reserves title after delivery to secure payment of the price. Only recently, with the adoption of The Personal Property Security Act, has this anomaly been removed. It may well be, however, that part of this anomaly continues to survive in cases where a bill of lading is issued in the seller's favour after shipment of the goods, and before the bill is endorsed to the buyer.

1. SECTION 19, RULE 2

JEROME v. CLEMENTS MOTOR SALES LTD.
See *supra*, chapter 9(A)

2. SECTION 19, RULE 5

CARLOS FEDERSPIEL & CO., S.A. v. CHAS. TWIGG & CO., LTD.
[1957] 1 Lloyd's Rep. 240 (QBD)

MR. JUSTICE PEARSON: In this case the basic facts are agreed and all the evidence is contained in agreed documents. The only remaining issues are (1) whether the ownership of certain goods passed from the defendant company, as sellers, to the plaintiffs, as buyers, in which case both defendants would be liable to the plaintiffs for conversion of their goods; (2) if there is liability, whether the sum described as loss of profit can, under any guise, be included in the damages. The defendant company has taken no part in the trial, and the contest has been between the plaintiffs and the second defendant, who is receiver for a debenture-holding company. The figures of damage, in the event of liability being established, are agreed at, I think, £646 5s. without the sum for loss of profit, and that sum, if it is to be added, is agreed at a figure which I think is £89 7s. 8d.

As stated in par. 1 of the statement of claim, the plaintiffs are a company incorporated in San Jose, Costa Rica, who were at all material times carrying on business as merchants in Costa Rica. The defendant company at all material times in the early part of 1953 carried on business as manufacturers of children's bicycles and tricycles at Lye in the County of Worcester. Then, as stated in par. 4 of the statement of claim, and admitted in the defence, in about June, 1953, the plaintiffs agreed to buy and the defendant company agreed to sell and deliver at a price of 1820 U.S. dols., certain goods which are set out in that paragraph of the statement of claim, namely, cycles, tricycles and certain accessories. As stated in par. 5 of the statement of claim and admitted in the defence, the agreement was contained in or evidenced by an order in writing from the plaintiffs to the defendant company dated June 16, 1953, and an acceptance in writing of the said order from the defendant company to the plaintiffs, dated June 25, 1953. Then it is also common ground that, as stated in par. 6 of the statement of claim, pursuant to the said agreement, the plaintiffs on or about July 1, 1953, paid the said price to the defendant company by cheque of that date, and the receipt of it was acknowledged by the defendant company on July 7, 1953. Then it appears from par. 2 of the defence which is similar to, but as to the date more accurate than, par. 3 of the statement of claim, that on July 28, 1953, the second defendant, Mr. H. J. Patience, was appointed receiver and manager of the defendant company by the debenture holders. Thereafter all goods belonging to the defendant company, which were charged to the debenture holders by virtue of their debentures, passed into his management and control. On Oct. 2, 1953, the second defendant, Mr. Patience, the receiver, refused to deliver to the plaintiff company any goods in fulfilment of the contract of sale which had been made in June, 1953. Then on Nov. 17, 1953, the company being insolvent, a compulsory winding-up order was made.

[Pearson J. reviewed the pleadings and continued:]

That, therefore, is the main issue: whether or not the goods were appropriated to the contract by the sellers with the consent of the buyers so as to pass the ownership to the buyers; and the buyers are the plaintiff company. I should have said that the defence to which I have referred is the defence of the defendant Patience only. As I have said, the defendant company have taken no part in the trial, and they did not even deliver a defence at the earlier stage.

. . .

Now I will come to the set of documents in this case which constitute the contract. First, there is the sellers' price list, which quotes the prices f.o.b. English port inclusive. That only states the price, so I think it is not of great significance. Then there is a letter of May 20, 1953, from the buyers to the sellers, saying:

> To-day we are able to inform you that we received your first shipment, according your invoice No. . . . and found that the cycles and tricycles are made of a good quality and are satisfactory.
>
> For the above mentioned, we would like to place a new order and would appreciate very much if you would send us by airmail, your last catalogue and complete price list. We do not have it complete and would like to place the new order for rush shipment.

The only significance of that is, I think, that at this early stage, as one will find throughout the correspondence, the emphasis is on shipment as indicating the intention of the parties that shipment should be a decisive act of performance by the seller.

Then there is the letter of June 6 from the sellers to the buyers, and they say, among other things:

> . . . as we should very much like to extend our business relationship with your goodselves, we have pleasure in offering you a commission of 5 per cent. (on the f.o.b. value exclusive of packing) on all orders which you place with us. This commission would be in addition to the 2½ per cent. cash discount which we allow for payment in advance or by confirmed irrevocable letter of credit.

On June 16, there is the offer. It is addressed by the buyers to the sellers, and it says:

> Gentlemen,
> Regarding to your letter dated June 6th, we are agree at the *present* with your indications in regard to the representation, but hope that in a very near future you are going to accede to our request naming us your exclusive agents for this territory.
> For the following order we beg you to send us two pro-forma invoices to be able to make advance payment reducing the 5 per cent. and 2½ per cent. discounts. Please prepare shipment to be able to ship with direct ship to our Port Limon, as soon as you receive our advance payment remittance.

Then they set out the goods for which the order is given, being cycles, and so on. Then there is the provision:

All boxes have to be marked: C. F. & Co., San Jose — Costa Rica, Port Limon.

The answer, which is the acceptance, is on June 25. There is a letter and an enclosed confirmation of export order and an enclosed pro forma invoice. The material parts of the letter from the sellers to the buyers are at the beginning:

Dear Sirs,

We thank you for your letter of the 16th June and are very pleased to have your second order for cycles and tricycles.

This has been entered by us under reference P/1052 and we are enclosing herewith our official acknowledgment form. Attached also is our pro-forma invoice, in duplicate, on which we have given the approximate c.i.f. charges and deducted the 5 per cent. commission and 2½ per cent. cash discount. This will enable you to remit to us, as suggested, and we look forward to receiving your cheque in due course.

Meanwhile, we have placed the order on our works and can assure you that we will have the goods ready for shipment at the earliest possible moment.

Confirmation of export order was enclosed, and it contains these provisions:

Shipping Marks: C. F. & Co., San Jose, Costa Rica, Port Limon.
Delivery: F.o.b. U.K. Port.
Packing: Extra. — No. 4. — As per our pro-forma invoice dated 25.6.53.
Freight: Extra.
Insurance: Extra.
Payment: In advance. — As per your letter dated 16.6.53.

The goods are set out, and there is the provision:

All shipments will be invoiced at prices ruling at the date of despatch, irrespective of anything shown to the contrary on your order sheet.

Then there is the enclosed pro forma invoice, which sets out the goods, sets out the shipping mark and numbers as before: "C. F. & Co., San Jose, Costa Rica, Port Limon. 1/up." Then certain packing charges are set out, and then there are these words: "Approximate c.i.f. charges — £60." Then there is a deduction made for the two commissions, 5 per cent. on the f.o.b. value, exclusive of packing, and 2½ per cent. cash discount on the same sum for payment in advance.

Then on July 1, there is a letter from the buyers to the sellers, saying:

To-day we received your letter dated June 25th from which we separate your two pro forma invoices.

To cover this pro forma invoices we are sending you herewith our cheque 2376 against our account at the National City Bank of New York in the amount of U.S.A. $1820.

We beg you to acknowledge receipt of this remittance any difference will be paid as soon as we receive your definitive invoices and two original shipping documents.

Please follow the shipping instructions given on our order of June 16 regarding marks, etc., etc.

> To avoid difficulties with the custom house it is indispensable that you send us with the five invoices, 5 packing lists indicating what contains on each box, with the indication of the No. of each cycle (serial No.) that would help us very much.
> Thanking you in advance for the soon shipment of that order, we remain,
> Yours truly,
> Carlos Federspiel & Co., S.A.

Then there is the receipt for the cheque, dated July 7, 1953.
Then on July 9 the sellers write to the buyers saying:

> We thank you for your letter of the 1st July together with cheque for the amount of $1820 and have pleasure in enclosing our official receipt.
> Your instructions regarding marks, etc., will be complied with and immediately we have some definite information as to the date of shipment we will write to you again.
> When we forward the documents we will let [you] have a statement showing the actual position of the account, and you can then remit to us any balance which may be due.
> You may be assured that the order is having our best attention, and we anticipate that the goods will be ready for despatch in the very near future.

That is the end of the contractual documents, and the question arises: what is the nature of this contract? I agree with Mr. Lyell that fundamentally it is to be regarded as an f.o.b. contract, but one has to add that it has some c.i.f. features attached to it. The delivery expressly is to be f.o.b., but freight and insurance are to be extras, and they are stated at an approximate figure of £60. It would seem that the intention is that the sellers are, in the first instance, to arrange the insurance and the contract of affreightment, and they are to pay the freight and insurance and charge them as extras: to the buyers; and the intention seems to be that they should charge the cost price to the buyers, so that any rise or fall in rates of freight or insurance would be for the account of the buyers and of no interest to the sellers. That seems to be the nature of the contract.

• • •

[Pearson J. reviewed the authorities on the time of transfer of the property in a contract for the sale of future or unascertained goods, and continued:]

On those authorities, what are the principles emerging? I think one can distinguish these principles. First, Rule 5 of Sect. 18 of the Act [Ont., s. 19, r. 5] is one of the Rules for ascertaining the intention of the parties as to the time at which the property in the goods is to pass to the buyer unless a different intention appears. Therefore the element of common intention has always to be borne in mind. A mere setting apart or selection of the seller of the goods which he expects to use in performance of the contract is not enough. If that is all, he can change his mind and use those goods in performance of some other contract and use some other goods in performance of this contract. To constitute an appropriation of the goods to the contract, the parties must have had, or be reasonably supposed to have had, an intention to attach the contract irrevocably to those goods, so that those goods and no others are the subject of the sale and become the property of the buyer.

Secondly, it is by agreement of the parties that the appropriation, involving a change of ownership, is made, although in some cases the buyer's assent to an appropriation by the seller is conferred in advance by the contract itself or otherwise.

Thirdly, an appropriation by the seller, with the assent of the buyer, may be said always to involve an actual or constructive delivery. If the seller retains possession, he does so as bailee for the buyer. There is a passage in *Chalmers' Sale of Goods Act*, 12th ed., at p. 75, where it is said:

> In the second place, if the decisions be carefully examined, it will be found that in every case where the property has been held to pass, there has been an actual or constructive delivery of the goods to the buyer.

I think that is right, subject only to this possible qualification, that there may be after such constructive delivery an actual delivery still to be made by the seller under the contract. Of course, that is quite possible, because delivery is the transfer of possession, whereas appropriation transfers ownership. So there may be first an appropriation, constructive delivery, whereby the seller becomes bailee for the buyer, and then a subsequent actual delivery involving actual possession, and when I say that I have in mind in particular the two cases cited, namely, *Aldridge* v. *Johnson*, (1857) 7 E & B 885 and *Langton* v. *Higgins*, (1859) 4 H & N 402.

Fourthly, one has to remember Sect. 20 of the Sale of Goods Act [Ont., s. 21] whereby the ownership and the risk are normally associated. Therefore as it appears that there is reason for thinking, on the construction of the relevant documents, that the goods were, at all material times, still at the seller's risk, that is *prima facie* an indication that the property had not passed to the buyer.

Fifthly, usually but not necessarily, the appropriating act is the last act to be performed by the seller. For instance, if delivery is to be taken by the buyer at the seller's premises and the seller has completed his part of the contract and has appropriated the goods when he has made the goods ready and has identified them and placed them in position to be taken by the buyer and has so informed the buyer, and if the buyer agrees to come and take them, that is the assent to the appropriation. But if there is a further act, an important and decisive act to be done by the seller, then there is *prima facie* evidence that probably the property does not pass until the final act is done.

Applying those principles to the present case I would say this. Firstly, the intention was that the ownership should pass on shipment (or possibly at some later date) because the emphasis is throughout on shipment as the decisive act to be done by the seller in performance of the contract. Secondly, it is impossible to find in this correspondence an agreement to a change of ownership before the time of shipment. The letters, especially those of Aug. 27 and Sept. 14, which are particularly relied on by the plaintiff, do not contain any provision or implication of any earlier change of ownership. Thirdly, there is no actual or constructive delivery; no suggestion of the seller becoming a bailee for the buyer. Fourthly, there is no suggestion of the goods being at the buyer's risk at any time before shipment; no suggestion that the buyer should insist on the seller arranging insurance for them. Fifthly, the last two acts to be performed by the seller, namely, sending the goods to Liverpool and having the goods shipped on board, were not performed.

Therefore, my decision that the *prima facie* inference which one would have drawn from the contract is that the property was not to pass at any time before shipment, is in my view not displaced by the subsequent correspondence between the parties. It follows, therefore, that there was no appropriation of these goods and therefore the action fails.

Judgment for defendants.

Notes:

1   As will be noted, the contest in this case was between a receiver of the seller and a buyer who had paid for the goods in advance and had nothing to show for it. This is not an uncommon situation, as is shown by a more celebrated case, in *In Re Wait, infra*, chapter 12(C). Do you think the courts in these cases reached a fair result? Could they have reached a result more favourable to the buyer and, if so, by what route? If you were acting for a buyer who was being asked to make advance payment, what advice would you give him?

2   The Uniform Commercial Code, in UCC 2-502, confers a highly circumscribed degree of protection on a buyer who has made payment to an insolvent seller. The OLRC (Sales Report, p. 265) was of the view that the section is of negligible practical value and that it is doubtful whether a province could constitutionally adopt a similar provision in Canada. Would an amendment to the Personal Property Security Act be a more promising avenue and, if so, how should it be framed?

CARADOC NURSERIES LTD. v. MARSH
(1959) 19 DLR (2d) 491, [1959] OWN 123 (Ont. CA)

MORDEN J.A: The defendant appeals from the judgment of His Honour Judge McCallum, sitting as Judge of the First Division Court of the County of Middlesex, awarding the plaintiff the sum of $123.75.

By a written agreement, dated October 22, 1957, the defendant agreed to purchase from the plaintiff specified quantities of various shrubs and trees. Sometime in the winter of 1958, the defendant called at the plaintiff's place of business at which time the contract was slightly varied by the substitution of two items for different types of trees. Except for a large silver maple which was on this occasion tagged by an employee of the plaintiff in the presence of the defendant, the contract was, in my view, one for the sale of unascertained goods. In April, 1958 the plaintiff sent the goods by its deliveryman to the defendant who refused to accept them. The plaintiff sued for the sale price. In his dispute and at the trial the defendant stated that the contract called for delivery in the fall of 1957 and as the goods were admittedly not tendered or delivered then, he was under no liability to the plaintiff. On the other hand, the plaintiff maintained that the parties had agreed upon a spring delivery. This was the sole issue raised at the trial and it was resolved by the learned trial Judge in the plaintiff's favour.

• • •

Mr. Rowan in an able and full argument submitted that s. 48(1) and (2) of the Sale of Goods Act, RSO 1950, c. 345 was applicable. On the other side, Mr. Shortt contended that the relevant provision was s. 47(1). I set them out: . . .

The determination of this appeal turns upon whether or not in the circumstances disclosed by the evidence the property in the goods passed to the defendant. If it did, then the plaintiff is entitled to the sale price; if it did not so pass, then there will have to be a new trial to ascertain the damages in accordance with s. 48(2). There is nothing in the written agreement expressing the intentions of the parties with respect to the passing of the property and it is therefore necessary to fall back upon s. 19 of the Act, particularly Rule 5(i) which is as follows: . . .

In this case upon the facts there was no appropriation by the buyer; if there was any it was by the seller. The buyer did not expressly assent but his assent can be implied from the terms of the contract — the plaintiff was obligated to deliver the goods to the defendant and before he could do this he had to select the various shrubs and trees to complete the order. Implied assent to appropriation is discussed in Benjamin on Sale of Personal Property, 8th ed, pp. 327 *ff*. and I quote from p. 328 the following extract from Lord Blackburn's authoritative treatise: " 'It follows from this, that where from the terms of an executory agreement to sell unspecified goods the vendor is to despatch the goods, or to do anything to them that cannot be done till the goods are appropriated, he has the right to choose what the goods shall be; and the property is transferred the moment the dispatch or other act has commenced, for then an appropriation is made finally and conclusively by the authority conferred in the agreement, and in Lord Coke's language, "the certainty, and thereby the property, begins an election" (*Heyward's Case* (1595) 2 Co. Rep. 37A). But, however clearly the vendor may have expressed an intention to choose particular goods, and however expensive may have been his preparations for performing the agreement with those particular goods, yet until the act has actually commenced the appropriation is not final, for it is not made by the authority of the other party, nor binding upon him.' " See also *Aldridge* v. *Johnson* (1857) 7 El. & Bl. 885 at p. 901, 119 ER 1476.

The appropriation by the plaintiff was not final, was not unconditional when the particular shrubs and trees were selected, nor when they were uprooted, nor when they were loaded on the plaintiff's truck and being carried to the defendant's house. During those times the plaintiff could have changed its mind, recalled the truck and substituted other shrubs and trees. But when the truck arrived at the defendant's house and the goods were tendered then I say the appropriation became unconditional and the property in the goods was transferred to the plaintiff. At that point of time the seller's election had become irrevocable. It is not essential for a final appropriation by a seller that the delivery be completed by the buyer's acceptance; tender is sufficient: *Mason & Risch Ltd.* v. *Christner* (1918) 46 DLR 710 at p. 716, 44 OLR 146 at p. 153 and *Scythes & Co.* v. *Dods Knitting Co.* (1922) 52 OLR 475 at pp. 477-8. There is no evidence, in fact no suggestion that the goods tendered were not those described in the contract.

The property in the goods having passed to the defendant, the plaintiff was entitled to the sale price which was what the learned trial Judge awarded him. Accordingly the appeal must be dismissed with costs including a counsel fee of $15.

Appeal dismissed.

[*Cf. Colley* v. *Overseas Exporters, infra,* chapter 11.]

Note on the Consequences of Passing of Property:

As Atiyah points out in *The Sale of Goods,* 5th ed., p. 144, so far as sales law is concerned, the passing of property between seller and buyer only has the following practical consequences:

(a)   the risk of loss or damage passes to the buyer (SGA s. 21);
(b)   the buyer may lose his right to reject the goods if the sale is one of specific goods (SGA s. 12(3)); and
(c)   generally speaking, the seller can only sue for the price where the property has passed (SGA s. 47(1)).

On the other hand, the passing of property does not affect the following questions:

(a)   The buyer's non-entitlement to possession until he has paid the price (SGA ss. 27, 39);
(b)   The power of a seller in possession to pass good title to a third party acting in good faith and without notice (SGA s. 25(1));
(c)   The seller's possessory lien for the unpaid price and the right to resell the goods in case of default (SGA s. 46(3));
(d)   The buyer's right to reject non-conforming goods (SGA ss. 33-34);
(e)   the locus of the risk of loss where delivery has been delayed through the default of one of the parties (SGA s. 21(b)).

Karl Llewellyn, the Chief Reporter of the Uniform Commercial Code and principal architect of Article 2, was averse altogether to the "lump concept" approach to title in the Uniform Sales Act (and therefore also in the SGA) on the grounds that such unrelated issues as the transfer of risk or the seller's rights to claim the price should not depend on the same metaphysical abstraction. He preferred "narrow issue thinking" in which the several questions were decided on their individual merits without reference to title. See K. N. Llewellyn, "Through Title to Contract and a Bit Beyond" (1938) 15 NYU L Q Rev. 159.

Despite Williston's objections (63 Harv. L. Rev. 561, 566 *et seq.*), the Code's sponsors approved Llewellyn's functional approach, as may be seen from the following Article 2 provisions:

    UCC 2-509 — 510 (risk of loss)
        2-501 — (insurable interest)
        2-722 — (right to sue for third party injury to goods)
        2-502 — (buyer's rights to goods on seller's insolvency)

2-709 — (seller's right to sue for price)

2-716 — (buyer's right to replevy identified goods and to sue for specific
performance).

The U.N. International Sales Convention has adopted a similar functional approach
(see Articles 67-69) and intentionally abstained from adopting any rules on the transfer
of title (see Article 4(b)). The OLRC Sales Report (pp. 280-282) supports the Code
solution and recommends it for adoption in a revised Ontario Act.

If the Code approach is adopted, does it dispense with the need to have general
title rules to govern situations not covered by specific rules, e.g., to determine tax
liabilities or tort liability in the case of a motor vehicle driven by a person with the
''owner's'' consent? Cf. UCC 2-401(1) which contains general rules for the passing of
title ''insofar as situations are not covered by the other provisions of this Article and
matters concerning title become material''.

B. THE TRANSFER (OR RETENTION) OF TITLE AND THE POSITION OF THIRD PARTIES: EXCEPTIONS TO THE "NEMO DAT" RULE

Introductory Note:

No property rule is more fundamental in the common law than that a seller can transfer
no better title than he himself has: *nemo dat quod non habet*. However, there are
numerous exceptions to the rule. The OLRC Sales Report, pp. 283-84, lists the following
as the most important in Ontario law:

1. conduct precluding the true owner of the goods from denying the seller's
    authority to sell [SGA s. 22];

2. sale pursuant to any special common law or statutory power of sale, or a sale
    pursuant to a court order [SGA ss. 22(a) and (b)];

3. sale under a voidable title [SGA s. 24];

4. sale by a seller or buyer in possession [SGA s. 25 (1) and (2)];

5. sale by a buyer in possession of a document of title, thus defeating the unpaid
    seller's right of lien or retention or stoppage *in transitu* [SGA, s. 45];

6. sale by a seller in possession in transactions subject to The Bills of Sale Act [RSO
    1970, c. 44 as am.];

7. sale by a mercantile agent in transactions subject to the provisions of The
    Factors Act [RSO 1970, c. 156];

8. dealings in negotiable warehouse receipts [RSO 1970, c. 489, s. 22];

9. sales subject to an outstanding security interest in the following circumstances:
    (a) unperfected security interest [PPSA, s. 22];
    (b) inventory held for sale [PPSA, s. 30(1)];
    (c) goods brought into Ontario from outside the Province [PPSA, s. 7]; and,
    (d) sale of chattel paper in the ordinary course of business [PPSA, s. 30(2)].

The exceptions are now so numerous that it is easy not to see the woods for the trees. It may be helpful to look for the following guidelines while threading one's way through the labyrinth:

i.   Is the exception based on the original owner's conduct or on the need to protect the security of commercial transactions, or both?

ii.   Do the exceptions draw a distinction between a commercial sale and a private sale? Should they?

iii. Do the statutory exceptions reflect a consistent principle or were they thrown together haphazardly? What is the distinction between them?

iv.   Is there a suitable *via media* between the retention of the *nemo dat* principle and its substantial rejection? Is a registration requirement the solution? Is registration always feasible? Can the third party, e.g. a buyer from a used car dealer, always be expected to make a search? If the question is one of allocation of risk, who is the better risk absorber?

1. SELLER IN POSSESSION

PACIFIC MOTOR AUCTIONS PTY., LTD. v. MOTOR CREDITS (HIRE FINANCE) LTD.
[1965] 2 All ER 105, [1965] AC 867 (PC)

LORD PEARCE: The present case is concerned with the title to certain motor cars which were sold to each party in turn by a dealer who became insolvent. In 1960, one Webb was carrying on a large, vigorous, and apparently thriving business as a dealer in motor-cars under the style of Motordom. The business was turned into a limited company in June, 1960; but this has no relevance to the issues and at all times the dominant personality was Webb. The respondent carries on the business of a hire-purchase finance house. In February, 1960, the respondent and Motordom made a written agreement called a "display agreement" (and referred to in evidence as a "floor plan"). The purpose of Motordom in making the agreement was to obtain cash to finance some of the stock which it had to buy from time to time; and the purpose of the respondent was to obtain hire-purchase contracts with Motordom's customers. The subsequent course of dealing changed the operation of the written agreement in important respects and superseded it. Under the original agreement in writing, Motordom, described as the agent, was, inter alia, to buy such used vehicles as the respondent might authorise in writing, but it might do so in its own name without disclosing its agency; and the respondent was to pay to Motordom ninety per cent of the purchase price of such cars. Cars so bought were to be on hire to Motordom, who was to be in possession of them as bailee only, and must keep them in good condition. Motordom was, however, to be at liberty to sell them on behalf of the respondent, and must in that case account to the respondent immediately, retaining for itself as commission any surplus obtained on the sale over and above certain sums. During the period in which it held the goods before selling them, it had to pay a certain rental. The respondent was entitled without notice to take possession of any cars so bought.

The agreement in practice, as found by the learned trial judge, was as follows. Motordom without any prior written authority from the respondent bought used cars in its own name and on its own account, so that the title in the cars passed to Motordom. It then got in touch with the respondent (as a rule by telephone), and asked that the cars so purchased should be "put on display plan". If they were accepted, a cheque for ninety per cent of the price which Motordom had paid for them was sent to it by the respondent with a list of the cars accepted. This procedure constituted an offer by Motordom to sell the cars to the respondent and, on acceptance, the respondent acquired the title to the cars. Motordom then had the right to retain the cars in its possession, and had a general authority to resell them in its own name and at such price as it should decide; it also had a right to receive the purchase money and retain it subject only to its obligation to account to the respondent. The general effect of this course of dealing was that Motordom would receive in cash ninety per cent of the price of stock purchased; and, after disposal of the stock, would repay the cash. If Motordom's customer bought the car on hire-purchase from the respondent, the money would be repaid without interest, but otherwise certain interest was payable. Motordom of its own volition decided what cars it would place "on floor plan" with the respondent, and only a proportion of its stock was so placed. On Nov. 2, 1960, the date of the transaction with which this appeal is concerned, about twenty cars were "on floor plan" out of a total stock of about eighty cars.

The appellant is an auctioneer and dealer in used motor cars. During 1960, it had various dealings with Motordom both in selling to it and buying from it used cars. In that year, up to Oct. 31, it sold to Motordom 264 cars in all at a total price of £143,854 and bought from Motordom 173 cars at a total price of £58,910. Early in November, 1960, Motordom was in financial difficulties. On the afternoon of Nov. 2, the respondent told it that Motordom's authority to handle the respondent's cars (that is to say any of Motordom's stock which was "on floor plan") was withdrawn. No notification of this withdrawal was given to the appellant or any other person with whom Motordom had dealings. The appellant also was having trouble with Motordom. A few days before Nov. 2, Motordom's cheques drawn in favour of the appellant for £6,965, £2,535 and £3,790 in respect of cars which it had bought from the appellant had been dishonoured. Motordom assured the appellant that this difficulty was temporary and could be surmounted. On the evening of Nov. 2, after ordinary working hours, the appellant's manager went to Motordom's premises and bought twenty-nine cars at specific prices which made a total of £16,510. In respect of each car Webb, on behalf of Motordom, signed a declaration that the car was the seller's sole property, free from any other interest, and that the seller had good right and title to sell it. It was arranged that the appellant would sell them back to Motordom if within seven days Motordom had paid off the dishonoured cheques. The appellant made out a cheque to Motordom for £16,510 which Motordom endorsed on the back in favour of the appellant. The appellant kept the cheque and took away the cars. Of the twenty-nine cars thus sold, nineteen had been purchased from the appellant shortly before, and only two had been paid for. Out of the twenty-nine, there were sixteen which had been "put on floor plan" and paid for by the respondent, and which were thus the property of the respondent. These sixteen cars are the subject-matter of the present dispute. Motordom did not surmount its financial difficulties. The respondent demanded the return of its cars. On refusal, it started these proceedings claiming return of the cars and damages for detention.

At the trial, there was much controversy over the details of the complicated events which led up to the situation in which one or other of the parties, by reason of Motordom's misbehaviour, must lose its money. . . . The trial judge accepted that the transaction on the appellant's part was done in good faith. He also held that, in spite of the unusual features of the transaction, it must be regarded as one of the sale and purchase of the cars in question. Further, the trial judge considered that it was not material if the transaction was not one " in the ordinary course of business", since

> that is a limitation applicable where the only basis of the apparent authority is the possession of the goods and where the Factors (Mercantile Agents) Act, 1923, is applicable.

Had that question been relevant, their lordships deduce that he would have held (and rightly held) that the transaction was not in the ordinary course of business.

The New South Wales Sale of Goods Act, 1923 to 1953, provides as follows:

> **26.** (1) Subject to the provisions of this Act, where goods are sold by a person who is not the owner thereof and who does not sell them under the authority or with the consent of the owner, the buyer acquires no better title to the goods than the seller had, unless the owner of the goods is by his conduct precluded from denying the seller's authority to sell.

> **28.** (1) Where a person having sold goods continues or is in possession of the goods or of the documents of title to the goods, the delivery or transfer by that person or by a mercantile agent acting for him of the goods or documents of title under any sale pledge or other disposition thereof to any person receiving the same in good faith and without notice of the previous sale shall have the same effect as if the person making the delivery or transfer were expressly authorised by the owner of the goods to make the same.

The appellant relied on each of these sections. The trial judge having considered s. 26(1) and the question of estoppel and *Eastern Distributors, Ltd.* v. *Goldring (Murphy, Third Party)* [1957] 2 QB 600, came to the conclusion that the respondent was, by its conduct in clothing Motordom with apparent authority to sell, precluded from denying Motordom's authority to sell. It was, therefore, not necessary for him to deal with the contention that the appellant had acquired a good title under s. 28(1). He accordingly dismissed the respondent's claim. On appeal to the High Court of Australia, the respondent succeeded by a majority. McTiernan, J., agreed with the learned trial judge. Taylor, J., however, distinguished the facts from *Eastern Distributors, Ltd.* v. *Goldring* on the ground that the transaction here was not in the ordinary course of the dealer's business and that the present case was not one of ostensible ownership, since the appellant was aware of the fact that Motordom was receiving "floor plan" finance from the respondent. In Taylor, J.'s view, Motordom's authority, even had it not been revoked, would not have covered the present transaction. On the point under s.

28(1) of the New South Wales Sale of Goods Act, 1923-1953, he took the view that Motordom did not continue in possession since the character of its possession had changed from that of a seller to that of a bailee (following *Staffs Motor Guarantee, Ltd.* v. *British Waggon Co., Ltd.* [1934] 2 KB 305 and *Eastern Distributors, Ltd.* v. *Goldring.* Owen, J., took the view that

> there can be no doubt that had Motordom sold the cars in the ordinary course of its business, the [appellant] would have got a good title to them notwithstanding the fact that the [respondent] had revoked Motordom's authority to sell,

since the Factors (Mercantile Agents) Act, 1923, would have applied. He also considered that the respondent held Motordom out as having authority to sell in the ordinary course of business, but that it had not held out Motordom as having authority to sell otherwise. For that reason he held that the respondent was not precluded from denying Motordom's authority to sell the cars under the circumstances in question. As to s. 28(1), he held the same view as Taylor, J.

The appellant contended before their lordships both that the respondent was estopped or precluded from denying Motordom's authority as the learned trial judge had found, and also that the appellant obtained a good title under s. 28(1) of the Sale of Goods Act, 1923-1953, of New South Wales. Owing to the view taken by their lordships on the effect of s. 28(1), it became unnecessary to consider the difficult question of estoppel. The point under s. 28(1) turns on the construction of the words "Where a person having sold goods continues or is in possession of the goods". Are those words to be construed in their full sense, so that wherever a person is found to be in possession of goods which he had previously sold he can, whatever be the capacity in which he has possession, pass a good title? Or is some, and if so what, limitation to be placed on them by considering the quality and title of the seller's possession at the time when he sells them again to an innocent purchaser? Section 28(1) does not limit its effect to a sale "made in the ordinary course of business", as does s. 5(1) of the Factors (Mercantile Agents) Act, 1923, and the corresponding English provision (3). Counsel for the respondent, however, urged their lordships to limit the application of s. 28(1) in a like manner, since Motordom was in fact a mercantile agent and, therefore, it was not right to attribute to it a wider authority than was provided by the section particularly directed to its activity. Their lordships are unable to accept this view. Section 28(1) is not limited to any particular class of seller; it applies to a purchase from any kind of seller made in good faith and without notice of the previous sale.

The English statutory provision (4) which was the origin of s. 28(1) was introduced in 1877 with the object of mitigating the asperity of the common law towards an innocent party purchasing goods from a person who has all the trappings of ownership but in truth has no proper title to the goods. Nemo dat quod non habet. The purchaser had no defence at common law against the true owner, subject to certain exceptions which are set out by Willes, J., in *Fuentes* v. *Montis* (1868) LR 3 CP 268 at 276-77. In *Johnson* v. *Credit Lyonnais Co.* (1877) 2 CPD 224 an innocent purchaser attempted to establish that the true owner had "so conducted himself as to have lost the right to follow his own goods into the hands of the purchaser or pledgee". The true owner had in that case left in the hands of the seller the documents of title to the goods which he had bought, and had failed to have an entry made in the books of the dock company which had custody of the goods, thus facilitating the fraudulent second sale. Denman, J., held that there was no estoppel. As a direct consequence statutory protection was given to purchasers by s. 3 of the Factors Act Amendment Act, 1877. When *Johnson's* case was dismissed on appeal, Cockburn, C.J., said (1877) 3 CPD 32 at 36:

> And I am strongly fortified in this view by the fact that, as soon as the decisions here appealed from had been made public, the legislature by statute (40 & 41 Vict. c. 39) at once proceeded to settle the question in that view in the future by applying the protection given by the Factors Acts to persons acquiring title from agents, to innocent parties purchasing or making advances in such cases as the present. Whether, prior to and independently of such legislation, the law as it stood would have afforded protection is a different matter.

There is thus no doubt about the general intention of the original provision and the general mischief at which it was aimed. It was intended as a protection to innocent purchasers in cases where estoppel gave insufficient protection.

Section 3 of the Factors Act Amendment Act, 1877, dealt only with sellers who continued in possession of documents of title, but later s. 8 of the Factors Act, 1889, which took its place, dealt with the seller's continued possession both of goods and of documents of title. The wording of this latter section was included in identical terms in the Sale of Goods Act, 1893 (s. 25 (1)). In the Sale of Goods Act, 1923-1953, New South Wales adopted the same form of words as that contained in two English sections. The first reported question that arose about the construction of those same words is to be found in *Mitchell* v. *Jones* (1905) 24 NZLR 932, a case under the New Zealand Sale of Goods Act, 1895. There the owner of a horse sold it to a buyer and some days later obtained it back from him on lease. Then, having possession of the horse in the capacity of lessee, he sold it a second time to an innocent purchaser. The full court held that the innocent purchaser was not protected. Stout, C.J., said (at 935):

> The point turns on how the words "or is in possession of the goods" . . . are to be construed . . . The meaning is — first, that if a person sells goods and continues in possession, even though he has made a valid contract of sale, provided that he has not delivered them, he may to a bona fide buyer make a good title; and, secondly, the putting-in of the words "or is in possession of the goods" was meant to apply to a case of this character: If a vendor had not the goods when he sold them, but they came into his possession afterwards, then he would have possession of the goods, and if he sold them to a bona fide purchaser he could made a good title to them. He would be in the same position as if he had continued in possession of the goods when he made his first sale. In such a case as that he could make a good title to a bona fide purchaser. That is not this case. In this case the person who sold the goods gave up possession of them, and gave delivery of them to the buyer. The relationship, therefore, of buyer and seller between them was at an end. It is true that the seller got possession of the goods again, but not as a seller. He got the goods the second time as the bailee of the buyer, and as the bailee he had no warrant, in my opinion, to sell the goods again, nor could he make a good title to them to even a bona fide purchaser.

And Williams, J., said (at 936) that the section "does not . . . apply where a sale has been absolutely final by delivery, and possession has been obtained by the vendee". It has not been doubted in argument nor do their lordships doubt that that case was rightly decided.

In 1934, however, MacKinnon, J., founding on that case, put a further gloss on the statutory provision in *Staffs Motor Guarantee, Ltd.* v. *British Wagon Co., Ltd.* [1934] 2 KB 305. In April, one Heap agreed with a finance company to sell his lorry to it and then to hire it from the company on hire-purchase terms. He filled up a proposal form which was accepted, and a hire-purchase agreement, dated May 2, was signed. During the term of the hiring he sold it to an innocent purchaser. It seems that there was an interval between the agreement to sell and the hire-purchase agreement, but it does not appear from the report that there was any physical delivery or interruption of Heap's physical possession. MacKinnon, J., held that:

> Heap's possession of the lorry [at the time of the second sale] . . . was not the possession of a seller who had not yet delivered the article sold to the buyer, but was the possession of a bailee under the hire-purchase agreement. . . .

Although the sale had not been completed by physical delivery nor had there been interruption of the seller's physical possession, he held that the case was covered by the principle in *Mitchell* v. *Jones*. In *Union Transport Finance, Ltd.* v. *Ballardie* [1937] 1 KB 510, du Parcq, J., while not doubting the correctness of the decision of MacKinnon, J., came to a contrary conclusion in slightly different circumstances. One Clark sold his car to a finance house with a view to its being let on hire-purchase to his employee. The employee signed the agreement, but the whole transaction was colourable and Clark at all times was intended to keep possession of the car. The learned judge held that, at different stages, the finance house and the employee had a right to the possession of the car but that neither had exercised the right at the date of delivery of the car to the innocent purchaser. Clark had never attorned to the employee so as to make his possession a bailment under the hire-purchase. The section, therefore, applied. This conclusion is, in their lordships' opinion, correct. In *Olds Discount Co., Ltd.* v. *Krett and Krett* [1940] 2 KB 117, Stable, J., accepted the decision of MacKinnon, J. There, a finance house agreed with Goldstein that it would buy his goods whenever he could negotiate a contract with somebody who would hire the goods on hire-purchase from the finance house. He did so. The finance house bought the goods from Goldstein and the hirer took possession of them. He defaulted, however, and Goldstein, as agent for the finance house, took possession and then dishonestly sold them to an innocent purchaser. Stable, J., rightly held that it was a mere accident that the agent to whom the finance house subsequently gave their mandate to hold the goods was the person who had sold them to the finance house. That decision, in their lordships' opinion, is clearly maintainable on the principle of *Mitchell* v. *Jones*. Finally, a judgment of the Court of Appeal delivered by Devlin, J., in *Eastern Distributors, Ltd.* v. *Goldring* [1957] 2 QB 600 on one point in a complicated case accepted and followed the decision in *Staffs Motor Guarantee, Ltd.* v. *British Wagon Co., Ltd.* without discussing it or questioning its validity.

There is thus no case which holds that the section does not apply where, after the sale, the seller simply attorns to the buyer and holds the goods as his bailee.

It is plainly right to read the section as inapplicable to cases where there has been a break in the continuity of the physical possession. On this point, their lordships accept the observation of the learned judges in *Mitchell* v. *Jones* as to the words "or is" which are the sole grounds for any doubt on this point. What is the justification, however, for saying that a person does not continue in possession where his physical possession does continue, although the title under or by virtue of which he is in possession has changed? The fact that a person having sold goods is described as *continuing* in possession would seem to indicate that the section is not contemplating as relevant a change in the legal title under which he possesses. For the legal title by which he is in possession *cannot* continue. Before the sale he is in possession as an owner, whereas after the sale he is in possession as a bailee holding goods for the new owner. The possession continues unchanged, but the title under which he possesses has changed. One may, perhaps, say in loose terms that a person having sold goods continues in possession as long as he is holding because of, and only because of, the sale; but what justification is there for imposing such an elaborate and artificial construction on the natural meaning of the words? The object of the section is to protect an innocent purchaser who is deceived by the vendor's physical possession of goods or documents and who is inevitably unaware of legal rights which fetter the apparent power to dispose. Where a vendor retains uninterrupted physical possession of the goods, why should an unknown arrangement, which substitutes a bailment for ownership, disentitle the innocent purchaser to protection from a danger which is just as great as that from which the section is admittedly intended to protect him? Since the original provision under the Factors Act Amendment Act, 1877 (s. 3), dealt only with the continuing in possession of documents of title to goods, it seems clear that it was intending merely to deal with the physical possession of the documents and that it did not intend that a consideration of the legal quality of the possession of the documents should have any relevance. When the Factors Act, 1889 (s. 8), added continuance in possession of the goods themselves to continuance in possession of the documents, it can hardly be suggested that the word "possession" was intended to have any more esoteric meaning in relation to goods than it had in relation to documents of title. Moreover, such a construction would be in direct conflict with the definition (s. 1(2) of the Factors Act, 1889) whereby

> A person shall be deemed to be in possession of goods or of the documents of title to goods, where the goods or documents are in his actual custody or are held by any other person subject to his control or for him or on his behalf.

When s. 8 of the Factors Act, 1889, came to be enacted again as s. 25(1) the Sale of Goods Act, 1893, the identical words cannot have been intended to bear a different meaning from that which by definition they bore under the Act of 1889.

Further, s. 25(1) of the Sale of Goods Act, 1893, was accompanied by sub-s. (2) which was in identical terms with s. 9 of the Factors Act, 1889 (originally s. 4 of the Factors Act Amendment Act, 1877), and dealt with a person who, having bought or agreed to buy goods, obtained possession of the goods. Possession under sub-s. (1) must surely mean the same as possession under sub-s. (2), which has been held to mean actual custody. In sub-s. (2) there is a reference to "mercantile agent" which, by sub-s. (3), "has the same meaning as in the Factors Acts". In *Hugill* v. *Masker* (1889) 22 QBD 364 at 370, Lord Esher, M.R., said of sub-s. (2):

> It is to be observed that the section is not dealing with the rights of the parties to that contract as against each other, but with the rights of third persons who enter into another transaction on the faith of the possession which the vendee under that contract has obtained of the documents of title.

Again in *Cahn and Mayer* v. *Pockett's Bristol Channel Steam Packet Co., Ltd.* [1899] 1 QB 643 at 658, Collins, L.J., with reference to sub-s. (2), said:

> "Possession" by the Factors Act, 1889, s. 1 (2), means actual custody. The Factors Act, 1889, which is thus referred to, and as to part of it in terms again enacted, in the Sale of Goods Act, is the last of a series of statutes whereby the legislature has gradually enlarged the powers of persons in the actual possession of goods or documents of title, but without property therein, to pass the property in goods to bona fide purchasers. Possession of, not property in, the thing disposed of is the cardinal fact. From the point of view of the bona fide purchaser the ostensible authority based on the fact of possession is the same whether there is property in the thing, or authority to deal with it in the person in possession at the time of the disposition or not.

The climate of legislative opinion was, at the time of the passing of the Factors Act, 1877 and 1889, favourable to legislation which would prevent the buyers or others from being misled by an apparent possession of goods which was belied by legal transactions, which were unknown to the world at large. In 1878, the Bills of Sale Act, 1878, destroyed the validity of assignments and the like without delivery unless registered, and in 1882, the Bills of Sale Act (1878) Amendment Act, 1882, made similar provisions in respect of agreements to secure money on goods remaining in the apparent possession of the borrower. The heredity of the section which their lordships are now considering can, therefore, be summed up as follows. Its words are identical with those of s. 8 of the Factors Act, 1889, where they first appeared in this exact form. In that Act, it was expressly deemed that "actual custody" should constitute possession. In the Sale of Goods Act, 1893, s. 25(1), the same form of words was again enacted. Part of that section (namely s. 25(2)) contains an implicit reference, and part of it (namely, s. 25(3)) an explicit reference, to the Factors Act. There was strong authority for saying that in part of the section (namely, s. 25(2)) "actual custody" constitutes possession. It had never been suggested by 1923, when the same form of words was first enacted in New South Wales, that there could be written into another part of s. 25 (namely, s. 25(1)) an implied proviso that actual custody should *not* constitute possession if the possession, though continuous, became attributable to a bailment — thus giving to possession a meaning different from that which it had under the rest of the section and different from that which it had under a previous and co-existing section in identical terms (Factors Act, 1889,

s. 8). There is, therefore, the strongest reason for supposing that the words "continues . . . in possession" were intended to refer to the continuity of physical possession regardless of any private transactions between the seller and purchaser which might alter the legal title under which the possession was held.

Their lordships do not think that such a view of the law which they believe Parliament to have intended could in practice create any adverse effect. It would mean that, when a person sells a car to a finance house in order to take it back on hire-purchase, the finance house must take physical delivery if it is to avoid the risk of an innocent purchaser acquiring title to it. In any event, however, such arrangements where there is no delivery are not without some jeopardy owing to the Bills of Sale Acts. It seems to their lordships that *Staff Motor Guarantee, Ltd.* v. *British Wagon Co., Ltd.* (and *Eastern Distributors, Ltd.* v. *Goldring* in so far as it followed it), was wrongly decided. Even if it were rightly decided, it would not cover the facts of this case. For, even assuming that a separate agreement of bailment, following a sale, without any break in the seller's physical possession, were sufficient to break its continuity for the purposes of the section, here there was no such separate bailment. Motordom's continued physical possession was solely attributable to the arrangement which constituted the sale. It was a term of the sale by Motordom to the respondent that Motordom should be entitled to retain possession of the cars for the purpose of selling them to customers. Motordom only received ninety per cent of the price on the sale to the respondent, and it cannot be argued that the sale ended at that stage. It would be absurd to suppose that either party intended Motordom to sell its stock for ninety per cent of its value without getting a right to any further benefit. The transaction by which Motordom sold the cars to the respondent was inextricably mixed with Motordom's right to keep the cars for display at its premises. In their lordships' opinion, Motordom, having sold the goods whose ownership is disputed, continued in possession of them. In spite of counsel for the respondent's arguments, their lordships cannot question the learned trial judge's conclusions as to the bona fides of the appellant and its lack of notice of the previous sale. No doubt those arguments were put to him at the trial, but, having heard and seen the witnesses, he did not accept the arguments.

Appeal allowed.

Notes:

1   Auto dealers have long looked to sales finance companies and other financial intermediaries to help them carry their inventory of new and used vehicles. In Canada the traditional instrument for providing inventory financing has been the wholesale conditional sale agreement in the case of new vehicles and chattel mortgage agreement in the case of used vehicles. See further J. S. Ziegel, "The Legal Problems of Wholesale Financing of Durable Goods in Canada" (1963) 41 Can. Bar Rev. 54; and R. M. Goode and J. S. Ziegel, *Hire-Purchase and Conditional Sale* (1965) ch. 17. Until recently both types of agreements were subject to registration and other requirements under their respective Acts. In Ontario, Manitoba and Saskatchewan these security agreements will now be governed by the personal

property security legislation of these provinces. The Australian states, like the U.K., have not adopted registration requirements for conditional sale agreements. They have adopted registration requirements for chattel mortgages (generally referred to as conditional bills of sale: do you see the relevance of the qualifying "conditional"?) but the bills of sale legislation has never been popular and, in the inventory financing field, lawyers have navigated their way around it by the use of various types of sale and lease back or bailment agreements such as were used in the *Pacific Motor* case, *supra*. See generally R. M. Goode, *Hire-Purchase Law and Practice*, (2nd ed., 1970) ch. 28. Such subterfuges would probably not withstand attack under the Canadian PPSA legislation (for the reason, see s. 2 of the Ontario PPSA) and are also open to scrutiny under the older bills of sale legislation, but that is another question. In the *Pacific Motor* case the proper characterization of the "floor plan" agreements does not appear to have been in issue.

2 Note the vitally important differences in language and scope between s. 2 of the Factors Act (Ont.) and s. 25(1) of the SGA (Ont.) — differences that were crucial to the outcome in *Pacific Motor*. Can the contrasting philosophies be justified and, if so, on what grounds? Historical? Functional?

3 *Pacific Motor* is authority for the proposition that the seller's possession of the goods after sale must be continuous. Does this mean that any interruption in his possession, however short, will exclude s. 25(1)? Does the underlying rationale of s. 25(1) require such a strict reading?

WORCESTER WORKS FINANCE LTD. v. COODEN ENGINEERING CO. LTD.
[1972] 1 QB 210, [1971] 3 All ER 708 (CA)

LORD DENNING M.R.: This case raises again the question of which of two innocent people should suffer owing to the fraud of a third. In June of 1966 the Cooden Engineering Co. Ltd., or their parent company, owned a Ford Zephyr motor car. A dealer called Griffiths (who turned out to be a fraud) wanted to buy it from the Cooden company. He said he had a customer to whom he wanted to resell it. The Cooden company agreed to sell it to Griffiths for the sum of £525. Griffiths gave them his cheque dated June 21, 1966, for £525. He took delivery of the car and the logbook with it. On July 14, 1966, he was registered with the registration authority as the owner of the car. In point of fact, he did not pay for the car. His cheque was returned dishonoured. But more of that hereafter.

While Griffiths still had the car, he made arrangements with a man called Millerick (whom one suspects was in the fraud) by means of which Griffiths got money from a finance company called Worcester Works Finance Ltd. Griffiths and Millerick filled up documents which on the face of them appeared to evidence the following transaction: on July 14, 1966, Griffiths invoiced this car to Worcester Works Finance Ltd. at a price of £645, less initial payment of £195, leaving £450. Worcester Finance paid the £450 to Griffiths and thus became the owners of the car. By a hire-purchase agreement dated July 18, 1966, Worcester Finance let the car on hire-purchase terms to Millerick at a total hire-purchase price of £757 7s. 6d. payable at £20 15s. 10d. a month for 26 months. Millerick signed a delivery receipt acknowledging that he had taken delivery of the car.

Those documents told a false story. Millerick never took delivery, never paid any deposit, or any instalment of hire charges. The truth was that Griffiths took the car to Millerick's house. He left it outside. He went in and got Millerick to sign the documents. Griffiths then went off in the car with the documents. He sent the documents up to the Worcester Finance company and got £450 from them on the faith of the documents. Worcester Finance did not see the car or have anything to do with it. They simply received the documents, assumed they were genuine, and paid out the £450. Griffiths retained the car in his own possession. Millerick never had it.

Let me return to the original transaction. The Cooden company had sold the car to Griffiths and received a cheque from him for £525. They presented the cheque for payment but it was dishonoured. It was re-presented and still dishonoured. It was dishonoured three times. As they had not been paid, the Cooden company on August 15, 1966, determined to repossess the car. They sent a man along to Griffiths' premises. The car was still in Griffiths' custody. So the Cooden company took possession of it. So far as the Cooden company were concerned, they thought that the cheque not having been met, they were entitled to retake possession, and they did so. The man who retook it said: "We all thought it belonged to the Cooden company, because the cheque had been dishonoured." After the Cooden company had got the car back, they used it in their own fleet of self-drive cars.

Now I must return to Griffiths again. He had, as I have said, received £450 from Worcester Finance, and paid out nothing. But he did not want his fraud to be discovered. So he — no doubt in league with Millerick — kept up the hire instalments for some months. He paid some £240, but then stopped altogether. (That still left Griffiths well in hand.) After that, Griffiths kept the finance company quiet for a time by asking for a settlement figure at which Millerick could buy the car. The finance company quoted £310, being the balance of the hire-purchase price. But nothing was ever paid.

I come back now to the Cooden company. They used the car in their own fleet for a time, but afterwards let it out on hire-purchase themselves: and they registered their interest with the Hire-Purchase Information Bureau. In consequence Worcester Finance got to know that the car was in the hands of the Cooden company. Thereupon Worcester Finance claimed that the car was theirs. Now they bring this action for damages for conversion. They have limited their claim to £315 0s. 10d., which was the balance of the hire-purchase price. Worcester Finance rely on the documents which were executed, which on the face of them give them the title to the car. They claim £315 which is the balance outstanding, recoverable in conversion.

The Cooden company in answer rely on the provisions of section 25(1) of the Sale of Goods Act 1893, which says:

> Where a person having sold goods continues or is in possession of the goods . . . the delivery . . . by that person . . . of the goods . . . under any sale, pledge, or other disposition thereof, to any person receiving the same in good faith and without notice of the previous sale, shall have the same effect as if the person making the delivery . . . were expressly authorised by the owner of the goods to make the same.

The Cooden company apply that section in this way: They say that Griffiths was a person who, having sold goods to the finance company, continued in possession of them.

The judge has found (and it is no longer disputed) that when the Cooden company delivered the car and logbook to Griffiths and received the cheque for £525, that was then a completed sale to Griffiths. That was in June of 1966. So Griffiths was the owner of thee car at that time and was in possession of it. Then when Griffiths on July 14, 1966, invoiced the car to Worcester Finance, he was "a person who had sold goods" to the finance company: and was thus within the opening words of section 25(1). So far there is no difference between the parties.

The question is whether Griffiths comes within the words: was he a person who "continues or is in possession of the goods." The material word here is "continues." The words "or is" have been explained in a New Zealand case — *Mitchell* v. *Jones* (1905) 24 NZLR 932 — which was approved by the Privy Council in *Pacific Motor Auctions Pty. Ltd.* v. *Motor Credits (Hire Finance) Ltd.* [1965] AC 867. They refer only to a case where the person who sold the goods had not got the goods when he sold them, but they came into his possession afterwards. Those words "or is" do not apply to this case, because Griffiths, at the time when he sold the car to Worcester Finance, was already in possession of it. The only relevant word is therefore "continues." Was Griffiths a person who, having sold goods, "continues in possession of the goods"?

Mr. Jacob, who appears for Worcester Finance, submits that the words "continues in possession" mean continues in *lawful* possession. He says that, after Griffiths sold the car to the finance company, he ought to have delivered it to the hirer Millerick: and that, by retaining it himself, he retained it unlawfully; and he was, vis-à-vis the finance company, a trespasser. He was in possession of it without their consent at all. In support of this contention Mr. Jacob relied on two cases: *Staffs Motor Guarantee Ltd.* v. *British Wagon Co. Ltd.* [1934] 2 KB 305, applied in this court in *Eastern Distributors Ltd.* v. *Goldring (Murphy, Third Party)* [1957] 2 QB 600. In those cases it was held that the words "continues in possession" mean continues in possession as seller and not as bailee: and accordingly, if the person who had sold goods continued in possession as a bailee, he did not "continue in possession" within the meaning of the section. But those cases are no longer good law. They were disapproved by the Privy Council in *Pacific Motor Auctions Pty. Ltd.* v. *Motor Credits (Hire Finance) Ltd.* [1965] AC 867: and, although decisions of the Privy Council are not binding on this court, nevertheless when the Privy Council disapprove of a previous decision of this court, or cast doubt on it, then we are at liberty to depart from previous decision. I am glad to depart from those earlier cases and to follow the Privy Council. The words "continues in possession" refer to

> the continuity of physical possession regardless of any private transactions between the seller and purchaser which might alter the legal title under which the possession was held: *per* Lord Pearce, at p. 888.

It does not matter what private arrangement may be made by the seller with the purchaser — such as whether the seller remains bailee or trespasser, or whether he is lawfully in possession or not. It is sufficient if he remains continuously in possession of the goods that he has sold to the purchaser. If so, he can pass a good title to a bona fide third person, and the original purchaser will be ousted. But there must be a continuity of physical possession. If there is a substantial break in the continuity, as for instance, if the seller actually delivers over the goods to a purchaser who keeps them for a time, and then the seller afterwards gets them back, then the section might not apply.

Applying these principles it is plain that Griffiths was a person who, having sold goods to the finance company, "continued in possession" of them until the time when they were retaken by the Cooden company.

The next question is whether the retaking by the Cooden company was "the delivery or transfer" by Griffiths of the goods to the Cooden company under a "disposition" thereof. Griffiths did not actually deliver or transfer the car to the Cooden company. But he acquiesced in their retaking it. That was, I think, tantamount to a delivery or transfer by him. But was it under a "disposition" thereof?

Mr. Jacob argued that there was no disposition here: there was, he said, only a retaking by the Cooden company. To my mind the word "disposition" is a very wide word. In *Carter* v. *Carter* [1896] 1 Ch. 62, 67, Stirling J. said that it extends "to all acts by which a new interest (legal or equitable) in the property is effectually created." That was under an entirely different statute, but I would apply that wide meaning in this section. When the Cooden company retook this car (because the cheque had not been met) there was clearly a transfer back to them of property in the goods. They would not thereafter be able to sue on the cheque. By retaking the goods they impliedly gave up their remedy on the cheque. That retransfer of the property back to the Cooden company was a "disposition" within the section.

The last question is whether at the time when the Cooden company retook the car they received "the same in good faith and without notice of the previous sale," that is, without notice of the sale by Griffiths to the finance company. The word "notice" here means actual notice, that is to say, knowledge of the sale or deliberately turning a blind eye to it. Our commercial law does not like constructive notice. It will have nothing to do with it. I am quite clear that the Cooden company acted in good faith without notice of the sale to the finance company. They had sold a car and been given a dud cheque for it; and were just retaking it.

So all the requisites of section 25(1) are satisfied. The retaking by the Cooden company has the same effect as if it was expressly authorised by Worcester Finance. It is equivalent to a transfer by Griffiths back to the Cooden company with the express authority of the finance company. So the Cooden company acquired a good title to the car.

This result is consonant with the object of section 25. Worcester Finance did not see the car at all. They did not take possession of it. They simply received documents from the dealer Griffiths and handed out money to him. They relied on his honesty. He was dishonest. He got £450 out of them by a trick. In contrast, the Cooden company actually had possession of the car, sold it to Griffiths, and when his cheque was dishonoured, they retook it. Plainly as a matter of commercial good sense the title should remain in the Cooden company and not in Worcester Finance. The Cooden company are protected by section 25. The car is theirs.

I think the judge was right in the conclusion to which he came, and I would dismiss the appeal.

Appeal dismissed.

[Concurring judgments were delivered by Phillimore and Megaw L.JJ.]

Notes:

1 SGA s. 25(1), unlike SGA s. 25(2), does not require the seller to be in possession of the goods with the buyer's permission or knowledge. Does this distinction make sense?

2 For an earlier British Columbia case anticipating the decision in the *Worcester Works* case, see *Vowles v. Island Finances Ltd.* [1940] 4 DLR 357 (BC CA), whose facts were the following.

M, an auto dealer, entered into a conditional sale agreement with H for the sale of a vehicle. M assigned the agreement to I and the agreement was registered under British Columbia's Conditional Sales Act. H did not take delivery of the car and M, in whose possession it remained, sold it to V under a cash sale. I seized the car from V and V sued for its recovery or alternatively its value. The B.C. Court of Appeal held inter alia that the assignment from M to I constituted a sale and that, since I had not taken possession of the vehicle, V was entitled to invoke s. 32(1) of the B.C. Sale of Goods Act, the equivalent of s. 25(1) of the British Act.

The court assumed, *semble* without argument, that s. 25(1) was intended to apply to the assignment of a financing agreement but this is debatable. Does the history of s. 25(1), as related in *Pacific Motors*, throw any light on the issue one way or the other? Does it matter that the seller under a conditional sale agreement merely retains a security title in the goods and that this is all that he purports to assign? Does the treatment of "chattel paper" in the PPSA (defined in s. 1(*c*) of the Ontario Act) assist in the exegesis of s. 25(1)? See particularly PPSA, ss. 29 and 63.

Note on Bills of Sale Legislation:

In the last century it was common for traders and other persons trying to raise funds to borrow money on the security of bills of sale covering their inventory or household goods. Sometimes these bills of sale were expressed to be absolute in character, and at other times they were conditional bills, more commonly called mortgages. (Conditional bills of sale must not be confused with conditional sale agreements.) In both cases the transferor remained in possession. Thus he was in a position to mislead his creditors or other third parties with respect to the state of title and his solvency.

In an age when credit reporting facilities were non-existent such secret bills of sale gave rise to loud complaints. As a result many common law jurisdictions adopted bills of sale registration requirements. Ontario adopted its first Act as far back as 1859. Like its British counterparts, the Ontario Bills of Sale and Chattel Mortgages Act covered absolute and conditional bills of sale. When the PPSA was proclaimed on April 1, 1976, the Bills of Sale and Chattel Mortgages Act was repealed. In its place there was proclaimed the Bills of Sale Act, S.O. 1967, c. 7, which, as its name implies, continues to impose registration requirements regarding absolute bills of sale. The chattel mortgage component of the old Act has now been absorbed by the PPSA. Section 3 of the Bills of Sale Act provides that every sale of goods, not accompanied by immediate delivery and followed by an actual and continued change of possession of the goods sold, is void as against creditors of the seller and as against subsequent buyers and mortgagees in good faith unless the sale is (i) evidenced in writing signed by the seller, (ii) accompanied by affidavits of execution and good faith, and (iii) registered in conformity with the Act. The Act applies to a sale of future goods as well as present goods (s. 5).

A logical inference might be that the BSA, being *lex specialis*, supersedes s. 25(1) of the SGA, or, in the alternative, that registration of a bill of sale constitutes constructive notice to third parties dealing with the seller in possession. However, in *Joseph* v. *Lyons* (1884) 15 QBD 280, 54 LJQB 31, an English decision, the Court of Appeal refused to apply the doctrine of constructive notice to a registration under the then British Bills of Sale Act. That case, and other cases to the same effect, have generally been followed in Canada, including Ontario, as is illustrated by the jurisprudence cited below in connection with SGA s. 25(2). The Saskatchewan Court of Appeal purported to distinguish *Joseph* v. *Lyons* in *Kozak* v. *Ford Motor Credit Co.* (1971) 18 DLR (3d) 735, foll'd in *Harvey Dodds Ltd.* v. *Royal Bank* (1979) 105 DLR (3d) 650, 1 SR 78 (CA), but the distinction is not convincing and the position must be regarded as unsettled in Ontario. See further *GMAC* v. *Hubbard* (*infra*, this chapter). Note also that s. 25(3) of the SGA only applies to security interests registered pursuant to the PPSA.

There have been several recommendations in favour of the repeal of the Bills of Sale Act. Their weakness has been that they failed to deal with the future of SGA 25(1), thus providing the buyer out of possession with no means to protect himself against a dishonest or careless seller who disposes of the goods for a second time even though the buyer out of possession has already paid for the goods.

What solution to this conundrum would you recommend? For the OLRC's recommendations, see Sales Report, pp. 302-05.

2. Buyer in Possession

CENTRAL NEWBURY CAR AUCTIONS LTD. v. UNITY FINANCE LTD.
[1957] 1 QB 371, [1956] 3 All ER 905 (CA)

HODSON L.J.: The plaintiffs' claim is for damages for conversion of a motor-car. In the event of the claim succeeding damages have been agreed at £240.

By their amended defence, the first defendants have alleged that the plaintiffs, by their conduct, are estopped from denying the authority of one Frank Cullis to sell the car in question because they permitted him, being a stranger to them, to take possession of the car and its registration book without having made any or sufficient inquiries about him and before he was accepted as a client by a hire-purchase company.

This defence succeeded before the county court judge, who gave judgment against the plaintiffs on the ground that this plea was established.

The facts were as follows: In September, 1955, the plaintiffs bought the car, a Morris, for £278 and received the registration book therewith.

On page 3, the column headed "Name and address of the person registered with the council whose date stamp is affixed hereto as the person keeping the vehicle the particulars of which are given on page 7," there appears this entry: "2nd change, C. Ashley, Bonniebrae, 11 Beaulieu Road, Christchurch" followed by the signature "C. Ashley." In the same space is the date stamp of the Hampshire County Council, dated January 22, 1955.

The probabilities are, though there is no specific evidence of this, that the date stamp and the whole of this entry except the signature, were on the book at the time of the purchase in September, 1955.

On November 4, 1955, a man who was a complete stranger to the plaintiffs, giving his name as Frank Cullis, arrived at the plaintiff's showroom in Newbury at about 4:30 p.m. in a Hillman car.

A deal was arranged on the terms that Cullis would hand over the Hillman to the plaintiffs at a price of £110 and the plaintiffs would sell the Morris to a finance company, and the hire-purchase company would enter into a hire-purchase agreement with Cullis. Cullis signed a proposal form addressed to the finance company giving the necessary particulars, including his address, which he gave as 32, George Road, Swindon, and that of his employers. Both of these pieces of information turned out to be false. Cullis was not the owner of the Hillman and disappeared, having been permitted by the plaintiffs to drive the Morris away and to take the registration book with it.

Cullis had also signed an undated printed memorandum of agreement between the finance company and himself whereby the company purported to sell the Morris car to the hirer upon the terms contained in the agreement. He also signed a receipt for the Morris car dated November 5, 1955. These forms were prepared by the plaintiffs in his presence in anticipation of the transaction going through.

The transaction fell through because the finance company discovered that Cullis was a rogue: but the plaintiffs had trusted Cullis. There was no contractual relationship between the plaintiffs and Cullis and they were the victims of larceny by a trick.

The plaintiffs had a good title to the Morris car and simply permitted Cullis to drive it away and take the registration book with him.

The subsequent history of the matter is that on November 7 a man driving a Morris car, no doubt the man who had called himself Cullis three days earlier, arrived at the Mercury Garage, Birkenhead, now passing under the name of Ashley, produced the registration book (presumably having himself signed "C. Ashley" in the appropriate space) and sold the car to the Mercury Garage for £200 in cash. The car was sold to the Unity Finance Company, the first defendants, who entered into a hire-purchase agreement with the second defendant, whose name appears now on the registration book in the space reserved for 3rd change.

The plaintiffs rely on the maxim "Nemo dat quod non habet."

The question for determination was thus stated by the county court judge: what representation did the plaintiffs make by the unconditional delivery of the car together with the registration book to a stranger?

First it is to be noticed that the registration book is not a document of title as defined by section 1 (4) of the Factors Act, 1889. This was pointed out by Croom-Johnson J. in *Joblin* v. *Watkins & Roseveare (Motors) Ltd.* [1949] 1 All ER 47.

An examination of the book shows that its primary purpose is to show who is the person liable to pay the road fund licence tax in respect of the vehicle. On pages three and four there is a column headed "Name and address of the person registered with the council whose date stamp is affixed hereto as the person keeping the vehicle the particulars of which are given on page 7," and at the foot of each of those pages in leaded type appear these words: "Important. The person in whose name a vehicle is registered may or may not be the legal owner of the vehicle."

It is true, as Croom-Johnson J. pointed out, that in the motor trade a wise purchaser of a car asks that the registration book may be handed over too as it is usually some evidence of bona fides unless the vendor has stolen both car and book at the same time. Since the keeper of the car is specifically instructed to keep the book in a safe place not in his car, a stolen car will not normally be accompanied by the registration book.

This point was emphasized in *Pearson* v. *Rose & Young Ltd.* [1951] 1 KB 275 (a case arising under the Factors Act, 1889), where the decision of the court was that a mercantile agent dealing with a car without the book was not dealing in the ordinary course of business.

The mere handing over of a chattel to another does not create an estoppel and there will be no estoppel unless the doctrine of ostensible ownership applies, as for example, when the owner gives the recipient a document of title or, as has often been said, invests him with the indicia of ownership.

This doctrine was first applied by a common law court to a commercial transaction by Ashhurst J., who pronounced in *Lickbarrow* v. *Mason* 2 Term. Rep. 63, 70 the famous dictum: "We may lay it down as a broad general principle, that, wherever one or two innocent persons must suffer by the acts of a third, he who has enabled such third person to occasion the loss must sustain it."

This dictum has been said to be too wide for general application. See the observations of Lord Lindley in *Farquharson Bros. & Co.* v. *King & Co.* [1902] AC 325, 343 where he pointed out that it could not be relied upon without considerable qualification. The noble Lord thought that the word "enable" introduced an element of error.

Lord Halsbury, in the same case, (at 332), speaking of the word "enabled" as used by an American judge (Savage C.J.) in like context, said: "in one sense every man who sells a pistol or a dagger enables an intending murderer to commit a crime; but is he, in selling a pistol or a dagger to some person who comes to buy in his shop, acting in breach of any duty?"

As Donovan J. pointed out in *Jerome* v. *Bentley,* [1952] 2 All ER 114, everything depends on the construction of the word "enabled" in the dictum of Ashhurst J., for if I carelessly leave my front door open so that a thief walks in and steals my silver I have in a sense enabled him to steal it by not locking my door; but that does not prevent my recovering it from some innocent purchaser from the thief otherwise than in market overt.

In *Lickbarrow* v. *Mason* the facts were that an unpaid vendor of goods shipped them to the purchaser and indorsed to him the bill of lading. The purchaser transferred the bill of lading to a sub-purchaser and became insolvent before the arrival of the goods. The vendor asserted a right to stop the goods "in transitu" but it was held that he could not assert this right against the sub-purchaser because by his conduct in endorsing over the bill of lading to the purchaser the vendor had enabled the purchaser to represent himself as the owner of the goods and so to deceive the sub-purchaser.

The word "enabled" was therefore not apparently used in any extended sense by Ashhurst J.

It is said that the negligence of the plaintiffs in parting with the registration book was a breach of a general duty owing to the whole of the public or at any rate that section of it who might become purchasers of motor-cars for, as Blackburn J. said in *Swan* v. *North British Australasian Co.*, (1863) 2 H & C 175, 182, there

> must be the neglect of some duty that is owing to the person led into that belief, or, what comes to the same thing, to the general public of whom that person is one, and not merely neglect of what would be prudent in respect to the party himself, or even of some duty owing to third persons, with whom those seeking to set up the estoppel are not privy.

This conception of duty was accepted by the Privy Council in *Mercantile Bank of India Ltd.* v. *Central Bank of India Ltd.* [1938] AC 287, where the topic of estoppel was discussed at length.

The plaintiffs do not deny that by negligently allowing the registration book to fall into the hands of the thief they facilitated his fraudulent conduct, but they deny that they were in breach of any duty owing to the general public any more than the man who leaves his house unlocked, as in the example given by Donovan J.

In my judgment the case fell to be determined not upon a consideration of negligence but upon what is the nature of the representation made by the delivery of the registration book. The book itself is not a document of title; its terms negative ownership and it contains no representation by the plaintiffs or anyone else that the thief was entitled to deal with the car as his own.

I think that Mr. Molony was right in saying that while a person in possession of a chattel may reasonably be thought to be the owner when he offers it for sale, the case of a person in possession of a motor-car does not differ in kind although the absence of the registration book detracts from the signification of possession.

The case is entirely different where, as in *Henderson & Co.* v. *Williams*, [1895] 1 QB 521, 525, in the words of Lord Halsbury:

> There may be a question where, although no property had in fact passed, yet the true owner has allowed another person to hold himself out as the owner in such a way as to make an innocent person enter into a contract, which contract being performed cannot be set aside.

An interesting example of the application of the same doctrine appears in the case of *Abigail* v. *Lapin*, [1934] AC 491, a case dealing with a conflict of equities.

The Privy Council rejected the view of the majority and accepted that of the minority of the High Court of Australia. In the dissenting judgment of two members of the High Court of Australia, Gavan Duffy and Starke JJ., there is found this passage (at 499):

> In our opinion, the Lapins are bound by the natural consequences of their acts in arming Olivia Sophia Heavener with the power to go into the world as the absolute owner of the lands and thus execute transfers or mortgages of the lands to other persons, and they ought to be postponed to the equitable rights of Abigail . . .

Applying the principle to the facts of this case, I cannot say that the plaintiffs armed the thief with the power to go into the world as the absolute owner of the Morris motor-car. This handing over of the registration book had no such effect.

Rimmer v. *Webster* [1902] 2 Ch. 163 is another example. That was a case where certain stock had been transferred to a broker by the owner with instructions to sell it, but the broker abused his position as transferee of the stock in order to borrow money for his own purposes on its security.

Sir George Farewell held that the borrower's equity must prevail, thus stating the principle (at 173):

> when . . . the owner is found to have given the vendor or borrower the means of representing himself as the beneficial owner, the case forms one of actual authority apparently equivalent to absolute ownership, and involving the right to deal with the property as owner, and any limitations on this generality must be proved to have been brought to the knowledge of the purchaser or mortgagee.

This decision was approved by the Privy Council in *Tsang Chuen* v. *Li Po Kwai*, [1932] AC 715 and also in *Abigail* v. *Lapin*.

In my opinion, in this case the plaintiffs did not give the thief the means to represent himself as the owner of the Morris car by handing him a document which stated the precise opposite.

Similarly, *Fuller* v. *Glyn, Mills, Currie & Co.*, [1914] 2 KB 168 discussed by the Privy Council in *Mercantile Bank of India Ltd.* v. *Central Bank of India Ltd.*, was a case where the plaintiff had left share certificates in the hands of the stockbrokers. The certificates were in the name of the person from whom the plaintiff had bought the shares and bore upon them an indorsed form of transfer executed by the seller. The stockbrokers used the certificates to obtain an advance for themselves. On their bankruptcy the plaintiff claimed the certificates from the pledgees but it was held that he was estopped from setting up his title as against them. The instrument was held to carry with it a representation of authority in the person entrusted with it to deal with it and, if produced to a third person, calculated to convey to that third person that such an authority existed.

Such cases lend no authority, in my view, for the proposition that a car registration book, if produced to a third person, is calculated to convey to that person that authority exists to deal with the car as owner.

I would allow the appeal.

Appeal allowed.

[Morris L.J. concurred with Hodson L.J.; Denning L.J. dissented.]

Notes:

1 Denning L.J., disssenting, accepted the proposition that the mere entrustment of possession of goods or the indicia of title thereto, even if done carelessly, was not sufficient to estop the owner from denying the authority of the person to whom the goods were entrusted to dispose of them. He felt however that the present facts were different and that Newbury Auction had in fact intended to part with the property in the goods, thus making applicable a different line of authority. He dealt with the difficulty that Newbury Auction intended to pass title to the finance company and not to Cullis as follows (*ibid.*, p. 383):

> . . . I think it is quite plain that when the Newbury Auction Co. handed the Morris car to Cullis they intended to part with all their property in it. Not to Cullis, of course, but only to the finance company, but that makes no difference. They intended to part with the property just as much as if they agreed to sell it to Cullis. They intended, of course, that the transaction should go through on hire-purchase terms: but that only meant that the sale was in law to the finance company, not to Cullis. The "dealers' statement" which they signed shows that they intended that the property should pass "as soon as the finance company accepted" the proposal. That condition about the finance company's acceptance was a private condition or reservation which did not derogate from the intention ot the Newbury Auction Co. to part with the property. It did not enter their heads that the finance company would refuse to accept the proposal. They assumed without question that the finance company would accept. That is why they handed over the car and log-book to Cullis without any thought of seeing him again. They did not verify his address. They did not even ask him where he was going. Once he left their showrooms he was gone beyond trace. So were the Morris car and log-book. . . .

Denning L.J. was also influenced by the fact that Newbury Auction still had the Hillman and had no intention of giving it up. Are you persuaded by this reasoning? Could Mercury Motors have made a valid claim to the Hillman and, if so, on what basis?

2 Why should an owner not be subject to a duty of reasonable care in entrusting possession of his property to another? Compare Devlin L.J.'s observations in *Ingram* v. *Little* [1961] 1 QB 31 with respect to the apportionment of loss where an owner is induced to part with his goods as a result of another's fraud. Would it lead to horrendous consequences? Are the courts capable of introducing this change themselves or does it require statutory initiative?

3 Log books, as a fiscal document, have no counterpart in Canada. Many American states have a system of certificates of title for motor vehicles but no Canadian province has so far copied it. A certificate of title system was recommended in the report of a Select Committee of the Ontario Legislature in 1955 but its recommendations were not implemented. For the details, see R. M. Goode and J.S. Ziegel, *Hire-Purchase and Conditional Sale* (1965) pp. 166-69. What we do have are certificates of transfer and, as in England with respect to log books, the question has arisen whether an owner who entrusts a vehicle to a dealer without the certificate is estopped from denying the dealer's authority to sell, at common law or under the Factors Act (the reasoning being that without the certificate the dealer has no effective power to deal with the vehicle or that the third party is put on notice that something is amiss). The courts have adopted conflicting positions: compare, for example, *Rider* v. *Bank of Montreal* [1965] 1 OR 69 (Co. Ct.) with *Durham* v. *Asser* (1968) 67 DLR (2d) 574 (NS CA).

NEWTONS OF WEMBLEY LTD. v. WILLIAMS
[1965] 1 QB 560, [1964] 3 WLR 888 (CA)

The plaintiffs sold a 1960 model Sunbeam Rapier to one Marks, who registered it on November 23, 1959. Marks sold the car back to the plaintiffs in part exchange for another car on January 22, 1962. On June 15, 1962, the plaintiffs sold the car to one Andrew in return for a cheque, for £735. The written contract of sale provided that the property in the car was not to pass to Andrew until the plaintiffs had received the whole of the purchase price, and if payment was made by cheque until clearance of the cheque. Andrew drove away the car, and was registered as owner of it with the Middlesex County Council on the same day. On Monday, June 18, 1962, the plaintiffs were told by their bank that Andrew's cheque would not be met. The plaintiffs sent a "stop" notice to the Hire Purchase Information Bureau and authorised two men to trace and seize the car. The men were not successful. The plaintiffs also informed the police.

In July, 1962, one Biss came to London from Wincanton in order to purchase a car for himself. He went to Warren Street which was a regular centre for dealings in used cars. Biss met Andrew, who was a complete stranger to him, and agreed to buy the car for £550, which he paid in cash. Biss took the car to Wincanton, and on July 12 sold it to the defendant, who was also a car dealer, in return for a cheque for £505. Later in July an employee of the defendant offered the car in part exchange to Douglas Seaton (Yeovil) Ltd., who communicated with the Hire Purchase Information Bureau. They informed the plaintiffs of the car's whereabouts. The defendant refused the plaintiff's demand for the return of the car. Andrew was sought by the police on a variety of charges and on September 14, he pleaded guilty to, inter alia, obtaining the Sunbeam Rapier from the plaintiffs by means of false pretences.

The plaintiffs brought action against the defendant in detinue for the return of the car or its value and, alternatively, for damages for conversion.

SELLERS L.J. stated the facts relating to the sale of the car to Andrew and continued: When the plaintiffs found on Monday, June 18, 1962, that the cheque was not to be met and that there was no probability of it being met as the bank account or accounts of the man Andrew were not in funds and there were many claims against them, they sought at once to recover the car and to rescind the contract. The judge found [1964] 1 WLR 1028, 1032 that they took all the available steps they could to recover the car and disaffirm the sale, and that the contract between the plaintiffs and Andrew was rescinded on or about June 20 — rescinded by the unequivocal acts or conduct of the plaintiffs, applying the decision of this court in *Car & Universal Finance Co. Ltd.* v. *Caldwell* [1964] 2 WLR 600: so that, whether the title to the car had ever passed to Andrew or not, it being a case clearly of false pretences as the judge found, the title had re-vested in the plaintiffs by June 20, 1962. It may well be that the intention of the parties, if this was viewed as a bona fide transaction, was that the property in the car, the title to the car, had not passed in any case because it was not to pass by reason of a clause which provided that payment should be made on or before delivery and that until clearance of cheque or receipt of cash for the full purchase price by the plaintiffs the vehicle would remain their property. But it matters not: by June 20 the ownership of the car was with the plaintiffs. [His Lordship stated the facts occurring after June 20, 1962, and continued:] Both parties have claimed the car in these proceedings, and the matter came for consideration before Davies L.J., sitting at first instance as an additional judge of the Queen's Bench Division. He found that the defendant was entitled to retain the car. The plaintiffs appeal from that decision and seek to establish before this court that the defendant has no title to the car. The title he seeks to advance is the title of Biss, when Biss was the buyer, or the purported buyer, of the car from Andrew in the Warren Street market on or about July 6, 1962.

Quite clearly, at common law, Andrew at that date had no title to give, and at common law Biss obtained no title. It was submitted before us that at that stage Andrew was a complete stranger in this matter, that the case is clear, and that possession should be given to the plaintiffs, or damages in lieu thereof. But in fact Andrew was not a complete stranger. Andrew had in fact the possession of the car, which had been given to him or which he had obtained when he acquired the car on the handing over of the cheque on June 15.

In those circumstances, notwithstanding the position at common law — or because of it — the defendant has relied on the Factors Act, 1889 [RSO 1970 c. 156]; and the question which arises in this case is whether the transaction between Andrew and Biss can be brought within the provisions of that Act.

I turn first to section 9. It is one of two sections, sections 8 and 9, dealing with dispositions by sellers and buyers of goods, section 8 dealing with the dispostion by a seller remaining in possession, section 9 with disposition by a buyer obtaining possession.* [His Lordship read section 9 and continued:] Andrew had bought the goods and obtained them with the consent of the plaintiffs. He had subsequently delivered them on a sale to Biss and, if Biss was a person receiving the same in good faith and without notice of any lien or other right of the original seller, then this section provides that the transaction shall have the same effect as if the person making the delivery, i.e., Andrew, were a mercantile agent in possession of the goods or documents of title with the consent of the owner. So the first part of section 9 is complied with on the facts of this case, and the question arises whether the second part, the receiving of the goods in good faith (and it is not suggested that Biss had notice of any lien or other right of the original seller), has been complied with, and whether, treating Andrew as a mercantile agent, the requirements of section 9 in that respect have been complied with.

That requires a consideration in the first place of the question: What is a mercantile agent? In section 1(1) [Ont., s. 1(1)(c)]:

> The expression "mercantile agent" shall mean a mercantile agent having in the customary course of his business as such agent authority either to sell goods, or to

---

* These sections do not appear in the Ontario Factors Act but almost identical provisions appear in the Ontario SGA s. 25(1) and (2). [Eds.]

consign goods for the purpose of sale, or to buy goods, or to raise money on the security of goods.

That description is to be applied to Andrew on the facts of this case.

Section 2(1) concerns the powers of a mercantile agent with respect to the disposition of goods thus.

> Where a mercantile agent is, with the consent of the owner, in possession of goods . . . any sale . . . made by him when acting in the ordinary course of business of a mercantile agent, shall, subject to the provisions of this Act, be as valid as if he were expressly authorised by the owner of the goods to make the same; provided that the person taking under the disposition acts in good faith, and has not at the time of the disposition notice that the person making the disposition has not authority to make the same.

One of the points taken by the plaintiffs was that although at the outset Andrew was a person who had obtained, with the consent of the seller, possession of the goods, at the time when this transaction took place that consent no longer operated: it had been withdrawn by the rescission of the contract. But Andrew was in possession of the goods of the plaintiffs, a possession which he had obtained at the outset with their consent. Section 2(2) provides that "Where a mercantile agent has, with the consent of the owner, been in possession of goods . . . any sale . . . which would have been valid if the consent had continued, shall be valid notwithstanding the determination of the consent. . . ." That is an express provision which altered the law as it had been laid down in an earlier case, *Fuentes* v. *Montis* (1868) LR 3 CP 268; aff'd LR 4 CP 93, some time in 1868. Notwithstanding that which the plaintiffs had done to terminate their contract and withdraw their consent, they had in fact — true, through inability to do otherwise — left the possession of their car with Andrew.

The only other question which arises is how far section 9, on its true construction, takes the ultimate sub-buyer (the defendant in the present case), relying, as he does, on what happened between Andrew and Biss. The judge treated section 9 as placing Andrew in the position of a mercantile agent, but with the obligation on the defendant of establishing not only that Biss took in good faith (I leave out the other requirement of no notice of the plaintiffs' rights; nothing arose on that), but also that in the transaction between Andrew and Biss (Andrew being treated as a mercantile agent in accordance with section 9), Andrew was "acting in the ordinary course of business of a mercantile agent." There is a possible construction, which was urged upon us by the defendant, that Andrew must be deemed to be acting under section 9 as a mercantile agent, that it must be assumed or deemed that he was acting in the ordinary course of business of a mercantile agent; and investigations were made in other parts of the Act of 1889, in particular section 8, to see whether any support could be had for that view.

Section 8 makes a different provision. It states that where a person, having sold goods, continues, or is, in possession of the goods and then sells them, then, providing the person who receives them does so in good faith and without notice of the previous sale, the transaction will have "the same effect as if the person making the delivery or transfer were expressly authorised by the owner of the goods to make the same." The words are different in section 9, and for myself I do not find much help, in constructing section 9, from looking at section 8, except for the fact that since they are different they are intended to have a different effect.

Before one takes too favourable a view for the sub-buyer and too harsh a view against the true owner of the goods as to the cases where section 9 can be invoked, one must remember that it is taking away the right which would have existed at common law, and for myself I should not be prepared to enlarge it more than the words clearly permitted and required. It seems to me that all section 9 can be said clearly to do is to place the buyer in possession in the position of a mercantile agent when he has in fact in his possession the goods of somebody else, and it does no more than clothe him with that fictitious or notional position on any disposition of those goods. Section 2(1) makes it clear that the sub-buyer from a mercantile agent, to whom that section applies, has in order to obtain the full advantage of the subsection, to establish that the mercantile agent was acting in the ordinary course of business. It is said that that is a somewhat vague phrase, and we have been referred to some authorities with regard to that. It may be that in some cases precisely what is in "the ordinary course of business" of a mercantile agent may call for some special investigation, but on the face of it it seems to me that it envisages a transaction by a mercantile agent and is to be derived from such evidence as is either known to the court or established by evidence as to what would be the ordinary course of business.

We were referred to *Oppenheimer* v. *Attenborough & Son* [1908] 1 KB 221 (CA). That was a case on a different point as to the range of the business, and the meaning of "in the ordinary course of business" was considered in the judgment, but I need not refer any further to it.

The question arises here on the evidence whether this transaction is to be said to have been in the ordinary course of business of a mercantile agent. Counsel for the plaintiffs sought to establish that a transaction taking place in this somewhat unusual market, the street kerb in Warren Street, was, on the face of it, something which was not an ordinary business transaction in any way, by a mercantile agent or anybody else, but was to some extent suspect. But the judge had evidence about this and he said and I think it is within the knowledge of the court, that there had been an established market in secondhand cars in this area on this very site for a long time. Although he said that he had some doubt at one time about the sale to Biss being in the ordinary course of business, for, as he pointed out, there were no business premises, the sale was in the street, and it was for cash, yet he came to the conclusion, which I think cannot be challenged, that there was in Warren Street and its neighbourhood an established street market for cash dealing in cars. When one looks at what took place in that area and finds the prospective buyer coming up and getting into contact with the prospective seller in regard to a car, with an offer and an acceptance, trial of the car and a looking over it and some questions asked and a delivery — I do not find anything to indicate that it was not in the ordinary course of business of a mercantile agent. It seems to me that the defendant has established that essential fact.

That leaves only the other matter which has to be proved, likewise by the defendant, as to whether Biss acted in good faith. If he did, then the requirements of section 9 are complete, and the result follows that he obtained a good title, as if the goods had been sold to him with the consent of the plaintiffs.

[Sellers LJ. reviewed the evidence and concluded:]

I think that that was established, and I would dismiss this appeal.

Appeal dismissed.

[Concurring judgments were delivered by the other members of the court.]

Notes:

1   For a discussion of *Newtons'* case from the Canadian point of view see Comment, (1965) 43 Can. Bar Rev. 639. See also *GMAC* v. *Hubbard, infra.*

2   In *Brandon* v. *Leckie; Avco Corp.* v. *Borgal* (1972) 29 DLR (3d) 633, [1972] 6 WWR 113 (Alta. SC), a mobile home was stolen from each of the plaintiffs. Subsequently, they were purchased by a Calgary auto dealer from one G. Young. The dealer in turn sold the mobile homes to the defendants who acquired them in good faith. The true owners sought to recover the homes in the hands of the defendants or damages in lieu thereof. It was admitted that the dealer was not a buyer in possession of the goods with the consent of the true owners, but it was argued that this did not matter because the concluding words of the Alberta equivalent of s. 25(2) provide that a disposition by a buyer in possession of the goods (which, it was argued, the dealer was, vis-à-vis the person from whom he bought the homes) has the same effect as if the person making the delivery were in possession of the goods "with the consent of the owner". The defendants contended that "owner" should be given its literal meaning. What result?

GENERAL MOTORS ACCEPTANCE CORP. OF CANADA LTD. v. HUBBARD
(1978) 87 DLR (3d) 39, 21 NBR (2d) 49 (NB CA)

BUGOLD J.A. (for the court): This is an appeal by the plaintiff, General Motors Acceptance Corporation of Canada Limited (GMAC), from a judgment pronounced by Mr. Justice Stratton on July 14, 1977, whereby the claim of GMAC was dismissed with costs.

GMAC alleges that the defendant (Mr. Hubbard) detained and continues to unlawfully detain a Chevrolet Impala automobile (the motor vehicle) despite oral and written requests by GMAC for its return and claims the return of the motor vehicle or its value and $500 damages for its detention, together with such sum as may be allowed on taxation for costs.

The following material facts were agreed to by the parties:

1. The Plaintiff is a body corporate having a branch office in the Province of New Brunswick.
2. The Defendant is a member of the Canadian Armed Forces presently stationed at C.F.B. Chatham, in the County of Northumberland and Province of New Brunswick.

3. On October 12, 1972, in Sudbury, Ontario, one Chevrolet Impala vehicle, having serial number IL69H3118009 was sold by Campbell Chevrolet Ltd. to Robert Kenney by contract of conditional sale.

4. The contract of conditional sale was ostensibly assigned by Campbell Chevrolet Ltd. to GMAC and registered in the Registry Office in the Personal Property Security District of Sudbury in the Province of Ontario as No. 7752 on the 16th day of October 1972.

5. The conditional sale included the following conditions:

    (a)   a condition that title ownership and the right of ownership in the car should not pass to the purchaser until the entire price had been paid.

    (b)   a condition that upon default by the purchaser on any payment when due under the contract or failure by the purchaser to comply with any condition of the contract the Seller should become entitled to take immediate possession of the car without demand.

    (c)   a condition that the purchaser should not at any time transfer any interest in the car or contract.

6. The conditional sale contract was filed in the Registry Office in the Personal Property Security District of Sudbury, Province of Ontario as No. 7752 on the 16th day of October, 1972 and was filed in the Registry Office in the County of Northumberland and the Province of New Brunswick as Number 29349 on the 25th day of July, 1974.

7. Possession of the aforesaid motor vehicle was delivered by Campbell Chevrolet Ltd. to Diane Kenney, wife of Robert Kenney, and Campbell Chevrolet Ltd. had the motor vehicle registered in the name of Diane Kenney and the new vehicle warranty prepared in the name of Diane Kenney.

8. The aforesaid Robert Kenney declared an Assignment in Bankruptcy subsequent to purchasing the subject motor vehicle from which he was eventually discharged.

9. The Trustee in Bankruptcy excluded the said motor vehicle from the bankruptcy proceedings on the grounds that it was not part of the property of Robert Kenney.

10. GMAC did not participate in the bankruptcy proceedings and did not share in the disposition of assets.

11. GMAC were unable to locate the subject motor vehicle and when it was located the party in possession refused to deliver it up.

12. The aforesaid motor vehicle was sold by Diane Kenney to John Kenney for valuable consideration, the said sale having taken place in Ontario. John Kenney is the brother of Robert Kenney.

13. The aforesaid motor vehicle was registered in New Brunswick in March 1974 by John Kenney who is stationed at C.F.B. Chatham.

14. The aforesaid motor vehicle was sold by John Kenney to Allan Hubbard for valuable consideration on June 12, 1974 at which time the motor vehicle was registered in the name of Allan Hubbard.

15. The Purchaser, Robert Kenney, is no longer is possession of the said car.

16. The defendant is now in possession of the said car.

17. The said conditional sale was signed for and on behalf of the seller, Campbell Chevrolet Ltd. by Brian W. Girdwood, the Secretary-Treasurer of Campbell Chevrolet Ltd.

At trial, two additional facts were agreed to by the parties as follows:

18. The original purchaser of the vehicle in question under the contract of conditional sale, Robert Kenney, has defaulted under that contract.

19. The plaintiff first had actual notice of the removal of the vehicle in question to the County of Northumberland in the Province of New Brunswick on June 25, 1974.

Based on the admitted facts, the trial Judge was satisfied and found that the required filing of the conditional sale agreement in the Northumberland County Registry Office in the Province of New Brunswick was proper and within the prescribed time, the conditional sale agreement was properly assigned by Campbell Chevrolet Ltd. to GMAC and Mr. Hubbard was a *bona fide* purchaser of the motor vehicle.

The following issues were raised both at trial and on the present appeal:

(1)   Do the provisions of the Sale of Goods Act, RSNB 1973, c. S-1 have any application to conditional sales agreements?

(2)   If so, what is the nature of the application in relation to the sale by a conditional vendee of goods subject to a conditional sale to a bona fide purchaser for value without notice?

(3)   If the Sale of Goods Act applies to such sales and protects the bona fide purchaser, then is the registration of a conditional sale agreement notice? and

(4)   If the Sale of Goods Act applies what is the meaning and effect of s. 24(2) of the Act?

To determine the above issues it is necessary to set out in full the relevant provisions of the Conditional Sales Act, RSNB 1973, c. C-15, the Sale of Goods Act, RSNB 1973, c. S-1, and the Factors and Agents, RSNB 1973, c. F-1.

Firstly, the Conditional Sales Act:

1. In this Act

· · ·

"conditional sale" means:

(a)   a contract for the sale of goods under which possession is or is to be delivered to a buyer and the property in the goods is to vest in him at a subsequent time upon payment of the whole or part of the price or the performance of any other condition, or

(b)   a contract for the hiring of goods under which it is agreed that the hirer will become or have the option of becoming the owner of the goods upon compliance with the terms of the contract;

· · ·

2. Where possession of goods has been delivered to a buyer under a conditional sale, every provision contained therein whereby the property in the goods remains in the seller is, unless this Act is complied with, void as against a creditor and as against a subsequent purchaser or mortgagee claiming from or under the buyer in good faith for valuable consideration and without notice; and the buyer shall, notwithstanding such provision, be deemed as against such persons to be the owner of the goods.

· · ·

5. Where goods are brought into the Province and are subject to an agreement made or executed outside the Province that provides that the right of property

therein, or the right of possession thereof, in whole or in part, remains in the seller notwithstanding that the actual possession of the goods passes to the buyer, then unless

    (a)   the agreement contains such a description of the goods that they may readily and easily be known and distinguished, and

    (b)   a copy of the agreement is filed with the proper officer of the registration district into which the goods are brought within thirty days after the seller has received notice of the place to which the goods have been brought,

the seller shall not be permitted to set up any right of property in or right of possession of the goods as against a subsequent purchaser or mortgagee claiming from or under the buyer in good faith for valuable consideration and without notice, or as against a creditor; and the buyer shall, notwithstanding such agreement, be deemed as against such persons to be the owner of the goods.

Secondly, the Sale of Goods Act:

[The court here quoted the New Brunswick equivalent of ss. 2 and 25(2) of the Ontario Sale of Goods Act and ss. 1(1), 2 and 12 of the New Brunswick Factors and Agents Act. Section 12 has no counterpart in the Ontario Factors Act, but is identical to s. 9 of the U.K. Factors Act and almost identical to s. 25(2) of the SGA.]

The trial Judge found that the conditional sale contract in the present case is an agreement to sell within the purview of the Sale of Goods Act and the Factors and Agents Act and he concluded that the provisions of those statutes apply to conditional sales.

Furthermore, relying on *Manchester Trust* v. *Furness* [1895] 2 QB 539 (CA) *per* Lindley, L.J., at p. 545, and *Vowles* v. *Island Finances Ltd.* [1940] 4 DLR 357, [1940] 3 WWR 177 55 BCR 362 (BC CA), the trial Judge advances the following proposition, which I would support [18 NBR (2d) 248 at p. 258]:

> The Conditional Sales Act does not contain an express provision that filing under it shall constitute notice to subsequent purchasers so as to prevent them taking advantage of section 24(2) of the Sale of Goods Act. Moreover, it has been held that the doctrine of constructive notice is inapplicable to commercial transactions where title cannot be leisurely investigated . . .

The trial Judge also states that the apparent conflict between the Conditional Sales Act and the Sale of Goods Act requires remedial legislation. He found that the equity of Mr. Hubbard was greater than that of GMAC and by virtue of s. 24(2) of the Sale of Goods Act, Mr. Hubbard acquired clean title to the motor vehicle.

In my view, the trial Judge did not err in his finding that the Sale of Goods Act has application to conditional sales. As stated in his judgment the Conditional Sales Act was first enacted in New Brunswick in 1899 while s. 24 of the Sale of Goods Act and s. 12 of the Factors and Agents Act were not enacted in New Brunswick until 1919. It is reasonable to conclude that the Legislature contemplated and was aware of the effect the two latter statutes would have on conditional sales. By virtue of s. 2(1) of the Sale of Goods Act a contract of sale includes a sale of goods and an agreement to sell goods and by virtue of s. 2(2) a contract of sale may be absolute or conditional. A conditional sale falls entirely within the definition of an agreement to sell in s. 2(3) of the Sale of Goods Act.

Prior to the enactment of the Conditional Sales Act the common law rule of *nemo dat quod non habet* applied to sales by a conditional vendee to a *bona fide* purchaser for value without notice so that the conditional seller's rights were protected as against the *bona fide* purchaser: see *Forristal et al.* v. *McDonald* (1883) 9 SCR 12.

With the introduction of the Conditional Sales Act, the conditional seller's common law rights were restricted. A failure to register the conditional sale agreement rendered conditions reserving title in the seller void as against creditors, subsequent purchasers or mortgagees claiming from or under the buyer in good faith for valuable consideration and without notice. If the conditional sale agreement were registered the seller's common law rights were preserved. This rule was later changed by s. 24(2) of the Sale of Goods Act and s. 12 of the Factors and Agents Act, the provisions of which clearly apply to sales by conditional vendees to *bona fide* purchasers without notice. Those provisions must be given some meaning and to rule that they do not apply in the case at bar would render the sections meaningless.

It appears the trial Judge examined the legislation in other Provinces: *viz.*, Alberta, British Columbia, Ontario and Manitoba, where special provisions were enacted to exclude conditional sales from the scope of the sections of the sale of goods legislation under which a buyer in possession of goods can pass a good title to an innocent third party purchasing from him. No such provisions have been enacted in New Brunswick and I agree with the trial Judge that, but for such provisions, the Sale of Goods Act and the Factors and Agents Act do apply to conditional sales: see Fridman, *Sale of Goods in Canada* (1973), pp. 277-8 and pp. 419-20; G. V. La Forest, "Filing Under the Conditional Sales Act: Is it Notice to Subsequent Purchasers?", 36 Can. Bar Rev. 387 (1958).

It is held in *Traders Finance Corp. Ltd.* v. *Dawson Implements Ltd.* (1958) 15 DLR (2d) 515, 26 WWR 561, [1956-60] ILR 1058*n* (BC SC), and *Century Credit Corp.* v. *Richard* (1962) 34 DLR (2d) 291, [1962] OR 815 (Ont. CA), that provisions of the Sale of Goods Act (Ont.), s. 25(2), and the Factors Act (Ont.), s. 2(1), applied to transactions between a conditional vendee and a *bona fide* purchaser so as to give the *bona fide* purchaser a good title to the goods.

In *Traders Finance Corp. Ltd.*, a corporation in Alberta sold a motor-car to P. under a conditional sales agreement by virtue of which the property in the vehicle was to remain in the vendor until the purchase price had been paid in full. The agreement was assigned to the plaintiff, and all provisions of the Alberta statute with regard to registration were duly complied with. P. removed the car to British Columbia (where no copy of the conditional sales agreement was registered pursuant to s. 3(5) of the Conditional Sales Act, RSBC 1948, c. 64) and sold the car to the defendant as a *bona fide* purchaser for value without notice. In an action for conversion the Court held the sale to the defendant of goods situate in British Columbia having taken place in that Province, the law of British Columbia governed, and the defendant acquired a valid title under s. 32(2) of the Sale of Goods Act, RSBC 1948, c. 294 (our s. 24(2)), which displaced the title reserved by the plaintiff in Alberta. Registration of the conditional sales agreement in Alberta was not notice to the defendant of the plaintiff's rights. In other words, the registration in Alberta was not constructive notice to residents of British Columbia.

The Court in *Traders Finance Corp. Ltd.* did not have to decide the question whether registration within the jurisdiction would be notice and thereby prevent a *bona fide* purchaser from relying on s. 32(2) of the British Columbia Sale of Goods Act (our s. 24(2)). However, the following comments of Whittaker, J., at pp. 519-20:

> A serious question may arise as to whether the framers of our Conditional Sales Act may have overlooked s. 32(2) of the Sale of Goods Act. The former Act does not say that filing shall be deemed notice to innocent third parties. There is clear authority that conditional sale statutes do not enlarge the rights of conditional vendors. Their purpose is to protect innocent third parties against the vendor's common law right of seizure by providing in effect that the vendor may not exercise such right unless he registers. Registration gives third persons dealing with the conditional buyer an opportunity to discover a lien which might otherwise remain secret . . .
>
> If the Act does not enlarge the rights of the conditional vendor as against innocent third persons, it may be arguable that it should not be so construed as to cut down rights already conferred on such persons by s. 32(2).

(albeit *obiter dicta*) suggests that if it had been necessary for the Court to decide the question, he would still have allowed the innocent purchaser the protection of the equivalent of our s. 24(2).

In *Century Credit Corp.* a vendor assigned a conditional sales contract made in the Province of Quebec to the plaintiff. The purchaser, without the knowledge of the plaintiff or the vendor, brought the car into the Province of Ontario and sold it to a dealer. The dealer sold it to a third party from whom it was purchased by the defendant without notice of the plaintiff's claim. On appeal from a judgment giving the plaintiff the possession of the car, the appeal was allowed. Although the title acquired under the contract had to be determined by Quebec law and was valid in Ontario as against the original purchaser in spite of the lack of registration, it was superseded by a new title acquired under the Ontario sale, which had to be determined under Ontario law. By virtue of s. 25(2) of the Sale of Goods Act, RSO 1960, c. 358 [now RSO 1970, c. 421] (our s. 24(2)), and s. 2(1) of the Factors Act, RSO 1960, c. 129 [now RSO 1970, c. 156] (our s. 2), the sale by the conditional purchaser to the dealer in Ontario was as valid as if it were expressly authorized by the owner, and the title subsequently acquired by the defendant was absolute. If the conditional sale contract had been registered in Ontario, the *bona fide* purchaser could not have claimed the benefit of s. 25(2) of the Sale of Goods Act because s. 10(3) of the Ontario Conditional Sales Act provided that registration is deemed to be actual notice. There is no such provision in the New Brunswick Conditional Sales Act.

Both *Traders Finance Corp. Ltd.* and *Century Credit Corp.* lend support to the view that conditional sales are agreements to sell within the meaning of the Sale of Goods Act and the Factors and Agents Act. These statutes are designed to protect a *bona fide* buyer of goods from a conditional vendee.

The *Century Credit Corp.* case stands for the proposition that the registration of a conditional sale contract within the Province is actual notice and in the absence of such registration the *bona fide* purchaser is protected by s. 25(2) of the Ontario Act (our s. 24(2)). The Conditional Sales Act of New Brunswick does not provide that filing is notice and in the absence of such provision it is difficult to envisage why a *bona fide* purchaser should not avail himself of s. 24(2) of the Sale of Goods Act of New Brunswick to protect his goods.

In *Kozak* v. *Ford Motor Credit Co. of Canada Ltd.* (1971) 18 DLR (3d) 735, [1971] 3 WWR 1 (Sask. CA), a conditional sale contract was executed and registered within the Province of Saskatchewan. Subsequent sales between the conditional vendee and a used car dealer and between the used car dealer and the plaintiff took place within the Province of Saskatchewan. The credit company seized the car from Kozak who brought an action against the used car dealer and the credit company. Kozak's action against the credit company was dismissed but he was awarded damages against the used car dealer. The trial Judge held that neither the conditional vendee nor the used car dealer nor Kozak had received title to the car so as to enable Kozak to resist the seizure by the credit company. On appeal by the used car dealer the appeal was dismissed. The Court of Appeal held that neither the Factors Act nor the Sale of Goods Act applied to conditional sales and the appellant could not therefore rely on their provisions. Furthermore, the appellant had, by virtue of the registration under the Conditional Sales Act, constructive notice of the agreement and of the credit company's interest thereunder, and was properly found liable to Kozak for breach of condition as to clear title.

In dismissing the appeal by the used car dealer, Hall, J.A. based his decision on three alternative grounds. Firstly, he found that the pertinent sections of the Factors Act, RSS 1965, c. 386, and the Sale of Goods Act, RSS 1965, c. 388, did not apply to conditional sales. Secondly, if the pertinent sections of the statutes did apply, he accepted the interpretation placed on s. 10 of the Factors Act (our s. 12), and s. 26(2) of the Sale of Goods Act (our s. 24(2)) as set out in *Newtons of Wembley Ltd.* v. *Williams* [1964] 3 All ER 532. In his opinion, that case required the buyer in possession to be acting in the ordinary course of business of a mercantile agent when the car was sold. Thirdly, if he were wrong in his understanding of *Newtons of Wembley Ltd.* v. *Williams* and its application to the instant (*Kozak*) case, there still remained the matter of registration under the Conditional Sales Act. The Act itself did not contain a provision specifically making registration notice. Maguire J.A., concurred with Hall, J.A. Woods, J.A., although agreeing with the result and with the first and second bases for the decision of the Court, had this to say at p. 740 in regard to registration being notice:

> My brother Hall has discussed another ground as an alternative, however. He finds that registration under the Conditional Sales Act constitutes notice. In *Bozsik* v. *Kaufmann, supra* [(1963) 45 WWR 316], I expressed the view that registration of a bill of sale served to preserve the common law interest of the vendor. The question has not hitherto been determined in any decision binding on this Court but the weight of the dicta and pronouncement on it have been to the effect that registration does not constitute notice. Section 3(1) of the Conditional Sales Act states:
>
> > 3.(1) Where possession of goods has been delivered to a buyer under a conditional sale,

unless the conditional sale is evidenced and is registered in accordance with, and within the times limited in, section 5, every provision contained therein whereby the property in the goods remains in the seller is void as against a creditor, and as against a subsequent purchaser or mortgagee claiming from or under the buyer in good faith, for a valuable consideration and without notice.

I do not read these words as intended to give a preference or priority to a registered conditional sale agreement. Failure to register subordinates the interest of the seller to that of creditors and certain subsequent purchasers and mortgagees. Registration preserves the rights of the seller and provides third parties with a means of discovering agreements relating to the chattels and their terms. In other words, it gives to the purchaser an avenue for avoiding the stringent consequences of the common law maxim: *nemo dat quod non habet*.

For the reasons already given I would, with respect, disagree with the first basis of the decision in the *Kozak* case and with the conclusion that registration is notice.

GMAC alleges that the most fundamental question in the case at bar is whether the Sale of Goods Act is applicable to conditional sales. The law on this point has been unanimously settled, with the exception of the *Kozak* dicta relied upon by GMAC.

An historical analysis supports the theory that conditional sales are covered by the Sale of Goods Act. At the risk of being repetitious, the Conditional Sales Act was enacted in New Brunswick in 1899 and had the effect of dramatically altering the common law doctrine of *nemo dat quod non habet*. The Sale of Goods Act was transported to the Canadian Provinces from Great Britain where it was enacted in 1893. It was first enacted in New Brunswick in 1919. It is of significance that the Sale of Goods Act was adopted chronologically after the Conditional Sales Act which implies that the framers of the legislation were aware of the manner in which the Sale of Goods Act would affect conditional sales.

Counsel for Mr. Hubbard submits that the system of filing conditional sale agreements in the Province of New Brunswick is irrelevant to a conditional sale filed in another Province as in the present case. At the time Mr. Hubbard purchased the motor vehicle in New Brunswick, the conditional sale contract was only registered in the Province of Ontario. It is further contended on behalf of Mr. Hubbard that a preposterous situation would be created if purchasers in New Brunswick were to be fixed with constructive notice of conditional sales registered throughout Canada.

Furthermore, there is no express provisions that filing under the Conditional Sales Act, constitutes notice. This may be contrasted with the Registry Act, RSNB 1973, c. R-6, and in particular s. 64 thereof which renders registration notice to subsequent purchasers. Under the Registry Act, the registration of a deed is actual notice as of the date of registration. Also I do not think filing constitutes constructive notice to a *bona fide* purchaser for value without actual notice.

Mr. La Forest in his article, *supra*, at pp. 388-9 is reported as follows:

But nowhere in the Act will one find a provision setting forth the effect of ordinary registration. It may, of course, be argued that since the Act declares that conditions reserving title in unregistered agreements are void against subsequent purchasers for value and without notice, then by implication it provides that such conditions in registered agreements are valid against innocent purchasers. But reading into statutes provisions that are not there is at best dangerous, and this is particularly so where it would take away the rights of innocent persons as it would here. Further, it is suggested that implying such a condition would fly in the face of the whole purpose and object of the Act as it appears from its provisions. The purpose of the Act is to limit the rights of conditional sellers, not to add to them. Thus the section already cited makes conditions reserving title in the seller void unless the agreement is registered or the Act is otherwise complied with, and a later section seriously curtails the seller's right of sale on repossession. It is submitted, therefore, that the legislature intended to make conditions reserving title void unless the agreement was registered, and not to interfere with them if registered, but rather to allow them whatever operation they had before. This, I suggest, is a fair inference to draw if one reads the Act without preconceived notions.

And at pp. 395-6 Mr. La Forest expresses the view that registration in New Brunswick has the following purpose:

> The Acts were not designed, then, to compel buyers to search the registry at their peril; they were aimed rather at preventing fraudulent and preferential agreements by making transactions that could be used for the purpose void unless made public. This is probably what Orde J. and other judges had in mind when they said that the rights of sellers were not increased by the Conditional Sales Act. It was true that when a conditional sale was registered the seller's rights prevailed over those of the buyer by virtue of the common law, but that rule was subsequently altered as we have seen, when section 9 of the Factors Act and section 25(2) of the Sale of Goods Act were reproduced in Canada. To argue otherwise one must assert that these sections were virtually meaningless from their inception.

The former *nemo dat quod non habet* rule or maxim which governed the operation of conditional sale agreements prior to the advent of the Conditional Sales Act was altered by s. 12 of the Factors and Agents Act and s. 24(2) of the Sale of Goods Act. The inconsistency between requiring a security interest to be registered on the one hand and still retaining a rule on the other that a buyer in possession should be deemed to have power to pass good title requires legislative reform. Several Provinces have recognized the anomaly and have eliminated it by (1) excluding the operation of s. 24(2) of the Sale of Goods Act, in regard to conditional sales or by (2) making registration actual notice. The *Kozak* case resolved the conflict through statutory interpretation and reliance on *Newtons of Wembley* case, *supra*. It is noted that the Province of Saskatchewan has a central registry for conditional sale agreements and bills of sale. No equivalent system exists in New Brunswick.

See also: *Commercial Credit Co. of Canada Ltd.* v. *Fulton Bros.* (1922) 65 DLR 699, 55 NSR 208 (NS SC); affirmed [1923] 3 DLR 611, [1923] AC 798; *Joseph* v. *Lyons* (1884) 15 QBD 280, *per* Cotton, L.J., at p. 286, and Lindley, L.J., at p. 287.

In *Manchester Trust* v. *Furness* [1895] 2 QB 539 (CA), the position is taken that the doctrine of constructive notice should not be extended to commercial transactions.

There now remains the issue whether the meaning and effect of s. 24(2) of the Sale of Goods Act is restricted to particular types of transactions of which the instant case does not form part.

GMAC contends that the words "has the same effect as if the person making the delivery or transfer were a mercantile agent in possession of the goods" (s. 24(2) of the Sale of Goods Act) should be construed to refer only to the disposition by a mercantile agent when "acting in the ordinary course of business of a mercantile agent" (s. 2 of the Factors and Agents Act).

In support of this argument GMAC relies upon the decision of the English Court of Appeal in *Newtons of Wembley Ltd.* v. *Williams, supra,* which stands for the proposition that a buyer in possession can only pass a good title to a *bona fide* purchaser under the equivalent of our s. 24(2) of the Sale of Goods Act and s. 2 of the Factors and Agents Act if the buyer in possession, when making the sale, is acting in the ordinary course of business of a mercantile agent.

I believe a logically incorrect result is derived from the GMAC reasoning and that the portion of the *Newtons of Wembley* decision relied upon is *obiter* since the Court found as a fact that the sale was made by a seller acting in the ordinary course of his business. GMAC's argument renders s. 24(2) of the Sale of Goods Act effectively sterile since it is impossible for a seller who is not in business to act in "the ordinary course of business".

It is obvious that s. 24(2) of the Sale of Goods Act was intended to apply to private individuals and not mercantile agents because of the wording "the delivery or transfer by that person or by a mercantile agent acting for him".

In the case at bar, GMAC advanced the same argument in reference to s. 24(2) of the Sale of Goods Act as the argument raised by the plaintiff in *Jeffcott et al.* v. *Andrew Motors Ltd.* [1960] NZLR 721 (CA), regarding the interpretation to be placed on s. 27(2) of the Sale of Goods Act, 1908, New Zealand (our s. 24(2)). The judgment of Gresson, P., and Cleary, J., was delivered by Gresson, P., in the *Jeffcott* case. Hutchison, J., agreed with the following interpretation and effect of s. 27(2) (our s. 24(2)) given by Gresson, P., at p. 729:

> Mr. Harding further argued that s. 27(2) could not be invoked to support the sale by Stevens to the respondent, because when Stevens made that sale he was not acting in the ordinary course of business of a mercantile agent, or, indeed, acting as an agent at all. He said that it was necessary for the buyer in possession to act as a mercantile agent because of the concluding words of s. 27(2), which provide that the delivery of the goods
>
> > shall have the same effect as if the person making the delivery or transfer were a mercantile agent in possession of the goods . . . with the consent of the owner.
>
> This is a novel argument, and seems to us to be quite unsound. The section operates to validate a sale as if the buyer in possession were a mercantile agent; it does not require that he should act as though he were a mercantile agent. The section is derived from sections of the Factors Act 1877 and 1889 which were enacted only because a buyer in possession was not a mercantile agent entrusted with the goods: *Chalmer's Sale of Goods Act*, 13th ed., 209-210; *Marten* v. *Whale* [1917] 2 KB 480, 486. Mr. Harding's construction would virtually deprive the section of any effect beyond the operation of s. 3 of the Mercantile Law Act 1908, and is contrary to the interpretation applied in a line of cases commencing with *Lee* v. *Butler* [1893] 1 QB 318.

See also *Langmead* v. *Thyer Rubber Co. Ltd.* [1947] SASR 29. Reed, J., states at p. 39:

> It will be observed that a sale by a mercantile agent is not valid under s. 4, unless it is made by him "when acting in the ordinary course of business of a mercantile agent." Section 25(2) of the Sale of Goods Act contains no stipulation that any sale etc. under which goods are delivered or transferred must, in order to be effective, be made in any particular manner, such as in the course of the business of a mercantile agent. The meaning of s. 25(2) appears to be that where, for example, a sale by a person who has bought or agreed to buy goods has taken place, if the conditions therein stated are satisfied, the delivery or transfer of the goods is to have the same effect as if a sale of the goods had been legally effected by a mercantile agent, i.e, made by him when acting in the ordinary course of business as a mercantile agent. This is in effect the construction that has been put on similar legislation: cf. *Martin* v. *Whale* (1917) 2 KB 480.

I would fully agree with the interpretation placed on the section of the Sale of Goods Act in the respective cases of *Jeffcott* and *Langmead*. Furthermore, the illogic of the *Newtons of Wembley* decision has been attacked by Fridman, *Sale of Goods in Canada, supra*, at p. 140:

> This seems a little restrictive. Its purpose, however, may be to apply the rules as to dispositions by mercantile agents to dispositions by buyers who are not within that category. If so, then it would seem either nonsensical to stipulate that transactions by such persons should only be effective if they act in the ordinary course of business, if they have no business, since they are not mercantile agents, or unnecessarily limited to treat such persons as having the power to transfer title effectively only where the disposition would have been good if the buyer had carried on a business and the transaction in question would have been valid as being in the ordinary course of such business.

Furthermore, the *Newtons of Wembley* decision, being *dicta*, was directed towards an interpretation of the Factors and Agents Act of Great Britain which is primarily concerned with commercial rather than private transactions.

In the result, I would dispose of the issues raised on this appeal as follows:
(1) The provisions of the Sale of Goods Act, are applicable to conditional sale agreements (which are agreements to sell).
(2) Section 24(2) of the Sale of Goods Act, applies to protect a *bona fide* purchaser for value without notice.

In the present case, the sale by Mr. John Kenney to Mr. Hubbard took place in New Brunswick and its effect must be decided according to New Brunswick law. The applicable statutory provisions are s. 24(2) of the Sale of Goods Act, and s. 2 of the Factors and Agents Act.

The sale by Mr. Kenney to Mr. Hubbard as purchaser, who received the vehicle in good faith and without notice of any lien or other right of the original seller, by reason of s. 24(2) of the Sale of Goods Act, has the same effect as if Mr. Kenney in making the delivery and transfer were a mercantile agent in possession of the goods with the consent of the owner. Applying s. 2 of the Factors and Agents Act, the sale by Mr. Kenney is as valid as if it were expressly authorized by the owner and the title acquired by the purchaser, Mr. Hubbard, is, by virtue of this sale, absolute. GMAC can stand in no higher position than the seller in

Ontario and therefore its title is displaced by the valid sale in New Brunswick.
(3) Registration under the Conditional Sales Act, is not notice so as to defeat a
bona fide purchaser's title acquired under s. 24(2) of the Sale of Goods Act.
(4) As to the meaning and effect of s. 24(2) of the Sale of Goods Act, see the last
paragraph of issue (2) above.

I am, therefore, of the opinion that the appeal should be dismissed with
costs.

Appeal dismissed.

Notes:

1   *GMAC* v. *Hubbard* is critically discussed in Ziegel, "GMAC v. Hubbard: Statutory
Conflict, Conditional Sales and Public Policy" (1979) 3 CBLJ 329. Professor Ziegel
argues, inter alia, that the provinces for the most part adopted their conditional
sales legislation well before the introduction in Canada of the British Sale of Goods
Act, that registration requirements were viewed as providing a reasonable accommodation of the conflicting interests of the conditional seller and third parties
dealing with the goods in the buyer's possession, and that there is no evidence that
the Canadian Uniformity Commissioners, in recommending the adoption of the
British SGA by the provinces, intended to nullify the scheme of the conditional sales
legislation. He also joins issue with the court's holding, notwithstanding the earlier
supporting precedents, that the doctrine of constructive notice does not apply to
SGA s. 25 and expresses his preference for the reasoning of the Saskatchewan
Court of Appeal in *Kozak* v. *Ford Motor Credit Co.* referred to in the judgment (and
recently following by the same court in *Harvey Dodds Ltd.* v. *Royal Bank* (1979) 105
DLR (3d) 650, 1 SR 78). Finally, Professor Ziegel argues that the New Brunswick court
misinterpreted the ratio in *Newtons of Wembley* v. *Williams* and that the sequence
of events did not in fact satisfy the requirements in s. 24(2) of the New Brunswick
Sale of Goods Act. Can you see why?

2   Following the decision in *Hubbard* the New Brunswick legislature amended its Sale
of Goods Act by adding the following provision to the Act:

   24.(4) For the purposes of subsection (1), the registration in accordance with the
   Bills of Sale Act of a bill of sale or other document under that Act, whether before or
   after the coming into force of this subsection, constitutes notice of the bill of sale or
   other document under that Act within the registration district in which it has been
   registered, from the time of registration to all persons claiming from or under the
   person who, having sold the goods, continues or is in possession of the goods or the
   documents of title to the goods.

   24.(5) For the purposes of subsection (2), the registration in accordance with the
   Bills of Sale Act of a bill of sale or other document under that Act, whether before or
   after the coming into force of this subsection, constitutes notice of the bill of sale or
   other document under that Act within the registration district in which it has been
   registered, from the time of registration to all persons claiming from or under the
   person who, having bought or agreed to buy the goods, obtains possession of the
   goods or the documents of title to the goods.

   24.(6) For the purposes of subsection (2), the filing in accordance with the

Conditional Sales Act of a conditional sale or other document under the Act, whether before or after the coming into force of this subsection, constitutes notice of the conditional sale or other document under that Act within the registration district in which it has been filed, from the time of filing to all persons claiming from or under the person who, having bought or agreed to buy the goods, obtains possession of the goods or the documents of title to the goods.

As will be observed, the amendment reverses *Hubbard* by providing that registration of a document under the Bills of Sale Act and the Conditional Sales Act constitutes notice of the document for the purposes of s. 24(1) and (2) of the Sale of Goods Act. The draftsman, it will be noted, chose not to exclude s. 24(1) and (2) entirely from transactions governed by the Bills of Sale and Conditional Sales Acts and in this respect the amendment differs from the approach adopted in the new personal property security legislation and the various Proposals discussed in Prof. Ziegel's article.

It will also be observed that constructive notice is only imputed "within the registration district" in which the document is registered. The onus is therefore placed on the secured party to monitor the location of the collateral or the residence of the debtor, as the case may be, and to effect a new registration when a change occurs. It will be equally evident that the amendment does not deal with the other difficulties surrounding the interpretation of s. 24(2) of the New Brunswick Sale of Goods Act discussed in the text.

3. BUYER'S POSSESSION AND THE PERSONAL PROPERTY SECURITY ACT

J.S. ZIEGEL
"GMAC v. Hubbard. . ."
(1979) 3 CBLJ 329, 347-56

Even before *Hubbard*, a number of provinces had adopted remedial legislation to resolve the conflict between their Conditional Sales Acts and the provisions in their Sale of Goods Acts corresponding to s. 25(2) of the British Sale of Goods Act. For the purpose of the ensuing discussion, it will be convenient to focus on the approach in the new personal property security legislation adopted in Ontario and Manitoba, and the Proposals for the adoption of such legislation in Saskatchewan, Alberta and British Columbia. It is also desirable to distinguish the general relationship between the personal property security legislation and s. 25 of the Sale of Goods Act from the separate rules applied in the legislation to wholly intraprovincial transactions and those that have a foreign element to them.

(a) *The general relationship*

Section 68 of the Ontario Personal Property Security Act (hereafter OPPSA) provides that where there is a conflict between its provisions and the provision of any other Act, other than The Consumer Protection Act, the provisions of the OPPSA shall prevail. A similar provision is found in the Manitoba Act and the various Proposals. Section 25(3) of the Ontario Sale of Goods Act also provides that s. 25(2) is not applicable to goods the possession of which has been obtained by a buyer under a security agreement governed by the OPPSA. However, s. 25(3) has so far not been proclaimed and will therefore be ignored in the ensuing discussion.

The relevant provisions, in the case of the OPPSA, include ss. 1(y), 2, 9, 21, 22, and 63. Section 1(y) defines the meaning of security interest; s. 2(a) defines the scope of the Act and makes it clear that it applies to a conditional sale agreement. Section 9 provides that, except as otherwise provided by this or any other Act, a security agreement is effective according to its terms between the parties and against third parties. Section 21 defines the meaning of a "perfected security interest". Section 22 determines the consequences of an unperfected security interest and provides that such an interest is subordinated, *inter alia*, to the interest of a transferee who is not a secured party to the extent (*sic*) that he gives value without knowledge of the security interest and before it is perfected. Sections 24 and 25 describe the primary routes that must be followed (perfection by possession or perfection by registration) to obtain more than a temporarily perfected security interest in collateral. If registration of a financing statement is the chosen route, then s. 53 is triggered. This provides that registration of a financing statement constitutes notice of the security interest to which it relates to all persons claiming any interest in such collateral during the period of three years following such registration.

It will, therefore, be seen that, apart from questions of priority between competing security interests and a number of other specialized situations not relevant to the present discussion, the rights of third parties with respect to goods subject to a prior security interest turn on whether or not the security interest was perfected at the material date. On this ground alone it may be argued that there is a fundamental repugnancy between the concepts of the OPPSA and the protection conferred on third parties under s. 25(2) of the Ontario Sale of Goods Act and that, pursuant to s. 68 of the OPPSA, the rights of the seller with a perfected security interest in the goods should prevail. The basic structure of the Manitoba Act and the Proposals is the same as the OPPSA and the same result should follow as under the Ontario Act. To the extent that there is any lingering doubt about the position, s. 53 of the Ontario Act gives the seller, who has perfected by registration, the benefit of a doctrine of constructive notice. Invoking s. 53, however, in a conflict between a conditional seller and a person claiming under the buyer in possession, involves the concession that, but for the section, s. 25(2) would apply. This seems an unwise admission and may create difficulties where the seller is only claiming a temporarily perfected security interest not supported by registration.

The aforegoing observations are subject to a number of important caveats. First, the OPPSA only applies where the seller is claiming a security interest in the goods in the buyer's possession. If his rights are of a different character (as, for example, where he claims the statutory lien of an unpaid seller under The Sale of Goods Act rather than the consensual lien of a secured seller) then s. 25(2) may still apply. Secondly, the OPPSA does not regulate absolute bills of sale, *i.e.*, sales in which the seller remains in possession after a sale. In Ontario, such transactions continue to be governed by The Bills of Sale Act. Like the Conditional Sales Acts, it has no constructive notice provision. Consequently, the conflict between The Bills of Sale Act and s. 25(1) remains and *Hubbard's* case and the earlier authorities remain relevant. Finally, the OPPSA and the other provincial Acts contain several important exceptions to the primacy of the seller with a perfected security interest. These will be considered hereafter.

(b) *Wholly intraprovincial sales*

The basic features of the OPPSA described above should apply without much difficulty to the typical conditional sale where the relevant facts all occur in the same province. Assume A delivers goods to B under a conditional sale agreement. A perfects his security interest by filing a financing statement. B purports to sell the goods to C without disclosing the subsisting security interest. Under one or both theories of the relationship between the OPPSA and s. 25(2) of The Sale of Goods Act discussed above, A's security interest should prevail over C's claim. Had C made a search of the registry he would have discovered A's security interest and if he failed to make a search the Act deems him to be the author of his own misfortune.

Section 30(1) of the OPPSA recognizes an important exception to the general rule where goods are bought in ordinary course from a seller who has created a security interest in them. This is the familiar inventory or "trader's" exception already well known at common law and reproduced in the provincial Conditional Sale Acts. Section 30(1) goes somewhat beyond the earlier provisions, but this is a separate question that need not detain us.

Another and somewhat broader exception to the general primacy of the perfected security interest is recognized in the Saskatchewan, Alberta and British Columbia Proposals. To a greater or lesser extent, each of the Proposals enables a buyer or lessee of consumer goods to acquire an interest in the goods free of a prior perfected security interest unless he had actual knowledge of the security interest. In Saskatchewan's case, the exception does not include a security interest in a motor vehicle, fixture, boat, vessel or aircraft, or to goods the purchase price of which exceeds $500 or, in the case of a lease, the value of which exceeds $500. The exception is, therefore, not as far reaching as may appear at first sight.

Its underlying rationale is that a buyer of consumer goods should not be expected to make a search except in those cases where the need to make a search is well known among consumers or it is customary to obtain legal assistance in the transaction. The proponents of the exception clearly felt that secured parties claiming a security interest in consumer goods are in a better position than the consumer to protect themselves and to absorb losses resulting from a wrongful resale to the innocent third party. In a losse sense, therefore, it may be said that the exception is a limited reincarnation of s. 25(2) of the Sale of Goods Act. It goes beyond it in one respect in so far as the exception covers any prior security interest, whether in the form of a conditional sale or otherwise. The exception also enures for the benefit of any subsequent buyer or lessee of the goods; he does not have to deal directly with the buyer under the original conditional sale agreement as is true in the case of s. 25(2).

(c) *Conditional sales with a foreign element*

The policy issues become substantially more complicated when goods, subject to a valid security interest in province X, are brought by the conditional buyer into province Y and there wrongfully disposed of by him to an innocent transferee. The resulting problems are dealt with in ss. 5 to 8 of the OPPSA. The Ontario Act distinguishes between mobile goods and other types of goods, mobile goods for this purpose being goods normally used by a business debtor in more than one jurisdiction if such goods are classified as equipment or classified as inventory because the debtor leases them to others. Security interests in such mobile goods are made subject to a separate conflicts of law rule and their validity and perfection is determined by the debtor's chief place of business. They have given rise to few reported conflict of laws problems in Canada and they are outside our present range of concerns.

A further exception is recognized in s. 6(2) of the Ontario Act in the case of goods originally sold in Quebec and subject to a seller's right of revendication or resilition under Quebec law. We may ignore this problem too as being of limited practical importance. We are then left with the stereotype *Hubbard* situation covered in ss. 7 and 8 of the Ontario Act.

These sections distinguish between goods subject to a perfected security interest in the first *situs* before being brought into Ontario and goods subject to a valid but unperfected security interest under the law of the first *situs*. Not surprisingly, the secured party with a perfected security interest under the law of the first *situs* is given more favourable treatment than the holder of an unperfected security interest. In the former case the security interest remains perfected in Ontario for a period of 60 days after the goods are brought into the province and also thereafter if the security interest is perfected in Ontario within the 60-day period. If the secured party learns of the removal before the 60 days have expired, then the security interest loses its perfected status in Ontario unless the secured party registers a financing statement in Ontario within 15 days of the notice. If the security interest was not perfected in the first *situs*, then it will also be treated as unperfected in Ontario but may be perfected in Ontario within 30 days from the date the collateral is brought into Ontario. However, even after the 30-day limitation has expired the secured party is entitled to apply under s. 63 for an extension of time for the perfection of his security interest. The Manitoba Act and the Proposals have adopted substantially similar provisions but with the one important difference that an unperfected security interest is not subject to the 30-day limitation: it may be perfected in the second *situs* at any time.

From the aforegoing summary it will be seen that the personal property security legislation has retained the requirement of the prior conditional sales legislation that the extraprovincial security interest must be reperfected in the second *situs* if it is to have a recognized status there. The novel feature is the discrepant treatment of a security interest according to its perfected or unperfected status under the first *lex situs*, but the novelty may be more apparent than real because the distinction was already drawn at common law by a substantial number of American courts and by at least one Canadian court. It will also be noticed that the new provisions are less favourable to the conditional seller than the earlier legislation since they impose an absolute obligation on the conditional seller to perfect his security interest in Ontario even though he is not aware that the goods have been brought into the province.

Assuming New Brunswick had adopted a Personal Property Security Act, this would have meant in *Hubbard* that Hubbard's claim would have prevailed. It would have prevailed, it is submitted, not on the ground that s. 24(2) of the New Brunswick Sale of Goods Act applied but because GMAC had apparently perfected its security interest in New Brunswick more than 60 days after the goods had been brought into the province and because the temporary period of perfection had lapsed at the time Hubbard bought the vehicle from John Kenney. Suppose, however, that he had bought the vehicle within the 60-day period. GMAC's security interest would then have prevailed. Would this have been a fair result? The answer depends in part on the kinds of inquiries Hubbard might reasonably be expected to have made before buying the vehicle and in part on the proper allocation of risks of loss between GMAC and Hubbard.

As previously noted, the vehicle was registered in New Brunswick at the time of Hubbard's purchase and the reported facts do not indicate whether he knew the vehicle had originated in Ontario. Even if he had known, it is unreasonable to expect a private purchaser to undertake extraprovincial searches. In *Hubbard*, the court noted that New Brunswick has no central registration system for liens against motor vehicles, the implication being that Hubbard would have had great difficulty in establishing whether a lien has been registered in one of the registration districts in New Brunswick. If this is true of a search inside New Brunswick, it must be that much more true of a search outside the province. Admittedly, in our assumed facts, GMAC had complied with the applicable requirements of Ontario and New Brunswick law and, let us further assume, had not been negligent in not learning earlier of the removal of the vehicle into New Brunswick. The equities therefore seem to be evenly divided. There is, however, the important difference that GMAC is in a much better position than the average consumer to assess the risk of loss arising from a wrongful conversion by its debtor and to internalize it as part of its costs of operation. Consequently, the more efficient solution is to impose the risk of loss on GMAC.

Other possible solutions also suggest themselves. One would be the introduction of a system of certificate of title for motor vehicles and another would be an independently operated insurance fund to protect private buyers of motor vehicles. However, there is no evidence of strong support for either of these solutions and this may be because the problem is not perceived to be sufficiently important to warrant major changes of this character. A more modest alternative would be to require proof of ownership and absence of encumbrances before an extraprovincial vehicle is registered within the province. Such requirements are already imposed in some American jurisdictions. Assuming their feasibility in the Canadian context then, once again, it may be said that the consumer finance industry is in a better position to press for their adoption than is the consumer. Imposing on the industry the risk of loss arising from the interprovincial movement of goods may in fact encourage the search for the most efficient solution.

The issue raised here is not novel. As noted earlier, the Saskatchewan and other Proposals favour the position of an innocent buyer of consumer goods subject to an undisclosed security interest even where the security interest has been perfected in the province. If this is true of a perfected security interest then an even stronger case can be made for protecting the consumer buyer of an extraprovincial vehicle where the security interest has not been reperfected in the second *situs* and regardless of its state of perfection under the first *lex situs*. This view was forcibly argued at the May, 1978 meeting of the Committee on a Model Uniform Personal Property Security Act (MUPPSA) and the committee approved an amendment to s. 7 of the Model Act to the effect that, vis-à-vis a buyer of consumer goods, no grace period should be allowed for the perfection of an extraprovincial security interest and that the buyer should be protected unless the security interest has been perfected within the jurisdiction at the time of his purchase.

If one accepts this, as the writer does, as a reasonable accommodation of the conflicting interests, then the decision in *Hubbard* can be justified though not for the reasons advanced by the court. It should be carefully noted that the amendment to s. 7 of the Model Act recommended by the MUPPSA Committee is only intended to enure for the benefit of a buyer of "consumer goods", *i.e.*, goods that are used or acquired for use primarily for personal, family or household purposes. The amendment would not, therefore, protect a dealer in the second *situs* since he would not be acquiring the goods for personal, family or household purposes. Even the protection afforded the consumer buyer will not be complete if the second *situs* has not adopted a central registration system for security interests in personal property and the foreign secured party has reperfected his security interest in a district other than the one in which the subsequent buyer conducted his search. This then reinforces the case for a central registration system.

Our discussion has focused on the consumer buyer of a motor vehicle who may reasonably be expected to make a search. In the case of other types of consumer goods, and particularly those of small unit value, the requirement may be unreasonable. Here the most efficient, and equitable, solution may be to follow the Saskatchewan precedent, and to protect the consumer buyer regardless of the state of perfection of the interest of the conditional seller or other secured party with a purchase money security interest.

4. Inventory Financing and the Buyer in Ordinary Course

See *infra*, chapter 22.

5. Proposals for Reform; Code Provisions

Notes:

From the foregoing materials in this chapter, it will be obvious that the SGA exceptions to the *nemo dat* rule are ripe for reform, both on questions of detail and on wider grounds of principle. Agreement on the former ground should not be too difficult to achieve but agreement on questions of principle is likely to prove more elusive. This distinction should be borne in mind in considering the notes that follow. Some important (though hardly revolutionary) changes have been effected by the Code; a large number of recommendations of varying importance were made in the 12th Report of the English Law Reform Committee on *Transfer of Title to Chattels* (1966), and an equally large number, though again not of a revolutionary character, appear in the OLRC Sales Report. It will be convenient to deal with each of these sources in turn.

1. *Code Provisions.* The basic *nemo dat* rule is retained subject to the following exceptions in Article 2:

a) *UCC 2-402(2)* entitles a creditor of the seller to treat a sale or an identification of goods to a contract for sale as void if as against him a retention of possession by the seller is fraudulent under any rule of law of the state where the goods are situated. However, retention in good faith and current course of trade by a merchant-seller for a commercially reasonable time after a sale or identification is not fraudulent. This provision substantially continues prior state law.

b) *UCC 2-403(1)* abolishes the common law distinction between void and voidable title and deems the purchaser to acquire a voidable title even though

> (a) the transferor was deceived as to the identity of the purchaser, or
> (b) the delivery was in exchange for a check which is later dishonored, or
> (c) it was agreed that the transaction was to be a "cash sale", or
> (d) the delivery was procured through fraud punishable as larcenous under the criminal law.

c) *UCC 2-403(2)* introduces the important proposition that "any entrusting of possession of goods to a merchant who deals in goods of that kind gives him power to transfer all rights of the entruster to a buyer in ordinary course of business." "Entrusting" is very broadly defined in 2-403(3) and includes any delivery and any acquiescence in retention of possession regardless of any condition expressed between the parties to the delivery or acquiescence. Note, first, that this provision substantially expands the scope of the old Factors Act and, secondly, that entrusting is not restricted to entrusting for purposes of sale. It embraces "*any* delivery and *any* acquiescence" and is thus wide enough to cover goods left with a merchant for repair or safekeeping. This feature of UCC 2-403(2) has attracted some criticism and a number of states have modified the definition of entrusting to restrict it to goods delivered or retained for purposes of sale. See further J.J. White and R.S. Summers, *Uniform Commercial Code*, pp. 142-46; *Anderson on the Uniform Commercial Code*, vol. II, p. 39, and Annual Supplement; and OLRC Sales Report, pp. 299-300.

d) *Miscellaneous sales provisions:* See UCC 2-502 (buyer's restricted right to claim goods identified in contract on seller's insolvency); and UCC 2-716 (buyer's remedy of specific performance and restricted right to replevy identified goods). It is not clear how far these provisions displace normal common law rules governing the remedies of a buyer who has acquired title to the goods.

e) *Article 9 provisions:* Article 9 systematically regulates the relationship between a secured party and a third party both of whom claim an interest in the collateral. In general the secured party's priority will depend on whether or not his security interest was perfected before the competing interest arose. Exceptionally however even a perfected security interest will be cut off in favour of an ordinary course buyer. See UCC 9-307(1) and compare OPPSA, s. 30(1); and see further *infra*, chapter 22 (G)(2).

2. Recommendations of the English Law Reform Committee. The Committee's recommendations with respect to the *nemo dat* rule are summarized below (Report, *op. cit.*, para. 40):

(1) We do not think it is practicable to introduce any system of apportioning the loss between persons who are the victims of theft, fraud or mistake affecting the transfer of a chattel (paragraphs 9-12).

(2) Where goods are stolen the owner should retain his title except where the goods are subsequently bought by a purchaser in good faith by retail at trade premises or at a public auction (paragraphs 14 and 33).

(3) Where goods are sold under a mistake as to the buyer's identity, the contract should, so far as third parties are concerned, be voidable and not void (paragraph 15).

(4) A voidable contract should be capable of being rescinded only by notice to the other contracting party (paragraph 16).

(5) We do not recommend any change in the law in regard to the effect of a disposition by a mercantile agent (paragraph 18).

(6) Sections 8 and 9 of the Factors Act 1889 should be repealed, in reliance on section 25 of the Sale of Goods Act 1893 (paragraph 19).

(7) Section 25(2) of the Sale of Goods Act should be amended so as to make it unnecessary for the buyer in possession of goods to have acted, in disposing of them, as if he were a mercantile agent (paragraph 23).

(8) A buyer who obtains goods under a voidable title which is effectively avoided by the seller should not be regarded as a buyer in possession after sale for the purposes of section 25(2) of the Sale of Goods Act (paragraph 24).

(9) We make no recommendation in regard to the power of a person in possession of goods under a hire-purchase agreement to pass a good title (paragraph 28).

(10) We do not consider that a bailee who is neither a mercantile agent nor a person to whom section 25 of the Sale of Goods Act applies should be able to pass a good title except in the case of a sale by auction or a retail sale at trade premises (paragraph 29).

It will be observed that the two most important recommendations concern the abolition of the distinction between void and voidable titles (recom. 3) and the elimination of the *market overt* exception in favour of a new provision extending protection to a person who buys goods from a retailer or at an auction. As in the case of the *market overt* exception, this protection would include the title to goods that have been stolen.

3. OLRC Recommendations. The Commission reviewed the existing SGA provisions and, after canvassing several alternatives, favoured a substantial modification of the existing exceptions to rejection of the *nemo dat* rule and its replacement by the principle adopted in many civil law jurisdictions that *en fait de meubles, possession vaut titre* (Art. 2279 of the French Civil Code). The Commission's recommendations are summarized below and, as will be seen, they were substantially influenced by the weaknesses in the existing provisions and the provisions in UCC 2-403:

OLRC RECOMMENDATIONS (pp. 316-18)

1. The revised Sale of Goods Act should not adopt a general *possession vaut titre* principle. Rather, the basic *nemo dat* doctrine should be affirmed.

2. The exceptions to the *nemo dat* doctrine contained in sections 22, 24 and 25 of the existing Sale of Goods Act should be retained in the revised Act, subject to the amendments and modifications set out below.

3. The *nemo dat* rule should not apply in the circumstances set out in section 22 of the existing Act. However, the exception to the rule now recognized in the case of conduct by the owner precluding him from denying the authority of the person in possession to sell the goods should be broadened to include cases where the owner has failed to exercise reasonable care in the entrustment of the goods and the buyer has exercised reasonable care in buying the goods and has acted in good faith.

4. As under section 24 of the existing Act, a seller who has a voidable title to goods should be able to pass good title to a person who buys in good faith and without notice of the seller's defective title. For purposes of this exception to the *nemo dat* rule, the distinction between void and voidable titles should be abolished. The revised Act should, accordingly, contain a provision stating that a purchaser of goods shall be deemed to have a voidable title notwithstanding that the transferor of the goods was deceived as to the identity of the purchaser or the presence of some other mistake affecting the validity of the contract of sale, and also in circumstances similar to those set out in UCC 2-403(1) (b), (c) and (d).

5. The revised Act should provide that, where the seller has or is deemed to have a voidable title, a purported avoidance of the contract by the owner of the goods shall have no effect on a third party, unless the goods are recovered by the owner before they are delivered to the third party by the person in possession of the goods.

6. Subject to the following amendments, the revised Act should contain a provision comparable to section 25 of the existing Sale of Goods Act, which recognizes an exception to the *nemo dat* rule in the case of a transfer of goods, or of a document of title, by buyers and sellers in possession:

    (a) The power of a seller in possession to transfer a better title to goods than he himself has should apply whether he is, or continues, in possession of the goods in his capacity as seller, or otherwise.

    (b) The power of a buyer or seller in possession to transfer a better title than he himself has shall not apply where a security interest governed by The Personal Property Security Act has been created in the seller or buyer out of possession, or where, prior to the disposition to the third party, a notice in the prescribed form has been filed under The Personal Property Security Act.

    (c) The power of a buyer or seller in possession to pass a better title to a third person than he himself has shall be contingent upon his originally being in possession of the goods, or of a document of title thereto, with the consent of the other party to the transaction; and in all other respects, the conditions governing the dispositive powers of buyers and sellers in possession should be the same.

    (d) The protection of the provision in the revised Act comparable to section 25 should be confined to a buyer or lessee who receives the goods in good faith and for value from the person in possession.

(e) The scope of the provision in the revised Act comparable to section 25 should be enlarged to cover a prospective buyer, as well as an actual buyer, in possession of the goods. A prospective buyer should be defined to mean a person who receives goods under a sale on approval or contract of sale or return or with an option to purchase, and a person whose offer to buy the goods has been accepted subject to the approval of a third person or the fulfilment of some other condition.

7.   The revised Act should not incorporate a general *market overt* rule with respect to sales, including sales of lost or stolen goods, made at retail premises.

8.   The revised Act should contain a further exception to the *nemo dat* doctrine, along the lines of UCC 2-403(2), in the case of goods entrusted to a merchant who deals in goods of the kind entrusted. Any entrusting of possession of goods to a merchant who deals in goods of that kind should give him power to transfer all rights of the entruster to a buyer or lessee in the ordinary course of business. "Entrusting" should be defined in the revised Act as in UCC 2-403(3).

9.   In light of recommendation No. 8, *supra*, The Factors Act should be reviewed with a view to determining the desirability of its retention.

10.   The ability of a buyer or seller in possession, or of a merchant to whom goods have been entrusted, to pass better title than he himself has should apply even though the owner has revoked his consent to possession of the goods by the other party, unless the goods are recovered by the owner before they have been delivered to the third party.

11.   Except in the case of entrustment of goods to a merchant who deals in goods of that kind, the court should be able, where it considers it fair, to order that the owner of goods may recover the goods from the person in possession upon repaying to the person in possession the price paid by the person in possession for the goods, together with such reliance losses as the person in possession would otherwise suffer and as the court may order to be paid.

12.   The Bills of Sale Act should be repealed.

[The Commission rejected the civilian approach for the following reasons (pp. 307-08):]

ARGUMENTS FOR AND AGAINST THE ADOPTION OF THE POSSESSION VAUT TITRE RULE IN ONTARIO

As previously noted, existing provisions of The Factors Act and The Personal Property Security Act, as well as a substantial body of case law, already favour a specialized aspect of the *possession vaut titre* rule (that is, a limited *market overt* principle) where goods are entrusted to a person who disposes of them in the ordinary course of his business. So too, we have seen that UCC 2-403(2) has adopted and restated the entrustment rule, but in somewhat broader language. It should also be noted that the English Law Reform Committee favoured the abolition of the *market overt* rule, which is part of English law, and its replacement by a new provision protecting good faith purchasers of goods bought in ordinary course at retail premises. This recommendation is not restricted to goods entrusted by the owner to a merchant, but it will, of course, include such situations.

The essential issue, therefore, is whether the mercantile rule should be extended to cover *all* forms of entrustment of goods, whether to a merchant or any other kind of person. The Law Reform Committee was opposed to such an extension because of the hardship it would cause to bailors who might not appreciate the risks they were running in entrusting their goods to a non-merchant bailee. To quote the Committee:

> ... it would have repercussions on a large variety of transactions of daily occurrence, such as the sending of goods to the laundry or the deposit of luggage in a station cloakroom, and we think it would generally be regarded as unsatisfactory if in cases of this kind the interests of the true owner were to be subordinated to those of the purchaser from the bailee.

We have reached the same conclusion as the Committee, but on somewhat broader grounds.

In the first place, we are not satisfied that a persuasive case has been advanced for making the entruster of goods to a non-merchant an insurer of the bailee's honesty, assuming that the owner has exercised reasonable care in the entrustment of his goods. The position is not the same as in the entrustment of goods to a merchant. The merchant is invested with an ostensible authority to deal with the goods, and it has generally been assumed that it would seriously impede the security of transactions to expect a buyer in ordinary course to investigate the origin of the goods and the merchant's authority to deal with them. These considerations do not apply in the case of entrustment of goods to non-merchants. There is no holding out by the owner, and commerce is not impeded. Admittedly, the third party may suffer a loss, but the loss derives from the fact that he thought he was dealing with an honest seller. At best the equities are even, and the loss should be divided equally between the owner and the third party, excluding, once again, any issue of negligence. However, apportionment principles have so far found little support in title cases where both parties are equally innocent.

Secondly, we have found no significant support in favour of a general adoption of the civil law principle; nor do we know enough about its practical operation in those jurisdictions that have adopted this principle. Finally, there is no evidence that conversions by simple bailees constitute a significant problem.[124] Other than in a business context, it is not customary to entrust valuable goods to complete strangers. If the bailee has a fixed place of business — a warehouseman, for example, or a drycleaner — he has little to gain by becoming dishonest. He can be caught too easily. Moreover, the goods are frequently of a used character, and have no ready market. To the extent that there is a serious risk that a professional bailee will dishonestly dispose of the goods, a preferable route would be to protect *both* the owner and the third party by imposing licensing or bonding requirements, or both.

There is one possible qualification to the above observations. This qualification concerns goods, particularly motor vehicles, entrusted under a conditional sale or other form of security agreement to a buyer who wrongfully disposes of the goods, within or outside the province of original purchase, without disclosing the outstanding security interest. Such transactions are covered by the registration requirements of The Personal Property Security Act. It may be that third parties are not always sufficiently aware of the need to search for liens and that, as previously

---

[124] We are aware, of course, that there is a high incidence of theft (in the common law sense, as opposed to the definition in section 283 of the Canadian Criminal Code) of goods of many kinds. For example, the Metropolitan Toronto Police *Annual Statistical Report (1973)*, indicates that in 1973, 6714 automobiles and trucks, 359 motorcycles and snow vehicles, and 8219 bicycles were stolen in Toronto. But this has no bearing on the allocation of risk arising from the entrustment of goods, and raises an entirely different issue.

discussed, the registration mechanism may need improvement. In any event, we do not think this particular problem provides sufficient justification for any general reversal of the *nemo dat* doctrine. Rather, it should be resolved within the context of The Personal Property Security Act.

The Commission was not persuaded that there was a need for a special rule governing retail buyers or that, as recommended by the Law Reform Committee, retail merchants should be able to pass good title to stolen goods. The Commission gave the following reasons (Report, pp. 312-13):

> The English Law Reform Committee apparently accepted the same principle as part of its wider proposal concerning sales at retail premises, but with one important restriction. A majority of the Committee recommended that section 22(1) of the U.K. Sale of Goods Act should be replaced by a provision to the effect that a person who buys goods by retail at trade premises or by public auction acquires a good title, provided he buys in good faith and without notice of any defect or want of title on the part of the apparent owner. The Committee recommended that "trade premises" should be defined as "premises open to the public at which goods of the same or a similar description to those sold are normally offered for sale by retail in the course of business carried on at those premises". It would therefore appear that a wide range of commercial transactions would be excluded from the Committee's recommendation. The Committee offered no reason for excluding such transactions, other than the common law concept of "market overt". In our view, the proposal of the Committee restricting protection to those who purchase at retail premises would create a new set of anomalies. We do not, therefore, favour this approach. Accordingly, we recommend that the revised Act contain an additional exception to the *nemo dat* rule, along the lines of UCC 2-403(2) and (3), in the case of entrustment of goods to a merchant. Our Draft Bill so provides. In light of this recommendation it will be necessary, as mentioned earlier, to review The Factors Act with a view to determining the desirability of its retention. We so recommend.
>
> A second aspect of the recommendation of the English Law Reform Committee concerns the sale of lost or stolen goods. As will have been noted, UCC 2-403(2) is based on a concept of entrustment, not on a principle of *market overt*, and therefore does not apply where the goods sold by the merchant are stolen from, or lost by, the owner. On the other hand, the recommendation of the Law Reform Committee to extend the concept of *market overt* to sales at retail premises would include the sale of lost or stolen goods. The civil law jurisdictions that have adopted the *possession vaut titre* principle are divided on this issue. Apparently only Italy fully protects the *bona fide* purchaser against the owner's claim. France and Quebec and other Civil Code systems that follow the Napoleonic model entitle the owner to recover the goods in the hands of a *bona fide* purchaser; but the owner is obliged to reimburse the purchaser the price he paid for the goods, if the purchaser bought the goods from a merchant acting in ordinary course, or in a similar commercial context. The status of stolen goods attracted intensive discussion among the Committee of Experts considering the draft Uniform International Law on the Protection of the *Bona Fide* Purchaser. The original draft made no exception to the *possession vaut titre* principle for stolen goods. The June 1974 version reversed the position; a majority of the delegates were apprehensive that an unqualified principle might encourage trafficking in stolen goods, particularly works of art. As a result, Article II of the final text provides that the "transferee of stolen movables cannot invoke his good faith".

Given the divided voices within the civilian world, it is a little surprising that the English Law Reform Committee should have voted in favour of extending its modernized *market overt* concept to stolen goods. It seems to us to be difficult to justify the proposal, and it is open to a large number of objections. Ontario has never adopted the *market overt* principle, even in its restricted common law form, and it would be anomalous if the Province were now to embrace it on a much more extended basis. We do not, therefore, recommend adoption of the Committee's proposal.

C. BULK SALES LEGISLATION

Introductory Note:

Bulk sales legislation is a North American phenomenon which is unknown in England and other parts of the Commonwealth. As Mr. Catzman points out in the article following this note, the legislation originated in the U.S. and was then copied in Canada. In both countries its object was (and remains) the protection of creditors of a business which might otherwise be sold without the creditors' claims being satisfied. It therefore differs fundamentally from the exceptions to the *nemo dat* rule considered in the previous part of this chapter, whose purpose is to enable a buyer, in the prescribed circumstances, to obtain a better title than his seller had. Bulk sales legislation, in contrast, seeks to prevent a buyer obtaining a good title unless he complies with the statutory requirements. In Canada the requirements generally are that the buyer of the business must satisfy himself either that there are no creditors (or no claims exceeding in the aggregate a prescribed amount) or to require him to use the purchase money to satisfy their claims.

As will readily be apparent, bulk sales legislation raises important questions of policy and many questions of detail. Mr. Catzman's article should be studied in conjunction with the Bulk Sales Act, RSO 1970, c. 52. In 1962 the Conference of Commissioners on Uniformity of Legislation in Canada (now known as the Uniform Law Conference) adopted a Uniform Bulk Sales Act. The Act has been enacted, with or without modification or by provisions with similar effect, in Alberta, Manitoba, New Brunswick, Newfoundland, Nova Scotia, Prince Edward Island, the Yukon and the North West Territories. In the U.S., Article 6 of the Code now supersedes prior state legislation on bulk sales in those states that have adopted the Article. Article 6 differs significantly in approach and detail from the Ontario Act. For a succinct description of the Code provisions, see J.J. White and R.S. Summers, *Uniform Commercial Code*, ch. 19.

CATZMAN
"Bulk Sales in Ontario"
(1960) 3 Can. Bar J. 28-38

Legislation governing bulk sales was first introduced in the provinces of Canada after the turn of the present century. It was borrowed from American legislation, there being no counterpart in English law. Uniformity of legislation in Canada was instituted in 1918 when the Conference of Uniformity of Legislation was formed and one of its projects was to prepare a Uniform Bulk Sales Act. The present Uniform Bulk Sales Act was adopted by the Commission in 1950. It has undergone and is still under continual study and revision. A number of suggestions contained in a paper which I was privileged to present to the annual meeting of The Canadian Bar Association at Toronto in 1950 have since been adopted and incorporated in the current draft. In one form or another the uniform statute has been enacted in the provinces of Alberta, British Columbia, Manitoba, New Brunswick, Prince Edward Island and the North West Territories.

In Ontario, bulk sales legislation was first enacted in 1917 and, except for one amendment in 1933, continued in force until last year insulated from the spirit of reform which permeated its sister provinces.

About a year ago Ontario decided to review its outmoded Bulk Sales Act and to join the march of progress. The writer was requested in collaboration with other interested groups, notably the Commercial Law Sub-section of Ontario of this Association, to draft new legislation. The terms of reference quite logically and properly provided that the current draft act prepared by the Commissioners of Uniformity of Legislation (which is termed "the model act") should serve as a foundation for any new legislation. However, it is fair to say, that in carrying out the mandate of Legislative Counsel of Ontario to prepare a new act, we introduced many innovations and changes in policy and draftsmanship so that our draft varied considerably from the model act.

• • •

Time will not permit an exhaustive analysis of the Ontario Bulk Sales Act 1959. I am therefore, constrained to review in brief the major principles embodied in the Act and to highlight the areas where they deviate from existing legislation.

I propose to deal with these under the following topics:

1. Scope of the Act
2. Creditors
3. Completion of Sale
4. Deposit
5. Trustee
6. Notice of Sale and Limitations
7. Consequences of Non-Compliance
8. Distribution of Proceeds of Sale.

SCOPE OF THE ACT

The scope of the Act is defined in section 2 which reads as follows:

> **2.** This act applies to every sale in bulk except a sale in bulk by an executor, an administrator, a receiver, an assignee or trustee for the benefit of creditors, a trustee under the Bankruptcy Act (Canada), a liquidator or official receiver, or a public official acting under judicial process.

Thus we begin with the principle that the Act is of general application to all bulk sales. The policy embodied in the model act of setting out a catalogue of businesses which are governed by the Act has been rejected. Any catalogue of businesses tends rapidly to become outdated by the variety of business changes generated by the ingenuity of the entrepreneur. Thus, for example, it was found necessary in British Columbia last year to amend the Bulk Sales Act by adding to the catalogue of businesses set forth in section 3 the words "motels, auto courts, apartment houses" (see B.C. 1958 Statutes, Chapter 6, Section 2).

The exclusion in the model act of "sales by a trader or merchant selling exclusively by wholesale" was omitted as anomalous in that it restricts the Act to the control of fraud at the retail level but not on a wholesale scale. It is a perversion of the established doctrine *de minimis non curat lex*.

The definitions of "sale", "sale in bulk", "stock" and "stock in bulk" which determine the scope of the Act have been considerably revised. Since these definitions do not accord with those in the model act, it is useful to note wherein they vary and I propose to deal with these variations from the viewpoint of their enlargement and contraction of the scope of the model act and the Old Ontario Act.

The scope of the Act is expanded
(1) by making the Act of general rather than limited application as previously explained;
(2) by including mixed sales of "stock" (as defined) with other property. Thus, if the subject matter of the sale is a business together with the realty in which it is conducted, or a sale of stock coupled with a transfer and assignment of leases, accounts receivable, franchises, patents, copyrights, good will or other intangible assets, the whole subject matter of the sale is governed by the Act. This eliminates the doctrine of severability which was applied by the Courts in the *Canadian Credit Mens Trust Association* v. *Westerguard* (1951) 1 WWR 822, New Series, wherein, in a mixed sale of land and chattels, the Court allowed evidence to be adduced to apportion the lump sum consideration for the sale, so as to validate the sale of the land and invalidate the sale of the chattels. Under the Ontario Act, the transaction must stand or fall as a whole and is not severable;
(3) by including in the definition of "sale" the words "barter or exchange" which, under the old Ontario Act, were held to be excluded as there was nothing in the nature of purchase moneys involved;
(4) by omitting from section 3 of the old Act the words "for cash or on credit" to avoid the implication that sales that are made partly for cash and partly on credit are not covered by the Act, and likewise that sales, where the consideration consists of neither cash nor credit, as in the case of a voluntary conveyance, or extinguishment of debt, do not fall within the ambit of the statute;
(5) by substituting "a person" for "he" in section 1(k)(iii) which now reads "the fixtures, goods and chattels with which a person carries on trade or business". The Act is thus extended to include equipment which the seller never used or discontinued using in the conduct of his business (see *Bank of Montreal* v. *Ideal Knitting Mills* (1924) 55 OLR 410). It is designed to plug the loophole whereby the seller could circumvent the

Act in two easy stages — first, by ceasing to use the equipment, and thereafter, by selling it off without restraint.

The scope of the Act is contracted as follows:

(1) by excluding sales of "an interest in business" through the elimination of these words from the definitions of "sale" and "seller". This amendment is in line with a judicial decision which held that a sale by a partner of his partnership share is not a sale of stock and that creditors are not affected thereby;

(2) by eliminating the words "or whenever substantially the entire stock of the vendor is sold and conveyed" from the definition of "sale in bulk" which are at best redundant and at worst ambiguous and confusing;

(3) by specifically excluding from the definition of sale "a pledge, charge or mortgage" on the theory that legitimate borrowing should not be hampered and does not properly come within the vice which the Act is designed to control.

There are two additional features which might be considered as indirectly contracting the scope of the Act.

(1) Section 3 provides for judicial exemption of a sale in bulk from the application of the Act where the judge is satisfied that the sale is advantageous to the seller and will not impair his ability to pay his creditors in full. It is intended to mitigate the rigour of the Act in those cases where strict compliance with the Act would be onerous, cumbersome or pointless, as, for example, where a substantial chain store owner disposes of one of his units, or a solvent manufacturer clears out obsolete or surplus merchandise, or discontinued or broken lines.

(2) Section 9, subsection 1, provides that where the seller has delivered to the buyer the statutory statement of creditors (Form 1) and has given notice of the intended sale by publication in the Ontario Gazette, and such statement discloses that the claims of the secured and unsecured trade creditors of the seller do not exceed a total of $5,000.00 (and the buyer has nò notice to the contrary), the buyer may pay the sale price to the seller and thereupon acquire the property of the seller in the stock in bulk.

This provision is designed to relieve against compliance with the formalities prescribed by the Act where, either the transaction is a comparatively small one, or, even if the transaction is substantial, the seller's debts to the trade are comparatively small.

CREDITORS

The Act differentiates between three classes of creditors:

(a) unsecured trade creditors (defined in S. 1(m));

(b) secured trade creditors (defined in S. 1(h)); and

(c) creditors generally (defined in S. 1(c)).

The purpose of this distinction can best be demonstrated by reference to the operative sections of the Act.

Thus, section 4 which requires the buyer to demand and receive from the seller a statement of creditors, limits the contents of the statement to a list of his secured and unsecured trade creditors. Eliminated from the statement are:

(a) non-trading creditors;
(b) persons with contingent claims;
(c) sureties and endorsers.

Their consents are no longer required to the completion of a sale or to the appointment of a trustee nor are their claims included in computing the majority of creditors required to consent to a sale. It should be noted, however, that where a trustee is appointed to receive and distribute the proceeds of sale, the statement of affairs prescribed by the Act requires the inclusion of all of the seller's creditors (including those not of a strictly trading character) (see Form 4) and they are entitled to share in the distribution of the proceeds of sale (Section 13). Similarly the right to demand particulars of the sale is extended to all creditors (S. 8).

In order further to trace the distinction made in the Act between the various classes of creditors, it is useful to pass on to the next topic — completion of sale.

COMPLETION OF SALE

Section 9 of the Act deals with completion of sale. It is divided into two main subsections, both of which are subject to the conditions that, prior thereto, the seller has delivered to the buyer a statement of creditors (S. 4), and has caused notice of the proposed sale to be published in the Ontario Gazette (S. 7).

Under subsection 1, the buyer may pay the seller the price (without the intervention of a trustee) and, by the express language of the statute, thereupon acquire the property of the seller in the stock in bulk in any of these three circumstances.

(a) if the claims of the secured and unsecured trade creditors do not exceed $5,000.00 (as disclosed in the statement of the seller, and the buyer has no notice to the contrary);
(b) if the seller produces evidence that the claims of all secured and unsecured trade creditors of which the buyer has notice have been paid in full.

    This contemplates a situation where the seller, having delivered a statement which disclosed claims of secured and unsecured creditors in excess of $5,000.00, has, before completion of sale, paid them in full. You will observe that it is not open to the seller to make partial payment to reduce the total of such claims under $5,000.00 and thereby to avoid the appointment of a trustee to receive the proceeds of sale. This might encourage fraudulent preferences and inequitable distribution;

(c) if adequate provision has been made for the immediate payment in full of all claims of the unsecured trade creditors of the seller of which the buyer has notice and of all claims of secured creditors of the seller which are or become due and payable upon completion of the sale of which the buyer has notice, so long as their claims are paid in full forthwith after completion of the sale, but, where any such creditor has delivered a waiver (Form 2), no provision need be made for the immediate payment of his claim.

This provision enables a buyer, instead of paying his purchase price to a trustee, to withhold from the purchase price an amount sufficient to pay off the claims of all unsecured trade creditors and those secured creditors whose claims have matured or whose claims are accelerated by virtue of the sale. The purchaser acquires the protection of the Act only if, in fact, he does forthwith after the sale pay such claims in full, except where the creditor delivers a written waiver dispensing with immediate payment. You will observe that the waiver of a creditor applies only to his own claim. We have eliminated the provision that waivers by a majority of creditors affect the claims of the minority who do not deliver waivers. Each creditor binds only himself. It should also be noted that, if the claim of the secured trade creditor is not or does not become (by virtue of any acceleration clause in the instrument which secures the debt) payable upon completion of sale, no provision need be made for its immediate payment. The buyer assumes the debt to be paid in accordance with the proviso for repayment precisely as in the case of a buyer of an equity in real property.

Under subsection 2, the buyer may pay the proceeds of sale to a trustee and thereupon acquire the property of the seller in the stock in bulk if the seller delivers to the buyer the following two documents.

(a) the written consent of unsecured trade creditors of the seller representing not less than 60% in number and amount of the claims that exceed $50.00 (of which the buyer has notice); and

(b) an affidavit of the seller that he has delivered to all his secured and unsecured trade creditors at least 14 days before the date fixed for completion of the sale
(i) copies of the contract of the sale in bulk;
(ii) the statutory statement of creditors;
(iii) a statement of affairs (in prescribed form — Form 4) with an affidavit that his affairs have not materially changed since it was made.

In this connection the following observations should be made.

The required consents are limited to unsecured trade creditors and are similarly limited to the appointment of the trustee. Secured trade creditors have been excluded on the grounds that, either, being secured, they will be unaffected by an improvident sale and may readily consent to it, or that, being secured, they have no interest in consummating the sale and may withhold consent to an advantageous sale and thereby jeopardize its approval. Consequently, provision for the valuation of securities by secured trade creditors has been eliminated as superfluous. The delays involved in valuing security and in disposing of any appeal from such valuation might jeopardize a pending sale, and it was concluded that it would not be unreasonable to bind all secured creditors (including those who are or consider themselves to be imperfectly secured) by the wishes of the majority of the unsecured trade creditors who have a real stake in the sale.

The seller is required to make full disclosure in advance of the sale of all the terms of the contract of sale so that, if the sale is considered improvident, an opportunity is given to institute bankruptcy proceedings against the seller and thereby to frustrate the sale. The seller must also make full disclosure of his affairs, and your attention is directed to Form 4 which requires the statement of affairs to reflect the seller's financial position as at a date not more than thirty days before the date of the affidavit to ensure that it is reasonably current.

Section 6, subsection 2 of the old Ontario Act has been eliminated for reasons which should be self-evident. It read as follows:

> Where the total amount of any sale in bulk is for a sum less than an amount sufficient to pay 60 per cent of the claims of all creditors of the vendor, from the proceeds of such sale, or where the term of payment extends beyond one year from the date of purchase and sale and there is not sufficient to pay 60 per cent of the claims of all the creditors of the vendor within the year, then in all such cases the sale shall be deemed to be fraudulent and void as against the creditors of the vendor; provided that a sale shall not be liable to be set aside or declared void under this Act, if the vendor submits to his creditors a statement of his affairs at the time of the proposed sale, verified by a statutory declaration of the vendor or his authorized agent, or if the vendor is a corporation, by the declaration of the president, secretary-treasurer or manager of the corporation, and thereafter produces and delivers to the purchaser the written waiver from his creditors having claims of $50 and over, representing 60 per cent in number and value of the claims of $50 and over.

DEPOSIT

The old Ontario Act imposed a limit of $50.00 on the amount permitted to be paid by way of deposit on account of purchase price (Section 2). The model act increased it to "a sum not exceeding five per cent of the purchase price or five hundred dollars, whichever is the lesser amount." (Section 5(5)). We have increased it further to "a sum not exceeding ten per cent of the purchase price" (Section 6) but at the same time have impressed the amount paid as a deposit with a trust, so that the seller holds the same in trust

> (a) for the buyer until completion of sale, or, if the sale is not completed and the buyer becomes entitled to repayment of it, until it is repaid by the buyer; or
> (b) where the sale is completed and a trustee has been appointed, for the trustee until the seller complies with clause (b) of section 11 (which requires the seller to pay the amount of the deposit to the trustee). (Section 6)

It was felt that the amount permitted to be paid by way of deposit should be enlarged so as to serve the twofold purposes of a deposit, namely, evidence of the buyer's good faith, and adequate security for the completion by him of the contract of purchase. Yet, at the same time, it was felt that the buyer should be accorded some protection to recover his deposit if the seller repudiates the contract or is adjudged bankrupt before completing it.

THE TRUSTEE

For some curious reason, the appointment of the trustee was covered (in unintelligible language) in the definition section of the old Ontario Act (S. 1(e)) and in somewhat more understandable language in the model act. The new Act contains a substantive section (Section 10) which deals with the manner of his appointment and the security to be given by him. As previously indicated, the trustee is appointed by the seller with the consent of 60% of his unsecured trade creditors. Some consideration was given to limiting the eligibility of trustees to those licensed under the Bankruptcy Act, but was abandoned because of valid objections that, outside of the large urban centres, such limitation might impose serious hardships.

It may be relevant at this point to draw your attention to the following additional provisions in the new Ontario Act relating to trustees:

(1) "Upon notice to the trustee within thirty days after the date of the filing of the documents mentioned in section 12 that a petition for a receiving order against the seller has been filed, the trustee shall not distribute the proceeds of the sale until the final disposition of the petition and, where a receiving order is made pursuant to the petition, the trustee shall pay the proceeds of the sale, after deducting therefrom his fee and disbursements, to the trustee appointed by the receiving order." (Section 13(3))

(2) The schedule of fees payable to trustees has been revised and is fully set out in section 15.

(3) The right to bring an action or proceeding to set aside or have declared void a sale in bulk has been conferred upon the trustee in bankruptcy of the estate of the seller, if the seller is adjudged bankrupt. (Section 18)

(4) Provision has been made that, "where the proceeds of sale exceed the amount required to pay in full all indebtedness of the seller to his creditors, the fee of the trustee together with any disbursements made by the trustee shall be deducted by him from the excess proceeds to the extent of that excess". (Section 15(3)). This eliminates the absurd provision in the old Ontario Act that the fees of the trustee "shall in no event be charged to the debtor".

In passing, may I deal with the problem of solicitor's costs of completing sale. In bankruptcy the sale of assets is made by the trustee and the costs of his solicitor constitute a proper disbursement in the administration of the estate. In a bulk sale, the trustee is not appointed until the sale has been completed. Accordingly, the definition of "proceeds of sale" has been amended by adding thereto the words "less the proper and reasonable costs of the seller's solicitor for completing the sale". (Section 1(e)). This provides for a deduction by the seller at source out of the purchase price of the amount required to pay the solicitor who might otherwise have to rank as a creditor.

NOTICE OF SALE AND LIMITATIONS

A glaring deficiency in the old Ontario Act was the failure to require notice to creditors of the bulk sale by registration or otherwise, and further, in imposing a limitations period to set aside the sale of 60 days from the date of the sale or from the date when the creditor attacking the sale first received notice thereof. (Section 8). The model act purported to remedy this latter defect by extending the period of limitations to "six months from the date of the completion of the sale". (Section 12).

The new Act requires the buyer within five days after the completion of sale to file in the office of the Court of the County or District where the seller's stock is located or where he carries on business an affidavit setting out the particulars of the sale and the name and address of the trustee and exhibiting thereto duplicate originals of the following documents:

 (i) the bill of sale;
 (ii) the statement of creditors;
 (iii) the affidavit proving publication of notice of sale in the Ontario Gazette;
 (iv) the statement, if any, that the claims of all unsecured and secured trade creditors have been paid in full;
 (v) the waivers, if any, of unsecured and secured creditors of their right to receive immediate payment of their claims upon completion of sale;
 (vi) the consent of unsecured trade creditors to the appointment of the trustee;
 (vii) the affidavit of the seller that he has delivered notice of the sale and statement of his affairs in advance of the sale. (Section 12)

Provision is made for the extension of the time limited for filing these documents, and conversely, upon failure of the buyer to file them, to compel him to do so.

The Act also includes a general provision that "any creditor of a seller is entitled to demand of the seller or the buyer, in which case, the seller or the buyer, as the case may be, shall forthwith deliver to the creditor, particulars in writing of the sale in bulk." (Section 8)

In the light of the foregoing, you will better appreciate the limitations section which requires action to be brought "within six months from the date on which the documents were filed under section 12". (Section 20)

You might also note that notice is required to be given of a proposed sale by publication in the Ontario Gazette so as to enable creditors to give the buyer notice of their claims. (Section 7(1)). No sale may be completed until after the expiry of at least five days following such publications (Section 7(2)). I entertain some doubt as to the value of this section in that it entails delay in completing a sale, and provides for notice in a manner which is not likely to come to the attention of creditors generally. It has been urged, however, that this requirement may deter a dishonest seller from delivering a false affidavit that he has no creditors, and that, where a trustee is appointed, it is better to require publication in the Gazette before completion of sale than after, as provided in the model act. (Section 8(4)).

CONSEQUENCES OF NON-COMPLIANCE

The only penalty imposed on a buyer for violating the requirements of the old Ontario Act was to render the transaction liable to be declared void as against creditors if it was attacked within the statutory period of limitations. This remedy usually proved ineffectual, as the subject matter of the sale was, in the meantime, dissipated.

The new Act provides that "if the buyer has received or taken possession of the stock in bulk he is personally liable to account to the creditors of the seller for the value thereof, including all moneys, security or property realized or taken by him, from, out of or on account of, the sale or other disposition by him of the stock in bulk. (Section 17). The burden of proof that the Act has been complied with is upon the person upholding the sale in bulk. (Section 19).

As previously stated, an action to enforce the consequences of non-compliance may be maintained by a trustee in bankruptcy who probably is better equipped than any individual creditor with a war-chest know-how and zeal to prosecute such an action.

DISTRIBUTION OF PROCEEDS OF SALE

The old Ontario Act provided that the proceeds of sale should be distributed in accordance with the provisions of the Assignments and Preferences Act. (Section 4). This Act has fallen into disuse and no one seems to know precisely what it provides. It differs from the Bankruptcy Act in at least one important respect in that the preferential claim of the landlord is limited to arrears of rent. It was deemed advisable to avoid any disparity between distribution under a bulk sale and bankruptcy. Accordingly, the new Act provides that the proceeds of sale shall be distributed in accordance with the provisions of the Bankruptcy Act with one notable exception. Section 95(e) of the Bankruptcy Act which deals with the claims of municipalities for taxes is poorly worded, and, understandably, the Bankruptcy Act, being federal legislation, assigns to claims of municipalities a lower place on the totem pole than the claims of Her Majesty in the right of the Dominion. Through the alertness of the Deputy City solicitor of Toronto, the municipalities (which are creatures of the Province) have been upgraded in priority under the Ontario Act by the enactment of section 14 which provides:

Nothing in this Act affects the rights of any municipality under the Assessment Act.

I am not too certain of the effect of this section, but I am advised and verily believe that it will be unsafe for trustees to make any distribution of the proceeds of a bulk sale until the claims of municipalities are paid in full.

I have previously mentioned that, although the Act makes a distinction between unsecured trade creditors and secured trade creditors, and other creditors, for the purposes of distribution all creditors are included.

Chapter 11
Buyer's Obligations and Seller's Remedies for Buyer's Breach

1. Introduction

Compared to the seller's obligations, the buyer's obligations in a typical cash sale are relatively simple and straightforward. His obligations are to accept delivery of the goods in accordance with the contractual terms, express or implied, and to pay for the goods. See SGA ss. 26-7.

As in the case of any other creditor, the seller's overriding concern is to procure payment of the goods or damages in lieu thereof. The position differs fundamentally depending on whether we are dealing with a cash sale or a credit sale. (''Cash sale'' is not a term of art but means a sale where payment is required on or before delivery of the goods: *cf.* SGA s. 27). The present chapter is only concerned with cash sales. The seller's rights and remedies in secured credit sales are dealt with *infra*, chapter 24.

Even in cash sales the position is not as simple as one might suppose. The SGA distinguishes between the seller's ''real'' rights and his ''personal'' remedies. Real rights are those which the seller may exercise against the goods and consist of the right to detain the goods, stoppage *in transitu*, and the right to resell for non-payment. See SGA s. 37-46. The first and third rights are still of great practical importance; stoppage *in transitu* on the other hand has lost much of its practical impact because of faster modes of transportation, modern credit techniques, and the ubiquitous use of letters of credit in international sales transactions.

As far as personal remedies are concerned, the seller will always be entitled to sue for damages. As in the converse case of damage claims by the buyer, the recoverable measure of damages will be governed by the rules in *Hadley* v. *Baxendale*. See SGA s. 48(2). The difference is that the seller will rarely seek to recover consequential damages (why not?), although in principle he should be entitled to do so. If there is an ''available market'' for the goods, the seller's damages will prima facie be governed by SGA s. 48(3). The seller would prefer of course to be able to sue for the price (because that spares him the onus of proving damages and disposing of the goods) but his right to do so depends on the circumscribed rules of s. 47. Finally, the seller may also be entitled to forfeit any deposit or part payments already made by the buyer and this may satisfy the seller if he has suffered only nominal damages. The table following this note illustrates in simplified form the seller's alternative remedies in the principal types of situation. The reader will note the heavy hand of property concepts in determining the seller's right of specific performance, i.e., to sue for the price.

SELLER'S REMEDIES FOR NON-PAYMENT OF PRICE (CASH SALES)

Real Rights   **Personal Remedies**

A. WHERE GOODS NOT YET IN BUYER'S POSSESSION

(1)   *Property has passed:*

(a) Vendor's lien: s. 39	(a) Action for price: s. 47(1)
(b) Stoppage *in transitu:* s. 42	(b) Acceptance of buyer's repudiation and rescission of contract:
(c) Right of resale: s. 46	i) claim for damages: s. 48(1)
	ii) forfeiture of deposit or part payment. Cf. SGA s. 57

(2)   *Property has not passed but goods are specific or ascertained:*

(a) Vendor's right of retention: s. 38(2)	(a) No action for price unless s. 47(2) applies
(b) Stoppage *in transitu:* s. 42	(b) Same as in (1)
(c) Right of resale: s. 46	

Sale of future or unascertained goods:

No real rights because no goods have been appropriated to the contract.	(a) Same as in (2)
	(b) Same as in (1)

B. WHERE GOODS IN BUYER'S POSSESSION

No statutory right to reclaim goods; seller's rights depend on terms of contract unless buyer has procured goods by fraudulent means.

(a)   Same as in (1)

Common Payment Terms in Ontario Manufacturing Contracts*

		Always or Often	% Mid	Rarely or Never
(a)	Payment in advance of delivery in one lump sum	0.4	8.0	91.2
(b)	Payment in instalments in advance of delivery as work on order progresses	2.3	14.1	83.7
(c)	Payment on delivery	3.9	31.6	64.6
(d)	Payment within 30 days of delivery	82.3	15.2	2.5
(e)	Payment within 60 days of delivery	13.4	28.3	58.3
(f)	Payment more than 60 days after delivery	1.8	15.8	82.5
(g)	Payment in instalments (types of usual arrangements to be detailed)	3.4	13.9	82.7
(h)	Other	5.5	4.9	89.7

Note on Documentary Draft Sales:

Even in Chalmers' day, except in retail sales, face to face sales were declining in importance in favour of shipment contracts, and the importance of shipments to a distant point has grown apace since then. In such circumstances, how is the seller to ensure in a cash sale that the goods are not released to the buyer without payment? If the seller uses his own carrier (an uncommon procedure in Canada for out of town shipments) there is no problem: he will simply instruct the driver to require cash on delivery. Theoretically, the C.O.D. method could also be applied to an independent carrier in inland transportation but apparently it is not used widely.

Instead, since the last century the more common method has been for the carrier to issue a bill of lading to the order of the seller. The seller endorses the bill of lading and forwards it through his bank to an agent (also usually a bank) located in the city of the

---

* Source: OLRC Sale of Goods Project. (The headings in the original table have been changed slightly.)

buyer's place of business. Attached to the bill of lading will be the seller's draft on the buyer for the price of the goods — a "sight" draft if payment is due on presentment of the draft; a "time" draft if payment is due at a later date. The agent will be authorized to release the bill of lading, and any other documents incidental thereto, on acceptance of the draft by the buyer in the case of a time draft and payment thereof if it is a sight draft. Documentary draft sales are no longer common in Canada in domestic sales, but they still retain their importance in overseas sales, usually in conjunction with letter of credit payment arrangements.

A distinctive feature of such documentary sales requiring payment against documents of title is that, by the express or implied terms of the parties' agreement, the buyer is not entitled to inspect the goods before payment of the price, whether or not the goods are available for inspection at the time. *Cf.* UCC 2-513(3), 2-319(4), 2-320(4); *E. Clemens Horst Co.* v. *Biddell Bros.* [1912] AC 18. This is a necessary provision because ordinarily the documents are presented to the buyer or his agent well before the goods reach their destination and the seller wants his money promptly. It also means however that the buyer runs the risk that the goods may be defective, although he can protect himself by requiring a "certificate of inspection" of the goods from an independent appraiser at the place of shipment as a condition of his payment. "Stand-by" letters of credit in favour of the buyer are also popular in export agreements with some Middle Eastern countries. See further *infra*, chapter 19(E).

The documentary sale therefore ensures that the seller does not lose control of the goods before he has been paid; it does not however ensure payment itself if the buyer has lost interest in the goods or has become insolvent. The seller would then have to try and find an alternate buyer for goods that may have no ready market and that are located perhaps thousands of miles from the point of shipment. It is the office of the letter of credit to insulate the seller from such not inconsiderable risks in overseas trade. The salient features of letter of credit law are examined *infra*, chapter 19. In the post-war period the governments of many exporting countries have become heavily involved in providing export credit insurance and guarantee facilities to their exporters where the importer is not able or willing to pay cash and insists on credit terms from the exporter. In Canada, federal assistance is provided through the Export Development Corporation (EDC), a Crown instrumentality established by the Export Development Act, RSC 1970, c. E-18, as am. See further Charles E. O'Connor, "Payment and Financing Mechanisms in International Trade", in *New Dimensions in International Trade Law* (Can. Bar Assoc. — Ontario and Univ. of Toronto, Joint Programme, Nov. 14, 1980).

COLLEY v. OVERSEAS EXPORTERS
[1921] 3 KB 302, [1921] All ER Rep. 596

McCARDIE J.: This action is brought upon a writ specially indorsed within Order XIV to recover the sum of 985*l*. 17*s*. 4*d*. alleged to be due from the defendants to the plaintiff as the price of goods. The only question is whether that liquidated sum is due. No question arises as yet as to damages against the defendants. The case raises a point of legal interest and practical utility as to the circumstances under which the purchase price of goods can be sued for. The facts are not in dispute. They can be briefly stated. The plaintiff is a leather merchant at Sheffield.

The defendants are merchants at Sheffield. On December 17, 1920, the plaintiff sold to the defendants a quantity of leather belting of stated sizes and qualities and at certain prices "F.O.B. Liverpool." The goods were not specific within the definition clause (s. 62) of the Sale of Goods Act, 1893. They were unascertained at the date of the bargain. On January 26, 1921, the defendants sent shipping instructions to the plaintiff. These directed that the goods should be packed for export and marked as ordered, and then said: "S/S. *Kenuta*. Closing despatch 2/2/21 and 5/2/21. Consign to Alexandra Dock Station, Liverpool, c/o Daniel Maccabe, Ltd., 17 Brunswick St., Liverpool, advising them of despatch." On February 3 the plaintiff wrote to Maccabe, Ld., who are shipping agents at Liverpool: "We have to day despatched by the Great Central Railway Co. (Alexandra Dock Station) to S/S. *Kenuta* to the order of Overseas Exporters Ltd. of Sheffield 7 cases of leather belting." The goods left Sheffield and reached their destination in Liverpool to be dealt with by Maccabe, Ld., in order to carry out the plaintiff's obligation to put them on board. A series of misfortunes then occurred. The *Kenuta* was withdrawn from service by her owners, who then proposed to substitute another ship. This second ship was however inadequate for the intended voyage. Then a third vessel was put forward as a substitute, but, an accident having occurred to a fourth vessel of the same owners, the third ship had to be used to replace that damaged vessel. So a further ship was put forward — namely, *The Sorata*, which was then at Glasgow. She however could not reach Liverpool because of a strike. The result was that on April 14, 1921, the day on which the writ was issued, the goods were still unshipped and the plaintiff was still unpaid. Prior to April 13 Daniel Maccabe, Ld., sent a note of their charges, amounting to 1l. 4s., to the plaintiff, and on April 13 he gave them a cheque for that sum. He of course was responsible for these charges, as the cost of getting the goods aboard fell on him under the contract. Such are the facts. The defendants committed no deliberate breach of contract; they suffered a series of misfortunes. They failed however to name an effective ship. The plaintiff on his part did all he could to carry out his obligations. Under these circumstances the plaintiff seeks to recover the price of the goods in question. The able argument of Mr. Willes for the plaintiff rested on two well-known passages in the judgment of Lord Blackburn in *Mackay* v. *Dick* 6 App. Cas. 251, 263, 264. The first passage is this: "I think I may safely say, as a general rule, that where in a written contract it appears that both parties have agreed that something shall be done, which cannot effectually be done unless both concur in doing it, the construction of the contract is that each agrees to do all that is necessary to be done on his part for the carrying out of that thing, though there may be no express words to that effect." The second passage is this: "It would follow in point of law that the defender having had the machine delivered to him, was by his contract to keep it, unless on a fair test according to the contract it failed to do the stipulated quantity of work, in which case he would be entitled to call on the pursuers to remove it. And *by his own default* he can now never be in a position to call upon the pursuers to take back the machine, on the ground that the test had not been satisfied, he must, as far as regards that, keep, and consequently pay for it." I will consider later on the facts in *Mackay* v. *Dick*. The contention of Mr. Willes before me was that inasmuch as the defendants' own fault had here prevented the goods from being put on board they were disabled from saying that the price, which would have been payable if and when the goods had actually been put on board, was not now due to the plaintiff. This is a novel and interesting submission. An action for the price of goods is, of course, essentially an action for a liquidated sum. It involves special and technical elements. By special bargain the price of goods may be payable before delivery or before the property has passed from vendor to buyer: see *Pordage* v. *Cole* (1669) 1 Wms. Saund. 320; *Leake on Contracts*, 6th ed., pp. 487-8; *Workman, Clark & Co.* v. *Lloyd Brazileño* [1908] 1 KB 968; and s. 49 of the Sale of Goods Act, 1893. In ordinary cases and unless otherwise agreed delivery of the goods and payment of the price are concurrent conditions: see s. 28 of the Sale of Goods Act, 1893. Now the full meaning of the word "price" is not actually defined by the Sale of Goods Act, except perhaps in s. 1, which says: "A contract of sale of goods is a contract whereby the seller transfers or agrees to transfer the property in goods to the buyer for a money consideration, called the price." The circumstances however under which a claim to the price may be made (as distinguished from a claim of damages for breach of contract) are indicated in s. 49 of that Act [Ont. s. 47(1)] . . . Here sub-s. 2 of s. 49 does not apply, as it apparently did in *Workman, Clark & Co.* v. *Lloyd Brazileño* [1908] 1 KB 968, where the price was payable by stated instalments on stated dates. The parties before me here made no special agreement as to the payment of the price. Nor can it be said that sub-s. 1 of s. 49 applies here, for the property in the goods has not in fact and law passed to the buyer. Several rules for the passing of property in sale of goods contracts are indicated in ss. 16, 17, 18, and also in s. 32. The Act does not deal specifically with f.o.b. or c.i.f. contracts. Judicially settled rules exist however with respect to them. I need only deal with f.o.b. contracts. The presumed intention (see s. 18 of the Act) of the parties has been settled. It seems clear that in the absence of special agreement the property and risk in goods does not in the case of an f.o.b. contract pass from the seller to the buyer till the goods are actually put on board: see *Browne* v. *Hare* (1859) 4 H & N 822; *Inglis* v. *Stock* (1885) 10 App. Cas. 263; *Wimble* v. *Rosenberg* [1913] 3 KB 743, 747; *Benjamin on Sale*, 6th ed., p. 785, where several useful cases are collected. Unless therefore the principle involved in the words of Lord Blackburn in the second passage cited from *Mackay* v. *Dick* applies here the plaintiff will fail. Does the principle go to the extent submitted by Mr. Willes? It is well to consider *Mackay* v. *Dick*. The headnote says: "If, in the case of a contract of sale and delivery, which makes acceptance of the thing sold and payment of the price conditional on a certain thing being done by the seller, the buyer prevents the possibility of the seller fulfilling the condition, the contract is to be taken as satisfied." If this headnote be given its full apparent effect then the principle it suggests would be most far reaching, and the results extraordinary. The facts in *Mackay* v. *Dick* must be remembered. Concisely put they were these. By a contract in two letters the seller agreed to sell and deliver at the buyer's works a digging machine. The price of 1125*l*. was payable after the machine had satisfactorily performed certain tests. If it failed to perform them the buyer was to remove the machine. The machine was actually delivered into the buyer's possession. Owing however to the buyer's own default it did not perform the tests. He refused to pay the price, and the seller thereupon brought his action for the 1125*l.* The plaintiff succeeded on the principle stated by Lord Blackburn. It is to be clearly noted that a specific machine was fully delivered by the seller to the buyer. Apparently the property in the machine actually passed to the buyer. It is true that *Mackay* v. *Dick* fell to be decided by Scotch law. The decision was given by the House of Lords in 1881, twelve years before the Sale of Goods Act, 1893. Scotch law then rested on the civil law and not on English common law, and the transfer of property in goods therefore possessed special features derived from Roman jurisprudence: see *Erskine's Principles of the Law of Scotland,* 19th ed., p. 322; *Chalmers' Sale of Goods,* 8th ed., p. 9; *Brown on Sale of Goods,* 2nd ed., p. 114. It seems clear however that under Scotch law the property in the digging machine had passed to the buyer on delivery: see Erskine (*sup.*), p. 322. Hence I think that the sale and delivery of the machine must in *Mackay* v. *Dick* be deemed to have been complete, and payment of the price was therefore subject only to the "resolutive condition" imposed by the clause as to the test: see *Chalmers' Sale of Goods,* 8th ed., pp. 6, 7, and the cases there cited as to resolutive conditions. Default by the buyer as to the test was proved, and thus the seller got his judgment for the price. The actual decision in *Mackay* v. *Dick* does not therefore aid the plaintiff here. The real question is as to the extent to which the principle indicated by Lord Blackburn in the second passage I have quoted operates to make a price payable which, apart from that principle, would not be payable. Although, as I have said, *Mackay* v. *Dick* turned on Scotch law yet I think that that principle is equally well settled in English law. It has frequently been asserted in well-known text books based on English law: see *Addison on Contracts,* 11th ed., p. 624; *Leake on Contracts,* 6th ed., p. 479. In *Chitty on Contracts,* 17th ed., p. 833, the matter is put very broadly thus: "If on a contract of sale payment is conditional on a certain thing being done by the seller, and the buyer prevents the possibility of the condition being fulfilled, the seller may recover the price." So too in *Benjamin on Sale,* 6th ed., p. 641, there is this passage: "As long ago as 1787 Ashhurst J. in delivering the opinion of the King's Bench in *Hotham* v. *East India Co.* (1787) 1 TR 638, 645 said that it was evident from common sense that if the performance of a condition precedent by the plaintiff had been rendered impossible by the neglect or default of the defendant 'it is equal to performance.'" The principle moreover has been frequently applied in the Courts and is illustrated by *Braithwaite* v. *Foreign Hardwood Co.* [1905] 2 KB 543. Nowhere is that principle more luminously dealt with or the English decisions more aptly cited than in *Pollock on Contracts,* 9th ed., 294-6. It is a corollary and amplification of the rule asserted in the first passage cited by me from Lord Blackburn's judgment. This rule is recognized by the text books as embodied in English law, and has been widely applied by high tribunals as of obvious justice and convenience: see, e.g., *Sprague* v. *Booth* [1909] AC 576, 580; *Kleinert* v. *Abosso Golld Mining Co.* (1913) 58 Sol. J. 45. I respectfully followed those authorities in *Harrison* v. *Walker* [1919] 2 KB 453. Now in deciding whether the argument of Mr. Willes in this case be sound, and in determining the extent to which the principle stated in the second cited passage from Lord Blackburn may be applied, it is necessary to remember the law which existed before the Act of 1893 was passed. In former days an action for the price of goods would only lie upon one or other of two counts. First, upon the *indebitatus* count for goods sold and delivered, which was pleaded as follows: "Money payable by the defendant to the plaintiff for goods sold and delivered by the plaintiff to the defendant": *Bullen and Leake, Precedent of Pleading*, 3rd ed., p. 38. This count would not lie before delivery: *Boulter* v. *Arnott* (1833) 1 Cr. & M. 333. The count was applicable where upon a sale of goods the property had passed and the goods had been delivered to the purchaser and the price was payable at the time of action brought. Secondly, upon the *indebitatus* count for goods bargained and sold, which was pleaded as follows: "Money payable by the defendant to the plaintiff for goods bargained and sold by the plaintiff to the defendant": *Bullen and Leake*, p. 39. This count was applicable where upon a sale of goods the property had passed to the purchaser and the contract had been completed in all respects except delivery, and the delivery was not a part of the consideration for the price or a condition precedent to its payment. If the property had not passed the count would not lie: *Atkinson* v. *Bell* (1828) 8 B & C 277. In my view the law as to the circumstances under which an action will lie for the price of goods has not been changed by the Sale of Goods Act, 1893. That enactment appears to crystallise and confirm the old law: *Chalmers' Sale of Goods*, 8th ed., p. 112. By the definition clause of that Act, s. 62, "sale" is to include a bargain and sale as well as a sale and delivery. A sale or, as it is called for distinction, an executed contract of sale is a contract plus a conveyance: *Chalmers* (*sup*.), p. 8. The existing condition of the law is put in *Benjamin on Sale*, 6th ed., p. 946, where it is rightly stated that the old principles "are by implication preserved by s. 49 of the code." And the learned editor adds: "Where the property has not passed, the seller's claim must, as a general rule, be special for damages for non-acceptance." An exception to the general rule is to be found in the cases provided for by s. 49, sub-s. 2, of the code. In my opinion (subject to what I say hereafter as to estoppel) no action will lie for the price of goods until the property has passed, save only in the special cases provided for by s. 49, sub-s. 2. This seems plain both on the code and on common law principle. I have searched in vain for authority to the contrary. A clear distinction exists between cases where the default of the buyer has occurred after the property has passed and cases where that default has been before the property has passed. To the former cases *Mackay* v. *Dick* may be applied on appropriate facts. To the latter cases *Mackay* v. *Dick* does not apply so as to enable the buyer to recover the price as distinguished from damages for breach of contract. To hold that *Mackay* v. *Dick* applies where the property has not passed would lead to extraordinary results. Here the substantial allegation against the defendants is that their default prevented the plaintiff from passing the property and so entitling him to the price. Just the same default however would, in substance, have been committed if the defendants had repudiated the contract before the goods had been sent from Sheffield. So too every buyer who refuses to take delivery of unascertained goods and thereby prevents the transference of property in them from the seller commits a similar default. If the ingenious contention of Mr. Willes were correct it would be difficult to imagine a case of sale of goods, even though unascertained, to which *Mackay* v. *Dick* would not apply. The pages of *Benjamin on Sale* will afford many appropriate illustrations of this. An interesting decision on the matter is that of Atkin J. in *Stein Forbes* v. *County Tailoring Co.* (1916) 115 LT 215. There the purchasers of goods under a c.i.f. contract (payment to be net cash against documents on arrival of steamer) refused to take up the documents when ready. Atkin J. held that s. 49, sub-s. 2, of the Code did not apply, and that as the property in the goods had not passed the sellers could recover damages only and not the price.

Judgment for the defendants.

Note on UCC 2-709:

The Code's approach to the seller's entitlement to sue for the price in cash sales is very different from the SGA approach. True to its general approach, the locus of title to the goods is irrelevant and the issue is whether the buyer has accepted the goods. If he has, he is liable for the price; but if he refuses to accept the goods the seller is remitted to a claim in damages: UCC 2-709(1)(*a*); 2-708. The theory of the Code is that the seller is usually in a better position to dispose of unwanted goods than is the buyer, and that it is economically wasteful to force goods on an unwilling buyer. There is an exception to the basic rule, in the case of goods identified to the contract, if the seller is unable after reasonable effort to resell them at a reasonable price or the circumstances reasonably indicate that such effort will be unavailing: UCC 2-709(1)(*b*). It will be seen therefore that the seller's right to claim the price is put on the same footing as the buyer's right in UCC 2-716 to claim specific performance of the seller's obligation to perform.

The OLRC Sales Report, while admitting that the Code had not found the complete solution to a difficult problem, nevertheless supported the thrust of UCC 2-709. The Report's reasons were as follows (p. 417):

> We support the thrust of UCC 2-709. We appreciate that it can be argued that the Code swings the pendulum too far in the buyer's favour, and that, at least in some circumstances, the seller should be able to sue for the price even though the goods have not been accepted by the buyer. For example, there may be concern about the inadequacy of remitting the seller to a claim for damages and the dilemma that may confront him where the goods are rejected at a distant place. We believe, however, that these apprehensions can be satisfactorily answered. So far as the first point is concerned (the inadequacy of damages), at least in theory the Code's damage provisions, like those in The Sale of Goods Act, attempt to make the seller whole. The real issue is whether it is the seller or the buyer who should have the burden of disposing of the goods. The Code answers this question in terms of a balance of convenience. It may be argued that a wrongly rejecting buyer does not deserve much sympathy; but this proves too much. The argument could lead to the seller's being entitled to sue for the price even where the goods are still in his possession, and this would be even more favourable to him than the present law. So far as the second point is concerned (the rejection of goods at a distant place), UCC 2-603 comes to the seller's assistance by requiring the buyer's co-operation in disposing of the goods where the seller has no agent or place of business at the market of rejection. It is also reasonable to expect that, in such a case, a court will be more inclined to find that the goods are not readily resaleable than would be the case where the goods have never left the seller's premises.

Why would a merchant seller want to force goods for which there is a ready market on an unwilling buyer? Is the Code's approach equally apt for private sales?

R.V. WARD LTD. v. BIGNALL
[1967] 1 QB 534, [1967] 2 All ER 440 (CA)

The following statement of facts is taken from the judgment of Sellers L.J.:

In May, 1965, the plaintiff seller, wished to sell two motor vehicles, a Vanguard Estate car and a Ford Zodiac, for which, by advertisement, it was asking £395 and £490 respectively. The defendant buyer, who is a dealer in motor vehicles, saw the advertisement and on May 6, 1965, he went to Mr. Ward's private house. There he examined both the vehicles and then offered Mr. Ward, for the seller, £850 for the two, which was accepted. No log books were produced or even mentioned. The buyer paid £25 in cash and went off to get the balance of £825 in cash from his bank, and it was arranged that he would return with the balance of the price and pay it to Mrs. Ward. Whilst away the buyer had second thoughts. The Vanguard had been advertised as 1962 and the buyer thought that so to describe it was a misrepresentation or a misdescription. He told Mr. Ward that he would not, in the circumstances, proceed with the purchase. The buyer offered to pay £800 instead of the £850. That was refused. The buyer then offered to take the Zodiac alone for £500 and that was refused.

On the same day the seller consulted its solicitors. They wrote a letter to the buyer in which they quoted what the buyer had written on the back of one of the seller's cards: "A. M. Bignall Purchased Vanguard Estate Ford Zodiac for sum of £850 [signed] A. M. Bignall £25 deposit paid as seen and approved." In view of the argument before this court it is necessary to quote further from the letter. It continues:

> In view of the foregoing it is our view that ownership of the said motor cars passed to yourself. Mr. Ward further states that you left his home for the purpose of obtaining the balance of the agreed purchase price in cash, but that on your return, you informed Mrs. Ward in the absence of Mr. Ward that you did not intend to purchase the Vanguard but would only purchase the Ford which conversation you later repeated to Mr. Ward over the telephone. As mentioned above, ownership of the two cars has now passed to yourself, and all that remains is for you to collect the same, and to pay to our clients the balance of the agreed purchase price. We have advised [the seller] that a binding agreement has been made by you to purchase the said motor cars, and that failure by you to take possession thereof, and to pay the balance of the agreed purchase price will place you in breach of the said agreement, and will entitle them to recover against you by way of damages, such sum below the price agreed by you, should it be necessary to sell them elsewhere. In these circumstances please accept this letter as notice calling upon you to take delivery of the said cars and to pay the balance due of £825, on or before Tuesday next May 11, failing which our clients will consider you in breach of the said agreement, will dispose of the said motor cars for the best price they can obtain, and in the event of them receiving a price below that agreed by yourself, will look to you for the difference after giving credit for the £25 already paid by you.

The buyer did nothing except to consult a solicitor and to maintain that there had been misrepresentation.

On Oct. 12, 1965, the seller's solicitors wrote to the buyer's solicitor and, after denying that there had been any misrepresentation and pointing out that the buyer had inspected both vehicles before arriving at the contract, the letter continues:

> In an effort to mitigate the damage following [the buyer's] repudiation [the seller] sold the said Vanguard for £350 but [its] efforts to procure a purchaser for the Zodiac have been completely fruitless.

The Vanguard was sold on or about May 24, 1965, without any further communication to the buyer up to that date than the letter of May 6. The seller also endeavoured to sell the Zodiac, but it has remained unsold and in the seller's possession throughout. Apparently without any further communication between the parties, the writ in this action was taken out on Feb. 9, 1966.

That in its terms was a claim for damages, being the balance of the contract price £825 less the £350 received from the sale of the Vanguard plus £22 10s. advertising expenses in respect of the two cars since the date of the contract, a total of £497 10s. When the matter came before Deputy Judge Ellison the buyer pursued two defences. First, . . .

Secondly, the defence relied on the buyer's offer to buy the Zodiac for £500 and the seller's refusal of it and said that the seller had failed to mitigate its loss. The judgment held that this was not an unfettered offer. It was to be substituted for the contract to buy the two vehicles. This was clearly right, but judgment was thereupon entered for the seller for £497 10s. damages and costs.

DIPLOCK L.J.: This is an appeal from a judgment of the deputy county court judge at Woolwich County Court in what appeared to be a simple action for damages for non-acceptance of goods. The appeal is as to quantum of damages only. [Sellers L.J.] has already stated the facts [see above]. The main issue in the action was whether it was a term of the contract that the Vanguard should be a 1962 model. The judge held that it was not, and there is no appeal from that decision. The legal consequence of that finding was that the buyer's refusal to go on with the contract was a wrongful repudiation of the contract. The seller could elect to treat that as rescinding the contract, giving him an immediate right to damages for non-acceptance. Alternatively, he could hold the buyer to the contract. That he chose to do, and communicated his intention to the buyer both orally and by a letter written by his solicitors on May 6 which my lord has already read. That letter states the opinion of the sellers' solicitors that the property had passed to the buyer. That opinion was no doubt based on section 18, r. 1, of the Sale of Goods Act, 1893. The governing rule, however, is in section 17, and in modern times very little is needed to give rise to the inference that the property in specific goods is to pass only on delivery or payment. I think that I should have inferred that in this case: but I do not find it necessary to form any final conclusion on the matter, on which the judge made no finding.

Whether or not the property had passed on May 6, 1965, the seller was only liable to deliver upon payment or tender of the balance of the purchase price (see the Sale of Goods Act, s. 28) and was entitled until then to retain possession, either by virtue of his lien as an unpaid seller if the property had passed (Sale of Goods Act, s. 39(1)), or by virtue of his right to withhold delivery if the property had not passed (subs. (2) of the same section). In either case, the unpaid seller has a right to resell the goods if he gives notice of his intention to do so and the buyer does not within a reasonable time pay or tender the price (Sale of Goods Act, s. 48(3)). The note in the current edition of *Chalmers* that the right of resale only arises where the seller exercises his right of lien or stoppage in transitu, that is, where the property has passed to the buyer, is in my view wrong. This subsection enables a seller in possession of the goods to make time of payment of the purchase price of the essence of the contract whether the property has passed or not. The seller cannot have greater rights of resale if the property has already passed to the buyer than those which he would have if the property had remained in him.

The letter of May 6, 1965, contained notice to resell on or after May 11. Whether that was a reasonable time or not does not matter. The buyer never tendered the price, and on or before May 24 the seller resold the Vanguard for £350. He advertised the Zodiac for sale, but failed to find a buyer at the advertised price, and on October 12, 1965, offered to deliver it to the buyer against payment of £475, being the balance of the original purchase price of £850 for the two cars less the deposit of £25 and the £350 received on resale of the Vanguard car.

The letter of October 12, 1965, in which that offer was made expressed the intention of the seller to institute proceedings against the buyer for the sum of £475 "as the balance of money due and payable . . . for goods bargained and sold." When the writ was issued on February 9, 1966, however, the cause of action was not framed as an action for the balance of the purchase price under section 49(1) of the Sale of Goods Act but as an action for damages for non-acceptance under section 50(1), although the particulars of damage were inappropriate to an action for damages for non-acceptance. In the particulars of damage in the statement of claim credit was given, against the balance of the purchase price of £825, for the sum of £350 for which the Vanguard had been sold, but no credit was given for the market price of the Zodiac.

At the trial neither party, nor the judge, seems to have given his mind to the question of where the property in the Zodiac lay by that date. The only argument as to the *quantum* of damages was based on the contention that the seller ought to have mitigated his damage by accepting the buyer's offer to purchase the Zodiac alone for £500 on May 6, 1965. That contention was ill-founded. At the date of that offer the contract of sale of the two cars was still in being. The offer to buy the Zodiac alone was a proposal by the buyer to rescind that contract by mutual consent coupled with an offer to enter into a fresh contract of sale of the Zodiac alone. The seller, as he was entitled to do, refused to rescind the existing contract of sale at that date, and no question of mitigating his damages then arose. The judge appears tacitly to have accepted the view that the seller was under a duty to mitigate his damage as soon as the buyer wrongfully repudiated the contract but to have taken the view that his rejection of the buyer's offer of £500 for the Zodiac was not a breach of that duty for the reason that the seller was entitled to test the market before accepting any offer to buy either or both of the cars. The judge awarded the seller the damages which he claimed and made no allowance for the value of the Zodiac, which the seller still retains.

If the seller, at the date of the issue of the writ, had been in a position to bring an action for the balance of the purchase price and had done so, the measure of damages awarded by the judge would have been correct and the seller would have been entitled to retain possession of the Zodiac by virtue of his unpaid seller's lien until the judgment was satisfied (Sale of Goods Act, s. 43(2)). If, however, he were only in a position to claim damages for non-acceptance, which was what he did, the *prima facie* measure of his damages would be the difference between the contract price and the market price of the two cars (Sale of Goods Act, s. 50(1) and (3)), and any reasonable costs, such as those of advertising, incurred by him in reselling the cars. The onus of proving the market price of both cars lay upon the seller. The evidence of the sale of the Vanguard at £350 on May 24, 1965, was evidence of the market price of the Vanguard. Evidence of the price at which he had advertised the Zodiac but failed to sell it was some evidence that its market price was less than those figures, which ranged from £490 on May 25, 1965, to £450 on July 1, 1965. The lowest figure at which it was offered was, however, rather late in date, and in order to avoid any necessity for a new trial the parties have very sensibly agreed on a figure of £450 as the market price of the Zodiac at about the end of May, 1965. If, therefore, the seller's only right at the date of the issue of the writ on February 9, 1966, was for damages for non-acceptance, the appeal must be allowed and the damages awarded reduced by £450 from £497 10s. to £47 10s.

In this court it has been contended on behalf of the seller that, when an unpaid seller who retains possession of goods the property in which has passed to the buyer exercises his statutory right of resale under section 48(3) of the Sale of Goods Act, he does not thereby elect to treat the contract as rescinded, but remains entitled to recover the purchase price from the buyer although he must give credit for the net proceeds of sale of any of the goods which he has sold. Authority for this proposition is to be found in the judgment of Finnemore J. in *Gallagher v. Shilcock* [1949] 2 KB 765 and the question in this appeal is whether that judgment is right or not.

Finnemore J. based his conclusion on his view as to the construction of section 48 of the Sale of Goods Act, and in particular upon the contrast between the express reference in subsection (4) of section 48 to the contract being rescinded when goods are resold under an express right of resale and the absence of any reference to rescission in subsection (3) of section 48. With great respect, however, I think that that disregards basic principles of the law of contract, and that there is another explanation for the contrast between the two subsections.

Rescission of a contract discharges both parties from any further liability to perform their respective primary obligations under the contract, that is to say, to do thereafter those things which by their contract they had stipulated they would do. Where rescission occurs as a result of one party exercising his right to treat a breach by the other party of a stipulation in the contract as a repudiation of the contract, this gives rise to a secondary obligation of the party in breach to compensate the other party for the loss occasioned to him as a consequence of the rescission, and this secondary obligation is enforceable in an action for damages. Until, however, there is rescission by acceptance of the repudiation, the liability of both parties to perform their primary obligations under the contract continues. Thus, under a contract for the sale of goods which has not been rescinded, the seller remains liable to transfer the property in the goods to the buyer and to deliver possession of them to him until he has discharged those obligations by performing them, and the buyer remains correspondingly liable to pay for the goods and to accept possession of them.

The election by a party not in default to exercise his right of rescission by treating the contract as repudiated may be evinced by words or by conduct. Any act which puts it out of his power to perform thereafter his primary obligations under the contract, if it is an act which he is entitled to do without notice to the party in default, must amount to an election to rescind the contract. If it is an act which he is not entitled to do, it will amount to a wrongful repudiation of the contract on his part which the other party can in turn elect to treat as rescinding the contract.

Part IV of the Sale of Goods Act, sections 38 to 48 [Ont., ss. 37-46], deals with the rights of an unpaid seller both before the property in the goods has passed to the buyer and after it has passed. The mere fact that a seller is unpaid does not necessarily mean that the buyer is in breach of the contract, or, if he is, that his breach is one which entitles the seller to exercise his right to treat the contract as repudiated. Section 39(1) and (2) states what the unpaid seller's rights are in relation to the possession of the goods before and after the property has passed to the buyer. Subsection (1)(c) provides that he shall have "a right of resale as limited by this Act." Sections 41 to 47 deal in greater detail with the exercise by the unpaid seller of his rights in relation to the possession of the goods after the property has passed to the buyer. Section 48 [Ont., s. 46] deals with several topics. Subsection (1) reads as follows: "Subject to the provisions of this section, a contract of sale is not rescinded by the mere exercise by an unpaid seller of his right of lien . . . or stoppage in transitu."

If the contract provided for delivery upon a specified date, the seller's conduct in failing to deliver on that date would put it out of his power to perform one of his primary obligations under the contract if time were of the essence of the contract. It was, therefore, necessary, or at least prudent, to provide expressly that if his failure to deliver were in the mere exercise of a lien or right of stoppage in transitu it did not discharge his liability to deliver the goods upon tender of the contract price, or the buyer's liability to accept the goods and to pay for them.

Subsection (2) deals with a different topic, videlicet, the title of a new buyer to whom the goods are resold by the seller. If the property in the goods at the time of the resale remained in the seller, the new buyer would obtain a good title at common law and would require no statutory protection. The subsection is, therefore, limited to cases where the property in the goods at the time of resale had already passed to the original buyer, and provides that, where the seller is in possession of the goods in the exercise of his unpaid seller's lien or right of stoppage in transitu, the new buyer shall acquire a good title, and this is so whether or not the seller had a right of resale as against the original buyer.

Subsection (3) reads as follows: . . .

This is the provision of the Act which confers "a right of resale as limited by this Act," referred to in section 39(1)(c) [Ont., s. 38(1)(c)]. The right dealt with in this subsection is a right as against the original buyer. As a stipulation as to time of payment is not deemed to be of the essence of a contract of sale unless a different intention appears from the terms of the contract (Sale of Goods Act, s. 10(1)), failure by the buyer to pay on the stipulated date is not conduct by him which entitles the unpaid seller to treat the contract as repudiated. He remains liable to deliver the goods to the buyer upon tender of the contract price (Sale of Goods Act, s. 28). Apart from this subsection, if the unpaid seller resold the goods before or after the property had passed to the original buyer, he would remain liable to the original buyer for damages for non-delivery if the original buyer tendered the purchase price after the resale, and if the property had already passed to the original buyer at the time of the resale he would be liable to an alternative action by the original buyer for damages for conversion. The purpose of the subsection is to make time of payment of the essence of the contract whenever the goods are of a perishable nature, and to enable an unpaid seller, whatever the nature of the goods, to make payment within a reasonable time after notice of the essence of the contract. As already pointed out, an unpaid seller who resells the goods before the property has passed puts it out of his power to perform his primary obligation to the buyer to transfer the property in the goods to the buyer and, whether or not the property has already passed, to deliver up possession of the goods to the buyer. By making the act of resale one which the unpaid seller is entitled to perform, the subsection empowers the seller by his conduct in doing that act to exercise his right to treat the contract as repudiated by the buyer, that is, as rescinded, with the consequence that the buyer is discharged from any further liability to perform his primary obligation to pay the purchase price, and becomes subject to the secondary obligation to pay damages for non-acceptance of the goods. If the contract were not rescinded by the resale the seller would still be entitled to bring an action against the buyer for the price of the goods although, no doubt, he would have to credit the buyer with the proceeds of the resale. If that were the intention of the subsection one would have expected it to provide this in express terms. That it was not the intention is, however, apparent from the words used to define the remedy of the unpaid seller who has exercised his right of resale, videlicet, to "recover from the original buyer damages for any loss occasioned by his breach of contract." It is, of course, well-established that where a contract for the sale of goods is rescinded after the property in the goods has passed to the buyer the rescission divests the buyer of his property in the goods.

Subsection (4) deals with the consequences of a resale by a seller, not necessarily an "unpaid seller" as defined in section 38, made in the exercise of an express right of resale reserved in the contract on the buyer making default. If such an express right were exercisable after the property in the goods had passed to the buyer, its exercise might, on one view, be regarded as an alternative mode of performance of the seller's primary obligation under the contract, and the resale as being made by the seller as agent for the buyer. It was, therefore, necessary to provide expressly that the exercise of an express power of resale should rescind the original contract of sale. That is, in my view, the explanation of the express reference to rescission in subsection (4). The absence of a similar express reference to rescission in subsection (3) is no sufficient ground for ascribing to subsection (3) a meaning which the actual words of the subsection would appear to contradict and which would, in my view, conflict with the general principles of the law of contract.

In the present case the unpaid seller only resold part of the goods which he had contracted to sell to the original buyer. This makes no difference, however. His primary duty under the contract was to deliver both cars to the buyer. If he delivered only one, the buyer would be entitled to reject it (Sale of Goods Act, s. 30(1)). By his conduct in selling the Vanguard on May 24, 1965, the unpaid seller put it out of his power to perform his primary obligation under the contract. He thereby elected to treat the contract as rescinded. The property in the Zodiac thereupon reverted to him, and his only remedy against the buyer after May 24, 1965, was for damages for non-acceptance of the two cars, of which the prima facie measure is the difference between the contract price and their market value on May 24, 1965.

I, too, would allow this appeal, and enter judgment for the plaintiffs for £47 10s. instead of £497 10s.

Appeal allowed.

[Sellers L.J. delivered a separate concurring judgment; Russell L.J. concurred without giving reasons.]

Notes:

1   Why should the exercise of the seller's right of resale necessarily be regarded as a rescission of the sale? Would it not be just as logical to treat it as an enforcement of the seller's security interest? For the Code's resale provisions, see UCC 2-706.

2   How would *Ward* v. *Bignall* be decided under UCC 2-709(1)(b)? Should a court, in applying the section, permit partial specific performance of the buyer's obligation to accept and pay for the goods?

3   The OLRC Sales Report (pp. 401-03) shows that SGA s. 46 is more conspicuous for the questions it fails to answer than for the questions it does answer. Do you agree with this analysis? Consider the following questions:

   a)   Absent s. 46, would the seller be entitled to cancel the contract and/or to resell the goods at common law?

   b)   If a seller sells pursuant to the statutory provision for less than the contract price, is he entitled to sue for the difference or must he prove his damages in the ordinary way under SGA s. 48?

   c)   Is the seller free to sue for damages under SGA s. 48 and to disregard the results of a favourable sale under SGA s. 46?

   d)   If the seller has sold at a profit, should he be accountable to the buyer for the surplus?

On all of these questions and for the corresponding position under UCC 2-706, see OLRC Sales Report, pp. 401-03 and pp. 408-15.

COMMISSION CAR SALES (HASTINGS) LTD. v. SAUL
[1957] NZLR 144 (SC)

The respondent Saul entered into a contract with the appellant company for the purchase of a Plymouth motor-car at a price of £1,200. The purchase price was to be paid by the trading-in of an Oldsmobile motor-car which was valued at £300 and was also treated as a deposit. The balance was to be paid in cash within a few days. The respondent returned the Plymouth car to the company, and refused to carry on with the purchase. A few days later, the company served upon the respondent a notice stated to be gaven under s. 49 of the (New Zealand) Sale of Goods Act [Ont., s. 46], indicating that if the balance of the purchase price was not paid within seven days the Plymouth car would be resold and that the respondent would remain responsible for any damages suffered by the company. The respondent ignored the notice. Eventually the Plymouth car was sold for £1,100.

The respondent brought action to recover the amount of the deposit. The company counterclaimed for £110 10s. 9d.,* being its loss on the resale of the Plymouth (£100); cost of repainting the car (£35); general loss of commission or profit on resale of the car (£110), and costs of serving the notice under s. 49 of the Sale of Goods Act 1908 (£5 10s. 9d.).

The Magistrate allowed the respondent's claim in full, and gave judgment on the counterclaim in favour of the appellant for the amount of its counterclaim, £110 10s. 9d. The appellant appealed against the judgment in favour of the respondent.

TURNER J.: When the respondent returned the Plymouth car to the appellant and intimated that he would not pay for it, he repudiated liability under the contract for its purchase. By accepting the car, the appellant must be taken to have treated the contract as discharged by breach. Doing this, the appellant was clearly entitled, as Mr. Monagan concedes, to treat any deposit as forfeited. This result follows equally when a deposit is (as here) also a payment on account of the purchase price. The Oldsmobile car, which had been traded in by the respondent, must be treated in precisely the same way as a monetary payment by way of deposit which is also a payment on account of purchase moneys: this follows in the present case from the form of the pleadings as finally amended, and from Mr. Monagan's concession at the hearing. The result must therefore be that, immediately after the return of the Plymouth, the appellant was entitled to keep the Oldsmobile (see, for instance, *Howe* v. *Smith* (1884) 27 Ch. D. 89); and, further, it would seem to follow from *Fitt* v. *Cassanet* (1842) 4 Man. & G. 898; 134 ER 369 that any final surplus on resale of the Plymouth also became the property of the vendor.

Different considerations apply to a case where a vendor, never having lost possession of the goods, resells them under his statutory power upon default

---

* The Report does not indicate how this sum was arrived at and it does not jibe with the break-down of the respondent's claim given in the Report. [Eds.]

being made in payment of the purchase price. In *Gallagher* v. *Shilcock* [1949] 2 KB 765; [1949] 1 All ER 921, Finnemore J. held that where this happens, the whole of the moneys received by the vendor — deposit and resale price combined — must be accounted for, and any net surplus over and above the original purchase price must be refunded. But that decision expressly depended upon the fact that where a purchaser defaults in payment upon a contract for the sale of goods, time is not of the essence, and his default does not result in rescission. It was deduced from this proposition that, there being no rescission, such a vendor does not resell "as the full and untrammelled owner", and that, therefore, he must account not only for the actual proceeds of the resale, but, necessarily, in doing so effectively, also for the deposit.

The present case is quite a different one. Here the vendor sold, to mitigate his damages, a car of which the ownership and possession had passed from him and had later been restored to him: his acts were those which the common law empowers him to do. I am perfectly clear, moreover, that the vendor in the case before me was not able, even if he wished to do so, to exercise the statutory power of sale given by s. 49 of the Sale of Goods Act 1908, for this power is given by the Act only to those vendors who have never lost possession of the goods sold: cf. *Chalmers on Sale of Goods*, 12th ed., 135. Mr. Monagan contends, however, that though as a matter of law the appellant did not at the time have the power to sell under s. 49, he must now be taken so to have sold (incurring thereby the responsibilities attaching to vendors so selling, as laid down in *Gallagher* v. *Shilcock*) by reason of the notice given on February 4, 1955. It was contended that the appellant, by intimating that he would hold the respondent liable for any final deficiency on resale pursuant to s. 49, became estopped thereby from refusing to give credit when actually a final surplus was realized.

It will perhaps be as well if I now set out the notice that was given on February 4. It was in the following terms:

To:
   Edgar Dalmage Saul,
   Farmer,
   Takapau.

COMMISSION CAR SALES LIMITED, a duly incorporated Company having its registered office in Karamu Road, Hastings, and carrying on business there as car salesmen HEREBY GIVES YOU NOTICE that it intends on or after the expiry of seven (7) clear days from the service of this notice upon you in exercise of its right as an unpaid seller to resell the 1952 "Cranbrook" Plymouth Sedan Motor vehicle Registered No. 358274 which you agreed to buy from it on the 27th day of January, 1955, AND TAKE FURTHER NOTICE that after the resale the said Company intends to take proceedings to recover from you damages for any loss occasioned by your breach of contract.

This Notice is given in terms of Section 49 of the "Sale of Goods Act 1908".

DATED at Hastings this 4th day of February, 1955.

   COMMISSION CAR SALES LIMITED by its Solicitor and duly authorised
agent.

I am of opinion that Mr. Monagan's submissions must fail. It must be remembered, I think, throughout their consideration that the appellant had, before giving the notice, already treated the contract as discharged by breach, and had accepted re-delivery of the Plymouth car. He thenceforward had the right to resell, and so to sue in damages for any net deficiency. It is true that if he so sued, he would have had to give credit for the deposit, for it would be unreal to allege a net deficiency unless the deposit was taken into account; but he could either (a) keep the deposit and resell, retaining the whole proceeds; or (b) resell, suing for any net deficiency after giving credit for the deposit: cf. *Howe* v. *Smith* (1884) 27 Ch. D. 89, 105 *per* Fry L.J. But he could not resell under s. 49; he had, and could have, no rights under that section, nor could the purchaser have any such rights. The section was simply inapplicable.

I think that the notice given by the appellant on February 4 must be treated simply as a nullity. It was given by a party who mistook his legal position and thought, erroneously as it turned out, that he was bound to give notice whereby time was made of the essence, when already the contract had been repudiated and treated as discharged by breach. The notice contains no express misrepresentation of fact upon which any estoppel could be founded; nor do I find that it contains any such implied representation of fact. Expressions of intention will not found an estoppel, nor will misrepresentations of law. Moreover, I do not see in any case that the respondent has shown, or can show, that he has moved to his detriment in reliance upon the notice.

Appeal allowed.

Questions:

1   It will be observed that *Commission Car Sales* v. *Saul* was decided before *Ward* v. *Bignall*. Would it have been decided differently if it had come later?

2   In *Saul*, upon the buyer's refusal to pay the balance of the price, would the seller have been entitled to repossess the Plymouth vehicle without the buyer's consent? *Cf.* UCC 2-702 and OLRC Sales Report, p. 398. Why should the seller's unpaid lien not extend, for a limited period at any rate, even after the buyer has acquired possession of the goods? Can the buyer's voluntary return of the vehicle, and its acceptance by the seller, be treated as an accord and satisfaction of all outstanding claims between the parties? Should it have been so treated here?

3   *Semble*, equity's power to relieve from forfeiture of payments, as accepted by Denning and Somervell L.JJ. in *Stockloser* v. *Johnson* (*infra*, this chapter) was not raised before Turner J. Would it have made a difference if it had been?

CHARTER v. SULLIVAN
[1957] 2 QB 117, [1957] 1 All ER 809 (CA)

The defendant Sullivan appealed from a judgment of Judge Rawlins in which the judge awarded the plaintiff Charter, a motor-car dealer, £97 15s. damages against the defendant for breach of a contract for the sale by the plaintiff to the defendant of a "Hillman Minx" motor-car. The contract was entered into on June 29 or 30, 1955, when the defendant called at the plaintiff's showroom and agreed to buy a new "Hillman Minx" de luxe saloon motor-car which the plaintiff had in stock, together with extras at a total price of £773 17s. At this price the sale, if completed, would have given the plaintiff a profit of £97 15s., of which £90 2s. 6d. was attributable to the car and the balance to the extras. A term of the bargain was that the plaintiff was to take in part exchange at the price of £350 a "Commer" van belonging to the defendant. On or about July 2, 1955, the defendant found that another dealer would be prepared to give him, as he thought, better terms, and on July 5, 1955, he wrote to the plaintiff a letter in which he refused to take the car. Some seven or 10 days later the plaintiff resold the car to another purchaser, Wigley, for the same price as the defendant had agreed to pay, namely, £773 17s., including the extras which had been fitted at the defendant's request.

The "Hillman Minx" car was a product of the motor manufacturing organization known as the Rootes Group, and the plaintiff was an area dealer for that organization, covering the North Hampshire area. In accordance with the usual practice in the trade, the retail price of the cars was fixed by the manufacturers, so that the profit realizable by a dealer on the sale of a new car remained constant.

No point was made on either side of the fact that the defendant was to give another vehicle in part-exchange, nor was any distinction drawn between the car itself and the extra items. The case was argued before the Court of Appeal on the footing that this was a sale for cash; and, although different considerations might apply to the extras as compared with the car itself, £773 17s. was treated as the fixed retail price simply of the car as supplied by the manufacturers and £97 15s. as the profit resulting from a sale of the car at that price.

The sole issue before the court was the measure of damages.

JENKINS L.J.: I turn now to consider what, on the undisputed facts of the case, is in the eye of the law the true measure of the damages, if any, over and above merely nominal damages, which the plaintiff has suffered through the defendant's failure to take and pay for the car he agreed to buy.

Consideration of this question must inevitably begin with a reference to section 50 of the Sale of Goods Act, 1893. [His Lordship read section 50 [Ont. SGA s. 48] and continued:] Mr. Collard, for the defendant, argued that in the present case there was an available market for "Hillman Minx" de luxe saloon cars within the meaning of section 50(3) of the Act, and accordingly that the measure of damages ought, in accordance with the *prima facie* rule laid down by that subsection, to be ascertained by the difference between the contract price and the market or current price at the time of the defendant's refusal to perform his contract.

The result of this argument, if accepted, would be that the plaintiff could claim no more than nominal damages, because the market or current price could only be the fixed retail price, which was necessarily likewise the price at which he sold to the defendant and resold to Wigley.

But the plaintiff is a motor-car dealer whose trade for the present purpose can be described as consisting in the purchase of recurrent supplies of cars of the relevant description from the manufacturers, and selling the cars so obtained, or as many of them as he can, at the fixed retail price. He thus receives, on each sale he is able to effect, the predetermined profit allowed by the fixed retail price, and it is obviously in his interest to sell as many cars as he can obtain from the manufacturers. The number of sales he can effect, and consequently the amount of profit he makes, will be governed, according to the state of trade, either by the number of cars he is able to obtain from the manufacturers, or by the number of purchasers he is able to find. In the former case demand exceeds supply, so that the default of one purchaser involves him in no loss, for he sells the same number of cars as he would have sold if that purchaser had not defaulted. In the latter case supply exceeds demand, so that the default of one purchaser may be said to have lost him one sale.

Accordingly, it seems to me that even if there was within the meaning of section 50(3) an available market for cars of the description in question, and even if the fixed retail price was the market or current price within the meaning of the same subsection, the prima facie rule which it prescribes should be rejected in favour of the general rule laid down by subsection (2); for it does not by any means necessarily follow that, because the plaintiff sold at the fixed retail price to Wigley the car which the defendant had agreed to buy at the selfsame fixed retail price, but refused to take, therefore the plaintiff suffered no "loss directly and naturally resulting, in the ordinary course of events" from the defendant's breach of contract.

This makes it strictly unnecessary to decide whether there was in the present case an available market for cars of the description in question within the meaning of section 50(3). But I would find it difficult to hold that there was. Given default by some purchaser of one of his cars of the relevant description, the plaintiff's only alternative mode of disposal would be to sell it at the fixed retail price to some other purchaser. He could endeavour to find another purchaser by displaying the car in his saleroom, circularising or canvassing old customers or the public at large, and advertising by posters or in newspapers. The car would obviously be of interest to retail customers only (i.e., the car-using public as distinct from the trade) and any purchaser he might succeed in finding would necessarily have to be a purchaser at the fixed retail price. At that price there might be no takers, in which case the plaintiff would be left with the car on his hands. Section 50(3) seems to me to postulate a market in which there is a market or current price, i.e., a price fixed by supply and demand at which (be it more or less than the contract price) a purchaser can be found. If the only price at which a car can be sold is the fixed retail price and no purchaser can be found at that price, I do not think it can reasonably be said that there is a market or current price or that there is an available market. If the state of the trade were such that the plaintiff could sell at the fixed retail price all the cars he could get, so that the defendant's default did not result in the plaintiff effecting one sale less than he would otherwise have effected, it may well be that the plaintiff could not make out his claim to anything more than nominal damages. I am, however, inclined to think that this would not be on account of the necessary equality of the contract price and the fixed retail price at which alone the car could be sold, taken for the present purpose as the market or current price within the meaning of section 50(3), but because on an application of the general principle laid down by section 50(2) the plaintiff would be found to have suffered no damage.

In *Thompson (W. L.) Ltd.* v. *Robinson (Gunmakers) Ltd.* [1955] Ch. 177, Upjohn J. had before him a claim for damages in a case resembling the present case to the extent that the damages were claimed in respect of the defendants' refusal to perform a contract with the plaintiffs for the purchase from the plaintiffs of a car (in that instance a "Standard Vanguard" car) which, like the car in the present case, could only be sold by the plaintiffs at a fixed retail price. It is, however, important to note that the case to which I am now referring proceeded on certain admissions, including an admission to the effect that in the relevant district at the date of the contract (which was also the date of the breach) "there was no shortage of 'Vanguard' models to meet all immediate demands in the locality," which I take to mean, in effect, that the supply of such cars exceeded the demand. In these circumstances the plaintiffs by agreement with their suppliers rescinded their contract with them, and returned the car. In the ensuing action the plaintiffs claimed from the defendants damages amounting to the profit the plaintiffs would have made on the sale of the car to the defendants if the defendants had duly completed their purchase of it, and the judge held them entitled to those damages. The defendants raised the same argument as has been raised by the defendant in the present case, namely, that there was an available market for a car of the kind in question, within the meaning of section 50(3), that there was a market or current price in the shape of the fixed retail price, and that as the fixed retail price was the same as the contract price the plaintiffs had suffered no damage. In the course of his judgment Upjohn J. at 185 Ch. referred to James L.J.'s definition of a market in *Dunkirk Colliery Co.* v. *Lever* (1878) 9 Ch. D. 20, 24, 25. James L.J. said this:

> Under those circumstances the only thing that we can do is to send it back to the referee with an intimation that we are of opinion upon the facts (agreeing with the Master of the Rolls in that respect), that the facts do not warrant the application of the principle mentioned in the award, namely, that there was what may be properly called a market. What I understand by a market in such a case as this is, that when the defendant refused to take the 300 tons the first week or the first month, the plaintiffs might have sent it in waggons somewhere else, where they could sell it, just as they sell corn on the Exchange, or cotton at Liverpool: that is to say, that there was a fair market where they could have found a purchaser either by themselves or through some agent at some particular place. That is my notion of the meaning of a market under those circumstances.

Upjohn J. (at 186 Ch.) also referred to the Scottish case of *Marshall & Co.* v. *Nicoll & Son*, 1919 SC (HL) 129 where it was held in the Court of Session that there was an available market within the meaning of section 51(3) of the Sale of Goods Act, 1893, for annealed steel sheets although they were not kept in stock and were not purchasable in the open market. In the House of Lords the decision was affirmed, but their Lordships would seem to have been equally divided on the question whether there was an available market for the goods. In this state of the authorities, the judge felt himself bound by *Dunkirk Colliery Co.* v. *Lever*, and held, in effect, that James L.J.'s definition in that case prevented him from holding that in the case then before him there was an available market within the meaning of section 50(3).

Upjohn J. (at 187 Ch.) went on to propound a more extended meaning for the phrase "available market" in these terms:

> Had the matter been res integra I think that I should have found that an "available market" merely means that the situation in the particular trade in the particular area was such that the particular goods could freely be sold, and that there was a demand sufficient to absorb readily all the goods that were thrust on it, so that if a purchaser defaulted, the goods in question could readily be disposed of.

He went on to say, in effect, that in the case then before him there was no available market because the supply of "Vanguard" cars at the material time exceeded the demand.

I doubt if James L.J.'s observations in *Dunkirk Colliery Co.* v. *Lever* should be literally applied as an exhaustive definition of an available market in all cases. On the other hand, I do not find Upjohn J.'s definition entirely satisfactory. I will not, however, attempt to improve upon it, but will content myself with the negative proposition that I doubt if there can be an available market for particular goods in any sense relevant to section 50(3) of the Sale of Goods Act, 1893, unless those goods are available for sale in the market at the market or current price in the sense of the price, whatever it may be, fixed by reference to supply and demand as the price at which a purchaser for the goods in question can be found, be it greater or less than or equal to the contract price. The language of section 50(3) seems to me to postulate that in the cases to which it applies there will, or may, be a difference between the contract price and the market or current price, which cannot be so where the goods can only be sold at a fixed retail price.

Accordingly, I am of opinion that whether there was in this case "an available market" within the meaning of section 50(3) or not, it is a case in which section 50(2) should be applied to the exclusion of section 50(3).

It remains, therefore, to ascertain the loss (if any) "naturally resulting, in the ordinary course of events" from the defendant's breach of contract, and the measure of that loss must, in my opinion, be the amount, if any, of the profit the plaintiff has lost by reason of the defendant's failure to take and pay for the car he agreed to buy. This accords with the view taken by Upjohn J. in *Thompson (W. L.) Ltd.* v. *Robinson (Gunmakers) Ltd.*, and also with the principle stated in *In re Vic Mill Ltd.* [1913] 1 Ch. 465 which Upjohn J. applied.

Appeal allowed.

[Hodson and Sellers L.JJ. delivered concurring judgments.]

Notes:

1   *Semble,* the only reported Canadian cases to date on the problem of the "lost volume" seller are *Victory Motors Ltd.* v. *Bayda* [1973] 3 WWR 747 (Sask. Dist. Ct.), followed in *Sanford* v. *Senger* [1977] 3 WWR 399 (Sask. Dist. Ct.) and *Canadian Union College* v. *Camsteel Indust. Ltd.* (1979) 9 Alta. LR (2d) 167 (DC). Should the principle in *Charter* v. *Sullivan* and the earlier cases also be applied to a contract by a car dealer for the sale of a used car? See *Lazenby Garages Ltd.* v. *Wright* [1976] 1

WLR 459 (CA). How would the principle in *Charter* v. *Sullivan* operate in the following circumstances:

a) there is a glut of new cars on the market and the dealer, in order to reduce his inventory, sells the car below the agreed price;

b) the market picks up strength and the dealer is able to sell the vehicle for a better price than agreed upon in his contract with the defendant?

2   In *Sanford* v. *Senger, supra*, defendant agreed to purchase a reconditioned cash register from plaintiff for $2,400. Plaintiff agreed to give defendant $600 credit on a trade-in and the balance was to be financed through a leasing company. Defendant repudiated the contract and plaintiff sold the register to another buyer for $1,600 after spending $201 to convert the machine to the second buyer's use. Plaintiff sued defendant for damages. Walker D.C.J., purporting to follow *Victory Motors* v. *Bayda*, assessed damages as folows (*ibid.*, at 409):

Agreed sale price	$2,400
Less cost of machine to the plaintiff	450
	$1,950
Less cost of conversion	715
Loss of profit	$1,235
Cost of conversion for sale to third party	201
Less labour on first conversion which was useful in the second conversion	10
	$1,426

Was this a proper case for applying the lost-volume principle and, if it was, did the court arrive at the correct mathematical result?

3   UCC 2-708(2) deals expressly with the assessment of damages in a lost-volume sale, but its wording has attracted much critical comment. See OLRC Sales Report, pp. 420-21, and the literature cited on p. 421, n. 130. Nevertheless the Report recommended the adoption of a modified version of UCC 2-708(2). *Ibid.*, pp. 421-22.

4   The market price test was developed at common law in the early part of the 19th century in the assessment of damage claims by seller or buyer and, as the OLRC Sales Report observes (p. 521), it has much to commend it. In optimum conditions it provides a ready yardstick for the ready quantification of damages, and at the same time it reaffirms the innocent party's obligation to mitigate his damages by taking those steps that a reasonably prudent person would take in his place. Nevertheless, the Commission felt the market price test had become encrusted with unnecessary technicalities and was too rigid in its statutory form. The Commission was particularly concerned about the unsettled meaning of "available market" and the uncertainties concerning the time and place for determining the market price. The Commission therefore favoured the adoption of a revised market price test to read as follows (Report, p. 527):

9.10(3) Where at the agreed time for performance and in circumstances amounting to a substantial breach the buyer wrongfully neglects or refuses to accept and pay for the goods and section 9.9 does not apply, the measure of damages is *prima facie* to be ascertained by the difference between the contract price and the price that could have been obtained by a commercially reasonable disposition of the goods within or at a reasonable time and place after the seller learned of the buyer's breach, less any expenses saved in consequence of the buyer's breach.

For further analysis of the market price test see R. Lawson, "An Analysis of the Concept of 'Available Market' " (1969) 43 ALJ 106, and D.W.M. Waters, "The Concept of Market in the Sale of Goods" (1958) 36 Can. Bar Rev. 360, and Fridman, 2nd ed., pp. 389-400.

5   An important feature of the market price test is that it is a hypothetical test — the question is not what damages has the seller (or buyer) actually suffered but what damages is he deemed to have suffered? This raises two important issues: (a) should the seller be entitled to recover his actual damages; and (b) should the buyer be entitled to show that the seller suffered less than the market price damages? UCC 2-706 and 2-712 answer the first question affirmatively (2-706 deals with a resale by the seller; 2-712 with a covering purchase by the buyer); but are markedly silent on the second. American authors are divided on the correct answer. See OLRC Sales Report, pp. 409-10. The SGA is silent on both points but the accepted learning is that the seller's actual resale price, where there is an available market, is only of evidentiary value and, conversely, when sued for the market price measure of damage the buyer is not entitled to prove that the seller suffered lesser damages. See OLRC Report, p. 501 (dealing with the converse case of a defaulting seller). The Privy Council's decision in *Wertheim* v. *Chicoutimi Pulp Co.* [1911] AC 301 (PC) runs counter to the current of authority and is reproduced below in chapter 12. Art. 75 of the UN International Sales Convention provides:

> If the contract is avoided and if, in a reasonable manner and within a reasonable time after avoidance, the buyer has bought goods in replacement or the seller has resold the goods, the party claiming damages may recover the difference between the contract price and the price in the substitute transaction as well as any further damages recoverable under article 74.

Art. 76 further provides that if the injured party "has not made a purchase or resale under article 75" and there is a current price for the goods he may recover the market-price/contract-price difference by way of damages. It will be seen therefore that under the Sales Convention the injured party is bound by his election although there is nothing in Art. 75 requiring him to give the other party notice of his election.

STOCKLOSER v. JOHNSON
[1954] 1 QB 476, [1954] 1 All ER 630 (CA)

The defendant was the owner of plant and machinery used in connection with the operation of two quarries, known respectively as the Washington and "Playhatch" quarries. The defendant let the Washington plant and machinery to the "Renown" company in exchange for royalty payments and subsequently entered into a similar arrangement with another company, Dow-Mac (Quarries) Ltd., with respect to the Playhatch plant and machinery.

In 1950 the plaintiff agreed to purchase from the defendant the plant and machinery at the two quarries together with the benefit of the hiring agreements. Payment was to be made by instalments. By clause 5 of the agreement it was provided that if the purchaser made default in an instalment for a period exceeding 28 days the vendor was entitled, on giving 14 days' notice to rescind,

> to retake possession of the plant, machinery and appliances specified in the schedule hereto and again to enter into enjoyment of the said agreement and the fruits thereof as though this agreement had never been executed. And in such event all payments made hereunder by the purchaser to the vendor shall be forfeited to the vendor who shall retain the same.

The plaintiff encountered difficulties from the outset and in December, 1951, he defaulted in the payment of instalments on both agreements. On February 25, 1952, the defendant gave notices rescinding both agreements.

The plaintiff at no time expressed his readiness or ability to make further payments if the defendant were willing to waive his right to rescind, but he brought the present action claiming the return of the instalments paid under the agreements. The plaintiff contended that the retention of the instalments by the defendant amounted to the exaction of a penalty, from which he was entitled to be relieved.

Hallett J. gave judgment refusing the plaintiff relief in respect of the instalment paid under the "Playhatch" agreement, but granting him relief, subject to certain deductions, in respect of the instalments paid under the Washington agreement.

The defendant appealed, and the plaintiff cross-appealed.

DENNING L.J.: There was acute contest as to the proper legal principles to apply in this case. On the one hand, Mr. Neil Lawson urged us to hold that the buyer was entitled to recover the instalments at law. He said that the forfeiture clause should be ignored because it was of a penal character, and once it was ignored, it meant that the buyer was left with a simple right to repayment of his money on the lines of *Dies* v. *British and International Mining and Finance Corporation* [1939] 1 KB 724 subject only to a cross-claim for damages. In asking us to ignore the forfeiture clause, Mr. Lawson relied on the familiar tests which are used to distinguish between penalties and liquidated damages, and said that these tests had been applied in cases for the repayment of money, citing *Barton* v. *Capewell* (1893) 68 LT 857 and *Commissioner of Public Works* v. *Hills* [1906] AC 368. In neither of those cases, however, was the point argued or discussed, and I do not think they warrant Mr. Lawson's proposition. There is, I think, a plain distinction between penalty cases, strictly so called, and cases like the present.

It is this: when one party seeks to exact a penalty from the other, he is seeking to exact payment of an extravagant sum either by action at law or by appropriating to himself moneys belonging to the other party, as in *Commissioner of Public Works* v. *Hills*. The claimant invariably relies, like Shylock, on the letter of the contract to support his demand, but the courts decline to give him their aid because they will not assist him in an act of oppression: see the valuable judgments of Somervell and Hodson L.JJ. in *Cooden Engineering Co.* v. *Stanford* [1953] 1 QB 86.

In the present case, however, the seller is not seeking to exact a penalty. He only wants to keep money which already belongs to him. The money was handed to him in part payment of the purchase price and, as soon as it was paid, it belonged to him absolutely. He did not obtain it by extortion or oppression or anything of that sort, and there is an express clause — a forfeiture clause, if you please — permitting him to keep it. It is not the case of a seller seeking to enforce a penalty, but a buyer seeking restitution of money paid. If the buyer is to recover it, he must, I think, have recourse to somewhat different principles from those applicable to penalties, strictly so called.

On the other hand, Mr. Beney urged us to hold that the buyer could only recover the money if he was able and willing to perform the contract, and for this purpose he ought to pay or offer to pay the instalments which were in arrear and be willing to pay the future instalments as they became due; and he relied on *Mussen* v. *Van Dieman's Land Co.* [1938] Ch. 253. I think that this contention goes too far in the opposite direction. If the buyer was seeking to re-establish the contract, he would of course have to pay up the arrears and to show himself willing to perform the contract in the future, just as a lessee, who has suffered a forfeiture, has to do when he seeks to re-establish the lease. So, also, if the buyer were seeking specific performance he would have to show himself able and willing to perform his part. But the buyer's object here is not to re-establish the contract. It is to get his money back, and to do this I do not think that it is necessary for him to go so far as to show that he is ready and willing to perform the contract.

I reject, therefore, the arguments of counsel at each extreme. It seems to me that the cases show the law to be this: (1) *When there is no forfeiture clause.* If money is handed over in part payment of the purchase price, and then the buyer makes default as to the balance, then, so long as the seller keeps the contract open and available for performance, the buyer cannot recover the money; but once the seller rescinds the contract or treats it as at an end owing to the buyer's default, then the buyer is entitled to recover his money by action at law, subject to a cross-claim by the seller for damages: see *Palmer* v. *Temple* (1839) 9 Ad. & El. 508; *Mayson* v. *Clouet* [1924] AC 980; *Dies* v. *British and International Co.* [1939] 1 KB 724; *Williams on Vendor and Purchaser*, 4th ed., p. 1006. (2) *But when there is a forfeiture clause or the money is expressly paid as a deposit, (which is equivalent to a forfeiture clause),* then the buyer who is in default cannot recover the money at law at all. He may, however, have a remedy in equity, for, despite the express stipulation in the contract, equity can relieve the buyer from forfeiture of the money and order the seller to repay it on such terms as the court thinks fit. That is, I think, shown clearly by the decision of the Privy Council in *Steedman* v. *Drinkle* [1916] 1 AC 275, where the Board consisted of a strong three, Viscount Haldane, Lord Parker and Lord Sumner.

The difficulty is to know what are the circumstances which give rise to this equity; but I must say that I agree with all that Somervell L.J. has said about it, differing herein from the view of Romer L.J. Two things are necessary: first, the forfeiture clause must be of a penal nature, in this sense, that the sum forfeited must be out of all proportion to the damage, and secondly, it must be unconscionable for the seller to retain the money. Inasmuch as the only case in which this jurisdiction has been exercised is *Steedman* v. *Drinkle,* I have examined the record and would draw attention to the circumstances of that case. The agreement was in effect a hire-purchase agreement of land. The purchase-money was payable by instalments over six years, completion to be at the end of the six years, and meanwhile the purchasers were to be let into possession of the land as tenants with the instalments ranking as rent. In case of default the vendor was at liberty to cancel the contract and retain the payments which had been made. The purchasers paid the first instalment and went into possession, but they failed to pay the second instalment which was due at the end of the first year. The value of the land had risen greatly during that year and the vendor seized upon the purchaser's default as giving him the opportunity to rescind the contract. Without previous warning, the vendor gave notice cancelling the contract. The purchasers at once tendered the amount due but the vendor refused to accept it. The purchasers issued a writ for specific performance and meanwhile remained in possession of the land taking the crops off it. They failed to get specific performance in the first court, then succeeded in the Court of Appeal, but failed again in the Privy Council on the ground that time was expressly of the essence of the contract. Nevertheless, the Privy Council relieved the purchasers from forfeiture of the sums already paid. The purchasers would no doubt have to give credit for the crops they had taken from the land during the three years or more that they had been in possession, but subject to that credit they would get their money back.

In the later case of *Mussen* v. *Van Dieman's Land Co.* [1938] Ch. 253 Farwell J. said that the whole basis of the decision in *Steedman* v. *Drinkle* was that the purchasers were ready and willing to perform the contract; but I think that that is much too narrow an explanation. Readiness and willingness is essential in specific performance, and in relief from forfeiture of leases, but not in relief from forfeiture of sums paid. The basis of the decision in *Steedman* v. *Drinkle* was, I think, that the vendor had somewhat sharply exercised his right to rescind the contract and retake the land, and it was unconscionable for him also to forfeit the sums already paid. Equity could not specifically enforce the contract, but it could and would relieve against the forfeiture.

In the course of the argument before us Somervell L.J. put an illustration which shows the necessity for this equity even though the buyer is not ready and willing to perform the contract. Suppose a buyer has agreed to buy a necklace by instalments, and the contract provides that, on default in payment of any one instalment, the seller is entitled to rescind the contract and forfeit the instalments already paid. The buyer pays 90 per cent of the price but fails to pay the last instalment. He is not able to perform the contract because he simply cannot find the money. The seller thereupon rescinds the contract and retakes the necklace and resells it at a higher price. Surely equity will relieve the buyer against forfeiture of the money on such terms as may be just.

Again, suppose that a vendor of property, in lieu of the usual 10 per cent deposit, stipulates for an initial payment of 50 per cent of the price as a deposit and a part payment; and later, when the purchaser fails to complete, the vendor resells the property at a profit and in addition claims to forfeit the 50 per cent deposit. Surely the court will relieve against the forfeiture. The vendor cannot forestall this equity by describing an extravagant sum as a deposit, any more than he can recover a penalty by calling it liquidated damages.

These illustrations convince me that in a proper case there is an equity of restitution which a party in default does not lose simply because he is not able and willing to perform the contract. Nay, that is the very reason why he needs the equity. The equity operates, not because of the plaintiff's default, but because it is in the particular case unconscionable for the seller to retain the money. In short, he ought not unjustly to enrich himself at the plaintiff's expense. This equity of restitution is to be tested, I think, not at the time of the contract, but by the conditions existing when it is invoked. Suppose, for instance, that in the instance of the necklace, the first instalment was only 5 per cent of the price; and the buyer made default on the second instalment. There would be no equity by which he could ask for the first instalment to be repaid to him any more than he could claim repayment of a deposit. But it is very different after 90 per cent has been paid. Again, delay may be very material. Thus in *Mussen's* case the court was much influenced by the fact that the purchaser had allowed nearly six years to elapse before claiming restitution. He had already had a good deal of land conveyed to him and, during his six years delay, values had so greatly changed that it may be that he had his money's worth. At any rate, it was not unconscionable for the defendant to retain the money.

Applying these principles to the present case, even if one regards the forfeiture clause as of a penal nature — as the judge did and I am prepared to do — nevertheless I do not think that it was unconscionable for the seller to retain the money. The buyer seems to have gambled on the royalties being higher than they were. He thought that they would go a long way to enable him to pay the instalments; but owing to bad weather they turned out to be smaller than he had hoped and he could not find the additional amount necessary to pay the instalments. The judge summarized the position neatly when he said that the purchaser "is in the position of a gambler who has lost his stake and is now saying that it is for the court of equity to get it back for him." He said, "if it is a question of what is unconscionable, or, to use a word with a less legal flavour, unfair, I can see nothing whatever unfair in the defendant retaining the money." With that finding of the judge I entirely agree and think that it disposes of the purchaser's claim to restitution.

Despite this finding, however, the judge did allow the buyer to recover the instalments he had paid on the Washington quarry. The reason was because, after the buyer made default, the seller bought up the interest of the Renown company in the quarry and thereby disabled himself from fulfilling the contract with the buyer if called upon to do so. I do not myself think that in this case that makes any difference. It might have done if there had been no forfeiture clause and the buyer was claiming at law for the return of his instalment; because then the buyer would have to show that the seller had treated the contract as at an end, see *Palmer* v. *Temple*, 9 Ad & El. 508, 521. But the buyer here cannot claim at law. There is a forfeiture clause which prevents him doing so. He can only claim in equity; and he does not gain an equity simply because the seller has bought up the quarry. I do not think therefore, that the judge was right in allowing the buyer to recover the instalments which he had paid on the Washington quarry. The buyer should not be allowed to recover anything. I agree that the appeal of the seller should be allowed, but the cross-appeal should be dismissed.

Appeal allowed;
cross-appeal dismissed.

[In a separate concurring judgment, Somervell L.J. expressed the same view of the law as Denning L.J. Romer L.J. agreed with the result but disagreed on the main question whether equity will grant relief from forfeiture of instalments paid under a contract of sale. He adopted the position that there was no justification for disturbing contractual stipulations between freely consenting parties where there are no elements of pressure or duress, and he thought that the precedents cited by Denning L.J. only stood for the proposition that the court will, in a proper case, give a defaulting purchaser further time to make the payments in arrear if he is able and willing to do so.]

Notes:

1   *Stockloser* v. *Johnson* involved a claim for relief from forfeiture of instalments. Denning L.J. does not state clearly whether equity's power applies equally to payments in the form of deposits. In principle it should make no difference and subsequent Canadian decisions (see *infra*, note 3) have not distinguished between these two situations. The broad equity is also supported in S.M. Waddams, *The Law of Contracts* (1977) pp. 277-78.

2   In only one reported case since *Stockloser* v. *Johnson* has an English court apparently been asked to grant equitable relief from forfeiture of monies paid: see *Galbraith* v. *Mitchenall Estates* [1965] 2 QB 473, [1964] All ER 653, which involved a hiring agreement for a caravan. In that case Sachs J. stated his preference for the approach taken by Romer L.J. in *Stockloser* and expressed the view that Denning L.J.'s discussion of the scope of equitable relief was obiter.

3   Canadian courts, in contrast, have generally favoured Denning L.J.'s approach. However, only two Canadian judgments, both from Nova Scotia, have actually applied the equitable doctrine to allow a defaulting payor to recover money paid under an agreement that was subsequently cancelled: see *Re Provinces and Central Properties Ltd. and City of Halifax* (1969) 5 DLR (3d) 28 (NS CA) and *Deber Investments Ltd.* v. *Roblea Estates Ltd.* (1976) 21 NSR (2d) 158 (SC). In the other reported Canadian cases the courts have recognized their jurisdiction to grant general equitable relief from forfeiture, but have refused to grant relief based on the facts involved. See, for example, *Hughes* v. *Lukuvka* (1970) 14 DLR (3d) 110 (BC CA); *Canadian Union College* v. *Camsteel Industries Ltd.* (1979) 9 Alta. LR (2d) 167, 17 AR 98 (Dist. Ct.); and *Buck* v. *Cooper* (1955) 1 DLR (2d) 282 (BC SC). It should be noted that, of the above cases, only the *Canadian Union College* case involved a sale of chattels. The majority of forfeiture cases seem to involve interests in land. Why should this be so?

4   For a comment on *Stockloser* v. *Johnson* and a discussion of the earlier Canadian cases, see Ryan, (1954) 32 Can. Bar Rev. 568. See also S.M. Waddams, *The Law of Contracts* (1977), pp. 277-81, and R. Goff and G. Jones, *The Law of Restitution*, 2nd. ed. (1978), pp. 382-84.

5   For the Code's treatment of the forfeiture problem, see UCC 2-718(2) and (3), and note its assimilation of the law of penalty and forfeiture clauses. The same approach appears in s. 2-516(c) of the (American) Uniform Land Transactions Act and, in a wider setting, in s. 388 of the Restatement of the Law of Contracts 2d, Tent. Draft No. 14. Do you prefer the Code's solution to the vaguer equitable doctrine enunciated in *Stockloser* v. *Johnson*? The Code's provisions are discussed in Robert J. Nordstrom, "Restitution on Default and Article 2 of the Uniform Commercial Code" (1966) 19 Van. L. Rev. 1113.

6   As will be noted, *Stockloser's* case involved a conditional sale of plant and machinery which, in Ontario, would be governed by the PPSA. Part V of the Act, discussed *infra*, chapter 24, deals with enforcement of the security interest and foreclosure of the debtor's equity. Does it supersede the equitable power to grant relief from forfeiture of payments?

7   The English Law Commission made the following recommendation in its Working Paper No. 61 on *Penalty Clauses and Forfeiture of Monies Paid* (1975):

> (ix)   The court's jurisdiction to grant relief against the forfeiture of a deposit or part payment should be reconsidered (paragraph 61).
>
> (x)   We put forward for consideration two possible ways of dealing with relief against forfeiture in place of the present law (paragraph 67).
>
> (xi)   One way would be to confer a general power on the court to grant such relief as it considers just, whether by allowing more time to perform a contract or by the return of money or property. The court would be empowered to grant relief if it was reasonable to do so, regard being had to —
>
> (1) the general practice in transactions of a similar nature, and
>
> (2) the reasonableness of the amount which is subject to forfeiture, and
>
> (3) all the circumstances of the case (paragraph 64).
>
> (xii)   The other way would be to apply to forfeiture the law regarding liquidated damages and penalties, but with a special rule applying to deposits on the sale of land (paragraphs 65 and 66).
>
> (xiii)   The special rule applying to deposits on the sale of land might enable the defaulting purchaser to challenge, on the same principles as apply in other cases, the forfeiture of a deposit exceeding a statutory percentage of the purchase price. We should welcome views as to what this statutory percentage should be. The court should in all cases relating to land continue to have jurisdiction to extend the time for completion (paragraph 66).
>
> (xiv)   Our provisional conclusion is in favour of the proposals in paragraphs (xii) and (xiii) above, but we should welcome views on this preference (paragraph 67).

What is the practical difference between recommendations (xi) and (xii)? Should deposits on the sale of land be subject to a separate rule?

Chapter 12
Buyer's Remedies For Breach of Seller's Obligations

As we have seen in earlier chapters, the law imposes heavy obligations on a seller, especially if he is a merchant-seller and therefore subject to the implied conditions in SGA ss. 15-16. The purpose of the present chapter is to examine the contractual remedies available to an aggrieved buyer and the important issues — exegetical and policywise — which they raise. As will be seen, from the seller's point of view, the remedial structure matches in severity the heavy substantive obligations imposed on the seller. In practice therefore a well drafted agreement will almost invariably modify, or perhaps exclude altogether, the statutory and common law remedies available to the buyer. (Disclaimer and exception clauses are considered in chapter 13). This important qualifier should be borne in mind in studying the materials in this chapter.

OLRC Sales Report
p. 433

Under existing law, an aggrieved buyer has a variety of remedies, not all of which are spelled out in the Ontario Sale of Goods Act. The nature of these remedies will vary with the nature of the breach and the time it comes to light, the type of goods and the nature of the damages. If the seller, prior to the delivery date, notifies the buyer that he will not meet his delivery obligation, the buyer is confronted with an anticipatory breach which, at his election, he may ignore or accept. If the buyer accepts the repudiation, the agreement, subject to the buyer's right to sue for damages, is deemed at an end. Where there is no anticipatory repudiation but the seller fails to deliver at the proper time, the buyer is usually limited to an action in damages for non-delivery. Exceptionally, however, he may be entitled to an order for specific performance or to other forms of specific relief. If goods are tendered but are non-conforming in character, the buyer usually has an option. If the non-conformity involves breach of a condition and the contract does not involve a sale of specific goods the property in which has passed to the buyer, the buyer may reject and once again, sue for damages for non-delivery or content himself with a restitutionary claim for the return of any payments he may have made. If he elects to retain the goods he does not waive his claim to damages. This will be equally true if the non-conformity does not come to light until after the buyer is deemed to have accepted the goods; Anglo-Canadian law does not recognize a general right to rescind on account of a latent defect, except where the seller has been guilty of fraud or, possibly, innocent misrepresentation. Where the buyer is entitled to sue for damages for breach of the contract of sale, his damages will be assessed on the same basis of compensation for loss as in claims by the seller in the reverse situation, and subject to the rules of foreseeability enunciated in *Hadley* v. *Baxendale*. The buyer may also be entitled to sue in tort if the defective goods have caused personal injury or damage to other property.

A. THE RIGHT TO REJECT AND STATUTORY LIMITATIONS THEREON

1. THE INTERACTION OF S. 12(3) AND S. 19, RULE 1

HOME GAS LTD. v. STREETER
[1953] 2 DLR 842, 8 WWR (NS) 689 (Sask. CA)

GORDON J.A. (for the court): The plaintiff is a company having what appears to be a head office or main office for Saskatchewan in the City of Saskatoon, with a local agent or representative in the City of North Battleford where it has a show-room. On May 18, 1951, the defendant and her husband went to the plaintiff's show-room in North Battleford for the purpose of buying a gas stove. Neither of them had any experience with gas stoves before. They did not like any on display and one Palmer, the plaintiff's agent, told them that he had a fully automatic demonstrator in his trailer, and the defendant's husband went to inspect it in the trailer. Palmer gave the defendant a description of the stove over the telephone and the defendant decided to buy it. Her husband completed the deal. The price installed was to be $398.21. The defendant's husband swears that the cost of installation was to be approximately $100. On May 19, 1951, the defendant gave a cheque to Palmer at her home for $75 as a deposit on the transaction. On September 29, 1951, more than 4 months after the order had been given this stove was installed at the defendant's home and connected up to two tanks of propane gas, the fuel used in the stove. After it was installed Palmer said that he required the balance in cash or a cheque and the cheque sued upon for $323.21 was given.

During the installation the defendant complained that she smelled gas in the room, but Palmer assured her that it was merely some gas that had escaped during the installation. At the conclusion Palmer said: Try it for 4 days and then I will be back and check it thoroughly again and will bring a thermometer to check the oven. No demonstration was made after installation but the next day the defendant tried to use it. The burners in the oven would not light at all. Eventually when they got them to light the oven would not bake properly, it burnt food being baked on the bottom and the top was uncooked. One top burner did not light at all and instead of the burners being lit by the pilot light they had to be lit with a match. The day that the stove was first used was a Sunday, it having been installed on Sunday. On the Monday following the defendant endeavoured to get in touch with Palmer on the telephone a number of times but could not get in touch with him. Trips to the plaintiff's show-room at North Battleford were likewise fruitless. According to the evidence the defendant and her husband have never seen it open since their first visit.

A month after the stove was installed the defendant's husband was in Saskatoon and called at the office of the plaintiff and saw the manager in charge, telling him all about his complaints. The manager then called up Palmer at North Battleford and asked him to go and see the stove and put it in proper operating condition.

During the first 3 weeks after the stove had been installed the defendant had used one of the tanks of gas endeavouring to get it to work and at Christmas time after the installation she again tried until the second tank of gas was exhausted. This was used in a period of about 3 weeks. On cross-examination of the defendant, counsel for the plaintiff brought out the fact that she had written four letters to the plaintiff, one of which was dated February 13, I presume 1952, in which she stated "unless I hear from you immediately we intend to take action against you". None of these letters was produced or filed as exhibits.

On the 26th or 27th of January, 1952, Palmer appeared with a Mr. Jones who was represented to be the plaintiff's manager at Winnipeg. I presume that his visit was that promised by the manager when the defendant's husband visited Saskatoon about a month after the installation, which would be about the end of October. They looked at the stove but did nothing to it. Jones and Palmer were then told all the defects of the stove. Jones told them that one burner would have to be replaced and Jones told Palmer to come back the following day to check the oven. He never came back.

The defendant then wrote the manufacturer of the stove on April 8th and on April 25th the defendant received a letter in reply from the distributors of this particular stove who have their office in Saskatoon. I do not name them because I do not think that they should be implicated in what I consider despicable treatment meted out to this defendant by the plaintiff company. The distributors promised that they would have a sales representative in the district and try and have the stove satisfactorily adjusted, although they stressed that it was not their responsibility. This representative of the distributors did call at the end of April and said that he would do anything that he could to have the plaintiff look after it.

Early in May, 1952, Mr. Olsen, stated to be a representative of the plaintiff from Saskatoon came and looked at the stove but did nothing to it although he was told all of the complaints. At the time of the visit from Mr. Olsen the stove had been disconnected and was in a different room from that in which it had been installed.

The evidence does not disclose the date on which the payment of the cheque was stopped, but attached to the cheque is a bank notation dated October 5, 1951, showing the reason for nonpayment was "payment stopped", so it would have been prior to that date. The above are the undisputed facts and on these facts the plaintiff asks the Court to give it judgment for the amount of the cheque.

It is now necessary to look at the pleadings. The statement of claim is a simple one asking for payment of the cheque. The statement of defence sets forth, first there was no consideration for the cheque, alternatively that the plaintiff "warranted that the goods were reasonably fit for the purpose that they were required", that there was a breach of the warranty and particulars as disclosed in the above are given. There was no reply.

On the argument before us counsel for the defendant who was not the counsel at the trial or the solicitor on the record took the position that the evidence clearly disclosed that the stove was sold on the condition that it would be a useful stove and that the defendant had rejected the stove and that the plaintiff could not succeed on the cheque. Counsel for the plaintiff, on the other hand, contends that the stove was accepted by the defendant at least by Christmas time 1951 when it was used while burning the second tank of gas and contends that as there is no counterclaim for damages or set-off against the cheque the plaintiff is entitled to judgment for the amount of the cheque and the defendant is entitled to nothing by virtue of the failure of his solicitor to set up a counterclaim.

The learned trial Judge held that the defendant accepted the stove which had been delivered to her and had used it for the two periods of time set forth and that she had no right to reject it or repudiate the contract. The learned trial Judge stated that he was following the decision of the Ontario Court of Appeal in *Sedgwick* v. *Lloyd* [1951] OWN 469, and gave the plaintiff judgment for its claim and costs.

I do not think for one moment that the defendant ever intended to accept the stove but it may be that she is bound by the authorities and is limited to her right to damages.

To analyze the evidence a little more carefully, it will be noted that 3 days after the stove was installed the defendant did her best to get in touch with Palmer and at various times until about the end of October when her husband went to Saskatoon and saw the plaintiff's manager at that city and that in his presence Palmer was called and asked to go and see the stove and put it in operating condition. Up to that time it could not be said that the stove had been accepted. Then following various other efforts to get in touch with Palmer, after waiting from this time until the day before Christmas, nothing was done, when another effort was made to get the stove to work unsuccessfully. On the 26th or 27th day of January Jones came from Winnipeg and stated that a burner would have to be replaced and that the oven would be checked. The letters written by the defendant are not produced and we only know that in the letter of February 13th the defendant threatened the plaintiff with action.

If there was ever a case where a purchaser was entitled to reject the goods this is it. On the other hand the law in respect to the rejection of goods is very clear. No particular form of notice of rejection is necessary. The buyer may return the goods or offer to return them and it is sufficient to signify his rejection of them by stating that they are not according to the contract and that they are held at the vendor's risk: see *Grimoldby* v. *Wells* (1875) LR 10 CP 391 at p. 395. As far as I can find from the evidence the defendant although trying desperately to have the stove put in order, did not reject it.

Further s-s. (3) of s. 13 of the Sale of Goods Act, RSS 1940, c. 284, provides as follows: [see Ont. SGA, s. 12(3)].

The stove in this case falls within the description of "specific goods" and there was no express or implied term in the contract of sale that it could be rejected. I have already stated that the stove was not rejected. This does not, however, fortunately for the defendant, mean that she has no redress.

The learned trial Judge stated that he was following the case of *Sedgwick* v. *Lloyd, supra*, but unfortunately he did not do it. In that case the Court of Appeal of Ontario while allowing the appeal referred the matter back to the trial Judge to determine the amount of damages caused by the breach of warranty.

Appeal allowed in part.

Notes:

1   Was the court's attention drawn to *Varley v. Whipp (supra,* chapter 6(B)(1))? Would it have made any difference if it had been? The rule in section 12(3) is usually ascribed to *Street v. Blay* (1831) 2 B & Ad. 456, 109 ER 1212. Do you think it is a sensible rule? Section 12(3) has now been amended by s. 4(1) of the English Misrepresentation Act, 1967. None of the Canadian provinces appears so far to have copied the English example.

2   Without referring to *Home Gas Ltd.* v. *Streeter*, in *Wojakowski* v. *Pembina Dodge Chrysler Ltd.* [1976] 5 WWR 97 (Man.) Morse J. refused to apply literally the Manitoba equivalent of Ont. SGA s. 12(3), although he also found that no property in the goods had in fact passed to the buyer. The case arose out of a contract for the sale of an automobile. The automobile was delivered by the seller but proved to be unsatisfactory. It was therefore agreed that the seller should provide another automobile. Certain defects were noticed at the time of possession or shortly afterwards, which the seller agreed to correct. The repairs were not made, or not made to the plaintiff's satisfaction; indeed the problems were aggravated by the drive shaft falling off while the plaintiff was driving the vehicle. Shortly afterwards the plaintiff refused to have anything further to do with the automobile and brought action claiming rescission of the agreement and the return of the purchase money. Morse J. allowed the claim and disposed of the SGA s. 12(3) issue as follows (at 102-03):

> I am of the view that the contract between the plaintiff and the defendant was for specific goods. Specific goods are defined by s. 2(1)(*n*) of the Act to mean: "goods identified and agreed upon at the time a contract of sale is made". There is no question that the second automobile purchased by the plaintiff was identified and agreed upon at the time the plaintiff agreed to buy it. However, I do not believe it can be said that the property in the automobile at any time passed to the plaintiff within the meaning of s. 13(3) of the Act. It is pointed out in Chalmers' Sale of Goods, 15th Ed., at p. 51, that: "A literal application of [the equivalent section in the English Act] might often mean that a purchaser of specific goods would be unable ever to

reject the goods and treat the contract as repudiated". I am of the view that a literal interpretation cannot and should not be given to the words in question and that, as is indicated in the authorities referred to in Chalmers (p. 51, footnotes (k) and (l)), until the goods are accepted by the purchaser, only a conditional property passes and that this is not a passing of property for the purpose of s. 13(3). See, for example, *Taylor* v. *Combined Buyers Ltd.* [1924] NZLR 627; *Leaf* v. *International Galleries* [1950] 2 KB 86, [1950] 1 All ER 693; and, to the contrary, 14 MLR 173. The evidence satisfies me that the plaintiff in this case never unconditionally accepted the second automobile (and see s. 37 of the Act). Even at the outset, plaintiff accepted the automobile on the basis that certain painting work was to be done by the defendant. Thereafter, the plaintiff made additional complaints which the defendant agreed to remedy. Up to the date on which the plaintiff elected to repudiate the contract, i.e., approximately 27th November 1975, the automobile had not been repainted, the leak in the trunk had not been repaired, and the rust in the trunk had not been removed. In my opinion, therefore, the plaintiff never accepted the second automobile and the property in that automobile never passed to her within the meaning of s. 13(3) of the Act. . . .

3   The student will note that, both at common law and under the SGA, the buyer's right of rejection is limited to breach of a condition; a breach of warranty is not sufficient. On the other hand, the right to reject does not depend on the gravity of the breach. *Cf. I.B.M.* v. *Shcherban, supra,* chapter 6(B)(2). Do these rules conform to reasonable commercial practices? What rules would you substitute in their place? *Cf.* the recommendations in the OLRC Sales Report, reproduced *infra,* this chapter, section 5.

For the Code's treatment of the buyer's right to reject, see UCC 2-508, 2-601, 2-606, and 2-608. And see further J. Honnold, "Buyer's Right of Rejection: A Study in the Impact of Codification Upon a Commercial Problem" (1948-49) U. Pa. L. Rev. 457, and G.L. Priest, "Breach and Remedy for Tender of Nonconforming Goods Under the Uniform Commercial Code: An Economic Approach" (1978) 91 Harv. L. Rev. 960.

2. THE INTERPRETATION OF SGA ss. 33 AND 34

HARDY & COMPANY v. HILLERNS AND FOWLER
[1923] 2 KB 490, [1923] All ER Rep. 275 (CA)

BANKES L.J.: This case raises a question of law as to the proper construction to be placed on s. 35 of the Sale of Goods Act. Messrs. Hillerns & Fowler bought a large quantity of Rosario or Santa Fé wheat to be shipped from a port in Uruguay to Hull at a certain price including freight and insurance, payment to be by cash in London against shipping documents. The ship sailed and arrived in Hull on March 18. On March 20 the buyers' bankers in London took up the shipping documents. On the 21st the ship commenced to discharge the wheat, and on the same day the buyers sold to sub-purchasers portions of the wheat so discharged, 200 qrs. to a purchaser at Barnsley, 100 qrs. to a purchaser at Nottingham, and 500 qrs. to a purchaser at Southwell. In order to fulfil those sub-contracts they on the same day, March 21, despatched the quantities so sold by rail to Barnsley and Nottingham respectively, and to Southwell by barge. They had taken samples of wheat on the 21st, which samples had raised a suspicion that the cargo was not according to the contract description. But they allowed the discharge to continue, and on the 22nd took further samples, which satisfied them that their suspicions were well founded, and on the 23rd they gave the sellers notice that they rejected the wheat. Upon those facts the sellers contended that under the terms of s. 35 the buyers must be deemed to have accepted the goods and lost their right of rejection. The arbitration tribunal found that the wheat was not in accordance with the contract, but that owing to the difficulty of getting a fairly representative sample until a considerable portion of the cargo had been discharged it was reasonable for the buyers to delay making up their mind to reject until the 23rd.

The question now arises whether the buyers by so reselling and forwarding to the sub-purchasers portions of the wheat had lost the right to reject and were confined to their remedy in damages. The construction which Greer J. has placed upon ss. 34 and 35 of the Sale of Goods Act [Ont., ss. 33-34] is one with which I entirely agree. Sect. 34 gives a buyer to whom goods have been delivered, which he has not previously examined, a reasonable opportunity of examining them before he shall be deemed to have accepted them. Then s. 35 [Ont., s. 34] provides as follows: [The Lord Justice read the section.] I understand that to mean that if during the currency of the reasonable time within which the examination is to be made the buyer does certain things, one of which is an "act in relation to (the goods) which is inconsistent with the ownership of the seller," he shall be deemed to have accepted them. Sect. 35 is, in my opinion, independent of s. 34, and it is quite immaterial for the purposes of that section that the reasonable time for examining the goods had not expired when the act was done. The finding therefore of the arbitration tribunal that in the present case that time had not expired may be disregarded.

It remains to be considered whether the act of reselling to the sub-purchasers was an act which was inconsistent with the ownership of the sellers. Mr. Le Quesne has argued that s. 35 has no application to this case, because the contract under which the wheat was sold to the buyers was a c.i.f. contract, and that upon the bank taking up the shipping documents upon March 20 the property passed to the buyers, and that consequently when they resold on the 21st there was no ownership left in the sellers with which that act of resale could be inconsistent. It seems to me that that is attempting to put a meaning on the language of the section which it cannot reasonably bear. I understand the section to refer to an act which is inconsistent with the seller being the owner at the material date; and the material date for the purposes of this case is not the date of the resale, but the date of the notice of rejection, upon receipt of which the ownership revested in the sellers. It is with that revested ownership that in my opinion the act of resale was inconsistent. And it was inconsistent with it for this reason: Where under a contract of sale goods are delivered to the buyer which are not in accordance with the contract, so that the buyer has a right to reject them, the seller upon receipt of notice of rejection is entitled to have the goods placed at his disposal so as to allow of his resuming possession forthwith, and if the buyer has done any act which prevents him from so resuming possession that act is necessarily inconsistent with his right. It is not enough that the buyer should, as in the present case, be in a position to give the seller possession at some later date, he must be able to do so at the time of the rejection. For these reasons I have come to the conclusion that the decision of Greer J. was right and that the appeal should be dismissed.

ATKIN L.J.: This case raises, not I think for the first time, an important question as to the relation of s. 34, sub-s. 1, of the Sale of Goods Act to s. 35.

[Atkin L.J. read the two sections (Ont. ss. 33-34) and continued:]

A possible view of those two sections is that s. 34 limits the provisions of s. 35, and that under the latter section the buyer is not, even in the events there specified, to be deemed to have accepted the goods unless he has had reasonable time and opportunity for examining them. That seems to have been the view taken by the editors of the two last editions of *Benjamin on Sale*. It is there said (6th ed., p. 857) that: "Section 35 contemplates a later stage of the transaction than s. 34(1.). Under s. 34(1.) where the buyer has not previously examined the goods, he is *not* deemed to have accepted them until he has been able to examine them. By s. 35 it is necessary to prove some further fact in order to show that the buyer *has* accepted them." Those words "some further fact" would seem to presume that it was necessary to prove that he had a reasonable opportunity of examination as well as that he did the act mentioned in s. 35. That is no doubt a possible view, but it seems to me to be incorrect. Indeed it was not so argued by Mr. Le Quesne. And I think the reason is obvious. It is that given by the learned judge. One of the acts upon the doing of which the buyer is deemed to have accepted the goods is that "he intimates to the seller that he has accepted them." I think it is plain that such an intimation may be made before he has had a reasonable opportunity of examination, and if such an intimation is made then it appears to me that without more s. 35 operates, and he is to be deemed to have accepted them. In the same way when he does an act in relation to the goods which is inconsistent with the ownership of the seller the section must be treated as coming into operation notwithstanding that the reasonable opportunity of examining them has not expired; as for instance where a man having had goods delivered to him turns them or part of them at once into his mill and uses them in the manufacture. In the present case the tribunal of appeal have found that the buyer had not had a reasonable opportunity of examination until March 23, a date which is subsequent to the act relied on by the sellers as being inconsistent with their ownership; but that finding is, in my opinion, immaterial. Therefore we have here to face the problem whether the act of the buyers in reselling and despatching the goods was inconsistent with the ownership of the sellers. If it was, they must be deemed to have accepted them. I should like to point out, in reference to that provision, that all the words of the section must have effect given to them. The words are: "When the goods have been delivered to him" — that is to the buyer — "and he does any act" of the kind specified. That means that the buyer must have got delivery before he does the act. Here the arbitrators have found the buyers did not obtain delivery of 1877 qrs. on March 21, and that it was out of the wheat so delivered to them that they on the same day forwarded the various parcels to their sub-purchasers. It was however said on behalf of the buyers that before they did so the property in the cargo had already passed to them, and that therefore the sub-sales by them could not be inconsistent with the ownership of the sellers. What is the precise position with regard to the passing of the property under a c.i.f. contract it is perhaps not necessary here to determine. My own view is that if the goods are not in accordance with the contract the property does not pass to the purchaser upon his taking up the documents if he has not had at that time an opportunity of ascertaining whether the goods are in conformity with the contract. Though it may be that the property passes subject to its being revested when the buyer exercises his right of rejection. But it does not seem to me to matter much for the purposes of this case which of those two views is correct. In either view what happened here was enough to take away the buyers' right of rejection. If the possession was transferred by the buyers to third persons in circumstances which were inconsistent either with the goods being the property of the sellers at the time of such transfer, or inconsistent with their being restored to the sellers upon the notice of rejection being given, it appears to me that the transfer was an act which was inconsistent with the ownership of the sellers; and under those circumstances I think that it is quite immaterial that the sub-purchasers may afterwards, by agreement or otherwise, have returned the goods to the buyers. Such return cannot avail to restore a right of rejection which has been lost. That being so I think that the buyers must be content with their claim in damages.

Appeal dismissed.

[Younger L.J. concurred without separate reasons.]

Note on Hardy's Case:

Hardy's case raises difficult issues of exegesis and policy:
a)   What was the ratio of the decision? The re-dispatch of the goods by the buyer? The passing of title? The fact that at the time of rejection the goods were (or were assumed to be) still in the sub-buyer's hands?
b)   Is there hardship to the seller in requiring him to take back goods at a place other than the place of delivery? Would the logic of this reasoning also lead us to the same conclusion where a buyer with many retail outlets distributes the goods within the chain before the defects come to light? *Cf.* UCC 2-513 which provides inter alia that, unless otherwise agreed, the buyer has a right before acceptance to inspect the goods at any reasonable time and place and in any reasonable manner.
c)   If the buyer were to sue for damages, would the quantum of his recovery be less than the cost to the seller of collecting the goods from the place of rejection? *Cf. Molling & Co.* v. *Dean & Son, Ltd.* (1901) 18 TLR 217 (DC).

   Hardy was distinguished by the Ontario Court of Appeal in *A.J. Frank & Sons Ltd.* v. *Northern Peat Co. Ltd.* (1963) 39 DLR (2d) 721, on the grounds that by the terms of the agreement the goods were to be inspected at the ultimate point of destination and that at the time of rejection they were still in the buyer's possession. For a similar decision see *Hammer and Barrow* v. *Coca-Cola* [1962] NZLR 723. *Hardy* was statutorily reversed in England by s. 4(2) of the Misrepresentation Act, 1967, but the drafting is unclear and is criticized in the OLRC Sales Report, pp. 470-71. For a post-1967 decision giving effect to the amendment (but without referring to it), see *Manifatture Tessile Laniera Wolltex* v. *J.B. Ashley Ltd.* [1979] 2 Lloyd's Rep. 28 (CA). No Canadian province has so far adopted a s. 4(2) type amendment and the Sales Report, p. 471, recommends the total deletion of the inconsistent act rule.

RAFUSE MOTORS LTD. v. MARDO CONSTRUCTION LTD.
(1963) 41 DLR (2d) 340, 48 MPR 296 (NS CA)

COFFIN J.: This appeal arises from an action on a promissory note made by the defendant to the plaintiff.

The plaintiff (appellant), a body corporate, whose chief place of business is Bridgewater in the County of Lunenburg, is a dealer and distributor for Ford Motor Co. and its subsidiaries, and the defendent (respondent), is a body corporate, whose president and general manager is Mr. George Zinck.

The defendant held a contract for a consolidated school at New Ross in the County of Lunenburg, and in order to complete this contract, Mr. George Zinck decided it would be necessary to use a tractor. Early in January, 1960, he was approached by Mr. Cliff Oxner, salesman for Rafuse Motors Limited, who wanted to sell a tractor. Mr. Zinck told him that the only tractor in which he would be interested was a Major tractor. As a result an order for a Major tractor was executed for the price of $4,673, of which $1,500 cash was to be paid on delivery, balance to be secured by a note.

Mr. Zinck was asked what discussions he had with Mr. Oxner relating to the use of this tractor by Mardo Construction Ltd.

> A. I told him that I had this contract at New Ross, which he was aware of, and I wanted this equipment of a certain type to be used on this job. I explained to him what I was going to do with it and what I wanted it for and why I wanted it.
>
> Q. Do you recall how the name Major or Fordson Major came into the conversation? A. Because I had a Fordson Major tractor before that — a couple of years.
>
> Q. What, if anything, did you say about it? A. I told him I wanted that tractor because I was acquainted with it and had good satisfaction with it prior to this.

A few weeks later Mr. Zinck was advised by Mr. Oxner that he could not get the front end loader for this tractor and that he could supply a Ford tractor complete with all the equipment made by the Ford Motor Co. that was equal to the Fordson Major.

Mr. Zinck said that Mr. Oxner told him: "It would do everything that the Fordson Major would do on this particular job. I told him I wouldn't buy it if he felt it wouldn't do the job because I was disappointed because I wanted the Fordson Major."

This suggested tractor was the 871 Ford tractor.

Mr. Zinck said that he told Mr. Oxner he would take this tractor if it was equal to the Fordson Major, and late in February, 1960, this tractor was delivered to Mr. Zinck's brother's home outside of Chester.

This history of the use of this equipment should be set out in some detail.

1. It was first used around the home outside of Chester to remove snow. Mr. Zinck found it did not do the job that he expected because it seemed too light. Mr. Oxner and Mr. McAfee of the Ford Motor Co. tried the tractor and suggested

tractor chains. They were unobtainable nor could Rafuse Motors supply half-tracks, so Mr. Zinck obtained half-tracks from Harbour Motors in Dartmouth, Nova Scotia.

He then found the tractor too light in the rear, and on Mr. Oxner's suggestion he had a set of wheel weights made by Hillis Foundry in Halifax.

The tractor remained in the Chester area until about April 5, 1960.

2. It was taken to New Ross to remove snow from a building that had just been steel framed for the New Ross school. There certain break-downs occurred in the tractor:

(a) The radius rod piece broke.
(b) Transmission failed and Mr. McAfee found that there was some foreign material under the valve. Mr. Zinck at this time pointed out that he thought the front end was too light but was assured by Mr. McAfee that it would stand.

The loss of time consumed by these two incidents was three to four days.

(c) The tractor was then put to work levelling off sand and gravel to get ready for the floors and around the school in general when the rear end collapsed. These repairs absorbed about 10 days at Seffern's garage.
(d) Next the front end bent down and broke the pump shaft and housing around the motor holding this pump heading. The repairs in this case took 14 days.

At this point Mr. Zinck said he complained to Mr. Oxner, Mr. L.S. Rafuse and Mr. McAfee who told him the difficulties were in the manufacture and they would "replace them, and they felt sure it would be all right from now on".

• • •

(e) Something broke in the rear end again. I quote Mr. Zinck on this point:

> I called Mr. Oxner at Bridgewater and told him the tractor was broken down, that I was finished with it and wouldn't accept it and couldn't accept it. It was a continual break-down and it was costing us money, plus the fact you couldn't get the parts without delay.

His evidence is that thereupon Mr. Oxner asked him to call Seffern's Garage to pick up the tractor which they did, and that he has had nothing to do with the tractor since that time. The tractor left his possession around the first of July having performed about 135 hours of work from the time it came on the site not earlier than April 5, 1960. It is apparent from the facts that the time lost in break-downs was approximately 27 days exclusive of the last collapse of the rear end.

The particulars of the sale of the tractor 871 and equipment are set out in ex. S/5, the total purchase price being $5,055, and on February 22, 1960, the defendant paid the plaintiff $1,500 and gave a promissory note for the balance of $3,555. The defendant (respondent) refused to pay the note, and the plaintiff (appellant) then launched this action on the note for $3,555 principal and $160.20 interest to October 14, 1960, together with interest on the principal at 7% per annum from that date.

534 CH. 12 BUYER'S REMEDIES FOR BREACH OF SELLER'S OBLIGATIONS

The defence alleged failure to deliver the tractor as agreed upon and total failure of consideration. In the alternative the defendant alleged that the consideration for the note was the delivery to the defendant of a Ford 871 tractor with equipment on the express condition that it was the equivalent of a Fordson Major tractor, and adequate for specific work by the plaintiff in carrying out a contract to construct a school building at New Ross, Lunenburg County.

The defendant counterclaimed alleging the contract to supply a Fordson Major diesel tractor and equipment, the failure to deliver, the agreement to substitute the Ford 871 tractor with equipment equivalent to the Fordson Major, the guarantee by the plaintiff that the Ford 871 would do the specific work required, and the acceptance by the defendant of the Ford 871 tractor subject to these conditions and on a trial basis $1,500 being paid as a down payment. The counterclaim further alleged that the defendant gave the tractor a reasonable trial and the plaintiff every opportunity to make good its deficiencies until its final rejection. The reply denied these allegations and the defence to counterclaim denied the surrender of possession and stated that the plaintiff had no knowledge of what happened to the tractor.

• • •

IV. Was there an acceptance of the 871 and equipment by the defendant? I now refer to the Sale of Goods Act, s. 36 [Ont., s. 34]:

• • •

There is no evidence that the defendant ever intimated to the plaintiff that he had accepted the unit.

The question here is whether the defendant did any act in relation to the unit inconsistent with the ownership of the seller or retained the unit for an unreasonable time without intimating to the plaintiff its rejection.

In the *Alabastine* case, *supra*, Meredith, C.J.O., said at pp. 819-20 DLR, p. 409 OLR:

> It is, I think, the proper conclusion on the evidence that the "trying out" of the engine was, as understood by both parties, to be for the purpose of discovering whether or not it answered the conditions of the contract, and what was done by the respondent in "trying out" the engine cannot be treated as an acceptance of it, or as evidence that it had been accepted by the respondent.

Brodeur, J., in *Schofield* v. *Emerson Brantingham Implement Co.* 43 DLR 509 at pp. 524-5, 57 SCR 203 at p. 225, [1918] 3 WWR 434 at p. 450 dealt with the matter of inducements and encouragements by the vendor:

> The company knew the purpose for which Schofield required the engine and he has certainly relied on their skill and ability to furnish him with an engine suitable for that purpose. The engine not having developed the quantity of horse-power for which it was sold, the respondent company has certainly not fulfilled its contract.
>
> It is true that there was a settlement made; but that settlement was obtained by continuous representation that the machine would develop the horse-power they contracted for. This engine, it was claimed, would get better with wear, etc. As a

question of fact, the company sent after that settlement some experts to try and make it right. They have never succeeded, and it seems to me that the machine, having never been fit for the purpose for which it was purchased, and the settlement having been obtained under certain representations which proved absolutely incorrect, the respondent cannot avail itself of that settlement and the plaintiff should succeed.

I should mention the remarks of Henderson J.A., in *Cork* v. *Greavette Boats Ltd.*, [1940] 4 DLR 202 at p. 206, [1940] OR 352 at p. 365, where the plaintiff "deferred the exercise of his right of rejection upon representations made to him that the boat would be made satisfactory. . . ."

In considering whether the time is or is not reasonable any inducement by the seller to extend the period of trial of the goods is relevant: 34 *Hals.*, 3rd., p. 112.

I agree with the learned trial Judge that Mr. Steele had encouraged Zinck to give the tractor a fair trial. Mr. Zinck said on cross-examination at pp. 85-6:

> Well, it was sometime before the tractor broke down the last time Mr Steele was to see me and told me he had got a call from Rafuse Motors and he was going to come to see me and I told him I was finished with the tractor and he explained to me why it broke down and it was part of the fault of the manufacturer and it was now cured and if I would give it a fair trial he assured me it would do the work.

In fact the whole history of the dealings between the plaintiff and the defendant as shown by the constant efforts to make the equipment work corroborated by the statements in the various letters from the plaintiff to the Ford Company, justify the findings of the learned trial Judge, that any delay in rejection and any acts inconsistent with the plaintiff's ownership were due to the inducements of the plaintiff.

From the time the defendant first operated the unit for snow removal in the Chester area to the final break-down, complaints were being made to the plaintiff. The defendant did everything possible to comply with the suggestions of both plaintiff and Ford Company officials to give the unit a fair trial.

Even before he gave his final notice of rejection, Mr. Zinck told Mr. Oxner that he would pay no more money unless they could prove "it was able to do the work I purchased it for".

I can find nothing in the evidence to persuade me that there was an acceptance under any of the elements contained in s. 36 of the Sale of Goods Act.

Appeal dismissed.

[Currie and MacDonald JJ. concurred; Ilsley C.J. and MacQuarrie J. dissented in part on another question.]

Notes:

1 The purchaser of a computer system informed the seller of the particular purposes for which he required the computer. The computer was delivered but, after several months of programming, it become obvious that the computer could not operate at the required speed. For the next six months the seller tried unsuccessfully to make the machine operate satisfactorily. Finally, the buyer told the seller he did not want the computer and that the seller should take it back, but not before the buyer

could replace it with another. Fourteen more months passed before the replacement was delivered. Seller now claims that the buyer has kept the goods too long to rescind. What result? See *Public Utilities Commission of City of Waterloo* v. *Burroughs Business Machines Ltd.* (1974) 6 OR (2d) 257, 52 DLR (3d) 481 (CA), and compare UCC 2-602(2) and OLRC Sales Report, pp. 471-72.

2 As the principal case illustrates, the courts are reluctant to find that the buyer has accepted the goods if the defect in the goods manifests itself from the beginning. Helpful though it is, this attitude does not resolve the buyer's dilemma where the defect is latent and only appears after a substantial period of time has elapsed. On this important issue, see the notes following *Hart-Parr Company* v. *Jones, infra.*

3 Under SGA s. 35 the buyer may rescind by intimating to the seller that the goods are rejected. Under the Business Practices Act, s. 4(5) and (6) the notice must be given in writing and delivered personally or by registered mail. But under the Consumer Protection Act, s. 33(2) (which deals with contracts not signed at the seller's place of business) notice is not sufficient and the buyer must return the goods to the seller, albeit at the seller's expense. Is there any reason for the lack of uniformity? Which method of rescission is best in the consumer context? For the commercial situation? Is there a conflict between the BPA and the CPA?

HART-PARR COMPANY v. JONES
[1971] 2 WWR 888 (Sask. SC)

LAMONT J.: By an order in writing dated August 1, 1913, the defendant requested the plaintiff company, who are the manufacturers of tractors, to ship to him one of their 30 brake, gas tractors and a 4 furrow 14 inch stubble bottom plough, for which he agreed to pay $2,755. Before giving the order the defendant made known to the plaintiffs that he wanted an engine that would operate satisfactorily his threshing separator and that would pull satisfactorily the ploughs which he contemplated purchasing. In pretended compliance with the order the plaintiffs shipped to him an engine of the size and shape of the one ordered, freshly painted so as to look like a new engine. The defendant and the plaintiffs' experts endeavoured in the fall of 1913 to make the engine satisfactorily drive the defendant's separator, but failed to do so. In November an expert named Ginter went to the defendant's to fix up the engine so that it would plough, but when he got the engine operating the ground was frozen so that ploughing was practically impossible. In March the defendant requested the company to send up an expert to start the engine ploughing. In April or the beginning of May the expert arrived and the defendant and the expert examined the engine. The paint in places, owing probably to winter weather, had come off and the parts of the engine thus exposed bore such evidence that the engine had not been a new one when delivered, that certain suspicions along that line which the defendant had entertained were confirmed. He asked the expert about it, but the expert replied that the company's manager at Regina had forbidden him to say whether or not the engine was a rebuilt one. The defendant, becoming satisfied that the company had delivered to him a second-hand engine, drew it to his barn and notified the representatives of the company that it was not the article he had ordered and that it was at his place at the company's risk.

Not receiving the purchase price, the plaintiffs have brought this action for the full amount. The defendant resists payment on the ground (1) that the engine delivered was not the one he ordered and that he refused to accept it, and (2) that there was a total failure of consideration.

On the evidence I find that the engine delivered was not new, but was a second-hand engine with some new parts put in, the whole being newly painted to look like a new engine. I accept the evidence of the defendant that he notified the company that it was an old engine as soon as he was really sure of that fact and that thereafter he made no use of the machine.

On the argument it was not disputed that both parties understood the order to call for a new engine. That such was the meaning of the order I have no hesitation in holding. The delivery of a second-hand engine was not therefore, a compliance with the order.

• • •

In this case, the engine ordered was not delivered. Did the defendant accept the second-hand engine in fulfilment of his order?

Secs. 33(1) and 34 of The Sale of Goods Act are as follows:

• • •

What took place in this case is very similar to what occurred in *Alabastine Co. v. Canada Producer & Gas Engine Co.* (1914) 30 OLR 394, 23 OWR 841, 4 OWN 486. There, the plaintiffs ordered from the defendants a three cylinder 19 x 20 natural gas engine and fittings, in accordance with specifications which were made part of the agreement, for $6,000. The specifications required the engine to develop 250 h.p. The title was to remain in the defendants until fully paid for. The engine was delivered in August and set up by the defendant company's engineer about September 8, and commenced to run September 10. From the start there was trouble with the engine and it could not be made to work satisfactorily. At times it would work fairly well for a while and then some part would go wrong. On March 25, 1912, the engine went to pieces. The plaintiffs had paid $5,500 of the purchase price. They sued for a rescission of the contract and a return of the money paid. In giving the judgment of the Court of Appeal, Meredith, C.J.O., at p. 406, said:

> It is reasonably clear, we think, that there was no such acceptance of the engine as precluded the respondent from rejecting it if it did not fulfil the requirements of the contract. It was being "tried out" from September, when it was set up in the respondent's factory, until the time of the break-down in the following March. The evidence, no doubt, shows that throughout this period the respondent's manager was hoping, and perhaps believing, that the appellant would succeed in making such changes in the engine as would put it in a condition to meet the requirements of the contract, but there is nothing to show that the respondent at any time accepted the engine as answering those requirements, and, besides this, by the terms of the contract, "the title to the machinery or material" furnished was to remain in the appellant until the purchase-price should be fully paid.

This case is authority for the proposition that, where the property has not passed, the receipt of the engine, payment of part of the purchase money and attempted use from September to the following March does not necessarily constitute acceptance. In the case at bar, also, the property had not passed. The defendant received the engine in August; he commenced to thresh in the fall and threshed in all about 30 days, threshing only 20,000 bushels. According to the plaintiffs' own letter they had an expert on the engine 14½ days in the fall. In the spring the defendant rejected the engine.

In November 1913, when the expert Ginter was out attempting to put the engine in shape so that it would plough, he obtained the defendant's signature to the following:

> Hart-Parr Co.
>   Charles City, Iowa.
> Gentlemen:
>   Your Mr. W.C. Ginter called at my request and has spent 4 days rendering the desired assistance on engine No. 2405 and leaves the same in good running order and it is satisfactory to me.
>
>   John Jones

This the defendant signed because the expert represented that it was necessary for him to obtain a voucher for the days that he had spent on the defendant's engine. I do not place any reliance upon it as an acceptance of the engine. It was not signed for that purpose, and at the very time it was signed the ground was frozen too hard to make any real trial of the ploughing capacity of the engine. Under the circumstances, this acknowledgement cannot, in my opinion, be considered as an intimation to the seller by the defendant that he accepted the engine. The property in the engine was and still is in the plaintiff company.

Then, did the defendant retain the engine an unreasonable length of time before he intimated that he rejected it?

Ordinarily, the receipt of an article and its retention for eight months would afford strong evidence of acceptance, although not necessarily conclusive. Along with the lapse of time the circumstances must be taken into consideration. In this case two circumstances must not be lost sight of: (1) that from the early part of November until April there was no opportunity of "trying out" the engine, (2) the conduct of the plaintiffs' agents.

In 25 *Halsbury*, at p. 231, the learned author says:

> **401.** In determining what is a reasonable time for the rejection of the goods by the buyer, regard is had to the conduct of the seller, as where he has induced the buyer to prolong the trial of the goods, or has by his silence acquiesced in a further trial.

In *Heilbutt* v. *Hickson*, LR 7 CP 438; 41 LJ CP 228, the plaintiffs contracted for the purchase of 30,000 pairs of army shoes as per sample, to be inspected and quality approved before shipment. The plaintiffs inspected, received, paid for and shipped to Lille, 4,950 pairs. It was then discovered that the soles of some of the shoes contained paper. The defendants then gave a letter to the plaintiffs agreeing to take back any shoes that might be rejected by the French authorities in consequence of containing paper. The plaintiffs then took delivery of 12,000 additional pairs. The French authorities rejected the whole. The plaintiffs sued for damages, which they claimed to be the whole cost of the shoes with freight, insurance and cartage added and loss of profit. They were held to be entitled. In appeal, the majority of the Court based its judgment on the fact that the letter gave the plaintiffs a right to reject the shoes at Lille, but Brett, L.J., while agreeing with the judgment, expressed a decided opinion that the right of the plaintiffs would have been the same under the original bargain and independently of the latter; holding that, where a buyer has a right to reject goods upon inspection at a certain place and the vendors or those for whose acts they are responsible prevent the buyer from making an effective inpsection at the place, he is not bound by such inspection. His Lordship, at p. 456, says:

> The defect, though known to the defendants' servants, was a secret defect, not discoverable by any reasonable exercise of care or skill on an inspection in London. By the necessary inefficacy of the inspection in London, an inefficacy caused by this kind of fault, *viz*: a secret defect of manufacture which the defendants' servants committed — the apparent inspection in London could be of no more practical effect than no inspection at all. If it could be of no practical effect, there could not, as has been observed, be any effective, and, therefore, any real practical inspection until an inspection at Lille.

This view seems to be approved of in *Halsbury's Laws of England*, vol. 25, p. 229. Applying the principles there laid down to the facts before us, it would justify the conclusion that the plaintiffs' servants by painting the engine made the inspection on the part of the defendant when it was delivered ineffective, and it was not until the spring of 1914 when the paint came off that an effective inspection could be made.

On the whole, I have reached the conclusion that what took place in this case was not such an acceptance of the engine as prevented the defendant from rejecting it when he did. If, however, what took place did amount to an acceptance, it seems clear to me that that acceptance was induced by the act of the plaintiffs' servants in concealing from the defendant the fact that he was not getting a new engine.

Action dismissed; counterclaim allowed.

Notes:

1   George purchased a school bus. Three months after the delivery of the vehicle he received a "recall" notice from the manufacturer advising him that the brackets supporting the exhaust system were not strong enough and needed to be replaced. Can George reject the vehicle and demand the return of his money?

2   *Hart-Parr* v. *Jones* seems to go a substantial distance towards recognizing a right of rejection because of a latent defect even after a substantial time for inspection has elapsed. Is this consistent with the history and rationale of ss. 33-34? Should such a right be expressly recognized as is true in UCC 2-608? Civil law systems which trace their roots to Roman law have long recognized such a right in the so-called

"redhibitory" action to rescind the transaction on the grounds of a latent defect. See e.g., Que. C.C. art. 1522 *et seq.* and *cf.* UN International Sales Convention, art. 38-40. Where lies the balance of convenience in such circumstances — the "allocative" and "distributive" costs, to borrow from the economists' lexicon? Or does it depend on the facts of each case? For an economic analysis of the Code's provisions and case law, see G.L. Priest, "Breach and Remedy for Tender of Nonconforming Goods under the Uniform Commercial Code: An Economic Approach" (1978) 91 Harv. L. Rev. 960. The OLRC supports the Code approach. See Sales Report, pp. 472-75.

3. Part Rejection and Part Acceptance in Indivisible Contracts

WILLIAM BARKER (JUNIOR) AND CO. LTD. v. ED. T. AGIUS, LTD.
(1927) 33 Com. Cas. 120, 43 TLR 751 (KB)

The buyers, William Barker (Junior) and Co., Limited, agreed to buy from the sellers, Ed. T. Agius, Limited, a quantity of German coal. The coal was shipped at Hamburg on a vessel chartered by the buyers, some of it being in the holds and the remainder on deck and covering the hatch covers. When the vessel reached Liverpool it had to wait for a discharging berth. The captain became alarmed because the cargo in the holds was heating. In order to reach it he offered to buy the cargo on deck. The buyers agreed to do so with a view to helping him, and to secure the safety of the ship. The captain had the cargo moved into the bunkers and the covers were taken off the hatches. Only then did the buyers for the first time inspect the cargo in the holds and they found that it was not of the contract description. They then gave notice of rejection of the *whole* cargo, but the sellers contended that as the buyers had dealt with part of the cargo by selling it to the captain the right to reject had been lost. The arbitrator decided in favour of the buyers, subject to the opinion of the court on a special case.

SALTER J.: The next question that is put is whether on the true construction of the documents and on the facts as found by me the applicants had and validly exercised a right to reject the under deck cargo. Those are two questions. Had they a legal right to reject this part of the delivery which is called the under deck cargo? If they had, did they validly exercise it? I will deal with the two questions in that order.

• • •

Now [the first question], I think, having regard to the authorities, is a question of some difficulty. I will deal with it first as if I were free from authority. It involves a consideration of three sections of the Sale of Goods Act: section 11, subsection 1(c) [Ont., s. 12(3)]; section 30, subsection 3 [Ont., s. 29(3)], and section 35 [Ont., s. 34]. It is convenient, I think, to look first at section 35: "The buyer is deemed to have accepted the goods" — I am reading only the material parts — "when he does any act in relation to them which is inconsistent with the ownership of the seller." I have no doubt that if a buyer takes part of the goods and sells them that he does an act in relation to the goods which have been delivered to him which is inconsistent with the ownership of the seller; he cannot have a right to deal with part of the goods. Now I turn to section 11, 1(c), and I will read the first subsection: "In England or Ireland (a) Where a contract of sale is subject to any condition to be fulfilled by the seller, the buyer may waive the condition, or may elect to treat the breach of such condition as a breach of warranty, and not as a ground for treating the contract as repudiated." Paragraph (c): "Where a contract of sale is not severable, and the buyer has accepted the goods, or part thereof" — I am again reading only the material words — "the breach of any condition to be fulfilled by the seller can only be treated as a breach of warranty, and not as a ground for rejecting the goods and treating the contract as repudiated." I should have thought, if I were free from authority, that that clause governs this case. In my opinion this is not a severable contract. It is a contract for the sale of a cargo of briquettes which, within small limits, may vary in amount but which will be ascertained on delivery on board the ship, for an agreed lump sum which will be ascertained by multiplying the tons by 34s., the price. It is one contract and it is not severable. The buyer has accepted part of the goods. He has sold and delivered 25 tons of it, and, therefore the breach of this condition to be fulfilled by the seller can only be treated as a breach of warranty and not as a ground for rejecting the goods and treating the contract as repudiated. I should like to say that it is clear that rejection in this connexion means rescission. If a seller tenders to a buyer goods which are not in accordance with the contract and the buyer says to the seller, "This is not a performance of the contract; go and get proper goods and perform your contract," in a sense he rejects those goods. But that kind of refusal is not what is meant by rejection in this Act. So far from being a rescission or treating the contract as repudiated, that is an insistence on the contract. "Rejection" here means that the buyer might say to the seller: "This tender in purported performance of the contract is a fundamental breach of the contract and it entitles me, if I please, to treat the contract as repudiated by you, and I do so treat it as rescinded." Now where a buyer has accepted the whole of the goods, there can be no question that after that he cannot claim to reject and rescind, and it seems to me that if this clause were concerned only with rejection of the whole of the goods it would have been unnecessary to say anything about severable contracts. The words "Where a contract of sale is not severable" must have been inserted in view of the words "or part thereof," and if I were left to myself I should say that that means that where the buyer of goods has so dealt with part of the goods that he has rendered it impossible for him to return the whole of the goods the subject of the one contract, so that the parties cannot be restored to their former position, he cannot then claim to return either the whole of the goods — which is obviously impossible here as the buyer has sold part of them — or the part which remains in his hands. Supposing he has had delivery to him in purported performance of a contract for an agreed lump sum 100 tons of goods 5 tons of which are of contract quality and 95 tons are not, if he sells and delivers the 5 tons to a sub-purchaser, keeping the 95 tons in his hands, he cannot after that claim to return to the seller the 95 tons, to recover from the seller 95 percent of the contract price, and to retain the 5 tons at a rate applicable to 100 tons which no one would think of applying to so small a quantity as 5 tons, and then leave the matter so that neither party has any further rights against the other, the contract having been neither repudiated nor rescinded nor performed as a whole. I should have thought that such a position was impossible and that the purchaser who has resold part of the goods delivered in performance of one inseverable contract cannot after that throw back that part which is bad upon the seller, but that he is remitted to his remedy in damages in respect of that part of the delivery which is not in accordance with the contract. That brings me to section 30, sub-section 3, and it is said that section 11, 1(c) and section 35 must be read in conjunction with and in the light of section 30, sub-section 3. Section 30 deals with such matters as delivery of the wrong quantity, delivery of too large a quantity, and, under sub-section 3, delivery of mixed goods. Sub-section 1 provides that where the seller delivers to the buyer a quantity of goods less than he contracted to sell, the buyer may reject them, but if the buyer accepts the goods so delivered he must pay for them at the contract rate. Sub-section 2 says, "Where the seller delivers to the buyer a quantity of goods larger than he contracted to sell, the buyer may accept the goods included in the contract and reject the rest, or he may reject the whole. If the buyer accepts the whole of the goods so delivered he must pay for them at the contract rate." Then sub-section 3 deals with mixed goods: "Where the seller delivers to the buyer the goods he contracted to sell mixed with goods of a different description not included in the contract the buyer may accept the goods which are in accordance with the contract and reject the rest, or he may reject the whole." If I were free to read that section as *res nova* I should have thought it referred only to the goods of surplus delivery and admixture. I should be disposed to give to the word "mixed" a much more definite meaning than was given to it by Rowlatt J. in the case of *Moore and Co.* v. *Landauer and Co.* [1921] 2 KB 519 reported in the Court below in 1921, 1 KB 73. He said in that case that he thought it meant no more than "accompanied by." I should have thought that it meant much more than "accompanied by." If a man buys a horse and the seller delivers a horse and a donkey it would not require an Act of Parliament, I should think, to say he must keep the horse and return the donkey. I think that a good deal was meant to depend here on the word "mixed." I should have thought that it refers to the case, and only the case, where the seller has delivered the whole of the goods he contracted to deliver, the whole quantity and all of the right description and quality, but he has intermixed with those goods goods which are wholly alien to the contract, goods of a different description not included in his contract. Then the position is that the goods which are in accordance with the contract mixed with those which are not, cannot be separated out without trouble and expense, and then the section would simply say if the buyer chooses to go to that trouble and expense he can accept the goods which are in accordance with the contract and reject those which are not, but that he need not go to that trouble and expense. The seller cannot say to him, "All the goods I contracted to sell of the agreed quantity are there and, therefore, you must taken them and sort them out for yourself." He cannot say that. The buyer may, if he pleases, reject the whole. That reading does not touch section 35 or section 11, and that is the way in which I should read it if I were free to read it for myself. But it has not been so read, and the question for me is whether the observations and decisions in three cases to which I now have to refer are such that it is my duty to read section 30, subsection 3, as giving to the buyers in this case a right to accept the 25 tons and to reject, in the sense in which I have defined that word, the balance; that is to say, the right to accept the 25 tons and to pay for them at 34s. a ton and no more, and to return to the sellers the rest of the goods and to recover from them the whole of the contract price except 25 tons at 34s. a ton, with the result that after that neither party has any right against the other. The contract is in a sense repudiated, in a sense performed; neither wholly repudiated nor wholly performed. That is the right which the buyers here are claiming and which it is said section 30, subsection 3, gives them; and the question is whether these three cases show that I ought so to hold.

Now the first of these cases is the case of *Moore and Company* v. *Landauer and Company* [1921] 2 KB 519. In that case there was one contract for the sale of canned fruit, "the buyers stipulated that they should be packed in cases containing 30 tins each, payment to be per dozen tins. The sellers tendered the whole quantity ordered, but about one-half was packed in cases each containing 24 tins only." Those were the facts. It was held that the buyers were entitled to reject the whole consignment. The question being considered was whether they were bound to accept the whole, but it is to my mind quite clear that Rowlatt J. regarded section 30, subsection 3, as being a section by which on facts such as exist in this case the buyer might accept the part of the goods in accordance with the contract and reject the part which was not, in the sense that he might make a partial rescission of the contract and accept part performance. That case went to the Court of Appeal, where the decision of Rowlatt J. was upheld, but the decision is not of much importance in this case. It was held that as part of the goods was not in accordance with the contract the buyers were entitled to reject the whole. But I think it is quite clear that the Court took the view that the meaning of section 30, subsection 3, is that where the seller delivers the whole quantity partly of the contract quality and partly not, the buyer is at liberty to accept the part which is of the contract quality and to reject the rest in the sense of rescinding the contract in respect of the rest. In that case section 11 was not referred to and there was no reason why it should be; and there was certainly no reason why section 35 should be referred to.

The next case is the case of *J. and J. Cunningham, Limited* v. *Robert A. Munro & Company, Limited* [1922] 28 Com. Cas. 42. That was a special case stated under section 19 for a Divisional Court. There was a contract for the sale of 200 tons of Dutch bran, f.o.b., Rotterdam, for October shipment. The buyers' ship was to be loaded at Rotterdam, and there was some delay. When loading began it was found that the bran was heated, and the buyers refused to accept any more than 384 bags which had already been put on board. The sellers contended that the buyers had no right to reject and that the bran remained at the risk of the buyers. Various other questions were raised there, but it is to my mind clear that the claim was to reject the portion other than the 384 bags; in fact, the buyers resold the 384 bags, just as in the present case, and they claimed to reject the balance. The first question was whether they were entitled to reject the balance and it was held that they were. In that case I should have expected section 11 and section 35 would have been considered, seeing that the buyers had exercised the rights of owners over part of the goods delivered, but I do not find that that was done. But it is quite clear that that Court considered section 30, sub-section 3, as a section which would give to the buyers the right which they claimed in this case, a right of partial rejection.

The third case contains a dictum of Greer J. It is the case of *E. Hardy & Company (London), Limited* v. *Hillerns and Fowler* [1923] 2 KB 490, reported in the Court below in 28 Com. Cas. 193. That was a case in which the buyers, when the cargo was in process of unloading, without waiting to make a complete inspection of the cargo, resold and delivered parcels of it to sub-buyers. They afterwards claimed to reject the whole; and it was held that they had no such right. That I should have thought was a fairly simple matter, but Greer J., on a further question of a right to reject part having been raised, said: "I shall only answer the question which is raised, not expressly but inferentially, by the case stated — namely, whether the rejection which in fact took place, rejection of the whole quantity, was or was not a valid rejection. If my view is desired on that other point, I should add that in my judgment there has not been an acceptance of part and a rejection of the balance; that can be done where part of the goods is obviously in accordance with the contract and part is not; but where the same objection applies to the whole quantity and notwithstanding the objection to the whole quantity a portion has been accepted, there cannot be a rejection of the remainder. As the point is not raised by the case stated my views on it are *obiter* and need not be regarded as any authority for the proposition." I think that considered observations by Greer J., even though *obiter*, are by no means to be neglected; and what is more, those observations were expressly approved, of course *obiter*, by Bankes L.J. when that case was considered in the Court of Appeal.

I have come to the conclusion that in view of these authorities, while it may be possible to say that they are not strictly speaking decisions which I am bound to follow, it would not be right for me to follow what would have been my own reading of these sections; and in view of those authorities and in deference to those authorities I hold that the buyers had in this case a right to accept the 25 tons and to reject the remainder.

[Salter J. went on to find, however, in response to the second question, that the buyers had not made an effective rejection since they had purported to reject the whole cargo and not merely the non-conforming part of it. He accordingly held that the buyers were restricted to a claim in damages for breach of warranty.]

> *Judgment for the buyers, except on the question*
> *whether they had validly exercised their right to reject.*

Notes:

1   For further discussion of the issues presented in this case see Sutton, *The Law of Sale of Goods in Australia and New Zealand,* 2nd ed. (1974), pp. 339-42 and *J.*

Rosenthal & Sons Ltd. v. *Esmail* [1965] 1 WLR 1117 (HL). With respect to the meaning of description in SGA s. 29(3) see *Runnymede Iron & Steel Ltd.* v. *Rossen Engineering & Construction Co.* (1961) 30 DLR (2d) 410 (SCC) (held that "relaying rails" unfit for relaying without repair were goods of a different description and not simply goods of inferior quality). Is there any justification for restricting s. 29(3) to goods of the wrong description?

2   The Uniform Sales Act did not expressly reject the partial acceptance rule but it was substantially undermined by the New York Court of Appeals in a leading case, *Portfolio* v. *Rubin* (1922) 125 NE 843, and the process has been completed in Article 2. UCC 2-601 provides *inter alia* that if the goods or the tender of delivery fail in any respect to conform to the contract, the buyer may reject the whole, accept the whole, or accept any commercial unit or units and reject the rest. "Commercial unit" is defined in UCC 2-105(6) as meaning "such a unit of goods as by commercial usage is a single whole for purposes of sale and division materially affects its character or value on the market or in use". The OLRC recommended adoption of the Code's approach where the non-conformity amounts to a substantial breach. See Sales Report, p. 447. Does UCC 2-601 mean that the buyer has complete freedom of action — that, for example, he can retain part of the conforming goods and reject the rest, or that he can retain only part of the non-conforming goods? How could the section be read to avoid such unreasonable results? Curiously, judging by the paucity of reported Code cases, the issue does not so far appear to have arisen for decision.

4. INSTALMENT CONTRACTS

MAPLE FLOCK CO. LTD. v. UNIVERSAL FURNITURE PRODUCTS (WEMBLEY) LTD.
[1934] 1 KB 148, [1933] All ER Rep. 15 (CA)

LORD HEWART C.J. (for the court): The appellant company are manufacturers of rag flock, and the respondents are manufacturers of furniture and bedding for which they use such flock. The action was brought by the appellants for breach by the respondents of a contract in writing, dated March 14, 1932, for the sale by the appellants to the respondents of 100 tons of black lindsey flock at 15*l*. 2*s*. 6*d*. per ton, to be delivered in three loads per week as required. It was further stipulated that there should be a written guarantee that all flock supplied under the contract should conform to the Government standard. The load was 1¹/₂ tons or 60 bags. The government standard was that required under the Rag Flock Act, 1911, which had been fixed by regulation under the Act at not more than 30 parts of chlorine in 100,000 parts of flock. The Act made it a penal offence punishable by fine for any person (*inter alia*) to sell or have in his possession for sale or use or to use flock not conforming to that standard. A person charged under the Act might, however, if he could prove that he bought it from some one resident in the United Kingdom under a warranty that it complied with the Government standard, and that he had taken reasonable steps to ascertain and did in fact believe in the accuracy of the warranty, bring the seller before the Court by information and transfer the burden of the offence to him.

The appellant company duly gave a written guarantee as required by the contract and deliveries were at once commenced and continued of $1^1/_2$ tons each. The sixteenth of these deliveries was made on April 28, 1932, and, according to the respondent's evidence, was duly accepted and the stuff put into use; a further delivery was made on April 29, 1932, and another on May 2, 1932. On that latter date the respondents notified the appellants that a sample drawn from the delivery of April 28, 1932, had been analysed and showed a contamination of 250 parts of chlorine, instead of the maximum allowed by law of 30 parts. The respondents thereupon claimed to rescind the contract; the appellants protested, and some negotiations took place, during which two more deliveries were tendered and taken, each of $1^1/_2$ tons. Eventually the respondents adhered to their claim that they were entitled to rescind, and the writ was issued by the appellants claiming damages on the ground that the refusal of the respondents to take further deliveries was wrongful.

• • •

The decision of this case depends on the true construction and application of s. 31, sub-s. 2, of the Sale of Goods Act, 1893, which is in the following terms: "Where there is a contract for the sale of goods to be delivered by stated instalments, which are to be separately paid for, and the seller makes defective deliveries in respect of one or more instalments, or the buyer neglects or refuses to take delivery of or pay for one or more instalments, it is a question in each case depending on the terms of the contract and the circumstances of the case, whether the breach of contract is a repudiation of the whole contract or whether it is a severable breach giving rise to a claim for compensation but not to a right to treat the whole contract as repudiated." That sub-section was based on decisions before the Act, and has been the subject of decisions since the Act. A contract for the sale of goods by instalments is a single contract, not a complex of as many contracts as there are instalments under it. The law might have been determined in the sense that any breach of condition in respect of any one or more instalments would entitle the party aggrieved to claim that the contract has been repudiated as a whole; or on the other hand the law as established might have been that any breach, however serious, in respect of one or more instalments should not have consequences extending beyond the particular instalment or instalments or affecting the contract as a whole. The sub-section, however, which deals equally with breaches either by the buyer or the seller, requires the Court to decide on the merits of the particular case what effect, if any, the breach or breaches should have on the contract as a whole.

The language of the Act is substantially based on the language used by Lord Selborne L.C. in *Mersey Steel and Iron Co.* v. *Naylor, Benzon & Co.*, 9 App. Cas. 434 where he said: "I am content to take the rule as stated by Lord Coleridge in *Freeth* v. *Burr* (1874) LR 9 CP 208, which is in substance, as I understand it, that you must look at the actual circumstances of the case in order to see whether the one party to the contract is relieved from its future performance by the conduct of the other; you must examine what that conduct is, so as to see whether it amounts to a renunciation, to an absolute refusal to perform the contract, such as would amount to a rescission if he had the power to rescind, and whether the other party may accept it as a reason for not performing his part" (at 438). In *Freeth* v. *Burr* Lord Coleridge C.J. stated the true question to be: "Whether the acts and conduct of the party evince an intention no longer to be bound by the contract" (at 213). These were both cases of breach by the buyer in not making punctual payment, and in each case it was clear that the buyer had some justification for the course he took. The case of breach by the seller in making defective deliveries may raise different questions. Lord Selborne in the passage above quoted did not refer to any questions of intention, but said that what is to be examined is the conduct of the party. Lord Coleridge in *Freeth* v. *Burr*, citing *Hoare* v. *Rennie* (1859) 5 H & N 19, on the question of a seller's breach, states thus one aspect of the rule: "Where by the non-delivery of part of the thing contracted for the whole object of the contract is frustrated, the party making default renounces on his part all the obligations of the contract" (at 214). In other words, the true test will generally be, not the subjective mental state of the defaulting party, but the objective test of the relation in fact of the default to the whole purpose of the contract.

Since the Act, the sub-section has been discussed by a Divisional Court in *Millars' Karri and Jarrah Company* (1902) v. *Weddel, Turner & Co.* 14 Com. Cas. 25, where the contract being for 1100 pieces of timber, the first instalment of 750 pieces was rejected by the buyers; an arbitrator awarded "that the said shipment was, and is, so far from complying with the requirements of the said contract as to entitle the buyers to repudiate and to rescind the whole contract and to refuse to accept the said shipment and all further shipments under the said contract." The Court upheld the award. Bigham J. thus stated what in his opinion was the true test. "Thus, if the breach is of such a kind, or takes place in such circumstances as reasonably to lead to the inference that similar breaches will be committed in relation to subsequent deliveries, the whole contract may there and then be regarded as repudiated and may be rescinded. If, for instance, a buyer fails to pay for one delivery in such circumstances as to lead to the inference that he will not be able to pay for subsequent deliveries; or if a seller delivers goods differing from the requirements of the contract, and does so in such circumstances as to lead to the inference that he cannot, or will not, deliver any other kind of goods in the future, the other contracting party will be under no obligation to wait to see what may happen; he can at once cancel the contract and rid himself of the difficulty" (at 29). Walton J. concurred.

This ruling was more recently applied in *Robert A. Munro & Co.* v. *Meyer* [1930] 2 KB 312, where under a contract for the sale of 1500 tons of bone meal, 611 tons were delivered which were seriously adulterated. The sellers were middlemen, who relied on their suppliers, the manufacturers, for correct delivery; when the buyers discovered that the deliveries did not conform to the contract they claimed that they were entitled to treat the whole contract as repudiated by the sellers. It was held that they were right in so claiming, on the ground that "in such a case as this, where there is a persistent breach, deliberate so far as the manufacturers are concerned, continuing for nearly one-half of the total contract quantity, the buyer, if he ascertains in time what the position is, ought to be entitled to say that he will not take the risk of having put upon him further deliveries of this character" (at 331). On the other hand in *Taylor* v. *Oakes Roncoroni & Co.* 27 Com. Cas. 261, Greer J., as he then was, and the Court of Appeal, declined to hold that the buyers were entitled to refuse to go on with the contract, but held that the breach was a severable breach, as it was a case "where the instalment delivered failed in a slight but appreciable degree to come up to the standard required by the contract description."

With the help of these authorities we deduce that the main tests to be considered in applying the sub-section to the present case are, first, the ratio quantitatively which the breach bears to the contract as a whole, and secondly the degree of probability or improbability that such a breach will be repeated. On the first point, the delivery complained of amounts to no more than 1½ tons out of a contract for 100 tons. On the second point, our conclusion is that the chance of the breach being repeated is practically negligible. We assume that the sample found defective fairly represents the bulk; but bearing in mind the judge's finding that the breach was extraordinary and that the appellant's business was carefully conducted, bearing in mind also that the appellants were warned, and bearing in mind that the delivery complained of was an isolated instance out of 20 satisfactory deliveries actually made both before and after the instalment objected to, we hold that it cannot reasonably be inferred that similar breaches would occur in regard to subsequent deliveries. Indeed, we do not understand that the learned Judge came to any different conclusion. He seems, however, to have decided against the appellants on a third and separate ground, that is, that a delivery not satisfying the Government requirements would or might lead to the respondents being prosecuted under the Act. Though we think he exaggerates the likelihood of the respondents in such a case being held responsible, we do not wish to underrate the gravity to the respondents of their being even prosecuted. But we cannot follow the Judge's reasoning that the bare possibility, however remote, of this happening would justify the respondents in rescinding in this case. There may indeed be such cases, as also cases where the consequences of a single breach of contract may be so serious as to involve a frustration of the contract and justify rescission, or furthermore, the contract might contain an express condition that a breach would justify rescission, in which case effect would be given to such a condition by the Court. But none of these circumstances can be predicated of this case. We think the deciding factor here is the extreme improbability of the breach being repeated, and on that ground, and on the isolated and limited character of the breach complained of, there was, in our judgment, no sufficient justification to entitle the respondents to refuse further deliveries as they did.

Appeal allowed.

Notes: Apart from the question of the right to cancel the whole contract for breach with respect to a single instalment, instalment contracts raise other questions of which the following is a sampling:

a) *The definition of "instalment contract".* The OLRC Sales Report, pp. 541-47, argues that the requirements in SGA s. 30(2) that the contract must envisage deliveries of "stated instalments" "to be separately paid for" are too rigid, and expresses a preference for the test in UCC 2-612(1), viz. whether the contract is one "which requires or authorizes the delivery of goods in separate lots to be separately accepted". Applying either of these tests, how would you characterize the following transactions: (i) a basketful of groceries tendered for purchase at the checkout counter of a supermarket; (ii) an order for a three-piece made to measure man's suit; (iii) an agreement to supply a restaurant with its daily requirements of bread, payment to be made at the end of each month?

b) *Effect of breach of the whole contract on previously accepted instalments.* Two questions arise under this head: (1) must the buyer be in a position to return any previously accepted instalments as a condition of his right to cancel the contract because of a subsequent breach? and (2) should the buyer be *entitled* to return any previously accepted instalments if he elects to do so?

The first question is much easier to answer than the second. (Can you see why?) Apropos the second question, the OLRC Sales Report observes (pp. 549-550):

> Under this heading, two separate questions must be considered. The first is whether the buyer must be in a position to return any previously accepted instalments as a condition of his right to cancel the contract because of a subsequent breach. The second question is whether the buyer is *entitled* to return any previously accepted instalments if he elects to do so.
>
> The first question is much easier to answer than the second. The buyer's right to cancel is not dependent on his ability to return previous instalments. This position can be justified by analogy to section 29(3) of the Ontario Sale of Goods Act. This subsection entitles the buyer to reject goods that do not conform to the contract description that have formed part of a single delivery, while retaining those goods that are conforming. More simply, this result can be justified on the basis that it is inherent in the concept of a divisible contract. Both The Sale of Goods Act and the Uniform Commercial Code appear to assume implicity that this is the position, and no contrary case law has appeared since 1893. The point would not appear, therefore, to call for specific treatment in the revised Act.
>
> The second question is much more difficult. At first glance, it might be thought that, if the contract is divisible, it should no more be possible for the buyer to force previously accepted instalments back on the seller than it should be possible for the seller to insist on complete rescission. The meagre case law appears to support this proposition. To the extent that they discuss the problem at all, textwriters appear to be divided in their views, and neither the Ontario Sale of Goods Act nor Article 2 of the Uniform Commercial Code addresses itself directly to the issue.
>
> The position is complicated because discussions of this question do not always observe the distinction between entire and divisible contracts. If the manufacturer of a machine delivers part of it and then repudiates, it can be persuasively argued that the buyer should be able to revoke his "acceptance" of the part that has already

been delivered. This conclusion rests, however, on the assumption that the machine constitutes a single functional unit and that the contract was indivisible. There was, in reality, no true "acceptance" of the part; at best there was only a conditional acceptance, dependant upon satisfactory performance of the balance of the contract. This example throws little light on what the rule should be where the instalment that has been delivered and accepted constitutes a commercial unit in its own right.

Nevertheless, on balance the Commission concluded that the equities favour the buyer and that he should be allowed to return previously delivered instalments provided certain conditions are met: Report, p. 550. Do you support this recommendation?

5. REFORM OF THE BUYER'S RIGHT TO REJECT AND THE SELLER'S RIGHT TO CURE A NON-CONFORMING TENDER

OLRC Sales Report
pp. 459-65

From the foregoing recital it will be obvious that, under existing Ontario law, there are serious shortcomings with respect to the buyer's right to reject. It will also be clear that there are at least two important models on which a recasting of the applicable rules may be based. However, before canvassing the alternative solutions and offering our own recommendations, it may be useful to inquire what interests the law seeks to protect in conferring the right to reject and what prejudice may be caused to the seller if this right is granted too freely.

The following interests have been identified as arguing in favour of the right to reject. First, in the case of cash sales, the denial of a right of rejection may impose a twofold hardship on the buyer: he would be required to become an involuntary creditor of the seller; and, he might experience difficulty in recovering damages from a defaulting seller who may be a long distance away. Secondly, it may be difficult for the buyer to compute damages accurately, even assuming the seller is within the jurisdiction or that the buyer has a right of set-off or reduction with respect to the unpaid balance of the price. Thirdly, there is the hardship to the buyer of requiring him to dispose of goods bought for use and not for resale. Finally, there is the danger that sellers will not take their contractual obligations seriously if there is no right to reject and if they can only be liable in damages.

A liberal right of rejection also poses difficulties from the seller's point of view that are at least as significant as, and perhaps more so than, those already identified as confronting the buyer. This is particularly true if the goods have been manufactured to the buyer's specification, if they have been shipped to a distant destination where there is no ready market for the goods or, if, in the case of commodities, there has been a substantial drop in price since the time of purchase. Even if the goods are of a standard type, the seller stands to suffer substantial distributive and allocative costs through being required to take back and dispose of goods that are no longer new, and, if the defect is only of a minor character, the loss to him may greatly exceed the diminution in the value of the goods in the buyer's hands. Not surprisingly, therefore, commercial sale agreements frequently contain important restrictions on the buyer's right to reject, or even deny this right altogether.

It will be obvious that the importance of these factors will vary greatly from case to case and that the picture will be further clouded by considerations such as the character of the buyer or seller, the nature of the goods, the terms of payment, and the time when the buyer seeks to exercise the right of rejection. It would be a Herculean task for a general sales act to be so sensitively calibrated that it could provide the right mixture of solutions to meet every possible contingency. An attempt to do so would involve the draftsmen in an excessive and self-defeating amount of detail. In our view, therefore, the search should be for a flexible formula, supported by ancillary rules designed to strike a fair balance in the great majority of cases. By "fair balance" we mean a balance that minimizes costs to both parties and seeks to save the bargain if this can be done on acceptable terms.

This approach is clearly inconsistent with the adoption or retention of a rigid perfect tender rule, however it is expressed. It is sometimes said that a perfect tender rule leads to greater certainty and promotes greater respect for bargains. While this may be true for some transactions and for certain types of obligation, we are not aware of any empirical evidence that supports the general proposition. Even if greater certainty could be demonstrated, the price would be unacceptably high, and this is shown by the increasing aversion of courts to attempts by buyers to reject for minor breaches, and by the frequency with which standard form contracts restrict the right to reject. A more serious alternative would be an Article 2 type solution; that is, the retention of a perfect tender rule coupled with exceptions to the rule. We are not, however, attracted by this solution either. If American observers are correct in claiming that the exceptions have to all intents and purposes destroyed the rule, it seems better to recognize realities and not to confuse form with substance.

Accordingly, we are led to the conclusion that the buyer's right to reject a non-conforming tender, in the absence of contrary agreement, should be confined to substantial breaches of the seller's obligations and we so recommend. We consider the desirable definition of "substantial breach" in chapter 18 of this Report. We would emphasize, however, that our recommendation, which is supported by a similar recommendation in the New South Wales Working Paper, is consistent with our earlier recommendation with respect to the abolition of the existing *a priori* classification of contractual obligations, and, subject to what we say hereafter about questions of cure, will place breaches by buyer and seller on the same footing. We are further of the opinion, as discussed earlier in this chapter, that the buyer's right to reject should not turn, as is the case under section 12(3) of the existing Sale of Goods Act, on whether, in a non-severable contract, the buyer has accepted part of the goods, or on whether the contract involves a sale of specific or non-specific goods or title has passed to the buyer. Accordingly, we recommend that the buyer should not lose his right to reject where he has accepted part of a nonseverable consignment of goods; rather the revised Act should provide that, where the non-conformity amounts to a substantial breach, the buyer may accept the whole, reject the whole, or accept one or more commercial units and reject the rest. In light of this recommendation, we recommend that section 29 of the existing Sale of Goods Act should be omitted from the revised Act. The Commission also recommends that the buyer should not lose his right to reject where the contract involves a sale of specific goods the title in which has passed to the buyer. Finally, a provision equivalent to section 12(3) of the existing Act should be omitted from the revised Act, and we so recommend.

(ii) Seller's Right to Cure and Buyer's Right to Demand Cure

The adoption of a substantial breach test to determine the buyer's right to reject a non-conforming tender does not end our inquiry. Two related matters need to be considered: namely, whether the seller, even after the buyer has exercised a right of rejection, should have an opportunity to cure the non-conformity; and, conversely, whether a buyer should be entitled to *demand* cure regardless of the gravity of the breach, and to reject the goods if the seller does not cure. While we are fully sensitive to the difficulties involved, we have reached the conclusion that both types of right should be recognized.

(1) Seller's Right to Cure

So far as the seller's right to cure is concerned, it has long been a common practice for contracts for the sale of durables and other types of goods to contain provisions entitling the seller to repair or replace defective goods and imposing corresponding restrictions on the buyer's right to reject. Table 1, which is based on an analysis of contract forms supplied to us by C.M.A. respondents, illustrates the widespread use of such provisions among Ontario manufacturers. A right to cure would, therefore, merely recognize an existing practice.

TABLE 1

VENDOR'S LIABILITY FOR DEFECTIVE GOODS AND
RIGHT TO CURE: INDUSTRY CLAUSES

Key to clauses: 10 — Liability limited to cost of goods.
11 — Liability limited to cost of repair of goods.
12 — Liability limited to replacement of goods.
13 — Vendor will at his option repair or replace parts proven defective.

Industries using these clauses:

Food and Beverage	10, 13
Rubber and Plastic	10, 13
Leather	10
Knitting Mills	—
Furniture and Fixtures	10
Paper	10
Printing, Publishing and Allied Industries	10
Primary Metal	13
Metal Fabricating	10, 11, 12, 13
Non-Electrical Machinery	10, 11, 12, 13
Electrical Products	10, 12, 13

Non-Metalic Mineral Products	—
Petroleum and Coal Products	—
Chemicals	10
Miscellaneous Manufacturing	13

Again, there are important precedents for conceding such a right, including UCC 2-508, the provisions in ULIS and the draft UNCITRAL Convention, and, in Canada, the farm implements and agricultural machinery legislation of the Prairie provinces and Prince Edward Island. We appreciate that each of these precedents contains restrictions with respect to the types of breach, the types of goods, or other circumstances in which the right may be invoked. The adoption of a broad right to cure, on the other hand, is recommended in the New South Wales Working Paper. The real question, it seems to us, is whether the statutory recognition of a general right to cure would militate unfairly against the buyer's interests and would add an element of uncertainty. We believe that, with proper safeguards, the right can be made to serve equitably the interests of both the buyer and the seller. Accordingly, subject to the recommendations made hereafter, we recommend that the revised Act should confer upon the seller a right to cure a non-conforming tender or delivery where the buyer has rightfully rejected or revoked his acceptance of the goods. The safeguards we propose are as follows: (i) that the seller must seasonably notify the buyer of his intention to cure the non-conformity, following the buyer's rejection; (ii) that the non-conformity can be cured without unreasonable prejudice, risk or inconvenience to the buyer; and (iii) that the type of cure offered by the seller is reasonable in the circumstances.

If the principle of a right to cure is conceded, then several consequential questions arise for decision. UCC 2-508, which is set out above, is the important provision of the Code that deals with the seller's right to cure an improper tender or delivery. In our discussion of these consequential issues, we make reference to this section.

(aa) *When Does the Right to Cure Arise?*

UCC 2-508(1) governs the right to cure a non-conforming tender or delivery that is made before the time for performance has expired. Section 2-508(2), on the other hand, confers a separate and more restricted right to cure when the contractual date for performance has expired. We do not think that this is a viable distinction. UCC 2-508(1), basing itself on common law precedents, seems to assume that no prejudice can be caused to the buyer by giving the seller an unqualified right to cure, provided that the conforming delivery is made within the contract time. As, however, the draft UNCITRAL Convention rightly perceives, this assumption may not be correct, and we would collapse the distinction in UCC 2-508(1) and (2). Accordingly, we recommend that, subject to our recommendation made below in respect of a late tender or delivery amounting to a substantial breach, the right to cure should arise where the buyer rightfully rejects a non-conforming tender or delivery, whether before or after the time for performance has expired. The safeguards that we have proposed would apply to each case. In practice, however, it may well be easier for the seller to discharge the onus imposed by the safeguards where the non-conforming delivery is made before, rather than at or after, the time for performance has expired; but this goes to proof and not to principle. We recommend that the right to cure should also arise where, in accordance with a later recommendation, the buyer exercises a right to revoke his acceptance. The right to cure in such a case is particularly important because, at the time of revocation, the buyer may already have had the goods for a considerable period of time.

We have concluded that the treatment accorded to the seller's right to cure a *late* tender or delivery should be different from that accorded to other non-conformities. We recommend that, if the late tender or delivery amounts to a substantial breach, then the seller, unlike the situation with other non-conformities, should not be allowed to cure. It is our view that in the case of late tender or delivery amounting to a substantial breach, the need for certainty as to the position of the parties outweighs any other considerations and, therefore, that no right to cure ought to be available.

Later in this chapter, we recommend that the buyer should have a right to demand cure and, where the seller fails to cure, that the buyer should be able to treat the seller's breach as amounting to a substantial breach and to reject the goods. In our view, where the seller has failed to cure in response to a demand by the buyer, and the buyer accordingly exercises his right to reject, the seller should not be permitted to cure, and we so recommend.

(bb) *Nature of Non-Conformity*

It will be noted that UCC 2-508 does not restrict the type of non-conforming tender that may be the subject of cure. Subject to what we have said above concerning late tender or delivery, we believe this approach to be the correct one. In particular there is no justification, in our view, for restricting the right to cure to physical or mechanical defects. The operative test should be, not the nature of the non-conformity, but whether the non-conformity can be cured without unreasonable prejudice, risk or inconvenience to the buyer. Accordingly, we recommend that, subject to our recommendation concerning the effect of a late tender or delivery on the seller's right to cure, the revised Act should not restrict the type of non-conforming tender that may be the subject of cure.

(cc) *Nature of "Cure"*

Given that the seller has a right to cure, there is the question of the nature or form that any adjustment or correction may take. As we have noted, UCC 2-508 is vague on this point and it seems desirable that the permissible types of cure should be spelled out in some detail. In our view, they should be sufficiently flexible to match the broad range of non-conformities to which they will be applied. The New South Wales Draft Bill contains an illustrative list, and we have adapted it to meet our own needs. Accordingly, we recommend that, for the purpose of the cure provisions, "cure" should mean:

(a) tender or delivery of any missing part or quantity of the goods;

(b) tender or delivery of other goods or documents which are in conformity with the contract;

(c) the remedying of any other defect, including a defect in title; or

(d) a money allowance or other form of adjustment of the terms of the contract.

Although the list seems to err on the side of generosity, we would emphasize that the seller will still be required to show that the proffered cure was reasonable in the circumstances.

Note: For further discussion of the above themes, see J. Honnold, "Buyer's Right of Rejection" (1948-49) 97 U. Pa. L. Rev. 457; G.H. Treitel, "Some Problems of Breach of Contract" (1967) 30 Mod. L. Rev. 139, 149 *et seq*; E.A. Peters (1963) 73 Yale LJ 199, 210 *et seq*; W.D. Hawkland (1962) 46 Minn. L. Rev. 697; and J.S. White and R.S. Summers, *Uniform Commercial Code*, 2nd ed. (1980), ch. 8.

B. THE MEASURE OF DAMAGES

Introductory Note:

Whether or not the buyer has a right to reject non-conforming goods, and chooses to exercise it, he is also entitled to claim damages. The SGA only concerns itself with damage claims sounding in contract but section 57(1) preserves the rules of the common law except insofar as they are inconsistent with the express provisions of the Act. Moreover, even the contractual damage provisions are incomplete.

Section 49 deals with damage claims arising out of the seller's failure to deliver and is the counterpart to the seller's right to damages for the buyer's failure to accept and pay for the goods. Section 51 is concerned with damage claims involving a breach of the seller's warranties or conditions where the buyer elects or is obliged to retain the goods. It will be seen therefore that the Act fails to deal explicitly with the right to claim damages following the rejection of non-conforming goods. A tender of non-conforming goods not accepted by the buyer is equivalent to no delivery at all and such a tender should, therefore, attract the provisions of section 49. Further, only by implication does the Act deal with the effect of a delayed delivery. It may also be noted that delayed delivery, breach of which is not waived, involves at least the breach of a warranty giving rise to a claim under section 51. (Can you see why?)

The present section examines, non-exhaustively, some aspects of the existing damage rules, all of which proceed from the general contract principle that, subject to the rules of remoteness and the duty to mitigate, the buyer is entitled to be put in the same position as if the seller had not breached his obligations. This principle is so fundamental, and so well established, that its soundness seems self-evident. It is obvious, however, from the pervasive use of disclaimer and limited liability clauses, that sellers do not share this view and it seems appropriate to conclude the section with a re-examination of the basic postulate and a brief inquiry as to possible alternatives.

1. THE COMPENSATORY BASIS OF DAMAGES AND THE MARKET PRICE MEASURE

WERTHEIM v. CHICOUTIMI PULP CO.
[1911] AC 301, [1908-10] All ER Rep. 707 (PC)

LORD ATKINSON: This is an appeal from the judgment of the Court of King's Bench for the Province of Quebec (Appeal Side), dated October 3, 1908, affirming in part and reversing in part a judgment of the Superior Court of that Province, dated November 12, 1907.

By the former judgment the respondent company was condemned in a sum of $2434 and costs.

The [respondent] company carry on the manufacture of wood pulp at the town of Chicoutimi, which is situate on the river Saguenay, a tributary of the St. Lawrence in the Province of Quebec. The [appellant] is the sole partner in a German firm of merchants carrying on business at Hamburg in Germany. He has an agent at Manchester named Reichenbach, where he trades in the pulp he imports from Canada and elsewhere, and an agent at New York named Goldman.

He claims in this action to recover damages from the respondents under three separate heads for three separate breaches of a contract entered into between them on March 13, 1900, to deliver at Chicoutimi f.o.b. 3000 tons of moist wood pulp between September 1 and November 1 in that year, at a price which was equivalent to 25s. per ton.

• • •

The first breach relied upon consists in the respondents having delayed the delivery of this quantity of pulp till the month of June, 1901; the second in the alleged inferior quality of the pulp actually delivered; and the third in its alleged deficiency in weight. In the view which their Lordships take of the appellant's claim under the second and third heads, it is unnecessary to deal with the amount demanded in respect of each. The first was the main claim. In respect of it the appellant claimed to recover 27s. 6d. per ton on the 3000 tons mentioned in the contract, that being the difference between the market price of such pulp at Manchester, the ultimate destination of the pulp, at the time it should have been delivered, namely, 70s. per ton, and its market price there at the time it was in fact delivered, namely, 42s. 6d. per ton; the differences between the market values of the pulp at these respective times being, according to Sir Robert Finlay's contention on behalf of the appellant, the well-established and indisputable measure of damages for delay in breach of contract in delivery of goods. The appellant in reality never sustained this loss nor anything like it, because he sold the goods under contracts, some anterior in date to the contract sued upon, the other anterior in date to the actual delivery, at the price of 65s. per ton, which is only 5s. per ton less than the top market price for which the pulp could presumably have been sold in Manchester had it arrived there in November, 1900, the contract time. Yet so rigid, it is insisted, is this formula or rule, that the resales must be ignored as collateral and irrelevant matters and damages be awarded for a loss which in reality has never been sustained. That, however, is not the only peculiarity of the appellant's claim. He admits that 13s. per ton would cover all the costs and expenses of the transport of the pulp from Chicoutimi to Manchester. It would thus cost him when delivered there 38s. per ton in all. If the pulp had been delivered in November and the appellant had sold it then at the highest market price, namely, 70s. per ton, he would have made a profit on it of 32s. per ton; but if the appellant was to succeed in this action, he would have received from the sub-vendees the price at which the goods were actually sold, namely, 65s. per ton, plus 27s. 6d. per ton, from the respondents in the shape of damages, making together 92s. 6d. per ton, or 22s. 6d. per ton more than if the contract had never been broken at all.

One cannot but feel that the reasoning which leads to results so unjust and anomalous must be fallacious.

On the assumption that by this delay in delivering of the pulp the respondents were guilty of a breach of their contract — a point to be dealt with presently — and that the appellant was therefore entitled to recover some damages in respect of it, the main question for decision is on what principle and by what rule those damages are to be measured under the circumstances of this case. That question has given rise, apparently, to much conflict of judicial opinion. By the judgment and decree appealed from, the damages seem to have been fixed at 5s. per ton, that being the difference between the full market value of the pulp at Manchester when it should have reached that town and the rate at which it was sold when it in fact reached it. The rate per ton so fixed is, in their Lordships' opinion, the highest rate at which it could properly be fixed, since it covers the loss actually sustained. And it is the general intention of the law that, in giving damages for breach of contract, the party complaining should, so far as it can be done by money, be placed in the same position as he would have been in if the contract had been performed: *Irvine* v. *Midland Ry. Co. (Ireland)* (1880) 6 LR Ir. at 63, approved of by Palles C.B. in *Hamilton* v. *Magill* (1883) 12 LR Ir. at 202. That is a ruling principle. It is a just principle. The rule which prescribes as a measure of damages the difference in market prices at the respective times above mentioned is merely designed to apply this principle and, as stated in one of the American cases cited, it generally secures a complete indemnity to the purchaser. But it is intended to secure only an indemnity. The market value is taken because it is presumed to be the true value of the goods to the purchaser. In the case of non-delivery, where the purchaser does not get the goods he purchased, it is assumed that these would be worth to him, if he had them, what they would fetch in the open market; and that, if he wanted to get others in their stead, he could obtain them in that market at that price. In such a case, the price at which the purchaser might in anticipation of delivery have resold the goods is properly treated, where no question of loss of profit arises, as an entirely irrelevant matter: *Rodocanachi* v. *Milburn* 18 QBD 67. The purchaser not having got his goods should receive by way of damages enough to enable him to buy similar goods in the open market. Similarly, when the delivery of goods purchased is delayed, the goods are presumed to have been at the time they should have been delivered worth to the purchaser what he could then sell them for, or buy others like them for, in the open market, and when they are in fact delivered they are similarly presumed to be, for the same reason, worth to the purchaser what he could then sell for in that market, but if in fact the purchaser, when he obtains possession of the goods, sells them at a price greatly in advance of the then market value, that presumption is rebutted and the real value of the goods to him is proved by the very fact of this sale to be more than market value, and the loss he sustains must be measured by that price, unless he is, against all justice, to be permitted to make a profit by the breach of contract, be compensated for a loss he never suffered, and be put, as far money can do it, not in the same position in which he would have been if the contract had been performed, but in a much better position.

The authorities cited, *Wilson* v. *Lancashire and Yorkshire Ry. Co.* (1861) 9 CB (NS) 632 and *Schulze & Co.* v. *Great Eastern Ry. Co.* (1887) 19 QBD 30, bear out this conclusion. In both these cases the goods, by reason of the delay in delivery, had become valueless or of less value to the purchaser. And it is clear from the judgments that the measure of damages in such a case is the difference between the contract price and the value of the goods to the purchaser when obtained. The same remark applies to the other cases cited.

Appeal dismissed.

Note: The general principle of the compensatory basis of damages for breach of contract enunciated in *Wertheim* is frequently quoted with approval. However, the decision itself has attracted much adverse criticism on the grounds, inter alia, that the plaintiff buyer's relationship with his sub-buyer was an irrelevant consideration or, alternatively, that the buyer was not legally obliged to use the pulp ordered from the defendant to satisfy his obligations with the sub-buyer — he might have gone into the market at the date of breach and purchased another consignment to satisfy his requirements. The basic issue then is whether the measure of damages for goods for which there is an available market should be deemed conclusively to be the market price differential or whether the defendant should be entitled to show that the buyer's damages were actually less. For the reasons explained in the following passage, the OLRC Sales Report, pp. 501-502, supported the *Wertheim* position:

> The second question is the extent to which the seller can take advantage of the buyer's actual resale or compensating purchase, as the case may be, in order to show that the buyer's actual loss was *less* than the figure that would otherwise be arrived at by the market price formula. The rule in the *Rodocanachi* case, just referred to, does not furnish an automatic answer to this question, because it fails to take into account the buyer's general obligation to mitigate his damages, which arises *after* he has learned of the seller's breach. The point does not appear to be covered by authority, but textwriters generally take a negative view. We have earlier recommended that a provision equivalent to UCC 2-712, which confers upon the buyer a right to "cover", should be incorporated into the revised Act. If this recommendation is accepted, then the mitigation issue will resolve itself in cases where the buyer has made a compensating purchase. The reason is that the covering price will measure the extent of the buyer's damages, whether the price is lower or higher than the prevailing market price.
>
> Our recommended right to cover does not, however, provide a complete answer to the broad policy issue presented by the question under discussion. The right to cover is by its nature limited to a post-breach event and does not relate to events that

occur prior to breach. To what extent should evidence of such pre-breach events be admissible? Our response to this policy issue is contained in our Draft Bill which, following the controversial decision of the Privy Council in *Wertheim* v. *Chicoutimi Pulp Co.* [1911] AC 301 limits the aggrieved party to such damages as he has actually suffered without distinguishing between events occurring before

breach. We have adopted this position because, in our view, the criticism of the *Wertheim* case confuses two separate issues. If the question is whether the aggrieved party should be entitled to recover enhanced damages because of loss of, or liability under, a sub-contract, the foreseeability of such damages is a relevant issue. But foreseeability has nothing to do with the question whether damages higher than those actually suffered should be recoverable. We agree with the Privy Council that the compensatory purpose of damages should be as applicable here as in other branches of contract law. Admittedly, this may lead to a lesser award than would otherwise be the case, but, in our view, this possibility is irrelevant. What is relevant is that the judgment leaves the aggrieved party inUapproximately the same position as if the contract had been performed, and this is what a damage award is supposed to do. We recognize that a market price test is easier to apply and that it has the appearance of being evenhanded. However, its equitable nature disappears once it is conceded that the buyer's damages may be based on the results of a covering purchase. The question then becomes whether only post-breach factors may be taken ino account, or whether the admissible evidence may also include antecedent events. For the reasons we have given we prefer the rule that is more generous to the seller. Accordingly, we recommend that the buyer should be limited to such damages as he has actually suffered without distinguishing between events occurring before or after the date of breach.

Questions: Would the adoption of the OLRC's proposal lead to too much uncertainty? Would it undermine the market price/contract price measure of damages by encouraging defendants to go on fishing expeditions? Some American authors have rationalized the market price rule on the footing that it is a convenient liquidated measure of damages test and should therefore be applied regardless of the plaintiff's actual loss. Do you find this a more convincing criticism of the decision in Wertheim's case than the reasons that are usually given?

2.   TYPES OF RECOVERABLE DAMAGES

BOWLAY LOGGING LTD. v. DOMTAR LTD.
[1978] 4 WWR 105, 87 DLR (3d) 325 (BC SC)

BERGER J.: The defendant Domtar Limited is a pole and pile manufacturer. It has a yard in Golden, British Columbia, where poles and piles are prepared for transportation to its wood treatment plants on the prairies. Until 1972 a local contractor logged Domtar's timber quota for it. Not all the timber was suitable for poles and piles, so the poles and piles were sorted from the other logs at the site and hauled to Domtar's yard in Golden. The sawlogs were hauled away to Briscoe Sawmills.

Domtar wished to increase its quota from 48,000 cubic feet to 1,750,000 cubic feet in order to establish a secure supply of timber, so it obtained Timber Sale

A03518 from the British Columbia Forest Service to be logged in 1972, additional timber sales to be obtained in subsequent years. Domtar expected to produce 10,000 cunits (1,000,000 cubic feet) from the timber sale. A series of meetings was held between Ron Dyck, of Domtar, and Donald Bremner, Clifford Bowles and Greg Lay. The outcome of the meetings was that the latter three established the plaintiff Bowlay Logging Limited to log Domtar's timber sale. Bremner was the principal financial backer. Lay, and then Bowles, ran the company's operations at the timber sale.

The parties entered into a contract under which Bowlay was to log Timber Sale A03518. Before the end of the year the arrangement was at an end. The timber sale had not been completely logged off. There were allegations of breach of contract. This lawsuit, brought by Bowlay, was the outcome.

[Berger J., after reviewing the evidence, found that Domtar was in breach in failing to supply an adequate number of trucks for the plaintiff's use and then turned to consider the question of damages:]

This brings me to the issue of damages. Bowlay's claim is not for loss of profits, but for compensation for expenditures made in part performance. Bowlay is not in a position to claim damages for loss of profits, because it cannot prove that if it had gone on to complete the contract it would have made any money. Bowlay, since it cannot prove any loss of profits, is seeking to recover its losses for actual outlay. These came to $232,905. The payments received from Domtar for deliveries of logs came to $108,128.57. Bowlay's claim is for the balance, $124,776.43.

While it is true that the parties contemplated that the contract might be renewed on an annual basis, I think Bowlay's claim for damages must be limited to damages in respect of Bowlay's losses on Timber Sale A03518. Any claim based on the loss of expected profits on future timber sales would be too uncertain and remote. In any event, Bowlay has limited its claim to compensation for expenditures made in part performance. It has not advanced any claim for loss of profits.

The cases say that a plaintiff can sue for expenses incurred in part performance of a contract when the contract has been ended by breach. In *Cullinane* v. *Br. "Rema" Mfg. Co. Ltd.* [1954] 1 QB 292, [1953] 2 All ER 1237 (CA), Lord Evershed said at p. 303:

> As a matter of principle also, it seems to me that a person who has obtained a machine, such as the plaintiff obtained, being a machine which was mechanically in exact accordance with the order given but which was unable to perform a particular function which it was warranted to perform, may adopt one of two courses. He may say, when he discovers its incapacity, that it was not what he wanted, that it is quite useless to him, and he may claim to recover the capital cost he has incurred, deducting anything he can obtain by disposing of the material that he got. A claim of that kind puts the plaintiff in the same position as though he had never made the contract at all. In other words, he is back where he started; and, if it were shown that the profit-earning capacity was in fact very small, the plaintiff would probably elect so to base his claim. But, alternatively, where the warranty in question relates to performance, he may, in my judgment, make his claim on the basis of the profit

which he has lost because the machine as delivered fell short in its performance of that which it was warranted to do.

See also *McRae* v. *Commonwealth Disposals Commn.* (1951) 84 CLR 377.

In *Anglia Television* v. *Reed* [1972] 1 QB 60, [1971] 3 All ER 690 (CA), Lord Denning M.R. held that a plaintiff had the right to sue for expenditures made in part performance. He said, at p. 64:

> If he has not suffered any loss of profits — or if he cannot prove what his profits would have been — he can claim in the alternative the expenditure which has been thrown away, that is, wasted, by reason of the breach. That is shown by *Cullinane* v. *Br. "Rema" Mfg. Co. Ltd.*, [*supra*, at pp. 303 and 308].

But Domtar has raised an issue not reached by these cases. Mr. Harvey says that even if there was a breach of contract Domtar is not bound to compensate Bowlay for their expenses — at any rate certainly not the full measure of those expenses — because the operation was losing money. If it had continued it would have lost more money. Domtar says that in fact Bowlay's losses on full performance would have exceeded its losses in expenses "thrown away". It is said that in these circumstances Bowlay cannot recover any damages.

May a claim for expenses made in part performance be sustained where the defendant shows that the plaintiff was engaged in a losing operation and, even if there had been no breach and the contract had been fully performed, would inevitably have suffered a loss on the contract? Should the defendant be entitled to have the losses that would have been incurred deducted from the plaintiff's claim for compensation for expenses made in part performance? What if the plaintiff's losses, in the event the contract had been fully performed, would have exceeded the claim for expenses? To what extent should the plaintiff be entitled to recover in such a case?

McGregor on Damages, 13th ed. (1972), p. 28, commenting on the *Anglia* case, said:

> This decision however does not cover the case where the plaintiff has made a bad bargain, and it is still an open question whether in such circumstances he should be allowed to opt for the alternative measure. The argument on the one side is that he should not be entitled to more than the normal measure would give him; the argument on the other is that a defendant in breach should not be entitled to object to a claim for the alternative measure even though not dictated by law or by the difficulties of proof.

Mr. Shaw says that the plaintiff should be entitled to recover all of its expenses by way of outlay, and that no deduction should be made even if the plaintiff would have suffered a net loss if the contract had been fully performed. He relies on a judgment of the United States Supreme Court: *U.S.* v. *Behan* (1884) 110 US 338. Bradley J., speaking for the court, said, at pp. 345-46:

> When a party injured by the stoppage of a contract elects to rescind it, then, it is true, he cannot recover any damages for a breach of the contract, either for outlay or for loss of profits; he recovers the value of his services actually performed as upon a *quantum meruit*. There is then no question of losses or profits. But when he elects to go

for damages for the breach of the contract, the first and most obvious damage to be shown is, the amount which he has been induced to expend on the faith of the contract, including a fair allowance for his own time and services. If he chooses to go further and claims for the loss of anticipated profits, he may do so, subject to the rules of law as to the character of profits which may be thus claimed. It does not lie, however, in the mouth of the party, who has voluntarily and wrongfully put an end to the contract, to say that the party injured has not been damaged at least to the amount of what he has been induced fairly and in good faith to lay out and expend, including his own services, after making allowance for the value of materials on hand; at least it does not lie in the mouth of the party in fault to say this, unless he can show that the expenses of the party injured have been extravagant and unnecessary for the purpose of carrying out the contract.

If it is only "extravagant and unnecessary expenses" that the defendant may insist be deducted from the plaintiff's claim, then what about expenses legitimately incurred, but in an unprofitable venture? The implication in the *Behan* case is that the defendant may not have them deducted from the plaintiff's claim for compensation for expenses. Bradley J. went on, at pp. 346-47:

> The party who voluntarily and wrongfully puts an end to a contract and prevents the other party from performing it, is estopped from denying that the injured party has not been damaged to the extent of his actual loss and outlay fairly incurred.

The *Behan* case was decided in the last century. It has been rejected in the United States in this century.

Professor L.L. Fuller and William R. Perdue, Jr., in "The Reliance Interest in Contract Damages": 1 (1936-37), 46 Yale Law Jour. 52, concluded that the principle enunciated in the *Behan* case compromised the basic notion of restitutio in integrum. They urged, at p. 79, that the law ought to reflect the following proposition:

> We will not in a suit for reimbursement for losses incurred in reliance on a contract knowingly put the plaintiff in a better position than he would have occupied had the contract been fully performed.

In *L. Albert & Son.* v. *Armstrong Rubber Co.* (1949) 178 F 2d 182, L. Hand C.J., speaking for the Circuit Court of Appeals, Second Circuit, held that on a claim for compensation for expenses in part performance the defendant was entitled to deduct whatever he could prove the plaintiff would have lost if the contract had been fully performed. Hand C.J. expressed his concurrence with the formula laid down by Professor Fuller. See also *Re Yeager Co.* (1963) 227 F Supp. 92.

It has been said by the United States Circuit Court of appeals in *Dade County* v. *Palmer and Baker Engineers Inc.* (1965) 339 F 2d 208, that, where the defendant alleges that full performance by the plaintiff would have resulted in a net loss to the plaintiff, the burden of proof is on the defendant. Accepting then that the onus is on the defendant, what has the defendant been able to prove in the case at bar?

Mr. Dunn, a chartered accountant called by Domtar, prepared a list of expenses of the Bowlay logging operation. The list is not complete. But Mr. Dunn says that when the revenues of the operation are measured against the expenses, whether on a cash basis or an accrual basis, there is no footing on which the operation could have been regarded as a profitable one. I think he is right about this.

* * *

The law of contract compensates a plaintiff for damages resulting from the defendant's breach; it does not compensate a plaintiff for damages resulting from his making a bad bargain. Where it can be seen that the plaintiff would have incurred a loss on the contract as a whole, the expenses he has incurred are losses flowing from entering into the contract, not losses flowing from the defendant's breach. In these circumstances, the true consequence of the defendant's breach is that the plaintiff is released from his obligation to complete the contract — or in other words, he is saved from incurring further losses.

If the law of contract were to move from compensating for the consequences of breach to compensating for the consequences of entering into contracts, the law would run contrary to the normal expectations of the world of commerce. The burden of risk would be shifted from the plaintiff to the defendant. The defendant would become the insurer of the plaintiff's enterprise. Moreover, the amount of the damages would increase not in relation to the gravity or consequences of the breach but in relation to the inefficiency with which the plaintiff carried out the contract. The greater his expenses owing to inefficiency, the greater the damages.

The fundamental principle upon which damages are measured under the law of contract is restitutio in integrum. The principle contended for here by the plaintiff would entail the award of damages not to compensate the plaintiff but to punish the defendant. So it has been argued that a defendant ought to be able to insist that the plaintiff's damages should not include any losses that would have been incurred if the contract had been fully performed. According to Treitel, *Law of Contract*, 3rd ed. (1970), at p. 798:

> It is uncertain whether the plaintiff can recover his entire expenses if those exceed the benefit which he would have derived from the contract, had there been no breach.

Ogus, in *Damages* (1973), has said that (p. 347), "it is not yet clear whether English law imposes this limitation".

The tendency in American law is to impose such a limitation. And I think Canadian law ought to impose it too.

The onus is on the defendant. But the onus has been met. The only conclusion that I can reach on the evidence is that if the plaintiff had fully performed the contract its losses would have continued at the rate that the figures show they were running at up to the time when the logging operation was closed down.

The case at bar takes the matter farther than any of the cases cited, because here the defendant has shown that the losses the plaintiff would have incurred on full performance exceed the expenditures actually made in part performance. No award for loss of outlay can therefore be made. There is no escaping the logic of this: see *Corbin on Contracts*, 1964 pp. 205-206:

If, on the other hand, it is proved that full performance would have resulted in a net loss to the plaintiff, the recoverable damages should not include the amount of this loss. *If the amount of his expenditure at the date of breach is less than the expected net loss, he should be given judgment for nominal damages only.* If the expenditures exceed this loss, he should be given judgment for the excess. (The italics are mine.)

On a conservative view of the evidence as a whole, the notional loss (had there been full performance) may be said to be in the amount of $124,653.60, calculated as follows:

A.   Plaintiff's claim $232,905.00
       Less: 108,128.57
                                                                                          $124,776.43

       Less: 28th March 1972 payment:
              see Ex. 39, Sched. I   179.34
                                                                                          $124,597.09

B.   Full Contract Price: See Ex. 38, Sched. IV $120,443.40
       Less: 2,793.24
                                                                                          $117,650.16

C.   Probable Loss on Full Performance of Contract
       Expenses on partial completion,
         i.e., incurred by Bowlay $232,905.00

       Rate of $3.50/ccf (W.C. Bowles' rate)
         applied to 2,283.23 ccf left cut but
         not skidded (2685.39 ccf × $3.50)   9,398.76
                                                                                          $242,303.76
       Less: Full contract price   117,650.16
       Loss there would have been on full performance $124,653.60

D.   Deduct Loss on Full Performance from
       Plaintiff's Claim for Part Performance
       Plaintiff's claim (A) $124,597.09
       Less: Loss (C)   124,653.60
       Amount Recoverable $ -   56.51

The plaintiff is entitled nevertheless to nominal damages for the breach of contract in the sum of $250.

Judgment for plaintiff for nominal damages.

Note: On the issues involved in this case see the Comment by Professor Baer in (1979) 3 CBLJ 198. Professor Baer raises the following issues:

(1) *Have some issues been overlooked?* Professor Baer finds it incredible that experienced loggers could so seriously misjudge their costs over such a short logging period. He also wonders whether the plaintiffs had incurred additional expenditures caused by the breach that are disclosed in the judgment. Would this have made a difference to the outcome?

(2) *The Relevance of Future Timber Sales.* Professor Baer conjectures that the plaintiffs might have been willing to undertake an unprofitable contract in the short term in the hope of long term benefits in the form of future profitable contracts. He notes that the contract was renewable annually subject to negotiation. Assuming this meant there was an obligation by Domtar to renew (does it?), he wonders whether Berger J. was correct in stating that "[a]ny claim based on the loss of expected profits on future timber sales would be too uncertain and remote." He notes that this would depend on the foreseeability rules in *Hadley* v. *Baxendale*.

(3) *Is the Corbin Formula Right?* Professor Baer queries whether the Corbin formula adopted by Berger J. (and incorporated in s. 333(*d*) of the *Restatement*; see now Rest. 2d, Tent. Draft No. 14, §363) is not too harsh and whether the plaintiff should not be entitled to recover at least at the contract rate for the work he has performed. "It is one thing to say that the innocent party should not get more than the contract rate and thereby pass onto the defendant his own improvident bargaining, inefficiency or risk. However, it is quite another thing to say that all losses should be deducted from a claim to expenses so as to give the plaintiff less than the rate for work performed" (at 205). Do you agree? Is a claim to be paid for part performance a claim for reliance losses? Professor Baer also notes that in the present case, applying the Corbin formula, Domtar had actually overpaid the plaintiffs and he asks whether Domtar would have been successful in a counterclaim to recover the difference.

(4) *Restitution.* Under this head Professor Baer considers the question whether the plaintiffs could have improved their position by framing their claim in restitution and seeking to recover the value of the benefits conferred on Domtar, thus by-passing the difficulties inherent in their damages claim. It is well settled in Anglo-Canadian law that a buyer can recover the purchase price where there has been a total failure of consideration regardless of any expectancy losses. Cf. *Rowland* v. *Divall, supra,* chapter 6(A). In other cases (such as the present), where the benefit conferred is of a non-pecuniary kind, the position is unsettled. American opinion favours the view that where the aggrieved party has fully performed his part of the contract and no performance by the other party remains due other than payment of a definite sum of money, the aggrieved party cannot recover more as restitution than he would have recovered in full performance: Restatement §§350-351; Rest. 2d, 14th Tent. Draft §387(2). If the aggrieved party has only partly performed, the American position is less clear. The first Rest., §347, Comment *c* made the contract price a relevant criterion but not a conclusive one; Rest. 2d, §387, Comment *d*, p. 230, firmly limits the aggrieved party's maximum restitutionary recovery to the contract price. Professor Baer regards the distinction between partly and fully performed contractual obligations as illogical. His concluding observation however is that "[i]f the plaintiff could at least get the contract rate by claiming restitution, it should get as much by claiming damages based on reliance" (p. 209). For

further discussion of these difficult issues see J.P. Dawson, "Restitution or Damages?" (1959) 20 Ohio SLJ 175; G.E. Palmer, "The Contract Price as a Limit on Restitution for Defendant's Breach" (1959) 20 Ohio SLJ 264; and English Law Commission, *Pecuniary Restitution on Breach of Contract* (W.P. No. 65, 1975) pp. 39-44, 65-6.

3.   ELECTION BETWEEN RECOVERY OF RELIANCE AND EXPECTATION LOSSES

CULLINANE v. BRITISH "REMA" MFG. CO. LTD.
[1954] 1 QB 292, [1953] 2 All ER 1257 (CA)

The plaintiff agreed to buy from the defendants a pulverizing and drying plant to be built according to specification. The defendants also warranted that the plant would be capable of pulverizing the plaintiff's clay at the rate of 6 tons per hour. The purchase price was £6,578. The plant was delivered about April 1, 1950, but it was never capable of pulverizing clay at the rate of 6 tons per hour. It could only handle 2 tons per hour and was therefore commercially useless to the plaintiff. The plaintiff kept the machine and brought an action for damages for breach of warranty. They computed their damages under five separate heads as follows:

PARTICULARS OF DAMAGE

A.   Cost of buildings erected and work done by the plaintiff to house, support, accommodate, and generally be ancillary to the plant supplied by the defendants.

	£	s.	d.	£	s.	d.
Total cost	4,559	1	5			
Subtract estimated break-up value of buildings	2,000	0	0			
				£ 2,559	1	5
B. Cost of plant supplied by the defendants	6,578	0	0			
Subtract estimated residual value of the plant	3,289	0	0			
				£ 3,289	0	0
C. Cost of associated and ancillary plant and charges —						
(Items) Total	3,343	0	0			
Subtract estimated residual value of the plant	1,671	0	0			
				£ 1,672	0	0

D.   Interest on capital at 4 per cent from April 1, 1950, to December 15, 1951 (and continuing until settlement of claim for damages) —

		£	s.	d.
	A.	4,559	0	0
	B.	6,578	0	0
	C.	3,343	0	0
		14,480	0	0

Subtract interest at 4 per cent for the same period on the balance of the purchase price	1,078	0	0			
	£13,402	0	0			
On which interest is				£ 915	16	0

E. Loss of profit.

(A) Per annum.

Receipts from warranted output of six tons per hour on a 47-hour week:

14,664 tons per annum at £1 17s. 6d. per ton				£27,495	0	0
Subtract						
Depreciation at 10 per cent and maintenance at 5 per cent on plant and buildings (on £14,480)	2,172	0	0			
Running costs	6,433	2	10			
Office expenses	1,030	0	0			
Interest on capital	579	4	0			
				£10,214	6	10
Estimated net profit per annum				£17,280	13	2

(B) From April 1, 1950, to December 15, 1951, and continuing

	£29,521	2	6
Total of A, B, C, D and E	£37,956	19	11
Subtract balance of the purchase price of the plant outstanding and due from the plaintiff to the defendants	£ 1,078	0	0
	£36,878	19	11

In reply to a request for further and better particulars, the plaintiff stated inter alia that under E.(B) the words "and continuing" covered the period from December 15, 1951, to the date of trial of the action. The defendants in their defence denied the warranty and any breach thereof and also alleged that the plaintiff had failed to mitigate his damages by failing to take steps to procure another plant.

The action was heard before an Official Referee and he found that the plaintiff was entitled to the following damages: Under A., £2,559 1s. 5d.; under B., £2,389 0s. 0d.; under C., £1,522 0s. 0d.; under D. (calculated to Apr. 1, 1953) £1,608 4s. 9d.; and under E., £8,913 1s. 0d. — Total, £ 17,891 7s. 2d. Less sum counterclaimed by defendants, £1,078 0s. 0d. — £16,813 7s. 2d.

The defendants appealed.

EVERSHED M.R.: This appeal relates only to the proper measure of the damages which flow from what has been found to be a breach of warranty in regard to certain plant manufactured by the defendants and supplied to the plaintiff. The nature of the plant and of the warranty alleged and found to have been broken is sufficiently stated in the statement of claim as amended thus: [see *supra*, statement of facts.] The plant was delivered about April 1, 1950.

It is, in my judgment, extremely important to have clearly in mind the nature of the contract and particularly of the warranty. The plant, I understand, was built according to a detailed specification, and there is no doubt that the plant as supplied conformed strictly with the specification. Unfortunately, however, as the official referee found, the plant did not satisfy the warranty, because it was incapable of producing dry clay powder at the requisite speed. The gist of the warranty lies in the last few words, which I read, "at the rate of six tons per hour." The machine was capable of handling the plaintiff's clay and of cutting, drying and grinding it so as to produce a dry clay powder, but not at the rate of six tons per hour. The productive capacity turned out to be at a considerably less rate, and I understand that the difference in rate, commercially speaking, was the difference between a profitable and an unprofitable commercial venture.

The plaintiff, in his statement of claim, further particularized the damage which he alleged he had suffered. [His Lordship referred to the particulars of damage set out above and continued:] It is, I think, obvious that damages of approximately £37,000 was a very large sum to claim for plant for which the purchase price was about £6,000 and which was to be used in an enterprise which seems (from my reading of the official referee's judgment) to have been of a somewhat speculative character. The total amount awarded was considerably less, namely, $16,813 odd. That reduction is attributable entirely, or almost entirely, to a reduction of the sum awarded for loss of profit. [His Lordship referred to the particulars of the award, and continued:] The argument in this court of the defendants has been that the award really involves giving damages twice over to the plaintiff. The machine was made precisely according to the specification. It was delivered and is now in the plaintiff's possession and it is working, though it does not perform its productive function in the way that was warranted. The principle upon which damages for breach of contract are awarded has been stated many times and was carefully considered by Asquith L.J. in delivering the judgment of this court in *Victoria Laundry (Windsor) Ld.* v. *Newman Industries* [1949] 2 KB 528, 539. The court has read passages from that judgment which are expository of the original principle laid down in *Hadley* v. *Baxendale* (1854) 9 Exch. 341, and it will, I think, suffice to quote the passage from *Hadley* v. *Baxendale* (at 354) which forms the text, so to speak, of Asquith L.J.'s later exposition:

> Where two parties have made a contract which one of them has broken, the damages which the other party ought to receive in respect of such breach of contract should be such as may fairly and reasonably be considered either arising naturally, that is according to the usual course of things, from such breach of contract itself, or such as may reasonably be supposed to have been in the contemplation of both parties, at the time they made the contract, as the probable result of the breach of it.

In the present case it is plain that to the knowledge of the defendants this machine was required to perform a particular function, and the warranty given shows what the function was that the machine was designed to perform. There is, therefore, no doubt at all that the plaintiff is entitled to rely on the second part of the passage I have read, and to claim as damages the business loss which must reasonably be supposed to have been, in the contemplation of both parties at the time when they made the contract, the probable result of the breach. In other words, this plaintiff is not confined to the loss which might be called the natural result of having a machine which turned out to be worth less than the purchase price he has paid for it.

Reference was made to the Sale of Goods Act, 1893; but that Act, which put into statutory form long established principles, does not for present purposes, to my mind, add anything to what I have already stated based on my citation from *Hadley* v. *Baxendale*. But it is perhaps right to note that section 53 of the Sale of Goods Act, 1893, is directed particularly to the remedy for breach of warranty. Subsection (2) provides: "The measure of damages for breach of warranty is the estimated loss directly and naturally resulting, in the ordinary course of events, from the breach of warranty." Subsection (3) provides: "In the case of breach of warranty of quality such loss is prima facie the difference between the value of the goods at the time of delivery to the buyer and the value they would have had if they answered to the warranty." Those two subsections do not, I think, assist, or qualify the general statement applicable here, that the plaintiff, who got a machine which in the event failed to live up to the performance warranted, should be put in the same position (so far as that can be done by money) as he would have been in if the machine had been as warranted.

I have read the material part of the statement of claim, and it is plain from the case as pleaded that the plaintiff was alleging entitlement to the total capital loss he had suffered by having laid out, approximately, £14,000 and then finding himself with material which was only worth £7,000, also to the loss of the profit which this machine, if it had been as warranted, would have brought him during its mechanical life. It is fair to say that in making his computation of damages for loss of profit, he did deduct from each annual sum a figure of 10 per cent of the total original capital outlay in respect of depreciation.

It appears from the finding of the official referee that the useful life of the machine was ten years — that is to say, it would have continued to perform its mechanical functions for a period of ten years: so that if there had been clay to grind and markets in which the ground clay could have been sold it would have brought emoluments to the plaintiff for that period. I base that statement on the passage of the judgment where the official referee said:

> If the plant had been as warranted Mr. Davies gave its probable life as ten years. I find that it was within the contemplation of the defendants that this plant would be used, not as a museum piece but as a means for making a profit by the sale of its products. If the plant had been as warranted the plaintiff's intention was to use it for its life, or for so long as it could provide profit. At the end of that time it would be useless.

It seems to me, as a matter of principle, that the full claim of damages in the form in which it is pleaded was not sustainable, in so far as the plaintiff sought to recover both the whole of his original capital loss and also the whole of the profit which he would have made. I think that that is really a self-evidence proposition, because a claim for loss of profits could only be founded upon the footing that the capital expenditure had been incurred. As I have said, however, there was a deduction made in respect of depreciation at 10 per cent; and if the estimated life of the plant is taken as ten years it follows that, during the period of ten years, while profits must be assumed to have been earned, the whole of the capital cost would have been written off. In other words, if the estimation of damages under head (E) had been carried on for the whole period of ten years, the sum total under heads (A), (B) and (C), having been elaborately worked out, would have all been deducted again in the course of calculating (E).

As a matter of principle also, it seems to me that a person who has obtained a machine, such as the plaintiff obtained, being a machine which was mechanically in exact accordance with the order given but which was unable to perform a particular function which it was warranted to perform, may adopt one of two courses. He may say, when he discovers its incapacity, that it was not what he wanted, that it is quite useless to him, and he may claim to recover the capital cost he has incurred, deducting anything he can obtain by disposing of the material that he got. A claim of that kind puts the plaintiff in the same position as though he had never made the contract at all. In other words, he is back where he started; and, if it were shown that the profit-earning capacity was in fact very small, the plaintiff would probably elect so to base his claim. But, alternatively, where the warranty in question relates to performance, he may, in my judgment, make his claim on the basis of the profit which he has lost because the machine as delivered fell short in its performance of that which it was warranted to do. If he chooses to base his claim on that footing, it seems to me that depreciation has nothing whatever to do with it.

During the course of the argument many analogies were taken, and I find some assistance from the simple agricultural analogy of the cow. If, for example, A sells to B a heifer for £100, and warrants that for the next five lactations she will produce milk at the rate of four gallons a day, but it is discovered that the cow's performance is not at the rate of four gallons a day but is only one gallon a day, and if a one-gallon-a-day cow is worth not £100 but £10, then the buyer might elect to follow one of two courses. He could claim to recover the difference between the £100 which he had paid for a four-gallon-a-day heifer and £10, the true value of the one-gallon-a-day heifer, and he could recover the difference, £90. That would put him in the position in which he would have been if he had bought, and intended to buy, the cow which in fact he got. Alternatively, he might say: "I keep this cow and I shall sue you for the loss I have suffered because her performance was not as warranted: I am getting not four gallons but one gallon a day, and, therefore, I am losing what I would have got on the sales (less necessary expenditure) of, approximately, an extra thousand gallons a year." If the latter course is chosen it seems to me, as I have indicated, that the depreciated or depreciating, value of the cow has nothing whatever to do with the claim. So much, I think, is conceded; and it has, therefore, seemed to the court that it would be impossible to combine in this case a claim for the capital loss with a claim for the total loss of profit; and it would be impossible to recover, in the hypothetical case, both the £90 (being the capital loss on the cow) and the full amount of the loss due to the shortage of milk.

But in the course of these proceedings there occurred an event which has given rise, as I think, to the whole difficulty. Head (E) of the statement of claim, subparagraph (B), reads: "From April 1, 1950, to December 15, 1951, and continuing," and the defendants asked the plaintiff to give particulars of the words "and continuing." They were asking the plaintiff to state for what period of time he was alleging and intending to prove loss of profit. The actual words of the request, which are of importance, are: "Of the words 'and continuing,' stating precisely what period is referred to and the amount of loss of profit (if any) claimed in respect of such period." The plaintiff's answer was: " 'and continuing' is the period from December 15, 1951, to the date of trial of this action." That seems to me to be a clear and unequivocal statement by the plaintiff that, so far as his claim was based on loss of profit, he was only claiming loss of profit up to the date of the trial and that he did not propose to claim or to seek to prove loss of profit beyond that date.

The effect of that statement in the particulars left the statement of claim as a claim for the full amount of the capital loss (arrived at by setting out under each head the total sum actually spent and deducting from that the estimated break-up, or residual, value of the buildings and plant at the date, I suppose, of the statement of claim plus a claim for loss of profit in addition; but subject to this qualification, that in the computation for loss of profit there remained in the statement of claim the item of depreciation at 10 per cent per annum on the original capital cost.

• • •

But whatever may be the answer to these problems, I come back to the point which I left a little time ago. I think that the plaintiff could choose to claim on the basis that he had wasted capital, and that he ought to be put in the position he would have been in if he had never bought this machine; or, alternatively, he was entitled to say: "I have got the machine: what I am claiming is the loss I have suffered because its performance falls short of that which was warranted; therefore I have not made profitable sales which I would have made, and I claim, accordingly, the loss of such profits." The second alternative being the larger, he was entitled to choose that; but, in my judgment, he should be limited to it. By stating that his claim for lost profit was limited to three years, he was not, in my judgment, then entitled to claim (as he, admittedly, could not claim if he had not placed the limitation on the profit) both for loss of capital *and* for loss of profit. It is said that he might do that if in the computation of profits he made due allowance for depreciation. But in my judgment depreciation has nothing to do with the profit which was lost as a consequence of the breach of warranty. And the effect of so reducing the profit would appear to be that the plaintiff first recovers for loss of capital and then has to bring into account against the profit part of what he has recovered for loss of capital.

Upon the question whether the plaintiff could have claimed for loss of profit up to the date of the hearing and have claimed an additional sum because he was at that date left with a machine which was less valuable than the machine as warranted, I say only that the plaintiff has not so claimed. If he had done so, the second part of the claim would appear to be no more than a method of computing profit for the possible profit-earning period after the date of the hearing.

MORRIS L.J. (dissenting): It seems to me that the basis on which the damages were pleaded on behalf of the plaintiff was permissible and logical.

Perhaps I can illustrate by figures why I express this view. Supposing that a machine cost £10,000 and had a life of ten years, and supposing it were found that there would be net profits of £2,000 a year. At the end of ten years, with fulfilment of the warranty, the purchaser would have received £20,000, and allowing for the £10,000 which he had spent in buying the machine he would make £10,000 profit. Supposing that the machine was delivered to him, and supposing he paid £10,000 for it, and supposing it is found to be entirely valueless, the purchaser might say: "I am claiming simply my profits, that is £20,000." But it seems to me that he could, alternatively, say: "out of £2,000 received by me each year I would have allocated £1,000 each year over the ten years to pay for the plant, and so my net profit would have been £1,000 a year. Instead of claiming £20,000 I put it in this way: I claim back the £10,000 I have paid for the plant, which is valueless, and I claim the profits which I would have made, that is £1,000 a year over ten years, £10,000." In either way of statement, the amount of the claim is exactly the same. It seems to me that in the statement of claim the matter was put in the latter way. It was pleaded on behalf of the plaintiff that, by reason of the breach of warranty, he was out of pocket. He had spent sums for the plant and for accessory plant and for buildings. He said: "I want those sums back, less, of course, the present scrap value of what I have got, and in addition I want the profits which I would have made, namely, my net profits: out of the profits that I would have received each year" (and the life of this plant was ten years) "I make an allocation of one-tenth and, making that allowance, I arrive at my net profits." It seems to me that it is permissible and logical to formulate the claim in that way.

Appeal allowed, judgment varied
by substituting £10,521 for £16,813.

H. STREET
Principles of the Law of Damages
(1962), p. 245

It is submitted therefore that in circumstances like the *Cullinane* case the plaintiff can always recover his expenditure (other than the purchase price of the warranted goods) contemplated by the parties. He can also always claim the difference between the price and the market value of the goods. If, however, it were reasonable for him to use the machine for a certain period in order to see whether it could measure up to the warranty then he could claim the difference between the profit he would have made had the machine been as warranted and that which he in fact made during this period. He could not recover in any event for loss of profit beyond the period when he ought reasonably to have ceased using the machine and either replaced it or discontinued his operation. In such a case, his loss of profit (struck after an allowance for depreciation) should be recoverable in addition to his reliance expenditures on other plant and his capital loss on the machine. In his dissenting judgment, Morris L.J. took a position not unlike that taken here. He appeared to treat the three years as a reasonable period during which the plaintiff tried to operate the machine with a view of profit, and justified an award of three years' loss of profits on that account.

R.G. McLEAN LTD. v. CANADIAN VICKERS LTD.
(1970) 15 DLR (3d) 15, [1971] 1 OR 207 (CA)

ARNUP J.A. (for the court): [This] action arises from the sale by the defendant to the plaintiff of a two-colour press. The plaintiff had previously purchased from the Mann company a two-colour press and, after considerable discussion between the parties, it was decided that the plaintiff should purchase a second press as identical as possible to the first one, with the idea of running them in tandem. By using both presses it would be possible to print two-colour material using one press and an additional two colours using the other, and thereby turn out a finished product in four colours. The parties entered into a written contract dated September 30, 1964, covering the sale by the defendant to the plaintiff of the second press at a price of $75,850, plus applicable taxes, with an adjustment in the price dependent upon the rate of exchange. The agreement was expressed to be "subject to the conditions of sale of goods attached hereto . . .".

• • •

The learned trial Judge correctly found on the evidence [[1969] 2 OR 249 at p. 251; 5 DLR (3d) 100 at p. 102] that "the new press was expected to turn out the highest quality offset lithographic printing. Anything less was not within the contemplation of the buyer or seller." Following the installation of the new press in the plaintiff's premises in Toronto, a long series of difficulties ensued. Some of these were capable of being repaired and were minor in nature, and were in fact repaired by the defendant or by the plaintiff itself. Problems continued, however, throughout the fall of 1965 and the early winter of 1966. Representatives of the defendant were sent out from England to try to locate the source of the trouble. Many things were tried but in the end it became obvious to the defendant that, whatever the trouble was, it could not be pinpointed and they were unable to fix it.

It was at this point (which was shortly before March 30, 1966) that the defendant finally offered to take back the press and to refund the payments made by the plaintiff. The plaintiff refused this suggestion, pointing out that it had already incurred more than $36,000 in expenses and direct losses. The offer, however, was not conditional upon the plaintiff agreeing to forego any claim for damages. This becomes significant in considering the question of damages, which I shall deal with later.

[Arnup J.A. reviewed the trial judge's finding that the defendants, by supplying a machine totally incapable of doing the job for which it was intended, had committed a fundamental breach of contract and considered the effect of this finding on the disclaimer clauses in the agreement. (For their terms see the judgment of Coffin J.A. in *Canso Chemicals Ltd.* v. *Canadian Westinghouse Co. Ltd., infra*, chapter 13.) Arnup J.A. held the disclaimer clauses inapplicable and continued:]

The next question therefore is: what damages should be awarded to the plaintiff on the basis of these findings? In effect, the award by the learned trial Judge in favour of the plaintiff falls into three categories:

(i) He dismissed entirely the claim of the defendant for the purchase price of the machine. This claim was for $59,782.75.

(ii) He awarded $50,549.47 in respect of a list of items which he appears to have thought were in the nature of special damages. These are as follows [[1969] 2 OR 249 at p. 261, 5 DLR (3d) 100 at p. 112]:

losses on Ontario 66 book	$18,338.25
losses due to lost press hours	6,968.00
" " " " "	5,769.79
losses incurred while Canadian mechanic of G. Mann Co. testing for print	643.50
loss incurred while mechanic from England G. Mann Co. working on press	8,190.00
13,750 sheets used in testing press	1,616.00
1,500 sheets used in testing press	129.59
plate making time, plate metal test plates	244.00
blankets spoiled	600.00
supervision and plant engineer's time spent with mechanics of George Mann Co.	2,286.27
installation cost on No. 7 press	4,542.46
loss incurred while press being tested during visit of L. Wright, George Mann. Co.	1,221.42
	$50,549.47

(iii) He allowed $50,554.50 for "loss of business profits".

Dealing with item (iii) first, the learned trial Judge stated [at p. 264 OR p. 115 DLR] that he had been furnished, during the trial, and after the accountants for both sides had examined the plaintiff's records, "with a statement (ex. 87) showing the various items of damage and the amounts, the amounts being agreed to, as I understand it, as accurate". He further said that that statement showed the loss of business as $50,554.50.

In this the learned Judge was clearly under a misapprehension. While the figure of $50,554.50 for loss of business profits continued to be shown in a column on ex. 87, it was made quite clear at the trial by counsel for the plaintiff that that amount was *not* being agreed to and that the issue with respect to it was at large. The learned trial Judge's allowance, under this heading, being based entirely upon a mistaken impression of the agreement between counsel, therefore cannot stand, and, while I have endeavoured on the basis of the record and the evidence as it exists to ascertain what a suitable allowance would be for loss of business profits, or indeed whether any such allowance should be made at all, I have found it impossible to do so on this record. This is partly due to the fact that in my view, as will appear, the basis upon which the over-all claim for damages was put forward is erroneous.

Turning next to the dismissal of the claim for the price, this could only have been done on the basis that a claim for breach of warranty had been established in an amount which exceeded the claim for the price. The plaintiff was quite entitled to set up the breach of warranty in diminution or extinction of the purchase price, and to claim any amount of damages over and above the amount of the price which he could establish, but in this case the learned trial Judge has not taken into account, in otherwise assessing the plaintiff's damages, the fact that he had in effect already allowed the plaintiff $59,782.75 by way of damages for breach of warranty when he dismissed the claim against the plaintiff for the price.

Since the damages are to be assessed on the basis that the contract was still in force, the plaintiff is entitled to be compensated (subject to questions of mitigation) to the extent that it will be in approximately the same position as it would have been in if the contract had been performed according to its terms: *Wertheim* v. *Chicoutimi Pulp Co.* [1911] AC 301 at p. 307, and see the cases referred to in *Sunshine Exploration Ltd. et al.* v. *Dolly Varden Mines Ltd. (N.P.L.)* [1970] SCR 2, 8 DLR (3d) 441, 70 WWR 418. If the contract had been performed, and profits earned by use of the machine, the plaintiff would have had to pay the purchase price. In any calculation of damages, on a basis as if the contract had been performed, the purchase price must stand as a debit against the plaintiff; any damages awarded in its favour can be used to extinguish the purchase price, but only the excess can then be allowed to the plaintiff by way of further damages.

This conclusion is supported by the judgment of the English Court of Appeal in *Cullinane* v. *British "Rema" Manufacturing Co. Ltd.* [1954] 1 QB 292. Mr. Starr attacked the reasoning of the majority of the Court in that case and invited us to adopt instead the reasons for judgment of Morris, L.J. (as he then was), in his dissenting judgment at p. 313. A close reading of the case does not indicate that the divergence of opinion between the majority and Morris, L.J., on the point involved here was as great as was indicated by Mr. Starr, but, in any event, I do not think that case assists Mr. Starr so far as the actual purchase price of the machine is concerned. There is a useful discussion of the case in Street, *Principles of the Law of Damages* (1962), at pp. 243-5. While the learned author criticizes the actual decision of the majority on the facts of that case, he does indicate at p. 244 that to give a purchaser both a refund of the purchase price and expenditures made would be double compensation.

Coming then to item (ii), it seems quite clear to me that there is overlapping as to at least three items in this list into the heading of damages "loss of business profits". These items are:

losses on Ontario 66 book	$18,338.25
losses due to lost press hours	6,968.00
losses due to lost press hours	5,769.79

These items in themselves total $31,076.04.

It was further argued before us that other items in this list, while treated by the plaintiff as being direct loss through expense incurred, or as outlays made for which no return was received, nevertheless included supervision and overhead (including supervision and overhead on the "Ontario 66 book job" itself), and hence further overlapping has taken place. There is much force in this argument but, since, for the reasons I have already stated, it is not possible for me to arrive at the assessment which I think would have been proper in this case, I do not pursue the mathematics of this matter further.

Before arriving at my final conclusion with respect to damages, I must deal with the arguments advanced to us that the plaintiff had failed to mitigate its damages. It was suggested that once the plaintiff had realized the difficulties being encountered with the new press, it should have run certain work on the old press instead of continuing to run it on the new one. I regard this as a counsel of perfection, particularly since some of these damages as claimed were sustained before it had become clear that nothing but trouble could ensue from further attempts to use the new press.

The more serious points of mitigation, however, arise from the argument of the defendant that by February, 1966, the plaintiff had concluded that there were serious problems with the press, yet went ahead knowing of these problems and of sufficient facts that any prudent person in the position of the plaintiff should have known that the press could never properly perform its function. The first proposition made by counsel for the defendant is founded on the offer of the defendant, already referred to, to remove the press and refund the purchase price. No evidence was referred to in the argument which would indicate that there was any condition, express or implied, that the plaintiff must accept such offer in full settlement and forego any claim for damages. The plaintiff's answer to this contention was that it had already spent so much money and had sustained such losses that it could not afford to buy another press to replace the one purchased from the defendant. In my opinion, this argument cannot prevail. The plaintiff could not refuse the unconditional offer made, retain the obviously defective press and "run up the damages" to the prejudice of the defendant. The frailties (if any) of the plaintiff's credit, or its inability to purchase a new press from available assets, cannot be set up to destroy the effect of the defendant's offer. If the plaintiff had a good cause of action for damages by March, 1966 (and I have already found that it had), any delay in actually collecting such damages would not in law be the fault of the defendant nor a valid excuse for the plaintiff's failure to mitigate its damages by accepting the offer.

The second point arises independently of the offer, but on facts existing at approximately the same time. As I have indicated, the plaintiff should have known by February or March, 1966, that the difficulties concerning the press were so serious that it was entitled to treat the breach of contract as a fundamental one, enabling it to treat the contract as at an end, and demand back its money (only a portion of the purchase price had then been paid), and sue for damages. In my opinion, once the innocent party is in a position to make this election, in a case where the other party has purported to complete its performance, he cannot make an election which has the effect of increasing the burden upon the wrong-doer. The effect in law is almost precisely the same as the effect of the offer, *i.e.*, the plaintiff could not elect to keep the press, knowing it could never properly perform its function and that its continued operation would only result in future losses, and thereby "run up the damages" against the defendant. This seems to me to be the clear and logical conclusion which follows from the conclusion that the right of election arose.

The situation would undoubtedly be different in a case of an instalment contract, or one requiring the performance of a series of future acts. In such case, when fundamental breach occurs, the innocent party may decide he wants the rest of the contract performed and he is entitled to require that that be done. In this case no further acts of performance on the part of the defendant were called for by the contract; it was what had already been done that either was, or was not, a performance of its contractual obligations.

I am therefore of the opinion that the plaintiff did fail to mitigate its damages and that in the assessment of damages a date which I will arbitrarily take as being March 30, 1966, should be treated as being the "cutoff date"; no damages should be payable by the defendant in respect of events occurring after that date.

Finally, it was argued before us that there was no evidence to show what work was lost to the plaintiff by reason of the press being shut down, or what work was available for tender by it. Instead, the accountant who gave evidence on behalf of the plaintiff appears to have based his figures on pre-contract estimates rather than actual contracts performed. He made estimates based on the number of available hours of press run and the estimated profit which might have been made by running at full capacity during those available hours, and from this he arrived at a mathematical conclusion. Furthermore, in taking into consideration the assessment of "loss of business profits", the profit picture for this company in the four years preceding 1966 was not such as to make certain by any means that the purchase of a second press identical to the one it already had was going to change its profit position (which had varied from small losses to small profits) into one of very substantial profit.

I therefore conclude that there must be a new assessment of damages in this case. Having regard to the extent to which the issues have already been canvassed with respect to damages, I see no reason to send this matter back to a trial Judge for a reassessment of damages, and I therefore would refer it to the Master at Toronto to assess the damages arising from the breach of contract. In so doing the Master will observe these principles:

1. The plaintiff is to be treated as being liable to pay the balance of the purchase price, if it elects to assert a claim for damages for breach of warranty in excess of the price.

2. No damages should be allowed in respect of any matter occurring subsequent to March 30, 1966.

3. The Master, when he comes to deal with "loss of business profits" generally, is to ensure that there is no duplication with items claimed for losses within the plant which include an allowance for supervision and overhead.

4. In assessing any claim that may be asserted for "loss of business profits" the Master will satisfy himself that work sufficient to earn the profits claimed was in fact available in the periods in question, and could have been obtained and performed by the plaintiff.

5. In assessing such loss of profits, the Master should take into account the work which was actually done, so that any estimate of the work which could have been done but for the defects in the machine will not include (as the estimates of the accountant at this trial clearly did include) the expenses and time of work actually done.

Appeal allowed in part.

SUNNYSIDE GREENHOUSES LTD. v. GOLDEN WEST SEEDS LTD.
(1972) 27 DLR (3d) 434, [1972] 4 WWR 420 (Alta. CA); aff'd 33 DLR (3d) 384n (SCC)

CLEMENT J.A. (for the court): This action arises out of a contract for the sale of goods by Golden West Seeds Ltd. to Sunnyside Greenhouses Ltd. Cullen, J., at trial found that there was implied in the contract a condition that the goods were reasonably fit for the purposes of Sunnyside and a condition that they were of merchantable quality, within s. 17(2) and (4) of the Sale of Goods Act, now RSA 1970, c. 327; and also an express warranty relating to the fitness for purpose. He further found that the condition and warranty were breached and awarded damages in the sum of $5,690. It was not open to Sunnyside in the circumstances to claim rescission of the contract by reason of the breaches of condition, and it sued for damages pursuant to s. 53 of the Act. Sunnyside has appealed the amount of the award, and Golden West has appealed against the finding that there was implied in the contract a condition that the goods were of merchantable quality.

Sunnyside carries on a business of producing and growing plants in greenhouses for sale to the public and to stores. The roof coverings of greenhouses, with which we are here concerned, require to be of a material that allows sunlight to pass through and reach the growing plants, in addition to protecting them from the weather and enabling the enclosed areas to be maintained at suitable temperatures. Golden West carries on the business of supplier of the requirements for the operation of commercial greenhouses, including roof coverings. It had been supplier to Sunnyside for many years and knew its operation and requirements, including those for roof coverings.

In 1965 Sunnyside moved its operation to a new site, on which it constructed 18 greenhouses 20 × 70 ft. in area with the long axis of each running east and west, together with a connecting house 20 × 250 ft. In the spring of that year Golden West had, in addition to an existing agency, taken on an agency for the sale of a relatively new greenhouse roof covering of plastic panels known as Takiron P.V.C. They were made of polyvinyl chloride. The salesman of Golden West brought this product to the attention of Sunnyside as suitable for the roof covering of its new greenhouses, and after discussions the latter ordered the panels at a cost of $10,472.82, together with amounts for fittings and hardware with which we are not concerned. Delivery was made at the end of October except for a small quantity delivered in February, 1966.

The length of time during which the plastic panels would maintain their transparency to sunlight was of major importance to Sunnyside and was a substantial part of the discussions leading to the order. Representations in this regard were made that the panels would have a useful life of fromm seven to ten years. In addition to finding the implied conditions above referred to, the trial Judge found that the representations amounted to an express warranty that the fitness of the panels in respect of transparency would endure for not less than seven years. On the facts it was reasonable for him to infer the warranty: *Traders Finance Corp. Ltd. v. Haley* (1966) 57 DLR (2d) 15 at p. 19 [aff'd *sub nom. Ford Motor Co. of Canada Ltd. v. Haley* (1967) 62 DLR (2d) 329, [1967] SCR 437, 60 WWR 497]. I agree with his conclusions both as to the implied conditions and the express warranty. In this view it is not necessary to deal with the appeal in respect of the implied condition of merchantable quality, although if it were I would affirm the finding of Cullen, J.

Installation of the panels on eight of the greenhouses was completed by December, 1965, when work shut down temporarily because of winter conditions. The remainder were completed by the end of April, 1966. The labour cost of installation of all of the panels amounted to $4,300.

Sunnyside grew two crops in the course of each year, one for the spring and one for the winter trade. The trial Judge found that the panels

> . . . functioned very well in 1966. In 1967 the panels on the southern exposure started to turn milky and hence became somewhat opaque, but the crops were average. In 1968 the panels on the south side became brownish. The crop was showing signs of "dropping off", although the year 1968 was a "reasonable" year. In 1969 the southern panels had reached such a stage of discolouration and opaqueness that it was necessary to move and manoeuvre the bedding plants from one position to another in order that they might utilize what sunlight was available. The Christmas crop of 1969 did not mature.

I should observe here that the increasing discolouration and opacity of the panels was caused by the action of the ultra-violet rays of sunlight (which is most powerful during the summer months) on their chemical composition. This may be categorized as a latent defect. Sunlight during the late fall and winter is weaker and of shorter daily duration, and the increased opacity of the south panels more effectively screened the required sunlight from the plants during this period. These could not then be manoeuvred as in the spring, since the manoeuvring had included moving them to outside cold frames which are unsuitable for winter conditions. At the end of October, 1969, Sunnyside had replaced the south panels of two greenhouses with fibreglass, and in July, 1970, it replaced all of the remaining south panels. The labour cost for this work amounted to $1,760.

The north panels did not deteriorate so rapidly. They received direct sunlight only during the early hours of the morning and the late hours of the afternoon in the summer months. They had gradually developed a discolouration which by the time of the trial in the spring of 1971 was described as markedly apparent; from which the inference is inevitable that their opacity had increased in like measure. Direct evidence was lacking to show what contribution, if any, this deterioration made to the failure of the winter crop of 1969 to mature, and there is evidence that the winter crop of 1970, after replacing the south panels with fibreglass, was normal in comparison with earlier years. Sunnyside gave evidence that it intended to replace these panels also in the summer of 1971 at a labour cost also of $1,760, although in fact it was stated on appeal that this had been postponed to 1972. The outcome of the winter crop of 1971 is, of course, not in evidence. I will return to this subject in discussing damages.

In assessing damages, Cullen, J., took into account s. 53 of the Sale of Goods Act: [Ont., s. 51] . . . He also referred amongst other authorities to *Ford Motor Co. of Canada Ltd.* v. *Haley* (1967) 62 DLR (2d) 329, [1967] SCR 437, 60 WWR 497, and *Massey-Harris Co. Ltd.* v. *Skelding* [1934] 3 DLR 193, [1934] SCR 431, discussed by this Division in *Evanchuk Transport Ltd.* v. *Canadian Trailmobile Ltd.* (1971) 21 DLR (3d) 246, [1971] 5 WWR 317. The principle there expressed is that upon a breach of an implied condition for fitness of purpose, where the buyer is compelled by the circumstances of the case to seek his remedy in damages rather than rescission, the damage is *prima facie* the amount of the full purchase price, subject to diminution by such residual value, if any, to the buyer that the seller may be able to establish. In so far as the panels alone are concerned, the evidence at trial was directed to assessment of damage on this principle.

In respect of the south panels, Cullen, J., held in effect that there had been no breach of the implied condition of fitness, nor of the related express warranty of duration of fitness, during the first three years of the prospective minimum of seven years of useful life, or, to put it another way, their residual value to Sunnyside was three years of useful life. He thus found that the recovery of the purchase price should be diminished by three-sevenths, which by calculation results in damages on this head of $2,992.23. Sunnyside does not seriously contend that this is an inadequate measure of its damage in respect of the south panels.

However, in respect of the north panels, Cullen, J., said:

> The panels on the northern exposure are still in use and are still performing whatever function northern-exposure panels are required to perform in this area.

With respect, to me the evidence falls short of showing that the north panels were of full value to Sunnyside throughout the whole of the seven years. As above noted, the discolouration of these panels had become markedly apparent by the spring of 1971. There is, I think, an almost irresistible inference that north light has some value in the growth of indoor plants. All greenhouses are so equipped, and it is common experience that some plants will grow satisfactorily with only north light. North panels should let in the light, for such growing powers as it has. They were no longer performing that function during the last two years of the seven-year expectancy, and Golden West has not established residual value to Sunnyside in respect of these two years. I would allow the appeal on this head and award damages, calculated in similar fashion, of $1,496.12.

As pointed out by Cullen, J., we are not concerned here with the principles applicable on rescission of a contract: the claim is for damages which are to be assessed in accordance with s. 53 of the Act. The recovery of the *prima facie* measure of damages prescribed by *Ford Motor Co. of Canada Ltd.* v. *Haley* does not exhaust the possibilities of recovery under the section, and several additional heads of damage have been put forward which require consideration.

The first head is the sum of $4,300 for installation of the panels. Cullen, J., allowed the portion of it attributable to the south panels, but in view of my opinion in respect of the north panels I am of opinion that the whole sum is assessable and should be allowed at $4,300 to Sunnyside. This was an expense that was unavoidable in order to make the intended use of the panels, and as the panels have to be replaced (including those of which the replacement was postponed), the expense was wasted by reason of the breaches. There is authority for such assessment. For example, in *McRae* v. *Commonwealth Disposals Commission* (1951) 84 CLR 377, the High Court of Australia, in circumstances treated as a case of breach by non-delivery of a stranded tanker, said at p. 415:

> ... we are of opinion that the plaintiffs were entitled to recover damages in this case for breach of contract, and that their damages are to be measured by reference to expenditure incurred and wasted in reliance on the Commission's promise that a tanker existed at the place specified.

Recovery was allowed of the purchase price of the tanker and also damages on several heads, including the expenses incurred and wasted in preparation for salvaging the tanker.

The next head of damage is the cost of removing the panels, for which Cullen, J., made an allowance in respect of the south panels, and if it is allowable counsel have agreed that the proper amount is $1,760. He made no allowance for the ultimate removal of the north panels since he had found there had been no breaches from which damage had resulted to Sunnyside in respect of them. The item is put forward as an expense caused by the breach, a subject which is discussed in *Mayne and McGregor on Damages*, 12th ed. (1961), para. 29, and dealt with in *Smeed v. Foord* (1859) 1 El. & El. 602, 120 ER 1035. It was contended on behalf of Golden West that this expenditure was not the direct and natural consequence of the breacch, since it was in contemplation by both parties that the panels would in any event have to be replaced after a period of time; and that if the matter were to be taken into account at all it should only be on the footing that the replacement was at an earlier date than contemplated and the proper compensation in that state of affairs is interest on the expenditures actually made in advance of the time at which they would otherwise be made. I am of opinion that this is the correct view. The expense was not caused by the breach: only the earlier outlay of the money. Interest will be allowed on the expenditure in respect of the south panels, amounting to $2,600, for four years at 5%. This amounts to $460. In respect of the north panels, the evidence warrants an allowance of interest for one year in the amount of $115. The aggregate on this head is $575, which is allowed.

The last head is the damage claimed in respect of the failure of the 1969 winter crop to mature. The trial Judge disallowed this claim, saying:

> There is a suggestion that the sales of the fall crop were down by $2,400 to $2,800 in

1969 as compared with 1966, 1967, 1968 and 1970. Whether this is attributable to the failure of maturity of the Christmas crop or to some other reason has not been made clear in the evidence.

The gross sales of the fall crop for those years, and the year 1969, are as follows:

1966	$6,684.35
1967	$7,141.35
1968	$6,654.00
1969	$4,274.00
1970	$7,181.00

The average gross sales for the years other than 1969 is $6,915, and the 1969 gross sales were below this average by some $2,640. The trial Judge found that the 1969 fall crop failed to mature by reason of the breach of condition of fitness for purpose, and I think he erred in rejecting the foregoing figures, and related evidence, as proof of damage. The related evidence was that the operating expenses in growing the 1969 fall crop which failed to mature, were exactly the same as if the crop had matured satisfactorily. The loss in gross sales resulted from Sunnyside being unable to supply its customers because of the crop failure. It is not put forward as special damage for loss of particular customers but rather as general damage arising from loss of crop with which to supply customers. Damages of this nature were allowed, for example, in *Gull* v. *Saunders & Stuart* (1913) 17 CLR 82.

The remaining issue for consideration is whether these damages, which are akin to loss of profit, can be given in addition to recovery of the capital loss through the breaches and the expenses wasted thereby. In so far as such damages fairly come within s. 53, I am of opinion that they can also be recovered. They were allowed in *Grosvenor Hotel Co.* v. *Hamilton* [1894] 2 QB 836, a case in which a tenant brought action against his landlord for the commission of a nuisance in respect of the demised premises of such extent that they became useless to the tenant and he moved out. The tenant claimed for the value of the term of the lease which he had thereby lost (*i.e.*, capital loss), and also for the consequential loss of expenses of moving and loss of profits occasioned by the move. Damages on these heads were awarded at trial, and were sustained on appeal although with some reduction in respect of the moving expenses. Lindley, L.J., said at p. 840:

> There being then a good cause of action, the question of damages arises. It is contended for the plaintiffs [the landlord who was suing for rent and against whom the tenant counterclaimed] that the damages consist solely in the loss of the term. If the term were of value the defendant could recover its value by way of damages; but to say that the damages are confined to the value of the term is erroneous in point of law. The damages are whatever loss results to the injured party as a natural consequence of the wrongful act of the defendant.

Similarly, in *Hydraulic Engineering Co. Ltd.* v. *McHaffie, Goslett, & Co.* (1878) 4 QBD 670, damages were assessed both for the expenses wasted by the purchaser and the profit he lost by reason of the seller's breach. In *Gull* v. *Saunders & Stuart*, damages were awarded in respect of capital loss, as well as for consequential loss of crops. I think that the correct principle is that loss of profit (or similar loss) which is the direct and natural consequence of the breach, may be claimed for the period during which the breach is the effective cause of the loss, in addition to other heads of damage which fairly come within s. 53.

In determining the period during which the breach is the effective cause of the loss, regard must be had to the duty of mitigation stated in the leading case of *British Westinghouse Electric & Mfg. Co., Ltd.* v. *Underground Electric Railways Co. of London Ltd.* [1912] AC 673. There Viscount Haldane, L.C., said at p. 689:

> The fundamental basis is thus compensation for pecuniary loss naturally flowing from the breach; but this first principle is qualified by a second, which imposes on a plaintiff the duty of taking all reasonable steps to mitigate the loss consequent on the breach, and debars him from claiming any part of the damage which is due to his neglect to take such steps.

When such loss is a direct and natural consequence of the breach, as it unquestionably is in the present case, then I am of opinion it may be assessed for such period of time as it is incurred before reasonable steps in mitigation of loss can become effective. It was not suggested that Sunnyside was dilatory in replacing the south panels and on cosidering the evidence I am clearly of opinion that they acted with reasonable dispatch in all of the circumstances. The loss of crop occurred during this period. Had they delayed unreasonably in replacing the panels, then I would have thought that a succeeding crop loss would not have been the direct and natural consequence of the breach, but rather the consequence of the default of Sunnyside in acting reasonably in mitigation.

Appeal allowed; cross-appeal dismissed.

[Clement J.A. concluded his judgment by discussing *Cullinane's* case, *supra*. He pointed out that the majority judgment in that case overlooked the plaintiff's duty to mitigate his damages, and that it was this duty to mitigate that affected the amount of damages recoverable by the plaintiff in the present case.]

Note on Measurement of Damages for Loss of Revenue Producing Property:

Cullinane, McLean and *Sunnyside* raise the following basic questions: (1) is the buyer bound to elect between recovery of his capital loss (i.e., diminished value of the equipment) and loss of prospective revenue from the property (ie., his expectancy); (2) how are the lost profits to be calculated; and (3) is impecuniosity a defence to the buyer's failure to mitigate his damages?

The first question is considered by Professor M.G. Baer in an admirable comment in (1973) 51 Can. Bar Rev. 490. He argues that the courts in *Cullinane* and *McLean* were mistaken in putting the buyer to his election and that there is no incompatibility in allowing the recovery of reliance and expectancy losses (ie., lost profits), provided lost profits are defined as those profits that remain after deduction of depreciation and all other relevant expenditures. In other words, he agrees with Morris L.J.'s approach in *Cullinane*. This approach also won the support of the High Court of Australia in *T.C. Industrial Plant Pty. Ltd.* v. *Robert's Queensland Pty. Ltd.* (1963-4) 37 ALJR 289. *Sunnyside* also shows the compatibility of combining reliance and expectancy losses. Can you see why?

The proper measure of expectancy losses is the subject of an important article by Professor Biger and Andrea Rosen, a substantial part of which is reproduced below. The third question, the issue of impecuniosity, is dealt with in a separate note following the extract from the Biger and Rosen article.

NAHUM BIGER AND ANDREA S. ROSEN
"A Framework for the Assessment of Business Damages for Breach of Contract"
(1981) 5 Can. Bus. LJ 302, 308-26

Two major concepts govern the accurate measurement of an injured party's expected and actual financial positions: cash flow analysis and the time value of money. Related to these concepts are two important subsidiary issues: depreciation and the residual value of capital assets. Although these principles are interconnected, it is helpful first to address each of them separately. Then they will be integrated for application to a practical example.

(1) Cash flow valuation

As Professor Baer has pointed out, much of the confusion surrounding the damage assessment issue stems from a loose use of the term "profits". What Professor Baer has not adequately appreciated, however, is that the problem extends beyond the definitional issue. In fact, the use of any accounting profit figures to measure business performance may lead to improper valuations of such performance. Accurate assessment of the damage to an injured party should be based not on the plaintiffs "book profits" (or "losses"), but rather on an analysis of his differential cash position. More colloquially put, the relevant questions are: What is the plaintiff's position at the bank now, and what would it have been had the contract been performed?

Accounting practices fail to provide direct answers to such questions. For instance, in accordance with Generally Accepted Accounting Principles (GAAP), many non-cash expenses, notably depreciation and amortization, are charged against revenues to arrive at a net income figure. The arbitrary nature of these allocations has led many accountants to question the usefulness of the income statement in analyzing a firm's performance. The result has been increased reliance on the "Statement of Changes in Financial Position", a relatively new financial report which does not require non-working capital expense allocations.

Just as the accounting profession has turned to cash flow analysis for a more objective evaluation of economic performance, so should the legal profession in assessing consequential economic damages. Indeed, where a contract breach results in loss of business earnings, a truly accurate measure of the damage to an innocent party can be determined only if the analytical focus is on the plaintiff's cash rather than "book profit" position.

Appropriate use of cash flow valuation for damages assessment can best be demonstrated in the context of an investment decision. After all, the whole question of assessing consequential business losses arises because an investment has been undertaken and then altered by a contract breach.

Any investment decision involves four elements: investment outlays, cash flows, investment project life and residual value of capital assets. Investment outlays are all expenditures made for the purpose of producing a stream of future earnings. These include not only capital equipment expenditures but also all outlays for labour when an enduring benefit in future earnings potential is created.

Investment outlays will give rise to a stream of revenues. That is, each year following the outlays, the investor will receive certain gross revenues. Also, each year the investor will incur certain operating expenses of a continuous nature in order to generate his revenues. The difference between revenues and operating expenses constitutes the investor's net operating income, or his cash flow.

Of course, the cash flow from a given investment will not continue indefinitely. Each investment has a "project life" at the end of which no operating revenues will be generated. Clearly, a project's life will expire when the assets originally invested in lose most of their productive ability. The investor will be left at the end of a project with some physical assets, the market value of which will be substantially less than what he originally paid for them. The extent of this asset deterioration will be reflected in the difference between the original outlay and the "salvage" or "residual value" of the investment assets. In other words, the assets will have depreciated in value through use and this depreciation will be evident when the residual value is measured at the end of the project life.

Thus, when an investment is undertaken, outlays are made in the expectation that annual cash flows will be received for a certain period and that investment assets will have a particular residual value at the end of that time. (Sometimes this residual value will be expected to equal zero.) When a contract affecting the investment project is breached, a different situation materializes. Cash flows different from those expected are received and a different residual value from that anticipated is realized. A simple example will clarify these points.

A manufacturer purchases a machine and erects a building to house it. Altogether, costs of the machine and the building, including labour for installation, amount to $100,000. The machine is expected to last for five years. During that time it is expected to generate $30,000 of revenue per year because it is warranted by the seller to produce widgets at the rate of six an hour. It is also expected that $10,000 a year in operating expenses will be incurred in the production process. At the end of the five-year period, the manufacturer expects the machine to have a salvage value of $6,000 and the building to have a salvage value of $8,000.

The expected cash flow profile of this investment is:

Time of Investment	Year 1	Year 2	Year 3	Year 4	Year 5	
($100,000)	$30,000	$30,000	$30,000	$30,000	$30,000	
	(10,000)	(10,000)	(10,000)	(10,000)	(10,000)	
					14,000	(residual value)
	$20,000	$20,000	$20,000	$20,000	$34,000	

This cash flow pattern does not materialize, however, because the machine does not produce at a rate of six widgets per hour, only four. Thus, there is a breach of an express warranty in the contract of sale. The breach does not affect the original outlay which remains at $100,000. Only the cash flows and residual value change. The machine is only two-thirds as productive as was warranted; hence, assume that revenues are only two-thirds of those otherwise expected, that variable expenses are reduced by a third and that the residual value of the machine is also reduced by a third. The residual value of the building is not altered. The *actual* cash flow profile thus turned out to be:

Start	Year 1	Year 2	Year 3	Year 4	Year 5	
($100,000)	$20,000	$20,000	$20,000	$20,000	$20,000	
	(7,000)	(7,000)	(7,000)	(7,000)	(7,000)	
					12,000	(residual value)
	$13,000	$13,000	$13,000	$13,000	$25,000	

The difference between the manufacturer's anticipated and actual positions can be computed on a yearly basis:

Start	Year 1	Year 2	Year 3	Year 4	Year 5
no difference	–$7,000	–$7,000	–$7,000	–$7,000	–$9,000

Even ignoring the manufacturer's duty to mitigate, the total damages cannot be properly assessed by simply adding all these losses together: the time value of money must be taken into account.

(2) *The time value of money*

In listing the issues involved in investment analysis, one crucial factor was ignored. This factor, the investor's "cost of capital", is related to a broader concept, that of the time value of money. Simply stated, $1 now is worth more than $1 to be received a year from now, and each is worth more than $1 due in two years. After all, $1 received now can be invested and earn interest for one or two years. For the moment, denote the best rate at which it can be invested as "k".

If we invest A_0 now and can get k, the value of A_0 one year hence is $A_1 = A_0(1 + k)$. If the investment is for two years and the first year's proceeds are invested for another year at k, the future value two years hence is: $A_2 = A_0(1 + k)(1 + k) = A_0(1 + k)^2$. In general, the future value of A_0, n years hence, is: $A_n = A_0(1 + k)^n$.

If k is assumed to be .10 (10%), then one dollar invested for one year will be worth $1(1.10) = $1.10 in one year. Invested for two years the dollar will be worth $1(1.10)^2 = $1.21, because the $1.10 is reinvested to earn 10% for one more year.

In the example of cash flow analysis presented above, the manufacturer received $7,000 less per annum for four years and $9,000 less for one year than he would have if the machine had performed as warranted. The $7,000 lost in the first year could have been invested for five years at "k", the $7,000 lost the second year could have been invested at "k" for four years, and so on. Investment opportunity at the rate of "k" was lost. Hence, "k" is termed the *opportunity cost* by economists. What "k" will be in any given situation will depend on circumstances specific to each investor. The "cost of capital", as k is more precisely described, varies from firm to firm. For the purposes of this article, however, "k" will be assumed to equal the interest rate the investor would obtain by depositing the funds in a bank savings account. Assuming an interest rate of 12%, the true loss suffered by the manufacturer, measured as of the end of year five is:

$$\$7,000(1.12)^4 + \$7,000(1.12)^3 + \$7,000(1.12)^2 + \$7,000(1.12)^1 + \$9,000 = \$46,470.$$

Thus, if the date of trial is at the end of year five the proper amount of damages to be awarded the manufacturer is $46,470. This figure is significantly greater than the $37,000 which would have been calculated by simply adding the annual differentials together. Failure to consider the time value of money would thus have grossly undercompensated the plaintiff in this case. Clearly, the higher the interest rate, the more crucial is the future value calculation. Indeed, at current high interest rate levels, the investment opportunity lost because of reduced cash flows will be substantial and must not be ignored if the injured party's economic loss is to be accurately assessed.

(3) Duty to mitigate

The foregoing example is completely correct only in so far as the plaintiff's duty to mitigate is not at issue. If the plaintiff's failure to mitigate were deemed unreasonable by the court, then it would be necessary to consider the potential for mitigation in the assessment of damages. Specifically, it would be necessary to adjust the measurement of the plaintiff's so-called actual position to reflect what it would have been had proper mitigation taken place. This presumed actual position, rather than that attained in the absence of mitigation would then be compared to the expected position to derive the measure of damages.

Consider again the manufacturer example above. Suppose the court has concluded that the plaintiff should have taken mitigating actions, and could reasonably have done so by undertaking major repairs to the machine in year 2 at a cost of $8,000. Suppose also that as a result of such repairs, the court estimates that the plaintiff would have been able to earn $27,000 revenues in each of years 3, 4, and 5, instead of the $20,000 earned without the repairs. The annual variable expenses would then have been $8,100 per year, and with $1,000 fixed cost total operating expenses would have been $9,100 per year. Furthermore, assume that with the value added by the repairs the residual value of the machine at the time of trial would have been $5,400 and with the building total residual value would have been $13,400. Under such circumstances the differential cash flow, computed with recognition of the plaintiff's duty to mitigate, would be as follows:

	Start	Year 1	Year 2	Year 3	Year 4	Year 5
Expected	($100,000)	$20,000	$20,000	$20,000	$20,000	$34,000
Presumed actual given mitigation	(100,000)	13,000	13,000	17,900	17,900	31,300
			(8,000)			
Difference	—	$ 7,000	$15,000	$ 2,100	$ 2,100	$ 2,700

Assuming as before an interest rate of 12%, the loss for which damage should be awarded is:

$$\$7,000(1.12)^4 + \$15,000(1.12)^3 + \$2,100(1.12)^2 + \$2,100(1.12)^1 + \$2,700 = \$39,774.80$$

Thus, as would be expected, the damage award computed with explicit consideration of the plaintiff's duty to mitigate and his failure to do so would be about $7,000 lower than otherwise.

(4) Depreciation

Since *Rema*, Canadian courts and commentators have been confused about the issue of depreciation. As the widget example above demonstrates, depreciation must be ignored when cash flow figures are constructed; the annual cash flow figures will represent net annual income from the project before depreciation. There are two reasons for this approach. The first is technical: depreciation allowance does not involve any cash flows and therefore depreciation is not to be subtracted from income. The second reason is more profound: each investment project is assumed to have some limited "useful life", at the end of which the value of the investment will be either zero or some greatly diminished salvage value. In assessing a plaintiff's financial position, consideration of the salvage value instead of the original investment already assures consideration of the loss of value of this investment. A further subtraction of depreciation charges against annual operating income figures would be tantamount to double-counting. Thus, the majority in *Rema* was basically correct in ignoring depreciation expenses, the fact that the capital assets had depreciated was already taken into account in the plaintiff's assessment of their break-up value. The break-up or salvage value was substantially less than the original capital investment in the assets; depreciation of the assets during three years of use is accounted for in the difference.

Whether or not there is a contract breach, assets usually deteriorate in value over time. Thus, at any point throughout their economic life, capital assets will have a market value lower than their original price. Although this residual asset value incorporates depreciation, it does not by itself, or in conjunction with the original value, define the injured party's loss in the event of a contract breach. Again, what is important is the difference between the plaintiff's actual and expected positions; that is, the difference between the actual residual value of the assets and what the residual value would have been if the contract had been performed. In *Rema*, for example, after three years of use, the actual break-up value of the capital assets was £6,960, or £7,520 less than the original investment. However, had the machines performed at the rate warranted, their residual value would have been considerably greater. Presumably a three-year-old, six ton-per-hour machine would have been worth considerably more than a three-year-old, two ton-per-hour machine. In other words, an accurate measurement of the plaintiff's loss would have had to account for the fact that the breach left the plaintiff with used defective assets instead of just used assets.

There are some significant measurement problems attached to the assessment of actual and expected residual asset values. These problems are elaborated upon below in a more detailed discussion of residual values.

(5) *Residual asset value*

The term "residual value" refers to the net market value of investment assets at any given point during the economic life of the assets. Clearly, in measuring an injured party's expected and actual economic positions, a cash value assessment of all assets must be made. In the case of capital assets, the relevant value is their net realizable value; that is, market value net of the removal and selling costs which may have to be incurred in order to dispose of the asset.

It seems elementary to insist that the value of an asset to an injured party is its market value (more precisely, its net realizable value) and not its book value. After all, book value is determined solely by the choice of depreciation method and reflects an arbitrary allocation of depreciation expenses against the asset's original cost. Yet this point has not been understood by either courts or commentators. For example, implicit in the dissent of Morris L.J. in the *Rema* case is the notion that an asset's residual value can be assessed on the basis of straight line depreciation. That is, where, as in *Rema*, an asset has an economic life of ten years and its value is assessed after three, this value is determined to be seven-tenths of the purchase price.

There are three major flaws in this valuation approach. In the first place, an asset will probably not deteriorate in an even pattern; however, this is the assumption inherent in straight line depreciation. In addition, straight line depreciation is based on the original cost of the asset. So even if an asset's value did diminish in equal amounts every year, it is incorrect to calculate residual value with reference to the asset contracted for instead of the asset actually received. After all, if the assets received were not defective in some way, there would be no claim for damages. The very fact that the asset was defective when purchased means that its true value when new was considerably less than the price paid for it. Hence, it is improper to determine residual asset values through use of a depreciation method based on this price. As noted above, the asset is not simply used; it is used *and* defective.

The third flaw in the use of straight line depreciation to measure residual asset value is its failure to account for the time value of money. This is the major error in the reasoning of Lord Justice Morris in his dissent in *Rema*. At any positive interest rate, deduction of depreciation expenses from annual revenues does not accurately account for an asset's deterioration in economic value, *even when its residual value is zero*. Thus, it is not correct to say as did the High Court of Australia that "x + y - x + x = x + y".

These conceptual problems are eliminated when an asset's residual value is defined in terms of its market value. Where a market for the asset in question exists, ascertainment of this value will be straightforward. Complications arise, however, when a market value cannot be easily determined. In such a case, the asset's worth must be defined in terms of its future productive ability. The asset will generate earnings in the form of net cash inflows. These cash flows must be evaluated as of a particular point in time using the firm's cost of capital. The capitalized value of the earnings, or their "present value", represents the asset's true worth. In essence, this is how the market establishes asset prices. The absence of a market means this value must be calculated with reference only to the asset's value to a particular firm instead of to the market as a whole.

This capitalization of income method of valuation is a fairly complex concept. It can best be understood in the context of an actual assessment problem. Indeed, at this point, it would be helpful to integrate all the relevant financial principles and apply them to a real case. This should not only further clarify the principles but also demonstrate the ease with which they can be used to measure consequential business losses. . . .

D. REASSESSMENT OF DAMAGES AWARDED IN SUNNYSIDE GREENHOUSES LTD. v. GOLDEN WEST SEEDS LTD.

[The authors review the facts in *Sunnyside* and the damages awarded by the Appellate Division, and continue:]

To summarize, then, the Appellate Division awarded the plaintiff total damages in the amount of $12,003.35: $4,488.35 for lost investment in panels, $4,300 for installation of the original roof, $575 for interest foregone in incurring removal costs earlier than anticipated, and $2,640 for lost profits. In fact, however, Sunnyside's *true* damage was only about two-thirds of the court's award; the company was significantly overcompensated. This can easily be shown by applying the measurement principles set out in this article.

To derive a measure of Sunnyside's true loss, three steps are necessary: First, assess what Sunnyside's financial position would have been at the beginning of 1973 (the time of trial) had the panels functioned as warranted. Then, assess Sunnyside's actual financial position at that time. Finally, compute the difference and account for the time value of money using the firm's cost of capital.

(1) Sunnyside's "expected" position

Sunnyside undertook an investment in roof panels. Its total investment was $14,772.82 by April of 1966. The panels should have lasted for seven years. It follows that at the end of 1972 these panels would have had no value; that is, their residual value would have been zero.

No information is available with regard to the operating costs of the greenhouses. However, since operating costs were established as fixed, they are not needed to calculate the difference between Sunnyside's actual and expected positions. Accordingly, Sunnyside's cash flow, had the roof panels lasted for the entire seven years, can be represented as follows:

Date	Amount ($)	Date	Amount ($)
October 1965	–6,565.70	December 1969	6,916.00
April 1966	–8,207.12	December 1970	7,181.00
December 1966	6,684.35	December 1971	6,916.00
December 1967	7,141.35	December 1972	6,916.00
December 1968	6,654.00	January 1973	0

The analytical context here is that of an investment in the panels. If the panels had functioned as promised, they would have lasted until the end of 1972. At that time, Sunnyside would have faced a decision whether or not to purchase new panels. This would be a new business decision which is not relevant to the analysis; revenues from the original investment would have been zero in 1973.

(2) Sunnyside's actual position

Now consider the actual cash flow over the period 1965-72. Sunnyside did invest a total of $6,565.70 in December, 1965, and $8,207.12 in April, 1966. In the years 1966-68, its revenues were equal to those cited above, but in 1969, total revenues were only $4,274. At the end of October, 1969, Sunnyside acted to mitigate the damage, replacing some panels. By April, 1970, all the south side panels had been replaced. In 1972, Sunnyside replaced the north side panels. Because the mitigation was undertaken in a timely fashion, no further crop loss occurred. Thus, revenues for 1971 and 1972 can be assumed, as above, to have been at the average level of $6,916.

As of the beginning of 1973, then, Sunnyside was presumably in a normal business position, but one substantially different from that where it would have been had the breach not occurred. Instead of having to replace the panels because their physical life of seven years had expired, Sunnyside was in possession of a roof of fiberglass panels which would serve for another five to seven years.

Of course, Sunnyside had been required to make additional investment outlays to obtain this new roof. No information is given regarding the price paid for the fiberglass panels. The only figures available are the related installation costs ($1,760 for the south panels and $1,760 for the north panels). Hence, the material cost of the panels must be assumed. For lack of a better figure this will be considered to have been the same as that of the original panels, or about $10,472. Thus, including installation costs, the total outlays for the new panels are assumed to have amounted to $1,554.66 at the end of October, 1969, $5,441.34 in April, 1970 and $6,996 in July, 1972.

In order to assess Sunnyside's actual financial position at the beginning of 1973, an estimate must be made of the residual value of the newer fiberglass panels it had on the roof at that date. Had the contract not been breached, the value of the roof panels in Sunnyside's possession on January 1, 1973, would have been zero; the original panels would have been obsolete since they were promised to function for seven years only. Conversely, the mitigation by Sunnyside, while requiring an outlay, left the company in possession of relatively new panels that will continue to function for several years. The value of these panels must be acknowledged in assessing Sunnyside's actual position since the fact that they continued to be useful as of January, 1973, partially offsets the financial effect of the expenditures made earlier to obtain them.

A January, 1973 market price for these partially used panels is not now available. None the less, it is possible to estimate their value to Sunnyside in terms of their residual productive ability. The estimation involves somewhat complex computations which take Sunnyside's cost of capital into account, and they are presented in the Appendix. As the Appendix shows, the residual value of the two-year-old south side panels was determined to be $4,038.97. The value of the new north side panels was determined to be $6,115.54.

Thus, Sunnyside's financial position following the breach and mitigation can be assessed in terms of the actual cash flows and residual asset values as follows:

Date	Amount ($)	Date	Amount ($)
October 1965	−6,565.70	April 1970	−5,441.34
April 1966	−8,207.12	December 1970	7,181.00
December 1966	6,684.35	December 1971	6,916.00
December 1967	7,141.35	July 1972	−6,996.00
December 1968	6,654.00	December 1972	6,916.00
October 1969	−1,554.66	Jan. 1, 1973	4,038.97
December 1969	4,274.00	Jan. 1, 1973	6,115.54

(The January, 1973 figures represent the value of the new panels as of this date.)

(3) The difference

The true loss suffered by Sunnyside as a result of the defective roof panels is represented by the difference between the expected and actual cash flows, with proper consideration of Sunnyside's possession of relatively new panels as of January, 1973.

The seven-year profile of the difference can be shown as follows:

Date	Amount ($)	Date	Amount ($)
Start	0	April 1970	−5,441.34
December 1966	0	December 1970	0
December 1967	0	December 1971	0
December 1968	0	July 1972	−6,996.00
October 1969	−1,554.66	December 1972	0
December 1969	−2,642.00	Jan. 1, 1973	10,154.51

These figures must now be adjusted to account for the time value of money. The court assessed Sunnyside's costs of capital to be 5% per annum. Using this interest rate, the total value of Sunnyside's loss as of trial date is:

$$(1,554.66)1.05^{3.25} + (2,642.00)1.05^3 + (5,441.34)1.05^{2.75} + (6,996.00)1.05^{0.5} - 10,154.51$$
$$= 1,821.80 + 3,058.44 + 6,222.67 + 7,168.77 - 10,154.51 = \$8,117.17$$

Thus, Sunnyside's true economic loss was only $8,117.17, about two-thirds of the $12,003.35 awarded as damages by the Appellate Division. While the difference in this case was only $3,886.18 and may seem trivial to some, the results will certainly not be trivial where the financial stakes are much greater. In large commercial damage actions the business losses claimed may amount to hundreds of thousands of dollars. In such cases, failure to apply appropriate assessment principles will result in errors involving substantial sums of money. The appropriate assessment principles are not unduly complex. Certainly, the concepts of cash flow analysis and the time value of money are less difficult to grasp than the *Rema* court's distinction between capital and profits. There is no reason why the legal profession should not use the same basic principles employed by the business community in investment analysis. Equitable law and sensible economics both depend on it.

Notes on the Duty to Mitigate Damages, Impecuniosity, and Contributory Negligence:

(a) *The duty to mitigate.* The aggrieved party's duty to mitigate his damages is as much a part of sales law as it is of general contract, and it underlies the market price damages rule in SGA ss. 48 and 49. As will have been seen, the mitigation rule was applied in both *McLean* and *Sunnyside* and explains why the buyer with defective goods on his hands cannot simply sit back and do nothing: he must act as a reasonable person would have acted to mitigate his damages.

Difficulties may arise because the buyer often cannot afford to buy substitutional goods or take other mitigating steps, or may not be able to do so until he recovers the purchase price or damages from the seller. Or again the buyer may suffer aggravated damages because he was relying on the expected stream of income from the seller's equipment to help pay for some of his other debts. This happened for example in *Freedhoff* v. *Pomalift Industries Ltd.* [1971] 2 OR 773 (CA). Nevertheless, in *McLean* the court held that impecuniosity is no defence to the buyer's failure to mitigate and in *Freedhoff* it denied damages ascribable to the buyer's impecuniosity on the grounds that they were too remote. However, this position may be too rigid and does not appear to be consistent with the views expressed in *Muhammad Issa el Sheik Ahmad* v. *Ali* [1947] AC 414, and *Trans Trust S.P.R.L.* v. *Danubian Trading Co. Ltd.* [1952] 2 QB 297 (CA). In the latter case, Denning L.J. observed (at p. 306):

> It was also said that the damages were the result of the impecuniosity of the sellers and that it was a rule of law that such damages are too remote. I do not think there is any such rule. In the case of a breach of contract, it depends on whether the damages were reasonably foreseeable or not. In the present case they clearly were.

(Somervell and Romer L.JJ. expressed similar views.) On the other hand, the Ontario position is consistent with the decision in ``*The Liesbosch*'' [1933] AC 449 (HL), a leading case on the assessment of damages in tort. See further, OLRC Sales Report, pp. 502-03, and note that American law appears to support Denning's dictum. Is the conflict one that can be resolved in logical terms?

(b) *Contributory Negligence.* Although the issue did not arise in *Cullinane, McLean,* or *Sunnyside* it may happen that the buyer has himself been negligent in his handling, maintenance or use of the goods. It happened for example in *Lambert* v. *Lewis* [1980] 2 WLR 299 (CA), discussed *supra*, chapter 5(A)(1), in which the trial judge found, in the action by the plaintiffs against the owner of the trailer and the manufacturer of the towing hitch, that the owner had been contributorily negligent in not discovering the defect before the time of the accident and held him responsible for 25 per cent of the damages. Not surprisingly, in the claim by the owner over against the retailer for breach of the implied conditions of quality (SGA s. 15), the retailer relied on these findings and sought an abatement of the damages for which he might be held responsible, if not indeed a full discharge. The trial judge responded favourably but the Court of Appeal unanimously reversed this part of his judgment.* The Court of Appeal's reasoning is summarized in the following extract from the headnote ([1980] 2 WLR 299, 300):

> although the negligence of the owner triggered off the accident, the basic cause of that accident was the faulty design of the towing hitch and, since the owner's conduct was neither so unreasonable as to be beyond the contemplation of the

---

* The decision was reversed by the House of Lords on 8 April 1981 on the issue of causation. The House, speaking through Lord Diplock, apparently held that the dealer's implied warranties did not endure beyond the time when the farmer became aware of the defective towing hitch, and that the farmer's negligence was an independent act which was not related to the dealer's original breach of warranty. At the time of writing (May 1981) only *The Times* summary of the judgment was available to us. [Eds.]

retailers nor such as to break the chain of causation between the warranty and the accident, the damage sustained was a natural consequence of the retailer's breach of warranty and accordingly they were liable to indemnify the owner to the extent that he had been found 25 per cent. liable to the plaintiffs in damages.

The court followed its earlier decision in the leading case of *Mowbray* v. *Merryweather* [1895] 2 QB 640, and subsequent decisions to the same effect. In *Mowbray* v. *Merryweather,*

> . . . a chain supplied by the defendants was defective and caused an accident to the plaintiff's servant, who recovered damages from the plaintiff. It was held that the plaintiff's liability to pay damages to the servant was a natural consequence of the defendant's breach of contract and was such as might reasonably have been supposed to have been in the contemplation of the parties when the contract was entered into and that accordingly the damages were not too remote.

The reasoning in *Mowbray* has been criticized by Glanville Williams, *Joint Torts and Contributory Negligence* (1951), pp. 219 *et seq.* as being illogical (can you see why?) and he argues strongly that contributory negligence should be a defence to an unintentional breach of contract regardless of the exact verbal mechanism by which the defence may be introduced: "the fact remains that whatever the language the subject of enquiry is whether the negligence of the plaintiff has concurred with that of the defendant to produce the misfortune for which damages are claimed" (p. 214). Other authors simply cite *Mowbray* v. *Merryweather* without questioning the soundness of the court's reasoning. See e.g., *McGregor on Damages*, 14th ed., §§638-639, 644; and *Benjamin's Sale of Goods*, §1315.

It will be observed that the Court of Appeal in *Lambert* v. *Lewis* did not preclude the buyer's negligence being a defence if the negligence was not reasonably foreseeable or if, as Stephenson L.J. put it (at 317), "the owner's carelessness was so unreasonable as to be beyond the contemplation of the retailers, or such as to break the chain of causation between their breach of warranty and the accident which resulted in the owner's liability to pay the plaintiffs damages". One obvious example, well substantiated by authority, is where the buyer resells the goods with knowledge of the defect. See e.g., *G. C. Dobell & Co. Ltd.* v. *Barber and Garratt* [1931] 1 KB 219 and *Benjamin's Sale of Goods*, §§1314, but such cases could also be explained on the ground of the buyer's failure to mitigate his damages after he became aware of the seller's breach. What is difficult to understand is why the court in *Lambert* v. *Lewis* thought that the seller's ability to foresee the buyer's negligent conduct should preclude him from seeking a reduction in the amount of damages payable by him.

One reason may be that none of the counsel had suggested that the court should apportion the damages as between the owner and the retailer — it was an all or nothing proposition. See [1980] 2 WLR at 310. Unfortunately none of the lord justices discussed the question whether the court had the power to apportion. So far as the answer depends on the construction of language substantially the same as that of the Ontario Negligence Act, RSO 1970, c. 296, the answer may well be no. It has been repeatedly held in Ontario that s. 2(1), which deals with claims for contribution between wrongdoers "whose damages have been caused or contributed to by the fault or neglect of two or more persons", is limited to claims between tortfeasors. See e.g., *Dominion Chain Co. Ltd.* v. *Eastern Construction Co. Ltd.* (1976) 68 DLR (3d) 385; (Ont. CA) aff'd

[1978] 2 SCR 1346. Presumably the same interpretation will be applied to s. 4, which deals with the defence of contributory negligence in actions based on "the fault or negligence" of the defendant. (Glanville Williams, *op. cit.*, ch. 11, argues for the applicability of the differently worded English Act; and see also *West Coast Finance Ltd. v. Gunderson, Stokes, Walton & Co. Ltd.* (1974) 44 DLR (3d) 232 (BC SC), rev'd on other grounds 56 DLR (3d) 460 (CA), and S. M. Waddams, *The Law of Contracts*, pp. 467-68).

4. The Foreseeability Test

KOUFOS v. CZARNIKOW LTD. ("THE HERON II")
[1967] 3 WLR 1491, [1969] 1 AC 350 (HL)

LORD REID: My Lords, by charterparty of October 15, 1960, the respondents chartered the appellant's vessel, *Heron II*, to proceed to Constanza, there to load a cargo of 3,000 tons of sugar; and to carry it to Basrah, or, in the charterer's option, to Jeddah. The vessel left Constanza on November 1, 1960. The option was not exercised and the vessel arrived at Basrah on December 2, 1960. The umpire has found that "a reasonably accurate prediction of the length of the voyage was twenty days." But the vessel had in breach of contract made deviations which caused a delay of nine days.

It was the intention of the respondents to sell the sugar "promptly after arrival at Basrah and after inspection by merchants." The appellant did not know this, but he was aware of the fact that there was a market for sugar at Basrah. The sugar was in fact sold at Basrah in lots between December 12 and 22, 1960, but shortly before that time the market price had fallen, partly by reason of the arrival of another cargo of sugar. It was found by the umpire that if there had not been this delay of nine days the sugar would have fetched £32 10s. 0d. per ton. The actual price realised was only £31 2s. 9d. per ton. The respondent claimed that they were entitled to recover the difference as damages for breach of contract. The appellant admits that he is liable to pay interest for nine days on the value of the sugar and certain minor expenses but denies that fall in market value can be taken into account in assessing damages in this case.

McNair J., following the decision in *The Parana* (1877) 2 PD 188 (CA), decided this question in favour of the appellant. He said [1966] 1 Lloyd's Rep. 259, 274:

> In those circumstances, it seems to me almost impossible to say that the shipowner must have known that the delay in prosecuting the voyage would probably result, or be likely to result, in this kind of loss.

The Court of Appeal [1966] 2 QB 695 by a majority (Diplock and Salmon L.JJ., Sellers L.J. dissenting) reversed the decision of the trial judge. The majority held that *The Parana* laid down no general rule, and, applying the rule (or rules) in *Hadley* v. *Baxendale* (1854) 9 Exch. 341 as explained in *Victoria Laundry (Windsor) Ltd.* v. *Newman Industries Ltd.* [1949] 2 KB 528 they held that the loss due to fall in market price was not too remote to be recoverable as damages.

It may be well first to set out the knowledge and intention of the parties at the time of making the contract so far as relevant or argued to be relevant. The charterers intended to sell the sugar in the market at Basrah on arrival of the vessel. They could have changed their mind and exercised their option to have the sugar delivered at Jeddah but they did not do so. There is no finding that they had in mind any particular date as the likely date of arrival at Basrah or that they had any knowledge or expectation that in late November or December there would be a rising or a falling market. The shipowner was given no information about these matters by the charterers. He did not know what the charterers intended to do with the sugar. But he knew there was a market in sugar at Basrah, and it appears to me that, if he had thought about the matter, he must have realised that at least it was not unlikely that the sugar would be sold in the market at market price on arrival. And he must be held to have known that in any ordinary market prices are apt to fluctuate from day to day: but he had no reason to suppose it more probable that during the relevant period such fluctuation would be downwards rather than upwards — it was an even chance that the fluctuation would be downwards.

So the question for decision is whether a plaintiff can recover as damages for breach of contract a loss of a kind which the defendant, when he made the contract, ought to have realised was not unlikely to result from a breach of contract causing delay in delivery. I use the words "not unlikely" as denoting a degree of probability considerably less than an even chance but nevertheless not very unusual and easily foreseeable.

For over a century everyone has agreed that remoteness of damage in contract must be determined by applying the rule (or rules) laid down by a court including Lord Wensleydale (then Parke B.), Martin B. and Alderson B. in *Hadley* v. *Baxendale*. But many different interpretations of that rule have been adopted by judges at different times. So I think that one ought first to see just what was decided in that case, because it would seem wrong to attribute to that rule a meaning which, if it had been adopted in that case, would have resulted in a contrary decision of that case.

In *Hadley* v. *Baxendale* the owners of a flour mill at Gloucester which was driven by a steam engine delivered to common carriers, Pickford & Co., a broken crankshaft to be sent to engineers in Greenwich. A delay of five days in delivery there was held to be in breach of contract and the question at issue was the proper measure of damages. In fact the shaft was sent as a pattern for a new shaft and until it arrived the mill could not operate. So the owners claimed £300 as loss of profit for the five days by which resumption of work was delayed by this breach of contract. But the carriers did not know that delay would cause loss of this kind.

Alderson B., delivering the judgment of the court, said (at 355-56):

> We find that the only circumstances here communicated by the plaintiffs to the defendants at the time the contract was made, were, that the article to be carried was the broken shaft of a mill, and that the plaintiffs were the millers of that mill. But how do these circumstances show reasonably that the profits of the mill must be stopped by an unreasonable delay in the delivery of the broken shaft by the carrier to the third person? Suppose the plaintiffs had another shaft in their possession put up or putting up at the time, and that they only wished to send back the broken shaft to the engineer who made it; it is clear that this would be quite consistent with the above circumstances, and yet the unreasonable delay in the delivery would have no

effect upon the intermediate profits of the mill. Or, again, suppose that at the time of the delivery to the carrier, the machinery of the mill had been in other respects defective, then, also, the same results would follow.

Then, having said that in fact the loss of profit was caused by the delay, he continued (at 356):

> But it is obvious that, in the great multitude of cases of millers sending off broken shafts to third persons by a carrier under ordinary circumstances, such consequences would not, in all probability, have occurred.

Alderson B. clearly did not and could not mean that it was not reasonably foreseeable that delay might stop the resumption of work in the mill. He merely said that in the great multitude — which I take to mean the great majority — of cases this would not happen. He was not distinguishing between results which were foreseeable or unforeseeable, but between results which were likely because they would happen in the great majority of cases, and results which were unlikely because they would only happen in a small minority of cases. He continued (at 354):

> It follows, therefore, that the loss of profits here cannot reasonably be considered such a consequence of the breach of contract as could have been fairly and reasonably contemplated by both the parties when they made this contract.

He clearly meant that a result which will happen in the great majority of cases should fairly and reasonably be regarded as having been in the contemplation of the parties, but that a result which, though foreseeable as a substantial possibility, would only happen in a small minority of cases should not be regarded as having been in their contemplation. He was referring to such a result when he continued (at 356):

> For such loss would neither have flowed naturally from the breach of this contract in the great multitude of such cases occurring under ordinary circumstances, nor were the special circumstances, which perhaps, would have made it a reasonable and natural consequence of such breach of contract, communicated to or known by the defendants.

I have dealt with the latter part of the judgment before coming to the well known rule because the court were there applying the rule and the language which was used in the latter part appears to me to throw considerable light on the meaning which they must have attached to the rather vague expressions used in the rule itself. The rule (at 354) is that the damages "should be such as may fairly and reasonably be considered either arising naturally, i.e., according to the usual course of things, from such breach of contract itself, or such as may reasonably be supposed to have been in the contemplation of both parties, at the time they made the contract, as the probable result of the breach of it."

I do not think that it was intended that there were to be two rules or that two different standards or tests were to be applied. The last two passages which I quoted from the end of the judgment applied to the facts before the court which did not include any special circumstances communicated to the defendants; and the line of reasoning there is that because in the great majority of cases loss of profit would not in all probability have occurred, it followed that this could not reasonably be considered as having been fairly and reasonably contemplated by both the parties, for it would not have flowed naturally from the breach in the great majority of cases.

I am satisfied that the court did not intend that every type of damage which was reasonably foreseeable by the parties when the contract was made should either be considered as arising naturally, i.e., in the usual course of things, or be supposed to have beenbin the contemplation of the parties. Indeed the decision makes it clear that a type of damage which was plainly foreseeable as a real possibility but which would only occur in a small minority of cases cannot be regarded as arising in the usual course of things or be supposed to have been in the contemplation of the parties: the parties are not supposed to contemplate as grounds for the recovery of damage any type of loss or damage which on the knowledge available to the defendant would appear to him as only likely to occur in a small minority of cases.

In cases like *Hadley* v. *Baxendale* or the present case it is not enough that in fact the plaintiff's loss was directly caused by the defendant's breach of contract. It clearly was so caused in both. The crucial question is whether, on the information available to the defendant when the contract was made, he should, or the reasonable man in his position would, have realised that such loss was sufficiently likely to result from the breach of contract to make it proper to hold that the loss flowed naturally from the breach or that loss of that kind should have been within his contemplation.

The modern rule of tort is quite different and it imposes a much wider liability. The defendant will be liable for any type of damage which is reasonably foreseeable as liable to happen even in the most unusual case, unless the risk is so small that a reasonable man would in the whole circumstances feel justified in neglecting it. And there is good reason for the difference. In contract, if one party wishes to protect himself against a risk which to the other party would appear unusual, he can direct the other party's attention to it before the contract is made, and I need not stop to consider in what circumstances the other party will then be held to have accepted responsibility in that event. But in tort there is no opportunity for the injured party to protect himself in that way, and the tortfeasor cannot reasonably complain if he has to pay for some very unusual but nevertheless foreseeable damage which results from his wrongdoing. I have no doubt that today a tortfeasor would be held liable for a type of damage as unlikely as was the stoppage of Hadley's Mill for lack of a crankshaft: to anyone with the knowledge the carrier had that may have seemed unlikely but the chance of it happening would have been seen to be far from negligible. But it does not at all follow that *Hadley* v. *Baxendale* would today be differently decided.

As long ago as 1872 Willes J. said in *Horne* v. *Midland Railway Co.* (1872) LR 7 CP 583, 590.

> The cases as to the measure of damages for a tort do not apply to a case of contract. That was suggested in a case in Bulstrode (*Everard* v. *Hopkins*, 2 Bul. 332) but the notion was corrected in *Hadley* v. *Baxendale*. The damages are to be limited to those that are the natural and ordinary consequences which may be supposed to

have been in the contemplation of the parties at the time of making the contract.

And in *Cory* v. *Thames Ironworks Co.* (1868) LR 3 QB 181, 190, 191 Blackburn J. said:

> I think it all comes round to this: The measure of damages when a party has not fulfilled his contract is what might be reasonably expected in the ordinary course of things to flow from the non-fulfilment of the contract, not more than that, but what might be reasonably expected to flow from the non-fulfilment of the contract in the ordinary state of things, and to be the natural consequences of it. The reason why the damages are confined to that is, I think, pretty obvious, viz. that if the damage were exceptional and unnatural damage, to be made liable for that would be hard upon the seller, becuase if he had known what the consequences would be he would probably have stipulated for more time, or, at all events, have used greater exertions if he knew that that extreme mischief would follow from the non-fulfilment of his contract.

It is true that in some later cases opinions were expressed that the measure of damages is the same in tort as it is in contract, but those were generally cases where it was sought to limit damages due for a tort and not cases where it was sought to extend damages due for breach of contract, and I do not recollect any case in which such opinions were based on a full consideration of the matter. In my view these opinions must now be regarded as erroneous.

For a considerable time there was a tendency to set narrow limits to awards of damages. Such phrases were used as that the damage was not "the immediate and necessary effect of the breach of contract" (*per* Cockburn C.J. in *Hobbs* v. *London and South Western Railway Co.* (1875) LR 10 QB 111, 118). *The Parana* was decided during that period. But later a more liberal tendency can be seen. I do not think it useful to review the authorities in detail but I do attach importance to what was said in this House in *R. & H. Hall Ltd.* v. *W. H. Pim (Junior) & Co. Ltd.* (1928) 33 Com. Cas. 324.

In that case Pim sold a cargo of wheat to Hall but failed to deliver it. Hall had resold the wheat but as a result of Pim's breach of contract lost the profit which they would have made on their sub-sale. Three of their Lordships dealt with the case on the basis that the relevant question was whether it ought to have been in the contemplation of the parties that a resale was probable. The finding (at 329) of the arbitrators was:

> The arbitrators are unable to find that it was in the contemplation of the parties or ought to have been in the contemplation of Messrs. Pim at that time that the cargo would be resold or was likely to be resold before delivery; in fact, the chances of its being resold as a cargo and of its being taken delivery of by Messrs. Hall were about equal.

On that finding the Court of Appeal (1927) 32 Com. Cas. 144, 151 had decided in favour of Pim, saying that, as the arbitrators had stated as a fact that the chances of the cargo being resold or not being resold were equal, it was therefore "idle to speak of a likelihood or of a probability of a resale."

Viscount Dunedin pointed out that it was for the court to decide what was to be supposed to have been in the contemplation of the parties, and then said (at 329-30):

> I do not think that "probability" . . . means that the chances are all in favour of the event happening. To make a thing probable, it is enough, in my view, that there is an even chance of its happening. That is the criterion I apply: and in view of the facts, as I have said above, I think there was here in the contemplation of parties the probability of a resale.

He did not have to consider how much less than a 50 per cent chance would amount to a probability in this sense.

Lord Shaw of Dunfermline went rather further. He said (at 333):

> To what extent in a contract of goods for future delivery the extent of damages is in contemplation of parties is always extremely doubtful. The main business fact is that they are thinking of the contract being performed and not of its being not performed. But with regard to the latter if their contract shows that there were instances or stages which made ensuing losses or damage a not unlikely result of the breach of the contract, then all such results must be reckoned to be within not only the scope of the contract, but the contemplation of parties as to its breach.

Lord Phillimore was less definite and perhaps went even further. He said (at 337) that the sellers of the wheat knew that the buyers "might well sell it over again and make a profit on the resale"; and that being so they "must be taken to have consented to this state of things and thereby to have made themselves liable to pay" the profit on a resale.

It may be that there was nothing very new in this but I think that *Hall's* case must be taken to have established that damages are not to be regarded as too remote merely because, on the knowledge available to the defendant when the contract was made, the chance of the occurrence of the event which caused the damage would have appeared to him to be rather less than an even chance. I would agree with Lord Shaw that it is generally sufficient that that event would have appeared to the defendant as not unlikely to occur. It is hardly ever possible in this matter to assess probabilities with any degree of mathematical accuracy. But I do not find in that case or in cases which preceded it any warranty for regarding as within the contemplation of the parties any event which would not have appeared to the defendant, had he thought about it, to have a very substantial degree of probability.

But then it has been said that the liability of defendants has been further extended by *Victoria Laundry (Windsor) Ltd.* v. *Newman Industries Ltd.* [1949] 2 KB 528. I do not think so. The plaintiffs bought a large boiler from the defendants and the defendants were aware of the general nature of the plaintiffs' business and of the plaintiffs' intention to put the boiler into use as soon as possible. Delivery of the boiler was delayed in breach of contract and the plaintiffs claimed as damages loss of profit caused by the delay. A large part of the profits claimed would have resulted from some specially lucrative contracts which the plaintiffs could have completed if they had had the boiler: that was rightly disallowed because the defendants had no knowledge of these contracts. But Asquith L.J. then said (at 543):

> It does not, however, follow that the plaintiffs are precluded for recovering some general (and perhaps conjectural) sums for loss of business in respect of dyeing

contracts to be reasonably expected, any more than in respect of laundering contracts to be reasonably expected.

It appears to me that this was well justified on the earlier authorities. It was certainly not unlikely on the information which the defendants had when making the contract that delay in delivering the boiler would result in loss of business: indeed it would seem that that was more than an even chance. And there was nothing new in holding that damages should be estimated on a conjectural basis. This House had approved of that as early as 1813 in *Hall* v. *Ross* (1813) Dow. 201.

But what is said to create a "landmark" is the statement of principles by Asquith L.J. (at 539-40). This does to some extent go beyond the older authorities and in so far as it does so, I do not agree with it. In paragraph (2) it is said (at 539) that the plaintiff is entitled to recover "such part of the loss actually resulting as was at the time of the contract reasonably foreseeable as liable to result from the breach." To bring in reasonable foreseeability appears to me to be confusing measure of damages in contract with measure of damages in tort. A great many extremely unlikely results are reasonably foreseeable: it is true that Lord Asquith may have meant foreseeable as a likely result, and if that is all he meant I would not object further than to say that I think that the phrase is liable to be misunderstood. For the same reason I would take exception to the phrase "liable to result" in paragraph (5). Liable is a very vague word but I think that one would usually say that when a person foresees a very improbable result he foresees that it is liable to happen.

I agree with the first half of paragraph (6). For the best part of a century it has not been required that the defendant could have foreseen that a breach of contract must necessarily result in the loss which has occurred. But I cannot agree with the second half of that paragraph. It has never been held to be sufficient in contract that the loss was foreseeable as "a serious possibility" or "a real danger" or as being "on the cards." It is on the cards that one can win £100,000 or more for a stake of a few pence — several people have done that. And anyone who backs a hundred to one chance regards a win as a serious possiblity — many people have won on such a chance. And the *Wagon Mound* (*No.* 2) [1967] AC 617 could not have been decided as it was unless the extremely unlikely fire should have been foreseen by the ship's officer as a real danger. It appears to me that in the ordinary use of language there is wide gulf between saying that some event is not unlikely or quite likely to happen and saying merely that it is a serious possibility, a real danger, or on the cards. Suppose one takes a well-shuffled pack of cards, it is quite likely or not unlikely that the top card will prove to be a diamond: the odds are only 3 to 1 against. But most people would not say that it is quite likely to be the nine of diamonds for the odds are then 51 to 1 against. On the other hand I think that most people would say that there is a serious possibility or a real danger of its being turned up first and of course it is on the cards. If the tests of "real danger" or "serious possibility" are in future to be authoritative then the *Victoria Laundry* case would indeed to be a landmark because it would mean that *Hadley* v. *Baxendale* would be differently decided today. I certainly could not understand any court deciding that, on the information available to the carrier in that case, the stoppage of the mill was neither a serious possibility nor a real danger. If those tests are to prevail in future then let us cease to pay lip service to the rule in *Hadley* v. *Baxendale*. But in my judgment to adopt these tests would extend liability for breach of contract beyond what is reasonable or desirable. From the limited knowledge which I have of commercial affairs I would not expect such an extension to be welcomed by the business community and from the legal point of view I can find little or nothing to recommend it.

Appeal dismissed.

[Concurring judgments were delivered by the other law lords, though the test of forseeability preferred by them was expressed in slightly different terms, viz., whether there was a "serious possibility" or a "real danger" of the type or damages occurring claimed to have been suffered by the plaintiff, or whether such damages were "liable to result" or "not unlikely to result".]

Notes:

1 As will be noted, *The Heron II* is essentially a gloss on *Hadley* v. *Baxendale*, the foundation of the modern rule governing the measurement of damages in contract cases. The House of Lords did not question the soundness of the rule itself. For a fascinating description of the legal and business matrix in which *Hadley* v. *Baxendale* was decided, see R. Danzig, "*Hadley* v. *Baxendale*: A Study in the Industrialization of the Law" (1975) 4 J. Leg. Studies 249. In view of the limited reach of *The Heron II*, will the decision make the damages assessment rules more acceptable to sellers?

2 Art. 74 of the UN International Sales Convention provides as follows:

> Damages for breach of contract by one party consist of a sum equal to the loss, including loss of profit, suffered by the other party as a consequence of the breach. Such damages may not exceed the loss which the party in breach foresaw or ought to have foreseen at the time of the conclusion of the contract, in the light of the facts and matters of which he then knew or ought to have known, as a possible consequence of the breach of contract.

Is its test of foreseeability the same as the tests favoured in *The Heron II*?

3 *Sub-contracts and the foreseeability test.* Predictably, the attempt to apply the *Hadley* v. *Baxendale* formula in the almost unlimited range of circumstances in which damage claims may be presented has given rise to much difficulty. Some of the problems — theoretical and practical — are illustrated in the cases that follow. One such question is whether an aggrieved buyer can claim enhanced damages on the ground that the seller's failure to perform caused him to lose a profitable sub-contract or that the seller's breach has involved him in damage claims brought by his sub-buyer. The unsettled state of the law is reviewed in the following passage in the OLRC's Sales Report (p. 500):

> . . . In *Williams Brothers* v. *Ed. T. Agius Ltd.* [1914] AC 510 the House of Lords approved the rule enunciated by the Court of Appeal in *Rodocanachi Sons & Co.* v. *Milburn Brothers* (1886) 18 QBD 67, 77 that "the law does not take into account in estimating

the damages anything that is accidental between the plaintiff and the defendant". This rule has been reaffirmed and followed in subsequent cases with the exception of the much discussed decision of the House of Lords in *Re R. & H. Hall Ltd. and W.H. Pim (Junior) & Co.'s Arbitration* [1928] All ER Rep. 763. The controversial judgments in the *Hall* case discussing the test of foreseeability under the rules in *Hadley* v. *Baxendale* were quoted with approval in *The Heron II*, although in the latter case Lord Reid [1969] 1 AC 350, 393 was careful to reserve his opinion with respect to whether a different test of foreseeability applies in sales cases than applies in contracts for the carriage of goods and other branches of contract law.

This, indeed, is the critical issue. It appears to be well accepted that if the seller knows that the buyer needs the goods to meet an existing commitment, or intends to resell them under a strong contract, he will be held responsible for the buyer's enhanced damages. Further, in *Patrick* v. *Russo-British Grain Export Co. Ltd.* [1927] 2 KB 535, esp. at 540 Salter, J., stated that it was sufficient if both parties contemplate that the buyer will "probably" resell on terms that will not enable the buyer to go into the market and replace the goods if the seller defaults, "and the seller is content to take the risk". On this basis it seems that the issue is narrowed to a choice between the test of "probable" resale and the broader test of "serious possibility", "real danger", "not unlikely occurrence" favoured by the members of the House of Lords in *The Heron II* [1969] 1 AC 350 (HL). It is understandable that the courts should be reluctant to saddle the seller with aggravated damages in the absence of compelling evidence that he appreciated the risk. At the same time it is difficult to justify a stricter test to measure the seller's liability for damages of this nature, than to measure his liability where other forms of damages are being claimed. Be that as it may, we are of the view that the discrepancy is one that is best left for judicial resolution. . . .

See also *McGregor on Damages* (14th ed., 1980) para. 206.

The above cases should be distinguished from those in which the buyer seeks to recover consequential damages for liability he has incurred to third parties (typically but not necessarily sub-buyers) because of the defective character of the goods. In the latter situation the buyer should be entitled to recover if the seller knew or ought to have realized that the goods were intended for resale, in their original or in a processed form. So typically a retailer will be entitled to recover indemnity from a manufacturer for damages caused to sub-buyers because of the defective goods and the manufacturer in turn may have a claim over against a parts manufacturer or the supplier of raw materials if the defect can be traced into their hands. The chain of liability may be broken however if the damages are too remote, if the description of the goods in the contract of resale or the warranties given by the buyer to the third party differ materially from the terms of the head contract, or if the buyer knew of the defect before he resold the goods or delivered them to the third party. See further *Benjamin's Sale of Goods*, paras. 1323, 1328-36; G.H.L. Fridman, *Sale of Goods in Canada* 2nd ed., pp. 437-43.

4   For a thorough discussion of the problems associated with the foreseeability test, see K. Swinton, ``Foreseeability: Where Should the Award of Contract Damages Cease?'' Study 3 in Reiter and Swan (eds.) *Studies in Contract Law* (1980), 61.

H. PARSONS (LIVESTOCK) LTD. v. UTTLEY INGHAM & CO. LTD.
[1977] 3 WLR 990, [1978] QB 791 (CA)

LORD DENNING M.R.: The plaintiffs, H. Parsons (Livestock) Ltd., have a fine herd of nearly 700 pigs at their farm in Derbyshire. They call it the Wayside Herd. They manage it most efficiently. They feed the pigs on special pignuts. They use about 10 tons a month of these pignuts. In order to store and handle the pignuts, the plaintiffs bought in 1968 a big hopper called a bulk feed storage hopper. They bought it from the makers, the defendants, Uttley Ingham & Co. Ltd., who are sheet-metal workers. The plaintiffs paid £270 for it. It was a huge round metal bin 28 feet high and 8 feet 6 inches in diameter. It was cylindrical at the top and tapering down into a cone. It had a lid on the top with a ventilator in it. The pignuts go into the top and come out at the bottom.

The first hopper was so successful that in 1971 the plaintiffs ordered a second one to be just the same as the first. It cost £275. The defendants accepted the order in a letter of April 23, 1971, in these terms:

> We are very pleased to book your order for one bulk hopper exactly as supplied in 1968. . . . Hopper fitted with ventilated top and complete with filler and breather pipes. . . . Ex works price £275. Carriage charges £15. We deliver in an upright position on your prepared concrete base and bolt down . . . tipping the hopper off the back of the vehicle.

On August 2, 1971, the defendants delivered the hopper to the site. It was exactly the same as the first, but when the delivery man erected it in position he forgot to adjust the ventilator. He left it closed. It was fastened with a piece of tape which had been put on so as to stop it rattling on the journey. No one noticed the mistake, because the ventilator was at the top of the hopper 28 feet above the ground. The delivery man went off. The plaintiffs used the hopper. They put pignuts into it just as they did with the first hopper. On August 12, 1971, they filled it with 9½ tons of pignuts; on September 10, 8½ tons; on October 1, 8 tons.

At first all was well. But on September 28 a small number of the nuts appeared to be mouldy. The plaintiffs did not think this would harm the pigs. So they went on feeding them. Early in October more nuts turned mouldy. But still the plaintiffs were not unduly concerned. As a rule, mouldy nuts do not harm pigs. On Saturday, October 9, there was a bigger proportion of mouldy nuts; and some of the pigs were showing signs of illness. About six of the 21 sows suckling litters were very loose, and about seven or eight were not eating all their ration of nuts. Over the weekend the plaintiffs became really concerned. They did not know the cause. They telephoned the suppliers of the nuts. They telephoned the veterinary surgeon. The suppliers of nuts came. The veterinary surgeon came. They stopped feeding the pigs with nuts from the hopper. They got some bagged foods and fed them from the bags. They telephoned the defendants. On Friday, October 15, a representative of the defendants came. He climbed up to the top of the hopper. He found the ventilator closed. He opened it. When he came down, he said to the plaintiffs: "That appears to be your trouble."

It was indeed the trouble. After much evidence by experts, the judge found that the closed ventilator was the cause. But the effects remained so as to affect the herd greatly. A large number of the pigs suffered an attack of E. coli, which is very bad for pigs. It was triggered off by the eating of the mouldy nuts. The infection spread rapidly; 254 pigs died of a value of £10,000. They also lost sales and turnover resulting in big financial loss. The total claim is £20,000 or £30,000. The question is whether that damage is recoverable from the makers of the hopper, or whether it is too remote.

The judge's findings

The judge had before him the speeches in the House of Lords in C. Czarnikow Ltd. v. Koufos [1969] 1 AC 350 about remoteness of damage. That case draws a distinction between contract and tort. Remoteness in contract depends on what the parties "reasonably contemplated at the time of the contract," whereas in tort it depends on what could "reasonably be foreseen at the time of the wrongful act or omission." But the judge did not think either of those tests was applicable. He based his decision on the implied term that the goods should be reasonably fit for the purpose under the implied condition of section 14(1) of the Sale of Goods Act 1893, as it then was. He held that this was an "absolute warranty" and that, in case of a breach, the seller was liable for all the damage of which the breach was a cause. The judge said, significantly:

> The plaintiffs do not have to prove that the toxicity or its results were foreseeable to either party . . . there is no need to have recourse to the question of the presumed contemplation.

But, in case he was wrong on this point and that, being a breach of contract, he ought to consider what was "reasonably contemplated at the time of the contract," the judge went on to consider the facts in regard to it. He inquired whether the "damage that occurred through the outbreak of E. coli was within the reasonable contemplation of the parties." After considering the evidence, he said:

> Although I sympathise with the plaintiffs, who have no doubt suffered heavy loss as a result in fact on my findings of a breach of contract, I would not consider that I would be justified in finding that in the spring of 1971 at the time of the contract either a farmer in the position of the plaintiffs or a hopper manufacturer in the position of the defendants would reasonably have contemplated that there was either a very substantial degree of possibility or a real danger or serious possibility that the feeding of mouldy pignuts in the condition described by Mr. Parsons would cause illness in the pigs that ate them, even on an intensive farm such as that of the plaintiffs.

Applying the speeches in C. Czarnikow Ltd. v. Koufos [1969] 1 AC 350, that finding would mean that the illness and death of the pigs was too remote to be an admissible head of damage.

The terms of contract

The judge derived his "absolute warranty" from section 14(1) of the Sale of Goods Act 1893 about reasonable reasonable fitness for the purpose. I agree that the warranty in section 14(1) is absolute in this sense: if the goods are unfit owing to a latent defect, which could not be discovered by any amount of care, nevertheless the seller is liable. But I do not think this absoluteness means that the seller is liable for all consequences of a breach, however remote the consequences may be. He is only liable, as section 53(2) of the Act of 1893 says, for "the estimated loss directly and naturally resulting, in the ordinary course of events, from the breach of warranty." That section is an attempted codification of the rule in *Hadley* v. *Baxendale* (1854) 9 Exch. 341 and should be so interpreted.

But I am not sure that section 14(1) was really appropriate here. The contract was divisible into two parts: the sale of the hopper and the erection of it. Under the second part, the maker was under a duty to use reasonable care in erecting the hopper. But even so, here again the maker would not be liable for all consequences. He would only be liable for such damage "as may fairly and reasonably be considered either arising naturally, i.e., according to the usual course of things, from such breach:" see *Hadley* v. *Baxendale,* 9 Exch. 341, 354. That is virtually the same as section 53(2).

On either view, therefore, the maker is not liable for all the consequences, but only for such damage as is not too remote in law. So I turn to examine the judge's findings of fact in regard to it.

The judge's findings of fact

As I read the judge's findings of fact, he was of opinion that the makers of the hopper could reasonably contemplate the following consequences as the result of the breach: (i) that the ventilator would remain closed whilst the hopper was in use; (ii) that the pignuts stored in it would become mouldy for want of proper ventilation; (iii) that the pignuts would be fed to the pigs in a mouldy condition.

But the judge, in the important extract I have already read from his judgment, was also of opinion that the makers would not reasonably contemplate that there was a serious possibility that the mouldy nuts would cause the pigs to become ill. There may have been a slight possibility, but not a serious possibility. It was so slight that the plaintiff pig farmers (who fed the nuts to the pigs knowing that they were mouldy) did not themselves feel any concern about feeding the mouldy nuts to the pigs.

By making that last finding the judge has presented us with a nicce problem of remoteness of damage. Mr. Drake submitted that it means that the plaintiffs should fail. The action is for breach of contract. It has, he says, been held by the House of Lords that a contract-breaker is only liable for the consequences which he may reasonably contemplate as a *serious* possibility and not for those which he can only foresee as a *slight* possibility.

There is no problem here about causation. The closed ventilator was clearly the cause, or one of the causes, of the deaths of the pigs. There was an unbroken sequence all the way. There was no intervening human action such as gave rise to the discussion on causation in *Weld-Blundell* v. *Stephens* [1920] AC 956 or *Dorset Yacht Co. Ltd.* v. *Home Office* [1970] AC 1004, 1030. The only problem here is with remoteness of damage.

The law as to remoteness

Remoteness of damage is beyond doubt a question of law. In *C. Czarnikow Ltd.* v. *Koufos* [1969] AC 350 the House of Lords said that, in remoteness of damage, there is a difference between contract and tort. In the case of a *breach of contract*, the court has to consider whether the consequences were of such a kind that a reasonable man, at the time of making the contract, would *contemplate* them as being of a very substantial degree of probability. (In the House of Lords various expressions were used to describe this degree of probability, such as, not merely "on the cards" because that may be too low: but as being "not unlikely to occur" (see pp. 383 and 388); or "likely to result or at least not unlikely to result" (see p. 406); or "liable to result" (see p. 410); or that there was a "real danger" or "serious possibility" of them occurring (see p. 415).)

In the case of a *tort*, the court has to consider whether the consequences were of such a kind that a reasonable man, at the time of the tort committed, would *foresee* them as being of a much lower degree of probability. (In the House of Lords various expressions were used to describe this, such as, it is sufficient if the consequences are "liable to happen in the most unusual case" (see p. 385) or in a "very improbable" case (see p. 389); or that "they may happen as a result of the breach, however unlikely it may be, unless it can be brushed aside as far-fetched" (see p. 422).)

I find it difficult to apply those principles universally to all cases of contract or to all cases of tort: and to draw a distinction between what a man "contemplates" and what he "foresees." I soon begin to get out of my depth. I cannot swim in this sea of semantic exercises — to say nothing of the different degrees of probability — especially when the cause of action can be laid either in contract or in tort. I am swept under by the conflicting currents. I go back with relief to the distinction drawn in legal theory by Professors Hart and Honore in their book *Causation in the Law* (1959), at pp. 281-287. They distinguish between those cases in contract in which a man has suffered no damage to person or property, but only *economic loss*, such as, loss of profit or loss of opportunities for gain in some future transaction: and those in which he claims damages for an *injury actually done* to his person or *damage actually done* to his property (including his livestock) or for ensuing expense (*damnum emergens*) to which he has actually been put. In the law of *tort*, there is emerging a distinction between economic loss and physical damage: see *Spartan Steel & Alloys Ltd.* v. *Martin & Co. (Contractors) Ltd.* [1973] QB 27, 36-37. It underlies the words of Lord Wilberforce in *Anns* v. *Merton London Borough Council* [1977] 2 WLR 1024, 1039 recently, where he classified the recoverable damage as "material, physical damage." It has been much considered by the Supreme Court of Canada in *Rivtow Marine Ltd.* v. *Washington Iron Works and Walkem Machinery & Equipment Ltd.* [1973] 6 WWR 692 and by the High Court of Australia in *Caltex Oil (Australia) Pty. Ltd.* v. *Dredge Willemstad* (1976) 51 ALGR 270.

It seems to me that in the law of *contract*, too, a similar distinction is emerging. It is between loss of profit consequent on a breach of contract and physical damage consequent on it.

Loss of profit cases

I would suggest as a solution that in the former class of case — loss of profit cases — the defaulting party is only liable for the consequences if they are such as, at the time of the contract, he ought reasonably to have *contemplated* as a *serious* possibility or real danger. You must assume that, at the time of the contract, he had the very kind of breach in mind — such a breach as afterwards happened, as for instance, delay in transit — and then you must ask: ought he reasonably to have *contemplated* that there was a *serious* possibility that such a breach would involve the plaintiff in loss of profit? If yes, the contractor is liable for the loss unless he has taken care to exempt himself from it by a condition in the contract — as, of course, he is able to do if it was the sort of thing which he could reasonably contemplate. The law on this class of case is now covered by the three leading cases of *Hadley* v. *Baxendale,* 9 Exch. 341; *Victoria Laundry (Windsor) Ltd.* v. *Newman Industries Ltd.* [1949] 2 KB 528; and *C. Czarnikow Ltd.* v. *Koufos* [1969] 1 AC 350. These were all "loss of profit" cases: and the test of "reasonable contemplation" and "serious possibility" should, I suggest, be kept to that type of loss or, at any rate, to economic loss.

Physical damage cases

In the second class of case — the physical injury or expense case — the defaulting party is liable for any loss or expense which he ought reasonably to have *foreseen* at the time of the breach as a possible consequence, even if it was only a *slight* possibility. You must assume that he was aware of his breach, and then you must ask: ought he reasonably to have foreseen, at the time of the breach, that something of this kind might happen in consequence of it? This is the test which has been applied in cases of tort ever since *The Wagon Mound* cases [1961] AC 388 and [1967] 1 AC 617. But there is a long line of cases which support a like test in cases of contract.

One class of case which is particularly apposite here concerns latent defects in goods; in modern words "product liability." In many of these cases the manufacturer is liable in contract to the immediate party for a breach of his duty to use reasonable care and is liable in tort to the ultimate consumer for the same want of reasonable care. The ultimate consumer can either sue the retailer in contract and pass the liability up the chain to the manufacturer, or he can sue the manufacturer in tort and thus by-pass the chain. The liability of the manufacturer ought to be the same in either case. In nearly all these cases the defects were outside the range of anything that was in fact contemplated, or could reasonably have been contemplated, by the manufacturer or by anyone down the chain to the retailers. Yet the manufacturer and others in the chain have been held liable for the damage done to the ultimate user, as for instance the death of the young pheasants in *Hardwick Game Farm* v. *Suffolk Agricultural Poultry Producers Association* [1969] 2 AC 31 and of the mink in *Christopher Hill Ltd.* v. *Ashington Piggeries Ltd.* [1972] AC 441. Likewise, the manufacturers and retailers were held liable for the dermatitis caused to the wearer in the woollen underwear case of *Grant* v. *Australian Knitting Mills Ltd.* [1936] AC 85, even though they had not the faintest suspicion of any trouble. So were the manufacturers down the chain to the sub-contractors for the disintegrating roofing tiles in *Young & Marten Ltd.* v. *McManus Childs Ltd.* [1969] 1 AC 454.

Another familiar class of case in where the occupier of premises is under the common duty of care, either in pursuance of a contract with a visitor or under the

Occupiers Liability Act 1957. If he fails in that duty and a visitor is injured, the test of remoteness must be the same no matter whether the injured person enters by virtue of a contract or as a visitor by permission without a contract. No matter whether in contract or tort, the damages must be the same. Likewise, when a contractor is doing work on premises for a tenant and either the tenant or a visitor is injured — the test of remoteness is the same no matter whether the person injured is a tenant under the contract or a visitor without a contract; see *A.C. Billings & Sons Ltd.* v. *Riden* [1958] AC 240.

Yet another class of case is where a hospital authority renders medical services in contract to a paying patient and gratuitously to another patient without any contract. The paying patient can sue in contract for negligence. The poor patient can sue in tort: see *Cassidy* v. *Ministry of Health* [1951] 2 KB 343, 359-60. The test of remoteness should be the same whether the hospital authorities are sued in contract or in tort: see *Esso Petroleum Co. Ltd.* v. *Mardon* [1976] QB 801, 802.

Instances could be multiplied of injuries to persons or damages to property where the defendant is liable for his negligence to one man in contract and to another in tort. Each suffers like damage. The test of remoteness is, and should be, the same in both.

Coming to the present case, we were told that in some cases the makers of these hoppers supply them direct to the pig farmer under contract with him, but in other cases they supply them through an intermediate dealer — who buys from the manufacturer and resells to the pig farmer on the self-same terms — in which the manufacturer delivers direct to the pig farmer. In the one case the pig farmer can sue the manufacturer in contract. In the other in tort. The test of remoteness should be the same. It should be the test in tort.

Conclusion

The present case falls within the class of case where the breach of contract causes physical damage. The test of remoteness in such cases is similar to that in tort. The contractor is liable for all such loss or expense as could reasonably have been foreseen, at the time of the breach, as a possible consequence of it. Applied to this case, it means that the makers of the hopper are liable for the death of the pigs. They ought reasonably to have forseen that, if the mouldy pignuts were fed to the pigs, there was a possibility that they might become ill. Not a serious possibility. Nor a real danger. But still a slight possibility. On that basis the makers were liable for the illness suffered by the pigs. They suffered from diarrhoea at the beginning. This triggered off the deadly E. coli. That was a far worse illness than could then be foreseen. But that does not lessen this liability. The type or kind of damage was foreseeable even though the extent of it was not: see *Hughes* v. *Lord Advocate* [1963] AC 837. The makers are liable for the loss of the pigs that died and of the expenses of the vet and such like, but not for loss of profit on future sales or future opportunities of gain: see *Simon* v. *Pawson & Leafs Ltd.* (1932) 38 Com. Cas. 151.

So I reach the same result as the judge, but by a different route. I would dismiss the appeal.

Appeal dismissed.

Note: Separate concurring judgments were rendered by Orr and Scarman L.JJ. but based on different reasoning. They did not agree with Lord Denning M.R. that the test of remoteness in contract to be applied with respect to physical damages differs from that with respect to claims for loss of profit. They reached the same conclusion as Lord Denning because (*per* Scarman L.J.) they approved of the following statement in *McGregor on Damages* (13th ed., 1972, pp. 131-32): ". . . in contract as in tort, it should suffice that, if physical injury or damage is within the contemplation of the parties, recovery is not to be limited because the degree of physical injury or damage could not have been anticipated." What then is the practical difference between the two approaches?

Cf. UCC 2-715(2), which provides that "Consequential damages resulting from the seller's breach include . . .

(b)   injury to person or property proximately resulting from any breach of warranty."

What justification is there for applying a different test of foreseeability for some types of damages? The seller's superior ability to insure against the loss? The need to maximize the deterrent against negligent conduct? Are you persuaded by Lord Denning's reasoning that claims arising out of physical injury should be governed by the same test of remoteness whether the claim sounds in contract or tort? If this reasoning is sound why are tort claims for defective goods still subject to proof of negligence?

5. DAMAGE CLAIMS IN PRIVATE SALES

OLRC Sales Report
pp. 489-91

The existing law in respect of the assessment of damages does not distinguish between different types of seller. *Prima facie*, it may seem anomalous that the law should place damage claims against a private seller on the same footing as damage claims against a merchant seller. It may be thought that a persuasive case could be made for restricting the liability of a private seller to restitutionary damages, or, at any rate, to protecting him against claims for consequential damages in the absence of wilful breach of the contract, fraud or negligence. We have recommended in an earlier chapter an expanded definition of express warranty. We noted that a representor (including a private seller) could be liable for expectation and reliance losses, and for consequential, as well as direct damages, should there be a breach of an express warranty as so expanded. We considered the implications of this change of definition in the case of representations made by a private seller and the possibility of drawing a distinction between commercial and private sales. For reasons stated, we decided not to recommend an adoption of this distinction. We pointed out, however, that it may be that a different rule of damages should be adopted generally in non-commercial sales, and that we would explore this possibility at a later stage of this Report. We have reached that stage of the Report and we now turn to consider this more general issue.

The possibility that a private seller may be held liable for expectation and other non-restitutionary claims is not confined to breaches of an express warranty. The possibility also exists where he is sued for breach of any other contractual obligation, such as late delivery or breach of the implied conditions of title and description. The suggestion that a distinction should be drawn between the measure of the damages recoverable from a merchant seller and non-merchant seller is not novel since, with respect to latent defects in the goods sold, such a distinction already appears to exist in substance, if not in form, in various civil law systems.

There are, however, persuasive reasons against the adoption of such a distinction in the revised Act. First, to the best of our knowledge, no other common law jurisdiction has so far introduced the distinction in its sales legislation and, in the context of express warranties, it was not supported in the New South Wales Working Paper. Secondly, there is little evidence that the problem is a significant one. Most of the heavy damage claims appear to involve breaches of the conditions of merchantability and fitness, and these implied terms do not apply to private sales. Again, in so sensitive an area as damages, a flexible approach is preferable to a rigid distinction between different types of sale. Finally, it may be thought that if different damage rules are to be applied to private transactions the distinction should be drawn across a wider contractual area and not confined to sales law.

We are ourselves divided about the merits of introducing the distinction in the revised Act, but we agree that this problem warrants further examination. Accordingly, we recommend that it be remitted for this purpose to the Law of Contract Amendment Project.

6. Envoi: Has the Pendulum Swung too far?

OLRC Sales Report
pp. 486-89

Whatever reservations one may have about the terminology of general and "special damages" in this context, it is abundantly clear that within generous limits the law seeks to protect the buyer's reliance, expectation and restitutionary interests. In practical terms this means that the seller may be liable for damages amounting to many times the price of goods, and many more times the profit he could hope to derive from the transaction. The law reports are replete with examples of such awards. Equally serious from the seller's point of view is the fact that this potentially oppressive liability is not predicated on any form of moral culpability. Breach of a warranty or condition is a species of strict liability. The seller cannot exonerate himself by showing that the breach could not have been prevented by the exercise of reasonable care on his part and, indeed, that the breach could not even have been anticipated given the existing state of knowledge at the time that the contract was made. Not surprisingly, sellers have an intense dislike for these principles of liability and seek to exclude or restrict them whenever they deem the danger of heavy damages sufficiently serious.

Has the pendulum swung too far in the buyer's favour? To put the issue on a broader footing, has the law erred in combining principles of strict liability for breach of contract with a concept of damages aimed at making the innocent party substantially whole? The answer to this question would involve an elaborate inquiry into society's reasons for enforcing contracts and the rationale of contract damages, an inquiry that is beyond the scope of this Report. It must suffice to indicate some of the relevant factors and some of the difficulties that are raised by this issue. It is frequently said that a modern economy could not function without the assurance that promises seriously made will be honoured and that the contract breaker will be held accountable in damages, or otherwise, if he violates his undertaking. In economic terms, the legal norm is buttressed by the argument that enforceable promises lead to a more efficient allocation of resources and reduce transaction costs. There are obvious weaknesses in these lines of reasoning. There is no necessary correlation between the enforceability of promises and the measure of damages awarded under the *Hadley* v. *Baxendale* principles. Nor is it true to say that an award of damages always promotes economic efficiency, or that such an award reflects a proper allocation of risks. In fact, the reverse may be true. If a small manufacturer is confronted with a large damage award in respect of a liability for which he is not insured, he may be forced into bankruptcy and his employees may lose their positions. It may be questioned whether such a result would necessarily promote economic efficiency or reflect proper allocation of risk. By the same token, resort to insurance principles as the basis for justifying heavy damage awards will not, for two reasons, pick up all the slack. The first reason is that insurance is not readily available for many types of pure economic losses. The second reason is that, at least in some instances, it may be easier and cheaper for the buyer to insure than for the seller.

Some of the early comments on the damage principles enunciated in *Hadley* v. *Baxendale* sought to allay these misgivings by arguing that the party in breach must be deemed to have assumed the risk of foreseeable damages. Indeed, there have been intermittent suggestions that the seller will not be held liable unless this assumption can be made. It is doubtful whether this is still the law, and the tacit agreement test has been clearly rejected in Article 2 of the Uniform Commercial Code. However, an attenuated form of the test can be discerned in the Code's requirement that the damages sought to be recovered must have been within the contemplation of the parties as a substantial possibility, the suggestion being that since the damages were foreseeable the party sought to be held liable could have refused to assume the risk. The notion that the seller's liability is based upon an implied assumption of risk raises difficult issues, but there is a more serious concern about the foreseeability tests. A seller can readily foresee that a defective machine will result in various types of loss to the buyer: what he cannot predict is the quantum of the prospective loss, a feature that, for legal purposes, is generally regarded as irrelevant. Unless the seller has this information, it will be difficult for him to absorb the potential liability as part of the cost of his operations. The difficulties are compounded when the product is mass produced and mass distributed.

The broad principle of liability enshrined in the *Hadley* v. *Baxendale* formula is, therefore, vulnerable to criticism on important grounds. It is, however, easier to expose the weakness of the formula than to suggest alternatives that are not open to even greater objections. This appears to be true of the following solutions that suggest themselves as alternatives to the present scope of damage awards.

(a) To disallow damage claims for breach of executory contracts, other than claims of a restitutionary character. Clearly, such a solution would be a regressive step in the evolution of contract law and would do nothing to encourage the observance of consensual obligations.

(b) In the case of executed contracts, to restrict recovery to restitutionary and reliance losses, and to disallow all expectation losses save possibly where the seller has been guilty of negligence or wilful breach. This solution has a double weakness. It presupposes that an easy line can be drawn between reliance damages and expectation losses, and this is an assumption that does not correspond to the facts. This solution also assumes that expectation losses constitute the most important component in a typical damage claim arising out of an executed contract, and this too is probably an overgeneralization.

(c) To restrict the maximum recoverable damages to the value of the price or a multiple thereof unless the parties have agreed to a higher figure. This approach finds a precedent in many domestic and international contracts of carriage. It is also reflected in many sales contracts for manufactured goods that restrict the seller's liability to the repair or replacement of the defective goods, or to the return of the purchase price. The objection to this solution is that it may leave the buyer with ruinous consequential losses that he is ill-equipped to absorb.

(d) To distinguish between consumer and commercial contracts and, on the ground that business buyers may be assumed to be capable of protecting their own interests, to allow a higher level of recovery for contracts of the former type. It is true that a distinction between consumer and non-consumer transactions has been widely drawn in recent consumer protection legislation. But this is done for the purpose of conferring *additional* protection on consumers, and not for the purpose of cutting down the rights that non-consumer classes enjoy under existing law.

(e) To distinguish between economic losses and claims arising from injury to persons or damage to property, and to disallow the former losses and to accept the latter claims. There may, for various purposes, be good reasons for distinguishing between these two types of claim. To disallow economic claims altogether, unless expressly agreed to by the seller, would, however, be a solution that is open to even more serious objections than the preceding alternatives.

Having regard to the difficulty of finding an acceptable substitute, our conclusion is that the revised Act should continue to hold the seller liable for all substantially foreseeable damages falling within the *Hadley* v. *Baxendale* formula and we so recommend. We have also concluded that this formula should apply to the buyer's liability for damages. Whether any changes are desirable in the statutory reproduction of the formula will be considered hereafter.

The effect of this recommendation is to maintain the *status quo* and to impose on the seller the onus of disclaiming or restricting his liability within the limits permitted by the new law contained in the revised Act. Though this is an imperfect solution, it seems to us to be fairer than imposing on the buyer the onus of bargaining for the recovery of damages for the occurrence of which, *ex hypothesi*, he was in no way to blame. This is particularly true where the seller is a merchant selling goods to a non-merchant and is, therefore, more likely to be conversant with potential defects and risks of loss than the buyer. In reaching our conclusion we have also been influenced by the consideration that a change in basic damage principles, not applied uniformly across the contractual field, would disturb the existing equilibrium and would create serious anomalies. It should be clear from the preceding discussion that, under the scheme we propose, it would not be disreputable for a seller to seek to limit his liability and, provided it is not procured by unconscionable means, such allocation of risks should be respected by a court.

Note: Professor Morris Shanker shares the OLRC's criticism of the rule in *Hadley* v. *Baxendale* but is less hesitant in recommending the elimination of lost profits as a head of recoverable damages by the buyer. See Morris G. Shanker, "A Retreat to Progress (A Proposal to Eliminate Damage Awards for Loss of Business Profits)" (1978-79) 3 CBLJ 363. Does this proposal satisfactorily meet the concerns expressed in the Sales Report? For a comparative study of the above questions, See J. Hellner, "Consequential Loss and Exemption Clauses" (1981) 1 Oxford JLS 13.

C. SPECIFIC PERFORMANCE, ACTIONS IN DETINUE AND RELIEF UNDER THE REPLEVIN ACT

1. SPECIFIC PERFORMANCE

IN RE WAIT
[1927] 1 Ch. 606, [1926] All ER Rep. 433 (CA)

The following extract only deals with the question of specific performance and the interpretation and application of the SGA, s. 50.

ATKIN L.J.: This case has resulted in a decision which if correct will have far-reaching effects upon commercial transactions. It has the support of the judgments of both learned judges below, and also of Sargant L.J., and therefore in expressing my opinion that it was wrongly decided I feel bound to examine in some detail the facts and contentions relied on by the parties.

   Both the debtor and the claimant are grain merchants in Bristol. On November 20, 1925, by a written contract on form 22 of the London Corn Trade Association Messrs. W. H. Pim, Junior, & Co., Ld., acting for Messrs. Balfour Williamson & Co., of London, agreed to sell to the debtor 1000 tons Western White wheat. Shipment was to be in good condition per motor vessel *Challenger*, expected to load between December 16–31, 1925, from Oregon and/or Washington as per bill or bills of lading to be dated accordingly when the goods were actually on board. ... [This] is an ordinary commercial contract for the sale c.i.f. of grain to be imported to England from the United States of America. It is a contract for the future shipment of grain not, at the time, ascertained. It is not the sale of a cargo. Apart from some appropriation of the goods to the buyer with his express or implied assent at or after shipment, which would, I think, be unusual, the buyer would acquire no property in any grain until he took up the documents in exchange for cash or acceptance.

On November 21, 1925, the debtor by a contract in writing agreed to sell to the claimants 500 tons Western White wheat per motor vessel *Challenger*, expected to load between December 16–31, 1925, bill of lading to be dated accordingly ...

It appears that by other contracts the debtors had agreed with other sellers for the purchase from them of further grain to be shipped per the *Challenger*. He had a contract for the delivery of a further 500 tons of Western White wheat and 1500 tons of No. 2 Northern wheat. All this wheat was shipped on the *Challenger* on bills of lading bearing dates that conformed to the contracts of sale. The wheat was shipped in bulk. Of the Western White wheat 1190 tons were shipped in the after-hold, and 310 tons in No. 2 hold. On February 28 the *Challenger* arrived at Avonmouth bringing the wheat as described above. Meanwhile other events material to this decision had occurred. On December 22 the debtor gave the claimants particulars of the date of the bill of lading for motor vessel *Challenger* to satisfy the contract of November 21. On January 4 the bills of lading arrived in this country and were sighted by the consignees making the prompt date under the contract February 6. On the same date the debtor rendered to the claimants a provisional invoice for 5933*l*. 5*s*., the price of the 500 tons less freight; on February 3 the debtors passed to the claimants a debit note for Western White wheat for 5933*l*. 5*s*. stating the prompt to be February 6, which was a Saturday, with a note appended: "Kindly let us have your cheque for the above amount on Friday morning, and oblige." And on the Friday, February 5, the claimants gave the debtor a cheque for 5933*l*. 5*s*., which was paid in to the general credit of the debtor's account with the Westminster Bank, Bristol. ...

On February 23 the debtor, who was in difficulties, called a meeting of his creditors, and on February 24 on his own petition a receiving order was made, and he was adjudicated bankrupt, Mr. Collins being appointed special manager of the estate. On March 5 he was appointed trustee in bankruptcy of the estate. On February 27 Mr. Collins took up from the bank the bills of lading, giving them a cheque for the full amount less the sum of 5933*l*. 5*s*., which the bank allowed to be treated as a credit against the advance. Having received the bills of lading he was able to deal with the wheat. Of the 1500 tons Western White wheat, 830 tons were delivered to Messrs. Spiller & Baker ex ship; some further wheat was delivered to the purchasers; and at the time the motion was launched the trustee had in warehouse 530 tons available for performance of the contract with the claimants, but which was in fact property of the debtor or possibly only of the trustee available for distribution amongst the creditors generally. ...

It will be noticed from the above statement of facts that no 500 tons of wheat have ever been ear-marked, identified or appropriated as the wheat to be delivered to the claimants under the contract. The claimants have never received any bill of lading, warrant, delivery order or any document of title representing the goods. Nor can 500 tons or any less quantity be ascertained by subtracting from the bulk in the trustee's possession known quantities the property of the purchasers. The trustee has in his possession in warehouse 530 tons of Western White wheat. It is not suggested that this is not an ordinary commercial commodity. It is, however, said: (*a*) that the claimants are entitled to have the contract of sale of November 21 specifically performed by a direction to the trustee to weigh out and deliver 500 tons to the claimants. . . .

The claim of the claimants to specific performance in their argument in the Courts below and before us was based solely on the provisions of s. 52 of the Sale of Goods Act, 1893. That section is a re-enactment in an amended form of s. 2 of the Mercantile Law Amendment Act, 1856, which gave the remedy in all actions and suits for breach of contract to deliver specific goods for a price in money. The present section gives the remedy "in action for breach of contract to deliver specific or ascertained goods." It is not easy to discover the reason for adding the words "or ascertained." It is, however, clear that "specific goods" bear the meaning assigned to them in the definition clause "goods identified and agreed upon at the time a contract of sale is made." "Ascertained" probably means identified in accordance with the agreement after the time a contract of sale is made, and I shall assume that to be the meaning. It seems to be beyond dispute that at the date of this contract there were no goods identified and agreed upon; and I think it equally clear that at no time were there any goods ascertained. For the purpose of this case it is unnecessary to consider whether this section was intended to give the purchaser a larger remedy than he had in Courts of equity before the section in the Act of 1856 was passed. Speaking generally, Courts of equity did not decree specific performance in contracts for the sale of commodities which could be ordinarily obtained in the market where damages were a sufficient remedy. Possibly the statutory remedy was intended to be available even in those cases. But the Code appears to have this effect, that in contracts for the sale of goods the only remedy by way of specific performance is the statutory remedy, and it follows that as the goods were neither specific nor ascertained the remedy of specific performance was not open to the creditors.

• • •

Without deciding the point, I think that much may be said for the proposition that an agreement for the sale of goods does not import any agreement to transfer property other than in accordance with the terms of the Code, that is, the intention of the parties to be derived from the terms of the contract, the conduct of the parties and the circumstances of the case, and, unless a different intention appears, from the rules set out in s. 18. The Code was passed at a time when the principles of equity and equitable remedies were recognized and given effect to in all our Courts, and the particular equitable remedy of specific performance is specially referred to in s. 52. The total sum of legal relations (meaning by the word "legal" existing in equity as well as in common law) arising out of the contract for the sale of goods may well be regarded as defined by the Code. It would have been futile in a code intended for commercial men to have created an elaborate structure of rules dealing with rights at law, if at the same time it was intended to leave, subsisting with the legal rights, equitable rights inconsistent with, more extensive, and coming into existence earlier than the rights so carefully set out in the various sections of the Code.

The rules for transfer of property as between seller and buyer, performance of the contract, rights of the unpaid seller against the goods, unpaid sellers' lien, remedies of the seller, remedies of the buyer, appear to be complete and exclusive statements of the legal relations both in law and equity. They have, of course, no relevance when one is considering rights, legal or equitable, which may come into existence dehors the contract for sale. A seller or a purchaser may, of course, create any equity he pleases by way of charge, equitable assignment or any other dealing with or disposition of goods, the subject-matter of sale; and he may, of course, create such an equity as one of the terms expressed in the contract of sale. But the mere sale or agreement to sell or the acts in pursuance of such a contract mentioned in the Code will only produce the legal effects which the Code states.

Appeal allowed.

[Lord Hanworth M.R. delivered a concurring judgment; Sargant L.J. dissented on other grounds.]

SKY PETROLEUM LTD. v. V.I.P. PETROLEUM LTD.
[1974] 1 All ER 954, [1974] 1 WLR 576 (Ch.)

GOULDING J.: This is a motion for an injunction brought by the plaintiff company, Sky Petroleum Ltd., as buyer, under a contract dated 11th March 1970 made between the defendant company, VIP Petroleum Ltd., as seller, of the one part and the plaintiff company of the other part. That contract was to operate for a period of ten years, subject to certain qualifications, and thereafter on an annual basis unless terminated by either party giving to the other not less than three months written notice to that effect. It was a contract at fixed prices, subject to certain provisions which I need not now mention. Further, the contract obliged the plaintiff company — and this is an important point — to take its entire requirement of motor gasoline and diesel fuel under the contract, with certain stipulated minimum yearly quantities.

After the making of the agreement, it is common knowledge that the terms of trade in the market for petroleum and its different products changed very considerably, and I have little doubt that the contract is now disadvantageous to the defendant company. After a long correspondence, the defendant company, by telegrams dated 15th and 16th November 1973, has purported to terminate the contract under a clause therein providing for termination by the defendant company if the plaintiff company fails to conform with any of the terms of the bargain. What is alleged is that the plaintiff company has exceeded the credit provisions of the contract and has persistently been, and now is, indebted to the defendant company in larger amounts than were provided for. So far as that dispute relates, as for the purposes of this motion it must, to the date of the purported termination of the contract, it is impossible for me to decide it on the affidavit evidence. It involves not only a question of construction of the contract, but also certain disputes on subsequent arrangements between the parties and on figures in the accounts. I cannot decide it on motion and the less I say about it the better.

What I have to decide is whether any injunction should be granted to protect the plaintiff company in the meantime. There is trade evidence that the plaintiff company has no great prospect of finding any alternative source of supply for the filling stations which constitute its business. The defendant company has indicated its willingness to continue to supply the plaintiff company, but only at prices which, according to the plaintiff company's evidence, would not be serious prices from a commercial point of view. There is, in my judgment, so far as I can make out on the evidence before me, a serious danger that unless the court interferes at this stage the plaintiff company will be forced out of business. In those circumstances, unless there is some specific reason which debars me from doing so, I should be disposed to grant an injunction to restore the former position under the contract until the rights and wrongs of the parties can be fully tried out.

• • •

Now I come to the most serious hurdle in the way of the plaintiff company which is the well-known doctrine that the court refuses specific performance of a contract to sell and purchase chattels not specific or ascertained. That is a well-established and salutary rule and I am entirely unconvinced by counsel for the plaintiff company when he tells me that an injunction in the form sought by him would not be specific enforcement at all. The matter is one of substance and not of form and it is, in my judgment, quite plain that I am for the time being specifically enforcing the contract if I grant an injunction. However the ratio behind the rule is, as I believe, that under the ordinary contract for the sale of non-specific goods, damages are a sufficient remedy. That, to my mind, is lacking in the circumstances of the present case. The evidence suggests, and indeed it is common knowledge, that the petroleum market is in an unusual state in which a would-be buyer cannot go out into the market and contract with another seller, possibly at some sacrifice as to price. Here, the defendant company appears for practical purposes to be the plaintiff company's sole means of keeping its business going, and I am prepared so far to depart from the general rule as to try to preserve the position under the contract until a later date. I therefore propose to grant an injunction.

Order accordingly.

Notes:

1   As has been previously observed (*supra*, chapter 10(A)(2)), the real issue in cases such as *In re Wait* is whether a buyer who has paid for goods should have a preferred claim against them in the event of the seller's insolvency or whether he should rank equally with the seller's general creditors.

2   The reason for the restriction of SGA s. 50 to a sale of specific or ascertained goods is unclear. Professor Treitel has argued that the restriction did not exist in the pre-1893 law: see G. H. Treitel, "Specific Performance in the Sale of Goods" [1966] JBL 211. The restriction was not copied in the Uniform Sales Act and does not appear in UCC 2-716, the Code provision on specific performance. The OLRC in its Sales Report (p. 443) has recommended liberalizing the language of SGA s. 50 so as to allow a decree of specific performance in respect of any type of goods, whether or not the contract involves a sale of specific goods. Assuming this recommendation is adopted, will it help a buyer in a future *In re Wait, supra,* or *Carlos Federspiel* (chapter 10(A)(2)) type of situation? Will he be able to persuade the court that damages are not an adequate remedy because the seller is insolvent? Is this what equity means by "inadequacy"? Will the buyer be in a stronger position if he can show that title to the goods had passed to him prior to the seller's insolvency? For the Code's approach see UCC 2-502 and OLRC Sales Report, pp. 441-43, and *cf. Cohen* v. *Roche, infra,* this chapter.

3   The decision in *Sky Petroleum* appears to be quite incompatible with the reasoning in *In re Wait.* Can you see why? It is striking that Goulding J.'s judgment makes no reference to *Wait's* case. A willingness to overlook the restriction in SGA s. 50 also appears in various Canadian cases but again without discussion of the statutory difficulties. See R.J. Sharpe, "Specific Relief for Contract Breach", Study 5 in *Studies in Contract Law,* B. J. Reiter and J. Swan, eds., (1980), 123 esp. pp. 131-132. *Cf.* the decision in *Humboldt Flour Mills Co. Ltd.* v. *Boscher* (1975) 50 DLR (3d) 477 (Sask. QB), in which Bence C.J.Q.B. refused to continue an interim injunction to restrain the defendant from selling mustard seed grown and produced in 1973 to anyone other than the plaintiff. The defendant had previously agreed with the plaintiff to plant 500 lbs. of mustard seed and to deliver on the demand of the plaintiff all the mustard produced. The court rested its decision on the absence of a contract for the sale of specific or ascertained goods; the judgment does not disclose whether damages afforded an adequate remedy.

4   Civil law jurisdictions, in contrast to the common law, frequently regard specific performance as a general remedy and leave it to the plaintiff to decide whether to make do with the substitutional damages remedy. This Romanist approach is also adopted in the International Sales Convention though in deference to common law sensitivities this rule does not apply where a court would not order specific performance under its own law in respect of a domestic contract. See art. 28 of the Convention. The contrast between the civilian and common law approach is not as marked as may appear at first sight because of weaknesses in the enforcement mechanism of civil law jurisdictions as well as for other reasons. See further J. P. Dawson, "Specific Performance in France and Germany" (1959) 57 Mich. L. Rev. 495, and *cf.* Treitel, "Remedies for Breach of Contracts" in *International Encyclopedia of Comparative Law,* (1976) vol. VII, ch. 16. The "orthodox" economic view is that the common law discretionary remedy is preferable because it promotes the more efficient use of resources. See R. Posner, *Economic Analysis of Law,* 2nd ed. (1977) pp. 95-97, and *cf.* A. T. Kronman, "Specific Performance" (1978) 45 U. Chi. L. Rev. 351.

2. ACTIONS IN DETINUE

COHEN v. ROCHE
[1927] 1 KB 169, 95 LJKB 945

The plaintiff, a dealer in antique furniture, was the successful bidder for a set of Hepplewhite chairs owned by the defendant, an auctioneer, and sold by him at a public auction. The defendant refused to release the chairs, alleging the existence of a "knock out" agreement between the plaintiff and another dealer. Consequently the plaintiff brought this action claiming specific delivery of the chairs or damages in lieu thereof. The following extract from McCardie J.'s judgment deals with the plaintiff's claim to have the chairs delivered to him.

McCARDIE J.: I now take the final point in the case. The plaintiff sued in detinue only. The writ and statement of claim contain no alternative demand for damages for breach of contract. They ask (*a*) for delivery up of the chairs or payment of their value, and (*b*) damages for detention. I have however allowed an amendment whereby the statement of claim asks damages for breach of contract. The plaintiff vigorously contends he is entitled as of right, once a binding contract is established, to an order for the actual delivery of the chairs, and that he is not limited to damages for breach of bargain. This point raises a question of principle and practice. Here I may again state one or two of the facts. The Hepplewhite chairs in lot 145 possessed no special features at all. They were ordinary Hepplewhite furniture. The plaintiff bought them in the ordinary way of his trade for the purpose of ordinary resale at a profit. He had no special customer in view. The lot was to become a part of his usual trade stock.

The form of order in detinue cases for the delivery of goods is, in substance, this: "It is this day adjudged that the plaintiff do have a return of the chattels in the statement of claim mentioned and described (here set out description) or recover against the defendant their value (here set out value) . . . and damages for their detention": see the observations of Rowlatt J. in *Bailey* v. *Gill* [1919] 1 KB 41, 42. By Order XLVIII., r. 1, however, the Court has power to direct that execution shall issue for the delivery of the goods, without giving to the defendant the option to retain the property upon payment of the assessed value. Now in the case before me, the plaintiff desires to secure a warrant for the compulsory and specific delivery of the chairs to him: see *Benjamin on Sale*, 6th ed., p. 1121 (n.). I do not doubt that upon the purchase of specific items in lot 145 the plaintiff gained the property in such items: see *Tarling* v. *Baxter* (1827) 6 B & C 360 and s. 18 of the Sale of Goods Act, 1893. Prima facie, therefore, he would be entitled to possession on payment or tender of the price. Here the plaintiff was willing to pay the price, and it seems clear that the defendant waived a formal legal tender. The defendant did not object to the cheque as a cheque, inasmuch as the plaintiff's credit was perfectly good: see *Polglass* v. *Oliver* (1831) 2 Cr. & J. 15, and *Jones* v. *Arthur* (1890) 8 Dowl. PC 442, and *Roscoe's Nisi Prius*, 19th ed., p. 594. Tender divests lien (see *Martindale* v. *Smith* (1841) 1 QB 389, and I will assume that waiver of tender will produce the same result as actual tender in divesting a defendant of his right to assert a vendor's lien: see the cases at pp. 886-889 of *Benjamin on Sale*, 6th ed. It therefore follows that the plaintiff here was entitled to launch his action of detinue: see *Benjamin on Sale*, 6th ed., pp. 1120 and 1081.

But at this point there arise other considerations. In *Chinery* v. *Viall* (1860) 5 HN 288 it was laid down that as between buyer and seller the buyer cannot recover larger damages by suing in tort instead of contract: see too *Benjamin on Sale*, 6th ed., p. 1080 (z). Bearing *Chinery* v. *Viall* in mind, it is necessary next to mention s. 52 of the Sale of Goods Act, 1893, which provides that in any action for breach of contract to deliver specific or ascertained goods the Court may, if it thinks fit, on the application of the plaintiff, direct by its judgment that the contract shall be performed specifically without giving the defendant the option of retaining the goods on payment of damages. It has been held that s. 52 applies to all cases where the goods are ascertained, whether the property therein has passed to the buyer or not:; see *per* Parker J. in *Jones* v. *Earl of Tankerville* [1909] 2 Ch. 440, 445. It seems clear that the discretionary provisions of s. 52 cannot be consistent with an absolute right of a plaintiff to an order for compulsory delivery under a detinue judgment in such a case as the present. How, then, does the law stand as to detinue? In my view the power of the Court in an action of detinue rests upon a footing which fully accords with s. 52 of the Sale of Goods Act, 1893. In *Whitely, Ld.* v. *Hilt* [1918] 2 K.B. 808,819 (an action of detinue) Swinfen Eady M.R. said: "The power vested in the Court to order the delivery up of a particular chattel is discretionary, and ought not to be exercised when the chattel is an ordinary article of commerce and of no special value or interest, and not alleged to be of any special value to the plaintiff, and where damages would fully compensate. In equity, where a plaintiff alleged and proved the money value of the chattel, it was not the practice of the Court to order its specific delivery: see *Dowling* v. *Betjemann*" (1862) 2 J. & H. 544 in its several parts. In the present case the goods in question were ordinary articles of commerce and of no special value of interest, and no grounds exist for any special order for delivery. The judgment should be limited to damages for breach of contract. The plaintiff in his evidence said that the chairs were worth from 70*l.* to 80*l.* With this I agree. I assess the damages at the sum of 15*l.*

Judgment for plaintiff.

Note: Actions in detinue have now been abolished in England by the Torts (Interference with Goods) Act 1977, s. 2(1), and replaced by an omnibus remedy in s. 3 for "wrongful interference" with goods. Section 3(2) enables the following relief to be given against the person in possession or control of the goods:

(*a*)   an order for delivery of the goods, and for payment of any consequential damages, or

(*b*)   an order for delivery of the goods, but giving the defendant the alternative of paying damages by reference to the value of the goods, together in either alternative with payment of any consequential damages, or

(*c*)   damages.

Section 1 defines "wrongful interference" or "wrongful interference with goods" as meaning (*a*)   conversion of goods (also called trover),

    (*b*)   trespass to goods,

    (*c*)   negligence so far as it results in damage to goods or to an interest in goods,

    (*d*)   subject to section 2, any other tort so far as it results in damage to goods or to an interest in goods.

3. THE REPLEVIN REMEDY

OLRC Sales Report
pp. 439-40

At common law, an action in replevin only lay where the person suing for replevin alleged a wrongful seizure of his goods. The restitutionary remedy could not be invoked where the seller merely refused to deliver goods that had been in his lawful possession all the time. In this respect, The Replevin Act [RSO 1970, c. 412] appears to have made an important change in the law. Section 2 of the Act permits the owner or other person capable of maintaining an action for damages to bring a replevin action for the recovery of goods "wrongfully . . . detained", as well as for those wrongfully distrained or otherwise wrongfully taken. Assuming that title has passed to the buyer, it would appear that he is entitled to compel delivery by a recalcitrant seller by following the prescribed procedure, and it has been so held on a number of occasions.[39]

The reason for the extension in Ontario of the common law remedy of replevin is obscure, and it is not clear whether the draftsman appreciated a potential conflict with the rules of specific performance and the action in detinue. Presumably, the extension reflects the judgment of the legislature that, where the person suing for replevin claims superior proprietary or possessory rights, the person resisting the order for replevin should not be given the option of paying damages. However this may be, it appears anomalous that a buyer to whom title has passed should be able to obtain relief in a replevin action, and yet not be able to obtain an order for specific performance under The Sale of Goods Act. The Replevin Act does not, however, fall within our terms of reference and we refrain from offering any recommendations for its amendment beyond drawing attention to this conflict.

---

39 For example, *O'Rourke* v. *Lee* (1859) UCQB 609; *Lee* v. *Ianson* (1910) 1 OWN 586; and compare *Van Hull* v. *Mancer* [1944] 1 WWR 114 (Man. C.A.).

Chapter 13

Contractual Limitations on the Buyer's Rights and Remedies

1. Introduction

As will have been gathered from the preceding chapters, the buyer's position under the Sale of Goods Act is generally very favourable and if its provisions were mandatory the story would have a simple ending. In fact the real position is much more complex.

The complications are caused by three factors. In the first place, the SGA provisions are only presumptive and can be freely varied or excluded by agreement between the parties (s. 53). Needless to say, sellers freely avail themselves of this right. Secondly, at the retail level the sale is frequently accompanied by some form of financing arrangement either directly between the buyer and the seller or between the buyer and a third party, with the seller only playing an indirect role. In either event, if the buyer's promissory note or the agreement evidencing the sale is held by a third party, the question arises whether the buyer is entitled to raise defences or claim a set-off because the goods are defective or the seller has committed some other breach of the sale agreement. Finally, in the consumer context there is yet another formidable barrier the buyer may have to surmount. If he cannot resolve his difficulties with the seller amicably, can he afford to litigate or are there other channels he can pursue to find a solution to his problem? The present chapter is only concerned with the effectiveness of disclaimer clauses; the problems created by the intervention of a third party financer are dealt with *infra,* chapter 16. Unfortunately space does not permit further treatment of the consumer's remedial and procedural problems beyond the incidental materials found *supra,* chapter 3.

It is a rare agreement which is reduced to writing that does not contain a disclaimer or limitation clause of some description. For a classification of the clauses, see OLRC Warranties Report, p. 47, and OLRC Sales Report, p. 462. In the retail field such clauses are usually coupled with a manufacturer's express warranty which is frequently less favourable to the buyer than the statutory warranties and conditions usually displaced by the express warranty. See *supra,* chapter 7.

The judicial and legislative response to disclaimer clauses constitutes one of the most remarkable chapters in modern contract law. Before the war the courts mainly limited themselves to constructional techniques in trying to blunt the sharp edge of such clauses and legislation, though not unimportant, was restricted to a few discrete areas. The absence of comprehensive legislation until recently (and in Canada there is still no comprehensive legislation) and growing judicial concern no doubt accounts for the much more complex judicial reaction in the post-war period.

It was inevitable that some courts would seek a more explicit policing tool than was covertly provided by constructional techniques and, not surprisingly, in England Lord Denning led the crusade. It was he who first announced the proposition in *Karsales (Harrow) Ltd.* v. *Wallis* [1956] 2 All ER 866 (CA) that no exception clause, however sweeping, could excuse a seller from fulfilling his fundamental obligations, thus ushering in the era of the doctrine of "fundamental breach" and "breach of a fundamental term".

The principal question before the House of Lords in the *Suisse Atlantique* case ([1967] 1 AC 361) was whether the doctrine was compatible with the concept of freedom of contract. The law lords said no and indicated that it was for Parliament, not the courts, to declare whether exception clauses should be banned on grounds of public policy. But the House of Lords had reckoned without Lord Denning's ingenuity and the ambiguities in several of the law lords' own judgments. Dicta by Lord Reid and Lord Upjohn in *Suisse Atlantique* were seized upon by Lord Denning and his fellow judges in *Harbutt's "Plasticine" Ltd.* v. *Wayne Tank & Pump Co. Ltd.* [1970] 1 QB 447 (CA) to justify their conclusion that a disclaimer clause ceases to have effect once the agreement is terminated because of breach of the contract by the party seeking to rely on the clause. The gap was enlarged still further as a result of the decision in *Wathes (Western) Ltd.* v. *Austins (Menswear) Ltd.* [1976] 1 Lloyd's Rep. 14 (CA) that the disclaimer clause was equally of no effect even though the innocent party had affirmed the contract after the breach. Thus, to all intents and purposes, *Suisse Atlantique* had been successfully undermined, a fact that Lord Denning demonstrated with his usual skill and clarity in the Court of Appeal's judgment in *Photo Production Ltd.* v. *Securicor Transport Ltd.* [1978] 3 All ER 146, which is reproduced later in this chapter. It was a challenge which, as will be seen, the House of Lords could not ignore, and did not ignore.

Prior to its reversal by the House of Lords the doctrine of *Harbutt's "Plasticine"* only exerted a modest influence on appellate decisions in Canada. However, this made little difference because, with almost unfailing regularity, the courts have managed to find, as a matter of construction, that the parties could not have intended the disclaimer clause to apply in the circumstances before them. No wonder then that some judges declared, prior to *Photo Production*, that "'the fundamental term' doctrine is 'alive and prospering' in Canada": *Heffron* v. *Imperial Parking Co.* (1974) 3 OR (2d) 722 at 731. See also *Murray* v. *Sperry Rand Corp.* (1979) 96 DLR (3d) 113, at 122 (Ont. H C J). It remains to be seen whether the law lords' attempt in *Photo Production* to reinstate *Suisse Atlantique* will succeed. In Canada, at any rate, the first omens are not auspicious in the light of the Supreme Court of Canada's decision in *Re Beaufort Realties (1964) Inc.*, referred to *infra*, this chapter, in notes following *Photo Production*. What lessons may be drawn from this protracted chapter of modern legal history?

In the interests of space, the cases reproduced in this chapter are limited to the post-*Suisse Atlantique* period. It is assumed that the student is familiar with *Suisse Atlantique* itself and with the earlier case law. The second part of the chapter examines the very complex body of statutory provisions on disclaimer clauses that has evolved in various common law jurisdictions in the post-war period.

2. JUDICIAL REACTIONS

CANSO CHEMICALS LTD. v. CANADIAN WESTINGHOUSE CO. LTD.
(1974) 54 DLR (3d) 517, 10 NSR (2d) 306 (CA)

The respondent, Canso Chemicals, purchased equipment from the appellant for use in a new chemical plant. The equipment, a large electrical rectifier with a contract price of $266,380, was "to be suitable for electrochemical service" and "shall carry its full rated capacity continually". The agreement contained the following warranty clause:

> The Company warrants the apparatus to be supplied hereunder to be of the kind designated or specified. The Company shall repair or replace any defective part or parts, f.o.b. the Company's factory, repair shop or warehouse, which prove to be defective under normal and proper use within one year from the date of shipment, provided that the Purchaser gives the Company immediate written notice of any such defect or defects. In no event (including, but not limited to the negligence of the Company, its employees or agents) shall the Company be liable for special or consequential damages or damages for loss of use and on expiration of the Warranty period, any liability of the Company shall terminate. This constitutes the only Warranty of the Company and no other warranty or condition, statutory or otherwise, shall be implied.

Westinghouse, being inexperienced in the production of rectifiers of the size involved, failed to anticipate certain electrical problems. As a result, many fuses failed when the unit was operated at the full rated capacity for a material length of time. The rectifier was still operational, but as full amperage rates were approached, fuses would blow and cut-backs were required. Until repairs were completed (a period of seventy-five days) the capacity of the rectifier, and therefore the productive capacity of the plant, was reduced by 22 per cent.

The plaintiffs, who alleged that the defendants had committed a fundamental breach of contract, brought an action for damages and succeeded before Hart J. The defendants appealed.

COFFIN J.A.: I turn first to a consideration of the vexatious question whether there was here a "fundamental breach" of the contract as found by the trial Judge. The nature of a fundamental breach, or putting it another way, what constitutes such a breach, has been considered by various authors and Courts. The following appears at pp. 566-7 of Cheshire and Fifoot's *Law of Contract*, 8th ed. (1972):

> Of what nature, then, must a breach be before it is to be called "fundamental?" There are two alternative tests that may provide the answer. The court may find the decisive element either in the importance that the parties would seem to have attached to the term which has been broken or to the seriousness of the conse-

quences that have in fact resulted from the breach. We have already suggested that the former is the happier approach to the matter. Not only is it more convenient to the parties, since it enables them to predict whether the breach of a particular term will justify the discharge of the contract, but it represents the general practice of the courts over many years.

Lord Reid in *Suisse Atlantique Société D'Armement Maritime S.A.* v. *N.V. Rotterdamsche Kolen Centrale* [1967] 1 AC 361, said at pp. 397-8:

> One way of looking at the matter would be to ask whether the party in breach has by his breach produced a situation fundamentally different from anything which the parties could as reasonable men have contemplated when the contract was made. Then one would have to ask not only what had already happened but what was likely to happen in future.

As to the meaning of "fundamental term" Lord Upjohn in the *Suisse Atlantique* case, *supra*, said at pp. 421-2:

> There was much discussion during the argument upon the phrases "fundamental breach" and "breach of a fundamental term" and I think it is true that in some of the cases these terms have been used interchangeably; but in fact they are quite different. I believe that all of your Lordships are agreed and, indeed, it has not seriously been disputed before us that there is no magic in the words "fundamental breach"; this expression is no more than a convenient shorthand expression for saying that a particular breach or breaches of contract by one party is or are such as to go to the root of the contract while entitles the other party to treat such breach or breaches as a repudiation of the whole contract. Whether such breach or breaches do constitute a fundamental breach depends on the construction of the contract and on all the facts and circumstances of the case. The innocent party may accept that breach or those breaches as a repudiation and treat the whole contract [as] at an end and sue for damages generally or he may at his option prefer to affirm the contract and treat it as continuing on foot in which case he can sue only for damages for breach or breaches of the particular stipulation or stipulations in the contract which has or have been broken.

In *Harbutt's Plasticine Ltd.* v. *Wayne Tank & Pump Co. Ltd.* [1970] 1 All ER 225, Widgery, L.J., in considering whether a particular breach was fundamental gave as a test the following [at pp. 239-40]:

> . . . the first step is to see whether an "event" has occurred which has deprived the plaintiffs of substantially the whole benefit which they were to obtain under the contract . . . if the event which occurs as a result of the defendants' breach is an event which would have frustrated the contract had it occurred without the fault of either party, then the breach is a fundamental breach for present purposes.

Whether a breach is fundamental or not must, in the last analysis, be decided by reference to the contract and the circumstances in each particular case. The factual background to the contract in this case has been set forth earlier in this opinion. I make reference now, however, to certain further factors that I consider vital in the determination of the issue whether there was indeed a fundamental breach of contract.

[Coffin J.A. went on to discuss certain other facts, then continued:]

I would crystallize the issue here by the following test — was the design error which resulted in the malfunction of the rectifier equipment such as to justify a repudiation of the contract by the respondent? I think under all the circumstances and in light of the authorities cited above that it was. Put simply, the respondent as of July 26, 1968, had received equipment which was essentially different from that contemplated by the parties. Certainly it could not be suggested that it was within the contemplation of the parties that the equipment would have the design error it did.

• • •

The trial Judge accepted the product loss calculations of Ross A. Ritchie. Based on a daily plant capacity of 55 tons of chlorine and 63.8 tons of caustic soda, the production loss, using Mr. Ritchie's figures, due to the malfunction of the rectifier was in the vicinity of 22%. The percentage is substantially higher if the production loss figures of the respondent are used.

Thus, although the rectifier equipment was operating at well in excess of 50% at all material times, this, in my opinion, on the facts of this particular case does not establish that no fundamental breach occurred. It was an express condition of the contract that the rectifier be capable of producing 92,000 amps. continuously plus overload. That is what the appellant undertook to design, manufacture, deliver and install and that is what the respondent expected, and was entitled to expect, to get. The fact remains that due to a design error the respondent did not receive equipment that would produce the rated amperage output as specified and the failure on the part of the respondent to provide properly designed equipment capable of producing such specified output, amounts, in my opinion, to a fundamental breach of the contract as of July 26, 1970, because on that day had the respondent known that the malfunction of the equipment was due to a gross design error it could have repudiated the contract.

Once the malfunction occurred the respondent did not repudiate the contract, but rather kept it "on foot". This it was entitled to do.

Lord Denning in *Harbutt's Plasticine Ltd.* v. *Wayne Tank & Pump Co. Ltd., supra,* said at p. 233 of the report:

> In cases where the contract is still open to be performed, the effect of a fundamental breach is this: it gives the innocent party, when he gets to know of it, an option either to *affirm* the contract or to disaffirm it. If he elects to *affirm* it, then it remains in being *for the future* on both sides. Each has a right to sue for damages for *past* or *future* breaches. If he elects to *disaffirm* it (i.e. accepts the fundamental breach as determining the contract), then it is at an end from that moment. It does not continue into the future. All that is left is the right to sue for past breaches or for the fundamental breach, but there is no right to sue for *future* breaches.

This Court speaking through Cooper, J.A., in *Blackwood Hodge Atlantic Ltd.* v. *Kelly* (1971) 3 NSR (2d) 49, said at p. 59:

> Where a fundamental breach has occurred the innocent party may elect to treat the breach as a repudiation, bring the contract to an end and sue for damages. The consequence is stated by Lord Reid in *Suisse Atlantique* at p. 398 AC:

> > Then the whole contract ceased to exist including the exclusion clause, and I do not see how that clause can then be used to exclude an action for loss which will be suffered by the

innocent party after it has ceased to exist, such as loss of the profit which would have accrued if the contract had run its full term.

On the other hand, if the innocent party has elected that the contract should continue in force the clause excluding liability must continue to apply and it becomes a matter of construction as to whether or not the clause will serve to overcome the breach.

I now quote with approval the words of Arnup, J.A., in *R.G. McLean Ltd.* v. *Canadian Vickers Ltd.* (1970) 15 DLR (3d) 15 at pp. 18-9, [1971] 1 OR 207:

A finding that a "fundamental breach" of contract had taken place does not by any means end the inquiry necessary to determine the rights of the parties. The next question is: assuming a fundamental breach had occurred, what were the rights of the plaintiff? The law on the subject of "fundamental breach" was reviewed in each of the judgments in the House of Lords in *Suisse Atlantique Société D'Armement Maritime S.A.* v. *N.V. Rotterdamsche Kolen Centrale* [1967] 1 AC 361. Not all of the learned law Lords expressed the matter in the same way, and undoubtedly difficulties will arise in future cases in endeavouring to apply to particular circumstances the various statements and principles there enunciated. However, it is clear from that case that, when a fundamental breach has occurred, and the innocent party has learned of it, he then has a right to accept the repudiation evidenced by the acts which constitute the fundamental breach, to treat the contract as at an end and to sue the other party to the contract for such damages as he may have sustained. It was conceded before us that in that event "the damages are at large", and this is undoubtedly so.

• • •

The judgments in the *Suisse Atlantique* case, *supra*, further make it clear that, if the innocent party does not accept the repudiation, then the contract continues in force and the problem becomes one of construction of the contract itself. Most of the cases, as this one does, involve a consideration of an "exclusion clause", as clauses such as cl. 12, quoted above, have been termed. Notwithstanding some earlier judgments which seemed to hold that such an exclusion clause, by application of a rule of substantive law, should be treated as nullified where there had been a fundamental breach of the contract, the House of Lords came to the conclusion that where the repudiation has not been accepted by the innocent party, all of the clauses of the contract, including the "exclusion clause" must be considered. However, as it was put by Lord Reid in the *Suisse Atlantique* case, *supra*, at p. 398, it may be possible to construe the exclusion clause as never having been intended to apply to a situation that neither party had in contemplation, *i.e.*, a breach so fundamental as to go to the root of the contract.

Turning now as one must to a construction of the entire contract including the warranty and *force majeure* clauses which I shall refer to as the exclusion clauses, and bearing in mind that we must try to give business efficacy to what the parties have stated they intended, I think the approach used by Arnup, J.A., in *R. G. McLean* v. *Canadian Vickers, supra*, is highly commendable. This is what he said [at p. 20]:

... I ask myself: did these parties contemplate that, if there were defects in the machine attributable to defective parts or faulty workmanship, the defendant was to be liable to the extent indicated in cl. 12(*a*), but, if the machine was so defective as to be quite incapable of performing the function which both parties contemplated it should perform, the defendant was to be under no liability at all? This latter alternative is the contention advanced on behalf of the defendant as to the appropriate meaning of the concluding sentence of subcl. (*e*) of cl. 12.

Notwithstanding the broad language of subcl. (*e*), I am unable to construe it in the way contended for. Such a construction would, for all practical purposes, render nugatory the prime contractual obligations of the defendant. It would make those ostensible obligations what Lord Wilberforce called "a mere declaration of intention": *Suisse Atlantique, supra,* at p. 432. In short, cl. 12 does not exclude liability for a fundamental breach of contract resulting in performance totally different from what the parties had in contemplation. The clause can be given business efficacy if its operation is limited to identifiable defects due to faulty workmanship or use of defective material, which defects can be rectified, and which do not prevent performance of the contract as contemplated by the parties.

Clauses 12(*a*) and (*e*) at issue in the *R. G. McLean* v. *Canadian Vickers* case, read as follows [at pp. 16-7]:

12. WARRANTY

(*a*) Subject to fair and proper use we undertake to repair or replace all parts of our manufacture which shall, during the twelve months immediately following the date on which the goods are despatched, be found to be defective due either to faulty workmanship or the use of defective material.

• • •

(*c*) This condition No. 12 is in substitution for and excludes all express conditions warranties or liabilities of any kind relating to the goods sold whether as to fitness or otherwise and whether arising under the Sale of Goods Act, 1893 or other statute or in tort or by implication of law or otherwise. In no event shall we be liable for any direct or indirect loss or damage (whether special, consequential or otherwise) or any other claims except as provided for in these conditions.

It will be noted that cl. 12 (*e*) above is markedly similar to the latter part of the warranty clause in the present contract.

I am of the opinion that the first exclusion clause in the present case can only be given business efficacy or indeed common sense if it is limited to liability to repair or replace parts that prove to be defective under normal and proper use within one year from the date of their shipment. Surely this is what the parties meant by the exclusion clauses and I think it is stretching one's imagination too far to say that in addition the parties intended the exclusion clauses to relieve the appellant from all liability arising out of a breakdown or malfunction of the equipment due to a design error.

MacKEIGAN C.J.N.S. (dissenting): The appellant undoubtedly breached the warranty contained in the first sentence of the above paragraph. The specifications "designated" and "specified" that the equipment would convert to 92,000 amps. D.C. and that "the equipment shall carry its full rated capacity continuously". This it failed to do, albeit only for 75 days and during that period only by a rate reduction of 22%.

The appellant is liable for that breach, and indeed does not dispute liability. It has remedied the defects, at a cost to itself of over $35,000. It is liable to the respondent for its direct damages, for purchases of fuses and other parts, and pay and expenses of certain C.I.L. employees who assisted in the repair operation, assessed by the learned trial Judge at $8,201.

The third sentence of the warranty clause, which, of course, applies to a breach of the warranty contained in it, states that "in no event . . . shall the Company be liable for special or consequential damages or damages for loss of use". The whole issue in this case is whether this sentence can be disregarded or overridden. This involves whether the breach was a "fundamental breach" of a nature that falls outside the scope of the contract.

The warranty is indeed a wide one and, I suggest, makes the appellant liable in damages for any inadequacies in the equipment supplied. The second sentence of the clause, respecting repair and replacement of parts found defective during the first year of service, does not limit liability, but rather widens it to cover an additional responsibility not fully covered by the first sentence. The clause is thus quite unlike that in the printing press case discussed by the trial Judge and my brother Coffin, *R. G. McLean Ltd.* v. *Canadian Vickers Ltd. et al.* (1970) 15 DLR (3d) 15, [1971] 1 OR 207 (Ont. CA). In that case, the *only* warranty was to replace defective parts for one year and all other warranties or conditions were excluded. In the present case, the warranty is wide, and, indeed, probably includes and certainly does not effectively exclude warranties under the Sale of Goods Act, RSNS 1967, c. 274, which are not inconsistent with its first sentence: *e.g.*, the implied condition that the goods are reasonably fit for the intended purpose where the buyer has relied on the seller's skill (s. 16(a)).

The warranty clause is thus not strictly an exclusion or limitation clause like those involved in most "fundamental breach" cases. It does not exclude or limit liability materially, but limits the quantum of damages by excluding special or consequential damages or damages for loss of use. In this respect it is more like the clause involved in the leading case of *Suisse Atlantique Société D'Armement Maritime S.A.* v. *N.V. Rotterdamsche Kolen Centrale* [1967] 1 AC 361 (HL), where the clause held unaffected by any fundamental breach merely limited the amount of damages recoverable as demurrage for delay. Or, the clause in *Hunt & Winterbotham (West of England) Ltd.* v. *B.R.S. (Parcels) Ltd.* [1962] 1 QB 617, [1962] 1 All ER 111 (CA), where the plaintiff sought damages because only 12 of 15 packages of a shipment arrived but was held bound by a clause limiting the amount recoverable (a permanent non-performance of 80% compared to the very temporary non-performance of 78% in the present case!).

The breach in the present case is *prima facie* one which the parties contemplated might happen; it was of the very kind specified in the warranty clause and one in which loss of use and consequential damages were incurred. Furthermore, the parties contemplated a similar limitation on damages if Westinghouse had delayed delivery; it would be liable for delay not caused by *force majeure*, but, under the *force majeure* clause which appears with the warranty clause, not "for special or consequential damages or damages for loss of use". The parties agreed to a similar limitation on damages on March 20, 1970, when the Westinghouse start-up engineer was hired. It was specified that:

> The liability of the Company with respect to the Field Personnel's service, shall not, in any event, exceed the cost of correcting defects in the equipment supplied; the Company shall not be liable for special and consequential damages, or for loss of use.

In determining whether the parties contemplated these clauses as having full effect, it is relevant that both of them, Westinghouse and C.I.L., are very large companies, with wide experience in selling and buying equipment and other products. This is not the typical case of conditions in fine print on the back of a ticket or bill of lading where ". . . the customer has no time to read them, and if he did read them he would probably not understand them. And if he did understand and object to any of them, he would generally be told he could take it or leave it" (*Suisse Atlantique, supra, per* Lord Reid at p. 406). It is rather a case "where parties are bargaining on terms of equality and a stringent exemption clause is accepted for a quid pro quo or other good reason". (*Idem.*)

The problem is entirely one of construction of the contract. The contract has not been repudiated by the respondent; it has been affirmed, with its warranty clause. The question then is — was the breach by Westinghouse within the scope of the contract, *i.e.*, within the contemplation of the parties, as being a kind of situation to which the warranty clause would apply.

Here we have no ambiguity which, as in so many exclusion clauses, requires application of the *contra proferentem* rule, no inherent injustice arising from inequality of bargaining power which might cause a Court to strain the language to protect the weaker party. Above all, we do not have here an exclusion clause which excludes all liability for the kind of breach involved (as was the situation in the *McLean* case, *supra*).

In *Suisse Atlantique, supra,* Lord Reid at p. 407 said:

> The appellants chose to agree to what they now say was an inadequate sum for demurrage, but that does not appear to me to affect the construction of this clause. Even if one assumes that the $1,000 per day was inadequate and was known to both parties to be inadequate when the contract was made, I do not think that it can be said that giving to the clause its natural meaning could lead to an absurdity or could defeat the main object of the contract or could for any other reason justify cutting down its scope. If there was a fundamental breach the appellants elected that the contract should continue and they did so in the knowledge that this clause would continue.

Lord Upjohn in the same case at p. 426 stated:

> Therefore, my Lords, as in my opinion the owners have expressly affirmed the contract they cannot escape from the consequences of the demurrage clause, unless as a matter of construction of that clause they can show that it has no application to the events of this case; this they cannot do for the reasons I have already given. Accordingly, upon the footing that the demurrage clause is a clause of exclusion or limitation, this does not avail the owners in this case.

In the present case, the respondent, having affirmed the contract with full knowledge of its rights, is "bound by the terms of the contract, including the exemption clause, so long as the clause on its true construction extends to the breach which has occurred". (*Chitty on Contracts*, 23rd ed. (1968), vol. 1, s. 737.)

I accordingly conclude that the breach was of a type contemplated by the parties and within the scope of the contract and its warranty clause, including the limitation on damages. This is merely saying indirectly, on the basis of construction of the contract, that the breach was not a "fundamental breach".

Assuming that "neither party had in contemplation a breach which goes to the root of the contract" (Lord Reid in *Suisse Atlantique, supra*, at p. 399) and therefore that neither had in mind that the limitation of damages would apply in the event of a fundamental breach, let us test the conclusion I have tentatively reached by considering how the breach in this case compares with what the Courts have defined or held to be fundamental breaches. (And for this purpose I shall assume what may be debated, namely, that the fundamental breach doctrine applies in all its strength to a contract that has not been repudiated and to an "exclusion clause" that limits only the type of damages without limiting liability for the breach in question.)

The phrase or concept has been defined or described as follows:

— "whether in consequence of it [the breach] the performance of the contract becomes something totally different from that which the contract contemplates" — Viscount Dilhorne in *Suisse Atlantique, supra*, at p. 393.

— "a situation fundamentally different from anything which the parties could as reasonable men have contemplated . . ." — Lord Reid in *Suisse Atlantique*, at p. 397.

— "a breach which goes to the root of the contract" — *idem*, p. 399.

— "when there is such a congeries of defects as to destroy the workable character of the machine" — *Pollock & Co.* v. *Macrae* [1922] SC (HL) 192 at p. 200 (quoted by Lord Hodson in *Suisse Atlantique* at p. 413).

— "destroying the whole contractual substratum" — Lord Wilberforce in *Suisse Atlantique* at p. 433.

— "totally different performance of the contract from that intended by the parties" and which will "undermine the whole contract" — Sellers, L.J., in *Hong Kong Fir Shipping Co., Ltd.* v. *Kawasaki Kisen Kaisha, Ltd.* [1962] 1 All ER 474 (CA) at p. 479.

— "an 'event' . . . which has deprived the plaintiffs of substantially the whole benefit which they were to obtain under the contract" — Widgery, L.J., in *Harbutt's Plasticine Ltd.* v. *Wayne Tank & Pump Co. Ltd.* [1970] 1 All ER 225 at p. 239.

— "so defective as to be quite incapable of performing the function which both parties contemplated it should perform . . . resulting in performance totally different from what the parties had in contemplation" — Arnup J.A., in *McLean, supra*, in 15 DLR (3d) at p. 20, [1971] 1 OR at p. 212.

— "an accumulation of defects which, taken en masse, constitute such a . . . breach going to the root of the contract, as disentitles a party to take refuge behind an exception clause intended to give protection only in regard to those breaches which are not inconsistent with and not destructive of the whole essence of the contract" — Pearce, L.J., in *Yeoman Credit, Ltd.* v. *Apps* [1961] 2 All ER 281 at p. 289.

The kind of test involved is illustrated by Lord Wilberforce in *Suisse Atlantique* at p. 432:

> In application to more radical breaches of contract, the courts have sometimes stated the principle as being that a "total breach of the contract" disentitles a party to rely on exceptions clauses. This formulation has its use so long as one understands it to mean that the clause cannot be taken to refer to such a breach but it is not a universal solvent: for it leaves to be decided what is meant by a "total" breach for this purpose — a departure from the contract? but how great a departure?; a delivery of something or a performance different from that promised? but how different? No formula will solve this type of question and one must look individually at the nature of the contract, the character of the breach and its effect upon future performance and expectation and make a judicial estimation of the final result.

I have found no case where a temporary partial failure of performance comparable to that in the present case has been held to be a "fundamental breach". The kind of breach necessary is illustrated in *McLean, supra*. The printing press sold *never* produced the quality of printing specified despite nearly a year's efforts at repair. "In short, the machine simply did not do the job which it had been purchased to do and could not be made to do it by all efforts of both parties." (Arnup, J.A., at p. 18 DLR, p. 210 OR)

Again, in *Western Tractor Ltd.* v. *Dyck* (1969) 7 DLR (3d) 535, 70 WWR 215 (Sask. CA), a tractor bought for land clearing kept breaking down and finally, over a year after it was bought, broke down completely after 1700 hours' performance. It could not be made to perform reasonably satisfactorily "even with the most extensive servicing and repairs" (p. 542 DLR, p. 222 WWR). The Court held the performance to be "something totally different from that which the contract contemplated" (p. 543 DLR, p. 223 WWR).

A similar total and permanent failure was held to be a breach permitting rescission or, if adopted, damages, despite an exclusion clause:

Schofield v. *Emerson Brantingham Implement Co.* (1918) 43 DLR 509 at p. 509, 57 SCR 203, [1918] 3 WWR 434 (buyer bought "one of your Big Four 30 h.p. Gas Traction Engines" which never produced 30 h.p.);

Harbutt's Plasticine, supra (defective pipe supplied causing fire);

Pippy v. *RCA Victor Co. Ltd.* (1964) 49 DLR (2d) 523 (radar supplied which *never* worked properly despite nine months' attempts to repair);

Knowles v. *Anchorage Holdings Co. Ltd.* (1964) 43 DLR (2d) 300, 46 WWR 173 (a boat engine which *never* worked despite frequent attempts to repair);

Peters v. *Irving Oil Co. Ltd.* (1970) 1 NSR (2d) 861 (a heating system which *never* heated the house properly).

On the other hand, fundamental breach has been held *not* to have occurred in cases which involved temporary or partial failure of performance, even though longer in duration and of more serious result than in the present case. For example: *Suisse Atlantique, supra; Hunt & Winterbotham, supra; Hong Kong Fir, supra*.

In *Kenyon, Son & Craven Ltd.* v. *Baxter Hoare & Co. Ltd. et al.* [1971] 2 All ER 708, a warehouseman contracted to store groundnuts, with a clause negativing any liability except for "wilful default". Through negligence not amounting to wilful default, 20% of the groundnuts were destroyed by rats. Donaldson, J., held that this very permanent partial performance was not in fundamental breach. He said at p. 721 that the performance, "whilst falling far short of what the plaintiffs were entitled to expect and had contracted for, was not so deficient as to remove the sub-stratum of the contract . . .".

A very helpful discussion of the *Kenyon* case and others is found in "Fundamental Breach: The Aftermath of *Harbutt's 'Plasticine'* ", by P.N. Legh-Jones and M.A. Pickering, 87 LQR 515 (1971).

In the present case, the buyer received a 92,000-amp. rectifier which could operate continuously, even though a 75-day delay intervened during which the buyer had a rectifier which could produce only 78% of its capacity. That, in my opinion, under the authorities cited above, was not a fundamental breach of the contract between the appellant and the respondent.

Appeal dismissed.

JACOB S. ZIEGEL
"The House of Lords Overrules Harbutt's Plasticine"
30 UTLJ 421, 435-37

A difficult question confronts the court when the exception clause is ambiguous or simply fails to address itself to the type of situation that actually arose. The accepted rule in such cases is that the party seeking to rely on the clause should not be given the benefit of the doubt: he will simply have to go back to the drawing board and do better on the next occasion. It may be questioned whether, in the light of *Securicor*, this is still a satisfactory approach, since it encourages an unsympathetic court to look for ambiguities or gaps.

The well-known decision of the Ontario Court of Appeal in *R.G. McLean Ltd. v. Canadian Vickers Ltd.* (1971) 15 DLR (3d) 15 illustrates the problem. The case involved the sale of a large and complex printing press. The machine never worked, and, when sued for direct and consequential damages, the defendant relied on clause 12 of the agreement. This read in part as follows: [see *supra*, p. 629]. The Court of Appeal held that the defendant had committed a fundamental breach of contract and that clause 12(a) did not apply because it contemplated parts that proved to be defective in use and could be repaired or replaced, neither of which was true in the present case. The court further held that the defendant could not rely on clause 12(e) because that would enable the company to escape all liability when the machine was so defective as to be incapable of functioning at all. Such a construction, in the court's view, would have reduced the defendant's obligation to a mere declaration of intention and would fail to give business efficacy to the contract. The court therefore held the defendant liable for direct and consequential damages.

Assuming the court was right in its construction of clause 12(a) (which is debatable), the court surely failed to give effect to the seller's clear intention in clause 12(e) that 'in no event' should he be liable to pay damages 'except as provided for in these conditions.' Had they directed their minds to the question the parties must have contemplated the possibility of a basic design or construction failure that would prevent the machine from functioning at all. The Ontario court was obviously impressed by the argument that the plaintiff would be worse off, under the construction of clause 12 urged upon it by counsel, where there was a total machine failure than where there was only a partial failure.

It seems to me that the difficulty was more apparent than real. First, clause 12(a) could have been construed to include every type of machine failure, large or small. Secondly, following other precedents, the court could have held the seller liable in damages for failure to honour its obligations under clause 12(a). Third, clause 12(e) did not preclude a restitutionary claim for total failure of consideration — indeed, the defendant had previously offered to refund the plaintiff's payments and to take back the machine. There was a further approach open to the court, and this was to apply clause 12(a) analogically, thus once again holding the seller liable if he was unable or unwilling to replace the defective machine with a functioning machine. Significantly the court showed little interest in interpreting clause 12 as an entirety and in assisting the seller's overall goal to shift the burden of economic loss from its shoulders onto the buyer's shoulders. Since a partial malfunction would have involved the buyer in (presumably non-recoverable) economic losses while repairs were taking place it is difficult to see why the apportionment of loss was less valid or had no 'business efficacy' where the malfunction was total. The distinction would make even less sense if the buyer's insurance covered both types of contingency.

Question: Do you agree with Professor Ziegel's observations?

PHOTO PRODUCTION LTD. v. SECURICOR TRANSPORT LTD.
[1978] 1 WLR 856, [1978] 3 All ER 146 (CA);
rev'd [1980] AC 837, [1980] 1 All ER 556 (HL)

COURT OF APPEAL:

LORD DENNING M.R.: It was a factory at Gillingham Kent. A firm called Photo Production Ltd., the plaintiffs, made Christmas cards there and the like. There was a lot of paper and cardboard about which would burn easily. The factory was shut up for the night, locked and secure. No one was supposed to go in except a man on night patrol. He came from a security firm called Securicor, the defendants. He had a bunch of keys. His duty was to go through the factory and see that all was safe and secure. No burglars and no fire.

On the night of October 18/19, 1970, the patrolman was George Musgrove. He was a young man only 23 years old, unmarried. He came of a respectable family and had satisfactory references. He had been with Securicor for some three months. Securicor cannot be blamed for employing him on the job.

At the dead of night — ten minutes before midnight — Musgrove went to the factory. He unlocked the front door and went through the factory, switching on the lights as he went. Then he lit a match and threw it on to a cardboard box. It burst into flames. He says that he only meant it to be a very small fire and intended to put it out within a minute or two. But it got beyond his control. He was terrified and dialled 999 for the fire brigade. He tried to stop it spreading. He lost his glasses and false teeth. His right hand and arm were burnt. He staggered out of the factory through the smoke and flames. By that time the firemen and police were there. They had answered the call with great promptitude. They were at the factory at three minutes past midnight. But they could not save it. There was already a wall of flame across the building. Flames were coming through the roof. The place was gutted. The damage to the building and stock was put at £400,000. The loss of business at £250,000. Musgrove was afterwards charged with arson. He pleaded guilty to malicious damage and was sentenced to three years' imprisonment.

The occupiers of the factory claim damages from Securicor for this loss. The judge has held that Securicor are exempted from liability by an exception clause in the contract. The factory occupiers appeal to this court.

[Lord Denning held that Securicor were vicariously responsible for Musgrove's actions and that their liability sounded both in tort and in contract. He agreed however that even if sued in tort Securicor were entitled to rely on an exemption clause in the contract if it was fair and reasonable for them to do so. He therefore proceeded to examine the exempting provisions:]

The contract

The contract was contained in one of the printed forms used by the Securicor Group. These terms were typed into the form:

> The company shall provide their night patrol service whereby four visits per night shall be made seven nights per week and two visits shall be made during the afternoon of Saturday, and four visits shall be made during the day of Sunday.

The standard conditions were printed overleaf, and were as follows:

> 1. Under no circumstances shall the company be responsible for any injurious act or default by any employee of the company unless such act or default could have been foreseen and avoided by the exercise of due diligence on the part of the company as his employer, nor in any event shall the company be held responsible for: (*a*) Any loss suffered by the customer through burglary, theft, fire or any other cause, except insofar as such loss is solely attributable to the negligence of the company's employees acting within the course of their employment . . . (*b*) Any failure of the company to carry out the service by reason of strikes, . . . or other cause beyond the company's control.
>
> 2. If notwithstanding the foregoing provision, any liability on the part of the company shall arise (whether under the express or implied terms thereof or at common law) for any . . . loss or damage . . . sustained by the customer, such liability shall be . . . limited to a maximum of £25,000 for the consequences of each incident involving fire . . .; and shall be further limited to a maximum of £250,000 . . . in respect of all claims . . . arising during any consecutive period of 12 months.

The wording of the condition

One of the traditional ways of avoiding the effect of an exemption or limitation clause is by subjecting it to a literal analysis, and saying that it is not clear enough to exempt or limit the liability in the particular case: or that it excludes absolute liability but not negligent liability: and so forth. That is one of the arguments which Mr. Wright put forward in the present case. It was a most attractive performance. For instance, he said that "injurious act or default" covered a negligent act or default, but not a deliberate one. That is the sort of argument which we used in former times. But it is a most unsatisfactory method. It becomes an exercise in semantics only. The courts twist the natural and ordinary meaning of the words so as to achieve a result which is fair and reasonable. It would be much better to be straightforward and to ask: is the clause fair and reasonable? Or, is it fair and reasonable to allow the party to rely on it?

In this case it seems to me that the words of this clause, taken in their natural and ordinary meaning, do give Securicor the exemption they claim: or, at any rate, limit their liability to £25,000. The judge so held: and I would not disagree with him on this point.

There are, however, two other ways of avoiding the impact of such an exemption or limitation clause.

Fundamental breach

The first is by way of fundamental breach. In this way the court itself deprives the party of the benefit of an exemption or limitation clause if he has been guilty of a breach of a fundamental term or of a fundamental breach of one of the terms of contract.

This is the way which found favour with Lord Atkin in *Hain Steamship Co. Ltd.* v. *Tate and Lyle Ltd.* (1936) 41 Com. 350, 354; and with Lord Reid and Lord Upjohn in *Suisse Atlantique Société d'Armement Maritime S.A.* v. *N.V. Rotterdamsche Kolen Centrale* [1967] 1 AC 361, 398 and 425 respectively; and with this court in *Harbutt's "Plasticine" Ltd.* v. *Wayne Tank and Pump Co. Ltd.* [1970] 1 QB 447 and *Farnworth Finance Facilities Ltd.* v. *Attryde* [1970] 1 WLR 1053. It applies whether or not the injured party affirms or disaffirms the contract, as this court held in *Wathes (Western) Ltd.* v. *Austins (Menswear) Ltd.* [1976] 1 Lloyd's Rep. 14.

Applying this first way, it is clear in this case that Securicor were guilty of a breach which went to the root of the contract. They were employed to safeguard the premises against damage by fire. Instead of doing so, they deliberately burnt it down. It is a far worse breach than in the deviation cases — it is a far worse departure than in the warehouse cases — or it is a far more deliberate wrong than in the cases about conversion or mis-delivery of goods. Securicor were not doing what they contracted to do. They were doing the complete opposite. Whatever formula be taken from the various cases, it is plain that they cannot rely on the exemption or limitation clause. Some attempt was made by Mr. Machin to distinguish between a fire lit by a senior officer of Securicor (for which Securicor would not be exempt) and a fire lit by a subordinate patrolman (for which Securicor would be exempt). But I can see no difference in principle. In either case the breach was so fundamental that at that very moment — the throwing of the match on to the cardboard box — the contract was ended in respect of all further performance from that moment onwards and Securicor cannot rely on the exemption clause so as to escape the consequences of it.

Construction of the contract

The second is by way of the construction of the contract. In this way the court gives effect to the supposed intention of the parties. It says that the parties cannot have intended that the party should be entitled to rely on the exemption or limitation clause in the situation that has happened.

So far as this second way is concerned, it found favour with Pearson L.J. in *U.G.S. Finance Ltd.* v. *National Mortgage Bank of Greece and National Bank of Greece, S.A.* [1964] 1 Lloyd's Rep. 446 speaking at p. 453 of "presumed intention" which was approved by Viscount Dilhorne in *Suisse Atlantique* [1967] 1 AC 361, 393 and by Lord Reid at p. 405: and was applied by Sir John Pennycuick in *Wathes (Western) Ltd.* v. *Austins (Menswear) Ltd.* [1976] 1 Lloyd's Rep. 14, 25.

In this second way, it is important to notice that, in order to decide whether the exemption or limitation clause applies, you must construe the contract, not in the grammatical or literal sense, or even in the natural and ordinary meaning of the words — but in the wider context of the "presumed intention" of the parties — so as to see whether or not, in the situation that has arisen, the parties can reasonably be supposed to have intended that the party in breach should be able to avail himself of the exemption or limitation clause. That was pointed out by Lord Wilberforce in *Suisse Atlantique* [1967] 1 AC 361, 434, coupled with his illuminating observation in *Reardon Smith Line Ltd.* v. *Yngvar Hansen-Tangen (trading as H. E. Hansen-Tangen), The (Diana Prosperity)* [1976] 1 WLR 989, 996.

> When one speaks of the intention of the parties to the contract, one is speaking objectively — the parties cannot themselves give direct evidence of what their intention was — and what must be ascertained is what is to be taken as the intention which reasonable people would have had if placed in the situation of the parties. Similarly when one is speaking of aim, or object, or commercial purpose, one is speaking objectively of what reasonable persons would have in mind in the situation of the parties.

In other words, in order to ascertain the "presumed intention" of the parties, you must ask this question: If the parties had envisaged the situation which has happened, would they, as reasonable persons, have supposed that the exemption or limitation clause would apply to protect the wrongdoer?

Suppose then that the question was asked of the parties here: what is to happen if Securicor or their servants burn down the factory? Can they take advantage of the exemption or limitation clause? The answer would, I suggest, be "Of course not."

The meeting of the ways

Both ways are to be found in the speeches in *Suisse Atlantique Société d'Armement Maritime S.A.* v. *N.V. Rotterdamsche Kolen Centrale* [1967] 1 AC 361; and sometimes in the same speech. In actual practice, it makes little difference: because, whichever way is taken, the courts reach the same conclusion on the facts of any particular case. It should be noticed that the House did not say that any of the previous cases in this court were wrongly decided.

It seems to me that the two ways can be seen to meet in practice so as to produce a result in principle which may be stated thus: although the clause in its natural and ordinary meaning would seem to give exemption from or limitation of liability for a breach, nevertheless the court will not give the party that exemption or limitation if the court can say: "The parties as reasonable men cannot have intended that there should be exemption or limitation in the case of such a breach as this." In so stating the principle, there arises in these cases "the figure of the fair and reasonable man"; and the spokesman of this fair and reasonable man, as Lord Radcliffe once said, is and "must be the court itself": see *Davis Contractors Ltd.* v. *Fareham Urban District Council* [1956] AC 696, 728-729.

Thus we reach, after long years, the principle which lies behind all our striving: the court will not allow a party to rely on an exemption or limitation clause in circumstances in which it would not be fair or reasonable to allow reliance on it: and, in considering whether it is fair and reasonable, the court will consider whether it was in a standard form, whether there was equality of bargaining power, the nature of the breach, and so forth.

This solution follows the lead given by the legislature in the Supply of Goods (Implied Terms) Act 1973, section 4 [providing a new section 55 (4) of the Sale of Goods Act 1893], which says that, in a contract for the sale of goods, an exemption clause shall, "not be enforceable to the extent that it is shown that it would not be fair or reasonable to allow reliance on the term." And somewhat similarly, sections 3 and 11 of the Unfair Contract Terms Act 1977: and my own suggestion in *John Lee & Son (Grantham) Ltd.* v. *Railway Executive* (1949) 65 TLR 604; *Gillespie Bros. & Co. Ltd.* v. *Roy Bowles Transport Ltd.* [1973] QB 400, 416; and in *Levinson* v. *Patent Steam Carpet Co. Ltd.* [1978] QB 69, 79.

Reasonableness

I turn, therefore, to the test of reasonableness. That is the test on which the judge applied this case. He said:

> Condition 1, as I construe it, is, I think, a reasonable provision . . . Either the owner of the premises, or the person providing the service, must bear the risk. Why should the parties not agree to its being borne by the owners of the premises? He is certain to be insured against fire and theft, and is better able to judge the cover needed than the party providing the service . . . That is only another way of shifting the risk from the party who provides the service to the party who receives it. There is, as I have said, nothing unreasonable, nothing impolitic, in such a contract.

Whilst the judge was, I think, right to apply the test of reasonableness, I do not agree with his application of it. I would point out that, whilst the owner of the premises insured against fire (save for £25,000), Securicor insured against liability for the acts of their servants (save for £10,000). So to my mind the insurance factor cancels out: and we are left with the question as between the two parties. Is it fair or reasonable to allow Securicor to rely on this exemption or limitation clause when it was their own patrolman who deliberately burned down the factory? I do not think it is fair and reasonable. I would, therefore, allow the appeal and enter judgment for the plaintiffs.

[Shaw and Waller L.JJ. delivered separate concurring judgments.]

HOUSE OF LORDS:

LORD WILBERFORCE: It is first necessary to decide upon the correct approach to a case such as this where it is sought to invoke an exception or limitation clause in the contract. The approach of Lord Denning M.R. in the Court of Appeal was to consider first whether the breach was "fundamental." If so, he said, the court itself deprives the party of the benefit of an exemption or limitation clause ([1978] 1 WLR 856, 863). Shaw and Waller L.JJ. substantially followed him in this argument.

Lord Denning M.R. in this was following the earlier decision of the Court of Appeal, and in particular his own judgment in *Harbutt's "Plasticine" Ltd.* v. *Wayne Tank & Pump Co. Ltd.* [1970] 1 QB 447. In that case Lord Denning M.R. distinguished two cases (a) the case where as the result of a breach of contract the innocent party has, and exercises, the right to bring the contract to an end, (b) the case where the breach automatically brings the contract to an end, without the innocent party having to make an election whether to terminate the contract or to continue it. In the first case the Master of the Rolls, purportedly applying this House's decision in *Suisse Atlantique Société d'Armement Maritime S.A.* v. *N.V. Rotterdamsche Kolen Centrale* [1967] 1 AC 361, but in effect two citations from two of their Lordships' speeches, extracted a rule of law that the "termination" of the contract brings it, and with it the exclusion clause, to an end. The *Suisse Atlantique* case in his view

> affirms the long line of cases in this court that when one party has been guilty of a
> fundamental breach of the contract . . . and the other side accepts it, so that the
> contract comes to an end . . . then the guilty party cannot rely on an exception or
> limitation clause to escape from his liability for the breach (*Harbutt's* case [1970] 1 QB
> 447, 467).

He then applied the same principle to the second case.

My Lords, whatever the intrinsic merit of this doctrine, as to which I shall have something to say later, it is clear to me that so far from following this House's decision in the *Suisse Atlantique* it is directly opposed to it and that the whole purpose and tenor of the *Suisse Atlantique* was to repudiate it. The lengthy, and perhaps I may say sometimes indigestible speeches of their Lordships, are correctly summarised in the headnote — holding No. 3 [1967] 1 AC 361, 362— "That the question whether an exceptions clause was applicable where there was a fundamental breach of contract was one of the true construction of the contract." That there was any rule of law by which exceptions clauses are eliminated, or deprived of effect, regardless of their terms, was clearly not the view of Viscount Dilhorne, Lord Hodson, or of myself. The passages invoked for the contrary view of a rule of law consist only of short extracts from two of the speeches — on any view a minority. But the case for the doctrine does not even go so far as that. Lord Reid, in my respectful opinion, and I recognise that I may not be the best judge of this matter, in his speech read as a whole, cannot be claimed as a supporter of a rule of law. Indeed he expressly disagreed with the Master of the Rolls' observations in two previous cases (*Karsales (Harrow) Ltd.* v. *Wallis* [1956] 1 WLR 936 and *U.G.S. Finance Ltd.* v. *National Mortgage Bank of Greece and*

National Bank of Greece S.A. [1964] 1 Lloyd's Rep. 446 in which he had put forward the "rule of law" doctrine. In order to show how close the disapproved doctrine is to that sought to be revived in *Harbutt's* case I shall quote one passage from *Karsales* [1956] 1 WLR 936, 940:

> Notwithstanding earlier cases which might suggest the contrary, it is now settled that exempting clauses of this kind, no matter how widely they are expressed, only avail the party when he is carrying out his contract in its essential respects. He is not allowed to use them as a cover for misconduct or indifference or to enable him to turn a blind eye to his obligations. They do not avail him when he is guilty of a breach which goes to the root of the contract.

Lord Reid comments at p. 401 as to this that he could not deduce from the authorities cited in *Karsales* that the proposition stated in the judgment could be regarded as in any way "settled law." His conclusion is stated on p. 405: "In my view no such rule of law ought to be adopted" — adding that there is room for legislative reform.

My Lords, in the light of this, the passage cited by Lord Denning M.R. [1970] 1 QB 447, 465 has to be considered. For convenience I restate it:

> If fundamental breach is established the next question is what effect, if any, that has on the applicability of other terms of the contract. This question has often arisen with regard to clauses excluding liability, in whole or in part, of the party in breach. I do not think that there is generally much difficulty where the innocent party has elected to treat the breach as a repudiation, bring the contract to an end and sue for damages. Then the whole contract has ceased to exist including the exclusion clause, and I do not see how that clause can then be used to exclude an action for loss which will be suffered by the innocent party after it has ceased to exist, such as loss of the profit which would have accrued if the contract had run its full term. (*Suisse Atlantique* [1967] 1 AC 361, 398).

It is with the utmost reluctance that, not forgetting the "beams" that may exist elsewhere, I have to detect here a mote of ambiguity or perhaps even of inconsistency. What is referred to is "loss which will be suffered by the innocent party after [the contract] has ceased to exist" and I venture to think that all that is being said, rather elliptically, relates only to what is to happen in the future, and is not a proposition as to the immediate consequences caused by the breach: if it were that would be inconsistent with the full and reasoned discussion which follows.

It is only because of Lord Reid's great authority in the law that I have found it necessary to embark on what in the end may be superfluous analysis. For I am convinced that, with the possible exception of Lord Upjohn whose critical passage, when read in full, is somewhat ambiguous, their Lordships, fairly read, can only be taken to have rejected those suggestions for a rule of law which had appeared in the Court of Appeal and to have firmly stated that the queston is one of construction, not merely of course of the exclusion clause alone, but of the whole contract.

Much has been written about the *Suisse Atlantique* case. Each speech has been subjected to various degrees of analysis and criticism, much of it constructive. Speaking for myself I am conscious of imperfections of terminology, though sometimes in good company. But I do not think that I should be conducing to the clarity of the law by adding to what was already too ample a discussion a further analysis which in turn would have to be interpreted. I have no second thoughts as to the main proposition that the question whether, and to what extent, an exclusion clause is to be applied to a fundamental breach, or a breach of a fundamental term, or indeed to any breach of contract, is a matter of construction of the contract. Many difficult questions arise and will continue to arise in the infinitely varied situations in which contracts come to be breached — by repudiatory breaches, accepted or not, by anticipatory breaches, by breaches of conditions or of various terms and whether by negligent, or deliberate action or otherwise. But there are ample resources in the normal rules of contract law for dealing with these without the superimposition of a judicially invented rule of law. I am content to leave the matter there with some supplementary observations.

1.   The doctrine of "fundamental breach" in spite of its imperfections and doubtful parentage has served a useful purpose. There was a large number of problems, productive of injustice, in which it was worse than unsatisfactory to leave exception clauses to operate. Lord Reid referred to these in the *Suisse Atlantique* case [1967] 1 AC 361, 406, pointing out at the same time that the doctrine of fundamental breach was a dubious specific. But since then Parliament has taken a hand: it has passed the Unfair Contract Terms Act 1977. This Act applies to consumer contracts and those based on standard terms and enables exception clauses to be applied with regard to what is just and reasonable. It is significant that Parliament refrained from legislating over the whole field of contract. After this Act, in commercial matters generally, when the parties are not of unequal bargaining power, and when risks are normally borne by insurance, not only is the case for judicial intervention undemonstrated, but there is everything to be said, and this seems to have been Parliament's intention, for leaving the parties free to apportion the risks as they think fit and for respecting their decisions.

At the stage of negotiation as to the consequences of a breach, there is everything to be said for allowing the parties to estimate their respective claims according to the contractual provisions they have themselves made, rather than for facing them with a legal complex so uncertain as the doctrine of fundamental breach must be. What, for example, would have been the position of the respondents' factory if instead of being destroyed it had been damaged, slightly or moderately or severely? At what point does the doctrine (with what logical justification I have not understood) decide, ex post facto, that the breach was (factually) fundamental before going on to ask whether legally it is to be regarded as fundamental? How is the date of "termination" to be fixed? Is it the date of the incident causing the damage, or the date of the innocent party's election, or some other date? All these difficulties arise from the doctrine and are left unsolved by it.

At the judicial stage there is still more to be said for leaving cases to be decided straightforwardly on what the parties have bargained for rather than upon analysis, which becomes progressively more refined, of decisions in other cases leading to inevitable appeals. The learned judge was able to decide this case on normal principles of contractual law with minimal citation of authority. I am sure that most commercial judges have wished to be able to do the same: see *Trade and Transport Inc.* v. *Iino Kaiun Kaisha Ltd.* [1973] 1 WLR 210, 232, *per* Kerr J. In my opinion they can and should.

2. The case of *Harbutt* [1970] 1 QB 447 must clearly be overruled. It would be enough to put that upon its radical inconsistency with the *Suisse Atlantique* case [1967] 1 AC 361. But even if the matter were res integra I would find the decision to be based upon unsatisfactory reasoning as to the "termination" of the contract and the effect of "termination" on the plaintiffs' claim for damage. I have, indeed, been unable to understand how the doctrine can be reconciled with the well accepted principle of law, stated by the highest modern authority, that when in the context of a breach of contract one speaks of "termination," what is meant is no more than that the innocent party or, in some cases, both parties, are excused from further performance. Damages, in such cases, are then claimed under the contract, so what reason in principle can there be for disregarding what the contract itself says about damages — whether it "liquidates" them, or limits them, or excludes them? These difficulties arise in part from uncertain or inconsistent terminology. A vast number of expressions are used to describe situations where a breach has been committed by one party of such a character as to entitle the other party to refuse further performance: discharge, rescission, termination, the contract is at an end, or dead, or displaced; clauses cannot survive, or simply go. I have come to think that some of these difficulties can be avoided; in particular the use of "rescission," even if distinguished from rescission ab initio, as an equivalent for discharge, though justifiable in some contexts (see *Johnson* v. *Agnew* [1980] AC 367) may lead to confusion in others. To plead for complete uniformity may be to cry for the moon. But what can and ought to be avoided is to make use of these confusions in order to produce a concealed and unreasoned legal innovation: to pass, for example, from saying that a party, victim of a breach of contract, is entitled to refuse further performance, to saying that he may treat the contract as at an end, or as rescinded, and to draw from this the proposition, which is not analytical but one of policy, that all or (arbitrarily) some of the clauses of the contract lose, automatically, their force, regardless of intention.

If this process is discontinued the way is free to use such words as "discharge" or "termination" consistently with principles as stated by modern authority which *Harbutt's* case [1970] 1 QB 447 disregards. I venture with apology to relate the classic passages. In *Heyman* v. *Darwins Ltd.* [1942] AC 356, 399 Lord Porter said:

> To say that the contract is rescinded or has come to an end or has ceased to exist may in individual cases convey the truth with sufficient accuracy, but the fuller expression that the injured party is thereby absolved from future performance of his obligations under the contract is a more exact description of the position. Strictly speaking, to say that on acceptance of the renunciation of a contract the contract is rescinded is incorrect. In such a case the injured party may accept the renunciation as a breach going to the root of the whole of the consideration. By that acceptance he is discharged from further performance and may bring an action for damages, but the contract itself is not rescinded.

And similarly Lord Macmillan at p. 373: see also *Boston Deep Sea Fishing and Ice Co.* v. *Ansell* (1888) 39 Ch.D. 339, 361, *per* Bowen L.J. In *Lep Air Services Ltd.* v. *Rolloswin Investments Ltd.* [1973] AC 331, 350, my noble and learned friend, Lord Diplock, drew a distinction (relevant for that case) between primary obligations under a contract, which on "rescission" generally come to an end, and secondary obligations which may then arise. Among the latter he includes an obligation to pay compensation, i.e., damages. And he states in terms that this latter obligation "is just as much an obligation arising from the contract as are the primary obligations that it replaces." My noble and learned friend has developed this line of thought in an enlightening manner in his opinion which I have now had the benefit of reading.

These passages I believe to state correctly the modern law of contract in the relevant respects: they demonstrate that the whole foundation of *Harbutt's* case [1970] 1 QB 447 is unsound. A fortiori, in addition to *Harbutt's* case there must be overruled the case of *Wathes (Western) Ltd.* v. *Austins (Menswear) Ltd.* [1976] 1 Lloyd's Rep. 14 which sought to apply the doctrine of fundamental breach to a case where, by election of the innocent party, the contract had not been terminated, an impossible acrobatic, yet necessarily engendered by the doctrine. Similarly, *Charterhouse Credit Co. Ltd.* v. *Tolly* [1963] 2 QB 683 must be overruled, though the result might have been reached on construction of the contract.

3. I must add to this, by way of exception to the decision not to "gloss" the *Suisse Atlantique* [1967] 1 AC 361 a brief observation on the deviation cases, since some reliance has been placed upon them, particularly upon the decision of this House in *Hain Steamship Co. Ltd.* v. *Tate and Lyle Ltd.* (1936) 155 LT 177 (so earlier than the *Suisse Atlantique*) in the support of the *Harbutt* doctrine. I suggested in the *Suisse Atlantique* that these cases can be regarded as proceeding upon normal principles applicable to the law of contract generally viz., that it is a matter of the parties' intentions whether and to what extent clauses in shipping contracts can be applied after a deviation, i.e., a departure from the contractually agreed voyage or adventure. It may be preferable that they should be considered as a body of authority sui generis with special rules derived from historical and commercial reasons. What on either view they cannot do is to lay down different rules as to contracts generally from those later stated by this House in *Heyman* v. *Darwins Ltd.* [1942] AC 356. The ingenious use by Donaldson J. in *Kenyon, Son & Craven Ltd.* v. *Baxter Hoare & Co. Ltd.* [1971] 1 WLR 519 of the doctrine of deviation in order to reconcile the *Suisse Atlantique* with *Harbutt's* case, itself based in part on the use of the doctrine of deviation, illustrates the contortions which that case has made necessary and would be unnecessary if it vanished as an authority.

4. It is not necessary to review fully the numerous cases in which the doctrine of fundamental breach has been applied or discussed. Many of these have now been superseded by the Unfair Contract Terms Act 1977. Others, as decisions, may be justified as depending upon the construction of the contract (see *Levison* v. *Patent Steam Carpet Cleaning Co. Ltd.* [1978] QB 69) in the light of well known principles such as that stated in *Alderslade* v. *Hendon Laundry Ltd.* [1945] KB 189.

In this situation the present case has to be decided. As a preliminary, the nature of the contract has to be understood. Securicor undertook to provide a service of periodical visits for a very modest charge which works out at 26p. per visit. It did not agree to provide equipment. It would have no knowledge of the value of the plaintiffs' factory: that, and the efficacy of their fire precautions, would be known to the respondents. In these circumstances nobody could consider it unreasonable, that as between these two equal parties the risk assumed by Securicor should be a modest one, and that the respondents should carry the substantial risk of damage or destruction.

The duty of Securicor was, as stated, to provide a service. There must be implied an obligation to use due care in selecting their patrolmen, to take care of the keys and, I would think, to operate the service with due and proper regard to the safety and security of the premises. The breach of duty committed by Securicor lay in a failure to discharge this latter obligation. Alternatively it could be put upon a vicarious responsibility for the wrongful act of Musgrove — viz., starting a fire on the premises: Securicor would be responsible for this upon the principle stated in *Morris* v. *C. W. Martin & Sons Ltd.* [1966] 1 QB 716, 739. This being the breach, does condition 1 apply? It is drafted in strong terms, "Under no circumstances" . . . "any injurious act or default by any employee." These words have to be approached with the aid of the cardinal rules of construction that they must be read contra proferentem and that in order to escape from the consequences of one's own wrongdoing, or that of one's servant, clear words are necessary. I think that these words are clear. The respondents in fact relied upon them for an argument that since they exempted from negligence they must be taken as not exempting from the consequence of deliberate acts. But this is a perversion of the rule that if a clause can cover something other than negligence, it will not be applied to negligence. Whether, in addition to negligence, it covers other, e.g., deliberate, acts, remains a matter of construction requiring, of course, clear words. I am of opinion that it does, and being free to construe and apply the clause, I must hold that liability is excluded. On this part of the case I agree with the judge and adopt his reasons for judgment. I would allow the appeal.

Appeal allowed.

[Lord Scarman and Lord Keith of Kinkel concurred without reasons. Lord Diplock and Lord Salmon concurred in separate reasoned judgments.]

Notes:

1   For an admirable comment on *Photo Production* see M.H. Ogilvie, "*Suisse Atlantique* Re-vindicated: How Long, O Lords, How Long?" (1980-81) 5 CBLJ 100, and compare J.S. Ziegel, "The House of Lords Overrules *Harbutt's Plasticine*" (1980) 30 UTLJ 421. Professor Ziegel suggests (at 433) that "In the ultimate analysis *Securicor* may turn out to be anti-climactic because, while the House of Lords may have managed to banish the heresy of *Harbutt's "Plasticine"*, the decision may not prove successful in preventing the resurrection of old attitudes under the guise of rules of construction. We could indeed witness a second *Suisse Atlantique* in which, after an initial period of hesitation, Canadian courts covertly reintroduce doctrines of

fundamental breach while faithfully, and no doubt quite sincerely, swearing allegiance to *Suisse Atlantique* and *Securicor*.'' Do you agree?

2   The accurary of this apprehension may be judged in the light of the Supreme Court of Canada's decision in *Beaufort Realties (1964) Inc.* v. *Belcourt Construction (Ottawa) Ltd. and Chomedy Aluminum Co. Ltd.* (1980) 33 NR 460, which was rendered in November 1980.

   Beaufort Realties involved a mechanics' lien action and at issue was the effect of a waiver of lien clause signed by the subcontractor Chomedy Aluminum Co. Limited, in favour of the contractor, Belcourt Construction (Ottawa) Limited. The relevant clause read in part as follows:

> ARTICLE 6. The Subcontractor hereby waives, releases and renounces all privileges or rights or privilege, and all lien or rights of lien now existing or that may hereinafter exist for work done or materials furnished under this Contract, upon the premises and upon the land on which the same is situated . . .

   Belcourt failed to pay the advances due under the contract, whereupon Chomedy filed a mechanics' lien and commenced action against Belcourt. The trial judge found that Belcourt, by failing to make its payments, had committed a fundamental breach of contract and that this precluded it from relying on the waiver clause. On appeal, the Divisional Court of Ontario agreed that there had been a fundamental breach but held that this did not affect the enforceability of the waiver. On a further appeal the Ontario Court of Appeal [*sub nom. Chomedy Aluminum Co. Ltd.* v. *Belcourt Construction (Ottawa) Ltd.* (1979) 97 DLR (3d) 170] reversed the decision of the Divisional Court on the latter point and reinstated the trial judgment. Madam Justice Wilson, writing for a unanimous court, held (1) that ''the *Suisse Atlantique* line of authorities'' applied and that this was so notwithstanding section 5(1) of the Mechanics Lien Act, and (2) that as a matter of construction article 6 of the agreement ceased to bind Belcourt when it was advised by Chomedy of its election to treat the contract as at an end.

   The Supreme Court of Canada affirmed unanimously. Mr. Justice Ritchie agreed, in his brief written reasons on behalf of the court, with both grounds of decision of the Ontario Court of Appeal. In particular, so far as the construction of article 6 was concerned, he was satisfied that ''considering the fundamental breach of the contractor (Belcourt Construction (Ottawa) Limited), in the context of the contract as a whole the true construction to be placed on Article 6 is that the waiver therein contained ceased to bind the respondent upon its having communicated to the appellant its election to treat the contract as at an end.''

3. LEGISLATIVE REACTIONS

a) Summary of Provisions

The following is an outline of some of the more important statutory attempts to cope with disclaimer clauses:

A. GENERAL REGULATION OF UNCONSCIONABILITY

1. *Sales legislation*

a. UCC 2-302 gives courts the power to refuse to enforce a contract or clause that is unconscionable.

b. The OLRC Sales Report recommends the adoption of a modified version of UCC 2-302, including a non-exhaustive list of considerations which a court may consider in determining whether a clause is unconscionable. See pp. 160-62, Draft Bill s. 5.2.

2. *Consumer legislation*

a. Sections 3, 2(*b*) of the BPA prohibit "unfair practices" which include "unconscionable consumer representations". Would an unconscionable exemption clause fall within this provision?

B. SPECIFIC REGULATION OF DISCLAIMER CLAUSES

1. *Contract legislation*

a. Section 2(1) of the Unfair Contract Terms Act 1977 (U.K.), c. 50, prohibits exclusionary clauses purporting to restrict or exclude liability for death or personal injury resulting from negligence. Section 2(2) provides for similar control over the exclusion of other types of loss or damage caused by negligence.

   Section 3 of the Act prevents one party from disclaiming contractual liability based on standard form clauses or where the other party is a consumer, unless the disclaimer clauses satisfy the requirement of reasonableness (as amplified in s. 11).

   Other relevant provisions in the Act are ss. 7 and 8.

2. *Sales legislation*

a. UCC 2-316 provides specific guidelines concerning the circumstances and manner in which express or implied warranties may be modified or excluded. UCC 2-719 governs the limitation or modification of contractual remedies. Consequential damages may be limited or excluded unless the limitation or exclusion is unconscionable. In cases of injury to the person by consumer goods, limitation of consequential damages is deemed to be *prima facie* unconscionable.

b. The Unfair Contract Terms Act 1977, s. 6, provides that liability for breach of implied terms under the SGA (U.K.) and Supply of Goods (Implied Terms) Act 1973 cannot be excluded by contractual clauses; implied terms as to description or sample, quality or fitness *are* excludable as against a non-consumer, subject to an overriding requirement of reasonableness.

c. The OLRC Sales Report (pp. 227-35, 241) recommended that Ontario not adopt provisions similar to UCC 2-316, but that it adopt a modified version of UCC 2-719(3), which deems an exclusion or limitation of damages for breach to·be prima facie unconscionable in the case of injury to person, extended to cover cases of personal injury caused by *any* type of goods. Clauses purporting to exclude liability for all negligent acts, it recommended, should be controlled by the general unconscionability provision (*supra*). The Report also contains recommendations relating to disclaimer clauses and privity of contract.

3. *Consumer legislation*

a.   Section 44a of the CPA provides that any term in a "consumer sale" contract which purports to vary or negate any of the implied conditions or warranties in the SGA is void.

b.   Section 8(1) of Bill 110, dealing with the sale of "consumer products", provided that "any warranty under this Act or the availability or scope of any remedy otherwise available for the breach thereof" could not be negatived, excluded, restricted or diminished by terms of acknowledgments — any such term would be void if it purported to do so.

c.   The Saskatchewan Consumer Products Warranties Act, s. 7, provides that (with the exception of used consumer products) the provisions of the Act and regulations cannot be waived, limited or modified in effect and that any agreement which attempts to do so is void. Subs. (2) creates the offence of attempting to exclude or limit the benefits of the Act to consumers. Section 8(2) provides that no express warranty shall "disclaim, exclude or limit a statutory warranty prescribed by section 11."

d.   Section 2(3) of the New Brunswick Consumer Product Warranty and Liability Act, SNB 1978, c. C-18.1, provides that the Act applies "notwithstanding any agreement, notice, disclaimer, waiver, acknowledgment or other thing to the contrary". Sections 24-26 govern the exclusion of warranties and remedies. In the case of a contract for the sale or supply of a consumer product, an agreement excluding or restricting remedies provided by the Act for breach of express warranties is subject to an overriding requirement of reasonableness and fairness. Remedies provided for breach of any part of an express warranty which forms part of the description of a consumer product cannot be excluded or restricted (s. 25(4)). Section 26 deals with the situation of a buyer acting in the course of a business and permits the exclusion or restriction of any warranty or remedy provided by the Act but such agreement is ineffective with respect to any "consumer loss" for which the seller would be liable if no such agreement had been made.

e.   Section 10 of the Quebec Consumer Protection Act, SQ 1978, c. 9, provides that: "Any stipulation whereby a merchant is liberated from the consequences of his own act or the act of his representatives is prohibited." Section 44 prohibits exclusion clauses in a "conventional warranty" unless "clearly indicated in separate and successive clauses".

Which of the above approaches do you prefer? What are the relative weaknesses of the various attempts to control the use of disclaimer clauses? There is a dearth of authority interpreting and applying the above provisions of the Canadian consumer legislation. Why should this be so? For an early decision applying the disclaimer clause provisions in the Saskatchewan Conditional Sales Act (see now RSS 1978, c. C-25, as am.), see *Relland Motors Ltd.* v. *Foy* (1959) 20 DLR (2d) 558 (Sask. CA).

C. DISCLAIMER CLAUSES IN PARTICULAR TYPES OF SALE AGREEMENT

The agricultural machinery and farm implement acts of the Prairie provinces (later joined by P.E.I.) have long regulated the use of disclaimer clauses in sale agreements for this type of product. For the details see OLRC Warranties Report, pp. 96-100.

b) Judicial Application

R.W. GREEN LTD. v. CADE BROS. FARMS
[1978] 1 Ll. L. Rep. 602 (QB)

The sellers, who were seed potato merchants, had over a period of years done a considerable volume of business with the buyers, who carried on a substantial farming business. The sales were subject to the sellers' standard conditions of sale which were based on a standard form of conditions produced by the National Association of Seed Potato Merchants in collaboration with the National Farmers Union.

In January 1974 the buyers ordered twenty tons of uncertified King Edward potatoes at a price of £28 per ton. The potatoes were delivered to the buyers' farm on February 5, 1974. On February 18 the buyers complained to the sellers about the condition of the potatoes, but the sellers persuaded the buyers that although the potatoes looked dull and there was a bit of gangrene, the percentage was within accepted limits of tolerance.

The sellers were mistaken and, after the potatoes were planted, it became obvious that they were inherently unhealthy. On October 9, 1974, an official report was obtained and this revealed that the potatoes were infected with a virus which could only be detected by examination of the growing crop in the previous season.

As a result of this infection the crop was very poor and the buyers suffered a heavy loss of profit.

The sellers brought action claiming £2,273 in respect of the seed potatoes they had sold the buyers. The buyers admitted the debt but raised a counterclaim for the loss of profits they had suffered. By way of defence to the counterclaim the sellers relied on clause 5 of the conditions of sale, which read as follows:

> If the Purchaser considers he has grounds for rejection of the Seed notwithstanding that the goods have passed in transit from the point of loading, he shall, if requested by the Seller clear the goods and take all necessary measures to mitigate damage or loss without prejudice to the claim of either party. Time being the essence of this Contract, however, notification of rejection, claim or complaint must be made to the Seller, giving a statement of the grounds for such rejection, claim or complaint within three days (within ten days in the case of rejection, claim or complaint specifically in respect of Skinspot, Gangrene or Dry Rot) after the arrival of the Seed at its destination. The place of rejection is the place of delivery in all cases. Notwithstanding the foregoing it shall not be competent to the Purchaser to reject, claim or complain for any reason unless the Seed Potatoes shall have been properly stored during the period after their arrival at their destination. The Seller shall replace any Seed properly rejected by the Purchaser unless otherwise agreed. It is specifically

provided and agreed that compensation and damages payable under any claim or claims arising out of this contract under whatsoever pretext shall not under any circumstances amount in aggregate to more than the contract price of the potatoes forming the subject of the claim or claims.

GRIFFITHS J.: The crop that was grown was of poor quality and fetched only £14.50 per ton, and was unfit for pre-packing. The market price of a healthy crop was £29.50 per ton, to which must be added a pre-packing profit of £7.41 per ton. Some small allowance must be made for the fact that even in a healthy crop not all the potatoes are fit for pre-packing. These basic facts are taken from the evidence of the defendants' accountant and the Cade brothers, and I accept it. After the arithmetic has been done, it shows a total loss of profit on the crop of £5822.00.

Can the farmers recover these damages from the seed potato merchants? The first ground upon which they rely in their pleadings depends upon establishing that Mr. Richardson sold the seed potatoes as corresponding to the original sample he produced in September, 1973, and further, that he gave Mr. Stanley Cade an oral warranty that the seed potatoes were as good as the others and would produce just as good results. On my findings of fact that way of putting the case fails. I find that there was no such oral warranty and that it was not a sale by sample related to the original 100 tons.

Alternatively the defendants rely upon the implied terms that the seed potatoes were of merchantable quality and were reasonably fit for their purpose — s. 14, Sale of Goods Act, 1893. As the consignment was infected with potato virus Y at the time of sale, they were not reasonably fit for growing a crop of potatoes; nor were they of merchantable quality. The plaintiffs do not seek to argue that there were not breaches of these two implied terms, but say that they are relieved of the liability to pay damages by virtue of cl. 5 of their conditions of sale.

On the pleadings the defendants disputed that this sale was made subject to the plaintiffs' standard conditions of sale, but in the light of Mr. Stanley Cade's frank admission that he understood that all his business with the plaintiffs was done upon their standard trading conditions, this line of defence has no longer been pursued. However, although the defendants concede that the sale was subject to the plaintiffs' standard conditions, they say that cl. 5 does not protect the plaintiffs from the consequences of their breaches. Firstly, they say that it would not be fair or reasonable to allow the plaintiffs to rely upon cl. 5 in the circumstances of this case, and they rely upon s. 55, sub-ss. (4) and (5) of the Sale of Goods Act, 1893, as amended by s. 4 of the Supply of Goods (Implied Terms) Act, 1973. Secondly they say that in any event, upon its true construction, cl. 5 is of no application to a latent defect such as the presence of virus Y disease in these potatoes. Thirdly, and finally, they say that the plaintiffs were in fundamental breach of the contract or alternatively in breach of a fundamental term of the contract, and thus not entitled to rely upon cl. 5 of the contract of sale.

This contract, like any commercial contract, must be considered and construed against the background of the trade in which it operates. The plaintiffs' conditions are based upon a standard form of conditions produced by the National Association of Seed Potato Merchants. They are used by a large majority of seed potato merchants and, apart from amendments to accommodate a change to metrication, they have been in use in their present form for over 20 years. They have evolved over a much longer period as the result both of trade practice and discussions between the Association and the National Farmers' Union. They are therefore not conditions imposed by the strong upon the weak; but are rather a set of trading terms upon which both sides are apparently content to do business.

It is also important to have in mind the distinction between certified and uncertified seed. The Ministry of Agriculture provides a service whereby its inspectors will inspect a potato crop during the growing season, and if it appears healthy will issue a certificate to that effect. There are various grades of certificate indicating the percentage of virus infected plants in the growing crop, ranging from an H certificate based on a tolerance of 2 per cent., to an FS certificate, based on a tolerance of 0.001 per cent. If a farmer buys certified seed, he pays a little more for it to cover the costs of the inspection and certification. The certificate cannot be an absolute guarantee that the seed will not be infected, but according to Mr. Cock it is on the whole a fairly reliable system, and I have no doubt provides a very real safeguard against buying an infected batch of seed. The farmer who buys uncertified seed does not have this safeguard which is provided by the independent examination of the Ministry, and must as a general rule be taking a greater risk of buying infected seed, but of course he gets it at a cheaper price.

With these considerations in mind, I now look at cl. 5; it is headed "REJEC-TION AND CLAIMS" and it reads: [see statement of facts].

On my findings no complaint was made about the potatoes until 13 days after delivery. The plaintiffs therefore say that the claim is out of time and barred by the condition that it must be made within three, or in certain cases 10, days of delivery. The plaintiffs' directors, in their evidence, explained that such a term was necessary in the trade because potatoes are a very perishable commodity and may deteriorate badly after delivery, particularly if they are not properly stored. So it was thought reasonable to give the farmer three days to inspect and make his complaint, and in the case of certain specific types of damage which might take longer to become apparent, 10 days. This appears to me to be a very reasonable requirement in the case of damage that is discoverable by reasonable inspection. But the presence of virus Y in the potatoes was not discoverable by inspection, and the complaint that was made did not relate to this defect, which neither the farmer nor the potato merchant suspected.

Section 55 sub-s. (4) of the Sale of Goods Act as amended by s. 4 of the Supply of Goods (Implied Terms) Act, 1973, provides as follows:

> In the case of a contract for sale of goods, any term of that or any other contract exempting from all or any of the provisions of section 13, 14 or 15 of this Act shall be void in the case of a consumer sale and shall, in any other case, not be enforceable to the extent that it is shown that it would not be fair or reasonable to allow reliance on the term.

Sub-section 5 provides:

> In determining for the purposes of subsection 4 above whether or not reliance

on any such term would be fair or reasonable regard shall be had to all the circumstances of the case and in particular to the following matters; [— and then, by provision (d): —] Where the term exempts from all or any of the provisions of section 13, 14 or 15 of this Act if some conditon is not complied with, whether it was reasonable at the time of the contract to expect that compliance with that condition would be practicable.

At the time this contract was made no one would expect it to have been practicable for the farmer to complain of virus Y in the potatoes within three days of delivery, for the simple reason that he would not know of its presence. It would therefore, in my judgment, not be fair or reasonable that this claim should be defeated because no complaint was made within three or 10 days of delivery. I therefore declare that that part of cl. 5 is unenforceable in this action and provides no defence to the plaintiffs.

Is the claim to be limited to the contract price of the potatoes? Mr. Harvey submits that upon its true construction, cl. 5 applies only to patent defects; he argues that as that part of the condition that deals with notification of complaints could only have been intended to apply to patent — that is, to reasonably discoverable — defects, it follows that the limitation of the damages in the latter part of the condition must also be similarly restricted to patent defects. I cannot accept this construction. In the first place I doubt if, as a matter of construction, the parts of the condition dealing with complaints is restricted to patent defects; it appears, as drafted, to cover all complaints, but the Court has avoided the harsh consequences of this construction by declaring it unenforceable pursuant to its statutory power. However, even assuming that it should be construed as limited to complaints in respect of patent defects, I can see no reason to read a similar restriction into the very wide wording of the final sentence of the condition, which I now repeat:

> ... It is specifically provided and agreed that compensation and damages payable under any claim or claims arising out of this contract under whatsoever pretext shall not under any circumstances amount in aggregate to more than the contract price of the potatoes forming the subject of the claim or claims.

This is clear language, easily intelligible, and I do not believe that any farmer who read it would say to himself "Ah; now that only applies to patent defects".

Furthermore, it is made clear by the terms of cl. 3(a) that the condition is intended to cover defects not patent at the time of delivery, for that condition provides:

> Seed potatoes sometimes develop diseases after delivery. It being impossible to ascertain the presence of such diseases by the exercise of reasonable skill and judgment the Seller cannot accept any responsibility should any disease develop after delivery other than as provided under clause 5.

In my judgment, as a matter of construction cl. 5 limits the defendants' claim to the contract price of the potatoes.

Should I exercise my discretion under s. 55, as amended, of the Sale of Goods Act and declare it to be unenforceable, because it would not be fair or reasonable to let the plaintiffs rely upon it?

I have considered the matters to which I am particularly directed to have regard by s. 55 (5), in so far as they are relevant in this case. The parties were of equal bargaining strength; the buyer received no inducement to accept the term. True, it appears that he could not easily have bought potatoes without this term in the contract, but he had had the protection of the National Farmers' Union to look after his interests as the contract evolved and he knew that he was trading on these conditions.

No moral blame attaches to either party; neither of them knew, nor could be expected to know, that the potatoes were infected. There was of course a risk; it was a risk that the farmer could largely have avoided by buying certified seed, but he chose not to do so. To my mind the contract in clear language places the risk in so far as damage may exceed the contract price, on the farmer. The contract has been in use for many years with the approval of the negotiating bodies acting on behalf of both seed potato merchants and farmers, and I can see no grounds upon which it would be right for the Court to say in the circumstances of this case that such a term is not fair or reasonable.

There remains to be considered Mr. Harvey's final argument based upon fundamental breach, or more strictly as he developed it, based upon breach of a fundamental term. His argument ran thus: A fundamental term of a contract is a term a breach of which entitles the other party to repudiate the contract. In a contract for the sale of goods, if there is a breach of the implied terms of merchantable quality or reasonable fitness for their purpose, the buyer may reject the goods and treat the contract as discharged; they are therefore fundamental terms in a contract for the sale of goods. If the buyer in this case had known that the potatoes were infected, he would have rejected them and treated the contract as discharged, in which case, says Mr. Harvey, the contract being at an end the exclusion clause will also cease to be of any application; and he relies upon the passage in the speech of Lord Reid in *The Suisse Atlantique* [1966] 1 Lloyd's Rep. 529; [1967] 1 AC 361 at pp. 544 and 398. The fact that the buyer did not repudiate the contract because he did not know of the breach, but now sues for damages, makes no difference to the consequences of the seller's breach of a fundamental term; it still disentitles the seller from relying upon the exclusion clause, and for this proposition Mr. Harvey cites the recent decision of the Court of Appeal in *Wathe (Western) Ltd.* v. *Austins (Menswear) Ltd.* [1976] 1 Lloyd's Rep. 14.

Much judicial ingenuity has been expended over the last 25 years to avoid the unjust results that would flow from the literal application of unfair trading conditions. It is over this period that the doctrine of fundamental breach of contract has evolved. There are many authorities dealing with the subject; they are not all easily reconciled one with the other. At one time it appeared that the Courts were saying that if a fundamental breach of contract was established, then as a matter of law the guilty party could not rely upon an exclusion clause: see, by way of example, *Karsales (Harrow) Ltd.* v. *Wallis* [1956] 1 WLR 936; *Charterhouse Credit Co. Ltd.* v. *Tolly* [1963] 2 QB 683 and *Yeoman Credit Ltd.* v. *Apps* [1962] 2 QB 508. But the weight of authority is against that view. The true rule is that in every case the question whether or not the exclusion clause applies depends upon the construction of the contract, but the Court will approach the question of construction leaning heavily towards the view that the parties could not have intended the exclusion clause to apply to circumstances giving rise to a so-called fundamental breach of contract. In *Wathe* v. *Austin,* Sir John Pennycuick said at p. 25:

> The current of authority has now set, . . . in favour of the view that where a contract is affirmed after fundamental breach an exemption clause is treated as inapplicable to liability resulting from that breach, not upon a substantive principle of law, but upon construction, the clause being construed in the absence of some plain indication of a different intention, as by implication inapplicable to such liability.

I do not therefore accept Mr. Harvey's submission that the plaintiffs' breaches of s. 14 of the Sale of Goods Act automatically disentitled them from relying upon that part of cl. 5 that limits their liability to the contract price. Nor do I find much help in approaching the question of construction by applying the label "fundamental" to the breach or to the term breached. The Court has to look at the facts that constitute the breach and the circumstances surrounding it and ask itself whether the clause could have been intended by the parties to apply in such a situation and the nature of the breach must loom large in such a consideration. In this case both parties to the contract must have realized that there was a chance that the potato merchants would be guilty of this very breach, namely that they would innocently sell infected potatoes. That which they must have anticipated might happen, has happened; why then should the Court say that a term in the contract that limits liability in such readily foreseeable circumstances is to be of no effect? In my view the limitation of liability in cl. 5 is clearly intended to cover the circumstances of the present case, and the plaintiffs are entitled to rely upon it. Furthermore, it appears to me that now Parliament has given the Judge a discretion to declare such a clause unenforceable if he thinks that it is not fair and reasonable, there will in the future be little need to resort to the doctrine of the fundamental breach in this type of action, and that the Court should not strain to give an artificially restricted meaning to an exclusion clause when it has the other remedy close at hand to do justice between the parties.

Judgment for plaintiff.

Note: Section 55(4) of the amended British Sale of Goods Act 1893 has now been replaced by ss. 6(2) and 11 of the Unfair Contract Terms Act 1977. None of the Canadian common law provinces has so far adopted an unconscionability provision similar to s. 55(4). Is this fatal? Could the doctrine be adopted judicially, as it has been in other parts of contract law, or by analogy with the statutory powers in s. 2 of the BPA? Can statutes serve as a source of new judicial law? On these questions see further Comment on *Green* v. *Cade Bros. Farms* (1979) 57 Can. Bar Rev. 105.

PART II

PAYMENT MECHANISMS

This part of the materials deals with payment by negotiable instruments (bills, cheques and notes), credit cards, electronic funds transfers and letters of credit. Particular attention is given to these payment mechanisms in conjunction with the sale of goods. The materials are concerned with the evolution of the law of negotiable instruments, types of negotiable instruments and their essential characteristics, liability on negotiable instruments, preservation of consumer defences against a third party financer (a subject which takes us into the effect of the selection of a payment mechanism on the preservation of a buyer's defences as well as into the law which governs credit card plans), use of electronic funds transfers in commercial and consumer transactions and rights of parties thereunder, and the letter of credit, its use as a payment device in documentary transactions and rights of parties thereunder.

Chapter 14
Negotiable Instruments Law: Introduction

A. THE EVOLUTION OF THE LAW OF NEGOTIABLE INSTRUMENTS

1. ORIGINS

Negotiable instruments governed by the Bills of Exchange Act, RSC 1970, c. B-5, are "bills of exchange" (including cheques) and "promissory notes".

Early bills of exchange were used in the Middle Ages in connection with long distance trade. They enabled funds to be transferred from one fair to another or from one country to another without the risk of carrying money *in specie*. Thus, the earliest bills of exchange were in the form of a letter addressed by B to C, asking C to pay to a third person D a sum of money which A has entrusted to B for this purpose. This letter is handed by B to A, who sends it on to D; and D presents it for payment to C (Holdsworth, *H.E.L.* viii, p. 131). The function of this letter was the transfer to D of B's funds in C's hands (or the transfer to D of C's debt to B) in payment of A's debt to D.

The following example will facilitate the understanding of the use of this type of an early bill of exchange. Suppose A, an Amsterdam merchant, owes money to D, a London merchant, for goods sold from D to A. Suppose B and C are in what we would call today the banking business. B is in Amsterdam and C is in London. Rather than transferring the funds from Amsterdam to London *in specie*, A (the Amsterdam merchant) either gives funds to B (the Amsterdam banker) or has his account with him charged, and obtains from him a bill of exchange, namely a letter addressed by B to C asking C to pay D, in the sum of his debt to D. A then sends the letter to D (the London merchant) who presents the letter to C (the London banker) and obtains payment in discharge of A's debt to him. C then charges B's account with him.

The same operation takes place in reverse when a London debtor pays an Amsterdam creditor using a letter addressed by C (the London banker) to B (the Amsterdam banker) asking him to pay an Amsterdam creditor. On payment to the

Amsterdam creditor, B charges C's account with him. B and C, together with other bankers, meet periodically in a fair (a predecessor of the modern clearing house) where they settle the accounts between them. Such settlement operates with a minimum transport of money *in specie*. Thus, if the balance is in favour of B, C could pay him by directing a Barcelona banker, whose account with him is in his (C's) favour, to pay directly to B. Of course, the account between C and the Barcelona banker is based on similar mutual payments of debts between London and Barcelona merchants.

English merchants have used bills of exchange from the middle of the 15th century onwards. Their transferability (as distinguished from the transfer of funds represented thereunder to a designated payee as explained above) was recognized only in the 17th century.

Promissory notes (or their predecessors, bills of debt or writings obligatory) had been incorporated into the customs of merchants by the mid-17th century. Malynes, *Lex Mercatoria* (1622) p. 74 reproduces the following form:

> I, A.B., merchant of Amsterdam, do acknowledge by these presents to be truly indebted to the honest C.D., English merchant dwelling in Middleborough, in the sum of five hundred pounds current money for merchandise, which is for commodities received of him for my contentment, which sum of five hundred pounds as aforesaid, I do promise to pay unto the said C.D. (or the bringer hereof) within six month next after the date of these presents. In witness whereof I have subscribed to the same at Amsterdam the 10 of July 1622, *stilo novo*.

See H.A. Street, *The Foundations of Legal Liability* (1906) II, p. 365 & n. 6, and J.M. Holden, *The History of Negotiable Instruments in English Law* (1955) p. 67.

English courts, while acknowledging the cause of action of the original promisee, were reluctant to recognize the transferability of promissory notes. Their transferability on the same footing as bills of exchange was recognized by statute (3 & 4 Anne, (1704) c. 9).

2.   NEGOTIABLE INSTRUMENTS AND ASSIGNMENT OF CHOSES IN ACTION

Medieval common law did not recognize the transfer of choses in action. As a result, the early bill of exchange (in the form set forth *supra*) or its transfer could not fit into the framework of contemporary general principles of law. Its recognition and development in England is thus attributed to another body of law (the law merchant) which was first developed in the Fair Courts and the Courts of Staples and then (since 1585) by the Court of Admiralty. During the late 16th and early 17th centuries the Common Law Courts took over much of the jurisdiction of the Admiralty Court. In the course of the 17th century the law of negotiable instruments was incorporated into the common law (especially by Lord Holt C.J. and Lord Mansfield C.J.) as a distinct branch that derived its authority from the customs of merchants.

While the law merchant was developing its own concepts of transferability, equity mitigated the rigour of the common law rule against transferability of choses. As Blackburn J. explained in *Crouch* v. *Credit Foncier of England* (1873) LR 8 QB 374, 380:

> The general rule is not disputed that a chose in action cannot be transferred at law at all, but that in equity it may be assigned, though the action at law must be brought by

the assignee in the name of the original contractee. .... Equity will compel the contractee, if he has assigned the contract, to allow his name to be used for this purpose on an indemnity against costs.

A statutory form of assignment was introduced in England by section 25(6) of the Judicature Act 1873, substantially reproduced in s. 54(1) of the Ontario Conveyancing and Law of Property Act, RSO 1970, c. 85 as follows:

Any absolute assignment, made . . . by writing under the hand of the assignor, not purporting to be by way of charge only, of any debt or other legal chose in action of which express notice in writing shall have been given to the debtor . . . is effectual in law. . . .

(The provision has been superseded in England by the slightly revised version contained in the Law of Property Act, 1925 (15 and 16 Geo. 5, c. 5) s. 136.)

Nevertheless, these equitable and statutory responses to the needs of commercial life in no way dispensed with the need for a law of bills of exchange. For "the general rule, both at law and in equity, is that no person can acquire title, either to chose in action or any other property, from one who has himself no title to it" (*Crouch* v. *Credit Foncier of England, supra* at 380). Likewise, under the statutory provisions cited above, the assignee takes the debt or chose in action "subject to all equities that would have been entitled to priority over the right of the assignee if this section had not been enacted". In other words, the vital difference between the transfer of a chose and the transfer of a negotiable instrument lies in the qualities of negotiability attached to the latter instrument.

3. THE QUALITIES OF NEGOTIABILITY

To be negotiable an instrument must be "transferable by any person holding it, so as by delivery thereof to give a good title to 'any person honestly acquiring it' " (*London & County Banking Co.* v. *River Plate Bank* (1888) 20 QBD 232 at 238). "Negotiability" is thus characterized by (a) the "reification" or "thingification" of the obligation embodied in the instrument so as to make it transferable by the physical delivery of the instrument (with or without any necessary endorsement) rather than by mere agreement or notification ("transferability" or "formal negotiability") and (b) the ability of a transferor with a defective title to the instrument to confer a good title thereto upon a bona fide transferee for value ("material negotiability").

Negotiability was designed to facilitate the use of the instrument as a mechanism for payment by equating the rules applicable to it with those applicable to money. Money has always been transferable by delivery and "the very act of circulation destroys the title of the former owner and creates a title '*de novo*' in the person acquiring the coins in discharge of a monetary obligation. The vulgar proverb 'money does not stink' may be a cynical estimate of society but it has a sound legal foundation": Crossely Vaines, *Personal Property* (5th ed., 1973) p. 161. As negotiable instruments "form part of the currency of the country" (*Foster* v. *Mackinnon* (1869) 20 LTR 887, 889), the same rules should apply to them as to currency.

The leading case of *Miller* v. *Race* (1758) 1 Burr. 452, 97 ER 398, involved a contest between the bona fide purchaser of a stolen bank note and its original owner. In holding for the purchaser on the basis of the negotiability of bank notes, Lord Mansfield commented (at 401, ER):

> Now they are not goods, not securities, nor documents for debts, nor are so esteemed: but are treated as money, as cash, in the ordinary course and transaction of business, by the general consent of mankind; which gives them the credit and currency of money, to all intents and purposes. They are as much money, as guineas themselves are; or any other current coin, that is used in common payments, as money or cash.
>
> They pass by a will, which bequeaths all the testator's money or cash; and are never considered as securities for money, but as money itself. Upon Ld. Ailesbury's will, 900£ in bank-notes was considered as cash. On payment of them, whenever a receipt is required, the receipts are always given as for money; not as for securities or notes.
>
> So on bankruptcies, they cannot be followed as identical and distinguishable from money: but are always considered as money or cash.
>
> It is a pity that reporters sometimes catch at quaint expressions that may happen to be dropped at the Bar or Bench; and mistake their meaning. It has been quaintly said, "that the reason why money can not be followed is, because it has no ear-mark:" but this is not true. The true reason is, upon account of the currency of it: it can not be recovered after it has passed in currency. So, in case of money stolen, the true owner can not recover it, after it has been paid away fairly and honestly upon a valuable and bona fide consideration: but before money has passed in currency, an action may be brought for the money itself. There was a case in 1 G. 1, at the sittings, *Thomas* v. *Whip*, before Ld. Macclesfield: which was an action upon assumpsit, by an administrator against the defendant, for money had and received to his use. The defendant was nurse to the intestate during his sickness; and, being alone, conveyed away the money. And Ld. Macclesfield held that the action lay. Now this must be esteemed a finding at least.
>
> Apply this to the case of a bank-note. An action may lie against the finder, it is true; (and it is not at all denied:) but not after it has been paid away in currency. And this point has been determined, even in the infancy of bank-notes; for 1 Salk. 126, M. 10 W. 3, at Nisi Prius, is in point. And Ld. Ch. J. Holt there says that it is "by reason of the course of trade; which creates a property in the assignee or bearer." (And "the bearer" is a more proper expression than assignee.)

4. SOURCES OF NEGOTIABILITY

There is authority for the proposition that qualities of negotiability can be attached to a chose in action by private agreement (negotiability by contract). See, in *Ex parte Asiatic Banking Corporation* (1867) LR 2 Ch. App. 391, at 397 *per* Cairns L.J.:

> Generally speaking, a chose in action assignable only in equity must be assigned subject to the equities existing between the original parties to the contract; but this is a rule which must yield when it appears from the nature or terms of the contract that it must have been intended to be assignable free from and unaffected by such equities.

And also in *Re Goy & Co. Ltd.* [1900] 2 Ch. 149, at 154:

> There is nothing . . . to prevent a debtor from contracting with his creditor that he

will not avail himself against a transferee of any rights which he may possess against the creditor. . . .

(*Cf.* ``negotiability by estoppel'' in *The Colonial Bank* v. *Cady* (1890) 15 App. Cas. 267.)

Nevertheless, the most important source of negotiability is the custom of merchants (*lex mercatoria*, or law merchant). This is the source through which negotiable instruments were originally introduced into England. (See the detailed account of Cockburn C.J. in *Goodwin* v. *Robarts* (1875) LR 10 Ex. 337 at 346.) It is also a source from which new types of negotiable instruments may evolve and be recognized. See e.g. *Goodwin* v. *Robarts, id.* and 1 App. Cas. 476; *Bechuanaland Exploration Company* v. *London Trading Bank Ltd.* [1898] 2 QB 658; and *Edelstein* v. *Schuler & Co.* [1902] 2 KB 144 where the court emphasizes at p. 154 that for recognition of a new mercantile usage ``more depends on the number of the transactions which help to create it than on the time over which the transactions are spread''. A modern mercantile custom will be accepted provided it can be shown that it is generally accepted among merchants. For this ``general usage'' requirement *cf. Easton* v. *London Joint Stock Bank* (1887) 34 Ch. 95, at 113 *per* Bowen L.J.

5. CODIFICATION

FALCONBRIDGE
The Law of Negotiable Instruments in Canada
(1967) p. 2

§3. *Codification in Great Britain.*

It was a matter of especial inconvenience to bankers and merchants that the law relating to negotiable instruments was difficult to ascertain and in some respects uncertain, and a remedy was at last furnished by a codification of this branch of the law.

In the year 1878, M. D. (afterwards Sir Mackenzie) Chalmers published a digest of the law in the form of a series of articles or propositions, supported by illustrative cases. Chalmers says that he found the law to be contained in some 2,500 reported cases and in 17 statutory enactments. His digest was subsequently made the basis of a bill which was introduced in the British Parliament and, after some amendment, enacted as an Act to codify the Law relating to Bills of Exchange, Cheques, and Promissory Notes—its short title being the Bills of Exchange Act, 1882.

The statute made little change in substance, but it effected a great improvement in form, by stating the existing law in a concise and orderly manner. Some points of difficulty were rendered clear, and some matters as to which there was no judicial authority were settled by statutory authority. Although it is impossible for any code to anticipate all questions of difficulty, this statute provides a clear rule for the ordinary questions likely to arise with regard to bills, cheques and notes. . . .

§4. *Adoption of the code in Canada.*

After the passing in the United Kingdom of the Bills of Exchange Act, 1882, the English-speaking provinces of Canada continued for some years to retain the uncodified English law. In Quebec the law on this subject was partially stated in statutory form in the Civil Code of Lower Canada, but even in that province the law of bills, cheques and notes was, generally speaking, English law, and in cases not provided for by the code, the code itself provided that recourse should be had to the law of England.

In the year 1890 an act based upon the Bills of Exchange Act, 1882, was adopted by the Parliament of Canada. When the bill was before Parliament, however, it was found that apart from certain differences between the law of Quebec and that of the other provinces, certain local customs had become established in some of the provinces, and in order to facilitate the adoption of the bill some changes were made in it with a view of perpetuating these local customs. The result is that there are some differences between the Canadian statute and the original statute.

Note: The Scope and Scheme of the Bills of Exchange Act (Canada):

Under s. 91(18) of the British North America Act, 1867 (30 & 31 Vic., c. 3 as amended), the Parliament of Canada has exclusive power to legislate in relation to bills of exchange and promissory notes.

The Bills of Exchange Act (BEA) was enacted pursuant to this authority. The Act applies to bills, notes and cheques, generically referred to (though not in the Act itself) as "negotiable instruments". Note, however, that this is an imprecise use of the expression, as the category of "negotiable instruments" is broader than bills, notes, and cheques governed by the Act. See "Sources of Negotiability", *supra*.

The BEA consists of five parts:

Part I   — General (ss. 3-16);
Part II   — Bills of Exchange (ss. 17-164);
Part III   — Cheques on a Bank (ss. 165-175);
Part IV — Promissory Notes (ss. 176-187); and
Part V   — Consumer Bills and Notes (ss. 188-190) (added in 1970).

Subject to the provisions of Part IV, "the provisions . . . relating to bills of exchange, apply, with necessary modifications, to promissory notes" (s. 186(1)). Also, "[a] cheque is a bill of exchange drawn on a bank, payable on demand. . . . Except as otherwise provided in [Part III] the provisions . . . applicable to a bill of exchange payable on demand apply to a cheque" (s. 165(1), (2)). Thus, with necessary modifications, Part II applies to all negotiable instruments governed by the BEA.

Bills, notes and cheques are not governed exclusively by the BEA. This is acknowledged in s. 10 of the Act, which provides that

> The rules of the common law of England, including the law merchant, save in so far as they are inconsistent with the express provisions of this Act, apply to bills of exchange, promissory notes and cheques.

The following section of this Casebook deals with the sources of the Canadian law of bills and notes and their interaction with each other. These sources are the BEA (a federal statute), rules of common law (including the law merchant) applicable to negotiable instruments, provincial statutes, and those general principles of law which are part of the law of property and civil rights in the various provinces.

6. The Law of Bills and Notes: Interaction Between Federal and Provincial Laws

The term "law of bills and notes" is ambiguous. A bill or note is an obligation (or obligations) contained in a chattel (a tangible piece of paper) as well as a negotiable instrument. As such it is subject to two main sets of laws. One is the general law dealing with property and obligations, the other is the special law (whose historical roots are in the old law merchant) dealing with the specific characteristics of the bill or note as a negotiable instrument. The former set of laws, dealing with the property and the obligatory elements of the instrument, is "the law of bills and notes in the wide sense". The latter set of laws, which includes the form, issue, negotiation and discharge of bills and notes, is "the law of bills and notes in the strict sense". The terminology is therefore confusing since "the law of bills and notes in the wide sense" does not include its counterpart "in the strict sense". Rather, both are separate categories. See in general Barak, "The Requirement of consideration for Bills or Notes in Israel" (1967) 2 Israel L. Rev. 499, at 500-05. See also *Falconbridge On Banking and Bills of Exchange* (7th ed., 1969) pp. 456-57.

Apparently, "matters coming within . . . Bills of exchange and promissory notes" assigned to the exclusive jurisdiction of the Parliament of Canada under s. 91(18) of the BNA Act include all subjects governed by the law of bills and notes, whether in the broad sense or in the strict sense. It is unlikely that the BNA Act intended to exclude matters related to the property and obligatory elements of the instrument from the legislative jurisdiction of the federal Parliament. Nonetheless, the "broad sense"/"strict sense" classification is helpful in determining the extent to which provincial laws apply in situations involving bills and notes.

There are three classes of situations where provincial law could apply:

1. The federal BEA often provides for the determination of certain questions (falling as a rule within the law of bills and notes in the wide sense) under provincial law. Thus s. 47(1) provides that "[c]apacity to incur liability as a party to a bill is coextensive with capacity to contract." Again, s. 53(1)(a) provides that "[v]aluable consideration for a bill may be constituted by . . . any consideration sufficient to support a simple contract." Capacity and consideration in relation to bills and notes are therefore determined under the general law of contract in each province (see Chapter 15(C)(1) *infra*).

2. As a matter of construction of the Bills of Exchange Act it has been held that subjects not provided for expressly in the Act, and not constituting part of the law of bills and notes in the strict sense, are governed by general provincial laws: see Falconbridge, pp. 456-57. Section 10 of the Act, which appears to conflict with this position, has been held to be restricted to the law of bills and notes in the strict sense. For example, in *Guy v. Paré* (1892) 1 Que. SC 443, it was held that whether an endorser is discharged by the

giving of time by the holder to the maker after the maturity of the note is to be determined according to the general law of the province governing rights of a surety.

3. In general, "subjects which in one aspect and for one purpose fall within [provincial jurisdiction under] s. 92 [of the BNA Act], may in another aspect and for another purpose fall within s. 91" (*Hodge* v. *The Queen* (1883) 9 AC 117 at 130 (PC)). This is the "double aspect doctrine". Thereunder, provincial legislation falling under "matters coming within . . . Property and civil rights in the province", assigned to the exclusive legislative power of each provincial legislature under s. 92(13) of the BNA Act, could also relate to bills and notes, in the wide or strict sense of the law applicable to them. Nonetheless, under the doctrine of "federal paramountcy", "where there are inconsistent or conflicting federal and provincial laws, it is the federal law which prevails": P.W. Hogg, *Constitutional Law of Canada* (1977) p. 102. This has the following consequences:

(a) Insofar as "matters coming within . . . Bills of exchange and promissory notes" are concerned, whether they are part of the law of bills and notes in the wide or in the strict sense, the express provisions of the BEA supersede any conflicting or inconsistent provincial law even when the provincial law is by itself a valid exercise of provincial legislative power. See *Attorney-General for Alberta and Winstanley* v. *Atlas Lumber Co.* [1941] 1 DLR 625 (SCC).

b) Common law rules which are part of the law of bills and notes in the strict sense (whose validity is provided for by s. 10 of the BEA: Falconbridge *supra* at pp. 456-57) prevail over valid provincial laws. This is true even where the latter are embodied in a provincial statute which purports to supersede such common law rules. An example of a common rule which prevails over inconsistent or conflicting provincial law is the finality of payment with respect to payment made by a payor bank in ignorance of a forged drawer's signature. This special rule differs from the general law which governs the recovery of money paid under a mistake of fact: *Barclays Bank* v. *W.J. Simms Son and Cooke (Southern) Ltd.* [1980] 2 WLR 218, 237 (QBD).

B. TYPES OF NEGOTIABLE INSTRUMENTS AND THEIR COMMON USES

Listed below are the most common types of negotiable instruments currently in use.

1. *Promissory Note.* A promissory note is an instrument which contains an unconditional promise in writing signed by the maker promising to pay a certain sum of money as defined in s. 176(1). A specimen promissory note is reproduced below:

3415 YONGE ST. & TEDDINGTON PARK AVE.
TORONTO, ONTARIO
M4N 2M9

$ _____   _____ 19___

ON DEMAND _____ PROMISE TO PAY

TO THE ORDER OF THE TORONTO–DOMINION BANK AT   **THE TORONTO-DOMINION BANK**   HERE,

THE SUM OF _____ DOLLARS
WITH INTEREST PAYABLE MONTHLY AT THE RATE OF   % PER ANNUM UNTIL PAID.

CANCELLED

John Smith

VALUE RECEIVED

FORM 11418 (5-73)

Here, John Smith is the maker and the T-D Bank is the payee. See s. 176 and s. 179. Can the maker and payee be the same person?

2. *Bill of Exchange.* Under s. 17(1), a bill of exchange is an unconditional order in writing, addressed by one person to another, signed by the person giving it, requiring the person to whom it is addressed to pay, on demand or at a fixed or determinable future time, a sum certain in money to or to the order of a specified person, or to the bearer. See specimen below:

DUE _____	FORWARDING BANK & NUMBER
_____ 19____	
_____ AFTER DATE FOR VALUE RECEIVED PAY TO	
THE ORDER OF _____ Ed Jones _____ THE SUM OF	
	RECEIVING BANK & NUMBER
TO ____ Jane Doe _____	
	John Smith
FORM 1/052 (9-65)	

Here, John Smith is the drawer, Jane Doe is the drawee, and Ed Jones is the payee (s. 17). If the drawee signifies his assent to the order in due form he is the acceptor (s. 35). Can. (1) a bill be made payable to the drawer or the drawee, or (2) the drawer and the drawee be the same person? (See ss. 19, 26, 20, and 18(2).)

It should be noted that for the purpose of the Act the maker of a note is deemed to correspond with the acceptor of a bill, and the first endorser of a note is deemed to correspond with the drawer of an accepted bill payable to the drawer's order [s. 186(2)].

3. *Bank Draft.* A bank draft takes the form of an order to pay a sum of money addressed by a banker to himself or another bank (see specimen below).

THE TORONTO-DOMINION BANK

_____ 19____

PAY TO THE ORDER OF ____ SPECIMEN ____ Jane Doe _____ $ _____

_____ **DOLLARS**

To: Iceland Bank _____

FOR **THE TORONTO-DOMINION BANK**

Mr. X ⃝   ⃝   ⃝

AUTHORIZED OFFICER   NUMBER

COUNTERSIGNED

Here, if John Smith as remitter purchased a bank draft, the T-D Bank is the drawer, the Iceland Bank is the drawee, and Jane Doe is the payee. Is this instrument contemplated by the Act? In the most usual case, a bank draft is drawn by a bank branch on its head office or on another branch. Is this instrument a bill of exchange *vis-à-vis* the bank? See s. 26.

4. *Cheque*. A cheque is a bill of exchange drawn on a bank payable on demand. See s. 165(1) and specimen cheque below.

THE TORONTO-DOMINION BANK

123 ANY STREET
CITY, PROVINCE

PERSONAL
CHEQUING
ACCOUNT

No. _____

_____ 19 ____

PAY TO THE
ORDER OF _____ $ _____

_____ DOLLARS

JOHN SPECIMEN

_____

4⑆ ⑈12345⑈004⑆ 0234⑈0234567⑈

---

5. *Traveller's cheque*. This is an instrument available in various denominations purchased by a traveller from an issuer and bearing an authorized signature of its issuer. It includes two blank spaces. In the first space the purchaser is required to sign his name at the time of the purchase of the instrument in the presence of the issuer. The second blank space will be signed by the purchaser-traveller when he cashes the instrument or negotiates it to a person of his choice. This second signature is called the "countersignature". The undertaking of the issuer is to pay the amount specified in the instrument when the instrument is presented for payment provided the "countersignature" is identical to the signature in the first blank space.

The following is a specimen of a traveller's cheque issued by the American Express Company. What is its legal nature? Is it a cheque? Bill of Exchange? Promissory note? See *Emerson* v. *American Express Co.* (1952) 90 A.2d 236 (DC Mun. CA); Ellinger, "Travellers' Cheques and the Law" (1969) 19 Univ. Tor. LJ 132; and Stassen, "The Legal Nature of Travellers' Cheques" (1978) 95 SALJ 180.

6. *Personal Money Order.* A personal money order is purchased from an issuer in a blank form made out for a specified amount. Unlike a traveller's cheque it does not bear the issuer's signature and the amount is not preprinted but rather is filled in by the issuer when the instrument is actually purchased. Having properly signed it, the purchaser (the "sender" in the specimen below) can use the instrument in payment to a payee of his choice.

The following is a specimen of a personal money order before its purchase from the Toronto Dominion Bank. What is its legal character? *Cf. Dominion Express Co.* v. *Krigbaum* (1909) 18 OLR 533, dealing with "express money orders", and *Fine Art Society* v. *Union Bank of London Ltd.* (1886) 17 QBD 705, dealing with post office orders.

PERSONAL MONEY ORDER   PERSONAL MONEY ORDER

THE TORONTO-DOMINION BANK

_____ 19 _____

PAY TO THE
ORDER OF_____

NOT EXCEEDING
FIVE HUNDRED
DOLLARS

SPECIMEN

ADDRESS OF SENDER   SIGNATURE OF SENDER

PERSONAL MONEY ORDER   PERSONAL MONEY ORDER

The Use of Negotiable Instruments in Payment of Goods

1. A promissory note is typically used for the payment of goods in a credit sale. The buyer makes the note payable to the order of the seller and promises to pay on stated dates.

2. A cheque is typically used in a cash sale. The buyer draws the cheque on a bank with whom he has an account payable to the order of the seller. A post-dated cheque (i.e., a cheque bearing a date later than the date of its issuance; see discussion in chapter 17 *infra*) is designed to be presented for payment on the date it bears. As such it serves the same function as a promissory note in a credit transaction. For more on cheques, see *infra*, chapter 17.

3. A bill of exchange drawn by a seller on the buyer (or the buyer's bank) to the seller's own order is a payment device in transactions between distant merchants. The seller forwards the bill to the buyer or his bank together with documents relating to the goods through banking channels. Unless the bill is accepted (or paid) by the drawee as agreed the buyer will not obtain possession of the goods. The transaction is called a "documentary sale". See further *infra*, chapter 19(A), and *supra*, chapter 11.

4. Bank drafts are used in cash purchases when the seller is not willing to rely on the buyer's credit. The instrument is payable to the seller's order (or to the buyer's order and then endorsed by him to the seller) and signed by a bank as a drawer. The buyer who purchases the instrument from the bank (and who does not sign the instrument) is called "remitter" (a term which goes back to the law merchant and does not appear in the BEA).

5. Personal money orders (further discussed in chapter 17(C), note 6 *infra*) and travellers' cheques are used in cash sales. They are hybrid forms of instruments whose legal character has not yet been fully settled.

C. ESSENTIAL CHARACTERISTICS OF A NEGOTIABLE INSTRUMENT

To be governed by the BEA an instrument must be a bill of exchange, a cheque, or a promissory note. Its form must comply with the requirement of s. 17(1) (if it is a bill), s. 165(1) (if it is a cheque), or s. 176(1) (if it is a note). In *Korea Exchange Bank* v. *Debenhams* [1979] 1 Ll. L. Rep. 100 at 102 (QBD), Mr. Justice Donaldson was of the opinion that where an instrument ''appears to be intended to be a bill of exchange . . . a Court should [not] be astute to detect ambiguities. . . .'' He was reversed by the Court of Appeal: ''The bill, to achieve the required certainty, must . . . contain provisions as [required by the Act]'': [1979] 1 Ll. L. Rep. 548 at 553 (*per* Megaw L.J.). ''[C]ertainty is a great object in commercial instruments; and unless they carry their own validity on the face of them they are not negotiable'': *Carlos* v. *Fancourt* (1794) 5 TR 482, 101 ER 272 at 274.

Where the formal requirements of the Act are met, the instrument will be governed by the BEA. The only possible exception is an instrument governed (or created?) by another statute which as a matter of statutory construction is excluded from the coverage of the BEA (see e.g. the majority decision in *Bank of Canada* v. *Bank of Montreal* [1977] 1 SCR 1148 dealing with pre-1967 Bank of Canada banknotes).

Even though the formal requirements are not satisfied, an instrument is not necessarily void or invalid. It is then simply not governed by the provisions of the Act. The instrument could still be effective under the general law of contract outside the Act.

The following is a discussion of the essential elements of a negotiable instrument.

1. EXPRESSION OF ORDER OR PROMISE

A bill or cheque is an order to pay and must be expressed in imperative terms (ss. 17(1), 165(2)). Hence a mere authority or permission to pay is not a bill: see *Rex* v. *Ellor* (1784) 1 Leach 323, 168 ER 264. The addition of such words as ''please'' or other terms of courtesy will not prevent a document from being a bill if it is in other respects an order.

A promissory note is a promise to pay (s. 176(1)). While the use of the word ''promise'' is not essential, there must be some words implying a promise to pay. Hence, a mere acknowledgement of indebtedness without words expressing or implying a promise is not a note (*Sheehan* v. *Mercantile Trust Co. of Can.* (1919) 45 OLR 422). Will the letters ''I.O.U.'' suffice?

2. UNCONDITIONAL ORDER OR PROMISE

A bill, cheque or note must be unconditional at its inception (ss. 17, 165(2), 176), and subsequent fulfillment of the condition does not make it unconditional. The instrument must *on its face* be payable absolutely and cannot be expressed as being subject to a condition or contain words which limit or modify the order or promise to pay. Does s. 18(1) add anything to the statutory definitions of bill and note?

While the order or promise to pay must be unconditional, it seems that the drawer is free to add a stipulation operative only as between himself and the payee. For example, a cheque bearing at the foot the words "receipt at back hereof must be signed, which signature will be taken as an indorsement of this cheque" (*Nathan v. Ogdens Ltd.* (1905) 93 LTR 553) or a cheque bearing on its face the words "to be retained" (*Roberts and Co.* v. *Marsh* [1915] 1 KB 42) have been held to be negotiable instruments. Does this reasoning also apply to a stipulation by the maker of a note (rather than the drawer of a bill) addressed to the payee and appearing on the instrument itself?

An order to pay out of a particular fund is conditional, but an unqualified order to pay, coupled with an indication of a particular fund out of which the drawee is to reimburse himself, or a particular account that is to be debited with the amount, is unconditional (s. 17(3)(*a*)). Hence a mere reference to a particular fund or account that is to be debited or charged will not render an order conditional if the order itself is not modified or limited, and the debiting or charging of the particular fund or account is only a matter between the drawer and drawee. An order to pay "out of money due to me on the first of June for materials furnished" is not a bill of exchange. (See *Ward* v. *Royal Can. Ins. Co.* (1892) 2 Que. SC 229 (CA). What is the function of s. 17(3)(*a*) today?

Similarly, an unqualified order to pay coupled with a statement of the transaction which gives rise to the bill is unconditional (s. 17(3)(*b*)). Hence a party could make an order to pay followed by the words "on account of lumber to be shipped" (*Merchants Bank of Canada* v. *Bury* (1915) 21 DLR 495), provided the order to pay is unqualified. One must look at the face of the instrument to see if the order is unconditional and not at the total contractual relationship of the parties. See e.g. *Williams & Glyn's Bank Ltd.* v. *Belkin Packaging Ltd.* (1979) 8 BLR 238 (BCSC).

If an instrument contains an order to perform any act in addition to the payment of money, it is not a bill of exchange even if there is an unconditional order (s. 17(2)). However, it appears that this provision has been severely limited so as not to prevent the mere addition of words to the face of the instrument as long as there is no order of any act to be done in addition to the payment of money. (See *Kirkwood* v. *Carroll* [1903] 1 KB 531.)

Under section 176(3) a note is not "invalid" by reason only that it contains a pledge of collateral security. (Query: is "valid" the right word to use here?) The instrument will still be a note under the Act even though there is a statement that collateral has been given to secure obligations of an obligor on the instrument, or that in default of those obligations the holder may realize on or dispose of the collateral. Section 176(3) does not mean that the note itself may be explicitly stated to be a security (as otherwise the promise is conditional: *Hall* v. *Merrick* (1877) 40 UCQB 566). Rather it means that a mere reference in the note to a pledge of collateral security does not render it conditional.

The use of lien notes, that is, integrated documents each purporting to combine a conditional sale agreement with a promissory note, has raised questions as to the existence of an "unconditional promise". The practice is described hereafter. Are the two cases which follow Professor Ziegel's comment reconcilable?

JACOB ZIEGEL
"Range v. Corporation De Finance Belvédère — Consumer Notes . . ."
(1970) 48 Can. B. Rev. 309 at 310

When lien notes were first introduced in Canada the draftsmen frequently copied the American device of introducing the agreement with a promise by the buyer to pay the purchase price by the agreed instalments. The promise itself satisfied the formal requirements of a promissory note in section 176 of the Bills of Exchange Act. The difficulty arose because the promise was usually followed by the recital of the other terms of the agreement, thus inviting the inevitable argument that the promise to pay was not unconditional and the document containing it not a negotiable instrument. Still, for reasons that are not altogether clear, the draftsmen were reluctant to abandon the concept of an integrated chattel paper which incorporated a negotiable promise and created at the same time a security interest in the goods sold in favour of the seller. Perhaps they still hoped to persuade the Canadian courts to attribute a negotiable quality to the whole lien note (obviously a very desirable step from the financial community's point of view), as happened in the United States of America. Or they may have felt that a separate promissory note would introduce new kinds of complications — the note might, mistakenly or otherwise, end up in different hands from the lien agreement or the note might be subject to one set of rules and the agreement to another. We really do not know.

In any event, the draftsmen retained the single sheet concept but introduced two minor and, as it transpired, crucial modifications. They required the buyer to sign the promise to pay separately from the lien agreement and they also pointedly referred in the lien agreement to the fact that the buyer had given a promissory note for the balance of his indebtedness. To fasten the hatch still more securely they also inserted what is commonly referred to as a "cut-off" clause, that is, a clause in which the buyer agrees that any holder of the note is not to be affected by any equities between him and the promisee of the note.

MONTICELLO STATE BANK v. KILLORAN
(1920) 3 WWR 542, 16 Alta. LR 341 (AD); aff'd 61 SCR 528, [1921] 57 DLR 359

IVES, J.: This is an appeal from the judgment of Walsh, J. [1921] 3 WWR 17. The plaintiff claims the price of a stallion conditionally bought by defendant from one Dygert under a conditional sale agreement and in the alternative the payment of two certain promissory notes made and given Dygert by defendant. Dygert has assigned his rights under the agreement to the plaintiff and has endorsed and delivered the two promissory notes. The learned trial Judge dismissed the action on the ground that as the property in the chattel had not passed the risk remained in the plaintiff and it could not recover, the horse being dead. With respect, I think that The Sale of Goods Ordinance, CO 1915, ch. 39, does not apply. In my opinion the issue is as to defendant's liability as the maker of the promissory notes. The only connection between these notes and the conditional sale agreement is that they are found on the same sheet of paper. But they are distinctly and separately signed and by the expressed intention of the parties intended to be separate from the agreement. The agreement begins:

"It is hereby agreed by and between (the parties) . . . that the goods and chattels (stallion) are received by the subscriber on the following terms and conditions; namely — that the price thereof, which is $1,700, and for which the *subscriber shall give his promissory notes to the promisee*, shall be payable as provided for in such notes which are as follows" (here follow dates, amounts and dates of maturity of the two promissory notes sued upon, and the agreement continues):

"That these notes or any of them as well *as renewals* thereof may be discounted, pledged or hypothecated by the promisee and in every such case payment thereof is to be made to the holder of the notes . . . and no holder of said notes or any of them . . . shall be affected by the state of accounts between the subscriber [the defendant] and the promisee or by any equities existing between the subscriber and the promisee but shall be and shall be deemed to be a holder in due course and for value."

In my opinion the notes are bills of exchange within The Bills of Exchange Act, RSC 1906, ch. 119, and this plaintiff is the holder for value. Admittedly here the only defence is absence of consideration and the facts clearly establish a sufficient consideration.

Appeal allowed.

ON APPEAL TO SCC: (1921) 61 SCR 528, 57 DLR 359:

IDINGTON J.: The appellant signed what are in due form two ordinary promissory notes for $700 each. That was followed on each of the same sheets of paper at the respective heads of which each of said promissory notes had been written and signed by appellant, by an agreement purporting to be made between said appellant and Dygert, the payee of each of the said promissory notes.

Each of these agreements was signed by appellant but not by Dygert.

Each of the same has indorsed on it an affidavit, purporting to have been sworn to by Dygert; first stating that he is the owner or bailor of the goods mentioned in the written agreement; that said copy of agreement is a true and correct copy of the agreement of which it purports to be a copy, and that

> 3. The said agreement truly sets forth the agreement between myself and the said F.V. Killoran the parties thereto, and that the said agreement therein set forth is *bona fide* and not to protect the goods in question mentioned therein against the creditors of the buyer or bailee.

These promissory notes were indorsed to another party who re-indorsed to respondent who sued to recover same.

The learned trial judge treated each of these promissory notes, and what followed, as one document, and together as an ordinary lien note.

He then applied or sought to apply sections 9 and 22 of the "Sales of Goods Ordinance" of Alberta thereto and found that the effect thereof, in the event of the death of the stallion, (which was the property agreed to be sold) and which event took place before payment of the said promissory notes, was that the obligation to pay ceased, and dismissed the action.

In the Appellate Division this judgment was reversed and judgment given for the respondent for the amount of the said promissory notes and interest with costs.

Against that judgment this appeal is taken.

The said alleged promissory notes I must hold to be in law promissory notes, and the respective agreements following each, a merely collateral agreement which may or may not have some operative effect between the parties thereto, but cannot effect, even with notice thereof to the respondent taking them in due course, its rights to recover.

In each of these agreements was a clause designed to stop the appellant from denying that indorsees in due course could be otherwise than such.

In my view it is not necessary to follow up all the manifold views that may be taken of the curiously worded agreement.

The respondent was not a party thereto. There was no proof of failure of consideration, nor could there be under such very peculiar circumstances.

The whole contrivance of each of the said supplementary documents and all that followed each, may, if persisted in as a mode of doing business, lead to much litigation, and may result in disappointment to those using it when that has run its course, but for the present case all that has to be determined is that each of the documents first signed is a promissory note, to the suit upon which no effectual answer has been set up.

Of the curiosities I have found in my search for what might be an answer, I may refer to the cases cited by Byles on Bills, 17th ed., page 251. And of these the case of *Salmon* v. *Webb* [(1852) 3 HL Cas. 510], in its essential features, including the non-execution of the agreement by the promisee, alike to this, determines in principle how a mere collateral agreement may fail to operate against those holding in due course.

I need not enlarge but may, in deference to the argument presented by counsel for appellant, say that I doubt if his contention for the narrow meaning he claimed for the phrase

> any equities existing between the subscriber and the promisee

used in the said agreements, so called, is tenable.

DUFF J.: I have no difficulty in concurring with the view of the Appellate Division that the instruments sued upon are promissory notes. In each case there is, it is true, on the same piece of paper one of these instruments and a collateral agreement, but the collateral agreement is no part of the instrument sued upon. By its express terms, indeed, it is not to qualify the absolute obligation of the promissor or to affect the contractual rights of the parties in such a way as to impair the negotiability of the note.

ANGLIN J.: Assuming in the appellant's favour, but without so deciding, that although there is much in the terms of the documents to support the contrary view, the instruments sued upon were not promissory notes, the agreements in my opinion make it clear that the respondent, as a holder with whom the notes had been discounted, is entitled to all the rights which would have attached to its position were the instruments promissory notes of which it was the holder in due course. I cannot understand for what other purposes it was stipulated that

> no holder of said notes by or to whom . . . said notes . . . have been discounted . . . shall be affected by the state of accounts between the subscriber and the promisee or by any equities existing between the subscriber and the promisee, but shall be and shall be deemed to be a holder in due course and for value of the notes held by him.

As "a holder in due course," the respondent is, in my opinion, entitled to recover, whatever might have been the rights of R. F. Dygert had the notes remained in his hands.

BRODEUR J.: Killoran agreed to purchase from a man named Dygert a horse for $1,700 on which he made a part payment of $300 and signed for the balance of the purchase price two instruments which I might, for the sake of this decision, call lien notes. There is a difference of opinion in the courts below as to whether these instruments should not be considered as promissory notes. But I do not feel obliged in view of the conclusion I have reached to decide this point.

These instruments stipulate that the property of the horse would not pass until the balance of the purchase price would be paid and they contain the following clause:

> These notes . . . may be discontinued, pledged or hypothecated by the promisee and in every such case payment thereof is to be made to the holder of the notes instead of the promisee, and *no holder* of the said notes . . . shall be affected by . . . any equities existing between the subscriber and the promisee, *but shall be, and shall be deemed to be a holder in due course* and for value of the notes held by him.

Dygert indorsed these instruments and besides made a written assignment of them to the plaintiff who now sues Killoran, who signed them.

Killoran contends that the sale of the horse has been avoided under the provisions of the "Sale of Goods Ordinance Act," which declares, in section 9, that

> where there is an agreement to sell specific goods and subsequently the goods, without any fault on the part of the seller or buyer, perish before the risk passes to the buyer, the agreement is thereby avoided.
>
> Unless otherwise agreed the goods remain at the seller's risk until the property therein is transferred to the buyer; but when the property therein is transferred to the buyer the goods are at the buyer's risk whether delivery has been made or not.

In the present case, the goods were delivered, but the property thereof remained with the vendor, they are at his risk and between the vendor and the purchaser the sale should be considered as avoided since the horse sold died before it became the absolute property of the purchaser. *Res perit domino.*

But as far as the transferee is concerned, the situation is different, in view of the provisions of the contract made by the appellant. The latter has agreed that the notes could be transferred and that the holder should be considered as a holder in due course in spite of the notice he might have of the contract between the vendor and purchaser. He contracted himself out of the right of resorting as against the assignee of the creditor to his equities against the creditor himself. (*Leake on Contracts*, 6th ed., page 865).

This holder should then be considered in the light of this agreement as if he were a holder in due course without notice under the provisions of the Bills of Exchange Act. He can recover the payment thereof, though the sale of goods which has brought the signature of these instruments is avoided.

I am of the opinion that the plaintiff is entitled to recover.

MIGNAULT J.: I have duly considered all that Mr. Scott said in his very able argument for the appellant and in the memorandum which he has since filed. Nevertheless, in my opinion, the appeal cannot be sustained.

The promissory notes sued on, although printed on the same sheet of paper as the agreement for the sale of the stallion, are, I think, severable from this agreement, and constitute perfectly valid promissory notes which could be transferred, as was done here, by indorsement. Consequently even if the contract was terminated between the parties by the death of the stallion, the rights of the respondent as holder in due course of these notes are unaffected thereby.

I also concur in the reasons for judgment of my brother Anglin, as a further ground for the dismissal of this appeal.

Appeal dismissed.

Questions:

1   What is the ratio of the *Killoran* case? Is it sound?

2   Is the cut-off clause relevant in determining the unconditionality of the engagement?

Note the treatment of the subject as well as the application of *Killoran* in the case which follows:

RANGE v. BELVÉDÈRE FINANCE CORP.
[1969] SCR 492, (1969) 5 DLR (3d) 257 (SCC)

PIGEON J. (for the court) (translation): On April 7, 1960, the appellant signed an order for a fur coat for his wife. The total price, including tax, was $792, payable in 24 instalments of $33 each, starting on May 10th. When signing this order, addressed to Durand Fourrures Inc., he also signed a "conditional sales contract" at the same time, using a printed form supplied by United Loan Corporation, a "finance company". In this document, the vendor was described as Durand & Coutu Enrg., and the first condition printed on the back of the form read as follows:

1. Title to the articles being sold pursuant to this contract shall remain in the vendor

until the full purchase price with respect to this conditional sale has been paid: in the event of default by the purchaser in making payments in accordance with the conditions contained herein, vendor shall have the option of demanding immediate payment of the instalments which have fallen due, or of repossessing the said articles without liability, and without being required to repay money already received by it on account of the purchase price under this conditional sale, in which case purchaser shall not be liable for the balance of the purchase price owing on this conditional sale.

The total amount of the deferred payments was shown as $792 payable at the office of United Loan in 24 monthly instalments of $33 each, beginning on May 10, 1960, with the following stipulation:

A negotiable promissory note has been delivered by the purchaser to the vendor as evidence of the said total deferred payments, but not in payment thereof.

In fact, there was only one document, the "note" comprising the lower portion of the page, the top portion of which was entitled "Conditional Sales Contract". There was only a perforated line separating the two portions. On the left-hand side, the words "Negotiable Instrument" were printed sideways on the "note", and on the back there was a printed endorsement to the order of United Loan Corp. The vendor's signature was inserted in the appropriate space, and below this can also be seen an endorsement in the name of United Loan Corp. Only when this action was commenced did the respondent detach the "note" from the contract.

When the order and the conditional sales contract were signed, the vendor verbally promised to deliver the fur coat in two or three weeks. In fact it was never delivered, and the vendor made an assignment in bankruptcy a few months later. On and after April 13th, however, the conditional sales contract, including the note, was in the possession of United Loan Corp. at its Montreal office. On April 26th the latter delivered it along with a large number of other similar instruments, to the Imperial Bank, as collateral security for loans exceeding one million dollars.

When signing the order and the conditional sales contract, the appellant also signed a series of cheques in the amount of $33 each, payable to the order of Durand & Coutu Enrg., on each of the instalment dates. These cheques (or, I should say, these drafts: *Leduc* v. *Banque d'Hochelaga* [1926] 1 DLR 433, [1926] SCR 76) were endorsed, and United Loan was in possession of them, thereby enabling it to cash the first two. After that, the appellant stopped payment on the remaining cheques, so that payment was refused, and threats of legal action obtained no result. It should be added that prior to the first payment falling due, United Loan knew that the coat had not been delivered; by telephone, one of its employees had asked the appellant's wife if her coat had been delivered to her, and she answered in the negative.

The following year, United Loan itself became insolvent, and on October 19, 1961, the trustee for the holders of its guaranteed notes, with the concurrence of the bank, sold to the respondent a certain number of claims, including the one against the appellant. Upon execution of this agreement, the conditional sales contract, along with the "note" which had never been detached therefrom, was delivered to the respondent. An account card was also delivered to it, indicating that only the first two monthly payments had been received, and the words "non-delivery" also appeared on the card. The respondent detached the "note", and began an action based solely on it, alleging that it was a holder in due course.

• • •

It must still be determined, therefore, whether or not the instrument forming the subject-matter of this action is truly a "bill of exchange" within the meaning of the Bills of Exchange Act. To so qualify, it must be unconditional (s. 176(1)). Clearly, however, the instrument in question is not unconditional, unless it is to be considered independently of the conditional sales contract. If, on the other hand, the note and the contract are considered as a whole, the first condition indicates that the promise to pay is conditional: in the event of repossession of the article sold, the purchaser is exonerated from further liability. There is no doubt that the same result must obtain in the event of non-delivery. The evidence indicates that the respondent acquired rights arising out of the conditional sales contract and the "note" considered as a whole. Notices were published by it as if it were a conditional sale. Clearly it wished to be in a position to exercise rights arising out of the contract of sale, as well as those arising out of the "note". Only when it contemplated instituting legal proceedings, did it detach the "note", in order to argue that it should be considered as a separate and unconditional contract. We need not inquire what the situation would be if the respondent, and the bank prior to it, had taken the "note" after it had been detached from the contract. What was transferred in this case was the entire documentation as a whole, and upon examining this, it is impossible to conclude that the purchaser's promise is unconditional. The instrument in question, therefore, is not a bill of exchange.

It must also be noted that the contract produced in the case at bar differs from the one which was associated with the note forming the subject-matter of the decision of this Court in *Killoran* v. *Monticello State Bank*, 57 DLR 359, 61 SCR 528, [1921] 1 WWR 988. That contract contains the following provision [p. 362 DLR, p. 532 SCR]:

> These notes . . . may be discounted, pledged or hypothecated by the promisee and in every such case payment thereof is to be made to the holder of the notes instead of the promisee, and *no holder* of the said notes . . . shall be affected by . . . any equities existing between the subscriber and the promisee, *but shall be, and shall be deemed to be a holder in due course* and for value of the notes held by him.

There, it was expressly stipulated that the obligation arising with respect to the note was unconditional, and would enure to the benefit of any holder of the note, notwithstanding anything which might take place between the purchaser and the vendor as a result of the conditional sale. No such provision appears in the case at bar, and I would even go so far as to say that the clause in the contract relating to the "note" implies the contrary.

For these reasons, I would allow the appeal, reverse the judgment of the

Court of Appeal, and affirm the judgment of the Superior Court dismissing the action, the whole with costs against the respondent in all Courts.

Appeal allowed.

Notes and Questions:

1   For a critical comment on this case, see Ziegel, (1970) 48 Can. B. Rev. 309.

2   *Range* was followed in *Traders Group Ltd.* v. *Fulkerth* (1972) 25 DLR (3d) 452 (Alta. AD). In that case, as construed by the court, the conditional sales contract relieved the buyer of any obligation to pay if the goods were not delivered. The majority of the court was also of the view that the parties did not intend the contract and the note to operate separately, with the result that the buyer's promise was not unconditional. Further reliance was put on the seize or sue provision of the Alberta Conditional Sales Act, which extinguished liability on the instrument on reposses-sion of the goods. Do you agree with this analysis? See also *Bank of Montreal* v. *White & White* (1976) 10 Nfld. PEI R 346 (Nfld. CA).

3   *Range* was distinguished, and not followed, in a case where the conditional sale contract contained a cut-off clause benefiting an assignee (*British Acceptance Corp. Ltd.* v. *Hansen* (1974) 44 DLR (3d) 421 (Alta. CA)), or where the promissory note and the conditional sale contract appeared as two separate documents (*I.A.C. Ltd.* v. *Donald E. Hirtle Transport Ltd.* (1977) 78 DLR (3d) 90 (NSSC TD); aff'd (1979) 92 DLR (3d) 87. See also *I.A.C.* v. *Richard* (1975) 51 DLR (3d) 559 (SCC) where de Grandpré J. explained (at 562) that in *Range*, "this Court considered the effect of a note made by a purchaser who had never received the thing promised in the conditional sales contract originally attached to the note, and the evidence showed that the promise to pay could not be treated separately from the conditional sales contract."

4   *Bank of Montreal* v. *Kon* (1978) 82 DLR (3d) 609 (Alta. SC TD) was concerned with promissory notes given in conjunction with chattel mortgages to secure a loan. The borrower argued that *Fulkerth* (discussed in note 2, *supra*) should be followed. Kirby J. was not convinced by the argument. After explaining *Fulkerth* (as well as some previous cases) "on the basis that the notes were given subject to express conditions which were not met", he added (at 614):

> In the instant case, the notes were not a part of the chattel mortgage contracts other than rendering them void upon being paid. The chattel mortgages did not affect the liability assumed under the notes. The Bank of Montreal was not required to redeliver the vehicles but only to release its security upon payment of the notes.

3.   ON DEMAND OR AT A FIXED OR DETERMINABLE FUTURE TIME

A bill of exchange or a promissory note may be payable on demand or at a fixed or determinable future time (ss. 17, 176). A cheque must be payable on demand (s. 165). Note that although section 176(1) "apparently permits a promissory note to be ex-pressed to be payable on demand or at some fixed or determinable future time, it clearly does not permit both of these alternative occasions to be recited in a single instrument capable of being a promissory note": *T.D. Bank* v. *Parkway-Holdings Ltd.* (1968) 1 DLR (3d) 716 (BC SC).

The computation of time is governed by ss. 42 to 46. Where a bill is not payable on demand, three days grace are added to the time of payment fixed by the bill, unless the bill itself provides otherwise (s. 42).

A bill is payable on demand if it is expressed to be payable on demand or on presentation, or if no time of payment is expressed (s. 23).

A bill is payable at a determinable future time if it is payable at sight or at a fixed period after date or sight (s. 24(*a*)) or is payable at a fixed period after the occurrence of a specified event that is certain to happen (s. 24(*b*)). Note that section 24 only qualifies the time requirement and not the unconditionality requirement (see s. 18(1)). Since a bill payable at sight is not a bill payable on demand it is in fact payable three days after presentment.

A bill providing for a date of maturity in the event of acceptable, but failing to provide for the date of maturity in the event of non-acceptance, fails "to achieve the required certainty" and is not a bill of exchange (*Korea Exchange Bank* v. *Debenhams (Central Buying) Ltd.* [1979] 1 Ll. L. Rep. 548 at 553 (CA)). Is this consistent with ss. 23-34?

4.   SUM CERTAIN IN MONEY

A bill (s. 17(1)), note (s. 176(1)) or cheque (s. 165(1), (2)) must be for a sum certain in money. The requirement is governed by s. 28(1), (3). The amount will be a sum certain if the sum is required to be paid with interest by instalments, with or without acceleration, or according to an indicated or ascertainable rate of exchange. Are acceleration clauses compatible with a sum certain? Consider also the following questions:

1   A document entitled "promissory note" and signed in connection with a loan contains the following provision:

> Should insurance requested in connection with this loan be renewed, the under-signed agrees to pay the renewal premium(s) therefor and agrees that the same may be added on to the account balance of this loan and to charge interest thereon as provided herein. . . .

Is the promise for "a sum certain in money"? See *Avco Delta Corp.* v. *MacKay* [1977] 5 WWR 4 (Alta. CA).

2   Is a promise to repay a debt at "least $1,000 per year starting with payment from 1969 crop" a "promissory note" under s. 176(1)? See *MacMillan* v. *MacMillan* (1977) 76 DLR (3d) 760 (Sask. CA).

3   Is a promise to pay "the sum of $16,589.75 with interest . . . on the unpaid principal *from the date of advance*" a promise to pay a sum certain within the definition of a promissory note in s. 176(1)? Should extrinsic evidence be admissible to show the date of advance? See *Macleod Savings and Credit Union Ltd.* v. *Perrett* [1978] 6 WWR 178.

4   Under UCC 3-106 a sum payable "with costs of collection or an attorney's fee or

both upon default" is a "sum certain". Is this consistent with Canadian law? See *A. Macdonald Co.* v. *Dahl* (1919) 46 DLR 250 (Sask. CA).

Where there is a discrepancy between words and figures, the words prevail (s. 28(2)). Hence a bill is valid in which the sum payable is only expressed in figures.

Section 28(2) was recently applied in *Dartmouth Community Credit Union Ltd.* v. *Smith* (1977) 24 NSR (2d) 541 (SC). The court held that when the figures express a larger sum than the words, extrinsic evidence designed to show that the agreed sum is expressed in figures is inadmissible. The court was satisfied that "there is no ambiguity in the words of s. 28(2) . . . and that no question arises as to the exercise of judicial discretion" (*id.* at 550).

A negotiable instrument must be payable in money — i.e., something which is legal tender. A promise to pay "in mercantile lumber . . ." is not sufficient (*Boulton* v. *Jones* (1860), 19 UCQB 517). An instrument providing for the employment and payment of staff in addition to the payment of money is not a promissory note: *Dickie* v. *Singh* (1974) Sc. LT 129.

5. IN WRITING

A bill of exchange must be in writing (s. 17(1)). "Writing" includes words printed, typewritten, painted, engraved, lithographed, photographed, or represented or reproduced by any mode of representing or reproducing words in visible form (Interpretation Act, RSC 1970, c. I-23, s. 28 as am.).

6. PROVISIONS AS TO DRAWEES AND PAYEES

a) Provisions as to Drawees

The drawee must be named or otherwise indicated in a bill with reasonable certainty (s. 20). See also ss. 18(2), 26.

b) Provisions as to Payees

A bill, cheque or note may be payable to order or bearer (s. 21(2)). Where the instrument is payable to order (s. 22(1), (2)) the payee must be named or otherwise indicated with reasonable certainty (s. 21(4)). A bill may be drawn payable to, or to the order of, the drawer, the drawee, or to the holder of an office for the time being (s. 19).

According to Falconbridge, "Extrinsic evidence is admissible to identify the payee when misnamed, or when designated by description only, but not to explain away an uncertainty patent on the bill. . . . [I]f a bill be drawn in the form 'pay — or order' evidence is not admissible to show that C was intended to be the payee, and the bill cannot be recovered on by the person to whom it was given . . . unless he inserts his name in the blank . . . (s. 31). [But *cf. Chamberlain* v. *Young* [1893] 2 QB 206; a bill payable to '. . . order' and endorsed by the drawer was held to be deemed to be payable to the drawer's order.] . . . If the payee is wrongly designated or his name is misspelt, he may endorse the bill as therein described, adding his proper signature; or he may endorse by his own proper signature (s. 64). An instrument payable to 'cash or order' is not a bill of exchange''. (See *Falconbridge On Banking* pp. 479-80.)

An instrument is payable to bearer "that is expressed to be so payable, or on which the only or last endorsement is an endorsement in blank" (s. 21(3); "bearer" is defined in s. 2. See also s. 21(5), discussed in chapter 17(D) *infra*). The effect of s. 21(3) is that if an instrument is originally expressed to be a bearer instrument, it cannot later be converted into an order instrument even if it is specially endorsed. However, if the instrument is payable to order originally, and the payee or any subsequent holder endorses it in blank (i.e., writes his name on the back without naming an endorsee), the instrument becomes payable to bearer. Does such an instrument permanently remain a bearer instrument or can it be reconverted to an order instrument?

Orbit Mining & Trading Co. Ltd. v. *Westminster Bank Ltd.* [1963] 1 QB 794 (CA) stands for the proposition that while a bill payable to "cash or order" is not payable to bearer, an instrument payable to "cash" is payable to bearer: "as 'cash' can give no order the effect is no doubt that it is equivalent to a payment to bearer": *supra* at 811 *per* Sellers L.J. Is this consistent with the language of s. 21(3)?

Chapter 15
Liability on Negotiable Instruments

This chapter deals with the following subjects:
A. The persons entitled to enforce payment against parties liable on an instrument.
B. The statutory liabilities of parties to an instrument and the formalities required to be observed by the holder in order to preserve their liability.
C. The requirement of an enforceable obligation as a prerequisite to the enforcement of liability on a bill or note and the power of certain parties to overcome some defences.
D. Liability on the instrument and the basic transaction — the effect of payment by bill or note.
E. How liability is discharged: discharge of parties and discharge of the instrument.

A. TO WHOM DOES LIABILITY RUN?

1. THE RIGHT AND POWER TO ENFORCE PAYMENT ON A BILL OR NOTE

"In truth, a bill or note . . . is both a chattel and a chose in action. . . . It is a chattel, a tangible scrap of paper. . . . Secondly, a bill or note is a bundle of contracts. Its ownership involves not only the right to possess a thing but the right to sue several persons — maker, drawer and acceptor, indorsers" (Chafee, "Rights in Overdue Paper" (1918) 31 Harv. L. Rev. 1104 at 1109).

A bill or note "may be transferred as a chattel" (*Chalmers On Bills of Exchange* (13th ed., 1964) p. 133). Its true owner "has all the powers of the owner of any other property" (Willis, *The Law of Negotiable Securities* (5th ed., 1930) p. 28). It is also a "chose in action; therefore it may be assigned as a chose in action" (Chalmers *supra* at p. 133). Yet, "[t]he promises and the chattel are inseparable. The right to hold the paper and the right to enforce the obligation are in the same person" (Chafee *supra* at 1109).

The identification of the right to possess a bill or note and the right to sue thereon corresponds to the double nature of a negotiable instrument as a chose in action and a chattel and is produced by the "reification" of the debt claim under the instrument or its ''merger'' into the paper embodying it. This identification is supported by pre-Act English case law: *Stone* v. *Rawlinson* (1745) Willes 558, 125 ER 1320; *Mason* v. *Morgan* (1834) 2 Ad. & E. 30, 111 ER 12; and *Milnes* v. *Dawson* (1850) 5 Exch. 948, 155 ER 413, and is a cornerstone of the concept of negotiable instrument.

Under the BEA, the one who ''may sue on the bill in his own name'' is the ''holder'' (s. 74(*a*)). ''Holder'' is defined in s. 2 as the person to whom the bill is by its terms payable who is in possession of it. He is thus either the payee or endorsee of a bill payable to order or the bearer of an instrument payable to bearer.

''Holder'' according to Chalmers (*supra* at p. 8) ''signifies the mercantile owner of the instrument, who may or may not be the legal owner of it''. An agent for collection of a bill payable to order and properly endorsed to him would thus qualify as a holder.

The Act does not appear to require that the holder's possession must be lawful. Indeed, ''the finder of a bill indorsed in blank . . . who nevertheless can give a valid discharge . . . and also a good title . . .'' (Chalmers *supra* at p. 8; see also ss. 139, 56) is an ''unlawful holder'' who ''must be distinguished from a mere wrongful possessor — for example, a person holding under a forged indorsement, or a person who has stolen a bill payable to the order of another'': Chalmers, *id.* On the other hand, a right to possession, or lawful possession, is essential to success in an action on a bill or note. Thus, while a ''holder . . . may sue on the bill [or note] in his own name'' (s. 74(*a*)), it is overwhelmingly accepted that this provision ''means merely that the holder in an action upon the instrument is not liable to be defeated on the ground that the action has been brought by the wrong party, not that he is entitled to succeed in the action'' (*Falconbridge On Banking and Bills of Exchange* (7th ed., 1969) p. 662). The holder's power to enforce payment on an instrument, as distinguished from his right to sue thereon, further depends on his good title. Lawful possession (derived from the holder's own ownership or from someone else's ownership) is thus essential to the holder's power to enforce payment on the instrument. As to the loss of possession, *cf.* ss. 156-157 dealing with lost instruments.

2.   NEGOTIATION AND TRANSFER OF AN INSTRUMENT

BEA ss. 60-73. See also s. 21(1-4) and s. 2 (definition of bearer, delivery endorsement and holder); *cf.* ss. 56-74.

a)   The Effect of Negotiation

''Negotiation'' is the transfer of a bill (or note) ''from one person to another in such a manner as to constitute the transferee the holder of the bill [or note]'' (s. 60(1)). The rights of a transferee who is a holder are governed by s. 74. Only a holder can be a ''holder in due course'' (s. 56) and take the instrument ''free from any defect of title . . . as well as from mere personal defences . . .'' (s. 74(*b*)).

An overdue instrument and an instrument that has been ''dishonoured'' (s. 95(1)) can be negotiated (ss. 70, 72). Nonetheless, a person who takes an overdue instrument, or with notice of dishonour, takes it ''subject to any defect of title'' (*id.*) and cannot become a holder in due course (s. 56(1)(*a*)).

An instrument can be negotiated back to a prior party who "may . . . reissue and further negotiate [it]". However, "he is not entitled to enforce . . . payment . . . against any intervening party . . ." (s. 73).

b) The Manner of Negotiation

Negotiation of an instrument payable to bearer (ss. 21(3)) can only occur by delivery. See s. 60(2). "Delivery" is defined in s. 2. Negotiation of an instrument payable to order (s. 21(2), (4)) is made by "endorsement" by the "holder" (s. 2) and completed by "delivery" (s. 2). See s. 60(3).

An endorsement may be either "in blank" (specifying no endorsee; s. 67(2)) or "special" (specifying the name of the endorsee; s. 67(3)). An endorsement in blank may be converted by the holder into a special endorsement "by writing above the endorser's signature a direction to pay the . . . [instrument] to or to the order of himself or some other person" (s. 67(5)). An instrument endorsed in blank becomes a bearer instrument (ss. 67(2), 21(3)). Can the holder of an instrument which is originally "expressed to be . . . payable" to bearer convert it into an instrument payable to order? Consider ss. 21 and 67.

c) Transfer Not Amounting to Negotiation: Transfer Without Endorsement of an Order Instrument

Transfer of an order instrument without endorsement is not negotiation (s. 60(3)). Transfer by the holder of an instrument payable to his order without endorsement is nonetheless not entirely ineffective. Such a transfer for value "gives the transferee such title as the transferor had in the . . . [instrument]" as well as "the right to have the endorsement of the transferor" (s. 61(1)). Consider the following questions in conjunction with this provision: (a) Can such a transferee become a "holder"? (b) Can he sue in his own name or transfer the instrument further? (c) Can he become a "holder in due course" (s. 56(1))? (d) What are the rights of one who receives an unendorsed instrument payable to order by gift or inheritance? (e) Is a transferee's status as "holder" determined at the time of transfer or endorsement? For some answers, see e.g., *Whistler* v. *Forster* (1863) 14 CB (NS) 248, 143 ER 441; *Aldercrest Dev. Ltd.* v. *Hamilton Co-Axial Ltd.* [1970] 3 OR 529 (Ont. CA); aff'd [1974] SCR 793.

d) Conditional Endorsement

While a bill or note must be unconditional in its original terms, it may be endorsed conditionally (s. 66). Note the scope of s. 66. The section does not say that the endorsee is entitled to enforce payment without proving performance of the condition. As between endorser and endorsee the condition is binding and, in the event of payment to the endorsee, the endorser is entitled to recover the proceeds paid to the endorsee if the condition is not fulfilled. Only the payor may disregard the condition and is protected under s. 66.

e)   Restrictive Endorsement

An instrument may be non-negotiable in its original state, and in that event no endorsement can have the effect of making it negotiable. However, if the instrument was originally negotiable, it can subsequently be rendered non-negotiable by a restrictive endorsement.

A restrictive endorsement on an instrument "prohibits . . . [its] further negotiation . . . or . . . expresses that it is a mere authority to deal with the . . . [instrument] as thereby directed, and not a transfer of the ownership thereof" (s. 68(2)). An endorsee under a restrictive endorsement has "the right to receive payment of the [instrument] and to sue any party thereto that his endorser could have sued". He has, however, "no power to transfer his rights as endorsee unless [the endorsement] expressly authorizes him to do so" (s. 68(3) and *cf.* s. 74). Where there is such authority to transfer "all subsequent endorsees take the [instrument] with the same rights and subject to the same liabilities as the first endorsee under the restrictive endorsement" (s. 68(4)).

A restrictive endorsement is designed to assure that the money received in respect of the instrument is applied as instructed. A bill endorsed "pay D for collection" must be paid to D personally for the account of the endorser. The only effect of adding "or order" after D's name is to obviate the inconvenience of D's having to attend in person to obtain payment, and to enable D by endorsing the bill to authorize another person to receive payment.

The relations between an endorser and endorsee under a restrictive endorsement "which expresses that it is a mere authority to deal with the bill as thereby directed and not a transfer of the ownership thereof" (s. 68(2)) "are substantially those of principal and agent": *Chalmers On Bills of Exchange* (13th ed., 1964) pp. 118, 121. Such a restrictive endorsement may be notice that no valuable consideration has been given by the endorsee: *Edie* v. *East-India Co.* (1761) 2 Burr. 1216, 1227, 97 ER 797. Can an endorsee for collection become a holder in due course if he gives value to the endorser before collection? The answer depends initially on whether "restrictive endorsement" is "negotiation". Does s. 69(*a*) provide the answer? Can it be said that the provision applies only to a restrictive endorsement "that prohibits the further negotiation of the bill" (s. 68(2)), or that an instrument only ceases to be "negotiable" under s. 69(*a*) until *after* delivery to the restrictive endorsee? *Cf.* Arthur Basse, "Restrictive Indorsements" (1943) 52 Yale LJ 890 at 894-95.

B.   THE STATUTORY CONTRACT UNDER THE BILLS OF EXCHANGE ACT

1.   LIABILITY OF PARTIES UNDER THE ACT

"No person is liable as drawer, endorser, . . . acceptor [or maker] of . . . [an instrument] who has not signed it as such": s. 131. See also ss. 127, 35-38. Liability on an instrument thus requires signature. Provisions governing "signature" are contained in sections 4 and 5. Signature can be "by procuration" (s. 51) or in a representative capacity (s. 52). There has been much case law as to the personal liability of an agent who fails to indicate his representative capacity sufficiently clearly.

See e.g.:

Loczka v. *Ruthenian Farmers Co-operative Co.* (1922) 68 DLR 535, [1922] 2 WWR 782 (Man. CA)

Alliston Creamery v. *Grosdanoff and Tracy* (1962) 34 DLR (2d) 189, [1962] OR 808 (Ont. CA)

H.B. Etlin Co. Ltd. v. *Asselstyne* (1962) 34 DLR (2d) 191, [1962] OR 810 (Ont. CA)

Albert Pearl (Management) Ltd. v. *J.D.F. Builders Ltd.* (1973) 31 DLR (3d) 690, [1973] 1 OR 594 (Ont. CA)

Glatt v. *Ritt* [1973] 2 OR 447, 34 DLR (3d) 295 (Ont. HC)

Royal Bank of Canada v. *Mendel* [1977] 6 WWR 10 (BC Co. Ct.)

Moir v. *Livingstone* (1977) 16 NBR (2d) 584 (NB Co. Ct.)

Law review literature includes:
Karp (1963) 21 Fac. L. Rev. U. of T. 153
Sheldon Esbin (1963) 2 Osgoode Hall LJ 496
Marvin Baer (1973) 51 Can. B. Rev. 666

Parol evidence explaining the real intention of the signer will be more easily admitted between the immediate parties to the transaction underlying the instrument. The following summary of Ontario case law by Wright J. in *Glatt* v. *Ritt, supra* at 454-455, deals with the admissibility of extrinsic evidence in cases of ambiguity.

(1) The general rule is that any person who signs a promissory note without indicating his representative status or that otherwise he has no personal liability, is personally liable on the note.

(2) Unless such a note is ambiguous on its face, no evidence may be led to establish the character in which the person signed or, adversely, to affect his personal liability.

(3) A note in which the company's name is followed by three signatures is unambiguous. Such evidence is not admissible and judgment will go against the three individuals even if it has already gone against the company: *Daymond Motors Ltd.* v. *Thistletown Developments Ltd. et al.* [1956] OWN 867.

(4) The same rule applies where there are two signatures and the company's name appears below them: *Alliston Creamery* v. *Grosdanoff and Tracey, supra.*

(5) The rule does not apply in Ontario where there is only one unexplained signature either on a corporate cheque form: *H.B. Etlin Co. Ltd.* v. *Asselstyne, supra,* or under a stamped name of a corporation: *Albert Pearl (Management) Ltd.* v. *J.D.F. Builders Ltd. et al., supra.*

(6) Such a cheque or note is ambiguous, and extrinsic evidence may be heard particularly if its denial would lead to a gross miscarriage of justice: *H.B. Etlin Co. Ltd.* v. *Asselstyne (supra,* at p. 812 OR, p. 193 DLR), and where there is a partial failure of consideration: *Albert Pearl (Management) Ltd.* v. *J.D.F. Builders Ltd. et al., supra.*

FALCONBRIDGE
The Law of Negotiable Instruments in Canada
(1967) pp. 63 *et seq.,* 129

§61. *Liability of drawer.*

The Bills of Exchange Act provides:

> **130.** The drawer of a bill, by drawing it,—
> (*a*) engages that on due presentment it shall be accepted and paid according to its tenor, and that if it is dishonoured he will compensate the holder or any endorser who is compelled to pay it, if the requisite proceedings on dishonour are duly taken.

The liability incurred by the drawer of a bill of exchange may be better understood if the example of a bill, already given in chapter 1, is reproduced here:

> $100   Toronto, 31st January, 1932.
>   One month after date pay to the order of Martin Chuzzlewit one hundred dollars.
> To John Alden, Esq.,
>   Kingston,   Adam Bede
>   Ontario.

It will be observed that Bede does not make any express promise to pay, but impliedly he engages that his order upon Alden will be honoured, that is, that it will be accepted and paid by Alden. Thus, the drawer's liability is conditional upon the drawee's default. It is also conditional upon the holder's doing certain things. Even if the drawee fails to pay, the drawer is to be required to pay only if the holder (1) has duly presented the bill, and (2) has duly taken the requisite proceedings on dishonour. As to due presentment, it has been already pointed out in chapter 3 that in some cases a bill must be presented for acceptance in order to preserve the liability of the drawer and endorsers. Presentment for payment will be discussed in chapter 7. The requisite proceedings on dishonour are either protest and notice of protest or notice of dishonour. These will be discussed in chapters 8 and 9.

In the case of a bill payable on demand or of a cheque, the drawer does not engage that it will be accepted and paid, but that it will be paid, the holder's right being to presentment for payment only.

Although a bill may not be drawn conditionally, that is, although the order to pay must be unconditional (as explained in chapter 2), the drawer may by an express stipulation negative or limit his own liability to the holder. (See §64).

§62. *Liability of acceptor or maker.*

The mere fact that Bede has drawn upon Alden the bill given as an example in §61 does not render Alden liable to anyone upon the bill. In order to make him so liable he must have accepted the bill. (See chapter 2, §22, and chapter 3, §31). We may now, for the purpose of illustration, suppose that Alden writes across the face of the bill the following acceptance:

Accepted payable at the Lawyers' Bank, Kingston.

John Alden.

This is equivalent to a promise to pay on the drawee's part, as is provided by the following section of the Bills of Exchange Act:

128. The acceptor of a bill, by accepting it, engages that he will pay it according to the tenor of his acceptance.

It will be observed that the acceptor's promise is absolute. It is not subject to any of the conditions attached to the liability of the drawer, referred to in §61. The acceptor thus becomes the person primarily liable to pay the bill, and is in effect in the same position as if he had made a promissory note.

The Bills of Exchange Act provides:

185. The maker of a promissory note, by making it,—
(a) engages that he will pay it according to its tenor.

The example of a promissory note given in chapter 1 is reproduced for the purpose of illustration:

$100
Kingston, 31st January, 1932.
One month after date I promise to pay to the order of Adam Bede one hundred dollars at the Lawyers' Bank, Kingston.

John Alden.

As has been explained in chapter 1 §17, if this note is endorsed by Bede in favour of Martin Chuzzlewit, the three parties are in substantially the same position relatively to each other as they are in the case of a bill of exchange drawn by Bede upon Alden payable to Chuzzlewit and accepted by Alden.

§63. *Liability of endorser.*

In the case of a note made by Alden in favour of Bede and endorsed by Bede to Chuzzlewit, or of a bill drawn by Bede upon Alden in favour of Chuzzlewit, or of a cheque upon a bank drawn by Bede in favour of Chuzzlewit, we may for the purpose of illustration suppose that the instrument bears the following endorsements:

Pay to John Doe
M. Chuzzlewit
John Doe

If we find the instrument in the hands of Robert Elsmere we may conjecture that it was negotiated by Chuzzlewit to Doe (by special endorsement and delivery) and by Doe to Elsmere (by endorsement in blank and delivery). Endorsement as an essential element in the negotiation of an instrument payable to order has already been discussed in chapter 5. In the present chapter we are concerned with the question of the personal liability incurred by the endorsers. The Bills of Exchange Act provides:

133. The endorser of a bill, by endorsing it, subject to the effect of any express stipulation hereinbefore authorized—

(*a*)   engages that on due presentment it shall be accepted and paid according to its tenor, and that if it is dishonoured he will compensate the holder or a subsequent endorser who is compelled to pay it, if the requisite proceedings on dishonour are duly taken.

It will be observed that under this section each endorser incurs the same kind of conditional liability to the holder as the drawer of a bill incurs (as explained in §61), and that as between two endorsers, the earlier is liable to the later, subject to the same conditions.

The words "subject to the effect of any stipulation hereinbefore authorized" refer to the provisions quoted in §64.

§64.   *Stipulations as to liability.*

The Bills of Exchange Act provides:

34. The drawer of a bill, and any endorser, may insert therein an express stipulation,—
(*a*)   negativing or limiting his own liability to the holder;
(*b*)   waiving, as regards himself, some or all of the holder's duties.

61. (2) Where any person is under obligation to endorse a bill in a representative capacity, he may endorse the bill in such terms as to negative personal liability.

The endorsements authorized under these provisions of the statute are to be distinguished from conditional or restrictive endorsements, discussed in chapter 5, §58.

For the purpose of illustration we have in §63 supposed that an instrument of which Chuzzlewit was the holder was endorsed and negotiated by him to Doe and by Doe to Elsmere. We may now suppose that the instrument bears the following further endorsements:

Pay to the order of
    Sir John Flagstaff
    (without recourse)
    Robert Elsmere.
Pay to Lemuel Gulliver
    (Notice of dishonour waived)
    John Flagstaff
    John Falstaff.
Pay to Sherlock Holmes
    L. Gulliver
    per Jonathan Swift.

It now appears that the instrument has been negotiated by Elsmere to Falstaff, by Falstaff to Gulliver, and by Gulliver to Holmes. The endorsements present several special features.

Elsmere endorses "without recourse." He thereby negatives his own liability to the holder, as he is permitted to do by s. 34, but his endorsement followed by delivery to Falstaff has the effect of transferring the instrument to Falstaff. The words "sans recours" (the equivalent in French of "without recourse") are sometimes used.

Falstaff's endorsement is peculiar in two respects. By the words "Notice of dishonour waived" he has, in accordance with s. 34, waived or renounced, as regards himself, the benefit of one of the holder's duties. He has said in effect that if the instrument is dishonoured, he will be bound although he receives no notice of dishonour. If he had said "Protest waived," the effect would have been to dispense with notice of dishonour as well as protest and notice of protest, as regards himself. By the double form of signature he has shown that he has been misdescribed in the previous endorsement as Sir John Flagstaff. He has signed first as described and has added his proper signature in accordance with s. 64 (quoted in chapter 5, §56).

The form of Gulliver's endorsement shows that it has been written not by his own hand but by an agent. If Swift had authority to sign for Gulliver, the latter is bound to the same extent as if he had signed with his own hand. (See chapter 16).

§65. *Anomalous endorsement.*

An endorsement, properly so called, must be made by the holder for the time being. It is part of the transaction by which the holder transfers the instruments to another person as holder, as in the case of each of the endorsements mentioned by way of example in §§ 63 and 64. It sometimes happens, however, that a person who is not the holder of an instrument writes his name on the back for the purpose of obtaining credit for another person and thus facilitating the negotiation of the instrument. He is not, strictly speaking, an endorser, but he may incur the same liabilities as an endorser.

The Bills of Exchange Act provides:

> **131.** No person is liable as drawer, endorser or acceptor of a bill who has not signed it as such: Provided that when a person signs a bill otherwise than as a drawer or acceptor he thereby incurs the liabilities of an endorser to a holder in due course and is subject to all the provisions of this Act respecting endorsers.

For example, a bank consents to discount a bill or note of which A is the holder, provided X endorses it. If A endorses to X, and X endorses to the bank, both A and X are liable as endorsers. On the other hand, if A endorses directly to the bank and X writes his name on the back, X is not an endorser, but under s. 131 he incurs the same liability as an endorser to the bank.

Again, if A, instead of making a note payable to X and getting X to endorse it to the discounting bank, makes the note payable to the bank and X writes his name on the back, X incurs the same liability as an endorser to the bank.

• • •

§67. *Transferor by delivery.*

An instrument which is originally payable to bearer or which is, by reason of an endorsement in blank, temporarily payable to bearer, may be negotiated by delivery without the endorsement of the holder. For instance, in the series of endorsements given as examples in §§ 63 and 64 there is at least one time in the history of the instrument at which there may have been several negotiations of which the endorsements contain no record, namely, immediately after John Doe's endorsement in blank. The instrument being at this time payable to bearer, it may have been negotiated by delivery to X, and may have been further negotiated by X to Y, and then by Y to Robert Elsmere. Neither X nor Y is liable on the instrument because neither of them has made himself a party to it by signing it. The position of X and Y in such a case is defined by the following provisions of the Bills of Exchange Act:

137. (1) Where the holder of a bill payable to bearer negotiates it by delivery without endorsing it, he is called a 'transferor by delivery.'
(2) A transferor by delivery is not liable on the instrument.

138. A transferor by delivery who negotiates a bill thereby warrants to his immediate transferee, being a holder for value,—
(a)   that the bill is what it purports to be;
(b)   that he has a right to transfer it; and,
(c)   that at the time of transfer he is not aware of any fact which renders it valueless.

For example, the transferor by delivery undertakes that the signatures which are on the instrument when he delivers it are genuine, that is, that they were written either by or by the authority of the persons whose signatures they purport to be. The transferor by delivery does not, however, undertake that the parties to the instrument will pay. He is not in the position of an endorser, who can be called upon to pay if, upon due presentment, the acceptor (or the maker) does not pay, and the requisite proceedings on dishonour are duly taken.

It will be observed also that under s. 138 the transferor by delivery is liable only to his immediate transferee, not to any person who may subsequently become the holder of the instrument.

• • •

§145. *Accommodation party.*
The Bills of Exchange Act provides:

55.(1) An accommodation party to a bill is a person who has signed a bill as drawer, acceptor or endorser, without receiving value therefor, and for the purpose of lending his name to some other person.
(2) An accommodation party is liable on the bill to a holder for value; and it is immaterial whether, when such holder took the bill, he knew such party to be an accommodation party or not.

The fact that the drawer or endorser of a bill is an accommodation party does not make the bill itself an accommodation bill. An accommodation bill is a bill whereof the acceptor, (that is, the principal debtor according to the terms of the instrument) is an accommodation party, that is, in effect, a mere surety for some other person who may or may not be a party to the bill. Any other bill is not correctly spoken of as an accommodation bill, although it may be signed by one or more accommodation parties. The distinction is important with regard to the discharge of the bill. An accommodation bill is dicharged when it is paid in due course by the party accommodated (s. 139, quoted in chapter 18, §181), although in form he may not be the principal debtor.

Problem: A draws a bill on B to the order of C. B accepts the bill. C negotiates the bill to D. The bill is then duly negotiated from D to E, from E to F, from F to G, and from G to H. On the maturity of the bill in H's hands, what are the rights and liabilities among all these parties? Will your answer be different if (a) D was not a party to any transaction with E but signed the bill as a surety to one Z (a party to a transaction with E), or (b) before delivery of the instrument from E to F one X added his signature to it, or (c) the bill was payable to bearer (and not to C's order)?

2. PRESERVING LIABILITY ON THE INSTRUMENT: THE HOLDER'S DUTIES

Those liable on an instrument are either "primary" or "secondary" parties. "Primary parties" are those liable to pay according to the tenor of their undertaking. These are the acceptor of a bill (s. 128) and the maker of a note (s. 185(a)). "Secondary parties" engage to pay only on the dishonour of the instrument. They are the drawer of a bill and the endorser of a bill or note (ss. 130(a) and 133(a)).

Nothing need be done by the holder to fix liability of primary parties. By contrast, various formalities are imposed on the holder in order to preserve his rights against secondary parties. Delay in carrying out these formalities results in the discharge of these parties from liability on the instrument as well as on the underlying transaction. There is a qualified exception to such a discharge with respect to the drawer of a cheque: where the delay in presentment for payment caused him damage he is discharged from his liability *pro tanto* (s. 166). Typically, such damage would be the result of the failure of his bank during the delay. Insurance of deposits by governments (of Canada, Quebec and Ontario, see: *Falconbridge On Banking and Bills of Exchange* (7th ed., 1967) p. 312) minimizes (if not eliminating altogether) the possibility of such damage. In the absence of damage, failure to present the cheque promptly for payment does not result in his discharge.

The following is an outline of the holder's duties. For a more detailed discussion, see A. Abel, "Presentment, Notice, Protest" (1974) 24 Univ. Tor. LJ 191.

a) Presentment

Presentment can be either for acceptance (governed by ss. 75-84) or for payment (governed by ss. 85-95, 180, 181, 183-184).

i) Presentment for Acceptance

Presentment for acceptance does not apply to cheques and notes and is generally unnecessary to fix the liability of those who have signed before acceptance. It is required (a) where a bill is payable "at sight" or so many days "after sight", (b) where a bill explicitly requires it, or (c) where a bill is payable not at the place of business or residence of the drawee. Upon being presented with the bill, the drawee has two days to make up his mind. His refusal or failure to accept results in the dishonour of the bill. For the possibility of acceptance by a stranger ("acceptance for honour") where the instrument has been formally protested for non-acceptance and is not yet overdue, see ss. 147-155 and s. 186(3)(c).

ii)   *Presentment for Payment*

Presentment for payment is required for all bills (including cheques) and notes. It is nonetheless dispensed with (a) where it cannot be effected after the exercise of reasonable diligence; (b) where the drawee is a fictitious person; (c) where the drawee or acceptor is not bound, as between himself and the drawer, to accept or pay the bill and the drawer has no reason to believe that the bill would be paid if presented. An example is where a person draws a cheque against insufficient funds in his bank account with no reason to expect that it will be honoured (in which case presentment is dispensed with as regards the drawer); (d) where the instrument was accepted or made for the accommodation of an endorser and he has no reason to expect that it would be paid if presented; and (e) where it has been waived, explicitly or implicitly.

Presentment for payment must be made by the holder by exhibiting the instrument to the person designated by it as payor. There is a conflict of authority as to the meaning of ''exhibit'' where the instrument is kept at the place of payment.

A demand instrument must be presented for payment within a reasonable time after its issue. An instrument payable at a fixed or determinable future time must be presented for payment on the day it falls due. Delay is excused when caused by circumstances beyond the control of the holder and not imputable to his default, misconduct or negligence. When the cause of the delay ceases to operate, presentment must be made with reasonable diligence thereafter.

Where the instrument specifies a place of payment (as to the meaning of ''place of payment'', see s. 90), presentment for payment must be made at that place. Otherwise it must be made at the address of the drawee or acceptor as given on the instrument, or as known if not given. While presentment is not necessary to crystallize the liability of a primary party, where the instrument specifies a place of payment, the costs of an action against a primary party on an instrument which has not been duly presented for payment are in the discretion of the court.

b)   **Notice of Dishonour and Protest**

Dishonour of an instrument occurs where the instrument is duly presented for acceptance or payment, and acceptance or payment is refused or cannot be obtained (s. 81, dishonour by non-acceptance; s. 95, dishonour by non-payment). The instrument is also dishonoured where presentment is excused and the instrument is either not accepted or has not been paid in time (*id.*).

Notice of dishonour (governed by ss. 96-108) must be given by the holder to the drawer of a bill (including the drawer of a cheque) and each endorser of a bill or note. Those benefitting from such notice are enumerated in s. 102. The notice may be either written or verbal, and in any terms that identify the instrument and intimate that it has been dishonoured.

Notice of dishonour must be given not later than the juridical or business day next following the dishonour. A recipient of the notice has the same time to give notice to prior parties. Delay in giving notice of dishonour is excused in the same manner delay in presentment is excused. Unless a specific place is designated in the instrument, notice of dishonour of any instrument payable in Canada is sufficiently given if it is addressed to the party's "customary address or place of residence or at the place at which [the instrument] is dated" (s. 103(1)).

The circumstances where notice of dishonour is dispensed with are governed by ss. 106-108. Circumstances are similar to those dispensing with presentment. They also include situations where the drawer and drawee are the same person, or where the drawee lacks capacity to contract.

Protest (governed by ss. 112-126) is a formal act on behalf of the holder by a notary public (or a justice of the peace where no notary is available). A protest must contain a copy of the instrument (or the original), must be signed by the notary public (or the justice of the peace), and must specify (a) the person at whose request the instrument is protested, (b) the place and date of protest, (c) the cause or reason for protesting the instrument, (d) the demand made and the answer given, if any, or (e) the fact that the drawee or acceptor could not be found. Where the Act requires an instrument to be protested within certain time, it is sufficient that the instrument has been noted for protest (by the notary's initials) within that time.

A protest is required only on the dishonour (by non-acceptance as well as by non-payment) of a foreign instrument. The holder of an inland instrument may protest it for evidentiary purposes, and may also add the expenses of doing so to the damage claim against secondary parties. As to the distinction between an "inland bill" and a "foreign bill", see s. 25. Don't overlook the presumption in s. 25(3).

C. ENFORCEABLE OBLIGATION

The holder's compliance with the formalities set forth by the BEA does not by itself charge a signing party with absolute liability on the instrument. There must also be an enforceable obligation on the part of the signor. Alternatively, the plaintiff must hold an elevated status which overcomes the objection to the enforceability of the signer's obligation. The enforceability of the obligation on a bill or note is discussed in this section from the following viewpoints: (1) the elements of enforceable obligation, (2) the holder in due course and his power to overcome most defences to liability on an instrument, and (3) the holder not in due course and his position towards the obligor's defences.

1. THE CONTRACT UNDER A BILL OR NOTE

a) Capacity of Parties

BEA, ss. 47-48.

Chalmers On Bills of Exchange
(13th ed., 1964) p. 62

Capacity and authority.

Capacity must be distinguished from authority. Capacity means power to contract so as to bind oneself. Authority means power to contract on behalf of another so as to bind him. Capacity to contract is the creation of law. Authority is derived from the act of the parties themselves. Want of capacity is incurable. Want of authority may be cured by ratification. Capacity or no capacity is a question of law. Authority or no authority is usually a question of fact. Again, capacity to incur liability must be distinguished from capacity to transfer. An executed contract is often valid where an executory contract is unenforceable. An indorsement usually consists of two distinct contracts — one executed, the other executory. It transfers the property in the bill, and it also involves a contingent assumption of liability on the part of the indorser.

Note the following points made by *Falconbridge* on *Banking*, Ch. 43:

(1) "Notwithstanding that as a general rule the contract of an infant or minor is by English law voidable not void, an infant or minor incurs no liability by signing a bill or note, even to a holder in due course, or even though the instrument is given for the price of necessaries supplied to him" (p. 547).

(2) "The insertion of the word 'such' in [s. 47(2)] was intended to make clear that the proviso referred to a special statute relating to any particular corporation in question as well as to the law respecting companies in general" (pp. 551-52).

(3) "A corporation incurs no liability by drawing, indorsing, or accepting a bill, unless expressly or impliedly empowered by its act of incorporation so to do. . . . In the case of a trading corporation the fact of incorporation for the purposes of trade would give capacity. In the case of non-trading corporations, the power must be expressly given, or there must be terms in the charter wide enough to include it" (p. 552, citing Chalmers, p. 65).

(4) "To the extent stated in s. 48 the drawing or endorsement of a bill by an infant, minor or corporation is effective without regard to the law of a particular province; and it has been held that the endorsement passes the property in the bill, though from want of capacity the infant, minor or corporation may not be liable as endorser" (p. 553).

b)   Consideration

BEA ss. 2, 27(b) and 53.

As Professor Geva has pointed out in his article, "Absence of Consideration in the Law of Bills and Notes" ([1980] Camb. LJ 360):

> By the latter part of the sixteenth century the theory of liability on bills of exchange had been adapted to common law theory of contract so as to lie *in assumpsit*. In 1787 it was fully settled by the House of Lords that all "contracts in writing [which are] merely written and not specialities . . . are parol" and require consideration. Promissory notes and bills of exchange fell into this category. Indeed, "bills and notes were contracts and being such there was no persuasive reason why the basis of liability on a bill or note should be any different from that on any other written contract for payment of money". While there is no provision in the Bills of Exchange Act . . . directly to the point, it is well established indeed that consideration of "value" is needed for the creation of an obligation under a negotiable instrument. According to Chalmers, "Where B, by way of gift, makes a note in favour of C, C cannot recover from B."

At common law "[a] valuable consideration . . . may consist either in some right, interest, profit, or benefit accruing to the one party, or some forbearance, detriment, loss or responsibility given, suffered, or undertaken by the other": *Currie* v. *Misa* (1875) LR 10 Ex. 153 at 162; SC *sub nom. Misa* v. *Currie* (1876) 1 App. Cas. 554. Consideration must move from the promisee but not necessarily to the promisor.

Is this type of common law consideration required under the BEA? The central provision is s. 53(1)(*a*). Its language is quite ambiguous as to whether "any consideration sufficient to support a simple contract" should be read in reference to the common law of England or to the general law of the province (a question which is particularly important in relation to Quebec). Falconbridge's opinion is (at pp. 606-07):

> that the question of consideration for a bill or note is part of the law of bills and notes in the strict sense and therefore under s. 10 is governed by the rules of the common law of England except insofar as they are inconsistent with the express provisions of the statute.

In support of this view Falconbridge cites the fact that specific exceptions for Quebec are expressly stated in ss. 43(*b*), 113 and 114 and "in s. 53 itself the phrases 'valuable consideration' and 'simple contract' are technical terms of English law unknown to Quebec law" (*id.* at 607). This view is, however, contrary to the weight of authority as summarized by Aharon Barak, "The Requirement of Consideration for Bills or Notes in Israel: (1967), 2 Israel L. Rev. 499 at 511:

> . . . The question arose whether, in regard to bills, the English law of consideration or the law of Quebec relating to contracts should be followed. The courts held that the contract law of Quebec should be followed and that a bill may be based on causa and need not be grounded on "English" consideration. In the leading case of *Stephen* v. *Perrault* (1918) 56 QSC 54 the defendant signed a note in favour of the plaintiff as compensation for injury caused to the latter. It was established that the defendant was not legally liable to pay damages and that the note had been given in discharge of a moral obligation only. The defendant was held to be liable on the note. There was no consideration as known to English law, but there was causa in the civilian sense, and this was sufficient to support the obligation on the note. In the words of Judge Lafontaine:
>
>> It is a matter beyond doubt that, although the law of bills of exchange and notes is in the form of a federal statute drawn largely from English law, it is neverthless our French law which applies in this matter , *in accordance with the express provision of that statute*, section 53 of which says that any consideration sufficient to give validity to a simple contract is consideration sufficient for a bill of exchange. Accordingly the English authorities which have been cited to us on this point have no application.

In *Rouleau* v. *Poulin* [1965] BR 292 the defendant was declared bankrupt and, after his debts were paid by his trustee in bankruptcy, he signed a note in favour of the plaintiff who was one of his creditors. The defendant's intention was to repay the plaintiff that part of the debt which had not been discharged by the trustee. The defendant was held liable on the note. Although there was no antecedent debt, the bankruptcy proceedings having cancelled it, there was good causa under Quebec common law.

Finally, section 53(1)(*b*) should be mentioned. "What is meant [by the provision] is that a promise on a bill to pay the promisor's own debt is valid without consideration." It is uncertain whether the words "or liability" were added to cover the case of an obligation not presently payable or to extend the scope of the section to cover also "an obligation which is not only not presently payable, but which will not become an absolute obligation or debt until the happening of a contingency or the fulfilment of a condition". It is noteworthy in the context of s. 53(1)(*b*) that "[t]he rule that a promise to pay the promisor's own debt requires no consideration is not limited to a promise on a bill or note. It is merely an example of a general and ancient rule, applicable to the subsequent promise which before the decision in *Slade's Case* [76 ER 1072] was essential to enable an action of *assumpsit* to be brought" (Falconbridge, pp. 610-13). "Liability" under s. 53(1)(*b*) must be the liability of the promisor or drawer, and not that of a stranger to the instrument: *Hasan* v. *Willson* [1977] 1 Ll. L. Rep. 431 (QBD).

c)   Delivery

The general rule is that delivery (as defined in s. 2) is essential to render effective a negotiable instrument or the contract of any party to it (ss. 2, 39, 178). In order that a party to an instrument may be liable on it, he must not only have signed it but must also have delivered it. Hence, until delivery to a holder, the contract on the instrument is incomplete and revocable.

"To constitute a contract [under a bill or note], there must be a delivery over the instrument by the drawer or endorser for a good consideration: and as soon as these circumstances take place the contract is complete . . .": *Abrey* v. *Crux* (1869) LR 5 CP 37 at 42. Accordingly, "in an action on a promissory note, upon which a party has written his name, and after his death his executrix delivers the note to the plaintiffs without indorsing it, so that there is a writing of his name by the deceased, and a delivery by his executrix" it was held that "[t]hose acts will not constitute an indorsement of the note: the person to whom it is so delivered has no right to sue upon it": *Bromage* v. *Lloyd* (1847) 1 Ex. 32, 154 ER 14 at 15. Also in *Chapman* v. *Cottrell* (1865) 12 LT 706, where a promissory note was signed in France but was delivered to the payee in England it was held that the cause of action arose in England. "Until delivery of the note to the [payee] . . . there is not the slightest ground for saying there was a contract, or that the [payee] had any title to the note" (*id.* at 707).

The requirement of delivery thus provides the linkage between the chattel quality of a bill or note and the validity of the contract thereunder. Delivery is excused when the obligor is not the owner of the chattel as is the case with an acceptor. In the latter case, notice of acceptance substitutes for delivery (s. 39). Thus, "it is not the mere act of writing on the bill, but the making a communication of what is so written , that binds the acceptor; for the making the communication is a pledge by him to the party, and enables the holder to act upon it": *Cox* v. *Troy* (1882) 5 B. & Ald. 474, 106 ER 1264 at 1266.

As against any holder of the instrument (other than a holder in due course), the signer of an instrument may show either that the instrument was never delivered by him or under his authority or that it was delivered conditionally or for a special purpose (ss. 40(1), 41).

2.   Enforcement by a Holder in Due Course

BEA ss. 56-59, 74, 2, 3. See also ss. 31, 32 and 40.

The person who holds an instrument "free from any defect of title of prior parties, as well as from mere personal defences available to prior parties among themselves" and who "may enforce payment against all parties liable on the [instrument]" (s. 74(*b*)) is called a "holder in due course". Prior to the BEA, he was referred to as a bona fide holder for value, bona fide holder for value without notice, or bona fide holder of the bill for value without notice before it is overdue. His position under the Act constitutes an important exception to the rule, *nemo dat quod non habet.*

At common law, in order to acquire a holder in due course status, it was sufficient to purchase an instrument bona fide and for value: *Miller* v. *Race* (1758) 1 Burr. 452, 97 ER 398. Under the Act a person must comply with eight separate and independent conditions specified in section 56(1):

1) He must be a "holder" (defined in s. 2) of an instrument
2) complete and regular on the face of it, and
3) have become the holder before the instrument was overdue, and
4) without notice that it had been previously dishonoured, and
5) have taken the instrument in good faith,
6) for value,
7) by negotiation, and
8) without notice of any defect in the title of the person who negotiated it. ("Defective title" is partly defined in s. 56(2).)

Under s. 58(2), "[e]very holder of a bill is prima facie deemed to be a holder in due course". Also, a holder "who derives his title to a bill through a holder in due course . . . has all the rights of that holder in due course" provided he "is not himself a party to any fraud or illegality affecting it" (s. 57).

"Good Faith" and "Without Notice"

"Good faith" under the Act requires honesty alone. In other words, one could act negligently and still be in "good faith" (s. 3). Likewise, "notice" is actual notice. Thus the test of the good faith and without notice element is subjective. Nevertheless good faith is defeated by one's suspicion combined with a wilful disregard of the means of knowledge, as when the circumstances invite inquiry; see e.g. *Jones* v. *Gordon* (1877), 2 App. Cas. 616; and *Benjamin* v. *Weinberg*, [1956] SCR 553.

In relation to defences arising from a contract under which a negotiable instrument has been given, neither mere suspicion of the existence of defences nor mere knowledge of the terms of the contract which are capable of giving rise to defences defeats the holder's good faith. On the other hand, "notice of a condition to liability on an instrument, as distinguished from notice of an executory consideration, prevents one from [becoming a] holder in due course" (11 *Am. Jur.* 2d Bills and Notes §460). The preventing "condition" is one which triggers liability on an instrument, as for example on an instrument given as collateral to secure a principal obligation under a contract. It is not a "condition" whose breach under the terms of an executory contract excuses liability on the instrument given in payment under that contract. For example, the seller's failure to deliver the goods to the buyer is typically in breach of a condition which under the sale agreement excuses the buyer from his duty to pay for the goods. Knowledge of the actual occurrence of such a failure is knowledge of the buyer's defences. Yet knowledge of this "condition" of the contract is not knowledge of a "condition to liability" but rather of the "executory consideration". As such it should not defeat the holder's good faith. A case which confuses the two meanings of "condition" is *First & Lumbermen's National Bank of Chippewa Falls* v. *Buchholz* (1945) 18 NW 2d 771 (Minn. SC).

Can a Payee Be a Holder In Due Course?

A holder in due course must be "a person to whom, after its completion by and as between *the immediate parties*, the bill or note has been negotiated": *Lewis* v. *Clay* (1897) 77 LT 653 at 656 (QBD) (emphasis added). He must, in other words, be a *remote party* to the transaction under which the instrument was issued. Ordinarily, therefore, a payee cannot be a holder in due course. Nor does he enjoy the presumption of s. 58(2): *Talbot* v. *Von Boris* [1911] 1 KB 854. The orthodox view is that a payee can never be a holder in due course due to the definition of "negotiation" (which is one of the requirements of acquiring holder in due course status) in s. 60(3). See in general, Aigler, "Payees As Holders in Due Course" (1927) 36 Yale LJ 608. A payee who was remote party to the underlying transaction was awarded a holder in due course status in *Johnson* v. *Johnson* [1928] 2 DLR 531 (Alta. CA), as well as in *Central Factors Corp. Ltd.* v. *Bragg* (1977) 76 DLR (3d) 585 (BC SC). A payee who was immediate party to the underlying transaction was held to enjoy the "sheltering" doctrine of s. 57 on the dishonour of the instrument and its renegotiation back to him by the holder in due course in *Jade International Steel Stahl und Eisen GmbH Co. K.G.* v. *Robert Nicholas (Steels) Ltd.* [1978] 3 WLR 39 (CA). See Thorneley's criticism in [1978] Camb. LJ 236.

Rights of a Holder in Due Course

Section 74(*b*) of the Act provides that a holder in due course holds the bill free from "any defect of title of prior parties, as well as from mere personal defences available to prior parties among themselves". (As to the scope of "defect of title", *cf.* examples set forth in s. 56(2) and see further discussion in §3, *infra*.) His freedom relates also to defences arising from the basic transaction.

   Real (or absolute) defences do not constitute a defect of title and are also available against a holder in due course. *Falconbridge on Banking* explains the meaning of "real defence" as follows (at p. 668):

> A real defence is so-called because, at least as regards a particular defendant who is entitled to set it up, it is based upon the nullity of the *res* without regard to the merits or demerits of the plaintiff. It is a good defence, so far as that defendant is concerned, even against a holder in due course, and as a general rule a holder cannot even claim title through the signature of that defendant.
>
> Examples of real defences are the absolute incapacity of the defendant to make a binding contract, the fact that a party's signature has been forged or has been written without his authority except in so far as he is estopped from denying the validity of

the signature, the absence of effective delivery of a blank or incomplete document, the material alteration of a document, the discharge by payment in due course, by renunciation at or after maturity, or by intentional and apparent cancellation, fraud or illegality of a nature to make the bill void and not merely voidable. The omission in s. 74 of any mention of defences of this class impliedly recognizes that they are good even against a holder in due course, so far as effect must be given to other provisions of the statute.

In *Foster* v. *Mackinnon* (1869) LR 4 CP 704 at 713, it was said that

> The defendant . . . never intended to put his name to any instrument that then was or thereafter might become negotiable. He was deceived, not merely as to the legal effect, but as to the *actual contents* of the instrument. [Emphasis in the original.]

As he "never intended to indorse a bill of exchange at all, but intended to sign a contract of an entirely different nature", (*id.* 712) the endorser in that case was permitted to raise the defence of *non est factum*. The case was later explained in *Nordic Acceptance Ltd.* v. *Switzer* (1965) 50 DLR (2d) 600 at 606 on the basis that "[t]here was never intention that [the] document should be converted into a bill".

This interpretation of the scope of the *non est factum* defence was severely challenged by Lord Denning M.R. in *Gallie* v. *Lee* [1969] 2 Ch. 17 (CA); affirmed by the House of Lords [1970] 3 All ER 961 (*sub nom. Saunders* v. *Anglia Building Society*) (see chapter 3, *supra*).

While delivery is an indispensable requirement for the enforceability of an obligation on a bill or note (see Section C(1) *supra*), where the instrument is in the hands of a holder in due course, it is "conclusively presumed" that it was validly delivered "by all parties prior to him: (s. 40(2)). Nonetheless, absence of "issue" (namely, "the first delivery of a bill or note, complete in form, to a person who takes it as a holder": s. 2) is not overcome even by a holder in due course: *McKenty* v. *Vanhorenback* (1911) 21 Man. R. 360. Absent initial delivery (or issue), "the instrument . . . was never a negotiable instrument. It . . . never came into existence as a cheque. The bill (or cheque) must pre-exist before sub-section 2 of section 40 applies. . . . [Otherwise] the instrument was, and in fact still is, a nullity. 'The presumption [of s. 40(2)] would not apply to an instrument never issued as a bill' '': *id.* at 365.

A holder in due course also overcomes the defence of unauthorized completion of an instrument "delivered by the signer in order that it may be converted into a bill" (ss. 31-32). Nonetheless, this protection is withdrawn when delivery of the blank instrument by the signer was for custody and safekeeping only (without authority to convert it into a bill or note). See *Smith* v. *Prosser* [1907] 2 KB 735 (CA); *Ray* v. Willson (1911) 45 SCR 401; *Campbell* v. *Bourque* (1914) 17 DLR 262 (Man. CA); and *Commercial Acceptance Corp.* v. *Paris* (1964) 45 DLR (2d) 493 (Ont. Dist. Ct.).

3. ENFORCEMENT BY ONE NOT A HOLDER IN DUE COURSE

a) "Defect of Title" and Contractual Defences

Sections 56(2), 70(1), 72 and 74(*b*) of the Bills of Exchange Act.

BENJAMIN GEVA
"Equities as to Liability on Bills and Notes: Rights of a Holder Not in Due Course"
(1980) 5 Can. Bus. LJ 53

Prima facie, the obligor's contractual defences fall within either "defect of title" or "mere personal defences". This stems from the scheme governing the position of a holder in due course towards the obligor's defences. Thus, it is well established, beyond the need to cite any supporting authority, that the obligor's contractual defences are not available against a holder in due course. The range of defences which are not available against a holder in due course are delineated under the Act by the categories of "defect of title" and "mere personal defences". The obligor's defences must therefore fall within the territory covered by these expressions.

Further examination reveals that in dealing with the availability of the obligor's defences against a holder not in due course, the critical expression is "defect of title". . . . [I]n providing for two specific situations of a holder not in due course, the Act omits any reference to "mere personal defences" and is explicit with respect to the holder's subjection only to "any *defect of title*". The consensus among the majority of textbook writers is accordingly that "whereas neither 'defect of title' nor 'mere personal defences' may be raised against a holder in due course, defects of title may be raised against a remote party who is not a holder in due course, but 'mere personal' . . . defences are not available against such a holder". "A mere personal defence" is good only "as between the two parties between whom it arises, that is, between immediate parties". Implicit in this summary is the subjection of an immediate party to his own defect of title. Thus, it is only "defect of title" which is central to the delineation of defences available against all holders not in due course. Whether the obligor's contractual defences do fall within its ambit will now be examined.

The term "defect of title" was introduced into the Act as the statutory equivalent of the common law expression "equity attaching to the bill". Possible grounds for a defect of title set forth in the Act are obtaining the instrument or its acceptance by fraud, by duress or force and fear, by other unlawful means, or by illegal consideration, as well as its negotiation in breach of faith or fraud. As the list is preceded by "in particular", it is overwhelmingly accepted that "the examples . . . do not exhaust the category".

Indeed, "why a breach of positive contract should not form as strong a defence as a breach of faith is hard to perceive". Yet, pre-Act cases involved "equities of the bill", "equities that attach to the bill itself", "equities affecting it", or equities "with which the bill is incumbered" or a narrower range than the entire scope of the underlying contract. Thus in *Holmes* v. *Kidd* (1858) 3 H & N 891 at 893 where "[u]pon the concoction of [the] bill it was agreed that it was not to be paid if [the] canvas was sold", it was held that "[t]hat agreement directly affects the bill and was part of the consideration for it". As "the incumbrance on the bill was part of the transaction out of which the bill arose" the agreement became an equity attaching thereto. Other examples enumerated in pre-Act case law were "the payment or satisfaction of the bill itself to [such] holder, or where the title of [such] holder was only to secure the balance of an account due". While the subjection of an immediate party not a holder in due course to the defence of total failure of consideration was explicitly recognized, this recognition was generally not made in conjunction with the broad principle of the holder's subjection to the equities of the instrument.

None the less, it is erroneous to put "defect of title" into the narrow perspective of specific direct cases decided prior to 1882. What constitutes "defect of title" is a function of the nature of the title to bills and notes. Thus, according to Professor Chafee, a bill or note is both a chattel and a chose in action. Its ownership "involves not only the right to possess a thing but the right to sue . . ." Corresponding "to the duplex nature of the negotiable instrument", equities affecting it "must [thus] be classified accordingly as they relate to the ownership of the chattel or to liability on [the] obligation". Under this classification, "equities" affecting the right to sue, side by side with those affecting the right to possess the piece of paper, constitute defects of title.

Indeed, the subjection of an assignee of a chose in action "to all defences existing in respect of the right assigned which would be available against the assignor seeking to enforce the right assigned", has long been "expressed by the statement that the assignee takes subject to all *equities*". In this framework *Young* v. *Kitchin* (1878) 3 Ex. D. 127 held in the late nineteenth century that an obligor under an assigned contract that had been broken by the obligee-assignor "has no claim to recover anything against the [assignee]; he only meets the [assignee's] claim by a counterclaim of damages arising out of the same contract". Shortly thereafter, in *The Government of Newfoundland* v. *The Newfoundland Railway Company* (1888) 13 App. Cas. 199 the Privy Council adhered to this principle and explained how the obligor could meet the assignee's claim with a counterclaim. The position that "a party to a contract may assign a portion of it, perhaps a beneficial portion, so that the assignee shall take the benefit, wholly discharged of any counterclaim by the other party in respect of the rest of the contract which may be burdensome" was considered by the court "a lamentable thing" and accordingly was rejected. It was thus held that "[u]nliquidated damages [entitling the obligor to a counterclaim] may . . . be set off . . . against an assignee if flowing out of and inseparably connected with the dealings and transactions which also give rise to the subject of the assignment".

The obligor's equities have thus been perceived quite broadly to include "the terms and conditions of the contract under which the indebtedness arose". The proposition which emerges from both leading cases is indeed that an obligor can recoup his damage arising from breach of any term of the assigned contract by meeting the assignee's claim thereon with a defence whose subject matter gives ground to a counterclaim arising from the breach. Depending on the size of the damages the effect of such defence is either to extinguish or to diminish the size of the assignee's right but not to charge him with liability.

Equities attaching to the instrument were contrasted in pre-Act case law with "equities of the parties", with "collateral matters, such as the statutory right of set-off", or with "a right of set-off . . . which is merely a personal right not affecting the bill". This formula appears to be adopted by the Act speaking of the holder in due course holding free from "any defect of title . . . as well as from mere personal defences". [. . .]

Strictly speaking, a "mere personal defence" is not a "defence". Rather, it is a claim of the defendant arising outside the underlying contract whose availability in the plaintiff's action depends on a specific statute. A "mere personal defence" is either the right to set off a separate liquidated claim, or the right to set up an independent counterclaim for unliquidated damages. Set-off has been available to a defendant since a 1729 statute and is given to him as of right. The right to assert a counterclaim was originally introduced by the 1873 Judicature Act. Permission to present it may be refused under Rules of Practice if in the opinion of the court it cannot be conveniently disposed of in the pending action.

The right to assert a "mere personal defence" is a mode of adjusting mutual claims or avoiding circuity of action. Being a separate cause of action against the immediate party rather than an answer to the claim on the underlying contract, a "mere personal defence" is confined to the relations between those immediate parties between whom it arose. It cannot be asserted against a remote party.

• • •

It may be concluded that in drawing a contrast between "defect of title" and "mere personal defences" the Act follows the pre-Act differentiation between an "equity attaching to the bill" and the "equities of the parties". On its part the latter differentiation is modelled on the contrast between an "equity relating to the assigned debt" and "a personal claim" which is "not connected with the chose in action assigned". The comprehensiveness of the equities "relating to the assigned debt" with respect to all "the terms and conditions of the contract under which the indebtedness arose" entails that all defences arising from the underlying contract are defects of title. This formula specifically excludes counterclaims arising from separate matters, whether in liquidated or unliquidated amounts.

Notes and Questions:

1   For another view on the scope of defect of title see R. Donald, "Negotiation of an Overdue Bill of Exchange or Promissory Note" (1970) 8 Alta. L. Rev. 75. His conclusion (at 86) is that "[i]n the development of the law prior to the enactment of the Bills of Exchange Acts, it is clear that the only equities that attached to the instrument were basically those that arose at its inception or subsequent negotiation. The defects of title enumerated in the legislation, while not exclusive of others, are all of the same character. Not all equities cling to the instrument and it is submitted that any extension to include all the equities that existed between the parties to the underlying contract is an erroneous interpretation of the law."

2   The plaintiff in *Edcal Industrial Agents Ltd.* v. *Redl and Zimmer* (1967) 60 DLR (2d) 289 (Alta. Sup. Ct.) was a remote party not a holder in due course. The defendant (maker of the note) purported to meet the action with a defence based on partial failure of consideration in a sum uncertain. The majority of the court (*per* Johnson J.A.) stated (at 297-298):

In the present case the [defendant maker of the note] did not file a counterclaim but included his claim in his defence. . . . [The payee] was not a party to the proceedings and I consider that [the payee] should have been a party to the counterclaim which ought to have been filed.

Was the case correctly decided?

3   As mere personal defence rather than an equity as to liability, the right of set-off is not available against a remote party even one not a holder in due course. It is, however, well established (and currently expressed in s. 40(1)(*b*) of the Ontario PPSA, RSO 1970, c. 344) that an assignee of a non-negotiable chose in action takes it subject to the debtor's right to set off a liquidated amount owing from the assignor under a separate transaction which accrues before the debtor receives notice of the assignment. See e.g.: *Cavendish* v. *Geaves* (1857) 24 Beav. 163, 53 ER 319; and *Roxburghe* v. *Cox* (1881) 17 Ch.D. 520 at 526. For further analysis and citations, see Geva, *supra* at 66 *et seq.* Note, however, the ambiguity in the use of the term set-off in Anglo-Canadian law. The set-off discussed in this note (i.e., a statutory right of set-off) is a right to a liquidated sum of money arising *outside* the underlying transaction. *Government of Newfoundland* v. *Newfoundland Railway Co.* (1888) 13 App. Cas. 199 (PC) used set-off in the passages reproduced above, in connection with damages for breach arising from the underlying transaction. This is more properly called "equitable set-off": *Morgan and Son, Ltd.* v. *S. Martin Johnson and Co. Ltd.* [1949] 1 KB 107 (CA); see also: *Gilbert-Ash (Northern) Ltd.* v. *Modern Engineering (Bristol) Ltd.* [1973] 3 All ER 195 at 212 (HL) (judgment of Lord Diplock) and the term "set up" in section 51(1)(*a*) of the Sale of Goods Act, RSO 1970, c. 421. The term used by the Americans to denote the defendant's right "to present in opposition to the plaintiff's claim, for its reduction or extinguishment, a right of action . . . for loss or damage sustained . . . in the same transaction . . ." is "recoupment": William Loyd, "The Development of Set-off" (1916) 64 U. Pa. L. Rev. 541 at 563.

4   *Falconbridge on Banking* (p. 619) concludes that "[o]riginal absence of consideration is not a defect of title or equity attaching to the instrument". He bases his view on pre-Act cases as well as on the fact that "absence of consideration is not one of the defects of title specified in [the Act]." He adds that "[t]he general principle, that absence of consideration is not a defect of title, seems to be implied in s. 54 which defines a holder for value." His summary is in line with Chalmers (p. 102): "[Original] absence of consideration . . . is a matter of defence against an immediate party or a remote party, who is not a holder for value, but it is not a defence against a remote party who is a holder for value." ("Holder for value" is a holder who either himself took the instrument for value, or who derives his title from one who had given value for it. He does not have to be a holder in due course.) Do you agree? Note that (as acknowledged by him at p. 619) the pre-Act leading cases referred to by Falconbridge involve accommodation parties. Does the case of an accommodation party involve absence of consideration? *Cf.* s. 55(2). For a critique of Falconbridge's position and a repudiation of the view that "holder for value" is an intermediate concept for a person who, though not a holder in due course, overcomes the

defence of absence of consideration, see in general Geva, ``Absence of Consideration in the Law of Bills and Notes'' [1980] Camb. LJ 360. Prof. Geva concludes there
as follows with respect to the position under s. 54(1):

> It is submitted here, that in its true sense the . . . provision means that absence of
> consideration is not an equity as to ownership. The provision does not deal with
> absence of consideration as an equity as to liability. Its effect is indeed that only
> inasmuch as a holder seeks to establish his property in the instrument rather than to
> charge a party with liability, absence of consideration is not a defect of title. Thus, as
> ``the outgrowth of the fundamental idea in the law of negotiable paper . . . that a bill
> or note is a species of property'', the provision means that once ``value has . . . been
> given for the instrument, it becomes the subject of gift''. Accordingly, ``[i]f a party
> gives to another a negotiable instrument, *on which other parties are liable*, the man who
> makes the gift cannot recover the bill back, and the man to whom the bill is given
> may recover against the other parties on the bill.'' As such [s. 54(1)] is merely a
> ``sheltering'' provision which is complementary to [s. 61(1)] conferring on the
> transferee for value ``such title as the transferor had,'' as well as to [s. 57] giving to
> ``[a] holder . . . who derives his title to a bill through a holder in due course'' the same
> ``rights of that holder in due course''. Its effect is thus to confer the endorser's title on
> a holder who took the instrument without giving value thereto, thereby giving him
> a cause of action against *prior parties already liable on the instrument*. This indeed means
> that absence of consideration is not an equity as to ownership of the instrument. But
> it falls short of providing that absence of consideration is also not an equity as to
> liability on the instrument. In fact, it is submitted, the section does not even deal
> with the latter.

b)   The Defence of Failure of Consideration

In the law of bills and notes, ``there is a failure of consideration where the performance is
either absent, incomplete, or defective'': Note, ``Failure of Consideration in Negotiable
Instruments'' (1925) 25 Colum. L. Rev. 83. ``Failure of consideration'' is thus interchangeable with the breach of the underlying contract.

BENJAMIN GEVA
"Equities as to Liability on Bill and Notes: Rights of a Holder Not in Due Course"
(1980) 5 Can. Bus. LJ 53 ff.

The following example will facilitate the understanding of the problem explored
in this article. A negotiable instrument is issued by a buyer to the order of a seller
in return for two machines sold to him. The seller breaks the contract. His breach
could take different forms. He can fail altogether to deliver the machines (total
failure of consideration), he can fail to deliver one out of the two machines
(partial failure of consideration in an ascertained or liquidated amount), or while
having provided both machines, he can be in breach of a warranty with respect to
them (partial failure of consideration in a sum uncertain). The instrument either
remains in the hands of the seller (the immediate party) or is negotiated by him to
a finance company (a remote party) which for one reason or another fails to be a

holder in due course. In either case the buyer is sued on the instrument by a holder not in due course. Having failed or chosen not to rescind or terminate the contract, or being not entitled to exercise this remedy in the first place, can the buyer assert his defences arising from the seller's breach in an action on the instrument? Stated otherwise, the issue is the buyer's ability to avoid circuity of actions as well as the risk of ultimately incurring loss, namely his power to litigate his liability in the action on the instrument instead of in a separate action brought by him after having been forced to pay the full amount of the instrument.

· · ·

The traditional summary of the rules which under Anglo-Canadian law determine the availability of the defence of failure of consideration to an action on a bill or note by a holder not in due course is inconsistent with the analysis made so far. . . . Under this summary, total failure of consideration is a defence against an immediate party and possibly against a remote holder for value with notice. *Quaere*, whether it is a defence against a remote party without notice who is none the less not a holder in due course. Partial failure of consideration is a defence *pro tanto* against an immediate party and is available only when the failure is in an ascertained and liquidated amount. It is not a defence against a remote party holder for value. "Holder for value" is a holder who either himself took the instrument for value, or who derives his title from one who had given value for it. He does not have to be a holder in due course.

The availability of the defence of failure of consideration against a holder not in due course depends under this summary first on whether the claimant holder for value is an immediate or a remote party. Secondly, it depends on whether the failure involved has been total or partial. The validity of these classifications will now be examined.

It appears that the immediate/remote party dichotomy can easily be dismissed as groundless. None of the leading cases cited by Chalmers and Falconbridge either turned on the identity of the plaintiff as a remote party not a holder in due course or otherwise purported to establish a distinction between different claimants who are not holders in due course. Thus, a leading case as to the availability of partial failure of consideration in an ascertained or liquidated amount involved a remote rather than an immediate party. Furthermore, support for the proposition that partial failure of consideration "is not a defence against a remote party who is a holder for value" is drawn by Chalmers and Falconbridge from a case which in fact turned on the type of defence involved rather than on the immediate/remote party dichotomy. Other cases holding that failure of consideration, whether partial or total, is no defence against a remote party turned on the holder in due course status of the remote party. Unfortunately, however, they often used the terms "indorsee for value", "holder for value", or "remote party" as interchangeable with "holder in due course". This inaccurate use of the terms has indeed been a source of confusion resulting in creating the erroneous impression that insofar as failure of consideration is concerned, a remote party, even when not a holder in due course, is in a better position than an immediate party. It is my thesis, however, that all parties who are not holders in due course, whether immediate or remote, are in the same position with respect to the defence of failure of consideration.

• • •

Chalmers and Falconbridge undermine the effect of the obligor's inability to raise partial failure in a sum uncertain as a defence against a holder not in due course. Their opinion is that following the Judicature Acts, it is possible to include such a failure of consideration in a counterclaim "which may have all the practical consequences of a defence to the claim". This view is none the less erroneous. The raising of a counterclaim contemplates the personal liability of the defendant thereunder (the plaintiff in the principal action). Yet an obligor "has no claim to recover anything against [a remote party]". The latter's subjection to a counterclaim arising from the breach of the underlying contract can mean no more than subjection to the obligor's power to meet the claim by a defence based on facts giving rise to the counterclaim. Thus, the immunity of a remote party from the defence of partial failure of consideration in a sum uncertain confers on him in relation to this defence an absolute right on the instrument as if he were a holder in due course. Chalmers' and Falconbridge's view may be relevant indeed only in the context of an immediate party who is personally liable on the counterclaim. Yet, even with respect to such a party, courts stress the fact that a counterclaim "is not an absolute right to set off damages against a debt" but "merely a right depending on the discretion of the judge". As against an action on a bill or note the prevailing tendency is to disallow a counterclaim for unliquidated damages based on the underlying contract. Underlying this tendency is, indeed, the belief in the existence of a substantive rule of law which gives the holder (whether an immediate or remote party) an absolute right to recover on the instrument. Thus, notwithstanding Chalmers' and Falconbridge's observation, the alleged holder's immunity cannot be circumvented by rules of procedure.

Note: What is meant by the holder's power to overcome the defence of partial failure of consideration in a sum uncertain is the defendant's inability to reduce or extinguish his liability by meeting an action on a bill or note with a defence based on facts giving rise to a claim for unliquidated damages stemming from the breach of the underlying contract. At the same time the defence of an effective repudiation of the underlying contract is available against a holder not in due course even when its ground is partial failure in a sum uncertain.

JAMES LAMONT & CO. LTD. v. HYLAND LTD. (No. 2)
[1950] 66 TLR (Pt. 1) 940, 1 All ER 929 (CA)

ROXBURGH J.: The plaintiffs' claim in this case was (i) for £20,000 (and £575 6s. 10d. interest) against the defendants as acceptors of a bill of exchange for that amount, and (ii) for £15,141 odd for work and materials. This court is not concerned with the second head of claim. As regards the claim on the bill of exchange, the plaintiffs, in proceedings for summary judgment under Ord. 14, swore a common form affidavit verifying the cause of action. The defendants put in an affidavit in opposition to judgment by one Lane (the contents of which will be considered later) indicating an intention to counterclaim. The master gave the plaintiffs liberty to sign judgment for £20,000, plus £575 interest, subject to a stay of execution pending trial of the defendants' counterclaim. Both parties appealed from the master's decision, the defendants asking for unconditional leave to defend, the plaintiffs asking that the stay pending trial of the counterclaim be removed. Lynskey, J., before whom these appeals came, dismissed the defendants' appeal and allowed the plaintiffs' appeal against the stay — that is to say, he gave the plaintiffs liberty to sign immediate judgment for the amount claimed on the bill and interest. From that decision the defendants appeal to this court, reiterating their request for unconditional leave to defend.

The affidavit in opposition to judgment which was before the master, sworn by Lane, the defendants' managing director, can be summarised as follows. He deposed that early in 1948 the defendants employed the plaintiffs to repair and alter a ship. There was a specification and estimate for £15,000. He alleges that it was a condition of this contract that the repairs and alterations should be completed in time for the ship to reach Palermo by Dec. 1, 1948. He says that later there was a contract to pay reasonable charges for repairs up to £40,000 subject to the same conditions, the reason for which was that the ship had been chartered to carry displaced persons at a very high profit (£100,000) conditionally on its being ready by Dec. 1, 1948. He goes on to say that it was later agreed to raise the maximum of the repairs, etc., to £50,000, of which the defendants paid the plaintiffs £30,000 on account, and have accepted a bill of exchange for £20,000 for the balance. He says the plaintiffs violated the condition — failed to complete the repairs within the stipulated time — and that the defendants have lost a profit of £100,000. The defendants, therefore, have a counterclaim for breach of contract far over-topping the claim on the bill of exchange and are entitled to set off a sufficient amount thereof to extinguish the claim. There was no affidavit in reply to this before the master, who, as has been seen, gave liberty to sign judgment on the bill of exchange subject to a stay of execution.

Before Lynskey, J., on appeal, there was an affidavit in reply sworn by one Raeside, secretary of the plaintiff company, which is completely at variance with the case set up in the defendants' affidavit. This deponent denies the successive sums of £15,000, £40,000 and £50,000 alleged as successive contractual maxima in that affidavit and alleges a contract to do the work contracted for, subject to the approval of the Ministry of Transport, on the plaintiffs' usual terms, that is to say, cost plus certain specified percentages. He denies that it was a condition of the contract that the ship should be ready to reach Palermo by Dec. 1, 1948. He says that Lane on Oct. 4, 1948, had said he had £200,000 worth of stores at Malta, much of which had been stolen, and requested that, to save further loss, the ship might be ready by Oct. 20. The plaintiffs never promised this, but had said they would do their best; and the ship would, so far as their part was concerned, in fact have been at Palermo before Dec. 1, 1948, but for circumstances such as running aground on Oct. 21 and losing her stern anchor in trials in early November — circumstances for which the plaintiffs were in no degree responsible. He says that Mr. Lane gave him the bill for £20,000, dated Nov. 1, on Nov. 5 or 6 as a payment on account. (No doubt part of the consideration was also release of the ship from the plaintiffs' lien as repairers).

The position in law arising on these affidavits is, therefore, shortly, that the plaintiffs sue on a bill of exchange and the defendants seek to prevent the plaintiffs from having liberty to sign immediate judgment without a stay by alleging that the bill was given in pursuance of a contract which the plaintiffs have broken and for which the defendants claim unliquidated damages in excess of the amount of the bill. On these materials the judge has given liberty to sign judgment for the amount of the bill with interest and without any stay. This court has recently decided in *Morgan & Son, Ltd.* v. *S. Martin Johnson & Co., Ltd.* [1949] KB 107 that where the matters relied on by the defendant, although not strictly matters of defence, would before the Judicature Acts have been regarded by a court of equity as ground for relief by way of equitable set-off, the proper order to make under Ord. 14 procedure as a general rule is that the defendant have unconditional leave to defend and not that the plaintiff recover judgment with execution stayed until the trial of the counterclaim.

The question raised in the present appeal is whether this rule applies to an action between immediate parties to a bill of exchange, where the matters relied on by the defendant afford no defence under the Bills of Exchange Act, 1882. In such cases, although it is not easy wholly to reconcile the authorities, a rule more favourable to the plaintiff has in general prevailed, the court treating the execution of a bill of exchange either as analogous to a payment of cash, or as amounting to an independent contract within the wider contract in pursuance of which it was executed, and not dependent as regards its enforcement on due performance of the latter. Counsel for the plaintiffs cited in particular three cases which illustrate this rule or tendency. Some of them are pre-Judicature Act and pre-Order 14 cases.

The first in order of time is *Glennie* v. *Imri* (1839) 3 Y & C Ex. 436, a case decided on the equity side of the Court of Exchequer in 1839, long before the days of Ord. 14. The plaintiff sued on a bill of exchange given for goods sold and delivered. The defendant, using the language of that day, set up that he had been

> fraudulently deceived in his contract, the goods delivered being inferior both in quality and quantity to what he had ordered: *Held*, that he could not maintain a bill for an account and for an injunction to restrain the action, inasmuch as his object was to reduce the amount of the bill of exchange by the damages which he claimed for the alleged breach of contract,

and that, as this was not the subject of set-off in law, it could not be the subject of an account in equity. "Courts of equity will not take an account of debts one way and damages the other." A court of law would say you must pay the bill first and then bring an action for the fraud, and, apparently, where a bill of exchange was concerned, equity in this matter followed the law.

The second case cited to us under this head was *Warwick* v. *Nairn* (1855) 10 Ex. 762. The plaintiff supplied the defendant with goods under a contract and drew a bill of exchange for £313 odd of which all but £108 odd was in respect of their price. The defendant pleaded that the plaintiff promised that the goods should be of a certain quality and that he accepted the bill of exchange on the faith of that promise, which, he alleged, had been broken. On demurrer this was held a bad plea. During the argument Pollock, C.B., said (10 Exch. 764):

> The payment by a bill of exchange is to be taken as the payment of so much cash; the defendant ought to satisfy the bill and proceed upon the remedy for the breach of warranty.

Counsel arguing in support of the demurrer contended that such a partial failure of consideration cannot be pleaded to a bill of exchange or promissory note. Parke, B., intervened and stopped him with the observation (*ibid.*):

> The subject-matter of the plea [the alleged inferior quality of the goods] has been held on several occasions to afford no defence to an action on a bill of exchange. *Morgan* v. *Richardson* (1806) 7 East 482n and *Trickey* v. *Larne* (1840) 6 M & W 278 are direct authorities against the plea.

There might, it appears, have been a defence if it had been alleged that the goods tendered had not been of the contract description and had been rejected for then there would have been no consideration and this is a defence to an action on a bill of exchange, but in the actual case the "inferior" goods were retained by the deliveree, and the failure of consideration, therefore, partial only. So also in the present case. The same principle was applied in *Jackson* v. *Murphy* (1888) 4 TLR 92. In *Court* v. *Sheen* (1891) 7 TLR 556, a different result was reached on similar facts, and the plaintiff was refused liberty to sign immediate judgment. But the case is even more shortly reported than *Jackson* v. *Murphy*, and it is difficult or impossible to say on what grounds it proceeded.

Lastly, among the bill of exchange cases is that of *Anglo-Italian Bank* v. *Wells* (1878) 38 LT 197. The plaintiffs, by specially endorsed writ, sued the defendants on certain promissory notes and took out a summons under Ord. 14. The defendants resisted on the ground that they had a good defence and a good counterclaim. Thesiger, L.J., said (38 LT 201):

> If the appellants had disclosed by their affidavits facts sufficient to establish a good ground of counterclaim, I think the counterclaim would have been sufficiently connected with the cause of action in the present case to justify its being set up as a defence even to a liquidated claim on a bill of exchange.

In the result, however, leave to defend on the bills was refused. And Sir George Jessel, M.R., anticipating the possibility envisaged by Thesiger, L.J., strikes rather a different note. He said (*ibid.*, 199):

> . . . I must say, speaking for myself, that I should hesitate long before I allowed a defendant in an action on a bill of exchange to set up a case for damages by reason of the breach by the plaintiff of some other contract or the commission of some tort.

Pausing there, it would seem that the learned Master of the Rolls means by "some other contract" some contract other than that constituted by the bill of exchange itself. He goes on:

I do not say that there cannot be a case where the two transactions may not be so connected, but at present I cannot even imagine the existence of such a special case.

Having regard to the tenor of the authorities summarised above in cases where the action is on a bill of exchange, it is impossible to say that in giving liberty to sign immediate judgment without a stay the learned judge in chambers was guilty of an improper exercise of the discretion vested in him. In our view, the appeal fails.

Appeal dismissed.

Notes and Questions:

1   Did the court in *Lamont* hold that failure of consideration is not a defect of title? In distinguishing between failure of consideration and damages for breach of contract the majority of the court in *Edcal Industrial Agents Ltd.* v. *Redl and Zimmer* (1967) 60 DLR (2d) 289 at 297 (Alta. Sup. Ct.) regarded the rules on the defence of failure of consideration as an historical anomaly and expressed the view that since the English Judicature Act "there is probably no longer a reason for continuing it". Is this view reconcilable with *Lamont*?

2   Historically, the obligor's inability to assert the defence of failure of consideration in a sum uncertain against a holder of an instrument coincided with the common law rule under which a breach of warranty with respect to goods sold could not be asserted to reduce the amount of the seller's action for the price. The common law rule in the sales area was reversed in *Mondel* v. *Steel* (1841) 8 M&W 858, 151 ER 1288. The weight of authority in the law of bills and notes declined to conform to this change in general contract law and did not reverse the promisor's inability to raise a partial failure of consideration in a sum uncertain against a holder not in due course. *Lamont* is thus in line with the accepted view on the subject and has since then been affirmed in *Brown Shipley & Co. Ltd.* v. *Alicia Hosiery Ltd.* [1966] 1 Ll. L. Rep. 668 (CA); *Fielding & Platt Ltd.* v. *Najjar* [1969] 2 All ER 150 (CA); *Cebora S.N.C.* v. *S.I.P. (Industrial Products) Ltd.* [1976] 1 Ll. L. Rep. 271 (CA); *Nova (Jersey) Knit Ltd.* v. *Kammgarn Spinnerei GmbH* [1977] 2 All ER 463 (HL); and *Montecchi* v. *Shimco (U.K.) Ltd.* [1980] 1 L1. L. Rep. 50 (CA). In *Nova (Jersey) Knit Ltd., supra* at 479-80 (cited with approval in *Williams & Glyn's Bank Ltd.* v. *Belkin Packaging Ltd.* (1980) 8 BLR 238, 254 (BC SC)) Lord Russell of Killowen referred to a "deep rooted concept of English commercial law" under which "the nature and function of . . . a bill" is,

> not merely to serve as a negotiable instrument; it is also to avoid postponement of the purchaser's liability to the vendor himself, a postponement grounded on some allegation of failure in some respect by the vendor under the underlying contract unless it be total or quantified partial failure of consideration.

3   The result of *Lamont* is criticised in Geva, 5 Can. Bus. LJ 53, *supra*, at 85 as follows:

> Yet, even if seen as an independent rule, the holder's power to recover over the defence of partial failure in a sum uncertain appears to stand on a tenuous footing. Both grounds underlying it, the "independent contract" and the "pay-

ment in cash" theories, are in fact the two sides of the same coin. While the former provides the *cause* of the holder's freedom, the latter is the *result* thereof [emphasis added]. It further appears that historically the "independent contract" theory preceded the "payment in cash" explanation and thus the latter is in fact an aftermath rationale to a rule which had already been perceived as existing. The holder's power to overcome the defence of partial failure in a sum uncertain appears then to be founded on the "independent contract".

• • •

Yet if the holder's power to recover over the partial failure in a sum uncertain is based on contract, it should not extend to cover situations where an actual agreement is lacking.

D. EFFECT OF A BILL OR NOTE ON THE UNDERLYING OBLIGATION

Chalmers on Bills of Exchange
(13th ed., 1964) p. 338 *et seq.*

Where a creditor has taken a bill or note from his debtor various questions may arise as to the effect of his so doing. A bill or note may be given by a debtor to his creditor either by way of payment or as collateral security; but the presumption is in favour of payment.

COLLATERAL SECURITY

If it is given by way of collateral security it does not suspend the creditor's right to sue for his debt. The creditor must use due diligence to collect it and give notice of dishonour, if necessary; otherwise it may be treated as so much money in his hands.

CONDITIONAL PAYMENT

Where a bill or note is given by way of payment, the payment may be absolute or conditional, the strong presumption being in favour of conditional payment. It is immaterial whether the instrument is payable on demand or at a future time. "The title of a creditor," says Lush J., "to a bill given on account of a pre-existing debt, and payable at a future day, does not rest upon the implied agreement to suspend his remedies. The true reason is that a negotiable security given for such a purpose is a conditional payment of the debt, the condition being that the debt revives if the security is not realised. This is precisely the effect which both parties intended the security to have, and the doctrine is as applicable to one species of negotiable security as another; to a cheque payable on demand, as to a running bill or a promissory note payable to order or bearer, whether it be the note of a country bank which circulates as money, or the note of the debtor, or of any other person."

The effect of a bill or note as conditional payment may be illustrated by the contract of sale. If a bill be taken for the price of goods sold, the seller's lien is gone during the currency of the bill, but revives on its actual or practical dishonour. Thus, in *Gunn* v. *Bolckow, Vaughan & Co.* (1875) 10 Ch. App. 491, where iron rails were sold to be paid for by buyer's acceptances of sellers' drafts against wharfinger's certificates, it was held that the giving of the acceptances was not an absolute payment, but conditional on the acceptances being met and that upon the insolvency of the acceptors the sellers' lien on the goods revived, and the fact that the sellers had negotiated the bills made no difference. "No doubt," says Mellish L.J., "if the buyer does not become insolvent then credit is given by taking the bill, and during the time that the bill is current there is no vendor's lien, and the vendor is bound to deliver. But if the bill is dishonoured before delivery has been made, then the vendor's lien revives; or if the purchaser becomes openly insolvent before the delivery actually takes place, then the law does not compel the vendor to deliver to an insolvent purchaser." The bills had been discounted but the seller was liable on them, with recourse over against only the insolvent buyer; otherwise the fact that the bills were in the hands of third parties would have been material. Where the seller of goods took the buyer's acceptance and then indorsed the bill to a third person and the bill was dishonoured, it was held that he could not sue the buyer for the price while the bill was outstanding in the hands of a third person, even though he got it back before the action came on for hearing.

Where a cheque has been given in part payment of a debt, the Limitations Act as to suing for the balance begins to run from the time when the cheque was given, and not from the time when it was paid. . . .

When the bill or note has been dishonoured it seems that the debt which had been conditionally paid may be treated as subsisting throughout. Thus, where a debtor gave his creditor a cheque, but on the debt being garnisheed, stopped the cheque, it was held that there was a good subsisting debt which could be garnisheed. Conversely, when the bill or note is duly honoured, the payment dates from the date of the receipt of the bill or note.

CREDITOR HOLDING HIGHER SECURITY

There is, however, a qualification of the rule that a bill or note operates as conditional payment in the case where the creditor already possesses a higher remedy. In *Belshaw* v. *Bush* (1851) 11 CB 191, 138 ER 444, where it was held that the acceptance of a third person operated as a conditional payment, Maule J. says: "The cases in which the giving of the bill has been held not to suspend the remedy on a demand by specialty, or for rent, may be accounted for on the ground that the legal implication of an assent that the bill shall operate as a conditional payment does not arise, where, if it did, the plaintiff would be deprived of a better remedy than an action on a bill, as in *Davis* v. *Gyde* (1835) 111 ER 240, in which the debt being for rent, the plaintiff would part with a remedy for distress; and, as in *Worthington* v. *Wigley* (1836) 3 Scott 558, where the demand being on a bond the plaintiff might in certain events have recourse to other funds than he could in an action on a simple contract." . . .

EFFECT OF LACHES

If a creditor takes a bill or note as conditional payment, and he is guilty of laches in respect of it, the bill or note is then treated as absolute payment, and as between debtor and creditor the debt is discharged.

Thus, if a bill be indorsed on account of a debt and dishonoured, and the holder omits to give notice of dishonour to the indorser, he cannot sue him for the debt any more than on the bill; and where a creditor took the cheque of his debtor's agent, and was an unreasonable time in presenting it, whereby his debtor's position was altered, it was held, that, as against the debtor, the cheque must be treated as absolute payment.

At common law if the creditor lost a negotiable bill which he had taken as conditional payment, he was deprived of his remedies, both on the bill and on the consideration, for "if the bill be lost the condition on which payment may be defeated does not arise." But this rigour is now abated by sections 156 and 157 of the Bills of Exchange Act, which authorize application for a new bill or an action on the lost bill. . . .

ABSOLUTE PAYMENT

Though the general effect of giving and taking a bill or note is that the debt is conditionally paid, there is nothing to prevent its being given and taken as absolute payment if the parties so intend, and the creditor may receive the bill or note in absolute discharge of the debt, trusting solely to his remedies on the instrument. The intention of the parties is a question of fact; thus, the creditor may be offered cash, but may prefer to take a bill instead. Where the debtor is not a party to the instrument, perhaps the inference of absolute payment more readily arises.

PAYMENT BY NEGOTIABLE SECURITY FOR LESSER SUM

Where there is a disputed liability, it may be compromised by the payment of a lesser sum than that claimed, but the general rule of law is that where a liquidated sum is due, it cannot be discharged by the payment of a lesser amount, for there is no consideration for the creditor's promise to forgo the balance. But by a strictly logical though curious refinement on this rule it has been held that a liquidated debt may be discharged by the acceptance in satisfaction of a negotiable security for a lesser sum, even if the debtor himself be the only person liable on the instrument.

CHEQUE SENT IN SETTLEMENT RECEIVED ON ACCOUNT

There must, however, be an acceptance in satisfaction. If a cheque for a smaller sum be sent in settlement of a larger sum, the creditor can refuse to receive the cheque in satisfaction, even though he does not return it; he may cash it and sue for the balance. In a case where the debtor sent his own cheque in settlement of a claim for damages for breach of contract, and the creditor retained the cheque, sending back a receipt on account, Bowen L.J. says: "If a person sends a sum of money on the terms that it is to be taken, if at all, in satisfaction of a larger claim, and if the money is kept, it is a question of fact as to the terms upon which it is so kept. Accord and satisfaction imply an agreement to take the money in satisfaction of the claim in respect of which it is sent." But transactions with a third party stand on a different footing. Thus where a father sent a cheque for a smaller sum to settle a debt incurred by his son, it was held that the creditor ought to have returned the cheque if he was not going to take it in satisfaction of the debt.

The mere signature to a receipt form on the back of a cheque stating "in full and final settlement" does not bind the creditor if the wording of the receipt form is inconsistent with the object and intention of the transaction. As Denning L.J. says: "Words of this kind on the back of a cheque cannot be made a trap for the unwary."

BILL OR NOTE AS EVIDENCE OF DEBT

When an action is brought by the holder of a dishonoured bill, note or cheque against an immediate party liable thereon, he may sue on the consideration as well as on the instrument, and use the instrument as evidence.

Note: Whether the cashing of a cheque marked "payment in full" discharges the entire obligation even where the cheque is for a lesser sum depends on whether, by cashing the cheque, the creditor accepts the part payment as payment in full. This is a question of fact which is not always easily determined. For example, in *Phillip* v. *Massey-Ferguson Finance Company of Canada Ltd.* [1973] 1 WWR 443 (Sask. DC) the court found accord and satisfaction where the debtor was led by the creditor's silence to believe that the cheque had been accepted on the terms on which it had been sent. On the other hand, in *Woodlot Services Ltd.* v. *Flemming* (1977) 83 DLR (3d) 201 (NB AD) the court found that the creditor did not intend to accept the cheque in full payment and, therefore, allowed him to sue the debtor for the balance of the debt even though he had cashed the cheque. Consider in this context s. 16 of The Mercantile Law Amendment Act (RSO 1970, c. 272). For a discussion from an American perspective, see Rosenthal, "Discord and Dissatisfaction: section 1-207 of the Uniform Commercial Code" (1978) 78 Colum. L. Rev. 48.

McGLYNN v. HASTIE
(1918) 46 DLR 20, 44 OLR 190 (Ont. SC AD)

MACLAREN J.A.: The defendant appeals from a judgment of the County Court Judge of Huron condemning him to pay the plaintiff $200.10 for 6 hogs, and the cost of protest of the cheque given in payment for them. The defendant claimed that he had bought the hogs as the agent of one Munro, and had so informed the plaintiff, and that the plaintiff accepted Munro's cheque in payment.

The evidence is that the defendant called at the plaintiff's house on the evening of the 17th October, 1917, and asked him if he had any hogs for sale. The plaintiff says that he answered that he "had 4 about ready." The defendant says that he told the plaintiff he was buying for a dealer named Munro, who was giving 17½ cents a pound, and was going to ship from the Gorrie station the following morning, and had given him blank cheques to fill up. The plaintiff says that Munro's name was not mentioned that evening. The defendant asked the plaintiff if he would bring his hogs to the station in the morning. The plaintiff says that his reply was, "If it is a fine morning I will fetch them down" (it was raining that evening). In the morning the plaintiff brought to the station 6 hogs, which were weighed, and a slip was given him by the weigher, which be presented to the defendant, who filled up a blank cheque of Munro's drawn on the Dominion Bank at Wingham for $198.50, and gave it to him.

The plaintiff admitted that he had, a few weeks previously, sold another lot of hogs to one Scott, another agent of Munro's, and received in payment a cheque of Munro's filled up by Scott, which was honoured.

A brother of the defendant swore that he was present when the plaintiff called to see his brother about the cheque, and that the plaintiff then admitted that the defendant had told him on the evening of the 17th that he was buying for Munro and not for himself.

The trial Judge, however, preferred the testimony of the plaintiff on this point, and I accept his finding.

He has further held that the sale was made on the evening of the 17th October. In this I am of opinion that he is clearly in error. The plaintiff's evidence is that he said he had about 4 hogs ready, and if the next morning was fine he would take them to the station. He himself says that he was under no obligation to take them, and he took 6, instead of the 4 he had spoken of the previous evening, and they had to be weighed and delivered before the sale was complete. It is worthy of note that the solicitor of the plaintiff, in endorsing the particulars of his claim on the back of the writ of summons, gives the proper date of the sale, viz., the 18th October. The materiality of this question of date will presently appear.

The cheque was presented at the bank on the 19th October, and noted for non-payment, and protested on the 20th. The defendant was advised of this within a reasonable time, so that no question of laches arises.

While the plaintiff denied that the name of Munro was mentioned on the previous evening, he noticed, when the defendant gave him the cheque, that it was signed by Munro and not by the defendant, and he went away without saying anything about it. He, no doubt, was satisfied, as Munro's cheque which he had received from Scott a few weeks previously had been duly paid.

The authorities shew that where a bill, note, or cheque is taken for or on account of a pre-existing debt, the presumption is that it is only conditional payment, and if it is dishonoured the debt revives; but, if it is given in exchange for goods or other securities sold at the time, the transaction amounts to a barter of the bill, with all its risks.

In *Fydell* v. *Clark* (1796) 1 Esp. 447, one of the earliest cases where this question arose, Lord Kenyon says (p. 448): "If, in the discount of the notes, he" (plaintiff) "took the bills and notes in question, he must be bound by it: the bankers parted with them, supposing them to be good; he took them under the same impression. Having taken them without endorsement, he has taken the risk on himself."

In *Camidge* v. *Allenby*, 6 B & C 373, at pp. 381, 382, 108 ER 489, Bayley, J., says:

> If the notes had been given to the plaintiff at the time when the corn was sold, he could have had no remedy upon them against the defendant. The plaintiff might have insisted upon payment in money. But if he consented to receive the notes as money, they would have been taken by him at his peril.

The law on the point is, in my opinion, correctly summed up in *Byles on Bills*, 17th ed., p. 182, where it says that where an unendorsed bill is given "not in payment of a pre-existing debt, but by way of exchange for goods ... such a transaction has been repeatedly held to be a sale of the bill by tne party transferring it, and a purchase of the instrument, with all risks, by the transferee."

See also *Roscoe's Nisi Prius Evidence*, 18th ed., p. 699, where it says: "A distinction has been drawn between the cases in which it" (a bill) "has been given in exchange for goods or other securities, sold at the time, and those in which it has been given in payment of a pre-existing debt. The former transactions amount, it is said, to a barter of the bill, with all its risks."

In my opinion, the judgment appealed from should be reversed and the action dismissed.

• • •

HODGINS J.A. (dissenting): The contest is whether the appellant bought the hogs as agent for one Munro, and whether the respondent accepted Munro's cheque as payment.

• • •

There is nothing in the testimony that would suggest that the learned trial Judge is wrong in adopting the version which he prefers. It must therefore be taken that the sale was made by the respondent to the appellant not as agent but as principal. I am not at all sure, after perusing the evidence, that the appellant was not simply picking up hogs on his own account, having some agreement with Munro to take them at a price sufficient to pay for the appellant's time and trouble. But the finding I refer to puts an end to any such question. It also renders unimportant the difference between the respondent and the appellant's brother as to the effect of a conversation between them relative to this point of disclosed agency.

Such being the case, then, upon the delivery into the pens, the price became payable by the appellant. Instead of paying cash, he filled up a blank cheque of Munro's, making it payable to the respondent, gave it to him, and he took it away with him. Nothing was said at the time by either party by way of comment or explanation.

On these facts, what is the effect of the giving and receiving of a cheque signed by Munro instead of one signed by the appellant?

If it had been the appellant's own cheque, it would be a conditional payment, and the right of action for the purchase-money would be suspended, but on the dishonour of the cheque would have revived: *Cohen* v. *Hale* (1878) 3 QBD 371.

The case of *Belshaw* v. *Bush* (1851) 11 CB 191, 138 ER 444, forms a good starting-point for ascertaining how far that principle applies where the cheque is that of a third person. There the plaintiff drew a bill upon a third party, William Bush, for part of the debt of the defendant. Maule, J., who delivered the judgment of the Court, said what follows, at pp. 206, 207:

> If a bill given by the defendant himself on account of the debt operate as a conditional payment, and so be of the same force as an absolute payment by the defendant, if the condition by which it is to be defeated has not arisen, there seems

no reason why a bill given by a stranger for and on account of the debt should not operate as a conditional payment by the stranger; and, if it have that operation, the plea in the present case will have the same effect as if it had alleged that the money was paid by William Bush for and on account of the debt. But, if a stranger give money in payment, absolute or conditional, of the debt of another, and the causes of action in respect of it, it must be a payment on behalf of that other, against whom alone the causes of action exist, and, if adopted by him, will operate as payment by himself.

In 1858 this decision was followed in *Bottomley* v. *Nuttall* (1858) 5 CBNS 122, 141 ER 48. It was there decided that drawing a bill of exchange on one partner did not shew an election to trust him and to release the firm — nor did the making out of invoices in his name.

Williams, J., said (p. 144):

> If the creditor accepts a bill or note for and on account of the debt, that operates as a conditional payment . . . If the bill has been returned to the creditor unpaid, without any laches on his part, the condition which was to defeat the payment has happened, and consequently it is no payment.

Crowder, J., agreed with Williams, J. Byles, J., said that taking a bill for and on account of the debt does not operate as an absolute discharge of the debt. It is at most a conditional payment.

In *Hopkins* v. *Ware* (1869) LR 4 Ex 268, the plaintiff lent £250 to one Ware. After his death, the solicitor of the executor of Ware sent the plaintiff his own cheque for £258, the amount due. The solicitor's cheque was dishonoured, and the trial Judge found for the plaintiff. On appeal the Court were of opinion that the plaintiff, by laches, had lost the chance of payment and could not recover from the estate. Channell, B. (pp. 271, 272), says:

> Certainly when the cheque was remitted it did not operate as payment; it only did so, if at all, on the duty to present in reasonable time being neglected.

The case of *Currie* v. *Misa* (1875) LR 10 Ex. 153, *Misa* v. *Currie* (1876) 1 App. Cas. 554, is of importance here because the majority of the Court of Exchequer Chamber point out that the true reason, as given by the Court in *Belshaw* v. *Bush*, 11 CB 191, and upon which its judgment is founded, is that a negotiable security given on account of a pre-existing debt is a conditional payment of the debt, the condition being that the debt revives if the security is not realised (p. 163). They then go on to add (p. 164) that "the doctrine is as applicable to one species of negotiable security as to another; to a cheque payable on demand, as to a running bill or a promissory note payable to order or bearer, whether it be the note of a country bank which circulates as money, or the note of the debtor, or of any other person."

The question involved in *Currie* v. *Misa* arose on the giving of a cheque, and the argument proceeded on the assumption that while, if a negotiable security payable at a future day had been given, the element of time during which suspension of the remedy would operate formed the consideration, the same result could not follow in case of a cheque which was payable on demand.

I find that in cases earlier than *Belshaw* v. *Bush* the giving of a negotiable instrument made or drawn by a third party has been considered as equivalent to the giving of such an instrument by the debtor.

The view held by Mr. Justice Maclaren in his work on *Bills, Notes and Cheques,* 5th ed., p. 368, is shewn in the following passage where the learned author draws his conclusion from *Currie* v. *Misa* and *Maxwell* v. *Deare* (1853) 8 Moore PC 363, 14 ER 138:

> A creditor is not bound to take a bill, note or cheque in payment of a debt; and if he does so it operates only as a conditional payment, unless he expressly agrees to take it in absolute payment, or unless there are special circumstances from which such an agreement may be implied.

See also *Falconbridge on Banking and Bills of Exchange,* 2nd ed., pp. 569, 570, *et seq.; Roscoe's Nisi Prius,* 18th ed., p. 700; Byles, 17th ed., p. 183; *Chalmers on Bills of Exchange,* 7th ed., pp. 338, 242.

Belshaw v. *Bush* has been followed in *Keay* v. *Fenwick* (1876) 1 CPD 745 (CA); *In re A Debtor* [1908] 1 KB 344; *In re J. Defries & Sons Limited* [1909] 2 Ch. 423.

It may be interesting to note that, earlier than 1851, the question had arisen in at least four cases where promissory notes or bills of exchange of a third person had been taken by the creditor. These are *Stedman* v. *Gooch* (1793) 1 Esp. 3; *Kearslake* v. *Morgan* (1794) 5 TR 513, 101 ER 289; *Camidge* v. *Allenby* (1827) 6 B & C 373; *Goodwin* v. *Coates* (1832) 1 Moo. & Rob. 221; and in each case the plaintiff had judgment.

These cases, as well as *Currie* v. *Misa,* are discussed by my brother Riddell in *Freeman* v. *Canadian Guardian Life Insurance Co.* (1908) 17 OLR 296.

The only remaining question on this branch of the case is whether a cheque under our law stands in the same position as in the English cases. I think it is clear from our Bills of Exchange Act, RSC 1906, ch. 119, sec. 53, and sec. 165, that a cheque, for the purposes of this case, must be treated as a negotiable instrument within the decisions which have been already cited.

Section 53, in providing that valuable consideration may be constituted by an antecedent debt or liability, says that such a debt or liability is so considered "whether the bill is payable on demand or at a future time".

By sec. 165, a cheque is a bill of exchange drawn on a bank payable on demand, and, except as otherwise provided in Part III of the Bills of Exchange Act, the provisions of the Act applicable to a bill of exchange payable on demand apply to a cheque. The exceptions may be found in *Maclaren on Bills, Notes and Cheques,* 5th ed., p. 425, and do not affect the question. See *McLean* v. *Clydesdale Banking Co.* (1883) 9 App. Cas. 95; *Trunkfield* v. *Proctor* (1901) 2 OLR 326.

Looking at the facts of this case, I think the situation may be described in the words of Sir John Jervis in *Maxwell* v. *Deare,* 8 Moore PC 363, 377, 14 ER 138:

> The object was to substitute a bill of exchange for a cash payment as a mode of payment, but only to be considered so if the bill was duly honoured at maturity.

The law applicable to the case is that where a negotiable instrument, including a cheque either of the debtor or a third party, is taken for an antecedent debt of the debtor, it is, unless special circumstances intervene, only conditional payment, and that, unless the receiver of it is guilty of laches, he can, upon non-payment of the security, look to his original purchaser.

What then is the evidence on the question of diligence or laches on the part of the plaintiff? The cheque in question is dated the 18th October, 1917, and is drawn on the Dominion Bank, Wingham. The respondent deposited it to his credit in the Bank of Hamilton in Wroxeter on the same day, and it reached the branch of that bank at Wingham on the 19th October. It was noted for non-payment also on the 19th and protested on the 20th October, 1917. The respondent learned of this on the 22nd, and at once called up the appellant's house. In his absence he left a message with the appellant's wife that Munro's cheque was protested, and was told by her to go and see Fells in Wingham. Fells was a partner of Munro. The respondent did not go, but he heard, shortly after, from the appellant by telephone and discussed the matter with him. The appellant promised to see Munro and communicate with the respondent, but did not do so, and the respondent then went to see him without any result. No laches is shewn, and the cheque is produced from the respondent's custody. The right of the respondent to sue the appellant has not been lost, and he is entitled to recover the amount sued for.

The appeal should be dismissed.

Since writing the above, I have had the advantage of reading the judgment of my brother Maclaren. While unable to agree with its conclusions, yet, on account of his authority upon questions of this nature, I feel I must venture to set out my reasons notwithstanding the small amount at stake.

I cannot bring myself to regard the transaction as a barter, or as the purchase of a negotiable security. The cheque was, until the moment before it was handed over, an incomplete instrument: *Hogarth* v. *Latham & Co.* (1878) 3 QBD 643. The appellant was, therefore, not the holder of a security which he desired to sell, and it was not until after the delivery and weighing was complete, and the sale of the hogs made, that the cheque became a valuable security.

To decide that, without a word being said, the respondent at that moment of time bought the cheque as a bill of exchange, and lost his right to be paid for the hogs if Munro had not enough money in the bank, is to go much further than I think the real transaction warrants. It is a question of intention, and therefore of fact, as is pointed out in *Chalmers*, 7th ed., p. 342.

I think there was an antecedent debt; for, as Lord Campbell observes in *Timmins* v. *Gibbins* (1852) 18 QB 722, 726, 118 ER 273: "In fact it is difficult to say that there can be any case in which the debt is not antecedent to the payment. Even where the money is paid over the counter at the time of the sale, there must be a moment of time during which the purchaser is indebted to the vendor."

Fydell v. *Clark*, cited by my learned brother, relates to unendorsed bills and notes given by a bank 2 years before to a customer for the proceeds of promissory notes for £8,000, and the action was by the customer's former partner, asserting liability in the bank to pay the value in cash of those securities, which proved worthless. It was properly held that the customer must have long since agreed to take the securities in the place of cash.

The case of *Camidge* v. *Allenby* was one of what were known as county bank notes. Its effect is set out in the following quotation from *Halsbury's Laws of England*, vol. 1, pp. 574, 575:

> If a bank note be given in payment for value received at the time, the payment is complete, and in the event of dishonour of the note, no recourse can be had against the transferor either on the note or the consideration for it (*Camidge* v. *Allenby* (1827) 6 B & C 373). But a note given for a pre-existing debt has been held to be only payment conditional on its being paid when presented. A note, however, must be presented or circulated within a reasonable time, otherwise, in the event of the bank failing, the loss will fall on the transferee. And in the event of the bank failing, or the note being dishonoured, the transferee, in order to preserve his right as against the transferor, must give him notice and offer to return the note.

It is also treated in the same way by Roscoe and by Byles, in the last editions of their works, where the decision is limited to bills or notes *payable to bearer*. Bramwell, B., in *Guardians of Lichfield Union* v. *Greene* (1857) 1 H & N 884, 156 ER 1459, deals with it as if confined to bank notes.

In *Roscoe's Nisi Prius*, 18th ed., p. 699, this statement is made:

> If a bill or note payable to bearer be delivered without endorsement, a distinction has been drawn between the cases in which it has been given in exchange for goods or other securities, sold at the time, and those in which it has been given in payment of a pre-existing debt. The former transactions amount, it is said, to a barter of the bill, with all its risks. *Fenn* v. *Harrison*, 3 TR 757, 759; *Ex p. Shuttleworth* (1797) 3 Ves. 368, 30 ER 1057; *Camidge* v. *Allenby, supra*. But when the security is delivered in payment of a pre-existing debt, the delivery does not operate as payment, unless the transferee makes the security his own by laches.

Byles on Bills, 17th ed., p. 182, puts it thus:

> If a bill or note, made or become payable to bearer, be delivered without endorsement, not in payment of a pre-existing debt, but by way of exchange for goods, for other bills or notes, or for money transferred to the party delivering the bill at the same time, such a transaction has been repeatedly held to be a sale of the bill by the party transferring it, and a purchase of the instrument, with all risks, by the transferee.

No doubt the statement by Bayley, J., if read as applying generally to all negotiable instruments, may bear the construction given to it. If so treated it would be inconsistent with *Currie* v. *Misa, ante*. But such a wide interpretation was not necessary to the decision, and I do not think that all the learned Judge's remarks have been treated by the text-writers as authoritative, or as expressing the judgment of the Court.

Park, J., at about the same time, in *Evans* v. *Whyle* (1829) 5 Bing. 485, 488, 130 ER 1148, said:

> If a party sells goods, and takes for them a bill of exchange which is not honoured, he is remitted to his original consideration.

In *Halsbury's Laws of England* the sale or transfer of a bill is spoken of in vol. 2, pp. 521, 522, in this way:

A transferor by delivery is in effect the vendor of an instrument precisely as he might be the vendor of any other chattel. Beyond the actual points in regard to it which he warrants he is in no way responsible for the value of what he sells. If, therefore, its value diminishes or even vanishes altogether, e.g., through the bankruptcy of any of the parties to it, he is not bound to compensate the transferee for his consequent loss (*Fydell* v. *Clark* (1796) 1 Esp. 447, 448). Where, on the other hand, the instrument is transferred, not by way of sale, but in payment of a debt, the transferor is liable on the consideration unless the instrument was taken in absolute satisfaction of the debt. *Camidge* v. *Allenby* (1827) 6 B & C 373, 108 ER 489.

And in vol. 7, pp. 447, 448, the general rule is thus stated:

A creditor is not bound to accept payment of a debt otherwise than in current coin, or, in the case of a debt exceeding £5, in notes of the Bank of England; and if he takes a bill, note, or cheque in payment,he may either accept it in satisfaction of the debt, in which case he takes the risk of its being dishonoured, or may accept it as a conditional payment only, the effect of which is to suspend his remedies during the currency of the instrument.

The presumption, in the absence of a clear indication of a contrary intention, is that payment by means of a bill, note, or cheque is a conditional payment only. If the security is paid when it becomes due, this is equivalent to payment of the original debt; and it is paid in part, the original debt is discharged *pro tanto*. If the instrument is dishonoured, payment of the original debt may be enforced as if no security has been taken, unless the bill has been negotiated and is outstanding at the time of action brought in the hands of a third party, in which case the creditor's remedy continues to be suspended.

I cannot find, in the evidence in this case, any clear indication that the cheque of Munro, when it became a completed instrument, was, without a word being said, purchased *eo instanti* by the respondent, and prefer to rest my conclusion upon the proposition as above laid down.

Appeal allowed.

[Meredith C.J.O. and Ferguson J.A. concurred with Maclaren J.A.; Magee J.A. concurred with Hodgins J.A.]

Note: The Uniform Commercial Code deals with this effect of payment in the following provision:

3 – 802. Effect of Instrument on Obligation for Which It Is Given
(1) Unless otherwise agreed where an instrument is taken for an underlying obligation
   (a) the obligation is pro tanto discharged if a bank is drawer, maker or acceptor of the instrument and there is no recourse on the instrument against the underlying obligor; and
   (b) in any other case the obligation is suspended pro tanto until the instrument is due or if it is payable on demand until its presentment. If the instrument is dishonored action may be maintained on either the instrument or the obligation; discharge of the underlying obligor on the instrument also discharges him on the obligation.

Would you recommend its adoption? How would *McGlynn* be decided under this section?

E. DISCHARGE OF PARTIES AND DISCHARGE OF THE INSTRUMENT

FALCONBRIDGE
The Law of Negotiable Instruments in Canada
(1967), pp. 150 *et seq.*

[i] *Discharge By Payment*

[The Bills of Exchange Act provides:]

139. (1) A bill is discharged by payment in due course by or on behalf of the drawee or acceptor.

(2) Payment in due course means payment made at or after the maturity of the bill to the holder thereof in good faith and without notice that his title to the bill is defective.

(3) Where an accommodation bill is paid in due course by the party accommodated, the bill is discharged.

140. Subject to the provisions aforesaid as to an accommodation bill, when a bill is paid by the drawer or an endorser, it is not discharged; but,—

(*a*)   where a bill payable to, or to the order of, a third party is paid by the drawer, the drawer may enforce payment thereof against the acceptor, but may not re-issue the bill;

(*b*)   where a bill is paid by an endorser, or where a bill payable to drawer's order is paid by the drawer, the party paying it is remitted to his former rights as regards the acceptor or antecedent parties, and he may, if he thinks fit, strike out his own and subsequent endorsements, and again negotiate the bill.

The discharge of the instrument is to be distinguished from the discharge of a party to the instrument. The former is a real defence available against everyone, the latter is a personal defence which is not good against a holder in due course.

An instrument is discharged by payment in due course by the party primarily liable to pay, that is, by the drawee or acceptor of a bill, or by the maker of a note, or by one of two or more joint acceptors or joint makers, or, in the case of an accommodation instrument, by the party accommodated. Except in the case of payment by the party accommodated, payment by the drawer or by an endorser does not discharge the instrument, but the instrument remains in force so as to enable the person paying to exercise the rights given to him by s. 140. Payment before maturity does not afford a good defence against a holder in due course. As to the discharge of a bill in a set, see chapter 3, § 37.

[ii] *Discharge By Merger*

The Bills of Exchange Act provides:

141. When the acceptor of a bill is or becomes the holder of it, at or after its maturity, in his own right, the bill is discharged.

If the present right to receive payment of an instrument and the liability to pay it become united in the same person, the instrument is discharged. It is no objection to the negotiability of an instrument that a party liable upon it becomes the holder of it before maturity. He may re-issue and further negotiate the instrument. (See s. 73, discussed in chapter 5, §60.) If, however, at or after maturity, the acceptor of a bill or the maker of a note, or one of two or more joint acceptors or joint makers, remains or becomes the holder of the instrument in his own right, the instrument is discharged.

[iii] Discharge By Renunciation

The Bills of Exchange Act provides:

> **142.** (1) When the holder of a bill, at or after its maturity, absolutely and unconditionally renounces his rights against the acceptor, the bill is discharged.
>
> (2) The liabilities of any party to a bill may in like manner be renounced by the holder before, at, or after its maturity.
>
> (3) A renunciation must be in writing, unless the bill is delivered up to the acceptor.
>
> (4) Nothing in this section shall affect the rights of a holder in due course without notice of renunciation.

As in the case of discharge by payment, discharge of the instrument is to be distinguished from discharge of a party to it. Renunciation at or after maturity of the holder's rights against the party primarily liable discharges the instrument, but renunciation of the holder's rights before maturity, or of the holder's rights against the drawer or an endorser, does not discharge the instrument and does not affect the rights of a holder in due course.

[iv] Discharge By Cancellation

The Bills of Exchange Act provides:

> **143.** (1) Where a bill is intentionally cancelled by the holder or his agent, and the cancellation is apparent thereon, the bill is discharged.
>
> (2) In like manner, any party liable on a bill may be discharged by the intentional cancellation of his signature by the holder or his agent.
>
> (3) In such case, any endorser who would have had a right of recourse against the party whose signature is cancelled is also discharged.
>
> **144.** A cancellation made unintentionally, or under a mistake, or without the authority of the holder, is inoperative: Provided that where a bill or any signature thereon appears to have been cancelled, the burden of proof lies on the party who alleges that the cancellation was made unintentionally, or under a mistake, or without authority.

An instrument is discharged by cancellation only if the cancellation is apparent on it. If the cancellation of the instrument or of some signature on it is not apparent, the instrument may, as has been pointed out in chapter 11, §113, come into the hands of a holder in due course, and as against him the cancellation would not be a good ground of defence.

[v] Discharge By Material Alteration

The Bills of Exchange Act provides:

145. (1) Subject to subsection (2) where a bill or acceptance is materially altered without the assent of all parties liable on the bill, the bill is voided, except as against a party who has himself made, authorized, or assented to the alteration and subsequent endorsers.

(2) Where a bill has been materially altered, but the alteration is not apparent, and the bill is in the hands of a holder in due course, such holder may avail himself of the bill as if it had not been altered, and may enforce payment of it according to its original tenor.

146. In particular any alteration,—
  (a) of the date;
  (b) of the sum payable;
  (c) of the time of payment;
  (d) of the place of payment;
  (e) by the addition of a place of payment without the acceptor's assent where a bill has been accepted generally;
is a material alteration.

Read grammatically, s. 145 would seem to say that a material alteration of an instrument has the effect of nullifying it, as against all parties except the party who made the alteration and such as, at the time of or before the making of the alteration, had authorized or assented to it, but in any case a subsequent ratification would not give validity to an alteration amounting to forgery.

Before the passing of the statute a material alteration rendered an instrument wholly void, but the proviso mitigates, in favour of a holder in due course, the rigour of the old law. For example, a cheque for $5 is certified by the drawee bank, subsequently raised by forgery to $500, cashed at another bank and by it presented to the drawee bank. The drawee bank having paid $500 by mistake, is in ordinary circumstances entitled to recover only $495 from the presenting bank, because under the proviso to s. 145 the cheque is, notwithstanding the alteration, valid according to its original tenor.

As has been pointed out in chapter 11, § 113, a person may be a holder in due course if he takes an instrument which is apparently complete and regular, and it has been held under s. 145 that an alteration is "apparent" if it is one which can be discerned by the holder, without the use of a microscope, and without any previous knowledge on his part of the contents of the instrument.

An alteration is material which in any way alters the operation of the instrument and the liabilities of the parties, whether the change be prejudicial or beneficial. For example, the alteration of the rate of interest, the interlineation of a rate of interest, the alteration of a cheque so as to make it payable to bearer instead of to order, the conversion of a joint note into a joint and several note, and even the addition of a new maker to a joint and several note, would all be material alterations.

Chapter 16
Consumer Defences and Financers

A. INTRODUCTION

Generally speaking, ''receivables financing'' is the advancing of money to a retailer against debts due to him by his credit buyers. Obviously, a financer's self-interest is to take receivables free from buyers' defences. His best course actually is to abandon altogether the receivables financing and lend money directly to retail buyers to enable them to buy for cash. As a borrower, the obligor would be liable to repay the loan regardless of any complaints the buyer may have with respect to his goods. On the other hand, by establishing an ongoing financing relationship with a retailer, receivables financing gives the assignee the assurance of a regular flow of business from sellers of goods as well as an easy means of securing a seller's liability as an endorser of the retail paper. Historically, in the U.S., instalment sales financing was not subject to state usury laws and further it gave the financer an advantageous position on the debtor's default. The business community was interested in a scheme which could operate uniformly in North America. All this prompted a solution that would not undermine the use of receivables financing.

JACOB ZIEGEL
"Recent Legislative and Judicial Trends in Consumer Credit in Canada"
(1970) 8 Alta. L. Rev. 59, 69-70

4. *Promissory Notes and Cut-off Clauses*

. . . [F]ew retailers carry their own paper and they usually discount it with a finance company or, occasionally, with one of the chartered banks*. For understandable though not always creditable reasons the assignee wants to be sure that he has a good claim and that he will not become involved in disputes between the seller and the buyer concerning the quality of the goods or any other aspect of the original transaction. If he simply had to rely on the common law position he would not secure this measure of isolation since the common law rule is that the assignee of a chose in action takes it subject to all equities. To overcome this obstacle finance companies regularly resort to the following three devices:

---

* The position has changed since this article was written and the banks in Canada now occupy a dominant position in the financing of consumer purchases. See further *infra*, chapter 25. [Eds.]

725

(a) They ensure that there is a disclaimer clause in the sales contract which excludes all implied warranties and conditions and all representations not incorporated in the written contract;

(b) They also ensure that the contract contains a "cut-off" clause. This clause notifies the buyer of the seller's intention to assign the contract and the buyer purports to agree that he will not raise any defences or other equities against any assignee of the paper;

(c) Finally, the buyer is required to sign a promissory note for the balance of the time sale price, and this is negotiated by the dealer to the finance company. In this way the finance company hopes to acquire the superior status of a holder in due course under section 56 of the Bills of Exchange Act.

The general question of disclaimer clauses will not be dealt with here and I will therefore proceed immediately to the two other devices. Until the decision of the Supreme Court of Canada in *Killoran* v. *Monticello State Bank* (1921) 61 SCR 528 there was considerable doubt in Canada about the effect of cut-off clauses in conditional sale agreements and the status of a promissory note which formed a physical part of the agreement and was separated from it only by a perforated edge. However, the Supreme Court dispelled the doubts and each of the devices received the blessing of a majority of the judges. No questions were raised in the case concerning the effect of a close relationship between the assignor and assignee, such as today typically exists between the dealer and his finance company, and having regard to the early date of the decision it would have been surprising if the question had been raised.

Note on Cut-off Clauses: The power of parties to a contract to make it by their own agreement "assignable free from and unaffected by . . . equities [existing between them]" goes back to *Ex parte Asiatic Banking Corporation* (1867) LR 2 Ch. 391, *per* Cairns L.J. This power was implicitly recognized in *Range* v. *Belvédère Finance Corp.* (1969) 5 DLR (3d) 257, 262 (SCC) (chapter 14, *supra*). The use of cut-off clauses in consumer sales was prompted in the U.S. at the turn of this century by doubts as to the negotiability of a promissory note used with a conditional sale contract. The practice subsequently spread into Canada (recall chapter 14(C), *supra*).

Unico v. *Owen* (1967) 232 A. 2d 405, 417-418 (NJ SC) dealt with the validity of such a clause in a consumer transaction and held it "void as against public policy" and unconscionable. See also *Dean* v. *Universal C.I.T. Credit Corp.* (1971) 275 A. 2d 154 (NJ SC); and *Fairfield Credit Corp.* v. *Donnelly* (1969) 264 A 2d 547 (Conn. SC). The clause, however, is often defended on the basis that it "does not exempt the wrongdoer himself from an action by the defrauded maker . . . [but rather] it is . . . a device for the protection of an innocent person": Frederick Beutel, "Negotiability by Contract: A Problem in Statutory Interpretation" (1934) 28 Ill. L. Rev. 205, 214. *Cf.* also *Block* v. *Ford Motor Credit Company* (1972) 286 A 2d 228 (DC).

CARL FELSENFELD
"Some Ruminations about Remedies in Consumer-Credit Transactions"
(1967) 8 Bos. C. Indus. & Comm-L. Rev. 535, 550-551

The clause has been criticized for the following reasons:

(a) The retail buyer rarely reads the contract. When he does, he still cannot be expected to understand the waiver-of-defense clause, usually written in the fine technical jargon of the finance-company lawyer. All that the ordinary buyer usually cares about is that he has bought something, and, if it is defective, that he should not have to pay for it.

(b) The clause is of little benefit to financers, since the typical assignment is accompanied by a seller's warranty that the retail buyer received what he bought and has no defense, set-off, or the like to his duty to pay. If such a defense is available, the financer may reassign the obligation to the original seller because of the breach of warranty, thereby placing the seller and buyer in the positions the buyer expected, with the buyer able to withhold payment.

(c) An adjunct to point (b) is that it is only the poor, weak, or dishonest sellers who cannot or will not honor their warranties. Therefore, where the waiver-of-defense clause matters most is in transactions affecting the poorer members of the community. The indigent consumer in this situation has not received a satisfactory product, but his claims against the seller are futile, and he has no defense when the finance company presses for the money. In other words, those most needy of protection are those who suffer the most under the clause.

(d) The only real protection a consumer has against improper sales is his power to withhold payment. A waiver-of-defense clause effectively precludes this.

(e) As between two presumably innocent parties, the financer rather than the consumer should bear the loss if the seller fails to satisfy the consumer. The financer is usually involved with the seller under some continuing arrangement, is often aware of the seller's general behavior and type of operation, and has some power to correct abuses. Also, the financer is in a better position to afford the loss.

(f) If the seller's responsibilities become those of the assignee, sales financers would tend to offer their services to only the stronger sellers. Credit might, therefore, tend to disappear for the more marginal sellers who are equally, if not more, in need of financing.

The waiver-of-defense clause has also been vigorously defended:

(a) The financer is only a source of credit. The economic effect of a "sales-finance" transaction is the same as if the buyer financed his purchase through a bank or a loan company. Certainly the fact that a commodity is defective should not vary the terms of a loan debt simply because the loan proceeds went to buy it. In fact, the difference between a direct loan for the purpose of making a purchase and an assignment of a retail sale obligation to a financer is often more a matter of form than substance: even the latter financer often has some form of contact, if not actual agreement, with the retail buyer before the sale is made. Furthermore, the two types of transaction are often given identical legal treatment.

(b) The warranties of seller and manufacturer are usually sufficient to protect the retail buyer. Therefore, there is no need to involve the financer in such
matters.

(c) Eliminating the waiver-of-defense clause would cut off the sources of
credit which depend upon its existence.

(d) Objection (f) above may also be an argument in defense of the clause.
Withholding credit from marginal sellers may be a social good; needy buyers
who would otherwise go to such a retail outlet would be diverted to more
responsible sellers who are able to stand behind their warranties.

(e) If the waiver-of-defense clause were eliminated, the ultimate result
might be to force financing agencies to change the form of the credit transaction
from a purchase of a time-sale account to a direct loan to the buyer (where they
would have no concern with the goods sold). The potency of this argument
depends, of course, upon the statutory requirements (licensing, etc.) imposed on
lenders.

(f) Under the doctrine of freedom of contract, there is no right to preclude
the parties from agreeing to a waiver-of-defense clause.

Note: It has always been assumed that an assignee who seeks to enforce a cut-off
clause (often called a waiver-of-defence clause) must take the contract in good faith so
as to be in an analogous position to that of a holder in due course. The discussion of the
financer's insulation from product-related defences should thus focus on (a) the conditions of acquiring a holder in due course status as applied in the financing of consumer
sales, (b) the denial by statute of a holder in due course status to a holder of consumer
bills and notes regardless of his meeting the conditions leading to this status, (c) the
subsequent nullification of the cut-off clauses by provincial legislatures, and (d) the
judicial and legislative response to attempts to circumvent this body of law by shifting to
direct loan financing. The chapter concludes with a discussion of the preservation of
consumer defences in credit card transactions.

ALBERT ROSENTHAL
"Negotiability — Who Needs It?"
(1971) 71 Colum. L. Rev. 375, 377-79

A Bank of England bearer note, while not yet legal tender in 1756,[9] was,
according to Lord Mansfield, "treated as money, as cash." In the leading case of
Miller v. *Race* (1758) 97 ER 398 (KB) he concluded that when such a bearer note
was stolen and subsequently sold to a bona fide purchaser, it had to belong to the
purchaser rather than to the previous owner, because of "the consequences to
trade and commerce ... which would be most incommoded by a contrary
determination."

While the negotiable character of certain kinds of instruments had earlier
been given some measure of protection in specialized commercial courts in
England, this decision seems to have been the first clear-cut holding of its kind by
a common-law court. Several points should be noted. (1) A claim of ownership

---

[9] Bank of England notes became legal tender only in 1833. 3 & 4 Wm. IV, c. 98. § 6.

was cut off — no defense against payment of the instrument was involved. (2) The note in question was of a type customarily passed from hand to hand, serving many of the purposes of paper money, which did not exist in England at the time. (3) Without the free circulation of such "money," business would have been impeded.

The negotiable promissory note of today is quite a different instrument, serving different purposes, and the consequences of its negotiability are quite different in impact. By far the most commonly employed variety of the species today is the note given by the installment purchaser of goods to reflect the unpaid portion of the purchase price. Typically, such a note is transferred just once, from the dealer to the lender (usually either a finance company or a bank), and thereafter remains in the possession of the latter or its lawyers until it is either paid off or offered in evidence in court. Its negotiable character is of no importance with respect to claims of ownership, as it is unlikely to be lost or stolen. Even if it is, the last indorsement will have been a special indorsement to the order of the lender; without the genuine further indorsement of the latter there can be no subsequent holder, much less a holder in due course.

The only significant consequence of the negotiability of such a note is that it cuts off the defenses of the maker. If, for example, the purchaser gives the note in payment for a refrigerator, the finance company is entitled to full payment regardless of whether the refrigerator fails to work or whether its sale was accomplished through fraudulent misrepresentations or, indeed, whether it was ever delivered at all. And it may be small comfort to the buyer, forced to pay the finance company in full, to know that he has a cause of action against the seller, which may at best be collectible with difficulty and may in many cases be worthless because the seller is insolvent or has left town.

A promissory note of this kind, and a consequence of negotiability that works in this fashion, are a far cry from the stolen Bank of England note, and the protection accorded its purchaser, in *Miller* v. *Race*. Whether the finance company should be allowed to prevail free of the maker's defenses raises questions that ought to be decided on their own merits, and not merely through the absent-minded application of a doctrine created to meet an entirely different situation.

The social evils flowing from negotiability in this circumstance have become manifest, and there has been a clear trend in both the courts and the legislatures toward amelioration of its consequences. In particular, the unfairness to the poorest members of the community of the law governing consumer installment purchases has generated a reaction that is giving rise to a major alteration in it.

NOTE
"Direct Loan Financing of Consumer Purchases"
(1972) 85 Harv. L. Rev. 1409, 1411-17

POLICY CONSIDERATIONS
A. Goals

The issues involved in cutting off consumer defenses in actions for collection by financers, whether by direct loan financing or otherwise, essentially concern the distribution of costs which arise from inadequacies in seller peformance. These costs may be the result of fraud, breach of warranty, or failure of consideration and will be hereinafter collectively referred to as the costs of "seller misconduct." If sales defenses are eliminated, such costs fall, in the first instance, entirely on the buyer, and if defenses are preserved, these costs are initially absorbed by the financer. The legal rules which regulate the rights of these parties, and thus effectively allocate the cost of seller misconduct, should be directed toward two goals. First, they should so influence behavior as to minimize the costs of seller misconduct to innocent parties. Minimizing costs to innocent parties can be accomplished in either of two ways: by discouraging seller misconduct in the first place or by returning its cost to the responsible seller and making whole the injured consumer or financer. Second, the cost of so minimizing the effect of seller misconduct on innocent parties, as well as the cost of seller misconduct to innocent parties which cannot be eliminated, should be regarded as a real cost of the consumer goods distribution industry which should be reflected in the price of consumer goods; when prices approximate real social costs, consumer choices tend to lead to a more efficient allocation of society's resources. The legal rules should allocate the burden of seller misconduct to that party who is able most efficiently to achieve these two goals.

In cash sales, the cost of seller misconduct necessarily falls, in the first instance, on the buyer. In order to return the cost to a seller who refuses to make the buyer whole, the buyer must bring an action for damages. To the extent that buyers are so able to shift these costs back to sellers, each of the two goals can be advanced. Returning costs will eliminate some of the effect seller misconduct has on innocent buyers, and the prospect of reversals, and in certain situations the possibility of criminal sanctions, will discourage seller misconduct before it occurs. Furthermore, when misconduct costs are returned to sellers, they can be expected to account for them in the prices which they charge. The actual ability of buyers to shift these costs to sellers, however, is limited; the financial and psychological burdens of litigation are likely to exceed the amount at stake, and it is possible that the seller will have disappeared or become insolvent. In such cases the entire cost of seller misconduct remains on the particular victimized consumer, and there are no feasible means of including that cost in the cash price of consumer goods.

A buyer in a three party credit sale, where the financer is insulated from sales-related defenses, is in the same position as a cash buyer who has already paid for the merchandise. In three party credit transactions, however, the financer's presence provides another alternative for the initial allocation of seller misconduct costs. It will be contended below that placing this burden on the financer by preserving defenses in three party consumer credit transactions, including direct loan financing, will most efficiently achieve both of the enunciated goals.

B. Reducing the Cost of Seller Misconduct by Preserving Defenses

By the very nature of his business, the financer is in a better position than the buyer to return the costs of seller misconduct to the responsible seller and to discourage in other ways the incidence of seller misconduct.

First, the financer is better able to return the costs to the seller. This will involve little difficulty when the financer has direct and continuous dealings with the seller and can set off his losses against the latter's account. Even in the absence of such a relationship financers may have at their disposal important means of persuasion, such as influence over credit ratings, not available to consumers. Finally, if the financer must resort to litigation his expenses are likely to be less than those of the consumer. Psychological barriers will tend to be lower for financers, and actual costs of litigation will tend to be less for creditors who have an ongoing need for legal services. Even if the consumer is eventually able to shift costs back to the seller, the swiftness with which the collection processes of the state serve the creditors and the delay in gaining redress from the seller may result in significant losses to the buyer in the interim. This would be particularly true of low income consumers for whom a temporary deprivation of income or property can involve long-lasting and irreparable harm. By comparison, the costs of delay to a financer will entail only the loss of interest.

Second, in addition to the deterrent effect which returning costs to delinquent sellers has on seller misconduct, initially placing the costs of seller misconduct on the financer will itself better cause seller misconduct to be discouraged than will placing such costs initially on the buyer. Whoever is forced to bear the costs of seller misconduct has an incentive to avoid dealing with offending merchants: buyers would avoid purchases from such merchants and financers would be reluctant to finance sales in which they foresee the likelihood of defenses which would thwart actions for collection. However, the policing of the market is likely to be more efficiently performed by financers than by careful buyers because consumers tend to lack the requisite machinery, available to financers, to investigate sellers and to gather information needed to make informed decisions.

Thus far the discussion has been concerned with the proper procedure for minimizing the effect of seller misconduct on innocent parties. The proffered solution of preserving consumer defenses may, however, aggravate the separate problem of what might be called "buyer misconduct," that is, the failure of consumers to compensate sellers for satisfactory goods and services. If defenses were preserved, financers would shift the costs of buyer misconduct to sellers rather than proceeding against the buyer in those cases in which it was more convenient for them to do so. The same factors which have been noted, which facilitate return of seller misconduct costs to sellers, would frequently lead to this result. The task of returning buyer misconduct costs to responsible buyers would in these cases then fall on sellers. The returning of buyer misconduct costs is currently accomplished more efficiently, however, by insulated financers who do not have to cope with unmeritorious consumer sales defenses. In addition, it is reasonable to assume that financers, who are in the business of collecting debts, are more efficient in this endeavor than are sellers.

The advantages of the financer, rather than the consumer, returning the costs of seller misconduct to responsible sellers, however, outweigh the advantages of the financer, rather than the seller, returning the costs of buyer misconduct to responsible buyers. Since sellers will tend to be relatively more efficient than consumers in pursuing their claims, a legal rule which causes financers to return seller misconduct costs and sellers to return buyer misconduct costs would be more desirable than one which causes financers to return buyer misconduct costs and consumers to return seller misconduct costs.

Although the above discussion indicates that financers should be used as a conduit for the minimization of seller misconduct costs, it must be recognized that financers will not be able to eliminate or return all such costs. Returning seller misconduct costs to responsible sellers and policing the market will themselves entail administrative costs. But so long as the cost of minimization is less than the cost to the financer of the seller misconduct which is eliminated, it will be in the financer's interest to attempt to investigate sellers before financing their sales and to chargeback losses.

The cost to the financers of charging back and otherwise discouraging seller misconduct is likely to vary directly with the remoteness of the seller and financer. The more closely related the seller and financer are, the easier it is for the financer to determine the character of the seller and thereby ascertain the probability of seller misconduct. As the relation becomes less intimate, the costs of such an investigation of the seller will increase. Furthermore, distant relationships will preclude the inexpensive and informal charging back of losses available during a well established and ongoing relationship. At some point of remoteness the costs of further investigation and litigation will exceed the gain from discouraging seller misconduct. At this point it would be rational for the creditor to absorb instead the remaining losses, regarding them, as well as the expenses which have been incurred to minimize and charge back seller misconduct costs, as a cost of his business, and therefore to account for them in his rates. The financers' ability to reflect the remaining costs of seller misconduct in the price of credit furthers the second goal which has been posited: more closely approximating real social costs in the price structure in order to allocate more efficiently society's resources. This point requires further comment.

C. Internalizing Seller Misconduct Costs
by Preserving Defenses

If individual consumption choices are to best allocate society's resources in a market system, the cost to a consumer of a given product must approximate the real social cost of providing him with that product. If financers are insulated from sales-related defenses, the real costs of a product sold on credit consist of the explicit price plus an undefined risk of seller misconduct. The risk component is extremely difficult for consumers to calculate and they are therefore unlikely to make an informed allocation of their resources. In constrast, as just noted, when defenses are preserved the social cost of seller misconduct which cannot be efficiently prevented or returned to the seller will necessarily be reflected in the price of credit. Since financers are better able to gather the information necessary to calculate the cost of the risk of seller misconduct, these prices will provide a more accurate basis for consumer choices.

The appeal to optimal resource allocation may seem inapposite in this situation since it appears that the cost of seller misconduct is to be reflected not in the price of goods sold but rather in the price of credit. This anomaly disappears, however, when consumer credit and sales are considered a single activity. The price for the goods produced by that activity consists of one charge for the goods and one for the credit. The cost of seller misconduct associated with goods financed by consumer credit can thus be accounted for in either component.

Since the seller misconduct costs will be reflected only in the total price of consumer credit goods rather than in the price of the goods sold alone, however, preserving defenses may have the effect of reallocating resources in favor of cash sales. The undefined risk of seller misconduct which has been internalized in the price of credit remains undefined in cash sales and the actual costs will continue to be shouldered by particular consumers. If consumers tend to underestimate such undefined risks, some shifting to cash purchases can be expected. The exact magnitude of this shift will depend on the capacity of consumers to evaluate and compare the relative risks and on their attitudes towards risky decisions.

In any event, preserving defenses advances the two goals of minimizing the costs of seller misconduct and internalizing the costs that remain in the price of consumer credit. It is important to note that the latter result is possible, however, only if financers are free to adjust their rates in response to changing costs. This adjustment may require the elimination of unrealistic interest rate ceilings.

Note: For further discussion of the policy issues, see Alan Schwartz, "Optimality and the Cutoff of Defenses Against Financers of Consumer Sales" (1974) 15 Bos. C Indus. & Comm.-L. Rev. 499 and B. Geva, "Optimality and Consumer Defenses — A Model for Reform" (1981) 31 Case W. Res. L. Rev. 51. Professor Schwartz finds consistency between the preservation of consumer defences and optimality where a seller and a financer are already in a bargaining relationship. Professor Geva's conclusion (at 73) is that:

> The pursuit of optimality supports a preservation of defenses rule which applies to a financer who is in a bargaining relationship with the seller. This includes a seller's assignee and a direct lender who is a party to an interlocking loan pattern. The rule should apply also to every restricted use loan given to a consumer-borrower by an institutional lender. Apart from specific situations covered by general principles of law, a financer's exposure should be confined to a consumer's right to withhold payment. This right to withhold payment from a financer should be coextensive with the right to withhold payment from a seller. It should thus encompass all types of defenses and should not be subject to time limitations or other preconditions. In the case of seller insolvency, where optimality considerations are equivocal, a financer's exposure to consumer defenses should increase. A financer should be subject to a consumer's defenses, with the exception of consequential loss, up to the value of the financed contract or the amount financed.

For contrary views, namely that "[t]he survival of the [holder in due course] doctrine in a highly competitive market . . . suggests that it is an efficient doctrine", see R. Posner, *Economic Analysis of Law* (2nd ed., 1977) p. 88 and R. Epstein, "Unconscionability: A Critical Re-appraisal", (1975) 18 J. of Law and Econ. 293 at 308-309.

B. JUDICIAL RESPONSE: THE "FEDERAL DISCOUNT" DOCTRINE

1. THE DOCTRINE AS APPLIED TO PURCHASER OF RETAIL PAPER

FEDERAL DISCOUNT CORP. LTD. v. ST. PIERRE
(1962) 32 DLR (2d) 86, [1962] OR 310 (Ont. CA)

KELLY J.A.: In this action tried on December 9, 1960 in the Ninth Division Court of the County of Wentworth, the plaintiff sought to recover from the defendants $273.30, the amount due on a promissory note dated October 8, 1959, signed by the defendants, of which the plaintiff claimed to be the holder in due course. In dismissing the plaintiff's claim the learned trial Judge held that payment could not have been enforced against the defendants by the original payee of the note and that the plaintiff was not a holder in due course.

The chain of events which culminated in the institution of this action began when the female defendant's attention was attracted by a newspaper advertisement inserted by one Pritchard who was a salesman of Fair Isle Knitting (Ontario) Limited and Yarncraft Industries Limited. Both these companies had identical shareholders and officers, occupied the same or adjacent office space and in their operation were associated as will be indicated. Fair Isle Knitting (Ontario) Limited, (hereafter referred to as Fair Isle) which was found by the learned trial Judge to have carried on business both under its own name and under the name of Fair Isle Knitting Company, was engaged in the retail door-to-door sale of hand knitting machines. Yarncraft Industries Limited (hereinafter referred to as Yarncraft) awarded home knitting contracts to purchasers of hand knitting machines from Fair Isle and sold or endeavoured to sell to retail or other outlets the goods knit by the purchasers of hand knitting machines. According to the evidence of Turack, one of the principal shareholders and officers of the two companies, the purpose for which the two companies had been incorporated was that one of them, Fair Isle, would sell knitting machines in conjunction with the giving of home knitting contracts by the other, Yarncraft. Later I will describe in more detail the activities of the female defendant in relation to her home knitting contract. Although the text of the newspaper advertisement referred to was not produced at trial, Pritchard admitted that its purport would lead a person reading it to believe that she could pay for the hand knitting machine out of the money earned from the sale of knitting done on it.

When Pritchard first visited Mrs. St. Pierre following her answer to the advertisement, she already was the owner of a knitting machine of a make other than that sold by Fair Isle; only by disposing of that knitting machine and purchasing a Fair Isle knitting machine could she become eligible for the home knitting contract which would have produced the earnings she was anxious to have.

In the interval between Pritchard's first and second visits, a matter of only a few days, the female defendant returned to Simpsons-Sears the knitting machine for which she had agreed to pay $130; by the time of Pritchard's second visit she had thus removed the only obstacle between her and the income she was led to believe would flow from her association with the companies Pritchard represented. At the second visit of Pritchard to the St. Pierre home, which took place on October 8, 1958, the document upon which the plaintiff relies, ex. 1, was signed along with a number of other documents, *i. e.*, a Questionnaire, ex. 4, a Conditional Sales Contract, ex. 2, an Application for Home Knitting Contract, ex. 6, a Purchase Order, ex. 5, a Receipt, ex. 7. Exhibits 1 and 2 were signed by the male defendant as well as by the female defendant; the Receipt, ex. 7, was signed by Pritchard on behalf of Fair Isle and he acted as witness to the signatures on, or as a representative of his employers with respect to, the other documents.

The Promissory Note and Conditional Sales Contract follow the form usually employed in instalment purchases, save in two particulars — although the vendor of the machine was Fair Isle Knitting (Ontario) Limited the payee and endorsee of the note was Fair Isle Knitting Company — the words "Federal Discount Corporation Limited" added in para. 10 of the Conditional Sales Contract, by rubber stamp, were not proven to have appeared on the contract when it was signed and in all probability were added subsequently. I do not think that the questions in issue are affected by either of these matters, especially since the plaintiff's counsel has not in his argument before this Court relied upon para. 10 of the Conditional Sales Contract, which purports to exonerate the plaintiff from "any equities existing between Vendor and Purchaser". . . .

In due course after having secured a credit report on the standing of the male defendant, Fair Isle delivered the note to the plaintiff in accordance with a pre-existing arrangement for the purchase by the plaintiff of notes and conditional sales contracts entered into in respect of the sale and purchase of home knitting machines. The note (ex. 1) was one of 24, each of a like amount, all set out on a sales report (ex. 8) a form furnished by the plaintiff to Fair Isle; the note was, before delivery, endorsed to the plaintiff by the payee. Exhibit 8 indicates that the plaintiff deducted a discount of 14% and a reserve of 25% in accounting to Fair Isle. Payment of the amounts due by the plaintiff to Fair Isle were made in due course. Contemporaneously with the delivery of the note, the Conditional Sales Contract was delivered to the plaintiff, accompanied by an assignment thereof executed by Fair Isle.

On receipt of the note the plaintiff sent to the female defendant an undated letter, ex. 25, reading in part as follows:

> On behalf of Fair Isle Knitting Company we wish to sincerely thank you for your recent purchase. As you are aware from your contract this account has been assigned to our firm. All payments are to be made only direct to our office at 185 Bay Street, Toronto, Ontario, unless otherwise notified by us.

Upon both of this letter and the account book, ex. 24, forwarded by the plaintiff to the defendants, the following words have been impressed by rubber stamp:

> Note — Payments must be made when due regardless of amount earned from knitting.

At about the same time the female plaintiff received, in a letter bearing the letterhead and superscription of Yarncraft, ex. 19, an impressive document printed in script type face and liberally decorated with red seals; this document which was introduced as ex. 3 reads as follows:

HOME KNITTING CONTRACT

Number 6829
Date Oct. 28, 1958

Mrs. E. St. Pierre
46 Parkdale N.
Hamilton, Ont.

has been duly approved and acccepted as to her general qualifications and is hereby granted the privileges, services and features outlined below for a period of two years from date.

(seal)   The privilege to purchase fine quality yarns at a substantial wholesale discount.

(seal)   All necessary instructions and patterns.

(seal)   The privilege to knit garments or knitted material using yarn purchased from us at a profit of 20¢ to 25¢ per ounce in accordance with patterns and orders supplied by us.

(seal)   On request sufficient orders which could reasonably be completed in spare time at home.

It is expressly understood and agreed that the contract holder is a separate business entity and is at no time to be considered an employee of the Company.

Yarncraft Industries Limited
(signed)   C. Harris
Executive Director

(seal)

The letter accompanying ex. 3 advised that the first cone of yarn and first pattern would follow in a few days.

Some time prior to December 4, 1958 the female defendant had been given her instructions and on that date received from Fair Isle a cheque for $2 representing the mileage payment referred to in the questionnaire, the cheque being made payable jointly to the female defendant and the plaintiff. The evidence does not directly disclose what became of this cheque but it can be assumed that it reached the plaintiff and that credit for it was given to the female defendant by the entry of January 9, 1959 in the account maintained by the plaintiff under the name of the female defendant.

Prior to the first week in December 1958 the female defendant started sending to Yarncraft garment pieces made on the hand knitting machine from yarns supplied to her, at her expense, by Yarncraft and knit according to patterns and directions furnished along with the yarn. A sample of these directions, ex. 7, is imprinted with the name of "Fair Isle Knitting Company" and no other name appears on it. The practice followed by the female defendant after the receipt of the first yarn for which she apparently paid cash, was to finish as many knitted garment pieces as could be made from the yarn on hand and to send the garment pieces and the unused yarn to Yarncraft; she would be credited at the rate of 60c per ounce for the finished pieces and at the rate of 35c per ounce for the unused yarn; against this credit she would be debited the price of new yarn at 35c per ounce and the net amount indicated as an amount due to her. However, the amounts due to her, save as for one cheque for $31, were not paid to her and she testified that she believes there is due to her for garment pieces and yarn shipped to Yarncraft the sum of $160. She is unable to verify this amount by any intelligible rcords but there is no evidence to the contrary save her own admission as to yarn she received on March 23, 1959 under circumstances which will be referred to later. . . .

On March 23, 1959 the female defendant, in company with the male defendant went to the premises occupied by Fair Isle and Yarncraft concerning the amounts due to her but was unable to see any one in authority; having left some finished knitted goods the female defendant took a quantity of wool, some of which she has since worked into a sweater for her own use. Shortly thereafter a circular letter was sent out by Yarncraft advising that it was suspending operations. A copy of this letter was received by the female defendant. After its receipt no further payments were made by the defendants. Obviously no payments were received by them. The machine is still in the possession of the female defendant and she has made some use of it on her own account.

On this appeal the plaintiff contended that it was a holder in due course of the note sued upon; that there was no evidence to support the finding that the plaintiff had at the time of negotiation notice of any defect of title of the payee; that there was no evidence the plaintiff knew anything of the specific transaction opposed to the general conduct of the business of its predecessor in title; and that as between the original parties there was no ground which would entitle the defendants to rescission of the contract of purchase.

The rights which accrue to a holder in due course of a bill of exchange are unique and distinguishable from the rights of an assignee of a contract which does not fall within the description of a bill of exchange. The assignee of a contract, unlike the holder in due course of a bill of exchange, takes subject to all the equities between the original parties, which have arisen prior to the date of notice of the assignement to the party sought to be charged.

The special privileges enjoyed by a holder in due course of a bill of exchange are quite foreign to the common law and have their origin in the law merchant.

There is little difficulty in appreciating how trade between merchants required that he who put into circulation his engagement to pay a specified sum at a designated time and place knowing that it was the custom of merchants to regard such paper much as we do our paper currency, should be held to the letter of his obligation and be prevented from setting up defences which might derogate from the apparently absolute nature of his obligation.

At first the customs prevailing amongst merchants as to bills of exchange extended only to merchant strangers trafficking with English merchants; later they were extended to inland bills between merchants trafficking with one another within England; then to all persons trafficking and finally to all persons trafficking or not.

Thus in time the particular conditions which were recognized as prevailing amongst merchants became engrafted onto the law generally applicable and came to be looked on as arising from the document itself rather than from the character of the parties dealing with the document. It is significant, however, that the transition did not affect the legal position as to one another of immediate parties and that as between any two immediate parties, maker and payee, or endorser and endorsee, none of the extraordinary conditions otherwise attaching to the bill, serve to affect adversely the rights and obligations existing between them as contracting parties. The document itself becomes irreproachable and affords special protection to its holder only, when at some stage of its passage from payee or acceptor to holder, there has been a *bona fide* transaction of trade with respect to it wherein the transferee took for value and without any notice of circumstances which might give rise to a defence on the part of the maker. Unless the ultimate holder or some earlier holder has acquired the instrument in the course of such a transaction the earlier tainting circumstances survive and the holder seeking to enforce payment of it must, on the merits, meet any defence which would have been available to the maker. Thus it appears that the peculiar immunity which the holding of a bill of exchange brings to the holder in due course arises not from the original nature of the document itself but from the quality which had been imparted to it by at least some one transfer of it. It follows that the transfer which is alleged to have given such a special character to the bill of exchange should be subject to more than a casual examination and that the true nature of that transaction be discovered.

There can be no doubt that everyday commercial life demands that the integrity of bills of exchange be recognized and that those acquiring them in good faith should not be required unnecessarily to make inquiries to establish their authenticity. Courts quite properly have refused to recognize that constructive notice has any place in the law of negotiable instruments: *London Joint Stock Bank* v. *Simmonds* [1892] AC 201 at p. 221. Any attempt to weaken the provisions of a valid bill of exchange duly launched into the stream of commercial life, should be avoided. To do so, however, does not require that a prospective purchaser of a bill of exchange who has knowledge of certain circumstances about the seller's business which puts him on inquiry can by avoiding making inquiries or drawing reasonable inferences from the circumstances known to him, improve his position beyond that which it would have been had he made the inquiries he should have made or drawn the inference he should have drawn. This is not charging the holder with constructive notice and does not go beyond the standard of conduct laid down by the House of Lords in *Earl of Sheffield* v. *London Joint Stock Bank* (1888) 13 App. Cas. 333.

It is not necessary for the support of ordinary commercial transactions that the holder of a bill of exchange should under all circumstances be permitted to shield himself behind the guise of a holder in due course and attempt to separate his character as holder in due course from the debilitating effect of facts and circumstances actually known to him at the time he acquired the bill or which were reasonably inferable from facts and circumstances which were brought to his knowledge.

In the examination of any transfer to decide if it constituted the transferee a holder in due course the plaintiff's actual involvement with the transferor will be a major factor; on this account the whole relationship between the plaintiff and its transferor must be examined and considered.

With the growth of the sale of household and personal goods on the extended payment plan, the promissory note, the conditional sales contract and the finance company have become inseparable parts of the procedure whereby the merchant realizes immediately cash from the extended obligation of the purchaser from him. The very existence of the seller's business depends on his ability to convert into cash these obligations and the finance company, standing ready and willing to buy them, has become not only an essential part of retail selling on the time payment plan but is in effect a department of the seller's business, exercising a measure of control over the seller's sales by the requirements laid down with regard to the negotiable paper proposed to be purchased.

In the course of this development an attempt has been made to project into the field of household law the law merchant originally designed for dealings between merchants. The fiction has been permitted to flourish that the finance company is a foreign and independent agency. When it does acquire the contracts which it was incorporated to buy and which it arranged to purchase before the contracts actually came into existence it attempts to shield itself behind the protection of the law merchant which can apply only, if at all, to one of the documents constituting the arrangement between the seller and the buyer; at the same time it takes unto itself all the advantages that can be drawn from the transaction out of which the note arose. It is beyond question that the promissory note is included in the documents required to be signed by the purchaser for the express purpose of enabling the finance company to avoid defences which would otherwise be available to the maker against his vendor and any assignee of his purchase obligation.

The plaintiff was in the business of discounting notes: it was its practice and policy where any note had relationship to a conditional sales contract that the conditional sales contract should also be purchased and assigned to it: when a dealer first approached the plaintiff with a view to having the plaintiff discount notes which were to arise from the dealer's sales, the plaintiff investigated the applicant as to its financial stability, moral responsibility and various other aspects which would qualify the applicant to be a dealer "with the plaintiff"; the plaintiff was interested in knowing the possible volume of the business of the dealer as in the words of the witness McGarry, the plaintiff's Credit and Collection Manager, "It's got to be worthwhile before you can go into business with them". It was also well known to the plaintiff that Fair Isle and Yarncraft were companies having the same principals and officers.

The plaintiff was informed of the manner in which Fair Isle intended to conduct its selling campaign for the distribution of home knitting machines and was told by Turack, an officer of both Fair Isle and Yarncraft, "What we were doing in the other company" (Yarncraft). In fact the form of purchase order, questionnaire, conditional sales contract, and application for home knitting contract which were used in the approach to the female defendant were shown to the plaintiff company at the inception of the dealings between the plaintiff and Fair Isle. The purpose of the incorporation of two distinct companies, Fair Isle Knitting (Ontario) Limited and Yarncraft Industries Limited, was stated by Turack to be that one, Fair Isle, would sell knitting machines in conjunction with the giving of home knitting contracts by the other, Yarncraft, and that the operation of Yarncraft and its home knitting contracts was something to facilitate the sale of home knitting machines by Fair Isle.

The plaintiff was fully aware of the general course of operation employed by Fair Isle and Yarncraft in their dealings with the purchasers such as the defendants. The words which were impressed by rubber stamp on exs. 24 and 25, "Note — payments must be made when due, regardless of the amount earned from knitting", proved beyond a shadow of a doubt that the plaintiff knew that the purchasers of home knitting machines would be or at least could have been left with the impression which was in the mind of the female defendant, that is, that the moneys to meet the instalments of purchase-price would be forthcoming from earnings under the home knitting contract.

According to the evidence of Barber, the association of the home knitting contract with the sale of home knitting machine was one of the reasons why the plaintiff dealt with Fair Isle because the plaintiff "felt that if a person could make money, sell their material back to Yarncraft Industries, they would be able to pay for the machine".

The course of dealings between the plaintiff and the officers of Fair Isle indicates a relationship much more intimate than that of endorsee or endorser in a normal commercial transaction. The company selling the home knitting machines in conjunction with the awarding by its associate of home knitting contracts and the plaintiff who made possible the operations of the seller by buying the purchaser's instalment obligation were more nearly engaged in one business, each one in the conduct of its particular phase being useless without the association of the other. To pretend that they were so separate that the transfer of each note constituted an independent commercial transaction not affected by the pre-existing arrangements between them would, in my view, be to permit the form to prevail over the substance.

My view of the relationship of the plaintiff and its endorser of the note sued upon is reinforced by the evidence as to the arrangement between the plaintiff and Fair Isle, which resulted in the writing of a letter of March 17, 1959, ex. 13. The conduct of the plaintiff and Fair Isle leading up to the despatch of this letter is of itself of such an extraordinary nature as to require no comment other than to say that it indicates a relationship somewhat beyond what would be expected of a financial institution and a merchant dealing in the ordinary course of business. Even granting that the plaintiff did not have actual notice of facts the knowledge of which would have prevented it from becoming a holder in due course, the transfer of the note to it by Fair Isle fell short of being the type of business transaction between two parties, dealing with respect to the note in complete good faith, which would have imparted to the note the power to endow with the character of holder in due course, one becoming a holder with complete knowledge of its history and the complete facts of the relationship between the maker and the payee.

There appear to be no Canadian cases which have held that the business relationship between a dealer and a finance company is an element to be considered in deciding finance company's claim to be a holder in due course; the question has been dealt with by American Courts in this manner and I would adopt the reasoning of the Judges who decided these cases: *Buffalo Industrial Bank* v. *De Marzio* (1937) 296 NY Supp. 783; *Commercial Credit Co.* v. *T. F. Childs* (1940) 128 ALR 726; *Taylor et ux.* v. *Atlas Security Co.* (1923) 249 SW 746.

Under the circumstances of this case I can find no error in the conclusion arrived at by the trial Judge, namely, that the plaintiff was not a holder in due course of the promissory note sued upon in this action.

Counsel for the plaintiff referred to *Commodity Discount Ltd.* v. *Baker* [1961] OWN 277, as authority for his contention that it could be no defence to an action by a holder in due course of a promissory note, that the note was given to the original payee as part of a conditional sales transaction. I have examined the Appeal Book and read the transcript of evidence in the case cited; in it the point at issue was whether the *mere* fact that the promissory note sued upon was part of a contract which had been entered into between the defendant and the payee of the promissory note, served to disqualify the endorsee of the note as a holder in due course. There was an absence of any evidence as to the relationship between the payee and the finance company and as to knowledge by the plaintiff of the circumstances under which the signature of the promissory note had been procured; the case is distinguishable upon the facts from the case now before this Court.

In view of my conclusion that the plaintiff is not a holder in due course, it falls to be considered whether the learned trial Judge erred in holding that the payee of note sued upon could not have payment from the defendants had it not assigned its rights to the plaintiff.

Those who conceived the scheme which led to Pritchard's activities as a salesman for Fair Isle and Yarncraft intended to achieve a twofold result — to lead prospective purchasers to believe, as actually happened in the case of the defendants, that they were purchasing a revenue-producing machine which could be paid for out of the proceeds of the work to be done on it and marketed by a means of the home knitting contract; and at the same time by the use of documents of an elaborate and confusing nature to secure a document from the purchasers which would accomplish a legal result quite foreign to the impression sought to be created in the purchasers' minds. The method employed displayed sales ability of a high degree and entailed the use of a series of documents which apparently confused even those responsible for their drafting and certainly confused the salesman through whom they were furnished to the defendants. A careful perusal of ex. 7 discloses that it was a blank form of receipt prepared to be given in respect of a full or partial payment on a home knitting contract. Although in the application for home knitting contract, ex. 6, readied by Pritchard for the signature of the female defendant, care was taken to have the application addressed to "Yarncraft Industries Limited", the receipt is headed "Official Receipt Fair Isle Knitting Company". Further the only payment required under the home knitting contract was a nominal one of $2. Pritchard in filling in the blanks in ex. 7 inserted the amount of $35, which was the down payment provided for in the purchase order ex. 5 and the conditional sales contract, ex. 2, both documents tendered in connection with the purchase of the home knitting machine. It is small wonder that the female defendant was unable to appreciate the fine distinction between the allegedly separate legal entities with which she was dealing, when the draftsman of the documents and the salesman who was trained in their use were unable to maintain the necessary separation which at least was essential to maintain that the right hand, Fair Isle, did not know what the left hand, Yarncraft, was doing and *vice versa*.

I find no difficulty in supporting the finding of the learned trial Judge that the female defendant believed what she was intended to believe, namely, that she was engaged in one transaction; the whole course of the conduct of Fair Isle and Yarncraft was to induce that belief, and it did so induce it.

Counsel for the appellant submitted that on two accounts the defendants were not entitled to rescission: first, that there had been no misrepresentation as to any existing fact, but only a statement as to future conduct; second, that the defendants having made payments and having used the machine, their only remedy lay in damages.

The female defendant by her earlier purchase of the machine she disposed of must be assumed to have wished to be the owner of a home knitting machine. She has admitted that the home knitting machine purchased from Fair Isle is still in her possession and that she has made use of it for the purpose of making knit goods for herself and the members of her family, the claim for rescission must be rejected; the defendants' only remedy would then be a counterclaim as to damages: *Kerr on Fraud and Mistake*, 7th ed., p. 529.

Even if there be accepted as evidence of the measure of damages, the very unsatisfactory testimony of the female defendant concerning the amount due to her for finished knit goods, her estimate would still have to be reduced by the value of the yarn admittedly taken from the premises of Fair Isle and Yarncraft on March 17, 1959. The evidence at trial, though voluminous and dealing at great length with matters of doubtful relevance leaves no sound basis for the assessment of damages. However, I hesitate to prolong further the course of these proceedings. Since the duty and power of the Division Court Judge is to hear and determine in a summary manner all questions of law and fact, and to make such order as appears to him just and agreeable to equity and good conscience, such an order should be made by this Court. I would avoid directing a reference to determine the measure of damages if there be any way in which this can be overcome. There will, therefore, be a reference to the Clerk of the Ninth Division Court of the County of Wentworth to take an account of the amount due the defendant by Fair Isle and Yarncraft for knit goods shipped by the female defendant over and above the value of the yarn obtained by her but only if either party demands it. In default of either party demanding such a reference within 15 days, the amount of the counterclaim is fixed at $140. In the result the appeal of the plaintiff will be allowed in part, and the judgment below varied to award to the plaintiff its claim of $273.30 with costs as fixed by the learned trial Judge and to allow the defendants' counterclaim at $140, or such amount as shall be fixed on the reference if there shall be one. If there shall be a reference, the costs of the reference will be in the discretion of the referee. As success of the appeal is divided, there will be no costs of the appeal.

Appeal allowed; counterclaim allowed.

Notes and Questions:

1 *Federal Discount* is analyzed in an excellent Comment by Ivan and Kristine Feltham in (1962) 40 Can. B. Rev. 461.

2 Were the circumstances of the close association between the endorsee and the payee in *Federal Discount* "such as to arouse suspicion of good faith" (*Falconbridge On Banking and Bills of Exchange* (7th ed , 1969) p. 632)? Is the result of the case consistent with a subjective standard of good faith? Indeed, it was stated in connection with U.S. cases denying a holder in due course status to holders of the consumer paper that "[t]he myth that the good faith test is a subjective one is just that — a myth. Courts have sought to determine what class of purchasers should enjoy the extraordinary protection and freedom from defenses which has its origin in the law merchant and is closely akin to similar protection given by courts of equity. In the run-of-the-mill commercial case, a test of actual knowledge has been adequate. The purposes of commercial paper supply the reasons for the extraordinary protection." Yet, in cases involving consumer paper, "a close connection between financing agency and the dealer in a consumer financing transaction will be grounds for finding a duty to police, inquire, or back-check." Accordingly, the general test of good faith includes "the observance of the reasonable commercial standards which are appropriate to the business in which the parties are engaged or to the transaction of which the purchaser is a part": N. Littlefield, "Good Faith Purchase of Consumer Paper: The Failure of the Subjective Test" (1966) 39 S. Cal. L. Rev. 48 at 74. Do you agree? Is an objective standard for measuring the good faith of a transferee of consumer paper consistent with section 3 of our Bills of Exchange Act?

3 "The basis of the *St. Pierre* case is that both the dealer and the finance company were engaged in one business": *Levenhurst Investments Ltd.* v. *Oakfield Country Club Ltd.* (1968) 68 DLR (2d) 79,88 (NS SC), *per* Coffin J., followed in *Williams & Glyn's Bank Ltd.* v. *Belkin Packaging Ltd.* (1979) 8 BLR 238 (BC SC). Likewise, in *Bank of Montreal* v. *Kon* (1978) 82 DLR (3d) 609, 630 (Alta. SC TD) Kirby J. stated that "[t]o bring the relationship [between a financer and seller] within the *Federal Discount* doctrine the evidence must establish or warrant the inference that the [financer] was a party to the wrongful acts of [the seller] or knew, or ought to have known, of the wrongful acts." Do you agree with any of these propositions? Other Canadian cases upholding the effectiveness of cut-off devices (by narrowly construing the close connectedness doctrine) are: *Prudential Finance Corp.* v. *Kucheran* (1964) 45 DLR (2d) 402 (Ont. CA) (commented on by N. Kessner, (1965) 11 McGill LJ 386); see also A. McMillan, (1965) 4 Alta. L. Rev. 166) and *Traders Finance Corp. Ltd.* v. *Edmonton Airport Hotel Co. Ltd.* (1964) 49 WWR 56 (Alta. SC). See in general: B. Crawford, "Consumer Instalment Sales Financing Since *Federal Discount Ltd.* v. *St. Pierre*" (1969) 19 Univ. Tor. LJ 353; J. Ziegel, "Recent Legislative and Judicial Trends in Consumer Credit in Canada" (1970) 8 Alta. L. Rev. 59, 70-71. See also *Bank of Montreal* v. *Kon, supra*, a direct loan case narrowly construing the close connectedness doctrine.

BENJAMIN GEVA
**"Close Business Relationship Between a Purchase Money Lender
and a Seller of Goods — Bank of Montreal v. Kon"**
(1978-79) 3 Can. Bus. LJ 90, 97-101, 105-06

In *Federal Discount* a promissory note evidencing a sale of a home knitting machine was negotiated by the payee-seller to the plaintiff finance company. Denying the finance company a holder in due course status the Ontario Court of Appeal, *per* Kelly, J.A., introduced into Canadian law what has been known in the United States as the "close connectedness" doctrine.

The doctrine originated and has primarily been applied in cases involving promissory notes issued by consumers in return for goods and then negotiated by the payees-sellers to sale finance companies. Upon the finding of a close business relationship between a payee-seller and a finance company taker-of-the-note, the effect of the doctrine has been to deny the latter a holder in due course status and thereby to subject it to the defences of the buyer arising from the sale agreement.

The exact elements of the close business connection have never been determined. The cases tend to consider combinations of certain factors, such as the drafting of the forms by the finance company, the approval or the establishment by it of the seller's sales practices and procedures, the substantial transfer of retail paper by the seller, a connected ownership or management or a family relationship, and more generally, the existence of mutuality of interest of the seller and finance company. What has always been emphasized, however, is the control by the finance company of the seller's scheme of selling on credit terms, which indicates the financer's involvement in the credit arrangement from its inception. Thus it was said in *Unico* v. *Owen* 232 A 2d 405 at 417 (1967, NJ SC), the doctrine will apply

> . . . when it appears from the totality of the arrangements between dealer and financer that the financer has had a substantial voice in setting standards for the underlying transaction, or has approved the standards established by the dealer, and has agreed to take all or a predetermined or substantial quantity of the negotiable paper which is backed by such standards. . . .

Some cases were concerned with situations where the close business association with the seller gave the finance company access to facts raising a suspicion of fraud. In denying a holder in due course status to the holder of the note, courts applied well established standards of knowledge and lack of good faith. Notwithstanding *Kon*, this situation has nothing to do with *Federal Discount* where Kelly, J., explicitly based his decision on the assumption that the finance company "did not have actual notice of facts the knowledge of which would have prevented it from becoming a holder in due course." Also, the close connectedness doctrine does not necessarily mean that an objective standard of good faith should be applied to a sale finance company having a close business relationship with the seller. As this explanation is contrary to the language of the Act, it has been criticized as unwarranted judicial legislation.

Indeed, the involvement in the arrangement from its inception is by itself the key to the doctrine. In order to invoke it, the buyer "must show that the seller contemplated that the credit would in fact be advanced by, and the note in fact held by, the particular financing institution involved." For, in addition to satisfying the statutory conditions of taking the note in good faith and for value and without notice of a defect of title, a holder in due course must be a *remote*, as distinguished from an immediate, party to the underlying transaction. Thus, in the landmark case of *Commercial Credit Co.* v. *Childs* (1940) SW 2d 210 (SC Ark.), the sale finance company "financed the deal, prepared the instrument, and on the day it was executed took an assignment of it from the . . . [seller]. Even before it was executed it prepared the written assignment thereon to itself." Under these circumstances, the plaintiff finance company was denied a holder in due course status since "Rather than being a *purchaser* of the instrument after its execution it was to all intents and purposes a *party* to the agreement and the instrument from the beginning."

Yet the close connectedness doctrine should not be taken to mean that the finance company becomes a party to the contract for sale. The doctrine is clearly distinguished from the line of cases holding that an owner of goods selling them through an agent acting in his own name cannot qualify as a holder in due course when the note evidencing the sale is negotiated to him. The owner in the latter situation is the "real vendor" of the goods, an original party to the sale transaction. The finance company on the other hand, being an original party to the credit-sale arrangement is better described as a *"participant"* in the sale, rather than being in privity under it. It is denied a holder in due course status by virtue of its *proximity* to the contract for sale to which it is none the less not a party. Indeed, "The basic philosophy of the holder in due course status is to encourage free negotiability of commercial paper . . . the closer his relationship to the underlying agreement which is the source of the note, the less need there is for giving him the tension free rights." In this framework, the close connectedness doctrine is an application of the spirit of the old distinction between a remote and an immediate party to an analogous new fact situation.

It is quite apparent that the pre-existing arrangement between the sale finance company and the seller under which the former undertook to finance the sale operation of the latter is the basis of the holding in *Federal Discount*. Thus, the court spoke there of the financer's exercise of "a measure of control over the seller's sales by the requirements laid down with regard to the negotiable paper". It also emphasized the fact that "The course of dealings between the . . . [finance company] and the . . . [seller] indicates a relationship much more intimate than that of endorsee or [*sic*, should read "and"] endorser in a normal commercial transaction." Under these circumstances, the court's conclusion was that "To pretend that they were so separate that the transfer of each note constituted an independent commercial transaction not affected by the pre-existing arrangements between them would . . . be to permit the form to prevail over the substance."

It would appear then that the conclusion of Kirby J. [in *Bank of Montreal* v. *Kon*], under which participation in or knowledge of wrongful acts is the basis of the *"Federal Discount* doctrine", is unsupported by the facts of the latter case as well as by the discussion of the court therein. Rather, it is the involvement of the finance company in the credit sale arrangement from its inception that makes it impossible to see it as a remote purchaser of the note contending to be a holder in due course.

• • •

Many aspects of the close connectedness doctrine have not been settled yet. For example, while some of the cases required only participation in the arrangement from its inception, others regarded the control of the financer over the credit terms, not merely as an indication of that involvement, but rather, as an independent additional prerequisite. Another problem stems from the fact that some of the leading cases that were decided under the doctrine could also be explained on a more traditional basis. Thus, in *Westfield Inv. Co.* v. *Fellers* 181 A 2d 809 at 818 (1962, NJ SC), the instrument evidencing the sale contained a printed assignment form designating the plaintiff finance company as the assignee. The finance company was denied a holder in due course status because "in delivery to its selected dealer of an instrument which for all practical purposes could be negotiated only to it, [it] became . . . inextricably a part of the original transaction with the purchaser. . . ." However, there were many circumstances in that case indicating actual knowledge on the part of the finance company of the activities of the seller. Also, in *Unico* v. *Owen,* though the court emphasized the control of the finance company on the "standards for the underlying transaction", the facts of the case disclosed a much more intimate relationship. The financer was "a partnership formed expressly for the purpose of financing" the seller involved; both seller and financer were subsidiaries in the same concern.

There are also uncertainties as to the scope of the doctrine. With few exceptions American courts applied it only with regard to consumers. In *Unico* v. *Owen* its range was explicitly confined to "consumer goods transactions". Moreover, in *Block* v. *Ford Motor Credit Co.* 286 A 2d 228 (1972, App. Ct., DC), in a situation that involved a consumer, the application of the close connectedness doctrine was rejected where the purchaser had capacity to understand the plain language of the instrument (he was a Ph.D. business executive), there was no claim of fraud, and the seller was still in business.

2.   THE APPLICATION OF THE DOCTRINE TO PURCHASE-MONEY LOAN

Note on Central Mortgage & Housing Corp. v. Graham:

In *Central Mortgage & Housing Corp.* v. *Graham* (1973) 43 DLR (3d) 686 (NS SC TD) an action was commenced by the Central Mortgage & Housing Corp. (CMHC) as mortgagee for foreclosure and sale of the mortgaged property (namely the Grahams' home). The home was part of a housing project in Sydney constructed by Bras D'Or Construction Ltd. and financed by CMHC. The Grahams admitted to withholding payments on the mortgage and claimed that the houses were improperly constructed. They maintained that the project was in fact a joint project by Bras D'Or and CMHC. They filed a defence and counterclaim joining CMHC and Bras D'Or.

The court reviewed the extensive American jurisprudence on joint ventures. A joint venture is an association of persons engaging in an *ad hoc* undertaking for joint profit by combining their respective resources without ostensibly forming a partnership. It contemplates a joint property interest in the subject matter of the venture, a right of mutual control or management of the enterprise and a right to participate in the profits. Jones J., after reviewing the American jurisprudence and the *Federal Discount* doctrine, concluded (at 709):

> I am satisfied on the evidence that Central Mortgage was involved in this project from the very start. Central Mortgage proposed the establishment of a shell housing project in Sydney. Agents of the corporation sought civic approval and directly enlisted Bras D'Or to carry out the project. The project was approved upon the submission of a proposal by Bras D'Or. Central Mortgage provided financing to cover the full cost of the project. The houses were sold to specified individuals only upon approval by Central Mortgage. Central Mortgage provided the plans and specifications and all necessary documentation.

> In terms of an agreement between Central Mortgage and Bras D'Or, the construction company agreed to erect 21 houses on lands which it provided according to plans and specifications provided by Central Mortgage at a fixed price. Central Mortgage agreed to provide total financing for the houses. Bras D'Or agreed to the sale of the houses to purchasers approved by Central Mortgage. Upon the execution of an assumption agreement by a purchaser satisfactory to both parties, Central Mortgage released Bras D'Or from any further liability for the funds advanced.

> In my view, there was a contribution by both parties of money, property, skill and knowledge to a common undertaking. There was a joint property interest in the subject-matter even though evidenced only in the mortgages. The parties had a mutual control and management of the enterprise during the construction of the houses and in the sales. The arrangement was limited to this project. There is no doubt that Bras D'Or intended a profit from the project. While there was [not]* a mutual sharing of the profits, Central Mortgage clearly had a financial interest at stake and was vitally concerned with the successful completion of the venture. . . . Based on the evidence, the arrangement between Central Mortgage and Bras D'Or can be characterized as a joint venture. To the extent that Bras D'Or in carrying on the venture incurred liabilities then both parties were bound.

BENJAMIN GEVA
"Close Business Relationship Between a Purchase-Money Lender and a Seller of Goods — Bank of Montreal v. Kon"
(1978-79) 3 Can. Bus. LJ 90-93, 101-05

Today, sixteen years after the landmark decision of *Federal Discount Corp. Ltd.* v. *St. Pierre* (1962) 3 DLR (2d) 86 and eight years after the enactment of Part V of the Bills of Exchange Act, thorny and fundamental issues relating to the subjection of a purchase-money lender to claims and defences arising from the financed contract for sale, have remained unresolved. Neither the doctrinal basis of this subjection, nor the range of circumstances where it operates, has been satisfactorily settled.

---

* The word "not" is erroneously omitted from the DLR report: see 13 NSR (2d) 183, at 212. [Eds.]

A recent reminder of this unsettled state of the law was given by the Trial Division of the Supreme Court of Alberta (Judicial District of Calgary) in *Bank of Montreal* v. *Kon* (1978) 82 DLR (3d) 609 where the facts were as follows:

> Maple Leaf, a private company . . . developed a plan whereby the company sold motor homes to purchasers who leased them back to the company. The purchase of the motor homes was financed by loans made by the [Bank of Montreal] to the various purchasers. The company rented the motor homes to users, applying the revenues from the rentals in part, on monthly payments to the bank on the various promissory notes evidencing the loans and in part on repairs, maintenance and other expenses for the motor homes. In a written agreement entered into between the purchasers and Maple Leaf it was provided that the loans were to be paid off out of the rentals over a four-year period, after which the company was entitled to rentals from the motor homes for one year and they would then revert to the purchaser. All of the loans were secured by chattel mortgages.
>
> In addition to financing the purchase of these motor homes, the bank granted commercial loans to Maple Leaf to finance its operations.
>
> In the fall of 1973 . . . Maple Leaf found itself unable to keep up the monthly payments to the bank on the various promissory notes.
>
> The bank proposed a six-month moratorium on payments on these loans to which the borrowers agreed. This required re-financing of the outstanding promissory notes. It was effected by their replacement with new promissory notes based on the amounts owing as at the date of the re-financing.

The financing of the purchases by the Bank of Montreal was made under an arrangement with Maple Leaf. Pursuant to that arrangement, the bank established a consumer lending branch one office space distant from Maple Leaf's premises. In some cases prospective borrowers were met by a bank officer on Maple Leaf's premises. Maple Leaf, on its part, referred the potential purchasers of motor homes to the bank and supplied it with basic credit information with respect to them. The refinancing documents were signed by the borrowers on Maple Leaf's premises on appointments made by Maple Leaf. To those borrowers who had received the original purchase-money loans from another bank, it was suggested by Maple Leaf that they refinance with the Bank of Montreal. Payments on the promissory notes were made to the Bank of Montreal by Maple Leaf.

Upon the failure of Maple Leaf and following its unauthorized sale of some of the motor homes and conversion of the proceeds, the Bank of Montreal moved to collect from the purchasers-borrowers themselves. Exercising a right under an acceleration clause inserted into each borrower's promissory note, it sued them all for the outstanding balances. The defence offered was that "The close connections between the Bank of Montreal and Maple Leaf deprives the Bank of Montreal of all defences to the equities of the respective transactions" and that "The notes were not endorsed 'consumer purchase' as required by the provisions of s. 190 of the Bills of Exchange Act and are therefore invalid." Rejecting these arguments and deciding for the plaintiff bank against the purchasers-borrowers, Kirby, J., held that as none of the purchases of the motor homes by the respective defendants was a "consumer purchase" the rights of the bank were not governed by Part V of the Act. Then, though conceding that apart from consumer purchases the *Federal Discount* doctrine "continues to apply", he went on to say that "[t]o bring the relationship within the *Federal Discount* doctrine the evidence must establish or warrant the inference that the Bank of Montreal was a party to the wrongful acts of Maple Leaf or knew, or ought to have known, of the wrongful acts; the wrongful acts being the conversion of the proceeds from the sale to the motor homes belonging to the respective defendants." Therefore, it was held, "the relationship beteen the bank and Maple Leaf does not come within the *Federal Discount* doctrine with respect to the transactions between Maple Leaf and the respective defendants."

• • •

Had the promissory notes of the debtors in *Kon* been issued to the order of Maple Leaf and then negotiated to the Bank of Montreal, the fact situation could have fitted easily into the close connectedness doctrine. The Bank of Montreal, by receiving the bulk of the business in the financing of the purchase of motor homes under a pre-existing arrangement with Maple Leaf, was involved in the scheme from its inception no less than the finance company in *Federal Discount*.

However, the bank and the seller chose to operate the scheme in a different manner. Cash was advanced to Maple Leaf not against buyers' obligations directed to it, but rather, against borrowers' obligations directed towards the Bank of Montreal.

Functionally, both methods of sales financing (purchase of retail paper and direct purchase-money loan) lead to the same result. In each case, goods move from the seller to the buyer, money moves from the financer to the seller, and the debt ends up running from the buyer to the financer.

Nevertheless, in theory the two financing patterns are entirely different. In the retail paper purchase situation, the financer sues the buyer on the obligation to pay for the goods. His title to the note is "derivative", and unless he is a holder in due course, he is subject to any defect in the title of a prior party. At the same time, in the direct purchase-money loan, the financer sues the buyer on a note expressing an obligation under the loan agreement which, conceptually, is separate and distinct from the contract for sale. In the latter situation, whether or not the lender is a holder in due course appears to be immaterial. The buyer-borrower "did get from the lender what he bargained for in exchange for his note." He is sued under an independent obligation and cannot interpose defences arising under his contract with the seller.

It would appear then that denial of holder in due course status, whether under the close connectedness doctrine or otherwise, would not affect the purchase-money lender's insulation from the buyer's defences against the seller. This, however, was not the view of two American cases, that treated the position of a purchase-money lender entirely as a holder in due course question. Finding in each case that in taking the note the payee-lender acted in good faith, each court found him a holder in due course taking the instrument free from all claims and defences of the buyer.

The same aproach, *i.e.*, treating the position of a direct purchase-money lender as a straight holder in due course question, was taken in Canada in

Beneficial Finance Co. of Canada v. *Kulig* (1970) 13 DLR (3d) 134. In that case, however, the court applied *Federal Discount* and found against the financer.

The result in *Kulig* commends itself at least for one reason: finding financers subject to buyer's defences only in the purchase of retail paper situation would encourage them to abandon that practice and set up purchase-money loans. An effective rule must lead to the same results under each mode of financing.

Yet, as explained, treating the position of the purchase-money lender as a holder in due course question is erroneous in principle. Notwithstanding *Kulig*, the close connectedness doctrine cannot be applied mechanically to the purchase-money loan situation.

To overcome the difficulty, suggestions have been made to treat the closely connected lender and the seller as principal and agent or as engaged in a joint business venture. Since the scope of the agency extends to the credit extension only, and the profits of the lender and the seller, though dependent on each other, are not "joint", these suggestions are open to criticism.

Another approach has been to see a financer involved in a scheme of selling goods as owing a duty of care to the buyers. Underlying the latter theory is *Connor* v. *Great Western Saving and Loan Ass'n.* 447 P 2d 609 (1969, SC Cal.) where a construction financer "became much more than a lender content to lend money at interest on the security of real property. It became an active participant in a home construction enterprise." Being found "well aware that the usual buyer of a home is ill equipped with experience or financial means to discern . . . structural defects", the lender was charged with a "duty to the buyers of the homes to exercise reasonable care to protect them from damages caused by structural defects".

Indeed, on the facts of *Kon,* where the loss was caused by a flaw in the scheme as well as by lack of capital in Maple Leaf, much could be said about the negligence of the Bank of Montreal. It is suggested, however, that apart from any of the above mentioned theories, the application of *Federal Discount* to the purchase-money lender situation can be rationalized on a basis analogous to that underlying its application in the holder in due course analysis. Indeed, it is the argument of involvement in the arrangement from its inception, or of "proximity" to the underlying sale transaction, that bars the financer-holder from being a holder in due course notwithstanding the appearance of a good faith purchase on his part. The apparent independence of the purchase-money loan transaction should be disregarded on the basis of the same argument. When the loan is offered through the seller as part and parcel of the sale, the arrangement is unitary and should be treated as indivisible. A lender participant thereto from its beginning, should be denied the benefit of what has only the appearance of an independent cause of action.

C.   LEGISLATIVE RESPONSES

Legislation governing the preservation of consumer defences developed in Canada along the lines established by the distribution of legislative powers under the BNA Act,

1867. Section 91(18) of the Act assigned to the Parliament of Canada the exclusive legislative authority in relation to bills of exchange and promissory notes. Under section 92(13), "matters coming within . . . Property and civil rights in the province" are subject to provincial jurisdiction. Accordingly, the federal Parliament has legislated in the area of negotiable instruments. Provincial legislation has dealt with waiver of defence clauses, and to some extent with purchase-money loans. See in general Buglass, "Consumer Notes, Holders in Due Course and Related Issues: Recent Judicial and Legislative Developments in Canada" in J. Ziegel (ed.) *Papers and Comments delivered at the Eighth Annual Workshop on Commercial and Consumer Law (1978)* (1980) p. 39; L. Milrod, "Part V of the Bills of Exchange Act: Effective Consumer Protection Legislation?" (1980) Ott. L. Rev. 319.

1.   PART V OF THE BILLS OF EXCHANGE ACT

a) Consumer Bills and Notes

Part V was enacted in 1970. It requires in s. 190(1) that "[e]very consumer bill or consumer note [as defined in s. 189] shall be prominently and legibly marked on its face with the words 'Consumer Purchase' before or at the time when the instrument is signed." Otherwise, the instrument "is void, except in the hands of a holder in due course without notice" that the instrument is consumer paper (s. 190(2)). The right of a holder of a properly marked consumer instrument "is subject to any defence or right of set off, other than counter-claim, that the purchaser would have had in an action by the seller on the consumer bill or consumer note" (s. 191).

Part V was enacted in 1970. It requires in s. 190(1) that "[e]very consumer bill or consumer note [as defined in s. 189] shall be prominently and legibly marked on its face

> the scope of "consumer purchase" as defined in s. 188 was read by the court quite narrowly. Finding that "the primary purpose underlying the purchase of the motor homes was to lease them to Maple Leaf to be rented out", that "[t]he defendants were all cognizant of the income tax benefits that were to be derived from the motor homes, and took advantage of them", and that "[t]he use of the particular motor home by a purchaser was an incidental benefit", the court concluded that the purchases "cannot be considered to have been 'consumer purchases' within the meaning of s. 188". Nevertheless, in defining "consumer purchase", s. 188 does not use language explicitly limiting its scope to a purchase of goods "for use primarily for personal, family, or household purposes". Instead, every purchase of goods "by an individual other than for resale or for use in the course of his business, profession or calling" is a "consumer purchase" under s. 188. This seems to cover a purchase relating to a business opportunity made not in the ordinary course of business of the purchaser. What is excluded from the coverage of the s. 188 definition is a purchase by an individual in the course of *his* business and not every purchase made for a business purpose. Moreover, on the facts of the case, the Maple Leaf plan was designed not to provide a source of income to the defendants, but rather, to enable them to pay for the motor homes that after five years were to revert to their own personal use.

(Geva (1978) 3 Can. Bus. LJ 90 at 94.)

b)   The Application of Part V to Bills and Notes Given to Sellers

As already noted, s. 190(1) requires the marking of a consumer bill or note with the words "Consumer Purchase". Otherwise, the instrument "is void, except in the hands of a holder in due course without notice that the bill or note is a consumer bill or consumer note" (s. 190(2)). Where the instrument is "void" under s. 190(2) the holder can presumably sue on the underlying transaction. (See Ziegel, "Consumer Notes — Bill C-208 — Bills of Exchange Amendment Act" (1971) 49 Can. Bar Rev. 121, 129.) In the action on the consumer sale the privilege of a holder in due course is obviously inapplicable. "Void" in s. 190(2) has therefore nothing to do with "void" bills and notes in the context of illegal consideration (discussed in *Falconbridge On Banking and Bills of Exchange* (7th ed., 1969) p. 677-80 (also 498-499). Nonetheless, may there not be some doubt as to the revival of the basic transaction upon non-payment of an instrument that has been voided by a statute? *Cf.* chapter 15(D) *supra.*

Section 191 governs the right of a holder of a consumer bill or note. It is modeled on s. 15, which governs the rights of a transferee of an instrument properly marked as given for a patent right. Both provisions are exceptions to the silence of the Act with respect to rights of a holder not in due course (chapter 15(C)(3) *supra*). As to the ultimate effect of each one of them, consider the following.

BENJAMIN GEVA
"Equities as to Liability on Bills and Notes — Rights of a Holder Not in Due Course"
(1979-80) 5 Can. Bus. LJ 53, 58 *et seq.*

[A] bill or note "the consideration of which consists, in whole or in part, of the purchase money of a patent right [must bear] prominently and legibly . . . the words *Given for a patent right*". Its "endorsee or other transferee" takes it under s. 15 "subject to any defence or set off in respect of the whole or any part thereof that would have existed between the original parties".

The scope of s. 15 depends on the meaning of its key terms. As " 'defence' includes counterclaim" some confusion may arise. Thus, according to Falconbridge, "claim and counterclaims are merely *independent cross-claims* made by the plaintiff and the defendant respectively in the same action." A counterclaim may arise under, but is not confined to, matters arising from the plaintiff's action. It "is the assertion by the defendant of a demand which does not answer or destroy the plaintiff's claim". It is unlikely, however, that "defence" in the context of s. 15 encompasses counterclaims arising outside the underlying transaction. At the same time, the right of "set-off" to which the holder is explicitly made subject under s. 15 relates to a separate transaction. Its assertion reduces the amount recovered under the plaintiff's claim in whole or in part. The overall effect of s. 15 under this construction is to put a remote party holder of an instrument governed thereby in the same position as an assignee of the underlying contract.

The second class of instruments whose holder appears to be exempt from the noncomprehensive coverage of the statutory scheme is governed by Part V of the Canadian Act. A bill or note issued by a buyer of consumer goods or services ("consumer bill" or "consumer note") is required thereunder to "be prominently and legibly marked on its face with the words 'Consumer Purchase' ". Under s. 191, the right of its holder "to have the whole or any part thereof paid by the purchaser . . . is subject to any defence or right of set-off, other than counterclaim, that the purchaser would have had in an action by the seller on the consumer bill or consumer note".

The exclusion of "counterclaim" side by side with the inclusion of "set-off" in s. 191 is probably designed to make clear that apart from the right of "set-off", a cross-claim arising out of a separate matter with the seller cannot be asserted by way of defence against an action by a remote party on the instrument. This results in avoiding the confusion mentioned above with respect to s. 15. Nonetheless, unlike s. 15, s. 191 does not turn out to be an exception to the noncomprehensiveness of the Act. The availability of defences against the holder of a consumer bill or note is not dependent under s. 191 only on the scope of "any defence or right of set-off, other than counterclaim". The holder's exposure is further limited thereunder to defences that "the purchaser would have had in an action by the seller *on the consumer bill or consumer note*". As our inquiry is directed to finding what defences are available against an action of a holder not in due course suing on a bill or note, this is rather unhelpful language. Apart from putting a remote party on the same footing as an immediate one, it falls short of delineating the defences applicable to an action on a consumer bill or consumer note.

c) The Application of Part V to Purchase-Money Loans

i) *Is Part V Limited to a Purchase-Money Lender Who Does Not Deal With the Seller at Arm's Length?*

JACOB S. ZIEGEL
"Consumer Notes and Part V of the Bills of Exchange Act — More Trouble Abrewing"
(1978) 2 Can. Bus. LJ 262, 263-66

In both *CIBC* v. *Langlois* (1977) 2 BCLR 83 (SC) and *CAC Ltd.* v. *Galbiati* [1977] 1 WWR 280 (Sask. Dist. Ct.) the primary issue was whether the definition of consumer purchase embraces a lender advancing a purchase money loan regardless of the intensity of his relationship with the seller. Both courts answered the question affirmatively albeit with very little reasoning. In the *Langlois* case, the plaintiff bank advanced a substantial sum of money to enable the defendant to purchase a mobile home. The proceeds of the loan were paid to the dealer, Pacific Mobilex Ltd., but the company went bankrupt before the home was delivered. In the *Galbiati* case the lender was a consumer loan company and the loan was sought, and used, to pay for the purchase of a second-hand automobile. The borrower took delivery of the car but then complained of an oil leak. The dealer had the car repaired at its own expense but the borrower refused to take it back. Forbes, D.C.J., found, without any elaboration of the facts, that the borrower had acted wrongfully and would not have been entitled to set up s. 190(2) by way of defence had the defence been relevant.

The major defence apparently advanced on behalf of the consumer-borrower in both cases was that the note signed by the borrower was void because it was not marked as required by s. 190(1). There was no doubt the lenders knew the purpose for which the money was required. There was also *prima facie* evidence in both cases that the lenders might not have been dealing at arm's length with the dealers and therefore fell within s. 189(3). However, this possibility is not pursued in the judgments. The *ratio* in both cases was that the borrower had executed a consumer note within the meaning of s. 189(2) which, not being marked as required by s. 190(2), was a complete nullity. In the *Galbiati* case Forbes, D.C.J., apparently deemed it so plain that Part V applies equally to a consumer note evidencing a purchase money loan as to a note given to a dealer for the balance of the purchase price that he did not find it necessary to go beyond a recitation of the statutory provisions. In the *Langlois* case, Anderson, L.J.S.C., was content to adopt the Saskatchewan court's language without adding reasons of his own.

Were the courts correct in their reading of the statutory provisions? There are at least three reasons which militate against such a construction. The first is that it is not consistent with the legislative history of Part V. The "Explanatory Notes" accompanying the original version of Bill C-208 explained the purpose of Part V in these terms:

> At the present time, where the purchaser in a consumer purchase gives the vendor a promissory note, the vendor may assign that note to a third party who may hold it free of any defence or right of set-off that the purchaser may have had against the vendor. The purpose of the new Part V is to provide the purchaser with such a defence or right of set-off against the third party.

A similar explanation was furnished by Mr. Thorson, Associate Deputy Minister of Justice, in explaining to the Standing Committee of the House of Commons on Justice and Legal Affairs the reason for the exclusion of "cash purchases" in the definition of consumer purchase in s. 189. It must be added however that under closer questioning he was prepared to concede that *some* types of lenders might also be caught by the definition of consumer purchase though he did not explain how he reconciled this result with the Explanatory Notes or indeed with the definition of consumer purchase.

The second reason is that if ss. 188 and 189(2) were intended to apply to all consumer instruments there would have been no need to add s. 189(3) at the Committee stage of the Bill. The amendment was added precisely because the members of the Committee were not satisfied that the existing definitions were broad enough to catch even those lenders who are in intimate relationship with the seller. Section 189(3) provides that:

> (3) Without limiting or restricting the circumstances in which, for the purposes of this Part, a bill of exchange or a promissory note shall be considered to be issued in respect of a consumer purchase, a bill of exchange or a promissory note shall be conclusively presumed to be so issued if
>
> (a)   the consideration for its issue was the lending or advancing of money or

other valuable security by a person other than the seller, in order to enable the purchaser to make the consumer purchase; and

(b) the seller and the person who lent or advanced the money or other valuable security were, at the time the bill or note was issued, not dealing with each other at arm's length within the meaning of the *Income Tax Act*.

Once again Mr. Thorson explained at the resumed hearings of the Committee that the purpose of the amendment was to incorporate the ratio of *Federal Discount* v. *St. Pierre* [1962] OR 310. This is a far cry from saying that all lenders who know the purpose of their loans are caught by Part V and had this been the draftsman's intention it would have been easy for him to say so.

Finally, the courts' reading of the scope of Part V ignores the mischief against which its provisions were aimed and may unfairly hold a lender responsible for the shortcomings of a seller over whose conduct he has no control at all. Both the original and the enlarged versions of Part V were designed to allow the borrower to retain the benefits of any defences he might have been able to raise in a claim on the instrument by the seller where there is either an intimate relationship between the seller and the financer in the *Federal Discount* sense or the holder of the note is put on notice about its origins. In the latter event the financer could either refuse to purchase the note or he could protect himself by means of a recourse agreement, the establishment of a dealer's reserve, and other well-known devices long in use between financers and the dealers whose paper they discount.

These mechanisms are not available to a lender who has no prior relationship with the seller. Suppose the dealer fails to deliver the goods or to render the promised service or that the goods or services are defective, how can the lender dealing at arm's length with the dealer force him to honour the terms of his contract with the borrower-buyer or to reimburse the lender for the amount of the loan? Presumably the lender could refuse the loan unless the dealer were willing to sign the note as an accommodation party or to provide some other form of guaranty. However, even ardent consumer advocates have hesitated to impose such extensive obligations on arm's length lenders.

ii) *The Meaning of "Consumer Purchase", of "Not Dealing at Arm's Length", and the Applicability of Part V to Purchase-Money Lenders of Non-Consumer Goods*

CANADIAN IMPERIAL BANK OF COMMERCE v. LIVELY
(1974) 46 DLR (3d) 432 (NS SC TD)

MORRISON J.: This is an action to recover the balance owing on the principal and interest of a promissory note dated April 27, 1971, made by the defendant, Havey Lively, and is against the defendant, Havey Lively, as the maker of the note and against the defendant, Lorne Richards, as guarantor of the note. It was agreed by counsel for all parties that the balance due and owing of principal and interest as of the date of the trial was $2,177.60.

An order of this Court adjourning the third party proceedings without day was granted on March 1, 1974.

At the conclusion of the plaintiff's case, the case against Lorne Richards was dismissed.

The defendant, Havey Lively, is a 51-year-old machine operator, residing at R.R. No. 1, Brookfield, Nova Scotia. In April, 1971, the defendant, Lorne Richards, made several trips to Lively's home in Brookfield to sell chinchillas to Lively's son, Gary, who was 27 years of age. Gary made a deposit of $100 on the purchase of some chinchillas but he could not raise the balance of the money and the deal fell through. The defendant, Havey Lively, however, was persuaded that it would be a good idea to raise chinchillas and agreed to purchase eight chinchillas, six female and two male, along with certain equipment and associated services from the defendant, Lorne Richards. Mr. Richards, at the time of the sale, was president of Seaboard Chinchilla Services Limited.

Mr. Lively did not have the funds to purchase the chinchillas but Richards suggested that the money could be borrowed from the plaintiff bank, and produced an application form and a form of promissory note for execution by Mr. Lively. The note was for a principal amount of $2,200, with interest thereon of $422.40, making a total of $2,622.40. This amount was to be repaid in monthly instalments of $72.65 until the full amount of $2,622.40 was paid.

Mr. Lively signed both the application and the note, which were actually reverse sides of the same form. The note was then taken to the plaintiff bank by Richards and he subsequently obtained the principal amount of the note from the bank. Lively never saw the money and never went to the bank at any time and never had any association with the bank. The note did not have the words "Consumer Purchase" prominently and legibly marked on its face either before or at the time of execution.

Lively admitted receiving from the bank a letter, which was introduced into evidence as ex. 2. This letter reads as follows:

April 20, 1971

Mr. Havey Lively,
R.R. #1,
Brookfield, N.S.

Dear Sir:

We record that your name appears as a borrower on a Commerce Bankplan Loan for $2,622.40 for a term of 36 months. The loan is required for the purchase of chinchillas and/or related equipment and services of the Seaboard Chinchilla Services Limited.

We should appreciate if you would sign the Declaration on the original of this letter and return to us at your earliest convenience, retaining the copy for your files. We enclose a stamped self-addressed envelope for your convenience when replying.

Yours truly
(Sgd.) E.M. Webber
Bankplan Officer

DECLARATION

I hereby certify that I did sign an application for a Canadian Imperial Bank of Commerce Bankplan loan in the amount of $2,622.40 which includes cost of borrowing charges of $422.40 at a rate of 11.78% per annum. I further certify that my present age is 48 years.

The bank is hereby directed to pay the proceeds of my Bankplan loan to Seaboard Chinchilla Services Limited.

Havey Lively
_____
(signed)   Borrower

At the same time the note was signed the conditional sale contract was entered into. This conditional sale contract was introduced into evidence as ex. 3, covering the purchase of the chinchillas. Mr. Lively testified that he intended to keep the animals and did not intend to sell them to anyone else. Exhibit 1, the form of promissory note and application was executed in respect to and in connection with ex. 3, the conditional sale contract. As far as Lively knew, all the money procured by his execution of the note was used to purchase the eight chinchillas and associated services.

Mr. Lively also testified that he received five females and three males instead of six females and two males. At the time that the sale was made Richards apparently told Lively that within three years he could make a lot of money from the sale of the chinchilla pelts and chinchillas for breeding purposes. Lively testified, however, that he was badly disillusioned as he spent $1,115 in addition to what he paid the bank, in endeavouring to make some profit off the animals.

Mr. Errol Mills Webber, presently unemployed, testified that from November, 1969, until February 1, 1974, he was an employee of the plaintiff company. Prior to that he had worked six months with Lorne Richards Enterprises. Lorne Richards Enterprises was an operation apparently carried on by Mr. Richards, engaged in the selling of chinchilla pelts and chinchilla breeding stock. When Mr. Webber worked for Richards he was a sales representative and was familiar with the business. He thought that a person who went into the raising of chinchillas might make, after one year, as much as $100 a month. However, as time progressed and his herd of chinchillas was built up he could make more money.

Mr. Webber was a consumer loan officer with the George and Granville Sts. branch of the Canadian Imperial Bank of Commerce, in Halifax, Nova Scotia, from November, 1969, to May or June, 1973.

He had dealings with the defendant, Lorne Richards, while working with the bank, and he arranged the financing for certain sales of chinchillas for Richards. At first he dealt with Mr. Richards as Lorne Richards Enterprises and then later on he dealt with Mr. Richards as representing Seaboard Chinchilla Services Limited.

He testified that when he became an employee of the Canadian Imperial Bank of Commerce, he discussed the financing of chinchilla sales with Richards and agreed to finance the sales. He knew the business because he had worked with Mr. Richards for six months prior to taking employment with the bank as a sales representative.

Webber then described the procedure which was used in arranging the financing of the sales of chinchillas. The defendant Richards would be supplied with application forms, on the reverse side of which were the promissory notes. Mr. Richards would take the forms to prospective customers and have them executed by the customer. He would then take the application and note into the bank. The bank would then check on the credit rating of the applicant. If his credit rating proved out the bank would then make the loan, but the money would never be advanced to the purchaser but rather to Mr. Richards, the bank first having obtained a signed letter, similar to ex. 2 herein, from the customer. He stated that the bank processed 15 or 20 of this type of loan. Webber testified that he did actually recall the Havey Lively loan and that he processed it.

Webber verified that Lively never entered the bank at all, and that no one who worked at the bank ever saw him. Mr. Richards' procedure was to have the application form and the promissory note signed by the purchaser, then he would witness the signature of the customer and sign as a guarantor of the note. He would then take the note and application form into the bank. The bank kept Mr. Richards supplied with an adequate supply of forms.

Webber also admitted that it was not a common practice to give out forms like this, that actually most people came into the bank to get their loans directly from the bank. He admitted that he and Richards were friends. They both lived in Dartmouth, Nova Scotia, and it was through a meeting that he had with Mr. Richards that Webber agreed to do the financing for the chinchilla sales through the Canadian Imperial Bank of Commerce. He also knew there was a contract for the sale of chinchillas and associated services between Lively and Richards. He was familiar with this type of contract. Mr. Webber ceased to be employed by the bank on February 1, 1974. Webber's title at the bank was consumer loan officer.

Following the execution of the note Mr. Lively attempted to raise the chinchillas but discovered, first of all, that the stock was not of good quality and, secondly, that he had received one less female and one extra male than had been bargained for. He found that the raising of chinchillas was not an easy business and that the animals required constant care and were prone to illness. He felt that Lorne Richards had misrepresented the business to him and discontinued payments on the promissory note.

Part of the defence to the action is raised under the provisions of the Bills of Exchange Act, RSC 1952, c. 15 [now RSC 1970, c. B-5], particularly the amendments to the said Act under the provisions of 1970, c. 48, s. 2, where ss. 188, 189, 190, 191 and 192 were added to the Act. Section 190 of the Bills of Exchange Act reads as follows:

> **190.**(1) Every consumer bill or consumer note shall be prominently and legibly marked on its face with the words "Consumer Purchase" before or at the time when the instrument is signed by the purchaser or by any one signing to accommodate the purchaser.
>
> (2) A consumer bill or consumer note that is not marked as required by this section is void, except in the hands of a holder in due course without notice that the bill or note is a consumer bill or consumer note or except as against a drawee without such notice.

If it is found that the promissory note, which is the basis of this action, is a "consumer note" then under the provisions of s. 190 the words "Consumer Purchase" must be prominently and legibly marked on its face, otherwise the note would be void.

Section 189(2) of the Bills of Exchange Act defines "consumer note" as follows:

> **189.**(2) A consumer note is a promissory note
> (a) issued in respect of a consumer purchase, and
> (b) on which the purchaser or any one signing to accommodate him is liable as a party.

Section 189(3) of the Bills of Exchange Act reads as follows:

> **189.**(3) Without limiting or restricting the circumstances in which, for the purposes of this Part, a bill of exchange or a promissory note shall be considered to be issued in respect of a consumer purchase, a bill of exchange or a promissory note shall be conclusively presumed to be so issued if
> (a) the consideration of its issue was the lending or advancing of money or other valuable security by a person other than the seller, in order to enable the purchaser to make the consumer purchase; and
> (b) the seller and the person who lent or advanced the money or other valuable security were, at the time the bill or note was issued, not dealing with each other at arm's length within the meaning of the *Income Tax Act*.

Section 188 of the Bills of Exchange Act reads as follows:

> **188.** In this Part
> (a) "consumer purchase" means a purchase, other than a cash purchase, of goods or services or an agreement to purchase goods or services
> (i) by an individual other than for resale or for use in the course of his business, profession or calling, and
> (ii) from a person who is engaged in the business of selling or providing those goods or services;

Section 188(a), (c), (d) and (e) define the meaning of "goods", "purchaser", "seller" and "services". Therefore a promissory note may be considered to be a consumer note if it falls within the provisions of s. 188, or it may be conclusively presumed to be a consumer note if it falls within the provisions of s. 189(3)(a) and (b).

To fall within the provisions of s. 188 the note would have to be issued in respect of a consumer purchase by "an individual other than for resale or for use in the course of his business, profession or calling".

It would seem that under the definition of "consumer purchase" contained in s. 188(a) that the defendant Lively was actually purchasing the goods for use in the course of his business.

The evidence of Havey Lively, both that contained in the examination for discovery and in that given at the trial of this matter, would indicate that the only reason he purchased the chinchillas and services from Richards was to make money out of them. In other words, he intended to operate a business of raising chinchillas for the sale of both their pelts and the animals themselves for breeding purposes.

I cannot read anything else into his evidence to convince me that he was only indulging in a hobby. All of his comments are to the effect that he was bitterly disappointed that he did not make money out of the transaction and that he was misled by Mr. Richards into thinking that he could make money. In other words, the business did not prosper as he thought that it would.

If one were forced to rely on the definition of consumer purchase (s. 188) and the definition of consumer note (s. 189(2)) as contained in the Act then one would be forced to conclude that the promissory note in question was not a "consumer note".

This, however, brings us to s. 189(3) of the Bills of Exchange Act, which reads as follows:

> 189.(3) Without limiting or restricting the circumstances in which, for the purposes of this Part, a bill of exchange or a promissory note shall be considered to be issued in respect of a consumer purchase, a bill of exchange or a promissory note shall be *conclusively* presumed to be so issued if
> (a)   the consideration for its issue was the lending or advancing of money or other valuable security by a person other than the seller, in order to enable the purchaser to make the consumer purchase;

(My emphasis.)

I am satisfied that the transaction entered into by Lively and Richards in the case at bar comes under the provisions of s. 189(3)(a); however, s. 189(3)(b) goes on to say:

> (b)   the seller and the person who lent or advanced the money or other valuable security were, at the time the bill or note was issued, not dealing with each other at arm's length within the meaning of the *Income Tax Act*.

In order to gain the protection of s. 190 of the Bills of Exchange Act the defendant Lively must establish that the promissory note in question was issued in respect of a consumer purchase, that is, that it was a "consumer note".

In my opinion the only way in which this can be done would be to establish that the transaction entered into by Lively and Richards falls under the provisions of s. 189(3)(b), that is, that the seller Richards and the plaintiff bank were at the time the note was issued not dealing with each other at arm's length within the meaning of the Income Tax Act, RSC 1952, c. 148 [am. 1970-71-72, c. 63].

Section 251 of the Income Tax Act reads as follows:

> 251.(1)   For the purposes of this Act,
> (a)   related persons shall be deemed not to deal with each other at arm's length; and
> (b)   it is a question of fact whether persons not related to each other were at a particular time dealing with each other at arm's length.

Section 251(2) of the Income Tax Act goes on to define the meaning of related persons.

It has not been suggested in this case that Richards and the Canadian Imperial Bank of Commerce are related persons within the meaning of the Income Tax Act. Rather it has been argued that there are situations where persons who are not related may be deemed to be dealing with each other not at arm's length, and that s. 251(1)(b) of the Income Tax Act is the basis for the proposition that it is a question of fact whether or not unrelated persons are dealing with each other at arm's length.

The language of s. 189(3)(b) of the Bills of Exchange Act provides that in interpreting the meaning of "at arm's length", one must do so "within the meaning of the Income Tax Act".

In the *Estate of Lillian Beckow Blank* v. *M.N.R.* (1969) 69 DTC 759, the Court said as follows, commencing at p. 768: "In the absence of a statutory provision defining who may or may not be deemed to deal at arm's length, the question becomes one of fact."

Black's Law Dictionary, 4th ed. (1951), at p. 159, contains the following passage:

"At arm's length". Beyond the reach of personal influence or control.

"Parties are said to deal 'at arm's length' when each stands upon the strict letter of his rights, and conducts the business in a formal manner, without trusting to the other's fairness or integrity, and without being subject to the other's control or overmastering influence."

Mozley and Whitely's Law Dictionary, 6th ed. (1950) puts it thus at p. 29:

When a person is not, or having been, ceases to be, under the influence or control of another, he is said to be 'at arm's length' with him, *e.g. cestui que trust and trustee.*

(My emphasis.)

The Shorter Oxford Dictionary, 3rd ed., defines "at arm's length' as meaning: "as far away from one as the arm can reach; away from familiarity," or "at a distance without fiduciary relations".

One of the clearest definitions is found in *Gatineau Westgate Inc.* v. *M.N.R.* (1966) 41 Tax ABC 440 at p. 457:

What does "at arm's length" mean? It is to stipulate in such conditions that the interests of each of the parties in a transaction are completely independent. In other words, the action of one party is independent of the action of the other in such a way as to make the interests of each, in the transaction entered into by the parties quite distinct.

In *M.N.R.* v. *Sheldon's Engineering Ltd.* [1955] 3 DLR 801, [1955] SCR 637, [1955] CTC 174, Locke, J., said as follows at p. 806:

The expression [at arm's length] is one which is usually employed in cases in which transactions between trustees and *cestuis que trust*, guardians and wards, principals and agents or solicitors and clients are called into question.

In my opinion "not at arm's length" within the meaning of the Income Tax

Act, applies to those situations where one person or corporation has control, direct or indirect over another person or corporation.

In the case at bar, I find that the plaintiff bank did not exercise such control or have such influence over the defendant, Lorne Richards. The interests of each of the parties are completely independent. The interest of each party in this transaction is quite distinct to the interest of the other party.

The bank made a loan to the defendant Lively, and Seaboard Chinchilla Services Limited made a sale to the defendant Lively. It is true that the sale would not likely have taken place unless Lively received the loan, but the bank had no other relationship to the sale of chinchillas. The supply of application forms by the bank to Richards was for his convenience only.

I find that the transaction involving the sale of chinchillas to the defendant Lively by Lorne Richards and Seaboard Chinchilla Services Limited was not a consumer purchase under the provisions of the Bills of Exchange Act. Therefore the words "Consumer Purchase" do not have to be prominently and legibly marked on the face of the promissory note.

Counsel for the defendant Lively also advanced the defence of fraudulent misrepresentation. He argued that (a) if the Court were to find as a fact that Richards was acting not only as agent for Seaboard Chinchilla Services Limited to obtain the contract but also as agent for the plaintiff bank to obtain the promissory note, and (b) that this was one continuous transaction, parts of which could not be severed, then the promissory note was void as well as the sales agreement. This argument is made primarily on the basis of agency, and defence argued that Richards was agent for both the plaintiff and the defendant Lively and therefore the promissory note could be set aside on the grounds of fraud.

With respect to this argument I am not satisfied that Richards was acting as agent for both Seaboard Chinchilla Services Limited and the plaintiff bank. I am satisfied that the relationship between Richards and the plaintiff bank was established solely for the convenience of Richards, in the submission of the loan applications of prospective purchasers to the bank. Nor am I satisfied that there was a single continuous transaction, but rather two transactions: (a) a purchase by Lively from Seaboard Chinchilla Services Limited, and (b) a loan by the plaintiff bank to Lively.

The defendant Havey Lively, is liable to the plaintiff bank for the sum (agreed upon between the parties) of $2,177.60.

Judgment for plaintiff.

Notes and Questions:

1   The draftsmen of the 1974 Official Text of the American Uniform Consumer Credit Code propose in s. 3.405 that in addition to an issuer of a lender credit card, a purchase money lender will be subject to consumer claims and defences arising from the sale in the following circumstances:

> (a) the lender knows that the seller or lessor arranged for the extension of credit by the lender for a commission, brokerage, or referral fee;

(b) the lender is a person related to the seller or lessor, unless the relationship is remote or is not a factor in the transaction;

(c) the seller or lessor guarantees the loan or otherwise assumes the risk of loss by the lender upon the loan;

(d) the lender directly supplies the seller or lessor with the contract document used by the consumer to evidence the loan, and the seller or lessor has knowledge of the credit terms and participates in preparation of the document;

(e) the loan is conditioned upon the consumer's purchase or lease of the property or services from the particular seller or lessor, but the lender's payment of proceeds of the loan to the seller or lessor does not in itself establish that the loan was so conditioned; or

(f) the lender, before he makes the consumer loan, has knowledge or, from his course of dealing with the particular seller or lessor or his records, notice of substantial complaints by other buyers or lessees of the particular seller's or lessor's failure or refusal to perform his contracts with them and of the particular seller's or lessor's failure to remedy his defaults within a reasonable time after notice to him of the complaints.

As a matter of construing the Bills of Exchange Act, could Canadian courts read such circumstances into the "not dealing with each other at arm's length" requirements of s. 189(3)?

2   Does *Lively* stand for the proposition that section 189(3) extends the coverage of Part V to *every* purchase-money loan given by a lender who does not deal with the seller "at arm's length" regardless of whether its proceeds were used to make a consumer purchase as defined in s. 188.? Is such a proposition supported by the language of s. 189(3)? It is definitely unsupported by the legislative history of Part V: *cf.* Ziegel, "Consumer Notes — Bill C-208 — Bills of Exchange Amendment Act? (1971) 49 Can. B. Rev. 121 at 124-126. In dealing with notes issued in respect to purchase money loans, *Bank of Montreal* v. *Kon* (1978) 82 DLR (3d) 609, 630 (Alta. SC TD) regarded Part V as limited to a "consumer purchase" as defined in section 188.

iii) *Some Final Observations*

BENJAMIN GEVA
(1978) 3 Can. Bus. LJ 90, 95-96

Confusion regarding the scope of consumer purchases that fall within the ambit of Part V of the Act has been added by a British Columbia County Court's recent holding that since a "cash purchase" is excluded from the s. 188 definition of "consumer purchase", Part V is inapplicable to situations "where payment for the goods was made and accepted as payment in full by the seller and the goods were delivered at that time and title thereto passed to the purchaser." This conclusion, the result of the reference to "consumer purchase" in s. 189(3)(*a*), would mean that the applicability of Part V of the Act to an instrument evidencing a purchase-money *loan*, depends on whether credit has also been extended to the consumer by the *seller*.

Last, but not least, even when Part V applies to the rights of purchase-money lenders, its effect on them is far from certain. Under s. 191, "the right of a holder of a consumer bill or consumer note that is marked as required by section 190 . . . is subject to any defence . . . that the purchaser would have had in *an action by the seller on the consumer bill or consumer note.*" This is something quite unintelligible, if not entirely meaningless, in the context of a bill or note evidencing a *loan.* Thus, due to the plain language of s. 191, notwithstanding the intention of its draftsmen, rights of the lender suing on an *instrument* covered by Part V, may turn on the applicability of the *Federal Discount* doctrine. Besides, as on the *dishonour* of an instrument the right on the basic transaction is revived, and as Part V is only concerned with the enforceability of the consumer instrument and does not purport to affect the right on the underlying debt, the lender may circumvent Part V by suing on the underlying loan transaction rather than on the instrument evidencing it. His rights will then be determined under the *Federal Discount* doctrine. This appears to be the law at least where the lender holds an instrument which has not been voided under s. 190(2), for this unquestionably is a situation where the instrument is said to be *dishonoured* by non-payment so as to revive the underlying obligation.

Notes:

1   The British Columbia County Courts decision referred to above is *Royal Bank of Canada* v. *Siemens* [1978] 2 WWR 298. It was followed in *Re Mclaren* (1978) 88 DLR (3d) 222 (NS SC). The court in the latter case also opined that where an unmarked note has been given not in payment of the loan, but rather in evidence of the indebtedness thereunder, the underlying indebtedness would have not been affected by s. 190(2) (rendering the instrument void). But *cf.* chapter 15 (D), *supra.* Both cases are reviewed by R. Diebolt, (1979), 13 UBC L. Rev. 401.

2   *Neptune Acceptance Ltd.* v. *Williams* (1974) 49 DLR (3d) 662 (Ont. Co. Ct.) held that the mere marking of a bill or note with "Consumer Purchase" is tantamount to an agreement as to the application of Part V. The case involved an action on the marked instrument (which was given under a sales transaction falling outside the definition of "consumer purchase" under s. 188(*a*)). Do the implications of the decision extend also to an action on the underlying transaction? Arguably, where a marked instrument is given in payment for a loan, the borrower who is sued on the underlying loan can use this case only by arguing that stamping the bill or note (so as to apply Part V by agreement) constitutes a "collateral contract" which induced him to enter into the main loan contract. Will the argument succeed?

2.   PROVINCIAL LEGISLATION

a)   Provisions Relating to Assignee's Rights

Provincial legislation is quite consistent in invalidating the effect of contractual waiver of defence clauses. Thus, s. 16 of the Personal Property Security Act provides explicitly in

Ontario (RSO 1970, c. 344 as amended) and Manitoba (SM 1973, c. 5) that such clauses are not enforceable in sales of "consumer goods". Furthermore, a standard provision in provincial legislation is s. 42a of the Ontario Consumer Protection Act (RSO 1970 c. 82 (as amended)) under which an assignee of a "lender" (broadly defined in s. 1(k) as "a person who extends credit" so as to cover the credit seller) "is subject to the same obligations, liabilities and duties as the assignor". Nonetheless, the consumer "shall not recover from, or be entitled to set off against, an assignee . . . an amount greater than the balance owing on the contract at the time of the assignment". In the case of successive assignments, payments made to an assignee "who no longer holds the benefit of the contract" set the ceiling to the amount recoverable from him.

The general rule under Ontario s. 42a is thus that the consumer's right to "recover . . . or . . . set-off" is limited to "the balance owing . . . at the time of the assignment". "Set off" is obviously used in the sense of "equitable set-off" or "recoupment" (see chapter 15(C)*supra*). What is the assignee's overall exposure under this section? Does the section speak of the consumer's right " to set off *and* recover up to the balance owing at the time of the assignment"? Does it speak of the consumer's right to "recover *in addition* to the right to set off"? Compare the language of Ont. CPA s. 42a to that of s. 4(4) of the Ontario Business Practices Act (SO 1974, c. 131):

> Notwithstanding subsection 2 of section 42a of the *Consumer Protection Act*, the liability of an assignee . . . is limited to the amount paid . . . under the agreement.

Does the time of notification of the assignment to the consumer affect the assignee's exposure under Ont. CPA s. 42a? Under s. 4(4) of the Ontario Business Practices Act? (Note that between assignment and notification, an obligor is authorized to pay the assignor: s. 40(2) of the Ont. PPSA.)

Problem: A consumer purchases a product for $6,000. He pays $1,000 in cash and undertakes to pay the $5,000 balance in monthly installments. The contract is immediately assigned to a finance company which collects directly from the buyer. The product breaks down (by virtue of the seller's breach) after payments totalling $2,000 are made to the finance company. The damage for which the seller is responsible is $10,000. It consists of past payments made to the seller and the finance company for a worthless product and consequential loss. Consider the following questions:

a) What are the buyer's rights against the finance company?

b) Assume that the buyer is not notified of the assignment to the finance company (which occurs before the first monthly installment is due) until he has paid the seller $500 of the monthly installments (in addition to the $1,000 down payment). The product breaks down after the consumer has paid the assignee $1,500. What are the buyer's rights against the finance company?

c) Assume that the buyer's undertaking to pay the $5,000 balance is embodied in a promissory note (properly stamped under Part V of the Bills of Exchange Act). Will this change your previous answers?

Note on Assignee's Rights under the UTRA:

A notable exception to the provincial anti-waiver-of-defence-clause provisions is section 5 of the Ontario Unconscionable Transactions Relief Act, RSO 1970, c. 472. Thereunder,

> Nothing in this Act affects the right of a *bona fide* assignee or holder for value without notice. . . .

The section was enacted before the rise of the anti-holder-in-due-course sentiment. What is the scope of this provision? Has it been superseded by Part V of the Bills of Exchange Act? By s. 42a of the Ontario Consumer Protection Act?

b)   Provisions Relating to Purchase-Money Lenders

Provincial legislatures have hardly dealt with preservation of consumer defences against purchase-money lenders.

Some protection is given by s. 69(1) of the Manitoba Consumer Protection Act. Under its provisions, where "the financing was arranged by the seller", a lender who has taken a chattel mortgage "is deemed to be an assignee of the seller". As an assignee, his position is governed by s. 67 of the Manitoba statute, which follows the model of s. 42a of the Ontario Consumer Protection Act.

The Quebec Consumer Protection Act deals with the purchase-money lender in a manner consistent with the current trend in the U.S. Section 116 provides:

> The consumer who has used the net capital of a contract for the loan of money to make full or partial payment for the purchase or the lease of goods or services, may, if the money lender and the vending or leasing merchant regularly work together with a view to the granting of loans of money to consumers, plead against the money lender any ground of defence that he may urge against the vending or leasing merchant.

The Act does not provide any assistance as to what types of business relations between a lender and seller fall within its framework. Nonetheless, in the face of the restrictive interpretation given by courts to the "Federal Discount" doctrine the provision is by no means superfluous.

A notably broad protection will be offered to consumers on the proclamation of section 8(1) of the B.C. Consumer Protection Act. Under this section (in conjunction with the definition of "purchase financing transaction" and "creditor" in section 1) a lender who "knows or ought to know that the credit proceeds will be used by the borrower to purchase [consumer] goods" is subject "to the same defences as may be raised against the seller." Unlike BEA s. 189(3)(b), the B.C. provision is not confined to a lender who has an ongoing relationship with the seller. Thus s. 8(1) will provide broader protection to consumers than any other enacted statute in North America. What is the lender's exposure under s. 8(1)? Compare the language of B.C. s. 8(1) with s. 191 of the BEA on the one hand, and with s. 3(1) of the B.C. CPA on the other. The latter provision is the same as Ontario's s. 42a so that an assignee of a seller "is subject to the same obligations, liabilities and duties, as the assignor", but is nonetheless not liable to the consumer for "an amount greater than the balance owing on the contract at the time of the assignment": s. 3(2).

D. CREDIT CARD TRANSACTIONS

1. INTRODUCTION

Under a credit card plan, cards are issued by a card issuer to selected customers (''card holders'') who are given a line of credit with maximum credit limits. The card can be presented in payment of goods or services. The card holder is billed periodically by the card issuer (for more on the use of credit card plans in consumer credit transactions, see chapter 25, *infra*).

In a two-party credit card plan the card issuer is a merchant and the card can be used for transactions between the merchant and the card holder (e.g., a department store credit card). In a multilateral credit card plan (e.g., Chargex/Visa plan), the issuer is typically a bank. The card can be used to purchase goods or services from any merchant who has signed a ''Merchant's Agreement'' with the card issuer or with another bank which is a member in the same interchange system. Payment to the seller is made by the issuer, directly or indirectly, upon the presentment of invoices or ''sales slips'' (through the interchange system where the seller's bank is not the specific card issuer). For further details of the mechanics of bank credit card plans and systems see Davenport, ''Bank Credit Cards and the Uniform Commercial Code'' (1968) 85 Banking L.J. 941, 950-961. Oil company credit cards and other credit cards issued by franchisors to be used for the purchase of goods and services from franchisees reflect a hybrid form of credit card plan. Formally, they are three-party plans but in substance the relationship between the issuer and each franchise may be so intimate as to blur the lines between their separate identities.

For a Canadian perspective on the legal framework for bank credit cards, see Government of Canada, *Changing Times: Banking in the Electronic Age* (1979, report prepared byy Stanley Goldstein) p. 131.

From the cardholder's point of view credit cards raise two major issues:

a) Defences arising from the seller's breach of the sales contract. This is the same question which was previously discussed in connection with promissory notes, waiver-of defence clauses and purchase-money lenders. The question arises only in the context of a multipartite credit card plan since in a two-party plan the issuer is himself the seller rather than a third-party financer. Absent direct legislation or effective contractual provisions, the answer to the question depends on the nature of the multipartite credit card transaction.

b) Defences arising from the unauthorized use of the credit card. This question (which raises similar issues to some of those involved in the allocation of cheque forgery losses discussed in chapter 17(D), *infra*) arises in connection with two-party as well as multipartite credit plans.

2. VISA CARDHOLDER AND MERCHANT'S MEMBER AGREEMENTS

Examine the following documents and consider the questions which follow.

Visa Cardholder Agreement

Merchant's Member Agreement ►

Your new Toronto Dominion Visa card

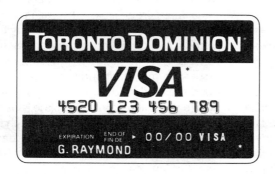

TORONTO DOMINION
CENTRAL VISA CENTRE
P.O. BOX 7050, STATION A
TORONTO, ONTARIO M5W 1X7

GENERAL ENQUIRIES
TEL. (416) 866-5042
TO REPORT A LOST/STOLEN CARD
TEL. (416) 866-5022

ACCOUNT NUMBER	CARD(S)	EXPIRATION	CREDIT LINE

Please sign your new card immediately. If you have received a duplicate Visa card this should be signed by the authorized user as indicated in the enclosed booklet. If this is a renewal card, please destroy your old card by cutting it up with a pair of scissors.

Please ensure that your name and address are correct, and that the account number on the enclosed Visa card is the same as that shown above.

If there is any error, or should you wish your credit line increased please contact your TORONTO DOMINION Visa Centre.

80026 - 1/80

Visa cardholder agreement

Signature on or use of any Chargex* Charge Card ("Chargex Card" hereinafter called the Visa* Card) supplied to the person whose name is embossed thereon ("Cardholder") or supplied to the Cardholder with the name of another person embossed thereon ("Secondary Cardholder"), by the Cardholder, by a person authorized by the Cardholder to use the Visa Card which is in the name of the Cardholder by having such person sign same in the space provided for signature on the back thereof, or by the Secondary Cardholder authorized by the Cardholder to use the Visa Card which is in the name of the Secondary Cardholder by having the Secondary Cardholder sign same in the space provided for signature on the back thereof will confirm agreement between the Cardholder and **THE TORONTO-DOMINION BANK** (the "Bank") as follows:

1. The Cardholder will pay to the Bank the amount of all sales drafts and cash advances in respect of which the Visa Card has been used (the "Indebtedness") and any interest accrued thereon within twenty-five (25) days from the date of every monthly billing statement sent by the Bank to the Cardholder either:-

a)   in full, in which case further interest may be payable only on cash advances as per clause 1b) (ii) hereof, or

b)   by an instalment payment which is at least 5% or greater of the Indebtedness and any accrued interest thereon set forth on the billing statement with a minimum instalment payment of $10; o by such other minimum instalment payment as may be notified to the Cardholder from time to time.

Interest on the Indebtedness will be accrued, calculated and payable as follows:

(i)   on the unpaid portion of Indebtedness (cash advances excepted) at the annual rate of 21% (1¾% per month, 0.05753% per day), or at such other rates as may be notified to the Cardholder from time to time. One month's interest will be calculated on each statement date on any unpaid portion of Indebtedness which was billed on the previous month's statement; interest will accrue daily, thereafter, until the date payment is received by the Visa processing office.

(ii)   on the entire Indebtedness relating to cash advances at the annual rate of 21% (0.05753% per day) from the date the advances were obtained until the date payment is received by the Visa processing office, or at such other rates as may be notified to the Cardholder from time to time.

2. The Visa Card may be used to incur indebtedness not in excess of the amount of credit extended by the Bank from time to time in respect of the use of the Visa Card, and not after the expiry date embossed on the Visa Card.

3. The Bank will not be liable if the Visa Card is not honoured at any time. In the event of breach of any obligation hereunder by the Cardholder, the entire balance of the Cardholder's indebtedness plus any accrued interest thereon shall, at the Bank's option, become immediately due and payable notwith-

standing the provisions of Clause 1 hereof, and the Bank in addition cancel this agreement and revoke the Visa Car or Cards, which shall at all times be and continue and rem the property of the Bank and the Bank or any agent thereo may immediately take possession of same.

4. Cardholder is responsible for all indebtedness resulting authorized use of the Visa Card and up to an aggregate maximum of $50, from unauthorized use until notification of loss or theft thereof has been received by the Bank. Cardholder agrees that no disclaimer of authorization of use Visa Card is an unauthorized use unless such Card is retrie and returned to the Bank.

5. If a merchant issued a Credit Voucher in respect of merchandise and/or services purchased through use of a Vi Card, the Bank will, upon receipt of such Credit Voucher, c the amount thereof to the Cardholder's account. Unless a C Voucher is received by the Bank, the indebtedness is payab to the Bank, as provided above.

6. All claims including any rights of set-off by any Cardholder and all disputes respecting any transaction evidence by a Sales Draft or Credit Voucher shall be settled directly between the merchant and the Cardholder.

* TD: Registered user of marks

MERCHANT'S MEMBER AGREEMENT

AGREEMENT between . . . . ("the Merchant")
and . . . . ("the Bank")
WHEREAS the Bank has undertaken to extend credit to holders of CHARGEX Charge Cards and the Merchant wishes to make available to its
customers a convenient means of acquiring merchandise and services:
NOW THEREFORE the parties hereto agree as follows: —
1.   The following terms used in this agreement shall have, except where inconsistent with the context, the following meanings:
(a)   "Charge Card" means an unexpired CHARGEX Charge Card or any other Charge Card bearing the distinctive Blue, White and Gold colour
bands identical to those appearing on the CHARGEX Charge Card (with which the Merchant hereby acknowledges he is familiar);
(b)   "Cardholder" shall mean the person whose name is embossed on a Charge Card;
(c)   "Authorized User" means a person, other than the Cardholder, whose signature appears on a Charge Card;
(d)   "Floor Limit" means the maximum amount authorized by the Bank in writing from time to time for which the Bank will be obliged to
credit the Merchant's account in respect of any single transaction.
2.   Upon presentation of a Charge Card by the Cardholder or an Authorized User, the Merchant agrees to sell merchandise to or perform services
for the account of the Cardholder at prices not in excess of the Merchant's ticketed or posted price for such merchandise or service.
The Merchant will invoice the Cardholder in respect of each transaction by completing a sales draft in form supplied by the Bank which
shall be signed by the Cardholder or Authorized User to whom the Merchant will hand one copy thereof, no attempt being made to diminish the
perceived amount of any transaction by the completion of more than one such sales draft.
3.   The Merchant will maintain an account with the Bank at its   branch, subject to the Bank's usual charges
and conditions. Upon delivery to such branch of one or more properly completed sales drafts accompanied by a deposit summary completed by the
Merchant, the Bank will immediately credit such account with the amount of such sales drafts. The Merchant agrees to deposit each sales draft at the
branch within three business days of the transaction evidenced thereby. All deposit figures are subject to final audit by the Bank and, in case of any
inaccuracies, the Bank shall charge or credit the Merchant's account, without notice, for any deficiencies or overages, as the case may be.
4.   The Bank may refuse to credit the account of the Merchant with or may charge back to the Merchant the total amount of any sales draft in
any of the following circumstances: —
(a)   The signature appearing on the sales draft is or is claimed by the Cardholder to be forged or unauthorized;
(b)   The merchandise referred to in the sales draft has been returned or claimed by the Cardholder to have been returned to the Merchant or the
services referred to in the sales draft are claimed by the Cardholder to have been unsatisfactory;
(c)   A sales draft exceeds the Floor Limit and has not been previously approved by or on behalf of the Bank which issued the Charge Card;
(d)   A sales draft is illegible;
(e)   A sales draft refers to a Charge Card which has expired or which the Bank has notifed the Merchant not to honour;
(f)   The transaction evidenced by a sales draft or any other credit extended in respect thereof includes a cash advance made by the Merchant to
Cardholder or Authorized User.
(g)   The transaction evidenced by a sales draft or any other credit extended in respect thereof is for any reason illegal, null or invalid.
(h)   The merchant can be shown to have attempted to reduce or disguise the amount of any one transaction by the use of multiple sales drafts
(known as split-ticketing); or
(i)   The Merchant shall have failed to comply with the terms of this agreement.
The Bank will give the Merchant details of any sales draft which it has refused to pay or has charged back to the Merchant.
5.   All fees, charges or adjustments payable by the Merchant and the amount of any charge-back to or credit voucher issued by the
Merchant shall constitute a debt payable on demand to the Bank for which the Bank may debit the Merchant's account, without prior notice. In
the event that any such debit results in an overdraft in the Merchant's account, the Merchant will, on demand, pay the Bank the amount of such
overdraft.
6.   All claims by any Cardholder and all disputes respecting any transaction evidenced by a sales draft shall be settled directly between the
Merchant and the Cardholder provided, however, that if any refund or other money adjustment is payable by the Merchant to the Cardholder, such
refund or adjustment shall be made (unless the amount of such transaction has not been credited to the Merchant's account by the Bank or has been
charged back to the Merchant) by means of the Merchant issuing a credit voucher in respect thereof which shall be delivered to the Bank within three
days of issuance.
7.   The Merchant agrees to pay on signing this Agreement, an initial sign-up fee.
The Merchant also agrees to pay in advance a rental fee per annum, to be agreed upon from time to time, to the Bank for each imprinter
required which rental may be debited automatically by the Bank to the Merchant's account, and the Merchant acknowledges that such imprinter(s)
will remain the exclusive property of the Bank.
The Merchant agrees to pay the Bank for its services hereunder fees in accordance with applicable Discount Schedule which has been
provided to the Merchant and which may be revised from time to time by mutual agreement of the parties.
The Bank shall not be entitled to any fee in respect of any amounts charged back to the Merchant or in respect of which credit vouchers
have been issued by the Merchant.
8.   The Merchant agrees to display prominently in his premises the availability of the Chargex Plan through the use of standard decals and signs
provided by the Bank. The Merchant also agrees to submit to the Bank for its prior approval any advertising by the Merchant which uses the Chargex
name, the blue, white and gold colour bands design or any representation of either of them.
9.   Except for sales drafts the amount of which the Bank has refused to credit or has charged back to the Merchant, the Merchant, shall have no
right to receive payment in respect of a transaction evidenced by a sales draft from any party except the Bank.
10.   This agreement shall remain in full force and effect unless terminated by either party upon at least five days' written notice of termination
to the other party. All obligations of both parties in respect of any particular transaction entered into prior to the date of such termination shall
survive such termination.
Upon such termination, all imprinters, forms and other material bearing the name or trade mark of the Bank or the name CHARGEX shall
be returned to the Bank forthwith and the Member thereafter shall not represent that he will honour Charge Cards.
11.   This agreement shall be binding upon the parties, their heirs, successors and assigns, provided however that the agreement shall not be
assigned by the Merchant without the written consent of the Bank.
12.   The Merchant will indemnify the Bank against and hold it harmless from all claims of whatsoever nature by any Cardholder or Authorized
User arising out of any transaction evidenced by a sales draft.
13.   The Bank may, from time to time, issue directions in writing regarding the procedure to be followed and prescribe forms to be used in
carrying out the present agreement and such directions and the terms of such forms shall be binding upon the Merchant upon receipt thereof unless
the Merchant elects to give immediate notice of cancellation of this agreement.
14.   Notices to be given hereunder shall be sent by prepaid mail to the parties at the following addresses:-

Merchant: . . . .

Bank: . . . .
Such notices shall be deemed to have been received on the day following the date of mailing.
15.   The present agreement is drafted in the English language at the specific request of the Merchant.

IN WITNESS WHEREOF, the parties have caused this agreement to be executed at
by their duly authorized officers on this   day of   19

. . . .
Merchant authorization   Bank authorization

C V   480

Questions:

1   What are the cardholder's rights where there has been an unauthorized use of the card? On asserting a defence arising from the sale? In rescinding or terminating the contract for sale? See clauses 1, 4, 5 and 6 of the cardholder agreement.

2   In terms of the agreements, what constitutes an unauthorized use of the credit card? See clause 1(c) of the merchant's member agreement and compare clause 4(a). Does the definition apply to the issuer-cardholder relationship?

3   What are the merchant's rights where the cardholder cancels the sale after a sale voucher has been completed? Where a claim or defence is asserted by the cardholder under the sale agreement? What legal leverage does the card issuer have over the merchant? Are the merchant's rights consistent with the cardholder's rights under the cardholder agreement? Can provisions of the merchants members agreement be relied on by the cardholder?

4   Consider the cardholder's rights in the following circumstances:
    a)   the cardholder wishes to cancel the sale before the seller has deposited the sales draft;
    b)   the cardholder claims breach of warranty by the seller with respect to the goods;
    c)   the card was used by a family member of the cardholder for a purpose other than that authorized by the cardholder;
    d)   a purchase was agreed upon between the merchant and the cardholder in a telephone conversation and was charged to the cardholder's account with his consent.

5   Do the contracts appeal to you as an effective and equitable way of regulating the parties' rights in a credit card transaction?

3.   THE COMMON LAW POSITION

The nature of a multilateral credit card transaction is discussed in the following case.

HARRIS TRUST AND SAVINGS BANK v. McCRAY
(1974) 316 NE 2d 209 (Ill. App. Ct.)

JOHNSON, Justice: This action was filed in order to recover a judgment for an amount of money allegedly due on a credit card account. The defendant filed a motion to dismiss the complaint, and the trial court denied the motion. The only question presented in this appeal is whether a credit card issuer may commence an action based upon the holder's failure to pay for the purchase of goods more than four years after the issuer's cause of action accrued.

The facts are undisputed. Defendant made two purchases with a credit card issued to her by the plaintiff. On December 14, 1966 she purchased goods for $400, and on December 19, 1966 she purchased additional goods for $102.27. She made no other purchase and incurred no other debts, except for interest, through the use of the plaintiff's card.

Defendant made three payments on her account with plaintiff: $20 in April 1967; $39.98 in June 1967; and $35 in March of 1968. Finance charges of $58.30 were charged to the account from February to September 1967. The defendant's account was "charged off" plaintiff's books in September 1967, when the balance due was $500.59. Defendant's final payment of $35 was made after her account was "charged off."

On June 13, 1972 plaintiff filed a complaint against the defendant seeking a judgment for the balance of $465.59 plus $77.32 attorney fees, for a total of $542.91. On January 16, 1973 the defendant filed a motion to dismiss which asserted that plaintiff's claim was barred by the four year limitation in Section 2-725 of the Uniform Commercial Code. (Ill. Rev. Stat. 1971, ch. 26, §2-725.) Plaintiff filed a counter petition on March 27, 1973, objecting to defendant's motion to dismiss on the ground that its cause of action was not brought upon a contract for sale but rather a debtor-creditor relationship. On April 24, 1973 the Honorable Joseph A. Solan denied the defendant's motion to dismiss.

On November 8, 1973 the cause was tried without a jury before the Honorable George W. Kasserman, who found for the plaintiff. Judgment was entered against the defendant in the amount of $542.91 and costs. On November 30, 1973 the defendant filed this notice of appeal.

Defendant argues that, when she purchased merchandise with a credit card issued by plaintiff, she entered a "contract for the sale of goods." She contends that plaintiff's cause of action is based upon a breach of this contract, which occurred when she failed to pay for the goods, and is thus governed by the four year limitation of Section 2-725 of the Uniform Commercial Code. That section provides:

> An action for breach of any contract for sale must be commenced within 4 years after the cause of action has accrued. By the original agreement the parties may reduce the period of limitation to not less than one year but may not extend it. Ill. Rev. Stat. 1971, ch. 26, §2-725.

Plaintiff's position is that the credit card transaction involved herein created a debtor-creditor relationship. It argues that the cause of action could not have arisen from the failure to pay for the goods because the goods were paid for by the bank. Instead, plaintiff urges, the cause of action arose when the defendant failed to repay the bank for funds advanced on her behalf to the merchant where the goods were purchased. Therefore, plaintiff argues, the applicable statute of limitations is that dealing with written contracts, including promises to pay money, which provides:

> Except as provided in Section 2-725 of the "Uniform Commercial Code," enacted by the Seventy-second General Assembly, actions on bonds, promissory notes, bills of exchange, written leases, written contracts, or other evidences of indebtedness in writing, shall be commenced within 10 years next after the cause of action accrued; but if any payment or new promise to pay shall have been made, in writing, on any bond, note, bill, lease, contract, or other written evidence of indebtedness,

within or after the period of 10 years, then an action may be commenced thereon at any time within 10 years after the time of such payment or promise to pay. Ill. Rev. Stat. 1971, ch. 83, §17.

Before discussing the specific question raised in this appeal, we deem it advisable to consider briefly the nature of the transaction involved herein.

The bank credit card system involves a tripartite relationship between the issuer bank, the cardholder, and merchants participating in the system. The issuer bank establishes an account on behalf of the person to whom the card is issued, and the two parties enter into an agreement which governs their relationship. This agreement provides that the bank will pay for cardholder's account the amount of merchandise or services purchased through the use of the credit card and will also make cash loans available to the cardholder. It also states that the cardholder shall be liable to the bank for advances and payments made by the bank and that the cardholder's obligation to pay the bank shall not be affected or impaired by any dispute, claim or demand by the cardholder with respect to any merchandise or service purchased.

The merchants participating in the system agree to honor the bank's credit cards. The bank irrevocably agrees to honor and pay the sales slips presented by the merchant if the merchant performs his undertakings, such as checking the list of revoked cards before accepting the card. The sales slips signed by the cardholder at the time of the purchase contain the following undertaking by the cardholder:

> I hereby authorize the Issuer of the Midwest Bank Card imprinted above to pay the amount shown as Total hereon upon presentation hereof to Issuer by a bank which is a member of the Midwest Bank Card system. I hereby promise to pay said Issuer the amount shown as Total hereon (together with other charges due thereon, if any) subject to and in accordance with the terms of the cardholder agreement governing the use of Issuer's Midwest Bank Cards.

These slips are forwarded to the member bank which originally issued the card. The cardholder receives a statement from the bank periodically and may then decide whether to make payment to the bank in full within a specified period, free of interest, or to defer payment and ultimately incur an interest charge.

Defendant contends that the foregoing transaction does not establish a debtor-creditor relationship between the issuer bank and the cardholder. She points out that no money was in fact loaned in this transaction, even though the agreement provides for cash advances. Defendant concedes that money advanced to her would be a loan, but she contends that money paid directly to merchants constitutes a sales contract for the purchase of goods.

We believe that money advanced to a merchant in payment for merchandise received by the defendant constitutes a loan. The defendant promised to repay the bank for money it paid to the merchant for her benefit. The credit card allowed defendant to make use of the resources of the issuer bank, and the merchant is in the same financial position as if he were receiving cash from the bank at a small discount for its service. Under this arrangement, the bank assumed the risk that the cardholder would not pay the debt and has no recourse against the merchant.

Defendant argues that the terms of the cardholder agreement itself recognize a difference between a cash advance made directly to the cardholder and payment for merchandise purchased through the use of the credit card. Thus, she urges, we should consider the former a loan and the latter an assignment of a retail installment sales contract from the merchant to the bank.

Plaintiff contends that it is not possible to read into this distinction the conclusion that the direct advance creates a loan and the indirect advance is the acceptance of an assignment of a retail installment sales contract. It urges, to the contrary, that the distinction is merely for the purpose of reflecting the different methods involved in disbursing these loans and computing the amounts necessary to repay them.

Defendant's argument is belied by the definition of a retail installment sales contract in effect at the time the transactions in question occurred in 1966. Although the act expired the following year, it is interesting to note that it stated:

> "Retail installment contract" or "contract" means and includes any agreement, negotiated or entered into in this state, including a chattel mortgage, conditional sale contract, or any other form of instrument evidencing an agreement to purchase goods for delivery to a person residing in the State of Illinois, other than for a commercial or business use [or] for the purpose of resale, by payment of the purchase price in two or more installments over a period of time and pursuant to which title to, or a lien upon the goods, which are the subject matter of the sale, is retained or taken by the seller as security, in whole or in part, for the buyer's obligation. Ill. Rev. Stat. 1965, ch. 121½, §223.

Title to the goods in the case at bar unquestionably passed to defendant when she signed the sales slip and took possession of them, no lien was retained thereon, and the payment of the purchase price did not involve two or more installments. Thus, the statutory definition of a retail installment sales contract, in effect at the time of the transaction in question, clearly did not include the tripartite agreement involved here.

We are not persuaded to reach a contrary conclusion by the two cases defendant cites in support of her argument. She relies upon *Johnson* v. *Sears Roebuck & Co.* (1973) 14 Ill. App. 3d 838, 303 NE 2d 627 as authority for the proposition that Illinois courts have rejected the notion that a credit card account is in substance a loan of money. However, *Johnson* involved a department store credit card, used solely for credit purposes, in which there were only two parties, the store and the customer. Here, there was a tripartite relationship in which the bank paid merchants for goods purchased by the cardholder, and the defendant agreed to repay the bank rather than the merchant. Thus, in our opinion, *Johnson* is not authority for defendant's contention that a three-party bank charge card transaction is in substance a loan of money.

Defendant also cites *Berry* v. *G.D. Searle & Co.* (1974) 56 Ill. 2d 548, 309 NE 2d 550, wherein the Supreme Court of Illinois held that §2-725 of the Uniform Commercial Code is applicable to the sale of birth control pills. We do not believe that *Searle* is applicable here because the relationship between the defendant and the bank was that of debtor-creditor.

In view of the foregoing, we conclude that the payments made by the plaintiff to the merchants pursuant to the cardholder agreement constituted a loan of money. Thus, plaintiff's cause of action was governed by the 10 year limitation applicable to written contracts, including promises to pay money. It was not barred by the expiration of the four year statute of limitations governing contracts for the sale of goods.

Affirmed.

Notes and Questions:

1   Suppose the defendant-cardholder in *McCray* had had defences arising from the sale; would she have been able to assert them against the plaintiff bank card-issuer?

2   For various alternative theories underlying the nature of the multilateral credit card transaction, see *inter alia* D. Maffly and A. McDonald, ''The Tripartite Credit Card Transaction: A Legal Infant'' (1960) 48 Cal. L. Rev. 459, 465-478; and Wohl, ''Three Credit Card Transactions: Legal Rights and Duties'', Legal Problems of Consumer Credit 357 (1971) 4 U. Cal. Davis L. Rev. 357. The alternative theories are that a credit card transaction triggers a direct loan, that it is an assignment of receivables, or that it is the equivalent of a commercial letter of credit.

3   The view has been expressed that ''[c]redit cards do not represent . . . a separate or unique type of consumer credit arrangement. . . . A credit card is merely the evidence of the existence of an arrangement between a credit institution and a consumer. The arrangement itself falls within one of the general categories of consumer credit arrangements. . . .'' (B. Curran, *Trends in Consumer Credit Legislation*, (1965) p. 12). Do you agree? How does this view affect the question of the preservation of consumer defences against the card issuer?

4   ''The relationship between a merchant who accepts the third party credit card as payment for goods and services and the issuer of the card is that of assignor and assignee. As such, it is parallel to the relationship between a merchant and the financers who purchases [*sic*] accounts arising out of contracts between the merchant and his customers. In each case, the financer is purchasing consumer accounts from the merchants'': R. Cuming, ''Legal Responsibility of Credit Card Issuers for Merchants' Defective Performance'' in J. Ziegel (ed.) *Papers and Comments delivered at the Eighth Annual Workshop on Commercial and Consumer Law: 1978* (1980) 64 at p. 65). Do you agree? Is it consistent with the analysis in *McCray*?

5   For policy discussions on the preservation of consumer defences against credit card issuers in the context of U.S. legislation, see e.g., Note, ''Preserving Consumer Defenses in Credit Card Transactions'' (1971) 81 Yale LJ 287; and N. Littlefield, ''Preservation of Consumer Defenses in Interlocking Loans and Credit Card Transactions — Recent Statutes, Policies and a Proposal'' [1973] Wis. L. Rev. 471. See also materials reproduced or cited in section (B)(2) *supra*.

Note on Indebtedness Resulting from Unauthorized Use of Credit Cards:

Prior to the enactment of U.S. federal legislation directly dealing with this question (reproduced in section (4) *infra*) most cardholder agreements imposed upon cardholders legal responsibility for all unauthorized charges incurred through use of the card prior to notification to the card issuer of the loss of the card. However

> [s]ome [American] courts refused to enforce the conditions of these contracts in the presence of negligence or bad faith on the part of card issuers or their agents. Other courts applied a more rigid standard by simply enforcing the issuer-holder agreements as written. As a result of this conflict of authority there exists no set of established judicial standards governing the circumstances under which credit card contracts will or will not be strictly enforced. Perhaps all that can be said is that in the absence of any evidence of negligence on the part of the issuer or its agents, liability will most likely fall on the cardholder who fails to report the disappearance of his credit card.

See Winford Richey, ``The Apportionment of Credit Card Fraud Loss'' (1971) 4 U. Cal. (Davis) L. Rev. 377, 388.

A widely adopted alternative to the common law position, though more in the U.S. than in Canada (see section (4) *infra*), is a statutory system of issuer's liability where the cardholder is liable only to a maximum of fifty dollars for charges resulting from the unauthorized use of the card. The rationale of such an alternative is explained by John Weistart, ``Consumer Protection in the Credit Card Industry: Federal Legislative Controls'' (1972) 70 Mich. L. Rev. 1475, 1509:

> A system of issuer liability is preferable because it stimulates more efficient precautions against losses. If issuers are made to bear fraud losses, they will implement procedures controlling such costs in order to preserve the profitability of their operations. The amount they spend for loss control is a function of the amount of loss experience: in an optimal situation, issuers will expend money for loss control as long as each additional expenditure results in the prevention of losses of a greater amount. If cardholders were to bear these losses individually, they, too, would respond with preventive measures. But their responses would not be economically efficient; their loss minimization measures would likely include unnecessary and ineffective devices. On the other hand, issuers have superior access to information about the cost, frequency, and causes of fraud losses. In addition, issuers are in a better position to control the occurrence of these losses. They not only select the merchants who may accept the card and the holders who may use it, but also design the security systems for card distribution, user identification and loss notification. Hence, the statutory choice of issuer liability assures that the problem of credit card loss is the responsibility of the party most likely to take efficient steps in its resolution.
>
> A system of issuer liability also ensures that fraud losses are spread over a large number of transactions so that the impact on any one cardholder is slight; the issuer initially accepts the loss and then spreads it back to cardholders or merchants in the form of increased service costs. Such a system is desirable because placing primary liability on the holder of a card that is fraudulently used may impose large, and potentially ruinous, costs on individuals. It is true that under a system of cardholder liability, cardholders could agree among themselves to spread fraud losses; this result is achieved when individual holders are joined together in an insurance plan.

However, insurance plans existing prior to the federal enactment indicate the undesirability of this technique, for the insurance cost per card was significantly higher than that incurred under a more perfect loss-spreading system. Therefore, in order to minimize the impact of each loss occurrence in the most effective manner, the issuer's superior knowledge and cost-spreading position are a more appropriate basis for a loss distribution scheme.

The new credit card law does not create an absolute issuer-liability system, for the cardholder may be held liable for up to fifty dollars resulting from unauthorized uses. This limited cardholder liability is commonly justified on two bases. First, the prospect of potential liability is intended to operate as an incentive to the cardholder to give the issuer prompt notice of loss. the incentive is provided by the fact that the cardholder may limit his liability to less than the statutory maximum; he bears liability only for unauthorized charges made *prior* to notification. Second, the provision for partial cardholder liability serves to encourage a cardholder to exercise proper care in the use and protection of his card; without such care the amount of fraud loss incurred by the issuer would increase.

For the voluntary adoption of this issuer liability scheme in a cardholder agreement, see the Visa cardholder agreement, section (2) *supra*.

4. LEGISLATION

Rights of parties to a credit card transaction are "matters coming within . . . Property and civil rights in the province" so as to fall within provincial jurisdiction under s. 92(13) of the British North America Act.

All ten provinces have provisions exempting a cardholder who has not requested or accepted the card from liability in respect of its use. See, for example, s. 46 of the Ontario Consumer Protection Act.

British Columbia (SBC 1977, c. 6, s. 31), Manitoba (RSM 1970, c. C-200 [as amended], s. 116), and Quebec (SQ 1978 c. 9, s. 123) have provisions governing the unauthorized use of credit cards. All provide for the notification of the loss by the cardholder to the issuer as the cut-off point. They further set $50 (or, in B.C. and Manitoba, the maximum credit available if it is less) as the maximum exposure of the cardholder for loss occurring prior to notification or in the absence of notification.

The availability of defences arising from an authorized sale has so far been neglected by Canadian legislation. A limited exception is s. 8(1) of the B.C. Consumer Protection Act dealing with the subjection of a purchase-money lender to consumer defences (see discussion in Section C (2)(b) *supra*). The section is broad enough to cover an issuer under a multilateral credit card. However, the provision excludes transactions where no "cost of borrowing" is incurred in connection with a particular purchase. The lender in s. 8(1) is a creditor in "a purchase financing transaction". Under s. 1a "purchase financing transaction" is a type of "extension of credit". "Credit" under s. 1 is "credit . . . for which a borrower incurs a cost of borrowing". Transactions where the cardholder pays the issuer without incurring a "cost of borrowing" are thus excluded.

Notwithstanding its broad language (see section C (2)(b) *supra*), s. 116 of the Quebec Consumer Protection Act does not appear to apply to multilateral credit card plans. Section 116 applies to loans but the Quebec Act does not treat a multilateral credit card transaction as involving a loan. Under s. 66, "contracts of credit" include "(*a*) contracts for the loan of money; (*b*) contracts extending variable credit; [and] (*c*) contracts involving credit". Contracts extending variable credit explicitly include "contracts made for the use of what are commonly called credit cards . . .": s. 118. They are thus a separate category from "contracts for the loan of money". Section 116 is one of a group of provisions subtitled "contracts for the loan of money". By its own terms it is limited to a "consumer who has used the net capital of a contract for the loan of money . . .". No provision corresponding to s. 116 appears under the subtitle of "contracts extending variable credit".

Consumer credit card defences are dealt with in the following provisions of the U.S. Consumer Credit Protection Act (15 U.S. Code §16.01 *et seq.*):

§132. Issuance of credit cards

No credit cards shall be issued except in response to a request or application therefor. This prohibition does not apply to the issuance of a credit card in renewal of, or in substitution for, an accepted credit card.

§133. Liability of holder of credit card

(a) A card holder shall be liable for the unauthorized use of a credit card only if the card is an accepted credit card, the liability is not in excess of $50, the card issuer gives adequate notice to the cardholder of the potential liability, the card issuer has provided the cardholder with a self-addressed, prestamped notification to be mailed by the cardholder in the event of the loss or theft of the credit card, and the unauthorized use occurs before the cardholder has notified the card issuer that an unauthorized use of the credit card has occurred or may occur as the result of loss, theft, or otherwise. Notwithstanding the foregoing, no cardholder shall be liable for the unauthorized use of any credit card which was issued on or after the effective date of this section, and, after the expiration of twelve months following such effective date, no cardholder shall be liable for the unauthorized use of any credit card regardless of the date of its issuance, unless (1) the conditions of liability specified in the preceding sentence are met, and (2) the card issuer has provided a method whereby the user of such card can be identified as the person authorized to use it. For the purposes of this section, a cardholder notifies a card issuer by taking such steps as may be reasonably required in the ordinary course of business to provide the card issuer with the pertinent information whether or not any particular officer, employee, or agent of the card issuer does in fact receive such information.

(b) In any action by a card issuer to enforce liability for the use of a credit card, the burden of proof is upon the card issuer to show that the use was authorized or, if the use was unauthorized, then the burden of proof is upon the card issuer to show that the conditions of liability for the unauthorized use of a credit card, as set forth in subsection (a), have been met.

(c) Nothing in this section imposes liability upon a cardholder for the unauthorized use of a credit card in excess of his liability for such use under other applicable law or under any agreement with the card issuer.

(d) Except as provided in this section, a cardholder incurs no liability from the unauthorized use of a credit card.

[For the purposes of s. 133, "unauthorized use" means "a use of a credit card by a person other than the cardholder who does not have actual, implied, or apparent authority for such use and from which the cardholder receives no benefit": s. 103(*o*).]

§170. Rights of credit card customers

(a) Subject to the limitation contained in subsection (b), a card issuer who has issued a credit card to a cardholder pursuant to an open end consumer credit plan shall be subject to all claims (other than tort claims) and defenses arising out of any transaction in which the credit card is used as a method of payment or extension of credit if (1) the obligor has made a good faith attempt to obtain satisfactory resolution of a disagreement or problem relative to the transaction from the person honoring the credit card; (2) the amount of the initial transaction exceeds $50; and (3) the place where the initial transaction occurred was in the same State as the mailing address previously provided by the cardholder or was within 100 miles from such address, except that the limitations set forth in clauses (2) and (3) with respect to an obligor's right to assert claims and defenses against a card issuer shall not be applicable to any transaction in which the person honoring the credit card (A) is the same person as the card issuer, (B) is controlled by the card issuer, (C) is under direct or indirect common control with the card issuer, (D) is a franchised dealer in the card issuer's products or services, or (E) has obtained the order for such transaction through a mail solicitation made by or participated in by the card issuer in which the cardholder is solicited to enter into such transaction by using the credit card issued by the card issuer.

(b) The amount of claims or defenses asserted by the cardholder may not exceed the amount of credit outstanding with respect to such transaction at the time the cardholder first notifies the card issuer or the person honoring the credit card of such claim or defense. For the purpose of determining the amount of credit outstanding in the preceding sentence, payments and credits to the cardholder's account are deemed to have been applied, in the order indicated, to the payment of: (1) late charges in the order of their entry to the account; (2) finance charges in order of their entry to the account; and (3) debits to the account other than those set forth above, in the order in which each debit entry to the account was made.

For discussion of these provisions, see generally B. Geva, "Preservation of Consumer Defences Against Third Party Financiers: Statutory Developments in the United States" in J. Ziegel (ed.) *Papers and Comments delivered at the Eighth Annual Workshop on Commercial and Consumer Law* (1980) p. 72.

Chapter 17
Cheques and Their Collection

A. PAYMENT BY CHEQUE AND THE COLLECTION SYSTEM — AN OVERVIEW

1. THE CHEQUE

A cheque is a bill of exchange drawn on a bank, payable on demand (BEA (s. 165(1)). A "bank" is "an incorporated bank or savings bank carrying on business in Canada" (s. 2). This falls short of covering all deposit institutions. Until recently "[t]he weight of authority [has accordingly been] that 'bank' in subsection 165(1) means chartered bank, and that similar instruments drawn upon a non-bank deposit institution are not cheques": Law Reform Commission of Canada, *The Cheque: Some Modernization* (1979) Report II, p. 4. Such non-bank deposit institutions include trust companies, credit unions and *caisses populaires*. A demand bill drawn on such an institution has been called "a demand bill of exchange" (*Duncan and Dist. Credit Union* v. *Greater Victoria Savings Credit Union* [1978] 3 W.W.R. 570 (BC SC)) or a "common law" cheque (*Sparkle Wash Ltd.* v. *Saskatoon Credit Union Ltd.* [1979] 2 WWR 320 (Sask. DC); *Royal Bank of Canada* v. *Lefaivre* [1979] 4 WWR 70 (Sask. CA)).

This anomalous distinction between "cheques" and "demand bills" or "common law cheques" has finally been abolished by s. 92 of the Canadian Payments Association Act (Part IV of the Banks and Banking Law Revision Act, SC 1980 c. 40). The Act amends Part III of the BEA "by adding thereto immediately preceding section 165 thereof", a new s. 164.1 which provides that for the purpose of Part III, "bank" includes every member of the Canadian Payment Association (namely every depository institution meeting certain requirements).

Cheques are governed by Part III of the BEA as well as by Part II, which governs bills of exchange in general. The following is an outline of the principal special provisions:

1. Section 165(3) contains a specific rule (to be dealt with hereafter) as to the holding in due course of a cheque delivered to a bank for deposit.

2. Section 166 contains a special rule as to the result of failure to present a cheque

779

for payment "within a reasonable time of its issue". The rule is that if the delay occasioned damage to the drawer he is relieved *pro tanto* from his liability on the cheque and the holder replaces him as creditor of the bank for the extent of the release. This alters the general rule under which a delay in performance of the holder's duties releases all secondary parties to a bill of exchange.

3. Section 167 deals with the determination of the bank's authority to pay by countermand of payment and notice of the customer's death.

4. Sections 168 to 175 deal with crossed cheques. The practice of crossing cheques may be broadly described as an instruction from the drawer to his banker that he is only to pay the instrument provided certain conditions are fulfilled. What these conditions are depends on the type of crossing used and whether it is general or special. A general crossing consists of two parallel transverse lines between which are often written the words "and company"; this is a shorthand method of instructing the payor bank to pay the amount of the instrument only to *a banker*. The special crossing consists of the name of a banker written across the face of the cheque, usually between two parallel transverse lines; this is a method of requiring the payor bank to pay the cheque only to *the banker* whose name appears upon it.

The crossing of a cheque has the effect of protecting the drawee bank as well as the collecting bank as against the true owner, provided payment is made strictly in accordance with the crossing. It also protects the drawer if the cheque has duly reached the payee.

The practice of crossing cheques is well known in England. It has never become common in Canada. In fact "[f]rom the customer's [drawer's] point of view it would . . . seem inadvisable to adopt the practice in Canada, in view of the protection given to a drawee bank in the case of forged endorsements of crossed cheques, and the omission from the Canadian statute of s. 60 of the [English Act] which gives protection to a bank in the case of uncrossed cheques": *Falconbridge On Banking and Bills of Exchange* (7th ed., 1969) at p. 876. (The lack of protection given to the drawee of an uncrossed cheque is discussed in section D of this chapter.)

2.   THE BANK-CUSTOMER RELATIONSHIP AND THE BANK'S DUTY TO HONOUR CHEQUES

Falconbridge On Banking and Bills of Exchange
(7th ed., 1969) pp. 275-80

A Bank is a debtor of its customer, not a bailee or a trustee, in respect of money deposited with it and not actually appropriated to a particular purpose. The money deposited becomes the property of the bank, and the bank owes an equivalent amount to the depositor.

• • •

The relation of bank and customer being that of debtor and creditor, it follows that the bank is discharged only by payments made to the customer, his agent or principal, or to some other person who can give a good discharge. It also follows that upon the insolvency of the bank the customer has, as a general rule, merely a right to prove as an ordinary creditor. The special rights and obligations arising out of the relation of banker and customer, however, are inconsistent with the ordinary rule that a debtor must seek out his creditor, and the customer has no right of action against the bank in respect of money deposited until after demand made. As a general rule a bank is obliged to pay its customer's cheque only at the branch on which it is drawn.

* * *

A bank must pay its customer's cheque on presentment at the branch on which it is drawn, if the customer has there sufficient funds at his credit.

There must, however, be sufficient funds to cover the whole amount of the cheque presented, for the bank is not obliged to pay part of a cheque for an amount exceeding the available balance, save under instructions. Probably if a cheque is presented for an amount greater than the amount at the credit of the drawer's account, the bank ought not to state the amount of the deficiency, or say more than "not sufficient funds".

Substantial damages may be given for the dishonouring of a customer's cheque, if he is a "trader" or engaged in business, even though proof of special damages is not adduced, or in the circumstances, is not admissible, whereas a non-trading customer is entitled to substantial damages only if he alleges and proves special damages.

* * *

If a customer's cheque is presented for payment, the bank must decide whether the state of the account between it and the customer will justify it in paying the cheque. If the cashier or teller counts out the amount of the cheque and places the money upon the counter or the ledge of the wicket in front of him, the payment is complete and cannot be revoked by the bank, even though the money has not been counted and accepted by the person presenting the cheque. The property in the money passes fron the bank to the payee of the cheque so that it can be attached as his property even before he has touched it with his hands.

A bank must pay cheques in the order of presentment, unless it has notice of the death of the customer or of a countermand of payment by him or has received other instructions from him. In the case of the simultaneous presentment of two cheques, each for less than the customer's credit balance, but added together, being for a sum greater than the credit balance, it has been held that the bank ought to refuse payment of both cheques.

It has been said that a bank is entitled to a reasonable time to satisfy itself of the genuineness of the signature to a cheque or bill of exchange, but in *Bank of England* v. *Vagliano Bros.* [1891] AC 107 at 157, Lord Macnaghten states that bankers who undertake the duty of paying their customers' acceptances cannot do otherwise than pay off-hand, and this reasoning would seem to apply equally to cheques.

3.   THE COLLECTION SYSTEM

PAUL THOMAS AND VINCENT ORCHARD
"The Presentment and Collection of Cheques in Canada"
(1976) 22 McGill LJ 203, 221-24

THE COLLECTION OF CHEQUES THROUGH CANADIAN BANK
CLEARING MACHINERY

The collection system in Canada is operated by the Canadian Bankers' Association, an organization of the chartered banks in Canada incorporated by Parliament in 1900. Section 7 of the incorporating statute confers on the Association the power to set up clearing houses in Canada and to make rules and regulations for the operation of such clearing houses. The Association has adopted in article 24 of its by-laws rules and regulations respecting clearing houses.

Historically, the idea of a clearing house originated in France during the Middle Ages, and early clearing operations took place at the great fairs. The birthplace of the modern clearing house, however, was London: Clerks would go from bank to bank in order to collect and present cheques and other items. Eventually, the clerks began to meet at public-houses to exchange cheques in an attempt to avoid the needless journey around the city to other banks. The next step was to simplify matters still further by appointing two or three of the clerks to deal with all the paper. This arrangement was formalized in 1805, when a committee of bankers "promulgated a set of rules for the clearing procedure, and in 1821 a permanent committee was appointed to assume the management of the clearing house". Finally, a permanent clearing house was erected in 1833.

Today, the following steps are normally taken for the simple deposit and collection of a cheque:

1. The payee deposits the cheque in his own bank (the collecting bank).
2. The bank gives its customer provisional credit pending collection of payment of the cheque by the drawee bank.
3. The collecting bank prepares the cheques for machine processing by encoding in magnetic ink the dollar amount of the cheque.
4. The collecting bank sorts the cheques. If the cheque is an "on-us" item (drawn upon the same bank where deposited) internal processing completes the transfer of the amount of the cheque from the drawer's account to that of the payee. If the cheque is drawn on another bank (which is normally the case) the cheque usually goes through the clearing house process.
5. In the larger Canadian centres, the cheques are processed and sorted at a data centre of the collecting bank. The bank then prepares cash letters, deposit tickets or computer printed lists for each category sorted, showing the total dollar amount of the cheques involved.
6. One or more representatives of the bank are then sent to the clearing house where they exchange debit and credit amounts with representatives from the other member clearing banks.

7. A list of the final balances due to or by each member is given to the local agency of the Bank of Canada and written direction is given to that agency for communication to the Bank of Canada where debits or credits are made to the members' accounts in Ottawa.

8. The cheques themselves (if not exchanged at the clearing house, and evidently this is not the practice at the larger centres) are delivered to the data centre of the drawee bank from where they are sent to the actual branch on which they were drawn.

9. The drawee bank on which the cheque was drawn verifies it. If it is an NSF cheque, or there is a stop-payment on it, or it is a forgery, the drawee bank does not pay the cheque and it must be returned within a specific length of time. If the drawee bank finds no reason to dishonour the cheque, it is posted to the drawer's account (if this has not already been done at the data centre), and is cancelled and paid.

10. The provisional credits given in the collecting process become final, or, in the case of a returned cheque, are reversed.

The chartered banks in Canada have developed a fairly comprehensive set of rules and procedures for governing the collection of cheques. Clearly the law must extend recognition to these rules of clearing usage unless they become unreasonable or unfair to the banking customer. In general the banks have provided a sound service with regard to the collection of cheques, and no advantage has seemingly been taken of the customer. It is also important that the law remain flexible with respect to the deposit and collection of cheques in view of the new banking practices being adopted to further increase the efficiency of the payments system.

Notes:

1   It is customary to designate banks participating in the collection process as follows:
   a) *Depositary Bank* (DB): The first bank to which a cheque is delivered for collection even when it is also the drawee.
   b) *Payor Bank* (PB): The drawee bank (whether or not it accepted (or certified) the cheque).
   c) *Intermediary Bank* (IB): Every bank involved in the process of collection except the depositary bank and the payor bank.
   d) *Collecting Bank* (CB): Any bank handling the cheque for collection except the payor bank. A "Presenting Bank" (PrB) is the last collecting bank that presents the cheque for payment.

   Typically, no intermediary bank is employed where both the depositary and the payor banks are chartered banks and members of the Canadian Bankers' Association. The only collecting bank is then the depositary bank (which is also the presenting bank). Intermediary banks (i.e., collecting banks which are not depositary banks) are involved in the process of collecting cheques drawn on foreign drawees but deposited for credit with a Canadian bank. Recall also "common law" cheques drawn on deposit institutions apart from chartered banks prior to the 1980 Canadian Payments Association Act.

2   Payment by the payor bank (if made in due course) discharges the cheque (s. 139). It also puts an end to the customer's right to countermand payment (s. 167(*a*)). If payment is refused, or cannot be obtained, a duly presented cheque is dishonoured (s. 95(1)). "Payment" is also crucial in determining creditors' competing claims to the customer's funds with his bank. For all these purposes, payment in cash is such payment: *Chambers* v. *Miller* (1902) 13 CBNS 125. Nonetheless, there is no direct provision in the BEA which provides for the precise moment of completion of payment where payment is made through the collection system. The Ontario Court of Appeal held that when a payor bank stamps a cheque as "paid" and makes out a credit slip, also stamped "paid", in favour of the depositary bank, there is an appropriation of the monies of the drawer to the cheque, which cannot be revoked on notice of the insolvency of the drawer (*White* v. *Royal Bank of Canada* (1923) 53 OLR 543; see also *Hall* v. *Hatch* (1902) 3 OLR 147). Case law on the time of completion of payment is far from comprehensive. Compare chapter 18 *infra*.

3   Time of payment of an "item" (defined in §4-104(*g*) as "any instrument for the payment of money even though it is negotiable but does not include money") is provided for by Article 4 of the American UCC as follows:

§4 – 109. Process of Posting
   The "process of posting" means the usual procedure followed by a payor bank in determining to pay an item and in recording the payment including one or more of the following or other steps as determined by the bank:
   (a)   verification of any signature;
   (b)   ascertaining that sufficient funds are available;
   (c)   affixing a "paid" or other stamp;
   (d)   entering a charge or entry to a customer's account;
   (e)   correcting or reversing an entry or erroneous action with respect to the item.

§4 – 213. Final Payment of Item by Payor Bank; When Provisional Debits and Credits Become Final; When Certain Credits Become Available for Withdrawal
   (1)   An item is finally paid by a payor bank when the bank has done any of the following, whichever happens first:
   (a)   paid the item in cash; or
   (b)   settled for the item without reserving a right to revoke the settlement and without having such right under statute, clearing house rule or agreement; or
   (c)   completed the process of posting the item to the indicated account of the drawer, maker or other person to be charged therewith; or
   (d)   made a provisional settlement for the item and failed to revoke the settlement in the time and manner permitted by statute, clearing house rule or agreement.
Upon a final payment under subparagraphs (b), (c) or (d) the payor bank shall be accountable for the amount of the item.
   (2)   If provisional settlement for an item between the presenting and payor banks is made through a clearing house or by debits or credits in an account between them, then to the extent that provisional debits or credits for the item are entered in

accounts between the presenting and payor banks or between the presenting and successive prior collecting banks seriatim, they become final upon final payment of the item by the payor bank.

§4—303. When Items Subject to Notice, Stop-Order, Legal Process or Setoff; Order in Which Items May Be Charged or Certified

(1) Any knowledge, notice or stop-order received by, legal process served upon or setoff exercised by a payor bank, whether or not effective under other rules of law to terminate, suspend or modify the bank's right or duty to pay an item or to charge its customer's account for the item, comes too late to so terminate, suspend or modify such right or duty if the knowledge, notice, stop-order or legal process is received or served and a reasonable time for the bank to act thereon expires or the setoff is exercised after the bank has done any of the following:

(a) accepted or certified the item;
(b) paid the item in cash;
(c) settled for the item without reserving a right to revoke the settlement and without having such right under statute, clearing house rule or agreement;
(d) completed the process of posting the item to the indicated account of the drawer, maker or other person to be charged therewith or otherwise has evidenced by examination of such indicated account and by action its decision to pay the item; or
(e) become accountable for the amount of the item under subsection (1)(d) of Section 4—213 and Section 4—302 dealing with the payor bank's responsibility for late return of items.

(2) Subject to the provisions of subsection (1) items may be accepted, paid, certified or charged to the indicated account of its customer in any order convenient to the bank.

4   A related issue to the time of payment of a cheque is the time of discharge of the underlying transaction by such payment. The question is whether on the payment of the cheque the transaction is discharged *ab initio* on the delivery of the cheque to the payee, or only at the time of the actual payment by the payor bank. *Re Hone, Ex parte the Trustee* v. *Kensington Borough Council* [1915] Ch. 85 stands for the proposition that the transaction is discharged at the time of the actual payment by the payor bank:

> . . . I cannot think that here the . . . [payees] did receive payment when the piece of paper passed to them. They received the money when they were richer by £55. It is quite true that, having accepted the cheque, they could not have sued for the debt unless and until the cheque was dishonoured. Nevertheless, it was not until the cheque was honoured that they were paid [*id.* at 89].

See also *Re Owen; Owen* v. *Inland Revenue Commissioner* [1949] 1 All ER 901. The latter case was partly decided on the basis that a cheque does not operate as an assignment of funds (see note 5 *infra*). However, the argument that payment subject to a condition subsequent (the honouring of the cheque) becomes valid *ab initio* upon fulfillment of this condition does not conflict with the no-assignment doctrine. See Lord Chorley, (1951) 14 Mod. L. Rev. 65.

Dicta of a unanimous Court of Appeal in *The Brimnes, Tenax Steamship Co. Ltd.* v. *The Brimnes (Owners)* [1974] 3 WLR 613 "may be regarded as pointing towards a reversal of the tendency of the Courts to regard the date of payment by the paying bank as the effective date upon which a debt is settled by cheque" (Lord Chorley and P.E. Smart, *Leading Cases in the Law of Banking* (4th ed., 1977) p. 41). In this case, "all three judges . . . accepted that payment would have been effected immediately upon receipt of a cheque by the beneficiary's bankers". This also appears to be the position in the U.S. See e.g. *Engstrom* v. *Wiley* (1951) 191 F 2d 684, 686-687 (CCA 9) where the sale of wheat for a cheque was considered to be a cash sale in which "wheat and the money are equivalent".

5 By itself a bill (including a cheque: s. 165(1)) "does not operate as an assignment of funds in the hands of the drawee . . . and the drawee of a bill who does not accept . . . is not liable on the instrument" (s. 127). There is no liability on an instrument without a signature (s. 131). Two results follow:

a) On the dishonour of a cheque for non-payment the holder's only rights are against the drawer and prior endorsers, if any. If the dishonour is wrongful, the only one who has a cause of action against the drawee bank is the customer. The holder of an uncertified cheque (see Section C note 5 *infra*) does not have a remedy against the drawee bank.

b) So far as the drawee bank is concerned, the order to pay embodied in the cheque is strictly a matter between itself and the customer. Therefore, until payment, the drawee bank must obey a stop payment order by the drawer, its customer (s. 167(*a*)). For more on the customer's right to countermand payment, see Section C *infra*. It should be noted, however, that the holder's rights on the cheque against parties liable thereon (i.e., the drawer and prior endorsers) are not prejudiced by the drawer's countermand of payment.

6 Cheques bearing dates later than the dates of their issue ("post-dated cheques") are frequently used as credit instruments (and as such are subject to the marking requirements of Part V: s. 189(1)). The intention of the parties to a post-dated cheque is that it will not be presented for payment before the date it bears. The BEA explicitly provides that a bill is "not invalid" by reason only that it is post-dated (s. 27(*d*)). Nevertheless, the opinion has been expressed that "[w]hile no doubt a 'cheque' is not invalid by reason of its being post-dated, yet it is not a cheque because it is not payable on demand": Rajanayagam, [1969] Jour. Bus. Law 33, at 34. Falconbridge's opinion, supported by case law (*Keyes* v. *Royal Bank of Canada* [1947] SCR 377, and *Shapiro* v. *Greenstein* (1970), 10 DLR (3d) 746 (Que. CA)) is, however, that "[a] cheque which is post-dated is nonetheless a cheque" (*Falconbridge On Banking and Bills of Exchange* (7th ed., 1969) p. 496).

7 A new legal framework for the administration of the collection of cheques was established by the recently adopted Canadian Payments Association Act (Part IV of the Banks and Banking Law Revision Act, SC 1980, c. 40). The objects of the Association (consisting of depositary of institutions in Canada) "are to establish and operate a national clearings and settlements system and to plan the evolution of the national payments system" (s. 58).

8 The bank-customer relationship is partly governed by their own contract, express or implied. See in general *Joachim* v. *Swiss Bank Corporation* [1921] 3 KB 110. No

specific statute governs this contract in Canada. *Cf.* the American position under UCC 4-103(1):

> no agreement can disclaim a bank's responsibility for its own lack of good faith or failure to exercise ordinary care or can limit the measure of damages for such lack or failure; but the parties may by agreement determine the standards by which such responsibility is to be measured if such standards are not manifestly unreasonable.

What is the effect of clearing house rules on bank customers parties to cheques handled in the collection system? *Sterling Bank* v. *Laughlin* (1912) 1 DLR 383 (Ont. Div. Ct.) stands for the proposition that "the dealings sanctioned as between the banks by their voluntary association in the clearing-house system . . . is a matter not binding per se on the public unless it can be assumed or proved that the party sought to be charged has been dealing with the bank subject to the usage of the clearing house." See also *Bank of British North America* v. *Haslip* (1914) 31 DLR 442, 450. This is unlike the current American position. UCC 4-103(2) provides that "clearing house rules . . . have the effect of agreements . . . whether or not specifically assented to by all parties interested in items handled."

The case which follows deals with the relationship between the depository bank and its customer in the collection process.

BANK OF NOVA SCOTIA v. SHARP
[1975] 6 WWR 97 (BC CA)

ROBERTSON J.A.: On 10th July 1972 the respondent Sharp opened a savings account at the Nanaimo branch of the appellant bank with a deposit of $10,000. Mr. Sharp was entitled to draw cheques on the account. No arrangement was made that, where cheques were credited to the account prior to the receipt of payment, Mr. Sharp would be entitled to draw on them before payment was received. He made two further substantial deposits in September and November 1972 and from time to time he made withdrawals from the account by cheque. On 15th September 1972 Mr. Tait, the manager of the branch, gave Mr. Sharp overdraft privileges up to an amount of $2,500 and by 20th September he had overdrawn. On 17th October 1972 Mr. Sharp endorsed and deposited in his account a cheque for $6,000, drawn in his favour by Mehan Lake Logging Limited ("Mehan") on the Langley branch of the bank. The bank did not give any valuable consideration for the cheque nor did it then do anything else that would make it the beneficial owner of the cheque. While the bank, in its own record of Mr. Sharp's account, showed the amount of the cheque as a credit, it is clear that Mr. Sharp deposited the cheque only for collection. In his evidence in chief Mr. Tait said:

> Q. What would you in the majority of occasions do when a cheque was returned back N.S.F.? A. We would charge it back to the customer's account.

And Mr. Sharp, in his cross-examination, said:

> Q. And what conclusion did you draw in your own mind as to what the situation would be if he couldn't collect the cheque? A. I thought that I would have to collect

by process of law from Mr. Sims (Mehan's president) and pay the bank if the bank couldn't collect it themselves.

Q. You never at any time thought that it was the responsibility of the bank to collect that cheque and if they did not — I'm sorry — collect the proceeds — and if they did not collect the proceeds, that was no concern of yours? A. Yes, I thought it was the responsibility of the bank.

Q. Well, let me put the question differently. Did you at any time think that if the bank failed to do so, that you were free and clear of any responsibility for repaying the bank — that you had no obligation to repay the bank? A. No, I never — that never passed through my mind.

The Nanaimo branch of the bank sent the cheque to the Langley branch of the bank but, there being insufficient funds in Mehan's account, the Langley branch returned the cheque to the Nanaimo branch N.S.F. on or about 19th October 1972. Upon receipt of the dishonoured cheque Mr. Tait telephoned the manager of the Langley branch asking information as to the likelihood of the cheque being honoured and, on being given a favourable reply, he sent the cheque to the Langley branch again, this time "on a collection basis", which meant that the Langley branch would hold the cheque against the event that sufficient funds were deposited in the account of the drawer, whereupon the cheque would be paid. Before doing this, Mr. Tait did not inform Mr. Sharp that the cheque had been dishonoured and so, of course, had no authorization from Mr. Sharp to send the cheque to the Langley branch a second time. Ultimately Mr. Tait informed Mr. Sharp that the cheque had been dishonoured and the learned trial Judge found that this was on or after — perhaps substantially later than — 26th October 1972. The cheque was never honoured and on 23rd November 1972 the Nanaimo branch debited Mr. Sharp's account in the sum of $6,000. The effect of this was to put Mr. Sharp's account into an overdraft position of $2,331.66. As a result of further withdrawals, by 11th January 1973 the overdraft stood at $3,602.40. At some unspecified time before the trial of this action, Mr. Sharp brought against Mehan an action upon the cheque for $6,000.

The bank brought this action against Mr. Sharp to recover the sum of $3,602.40 owing on the overdrawn account and interest. Mr. Sharp counterclaimed for $6,000, alleging that the bank had failed to notify him promptly of the dishonour of the cheque, alleging that he thereby suffered damage and alleging that, as a result of the bank's failure to give him notice of dishonour, he was discharged of any liability under the cheque. (Nothing was said about notice of dishonour to Mehan.)

In the result the trial Judge both dismissed the bank's claim for $3,602.40 and gave Mr. Sharp judgment against the bank for $6,000; and a formal judgment was entered accordingly. Upon the hearing of the appeal it was conceded by counsel for Mr. Sharp that the dismissal of the bank's claim was a mistake, as it clearly was.

The applicable law is in my opinion correctly set out in 2 Hals (3d) in the following passages [pp. 176-78]:

> 334. As agent of customer. Collection, strictly speaking, is the conduct of a banker who acts as a mere agent or conduit pipe to receive payment of the cheque

from the banker on whom it is drawn and holds the proceeds at the disposal of his customer.

As agent for collection he is bound to exercise diligence in the presentation of the cheque for payment. He fulfils his duty if, when the cheque is drawn on a bank in the same place, he presents it the day after receipt, or, when on a bank in another place, he either presents it or forwards it on the day following receipt. The forwarding may be to another branch or to an agent of the bank, who has the same time after receipt in which to present . . .

If the banker fails to present the cheque within the allotted time after it reaches him, he is liable to his customer for loss arising from the delay. The endorsers, if any, are discharged, . . .

335. Effect of notice of hishonour. If a cheque is dishonoured on presentment, the collecting banker can debit the customer's account with the amount. He must give due notice of dishonour either to the parties liable on the cheque, or to his customer. The latter is the usual course. Return of the cheque to the customer is deemed sufficient notice of dishonour, if the customer has endorsed it. Branches of the same bank are held to be separate persons for the transmission of notice of dishonour . . .

336. When proceeds available. Where cheques are collected, the banker has a reasonable time, consistent with ordinary bookkeeping, in which to pass the proceeds to current account before they are available for drawing against. Where cheques are credited as cash prior to receipt of payment, the customer is only entitled to draw on them at once if there is an agreement, express or implied, to that effect. If the cheque is dishonoured, the banker is entitled to debit the customer's account.

In *Falconbridge on Banking and Bills of Exchange,* 7th ed. (1969), this appears at p. 269:

> If a cheque is deposited and presented with due diligence to the drawee bank and dishonoured, the mere fact that the collecting bank has credited the payee with the amount of the cheque is not sufficient proof that the cheque was intended to be discounted, and the entry in the books of the collecting bank may be reversed and the payee of the cheque charged with the amount: *Regina* v. *Bank of Montreal* (1886), 1 Exch. C.R. 154.

As to proof, at p. 163 in the case cited, Strong J. said

> The question of the real relation between the bank and the Crown arising out of this particular transaction, is not a question of law, but one purely of fact . . . and as a question of fact, it is not concluded by an entry in the books, — such entry being susceptible of explanation, and being, as I hold, in the present case sufficiently explained by the evidence of . . . and by the attendant circumstances, and therefore to be construed in the way already indicated.

Merely for the purpose of illustrating how old in Canada is the practice of a customer being credited with the amount of a cheque that he has deposited in his bank account and then later being debited with the same amount after the cheque, presented by the bank for payment, has been dishonoured, I cite *Owens* v. *Quebec Bank* (1870) 30 UCQB 382 (CA), to which the learned Judge referred.

Applying the law as I have outlined it, I am of the opinion that the bank, having credited Mr. Sharp's account with $6,000 when he deposited the cheque, was entitled to debit his account with the same amount after the cheque was dishonoured. On the other hand, the bank owed a duty to Mr. Sharp to give him prompt notice of the dishonour of the cheque at its Langley branch on 19th October 1972. Its failure to do so was a breach of its duty and Mr. Sharp is entitled to recover any damages that he can prove resulted from the breach of that duty. At the same time, the breach of duty did not change the relationship between the parties so as to convert the bank from an agent for collection into beneficial owner of the cheque. The only section of the Bills of Exchange Act, RSC 1970, c. B-5, that may have direct application here is this one:

> 100.(1) Where a bill when dishonoured is in the hands of an agent he may himself give notice to the parties liable on the bill, or he may give notice to his principal, in which case the principal upon receipt of the notice has the same time for giving notice as if the agent had been an independent holder.
>
> (2) Where the agent gives notice to his principal he must do so within the same time as if he were an independent holder.

The learned trial Judge took a different approach. After citing some authorities and referring to ss. 85, 86, 96, 97 and 165 of the Bills of Exchange Act, among which there are included these provisions:

> 85.(1) Subject to this Act, a bill must be duly presented for payment.
>
> (2) If it is not so presented, the drawer and endorsers are discharged . . .
>
> 96.(1) Subject to this Act, when a bill has been dishonoured by non-acceptance or by non-payment, notice of dishonour must be given to the drawer, and each endorser, and any drawer or endorser to whom such notice is not given is discharged.

The Judge said [[1974] 6 WWR 481 at 487-89, 48 DLR (3d) 382]:

> The "notice of dishonour" provisions applicable are to be found in ss. 96 to 108 inclusive. I find, as a fact, that no such notice of dishonour as anticipated in those sections was given to the defendant Sharp within the time limited in s. 97(a), hereinbefore reproduced, and accordingly the defendant Sharp is discharged from liability as an endorser of the $6,000 cheque.
>
> By virtue of s. 165(2), ss. 133 to 135 inclusive also have application to the issue I must decide which are reproduced herein in part:
>
>> 133. The endorser of a bill by endorsing it, subject to the effect of any express stipulation hereinbefore authorized,
>>
>> (a) engages that on due presentment it shall be accepted and paid according to its tenor, and that if it is dishonoured he will compensate the *holder* or subsequent endorser who is compelled to pay it, if the requisite proceedings *on dishonour* are duly taken;
>>
>> (b) is precluded from denying to *a holder in due course* the genuineness and regularity in all respects of the drawer's signature and all previous endorsements; . . .
>>
>> 134. Where a bill is dishonoured, the measure of damages, which shall be deemed to be liquidated damages, are
>>
>> (a) the amount of the bill; . . .
>>
>> 135. In case of the dishonour of a bill the holder may recover from any party liable on the bill, the drawer who has been compelled to pay the bill may recover from the acceptor, and an endorser who has been compelled to pay the bill may recover from the acceptor or from the drawer, or from a prior endorser, the damages aforesaid. (The italics are mine.)

I find as a fact that the defendant Sharp endorsed the cheque on the reverse side in the appropriate place (see Ex. 4). In my opinion, it does not matter whether on or shortly after 19th October 1972 the plaintiff changed its status from a mere holder (i.e., an agent for collection) to a holder in due course because the reference in s. 133(*a*) is to a holder as distinguished from a holder in due course as referred to in s. 133(*b*).

Neither counsel relied or alluded to ss. 133 to 135 inclusive in their arguments, however, it is my view that pursuant to s. 133(*a*) the defendant Sharp would only become liable to compensate the holder, i.e., the plaintiff bank if *"requisite proceedings on dishonour"* had been properly taken. If I am wrong in that conclusion, the law merchant should govern. Section 10 of the Act reads as follows:

> **10.** The rules of the common law of England, including the law merchant, save in so far as they are inconsistent with the express provisions of this Act, apply to bills of exchange, promissory notes and cheques.

(I interject here that the learned Judge did not refer to the aspects of the common law to which I have referred earlier.)

> It is my considered opinion that the plaintiff bank was negligent on or about 19th October 1972 in failing to promptly notify the defendant Sharp of the dishonour of the $6,000 cheque. Accordingly, I find that the plaintiff was not entitled to reverse the $6,000 credited to the defendant Sharp's account as they purported to do on 23rd November 1972. The damages suffered by the defendant are in the amount of $6,000 and the plaintiff is, of course, entitled to continued possession of the original $6,000 cheque to take such steps, as it may be advised, against the drawer Mehan Lake Log Ltd.

In my respectful opinion the learned Judge went wrong in treating the bank's assertion of a right to reverse the credit in its accounts upon the basis that it was asserting the rights under ss. 133 and 134 above of the holder of the bill against an endorser thereof. This was not the basis of the bank's claim to reverse the credit. Its claim arose from the common law and its position as collection agent. When s. 85(2) says that, if a bill is not duly presented, the endorsers are discharged, it speaks of them being discharged in their capacity as endorsers, and not otherwise. When s. 96(1) says that "any . . . endorser to whom such notice is not given is discharged" it means that he is discharged qua endorser. Paragraph (*a*) of s. 133 says what the endorser of a bill "engages" "by endorsing it", if the requisite proceedings on dishonour are duly taken, and it does not extend to engagements that flow from some source other than the endorsement of the bill. Section 134 has to do with the measure of damages against a person who is liable in damages because of the dishonour of a bill on which he is liable, and it does not apply to the damages payable by an agent for collection to his principal because the agent has failed to give due notice of dishonour to the principal.

As I have said, Mr. Sharp is entitled to recover such damages as he can prove resulted from the bank's breach of duty; but that is all he can recover. On the trial, as part of its case, counsel for the bank put in these portions of the examination of Mr. Sharp for discovery:

> Q. 247. Now, in the next paragraph, paragraph 3, of your counter-claim, you allege and I am talking about half way down — that by reason of the failure of the

bank to notify you that the cheque was not honoured by Mehan Lake Log that you have suffered damage. Now, can you tell me what is the damage that you consider you have suffered as a consequence of this failure on the part of the bank? In what way have you suffered? A. Yes. I had my bank account closed off. I had the embarrassment of going around redeeming cheques. I felt hurt by the bank's action — their negligence in informing me.

Q. 248. Are you out of pocket in any way due to this failure and if so, how? A. Well, I am out of pocket because they mishandled the cheque. They mishandled the whole affair.

Q. 249. You say that by his late notifying you of the fact that this cheque was N.S.F. that you are out of pocket and can you explain to me in what way you are out of pocket and how much? What have you lost as a result? A. Well, I think that my greatest or — I should say I think my loss is in being hurt by the bank.

Q. 250. Would you agree with me that you are not out of pocket? You have not lost any money which you might otherwise have had? A. It's hard to say.

Q. 251. Well, you are the one who is saying it in your counter-claim and I am entitled to understand your counter-claim. Would you explain to me if you can how you have lost $6,000? A. Well —

Q. 252. Which is what you are claiming? A. Yes. I've lost $6,000 because they were negligent in honouring that cheque.

At the trial only Mr. Sharp gave evidence on his behalf and he said nothing about any damage he had suffered. The damages must then be assessed solely on the evidence afforded by his examination for discovery put in by the bank. Upon this evidence I think that no more than normal damages can be awarded, and I would assess them at $100.

In the result I would allow the appeal, give the bank judgment for $3,602.40 with interest at 12 per cent per annum, and reduce the damages awarded Mr. Sharp on his counterclaim from $6,000 to $100. The $100 should be set off against the amount for which the bank is given judgment.

Appeal allowed.

Questions:

1   Was the case correctly decided? What steps could respondent Sharp take against the drawer of the cheque following the Court of Appeal's decision?

2   May a depository bank effectively contract out of the duty to give its customer a notice of dishonour with respect to cheques delivered for deposit to the customer's account? See ss. 34 and 106.

B.   THE DEPOSITARY BANK AS A HOLDER IN DUE COURSE

To become a holder in due course of a cheque delivered for deposit to a customer's credit, a depository bank had, prior to the enactment of s. 165(3), to satisfy the requirements of s. 56(1). So far as the requirement of value is concerned, Falconbridge summarizes the law as follows:

If a customer endorses cheques to his bank for collection, the mere fact that the bank in its books enters the amount of the cheques to the customer's credit as soon as they are received and before they are cleared, does not make the bank a holder for value.To make the bank a holder for value there must be a contract express or implied between bank and customer that the bank will, before receipt of the proceeds, honour cheques of the customer drawn against the credit balance. Such a contract may be established by course of business or by entry in the customer's pass book, communicated to the customer and acted upon by him, or may be negatived by the terms of the paying-in slips.

(*Falconbridge On Banking* p. 615).

According to Falconbridge (*id.* at p. 860), s. 165(3) was added to the BEA in 1966 "after an Alberta decision that a cheque endorsed 'Deposit only to the account of' "A", and signed "A" was a restrictive endorsement, and that the bank in which it was deposited was not a holder in due course". In this case (*Imperial Bank of Canada* v. *Hays and Earl Ltd.* (1962) 35 DLR (2d) 136; see also *Bank of Nova Scotia* v. *Budget Motors Ltd.* [1966] Que. SC 272) the plaintiff depositary bank received from its customer a cheque restrictively endorsed for deposit. The bank credited the customer's account before the cheque had been cleared, and allowed him to draw on his account. Upon the dishonour of the cheque, the drawer was allowed to assert against the bank a defence available to him against the payee-customer of the plaintiff depositary bank.

Needless to say, the language of s. 165(3) covers more than the case of a cheque restrictively endorsed for deposit. According to Professor Scott, "[t]he history of [s. 165(3)] does not reflect a great deal of credit on the Canadian parliamentary process." He further states that "[a]t the request of the banking industry, but without understanding what it was doing, the Parliament of Canada in 1966 subverted the structure of the Bills of Exchange Act by adding section 165(3)": Stephen Scott, "The Bank is Always Right: Section 165(3) of the Bills of Exchange Act and Its Curious Parliamentary History" (1973) 19 McGill LJ 78.

On the dishonour of a cheque deposited to the credit of its customer, a depositary bank is not limited to its remedies against the drawer of the cheque. The depositary bank could debit the account of its customer (the payee or endorsee of the cheque) according to the deposit agreement or, alternatively, sue him on his endorser's contract (s. 133(*a*)). Note that in accepting unendorsed cheques from a customer for deposit, the "usual banking practice" of a depositary bank is for the teller to endorse the name of the customer on the cheque. "In so doing, the bank . . . [is] acting as agent for its customer" (*Keyes* v. *Royal Bank of Canada* [1974] SCR 377, 384); *cf.* s. 61(1)).

As to the relationship between the remedies of the depositary bank against the drawer and the endorser, it was stated in *Royal Bank of Canada* v. *Wild* (1974) 51 DLR (3d) 188, 190, (Ont. CA) that,

> [w]hen the cheque was dishonoured the [depositary bank], in its capacity as a holder in due course had the right to proceed against either or both . . . drawer and . . . payee. Neither in its efforts to collect from the payee . . . nor in any other conduct with respect to the cheque was there an election on the Bank's part to look to its customer to the exclusion of [the drawer] . . . .

Whether the depositary bank sues the drawer or the endorser (its customer) it must give the defendant prompt notice of dishonour (ss. 96 *et seq.*): "any drawer or endorser to whom such notice is not given is discharged" (s. 96(1)). According to Falconbridge (*id.* at 734), "[i]t is anomalous that the drawer of a cheque should ever be entitled to notice of dishonour . . . but it seems clear that he is a drawer . . . and therefore entitled to notice". Notice of dishonour is dispensed with as regards the drawer where inter alia "the drawer has countermanded payment", (s. 107 (*e*). For the effect of a depository bank's failure to give its customer, the endorser of a cheque, a prompt notice of dishonour, see *Bank of Nova Scotia* v. *Sharp*, section (A) *supra*.

A bank branch has a separate identity in the collection system for the purpose of attaining a holder in due course status as well as for other purposes. It was thus stated in *Bank of Nova Scotia* v. *Gould* (1978) 79 DLR (3d) 473, at 476 (Ont. Co. Ct.) that "two branches of the same bank . . . are in essence separate agencies and the knowledge of one is not the knowledge of the other." See also *William Ciurluini Ltd.* v. *Royal Bank of Canada* (1972) 2 OR 748 (Ont. HC). As to the separate identity of a bank branch and its relationship to the legal personality of the banking corporation, see in general *Canadian Life Assurance Co.* v. *Canadian Imperial Bank of Commerce* (1975) 8 OR (2d) 210, at 216-220 (Ont. HC); rev'd on other grounds, 74 DLR (3d) 599, 602-03 (Ont. C.A.). Note also that crediting the depositor's account with the amount of a cheque drawn against another account in the same bank branch is not payment of the cheque. Following the deposit and prior to payment (namely the irrevocable debit entered into the drawer's account), the bank branch (in its capacity as a depositary bank) is nonetheless a holder in due course. See e.g. *Capital Associates Ltd.* v. *Royal Bank of Canada*, reproduced *infra*.

It follows from the preceding discussion that the drawer's countermand is of no avail as against the depositary bank which, as a holder in due course, overcomes the drawer's defences against the payee. See e.g. *Caisse Populaire (St. Jean-Baptiste) Belle Rivière Ltd.* v. *A & L Auto Wreckers Ltd.* (1978) 82 DLR (3d) 766 (Ont. HC). This is true even where the cheque is drawn on the depositary bank itself and the notice of countermand reaches it after it has credited the account of the holder with the account of the countermanded cheque.

A current cheque is not a "consumer bill" under s. 189(1). The holder in due course status of a depositary bank is, therefore, not denied by Part V of the BEA.

Note: The following statutory changes are recommended by the Law Reform Commission of Canada in *The Cheque: Some Modernization* (Report II, 1979) pp. 31-33:

Cheque defined.

165. (1) A cheque is a bill of exchange, payable on demand and drawn upon a deposit institution. (*New*)

Provisions as to bills apply.

(2) Except as otherwise provided in this Part, the provisions of this Act applicable to a bill of exchange payable on demand apply to a cheque. (RSC 1970)

Meaning of deposit institution.

(3) In this section, deposit institution includes a bank, a credit union, a trust or loan company incorporated under the law of Canada or a province, an instrumentality of the Crown that accepts deposits from the public and any other organization, whether or not a legal entity, that accepts deposits from the public and that has the right to apply for membership in the Canadian Payments Association under the

statute establishing that Association. (*New*)

Endorsement for deposit: effect on certain collecting institutions.

(4) Endorsement of a cheque "for deposit", "for deposit to the account of the payee", or to like effect does not prevent a member of the Canadian Payments Association which is acting consistently with the emdorsement from acquiring the rights and powers of a holder.

Missing endorsement of payee — effect on certain collecting institutions.

(5) A member of the Canadian Payments Association, in collecting a cheque deposited for credit to the account of the payee without endorsement, for which it has given value as provided in this section, has such (if any) rights as it would have if, upon delivery, the payee had endorsed the cheque in blank. (*New*)

—joint accounts.

(6) Nothing in subsection (5) shall affect any claim or defence which could otherwise be asserted by a payee in respect of cheques deposited without his endorsement to an account over which another person or persons exercise signature authority. (*New*)

Security interest — certain collecting institutions.

(7) A member of the Canadian Payments Association has a security interest in a cheque deposited to an account to the extent to which credit given for that cheque is withdrawn or applied, or to which certification in reliance on such credit is made at the customer's request in respect of a cheque drawn by him. (*New*)

— partial withdrawal or application.

(8) Where credit is given for several cheques on a deposit, any withdrawal, application or certification mentioned in subsection (7) creates a security interest in all cheques in the deposit to the extent there stated, and the interest continues until the collection of all is complete. (*New*)

— enforceability and perfection.

(9) The security interest created by subsection (7) or (8) is enforceable without written security agreement, and is perfected by possession of the member or another member or deposit institution acting under the clearing by-laws of the Canadian Payments Association.

Value given by certain collecting institutions.

(10) A security interest under subsection (7) or (8) is value, to the extent of the interest, for the purpose of determining whether a member of the Canadian Payments Association is a holder in due course or for value. (*New*)

Status of certain credit unions.

(11) For the purposes of this section, a credit union which is a member of a central which is a member of the Canadian Payments Association is deemed to be a member of that Association. (*New*)

Consequential Amendments

As consequential amendments resulting from the re-definition of "cheque" proposed above, the Commission recommends that in subsection 166(1) and section 167 of the Bills of Exchange Act, the word "drawee" be substituted for the word "bank" wherever the latter occurs. In subsection 166(2) the phrase "usages of trade and of the members of the Canadian Payments Association" should replace "usage of trade and of banks". Paragraph 189(1)(*d*) of the Act should be deleted as super-fluous, together with the words "or (*d*)" in lines 3 and 4 of subsection 192(1) of the Act.

Note: The recommendations embodied in proposed s. 165(1) and (3) have now been implemented in s. 92 of the Canadian Payments Association Act. See introductory text to chapter 17(A), *supra*.

CAPITAL ASSOCIATES LTD. v. ROYAL BANK OF CANADA
(1971) 15 DLR (3d) 234 (Que. SC); aff'd (1973) 36 DLR (3d) 579 (Que. CA);
(1976) 65 DLR (3d) 384 (SCC)

MACKAY J.: This is an action for $109,990.92 being the amount of a cheque drawn on defendant's Montreal branch by All-Canadian Group Distributors Limited on June 30, 1965, and payable to the order of plaintiff Capital Associates Limited and deposited on the same day in plaintiff's account in the same branch and the proceeds of which cheque were not ultimately paid into plaintiff's account by defendant.

The plaintiff claims that it deposited the cheque in its account in defendant's Montreal branch; that defendant duly paid the said cheque and credited the proceeds thereof to plaintiff's account; that subsequently defendant illegally withdrew the amount of the cheque from plaintiff's account thereby causing it damages in the amount of the cheque.

Defendant pleads that when the cheque was deposited by plaintiff it was credited to plaintiff, subject to being debited, in accordance with normal banking practice and the specific banking agreement between plaintiff and defendant, should the cheque be dishonoured by the drawer; that after the cheque was deposited the drawer stopped payment; that the stop-payment order was imme-diately programmed into a computer which effects the debiting of cheques drawn on customers' accounts and therefore the cheque was effectively stopped before it was debited to the account of All-Canadian Group Distributors Ltd.; that the cheque being dishonoured was thereupon debited to plaintiff's account in accordance with the laws and customs of banking and the contractual agreement between plaintiff and defendant.

The facts giving rise to the present action, in addition to those set out in the foregoing pleadings, are these:

At all relevant times, the bank accounts of the plaintiff and of All-Canadian Group Distributors Ltd. were held in the same branch — the Montreal branch of defendant's bank. On October 12, 1961, plaintiff, by its president, Ira Van Vogt and its secretary, Michel de Martigny, agreed with the bank, *inter alia*, that:

> In consideration of THE ROYAL BANK OF CANADA (hereinafter referred to as the "Bank") taking on deposit from the undersigned, cheques or other instruments whether or not the undersigned is a party thereto (the whole hereinafter referred to as "instruments", which shall be deemed to include instruments drawn on any branch of the Bank), the undersigned hereby agrees with the Bank as follows:

• • •

(4) That the Bank is authorized to debit the account of the undersigned with any of the instruments, or any of the evidences of payment referred to in Section (2) hereof, which are not paid on presentation or which if paid the Bank may be called upon to refund, or which may be dishonoured by non-acceptance or non-payment or any party to which is bankrupt or insolvent or which, or the proceeds of which, through no fault of the Bank have been lost, stolen or destroyed, or which, or the proceeds of which, for any reason the Bank is unable to collect or withdraw, together with all costs, charges and expenses incurred by the Bank in connection therewith and/or to debit the account of the undersigned with any cheques drawn on the branch of the Bank at which the account of the undersigned is being carried and which have been cashed, negotiated or credited to the account of the undersigned but which have not been found good.

• • •

(6) That the undersigned will repay to the Bank all amounts debited to the account of the undersigned in accordance with the provisions of the agreement.

• • •

(8) That this is to be a continuing consent and agreement and shall bind the undersigned and the heirs, executors, administrators, successors and assigns of the undersigned.

On June 30, 1965, Van Vogt, in addition to being plaintiff's president, fulfilled the same function for All-Canadian Group Distributors Ltd. and in that capacity he, together with one J. E. Prefontaine, signed on behalf of All-Canadian Group Distributors Ltd. the cheque which is the source of this litigation. At noon on that day, the cheque bearing the endorsement "Deposit only to Capital Associates Limited", was taken to defendant's Montreal branch together with a deposit slip by Van Vogt's secretary, where they were presented to defendant's current accounts' teller who stamped the deposit slip and then sent them to the branch's proof teller. The latter scrutinized the cheque, stamped it with the endorsement "Pay to the order of any bank or banker — The Royal Bank of Canada" and the indication that it belonged to defendant's Montreal branch and then forwarded it to the bank's regional proof centre at the head office of the bank for further processing, after crediting plaintiff's account with the proceeds (ex. P-3).

The defendant's regional proof centre is a computerized regional posting operation referred to as the computer programme up-date, which posts all cheques drawn on any of defendant's branches within the region comprising Montreal Island. It acts as a clearing house for defendant's branches in the Montreal region.

In the normal course of events the computer, during the night, would debit the drawers' accounts and credit the payees' accounts with the proceeds of the cheque by effecting a transfer of the item from one account to the other and the information thus produced by the computer would be available to defendant's employees on the following banking day, which in this case would have been Friday, July 2nd, the first being Dominion Day.

However, unhappily for the plaintiff, events did not follow their normal course. For reasons which were never explained nor in fact have any relevance, Van Vogt and the directors of All-Canadian Group Distributors Ltd. found themselves in disagreement. Harold Hampson, a director and member of the executive committee, called a meeting of the company's board of directors for 12:30 p.m. on June 30th. Prior to the meeting he spoke on the telephone with the manager of defendant's branch and requested information as to what documents the bank would require in order to give effect to certain changes which he contemplated would be made by the board in the executive committee of the company. He also informed the manager that a letter countermanding payment of the cheque would probably be forthcoming.

The meeting of the board was then held and the board proceeded to replace the existing officers including Van Vogt and Prefontaine, and elected Hampson as president and others as officers of the company. At the same time new banking resolutions were adopted and the previous resolutions rescinded. Hampson then sent a new list of officers and directors to defendant's manager, and presumably a copy of the new banking resolution. He also wrote as follows (ex. D-1):

> Would you please stop payment on any cheque drawn by All-Canadian Group Distributors Limited payable to any one of the following:
> Capital Associates Ltd.
> Ira Van Vogt
> Edmond Van Vogt
> Michel L. de Martigny.

The letter and enclosed documents were taken to defendant's branch by hand and acknowledged as follows (ex. D-3) on the same day:

> Your instructions included therein with respect to cheques of the company payable to any one of the following will be carried out:

and there then followed those named in Hampson's letter to the bank.

The letter countermanding payment was then handed to the assistant manager of the current accounts department, Charles Dunseath, who was told to see that the order was effected. Dunseath thereupon caused to be prepared a memorandum (ex. D-6) for the staff of defendant's branch, to which was attached the letter (ex. D-1), instructing the staff to comply with the instructions contained in that letter. At the same time, a restraint order was prepared and fed into the computer programme up-date (ex. D-5).

It might perhaps be useful to outline briefly the system which defendant has adopted for its own convenience, if not its customers', in order to facilitate the receiving of deposits from its customers and the payment of its customers' cheques.

Deposits received during the day by the branch teller, and where he or she is not requested to pay out cash, are sent with the cheques deposited and a deposit slip to the regional proof centre where a proof teller verifies each cheque for proper endorsement and exchange charges and endorses the cheques with a stamp which indicates from which branch within the region the cheque came. The deposit is then credited to the depositor's account. If the cheque is drawn on a branch of another bank or on one of defendant's branches in another region, it is then sent to the clearing house. If, as in the present case, it is drawn on a branch within the region, then it is sent to the computer programme up-date at defendant's regional head office, where the information in the deposit is transcribed on a magnetic tape and then fed into a master file where it would normally be included in a "posted items report". When, however, an order is received countermanding payment, the current accounts department sends the order to the computer centre where it is transcribed on a second magnetic tape which is also fed into the master file, which then rejects all items on the first tape subject to such order. These items are then included in an "unposted items report". The reports are returned to the branch on the following banking day. Upon receipt of the unpostable items report, the items subject to the restraint order are scrutinized, and if payment had been stopped on any one item, it is charged back to the account into which it has been deposited and the cheque returned to the customer who presented it for deposit.

It was explained that the restraint order issued following receipt of Hampson's instructions would cover all cheques drawn by All-Canadian Group Distributors Ltd. on its accounts with defendant's Montreal branch and which had been fed into the computer that day, because no amounts had been given in Hampson's letter and the computer would not therefore be able to distinguish between the payees mentioned in the letter and any other payees who might have presented cheques on that day.

As a result of the restraint order all cheques of All-Canadian Group Distributors Ltd. drawn on its account and fed into the computer remained unposted. The cheques were handed to Dunseath on the following business day — July 2nd, and he removed the one cheque (ex. P-1) upon which payment had been stopped. He thereupon overstamped the proof teller's paid stamp — with a cancellation stamp and further stamped the cheque "Payment stopped". Dunseath then debited plaintiff's account with the amount of the cheque, $109,990.92.

At the trial, Van Vogt attempted to show by means of the books of accounts of All-Canadian Group Distributors Ltd. that its accounts in defendant's branch had been debited on July 2nd with the amount of the cheque payable to plaintiff. Objection was taken to this proof which was then admitted under reserve. In the event the plaintiff failed to establish that in fact the account of All-Canadian Group Distributors Ltd. had ever been debited with the specific item represented by the cheque (ex. P-1). It is unnecessary therefore to rule on the objection.

The issue therefore is whether or not the defendant committed a fault in charging back to plaintiff's account the amount of the cheque which the maker refused to pay.

It is the plaintiff's proposition that where both the drawer and the payee of a cheque have their accounts in the same branch of a bank, if the payee deposits the cheque in his account he is presenting it for payment and regardless of whether he is paid the proceeds in cash or certifies the cheque or deposits the proceeds in his account, the bank has effectively paid the cheque and any stop-payment order subsequently received from the maker cannot affect his right to receive the proceeds, for at this moment the bank is fully aware whether or not the cheque is good.

From which it follows that the defendant, in debiting plaintiff's account in the amount of the cheque after the amount had been deposited in its account, acted illegally and is bound therefore to reimburse plaintiff the amount so debited.

The defendant contends, on the other hand, that the situation is no different from that which it would have been had the two accounts been held in separate branches. That the proceeds of the cheque, not having been paid out of the account of All-Canadian Group Distributors Ltd. prior to the receipt of an order countermanding payment and which had been credited to plaintiff's account when the cheque was deposited, were properly debited to that account in accordance with the contractual agreement between plaintiff and defendant and the customs of banking.

If plaintiff's contention be correct, then it must establish that its relationship with defendant on June 30th was that of payee-drawee. That is to say that it was in the same position as any payee of a cheque attending at the drawer's bank and presenting that cheque for payment. For if its relationship with defendant was that of creditor-debtor, then it was negotiating a cheque to defendant with instructions to deposit the proceeds to its credit in its account, and in such event the bank became a holder in due course of the cheque: s. 165(3) . . . If the cheque was dishonoured before it was paid or when it was presented for payment, then the plaintiff as endorser would be liable to compensate the defendant as endorsee the amount which the endorsee had paid for the cheque: Bills of Exchange Act, ss. 133 and 134.

Was it also entitled to debit plaintiff's account by virtue of the banking agreement (ex. D-2) which existed between plaintiff and defendant? By that agreement plaintiff authorized defendant to debit its account "with any cheques drawn on" the Montreal branch and which had been credited to plaintiff's account "but which have not been found good".

The plaintiff submitted the argument that a cheque the payment of which has been stopped by the drawer prior to its payment from the drawer's account is not a cheque "which has not been found good" and that therefore the agreement cannot apply in the present case. It was contended that these words can only include a cheque drawn on accounts which are without sufficient funds to pay them, or cheques which are stale dated or which bear irregular signatures. In the opinion of the undersigned, the words include any cheque which has not been paid regardless of the reason. For no matter what rule of construction be applied to them, they must mean any cheque which upon presentation for payment has not been honoured and paid. The contrary would be a bad cheque and a bad cheque must mean any cheque which upon presentation for payment has been dishonoured. It may have been dishonoured for any number of reasons including the drawee's refusal to pay it upon instructions from the drawer (s. 95). It would distort the meaning of the words to hold that a cheque which is dishonoured and unpaid by reason of an order from the drawer countermanding payment is a "good" cheque.

Therefore, the defendant was also entitled to debit plaintiff's account with the amount of the cheque in virtue of the agreement.

Action dismissed.

Notes and Questions:

1 The Quebec court found that "the defendant took the cheque as a holder in due course": *supra*. Was this finding necessary for the ultimate decision? In affirming the decision, the Quebec Court of Appeal (1973) 36 DLR (3d) 579 at 584 preferred to rely on *Falconbridge on Banking*, pp. 276-77, where it is stated that "the mere fact that the collecting bank credits the customer with the amount of the cheque does not prove that the bank has discounted or bought the cheque so as to make the bank the debtor of its customer in respect of the amount of the cheque". The Supreme Court of Canada "agree[d] with the Courts below that the cheque in question . . . could not be treated as presented for payment and that the respondent bank, not having debited the drawer's account, was entitled to act on the stop payment": (1976) 65 DLR (3d) 384 *per* Laskin C.J.C.

2 Defendant bank argued "that after the cheque was deposited the drawer stopped payment": *supra*. Under these circumstances, did defendant bank have to debit plaintiff's account? Could defendant bank have proceeded against All-Canadian as drawer of the cheque? Would the success of this latter option depend on the position of defendant bank as holder in due course of the cheque?

C. COUNTERMANDING PAYMENT

Bills of Exchange Act, s. 167(*a*)

1. EFFECTIVE COUNTERMAND AND ITS EFFECT

SANDA RODGERS MAGNET,
"Inaccurate or Ambiguous Countermand and Payment over Countermand"
(1980) 4 Can. Bus. LJ 297, at 298, 300

As the customer by his cheque may order the drawee bank to pay so may he revoke his order, so long as the instrument has not been paid in the interim. As early as 1813, Lord Ellenborough held that "If I give a draft upon a condition, and I find the condition is to be eluded, I may stop the payment" and added that as a result "the draft . . . had become a piece of waste paper". The common law right of the drawer to countermand the order to his banker received codification in s. 167 of the Act.

Thus, the banker is bound strictly to observe his customer's order. He must pay the customers' cheques and pay damages for any failure so to do. But he must also give strict regard to his customer's countermand or again find himself in breach of the Act and of the terms of his contract with the drawer. For this reason courts have consistently required that the terms of the countermand be clear and unambiguous.

• • •

[There has been] a consistent line of cases requiring that the information given by the customer as to account number, payee, date and amount of the cheque he wishes to countermand be exact. Any discrepancy has resulted in the exoneration of the bank that pays a cheque which differs in any particular from the one described by the customer, although in fact the cheque paid was the one the customer intended to stop.

• • •

All the banks and near banks contacted by the writer have adopted virtually identical countermand procedures. The customer must indicate in writing the date of the cheque, payee, account number, amount and, if available, cheque number. He must indicate the date and time of his order to countermand. The computer is then programmed to flag any cheque of an amount identical to the amount given for the countermanded cheque. A daily computer print out of all posted cheques is manually compared with the cheques themselves. Those cheques flagged by the computer as possible countermands are specifically compared with the countermand form itself. Such a system requires that the information given by the drawer concerning the amount of the cheque be entirely accurate. In most institutions no other procedure to catch the countermanded instrument is utilized. None the less, the banks and near banks consulted indicated that they find that customers often err as to the exact amount.

REMFOR INDUSTRIES LTD. v. BANK OF MONTREAL
(1978) 21 OR (2d) 225, 5 BLR 22 (Ont. CA); 25 NR 450 (SCC)

DUBIN J.A.: The issue on this appeal is whether the defendant bank was liable for certifying a cheque of the plaintiff company, a customer of the said bank, following a direction given to it to stop payment on the cheque. The learned trial Judge held that the direction was not an effective countermand, but nevertheless the bank was negligent under the circumstances. It is from that judgment that the bank appeals on the issue of liability; no question being raised as to the amount of damages assessed against it.

On or about July 12, 1972, the plaintiff company drew a postdated cheque in the amount of $10,853, dated September 12, 1972, against a line of credit which it had with the defendant. On September 6, 1972, the president of the plaintiff company called the account manager of the branch of the defendant with which the plaintiff company had its account advising the bank to stop payment on the cheque since the plaintiff company was no longer indebted to the payee. The account manager was advised of the date of the cheque, the cheque number, and the name of the payee. He was advised that the cheque was in the amount of $10,800, and in this respect the president of the plaintiff company was in error.

In accordance with the standard practice of the bank a stop payment order on a cheque for $10,800 was programmed into a central computer. The information processed was limited to the amount of the cheque and the account number only. Because of the manner in which the computer was programmed the clerks of the bank would only be alerted to stop payment if the amount of the cheque presented for payment was exactly the same as was programmed into the computer.

The cheque was presented for certification on September 25, 1972, and since the amount of the cheque was not the exact amount as was recorded, the clerk was unaware of the direction given by the customer and the cheque was certified without any further inquiry.

As I have already observed, the learned trial Judge held that the instructions given to the bank did not constitute an effective countermand. In arriving at that conclusion, he felt the issue was resolved by what was stated by this Court in the case of *Giordano* v. *Royal Bank* [1973] 3 OR 771, 38 DLR (3d) 191 [reversed at p. 191n (SCC)]. On that issue Kelly J.A., speaking for the Court, stated at p. 774:

> When a customer issues a cheque he has given a formal order to the bank to pay to the payee the face amount of the cheque out of funds held by the bank for the account of the customer. This order, by the very nature of the cheque, is an unconditional one and one which the bank may not disregard without subjecting itself to liability to its customer.
>
> In order that a bank may with impunity refuse to follow the prior instructions of its customer contained in a cheque, s. 167 [of the Bills of Exchange Act, RSC 1970, c. B-5] lays down conditions under which a bank may disregard the order conveyed to it by the cheque and act upon the subsequent direction to stay payment. . . .
>
> If the bank is to be able to rely on the countermand as a termination of its duty to pay a cheque, the cheque countermanded must be identified by particulars furnished in the countermand. Date of issue, payee and amount, as well as the number when there be one, are well known features identifying the cheque to be countermanded. *Since the bank may incur liability by refusing to pay, it is entitled to have an unambiguous description of the cheque set out in the countermand*, for if the customer has given instructions which are ambiguous, the customer cannot hold the bank liable for proceeding on the basis of an interpretation which the bank fairly and honestly assumes it to bear: *Westminster Bank Ltd.* v. *Hilton* (1927) 43 TLR 124 at p. 126. [The italics are mine.]

And at p. 775 he concluded as follows:

> In the instant case, due to the discrepancy in the name of the payee and in the amount of the cheque sought to be countermanded, the notice of countermand did not carry to the bank notification of the change of purpose of the customer as to the exact order he had given in issuing the cheque in question. On this account, I am of the opinion that the customer did not countermand the cheque within the meaning of that term as used in s. 167 and that the bank was therefore not required to treat his instructions as a countermand.

It is to be observed that in the *Giordano* case, *supra*, there was a discrepancy in the name of the payee as well as in the amount of the cheque.

In the case of *Westminster Bank Ltd.* v. *Hilton, supra*, the customer had telegraphed the bank to stop payment on a cheque, the number of which he had misdescribed. It was also, however, of significance that the bank was not alerted to the fact that the cheque was postdated. When the cheque was tendered for payment, it was paid. In exonerating the bank, Viscount Dunedin concluded as follows at p. 126:

> It must always be remembered that a bank can be sued just as much for failing to honour a cheque as for cashing a cheque that had been stopped. Under the regula-

tions the bank had to inform the clearing house by 3.30 p.m. whether they honoured the cheque or not. They did not know the plaintiff's address, and *when it comes to a question of identification it must always be remembered that the number of a cheque is the one certain item of identification.* There can be only one cheque bearing a printed number; there may be many cheques in favour of the same drawee and for the same amount. I was at one time inclined to think that, inasmuch as both the cashier and the manager knew that there was a stop on a cheque they ought, on August 6, to have made certain investigations, but I find that they did do so. They followed the ordinary practice. They looked at the ledger, and the ledger showed that no cheque in favour of Poate had come in. *I think, therefore, that the view of the officials was correct that the cheque presented being subsequent to the date of the stop instructions might be a duplicate cheque, and that they were bound to cash it.* [The italics are mine.]

Lord Shaw of Dunfermline, in the same case, made the additional following observations at pp. 129-30:

My Lords: I concur. The case has reference to the stoppage of a cheque of a particular number, name, date, and amount. When a banker is in possession of sufficient funds to meet such a cheque from a customer, the duty of the bank is to honour that cheque by payment, and failure in this duty may involve the bank in serious liability to its customer.

This duty is ended, and on the contrary when the cheque is stopped another duty arises — namely, to refuse payment. In a case of that character *it rests upon the customer to prove that the order to stop reached the bank in time and was unequivocally referable to a cheque then in existence, and signed and issued by the customer before the notice to stop.*

It would, of course, be intolerable in business to permit the form of stoppage to be applied to a non-existent and non-issued cheque. *Further, in the ordinary course of trade a cheque is signed on the date it bears. This being so the notice of stoppage on reaching the bank will properly be treated as only applying to a cheque bearing a date the same as, or anterior to, the date of stoppage.*

To carry the scope of stoppage further and to make it apply to the case (exceptional and out of the ordinary course of business transactions) — *the case of cheques which though subsequent to stoppage in date were yet anterior to stoppage at the time of signature and issue, namely, post-dated cheques* — it is, in my view, necessary for the customer to prove and explain the post-dating, but further to prove that this fact was brought clearly home to the mind of the banker so as to bring the post-dated cheque within the order of stoppage. [The italics are mine.]

And further at p. 130:

The perplexity arose from the fact that the cheque as presented was for the same sum and to the same payee. But this perplexity arose not from any act of the bank but was actually caused by the acts of the customer, and *Ireland* v. *Livingston* (LR 5 HL 395) clearly applies. In the circumstances stated, was the banker to enter into a conjecture that the stopped cheque was the same cheque as one bearing a different number and appearing to have come into existence after the date of stoppage? And did he fail in his duty by not coming to a conclusion of identity? I do not see my way so to affirm, and for myself, I should have thought it highly dangerous in business to act upon any conjecture of the kind, or to dishonour such a cheque except upon clear and unmistakable instructions.

In the instant case, the bank was aware that the cheque referred to by the customer was postdated. It was also aware of the number of the cheque itself, the account number, and the payee. The case is, therefore, distinguishable from the *Giordano* and *Westminster Bank* cases.

In the case of *Shude* v. *Amer. State Bank*, 248 NW 886 at 889 the following statement appears:

> The law does not require a perfectly detailed description, but instead the notice is sufficient if the check is described with reasonable accuracy.

In my opinion, notwithstanding the minor discrepancy with respect to the amount of the cheque, the detailed information provided by the customer so clearly identified the cheque which was presented for certification that the customer's instructions constituted an effective countermand, and, with respect, the learned trial Judge erred in holding to the contrary. The bank was, therefore, unauthorized to certify the cheque.

In any event, even if there were no effective countermand in this case, I am of the opinion that the learned trial Judge was correct in holding that having regard to the information given to it by the plaintiff, the bank was under a duty to inquire from its customer as to whether the cheque presented for certification was the cheque with respect to which the direction to stop payment had been given. The bank's failure to do so constituted negligence. The information given to the bank was correct in every respect other than the amount. The instructions clearly related to the cheque, the number of which had been given to the bank. The bank's internal procedure in limiting the information supplied to its computer, by reference to account number and the amount of the cheque only, cannot relieve the bank of its duty where the customer has supplied such precise additional information. In that respect what was said by Kelly J.A. in *Giordano* v. *Royal Bank, supra,* at p. 776, is on point:

> It is my opinion that the bank's duty to its customer under the foregoing circumstances required it to use ordinary diligence to enlist the assistance of the customer before making the decision to pay the cheque: *Marsh* v. *Keating* (1834), 1 Bing. (NC) 198 at p. 220, 131 ER 1094. It is not necessary to consider what might have been the result if steps had been taken by the bank to speak to the customer and they had proven abortive, since no efforts at all were made to get into communication with the customer. Admittedly the bank did not attempt to reach the customer. In this respect the bank failed in the duty it owed the customer and its breach of that duty resulted in the payment of the cheque.

Appeal dismissed.

Notes and Questions:

1   For the proposition that an effective "countermand must not be expressed in ambiguous terms" but "must unequivocally refer to the particular cheque which is stopped", see *Shapera* v. *Toronto Dominion Bank* (1970 13 DLR (3d) 122 (Man. QB). *Giordano* v. *Royal Bank of Canada* (1973) 38 DLR (3d) 191 (Ont. CA) pur-

ported to follow this rule but then found it to be qualified by "the bank's duty to its customer . . . to use ordinary diligence to enlist the assistance of the customer before making the decision to pay the cheque". The court further concluded that "[a]lthough it is clear that if a bank pays a countermanded cheque, the customer has a claim for money had and received for the face amount of the cheque, where . . . the liability of the bank arises not from an unauthorized payment of a countermanded cheque but from some breach of its duty, the action lies in negligence and the measure of damages is the loss proven to have been suffered as a result of that breach of duty": *id.* at 196.

2   Professor Rodgers Magnet commented on the effect of the "reasonable accuracy" test outlined in *Remfor* as follows:

> Of the major banks consulted, it appears that all but the Royal Bank are employing countermand procedures that would fail to meet the requirements of the Ontario Court of Appeal. Procedures for countermand at the Bank of Montreal, Provincial Bank, Bank of Nova Scotia, the Toronto Dominion Bank and the Canadian Imperial Bank of Commerce are premised on a computer entry which will flag a potential countermand only if the amount given for the cheque is absolutely accurate. At the Royal Bank the computer is programmed to flag all cheques on the particular account.
>
> In the light of these recent developments banks might well reassess the procedure to be utilized whenever a customer countermands his order to pay. To meet the legal requirements several additional items of information ought to be programmed into the computer. The difficulty in so doing is that for the purposes of payment of cheques, only the account number and amount need be entered. To require additional information to be manually encoded on all cheques simply to catch the occasional countermand, would be prohibitively expensive. Undoubtedly, banks would prefer to absorb the cost of paying over countermand in most cases. Alternatively, data systems could be programmed to flag all cheques on the given account, or all cheques on the account that fall within a range of amounts, although this second course might not satisfy the Court of Appeal. These solutions seem feasible, are not prohibitively expensive and would solve the dilemma of a bank faced with a situation such as occurred in *Remfor* ((1980) 4 Can. Bus. LJ 297, 306-07).

3   In *Sparkle Wash Ltd.* v. *Saskatoon Credit Union Ltd.* [1979] 2 WWR 320 (Sask. DC), the plaintiff issued a cheque for $3,642 on his account with the defendant. Subsequently, the plaintiff advised the defendant that he wished to stop payment on the cheque, and attended at the branch, filling in a form in the incorrect amount of $3,612. The form also contained a clause purporting to hold the defendant harmless from inadvertent payment. On the improper payment by the defendant, the plaintiff sued for the improper debit. In holding for the plaintiff, the court held: (1) a countermand need not be in writing although writing is helpful; and (2) that in any event the error on the written countermand was made by the clerk of the defendant; and (3) that as the operative act was the oral advice, the "hold harmless" clause was of no effect. What are the implications holding (3)? Can a bank require its customer to sign a waiver form as a condition of accepting a countermand of payment order?

4   The customer's right to countermand payment follows from the absence of liability
on the part of the drawee bank to the holder of the cheque. See sections 127 and
131. Also, the right to countermand payment does not release the drawer from his
engagement on the cheque under s. 130(a). The drawer's liability ultimately depends on his defences as well as the status of the holder (whether or not he is a
holder in due course). It follows that the purchaser of a bank draft (also referred to
as a "remitter") is not entitled to countermand payment. The bank, as a drawer of
the instrument, is liable on it to the holder (s. 130(a)). Its duty to pay is derived not
from the customer's order but rather from its own signature (see also s. 131). In
practice, the drawer of the bank draft will follow a stop order payment at the
request of the purchaser of the draft if it is convinced that the draft has been lost. In
so doing, the drawer-bank protects itself from payment over a forged endorsement: *cf.* section (D) of this chapter. In reimbursing the remitter, the bank honours
his continuing ownership in the instrument; *cf.* s. 156. As to the remitter's power to
block payment on a bank draft on the basis of his defences against the holder, see
chapter 19 (F), note 10, *infra*.

5   The customer's right to countermand payment is brought to an end on the
certification of the cheque by the drawee-bank. "Certification" is the name given
to the marking of a cheque by the drawee bank to show that it was drawn by the
person purporting to draw it, that it is drawn upon an existing account with the
drawee, and that there are funds sufficient to meet it. As for the proper procedure,
"it has been suggested judicially that merely having a cheque initialed by the
drawee branch's manager is not sufficient formality without evidence of a local
custom to that effect, and the better practice appears to be for the bank to rubber
stamp the cheque 'certified' and to withdraw the sum payable from the account of
the drawer at that time": 3 CED (Ont. 3rd) Title 17, Bills of Exchange §270.
Certification may be procured by the drawer because he wishes or is required to
add the credit of the bank to his own liability, or by the holder because he wishes to
ensure payment but prefers to collect the proceeds of the cheque through the
collection system rather than over the counter. Certification of cheques is a well
established practice in Canada and the U.S. but not in England. It is not provided for
explicitly in the BEA. It signifies either acceptance by the drawee bank (see ss. 35(1),
36, 38 and 128) or actual payment into a specific item account to be collected later.
Alternatively, it can be seen as an agreement by the drawee bank to pay the
cheque. Any of these theories explains why certification puts an end to the
drawer's right to countermand payment. Do you see why? What is the effect of
certification on the drawer's own liability on the cheque? Does it depend on which
theory underlies certification?

    Falconbridge (*On Banking and Bills of Exchange* (7th ed.) at p. 865) claims that
"the [drawee] bank would not be justified in certifying a post-dated cheque before
its ostensible date, at least if the certification is requested by any person other than
the drawer. . . ." Do you agree? In *Keyes* v. *Royal Bank of Canada* [1947] SCR 377,
where at the holder's request the drawee bank certified the cheque before its
ostensible date, the drawer was held entitled to countermand payment before the
designated time. As to the priority in the case of a bank's insolvency of certified

cheques and of instruments issued by a bank (note 4, *supra*), see s. 85 of the Canadian Payment Association Act, SC 1980 c. 40 (Part IV).

6   There are different views as to whether the purchaser of a personal money order can effectively countermand payment. A personal money order bears the name of the bank but, unlike a bank draft, is signed by the purchaser. *Garden Check Cashing Service Inc.* v. *First National City Bank* (1966) 267 NYS 2d 698, 702 (NY SC AD); aff'd 277 NYS 2d 141, supports the purchaser's right to countermand payment on such an instrument:

> We see small difference between the present transaction and one where a person deposits with a bank a sum of money and receives a quantity of blank checks. The obvious difference is that here a single deposit was made and a single blank check received with the amount of the deposit inserted therein. Thereafter the procedure followed the normal and customary pattern — the purchaser filled in the name of a payee, signed his name and address and delivered the instrument. . . .
>
> The purchaser under his contract with . . . [the bank] was the sole person who might draw on the fund and he had the clear right to stop payment prior to acceptance by the bank. . . . This conclusion is fortified by decisions in another jurisdiction where, unlike this case, a legal "bank money order" signed by an officer of the issuing bank was held to be the equivalent of a [bank draft].

Under this analysis, what is the advantage of such an instrument in comparison to a cheque drawn on the customer's current account? Is the payee of a personal money order exposed to the risk of the instrument being dishonoured by reason of NSF?

A different viewpoint on a personal money order was expressed by the Quebec Provincial Court in *Mohan Goberdhan* v. *Banque Canadienne Nationale* [1978] CP 340. The court regarded the bank as an acceptor and observed (at 341):

> The juridical nature of this personal money order places it in the same category as a cheque under article 165 of the Bills of Exchange Act. In this case the drawer is . . . [the purchaser of the instrument], the beneficiary is . . . [the payee], and Bank is the drawee. This is like a certified cheque because the Bank in inserting the amount in the instrument by its protectograph machine undertakes to pay any holder who presents this for payment the amount indicated on its face.

The court concluded that "once the instrument has been accepted by the Bank and the Bank has guaranteed payment as in the present case, you cannot have a stop payment on a personal money order anymore than you can on a certified cheque. Even if the drawer gave an order to the Bank to stop payment, the Bank cannot refuse to pay" (*id.* at 342).

7   Another event, besides countermand, which determines the bank's authority to pay a cheque drawn on it by its customer is notice of the customer's death (s. 167(*b*)). *Duplisea* v. *T. Eaton Life Assur. Co.* (1979) 7 BLR 24 (SCC) held that s. 167(*b*) does not affect rights on the underlying transaction. Does the provision affect the drawer's liability on the cheque? *Cf.* note 4, *supra*.

2.   PAYMENT OVER EFFECTIVE COUNTERMAND

BARCLAYS BANK LTD. v. W.J. SIMMS SON & COOKE (SOUTHERN) LTD.
[1980] 2 WLR 218, [1979] 3 All ER 522 (QBD)

GOFF J.: This case raises for decision the question whether a bank, which overlooks its customer's instructions to stop payment of a cheque and in consequence pays the cheque on presentation, can recover the money from the payee as having been paid under a mistake of fact. The point is one on which there is no decision in this country; and it is a point, I was told, of considerable importance to bankers, not only because it is an everyday hazard that customers' instructions may be overlooked, but because modern technology, rather than eliminating the risk, has if anything increased it.

The matter comes before the court on agreed facts, which I now propose to set out in this judgment. On June 10, 1971, W.J. Simms Son & Cooke (Southern) Ltd. (which I shall call "the company") granted to National Westminster Bank Ltd. a mortgage debenture which provided, inter alia:

> 2. The company as beneficial owner . . . (v) charges by way of floating security its undertaking and all its other property, assets and rights whatsoever and wheresoever present or future.
>
> 7. At any time after this security shall have become enforceable [National Westminster] may by writing . . . appoint any person . . . to be a receiver of the property hereby charged . . . Any receiver so appointed shall be the agent of the company and the company shall be solely responsible for his acts or defaults and for his remuneration and any receiver so appointed shall have power: (i) to take possession of, collect and get in the property hereby charged and for that purpose to take any proceedings in the name of the company or otherwise . . . (v) to do all such other acts and things he may consider necessary or desirable for the realisation of any property hereby charged.
>
> 8. All moneys received by any receiver shall be applied by him in the following order: (i) in payment of the costs charges and expenses of and incidental to the appointment of the receiver and the exercise of all or any of his powers and of all outgoings paid by him; (ii) in payment of remuneration to the receiver at such rates as may be agreed between him and the bank at or at any time after his appointment; (iii) in or towards satisfaction of the amount owing on this security; (iv) the surplus (if any) shall be paid to the company or other person entitled to it.

The mortgage debenture was registered pursuant to section 95 of the Companies Act 1948, on June 24, 1971.

On June 21, 1976, the company entered into a contract in the R.I.B.A. Standard Form of Building Contract, 1963 edition with the Royal British Legion Housing Association Ltd. (which I shall call "the association") to perform certain works for the association at Borstal Road, Rochester, Kent, for the total sum of £699,024. Clause 25 of the building contract provided:

> (2) In the event of a receiver or manager of his business or undertaking duly appointed, or possession taken, by or on behalf of the holders of any debentures secured by a floating charge, of any property comprised in or subject to the floating

charge, the employment of the contractor under this contract shall be forthwith automatically determined but the said employment may be reinstated and continued if the employer and the contractor his . . . receiver or manager shall so agree. (3) In the event of the employment of the contractor being determined as aforesaid and so long as it has not been reinstated and continued, the following shall be the respective rights and duties of the employer and contractor: (a) The employer may employ and pay other persons to carry out and complete the works . . . (b) The employer may pay any supplier or sub-contractor for any materials or goods delivered or works executed for the purposes of this contract (whether before or after the date of determination) in so far as the price thereof has not already been paid by the contractor. The employer's rights under this paragraph are in addition to his rights to pay nominated sub-contractors as provided in clause 27(c) of these conditions and payments made under this paragraph may be deducted from any such due or to become due to the contractor . . . (d) The contractor shall allow or pay to the employer in the manner hereinafter appearing the amount of any direct loss and/or damage caused to the employer by the determination. Until after completion of the works under paragraph (a) of this sub-clause the employer shall not be bound by any provision of this contract to make any further payment to the contractor, but upon such completion and the verification within a reasonable time of the accounts therefor the architects shall certify the amount of expenses properly incurred by the employer and the amount of any direct loss and/or damage caused to the employer by the determination and, if such amounts when added to the moneys paid to the contractor before the date of determination exceed the total amount which would have been payable on due completion in accordance with this contract, the difference shall be a debt payable to the employer by the contractor; and if the said amounts when added to the said moneys be less than the said total amount, the difference shall be a debt payable by the employer to the contractor.

On September 2, 1977, Messrs. Michael Aukett Associates, the architect under the building contract, issued an interim certificate based on a valuation of works performed at August 25, 1977, certifying that £24,000 was payable under the building contract by the association to the company.

At all material times the association has been a customer of the plaintiffs, Barclays Bank Ltd. at their branch at 78, Victoria Street, London S.W. 1 (which I shall call "the branch").

On Monday, September 12, 1977, the association drew a cheque for £24,000 on its account with Barclays at the branch in favour of the company in payment of the interim certificate. At all material times there were sufficient funds in the account to meet the cheque.

On Tuesday, September 13, 1977, pursuant to the terms of the mortgage debenture, National Westminster appointed Mr. William Sowman, a chartered accountant, to be receiver of the undertaking, property and assets of the company.

On Thursday, September 15, 1977, at 9.20 a.m. the association telephoned the branch and instructed Barclays to stop payment on the cheque. The branch immediately prepared that instruction for the computer which was then programmed accordingly. On the morning of Friday, September 16, 1977, a member of the branch staff checked the computer amendment applied report to ensure that the stop details had been recorded correctly. The association subsequently confirmed its telephone instructions in writing to Barclays.

The cheque was received by Mr. Sowman in the ordinary course of post and his assistant paid in the cheque at the Waddon branch of National Westminster with a direction that the cheque be specially cleared. It is not suggested that in giving such instruction for special clearance or at any time prior to the cheque being specially cleared, Mr. Sowman, or his assistant or the company was aware of the instructions given by the association to Barclays on Thursday, September 15, 1977.

Late on Thursday, September 15, or early on Friday, September 16, 1977, a special presentation from the Waddon branch of National Westminster was received by the branch enclosing the cheque. Details of its presentation were recorded in the Branch Register on Friday, September 16, 1977, and the cheque was paid by the branch that day due to a mistake by the paying official at the branch who overlooked the stop instruction. A credit for National Westminster's special presentation account was sent to National Westminster in the branch credit transfers that evening.

The cheque was rejected by Barclays' computer on Monday, September 19, 1977, the next business day, and was placed to the debit of the computer's suspense account for the work of September 16, 1977. The cheque was subsequently filed with the association's vouchers and its omission from the association's statement was discovered at Barclays' central accounting unit, on Monday, September 19, 1977. On September 27, 1977, Barclays' head office telephoned the branch to state that there was an outstanding item for £24,000. The branch then telephoned the association to establish the reason for payment being countermanded. The association have since confirmed to Barclays, (1) that they heard of the receiver's appointment on about September 14, 1977, and (2) that they decided to stop the cheque in the belief that they were entitled so to act under the building contract.

Barclays subsequently demanded repayment of the cheque from Mr. Sowman who declined to make such repayment. Correspondence ensued between Barclays and its solicitors and Mr. Sowman and his solicitors. The bank subsequently commenced proceedings claiming repayment of the £24,000 from the company and/or Mr. Sowman as moneys paid under a mistake of fact. Mr. Sowman has at all times since December 1977 held £24,000 in a separate account pending a decision in these proceedings.

In the receivership there is likely to be a deficiency as regards the preferential creditors. There will certainly be a substantial deficiency in the receivership for National Westminster, the mortgage debenture-holder.

In the action as constituted, the plaintiff bank claimed to be entitled to recover the money from the first defendants (the defendant company) and the second defendant (the receiver) as money paid under a mistake of fact. Pleadings were served: in the defence, apart from certain non-admissions of fact (which were subsequently resolved in the agreed facts), the substantial point taken by the defendants was that the plaintiff bank were not entitled to recover because there was no mistake of fact between the plaintiffs and the defendants or either of them, alternatively that any mistake or misapprehension of fact was confined to the plaintiffs. This point went to the nature of the mistake necessary to ground recovery, the matter to which the greater part of the argument in the case was devoted; and the defendants' argument on this point was (as will be seen) the subject of some development. . . .

I propose to deal with the matter as follows. I shall first consider the principles upon which money is recoverable on the ground that it has been paid under a mistake of fact. Next, I shall consider the application of those principles to a case where a bank has paid, under a mistake of fact, a cheque drawn upon it by a customer. Third, I shall consider how far the defence in *Cocks* v. *Masterman*, 9 B & C 902 is available to defeat a claim brought by a bank which has paid a cheque under a mistake of fact. Lastly, I shall consider the application of these principles to the present case.

I. *The principles upon which money is recoverable on the ground that it has been paid under a mistake of fact.*

[Goff J. discussed at length the authorities on the subject and continued:]

From this formidable line of authority certain simple principles can, in my judgment, be deduced: (1) If a person pays money to another under a mistake of fact which causes him to make the payment, he is prima facie entitled to recover it as money paid under a mistake of fact. (2) His claim may however fail if (a) the payer intends that the payee shall have the money at all events, whether the fact be true or false, or is deemed in law so to intend; or (b) the payment is made for good consideration, in particular if the money is paid to discharge, and does discharge, a debt owed to the payee (or a principal on whose behalf he is authorised to receive the payment) by the payer or by a third party by whom he is authorised to discharge the debt; or (c) the payee has changed his position in good faith, or is deemed in law to have done so.

To these simple propositions, I append the following footnotes: (a) *Proposition* 1. This is founded upon the speeches in the three cases in the House of Lords, to which I have referred. It is also consistent with the opinion expressed by Turner J. in *Thomas* v. *Houston Corbett & Co.* [1969] NZLR 151, 167. Of course, if the money was due under a contract between the payer and the payee, there can be no recovery on this ground unless the contract itself is held void for mistake (as in *Norwich Union Fire Insurance Society* v. *Wm. H. Price Ltd.* [1934] AC 455) or is rescinded by the plaintiff. (b) *Proposition* 2(*a*). This is founded upon the dictum of Parke B. in *Kelly* v. *Solari*, 9 M & W 54. I have felt it necessary to add the words "or is deemed in law so to intend" to accommodate the decision of the Court of Appeal in *Morgan* v. *Ashcroft* [1938] 1 KB 49, a case strongly relied upon by the defendants in the present case, the effect of which I shall have to consider later in this judgment. (c) *Proposition* 2(*b*). This is founded upon the decision in *Aiken* v. *Short*, 1 H & N 210, and upon dicta in *Kerrison* v. *Glyn, Mills, Currie & Co.*, 81 LJKB 465. However, even if the payee has given consideration for the payment, for example by accepting the payment in discharge of a debt owed to him by a third party on whose behalf the payer is authorised to discharge it, that transaction may itself be set aside (and so provide no defence to the claim) if the payer's mistake was induced by the payee, or possibly even where the payee, being aware of the payer's mistake, did not receive the money in good faith: cf. *Ward & Co.* v. *Wallis* [1900] 1 QB 675, 678-679, *per* Kennedy J. (d) *Proposition* 2(c). This is founded upon the statement of principle of Lord Loreburn L.C. in *Kleinwort Sons & Co.* v. *Dunlop Rubber Co.*, 97 LT 263. I have deliberately stated this defence in broad terms, making no reference to the question whether it is dependent upon a breach of duty by the plaintiff or a representation by him independent of the payment, because these matters do not arise for decision in the present case. I have however referred to the possibility that the defendant may be deemed in law to have changed his position, because of a line of authorities concerned with negotiable instruments which I shall have to consider later in this judgment, of which the leading case is *Cocks* v. *Masterman*, 9 B & C 902. (e) I have ignored, in stating the principle of recovery, defences of general application in the law of restitution, for example where public policy precludes restitution. (f) The following propositions are inconsistent with the simple principle of recovery established in the authorities: (i) That to ground recovery, the mistake must have induced the payer to believe that he was liable to pay the money to the payee or his principal. (ii) That to ground recovery, the mistake must have been "as between" the payer and the payee. Rejection of this test had led to its reformulation (notably by Asquith J. in *Weld-Blundell* v. *Synott* [1940] 2 KB 107 and by Windeyer J. in *Porter* v. *Latec Finance (Qld.) Pty. Ltd.* (1964) 111 CLR 177, 204) in terms which in my judgment mean no more than that the mistake must have caused the payment.

In the case before me, Mr. Evans Lombe submitted on behalf of the defendants that I could not proceed on the basis of the simple principles I have stated, because I was precluded from so doing by binding authority, viz. the decision of the Court of Appeal in *Morgan* v. *Ashcroft* [1938] 1 KB 49. That case came on appeal from the county court. The respondent was a bookmaker, with whom the appellant was in the habit of making bets. The respondent claimed that his clerk mistakenly credited the appellant twice over with a sum of £24 2s. 1d., and claimed to recover that sum from the appellant as having been paid under a mistake of fact. The county court judge held that the respondent was entitled to recover the money. The Court of Appeal allowed the appeal, holding that the money was not recoverable. The first ground of the court's decision was that, in order to ascertain whether there had been an overpayment, it would be necessary for the court to examine the state of account between the parties, and that the court could not do, by reason of the Gaming Act 1845. However the court also held that the money was in any event not recoverable as having been paid under a mistake of fact. Mr. Evans Lombe relied in particular on a passage in the judgment of Sir Wilfrid Greene M.R., in which he stated, at p. 66:

> . . . a person who intends to make a voluntary payment and thinks that he is making one kind of voluntary payment whereas upon the true facts he is making another kind of voluntary payment, does not make the payment under a mistake of fact which can be described as fundamental or basic.

That passage Mr. Evans Lombe identified as being the crucial passage in Sir Wilfrid Greene M.R.'s judgment on this point; and he submitted further that the expression "voluntary payment" must here be understood as a payment made without legal obligation, so that, generally speaking, a person who makes a payment without the intention of discharging a legal obligation cannot recover the money from the payee although it has been paid under a mistake of fact except possibly in circumstances where the mistake can be described as fundamental, for example where the mistake is as to the identity of the payee.

It is legitimate to observe the consequences of Mr. Evans Lombe's submission. If he is right, money would be irrecoverable in the following, by no means far-fetched, situations. (1) A man, forgetting that he has already paid his subscription to the National Trust, pays it a second time. (2) A substantial charity uses a computer for the purpose of distributing small benefactions. The computer runs mad, and pays one beneficiary the same gift one hundred times over. (3) A shipowner and a charterer enter into a sterling charterparty for a period of years. Sterling depreciates against other currencies; and the charterer decides, to maintain the goodwill of the shipowner but without obligation, to increase the monthly hire payments. Owing to a mistake in his office, the increase in one monthly hire payment is paid twice over. (4) A Lloyd's syndicate gets into financial difficulties. To maintain the reputation of Lloyd's, other underwriting syndicates decide to make gifts of money to assist the syndicate in difficulties. Due to a mistake, one syndicate makes its gift twice over. It would not be difficult to construct other examples. The consequences of Mr. Evans Lombe's submission are therefore so far-reaching that it is necessary to examine the ratio decidendi of this part of the decision in *Morgan* v. *Ashcroft* to ascertain whether it produces the result for which Mr. Evans Lombe contends.

Only two judges sat to hear the appeal in *Morgan* v. *Ashcroft* [1938] 1 KB 49 — Sir Wilfrid Greene M.R. and Scott L.J. Furthermore, there are considerable differences between their two judgments on this part of the case. First, there was a difference in the basic philosophy expounded by the two judges. Sir Wilfrid Greene M.R. favoured the so-called "implied contract" theory as the basis of recovery of money paid under a mistake of fact. Citing a well-known dictum of Lord Sumner from *Sinclair* v. *Brougham* [1914] AC 398, 452, he rejected the principle of unjust enrichment and stated that the claim was based upon an imputed promise to repay: [1938] 1 KB 49, 62. Scott L.J. adopted a less restricted view. While accepting that the moral principle of unjust enrichment had been rejected as a universal or complete legal touchstone whereby to test the cause of action, he referred to passages from the works of eminent jurists and concluded, at p. 76, that his citations emphasised:

> the importance of trying to find some common positive principles upon which these causes of action called "implied contracts" can be said to rest, and which will not altogether exclude that of unjust enrichment embodied in those citations.

Scott L.J.'s approach has been amply vindicated by subsequent developments in the law, as is shown in particular by authoritative statements of principle in the House of Lords by Lord Atkin in *United Australia Ltd.* v. *Barclays Bank Ltd.* [1941]

AC 1, 28-29 and by Lord Wright in *Fibrosa Spolka Akcyjna* v. *Fairbairn Lawson Combe Barbour Ltd.* [1943] AC 32, 61.

How far Sir Wilfrid Greene M.R.'s narrower philosophic approach affected his analysis in *Morgan* v. *Ashcroft* [1938] 1 KB 49 is difficult to tell; but there was a further difference between him and Scott L.J., in their view of the nature of the mistake which will ground recovery of money paid under a mistake of fact. Again, Sir Wilfrid Greene M.R. adopted a more restricted view. He founded himself upon the dictum of Bramwell B. in *Aiken* v. *Short*, H & N 210, which he accepted as an authoritative statement of law "so far as regards the class of mistake with which he was dealing," i.e. in "cases where the only mistake is as to the nature of the transaction." From that dictum he deduced the conclusion on which Mr. Evans Lombe relied before me, viz. that if a person thinks that he is making one kind of voluntary payment, whereas on the true facts he is making another kind of voluntary payment, his mistake is not fundamental or basic and therefore cannot ground recovery: see pp. 65-67 of the report. Scott L.J., on the other hand, was not prepared to accept Bramwell B.'s dictum as authoritative; in particular, he referred to *Kerrison* v. *Glyn, Mills, Currie & Co.*, 81 LJKB 465 and said that the decision of the House of Lords in that case seemed to him "conclusive that the rule as stated in *Aiken* v. *Short*, 1 H & N 210 cannot be regarded as final and exhaustive in the sense that no mistake, which does not induce in the mind of the payer a belief that payment will discharge or reduce his liability, can ground an action for money had and received": see pp. 73-74 of the report. In these circumstances it is by no means easy to determine the ratio decidendi of this part of the case. It may well be found in the opinion of both judges that an overpayment of betting debts by a bookmaker is not made under a mistake of fact sufficiently fundamental to ground recovery, apparently on the basis that the payment is in any event intended to be a purely voluntary gift, because "the law prevents the plaintiff from saying that he intended anything but a present" (see p. 77, *per* Scott L.J.), and the plaintiff is therefore deemed in law to intend that the payee shall be entitled to retain the money in any event.

That the ratio decidendi is not to be found in the passage from Sir Wilfrid Greene M.R.'s judgment on which Mr. Evans Lombe relied is shown by the fact that the subsequent decision of the Court of Appeal in *Larner* v. *London County Council* [1949] 2 KB 683 is, in my judgment, inconsistent with that passage. In that case, the London County Council had resolved to pay all their employees who went to the war the difference between their war service pay and their civil pay until further order. Mr. Larner was an ambulance driver employed by the council, who was called up in 1942. As a result of his failure to keep the council accurately informed about changes in his war service pay, the council overpaid the difference. In contending that the overpayment was irrecoverable, Mr. Larner's counsel relied upon the dictum of Bramwell B. in *Aiken* v. *Short*, 1 H & N 210. The Court of Appeal however held that the money was recoverable. Denning L.J., who delivered the judgment of the court, declined to follow that dictum, because he said, at p. 688, ". . . that dictum, as Scott L.J. pointed out in *Morgan* v. *Ashcroft*, cannot be regarded as an exhaustive statement of the law." He pointed out that the council made a promise to the men which they were in honour bound to fulfil. The payments made under that promise were not mere gratuities. They were made as a matter of duty. . . .

but he went on to state that it was irrelevant that the council's promise was unsupported by consideration or unenforceable by action. It was enough that the council would never have paid the money to Mr. Larner had they known the true facts: see p. 688 of the report. It is doubtful if the decision in *Larner* v. *London County Council* [1949] 2 KB 683 is one of which Sir Wilfrid Greene M.R. would have approved; but, if I may say so with respect, it is entirely consistent with the principles of recovery established in the earlier decisions of the House of Lords to which I have referred. Accordingly it is those principles which I intend to apply in the present case.

II. *Where a bank pays a cheque drawn upon it by a customer of the bank, in what circumstances may the bank recover the payment from the payee on the ground that it was paid under a mistake of fact?*

It is a basic obligation owed by a bank to its customer that it will honour on presentation cheques drawn by the customer on the bank, provided that there are sufficient funds in the customer's account to meet the cheque, or the bank has agreed to provide the customer with overdraft facilities sufficient to meet the cheque. Where the bank honours such a cheque, it acts within its mandate, with the result that the bank is entitled to debit the customer's account with the amount of the cheque, and further that the bank's payment is effective to discharge the obligation of the customer to the payee on the cheque, because the bank has paid the cheque with the authority of the customer.

In other circumstances, the bank is under no obligation to honour its customer's cheques. If however a customer draws a cheque on the bank without funds in his account or agreed overdraft facilities sufficient to meet it, the cheque on presentation constitutes a request to the bank to provide overdraft facilities sufficient to meet the cheque. The bank has an option whether or not to comply with that request. If it declines to do so, it acts entirely within its rights and no legal consequences follow as between the bank and its customer. If however the bank pays the cheque, it accepts the request and the payment has the same legal consequences as if the payment had been made pursuant to previously agreed overdraft facilities; the payment is made within the bank's mandate, and in particular the bank is entitled to debit the customer's account, and the bank's payment discharges the customer's obligation to the payee on the cheque.

In other cases, however, a bank which pays a cheque drawn or purported to be drawn by its customer pays without mandate. A bank does so if, for example, it overlooks or ignores notice of its customer's death, or if it pays a cheque bearing the forged signature of its customer as drawer, but, more important for present purposes, a bank will pay without mandate if it overlooks or ignores notice of countermand of the customer who has drawn the cheque. In such cases the bank, if it pays the cheque, pays without mandate from its customer; and unless the customer is able to and does ratify the payment, the bank cannot debit the customer's account, nor will its payment be effective to discharge the obligation (if any) of the customer on the cheque, because the bank had no authority to discharge such obligation.

It is against the background of these principles, which were not in dispute before me, that I have to consider the position of a bank which pays a cheque under a mistake of fact. In such a case, the crucial question is, in my judgment, whether the payment was with or without mandate. The two typical situations, which exemplify payment with or without mandate, arise first where the bank pays in the mistaken belief that there are sufficient funds or overdraft facilities to meet the cheque, and second where the bank overlooks notice of countermand given by the customer. In each case, there is a mistake by the bank which causes the bank to make the payment. But in the first case, the effect of the bank's payment is to accept the customer's request for overdraft facilities; the payment is therefore within the bank's mandate, with the result that not only is the bank entitled to have recourse to its customer, but the customer's obligation to the payee is discharged. It follows that the payee has given consideration for the payment; with the consequence that, although the payment has been caused by the bank's mistake, the money is irrecoverable from the payee unless the transaction of payment is itself set aside. Although the bank is unable to recover the money, it has a right of recourse to its customer. In the second case, however, the bank's payment is without mandate. The bank has no recourse to its customer; and the debt of the customer to the payee on the cheque is not discharged. *Prima facie*, the bank is entitled to recover the money from the payee, unless the payee has changed his position in good faith, or is deemed in law to have done so.

It is relevant to observe that if, in *Chambers* v. *Miller*, 13 CBNS 125, the action had, instead of being a claim by the bearer for damages for false imprisonment, taken the form of a claim by the paying bank for recovery of the money as having been paid under a mistake of fact, that claim would, on the foregoing analysis, have failed, because the mistake of the bank in that case was a mistaken belief that there were sufficient funds in the customer's account to meet the cheque. Similarly in *Pollard* v. *Bank of England* (1871) LR 6 QB 623, where a bank paid a bill of exchange accepted by one of their customers payable at the bank, in ignorance of the fact that the balance of the credit of the acceptors at the bank was insufficient to meet the bill and indeed that the acceptance had, in the general sense, stopped payment (and so were unable to pay their debts, when they fell due), the bank was held to be unable to recover from the payee the money so paid: see p. 631 of the report, *per* Blackburn J., who delivered the judgment of the court. In both these cases, the bank acted within its mandate; but where the bank's mistake relates not to sufficiency of funds in its customer's account, but arises from ignorance or oversight of a notice of countermand, the bank acts without mandate, and the money is in my judgment *prima facie* recoverable.

• • •

IV. *Application of the foregoing principles to the present case.*

In the light of the above principles, it is plain that in the present case the plaintiff bank is entitled to succeed in its claim. First, it is clear that the mistake of the bank, in overlooking the drawer's instruction to stop payment of the cheque, caused the bank to pay the cheque. Second, since the drawer had in fact counter-manded payment, the bank was acting without mandate and so the payment was not effective to discharge the drawer's obligation on the cheque; from this it follows that the payee gave no consideration for the payment, and the claim cannot be defeated on that ground. Third, there is no evidence of any actual change of position on the part of either of the defendants or on the part of the National Westminster Bank; and, since notice of dishonour is not required in a case such as this, the payee is not deemed to have changed his position by reason of lapse of time in notifying them of the plaintiff's error and claiming repayment.

I must confess that I am happy to be able to reach the conclusion that the money is recoverable by the plaintiff bank. If the bank had not failed to overlook its customer's instructions, the cheque would have been returned by it marked "Orders not to pay," and there would have followed a perfectly bona fide dispute between the association and the receiver on the question, arising on the terms of the building contract, whether the association was entitled to stop the cheque — which ought to be the real dispute in the case. If the plaintiff bank had been unable to recover the money, not only would that dispute not have been venti-lated and resolved on its merits but, in the absence of ratification by the associa-tion, the plaintiff bank would have had no recourse to the association. Indeed, if under the terms of the building contract the money had not been due to the defendant company, non-recovery by the plaintiff bank would have meant quite simply a windfall for the preferred creditors of the defendant company at the plaintiff bank's expense. As however I have held that the money is recoverable, the situation is as it should have been; nobody is harmed, and the true dispute between the association and the receiver can be resolved on its merits.

I have however to consider the identity of the party against whom the plaintiff bank is entitled to judgment. As at present advised I am reluctant to enter judgment against the defendant company without further argument. I say that because the argument before me was concentrated on the right of recovery generally, and there was not fully canvassed before me the question whether, assuming that the National Westminster Bank received the payment as agent for the defendant company, an action will lie against its principal to whom the bank had neither paid the money nor done anything equivalent to payment. I will be glad, therefore, to hear submissions from counsel as to how the parties wish the matter to be taken from here.

Judgment for the plaintiff against first defendants.
Action against second defendant dismissed.

Notes:

1   *Shapera* v. *Toronto Dominion Bank* (1970) 13 DLR (3d) 122, 127 (Man. QB) held in favour of a payor bank which had paid over an effective countermand of the customer on the basis inter alia of "equitable doctrines under which a person who pays the debt of another without authority may be allowed the advantage of the payment". The court added that "[t]his equity may be extended, if the circum-stances justify, to a banker who pays a cheque without authority if it is shown that

the payment discharged a legal liability of the customer." In considering the implications of this statement take into account section 165(3) of the BEA. Consider also the following solution in Article 4 of the Uniform Commercial Code:

§4-407. Payor Bank's Right to Subrogation on Improper Payment

If a payor bank has paid an item over the stop payment order of the drawer or maker or otherwise under circumstances giving a basis for objection by the drawer or maker, to prevent unjust enrichment and only to the extent necessary to prevent loss to the bank by reason of its payment of the item, the payor bank shall be subrogated to the rights

(a) of any holder in due course on the item against the drawer or maker; and

(b) of the payee or any other holder of the item against the drawer or maker either on the item or under the transaction out of which the item arose; and

(c) of the drawer or maker against the payee or any other holder of the item with respect to the transaction out of which the item arose.

Compare the theories of *Shapera*, UCC 4-407, and *Simms*. Which do you prefer?

2   Related to the issue of a mistaken payment is the question of certification of a cheque by mistake. For certification in general, see note 5, following *Remfor Industries Ltd.* v. *Bank of Montreal, supra. Falconbridge on Banking*, p. 865, summarizes the position as follows:

> Where a cheque is certified by a bank in error, it may be revoked before there is any change in the position of the parties because of the certification (*v*), where, however, a cheque certified by mistake is in the hands of a holder in due course, who is unaware of any fraud, forgery, etc., the bank is liable (*w*).

Thus, in the absence of a change in the position of the holder, revocation of certification was allowed as against one not a holder in due course where the drawee bank overlooked an effective countermand given by its customer prior to the certification of the cheque, as well as where the drawee bank certifed the cheque while overlooking the fact that the customer had previously closed the account. See *Ken Halnan Motors Ltd.* v. *Imperial Bank* [1963] 1 OR 135 (Co. Ct.); *Nichols* v. *Bank of Montreal* [1963] 1 OR 132 (Dist. Ct.); and *Swartz* v. *Toronto Dominion Bank* (1972) 27 DLR (3d) 42 (Ont. Co. Ct.). According to dictum in the latter decision, the case "where the drawer lacks sufficient funds to cover the amount of the cheque" is an example of a certification by mistake whose revocation is governed by Falconbridge's summary.

What is the effect, if any, of *Barclays Bank* v. *Simms* on this line of cases?

D. ALLOCATION OF FORGERY LOSSES

1. THE BASIC SCHEME

a) The Effect of a Forged Signature

The general rule, provided for in BEA s. 49(1), is that a "forged . . . signature is wholly inoperative, and no right to retain the bill or to give a discharge therefor or to enforce payment thereof against any party thereto can be acquired through or under that signature. . . ." Four results should be noticed:

1.   A person whose signature has been forged is not liable on the instrument (*query:* whether the forger himself is liable). This also follows from s. 131: "No person is liable . . . [on the bill] who has not signed it. . . ."

2.   A forged endorsement does not pass title, or lawful possession, to the transferee. Title and right to possession remain with the holder whose signature has been forged.

3.   A transferee who derives his title, directly or indirectly, through a forged endorsement is not a "holder" in relation to parties whose signatures on the bill preceded the forgery: one cannot be holder without "negotiation" (s. 60(1)); negotiation of a bill payable to order is by "the endorsement of the holder" (s. 60(3)). The forger (and hence anyone who derives title from him) is not a holder. It follows that irrespective of good faith and the giving of value, one who takes the instrument subsequent to a forgery cannot be a "holder in due course" in relation to parties whose signatures preceded the forgery. It is frequently said that forgery is a "real defence" which cannot be overcome by a holder in due course. While this proposition describes correctly the effect of forgery or rights of subsequent parties, it contains a misleading element: insofar as parties whose signatures preceded the forgery are concerned, a party subsequent to the forgery cannot be properly called a "holder in due course". Note however that s. 165(3) can be read (and in fact was read in *Groves-Raffin Construction Ltd.* v. *C.I.B.C.* (1976) 64 DLR (3d) 78 (BC CA)) as changing this result with respect to a depositary bank. It is submitted that this is an erroneous construction of s. 165(3) and that in its true sense the provision has nothing to do with the allocation of forgery losses. *Cf.* Law Reform Commission of Canada, *The Cheque*, Report 11 (1979) p. 14.

4.   The possessor of a bill bearing a forged signature is not entitled to obtain payment from the drawee bank. Nor does payment to him (though made by mistake without notice of the forgery) effectively comply with an order of the customer to the payor bank. Since payment was not made to a "holder", it is not "payment in due course" which discharges the bill (s. 139). Having paid a cheque bearing a forged signature the payor bank cannot lawfully debit the customer's account.

In dealing with allocation of forgery losses it is assumed that the forger himself is unavailable to answer for his wrong-doing. He has either absconded or is insolvent. Alternatively he is unknown. The issue is therefore which of several innocent parties shall absorb the loss.

b)   Detecting the Forgery Before Payment

i)   *Allocation of Loss Created By a Forged Endorsement*

As already noted, a holder from whom an instrument has been stolen, and whose endorsement has been forged, remains the "true owner" of the instrument. Under general principles of law he can sue in conversion, or for money had and received, every person, including every collecting bank, through whom the instrument has passed subsequent to the forgery, whether or not such a person is in posssession of the bill at the time of the action. The issue which arises then is who, as among the parties subsequent to the forgery, bears the ultimate loss.

Where the bill has not been paid, the answer lies in s. 133. An endorser of a bill is precluded from denying "the genuineness and regularity . . . of . . . all previous endorsements" (s. 133(*b*)) as well as that "at the time of his endorsement . . . he had . . . a good title" (s. 133(*c*)). The former preclusion (s. 133(*b*)) runs in favour of a "holder in due course". The latter (s. 133(*c*)) runs in favour of "his immediate or a subsequent endorsee". In relation to prior parties who signed the instrument subsequent to the forgery, the possessor of a bill bearing a forged endorsement is an "immediate or . . . subsequent endorsee" as well as (depending on his compliance with the good faith purchase requirements of s. 56(1)) a potential "holder in due course". The effect of s. 133(*b*) and (*c*) is thus to give the possessor a cause of action on the bill against parties who signed the instrument prior to him but subsequent to the forgery. The one who ultimately bears the loss is therefore the party who took the bill directly from the forger. He is liable on his signature to subsequent parties and is liable in conversion or for money had and received to the one from whom the bill was stolen and whose signature has been forged. Where the forger collected the cheque through the collection system so that the forged endorsement was the last endorsement on delivery of the cheque to the depositary bank, the loser will be the depositary bank.

ii) *Allocation of Loss Caused By a Forged Drawer's Signature*

Insofar as the cheque has not been paid, the taker from the forger also bears the loss in the case of a forged drawer's signature. The preclusion under s. 133(*a*) includes "the genuineness and regularity in all respects of the drawer's signature". The payee (the taker from the forger in the case of a drawer's signature) is the one who is eventually left with this liability.

c) Detecting the Forgery After Payment

i) *Payment Against a Forged Endorsement*

Payment against a forged endorsement makes the payor bank liable to the "true owner" (the person from whom the cheque was stolen and whose endorsement thereon has been forged) in conversion as well as in a claim for money had and received. As payment over a forged endorsement is contrary to the drawer's order, it does not entitle the payor bank to debit the drawer's account with the amount of the instrument. Whether or not the payor bank meets its liability to the true owner, and then lawfully debits the drawer's account, the loss is initially allocated to the bank. Its remedy is provided by s. 50(1): where a cheque bearing a forged endorsement is paid "in good faith and in the ordinary course of business", the payor bank "has the right to recover the amount so paid from the party to whom it was so paid or from any endorser who has endorsed the bill subsequently to the forged . . . endorsement". Under s. 50(2), "[a]ny such person or endorser from whom such amount has been recovered has the like right of recovery against any prior endorser subsequent to the forged . . . endorsement". Alternatively, such a person could sue prior endorsers under s. 133(*b*) and (*c*). See the discussion in 1(b)(i) *supra*. The party who ultimately bears this loss is, again, the taker from the forger. He does not have a "prior endorser subsequent to the forged . . . endorsement" whom he could sue under s. 50(2). Nor can he find any intermediary party against whom he could invoke the estoppel under s. 133(*b*) and (*c*).

Where the payor bank has paid the forger directly, without the intervention of a collecting bank, its only recourse is against the forger. This result is supported by s. 50(1), which speaks of liability of parties who are subsequent to the forgery. Likewise, s. 133(*b*) and (*c*) cannot be invoked in favour of the payor bank and in any event only imposes liability on parties subsequent to the forgery.

ii) *Payment over a Forged Drawer's Signature*

Payment over a forged drawer's signature introduces more complexity. The payor bank is bound to recredit the account of its customer. No right to recover the amount paid on the cheque is specifically provided for under the Act. Section 50(1) is limited to a "bill bearing a forged . . . endorsement". The estoppel under s. 133 does not run in favour of the payor bank. As for general principles of law, presentment of a bill for payment is not a sale of the instrument. No "vendor's warranty" (*cf.* s. 138) therefore runs in favour of the payor bank. The only potential cause of action available to it is a restitutionary claim for monies paid under a mistake of fact. Nonetheless, this course is fraught with difficulties. For more than two hundred years it has been thought that a drawee pays or accepts at his peril. He cannot recover from a bona fide recipient an amount paid on an instrument bearing a forged drawer's signature. This is the doctrine of *Price* v. *Neal* (after *Price* v. *Neal* (1762) 3 Burr. 1354, 97 ER 871) or the principle of finality of payment, applied in Canada in *Bank of Montreal* v. *The King* (1907) 38 SCR 258. See also *Arrow Transfer Co. Ltd.* v. *Royal Bank of Canada* [1972] SCR 858, 878.

The scope of *Price* v. *Neal* and its doctrinal basis were recently curtailed in *National Westminster Bank Ltd.* v. *Barclays Bank International Ltd.* [1975] 1 QB 654, approved in *Barclays Bank Ltd.* v. *W.J. Simms Son & Cook (Southern) Ltd.* [1980] 2 WLR 218 (QBD).

In the *National Westminster Bank* case the court rejected the existence of an absolute duty on the part of a payor bank to know the signature of its customer as well as a duty of care owed by a payor bank to the holder in honouring cheques. The court thus held that a payor bank could recover from a recipient who had not lost a recourse right by virtue of the payor bank's original payment. The court explained and distinguished *Price* v. *Neal* by saying that the recipient there was a subsequent endorsee rather than the original payee on the instrument. The fact that the recipient in *National Westminster Bank* had parted with valuable consideration on the basis of the bank's payment was considered by the court to be immaterial. Payment by a payor bank of an undetectable forged cheque is no representation that the drawer's signature is genuine. It is merely a representation as to the availability of funds in the customer's account. In the absence of negligence, no estoppel by representation could arise on the bank clearing such a cheque whether presented for special collection or cleared in the normal way. Since an endorser is entitled to immediate notice of dishonour (s. 96 *et seq.*) and is released if he is not given it (s. 96(1)), the holder is also entitled to know immediately whether the bill is honoured or dishonoured so that he can give his notice. If the holder is allowed by the drawee to suppose that the bill has been honoured and is deprived of the opportunity to give notice, he is prejudiced by the loss of recourse. (Do you agree? See s. 105.) Payment by the drawee then is final only where made to a recipient who is under a duty to give notice of dishonour. Where no loss of recourse (by virtue of failure to give a timely notice of dishonour) is involved, the payor bank is free to go ahead and recover from the recipient. The only recipient without a recourse right (and hence without a duty to give notice of dishonour) is ultimately the payee.

Is a payee who collects through a collecting bank entitled to notice of dishonour? See *Bank of Nova Scotia* v. *Sharp*, chapter 17(A) *supra*.

2. Exceptions to the Basic Scheme

The scheme so far discussed is subject to the following exceptions:

a) Payment over a Forged Endorsement: The Drawer's Duty To Give Notice Under s. 49(3)

A payor bank which has paid a cheque "upon a forged endorsement out of the funds of the drawer" is not liable to the customer-drawer "unless [the drawer] gives notice in writing of such forgery to the drawee within one year after he has acquired notice of the forgery" (s. 49(3)). Absent the giving of this notice, the loss is allocated to the drawer: the "cheque shall be held to have been paid in due course as respects every other party thereto or named therein, who has not previously instituted proceedings for the protection of his rights" (s. 49(4)). Note that s. 49(3) and (4) only applies to cheques. The other provisions governing the allocation of forgery losses deal with bills. By virtue of s. 186 they apply to promissory notes as well. Section 49(3) and (4) does not apply to promissory notes or bills of exchange which are not cheques as defined in s. 165(1).

b) Payment over a Forged Endorsement: The Payor Bank's Duty To Give Notice Under s. 50(1)

Recovery by the payor bank under s. 50(1) is subject to the giving of notice "of the endorsement being a forged . . . endorsement" to the party from whom recovery is sought (s. 50(1)). The notice "shall be given within a reasonable time after the . . . [payor bank] has acquired notice that the endorsement is forged . . .and may be given in the same manner, and if sent by post may be addressed in the same way, as notice of protest or dishonour of a bill may be given or addressed . . ." (s. 50(3)). Absent the giving of such notice, the loss remains with the payor bank.

c) The Fictitious Payee Exception: s. 21(5)

A bill whose payee is "a fictitious or non-existing person . . . may be treated as payable to bearer: (s. 21(5)). The possessor of a stolen bill payable to bearer ("the bearer thereof'') may be a "holder" (see definition of "holder" in s. 2 and s. 60(2)). Hence he can be a "holder in due course" with a good title thereto (s. 74(*b*)). As a holder in due course he is not liable to the person from whom the bill was stolen. Payment to such a holder in due course discharges the bill and entitles the payor bank to debit the account of its customer. The loss is thus borne by the person from whom the instrument was stolen. The effect of s. 21(5) is thus to equate the forgery of an endorsement of "a fictitious or non-existing person" to the theft of a bill payable to bearer.

While the effect of s. 21(5) is quite clear, there is no indication in the Act as to when a bill falls within the ambit of the provision. The rules developed in the case law go back to *Bank of England* v. *Vagliano* [1891] AC 107 (HL). They provide that a payee who is either a creature of imagination or a dead person is "non-existing". A payee who is a real person and whose name is inserted by the drawer by way of pretence, with no intention that he will receive payment, is "fictitious". A payee who is a real person and is intended by the drawer to receive payment, but whose name is inserted because of the fraud of a third person who falsely represents that the drawer is indebted to such payee, is neither "fictitious" nor "non-existing". A bill payable to such a person falls outside s. 21(5). Where the payee's endorsement on such a bill is forged (typically by the third person who induced the drawer to draw the instrument), the case is governed by the general scheme applicable to forged endorsements. The intention of the drawer (or more accurately, of the one who signs as a drawer) determines whether the payee is "fictitious" but not whether he is "non-existing". "Existence" is an objective fact which has nothing to do with the drawer's intention. For recent critical analyses of the fictitious payee section, see: B. Geva, "The Fictitious Payee and Payroll Padding: (1978) 2 Can. Bus. LJ 418 (a commentary on the decision of the Supreme Court of Canada in *Royal Bank of Canada* v. *Concrete Column Clamps (1961) Ltd.* (1976) 74 DLR (3d) 26) and generally Peter Salvatori, "*Vagliano's Case* Revisited" (1979) 3 Can. Bus. LJ 296.

d) Preclusion from Setting Up Forgery: s. 49(1) Estoppel

A party to a cheque may be estopped from raising the defence of forgery. This is provided for in s. 49(1) itself: "where a signature on a bill is forged . . . the forged . . . signature is wholly inoperative . . . unless the party against whom it is sought to retain or enforce payment of the bill is precluded from setting up the forgery. . . ." The following types of estoppel should be considered:

i) *Estoppel by Representation or Conduct*

Failure to notify the drawee bank or the holder of the forgery was the ground of estoppel in *Greenwood* v. *Martins Bank Ltd.* [1933] AC 51 (AC); *Ewing* v. *Dominion Bank* (1904) 35 SCR 133; and *Ontario Woodsworth Memorial Foundation* v. *Grozbord* (1966) 58 DLR (2d) 21 (Ont. CA); aff'd [1969] SCR 622. The essential elements of such an estoppel are:

(1) A representation or conduct amounting to representation intended to induce a course of conduct on the part of whom the representation is made.

(2)   An act or omission resulting from the representation, whether actual or by conduct, by the person to whom the representation is made.

(3)   Detriment to such person is a consequence of the act or omission.

(*Greenwood* v. *Martin Bank Ltd. supra* at 57). While admitting that "[m]ere silence cannot amount to a representation", the court added that "when there is a duty to disclose . . . deliberate silence may become significant and amount to representation": *id.* at 57. Such a duty is easily admitted in the case of a customer-drawee bank relationship. It is less apparent when the duty is sought to be invoked in favour of a holder.

ii)   *Estoppel by Negligence*

The authority of a drawee bank to debit the account of the drawer for the full amount of a cheque that was negligently drawn so as to permit its subsequent alteration by the insertion of words and figures without erasures was established in England in *Young* v. *Grote* (1827) 4 Bing 253, 130 ER 764. It was later on stated by the House of Lords that the "sole ground upon which *Young* v. *Grote* was decided . . . was that Young was a customer of the bank owing to the bank the duty of drawing his cheque with reasonable care" (*London Joint Stock Bank* v. *MacMillan* [1918] AC 777, 793 *per* Lord Finlay L.C.). Estoppel by negligence presupposes the existence of a duty of care: *Swan* v. *North British Australasian Co.* (1863) 2 HC 175, 192, 159 ER 73 (Ex. Ct.) *per* Blackburn J.

English courts have confined the drawer's duty of care to the customer-drawee bank relationship. As a result the duty cannot be invoked in favour of a subsequent holder, including a subsequent holder that is a collecting bank. The duty of care has also been confined to acts or omissions with regard to the drawing and signing of cheques: "the negligence must be in the transaction itself, that is, in the manner in which the cheque is drawn": *London Joint Stock Bank* v. *MacMillan, supra,* at 795. No duty has been recognized in the English cases, even towards the drawee bank, to exercise reasonable care (a) in the general course of carrying on business (including in the selection of employees) so as to detect and prevent forgeries, or (b) in relation to the examination of the periodical bank statements, so as to discover and report forgeries and prevent a repetition thereof. A drawer is also not required to conduct his business in such a way so as to prevent the forgery of the payee's endorsement (before the delivery of the cheque to the payee) by the drawer's own employee. For a critique of these rules, see Geva, "The Fictitious Payee and Payroll Padding" (1978) 2 Can. Bus. LJ 418, 426 *et seq.*

The minority opinion of Laskin J. (as he then was) in *Arrow Transfer Co. Ltd.* v. *Royal Bank of Canada* [1972] SCR 845 (*infra*) represents a significant departure from the traditional narrow perspective given to the drawer's duty of care. Laskin J. opined there that the imposition of a bank customer's duty "to examine bank statements with reasonable care and to report account discrepancies within a reasonable time" was overdue (*id.* at 873). On the facts of the case, Laskin J. found the customer negligent in employing an untrustworthy employee in a sensitive position as well as in employing inadequate procedures for discovering fraud. See also the dissent of Spence J. in *Royal Bank of Canada* v. *Concrete Column Clamps (1961) Ltd.* (1976) 74 DLR (3d) 26 (SCC), finding a drawer liable for the loss caused by the forgery of the payee's endorsement by a dishonest clerk of the drawer on the basis that "it would have been quite easy [for the drawer] in proper office management to have designed sufficient methods of checking and verifying to have defeated [the drawer's dishonest clerk's] scheme" (*id.* at 46). Likewise, in *Number 10 Management Ltd.* v. *Royal Bank of Canada* (1976) 69 DLR (3d) 99 (Man. CA), Monnin J.A. spoke of "a duty on a bank's customer to examine bank documents regularly and to report discrepancies in such documents within a reasonable time of any discovery of error or forgery".

It remains to be seen whether this departure from the traditional restrictive view on the drawer's duty of care will gain universal acceptance.

iii) *Estoppel by Contract*

In *Arrow Transfer Co. Ltd.* v. *Royal Bank of Canada* [1972] SCR 845 *infra*, the majority of the Supreme Court (*per* Martland J.) read a verification agreement between the customer and the drawee bank as precluding the customer from setting up the forgery of his own signature. The verification agreement used broad language: it required the customer to notify the bank of any debits wrongly made in the account within a specified period after the receipt of each periodical statement of account from the bank. Unless the customer gave such notification, at the end of the stipulated period the account presented by the bank became conclusive. In his dissent, Laskin J. held that the language of the agreement was not sufficiently unambiguous to protect the bank in the event of a forged drawer's signature. The other justices relied on the agreement as a means of circumventing the effect of their own refusal to recognize a customer's duty of care to examine bank statements and to report forgeries that should have been discovered by such an examination.

3. THE CUSTOMER AND THE DEPOSITARY BANK: CAN THE CUSTOMER CIRCUMVENT THE ESTOPPEL EXCEPTION?

A customer whose signature as a drawer was forged, and who had failed to examine properly the bank statements and report the forgery, attempted in *Arrow Transfer* and in *Number 10 Management* to sue the depositary bank in conversion or for money had and received. The attempts failed. The courts reasoned that no valuable assets of the customer (namely cheques having their own value) passed through the collecting bank. As explained by Laskin J., in order to succeed the plaintiff must be the true owner of the piece of paper *qua cheque*, not merely *qua piece of paper*. In both these cases, therefore, a customer who lost against the payor bank was unsuccessful in seeking to shift the loss onto the depositary bank.

A similar result was reached in the U.S. in a case involving a cheque, bearing a genuine drawer's signature, that was stolen from the drawer by an unfaithful employee of the drawer. The unfaithful employee forged the payee's signature and collected the proceeds of the cheque from the payor bank through a depositary bank. In dismissing the drawer's action against the depositary bank the court opined that since the drawer did not have the right of a holder to present the cheque to the drawee for payment, he had no "valuable rights" in it and therefore was not entitled to sue in conversion. The "value of [the drawer's] rights was limited to the physical paper on which [the cheques] were written": *Stone & Webster Engineering Corp.* v. *First National Bank & Trust Co.* (1962) 184 NE 2d 358 (Mass.). For a recent discussion, see Williams, (1980) 31 Hastings LJ 221.

On the other hand, in a similar fact situation an Ontario High Court judge upheld the drawer's action against the collecting bank in conversion as well as for money had and received; *Jervis B. Webb of Canada Ltd.* v. *Bank of Nova Scotia and Reid* (1965) 2 OR 100 (Ont. HC). "As a matter of first impression", Fraser J. "was disposed to be of the opinion that the plaintiff [drawer] could have no right to recover directly against the defendant [depositary] bank as in the absence of . . . estoppel the . . . [payor bank] had no prima facie right to debit the account of the plaintiff with amounts paid or forged endorsements." However, after considering numerous authorities, Fraser J. became "satisfied that where, as here, the defendant has wrongfully appropriated cheques of the plaintiff, the plaintiff is entitled to recover the amount of the cheque as damages for the conversion, or, in the alternative, for monies had and received to the use of the plaintiff unless the plaintiff has in some ways precluded or estopped itself from setting up that forgery": *id.* at 107. It would appear, however, that none of the authorities relied on by Fraser J. actually compelled this result.

For a recent discussion of forged cheques see Rafferty, "Forged Cheques: A Consideration of the Rights and Obligations of Banks and Their Customers" (1980) 4 Can. Bus. LJ 208.

ARROW TRANSFER CO. LTD. v. ROYAL BANK OF CANADA
[1972] SCR 845, 27 DLR (3d) 81

MARTLAND J.: This is an appeal from the unanimous judgment of the Court of Appeal for British Columbia, which dismissed the appellant's appeal from the trial judgment.

The appellant's claim was made in respect of 73 forged cheques which, over a period of five years, had been paid out by the respondent, the Royal Bank of Canada, hereinafter referred to as "Royal", and which had been debited to the appellant's account with that bank. The total amount of these cheques was $165,109.03. Of these cheques, the forger, Seear, an employee of the appellant, had deposited with the respondent, Bank of Montreal, hereinafter referred to as "Montreal", cheques in the total amount of $128,418.23, on which Montreal had collected that amount from Royal.

Seear, in 1963, had become chief accountant and office manager of the appellant. His practice was to use the appellant's printed blank cheque forms, by filling in the name of a payee, or cash, and an amount. He would forge the signatures of the appellant's officers authorized to sign its cheques. He cashed the cheques made payable to cash at the Royal. Some of the others were deposited with Montreal to the credit of certain trade names adopted by Seear. From time to time he withdrew the moneys in these accounts. It was not until May, 1968, that an audit revealed that the 73rd of the cheques above mentioned, in the amount of $9,077.14, was a forgery, and notice was then given to Royal.

In 1962, the appellant had entered into an agreement with Royal in the following terms:

> In consideration of THE ROYAL BANK OF CANADA (hereinafter called the "Bank") opening or continuing an account with the undersigned, the undersigned hereby agrees with the Bank in respect of each account with the undersigned now or hereafter kept by the Bank at any of its branches or agencies to verify the correctness of each statement of account received from the Bank and if a statement of account and relative vouchers are not received by the 10th day after the end of each month or, if statements are not to be prepared monthly, by the 10th day after the end of the term agreed on for their preparation to obtain them from the Bank and within 30 days after the time when they should have been received to notify the Bank in writing at the branch or agency where the account is kept of any alleged omissions from or debits wrongly made to or inaccurate entries in the account as so stated and that at the end of the said 30 days the account as kept by the Bank shall be conclusive evidence without any further proof that except as to any alleged errors so notified and any payments made on forged or unauthorized endorsements the account contains all credits that should be contained therein and no debits that should not be contained therein and all the entries therein are correct and subject to the above exception the Bank shall be free from all claims in respect of the account.
>
> Dated at .... Vancouver ...., this .... 6th .... day of .... August 1962
>
> ARROW TRANSFER CO. LTD. General A/C
> (Sgd.) J. W. Charles
> (Sgd.) G. T. Campbell
>
> ....

The primary claim of the appellant against Royal was that it had paid out the total amount in question without authority from the appellant. Royal's defence to this claim was based upon the agreement set out above, hereinafter referred to as the "verification agreement". No notice to Royal had been given by the appellant within the time prescribed in the agreement in respect of any of the forged cheques, except only the last one. The appellant recovered judgment in the amount of that cheque, i.e., $9,077.14, but its action in respect of the remainder of its claim, i.e., $156,031.89, was dismissed.

The claim of the appellant against Montreal was for $128,418.23 as money had and received by it to the use of the appellant, or alternatively, as damages for conversion of that amount. This claim was dismissed.

I agree with the opinions expressed in the Court of Appeal that the verification agreement provided Royal with a complete defence to the action. That agreement is a contract, defining the terms upon which the bank continued the account of the appellant. The appellant agreed to verify each statement of account which it received from the bank, and, within the period specified, to notify the bank of debits wrongly made in the account. At the end of the stipulated period the account as kept by the bank became conclusive evidence that it contained no debits that should not be contained in it, subject to only two exceptions:

1. errors of which timely notice had been given to the bank;
2. payments made on forged or unauthorized endorsements.

The debits entered in the appellant's account in respect of the forged cheques paid by Royal were "debits wrongly made". The payment was not made on a forged endorsement. Except as to the last of the 73 cheques, the appellant failed to give the required notice as to debits wrongly made. As to the first 72 cheques, the account became conclusive evidence that it contained no debits that it should not have contained, and Royal was freed from any claim in respect of them.

I do not agree with the contention that the words "debits wrongly made" do not apply in respect of a forged cheque. The obligation of the customer to give notice to the bank within the prescribed period relates to any debit wrongly made, and it is clear that it is wrong for a bank to debit a customer's account in respect of the payment of a forged cheque. In the absence of the verification agreement, a bank which debited a customer's account in respect of a forged cheque would be liable to him. The agreement furnishes some protection to the bank in that the customer must check the account and the relevant vouchers and give prompt notice if he is to enforce that liability against the bank. I see no reason to limit the meaning of the words "debits wrongly made". They apply to any debit to the account which the bank was wrong in making.

There is the further fact that the verification agreement does refer to forgery, in relation to payments made on forged endorsements. Such payments are within one of the two exceptions to the conclusive nature of the account. The fact that a specific exception was created in respect of a forgery of that kind indicates that the agreement is applicable in respect of a debit wrongly made in relation to a cheque on which the signature of the drawer is forged. . . .

The verification agreement in question in the present case is not ambiguous. It is a contract under which the customer undertakes a duty to the bank to disclose within a limited period, among other things, debits wrongly made. In the present case, the appellant received the statements and the relevant vouchers. Having failed to perform his contractual duty, the agreement made the statements conclusive evidence against him. . . .

There has been one case in this Court dealing with the liability of a bank which had charged its customer's account with the amounts of forged cheques, i.e., *Bank of Montreal* v. *The King* (1906) 38 SCR 258. The cheques had been forged by a clerk employed by the Government of Canada. Periodically, the cheques, after payment, were received by the Government and a receipt was given to the bank therefor, together with an acknowledgment of the correctness of the balance as shown by the bank's statement. While the bank was held liable in that case, it does not, in my opinion, have any bearing in the present appeal. The essential distinction is that there was no contract on the part of the customer in that case to verify the statement of account, and to accept it as conclusive unless any errors were notified to the bank within a stipulated period. The bank relied on the signed acknowledgments, not on the basis of contract, but as creating an estoppel. The majority of the Court based their decision on the proposition that estoppel could not be invoked against the Crown. . . .

In my opinion the claim against Royal in respect of the first 72 cheques is completely answered by the verification agreement.

With respect to the claim against Montreal, I am in agreement with the reasons of Robertson, J.A., in the Court of Appeal, and with the reasons of my brother Laskin in this Court. In so far as the claim is for moneys had and received, the moneys received by Montreal in respect of the forged cheques were not those of the appellant, but were paid to Montreal by Royal. Royal was not entitled to charge those moneys to the appellant's account, and would have had to assume responsibility for their payment, save for the protection afforded to it by the verification agreement.

The claim for conversion has to be based upon the conversion of a valuable instrument of the appellant (*Morison* v. *London County and Westminster Bank, Ltd.* [1914] 3 KB 356 at p. 365; *Lloyd's Bank, Ltd.* v. *Chartered Bank of India, Australia and China* [1929] 1 KB 40 at p. 55). In this case, however, there was no conversion of the appellant's cheques. There was a conversion by Seear of the blank cheque forms of the appellant, but the signature of the drawer was a forgery, and the cheques were not payable to the appellant. Montreal did not convert cheques of the appellant.

For the same reasons the alternative claim in conversion against Royal also fails.

LASKIN J.: This [verification] . . . agreement replaced an earlier practice under which the appellant signed a verification form only after it had picked up or had delivered to it a statement of account and related cheques or vouchers. This form also provided for a 30-day period within which the bank was to be notified of errors, omissions or irregularities on pain, save as to forged or unauthorized endorsements, of the appellant being conclusively bound by the statement thereafter. I do not find much profit in disputation on whether the verification agreement in issue here was simply part of the contractual arrangement between the parties thereto or whether it was an exemption provision in their contractual relations. What is plain is that the verification agreement does not embrace the whole of the contractual relationship of the parties; it focuses on a part of it, albeit an important part, and in so doing it modifies the liabilities of the bank to its customer that would otherwise arise out of the fact of their relationship. That relationship is itself, of course, founded upon agreement but there was no suggestion before this Court that, apart from the verification document, the agreement was anything more than the manifested willingness of the one party to open an account for the other at the latter's request.

The issue, therefore, which the verification agreement raises is the extent to which it has modified liabilities of the bank which would have existed without it; and particularly, whether it relieves the bank of liability to answer for the consequences of successfully executed forgeries of a customer's signature as drawer of cheques against its account which the bank honours, where the customer does not give notice of such forgeries to the bank within the prescribed 30-day period. It is, of course, part of the bank's case that if the verification agreement includes in its scope forgeries of the customer's signature as drawer, there is no alleviation in the fact that the forgeries were not discovered nor reasonably discoverable within the said 30-day period.

The Royal Bank invokes in its favour a line of cases beginning with *Columbia Graphophone Co.* v. *Union Bank of Canada* (1916), 34 DLR 743, 38 OLR 326.

• • •

One distinction that emerges from the run of cases is that between a mere signed acknowledgment of the correctness of the account as a periodic settlement and a specific undertaking by the customer to examine the statement and vouchers and to make timely objection; it is the distinction between the form in *Bank of Montreal* v. *The King, supra* (and see also the earlier case of *Agricultural Investment Co.* v. *The Federal Bank* (1880) 45 UCQB 214; aff'd (1881) 6 OAR 192 *sub nom. Agricultural Savings & Loan Ass'n* v. *Federal Bank*), and that in the *Columbia Graphophone* case. I have no doubt of the significance of the distinction; it depended, however, on a strict view of the acknowledgment form. In the *Agricultural Savings* case, Burton, J.A., referred to the form therein as "at most a mere acknowledgment of the correctness of the balance on the assumption that the cheques issued by the plaintiffs had been paid to the proper parties" (6 OAR at p. 200). The question here is whether that very fact does not make it evident that if the bank is to rely on a verification contract it must be able to point to words in the contract that leave no doubt of the scope of the protection which it claims.

That this is the proper answer to the question finds some support in s. 49(1) of the Bills of Exchange Act. That clause provides that a forged signature on a bill is wholly inoperative, and no right to enforce payment of the bill can be acquired through such a signature unless the party against whom it is sought to enforce payment is precluded from setting up the forgery. It is not that s. 49(1) is of that class of statutes from whose terms there can be no contractual departure. Rather, its express reference to a forged signature appears to me to oblige those who would contract out to make it quite clear that forgery of a drawer's signature on a cheque is within the scope of the protection that a drawee bank has obtained under its self-protecting contractual arrangements with its depositors.

Apart from any verification agreement, a bank would be answerable for depletion of a customer's account by reason of any unauthorized dealing, including forgery, unless the drawer was precluded from setting up the want of authority, and the bank would be protected to the degree to which any such preclusion extended. Similarly, apart from a verification agreement, the bank would be answerable for forgery or unauthorized milking of a customer's account by an employee of the bank; and in this latter respect, the matter would not necessarily depend on principles of vicarious liability but rather would stem from the bank's obligation to maintain the integrity of a customer's account against unauthorized withdrawals.

The Royal Bank's position on the verification agreement is such that it would place upon a customer the duty to detect within the prescribed 30-day period not only forgeries of the customer's signature by the latter's employees or by third parties, but also by employees of the Royal Bank. There is the further hurdle, if literalness is to prevail, that it is the account as kept by the bank that has the conclusive effect, regardless of what may have been delivered or not delivered to the customer by way of statements or vouchers.

Forgery and unauthorized debits to a customer's acount owing to the forgery or fraud of third persons or of employees do not exhaust a bank's liability. There is the quite ordinary case of arithmetic error, of failure to credit sums to an account, of wrongful albeit innocent attribution of debits to an account. These are possible, even if infrequent; perhaps as infrequent as forgery and fraud. These instances of breach of obligation to a customer relate directly to what the bank has sought to achieve through the verification agreement. In my opinion, the principal question is not whether the bank has sought to protect itself against its breach of a fundamental term of its relationship with its customer, but rather what is the scope of protection which it has achieved under a document which is more a contract of adhesion than a bargained arrangement.

Neither forgery nor fraud are expressed as risks of the customer. The key words are "verify the correctness" of statements of account received from the bank; "notify the bank in writing . . . of any alleged omissions from or debits wrongly made to or inaccurate entries in the account". It is in respect of these, unless there is timely notice, that "the account as kept by the bank shall be conclusive evidence" that it is correct, and that, subject to what is excepted (this includes "payments made on forged or unauthorized endorsements"), the bank is to be free "from all claims in respect of the account".

I find it strange that a bank which seeks by contract to throw the risk of all forged drawer signatures upon its customer should be so reticent about referring expressly to such an eventuality. It is not as if its verification form lacks subject-matter without it. The verification form, as a matter of words, encompasses the situation which arose in *Union Bank of Canada* v. *Wood*. Beyond this or related situations, it surely is, to say the least, "ambiguous" (to use the term applied by Duff, J., in the *Stewart* case) in any suggested application to forgery or fraud. There is every reason to construe it *contra proferentem*, and I would therefore conclude that its words do not provide protection against the forgery of the drawer's signature.

The construction that I would put on the verification agreement is consistent with the approach to contractual limitations of liability in other kinds of relationships, such as bailee and bailor, carrier and consignor, retailer and purchaser. Risks that are by contract to be passed by a party, upon whom they would otherwise rest, to the other party to the relationship must be brought home expressly if they are to be effective; at least this is so when the limitation would still have subject-matter if unexpressed risks be found to be outside its general language.

There remains on this phase of the case the question whether the bank is in any event entitled to rest on the principle of an account stated or a settled acount or whether, if the relations between the parties do involve a stated or settled account, the appellant is entitled to reopen it to show unauthorized debits. The trial Judge dealt with this issue by declaring that "[the verification] contract does much more than create settled accounts . . .If this case involved a mere settled acount I would not think the injustice necessary to open such an account has been displayed". The key to this conclusion appears to be in the trial Judge's finding that "there was no step the bank could have taken to guard against this loss and there were many steps the plaintiff could have taken, any one of which would have discovered the earlier losses and prevented the later large losses" [see 9 DLR (3d) 693 at pp. 697-8, 72 WWR 19]. The basis of this finding is not spelled out until a later part of his reasons where the trial Judge dealt with a claim in negligence against the Bank of Montreal (a claim not pursued on appeal), and indicated that he would have found (were it necessary to do so) that the appellant's negligence was the primary cause of its loss. I shall return to this point later in these reasons.

In the course of his reasons for judgment in the House of Lords' decision in *Camillo Tank Steamship Co. Ltd.* v. *Alexandria Engineering Works* (1921) 38 TLR 134 at p. 143, Lord Cave classified three types of accounts stated. His third class was one "where a claim has been made by one party, and the other party has for valuable consideration agreed to accept it as correct. . . . This is a real agreed account, and . . . cannot be reopened except for fraud or on some other ground which would enable a party to an agreement to have it set aside". Lord Wright speaking for the Judicial Committee in *Firm Bishun Chand* v. *Seth Girdhari Lal* (1934) 50 TLR 465 at pp. 468-9, was more pointed in asserting that "it has not been doubted that in law there can be a settled or stated account between banker and customer". He went on to say that "what has been questioned is whether the acceptance by the customer without protest of a balance struck in the passbook constitutes a settled account, but the question has had reference merely to the issue whether such a settlement can be inferred as a matter of fact from the passing backward and forward of the pass-book. The legal competence of such a settlement, if made, is not questioned".

In the present case, the reliance on the verification agreement as establishing a settled account which is unchallengeable must fail because, on the construction I have put on the agreement, there was no settlement made that covered forgery of the drawer's signature. The settlement could go no farther than the document under which it was asserted.

Is then the Royal Bank's only defence to the claim of the appellant that the latter is (to refer to what is stated in s. 49(1) of the Bills of Exchange Act) precluded from setting up any or all of the forgeries? In examining the scope of this defence and in bringing the facts of this case into relation thereto, I begin by saying here what I might have said as conveniently much earlier in these reasons, that the adoption of verification receipts and verification agreements in this country appeared to be a response to judicial reluctance to impose upon a depositor a duty to examine bank statements and to report any discrepancies within a reasonable period.

Such a duty was imposed in the United States, the leading authority being *Leather Manufacturers' National Bank* v. *Morgan* (1885) 117 US 96. It goes beyond the holding of a customer to answer for a forgery of which he had knowledge and failed to inform the bank. The Uniform Commercial Code, of almost universal application in the United States, has spelled out this duty in some detail in s. 4-406. . . . *Halsbury's Laws of England*, 3rd ed., vol. 2, at p. 210, states that the authorities in England are conflicting on "whether there is or is not a duty on the part of the customer to examine the pass-book and paid cheques, if returned with it, and to communicate to the banker within reasonable time all debits which he does not admit". *Kepitigalla Rubber Estates, Ltd.* v. *National Bank of India, Ltd.* [1909] 2 KB 1010, is cited as supporting the view that there is no such duty, unless it is imposed by express stipulation. It was a case where a company, a customer of defendant bank, recovered the amounts of a number of cheques on which the drawer signatures were forged by the company's secretary and which had been debited to the company. The significance of the *Kepitigalla* case for Canada is that it was referred to with approval by Middleton, J., in the *Columbia Graphophone* case. There Middleton, J., noted that a duty to the bank may arise after a customer has knowledge of a forgery. *Ewing* v. *Dominion Bank* (1904) 35 SCR 133 (leave to appeal refused [1904] AC 806) goes far in this respect in its holding, by a bare majority, that a person may come under a duty to a bank where he is informed that a note of his, which was in fact forged, and which the bank had discounted, was coming due; and he may incur liability if he does not respond and in the result the proceeds thereof are withdrawn. I point out that the case was dealt with in terms of estoppel which involved turning the so-called duty into a representation by silence.

I do not think it is too late to fasten upon bank customers in this country a duty to examine bank statements with reasonable care and to report account discrepancies within a reasonable time. The Supreme Court of California in *Pacific Coast Cheese, Inc.* v. *Security First National Bank of Los Angeles* (1955) 286 P 2d 353, has stated the applicable principle as follows (at p. 355):

> The general rule is that a bank may not charge its depositor's account with payments made on altered or forged checks unless some conduct of the depositor falling under the principles of negligence or estoppel contributed to the loss *and* the bank was itself free from negligence. . . . This rule has been applied where, as here, the alteration or forgery was committed by an employee of the depositor. . . . When it appears that a bank has made payment on the basis of an altered or forged check, the burden is on the bank to justify the charge by establishing, as an affirmative defense, both that it was free from negligence and that the depositor was negligent or was estopped to deny the correctness of the payments.

This principle would be consistent with the duty of which I speak, a duty that would not, however, be as Draconian as that which the bank has sought to fasten upon the appellant under the verification agreement. . . .

The facts found in the present case go, however, beyond any failure to meet the duty that I have suggested, and hence make it unnecessary for me to determine how many of the forgeries would have to be borne by the bank by reason of a breach of duty which arose only in relation to the submission of statements of account to the appellant. The trial Judge absolved the bank of any negligence in relation to the forgeries, which were skilfully executed, and dealing with the appellant's conduct of its business, he made the following findings [9 DLR (3d) 693 at pp. 705-6, 72 WWR 19]:

> The plaintiff employed a person they knew had been found to be untrustworthy in the past and placed him in a position of complete trust where no one checked upon

his work adequately. The procedures followed by the plaintiff and its auditors were inadequate to discover the fraud and to discover that its books had not balanced for a number of years. Cheques remain today in which the duplicate shows one payee and the original another. The accounts payable had not balanced for years. In each of the months in which there was a forged cheque Mr. Seear was permitted to extract the cheque and complete the balancing. He was a very personable fellow, well trained in accounting. If the plaintiff had employed proper procedures it seems reasonable to expect that it would have discovered some of the forgeries, that its bank's returns did not balance in many months, that its accounts payable did not balance, or that its cheques were not in accordance with the duplicate register. One would have expected that in an organization handling money in the amounts that this plaintiff handled, no person would be so wholly entrusted with responsibility that no other person's duties would involve a check upon him. In this case the plaintiff knew that the person in that position had been discharged from his former employment because it was found that he could not be trusted.

On these findings, relating as they do to the particular facts of this case, I am of the opinion that the appellant is precluded from claiming against the Royal Bank on any of the seventy-two cheques which are the subject of its action.

This conclusion is enough to dispose of the alternative claims against this bank for money had and received and for conversion. I do not pause to examine the appropriateness of these causes of action to a claim made by a customer against its bank. What is obvious is that the appellant cannot be in any better position on his alternative causes of action than he is on his main allegation. It would require mounting fiction upon fiction by way of ignoring the findings of fact to conclude that the bank has improperly retained money (or improperly debited the account) of the appellant, or has made a wrongful appropriation of assets of the appellant so as to be guilty of tortious conduct.

The claim of the appellant against the Bank of Montreal, the collecting bank, for conversion, or alternatively, for money had and received, was rejected by the trial Judge on the ground that the principle of *Price* v. *Neal* (1762) 3 Burr. 1354, 97 ER 871; (1761) 1 Black W. 390, 96 E. 221, applied to bar a drawer, who must be taken to know his own signature, from throwing upon an innocent third party the loss resulting to him from the payment out of his account of the amounts of the forged cheques. He distinguished the present case from one where the drawer's signature was genuine but the amount of the cheque was wrongly raised. In his view, "The drawer's cause of action against his own bank gives him adequate protection. If he chooses to bargain that cause of action away or allow it to lapse, the loss should not be imposed on an innocent third party." This last statement referred, of course, to the trial Judge's appreciation of the effect of the verification agreement [at p. 704].

In the Court of Appeal [19 DLR (3d) 420, [1971] 3 WWR 241], Robertson, J.A., with whom Taggart,. J.A., agreed, said in summation (after exploring the theory upon which conversion lies for the value represented by a bill of exchange) that [at p. 438] "In order to succeed on a claim of this kind the plaintiff must be the true owner of the piece of paper *qua* cheque and not simply the owner of the piece of paper *qua* piece of paper." Nemetz, J.A., in concurring reasons rejected the claim for conversion because the so-called cheques were admittedly not bills of exchange, as defined in the Bills of Exchange Act; and hence the collecting bank could not be guilty of conversion so as to be answerable for the face value of the forged cheques for which it had received payment from the drawee bank.

The technical result of the forgeries in destroying the "bills of exchange" character of the documents in this case does not make it any less true that the value of the appellant's chose in action against the Royal Bank had been considerably diminished by the action of the collecting bank. But this is so in the present case only because the drawer's bank was, on the facts, not liable to make good to the drawer the amounts of the forgeries. The collecting bank was merely carrying out its duty to its customer; and the fact that he was the forger would not, on that ground alone, affect its position unless it knew or could reasonably be fixed with knowledge of the forgeries, and only to the extent of such knowledge or attribution thereof. The overriding question here is whether, despite want of knowledge or want of any basis of attribution thereof, a collecting bank is at the peril of a successful claim by the drawer whose signature has been forged because that bank has received money on the presentation of worthless documents and thus has reduced the credit position of the drawer with its own bank. The issue arises only because the collecting bank had both surrendered the documents and had in turn paid out to its fraudulent customer what it collected before having any knowledge of his criminal actions; and, above all, it arises because the drawer finds himself without recourse against the paying bank.

There is in this case no tenable claim for money had and received if there is no recovery for conversion. Although the former is not tied to conversion — it may, for example, arise where there has been a failure of consideration — the basis of the claim here for money had and received is the allegedly tortious conduct of the collecting bank, and the claim would arise upon a waiver of the tort. What, then, is the tort, with ensuing damage, which the collecting bank has committed against the appellant? It has not deprived the appellant of the fruits of bills of exchange to which the appellant was entitled. It has not knowingly assisted in perpetrating a fraud through which the appellant suffered a loss. It was not fixed with notice of the forgeries, or any of them, at a time when the forger's accounts with it were still on the credit side, so as to support a claim to follow the money.

I do not find it necessary to consider the Bank of Montreal's position as a holder for value. Certainly, in such a case, the doctrine of *Price* v. *Neal, supra,* would protect it against a claim by the drawee; and equally, it seems to me, against a claim by the drawer who would be expected to have recourse against the drawee. I look upon the present case as one where, as between the appellant and the collecting bank, the loss suffered as a result of the forgeries must lie where it has fallen.

Appeal dismissed.

Note: There is no disagreement between Martland and Laskin JJ. with respect to the position of the payor bank's customer towards the collecting bank. Their opinions differ as to the nature of the payor bank's defence against the customer. The decision of Mr.

Justice Martland represents the majority opinion of the court. From the viewpoint of a customer who received bank statements accompanied by cancelled forged cheques drawn on his account, and who failed to notify the payor bank of the forgery, is there a practical difference between the two approaches? Does it make any difference to such a customer whether the theory which can bar his action against the payor bank is based on the verification agreement (Martland J.'s view) or on his failure to exercise ordinary care in examining the bank statements and the attached cheques (Laskin J.'s view)?

Problems:

1   A drew on PB a cheque payable to B and delivered it to B. B endorsed the cheque to C and delivered it to him. The cheque was stolen from C and, bearing C's forged endorsement, was delivered to D who took it in good faith and for value. D deposited the cheque in his bank account with DB and drew funds against it. DB presented the cheque and obtained payment from PB. Consider the rights of the parties (a) prior to the deposit of the cheque by D in his account, and (b) after payment on the cheque by PB.

   Consider also the parties' positions on the alternative assumptions that the cheque (drawn by A on PB and delivered to B) was a cheque payable to bearer, that it bore no endorsements, and that, having been stolen from C, it was delivered to D who took it in good faith and for value.

2   A blank cheque, stolen from a customer of PB, was made payable to Ismail and, bearing the sum of $8,000 and a forged drawer's signature, was delivered to him for good consideration to be given after payment of the cheque. Ismail deposited the cheque in his bank account with DB and parted with the consideration only upon payment of the cheque by PB. On learning of the forgery, can PB recover from DB? From Ismail?

3   A promissory note purporting to be issued by A to the order of B and payable on December 1, 1980, was endorsed and delivered by B to C. C endorsed it and delivered it to D on August 1, 1980, for consideration to be given on November 1, 1980. D notified A on August 2, 1980, that his note would fall due on December 1. In fact, A's signature on the note had been forged by his nephew. A communicated immediately with his nephew (whom he suspected of the forgery) but communicated with D only at the end of November, having failed in the meantime to settle the matter privately with his nephew. On November 1, 1980, D gave the agreed consideration to C. What are D's rights?

4   A payroll clerk, whose normal duty is to prepare wage or salary cheques for employees of a company, perpetrates a fraud by including among the cheques presented to the authorized signing officers of the company a number of cheques payable to persons who were not owed any wages, some being former employees, and the other payees having names invented by the fraudulent clerk. The fraudulent clerk extracts these cheques, forges the endorsements and obtains payment from the company's bank, which debits the company's account accordingly. As between the company and the bank, who should bear the loss?

5   A cheque payable to the order of corporation B is stolen from it by an unfaithful employee. Taking advantage of careless office procedures, he also steals the corporate stamp. With the aid of the stamp and by forging the signatures of the authorized signing officers, the unfaithful employee endorses the cheque to his order, deposits it in his bank account with DB, and draws funds against it. DB presents the cheque to PB and obtains payment. Discuss the rights of the parties in this fact situation.

6   F is the bookkeeper of corporation A. From time to time he takes a blank cheque from the corporation's cheque book, makes it payable to himself and, after forging the signatures of the signing officers of the corporation and imprinting the corporate stamp on the cheque, deposits it in his bank account with DB. Amounts so deposited are later on withdrawn by F. Each cheque (bearing the drawer's forged signature) is paid to DB by PB. Monthly statements, together with all cancelled cheques, are sent by PB to corporation A where they are brought only to the attention of F (in his capacity as a bookkeeper). The scheme works for years. On discovering the forgeries, can corporation A recover from PB the amounts paid on cheques forged by F? Can PB rely on a term in its contract with corporation A under which the account stated in each monthly statement becomes conclusive within 30 days after its receipt by the corporation unless challenged within this period? Does PB have to rely on this contractual term?

7   A draws a cheque on PB payable to B. The cheque is stolen from A, before delivery to B, by an unfaithful employee of A who forges B's endorsement, deposits the cheque in his bank account with DB, and withdraws funds against it. DB obtains payment from PB. Discuss the parties' rights.

Chapter 18
Electronic Funds Transfers

A. CREDIT TRANSFERS IN COMMERCIAL TRANSACTIONS

BRADLEY CRAWFORD
"Credit Transfers of Funds in Canada: The Current Law"
(1979) 3 Can. Bus. LJ 119, 120-38

1. DEFINITION OF TERMS

There is no official definition of either "credit transfer" or "debit transfer" as terms describing payment systems but one author has suggested that:

> A "debit transfer" is one in which an item containing a request or order for the payment of money is received by the banking system from a depositor who is to receive payment if the item is honored by the drawee after receipt: and a "credit transfer" is one in which the first impact on the banking system is the receipt by the paying bank from its depositor of an order to pay money, to the debit of his account, and to the credit of an identified account in the same or another bank, which is also identified.

The usage is, however, not settled. Another author states:

> ... the present payment mechanism ... is essentially a "credit" transfer system wherein each holder of a check deposits it in a bank and receives credit for each successive stage of the collection process.

The cause of the ambiguity is clearly the fact that both a credit voucher and a debit voucher may be used to transfer value. In these comments I shall use the term "credit transfer" to mean a transfer accomplished by use of a credit voucher. Thus examples of credit transfer are the direct deposit by an employer of payroll payments into accounts held for employees, and the receipt of cash by a banker in payment of a utility account. Working Paper 21 restricts itself to consideration of the former type of transfer by corporations or governments (pensions etc.) to individuals.

2. BANKS' POWERS TO OPERATE CREDIT TRANSFER SYSTEM

No question arises concerning the powers of the Canadian chartered banks to transfer credits for customers and others. Although the matter has not been before a Canadian court, it is clear enough that transfers are a "dealing in" money and comfortably within "such business generally as appertains to the business of banking", within the meaning of s. 75(1) of the Bank Act. Certainly it appears from reported litigation that credit transfer services, both within the country and from overseas, have been part of Canadian bankers' business since at least the 1840's. As well, the banks' practice of accepting deposits by others to the credit of their customers has gone on for about the same time, without attracting adverse comment. Although the British author, Holden, dates the present well-developed system of "traders' credit" transfer in England "from about the beginning of the present century" (with facilities for credit clearing established in 1960), passing references to credit transfers and deposits to the accounts of others may also be found in reported English litigation dating from the early 19th century. Finally, *Corpus Juris Secundum* states that in America as well "It is an established custom among banks and financial institutions to transmit money and credit."

3. NATURE OF THE RELATIONSHIPS CREATED BY CREDIT TRANSFERS

There are at least two, and in some cases three, material legal relationships involved in a credit transfer. They are:
(a) between the payee and the one or more transferring fundholders;
(b) between the payer and the fundholders; and
(c) between the fundholders themselves, if more than one.
Of course, the existence of a contract between two of the participants may, but does not necessarily, affect the nature of the relationships between other participants, either with either of the contracting parties or with each other. Because of the potential importance of these relationships in the determination of the rights and duties of the participants at various stages of the credit transfer transaction, it will be necessary to consider each of them briefly.

(a) Between payee and transferring fundholder

A comparatively recent case in the Ontario Court of Appeal* indicates that in dealing with some payees fundholders may be acting as agents expressly appointed under letter agreements. The case was an unusual one in which a general merchant at Long Sault, Ontario, had been appointed an agent of the Hydro Electric Power Commissioners to receive payment of utility accounts on their behalf from local residents. The litigation arose following a break-in at the shop in which the monies received on behalf of Hydro, which had been carefully segregated from the merchant's own funds in a locked box, were stolen. The merchant claimed that the separated monies were the property of Hydro and had been taken without fault on his part. The Ontario Court of Appeal examined the terms of the contract by which the merchant had been authorized to collect and,

---

*   *Hydro-Electric Power Comm. of Ont.* v. *Brown* (1959) 21 DLR (2d) 551 (Ont. CA). [Eds.]

finding that he was under no obligation to segregate the money, held that he was a debtor of the utility rather than a trustee and remained indebted regardless of the theft.

For the present purposes, the importance of the case is twofold: (i) to confirm the capacity of the payee and the fundholder to affect their relationship by private contract, and (ii) to serve as a useful reminder that the terms of such written or oral agreements could affect the legal analysis of the relationship. Where such arrangements exist it would be necessary to analyze them in detail to determine their precise effect.

Standards and procedures of the Canadian Bankers' Association establish guidelines for such arrangements when involving banks, but the procedure is administrative only and does not purport to characterize the relationship or settle its incidents. Presumably in each case there would be some form of agreement which might do so, although a recent case in England indicates that not all such agreements would necessarily address the point. In *Midland Bank Ltd.* v. *Conway Borough Council* [1965] 2 All ER 972 (QB) a bank had accepted rents from tenants living in the borough and made certain payments of rates in respect of the rented premises, all on behalf of the landlord which was the bank's customer. The borough council sought to characterize the bank as an agent of its customer and, as such, to charge it with certain statutory responsibilities for repairs and improvements imposed upon owners and their agents by tenant protection legislation. The claim failed when the English court concluded that the only legal relationship created had been that of banker and customer. If the account management agreement contained any provisions material to the nature of the relationship there is no indication that they were relied upon in argument or even placed in evidence. The court treated the matter as one of principle, characterizing the receipt of credits for a customer as a normal incident of banking.

This reasoning would also tend to indicate that if the receipt of credit transfers for the account of customers is merely another incident in a normal banking relationship, the receiving bank would be liable to its customer in contract damages for any failure by it to perform its responsibilities in connection with the transfer in accordance with the duty of care required by law or as modified by the banking contract in any particular case.

Where the transferring fundholder has not previously been appointed a banker of the payee, the weight of authority is to the effect that there is no legally enforceable relationship between them created merely by the fundholder's receipt of a credit for transfer.

> In *Williams* v. *Everett*, one Kelly sent certain bills to the defendants, who were his bankers, instructing them to pay the plaintiffs, his creditors, whom he informed what he had done. The plaintiffs claimed that the defendants held the bills to their use. Lord Ellenborough thought that privity between the parties was necessary and would be satisfied by an "assent express or implied" on the defendants' part. But, on the facts, he found that there was no such assent, nor was there any "engagement entered into by themselves with the person who is the object of the remittance." The claim, therefore, failed.

But there are also reported cases deciding the other way and the leading text-writers' opinion is that "the law cannot be regarded as settled." The practical importance of the point is small as the transferring fundholder must be liable to one or the other of the payer and payee, either on its undertaking to the payee to remit, or on a constructive trust for the payer.

(b) Between payer and transferring fundholder

There is also considerable uncertainty concerning the nature of the legal relationship created between the person initiating a credit transfer and the transferring fundholder. There have been several reported cases attempting to characterize it variously as agency, trust and debt arising out of simple contract, among others.

(i) *Trust.* In several American cases plaintiffs have sought to characterize the relationship as one of trust — or at least fiduciary obligation. A typical example is *Beecher* v. *Cosmopolitan Trust Co.* 131 NE 338 (1921, Mass.), in which plaintiff paid cash to defendant in Boston, to be transferred to the credit of a named payee in Roumania. The transaction was aborted by the insolvency of the defendant and the seizure of its assets by an official receiver. Although the memorandum of the transaction prepared by defendant had asserted that defendant was acting only as an agent for the payer, plaintiff alleged a trust and sought restitution of the initial value given for the credit. This failed upon the finding that there was no obligation to keep the initial value separate. The court remarked:

> . . . what the plaintiff accomplished by the payment of the money was the receipt of an agreement by the defendant trust company that it would procure and provide funds in Roumania to meet the order which it had sold and delivered to the plaintiff. . . . It was not contemplated by the plaintiff that the money itself should be remitted or that the trust company should not use the money paid to it as its own pending the performance of its agreement with the plaintiff. Its failure to perform gave rise to an action in contract and not to a suit cognizable in court of equity.

In contrast, in a similar case, a Manitoba court created a constructive trust of at least a portion of the initial value paid to a financial intermediary for exchange and transfer to the credit of a named payee in Poland. Upon the failure of the financial intermediary the plaintiff's evidence had traced the initial payment to a "foreign exchange account" held in the name of the defendant by a Winnipeg chartered bank and on the strength of that (and perhaps also the absence of other claimants or opposition by the trustee in bankruptcy) ordered its repayment to the plaintiff.

Notwithstanding the latter decision, which may have been necessary in equity and good conscience, but which is surely not typical, the American decisions refusing to complicate credit transfer transactions with unnecessary concepts of trust are greatly to be preferred and more likely to be followed by a modern Canadian court in the absence of some unusual circumstances calling for restitution of unjustified enrichment. The inconvenience of a rule characterizing the credit as trust funds could not be overstated.

(ii) *Simple contract debt.* There is not strong support for this theory, although the *Beecher* decision previously noted and several other Massachusetts and New York decisions, in rejecting arguments seeking to establish a trust, concluded that a simple contract debt was created, although perhaps payable in another currency or at a distance place. A similar approach appears in an early Ontario case in which the Bank of British North America received money from its customer in England for transfer to his account with the Bank at Blenheim in what was then Upper Canada. The notification of the credit was intercepted in the post and the money claimed by an imposter. Robinson, C.J., in giving judgment for the customer's executrix remarked:

> I think when the Bank of British North America took the money in England and engaged to remit to White in Canada, they in effect promised to pay him in Canada the sum they had received. It is not like [a cited precedent] because there is no third party intervening, no agent, between whom and White it might be said there was no privity. *It is the Bank all the way through;* and as White could have had an action against the Bank in England, if they had given no direction, so might he sue them. . . . in Canada, for a sum which they had undertaken to pay there. The Bank is to be looked upon as having received this money to be paid to White in Canada, and liable to an action in Canada, where the demand arises and is to be enforced. [emphasis added.]

Another early case analyzing a credit transfer as creating a simple contract debt is *Smythies* v. *Bank of New Zealand* [1878] 3 JRNS 23 (NZ CA). It appears that a telegraphed credit transfer from plaintiff's agent in London to plaintiff in Dunedin aborted when defendant's London branch misspelled plaintiff's name and their Dunedin branch refused to pay before mailed confirmation could be obtained. Plaintiff claimed general and special damages for breach of contract and succeeded at trial. However, the award of general damages was lost on appeal. The reasoning of the majority is adequately summarized in the headnote as follows:

> 1. That a contract to transmit money by telegraphic advice differs in no respect from a contract to transmit by letter of advice, and in no essential respect from an ordinary contract for the purchase of a letter of credit or Bank draft;
> 2. That in these cases, the contract creates the relation of debtor and creditor, and on the breach of such a contract the ordinary measure of damages must be applied.

In the result, plaintiff recovered only interest for the time he had been without the money. Johnston, J., who had tried the case would have returned the costs of the telegram and foreign exchange but agreed with the majority that notwithstanding the air of urgency about a telegraphic transfer requested and paid for on behalf of plaintiff, the losses suffered by plaintiff in his business interests, by reason of being without money, were too remote. The reasoning clearly leaves open the possibility of a transferring fundholder becoming liable for heavy damages in consequence of failing to produce funds at a specific time and place in order to avert a consequence known to be contingent upon their timely arrival. Conversely, as the matter is one of contract only, such damages might also be avoided by an effective disclaimer.

(iii) *Agency.* According to *Corpus Juris Secundum* the weight of American authority is strongly in favour of an analysis in terms of agency. Basing themselves on those principles, American courts have reasoned that the transferring bank is not, in the ordinary case, under an absolute duty to complete the transaction. If it acts reasonably and prudently in strict accordance with its instructions it will not be liable even though the credit fails to reach the hands of the intended transferee. If it is authorized, either expressly or by necessary implication, to act through other banks or financial institutions, it makes those contracts on behalf of its principal and is not responsible for their defaults in the absence of proven want of care in selecting reasonably competent sub-agents. Other extensions of these principles are cited by the Atlanta Payments Study, together with an argument that Art. 4 of the Uniform Commercial Code might be applied by analogy in order to provide an even fuller statement of the rights and duties of the parties.

A Quebec Court recently characterized a bank as a "mandatory" when undertaking to hold a customer's cheque and, when it became payable, to credit its proceeds to a particular account. This is a relationship similar to agency in common law and therefore supports the American majority position.

Two *obiter dicta* in the English Court of Appeal have indicated that some modern English judges also tend to view the credit transfer as an agency of the transferring bank for its customer as a principal. But as no case has yet raised a difficult question of law, it is not clear whether this analysis is to be applied to its logical conclusions. As learned English authors on the laws of banking have observed:

> An agent holding the moneys of his principal is under very strict obligations, and in particular must meticulously account for its use within the terms of his authority. If bankers had so to account the practice of banking as we know it today would be hardly possible.

Although more recent Canadian precedents have relaxed the old law by which all agents were tacitly assumed to be fiduciaries of all funds coming to their hands and thus destroyed the value of the specific example chosen, there is still considerable force in the observation. For example, in the *Dominion Ticket* case noted earlier [[1924] 2 DLR 807] although Dysart, J., of the Manitoba court referred to the credit transferring corporation as an "agent" for the payer, it is not clear that all the normal incidents of a true agency relationship would necessarily have been applied. For example, an agent is prohibited by law from selling his own property to his principal without elaborate disclosure. Would that prohibition apply if the zloty purchased by the customer for transfer to Poland had come from the corporation's foreign cash on hand rather than a market purchase? If, before the transaction was consummated, the market rate of zloty had slumped, or if a black market supply at a greatly improved rate of exchange had suddenly become available, would the corporation have been obliged to share its windfall profits with the payer as a true agent would with his principal? It is surely doubtful, and until such cases arise, it is perhaps as well not to take too seriously the English dicta and U.S. courts' characterization of the relationship as one of agency. Perhaps a better way to express the point is to note the bankers are often loosely stated to have undertaken a specialized, restricted kind of agency for their customers, as where a negotiable instrument is endorsed and delivered to them "for collection only". The courts' acceptance of such use of the term agency has never led to extreme consequences such as those envisioned by the learned authors quoted. Similarly, in appropriate circumstances bankers have been held liable for their "negligence" in carrying out credit transfer instructions without being held accountable for damages according to the normal measure for the law of torts. The use of the term in the context of credit transfers, if similarly kept free from the further extremes of its purely logical consequences, would be unobjectionable on all but pedantic grounds.

(iv) *Other.* A further possibility is that a credit transfer, in addition to being a normal incident of the banker-customer relationship between payee and transferring fundholder, might also be within the normal scope of that relationship between the payer and his banker as well. It is remarkable to review, with credit transfers in mind, the opening lines of the judgment of Atkin, L.J., in *Joachimson* v. *Swiss Bank Corporation* [1921] 3 KB 110 at 127, the *locus classicus* of the basic principles of English banking law:

> I think that there is only one contract made between the bank and its customer. The terms of that contract involve obligations on both sides and require careful statement. They appear upon consideration to include the following provisions. The bank undertakes to receive money and to collect bills for its customer's account. The proceeds so received are not to be held in trust for the customer, but the bank borrows the proceeds and undertakes ... to repay any part of the amount due [deposited] against the written order of the customer addressed to the bank at the branch [where the account is kept].

Doubtless the learned Lord Justice was thinking more of cheques than credit transfers but the terms in which he expressed himself are broad enough to include the latter. Moreover the practice of English banks paying traders' credits was sufficiently well established by 1921 to make the dictum *some* little support for including the acceptance of credit transfers as falling impliedly within the banker-customer relationship, at least where a bank has accepted such instructions and proceeded to act upon them. It is, however, doubtful that it could be sufficient to create even a limited kind of banker-customer relationship between the payer and the transferring bank where none had existed before. Notwithstanding the precedents to the effect that it is not strictly necessary for a person to have an account with a bank in order to give rise to a banker-customer relationship, the level of formality of the proposed relation, the documentation exchanged and the normal expectations of the parties all must be considered, and indicate a less intensive and more informal relationship in the case of a simple request to initiate a credit transfer. It may be that the other suggested characterizations are chiefly useful as aids to analysis of legal consequences in cases where no pre-existing banking relationship exists between the payer and the credit transferor. In such cases it is clearly in the best interests of both parties to clarify their respective responsibilities by some form of agreement, however short and simple.

One remaining difficulty with all of the foregoing is to ascertain whether the true characterization of the relationship is a matter of law or of contract. In only one of the cases reviewed did a court even examine the terms of the credit transfer memorandum or agreement, and in that case that court completely disregarded the parties' invocation of agency in favour of its own analysis of simple contract debt. If the analysis of this memorandum characterizing the relationship as one of contract is correct, then it ought to be judicially recognized that the parties have the power to determine its incidents.

(c) Between fundholders

There has been less litigation concerning these relationships than the former pairings, probably reflecting the fact that the potential for variety is not great. If the fundholder receiving the initial value undertakes *as a principal* to transfer it to the payee his delivery of value to the payee's fundholder (or the acceptance by the latter of the former's payment message or request for credit) might be

> (i)   simple performance of its contract with the payer;
> (ii) a transaction within the ambit of a pre-existing correspondent relationship between the fundholders; or
> (iii) the creation of a new agency of the latter for the former.

If the transfer is viewed as being made by an agent for the payer, to the former range of relationships must be added the possibility that an agency might be created directly between payer and receiving fundholder, brought about by the express or implied authority of the payer to the transferring fundholder to create it. The characterization of the relationship between the transferring fundholder and the payer is of obvious importance to the process of characterizing the ensuing relationship between the fundholders. As we have seen from the preceding section, the former has not yet been settled. It is, therefore, hardly surprising that the law on the latter has also remained unsettled. The different results produced by the various possible analyses in questions involving the misdirection of the funds, their interception by unauthorized persons, their loss through insolvency of the receiving fundholder or the payment of the wrong amount are obvious. There would appear to be no need to investigate the precedents in detail at this time, as the relationship is clearly capable of precise definition and content in the contracts, both between the payer and the transferring fundholder, and between the fundholders themselves.

The authors of the Atlanta Payment Study state that:

> . . . in the ordinary agreements to transfer credit . . . the transferree bank is regarded as a subagent . . . thus there is no liability [on the transferring bank] for negligence of an agent bank. . . .

Although they consider that parts of Art. 4 of the Uniform Commercial Code might apply to regulate the rights of the fundholders, they are unequivocal in their recommendation that a master agreement among the participating fundholders be attempted.

4. AUTHORIZATION TO TRANSFER

As disinterested intermediaries the fundholders requested to transfer a credit will be well advised to obtain either a direct authorization from both the payer and the payee, or at the least a representation of such authorization from some financially responsible person.

(a) Payer's authorization

The kinds of questions which would be likely to arise concerning the payer's authorization would not be significantly different from those which arise now in respect of other media of payment. An example is provided by the liability recently sought to be imposed upon The Bank of Nova Scotia in the *Groves-Raffin* case [51 DLR (3d) 380]. The trial judge found the bank liable to reimburse its customer on the grounds that it ought to have been put upon inquiry by the unusual nature of certain cheques and transactions by which monies standing to the credit of the customer (a corporation) were transferred to another bank account held by a signing officer in his personal capacity. This was reversed on appeal since it had not been shown that the bank officers knew any fact indicating a breach of trust was being committed and did not participate in the fraud other than by honouring the apparently regular payment instruments. This places the case in line with earlier authority that agents retained to transmit funds are not liable for any consequences of fraud committed by their principals in ordering the transfer and appropriating the proceeds, in the absence of actual or constructive knowledge and participation by them. The danger to the banks posed by unauthorized credit transfer is clear, but no different from that presented by unauthorized debit transfers.

The form of authorization required will vary with the form of initial value offered by the person seeking to initiate the transfer. In each case, the same precautions now taken before value is given irrevocably would be advisable before a transfer is effected. Although a credit transfer is not necessarily irreversible, as will subsequently appear, it may be, and the prudent course for the fundholders would be to treat it as such.

(b) Payee's authorization

(i) *Generally.* Halsbury states that a banker is ordinarily bound to accept deposits by others to accounts held by him for customers and notes that it is common practice in the bank giro system. The one limitation recognized by Halsbury is rather exceptional. He cites authority for the proposition that the banker to whom there has been presented an instrument too large to be honoured by the balance in the account ought not not to accept a small deposit sufficient to enable the instrument to pass, on the grounds that there would be a breach of confidentiality and possibly a fraud on creditors. That might be so, but the breach would appear to be in the disclosure of the amount required to be made up before the presented instrument could be honoured rather than in the acceptance of the actual deposit.

I am not aware of any authoritative support in Canadian or American case law for a proposition as broad as that stated by Halsbury, and therefore conclude that it would probably be advisable for a credit transfer system to be administered in such a way that some evidence of authorization will be required of each person proposing to make a credit transfer to the account of another. Wholesale transfers such as payrolls no less than random cash payments made over the counter for transfer to the accounts of others, would be an expensive nuisance if the destination information were not reliable. There are, as well, some slight indications that it would be advisable as a matter of law, to require some evidence of authorization — in the interests of all parties.

(ii) *Payee's interest.* The payee's interest in remaining in control of his own fund is obvious. Even if the occurrence of unauthorized credit transfers were rare, individuals would be obliged to pay more attention to their financial records than they appear to do at present. The potential nuisance and liability of having to return payments should be avoided. Persons with public offices or other fiduciary responsibilities might be jeopardized by unauthorized and unexplained receipts. Lord Denning, M.R., has suggested in a recent case that a customer might validly instruct his banker not to accept credit transfers from specified persons in order to avoid having his rights against such persons affected — *e.g.*, by late receipt of a payment from another when the customer wished to allege default in order to terminate a contract with the other or to claim a forfeiture or some other advantage. As the relationship of banker and customer is contractual it could include such a duty. Although there is no case on the point, a banker failing to act in accordance with his undertaking to obey such an instruction might well be liable in damages for breach of that contract. The measure of the customer's recovery would probably be the loss directly and naturally resulting in the ordinary course from the breach as well as any special losses or damages actually within the contemplation of the parties when the "stop credit" order was accepted.

In the nature of credit transfers, the receiving fundholder will likely not be able to check for authorization at the place and time of his receipt of the initial value. It is also probable that it would not be feasible to attempt to conduct such a check during bulk processing of the credit transfer media (whether still in paper form or transferred to computer tape). Thus the receiving fundholder will have to incur all the costs associated with processing the credit, including a trial posting to the payee's account before discovering the prohibition. It will then also be necessary for him to incur the additional costs of reversing the transaction. Those might be great or small depending upon whether there was some pre-existing relationship between the payer and the transferring fundholder or fundholders, and whether the initial value was a debit memo on an established account or cash or negotiable instrument paid over the counter by an unknown member of the public.

(iii) *Payer's interests.* As far as the payer's interest is concerned, although perhaps not generally understood by the public, the law is that unauthorized payments may fail to have their intended effect and still be unrecoverable. In technical terms, the basic problems are the weakness of a claim for restitution of a voluntary payment and the judicial aversion to officious conduct. The latter has been typified for nearly a century by the trenchant observation of Bowen, L.J.:

> Liabilities are not to be forced on people behind their backs any more than you can confer a benefit upon a man against his will.

Transfers to accounts that are not in funds but that are overdrawn or more than offset by loan debts are, in effect, a purported payment by the credit transferor of the debt of the payee to his fundholder. As noted, such payments may fail to take their desired legal effect and not be recoverable. Some of the ramifications of this notion are elaborated by the leading text on the law of restitution as follows:

> In spite of dicta to the contrary . . . it is probably now settled that if A, a stranger, pays B's debt to C, such payment will not of itself discharge B's liability to C, unless it has been made on B's behalf and has been subsequently ratified by him. . . . It is *prima facie* still open to C to sue B for his debt despite A's payment . . . unless such an action would be a fraud on A or would constitute an abuse of the process of the court, or for some other similar reason. . . . If it is open to C to sue B and he does so, B will in all probability ratify A's payment, but if he does not do so and pays C's claim, A should be entitled to recover his money from C on grounds of total failure of consideration, or alternatively to recover B's payment from C on the grounds that C received it as trustee for him. . . . Even if C simply keeps A's payment and does not sue B, A can claim reimbursement from B, and if B refuses to ratify A's payment A may be entitled to recover his money from C on grounds of total failure of consideration . . . in other cases A may protect himself by taking an assignment from C of B's debt. Williston . . . concludes, on the weight of American authority that C, after accepting A's tender, cannot sue B; but the basis of his conclusion is accord and satisfaction, not legal discharge.

It is not necessary to scrutinize the reasoning supporting these conclusions or the many decided English and American cases cited as authority. From the point of view of payment systems design, the implications of this much legal uncertainty are clear, especially when it is appreciated that none of the difficulties adverted to arise if only authorized payments are accepted for credit transfer.

5. IMPLEMENTATION

(a) Time of payment — old law

A number of legal questions arise concerning the implementation of the credit order by the transferee fundholder. It may be important to ascertain with considerable precision the actual time the payment is legally considered to have been "made" or completed. This would have obvious implications for questions which might arise as to when the fund became available to the payee, or to an attaching creditor of the payee. Conversely, it should be possible for the users of the system to ascertain when the credit transfer becomes irrevocable, beyond the control of the payer to revoke or redirect.

In the older cases, the determination of the time of payment was fairly unsophisticated. When bankers received items to the credit of a customer's account they were usually afforded "a reasonable time" in which to process the entries and bring their ledgers up to date. If they dishonoured cheques drawn against the account after having had a reasonable processing time, they might be held liable in damages. What might qualify as a reasonable time was a question of fact and a matter for evidence in the absence of some provision in the banking contract concerning it. That the matter is still one which may be affected by contract seems clear from the cases giving effect to provisions prohibiting drawings against "uncleared effects" — *viz.*, debit orders of third parties deposited but not yet presented for payment. Similarly, the custom of bankers may have an effect, as evidenced by a recent decision of the English Court of Appeal which accepted and acted upon a proven custom of the London "walks clearing" banks to regard credit vouchers handed in over the counter as the equivalent of cash.

Where there was a transmittal of the credit order, and the question was not when the customer might draw on the deposited funds, but when the transfer was beyond the reach of the payer's creditors, it had been decided in Ontario by 1900 that payment was made at the latest when the voucher was received by the payee's fundholder through the mail. There was even reliance by one judge upon a section still to be found in the federal Post Office Act to the effect that property in mail passes to the addressee when it is posted. In a subsequent case involving a credit transfer between the Bank of Hamilton and the Home Bank on the very day of the failure of the latter, the Ontario Court of Appeal ruled that the transfer was complete when the Home Bank posted the credit to the account of the payee even though it would not, in the ordinary course, have presented the settlement voucher to the transferring bank through the normal debit clearing until the following business day.

There was a conflict among the older cases whether a notice to the payee was necessary in order to complete the transaction. *Eyles* v. *Ellis* (1827) 4 Bing. 112 was the first case to raise the point and was decided in 1827. The court then decided that a notification to the payee was not necessary. The credit was of an amount owing for rent from one customer to another, both having the same banker. An attempt by a creditor of the transferor to recover the credit failed on a showing that the process of posting to the two accounts had been completed. The rule there laid down was not regarded as contentious until 1933 when a foreign national in England sought to prevent an anticipated execution by creditors against his bank account by transferring the fund to the account of his embassy with the same bank. The credit had been requested and the accounts of the two customers adjusted when the anticipated seizure was attempted. The court ought perhaps to have decided that a sham transaction could not prejudice the rights of creditors, and may in fact have done so, but it chose to express that conclusion in other terms. Apparently, in ignorance of the 1827 precedent, it held that the process of posting was not complete and the payment therefore not final until notification to the payee. It had been held a century before that, in the absence of a contract to bind the transferring fundholder, no action would lie by the intended payee to enforce a credit transfer until the fundholder actually received the value for transfer and communicated its undertaking to hold it on behalf of the payee and to transfer it in accordance with the payer's instructions. However, a very different point is involved in these later cases. The matter appears now to have been set right. In a very recent case arising out of the failure of the Bank Herstatt Kerr, J., in the High Court of England, applied the 1827 case and concluded that where there was a genuine transaction underlying the credit transfer, the process was complete and the payment irrevocable when the payee's account was posted.

MOMM v. BARCLAYS BANK INTERNATIONAL LTD.
[1976] 3 All ER 588 (QBD)

KERR J.: The plaintiffs are a German banking partnership with offices in Cologne and Hamburg. They claim £12,000 from the defendants on the ground that on 27th June 1974 this sum was wrongfully debited from their account at the defendants' branch at 168 Fenchurch Street, in the City of London. The defendants deny liability and say that the case raises an important issue of banking law following on the computerisation of customers' accounts. It arises out of the failure of another German bank, Bankhaus ID Herstatt KGaA which also had an account at the same branch. On 24th June 1974 the plaintiffs and Herstatt concluded a contract for a normal currency exchange transaction whereby the plaintiffs agreed to transfer to Herstatt a quantity of deutschmarks against the transfer by Herstatt to the plaintiffs of £120,000 in sterling. Both transfers were on the basis of "value 26th June 1974". This meant that the payments had to be made on that date. Herstatt designated an account at a Hamburg bank to which the deutschmarks were to be credited and the plaintiffs designated their account at the defendants' branch to which the sterling was to be credited. The plaintiffs may have known from previous transactions that Herstatt also had an account at this branch, but they did not of course know — nor were they concerned — whether the payment would be made by a transfer from that account or in some other way. On the following day Herstatt instructed the branch by telex to make certain payments including this one "value 26th June". They instructed the defendants to pay two sums of £10,000 and £5,000 respectively into two accounts which Herstatt had with other London banks, and they also instructed them to transfer £120,000 from their account to the plaintiffs' account at the same branch. The latter payment was accordingly an "in-house" payment, as it was called in the evidence, whereas the others were "out-house" payments.

In order to follow what happened next it is necessary to refer to two background matters. The first concerns Herstatt's account at this branch. The second concerns the procedure within the so-called inward sterling transfer department of the branch — and no doubt also at other branches of the defendants — for in-house and out-house payments. Herstatt had no overdraft facilities on this account. In the case of "external" accounts, as this was, the Bank of England imposes stringent restrictions on the grant of overdraft facilities for more than 24 hours, though in practice these may be interpreted somewhat elastically, particularly if the account-holder is a bank. But from about November 1973 the defendants' international division, which is in the same building as this branch, had given instructions that no overdraft facilities were to be granted to

Herstatt, because their financial position had become somewhat suspect. However, overdraft positions nevertheless arose on Herstatt's account for a day or two from time to time, in particular in December 1973 when the debit balance exceeded £50,000 on two occasions and £40,000 on another, and again in May 1974 when it was about £19,000. Whenever this happened the branch drew Herstatt's attention to the position by telephone or telex, and the matter was soon put right. No payment orders from Herstatt were ever refused; nor was there ever any occasion — as happened in the present case — when a payment order was first carried out but subsequently reversed.

The procedure for dealing with payment orders of the kind with which I am here concerned is shortly as follows. Out-house payments to other banks for £5,000 or more are made by means of banker's payments despatched by messengers during bankers hours on the "value" date. If the account is overdrawn on that day, or may turn out to be overdrawn at the end of the day, it is therefore necessary to make a once-and-for-all decision whether to make the payment or not. In relation to in-house payments the position is more flexible, since the decision whether or not to make the payment can be deferred a little longer, or — in the view of the defendants' witnesses — can even be reversed in the accounts on the following day. The effect of such a reversal is a crucial issue in this case. I should add for the sake of completeness that transfers between different branches of the defendants are treated in the same way as ordinary out-house payments.

In relation to some accounts on which there may be numerous and substantial debits and credits in the course of a single day, such as with banking customers, problematic decisions may of course arise if the credit-worthiness of the customer is suspect or if an overdrawn position at the end of the day is for some other reason to be avoided. A funds control unit in the department is able to keep some approximate check on the movements in and out of particular accounts, but for various reasons it is impossible to monitor the position to any reliable extent. This problem has been accentuated by the introduction of computerisation to which I turn in a moment. But before doing so I must explain how, on the evidence, the problem was dealt with when customers' accounts were kept in ledgers. The position concerning out-house payments was then the same as it is now in that a once-and-for-all decision had to be made during banking hours. But the position was different in relation to in-house payments. The debits and credits were posted during the day in the appropriate ledgers as they arose. It was then possible to see the final position shortly after the close of banking hours before the staff left. If a customer's account then showed an unacceptable debit position certain entries might be reversed as between two in-house accounts before the end of the working day. In effect, therefore, the branch then sometimes availed itself of the opportunity, but still on the same "value" date, to decline to comply with one or more payment orders. The relevant entries in the customers' ledgers would then be reversed by appropriate deletions and corrections. This would be done without the knowledge of the customers concerned, and the statements subsequently sent to them would not show that it had happened. But the bank's books would show a final position for each customer at the end of each day which was treated as unalterable. Accordingly, at the end of each day it would be certain, as one would expect, whether a particular payment had or had not been made on that day, and on this basis there would therefore be no difference between in-house and out-house payments. The defendants, like all bankers, are fully aware of the importance to customers, whether they be payers or payees, of the "value" date specified in their transactions. It is the date of contractual payment. If payment is not made on that date then the payer will be in breach and his credit may suffer accordingly. Conversely, the payee relies on the payer's compliance with the obligation to make or to cause to be made the payment on that date and on the availability of the funds in his account on that date.

The difficulty produced by computerisation — at any rate under the defendants' procedure — is that a customer's final balance is not known until it has been produced by computer during the night and is available on the following morning. The defendants' procedure is as follows. The manager of the inward sterling transfer department at the time was a Mr. Dunn and his assistant a Mr. Bass. Whenever a payment order was received from a customer whose account was overdrawn without appropriate overdraft facilities by compliance with the order, the matter was referred to one of them. A decision was then made whether to comply with the order or to refuse to comply or to refer it to higher authority. The latter is the international division in the same building. One of the managers concerned with such inquiries in the international division, and also concerned in the present case, is a Mr. Delf. If compliance with the order is authorised, either within the branch or by the international division, then the appropriate action is taken at once. In the case of out-payments of £5,000 or more, banker's payments are then prepared manually and irrevocably despatched by messenger during banking hours. The appropriate debit is also put on the computer, but for present purposes it is only necessary to explain the computer procedure in relation to in-house payments.

In relation to in-house payments the computer process is set in operation at once in the same way as in relation to out-house payments. Cards are punched out so that the appropriate debits and credits of the two customers' accounts can be produced by the computer. There is a small computer in the branch which produces the cards during the day, and these are taken in batches to the defendants' central computer in another part of the City for processing during the night. The small computer within the branch does three things during the night. First, it produces an advice note and a duplicate concerning every transaction which has taken place during the day. Secondly, though this is not relevant for present purposes, it produces banker's payments for sums under £5,000 to be despatched on the following day. Thirdly, it reconciles and balances all transactions within the branch which have taken place during the day.

The central computer gets through a staggering amount of work during the night. First, it produces a list showing the credit or debit balance of each customer's account at the end of the previous day in all of the defendants' branches.

Secondly, it produces a list of accounts which should have the manager's attention: these are called "manager's refers" and indicate excess borrowings. Thirdly,
in relation to these accounts it produces a so-called disposable disposition sheet
(indicating that it is a disposable duplicate) showing recent transactions on these
accounts. Fourthly, it produces statements for every customer to whom a statement is due to be despatched on or about that date. Fifthly, it produces a ledger
sheet for every customer's account whenever 40 lines on such sheets have been
completed; meanwhile, these sheets are being printed on a continuous basis
inside the computer recording the previous day's debits and credits. The ledger
sheets are for the branch's internal use and are in effect the only thing which can
nowadays be described as the bank's books. Apart from entries of an administrative nature, mainly concerned with the timetable for sending out statements, the
ledger sheets contain precisely the same entries as the statements themselves.

At about 9 a.m. on the following morning the "manager's refers" are considered both in the international division and in the inward sterling transfer
department. If necessary, the disposable disposition sheets are referred to. Someone in the position of Mr. Delf or higher in the international division may then
speak to Mr. Dunn or Mr. Bass on the telephone and give instructions about
particular accounts if the previous day's transactions or debit balances give cause
for concern or warrant some action. In the vast majority of cases, if action is to be
taken, this takes the form of a telephone call or telex to the customer concerned,
drawing his attention to the state of his account, asking him to remedy the
position, and possibly sounding some warning note about the future. In some
cases, however, though no witness could remember it ever having happened in
relation to a banking customer, the previous day's transactions might be
"reversed".

Reversals can of course only be made in relation to in-house transfers. Their
effect would be to delete one or more of the previous day's debits made by the
computer in the relevant customer's ledger sheet and statement (if one had been
printed overnight) and similarly to delete the corresponding credits in the
account of the other customer or customers concerned. The computer can be
instructed to do this on the following day in one of three ways. First, in theory, it
could be instructed to delete the entries completely as though they had never
been made, but in practice this would be extremely difficult and appears in fact
never to have been done. Secondly, by using the so-called "one day back-value
code", the computer could be instructed to reverse the entry under the date of the
previous day. As I understand it, it would then appear as though the reversal had
in fact taken place on the previous day. In practice, however, this method also
involves considerable problems, since the computer would then reprint and
reproduce everything else which had taken place on the previous day. The
normal method, insofar as reversals were normal at all, was accordingly simply to
reverse the entries under the date of the following day. This is what happened in
the present case.

In the rare cases in which such reversals occur — though no specific instance
was referred to in the evidence — steps would then be taken to ensure that the
customers concerned did not get to know about the reversals having taken place.

In saying this, I am not implying that anything underhand takes place or making any criticism, but this is what would in fact happen. First, the relevant advice notes and duplicates relating to the transactions in question would be sorted out and not despatched to the customers concerned. In all other cases the advice notes printed overnight would be despatched on the following day and the duplicates would be sent together with the next statement. Secondly, the pages of the statements in which the original and reverse entries appeared, as and when produced by the central computer, would be retyped so as to omit these, but they would of course continue to appear in the ledger sheets. All this also happened in the present case. Finally, I should add, for the sake of completeness, that the rare cases of reversal such as I have been describing must of course be distinguished from the ordinary cases of wrong debits and credits which simply result from some human error. These would appear in the customer's statements and would also be covered by advice notes in the usual way. One sees these in one's own bank statements from time to time, and minor examples of them also appeared in the plaintiffs' statements which were in evidence.

The issue in the present case is shortly whether the debit of Herstatt's account of £120,000 on 26th June 1974, and a corresponding credit in the plaintiffs' account on the same day, which were processed by the central computer overnight but reversed on the following day, constituted a completed payment on the first day, followed by an unauthorised debit on the second day, or whether no completed payment was ever made. The defendants contend that for either or both of two reasons there was no completed payment. First, because no advice note was sent, or other communication made, to the plaintiffs before the credit on their account was reversed. Secondly, because the defendants maintain that the decision to credit the plaintiffs' account was only provisional on 26th June, and that the final decision against making the payment was made on 27th June by reversing the entries. The latter submission is made in particular in the context of a number of recent shipping cases to which I shall have to return, in which the time of decision was treated as the relevant time.

I must next complete the history. As already mentioned, on 25th June 1974, pursuant to their contract, Herstatt instructed the defendants' branch to transfer the sum of £120,000 "value June 26th" to the plaintiffs' account at this branch, and also gave instructions for two out-payments on the same day totalling £15,000. This telex was submitted to Mr. Bass at about midday on 26th June. The reason for consulting him was that on the morning of 26th June the computerised balance of Herstatt's account at the close of business on the previous day showed a debit of about £4,650. This fact in itself had caused no concern to anyone, since there had been no communication about it between Mr. Delf, Mr. Dunn or Mr. Bass. Nor had there been any communication with Herstatt about it, as there had been on previous occasions when they had been overdrawn. This is perhaps not surprising, since there had been considerable movements on Herstatt's account during the previous days without any resulting debit balances. A transfer from the plaintiffs of £150,000 and to the plaintiffs of £160,000 had taken place between these parties on 24th June. But since Herstatt's account was overdrawn on the morning of 26th June, though only to a small extent, the telex instructions for further payments totalling £135,000 "value 26th" were referred to Mr. Bass. He had to make a decision. He could comply with the instructions or he could refuse to comply with them wholly or in part, or he could consult Mr. Delf. His difficulty was, as on every such occasion, that he could not know whether or to what extent these payments would be covered by credits coming in during the day. In fact, though he did not then know it, £140,000 was received for Herstatt's credit at some unknown time on the same day. However, there were also some smaller further debits, with the result that the opening debit balance of about £4,650 rose to about £15,350 by the end of the day. But in the context of the history of the account as a whole over the last six months this was by no means alarming, and in itself hardly significant. At any rate, and in all the circumstances not surprisingly, Mr. Bass decided to allow the payments to be "actioned" without reference to higher authority. He accordingly gave instructions that all three payments, the in-house transfer of £120,000 and the two out-house payments of £10,000 and £5,000 respectively, were to be made. Banker's payments for the latter two sums were prepared and despatched. As regards the £120,000 the appropriate computer processes were set in motion to debit Herstatt's account, credit the plaintiffs' account, and to produce the corresponding advice notes.

Now, Mr. Bass said in evidence that he distinguished in his mind between the out-payments of £15,000 and the in-house transfer of £120,000. He said that he decided to "action" the latter payment only on a provisional basis. This is where it is necessary to choose one's words with care in determining what Mr. Bass's mental process was, insofar as this may be relevant. It was in no way an unusual situation. Mr. Bass and Mr. Dunn, as well as Mr. Delf, were continually making decisions of this kind several times a day. They were fully conscious of the importance of making payments on the "value" day. There was nothing unusual or particularly difficult about this decision; indeed, Mr. Bass did not even refer it to Mr. Delf. I think that his decision to sanction the transfer without reference to Mr. Delf may to some extent have been influenced by the thought at the back of his mind that if it should unexpectedly appear from the balance on the following morning that this payment had remained substantially uncovered by credits during the day, and if Herstatt were then unable to provide some satisfactory explanation or promise to remedy the situation quickly, there was always the possibility of reversing the entries on the following day. Mr. Bass had this at the back of his mind in relation to all substantial in-house payments which might produce an impermissible overdraft. However, on my impression of the witnesses and of the evidence as a whole, it was only to this very limited extent that Mr. Bass — or for that matter Mr. Dunn or Mr. Delf — would have regarded the transfer as "provisional". Thus, the plaintiffs would have been allowed to draw against it at once. If they had enquired whether the payment had been made, they would have been given an affirmative and not an equivocating answer, and I do not accept the evidence insofar as it suggested otherwise. No instructions would have been accepted from Herstatt to revoke the payment after the computerisation processes had begun. To express the position in legal terms, I do not accept that this was merely a conditional transfer in the sense that whether or not it stood depended on what might or might not happen on the following morning. It was an unconditional transfer, but subject to the remote possibility of the entries being reversed on the following day. This possibility, however remote and indeed unprecedented in the case of a banking customer, merely had the effect that the decision whether or not to make certain in-house payments was somewhat easier than in relation to corresponding out-house payments. But apart from this, the decision-making process itself, and all the physical processes in "actioning" such payments on the "value" date, were precisely the same.

However, at about 4.15 p.m. on 26th June it was announced that Herstatt had ceased trading and were going into liquidation. But for this, this action would never have seen the light of day. Mr. Delf got to hear about it shortly thereafter by telephone from Germany. His recollection is that he then gave instructions either to Mr. Dunn or to Mr. Bass that the entries relating to the transfer of £120,000 should be reversed *on that day*. I emphasise these words because he emphasised them in the way in which he gave his evidence, and he clearly recognised the importance of arriving at a final position on the "value" date itself. However, neither Mr. Dunn nor Mr. Bass had any recollection of this having happened. I cannot accept the accuracy of Mr. Delf's recollection on this point. Both Mr. Dunn and Mr. Bass only heard about Herstatt's failure when they read about it in the press early the following morning. They then spoke to Mr. Delf on the telephone. Even then, as I am satisfied on their evidence, the position remained fluid for some little time while further enquiries were being made. At first the only decision was to hold up the despatch of the advice notes concerning the debit and credit of the £120,000. Shortly thereafter Mr. Delf gave instructions for the entries to be reversed, and this was done by instructing the computer to debit the plaintiffs' account and to credit Herstatt's account with £120,000 on 27th June. Mr. Delf also gave instructions that the relevant pages in the statements of Herstatt and the plaintiffs should be retyped before being sent to them, omitting the original entries and their reversals. Insofar as it might be relevant — though in my view it is not — I find that none of this would have happened if Herstatt had not ceased trading and if there had merely been a debit balance of about £15,350 on their account on the morning of 27th June. The reason why it was done was that the defendants did not wish an unauthorised debit balance to appear in Herstatt's account at the time when they went into liquidation.

The subsequent events are of little importance. The plaintiffs made various enquiries directed to ascertain whether or not the £120,000 had been paid. They were told that it had not, "due to the present position of Herstatt's account". However, when they asked to see the branch's internal records, the photostat copies of the ledger sheets relating to their account were at once sent to them without any prevarication. These clearly showed the original entries on 26th June and their reversal on 27th June, but for some reason these passed unnoticed. It was only several months later, when the plaintiffs came to see photostat copies of Herstatt's ledger sheets, which had apparently equally readily been sent to Herstatt, that they realised what had happened. They then brought this action.

The issue is whether or not a completed payment had been made by the defendants to the plaintiffs on 26th June. This is a question of law. If the answer is Yes, then it is not contested that the plaintiffs have a good cause of action. If there were no authorities on this point, I think that the reaction, both of a lawyer and a banker, would be to answer this question in the affirmative. I think that both would say two things. First, that in such circumstances a payment has been made if the payee's account is credited with the payment at the close of business on the value date, at any rate if it was credited intentionally and in good faith and not by error or fraud. Secondly, I think that they would say that if a payment requires to be made on a certain day by debiting a payer customer's account and crediting a payee customer's account, then the position at the end of that day must be in fact and in law that this has either happened or not happened, but that the position cannot be left in the air. In my view both these propositions are correct in law.

The only authorities which are of any assistance are those concerning so-called in-house payments. The oldest of them was decided by the Court of Common Pleas nearly 150 years ago. It is indistinguishable on its facts, unless the process of computerisation has changed the law, which the defendants do not contend. It was an action between payer and payee, but it was rightly not suggested, if there was a completed payment as between them, that the position could be different as between the customers and the bank. In *Eyles* v. *Ellis* (1827) 4 Bing. 112 the plaintiff and the defendant had accounts at the same bank. The plaintiff sued the defendant for rent. The defendant contended that he had paid it. What happened was this. The defendant instructed his banker to transfer the amount of the rent to the plaintiff's account on a Friday, 8th October, the banker having omitted to do so on a previous occasion. The defendant's account was then overdrawn, but the banker complied with the plaintiff's instructions on that Friday by transferring the amount in his books from the defendant's account to the plaintiff's account. On the same day the defendant wrote to the plaintiff to inform him that the mistake had been rectified, but this letter did not reach the plaintiff until the Sunday. Meanwhile the banker failed on the intervening Saturday. The short judgment of the court was given by Best C.J. [at 113] and is worth quoting in full:

> The learned serjeant was right in esteeming this a payment. The Plaintiff had made the *Maidstone* Bankers his agents, and had authorized them to receive the money due from the Defendant. Was it then paid, or was that done which was equivalent to payment? At first, not; but on the 8th a sum was actually placed to the Plaintiff's account; and though no money was transferred in specie, that was an acknowledgment from the bankers that they had received the amount from *Ellis*. The Plaintiff might then have drawn for it, and the bankers could not have refused his draft.

The rest of the court concurred. *Eyles* v. *Ellis* has been referred to with apparent approval in a number of subsequent cases, and its correctness has never been questioned: see per Lopes L.J. in *Re Land Development Association, Kent's case* (1888) 39 Ch. D. 259; per Sankey J. in *British and North European Bank Ltd.* v. *Zalstein* [1927] 2 KB 92; and per Mocatta J. in *Zim Israel Navigation Co.* v. *Effy Shipping Corpn.* [1972] 1 Lloyd's Rep. 18. The important feature of the case for present purposes is that the payment was held to be complete when the payee's bank account was credited and before the payee had had any notice that this had happened.

I then turn to a case on which counsel for the defendants relied strongly. This was *Rekstin* v. *Severo Sibirsko and Bank for Russian Trade* [1933] 1 KB 47, a decision of the Divisional Court and the Court of Appeal. The facts were very unusual. I will refer to the first defendants, a Russian trading organisation, as "Severo" and to the second defendant as "the bank". The plaintiffs had obtained a judgment against Severo who had an account at the bank. Severo clearly wished to prevent the plaintiffs from levying execution against the moneys in that account. A Russian trade delegation with diplomatic immunity also had an account at the bank. The plaintiffs therefore decided, without the knowledge or consent of the delegation, to close their account and to transfer all the moneys in it to that of the delegation. The plaintiffs so instructed the bank by letter. On receipt of the letter a clerk of the bank made the necessary book entry to close Severo's account and also prepared a slip preparatory to crediting the delegation's account with the equivalent sum. However, the corresponding credit entry in the delegation's account had not yet been made when the plaintiffs served on the bank a garnishee order nisi in respect of their judgment against Severo. Insofar as the headnote of the report suggests that all relevant entries had then already been made to credit the delegation's account, it is inaccurate. The following three questions arose. (1) Was the mere notice to the bank to close Severo's account sufficient to bring to an end the relation of banker and customer between Severo and the bank? This was answered in the negative, because the bank continued to owe the moneys in the account to Severo until it had either paid them to Severo or to their order. (2) Was the mandate to the bank to transfer the moneys to the account of the trade delegation still revocable in the circumstances? This was answered in the affirmative and is relevant to the present case. (3) If so, did the garnishee order operate as a revocation? This was also answered in the affirmative and is irrelevant here.

It is not easy to extract from the judgments any clear ratio decidendi underlying the answer to the second issue. Counsel for the defendants submitted that the ratio was simply that payment to the trade delegation had not been completed because it had not received any notice of the payment. This was said in *Continental Caoutchouc & Gutta Percha Co.* v. *Kleinwort Sons & Co.* (1904), 90 LT 474 where money was paid to the defendant bank under a mistake by the payer of which the payee was aware. It was held that in these circumstances the payer could recover the money from the bank as money received to the payer's use — a result which might well have followed even after the bank had given notice of the mistaken payment to the payee. However, at any rate in the absence of any mistake, a requirement of notice to the payee would be in direct conflict with *Eyles* v. *Ellis* (*supra*) which does not appear to have been cited in either of these cases and is not referred to in the judgments. I cannot accept this analysis of the effect of the decision in *Rekstin* v. *Severo Sibirsko and Bank for Russian Trade* (*supra*). I think that the majority of the judgments show that the decision was based on either or both of two grounds. First, that there had been no final appropriation of the money to the credit of the trade delegation. Secondly, and evidently of greater importance in the minds of the members of the two courts, the fact that the trade delegation knew nothing of the proposed transfer, that there was no transaction between Severo and the delegation underlying it, and that the delegation had accordingly never assented to its account being credited with these moneys. Both these reasons distinguish the case from the present one. In my view this decision should be treated as confined to its special facts. As counsel for the plaintiffs submitted, I think that it merely decided that payment by means of an in-house transfer has not taken place if the payee has not assented to it, and perhaps also if the transfer has not been completed. I therefore reject counsel for the defendants' submission that for present purposes *Rekstin* v. *Severo Sibirsko and Bank for Russian Trade* decides that there could not have been any completed payment to the plaintiffs unless and until an advice note recording the credit to their account had been despatched to them or had been received by them. Counsel for the defendants preferred to rely on the time of despatch rather than on the time of receipt, because the evidence showed, as indeed one knows from one's own experience, that in practice some days may elapse before an account holder receives notice of a debit or credit to his account. But in my view the time of despatch would in any event be logically unjustifiable as the relevant time. If notice to the account holder is required, then it seems to me that only the receipt of the notice will do. However, apart from the fact that this would be wholly inconsistent with *Eyles* v. *Ellis*, such a rule would create all sorts of commercial difficulties and would also put a large question mark against the point of time up to which a payer could countermand his instructions. What would happen, for instance, if he instructed the bank to revoke notice of the payment to the payee by telex or telephone between the despatch of the advice note by post and its receipt? The evidence showed, in my view rightly as a matter of law, that the defendants would not have accepted countermanding instructions from Herstatt once the process of crediting the plaintiff's account had been set in motion pursuant to Herstatt's telex instructions.

This analysis of the legal position is strongly supported by one of the recent shipping cases to which I have already referred. They all concerned situations in which charterers made or purported to make a late payment of time-charter hire and the shipowners claimed to have validly withdrawn the vessel from the charterers' service before the payment was made. The issue was accordingly always a race between the effective time of payment and the time of withdrawal. The only one of these cases which is of direct assistance for present purposes is *The Brimnes, Tenax Steamship Co. Ltd.* v. *Owners of the motor vessel Brimnes* [1974] 3 All ER 88, [1975] 1 QB 929 since this concerned an in-house payment. The relevant facts were as follows. The charterers' bankers, Hambros, were instructed to pay the hire to the shipowners' bankers, MGT in New York, where Hambros also had an account. To pay the hire, Hambros instructed MGT by telex to transfer the appropriate amount from Hambros' account to that of the owners. The position was complicated by the fact that the owners had previously assigned the hire to MGT, with the result that there was some difference of opinion in the Court of Appeal whether MGT were acting as payees or as the owners' bankers in receiving the hire, but this is irrelevant for present purposes. All the members of the Court of Appeal clearly considered that payment was complete when MGT decided to credit the shipowners' account and acted on that decision. In a later case, which concerned an out-house payment before a differently constituted Court of Appeal, *Mardorf Peach & Co. Ltd.* v. *Attica Sea Carriers Corpn of Liberia, The Laconia* [1976] 2 All ER 249, this point was taken a little further by making it clear that the time of payment was the time when the bank accepted the payment order and decided to act on it, irrespective of the time which had to elapse before the bank's internal accounting processes had been completed.

Counsel for the defendants' answer to *The Brimnes* was that it was never argued, nor necessary to argue, that the time of payment was later than the time when the bank decided to act on the instructions to credit the shipowners' account and began to act on that decision, and that this point was also not argued in any of the other cases. This is correct. He also relied on a passage in the judgment of Megaw LJ where he said that "the time of payment could not be earlier than the time when MGT made their decision to debit Hambros' account. . . ." But taking the judgments as a whole, it is clear that it never occurred to anyone that notice to the payee was an essential ingredient of a completed payment. Both *Eyles* v. *Ellis* and *Rekstin* v. *Severo Sibirsko and Bank for Russian Trade* were cited in argument, but neither was mentioned in the judgments. The judgments are wholly consistent with *Eyles* v. *Ellis* but do not in any way reflect what counsel for the defendants seeks to extract from *Rekstin* v. *Severo Sibirsko and Bank for Russian Trade*. I therefore conclude that the authorities clearly support the contention that payment in the present case was complete when Mr. Bass decided to accept Herstatt's instructions to credit the plaintiffs' account and the computer processes for doing so were set in motion. Indeed, the present case is a fortiori to *The Brimnes* and *The Laconia*, because these processes were in fact completed before the defendants purported to revoke the payment by reversing the entries on the following morning.

This only leaves one further point with which I have to some extent already dealt. The defendants' witnesses said that they acted on the basis that the following morning was to be treated as an extension of the "value" day, because the final balances for that day are not available from the computer until then, and because they always had in mind the possibility of being able to reverse the entries. I cannot accept this. A day is a day. For banking purposes it ends at the close of working hours, and otherwise at midnight. Commerce requires that it should be clearly ascertainable by the end of a day whether a payment due to be made on that day has been made or not. Whether this has happened or not cannot be held in suspense until the following morning. In this case the payment was made on the due day. What happened on the following morning was that the defendants made an unauthorised reverse payment by the plaintiffs to Herstatt.

The defendants suggest that this result will send their system into disarray. But I do not see why, even if this were relevant. It is no more difficult to decide whether to make an in-house payment than an out-house payment, nor to set the necessary processes in motion if the payment is to be made. The consequences of an affirmative decision should be the same in both cases. The only result will be that the defendants will no longer be able to rely, as against their own payee customers, on the possibility of having second thoughts on the following morning.

Judgment for plaintiffs.

Notes:

1   In *The Brimnes, Tenax Steamship Co. Ltd.* v. *The Brimnes (Owners)* [1974] 3 All ER 88 (CA), referred to in *Momm's* case *supra*, the debtor's bankers instructed the creditor's assignee by telex to transfer the appropriate amount from their account to another account controlled by the creditor's assignee. The debtor was a charterer, the creditor was a shipowner, and the creditor's assignee was a bank. In the course of his decision, Megaw L.J. observed (at 111-112):

> I think that the shipowners are right in their contention that there is no useful analogy between, on the one hand, a payment made by delivery of cash or of a cheque (where a cheque is a permissible method of payment) and, on the other hand, telex instructions to pay, such as were given in this case. The receipt of a cheque is not the receipt of mere instructions. It is the receipt of an instrument — a chose in action — which has an inherent value, because the holder of it obtains, by virtue of his holding of the document, a legal right to a sum of money, which right he can enforce, if necessary by action. The receipt of a telex containing instructions to transfer funds from one account into another account confers on the holder of the telex no such right. It is instructions to pay, not a payment. . . . There might, I suppose, in a case such as this be evidence that such instructions from one banker to another have as a matter of banking or commercial practice the same status, generally or subject to qualifications, as bankers' cheques or drafts, that they are treated as being irrevocable, and that they are treated as constituting "payment" as soon as the instructions are received. But the weight of the evidence of witnesses for the shipowners, as accepted by the judge, and I think rightly accepted, was to the contrary. There was a notable absence of evidence from the charterers, or their bankers, on any such topic. On the evidence, and the absence of evidence, in this case, in agreement with Brandon J, I see no ground for holding that telex instructions such as were here given themselves constitute, or effect, "payment" by the mere receipt of the document containing the instructions.

2   In *Zim Israel Navigation Co. Ltd.* v. *Effy Shipping Corporation* [1972] 1 Ll. L. Rep. 18 (also referred to in *Momm's* case *supra*), Mocatta J. concluded in a fact situation similar to the one involved in *The Brimnes*, that payment was not finally made until the payee was in a position to draw on the balance created by the transferred credit. Megaw L.J., dissenting in *The Brimnes*, agreed with Mocatta J.'s view, and argued that " 'payment' is not achieved until the process has reached the stage that the creditor has received cash or that which he is prepared to treat as the equivalent of cash, or has a credit available on which, in the normal course of business or banking practice, he can draw, if he wishes, in the form of cash": [1974] 3 All ER 88, 110. Brandon J., the trial judge in *The Brimnes* (with whom the majority of the Court of Appeal agreed) referred, however, to "the time of the decision to debit the one account and credit the other" as well as to "the effective time of execution of the order": [1973] 1 All ER 769, 784. His reference was, however, made "without apparently considering that they might be very different, even though they had seemingly been more or less simultaneous in the case before him": Crawford *supra* at 140.

The weakness of the majority and minority positions are exposed in Lord Denning's judgment in *The Laconia* [1976] 2 All ER 249. Noting that the "processing" of the credit voucher by the payor bank "was a piece of mechanism inside the bank itself, which worked fast or slow according to the power put behind it", he stated that "[i]ts speed should not affect the legal position of the parties making or receiving payment . . . parties in the business must know where they stand." Note also the concern of the court in *Westminster Bank Ltd.* v. *Zang* [1965] 1 All ER 1023 (CA) to preserve for bankers the contractual freedom to decide whether or not to give immediate credit for "uncleared effects" (i.e., debit orders of third parties deposited but not yet presented for payment).

3   *Momm* and the other cases are discussed by Alan Tyree, "Electronic Funds Transfer in New Zealand" (1978) 8 NZU L Rev. 139, 145-150. He summarizes the current position as follows:

> *Momm* represents the most complete review yet of the law concerning time of payment. Kerr J. concludes that payment was complete when the bank officer "decided to accept Herstatt's instructions to credit the plaintiff's account and the computer processes for so doing were set in motion". The principle which emerges from the cases is that payment is complete when the appropriate person decides to honour the payment order and (possibly) acts upon that decision. This principle is subject to the following observations:
>
> 1. The proposition is not strictly speaking the *ratio decidendi* of any of the decided cases: in *Momm*, all of the accounting procedures had been completed; in *The Brimnes* it was only necessary to decide that the mere receipt of the Telex order was not completed payment; the payment in *Mardorf Peach* was an "out-house" payment. However, the time of payment was carefully argued in each of the cases; an argument in favour of some other time of payment would need to be very persuasive to succeed.
>
> 2. In each of the cases, bank practice was relevant but not always decisive. In *The Brimnes*, for example, the evidence of the bank established that there actually was a time of "decision" on the Telex message and that such payments were not, as claimed by the charterers, the result of a "continuous processing". However, in *Momm* itself, the bank attempted to show that it was the practice of the bank to reverse accounts on occasion on the following day. Kerr J. may not have been entirely convinced of the practice; no actual instances of such a reversal could be produced, but toward the end of his judgment it is clear that he did not accept such a practice as valid in any case.
>
> 3. The rule applies only when the receiving bank is authorised to receive payment on behalf of the payee.
>
> 4. In each of the cases, the accounting procedure followed the time of decision.
> . . .
>
> 5. The problem of obtaining evidence showing the exact time of payment is a difficult one under the above rule. Bankers might be advised to keep better records regarding the times of such "decisions". Each of the cases were "special" payments in that the matter did indeed come before an officer of the bank for consideration. In the vast majority of payments this will not be the case. The accounts will be credited

and debited, the payor's account will cover the transaction, and the question of payment will not, in fact, come to the explicit attention of any of the bank's employees. When, in such a circumstance, is the "decision" made? There are only two possibilities: the time when the accounts are changed or the close of the business day. The latter seems preferable, since until that time the bank clearly has the right to give the transaction special consideration and to "decide" in the above sense.

6. The dicta are not clear concerning the need for actions upon the decision to pay. Presumably, the "action" required is that necessary to establish objectively that the decision to pay has been made. If that is correct, then the question of necessity of the "action" is probably an academic one, for it is hard to imagine a contested case where the bank would admit the decision to pay but deny the "action".

4   The following is Crawford's observation (3 Can. Bus. LJ 119, 142-143) on Mr. Justice Kerr's decision in *Momm*:

> No doubt there is an appealing appearance of certainty about Mr. Justice Kerr's ruling that a payment is complete when a bank makes the decision to act. But on examination it too contains ambiguities. How often will there be credible evidence of the bank's decision apart from the record of the various "internal accounting processes"? If a decision by one level of the executive is overruled by a superior, is there one decision or two? What is the effective time of the controllng decision? The influence of, and upon, persons not privy to the payment is also important as may be illustrated by the *Rekstin* case, distinguished by Kerr, J. No change of mind occurred within the paying bank, but a garnishee order was served after the debiting of the payer's account on an in-house credit transfer, but before the credit to the payee's account had been physically made. The court held that the payment was not yet complete and the debt was properly attached by the garnishee order. As the only necessary decision had already been made, Kerr, J., would have ruled otherwise.

5   For further discussions of the legal aspects of credit transfers in the electronic age, see Law Reform Commission of Canada, *Commercial Law: Payment by Credit Transfer* (1978) Working Paper 21; and Government of Canada, *Changing Times: Banking in the Electronic Age* (1979, report prepared by Stanley Goldstein).

B.   ELECTRONIC FUNDS TRANSFERS IN CONSUMER TRANSACTIONS

1.   THE OPERATION OF THE SYSTEM

FRED GREGURAS
"Electronic Funds Transfers and the Financial-Institution/Consumer Relationship"
(1978) 10 UCC LJ 172, 175-76, 178-80, 206-08

Model for EFT Use

The model envisioned for the nationwide configuration of this telecommunications network includes the following operational process: The person desiring to make a purchase, effect a withdrawal, utilize a preauthorized line of. credit, or complete another type of financial transaction will initiate the transaction by presenting a plastic, personal identification card to a communications terminal operator or by inserting the card into a slot on an unmanned terminal. A single card will be utilized for both payment and credit transactions. The terminal could be located at a place of business, in the common area of a shopping center, or even in a home. The person presenting or inserting the card must in some way authenticate that the card is his or that he is authorized to use it.

Once authentication occurs, the type of transaction and the amounts are keyed. At this point the cardholder's account is queried at the card-issuing financial institution, through the communications network, to determine whether the specified type of transaction in the designated amount is authorized. For example, in a payment transaction the payor's funds transfer account is queried to determine if sufficient funds are available. In a credit transaction the credit account is queried to determine if a sufficient line of credit is available. The transaction may be partially payment and partially credit, analogous to the credit reserve accounts appended to checking accounts. The essential elements of the transaction message (cardholder, card-issuing financial institution and payee identification, type and amount of transaction, etc.) are transmitted to a local or regional computer-controlled message-processing center. From there, the message will either be sent directly or relayed (switched) through other processing centers to the relevant financial institutions for entry of the proper debits and credits. In its advanced stages the clearing process will likely occur on a completely on-line, real time basis with large financial institutions serving as correspondents for smaller ones. The authentication-authorization-transaction completion cycle will have to occur within seconds of the time at which the transaction is initiated in order to be acceptable to the consumer. The cardholder waits at the terminal for the message indicating successful completion. The cardholder probably will have to be provided some form of paper receipt for most transactions although no other paper flow will be involved.

The Hinky Dinky Pilot Project

The event that provided the impetus for much of the current EFT activity was the well-publicized and now almost legendary pilot project in Nebraska involving First Federal Savings and Loan of Lincoln and area Hinky Dinky grocery stores. As authorized by the Federal Home Loan Bank Board (FHLBB), this computer-assisted financial service, currently called The Money Service (TMS), allows First Federal depositors to deposit or withdraw money from a savings account or to make a loan or mortgage payment at a retail store via a telecommunications system. To utilize the service, the account holder proceeds to the convenience counter in a retail store where a communications terminal is located. The customer completes the TMS form and presents the form and his TMS plastic card to the employee operating the terminal. The operator activates the terminal and inserts the account card and a merchant identification card. For authentication, the customer is required to personally key or to provide the operator with a preassigned secret code called a personal identification number (PIN). The operator then keys the transaction code and the amount. If the transaction is authorized, the proper accounts are debited and credited and the customer receives a receipt. In the case of a withdrawal, the customer can then proceed with cash in hand. To a great extent, the use of an interest-paying savings account in this manner makes it the functional equivalent of a checking account.

• • •

Other Developments

Among other events that signal the evolution toward a comprehensive EFTS are the following. The expansion of the computer's use in transmission facilities such as the Federal Reserve Communications System (Fed Wire) and Bank Wire and the national authorization communications networks by National Bank-Americard (NBI) and Interbank Card Association (Master Charge) is a key step in the utilization of communications and computer switching facilities. The bank card authorization networks will eventually eliminate the flow of paper credit card drafts processed through the banking system. The use of detailed descriptive credit card statements in billing without returning copies of the associated drafts is another significant step. Experience gained through the use of the credit card descriptive statement is of assistance in designing descriptive statements that will meet the needs of consumers and other customers when cancelled checks are no longer returned, or become nonexistent. Exposure to the descriptive statement is a conditioning step designed to optimize customer acceptance of a less-paper payments system.

The introduction of point-of-sales communications terminals that capture data related to business system operations and provide check verification service is an important building block toward the creation of large numbers of EFT transaction points. Other significant progress toward establishing a network of terminals at retail locations include the use of communications terminals solely for check verification and credit authorization inquiry and the placement of automated teller machines (ATMs) and cash dispensers. If implemented and utilized properly, these devices will improve both consumer and merchant acceptance of EFT.

The links essential to these related developments may be emerging. As of mid-1977 there were at least thirty operational automated clearinghouses (ACHs) throughout the country. ACHs are commercial bank organizations which facilitate the exchange (clearing) of electronic debits and credits on magnetic tape authorized by a depositor of one member financial institution and posted to the account of another depositor in the same or another financial institution. Currently, the ACHs process only preauthorized, recurring payment transactions of consumers such as mortgage and installment loan payments and insurance premiums on a scheduled basis in batch mode. There are no major computer-to-computer links. The federal government is a major stimulus of ACH development through its massive direct payroll and payment deposit programs. Valuable experience concerning commercial and consumer customer acceptance and organizational structure and working relationship requirements is being gained.

• • •

THE OPERATIONAL SETTING

Authentication

Currently, an EFT transaction is authenticated when the consumer presents a card and knowledge of his PIN. The elements needed for access to an account are possession of the plastic card and knowledge of the PIN associated with it. To further limit the risk of loss, the amounts involved in single and cumulative daily transactions are restricted.

"Who the person is" can also be an important element of authentication. Although techniques such as fingerprint, voice print, and signature analysis are being tested for EFT use, no totally reliable or cost-effective method has yet been operationalized. In the check payments mechanism, absolute identification through drivers' licenses in the case of over-the-counter transactions and situational determinants in other settings provide a measure of "who a person is." It is unlikely that photo identification and other such means can be applied in an EFT setting because of the degree of inconvenience it would cause. The delay in completing transactions would be at least as great as for a check.

Thus, a fast means of authentication is crucial to consumer acceptance if any additional procedures are to be used. The method also must be reliable. The extent of reliability cuts both ways. It makes a system more secure, but at the same time inconsistent identifications can reduce convenience and increase the chance of consumer embarrassment and frequency of wrongful dishonor. Not only must access to unauthorized users be prevented but access must be virtually guaranteed to authorized users. Given the need for an increasingly large number of EFT terminals, it is highly improbable that a third measure of authentication will be implemented in the near future. But limiting the amount of funds involved in a transaction can only be an interim means of minimizing the risk of loss if EFT use is to expand. The point of removing the amount of restriction could arrive before an acceptable means of authentication is developed. For the foreseeable future, the elements of possession and knowledge will prevail. If financial institutions do not provide a better means of authentication, then the consumers' standards of care can be defined only in relation to those two elements and to the duty of notification.

Mechanics of the Transaction

The account holder inserts the card into an ATM or cash dispenser and personally keys his PIN, type of, and amounts involved in, the transaction in a current EFT transaction. No receipt is normally issued; the consumer must note the transaction in a register or other record book.

In the current manned terminal setting, the consumer typically directs the operator by completing a form in which the amount and type of the transaction is indicated. PIN identification occurs in one of two ways. A separate data entry terminal may be used through which the consumer can personally key his PIN. At other transaction stations, the consumer must verbally or in writing provide the operator with his PIN. The operator then keys each element of the transaction. The receipt provided in the manned terminal setting is generally a copy of the consumer's order to the terminal operator. The communications terminal usually does not verify the type or amount involved in the transaction by printing on the receipt. The consumer can not determine the accuracy of the communication until his statement arrives.

As EFT networks grow the trend will be that the consumer will become less involved in the operational actions of a transaction at a manned terminal. Speed and efficiency will dictate that an operator key the elements of the transaction rather than the consumer.

Note on the NCEFT Report and the EFT Act:

Guidelines designed to be a basis for a "Model EFT Consumer Code" were established in the U.S. by the National Commission on Electronic Fund Transfer (NCEFT) in its report to Congress (October 78). The Commission recommended that federal legislation be enacted to implement its Model Code in the areas of allocation of liability, written disclosures concerning an EFT account, the issuance of a receipt, the timing and content of descriptive statements, and procedures for error resolution and system malfunctions. It was recommended that the consumer responsibilities and liabilities under the Model Code could not be increased by contract.

During its final day the 95th Congress enacted the Electronic Fund Transfer Act, 15 USC §1693 (forming Title IX of Consumer Credit Protection Act). The statute establishes the rights, liabilities and duties of the consumer and the financial institution in electronic funds transfer transactions. It covers

(1)   Point-of-sale (POS) transfers;
(2)   Automated teller machine (ATM) transactions;
(3)   Transfers initiated by phone; and
(4)   Automated clearing house transactions.

Its provisions deal with choice of payment systems, federal preemption, variance by contract, advertising, distribution of cards, disclosure, receipts, account statements, liability for unauthorized transfers, burden of proof, liability for failure to comply with a proper order, error resolution, reversibility, preauthorized transfers, enforcement and informational privacy. For the EFT Act generally, see e.g. F. Greguras and A. Wright, "How the New EFT Act Affects the Financial Institution/Consumer Relationship" (1979) 11 UCC LJ 207; F. Greguras and A. Wright, "The Preemption Dilemma Under the New EFT Act" (1979) 12 UCC LJ 3; and Brandel and Olliff, "The Electronic Funds Transfer Act: A Primer" (1979) 40 Ohio St. LJ 531.

Bibliographical Note:

For further discussions of the consumer aspects of EFTs, see Paul Brace, "Electronic Funds Transfer System: Legal Perspectives" (1976) 14 Osgoode Hall LJ 787, and Government of Canada, *Changing Times* (*supra*). Privacy issues are canvassed in "Public Government for Private People", *The Report of the Commission on Freedom of Information and Individual Privacy* (Queen's Printer of Ontario: 1980, 3 vols.).

Chapter 19

Documentary Drafts and Letters of Credit

A. USE IN INTERNATIONAL TRADE

The most widely used type of contract for sale in international trade is the c.i.f. contract. Its main features were described by Lord Wright in *Smyth & Co. Ltd.* v. *Bailey Son & Co. Ltd.* [1940] 3 All ER 60, 67-68 (HL). Note also his brief discussion as to the practice of raising money on the documents executed in connection with such a contract:

> The contract in question here is of a type familiar in commerce, and is described as a c.i.f. contract. The initials indicate that the price is to include cost, insurance and freight. It is a type of contract which is more widely and more frequently in use than any other contract used for purposes of sea-borne commerce. An enormous number of transactions, in value amounting to untold sums, are carried out every year under c.i.f. contracts. The essential characteristics of this contract have often been described. The seller has to ship or acquire after that shipment the contract goods, as to which, if unascertained, he is generally required to give a notice of appropriation. On or after shipment, he has to obtain proper bills of lading and proper policies of insurance. He fulfils his contract by transferring the bills of lading and the policies to the buyer. As a general rule, he does so only against payment of the price, less the freight, which the buyer has to pay. In the invoice which accompanies the tender of the documents on the "prompt" — that is, the date fixed for payment — the freight is deducted, for this reason. In this course of business, the general property in the goods remains in the seller until he transfers the bills of lading. These rules, which are simple enough to state in general terms, are of the utmost importance in commercial transactions. I have dwelt upon them perhaps unnecessarily, because the judgment of the Court of Appeal might seem to throw doubt on one of their most essential aspects. The property which the seller retains while he or his agent, or the banker to whom he has pledged the documents, retains the bills of lading is the general property, and not a special property by way of security. In general, however, the importance of the retention of the property is not only to secure payment from the buyer but for purposes of finance. The general course of international commerce

involves the practice of raising money on the documents so as to bridge the period between shipment and the time of obtaining payment against documents. These credit facilities, which are of the first importance, would be completely unsettled if the incidence of the property were made a matter of doubt. By mercantile law, the bills of lading are the symbols of the goods. The general property in the goods must be in the seller if he is to be able to pledge them. The whole system of commercial credits depends on the seller's ability to give a charge on the goods and the policies of insurance. A mere unpaid seller's lien would, for obvious reasons, be inadequate and unsatisfactory. I need not observe that particular contracts may contain special terms, or otherwise indicate a special intention, taking the contract outside these rules. . . .

HAROLD BERMAN AND COLIN KAUFMAN
"The Law of International Commercial Transactions (Lex Mercatoria)"
(1978) 19 Harv. Int'l LJ 221, 237-251

THE DOCUMENTARY CHARACTER OF AN INTERNATIONAL SALE

Bills of Lading

Under the typical c.i.f. or other "shipment" contract, the seller is required to select a vessel, to secure the necessary shipping space, and to see to it that the goods are placed on board. At that point the seller normally receives from the carrier a bill of lading. This document has a threefold character: (1) it is the carrier's acknowledgement of receipt of the goods; (2) it embodies the terms of the contract of carriage; and (3) it is a document of title, that is, the person rightfully in possession of it is entitled to possess, use, and dispose of the goods represented by it.

Two kinds of bills of lading should be distinguished: the straight (non-negotiable) bill and the order (negotiable) bill. A straight bill obliges the carrier to deliver the goods to the named consignee whether or not he surrenders the bill of lading. Transfer of a straight bill under the general principles of contract law gives the transferee no greater rights than those of his transferor. A negotiable bill, on the other hand, conveys greater rights, which are generally defined in special legislation.

• • •

Other Documents of Title

In the course of time, merchants have devised other documents of title, in addition to the bill of lading. When goods are stored not on a vessel but on land, it is usually convenient to treat the warehouse receipt as the symbol of ownership. Where goods are left at a dock preparatory to shipment to sea, it is sometimes convenient to use the dock receipt as the document of title. Where it is desired to transfer rights in a portion of goods held under a bill of lading or warehouse (or dock) receipt, the practice has developed of using so-called delivery orders as a means for transferring ownership of such portions. . . .

Payment Against Documents in a C.I.F. Contract

There exist other factors that may diminish even the value of the rights possessed by the holder of a bill of lading. One such factor is the possible loss of the goods or damage to them while they are in transit. The bill of lading makes the carrier liable for such loss or damage only under certain circumstances and only within certain financial limits. Therefore, before an importer (or his bank) will pay for the goods, he (or it) will want to receive not only the bill of lading but also a policy or certificate of marine insurance naming the holder of the bill of lading as its beneficiary. He will also want an invoice as well as any other documents that may be required for exportation and importation, such as export license, import license, consular invoice, certificate of origin, and others. Under a typical c.i.f. contract, it is this entire package of documents that must be transferred by the seller to the buyer, or to the bank appointed by the buyer, before payment is made. Indeed, the typical documentary transaction calls for multiple copies of the documents — the commercial invoice in triplicate, a "full set" of bills of lading (one to be sent by ocean mail, one by air, and perhaps one by land), and sometimes multiple copies of other documents as well.

Payment under a c.i.f. contract is to be made against documents only, unless otherwise agreed. The Uniform Commercial Code expressly forbids the seller to tender the goods themselves instead of the documents. The reason for this is that banks normally play an important role in financing documentary transactions in international trade, and a bank that pays money to an exporter on behalf of an importer is better able to protect its security interest if the exporter is not permitted to avoid the tender of documents. Otherwise, possibilities of fraud may arise. For example, the importer who receives the goods may mortgage them to another lender, free of the bank's lien, or the exporter may supply goods of lower quality and value than the contract requires. Without the disclosures provided by the documents, the bank will not be alerted to obtain the exporter's check to the importer for the difference in value or to take other measures to reduce its loan. Essentially, the requirement in a c.i.f. contract that documents be transferred meets the same need as the requirement in a face-to-face transaction — for example, the sale of an automobile — that title documents go to the lender before the product goes to the buyer.

The documentary aspect of the c.i.f. transaction leads to the substitution of documents for goods in so many respects that it may also lead to the conclusion that the substitution is intended to be complete. Indeed, in one case, a great English commercial judge, Lord Scrutton, suggested that many of the difficulties arising from c.i.f. contracts could be resolved if the c.i.f. sale were understood not as a sale of goods but as a sale of documents relating to the goods: "he [the buyer] buys the documents, not the goods." This statement was sharply disputed in the same case by other English judges, who described the c.i.f. contract as "a contract for the sale of goods to be performed by the delivery of documents." Yet in a later case, another English judge stated: "the obligation of the vendor is to deliver documents rather than goods — to transfer symbols rather than the physical property represented thereby. . . ."

Non-Maritime Shipments

Although the above discussion is addressed to carriage of goods by sea, much of what has been said is equally applicable to international shipments by rail. The seller under an f.o.r. ("free on rail") clause, for example, must load the goods onto a railway. He is normally entitled to the purchase price when the goods are placed in the custody of the railway authority. C.i.f. terms are also used in shipments by rail.

Shipments by air also play a major role in international commerce. Since the period of risk and inaccessibility of the goods on such shipments is much shorter than in the case of rail or ocean shipments, the concept of symbolic delivery of goods by transfer of documents has not been applied to them. The air consignment note (or air waybill), for example, is not a document of title and cannot be transferred free of personal defenses.

FINANCING INTERNATIONAL SALES

In documentary sales transactions typical of international trade, the tender of the shipping documents usually fixes the time of payment. Of course, the parties may make other arrangements. In most types of international trade, however, the seller has strong incentives not to wait until the goods have arrived before requiring payment, and the buyer does not want to pay before he has received documents giving him control of the goods; hence, the popularity of the c.i.f. contract and its variants.

But the provision for payment against documents, while fixing the time of payment, leaves open the question of method of payment. If it is payment in cash, there is the problem of choice of currency. Moreover, the seller may not be in a position to insist on cash since buyers usually prefer suppliers who will meet their reasonable credit needs.

Documentary Drafts

In documentary international sales, the technique of payment usually involves the presentation of a draft, that is, of a written order addressed by the exporter-seller to the importer-buyer (or to a bank designated by the importer) requesting the addressee to pay a certain sum of money to, or to the order of, a specific person, or bearer, on presentation of the draft ("sight draft") or at a particular time in the future ("time draft").

Often the payee of the draft is the drawer himself — the exporter. Since the exporter and importer are almost always residents of different countries using different currencies, payment usually involves a currency conversion in one country or the other; and for such a conversion and for a remittance of foreign exchange, the services of a bank are invariably required. Thus, where the exporter draws a draft on the importer, he will usually endorse it to the order of a bank for collection; or he may draw it in the first instance to the order of a bank. The collecting bank will then endorse the draft "for collection" to the order of its foreign correspondent bank in the country of the importer. Typically, the draft will be accompanied by the complete set of documents — bill of lading or delivery order, marine insurance policy or certificate, invoice, etc. — required to effectuate delivery. A draft to which the shipping documents required by the underlying sales contract are attached is called a "documentary draft," as contrasted with a "clean draft," that is, one forwarded without shipping or other documents.

If the draft is payable at some time in the future, the drawee writes the word "*Accepted*" and the date across the face of the draft and signs his name underneath. With this, the drawee unconditionally accepts the obligation to pay the draft. It should be noted that even before such an acceptance, the draft is an obligation of the drawer and of the payee who has endorsed it and any other endorser.

Let us take as an example a shipment of goods by sea from New York to London. The New York seller draws his draft on the London buyer to the order of a bank in New York. The New York bank endorses the draft to the order of its London correspondent for collection by presentation to the buyer for payment (if it is a sight draft) or acceptance (if it is a time draft). If the contract is on c.i.f. terms, the seller will transmit to his New York bank a complete set of shipping documents which, with the draft, will be forwarded to the London bank. The New York bank will usually forward the documents by air and the London bank will present them to the buyer as soon as they are received. Thus, the buyer will pay or accept the draft at some time before the arrival of the goods.

If the draft is a sight draft drawn in American dollars, the buyer will usually pay the London bank a sufficient quantity of English pounds to pay the seller. If the draft is a time draft, the buyer will accept it and the bank will release the shipping documents to him. If so instructed, the London bank will hold the draft until maturity and then present it to the drawee (buyer) for payment, or else it may "discount" the draft, that is, lend money against it. . . .

International drafts are drawn in duplicate or triplicate, and a part is attached to each copy of the bill of lading, insurance document, and invoice, which are also commonly issued in multiple copies. The original, known as the first of exchange, is sent with the other documentary originals at the time of shipment. The remaining sets are sent by later mail. . . .

Trade and Banker's Acceptances

If a time draft is drawn on a merchant and accepted by him, it is known as a trade acceptance. If it is drawn on a bank and accepted by the bank, it is known as a banker's acceptance. The banker's acceptance adds the bank's credit to that of the seller-drawer, and it is obviously more readily marketable than the trade acceptance of all but the largest mercantile concerns. Financing drafts on the basis of bankers' acceptances is most frequently used by companies that have a substantial volume of export business and an even flow of export bills over the course of a year. Collections outstanding are accumulated to a point where the seller can draw a time draft on his bank for round amounts at 30, 60 or 90 days' sight. The collections serve as collateral and have to be of an amount sufficient to cover outstanding acceptances at all times. The bank will accept the time draft and discount it at a rate based on the acceptance commission plus the discount rate for prime bankers' acceptances.

Bankers' acceptances can also be used to refinance importations when the exporter has drawn a sight draft on the importer. If the importer finds that additional financing is necessary, he may draw a draft on his bank payable at 30, 60 or 90 days, depending on the period required to liquidate the underlying transaction. The bank will accept the draft, and the proceeds from discounting it will be used to pay the sight draft. This kind of arrangement is subject to the conditions of an acceptance agreement executed by the importer in favor of the bank. The importer holds the goods or the proceeds from the sale of the goods at the disposal of the bank, and he must meet his obligation not later than the date on which the draft matures.

Letters of Credit

Time drafts and, to a lesser extent, sight drafts drawn on an importer represent a credit risk to the exporter. The risk of exchange fluctuation, even where it falls on the importer, extends the exporter's credit risk. And the risk of foreign exchange restrictions falls immediately on the seller. For these reasons, unless the buyer is a very good credit risk and unless economic and political conditions in the country of importation negate the risks both of exchange fluctuation and foreign exchange restrictions, the typical United States exporter will prefer to sell on letter of credit terms. We shall confine our attention in this discussion to so-called commercial documentary letters of credit as distinct from travellers' letters of credit and other devices not used primarily in connection with export-import transactions.*

The commercial documentary letter of credit is an undertaking by a bank to honor the seller's drafts upon compliance with the conditions specified in the credit. The bank's undertaking runs to both the seller and the buyer. Thus, the bank lends the use of its name and credit standing to the buyer in order to induce the seller to part with his goods in exchange for the buyer's promise to pay for them; at the same time, it assures the seller of payment by a bank — often in his own country — upon presentation to it of the shipping documents.

Suppose a seller in New York enters into an export-import contract with a buyer in London calling for payment by letter of credit of a London bank, confirmed by a New York bank. In a normal transaction of this kind, the buyer will arrange for a line of credit with his bank in London (the "opening bank") which will carefully examine the buyer's financial condition and the state of the local market for the goods to be imported. If the results of such examination are satisfactory, the bank will then require the importer to submit an application stating the nature of the transaction, the amount to be paid, the merchandise to be shipped, the documents required, and the expiration date, so that the credit can be established to conform to the requirements of the contract of sale. The buyer's bank will then establish the amount it will make available to the importer for letters of credit at any one time.

When it has the necessary details, the London bank will "open" a credit on

---

*   Documentary collections diagrams are reproduced *infra*, following this article. [Eds.]

behalf of the New York exporter and will write or cable its New York correspondent bank asking it to "notify" the seller of the credit established for his benefit and the terms and conditions with which he must comply; or else it will ask the New York bank to "confirm" the credit, that is, to add its own undertaking to honor the seller's drafts drawn under it. In the case of a "confirmed" credit, the seller ("beneficiary"), upon shipment of the goods, will draw a draft on the New York bank ("confirming bank") and will attach to it the necessary documents. The New York bank, before paying or accepting the draft, will examine all documents with great care in order to verify that they conform with all the terms and conditions of the letter of credit. It can not waive the requirements of a credit without specific authority from its London correspondent, which must in turn obtain the consent of the buyer.

The New York bank will send the documents to the London bank, which will in turn transfer them to the buyer. The buyer, of course, will have provided, or will provide, the opening bank with the funds to meet the draft, and the opening bank will credit the confirming bank with the amount of the draft once it has been informed of the payment. All the banking transactions will be carried out for small fees based on commercial interest rates.

If the New York bank acts solely as a "notifying" (or "advising") bank, the New York seller-beneficiary will draw his drafts on the London bank, and the New York bank will have no obligation to honor them. In other words, the notifying bank is simply a conduit for the transmission of instructions. If, in addition, it honors the seller's drafts, it does so only as a paying agent for the opening bank, or acts independently on the basis of its own willingness to negotiate the draft and the shipping documents.

A letter of credit may be revocable, that is, the opening bank may modify or cancel it at any time without any obligation on its part, or on the part of the notifying bank, to inform the beneficiary of such modification or cancellation. Revocable letters of credit are rarely confirmed by United States banks. They serve only as a means of arranging payment. It is important to distinguish between the terms "confirmed" and "unconfirmed," on the one hand, and "irrevocable" and "revocable," on the other. "Revocable" and "irrevocable" relate to the opening bank's power to modify or cancel the credit. "Unconfirmed" and "confirmed" relate to the absence or presence of an obligation by a second bank, in addition to the opening bank, to fulfill the terms of the credit. An unconfirmed irrevocable credit is one which the opening bank has undertaken not to revoke but under which there is no direct liability to the exporter on the part of a correspondent bank.

Under the confirmed irrevocable letter of credit the seller has virtually eliminated the credit risk and normally need not concern himself with foreign exchange restrictions in the country to which the goods are to be exported. The time of receipt of the letter of credit may be of some importance to him in regard to his contract risk with the buyer; he incurs the risk that the buyer will default during the period between the date of sale and the date on which he receives the letter of credit. If the exporter considers that that is a substantial risk, he will insist on the issuance of the letter of credit at the time that the deal is closed.

The Letter of Credit as an Exporter's Financing Device

Although commercial documentary credits are principally used to finance individual export sales, they can be also used for financing a combined sale and supply transaction. If, for example, a New York seller has agreed to sell 500 bags of Brazilian coffee to a London buyer and has arranged with the buyer for payment at a bank in New York under a letter of credit, the credit in favor of the New York seller can sometimes serve as a means of effecting his purchase of coffee in Brazil.

One possibility is for the New York seller to assign the credit to his Brazilian supplier. However, international banking practice and national law impose severe limitations on the assignability of letters of credit. To be assignable, a letter of credit must expressly provide that the beneficiary may assign it. The credit may not be reassigned by the assignee. The assignee is bound by all the terms and conditions of the letter of credit. Indeed, even if the letter of credit is expressly assignable, there is some question whether the assignor may, by assignment, relieve himself from liability under it. However, the beneficiary of the letter of credit may always assign his right to the proceeds of drafts drawn under the credit, even where the credit specifically states that it is non-assignable.

As an alternative to assignment, the New York seller may seek to use the security of a letter of credit of which he is the beneficiary to open a separate credit in favor of the Brazilian seller. The second letter of credit, called a "secondary" credit or "back to back" credit, will contain all the terms and conditions of the first letter of credit, called the "prime" credit. The Brazilian beneficiary tenders shipping documents and receives payment under the secondary credit issued in his favor. If the New York exporter has arranged for the confirming bank to issue the second letter of credit, he will receive from the confirming bank any difference between the amount due to him under the prime credit and the amount paid to the supplier under the secondary credit. If he uses a different bank to issue the secondary credit, he will usually be required to reimburse it immediately after he collects under the prime credit. The second bank might insist that the exporter assign the proceeds of the original letter of credit to it in return for its issuance of the secondary credit, in which case the bank will later credit the seller with the diffrence due him.

In order for the prime credit to serve as security for the secondary credit, the documents required under the two credits should be literally identical, except for the price term and invoices. Regardless of the method employed, the use of a secondary credit will not of itself inform the Brazilian supplier of the price term under the original credit, i.e., of the seller's resale profit.

The Uniform Customs for Documentary Credits

A world wide unification of banking practices concerning documentary credits was first proposed in 1926 by the American National Committee of the International Chamber of Commerce (I.C.C.). A final draft was submitted to all I.C.C. Committees in 1927. These groups, in turn, were requested to consult with various banking associations in their countries. After a prolonged and careful study, the final version of the Uniform Customs and Practice for Commercial Documentry Credits (Uniform Customs) was approved by the Congress of the I.C.C. in Amsterdam in 1933. A revision of the Uniform Customs, adopted by the I.C.C. in 1951 and adhered to by United States banks since January 1, 1952, was designed to clarify and supplement the 1933 version.

English bankers, despite much pressure from their colleagues in other countries, refused to accept either the 1933 or the 1951 Uniform Customs. Primarily in order to induce the adherence of the British banks, the I.C.C. revised the Uniform Customs in 1962. The 1962 Revision took account of misgivings which had been expressed by various English bankers on different public and private occasions and also contained some changes proposed by non-British banks. The Uniform Customs were further revised in 1971 and 1974.

The banks of almost all countries of the world have given legal effect to the Uniform Customs by notifying their foreign correspondents that credits requesting either confirmation or notice of their issuance to local beneficiaries would be subject to these rules, and by incorporating the Uniform Customs into advices of credit sent to such beneficiaries. Partly to protect its large banking community from potential legal conflicts, and partly to avoid the slightly more stringent requirements of article 5 of the Uniform Commercial Code, New York enacted a law excluding the application of that article to any letter of credit which by express agreement or course of dealing was subject to the Uniform Customs. Thus, in effect, the Uniform Customs of the International Chamber of Commerce constitutes the New York law of letters of credit.

CANADIAN IMPERIAL BANK OF COMMERCE
Documentary Collection Operations: A Commerce International Service for Business
(1980)

Diagram of Procedures and Responsibilities of Export Collections

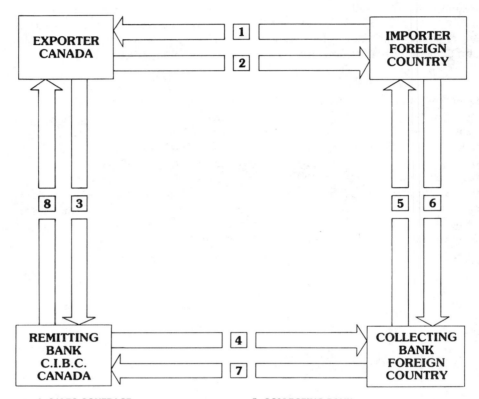

1. SALES CONTRACT
The sales contract or agreement provides for payment by way of documentary collection, draft at sight.

2. GOODS SHIPPED
The goods are shipped to the importer.

3. EXPORTER
The exporter sends the draft and documents with covering instructions to the remitting bank.

4. REMITTING BANK
The remitting bank sends the draft and documents registered airmail to a correspondent bank (collecting bank) with instructions for their release.

5. COLLECTING BANK
The collecting bank advises the importer that the documents have arrived and releases the documents against payment.

6. IMPORTER
The importer pays the collecting bank for release of the documents.

7. REMITTING BANK PAID
The collecting bank remits the net amount to the remitting bank.

8. EXPORTER PAID
The remitting bank pays or credits the account of the exporter.

Diagram of Procedures and Responsibilities of Import Collections

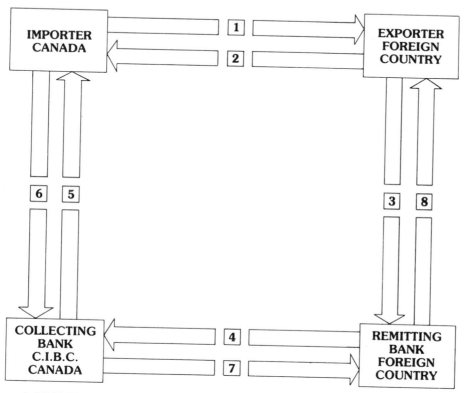

1. SALES CONTRACT
The sales contract or agreement provides for payment by way of documentary collection. draft at sight.

2. GOODS SHIPPED
The goods are shipped to the importer.

3. EXPORTER
The exporter sends the draft and documents with covering instructions to the remitting bank.

4. REMITTING BANK
The remitting bank sends the draft and documents registered airmail to a correspondent bank (collecting bank) with instructions for their release.

5. COLLECTING BANK
The collecting bank advises the importer that the documents have arrived and releases the documents against payment.

6. IMPORTER
The importer pays the collecting bank for release of the documents.

7. REMITTING BANK PAID
The collecting bank remits the net amount to the remitting bank.

8. EXPORTER PAID
The remitting bank pays or credits the account of the exporter.

B. DOCUMENTARY CREDIT OPERATIONS

CANADIAN IMPERIAL BANK OF COMMERCE
Commerce International Services: Documentary Credit Operations
(1979)

[a. THE PARTIES]

Applicant

When a bank issues a credit at the request of a customer the customer is the Applicant. The term "APPLICANT", "BUYER" and "IMPORTER" in this context are one and the same.

Beneficiary

When a bank issues a credit it is in favour of a Beneficiary. The term "BENEFICIARY", "SELLER" and "IMPORTER" in this context are one and the same.

Bank

When a sales contract between a buyer and seller provides for payment by way of a documentary credit, banks act on behalf of both parties in the following capacities:

Issuing Bank

The bank that opens a credit at the request and in accordance with the instructions of a customer (the applicant). The Issuing Bank is usually the importer's own bank.

Advising Bank

The bank that receives notification from an issuing bank that a credit is open, and subsequently advises the beneficiary of the details. The Advising Bank is frequently the exporter's own bank. Unless it has added its confirmation to the credit . . . the Advising Bank has no obligation to the beneficiary to pay, accept or negotiate drawings. It is, however, rare that the Advising Bank would refuse to do so.

Paying Bank/Accepting Bank

The bank designated to pay or accept drafts drawn under the credit. It is generally the issuing or the advising bank, but in certain cases it may be a third party in a large financial centre like London or New York depending on the foreign currency denominated in the credit.

Negotiating Bank

When the paying or accepting bank on which drafts are to be drawn is located, say, in another country to that of the beneficiary, the credit expressly or by implication allows the beneficiary's bank to negotiate drawings under the credit by giving value for the draft "with recourse" to the drawer.

Acceptance

When a draft is drawn under a documentary credit at a specified term on the issuing, advising or another bank that bank is designated the accepting bank. In accepting the draft, the bank signifies its commitment to pay the face value at maturity to a "bona fide" holder presenting it for payment at the appropriate time. The draft when accepted becomes a "bankers' acceptance" and may be discounted at the prevailing rate.

The purpose of an acceptance is primarily to provide short-term credit on behalf of the applicant (buyer) by deferring his ultimate payment date. On the other hand, when term drafts are discounted on behalf of the beneficiary (seller) the proceeds provide the beneficiary with working capital by replenishing his cash flow previously reduced by the value of the goods being delivered but not yet paid for by the buyer. This form of financing is known as "acceptance financing" under documentary credits.

[b. SPECIAL CREDITS]

[As was noted by Professors Berman and Kaufman in their article *supra*, letters of credit are either confirmed or unconfirmed, as well as either irrevocable or revocable. There are, however, various styles of such credits, as outlined below.]

Irrevocable Credit and Transferable Credit

In cases where the irrevocable documentary credit (confirmed or not) stipulates that it is "transferable" the exporter (beneficiary) has the right to instruct the advising bank to make the credit available *in whole* or *in part* to one or more third parties (second beneficiaries) according to whether or not part shipments are permitted. The amount of the credit so transferred, and unit prices, may be reduced, and the expiry and shipping dates shortened. The second beneficiary or transferee however cannot make transfers to a third beneficiary. . . .

Revolving Credit

A Revolving Documentary Credit can be irrevocable or revocable. It provides for continuous drawings for specific amounts within a specified period. When a drawing is made the amount of the credit is automatically reinstated under the same conditions, but when the credit is in revocable form it may also be cancelled. The purpose of a revolving credit is to replace a series of credits to the same beneficiary with similar requirements, and/or control the size of shipments at any one time.

Red Clause Credit

This special clause, which can vary, has been used mainly in the Australian wool trade and sometimes in connection with rubber shipments from the Far East (its description stems from the practice of "red inking" its special provisions). It enables the bank acting as the negotiating or paying agent of the issuing bank to provide the seller (the beneficiary of the credit, and perhaps the buyer's agent) in the country of shipment with funds to buy or accumulate the required merchandise from a number of different suppliers and to arrange shipment in accordance with the credit terms. Needless to say, any advances made will be deducted from the amount due to be paid when the full set of documents are presented under the credit, so invariably "Red Clause Credits" are restricted to one paying or negotiating bank abroad for obvious control and endorsement purposes.

Variations of the "Red Clause" provisions may also require that advances thereunder be secured by temporary warehouse receipts until such time as shipment is to take place. It might be added further that the beneficiaries of "Red Clause" credits are invariably brokers or agents of high standing and, of course, competent buyers of merchandise in their own particular field.

Back-to-Back Credit

The expression "Back-to-Back" is a feature used in special transactions involving two irrevocable documentary credits, but is never recorded on a credit.

The special transaction arises when a credit is issued by a foreign bank in favour of an exporter who is not in a position to furnish the goods required and has to purchase them from another supplier. In doing so the exporter may face difficulty in arranging credit terms or payment with his suppliers. The exporter therefore may arrange for his own bank to issue an irrevocable credit (counter credit) in favour of the supplier, using an assignment of proceeds payable under the foreign bank credit as backing. The terms of the counter credit are based on the foreign bank credit and call for documents evidencing shipment of the goods stipulated. The exporter will later substitute his own invoice for that of the supplier under the counter credit which is usually for a lesser amount.

Various types of technical problems can arise, however, in "back-to-back" situations and banks will carefully examine all aspects of the transaction before proceeding. This facility is not generally encouraged by banks, particularly where there is evidence that the exporter is trading in excess of his own financial resources.

Assignment of Proceeds

On occasions the beneficiary of an export credit which is not transferable will not be able to arrange the issuance of a "back-to-back" credit in favour of his actual supplier. Delivery by the supplier may, however, be arranged in such circumstances providing he is prepared to accept an advice from the drawee bank that they have recorded the beneficiary's instructions to pay the supplier a certain portion of the proceeds of the beneficiary's export drawing on the bank, relative to shipment of the goods in question. Suppliers sometimes control the bill of lading or other document of title until paid, where practicable.

[c. THE MECHANICS OF LETTERS OF CREDIT]

[The mechanics is demonstrated and explained by the following forms, diagrams of procedures, and shipping documents.]

Application for Import Credit

To The Manager
Canadian Imperial Bank of Commerce
Main Branch, Commerce Court
Toronto, Ontario ....

APPLICATION FOR
IRREVOCABLE DOCUMENTARY CREDIT

Date **January 2, 1979**

(1) OPEN:
☒ By Mail   ☐ By Mail With Cable Advice   ☐ By Cable
the following Irrevocable Documentary Credit.

(2) Your Name and Address
The Toronto Co. Ltd.
25 King Street West
Toronto, Ontario
M8W 2R9   Canada

(3) In Favour Of
The Export Co.
10-400 Des Voeux Road Central
Hong Kong, Hong Kong

(4) Amount: **CAN$42,350.00**

(5) Currency: **CANADIAN DOLLARS**

(6) Credit to Expire: **February 25, 1979**

(7) Drafts To Be Drawn At: ☒ Sight   Other _____

ACCOMPANIED BY THE FOLLOWING DOCUMENTS:

(8) Commercial Invoices: **three** Copies

(9) Canadian Customs Invoices Fully Completed and Signed: **four** Copies

(10) Bills of Lading: **Full set Clean 'On Board' Ocean Bills** of Lading to shippers order blank endorsed marked "Notify The Toronto Co. Ltd., Toronto" and "Freight Prepaid to Toronto, Ontario".

(11) Insurance   :   **Marine Insurance Policy or Certificate in duplicate, blank endorsed, for 110% of CIF Value covering all risks including war risks, strikes, riots and civil commotion, loss if any payable in Toronto, Canada.**

(12) Other   :   **Certificate of Origin Form "A".**
Detailed Packing List.
Special Exporters Declaration (Canadian Customs Form B31) required for shipment value CAN$10,000.00 or more.

(13) Covering: **Toys as per Buyer's Order No. 18348.**
C.I.F. Toronto, Ontario.
Latest date for shipment February 15, 1979.

(14) Shipment From: **Hong Kong**   To: **Vancouver, B.C.**

In Transit To: **Toronto, Ontario**

(15) Partial Shipments   ☒ Allowed   ☐ Not Allowed

(16) Transhipments   ☒ Allowed   ☐ Not Allowed

(17) Special Conditions:
Documents must be presented not later than **10** days after shipment.

(18)
Branch Confirmation

(19) I/WE HEREBY APPLY FOR THE ABOVE IRREVOCABLE DOCUMENTARY CREDIT WHICH CREDIT IS, EXCEPT SO FAR AS OTHERWISE EXPRESSLY STATED, SUBJECT TO THE "UNIFORM CUSTOMS AND PRACTICE FOR DOCUMENTARY CREDITS" (1974 REVISION) INTERNATIONAL CHAMBER OF COMMERCE (PUBLICATION NO. 290) IN CONSIDERATION OF YOUR ESTABLISHING THIS LETTER OF CREDIT, THE UNDERSIGNED AGREES TO COMPLETE YOUR FORM OF CONTRACT.

SPECIMEN
Signature

FORM 437 75

PART 1 - INTERNATIONAL DEPARTMENT COPY
(OR ISSUING CENTRAL BRANCH, WHERE APPLICABLE)

Import Credit

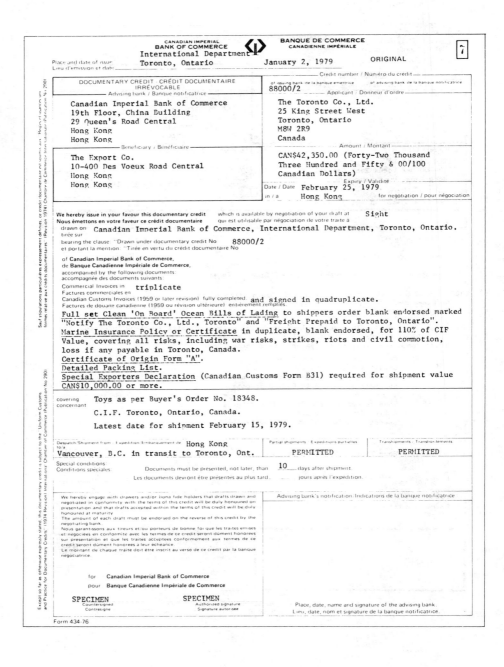

Export Credit

	Form 461-76
CANADIAN IMPERIAL BANK OF COMMERCE — BANQUE DE COMMERCE CANADIENNE IMPERIALE	

Place and date of issue
Lieu et date d'émission __International Department, Toronto, Ontario.   January 15, 1979.__

DOCUMENTARY CREDIT — CRÉDIT DOCUMENTAIRE
IRRÉVOCABLE

Credit number / Numéro du crédit
of issuing bank / de la banque émettrice | et advising bank de la banque notificatrice
ABC 5678 | IDT 12500/8

Issuing Bank / Banque émettrice

Korea Bank

Seoul, Republic of Korea

(South Korea)

Applicant / Donneur d'ordre

Industrial Co. Ltd.
P.O. Box 1745
Seoul, Republic of Korea
(South Korea)

Beneficiary / Bénéficiaire

The Metal Company
1935 Queen's Quay
Toronto, Ontario
M8W 9R2
Canada

Amount / Montant

US$112,000.00 (One Hundred and Twelve Thousand & 00/100 United States Dollars)

Expiry / Expiration
Date   Date   **March 15, 1979**
in   à   **Toronto, Ontario** for negotiation · pour négociation

We are pleased to advise that the above mentioned issuing bank has issued their documentary credit in your favour which is available against presentation of your following documents.
Nous vous informons que la banque émettrice précitée a ouvert un crédit documentaire en votre faveur, disponible sur présentation des documents suivants:

- Drafts drawn at 180 days sight on Canadian Imperial Bank of Commerce, International Department, Toronto, Ontario, enfaced "Drawn under Korea Bank, Seoul, Republic of Korea, (South Korea), Letter of Credit No. ABC 5678, dated January 5, 1979."
- Signed Commercial Invoice in quintuplicate.
- Packing List in duplicate.
- Certificate of Origin in duplicate.
- Weight Certificate in duplicate.
- Marine Insurance Policy or Certificate in duplicate, endorsed in blank for 110% of the Invoice value covering Institute Cargo Clauses All Risks, Institute War, S.R. & C.C. clauses.
  Insurance must stipulate that claims are payable in the currency of the draft, and must indicate a claims settling Agent in Korea.
- Full set Clean 'On Board' Ocean Bills of Lading issued to order and blank endorsed marked "Notify Industrial Co. Ltd., P.O. Box 1745, Seoul, Republic of Korea, (South Korea).

ALL DOCUMENTS MUST INDICATE L/CREDIT NO. ABC 5678.
THIS LETTER OF CREDIT IS PAYABLE AT SIGHT AS DISCOUNT CHARGES AND ACCEPTANCE COMMISSION ARE FOR ACCOUNT OF BUYERS.
ALL OTHER CHARGES OUTSIDE KOREA ARE FOR YOUR ACCOUNT.
DOCUMENTS MUST BE PRESENTED NOT LATER THAN 15 DAYS AFTER BILL OF LADING DATE.

covering
concernant   100 M/TONS OF SCRAP METAL OF CANADIAN ORIGIN

C.I.F. INCHON

LATEST DATE FOR SHIPMENT: MARCH 1, 1979.

Despatch/Shipment from / Expédition/embarquement de **U.S. OR** to / à **INCHON, KOREA** **CANADIAN PORT**	Partial shipments / Expéditions partielles **PERMITTED**	Transhipments / Transbordements **PROHIBITED**

Special conditions:
Conditions spéciales: Please present your documents to Canadian Imperial Bank of Commerce **Int'l Dept., Toronto, Ontario**
Veuillez présenter vos documents à la Banque Canadienne Impériale de Commerce . . . .
This advice must accompany your documents.
Le présent avis doit être annexé à vos documents.

The above credit carries our confirmation and we hereby engage that payment will be duly made provided that all terms and conditions of the credit have been complied with.
Le crédit ci-dessus comprend notre confirmation, et nous nous engageons, par les présentes, à ce que le paiement soit dûment effectué, pourvu que toutes les conditions régissant le crédit soient respectées.

Yours faithfully
Veuillez agréer l'expression de nos sentiments distingués.

SPECIMEN   SPECIMEN
. . . .
countersigned / contreseing   Authorized signature   Signature autorisée

Diagram of Procedures and Responsibilities of Import Credits

Note:

This diagram is intended to simply show the procedures and responsibilities of an irrevocable documentary credit when the credit stipulates that drafts are drawn on the

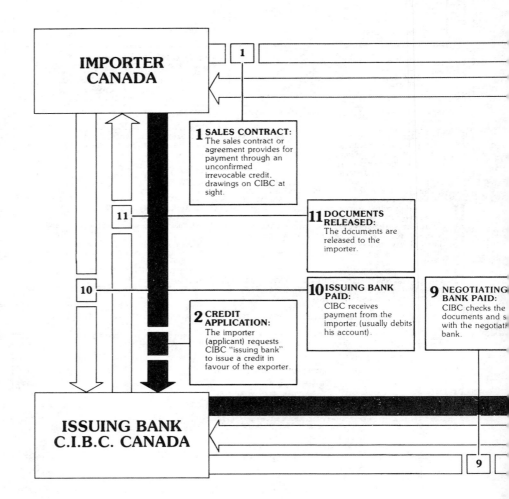

issuing bank at sight, which is generally the case. The procedures and responsibilities change slightly when a term draft is stipulated and/or if the drafts are drawn on a foreign bank . . . However, the flow as shown in the diagram is representative of documentary credit transactions.

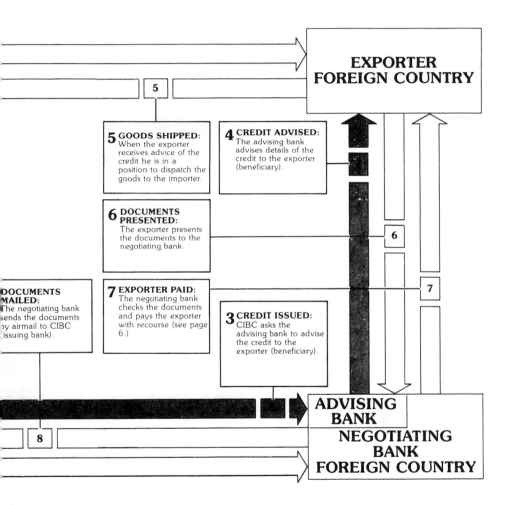

EXPORTER
FOREIGN COUNTRY

5

5 GOODS SHIPPED:
When the exporter receives advice of the credit he is in a position to dispatch the goods to the importer.

4 CREDIT ADVISED:
The advising bank advises details of the credit to the exporter (beneficiary).

6 DOCUMENTS PRESENTED:
The exporter presents the documents to the negotiating bank.

6

DOCUMENTS MAILED:
The negotiating bank sends the documents by airmail to CIBC (issuing bank).

7 EXPORTER PAID:
The negotiating bank checks the documents and pays the exporter with recourse (see page 6.)

3 CREDIT ISSUED:
CIBC asks the advising bank to advise the credit to the exporter (beneficiary).

7

ADVISING BANK
NEGOTIATING BANK
FOREIGN COUNTRY

8

Diagram of Procedures and Responsibilities of Export Credits

Note:

This diagram is intended to simply show the procedures and responsibilities of a confirmed irrevocable documentary credit when the credit stipulates that drafts are

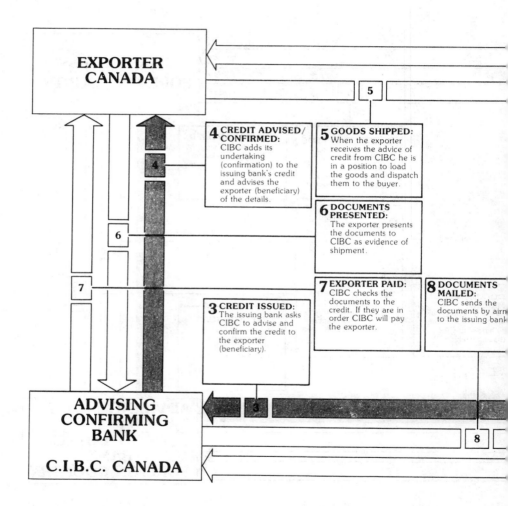

drawn on the confirming bank at sight, which is generally the case. The procedures and responsibilities change slightly when a term draft is stipulated and/or if the drafts are drawn on a foreign bank . . . However, the flow as shown in the diagram is representative of documentary credit transactions.

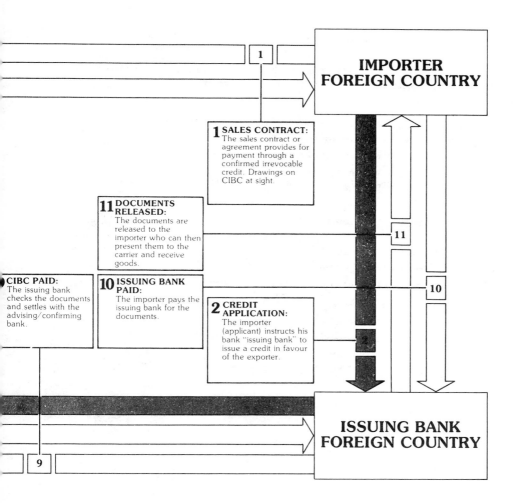

IMPORTER FOREIGN COUNTRY

1 SALES CONTRACT:
The sales contract or agreement provides for payment through a confirmed irrevocable credit. Drawings on CIBC at sight.

11 DOCUMENTS RELEASED:
The documents are released to the importer who can then present them to the carrier and receive goods.

CIBC PAID:
The issuing bank checks the documents and settles with the advising/confirming bank.

10 ISSUING BANK PAID:
The importer pays the issuing bank for the documents.

2 CREDIT APPLICATION:
The importer (applicant) instructs his bank "issuing bank" to issue a credit in favour of the exporter.

ISSUING BANK FOREIGN COUNTRY

Draft (Bill of Exchange)

Form 10-61

Toronto, Ontario   February 15, 1979   US$56,000.00
        Domicile   Date   (Amount in figures)

                                                                    after

    Sight   of this **FIRST** of Exchange *(Second unpaid) pay to the order of*

Canadian Imperial Bank of Commerce / (or "The Metal Company")   *the sum of*

Fifty-Six Thousand & 00/100 United States Dollars-------------------------
                              (Amount in words)

Value received, and charge to the account of   THE METAL COMPANY

To Canadian Imperial Bank of Commerce

              International Department   SIGNATURE

              Toronto, Ontario

    No.   Drawn under Korea Bank, Seoul, Republic of Korea, (South Korea),
                Letter of Credit No. ABC 5678.

Form 10-61

Toronto, Ontario   February 15, 1979   US$56,000.00
        Domicile   Date   (Amount in figures)

                                                                    after

    Sight   of this **SECOND** of Exchange *(First unpaid) pay to the order of*

Canadian Imperial Bank of Commerce / (or "The Metal Company")   *the sum of*

Fifty-Six Thousand & 00/100 United States Dollars-------------------------
                              (Amount in words)

Value received, and charge to the account of   THE METAL COMPANY

To Canadian Imperial Bank of Commerce

              International Department   SIGNATURE

              Toronto, Ontario

    No.   Drawn under Korea Bank, Seoul, Republic of Korea, (South Korea),
                Letter of Credit No. ABC 5678.

DOCUMENTARY CREDITS AND SHIPPING DOCUMENTS

Documents

A general term to denote the relative papers or forms which may accompany a draft (bill of exchange) arising out of an international commercial transaction. They primarily include: bills of lading, marine insurance policies or certificates, commercial invoices, appropriate customs invoices and perhaps certificates of weight and inspection. In the strict sense, however, documents are likely thought of as those instruments which convey title to the goods that secure the draft (bill of exchange). The following is a brief explanation of the more widely used documents. . . .

Bill of Lading (Ocean)

The Bill of Lading is a document of title to the goods contracted for by the buyer and seller. It is also a receipt and contract of carriage issued by the carrier to the shipper certifying that it has received the goods for transportation to a specified destination. In addition it can serve as a source of data for the preparation of other documents.

As a document of title, it can be transferred by endorsement. When the Bill of Lading is consigned to the "Shipper or Order" it may be endorsed in favour of the buyer on the reverse by the shipper, or simply endorsed by the latter in blank, which would make the bill of lading negotiable and enable title to the goods to be transferred to any holder of the document.

The latter method is the more usual, in that the transfer of title is thereby controlled by the negotiating and issuing banks, until the draft is paid or accepted, after which the Bill of Lading together with the other shipping documents are released to the importer so he can clear the goods on arrival.

If the goods are consigned to a specified consignee they will only be released to that person. In such a case the document is *not* in negotiable form, and therefore negotiating banks and others will not have title to the goods in any stage of the transaction. This is known as a "Straight" Bill of Lading and is not always acceptable to the banks in financing documentary credit transactions as it removes the possibility of the goods forming collateral security to them (goods may even be released to the consignee without the production of a "straight" bill). As a general rule documentary credits will stipulate that the Bill of Lading is to be consigned to "order" and "blank endorsed" with the notify party usually being either the buyer or his agent (or shipping broker).

As a receipt, the Bill of Lading should contain a general description of the goods so that they can be identified. It should be free from any superimposed clause or notation which expressly declares a defective condition of the goods or the packaging; in other words a Bill of Lading should be "clean". An "On Board" Bill of Lading indicates that the goods have been loaded on board the ship. On standard bills of lading it is usually incorporated in the text "shipped on board".

A "Received for Shipment" bill of lading is a receipt showing that the issuer has the goods in his custody, but they have not been placed on board a vessel. A

"Received for Shipment" Bill of Lading can be marked "On Board" by the carrier or their agents once the goods have been loaded on the vessel.

Unless otherwise specified in the credit, Bills of Lading of the following nature will be accepted:

1) "Through" Bills of Lading issued by shipping companies or their agents even though they cover several modes of transport.
2) "Short Form" Bills of Lading, issued by shipping companies or their agents which indicate some or all of the conditions of coverage by reference to a source or document other than the Bill of Lading.
3) "Container" Bills of Lading issued by shipping companies or their agents covering unitized cargoes, such as those on pallets or in containers.

A clean "On Board" Bill of Lading issued by a shipping company or its agent is the most widely used document of title in international transactions (see Exhibit 6, page 33).

Charter Party Bills of Lading

Unless specifically authorized in the credit, bills of lading which are subject to the conditions of a Charter — Party are not normally acceptable in documentary credit practice. Such bills of lading are not usually issued by or on behaf of the owners of a vessel but by a shipper or group of shippers who have leased or chartered the vessel from the owners for a designated trip or time period.

Accordingly, owners and charterers may have differing responsibilities regarding the operation or operating conditions of the vessel which would only be disclosed in full in the contract or lease executed between them; such a contract is called the "charter party". The charterers are normally free to sub-lease space in the vessel to other shippers and any bill of lading the charterers issue will be subject to the terms and conditions of the charter-party, possibly on a basis considerably different from that encountered in the direct owner/shipper contract in an ocean bill of lading.

Air Waybill

An Air Waybill covers goods transported by air, and takes the place of a bill of lading. It is only a receipt of goods despatched and is not usually a document of title. It is also known as an "Air Consignment Note".

Marine Insurance Policy or Certificate

After the ocean bill of lading, a Marine Insurance Policy or Certificate is the most important shipping document. Without it either one of the contracting parties and/or the bank financing the transaction would take all the risks involved in overseas shipments.

Each ocean shipment should be covered against general marine risks on warehouse-to-warehouse basis, and for those additional risks for which cover may be desirable because of the nature of the goods or other factors, and which should be stipulated in the credit.

The amount of the insurance should cover at least the amount of the shipment. However, it is advisable to obtain coverage for *110%* of the CIF value, to cover anticipated profit and/or additional expenses that may be incurred. A Marine Insurance Policy may only be issued by the insurer, and is usually on standard form with customary risks. Separate "policies" for different shipments are not always used by exporters as they would have to obtain a new policy for each shipment. Therefore, major companies are usually insured under a "Floating Policy" from which they are able to issue "certificates" covering their shipments all over the world. . . .

"Extension" clauses, of which a great variety are available at additional premium, should be considered and discussed with your marine insurance brokers to provide protection against risk elements other than simple "perils of the sea". "Cover Notes" issued by brokers are not acceptable, unless specifically authorized in the credit.

Commercial Invoice

An itemized bill given by the seller to the buyer showing all the particulars of sale, which should include: the date, name and address of the buyer and seller, quantity and description of goods, unit prices, trade terms, charges, extensions, etc. It should conform to the terms and conditions of the credit and be issued in the stipulated number of copies. . . .

Canada Customs Invoice

Effective June 1978, new customs invoices have been introduced, incorporating the MA and MB customs invoices. All import shipments in excess of Can. $200 require a Canada customs invoice. . . . The most careful completion of these forms is invariably necessary.

Inspection Certificate

This certificate, or combined certificate of weight and inspection, is sometimes required by an importer. It is prepared by a trade association or other organization authorized to make inspection and tests, and gives a description of the goods shipped by packages, boxes, barrels, contents, markings, etc., but without prices. . . .

Other Documents

From time to time, the exporter may be requested in the credit to furnish various other documentation, depending on the country the merchandise is being exported to and the type of merchandise. The following is a list of the more prominent documents that may be requested.

- Certificate of origin
- Consular invoice
- Health certificate
- Certificate of analysis
- Packing lists
- Weight lists
- Special expenses declaration (Canada Customs Forms B31 required for shipments value $10,000 or more)

SPECIMEN DOCUMENTS*

Bill of Lading

---

* In the interests of space, specimen forms of Marine Insurance Policy, Commercial Invoice, and Inspection Certificate have been omitted from the following documents.

Air Waybill

COMPLETE BY TYPEWRITER ONLY
DO NOT TYPE IN SHADED AREAS

À REMPLIR UNIQUEMENT À LA MACHINE
NE RIEN INSCRIRE DANS LES CASES OMBRÉES

AIR CANADA ✈ CARGO

SYSTEMS EQUIPMENT LIMITED TR5895-79

AIR CANADA ✈ CARGO

014-

014-

| Airport of departure | Execution date Date d'émission | TC | Charges Frais | Currency code Indic. monnaie |
| | Day Month Year Jour Mois Année | | | |

Airport of destination Aéroport de destination

③

Routing and destination / Itinéraire et destination

To · À | By first carrier Par 1er transporteur | By · Par | | To · À | By · Par | To · À | By · Par

NOT NEGOTIABLE
AIR WAYBILL
(AIR CONSIGNMENT NOTE)
ISSUED BY

NON NÉGOCIABLE
LETTRE DE TRANSPORT AÉRIEN
ÉMISE PAR

① **AIR CANADA**
1 PLACE VILLE MARIE, MONTREAL, P.Q. CANADA H3B 3P7
Incorporated in Canada with limited liability Compagnie canadienne à responsabilité limitée

MEMBER OF MEMBRE DE
IATA   L'IATA

Consignee's account number · N° de compte du destinataire

Consignee's name and address
Nom et adresse du destinataire

⑤

If the carriage involves an ultimate destination or stop in a country other than the country of departure, the Warsaw Convention may be applicable and the Convention governs and in most cases limits the liability of carriers in respect of loss of or damage to cargo. Agreed stopping places are those places (other than the places of departure and destination) shown under requested routing and/or those places shown in carriers' timetables as scheduled stopping places for the route. Address of the first carrier is the airport of departure.

Tout transport comportant une destination finale ou une escale dans un pays autre que celui du départ peut être régi par la Convention de Varsovie qui, en général, limite la responsabilité du transporteur en cas de perte ou d'avarie des marchandises. Les arrêts prévus sont les lieux autres que ceux de départ et de destination, indiqués à l'itinéraire et ceux qui figurent aux horaires du ou des transporteurs comme arrêts réguliers. L'adresse du 1er transporteur est celle de l'aéroport de départ.

SEE CONDITIONS ON REVERSE HEREOF – VOIR CONDITIONS AU VERSO

Shipper's Account Number · N° de compte de l'expéditeur

Shipper's name and address
Nom et adresse de l'expéditeur

⑥

The shipper certifies that the particulars on the face hereof are correct and agrees to the CONDITIONS ON REVERSE HEREOF, accepts the carrier's liability as stated in this AWB. Agreed on the reverse hereof, accepts such value unless a higher value for carriage is declared on the face hereof subject to additional charge and that packaging is subject to item 11 on the reverse hereof.

L'expéditeur certifie que les indications portées au présent document sont exactes; il accepte les CONDITIONS SPÉCIFIÉES AU VERSO, reconnaît que la responsabilité du transporteur est limitée à la valeur stipulée au paragraphe 4 ci-dessus, accepte cette valeur sauf déclaration si contre d'une valeur supérieure entraînant versement d'une surtaxe et reconnaît que le conditionnement est soumis aux dispositions de l'article 11 desdites conditions.

SPECIMEN ⑦

SIGNATURE OF SHIPPER OR HIS AGENT   SIGNATURE DE L'EXPÉDITEUR OU DE SON AGENT

Carrier certifies goods described below were received for carriage subject to the CONDITIONS ON REVERSE HEREOF, the goods then being in apparent good order and condition except as noted hereon.

Le transporteur certifie que les marchandises décrites ci-après ont été reçues en bon état apparent sauf indications portées d'autre part et que, pour le transport, elles sont soumises aux CONDITIONS SPÉCIFIÉES AU VERSO.

Issuing carrier's agent, account no.
N° de compte de l'agent du transporteur émetteur

Issuing carrier's agent, name and city
Nom et adresse de cet agent

⑧

EXECUTED ON – ÉTABLIE LE   (Date)   AT · À   (Place – Lieu)
⑨

Agent's IATA code · Indic. IATA de l'agent

SIGNATURE OF ISSUING CARRIER OR ITS AGENT – SIGNATURE DU TRANSPORTEUR ÉMETTEUR OU DE SON AGENT

Copies 1, 2 and 3 of this Air Waybill are originals and have the same validity

Les exemplaires 1, 2 et 3 de cette lettre de transport sont originaux et ont la même validité

| Currency Monnaie | Declared value for carriage · Valeur déclarée au Départ | | Declared value for customs Valeur déclarée pour la douane | Amount of insurance Montant de l'assurance | INSURANCE - If shipper requests insurance in accordance with conditions on reverse hereof, indicate amount to be insured in figures in box marked 'Amount of insurance' |
| ⑪ | | | ⑩ | | ASSURANCE - Si l'expéditeur demande que la marchandise soit assurée conformément aux conditions définies au verso, indiquer le montant de l'assurance dans la case ci-contre |

Weight charge and valuation charge Prepaid Payé Collect Dû

All other charges at origin Tout autres frais à l'origine Prepaid Collect

Accounting information · Renseignements comptables

| Number of Packages Nombre de colis R.C.P. | Actual gross weight Poids brut | Kg Lb | Rate Class Classe du tarif Commodity item no. Reference de l'article | Chargeable weight Poids de Taxation | Rate / Charge Tarif / Montant | TOTAL | Nature and quantity of goods (incl. dimensions or volume) Nature et quantité des marchandises (avec dimensions ou volume) |
| ⑫ | ⑬ | | | | | | ⑭ |

| PRE PAID PORT PAYÉ | Prepaid weight charge Taxation au poids payé | Prepaid valuation charge Taxation à la valeur payée | Due carrier Dus au transporteur | Total other prepaid charges Total des autres frais prépaid | Due agent Dus à l'agent | Total prepaid · Total port payé ⑮ | FOR CARRIER'S USE ONLY AT DESTINATION RÉSERVÉ AU TRANSPORTEUR À DESTINATION |

Other charges (except weight charge and valuation charge) · Autres frais (sauf taxation au poids et à la valeur)

COLLECT CHARGES IN DESTINATION CURRENCY À ENCAISSER EN MONNAIE DU PAYS DE DESTINATION

| PUP | DEL | INS | COD amount · Montant C.R. |
| Prepaid carrier's pick up Payé ramassage par le transporteur | Prepaid carrier's delivery Payé livraison par le transporteur | Prepaid carrier's insurance Assurance du transporteur payée | |

Total charges · Total des frais

| PUP | DEL | | |
| Collect carrier's pick up Dû ramassage par le transporteur | Collect carrier's delivery Dû livraison par le transporteur | | |

| COL LECT PORT DÛ | Collect weight charge Taxation au poids dû | Collect valuation charge Taxation à la valeur dû | Due carrier Dus au transporteur | Total other collect charges Total des autres frais dus | Due agent Dus à l'agent | COD amount · Montant C.R. | Total collect · Total dû ⑯ |

Handling information · Précisions pour la manutention

014-

ACF 294 (9-78)

THE EXPORT DEVELOPMENT CORPORATION

EDC Information Circulars 80-1 and 80-2

What is EDC?

The Export Development Corp. (EDC) is a Canadian Crown corporation that provides financial services to Canadian exporters and foreign buyers in order to facilitate and develop export trade. It does this through a wide range of insurance, guarantee and loan services not normally provided by the private sector.

EDC services are provided to assist Canadian exporters who are offering competitive products in terms of price, quality, delivery and service, to compete internationally. Exporters in other countries have access to similar support facilities from their governments. . . .

HISTORY

EDC is the successor to the Export Credits Insurance Corporation (ECIC), which was established by Act of Parliament in 1945.

In the immediate post-war period, the demand for goods and services far outstripped availability and, in the resulting sellers' market, credit terms tended to be well within the financing capacity of commercial banks. This was reflected in the corporation's original program, export credits insurance, which provided protection against non-payment by foreign buyers, and thus facilitated bank financing.

By passing the Export Credits Insurance Act, Parliament anticipated the re-emergence of a buyer's market, when normal trading conditions would re-assert themselves and the ability to provide credit terms would be a necessary competitive tool.

By 1960, the demand for long-term credit for capital projects led Parliament to amend the Act by adding a long-term financing facility to the corporation's powers. This service was established to help Canadian capital goods manufacturers and consulting engineers to retain their competitiveness in world markets.

Throughout the 60s, the changing demands of Canadian exporters required several amendments to the Act to allow the corporation to increase its financial ceilings and augment its services. The culmination of these changes and diversification of services was the decision to provide a new Act and a new corporation. Parliament passed the Export Development Act in June, 1969; it was proclaimed on Oct. 1, 1969. Notably changed under the new Act was the EDC financing facility. All loans prior to Oct. 1, 1969 were made for government account and funded by borrowings from the Consolidated Revenue Fund. Under the Export Development Act, the loan service became the responsibility of the Board of Directors of EDC. The government account remained for "national interest" lending to be administered by EDC. The Act also added a new service: foreign investment insurance.

During 1977 and 1978, two other major facilities were added: insurance and guarantees were provided with respect to bid and performance securities provided by banks and surety companies.

The effectiveness of EDC as a mechanism for facilitating exports is shown in the steady growth of its facilities and the demand for its services. It has grown from a corporation in 1945 which could assume financial commitments for $50 million to one which can today assume outstanding liabilities of $26 billion.

[The activities of the EDC are in the areas of insurance, guarantees, and loans. The following is a description of the insurance and guarantees activities.]

Insurance

Canadian firms of any size can insure their export sales against non-payment by foreign buyers. EDC normally assumes 90 per cent of the commercial and political risks involving insolvency or default by the buyer as well as blockage of funds, war or rebellion, cancellation of import licences, and the like, in a foreign country, and cancellation of export permits in Canada.

Almost any kind of transaction involving the export of goods, services or technology may be insured. Insurance is available to cover sales of general commodities and services normally made on short credit terms of up to 180 days, and capital goods and services made on medium-term credit of up to five years. It is also available to cover performance bonds, cross-liabilities in consortia and foreign investments of various types. . . .

EDC performance-related Insurance and Guarantees

INTRODUCTION

In many international transactions, particularly projects or construction works, the buyer requires the exporter to post security guaranteeing that he, the exporter, will perform satisfactorily, i.e., live up to the terms of the bid and/or contract.

In North America, this security usually is provided in the form of a bond issued on behalf of the exporter by a domestic surety company.

In transactions outside North America, it usually is provided by way of guarantee in the form of an Irrevocable Letter of Credit, or ILC.

An ILC is issued by the exporter's bank on behalf of the exporter and promises to pay the buyer on demand the amount of money stipulated in the letter.

The difference between a domestic bond and a guarantee under an ILC is that the domestic bond requires the buyer to prove non-performance under a contractual obligation whereas the ILC is payment on simple demand without such proof.

Since the ILCs required usually range between 5% and 25% of the contract value, not only are considerable amounts of money placed at risk, but the resultant holdings can impinge directly upon the exporter's working capital.

THE PROGRAM

In order to provide the requisite assistance, and to foster the ability of firms selling Canadian goods and services to compete effectively abroad, the Export Development Corporation has developed a five-tier program to protect Canadian exporters and financial institutions and surety companies which issue ILCs and domestic surety bonds to foreign buyers.

The five services provided are:

1. *Performance Security Insurance,* which covers an exporter against a wrongful call on an ILC issued by a bank or other financial institution on his behalf in favor of a buyer.
2. *Performance Security Guarantees,* which cover banks and other financial institutions against both rightful and wrongful calls on ILCs they have issued in favor of buyers on behalf of exporters as security for performance.
3. *Consortium Insurance,* which protects members of an exporting consortium against a rightful call by a buyer resulting from the non-performance of one or more members of the consortium.
4. *Surety Bond Insurance,* which covers a domestic surety company that has provided a performance bond in favor of a buyer on behalf of an exporter.
5. *Bid Security Guarantees,* which cover banks and other financial institutions against both rightful and wrongful calls on ILCs they have issued in favor of buyers on behalf of exporters as security for bids.

For a comprehensive discussion of current EDC financing practices and law, see Charles O'Connor, "Payment and Financing Mechanisms in International Trade", a paper delivered at *New Dimensions in International Trade Law,* a joint program by the University of Toronto and the Canadian Bar Association (Ontario), Toronto (November, 1980).

C. COMPLIANCE WITH THE TERMS OF THE CREDIT

An issuer of a letter of credit must honour a draft or demand for payment which complies with the terms of the credit. Where he has duly honoured a draft or demand for payment, the issuer is entitled to reimbursement from his customer (together with commission and interest as agreed). "In Anglo-American law, the bank's reimbursement has been treated variously as the result of an express promise to reimburse, as part of the performance of a contract implied in fact or as a quasi-contractual relationship for services rendered or money lent": Boris Kozolchyk, Chapter 5, "Letters of Credit", in J. Ziegel (ed.) vol. 9, *Intl. Ency. of Comparative Law* (1979) p. 46.

The issuing bank's right to reimbursement is typically secured by (a) the deposit of the stipulated amount, (b) a blocked account to which the amount is debited or (c) the pledge or hypothecation of the documents of title to the goods involved in the transaction. For further details, see Kozolchyk, *op. cit.* at 51 *et seq.*

"Compliance" with the terms of the credit is thus the key both to the duty of the issuing bank and to its right to reimbursement. The case and the notes which follow deal with the meaning of "compliance". The discussion stresses the documentary nature of the letter of credit transaction.

J.H. RAYNER & CO. LTD. v. HAMBROS BANK LTD.
(1942) 59 TLR 22 (CA)

MacKINNON, J.: This is an appeal from a judgment of Mr. Justice Atkinson in favour of the plaintiffs in the action. On March 29, 1940, the defendants received a cable from correspondents of theirs in Aarhus in these terms:

> Open irrevocable sight credit 3933 expiring June 1 next favour J.H. Rayner and Company 112/114 Fenchurch Street account Aarhus Oliefabrik for about 16975 pounds against invoice full set straight clean bills of lading to Aarhus Oliefabrik dated Madras during April 1940 covering about 1400 tons Coromandel ground-nuts in bags at £12 2s. 6d. per ton f.o.b. Madras shipment motorship Stensby to Aarhus.

Having received that cable on March 29 or 30, the defendants on April 1 issued to the plaintiffs a letter of credit which stated:

> We beg to inform you that a confirmed credit has been opened with us in favour of yourselves for an amount of up to about £16,975 account of Aarhus Oliefabrik available by drafts on this bank at sight to be accompanied by the following documents: invoice, marine and war insurance policy covered by the buyers, clean on board bills of lading in complete set issued to order Aarhus Oliefabrik, dated Madras during April, 1940, covering a shipment of about 1,400 tons Coromandel ground-nuts in bags at £12 2s. 6d. per ton f.o.b. Madras per m.s. "Stensby" to Aarhus. As our instructions to open this credit were by cable, we reserve the right to make any alterations that may be necessary upon receipt by us of our principals' written confirmation. This credit is valid until June 1, 1940. All drafts drawn here against must contain the clause "Drawn under Confirmed Credit No. 14597." We undertake to honour drafts on presentation if drawn in conformity with the terms of this credit.

On April 15 the plaintiffs presented to the defendant bank what they thought or claimed to be documents within the terms of that letter of credit and asked for payment of their draft. The documents presented consisted of an invoice and a bill of lading. The bill of lading describes the goods in these terms. In the margin are the marks "O.T.C. C.R.S. Aarhus," and it then states: "6,330 bags machine-shelled ground-nut kernels, each bag said to weigh 177 lb. net." Then, lower down: "Country of origin: British India. Country of final destination: Denmark. Goods are Danish property." The second document was a provisional invoice prepared by the plaintiffs in London, dated April 15. It is an invoice of "17.724 bags Coromandel ground-nuts, P.B.," which we were told is "pure basis," and states: "Bill of Lading dated 2.4.40."

Those two documents were presented to the defendants and under the letter of credit they were asked to accept the accompanying sight draft. After some negotiations, the defendants refused to accept the draft, and they did so on the ground that the terms of the letter of credit called for documents; an invoice and a bill of lading, both of which covered a shipment of goods described as "Coromandel ground-nuts," whereas the bill of lading only described the goods as "machine-shelled ground-nut kernels. Country of origin: British India." The plaintiffs alleged that that refusal was wrongful and in breach of the undertaking in the terms of the letter of credit.

There are various cases in which the legal result of a banker issuing a letter of credit of this type has been considered. As to the general observations with regard to such a document, and the obligations which it creates, there are two passages which seem to me to sum up the position with the greatest accuracy. One is in the judgment of Mr. Justice Bailbache in *English, Scottish and Australian Bank, Limited* v. *Bank of South Africa* ((1922) 13 Ll. L. Rep. 21, at p. 52):

> It is elementary to say that a person who ships in reliance on a letter of credit must do so in exact compliance with its terms. It is also elementary to say that a bank is not bound or indeed entitled to honour drafts presented to it under a letter of credit unless those drafts with the accompanying documents are in strict accord with the credit as opened.

The other passage is in the opinion of Lord Sumner in *Equitable Trust Company of New York* v. *Dawson Partners, Limited* ((1926) 27 Ll. L. Rep., at p. 52):

> It is both common ground and common sense that in such a transaction the accepting bank can only claim indemnity if the conditions on which it is authorized to accept are in the matter of the accompanying documents strictly observed. There is no room for documents which are almost the same, or which will do just as well. Business could not proceed securely on any other lines. The bank's branch abroad, which knows nothing officially of the details of the transaction thus financed, cannot take upon itself to decide what will do well enough and what will not. If it does as it is told, it is safe; if it declines to do anything else, it is safe; if it departs from the conditions laid down, it acts at its own risk.

The defendants were told by their Danish principals to issue a letter of credit under which they were to accept documents — the invoice and the bill of lading — covering "Coromandel ground-nuts in bags." What was offered to them was a bill of lading covering machine-shelled ground-nut kernels. There was the statement that its country of origin was British India. Those words in that bill of lading clearly are not the same as those required by the letter of credit. The whole case of the plaintiffs is that they will do just as well; that they are almost the same. If the defendants had accepted that proposition they would have done so at their own risk. I think that on pure principle they were entitled to refuse to accept this sight draft on the ground that the documents tendered, the bill of lading in particular, did not comply precisely with the terms of the letter of credit which they had issued.

The Judge in giving judgment said this:

> A sale of "Coromandel ground-nuts" is universally understood to be a sale of machine-shelled kernels, that is dry decorticated, and there is a standard form of contract, No. 37, used in the trade. The marking "C.R.S." is short for "Coros," which is itself an abbreviation of "Coromandels." If a bag of kernels is marked "C.R.S." it means that it is a bag of Coromandel ground-nuts.

That is stating the fact of evidence which was given by men who deal with ground-nuts in Mincing Lane, and when the Judge said that it was universally understood he meant that these men from Mincing Lane had told him:

> We dealers in Mincing Lane all understand these things. We understand that

Coromandel ground-nuts are machine-shelled ground-nut kernels, and we understand when we see "C.R.S." that that means Coromandels.

But it is suggested that as a consequence the defendants, when the bill of lading was brought to them for machine-shelled ground-nut kernels with "C.R.S." in the margin, ought to be affected with that special knowledge of the men who deal in these things on contracts in Mincing Lane. I think that that is an impossible suggestion. To begin with, this transaction does not concern any transaction in Mincing Lane; it is a transaction with Denmark, and for aught I know, and for aught the evidence provided, the people in Denmark know nothing about this practice or usage in Mincing Lane. Quite apart, however, from that special application of the relevant considerations, it is quite impossible to suggest that a banker is to be affected with knowledge of the customs and customary terms of every one of the thousands of trades with regard to the dealings in which he may issue letters of credit. As a homely illustration, suggested by the books in front of me, if a banker was ordered to issue a letter of credit with respect to the shipment of so many copies of the 1942 Annual Practice, and he was handed a bill of lading for so many copies of the 1942 White Book, it would be entirely beside the mark to call a lawyer, if that were necessary, to say that all lawyers know that the 1942 White Book means the 1942 Annual Practice. It would be quite impossible for business to be carried on, and for bankers to be in any way protected in such matters, if it was said that they must be affected by a knowledge of all the particular details of the way in which particular traders carry on their business.

As a second argument, Sir Robert Aske suggested that it was unnecessary under the terms of this letter of credit that the bill of lading should contain the description of Coromandel ground-nuts, and that it was sufficient if the bill of lading merely said so many bags of merchandise, provided that the invoice described the goods as Coromandel ground-nuts. In support of that argument he sought to rely on the letter of Aarhus Privatbank of March 29, in which, confirming their previous cable, they said that the credit was to be "available by sight draft on you against delivery of the following documents: Straight, clean bill of lading" and an invoice for Coromandel ground-nuts. He suggested therefore that it was only the invoice which need contain the description of Coromandel ground-nuts. There is nothing in that. In point of fact the letter of credit was issued in precise compliance with the previous cable, but whether that is so or not, the instructions to the defendants in pursuance of which they issued the letter of credit to the plaintiffs is entirely immaterial. The question is whether, on the terms of the letter of credit of April 1 addressed to the plaintiffs, the plaintiffs can allege that the defendants have broken their promise to honour their sight drafts.

There is one final incident which I think is of significance. It is a matter of evidence as to the reasonableness of the action of the defendants in refusing to pay the draft. They offered to pay it if the plaintiffs would furnish a bank guarantee absolving the defendants from the possible liability which they would incur by acting not in strict accordance with the terms of the letter of credit. They suggested that they would pay if the Eastern Bank, on behalf of the plaintiffs, would sign this guarantee: "In consideration of your, at our request, paying the sight drafts of Messrs. J.H. Rayner and Co., Limited, London, for £16,981 4s. 3d., in respect of a shipment of ground-nuts per the s.s. 'Stensby' from Madras to Aarhus under your confirmed credit No. 14597 dated April 1, 1940, notwithstanding the discrepancies mentioned in the schedule hereto" — the schedule stating, "The credit calls for the description 'Coromandel ground-nuts' whereas the relative bills of lading describe the goods as 'Machine-shelled ground-nut kernels' " — "we hereby guarantee that should your Danish banking principals eventually decline to confirm your action in paying the said drafts for their account by reason of such discrepancies we will repay to you," and so on. The plaintiffs, on that being submitted to them, refused to allow the Eastern Bank to sign that guarantee in those terms and said that they did so on legal advice.

The only materiality of that, as it seems to me, is not any question of which side was acting reasonably or otherwise, but as showing that the plaintiffs were advised that there was a serious possibility that if the defendants' payment of the draft was not in strict accord with the terms of the letter of credit, it might result in disputes and possibly in litigation with the Danish principals; that is to say, that it was not a matter universally known in the trade that this was a good bill of lading for Coromandel ground-nuts, and that no purchaser could possibly take any objection to such a discrepancy. There was a sufficiently serious danger of such objection being taken to make the plaintiffs under the advice of their legal advisers decline to give that guarantee. That seems to me to be in itself an incident which shows that the defendants were justified in saying: "We are not going to take this risk with our letters of credit." Paraphrasing the words of Lord Sumner in *Equitable Trust Company of New York* v. *Dawson Partners, Limited (supra)*, the defendants in effect said: "If we do as we are told, we are safe; if we decline to do anything but what we are told, we are safe, but if we depart from the conditions laid down, we act at our own risk." They would have acted at their own risk, and the plaintiffs knew it, because if the risk was negligible they themselves would have readily given that guarantee. The defendants are not called on to take, and the plaintiffs cannot insist that the defendants should take, that risk. Therefore the defendants were right in acting as they did and in refusing to pay the draft.

Appeal allowed.

Notes:

1   The principle that "when a banker . . . is given instructions or a mandate [to open the credit] they must be given to him with reasonable clearness" was restated by Devlin J. in *Midland Bank Ltd.* v. *Seymour* [1955] 2 Ll. L. Rep. 147, 153 (QB). "The banker is obliged to act upon them precisely. He may act at his peril if he disobeys them or does not conform with them": *id.* Yet, in the case of ambiguous instructions, the banker's position is analogous to that of an agent: "he is not in default if he can show that he adopted what was a reasonable meaning": *id.*

2   The following was said about documents under documentary sales (*Hansson v. Hamel and Horley Ltd.* [1922] 2 AC 36, 46, *per* Lord Sumner):

> When documents are to be taken up the buyer is entitled to documents which substantially confer protective rights throughout. He is not buying a litigation, as Lord Trevethin (then A.T. Lawrence J.) says in the *General Trading Co.'s Case*. These documents have to be handled by banks, they have to be taken up or rejected promptly and without any opportunity for prolonged inquiry, they have to be such as can be re-tendered to sub-purchasers, and it is essential that they should so conform to the accustomed shipping documents as to be reasonably and readily fit to pass current in commerce.

3   The importance of the bank's strict adherence to the terms of the credit in paying drafts drawn thereunder was noted by Viscount Sumner in *Equitable Trust Company of New York* v. *Dawson Partners Ltd.* (1927) 27 Ll. L. Rep. 49, 52:

> It is both common ground and common sense that in such a transaction the accepting bank can only claim indemnity if the conditions on which it is authorised to accept are in the matter of the accompanying documents strictly observed. There is no room for documents which are almost the same, or which will do just as well. Business could not proceed securely on any other lines. The bank's branch abroad, which knows nothing officially of the details of the transaction thus financed, cannot take upon itself to decide what will do well enough and what will not. If it does as it is told, it is safe; if it declines to do anything else, it is safe; if it departs from the conditions laid down, it acts at its own risk. The documents tendered were not exactly the documents which the defendants had promised to take up, and *prima facie* they were right in refusing to take them.

See also *Donald H. Scott & Co. Ltd.* v. *Barclays Bank Ltd.* [1923] 2 KB 1 where the Court of Appeal upheld the issuing bank's refusal to honour a draft drawn on the credit because the documents did not include an insurance policy as had been required by the terms of the credit.

4   However, the duty of the paying bank to inspect documents does not extend beyond reasonable care. "I doubt whether banks are under any greater duty to their correspondents than to satisfy themselves that the correct documents are presented to them, and that the bills of lading bear no indorsement or clausing by the shipowners or shippers which could reasonably mean that there was, or might be, some defect in the goods or their packing": *British Imex Industries Ltd.* v. *Midland Bank Ltd.* [1958] 1 QB 543, 552, *per* Salmon J. Likewise, "to assume that for one-sixteenth per cent of the amount he advances, a bank is bound carefully to read through all bills of lading presented to it in ridiculously minute type and full of exceptions, to read through the policies and to exercise a judgment as to whether the legal effect of the bill of lading and the policy is, on the whole, favourable to their client, is an obligation which I should require to investigate considerably before I accepted it . . .": *National Bank of Egypt* v. *Hannevig's Bank* (1919) 3 LDB 213, 214, *per* Scrutton L.J., cited in Chorley & Smart, *Leading Cases In the Law of Banking* (1977) p. 213.

5   Undue delay may forfeit the right of the issuing bank to reject documents against which the confirming bank has paid; *cf. Bank Melli Iran* v. *Barclays Bank (D.C. & O.)*

[1951] 2 TLR 1057 (KB). As to the bank's position in case of ambiguity, note the following excerpt from *Commercial Banking Co. of Sydney Ltd.* v. *Jalsard Pty. Ltd.* [1973] AC 279, 285-286 (PC) *per* Lord Diplock:

The contention of the buyer was that a document does not satisfy the description of "Certificate of Inspection" as that expression is used in a documentary credit unless it certifies that in the opinion of the inspector the goods are of an acceptable standard, i.e., that they conform to the requirements of the contract under which they have been sold. No evidence was called, however, to prove any usage either in the export trade generally or in the trade of exporting goods from Taiwan by which the ordinary English words "Certificate of Inspection" bear some special meaning. The respondent's claim in contract therefore turns upon the ordinary meaning of these words.

"Certificate of Inspection" is a term capable of covering documents which contain a wide variety of information as to the nature and the results of the inspection which had been undertaken. The minimum requirement implicit in the ordinary meaning of the words is that the goods the subject-matter of the inspection have been inspected, at any rate visually, by the person issuing the certificate. If it is intended that a particular method of inspection should be adopted or that particular information as to the result of the inspection should be recorded, this, in their Lordships' view, would not be implicit in the words "Certificate of Inspection" by themselves, but would need to be expressly stated.

It is a well-established principle in relation to commercial credits that if the instructions given by the customer to the issuing banker as to the documents to be tendered by the beneficiary are ambiguous or are capable of covering more than one kind of document, the banker is not in default if he acts upon a reasonable meaning of the ambiguous expression or accepts any kind of document which fairly falls within the wide description used: see *Midland Bank Ltd.* v. *Seymour* [1955] 2 Lloyd's Rep. 147.

There is good reason for this. By issuing the credit, the banker does not only enter into a contractual obligation to his own customer, the buyer, to honour the seller's drafts if they are accompanied by the specified documents. By confirming the credit to the seller through his correspondent at the place of shipment he assumes a contractual obligation to the seller that his drafts on the correspondent bank will be accepted if accompanied by the specified documents, and a contractual obligation to his correspondent bank to reimburse it for accepting the seller's drafts. The banker is not concerned as to whether the documents for which the buyer has stipulated serve any useful commercial purpose or as to why the customer called for tender of a document of a particular description. Both the issuing banker and his correspondent bank have to make quick decisions as to whether a document which has been tendered by the seller complies with the requirements of a credit at the risk of incurring liability to one or other of the parties to the transaction if the decision is wrong. Delay in deciding may in itself result in a breach of his contractual obligations to the buyer or to the seller. This is the reason for the rule that where the banker's instructions from his customer are ambiguous or unclear he commits no breach of his contract with the buyer if he has construed them in a reasonable sense, even though upon the closer consideration which can be given to questions of construction in an action in a court of law, it is possible to say that some other meaning is to be preferred.

Their Lordships are of opinion that the documents tendered by the two surveyors in the instant case clearly fall within the generic description "Certificate of Inspection." They record that the goods themselves, as well as the packages, were inspected. This, in the Board's view, would itself be sufficient to comply with the requirements of the credit. In addition, they contain an express statement as to the condition of the cases and an implied statement that the goods contained in the cases were in apparent good condition so far as could be seen in the course of supervising the packing of them.

6 The terms of a credit frequently call for payment against "clean bills of lading" (see e.g. the *Rayner* decision, *supra*). The meaning of this term was recently discussed by Donaldson J. in *M. Golodetz Et. Co.* v. *Czarnikow-Rionda Co.* [1979] 2 All ER 726 (QBD)); *aff'd* [1980] 1 All ER 501 (CA). The case involved a contract under whose terms the sellers were entitled to be paid the price on tender of "clean 'On Board' bills of lading evidencing freight having been paid". The particular bill of lading relating to 200 tonnes of sugar acknowledged in the printed clauses shipment of the goods in apparent good condition and order. In addition, it contained a typewritten notation that the cargo covered by the bill had been discharged because it had been damaged by fire and/or the water used to extinguish the fire. This damage occurred after the sugar had been loaded on board. The bill of lading was issued after the occurrence of the damage. It was rejected by the buyer on the grounds that it was not a "clean" bill of lading by reason of the typewritten notation. The issue is discussed by the court as follows (at 737):

(a) *That the bill of lading was not "clean"*: (i) *The practical test*

Counsel for the buyers submits that there are two possible tests to be applied, the practical and the legal. The practical test is whether a bill of lading in this form is acceptable to banks generally as being a "clean" bill of lading. Since 1962, virtually all banks have accepted the international rules set out in a document issued by the International Chambers of Commerce entitled Uniform Customs and Practice for Documentary Credits ("UCP rules"). Rule 16 provides as follows:

> A clean shipping document is one which bears no superimposed clause or notation which expressly declares a defective condition of the goods and/or the packaging. Banks will refuse shipping documents bearing such clauses or notations unless the credit expressly states clauses or notation which may be accepted.

This definition fails to specify the time with respect to which the notation speaks. The bill of lading and any notations speak *at* the date of issue, but they may speak *about* a state of affairs which then exists or about an earlier state of affairs or both. If the rule refers to notations about the state of affairs at the time of the issue of the bill of lading or, indeed, at any time after shipment of the 200 tonnes was completed, the bill of lading is not "clean" within the meaning of that word in the rule for the notation clearly draws attention to the cargo being damaged. If, however, it refers to notations about the state of affairs on completion of shipment, the bill of lading is equally clearly clean for it shows that the goods were in apparent good order and condition on shipment and suggests only that they were damaged after shipment.

Counsel for the buyers draws attention to the fact that this bill of lading was rejected by two different banks. The first rejection was by the sellers' own bank when the bill of lading was tendered by the shippers under the f.o.b. supply contract. The second rejection was by the buyers' sub-purchasers bank when it was tendered to them by the buyers without prejudice to the rights of the parties as between sellers and buyers. On these facts, counsel for the buyers invites me to hold that this bill of lading is not a "clean" bill in commercial or practical terms.

• • •

It is clear that the sub-buyers' bank thought that a letter of credit incorporating the UCP rules and calling for "clean" bills of lading was only satisfied if the bills were wholly unclaused. This goes further than the UCP rules justify since they appear to take exception only to a "superimposed clause or notation which expressly declares a defective condition of the goods and/or the packaging", whatever that may mean.

There is, I think, more than one answer to this "practical test" objection. First, the contract called for cash against documents, which no doubt assumes a documentary credit. But the board has not found that it was a custom of the trade, and the contract does not provide, that the documents shall be such as to satisfy the UCP rules as to "clean" bill of lading, which rules do not have the force of law. Furthermore, if there is ambiguity as to the meaning of those rules, that ambiguity should if possible be resolved in a way which will result in the rules reflecting the position under general maritime and commercial law. So construed they add nothing to the legal test which I consider hereafter.

Second, the evidence does not disclose that banks generally would reject such a bill of lading as that relating to the 200 tonnes as not being a "clean" bill of lading or that, if they would do so, it would be for any better reason than that they were applying what they thought the UCP rules required.

Third, I am not satisfied that it is right to apply a practical test, other than in the context of merchantability of the documents to which I will return hereafter. What is really being said here is that the very fact that the buyers and two banks rejected these documents proves that they are not "clean". This is a proposition which I decline to accept.

(ii) *The legal test*

I, therefore, proceed to apply the legal test. As Salmon J. remarked in *British Imex Industries Ltd.* v. *Midland Bank Ltd.* [1958] 1 QB 542, a "clean bill of lading" has never been exhaustively defined. I have been referred to a number of textbooks and authorities which support the proposition that a "clean" bill of lading is one in which there is nothing to qualify the admission that the goods were in apparent good order and condition and that the seller has no claim against the goods except in relation to freight. Some clearly regard the relevant time as being that of shipment. Some are silent as to what is the relevant time. None refers expressly to any time subsequent to shipment.

As between the shipowner and the shipper (including those claiming through the shipper as holders of the bill of lading) the crucial time is shipment. The shipowners' prime obligation is to deliver the goods at the contractual destination in the like good order and condition as when shipped. The cleanliness of the bill of lading may give rise to an estoppel and the terms of the bill of lading contract may exempt the shipowner from a breach of this obligation, but everything stems from the state of the goods as shipped. As between seller and c.i.f. or c. and f. buyer, the property and risk normally pass on the negotiation of the bill of lading, but do so as from shipment. Thus, the fact that the ship and goods have been lost after shipment or that a liability to contribute in general average or salvage has arisen is no reason for refusing to take up and pay for the documents.

In these circumstances, it is not surprising that there appears to be no case in which the courts or the textbook writers have had to consider a bill of lading which records the fate of the goods subsequent to shipment and, indeed, I have never seen or heard of a bill of lading like that in the present case. Nor is it surprising that some of the judgments and textbooks do not in terms say that when reference is made to the condition of the goods what is meant is their condition on shipment.

However, I have no doubt that this is the position. The bill of lading with which I am concerned casts no doubt whatsoever on the condition of the goods at that time and does not assert that at that time the shipowner had any claim whatsoever against the goods. It follows that in my judgment this bill of lading, unusual though it is, passes the legal test of cleanliness.

D. PAYMENT BY LETTER OF CREDIT

W.J. ALAN & CO. LTD. v. EL NASR EXPORT AND IMPORT CO.
[1972] 1 Ll. L. Rep. 313 at 321, 2 QB 189 (CA)

LORD DENNING M.R.:

THE EFFECT OF A LETTER OF CREDIT

When an irrevocable letter of credit is issued by one bank and confirmed by another, it may be a "conforming" credit; that is, one which conforms exactly to the contract of sale: or it may be a "non-conforming" credit; that is, one which does not conform exactly to the contract of sale, but is afterwards modified or accepted as being satisfactory to all concerned. It then becomes equivalent to a "conforming credit". In any such case the question arises whether the credit is to be regarded as absolute payment of the price, or as conditional payment of it, or as no payment at all but only a means by which payment may be obtained; i.e., as collateral security.

This must be a matter of the true construction of the contract: but, in order to construe it, it is important to bear in mind what the consequences are in each case.

ABSOLUTE PAYMENT

If the letter of credit is *absolute payment* of the price, the consequences are these: The seller can only look to the banker for payment. He can in no circumstances look to the buyer. The seller must present the documents to the banker and get payment from him in cash or get him to accept sight or time drafts. If the banker does not take up the documents, the seller will retain them, resell and sue the banker for damages. If the banker takes up the documents in exchange for *time* drafts, and the banker afterwards becomes insolvent, the seller must prove in the liquidation. He cannot sue the buyer.

There is an observation in the High Court of Australia which suggests that a confirmed irrevocable letter of credit may amount to absolute payment. In *Saffron* v. *Société Minière Cafrika* (1958) 100 CLR 231, at p. 243, the High Court said that

... a provision for payment by irrevocable and confirmed letter of credit ... might not unreasonably be regarded as a stipulation for the liability of the confirming bank in place of that of the buyer.

And in *Soproma S.p.A.* v. *Marine & Animal By-Products Corporation* [1966] 1 Lloyd's Rep. 367, at pp. 385-386, Mr. Justice McNair said:

Under this form of contract, as it seems to me, the buyer performs his obligation as to payment if he provides for the sellers a reliable and solvent paymaster.

Mr. Justice McNair did not, however, have all the arguments before him.

In my opinion a letter of credit is not to be regarded as absolute payment, unless the seller stipulates, expressly or impliedly, that it should be so. He may do it impliedly if he stipulates for the credit to be issued by a particular banker in such circumstances that it is to be inferred that the seller looks to that particular banker to the exclusion of the buyer. There are some cases in the United States which are to be explained in this way, such as *Vivacqua Irmaos S.A.* v. *Hickerson*, (1939) 190 So. 657; *Ornstein* v. *Hickerson*, (1941) 40 F. Supp. 305. And in the *Soproma* case, [1966] 1 Lloyd's Rep. 367, there was a stipulation for a particular banker, which may account for Mr. Justice McNair's observation.

CONDITIONAL PAYMENT

If the letter of credit is *conditional payment* of the price, the consequences are these: The seller looks in the first instance to the banker for payment: but, if the banker does not meet his obligations when the time comes for him to do so, the seller can have recourse to the buyer. The seller must present the documents to the banker. One of two things may then happen: (1) The banker may fail or refuse to pay or accept drafts in exchange for the documents. The seller then, of course, does not hand over the documents. He retains dominion over the goods. He can resell them and claim damages from the buyer. He can also sue the banker for not honouring the credit: see *Urquhart Lindsay & Co. Ltd.* v. *Eastern Bank Ltd.* [1922] 1 KB 318; (1921) 9 Ll. L. Rep. 572. But he cannot, of course, get damages twice over. (2) The bank may accept time drafts in exchange for the documents, but may fail to honour the drafts when the time comes. In that case the banker will have the documents and will usually have passed them on to the buyer, who will have paid the bank for them. The seller can then sue the banker on the drafts: or if the banker fails or is insolvent, the seller can sue the buyer. The banker's drafts are like any ordinary payment for goods by a bill of exchange. They are conditional payment, but not absolute payment. It may mean that the buyer (if he has already paid the bank) will have to pay twice over. So be it. He ought to have made sure that he employed a "reliable and solvent paymaster".

There are several cases which show that in the ordinary way a letter of credit is conditional and not absolute payment. But, as Mr. Tapp properly observed, they are all concerned with the time drafts. Thus, in New Zealand, *Hindley* v. *Tothill* (1894) 13 NZLR 13, at p. 23, the Court of Appeal said that the seller had the liability "of the bank in the first instance, and on the bank's default, that of the defendants (the buyers)". In the United States, *Greenough* v. *Munroe* (1931) 53 F.

2d. 362, at p. 365, the United States Court of Appeals for the 2nd Circuit (New York) said that

> ... the authorities favor the view that there is no presumption that the seller takes a draft drawn under a letter of credit in absolute payment of the buyer's obligation to pay for the merchandise; hence upon default by the bank upon its draft the seller may look to the buyer.

Finally, in England, in *Newman Industries Ltd.* v. *Indo-British Industries Ltd.,* [1956] 2 Lloyd's Rep. 219, at p. 236, Lord Justice Sellers said, in regard to a time draft:

> ... I do not think there is any evidence to establish, or any inference to be drawn, that the draft under the letter of credit was to be taken in absolute payment. I see no reason why the plaintiffs ... should not look to the defendants, as buyers, for payment.

Many of the textbooks treat a letter of credit as conditional payment. Thus, Professor Davis in 1953 said that

> ... such authority as there is supports the view that the letter of credit constitutes conditional, and not absolute, payment. Therefore, should the issuing bank fail to honour the seller's drafts, drawn in conformity with the terms of the letter of credit, the rights of the seller against the buyer will revive,

see his book on commercial credit, 2nd ed. (1954) at p. 46; 3rd ed. (1963) at p. 48; Megrah in the 4th ed. of Gutteridge (1968) pp. 29 to 33; and in 7th ed. of Paget (1966) pp. 620 to 622 is to the same effect.

NO PAYMENT AT ALL

If the letter of credit is *no payment at all,* but only a means by which payment may be obtained, i.e. if it is only collateral security, the consequences are these: The seller ought to present the documents to the banker. If the seller does not do so, he will be guilty of laches in enforcing his security and the buyer will be discharged — see *Peacock and Another* v. *Pursell* (1863) 14 CBNS 728. But if on presentation the banker fails or refuses to take up the documents, then (if the letter of credit is only collateral security) the seller will be entitled to take the documents round to the buyer (or send them to him) and demand that he take them up and pay the price. This situation finds no place in any of the authorities. There is a statement in an old case in Pennsylvania, *Bell and Others* v. *Moss and Another* (1840) 5 Wharton 189, at p. 203, when it was said that

> ... A credit with a banker is not payment, but a means of payment, more or less secure according to the solidity of the depositary; and the greater or less certainty of the security cannot affect the question of its character: it is but a security still ...

That statement was quoted with approval by Finkelstein in 1930 (*Commercial Letters of Credit,* at p. 156), who says that the seller "desires additional security without the surrender of any rights that he may have against the buyer". But the complete answer was given by Mr. Justice McNair in *Soproma S.p.A.* v. *Marine & Animal By-Products Corporation* [1966] 1 Lloyd's Rep. 367, at p. 386:

. . . It seems to me to be quite inconsistent with the express terms of a contract such as this to hold that the sellers have an alternative right to obtain payment from the buyers by presenting the documents direct to the buyers. Assuming that a letter of credit has been opened by the buyer for the opening of which the buyer would normally be required to provide the bank either with cash or some form of authority, could the seller at his option disregard the contractual letter of credit and present the documents direct to the buyer? As it seems to me, the answer must be plainly in the negative.

CONCLUSION AS TO PAYMENT

As a result of this analysis, I am of the opinion that in the ordinary way, when the contract of sale stipulates for payment to be made by confirmed irrevocable letter of credit, then, when the letter of credit is issued and accepted by the seller, it operates as conditional payment of the price. It does not operate as absolute payment.

It is analogous to the case where under a contract of sale, the buyer gives a bill of exchange or a cheque for the price. It is presumed to be given, not as absolute payment, nor as collateral security, but as conditional payment. If the letter of credit is honoured by the bank when the documents are presented to it, the debt is discharged. If it is not honoured, the debt is not discharged: and the seller has a remedy in damages against both banker and buyer.

Notes:

1   For an extensive discussion on *El Nasr*, see Malcolm Clarke, "Bankers' Commercial Credits Among the High Trees" [1974] Camb. LJ 260. On the effect of payment by letter of credit, the author agrees with Lord Denning: *id.* at 269-76. Lord Denning's conclusion as to payment was followed in *Maran Road Saw Mill* v. *Austin Taylor & Co. Ltd.* [1975] 1 Ll. L. Rep. 156 (QB).

2   The dispute between the buyer and the seller in *E.D. & F. Man Ltd.* v. *Nigerian Sweets & Confectionery Co. Ltd.* [1977] 2 Ll. L. Rep. 50 (QB) was originally referred to arbitration. The arbitrators found as a fact that there was no express stipulation that the opening of the credit was to be treated as absolute payment. Nonetheless, buyer's counsel (Mr. Evans) argued in court that as a matter of law the opening of the credit was to be treated as absolute payment. The point is discussed by Ackner J. in the following extract from his judgment (at 56):

> Mr. Evans sought to submit as a proposition of law, that where the identity of the bank is agreed between the parties, and not left to the choice of the buyers, it must follow that the sellers impliedly agree that the liability of the issuing bank has been accepted by them in place of that of the buyers. I do not think that this is correct. The fact that the sellers have agreed on the identity of the issuing bank is but one of the factors to be taken into account when considering whether there are circumstances from which it can be properly inferred that the sellers look to that particular bank to the exclusion of the buyer. It is in no way conclusive. In this case, unlike the United States case of *Ornstein* v. *Hickerson* referred to by Lord Denning, M.R., which was the basis of Mr. Evans's submission, there were other circumstances

which clearly supported the presumption that the letters of credit were not given as absolute payment but as conditional payment.

It follows from the finding that the letters of credit were given only as conditional payment, that if they were not honoured, the respondents' debt has not been discharged. This is because the buyers promised *to pay* by letter of credit, not to provide by a letter of credit the source of payment which did not pay. See *W.J. Alan & Co. v. L. Nasr Export* [1972] 1 Lloyd's Rep. 313 *per* Lord Justice Stephenson at p. 329. The sellers' remedy in such circumstances is to claim from the buyers either the price agreed in the contract of sale or damages for breach of their contractual promise to pay by letter of credit.

Mr. Justice Ackner further held that the analogy between a letter of credit and a bill of exchange "does not . . . provide any warrant" for holding that the buyer (who opened the credit) is discharged from his "primary liability to pay the purchase price of the goods" on the failure of the seller to give him a notice of dishonour (on the credit issuer's default); *id.* at 56-57.

3   The UCC deals with the effect of payment by letter of credit in §2-325(2). Under this subsection, "[t]he delivery to seller of a proper letter of credit suspends the buyer's obligation to pay. If the letter of credit is dishonored, the seller may on reasonable notification to the buyer require payment directly from him."

According to the official Comment, the subsection reflects "the established commercial understanding". Expressing its opinion that the subsection "conform[s] to existing law", the Ontario Law Reform Commission recommended that "the revised Act incorporate a [comparable] provision." See *Report on the Sale of Goods* (1979) p. 357 and s. 5.25 of the Draft Bill to Revise the Sale of Goods Act.

E. THE STANDBY LETTER OF CREDIT

E.P. ELLINGER
"Uses of Letters of Credit and Bank Guarantees in the Insurance Industry"
(1978) 6 Int. Bus. Lawyer 604, 609-22, 638-40

Standby letters of credit (which are also known as performance and guarantee letters of credit) serve a function altogether different from that of travellers' credits, acceptance credits and commercial credits. The last three types are, primarily, used for raising money or for facilitating payment. In each of them, the issuer undertakes to pay a certain amount of money when a given act — such as the drawing of a bill of exchange or the tender of stipulated documents — is performed. The standby letter of credit is a document issued to safeguard the position of the beneficiary if another person fails to perform an undertaking. By way of illustration, take a contract in which a builder agrees to complete a house on a given date and promises to pay a certain sum, by way of liquidated damages, if he fails to do so. To secure the payment of this amount, the builder may be asked to furnish a standby letter of credit, in which his bank promises to pay the agreed amount against a certificate in which the land-owner, or an architect, attests that the builder has failed to complete the house on time. It follows that the standby credit has a function similar to that of a guarantee or of an indemnity: it protects the beneficiary against loss incurred from the default of the "account party, i.e. the person who instructs the bank to furnish the credit. . . ."

The reason for the employment of letters of credit in place of guarantees is the restrictive scope of the powers conferred on American banks by statutes and by charters. As from about the middle of the 19th century, it has been accepted that American banks are not entitled to pledge their credit by acting as sureties and that guarantees issued by them are ultra vires and hence void. American banks are thus, in a different position from bankers in the rest of the world, who have traditionally regarded the issuing of guarantees as an accepted facet of banking business. Contradistinctively, the suretyship business in the United States has remained, primarily, the business of a separate branch of the business community.

• • •

2. Current Practice

In the United States standby credits are utilised in respect of a remarkable variety of legal transactions. This is evidenced, inter alia, by the cases which have come before the courts. In transactions concerning real property, standby credits have been used to secure the payment to a lender of a penalty accruing if the developer failed to take up the loan; to cover loss incurred by the land-owner where the builder failed to complete the construction of the building, and to secure repayment of a loan covered by a mortgage. They have been used in connection with business loans. In transactions involving the manufacturing or the sale of goods, standby credits have been used to secure the payment of the price, the payment of liquidated damages for defective performance, and to cover a deposit (or advance) repayable in the event of the non-performance of the underlying contract. Losses which could be incurred in the take-over of a company and arising from the non-payment of promissory notes, the payment of rentals, and the payment of an amount contested in an admiralty action brought against a ship have been, likewise, secured by standby credits. A somewhat less mundane function of this adaptable instrument was to secure the payment of wages payable to a football player and, surprisingly enough, to facilitate the payment of a ransom. One shudders to think that this apparently harmless banking facility of Wall Street, could, in due course, become a hijacker's dream!

The wide use of standby credits is a characteristic of the American business worlds. In other countries, including the United Kingdom, France, Germany and Australia, the function of standby credits is served by "first demand guarantees" and by performance bonds, which the banks, in these countries, are empowered to issue; but standby credits are not *terra incognita*.

In the United Kingdom, standby credits are used occasionally in respect of overseas transactions such as international loans, sales of goods and contracts for the supply of petroleum. A perusal of some recent forms disclosed that, usually, the issuing bank's engagement assumed the form of an undertaking to pay a sight draft, drawn under the letter of credit, and accompanied by two documents: (a) a matured bill of exchange for a given amount drawn by the beneficiary on the account party and (b) a certificate signed by a third party attesting the dishonour of the bill. In some cases, though, the standby credit stipulated for the tender of a notarial protest of the bill drawn on the account party instead of the default certificate. In only one specimen did the bank stipulate for the payment of a designated amount described as a debt and not covered by a negotiable instrument.

As would be expected, many of the standby credits opened by British banks related to transactions involving American merchants. But some standby credits were opened in favour of beneficiaries residing in Australia, in Libya, in Portugal, in Romania, in Sweden and in Switzerland. The sample studied was, unfortunately, too limited to draw any conclusion about the volume of business transacted in this manner. The general information obtained suggests, however, that in the United Kingdom both documentary credits and first-demand guarantees are used far more frequently, and are far better understood, than standby credits.

The position appears to be similar in Australia although there is an indication that financial stringency has encouraged the utilisation of letters of credit as a means of financial accommodation. Forms studied indicate that standby credits have been opened by American banks and by American branches of French banks in favour of local banks to back loans granted in respect of major commercial projects. Payment is usually against a sight draft accompanied by a certificate of the beneficiary, the local bank, attesting the borrower's default. One transaction, involving a loan granted by an Australian firm to an Australian subsidiary of an American Corporation and backed by a standby credit issued by an Australian bank, became the subject of litigation in the Supreme Court of New South Wales.

The very limited information available on the relevant banking practice of France and of Germany suggests that standby credits have not gained popularity in Western Europe. They are, again, used to a certain extent in substantial transactions involving overseas parties. The first demand guarantee appears to have remained dominant.

III. LEGAL ANALYSIS OF STANDBY CREDITS

1. Legal Nature of Standby Credits

The legal nature of a standby credit depends on whether it is revocable or irrevocable. A revocable standby credit may be cancelled or modified by the issuing bank at any time prior to the acceptance of documents tendered thereunder. It has been suggested that it is, nevertheless, of some value to the beneficiary because it constitutes an undertaking by the issuing bank to pay subject to cancellation. However, as the bank need not give any reasons for its decision to revoke, such a credit is, from a commercial point of view, an extremely poor assurance of payment. It is even less binding on the issuing bank than a simple offer to enter into a contract, which cannot be cancelled by the offeror after the communication of its acceptance by the offeree.

The nature of an irrevocable standby credit is altogether different. It constitutes a binding undertaking of the issuing bank and may be cancelled or modified by it only with the consent of all the parties, including the beneficiary. An irrevocable standby credit has been described as "a method of payment through banking chanels [that] defines the terms and conditions upon which payment will be made."

A standby credit — just as any other letter of credit — need not be in any specified form; but it must include the issuer's undertaking to pay. This point is illustrated by two recent American decisions. In the first, *Johnston* v. *State Bank* 195 NW 2d 126, a developer agreed to construct a house on a plot of land sold to a client. To enable the developer to obtain a construction loan, the client's bank wrote a letter, addressed to the developer, indicating that it would grant the client a long term loan upon the completion of the house, provided a clear title was issued by the local authority. As no such title was issued, the bank refused to effect the loan. An action brought against the bank jointly by the developer and the client, in which it was argued, inter alia, that the bank's letter to the developer constituted a letter of credit, was dismissed. The Supreme Court of Iowa observed: "The essential element of a letter of credit which is absent here is a direct promise by the bank to pay the addressee of the letter."

In the second case, *Dodge Motor Trucks Inc.* v. *First National Bank* 519 F 2d 578, the bank replied to Dodge's enquiry, regarding the availability of finance for the purchase of Dodge's trucks by F., that "we do have a commitment to [F.] that will take care of his needs. While we are not able to set a specific amount, [we] are sure that we will be able to handle any purchase he may make from your firm." It was held that this document did not constitute a letter of credit. "While no set form is necessary to create a letter of credit, it must contain the essential elements. . . . It must fulfil the office of a request, general or special, to pay the bearer or person named money or sell him some commodity on credit, or give him something of value, and look to the drawer of the letter for recompense . . .". The Circuit Court of Appeals based its conclusion that the bank had not issued a letter of credit on the fact that, in its course of dealings, Dodge did not expect to obtain direct payment from the bank. In a sense, this finding begged the question. The fact that Dodge sued the bank when F. was unable to pay might have implied that it had expected the bank to pay in the event of F.'s default. On that basis the bank's letter could have been regarded by Dodge as a standby credit. Moreover, it could have been so construed by other business firms. The decision is, however, supportable on a somewhat different reasoning based on the fact that the bank's letter did not make any express promise to Dodge. It was, in reality, akin to an ordinary bank reference.

The legal nature of a standby credit is further illustrated by its comparison with first demand guarantees and performance bonds.

2. Comparison with Guarantees and Performance Bonds
As already observed, an irrevocable standby credit has to include an express promise to pay. The issuing bank's liability is, however, contingent. It becomes absolute only if the beneficiary tenders the specified documents, which evidence the account party's non-performance of the underlying contract. The similarity between the function of the bank's undertaking in a standby credit and its

obligation under a performance bond or a first demand guarantee is well recognised. The conceptual distinction between the two types of instrument is best illustrated by a leading case.

In *Wichita Eagle and Beacon Publishing Co. Inc.* v. *Pacific National Bank* 343 F supp. 332 (1971); rev'd 493 F 2d 1285 (1974) a lessee, who had no further use for premises over which he had a long term lease, arranged for the lessor to sublet them to a construction firm, who undertook to erect a multi-storey garage on the land. At the instruction of that firm, the bank issued, in favour of the lessee and lessor, an irrevocable standby credit which was payable in the event the construction firm — the account party — did not erect the building. The standby credit could, however, be cancelled if the construction firm failed to acquire the necessary building permit. No indication was given in the credit as to how the construction firm's default, or its inability to obtain the permit, was to be established. When difficulties arose in respect of the permit, the bank informed the beneficiaries that the credit was cancelled. The lessee, who had to continue paying rent to the lessor during the prolonged period of delays, refused to accept the cancellation and presented a draft drawn under the letter of credit. When this was dishonoured, the lessee brought an action on the letter of credit to recover the loss sustained.

The District Court held that the document in question had not been validly cancelled as the local authority had not refused to issue the permit. The bank was therefore liable. To determine the measure of damages, the Court discussed whether the instrument constituted a letter of credit or a guarantee. Finding it to be a letter of credit, Levin J. said:

> While in a sense every letter of credit is a form of guarantee, the letter of credit differs from the classical surety undertaking in that it is a primary obligation between the issuer and the beneficiary. . . . The issuer of the credit is not concerned with the arrangements existing between the beneficiary and the issuer's account party.

The learned Judge thought that it was irrelevant that the letter of credit was neither documentary nor clean but payable upon the occurrence of a given event, i.e. if the construction firm failed to perform its contract with the lessor and the lessee. As the instrument was considered to be a letter of credit, the lessee was awarded the amount of the dishonoured draft less the profit made by him when the property in question was leased to another sub-lessor.

The Ninth Circuit reversed the decision on this point, holding the instrument to be a guarantee. The Court observed:

> We do not base our holding that the instrument is not a letter of credit on the fact that payment was triggered by default rather than performance . . . for we recognise that the commercial use of letters of credit has expanded far beyond the international sale context in which it originally developed. . . .
>
> The instrument involved here strays too far from the basic purpose of letters of credit, namely, providing a means of assuring payment cheaply by eliminating the need for the issuer to police the underlying contract.

The ratio of the decision is clear. The instrument constituted a guarantee and not a letter of credit because it was very closely related to the underlying contract made between the construction firm and the lessor and lessee. It terminated if the required building permit was not granted and not upon the tender of an agreed document attesting this fact; similarly, payment was due upon the occurrence of a specified event, i.e. the default by the construction firm, and not upon the tender of a certificate evidencing this fact. As the document was held to be a guarantee, the lessee was awarded the full amount of the draft, no allowance being made in respect of the mitigation of his loss. The Court was able to uphold the validity of the guarantee as the bank's power to open it was not in issue.

An English or an Australian lawyer may be perplexed by the *ratio decidendi* concerning the quantum of damages. As a letter of credit is not qualified by the underlying contract between the account party and the bank, why should the damages awarded to the beneficiary for the bank's dishonour of his draft be reduced by a sum based on the mitigation of his loss? Moreover, if this element is taken into account in respect of an action based on a letter of credit, should it not, *a fortiori*, be applicable in the case of the enforcement of a guarantee which, unlike a letter of credit, is ancillary to the underlying contract?

The conceptual distinction drawn in *Wichita*'s case between a standby credit and a guarantee is, probably, valid. The autonomous nature of a letter of credit is considered to be the main distinction between it and a guarantee. Whilst a mere recital of the nature of the underlying transaction in the letter of credit may have the purpose of identifying the transaction and, therefore, does not render the instrument a guarantee, an explicit incorporation of the contract between the account party and the beneficiary in the letter of credit destroys the credit's independent nature. It becomes, thereupon, indistinguishable from a guarantee.

The finding, that — unlike a guarantee — a standby credit is a primary and autonomous undertaking of the issuing bank, constitutes the basis for regarding the issuing of a standby credit as being within the powers of American banks. In other jurisdictions the conceptual distinction between the two types of instrument is of lesser importance. Indeed, the function of standby credits can be equally served by performance bonds or by guarantees payable on first demand. Thus, in *Bache & Co. (London) Ltd.* v. *Banque Vernes et Commerciale de Paris S.A.* [1973] Ll. L. Rep. 437, a French bank, at the request of French importers, issued a guarantee securing English commodity brokers in respect of orders placed by them with vendors at the importers' request. The guarantee included a clause, under which "[n]otice of default shall from time to time be given by [the commodity brokers] to [the bank] and on receipt of any such notice [the bank] will forthwith pay . . . the amount stated therein as due, such notice of default being . . . conclusive evidence that [the bank's] liability thereunder has accrued in respect of the amount claimed." Before the expiry of the guarantee, the commodity brokers served such a notice on the bank. The latter refused to pay, arguing that the French importers were not in default and assailing the validity of the conclusive evidence clause on the ground of its being contrary to public policy. The Court of Appeal held that the commodity brokers were entitled to enforce the guarantee. Adopting the reasoning of an earlier Australian decision, Lord Denning said:

> . . . it seems to me the notice of default given by the English brokers is perfectly good. There is no public policy against it. On the contrary, public policy is in favour of enforcing it. The evidence shows that "it is customary within the trade for a member of the association, dealing with a principal who is foreign, or whose reserves are uncertain, to demand a bank guarantee, not only to protect himself against his principal's possible impecuniosity, but also so as to be able to put himself in funds straight away in the event of his being called upon to honour his personal liability on his principal's behalf. This was such a guarantee and was called upon only when the plaintiffs were themselves called upon to account to the clearing house which they did."
>
> Such being the commercial practice, it is only right that brokers should be able to turn to the French bank and say: "On our giving you notice of default, you must pay."
>
> The French bank can in turn recover the sum from their own customer, the French trading company. No doubt they have taken security for the purpose.
>
> This does not lead to any injustice because if the figure should be erroneous, it is always open to the French trading company to have it corrected by instituting proceedings against the brokers, in England or in France, to get it corrected as between them.

Megaw and Scarman L.JJ. expressed similar views. This decision was followed in *Howe Richardson Scale Co. Ltd.* v. *Polimex-Cekop* [1978] 1 Ll. L. Rep. 161. A contract for the supply of valuable equipment, made between English manufacturers and Polish importers, stipulated for a bank guarantee assuring the importers of the repayment of a deposit, paid on account of the price, if the manufacturers failed to dispatch the goods. After supplying a portion of the goods, the manufacturers refused to send the balance as the Polish importers had failed to open an irrevocable credit agreed upon in the contract of sale. The importers reacted by claiming payment under the first demanded guarantee furnished by the bank at the manufacturers' instruction. The manufacturers applied for an injunction to restrain the importers from making this claim. Refusing to grant such an injunction, Roskill L.J., in the Court of Appeal, said [at 165]:

> The bank, in principle, is in a position not identical with but very similar to the position of a bank which opened a confirmed irrevocable letter of credit. Whether the obligation arises under a letter of credit or under a guarantee, the obligation of the bank is to perform that which it is required to perform by that particular contract, and that obligation does not in the ordinary way depend on the correct resolution of a dispute as to the sufficiency of performance by the seller to the buyer or by the buyer to the seller as the case may be under the sale and purchase contract; the bank here is simply concerned to see whether the event has happened upon which its obligation to pay has arisen. The bank takes the view that that time has come and that it is compelled to pay; in my view it would be quite wrong for the Court to interfere with [the Polish importer's] apparent right under this guarantee to seek payment from the bank because to do so would involve putting upon the bank an obligation to inquire whether or not there had been timeous performance of the sellers' obligations under the contract.

These decisions demonstrate that, despite the general, conceptual, difference between letters of credit and guarantees, it is difficult, from a functional point of view, to draw a distinction between standby credits and first demand guarantees. The point is highlighted by a ruling of the Comptroller of Currency of the United States, defining the elements of a letter of credit with the object of determining the scope of the instruments which are within the powers of an American bank. It will be useful to quote this ruling in full:

Letters of Credit Distinguished from Guaranty.

A national bank may issue its own letters of credit to or on behalf of its customers in the normal course of its business: *Provided,* That the bank's obligation may legally be described as a letter of credit and not as a mere guaranty. In order to constitute a true letter-of-credit transaction, the following elements must all be present: (a) The bank must receive a fee or other valid business consideration for the issuance of its undertaking; (b) the bank's undertaking must contain a specified expiration date or be for a definite term; (c) the bank's undertaking must not be unlimited but be up to a stated amount; (d) the bank's obligation to pay must arise only upon the presentation of specific documents and the bank must not be called upon to determine disputed questions of fact or law; (e) the bank's customer must have an unqualified obligation to reimburse the bank on the same condition as the bank has paid.

The first, second, third and fifth elements are just as applicable to first demand guarantees as to standby credits. Banks are not philanthropists and, therefore, expect to obtain a fee when they furnish a guarantee. Moreover, it is contrary to good banking practice to issue a guarantee which fails to specify an expiry date and a fixed ceiling amount or to effect a guarantee without obtaining the account party's promise to reimburse the bank for any amount paid to the beneficiary. The only apparent distinction between the two types of instrument relates to the fourth requirement listed by the Comptroller, according to which the bank's promise to honour its standby credit "must arise only upon presentation of specific documents", the bank not being called upon to determine questions of law or disputes between the account party and the beneficiary. Whilst a first demand guarantee does not call for the presentation of a specific document it is, invariably, payable against a demand in writing made by the beneficiary. This demand confirms the account party's default and is therefore singularly similar to the "certificate of default", which is the usual document required in a standby credit. It is true that the standby credit calls, in addition, for a bill of exchange, which is not stipulated for in the first demand guarantee. In reality, though, the bill is nothing more than a mode of determining the amount due. The second branch of the fourth requirement, according to which the issuer of a standby credit must not be called upon to determine disputes between the parties or questions of law, is equally attained in first demand guarantees by means of the conclusive evidence clause. It would appear to follow that the distinction between standby credit and first demand guarantees is largely illusory or, perhaps, of a semantic nature.

The similarity of the legal principles pertaining, respectively, to standby credits and to first demand guarantees will be further illustrated by a discussion of the autonomy of standby credits and of the fraud rule. It will, however, be convenient to consider, first, the application to standby credits of the Uniform Customs of the International Chamber of Commerce.

• • •

IV. ALLOCATION OF RISKS

Having discussed the legal aspects of standby credits, it appears appropriate to conclude this paper with an analysis of the risk incurred by each of the parties to the transaction.

The most favoured party is, undoubtedly, the beneficiary. He is in a much more advantageous position than the beneficiary of a commercial credit, who has to procure the shipping documents and, frequently, is also required to tender a surveyor's certificate attesting the quality or the origin of the goods. All that the beneficiary of a standby credit has to do, is to execute the default notice and the bill of exchange. The bank is not expected, or indeed permitted, to verify the truthfulness of the statement made in the default notice.

In reality, the beneficiary of a standby credit is in as favourable a position as the beneficiary of a first demand guarantee. Whilst the documents required in the standby credit may be slightly more complex than the demand-in-writing required under the guarantee, the distinction is minute.

Both standby credits and first demand guarantees are the subject of constant abuses of rights. It is not surprising to read Lord Denning's observation to the effect that "such guarantees are sometimes drawn upon, partly or wholly, without any or any apparent justification, almost as though they represented a discount in favour" of the beneficiary. The case law discussed in the third Part of this paper suggests that the very same observation is true in respect of standby credits. It is noteworthy that this result is attained, respectively, by means of the elegant "conclusive evidence clause" used in first demand guarantees and by the equally attractive doctrine concerning the autonomy of irrevocable credits; but this is of little consolation to an account party who, having meticulously performed his contract with the beneficiary, finds that the latter has nevertheless utilised the standby credit or the first demand guarantee.

The account party is frequently in the unhappy position of having the court's sympathy but no effective remedy. Undoubtedly, he can bring an action in damages against a beneficiary who has, improperly, obtained payment under a standby credit or a first demand guarantee. The proceeding, however, may have to be brought in the beneficiary's country. If this is a jurisdiction which is not renowned for its adherence to the mores of international commerce, the prospect of success is dim. Moreover, the expenditure involved renders such an action unattractive even if the beneficiary resides in a country with an outstanding legal machinery.

Under existing law the account party can do little to improve his position. The fraud rule, as has been shown, is of extremely narrow application. An attempt to incorporate the terms of the underlying contract in the standby credit or in the first demand guarantee is bound to be resisted by both the bank and the beneficiary. Banks dislike guarantees or letters of credit which become payable upon an actual default arising under a contract between the beneficiary and the account party. Banks are unwilling to get involved in disputes of this type. The beneficiary's reason for rejecting a proposal for a standby credit or a guarantee linked with the underlying contract is based on the fact that such an undertaking can encourage litigation in the event of a dispute.

An alternative, which is quite attractive from the account party's point of view, is the inclusion of a cancellation clause in the standby credit or in the first demand guarantee. Such a clause enables the account party to instruct the bank to cancel the credit or the guarantee upon the occurrence of some prescribed events, such as the beneficiary's bankruptcy or his failure to open an irrevocable commercial credit. However, in the majority of cases such a clause is likely to be resisted by the beneficiary. The reason is obvious. Under such a clause the cancellation of the credit or of the guarantee is effected against the account party's certification of the occurrence of the agreed event. In such a case the beneficiary is in as unenviable a position as that of the account party in the case of an ordinary standby credit or a first demand guarantee.

A more realistic solution is the stipulation in a standby credit for a certificate to be issued by an independent third party. Where the standby credit covers deficiencies in the manufacturing of goods or in the performance of services, a suitable certificate attesting defects is obtainable from qualified professional people such as engineers or surveyors. An architect's certificate is appropriate in respect of a standby credit covering a construction contract. It is difficult to envisage a transaction in which no certificate of this type is available. Moreover, such certificates may also be utilised in respect of first demand guarantees. The instrument would, in such a case, assume the form of an undertaking to pay against a written demand accompanied by the required expert's certificate.

It is submitted that such a clause ought to be acceptable to an honest beneficiary. Likewise, its demand is not contrary to the interest of the bank. Instruments stipulating for payment against designated certificates are common in commercial credit transactions. Banks are, therefore, familiar with certificates of this type and have experience in assessing their conformity with the terms of a letter of credit. Moreover, even where such a certificate is stipulated for, the risk of forgery or of fraud remains with the account party. It follows that such a requirement does not create a hazard from the bank's point of view. As regards the beneficiary, the tender of a certificate, issued by a third party, is a step in the direction of safety. Whilst a beneficiary may be sufficiently unscrupulous to make an unjustified demand under an ordinary standby credit or first demand guarantee, he is unlikely to resort to forgery.

It is noteworthy that, in certain cases, the stipulation for a third party's certificate may be of benefit to the issuing bank. The reason for this is related to an important practical distinction between a commercial credit and a standby credit. In a commercial credit transaction, the bank obtains a security for the amount paid to the seller by acquiring the possession of the documents of title tendered to it. The default certificate tendered by the beneficiary of a standby credit does not confer such security rights on the issuing bank. It follows that in a standby credit the bank relies far more heavily on the account party's solvency than in the case of a commercial credit. If the account party is forced to seek refuge in bankruptcy or to wind up, the bank may be unable to recover an amount advanced to the beneficiary under a standby credit or a first demand guarantee. Unless the bank obtains some independent security at the time it agrees to open the standby credit, it may be in the unfavourable position of an unsecured creditor in the account party's insolvency proceedings.

Obviously, the tender of a certificate of default issued by a third party does not protect the bank against the account party's insolvency. It does, however, protect the bank against the beneficiary's unjustified demand. In certain cases such an unjustified demand, followed by the account party's inability to reimburse the amount paid by the bank, culminates in the account party's insolvency. The bank has, therefore, an indirect interest in preventing such a state of affairs.

The stipulation for the tender of a certificate, signed by an independent third party, as a prerequisite of payment under a standby credit or a first demand guarantee is, accordingly, of some advantage to the bank. A policy encouraging the use of such certificates should be supported by banks and by their legal advisers.

F. THE AUTONOMY OF THE LETTER OF CREDIT

BENJAMIN GEVA
"Contractual Defenses As Claims to the Instrument:
The Right to Block Payment On a Banker's Instrument"
(1979) 58 Oregon LR 283, 288-92

A letter of credit is an engagement by a bank or other person, made at the request of a customer, that as issuer it will honor drafts or other demands for payment upon compliance with the conditions specified in the letter. In the context of sales financing, it is a promise by the issuer made at the request of the buyer to pay to the seller the price of the goods or to accept a draft drawn by the seller for that amount, provided that the shipping documents representing the goods are tendered to the banker before a specified date. Letters of credit are most commonly used in financing inventory purchases by merchants.

The issuance of a letter of credit involves three legal relationships: (1) the contract for sale between the seller and the buyer, calling for payment by the letter of credit; (2) the financing transaction between the buyer and the issuer, where the former undertakes to reimburse the latter for the advances made to the seller under the letter; and (3) the undertaking of the issuer towards the seller embodied in the letter itself.

It is a fundamental rule that the letter of credit is autonomous in relation to the contract for sale that it finances. The issuer's engagement towards the seller "is quite independent of the primary agreement" between the seller and the buyer. It "constitutes a bargain between the banker and the vendor of goods, which imposes upon the banker an absolute obligation to pay, irrespective of any dispute there may be between the parties as to whether the goods are up to contract or not."

The independence of the issuer's engagement is the letter of credit's primary feature and distinguishes it from a guaranty, which is secondary to the buyer's promise to pay the price. The absolute nature of the obligation is based on the terms of the letter of credit as agreed upon by the buyer and the issuer and as accepted by the seller. The characteristics of independence and absolute nature are fundamental to the concept of letters of credit. Thus, "where . . . the substantive provisions require the issuer to deal *not simply in documents alone, but in facts relating to the performance of a separate contract* . . ., all distinction between a letter of credit and an ordinary guaranty contract would be obliterated by regarding the instrument as a letter of credit."

Fraud is the only exception to the autonomy of the letter of credit. "[T]he principle of the independence of the bank's obligation under the letter of credit should not be extended to protect the unscrupulous seller." This is, however, a rule of public policy that "must be narrowly limited to situations . . . in which the wrongdoing . . . has so vitiated the entire transaction that the legitimate purposes of the independence of the issuer's obligation would no longer be served." Thus, fraud must be "very clearly established" and not merely alleged. In its proper sense, the exception does not apply to a breach of warranty, though made fraudulently, but rather is limited to situations of total failure of consideration, where "[t]he facts . . . speak for themselves."

• • •

The fraud exception to the autonomy of the letter of credit can be explained, not by the conduct of the seller towards the buyer, but by the seller's conduct towards the issuer. Thus, in making advances under the letter of credit, the issuer "acts not merely upon the credit of its customer, but upon the credit also of the merchandise which is to be tendered as security." Therefore, in misrepresenting or failing to provide to the issuer "the security upon which the advances are demanded," the seller commits a breach of his contract with the issuer. Since forfeiture of the seller's right depends on the worthlessness of the goods as security, and not on their conformity to the terms of the contract for sale, the fraud exception does not undermine the autonomy of the letter of credit. . . .

To justify the autonomy of the letter of credit, it is said that the "elaborate commercial system" of financing sales of goods by irrevocable credits "would break down completely if a dispute as between the vendor and the purchaser was to have the effect of 'freezing' . . . the sum in respect of which the letter of credit was opened." Underlying this observation are the large sums involved in the typical letter of credit, the distance between the seller and the buyer, and the function of the letter of credit as a source of credit to the seller.

Notes:

1   There has been a lengthy and inconclusive academic discussion on the theory underlying the enforceability of the issuing-bank undertaking by the promisee-seller. In particular, difficulties have arisen in trying to identify consideration moving from the promisee-seller. The following suggestions have been made:

a) There is a detriment to the promisee-seller in that the actual performance of an existing duty (under the contract for sale) may leave him worse off than he would be if he defaulted and faced an action for breach by the buyer.

b) There is a detriment in that the seller loses his chance to negotiate a discharge of the contract of sale with the buyer.

c) The seller provides consideration by forbearing from claiming the price of the goods from the buyer as well as by forbearing from attempting to find another market for the contract goods.

d) The buyer's obligation to procure an irrevocable credit is a condition precedent to the seller's duty to perform his bargain. The commencement of the irrevocability of the letter of credit and the maturity of the seller's obligation to perform the sale contract are thus simultaneous. The seller's duty to perform under the contract for sale is thus the consideration for both the buyer's contract and the issuing bank's undertaking.

None of these theories is entirely satisfactory: see M. Clarke, "Bankers' Commercial Credits Among the High Trees" [1974] Camb. LJ 260.

2   The validity of the fourth theory as to the seller's consideration (hereafter: "Ellinger's view") depends on the buyer's duty to procure the opening of the credit being a condition precedent. Case law is quite uniform in establishing that in the absence of express stipulation, "credit must be made available to the seller at the beginning of the shipment period. The reason is because the seller is entitled, before he ships the goods, to be assured that, on shipment, he will get paid": *Pavia & Co. S.P.A.* v. *Thurmann-Nielsen* [1952] 2 QB 84, 88. As to the theory underlying the buyer's obligation to procure the opening of the credit, note the following discussion by Clarke, *supra* at 264:

> There are broadly three possibilities. (i) The opening of the credit is a condition precedent to the existence of any contract between buyer and seller. Until the credit is opened, there is no contract, no obligation, either party may withdraw. (ii) The opening of the credit is a condition precedent that does not negative the existence of the contract, but suspends the seller's duties under the contract until it is met. Here there is a contract. (iii) The performance of his duty to procure the opening of the credit is a condition precedent to the buyer's right to enforce the seller's duties and a term of the contract, breach of which entitles the seller to his remedies. In other contexts this would be the most likely analysis and it is doubtful whether it is proper to call it a condition precedent at all although, as we shall see, the courts have undoubtedly done so.
>
> The difference between possibility (i) and possibility (ii) is the important one that in the former either party is free to withdraw from the arrangement until the condition is satisfied. The practical difference between possibility (ii) and possibility (iii) is less clearcut. The existence of possibility (ii) enables Ellinger to contend that the seller is under no duties normally until the buyer has opened the credit. Further, whether or not the seller has duties, it may be that he need do nothing towards fulfilling his contractual obligations other than, perhaps, to refrain from conduct likely to prevent or impede its eventual performance.

His conclusion (at 269) is however:

that the obtaining of the requisite credit may be a condition precedent in the sense of either possibility (i) or possibility (ii), if the parties expressly say so. . . . Normally however it will be an ordinary essential term of the contract, possibility (iii). It might still be otherwise if the opening of the credit is likely to be very difficult and appears to be an obstacle to the rest of the deal, in which event the parties may in effect say: "Everything hangs on this, let's wait and see if it goes through before we commit ourselves to performing the rest of the agreement." Accordingly, Ellinger's view that the seller who contracts with the issuing bank has no previous duty to the buyer will rarely be correct; his view does not therefore materially assist the search for consideration moving from seller to bank. The difficulties in analysing the seller-banker relationship in terms of contract remain.

3   The view that the obtaining of the requisite credit is normally an essential term of the contract is consistent with the position taken by UCC 2-325(1): "[f]ailure of the buyer reasonably to furnish an agreed letter of credit is a breach of the contract for sale". In the opinion of the Ontario Law Reform Commission, such a provision "conform[s] to existing law" and should be incorporated in the revised Act. See *Report on the Sale of Goods* (1979) p. 357 and s. 5.25 of the Draft Bill to Revise the Sale of Goods Act.

EDWARD OWEN LTD. v. BARCLAYS BANK
[1977] 3 WLR 764 at 766, [1978] 1 All ER 976 (CA)

LORD DENNING M.R.: This case concerns a new business transaction called a "performance guarantee" or "performance bond." In order to show the nature of the transaction, I will describe the documents in some detail.

The contract between suppliers and customers
    First, I will describe the principal contract between suppliers and customers. The suppliers are Edward Owen Engineering Ltd., the plaintiffs, who carry on business at Alton in Hampshire. The customers are the Agricultural Development Council of Libya which is a state enterprise of the Libyan Arab Republic whose full title is the Executive Authority for Jabel el Akhdar el Marj, (the "Executive Authority"); sometimes called the Green Mountain Project.
    In November 1976 a contract was made by which the English suppliers agreed to supply and instal glasshouses for the Libyan customers. The glasshouses were to be very extensive. They were to cover two hectares (about five acres) and were to be equipped with a complete irrigation system. The materials were to be sent from England to Benghazi on c. and f. terms: and skilled erectors were to go out from England to Libya to erect the glasshouses and instal the equipment. The total contract price was £502,030, payable in Libyan dinars. The shipment of the materials was to be by the end of April 1977, and erection was to be completed by the end of August 1977. Payment was to be made by the Libyan customers as follows: 20 per cent payable in advance of delivery: 50 per cent payable on the presentation of the shipping documents; 10 per cent when the materials were on the site; 15 per cent when there was a provisional handing-over, and 5 per cent on final handing-over; thus making it the full 100 per cent.

Those instalments were to be payable by an irrevocable confirmed letter of credit which was to be opened in favour of the English suppliers payable at Barclays Bank International Ltd. (the first defendant). There was an express clause which said:

> The contract is construed in accordance with Libyan law. Any dispute arising between the two parties shall be referred to the competent Libyan court. . . .

The Libyan customers instructed the Umma Bank at Benghazi (the second defendant), which is a state bank of Libya, to open an irrevocable documentary credit in favour of the English suppliers for payment of those instalments. The letter of credit was sent by the Umma Bank in Libya to their London correspondents, who sent it on January 6, 1977, through Barclays Bank International Ltd. to the English suppliers. But it did not comply with the contract. It was not a confirmed letter of credit. It was not confirmed by a bank. This was made clear by the advice itself. The correspondents in London said:

> Although our principals make provision for us to add our confirmation to this credit kindly note that we are unable to effect such action in view of the payment terms which are subject to instruction from our principals, upon presentation of documents.

That was indeed the case. The letter of credit expressly provided that payment was only to be made when the Libyan customers authorised it. So the letter of credit was plainly not a confirmed letter of credit.

As soon as the English suppliers got that notification, they made every effort to get the Libyan customers to amend the letter of credit so as to enable the contract to be fulfilled. They sent a long telex on January 18, 1977. They sent one of their staff, a Mr. Cowley, out to Libya to press the Libyan customers to make the required amendments to the letter of credit. But he was unable to get it amended. On his return, the English suppliers consulted their bankers, Barclays, and wrote a letter which was drawn up with the assistance of those bankers. It was dated March 29, 1977, by the English suppliers to the Libyan customers and is of much importance. It said:

> . . . The letter of credit is still not acceptable to us for three main reasons — (1) Our contract with you dated November 9, 1976, provided for the letter of credit to be confirmed. The advising bank in London refuses to confirm the letter of credit because of the way in which it is drawn up.

There follow two other reasons and then this significant paragraph: "Since the letter of credit is not operative, it obviously follows that our guarantee has no effect." That is a reference to the performance guarantee to which I will come shortly.

So there is the position. The English suppliers quite reasonably said:

> We cannot go on with any obligations under this contract because the letter of credit which would guarantee us payment has not come forward. We have not even got the 20 per cent in advance.

It looked very much as if the Libyan customers were in default. They had not provided the stipulated letter of credit. That is why the contract went off.

The performance guarantee

Second, I will deal with the contract between the banks. This is where we come to the "performance guarantee" or "performance bond." That is a guarantee by a bank that the suppliers will perform their obligations under the contract. The Libyan customers, before any contract was concluded, stipulated that there should be a performance guarantee. It was to be a condition precedent to their entering into any contract at all. The English suppliers wrote this letter on November 4, 1976, to the Libyan customers:

> Upon agreement of the final contract sum and approval of a draft contract, we will arrange for a letter of guarantee to be issued by Barclays Bank International and lodged at the Umma Bank, Benghazi, for 10 per cent of the total contract price and valid up to the final delivery date. On receipt of the letter of guarantee at the Umma Bank, Benghazi, we will sign the contract and the authority [the Libyan customers] will immediately open a letter of credit to our benefit for the full contract price.

So even before the contract was actually signed, the English suppliers agreed to arrange for a performance guarantee to be given for 10 per cent of the contract price. The contract was signed on November 9, 1976, and the performance guarantee given on November 15, 1976. It was given in this way: the English suppliers instructed their bankers, Barclays Bank, to give the performance guarantee. Acting on those instructions, on November 15 Barclays Bank International in England sent a cable to the Umma Bank in Benghazi in these words:

> Upon our responsibility and on behalf of Edward Owen Engineering Ltd. . . . please issue, in form required, performance bond in favour of Executive Authority for Jabel el Akhdar el Marj Libyan Arab Republic for pounds sterling 50,203 . . . being 10 per cent of total contract value for supply of greenhouse equipment with drip-overhead irrigation system contract dated November 9, 1969. Performance bond to be valid for claims on you until August 31, 1978, and is to be handed to Mr. N. Cowley, accredited representative of Edward Owen Engineering Ltd., who will contact you: we confirm that United Kingdom exchange control regulations satisfied and that our maximum liability is limited to the sum of pounds sterling 50,203. . . .

On November 17, 1976, Barclays Bank International confirmed that cable by letter to the Umma Bank and added: "We look forward to receiving in due course two translated copies of the actual guarantee issued." (It was not in fact received until May 1977.)

The Umma Bank wanted, however, a further assurance before issuing the performance guarantee. On November 22, 1976, they sent a telex to Barclays Bank International containing this request: "Please confirm that you will pay total or part of said guarantee on first of our demand without any conditions or proof . . ." On the same day, November 22, Barclays Bank International replied to Umma Bank: "We confirm our guarantee . . . payable on demand without proof or conditions."

So there it is. Barclays Bank International asked the Umma Bank (the state

bank in Libya) to issue the guarantee, and Barclays Bank promised to pay it on
first demand by Umma without any conditions or proof.*

On receiving that promise, the Umma Bank did issue a guarantee bond in
favour of the Libyan customers. It was written in Arabic, but we have a translation of it. It is dated November 23, 1976, Benghazi. It is addressed by the Umma
Bank to the Libyan customers under the name of the Green Mountain Project. It
says:

> Considering the fact that the contract relating to this transaction calls for the issue of
> a bank guarantee, for an amount of £50,203 . . . We, the undersigned, guarantee to
> you the firm "Edward Owen" to the extent of the above mentioned amount and it is
> understood that the said amount will be paid on your first demand, which must
> reach us within the period of validity of the letter of guarantee. This guarantee is
> valid until August 31, 1978, after which its validity will expire and the letter of
> guarantee will have to be returned to this bank.

This is the performance guarantee. It was handed by the Umma Bank to Mr.
Cowley in Libya. He was there as the representative of the English suppliers. He
handed it to the Libyan customers. Thereupon the English suppliers had done
everything necessary on their part to make the contract bindingg on the Libyan
customers. It was then for the Libyan customers to arrange for the confirmed
letter of credit for the price. But that they never did. On that account the English
suppliers on March 29, 1977, wrote the letter (which I have read) saying that the
guarantee had no effect.

It is obvious, of course, that Barclays would only give their guarantee on
getting a counter-guarantee from the English suppliers. It is on a printed form
dated December 17, 1976, signed by Edward Owen Engineering Ltd. It reads as
follows:

> In consideration of your procuring the giving by Barclays Bank International Ltd. of
> a . . . guarantee in the terms of the copy . . . attached hereto [that is the one of
> November 15, 1976] . . . we . . . agree to keep you indemnified . . . and . . . irrevocably
> authorise you to make any payments and comply with any demands which may be
> claimed or made under the said . . . guarantee . . . and agree that any payment which
> you shall make . . . shall be binding upon . . . us and shall be accepted by . . . us as
> conclusive evidence that you were liable to make such payment or comply with such
> demand.

It appears therefore, that, if Barclays Bank International paid under the guarantee, the English suppliers were to indemnify them.

So there was a string of guarantees. The English suppliers guaranteed Barclays Bank International, Barclays Bank International guaranteed the Umma
Bank in Libya, and the Umma Bank guaranteed the Libyan buyers.

The claim on the performance guarantee

On the facts so far known, it appears that the English suppliers had not been

---

* There is an error at this point in the WLR version of the judgment. We have used the All England Version to
supply the missing part of the sentence. [Eds.]

in default at all. The only persons in default were the Libyan customers. They had not issued the confirmed letter of credit as they should have done. Yet the Libyan customers appear to have demanded payment from the Umma Bank on their guarantee. The Umma Bank then claimed on Barclays Bank International. They did so by their telex of May 16, 1977, by Umma Bank to Barclays Bank:

> . . . we would inform you that beneficiaries request liquidation the amount of said guarantee being STG pounds 50203 stop Please credit our Tripoli head office account with Midland Bank London . . . We issued said guarantee under your full responsibility and your confirmation towards us dated November 22, 1976. Therefore any discussions concerning said guarantee must take place between the concerned parties and our bank not involved in the matter stop Awaiting your urgent tested cable confirmation regards.

On hearing of that demand, the English suppliers issued a writ in the High Court against Barclays Bank International. They obtained an interim injunction ex parte — to prevent Barclays Bank paying the Umma Bank. Barclays sent a telex telling Umma of the injunction. The Umma Bank replied on May 31:

> We are not in a position to comply with its contents. Subject matter must be settled between the concerned parties. We [were] astonished from your mentioned cable as we issued said guarantee according [to] your clear confirmation that you will pay total or part of said amount . . . without any conditions or proof if requested. . . . Please authorise us urgently . . . regret we hold you responsible for any consequences resulting from non-execution. Regards.

So there it is. The long and short of it is that although prima facie the Libyan customers were in default in not providing the letter of credit, nevertheless they appear to have claimed against the Umma Bank on the performance bond issued by them; in turn the Umma Bank claimed upon Barclays Bank: who claimed upon the English suppliers.

A little later Barclays applied to discharge the injunction. After hearing argument Kerr J. held that these performance bonds must be honoured as between the banks; and that the relations between the English suppliers and the Libyan customers were no concern of the banks. He held that Barclays Bank International ought to pay the Umma Bank and leave the English suppliers to claim damages against the Libyan customers, presumably in the courts of Libya, because the contract contained a clause giving exclusive jurisdiction to the courts of Libya.

The English suppliers appeal to this court. They ask us to restore the injunction. They say that there is no practical remedy for them in the Libyan courts. The Libyan customers are a department of the Libyan state: the Umma Bank is a state bank. It would be in practice impossible to obtain a visa for the purpose of bringing a claim against the Libyan customers and the Umma Bank.

So the English suppliers ask us to order that Barclays Bank should not pay this amount to the Umma Bank. They wish to join the Umma Bank and the Libyan customers as defendants to the action: for by so doing all the matters can be resolved here as to whether or not the Libyan customers should be paid this amount.

The law as to performance bonds

A performance bond is a new creature so far as we are concerned. It has many similarities to a letter of credit, with which of course we are very familiar. It has been long established that when a letter of credit is issued and confirmed by a bank, the bank must pay it if the documents are in order and the terms of the credit are satisfied. Any dispute between buyer and seller must be settled between themselves. The bank must honour the credit. That was clearly stated in *Hamzeh Malas & Sons* v. *British Imex Industries Ltd.* [1958] 2 QB 127. Jenkins L.J., giving the judgment of this court, said, at p. 129:

> . . . it seems to be plain enough that the opening of a confirmed letter of credit constitutes a bargain between the banker and the vendor of the goods, which imposes upon the banker an absolute obligation to pay, irrespective of any dispute there may be between the parties as to whether the goods are up to contract or not. An elaborate commercial system has been built up on the footing that bankers' confirmed credits are of that character, and, in my judgment, it would be wrong for this court in the present case to interfere with the established practice.

To this general principle there is an exception in the case of what is called established or obvious fraud to the knowledge of the bank. The most illuminating case is of *Sztejn* v. *J. Henry Schroder Banking Corporation* (1941) 31 NYS 2d 631 which was heard in the New York Court of Appeals. After citing many cases Shientag J. said, at p. 633:

> It is well established that a letter of credit is independent of the primary contract of sale between the buyer and the seller. The issuing bank agrees to pay upon presentation of documents, not goods. This rule is necessary to preserve the efficiency of the letter of credit as an instrument for the financing of trade.

He said, at p. 634, that in that particular case it was different because:

> on the present motion, it must be assumed that the seller has intentionally failed to ship any goods ordered by the buyer. In such a situation, where the seller's fraud has been called to the bank's attention before the drafts and documents have been presented for payment, the principle of the independence of the bank's obligation under the letter of credit should not be extended to protect the unscrupulous seller.

That case shows that there is this exception to the strict rule: the bank ought not to pay under the credit if it knows that the documents are forged or that the request for payment is made fraudulently, in circumstances when there is no right to payment.

I would in this regard quote the words of Browne J. in an unreported case when he was sitting at first instance. It is *Bank Russo-Iran* v. *Gordon, Woodroffe & Co. Ltd.* (unreported), October 3, 1972. He said:

> In my judgment, if the documents are presented by the beneficiary himself, and are forged or fraudulent, the bank is entitled to refuse payment if it finds out before payment, and is entitled to recover the money as paid under a mistake of fact if it finds out after payment.

But as Kerr J. said in this present case:

In cases of obvious fraud to the knowledge of the banks, the courts may prevent banks from fulfilling their obligation to third parties.

Such is the law as to a confirmed letter of credit. How does it stand with regard to a performance bond or a performance guarantee? Seeing that it is a guarantee of performance — that is, a guarantee that the supplier will perform his contracted obligations — one would expect that it would be enforced in such a case as this: suppose the English supplier had been paid for the goods and had delivered them, but that the Libyan customer then discovered that they were defective and not up to contract or that they had been delayed. The Libyan customer could then claim damages for the breach. But instead of coming to England to sue for the breach, his remedy would be to claim payment under the guarantee — of the 10 per cent or the 5 per cent of the price — as liquidated damage, so to speak. He claims payment from the Umma Bank. The Umma Bank pay him "on first request." They claim on Barclays Bank International. Then Barclays pay "on first demand without proof or conditions." And Barclays claim against the English suppliers, the payment being "conclusive evidence."

It is obvious that that course of action can be followed, not only when there are substantial breaches of contract, but also when the breaches are insubstantial or trivial, in which case they bear the colour of a penalty rather than liquidated damages: or even when the breaches are merely allegations by the customer without any proof at all: or even when the breaches are non-existent. The performance guarantee then bears the colour of a discount on the price of 10 per cent or 5 per cent or as the case may be. The customer can always enforce payment by making a claim on the guarantee and it will then be passed down the line to the English supplier. This possibility is so real that the English supplier, if he is wise, will take it into account when quoting his price for the contract.

Take the case one stage further. The English supplier is not in default at all. He has not shipped the goods because he has not been paid. The Libyan customer has not provided the confirmed letter of credit. It is still open to the Libyan customer to make some allegation of default against the English supplier — as for instance not doing the preliminary work or not being ready and willing — and on that allegation to claim payment under the performance guarantee. On that request being made, payment will be made by the banks down the line: and be made by them "on demand without proof or conditions."

So, as one takes instance after instance, these performance guarantees are virtually promissory notes payable on demand. So long as the Libyan customers make an honest demand, the banks are bound to pay: and the banks will rarely, if ever, be in a position to know whether the demand is honest or not. At any rate they will not be able to prove it to be dishonest. So they will have to pay.

All this leads to the conclusion that the performance guarantee stands on a similar footing to a letter of credit. A bank which gives a performance guarantee must honour that guarantee according to its terms. It is not concerned in the least with the relations between the supplier and the customer; nor with the question whether the supplier has performed his contracted obligation or not; nor with the question whether the supplier is in default or not. The bank must pay according to its guarantee, on demand, if so stipulated, without proof or conditions. The only exception is when there is a clear fraud of which the bank has notice.

Such has been the course of decision in all the cases there have been this year in our courts here in England. First of all, there was *R.D. Harbottle (Mercantile) Ltd. v. National Westminster Bank Ltd.* [1977] 3 WLR 752, before Kerr J. The judge considered the position in principle. I would like to adopt a passage from his judgment, p. 761E-G.

> It is only in exceptional cases that the courts will interfere with the machinery of irrevocable obligations assumed by banks. They are the life-blood of international commerce. Such obligations are regarded as collateral to the underlying rights and obligations between the merchants at either end of the banking chain. Except possibly in clear cases of fraud of which the banks have notice, the courts will leave the merchants to settle their disputes under the contracts by litigation or arbitration. ... The courts are not concerned with their difficulties to enforce such claims; these are risks which the merchants take. In this case the plaintiffs took the risk of the unconditional wording of the guarantees. The machinery and commitments of banks are on a different level. They must be allowed to be honoured, free from interference by the courts. Otherwise, trust in international commerce could be irreparably damaged.

Since that time there has been before Donaldson J. and afterwards in this court *Howe Richardson Scale Co. Ltd.* v. *Polimex-Cekop and National Westminster Bank Ltd.,* June 23, 1977; Bar Library Transcript No. 270. In that case Roskill L.J. spoke to the same effect. He said:

> Whether the obligation arises under a letter of credit or under a guarantee, the obligation of the bank is to perform that which it is required to perform by that particular contract, and that obligation does not in the ordinary way depend on the correct resolution of a dispute as to the sufficiency of performance by the seller to the buyer or by the buyer to the seller as the case may be under the sale and purchase contract; the bank here is simply concerned to see whether the event has happened upon which its obligation to pay has risen.

So there it is: Barclays Bank International has given its guarantee — I might almost say its promise to pay — to Umma Bank on demand without proof or conditions. They gave that promise, the demand was made. The bank must honour it. This court cannot interfere with the obligations of the bank.

This case is altogether different from *Mareva Compania Naviera S.A.* v. *International Bulkcarriers Ltd.* [1975] 2 Lloyd's Rep. 509 and the *Siskina (Owners of cargo lately laden on board)* v. *Distos Compania Naviera S.A.* [1977] 3 WLR 532. In those cases we stopped money in this country from being paid out to a debtor who was likely to take his assets away from England so as to avoid paying his debts. It is also different from the other cases which were cited to us, such as *Elian and Rabbath* v. *Matsas and Matsas* [1966] 2 Lloyd's Rep. 495. This is a new case on a performance bond or guarantee which must be decided on the principle applicable to it. I think Kerr J. was quite right in discharging the injunction. The bank must honour its bond.

Seeing that the bank must pay — and will probably come down on the English suppliers on their counter-guarantee — it follows that the only remedy of the English suppliers is to sue the Libyan customers for damages. The contract contains a clause giving exclusive jurisdiction to the courts of Libya. But we are told that it is not practicable for the English suppliers to invoke the jurisdiction of the Libyan courts. So the English suppliers wish to join the Libyan customers as defendants to this action and to get leave to serve them out of the jurisdiction. We will be ready to consider that application when it is made. But meanwhile the injunction against the bank must be discharged.

Appeal dismissed.

[Concurring opinions were delivered by Browne and Geoffrey Lane L.JJ.]

Notes and Questions:

1   "It would be reasonable to suppose that, if the person claiming to be creditor had no legally enforceable claim against the alleged principal debtor, there would also be no claim against the guarantor of the payment that the alleged principal debtor may have promised to make": L.A. Sheridan, *Rights in Security* (1974) p. 288. See also *Coutts & Co.* v. *Browne-Lecky* [1947] KB 104. Is *Edward Owen, supra,* reconcilable with this view?

2   A modified opinion on the guarantor's position was expressed in *Heald* v. *O'Connor* [1971] 1 WLR 497 (QB). Fisher J. thought that the guarantor's ability to assert the principal debtor's defences is a question of construing the guarantor's undertaking in each individual case. The question is:

> Did the guarantor undertake to pay only those sums which the principal debtor could lawfully be called to pay but had not duly paid, or did he promise to pay those sums which the principal debtor had promised to pay but had not paid whether the principal debtor could lawfully be called upon to pay them or not?

(*id.* at 506). Is *Edward Owen* better explained in light of this opinion?

3   The proposed Uniform Rules for Contract Guarantees (ICC Doc. 460/ 228-470/329, 25 June 1978), art. 2, defines the three most common types of guarantees as follows:

> For the purposes of these Rules:
> a) "tender guarantee" means an undertaking given by a bank, insurance company or other party ("the guarantor") at the request of a tenderer ("the principal") or given on the instructions of a bank, insurance company, or other party so requested by the principal ("the instructing party") to a party inviting tenders ("the beneficiary") whereby the guarantor undertakes — in the event of default by the principal in the obligations resulting from the submission of the tender — to make payment to the beneficiary within the limits of a stated sum of money;
> b) "performance guarantee" means an undertaking given by a bank, insurance company or other party ("the guarantor") at the request of a supplier of goods or services or other contractor ("the principal") or given on the instructions of a bank, insurance company, or other party so requested by the principal ("the instructing

party") to a buyer or to an employer ("the beneficiary") whereby the guarantor undertakes — in the event of default by the principal in due performance of the terms of a contract between the principal and the beneficiary ("the contract") — to make payment to the beneficiary within the limits of a stated sum of money or, if the guarantee so provides, at the guarantor's option, to arrange for performance of the contract;

     c) "repayment guarantee" means an undertaking given by a bank, insurance company or other party ("the guarantor") at the request of a supplier of goods or services or other contractor ("the principal") or given on the instructions of a bank, insurance company or other party so requested by the principal ("the instructing party") to a buyer or to an employer ("the beneficiary") whereby the guarantor undertakes — in the event of default by the principal to repay in accordance with the terms and conditions of a contract between the principal and the beneficiary ("the contract") any sum or sums advanced or paid by the beneficiary to the principal and not otherwise repaid — to make payment to the beneficiary within the limits of a stated sum of money.

See also Kozolchyk, at 28-29 and n. 135. Does the "performance guarantee" dealt with in *Edward Owen* fall into any of these guarantees? Does the guarantor's ability to assert the principal debtor's defences depend on your answer?

4   *Edward Owen* was recently relied on by Henry J. in *Aspen Planners Ltd.* v. *Commerce Masonry and Forming Ltd.* (1979) 7 BLR 102 (Ont.). The plaintiff in this case entered into a building contract with the defendant contractor. To ensure payment of the contract instalments, the plaintiff had its bank issue irrevocable letters of credit to the contractor. The terms of the letters of credit provided that the bank was to pay to the contractor the amount due under each letter of credit against receipt of a certificate of the contractor confirming that the moneys drawn pursuant to the letter of credit had been or would be expended pursuant to the building contract. On the collapse of the building during construction and prior to the submission of the final certificates of entitlement by the contractor to the bank, the plaintiff brought an application for an interim injunction to restrain the contractor from drawing down the final payments of the contract price under the letters of credit and for an interim injunction to restrain the bank from paying on the letters of credit. The application was dismissed. Citing heavily from *Edward Owen,* Henry J. held (at 110) that "the bank is obligated to pay the contractor under the letter of credit against a certificate that is not fraudulent to its knowledge, regardless of any dispute between the plaintiff and the contractor under the building contract. It is not within the plaintiff's power to revoke or alter the terms of the letter of credit nor is the bank entitled to do so. The bank cannot refuse payment at the instance of the plaintiff. Entitlement is a matter between the bank and the contractor". The court also held (at 111) that the plaintiff could not enjoin the contractor from drawing on the letter of credit "so long as the contractor does not create a fraudulent certificate to the knowledge of the bank". Enjoining the contractor "from applying for and receiving a payment from the bank under the letter of credit — a transaction to which the plaintiff is virtually a stranger" amounts, under Henry J.'s view, "to freezing a potential asset of the contractor as security to satisfy a potential judgment. In effect it is tantamount to execution before judgment". In these circumstances, he could not "consider that such an interim injunction should issue".

5   The relationship between the autonomy of the letter of credit (also known as the abstraction of the credit promise) and the documentary nature of the transaction was also noted in *Urquhart Lindsay & Co.* v. *Eastern Bank Ltd.* [1922] 1 KB 318. By authorizing the issuer "to undertake to pay the amount of the invoice as presented", the buyer "is taken for the purposes of all questions between himself and his banker or between his banker and the seller to be content to accept the invoices of the seller as correct": *id.* at 323.

6   Unfortunately, the exact scope of the fraud exception has not always been properly understood. In *NMC Enterprises, Inc.* v. *Columbia Broadcasting Sys., Inc.* (1974) 14 UCC Rep. Serv. 1427 (NY Sup. Ct.), the court awarded an injunction against an issuing bank on the basis of a fraudulent warranty by the seller. The case is criticized convincingly, together with other recent deviations from the rule of the autonomy of letters of credit, in Jack Justice, "Letters of Credit: Expectations and Frustrations — Part 2" (1977) 94 Banking LJ 493, 502-03.

7   The issuing bank in *Etablissement Esefka International Anstalt* v. *Central Bank of Nigeria* [1979] 1 Ll. L. Rep. 445 (CA) refused payment against documents complying with the terms of the irrevocable credit and counterclaimed for damages on the ground that documents relating to previous shipments presented by the seller under the letter of credit (against which the bank had paid) had been forged. Upholding the issuing bank's position, Lord Denning M.R. stated (at 447-48):

> Now certain points of law emerge on that matter. First of all, it seems to have been one transaction. The whole letter of credit covered all the 240,000 tonnes. The documents ought to be correct and valid in respect of each parcel. If that condition is broken by forged or fraudulent documents being presented — in respect of any one parcel — the defendants have a defence in point of law against being liable in respect of that parcel. And they have a claim, not only as to any outstanding claim but also they have a counterclaim for the money which they have overpaid and which they paid on false documents. We said as much in *Edward Owen Engineering Ltd.* v. *Barclays Bank International Ltd. & anr.* [1978] 1 Lloyd's Rep. 166; [1978] 1 QB 159 at pp. 171 and 169 to 170, in which I quoted what Lord Justice Browne said:

>> In my judgment, if the documents are presented by the beneficiary himself, and are forged or fraudulent, the bank is entitled to refuse payment if it finds out before payment, and is entitled to recover the money as paid under a mistake of fact if it finds out after payment . . .

> I should have thought that that was the good sense of the matter. That is so far as the actual payment and recovery are concerned.

> Then it is said, and I think this influenced the Judge, that these were separate transactions. Each shipment and each bill of lading could be considered separable from the rest. But I should have thought under this letter of credit that it was all one transaction. As to the cross-claims, it seems to me that this may well be a case for an equitable set-off because in *Federal Commerce & Navigation Co. Ltd.* v. *Molena Alpha Inc.* [1978] 2 Lloyd's Rep. 132; [1978] 3 WLR 309 I said at pp. 140 and 338:

>> It is only cross-claims that arise out of the same transaction or are closely connected with it. And it is only cross-claims which go directly to impeach the plaintiff's demands, that is, so closely connected with his demands that it would be manifestly unjust to allow him to enforce payment without taking into account the cross-claim. . . .

It seems to me in a way that the claim for demurrage for these other shipments (which were made) is so closely connected with the cross-claim in respect of these forged or fraudulent documents that it may well be a case for an equitable set-off. If so, this $6,000,000 odd which is claimed in respect of the money paid under the forged documents (if they were forged) over-tops any claim by the plaintiffs either in regard to the legitimate demurrage or as to damages.

I think I have said enough about the case to show that in regard to the claim there is a good arguable defence on account of the forged or fraudulent bills of lading to show that the claim is not well-founded. Alternatively there is an equitable set-off which more than over-tops the claim itself.

8   *Edward Owen* was distinguished and the fraud exception not applied in *The "American Accord"* [1979] 1 Ll. L. Rep. 267 (QB) where the plaintiffs presenting the fraudulent documents did not know of the fraud. Mocatta J. (at 278) held in these circumstances that:

> The case is, therefore vitally different from the *Sztejn* v. *Schroder* case approved by the Court of Appeal in the recent *Edward Owen* v. *Barclays Bank* case. Where there has been personal fraud or unscrupulous conduct by the seller presenting the documents under the letter of credit, it is right that a bank should be entitled to refuse payment against apparently conforming documents on the principle *ex turpi causa non oritur actio*. But here I have held that there was no fraud on the part of the plaintiffs, nor can I, as a matter of fact, find that they knew the date on the bills of lading to be false when they presented the documents. Further, there is no plea either by way of an implied term or by way of a warranty imposed by the law that the presenter of documents under a letter of credit warrants their accuracy. Accordingly, I take the view, on the principle so recently affirmed by the Court of Appeal, that the plaintiffs are, on the matters which have so far been argued before the Court, entitled to succeed.

9   A new procedure of considerable importance in international trade and letter of credit litigation has recently been developed by U.K. courts under the name of "Mareva injunction" (after *Mareva Compania Naviera S.A.* v. *International Bulkcarriers S.A.* [1975] 2 Ll. L. Rep. 509 (CA)). See C. Schmitthoff, "Export Trade" [1977] Jour. Bus. Law 264, and D. Powles, "The Mareva Injunction" [1978] Jour. Bus. Law 11. Under this procedure, a foreign defendant who has assets in the U.K. can be compelled, by way of an injunction, to leave them in the country until the British courts have disposed of the claim made against him. The *Mareva* injunction is only to be granted on a showing of good grounds for success in the case and where there is a danger of the money being taken out of the jurisdiction: *Etablissement Esefka Int. Anstalt* v. *Central Bank of Nigeria, supra*. A Mareva injunction was granted in *Liberty Nat. Bk. & Trust Co.* v. *Atkin* (Ont. SC, Jan. 28, 1981).

10   It is not uncommon for a buyer from a retailer (as, for example, a consumer who borrows money from a bank to pay for the purchase of a car) to pay for the goods with a bank draft (i.e., a bill of exchange whose drawer is a bank). The obligation of a drawer bank on a bank draft is often treated as analogous to the issuing bank's undertaking under a letter of credit. By analogy to the autonomy of the letter of credit, it is sometimes said that a direct "debtor-creditor relationship [exists] between the [drawer] issuing bank and the payee [seller]" (*Moon Over the Mountain Ltd.* v. *Marine Midland Bank* (1976) 386 NYS 2d 974, 975 (NY Cty. Civ. Ct.)); that the drawer bank's obligation under a bank draft "stands on its own foundation as an independent, unconditional and primary obligation of the bank" (*Pennsylvania* v. *Curtiss National Bank* (1970) 427 F. 2d 395, 400 (CCA 5)); and that "[t]o allow the bank to stop payment on such an instrument would be inconsistent with the representations it makes in issuing the check" (*National Newark & Essex Bank* v. *Giordano* (1970) 268 A. 2d 327, 329 (NJL Div.)). "Payee and drawer . . . have an implied contractual relationship: payee has a duty to present the check and the right to receive payment, while drawer . . . has a duty to pay the check upon present-ment": M. Cohen, "Drawer-Bank of Teller's Check Cannot Stop Payment When Not Party to Underlying Transaction" (1966) 15 Buff. L. Rev. 193, 195-96.

However, the possibility of a direct "debtor-creditor relationship between the [drawer] issuing bank and the payee" of a bank draft is actually inconsistent with the law of negotiable instruments. The idea that one who procures the issuance of a bank draft payable to the order of another (the "remitter") is the first owner and in a position "to confer a title upon the payee" (*Munro* v. *Bordier* (1849) 8 CB 862, 875; 137 ER 747) preceded the enactment of the English Bills of Exchange Act. Accordingly, in suing the drawer, the seller-payee acts not as a direct party to the promise but rather as one having a derivative title to the instrument embodying it.

It therefore follows that, as its previous owner, the remitter-buyer can claim the instrument back from the seller on the effective rescission of the contract or rejection of the goods. This is because "[t]o rescind a contract is . . . to abrogate and undo it from the beginning" (*Sylvania Industrial Corp.* v. *Lilienfeld's Estate* (1943) 132 F. 2d 887, 892 (4th Cir.)). As rescission "has the legal effect of entitling each of the parties to be restored to the condition in which he was before the contract was made" (*Hayes* v. *City of Nashville* (1897) 80 F. 641, 645 (6th Cir.)), it "requires the surrender of any consideration or advantage secured by either party" (*May* v. *Rice* (1954) 118 F. Supp. 331, 334 (S.D. Cal.)). Thus by rescinding the contract (or rejecting the goods) the buyer can claim the banker's instrument back from the seller and prevents its payment.

For a discussion on the "autonomy of a banker's instrument" from an American perspective, see B. Geva, "Contractual Defenses As Claims to the Instrument: The Right to Block Payment on a Banker's Instrument" (1979) 58 Oregon L. Rev. 283. The absence of autonomy of the banker's instrument and the rejection of the analogy to a letter of credit is explained there (at 292) as follows:

> To justify the autonomy of the letter of credit, it is said that the "elaborate commercial system" of financing sales of goods by irrevocable credits "would break down completely if a dispute as between the vendor and the purchaser was to have the effect of 'freezing' . . . the sum in respect of which the letter of credit was opened." Underlying this observation are the large sums involved in the typical letter of credit, the distance between the seller and the buyer, and the function of the letter of credit as a source of credit to the seller. These factors seldom exist in connection with banker's instruments, which are used most commonly to finance retail purchases from merchants who are in the same general geographic area as the buyers: Nonpayment neither puts the seller under credit strain nor forces him to pursue the buyer into a remote jurisdiction. As an obligation under a banker's instrument is backed by the bank's credit, the utility of the instrument is not necessarily dependent only on the autonomy of the obligation on it.

PART III
FINANCING COMMERCIAL AND CONSUMER TRANSACTIONS

Chapter 20

Security Devices
and the PPSA

This chapter deals with security devices, their evolution under pre-PPSA law and their treatment under the PPSA. It presents an outline as to the scope of the PPSA as well as to its scheme.

A. EVOLUTION OF SECURITY DEVICES UNDER CANADIAN LAW

JACOB S. ZIEGEL
"Canadian Chattel Security Law: Past Experience and Current Developments"
in J.G. Sauveplanne (ed.), *Security Over Corporeal Movables*
(Leiden: Sijthoff, 1974) pp. 78-87

The Different Types of Secured Financing
It is customary to distinguish between the different forms of secured and unsecured financing. Easily the most important distinction, at least from the economic and social points of view, is the distinction between consumer and business financing. As previously stated, consumer credit in Canada has grown prodigiously since the end of the war and the balance of outstanding credit currently exceeds $11 billion, thus placing Canadians among the largest users of consumer credit in the Western world.*

. . . Consumer credit may be extended for one of two principal purposes: either to pay for the acquisition of new goods or services or to discharge an existing indebtedness. The acquisition of new goods may be financed by the seller himself or the consumer may prefer to obtain a "purchase money loan" from a lender such as a bank, consumer loan company, or a credit union. Whether any, and what type of, security is taken by the financer (vendor or lender) will

---

* The figure currently stands at around $40 billion. See further *infra*, chapter 25. [Eds.]

depend on a variety of circumstances. If the seller provides the financing and a large amount is involved as, for example, in the case of the purchase of an automobile, he will usually reserve title in the chattel by means of a conditional sale agreement. He could also secure himself by means of a chattel mortgage but in Canada this is unusual. Often title is also reserved in the case of the sale of smaller durable goods such as furniture and home appliances, and even in the case of soft goods which are sold under a revolving line of credit, but repossessions for non-payment of such purchases are infrequent and the power is retained principally for its *in terrorem* impact.

If the buyer borrows the purchase price of the goods, the lender will frequently secure himself by means of a chattel mortgage unless the loan is made pursuant to some revolving loan or credit card arrangement. The chattel mortgage may be limited to the goods whose acquisition is being financed or it may extend to all the borrower's present and future household goods. The chattel mortgage is also frequently used to secure a general non-purchase money loan. The relative importance of the conditional sale and chattel mortgage as security devices may be gauged from the following figures which show the number of registrations for all types of security agreements filed in British Columbia in 1969:

	Filed in Central Registry	Filed with Registrar of Companies	Total
Conditional Sale Agreements	84,166	5,158	89,324
Bills of Sale	134,819	2,468	137,287
Assignment of Book Accounts	394	2,092	2,486
Land Mortgages, Debentures and Trust Deeds filed under Companies Act	—	12,438	12,438
TOTAL	219,379	22,156	241,535

The different forms of business financing and their related security devices are much more complex. Here again there are some basic distinctions which need to be drawn, of which the following are the most important:

1. *The Financing of Goods for Use.* This covers the type of situation in which the debtor wishes to acquire equipment for use in connection with his business, trade or profession. The legal position here is not very different from the acquisition of consumer goods, and the conditional sale and chattel mortgage are the two principal security devices in use, depending on whether it is the seller or an institutional lender who is doing the financing. Equipment leases, with or without an option to purchase, are also growing rapidly in importance. Hire-purchase agreements of the English type are rare. A fixed and floating charge may sometimes be used but usually only in conjunction with the issue of a corporate debenture and to secure a medium or long term loan.

2. *Inventory and Accounts Receivable Financing.* Both these types of financing are of major importance in Canada and, for large and many medium sized enterprises, represent the most usual forms of raising loan capital for working purposes. The feature that is common to both inventory and accounts receivable

financing is that the underlying security is of a shifting character and thus legally and factually provides the financer with a unique set of problems.

The banks are the most important source of these types of working capital, although sales finance companies and suppliers of all descriptions also provide large volumes of inventory credit. The banks secure most inventory loans by means of a statutory security sanctioned by the Canadian Bank Act and generally referred to as a Section 88 security. Manufacturers and other suppliers usually secure themselves by means of a wholesale conditional sale agreement and a "proceeds" clause obliging the debtor to hold the proceeds arising from the disposition of the collateral on trust for the inventory financer. Where the credit takes the form of a loan, a wholesale chattel mortgage with a similar clause will be the usual form of security. An assignment of book debts (again coupled with a proceeds clause) will frequently accompany an inventory loan by a bank and in any event may be the only valuable form of security available where the debtor is engaged in a service industry. As will be seen, such assignments are governed by separate common law and statutory principles.

3. *Possessory and Non-Possessory Secured Financing.* Most pledge financing is done by the banks and is usually of a short term character. The pledge usually consists of negotiable instruments, securities, or documents of title (e.g., bills of lading or warehouse receipts). This branch of secured financing has remained almost static throughout this century and continues to be governed largely by common law principles. As in other legal systems, possessory security devices in Canadian law are subject to a different set of rules from those which apply to non-possessory security devices. The most important single distinction is that a security interest of a non-possessory character can usually only be perfected by complying with a registration requirement.

III. *Evolution of Canadian Chattel Security Law*

Jurisdiction in the chattel security area is divided between the provinces and the federal government. The provinces derive their power from their general competence to regulate property and civil rights within their territories; the federal power is ancillary in nature and rests on several of the specific headings in Section 91 of the British North America Act and on Section 92(10)(*a*). These include banks and banking, interest rates, bills of exchange and promissory notes, patents, trademarks and copyrights, bankruptcy, shipping, and interprovincial undertakings and lines of communication. To these must be added the power to incorporate and regulate federal corporations, which is derived from the so-called peace, order and good government clause in the British North America Act. There are more than a dozen federal acts which regulate some aspect of chattel security law, but only two of them have exercised any significant influence on the general course of development of Canadian law. These are the provisions in the Bankruptcy Act and in the Bank Act.

As a result it has been left largely to the provinces to shape the character of the chattel security law. I will discuss the special position of Quebec presently. So far as the common law provinces are concerned, the principal outside influences have been those from England and the U.S. To this must be added a substantial indigenous element. Here then, as in so many other branches, Canadian law represents a mosaic.

The influence of English law has been felt mainly through our inheritance of the common law and equitable rules relating to secured financing and, to a lesser extent, from a number of the earlier statutes including the Bills of Sale Act, 1878, the Moneylenders Act of 1900 and the Bankruptcy Act of 1914. The American influence has been almost entirely statutory in character. The first Canadian Uniform Conditional Sales Act was substantially influenced by the American Uniform Conditional Sales Act of 1918. The early Bills of Sale Acts may also have been influenced by American precedents as may the notice filing provisions in Section 88 of the Canadian Bank Act. Easily the most important influence, however, has been Article 9 of the Uniform Commercial Code. Both the Ontario Personal Property Security Act 1967 and the Model Uniform Personal Property Security Act adopted by the Canadian Bar Association in September 1970 are largely copies of Article 9.

The indigenous Canadian contribution in the chattel security field has consisted of a very simple federal inventory financing law for banks, generally referred to as the Section 88 security, which was adopted long before any other common law jurisdiction appears to have done so, and in the formulation of enlightened statutory rules in such specific areas as fixtures and the conflict of laws — again at a very early date.

American chattel security law has of course undergone an almost total revolution since the war and Canada and the United Kingdom are also on the threshold of radical changes. This must be borne in mind when comparing the salient features of the law of these jurisdictions. However, there is still some merit in indicating what historically have been some of the principal differences between Canadian law and the laws of the U.S. and the U.K. So far as the comparison with American law is concerned, the Canadian rules concerning the creation of security interests and the range of collateral covered by them have generally been much more liberal. This has been notably true with respect to floating charges (American style) involving inventory and accounts receivable financing. Our concept of what constitutes a fraudulent preference in bankruptcy is also less rigid and complex than the rules in the American Bankruptcy Act and, mercifully, we have never adopted a Section 60(*a*) type provision.

The major differences between Canadian chattel security law and the present English law are these. First, most of the Canadian security devices are subject to a greater degree of statutory regulation than in England. (Bills of sale are an important exception.) This is notably true with respect to registration requirements. Secondly, little stigma attaches in Canada to the granting of chattel mortgages, whether by individuals or by trading concerns, and this security device is used much more widely in Canada than in England. Thirdly, non-bank lenders granting loans over fifteen hundred dollars are generally not required to be licensed and we have no counterpart to the onerous requirements of the Bills of Sale (1878) Amendment Act 1882 or the Moneylenders Act of 1927. Finally, our workhorse to secure working capital for business enterprises is the Section 88 security and a specific assignment of accounts and not the fixed and floating charge as in England.

From what has been said so far, it will be obvious that Canadian law at the federal level and in the common law provinces also differs materially from French law and those jurisdictions following the Napoleonic Code. We have never entertained any hesitation about recognizing non-possessory security devices and there has never been any serious movement to inhibit the growth of this form of secured financing. Leaving aside some possible consumer problems, there is no evidence that the permissiveness of Canadian law has led to widespread abuses. The evidence rather points to the beneficial effects of secured financing for those types of enterprises for whom credit would otherwise not have been available or not available in the same amounts.

IV. *Status of Particular Security Devices*

I have already described the use to which particular security devices are put in Canada. In the present section I should like to draw attention to some of the more salient features of the principal devices and the extent to which they are subject to statutory regulation. This brief discussion will also provide an introduction to the shortcomings of the existing Canadian law, a theme that is more fully developed in a subsequent section.

1. *The Pledge.* As elsewhere, this is the oldest of our security devices and, as has been previously explained, documentary pledges still serve an important role in short term financing. Their importance is partly recognized in the Uniform Warehouse Receipts Act which was adopted by the Canadian Uniformity Commissioners in 1945 and is now in force in six provinces. The Act explicitly establishes a negotiable type of receipt when the receipt is so marked and spells out the consequences of its negotiability.

Apart from these exceptions, there has been little attempt to put the documentary pledge to new uses. The ingenious field warehousing receipt invented in the U.S. is sparingly used in Canada and its status is still unsettled. A probable reason for this reticence is that less expensive and reasonably effective security devices are available for inventory financing purposes, which was not true of American law at the time when field warehousing was first introduced there. For obvious reasons the pledging of chattels for commercial purposes has disappeared almost completely. Even pawnbroking has suffered a marked decline as standards of living have improved and more sophisticated methods of consumer financing have taken its place.

2. *Conditional Sale Agreements, Hire-Purchase Agreements, and Equipment Leases.* The conditional sale agreement first became common in Canada around the 1860's and it still enjoys high popularity among sellers and sales finance companies as a purchase money security device. The Canadian common law early adopted the principle of English law that the parties to a sale agreement are free to postpone the vesting of title of goods in the buyer until a future time and this rule was subsequently enshrined in the provincial Sale of Goods Acts. However, it seemed wrong to the commercial community that a buyer should enjoy the

appearance of ownership without its reality and thus from 1882 onwards legislation was adopted by the provinces requiring conditional sale agreements to be registered in a designated public office. These requirements still exist. Some provinces permitted the seller to attach his name and address to the goods as a substitute for registration but this alternative fortunately has now been dropped. In 1922 the Conference of Commissioners on Uniformity of Legislation in Canada adopted a Uniform Conditional Sales Act and this Act was subsequently revised in 1947 and 1955. In its original or revised form the Uniform Act has been copied, wholly or in part, by many of the provinces.

The major difficulty about the conditional sale agreement has been with respect to its characterization. From the start there has been an almost continuous seesaw battle between those courts that regarded it as merely a short form of chattel mortgage, those who saw it as an executory agreement of sale, and those courts who could not quite make up their minds one way or the other. Surprising as it may seem, the various conditional sales acts never put to rest this important controversy.

The definition of conditional sale agreement in most of the provincial acts is wide enough to catch any bailment of goods with an option to purchase, but hire-purchase agreements of the English type are not common in Canada. Equipment leases, on the other hand, have grown rapidly in popularity and the courts have held that they are not governed by the conditional sales acts in the absence of an option to purchase even though in other respects the lease may be only a disguised conditional sale. As in the U.K., lessors have sought to protect themselves against premature termination of the agreement by various types of deficiency or minimum payment clauses. By and large the Canadian courts have uncritically applied the English jurisprudence and in this way reached the same unsatisfactory results.

3. *The Chattel Mortgage and Floating Charge.* The chattel mortgage is a much more flexible instrument than the conditional sale agreement since, first, it can be used to secure a sale on credit as well as a straight loan, secondly, because it is available to cover future as well as present advances and, thirdly, because it may cover after-acquired as well as existing collateral. These features are of course very important in inventory financing where the parties are engaged in a continuous series of transactions and there is a constant flow of goods in and out of the debtor's premises.

The disadvantages of the chattel mortgage as it has evolved in Canada are almost as great as its advantages. Registration requirements began to be adopted in Canada as early as 1849 and were subsequently enshrined by the Uniformity Commissioners in the Uniform Bills of Sale and Chattel Mortgage Act of 1928. What made the statute particularly onerous was the necessity to append to each agreement two highly technical affidavits of bona fides and execution. The courts have often applied the affidavit requirements with Draconian severity and many a secured lender has met his Waterloo on this particular battleground! A second shortcoming was the doubt, which still exists, whether and to what extent future advances can be secured under the Acts and the need to file a new document each time a new agreement is concluded between the parties. A further and equally serious shortcoming arises out of the decision in *Joseph* v. *Lyons* (1884) 15 QBD 280 (CA), which has been followed in Canada.

It was held by the Supreme Court of Canada in *Gordon Mackay & Co. Ltd.* v. *J.A. Larocque Ltd.* [1927] SCR 374 that the Ontario Bills of Sale Act then in force applied to a corporate debenture secured by a fixed and floating charge. This result was felt to be inconvenient. All the provincial acts require chattel mortgage filings to be renewed every two or three years whereas many corporate securities are of a long term character and may not mature for twenty years or more. To overcome the effects of the decision the Uniformity Commissioners adopted in 1931 a Uniform Corporation Securities Registration Act. This does not however dispose of all the problems. One of the persistent difficulties which the Canadian courts have experienced is to draw a satisfactory distinction between a specific mortgage coupled with a licence to carry on business by the debtor and a floating charge in the English sense. The difference may materially affect the position of the secured creditor vis-à-vis third parties. In my opinion, the problem can only satisfactorily be dealt with by legislation, although it is by no means clear that this has happened in the Ontario Personal Property Security Act.

4. *Inventory Financing and the Section 88 Security.* The American trust receipt was never adopted in Canada but we have a close analogue in Section 88 of the federal Bank Act. In several respects it is a superior instrument to the inventory financing device sanctioned in the Uniform Trust Receipts Act because it is much less technical and more flexible.

It was a widely held dogma in Canada in the last century that the only forms of security suitable for banking loans were those which were highly liquid in character and easily realizable in an emergency. Goods and merchandise not represented by documents of title or warehouse receipts did not fall into this category and the banks were prohibited from taking this form of collateral as security. The prohibition threatened to impede the development of the important agricultural, lumber and extractive industries. To meet their needs for working capital a series of exceptions were made beginning in 1861. The earliest exceptions made use of a fiction and permitted a warehouseman and other specified classes of persons to issue and pledge warehouse receipts even though the issuer of the receipt was also the owner of the goods. In 1890 the fiction was abandoned and banks were now permitted to grant loans against the security of the inventory of manufacturers and certain types of wholesalers without the pretence of a documentary pledge. Over the next seventy years the range of acceptable collateral was gradually expanded to include various forms of farmers' and fishermen's assets but the stock-in-trade of merchants and retail stores generally remained outside the charmed circle.*

The section of the Bank Act containing these exceptions is Section 88 and the security taken pursuant to it is generally referred to as a "Section 88" security. The Bank Act was completely revised in 1967, but the Section 88 provisions were left unaltered.**

---

* See now, however, the Banks and Banking Law Revision Act, 1980, s. 178(1)(a). [Eds.]

** See previous footnote and Comment (1981) 5 Can. Bus. LJ 238, 243. [Eds.]

From the legal point of view the special significance of the section resides in its perfection requirements. Originally all that was required was a short document signed by the borrower granting the bank a Section 88 security interest in the goods, present or future, which could be described in the most general terms. The effect of the agreement was to vest in the bank a legal title in the collateral which took priority over all subsequently created security interests. Until 1923 nothing was required to be filed, but since that time the bank's security interest is not perfected until a "notice of intention to give a Section 88 security" has been filed in one of the regional offices of the Bank of Canada. This one-page document is even briefer than the agreement to which it relates and is a model of simplicity. It represents in fact the Canadian counterpart of notice filing and corresponds closely to the Notice of Intention formerly required to be filed under the Uniform Trust Receipts Act and now continued in Article 9 of the Uniform Commercial Code.

One of several shortcomings about Section 88 is that it does not deal with the bank's rights with respect to the proceeds of the disposition of the inventory. However, a recent decision of the Supreme Court of Canada [*Flintoff* v. *Royal Bank of Canada* [1964] SCR 631] has bridged the gap to some extent by holding that the bank's security shifts automatically from the inventory to the proceeds and is not dependent on any new agreement between the parties.

5. *Assignment of Book Debts (Accounts Receivable Financing)*. Reference has already been made to the important position which accounts receivable financing occupies in Canada. Its popularity is explained in part by the liquid character of the security and the relative simplicity of the statutory formalities. Until 1919 such assignments were not subject to any registration requirement although the secured party's priority was (and still is) liable to be defeated under the rule in *Dearle* v. *Hall* (1823) 3 Russ. 1. An amendment to the federal Bankruptcy Act adopted in that year avoided general assignment of book debts against a trustee in bankruptcy unless the debt had been paid at the time of the bankruptcy or the assignment had been registered in accordance with provincial requirements. The provinces responded with a Uniform Assignment of Book Debts Act which was first adopted by the Uniformity Commissioners in 1928. This Act, like Section 43 of the English Bankruptcy Act, applies to any assignment of present and future book debts other than an assignment of book debts due at the date of assignment from specific debtors "or becoming due under specified contracts".

Two major difficulties confront the accounts receivable financer under existing Canadian law. The first is to know whether the courts will treat the assignment as a floating charge or as a specific charge. As we have seen, the identical problem arises in the inventory financing field. The second is the rule in *Dearle* v. *Hall*, which may cause him to lose his priority to a subsequent assignee who gives notice of the assignment to the account debtor before he does. Obviously the general assignee cannot be expected to give notice to an account debtor who may not even exist at the time of the original assignment. Even if he could give notice the common law requirement is commercially quite unreasonable. The failure to deal with this hiatus constitutes a serious blemish on the Canadian law. A further difficulty may be mentioned and this is that the accounts receivable financer may not always have notice of a proceeds clause under an inventory financing agreement since, as previously noted, the agreement does not have to be registered under the Assignment of Book Debts Acts.

Note on Canadian PPSA Legislation:

Modelled on Article 9 of the American Uniform Commercial Code (hereafter UCC or Code), the Ontario Personal Property Security Act (now RSO 1970 c. 344, as amended; hereafter PPSA or Ont. PPSA) was adopted in 1967. It became fully effective on April 1, 1976. In the years which followed, Manitoba and Saskatchewan adopted their own Personal Property Security Acts (SM 1973, c. 5 [continuing consolidation, c. P35] as amended, and SS 1980, c. P-6.1; Royal Assent given on June 17, 1980; hereafter Sask. PPSA). The Yukon Territory also adopted a Personal Property Security Ordinance, closely modelled on the Saskatchewan precedent, late in 1980. See YTO 1980 (2nd Sess.) c. 20. British Columbia and Alberta are actively working on their own Acts and have already produced exposure drafts. In Quebec the Civil Code Revision Office has recommended the incorporation of important aspects of Article 9 in the Revised Quebec Civil Code. There is also a movement to provide uniform legislation in this area. The Commercial Law Section of the Canadian Bar Association established a Committee as far back as 1963 to follow the provincial developments and to make recommendations with respect to model legislation. The Committee drafted a Model Uniform Personal Property Security Act (hereafter MUPPSA), based largely on the Ontario precedent, and this was adopted by the association in 1970. Since 1976 the Committee has been working on a revised model act. It has now substantially completed its task.

    The Ont. PPSA is drafted against the background of the 1962 Official Text of Article 9. The later statutes (as well as a draft bill to amend the Ont. PPSA circulated by the Ministry of Consumer and Commercial Affairs in September 1980) took into account changes introduced in the 1972 Official Text of the UCC (the Revised Code). Subsequent revisions of Article 9 (aimed at excluding transactions with securities from its coverage) took place in 1978. They are not reflected in any of the Canadian versions of the PPSA. Nor were they widely adopted in the U.S. where every state, with the exception of Louisiana, has adopted one or other version of Article 9.

B. THE COMPREHENSIVENESS OF THE ONT. PPSA

The PPSA attempts to provide a simple but integrated framework within which the large variety of present-day security transactions can be conducted at less cost and with greater certainty than that which existed under the prior law.

BRADLEY CRAWFORD
"A Practitioner's Notes Upon the Ontario Personal Property Security Act"
(1975-76) 1 Can. Bus. LJ 269, 269-70

A. CONCEPTS AND DEFINITIONS

The basic purpose of the Act is to reform — by simplifying and modernizing — the laws governing the creation and preservation of the various kinds of security interests that may exist in personal property. Under the old system of discrete security devices, assignments of book debts were governed by the Assignments of Book Debts Act, bills of sale and chattel mortgages by the Bills of Sale and Chattel Mortgages Act and conditional sales by the Conditional Sales Act. F.M. Catzman, Q.C., chairman of the committee which has promoted and stimulated these reforms for nearly 15 years, recently summarized the defects of that system as follows: despite the similarity of the basic intention of all elements of the system to take effect as security devices, there was little uniformity among the documentary requirements; new and combined forms were discouraged; elaborate formalities of execution and attestation, designed to prevent frauds, were inconvenient to the honest, a trap for the unwary and did not deter the fraudulent; the time and place for registration varied: searching the registers was difficult and time consuming; and when the whole process was complete, the rights of the parties and priorities among competing interests were nowhere clearly stated.

JACOB S. ZIEGEL
"The Draft Ontario Personal Property Security Act"
(1966) 44 Can. B. Rev. 104, 109-11

II. *The Structure of the Ontario Bill.*
The basic concepts of the Ontario Bill, like those of article 9 of the Uniform Commercial Code, are as simple as they are effective. The first concept is that every security agreement serves an identical object — to secure performance of a debt or obligation by a debtor. There is no need for a proliferation of acts all dealing with the same phenomenon. One act will suffice and it can cover all security agreements, regardless of the nature of the collateral involved (so long as it is still personal property or fixtures), the form of security device used, or the identity of the debtor. Section 2 of the Bill accordingly provides that,

> ... this Act applies to every transaction without regard to its form and without regard to the person who has title to the collateral that in substance creates a security interest, including, without limiting the foregoing,
>
> (a) a chattel mortgage, conditional sale, equipment trust, floating charge, pledge, trust deed or trust receipt; and
>
> (b) an assignment, lease or consignment intended as security.

"Security interest" is defined in section 1(*w*) as,

> an interest in goods, other than building materials that have been affixed to the [*sic*] realty, fixtures, documents of title, instruments, securities, chattel papers or intangibles that secure payment or performance of an obligation ...

The Bill applies to *consensual* transactions and therefore security interests arising by operation of law are not regulated by it, save with respect to the question of priorities in the case of artisans' liens. Excluded also is the transfer of an interest or claim in or under any policy of insurance or contract of annuity and transactions regulated by the Pawnbrokers Act. Security interests regulated by federal law are of course automatically excluded. Generally speaking, the Bill does not regulate the absolute transfer of an interest in personal property, even though the transferor remains in possession of the goods. Such transactions will continue to be governed by such legislation as the Bills of Sale Act and section 25(1) of the Sale of Goods Act. There is one exception to this rule in the case of book debts or "accounts receivable" as they are generally called in the United States. All assignments of book debts, whether absolute or only by way of security, are regulated by the Bill, the reason being that an absolute assignment especially when accompanied by a "recourse" or similar agreement, is indistinguishable in its practical effect from a security agreement.

The practical result of the comprehensive scope of the Bill will be twofold. Firstly, it will eliminate the four principal security acts and a host of provisions in other statutes which occupy the field at the moment. Gone, too, will be the pigeon-holing and labelling of security agreements which currently occupies so much of the practising lawyer's time. If the parties wish to include different types of collateral in the same agreement, they will be free to do so. The second practical result stems from the flexibility of the concept of a "security interest". The definition is wide enough to catch not only all the existing security interests, but also any new devices which ingenious counsel may conjure up in the future. Form will no longer count; it will be the substance and object of the agreement in each case that will matter. Our courts will therefore no longer have to struggle with the proper classification of the conditional sales agreement, and such anachronisms in the common law as the English form of hire-purchase agreement will cease to exist.

Note on the Scheme of the Act:

The PPSA is divided into six parts preceded by a definition section (s. 1):

Part I (ss. 2-8) "General", deals with the scope of the Act and conflict of laws rules.

Part II (ss. 9-20) "Validity of Security Agreements and Rights of Parties", deals with the creation of the security interest.

Part III (ss. 21-40) "Perfection of Interest", deals with the steps required to make a security interest effective against a third party and with the priority rules among competing security interests or between a security interest and a third party.

Part IV (ss. 41-54) "Registration", sets up a province-wide unified system for the registration of financing statements.

Part V (ss. 55-62) "Default Rights and Remedies", sets out the secured party's rights and remedies on the debtor's default.

Part VI (ss. 63-71) "Miscellaneous", deals with transition, interpretation, regulation, administration, etc.

BRADLEY CRAWFORD
"A Practitioner's Notes Upon the Ontario Personal Property Security Act"
(1976) 1 Can. Bus. LJ 269, 272-74

TYPES OF COLLATERAL

The Act makes functional distinctions among the various types of collateral.

Collateral, which is defined [in s. 1(*d*)] as "property that is subject to a security interest", may be of the following types:

(*a*) "goods" — all chattels personal, other than choses in action and money.

The definition follows the outlines of the definition of the term in the Sale of Goods Act, with the exception of the final conjunctive clause which provides that for the purposes of the Act, goods are one of,

(i) "consumer goods" — used or acquired for use primarily for personal, family or household purposes.

(ii) "inventory" — held by a person for sale or lease, or that are to be furnished or have been furnished under a contract of service, or that are raw materials, work in process or materials used or consumed in a business or profession.

or

(iii) "equipment" — all other goods.

These definitions of the types of goods are functional. The same television set may be "inventory" when it is "held . . . for sale", and after sale to a user either "consumer goods" because "used or acquired for use" for personal, etc., use, or "equipment" because installed in a tavern for the use of patrons. The function at the time of the transaction determines the classification. That may be changed in subsequent transactions involving the same goods. It may be desirable in some cases to obtain a covenant from the debtor concerning the continuance of the original classification, for example, to preclude a dealer from claiming the protection of classification as "consumer goods" for a car originally obtained by him as "inventory" but later used for personal purposes. Changes after perfection if not constituting amendments within the scope of s. 50(*a*) may be disregarded until the time of the next transaction creating a security interest in them, but remember, when searching the register, not to accept the debtor's assertion of the classification unquestioningly.

(*b*) "chattel paper"

(*c*) "document of title" — may be negotiable (by statute or custom), or non-negotiable

(*d*) "instrument"

(*e*) "intangible"

(*f*) "proceeds"

(*g*) "securities"

The foregoing list is not exhaustive. Note the reference to "fixtures" in the definitions of "proceeds" and of "security interest". As the term is not defined in the Act it probably retains its common law meaning. It is referred to in three other sections. "Building materials" are only mentioned once in the Act — to be excluded from the scope of "goods" in the definition of "security interest". It appears that a security interest under the Act may be retained in such materials only up until the time they are "affixed to the realty". If in that process they have become "fixtures" the security interest may be continued by compliance with the provisions concerning fixtures already noted. If they have simply been consumed in the process of construction, the supplier presumably may be secured for their price by a materialmen's lien pursuant to the Mechanics' Lien Act, or by realty mortgage.

——————————

The following chart presents the classification of "collateral" under the PPSA.

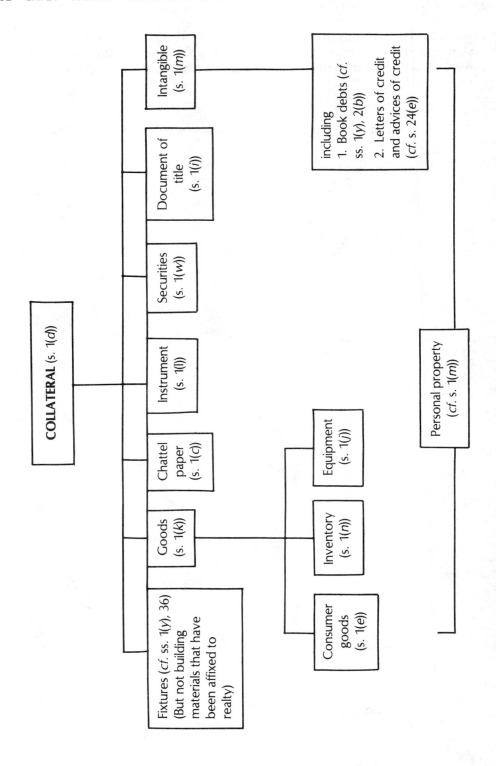

Problems:

1   A car dealer uses the proceeds of a bank loan to purchase a stock of new cars. The bank takes a security interest in the cars. The cars are sold on secured credit by the dealer as follows:

a)   to a businessman for use in his business;
b)   to an individual for family purposes;
c)   to a doctor for use partly for family purposes and partly in his profession;
d)   to another car dealer for the purpose of resale;
e)   to a rental company for the purpose of renting out to customers.

What is the PPSA classification of the cars in the hands of the original car dealer? Of each car in the hands of each purchaser?

2   A refrigerator is sold on credit in return for:
a)   a promissory note signed by the buyer;
b)   a promissory note signed by the buyer, taken together with a security agreement signed by the buyer giving the seller a security interest in the refrigerator;
c)   a contract obligation by the buyer to pay the price;
d)   a "conditional sale contract" under which the seller retains full title to the refrigerator until complete discharge of the buyer's obligation.

How is each of the four items characterized as "collateral" under the PPSA?

Notes and Questions:

1   In *Re Berman* (1979) 24 OR (2d) 79 (HC in Bkcy); rev. (1980), 26 OR (2d) 389, 8 BLR 134 (CA) (see this chapter, Section C(1) *infra*), a lender claimed a security interest in a fund representing the debtor's rights in a savings plan established by the lender. The rights in the plan were acquired by the debtor with the proceeds of the loan. In rejecting the existence of such a security interest, Steele J. held (at 83):

> Under section 12, a security interest attaches only if the debtor has a right in the collateral. The term "collateral" is defined in section 1(*d*) of the Act. . . .
>   This definition is sufficiently wide to include money. However, in *Jowett's Dictionary of English Law*, 2nd ed., the word "collateral" is defined as "that which is by the side of or distinct from, a certain thing. "I am of the opinion that the definition in the Act does not detract from this basic meaning. The money in question is the very money that was loaned by [the lender]. It is not something distinct from it. . . . There is therefore no collateral to which the security interest may attach. Under these circumstances, there can be no effective security interest within the scheme of the Act.

Do you agree?
     The draft Bill to amend the PPSA (*supra*) "clarifies that money is a separate class of property. At present, it would appear that money comes within the definition of an intangible." This is of course consistent with Steele J.'s view that the present definition of "collateral" is "sufficiently wide to include money".

2 The demarcation line between "goods" (defined in s. 1(*k*) and "intangible" (s. 1(*m*)) is not always obvious or clear. This can be seen, for example, from *United States* v. *Antenna Systems, Inc.* (1966) 251 F. Supp. 1013 (DNH). Dealing with "the blueprints and technical data produced when the company's engineering staff designed a product", the court observed that "these blueprints, drawings, etc. in reality [are] the visual reproductions on paper of engineering concepts, ideas and principles, [and as such] are . . . intangibles. . . ." At the same time patterns used in the production process by the debtor-company were held to fall into the category of "goods". Are "patterns" distinguished from "blueprints and drawings"? What is the main weakness of the definitions of "goods" and "intangible"?

As to the scope of the Act (s.2), see the following excerpts from Crawford.

BRADLEY CRAWFORD
"A Practitioner's Notes Upon the Ontario Personal Property Security Act"
op. cit. 274-79

1. GENERAL

The Act applies (subject to certain exceptions),
- (*a*) to every transaction that creates a security interest; and
- (*b*) to every assignment of book debts.

A list including all of the old security devices which are thus subsumed is given as indicative of the intended scope of the legislation. But the list is expressly not definitive. It is anticipated that new forms will be devised and some old forms — such as the "trust receipt", common in the United States and England — will be revitalized.

2. NEW APPLICATIONS

Some transactions previously exempt from registration requirements will be caught for the first time. The following may be noted.

(1) *Consignment*

This may affect the form of distributorship agreements. Simple agencies and simple bailments for storage will probably not be affected. The question will become one of ascertaining whether the transaction was "intended as security". Was it the real *purpose* of the parties (or is it the necessary consequence of the transaction — *i.e.*, was it "in substance") *regardless of the particular form employed*, intended to create an obligation upon the consignee and to secure its performance by reserving to the consignor a power over the disposition of the goods?

Although it is a form of consignment and is intended as security, the Act probably does not extend to the case in which a distant seller of goods, having reserved the right of disposal as permitted by s. 20 of the Sale of Goods Act (by obtaining a bill of lading to his own order, or to the order of his bank or his agent), sends the goods by common carrier "consigned" to the bank. Even though the intent of this transaction is to secure the seller by not transferring the bill of lading (hence the control over the goods) to the buyer by endorsement of the agent until acceptance by the buyer of the bill of exchange for the price of the goods, it is probably excluded by s. 3(2) which preserves "the rights of buyers and sellers". Since no right of a third party creditor of buyer could be asserted without derogating from the right of the seller, the exemption is probably completely effective.

(2) *Chattel Leases*

Although the Act does not qualify its use of the term "lease", obviously only leases of personal property are directly within its scope. Indirectly, an assignment of the rentals falling due under a lease of premises could be affected. Under the old law, the distinguishing feature which brought a lease, or any contract for the hire of chattels, within the expanded definition of a "conditional sale" in the Conditional Sales Act, was the presence of an option to purchase. This feature is no longer controlling, and may in fact not even be material. Registration is now required if the leasing transaction "is intended as security". The criteria established by IT-233 may be of assistance. Although they were developed by the Department of National Revenue to distinguish payments of rent (deductible expense) from payments on account of the purchase price of property, or in the case of sale and lease back the repayment of a loan, to the extent they assist in locating the beneficial interest, they also may assist in detecting a "security" intent. A sale and lease back, where the lessee is required to buy at the end of the term or to guarantee a minimum return, is almost certainly a loan secured by a charge on the equipment leased. A six-month rental with a bare option to purchase at fair market value is almost certainly not. The security intent of a transaction between such extremes becomes increasingly apparent where the lessor which, however great its volume of lease transactions, has no stock in trade of equipment which it leases to all applicants, but, rather, acquires specific items at the direction of proposed lessees, leases them for their estimated useful life to those lessees, with the lessees paying in addition to the costs usually considered incidental to ownership, such as taxes, insurance and maintenance, rents totalling the price of the equipment plus interest or financing charges. As in the case of consignments, the question will probably have to be resolved in difficult cases by attempting to ascertain whether the transaction creates an obligation on the lessee and a power in the lessor over the chattels as security for its performance.

But for one consideration, the prudent course would appear to be always to resolve doubt by registering a financing statement since only a $3 fee is involved, and by registering, notice of the lessor's interest is given to all persons claiming any other interest in the collateral. That one consideration is that by registering the lessor may preclude itself from later denying that the lease transaction was intended as security. Such a characterization of the lease would impose upon the lessor all of the duties of s. 19 and Part V of the Act, which would otherwise not apply. To the extent that such duties do not appear to individual lessors to be unduly onerous, registration will appear the more attractive. It is not, in any event, certain that registration will necessarily result in characterizing leases as security agreements.

(3) *Assignments*

The Act catches assignments in two subsections. It applies to every transaction of assignment "intended as security" and also "to every assignment of book debts not intended as security". The definition of "security interest" expressly includes "an interest arising from an assignment of book debts". It seems probable that the Act, in referring to the plural "book debts" will not be construed as excluding an assignment of a single book debt since nothing in the context appears to indicate a "contrary intention" precluding the deemed inclusion of the singular in the plural by s. 27(*j*) of the Interpretation Act. Even if that is not so, the old exemptions in s. 2 of the Assignment of Book Debts Act for assignments of book debts "due at the date of the assignment from specified debtors"; "growing due under specified contracts"; and "included in a transfer of a business" are no longer available. However, since the "debtor" in the transaction transferring the book debts is the assignor rather than the account debtor, one registration of a financing statement naming "book debts" as the collateral would appear to satisfy the Act.

Assignments for the general benefit of creditors pursuant to the Assignments and Preferences Act and, presumably, proceedings under the Bankruptcy Act remain exempt, as are assignments of any interest or claim in or under any policy of insurance or contract of annuity and any assignment whose registration is provided for in the Corporation Securities Registration Act.

It may become material to determine the distinction (if any) between a "book debt" and other choses in action, since the Act, unlike the old legislation, does purport to affect the rights of the parties to the contracts of assignment which are subject to it. The case law after the enactment of the provisions now found in s. 54 of the Conveyancing and Law of Property Act, enabling the legal assignment of any debt or legal chose in action, developed a scheme of priorities dependent upon the order in which the notices of the assignments were given to the account debtor to determine the relative rights of persons claiming competing interests in the assigned debt or chose in action. The Act now provides a different scheme dependent upon the dates of registration to determine these priorities. But the new scheme applies unevenly. It is extended, by s. 2(*b*) to *every* assignment of book debts, but governs other assignments (presumably of the other "intangibles") only if caught by s. 2(*a*) as having a security purpose. Section 40(2) in providing that the account debtor may pay the assignor until notice is given to him of the assignment, does not appear to speak to the priorities among competing assignees.

Thus, if an assignee wrongly characterizes the property assigned as an "intangible" and fails to register on the ground that the assignment was not for a security purpose, it might be that a second assignee of the same chose in action, correctly characterizing the property as a "book debt" and perfecting by registration, might take priority (if not acting with the intention of defrauding the former encumbrancer) notwithstanding the prior notification of the account debtor by the first assignee. Such a capricious, undesirable result argues strongly for either the repeal of s. 2(*b*) or its amendment to substitute "intangible" for "book debts" in order to give equal treatment to both. A further undesirable consequence of confusion between the two might arise if a financing statement were held to be misleading if it disclosed an interest in "book debts" when only "intangibles" (classified as "other" on line 10) were involved.

While the distinction remains, the question remains how to distinguish between "book debts" and other intangibles.

Although the terms "book debt", "debt" and "chose in action" are all used in the Act, they are not defined. Even if it is not destroyed as an aid to interpretation by the repeal of the Assignment of Book Debts Act, the definition of "book debts" found in s. 1(*d*) of that Act — *viz.*:

> (*d*) "book debts" means all such accounts and debts whether existing or future as in the ordinary course of business would be entered in books, whether actually entered or not, and includes any part or class thereof;

being expressed in terms of "books" seems hopelessly antiquated in an age of accounting machine methods, to say nothing of the age of computerization.

One practical distinction might be to emphasize the "commercial" connotation of "book debts", to assert that every debt owed to a business however atypical the transaction giving rise to it, should be characterized as a "book debt", if it is recorded (by whatever process) in the accounts of such business. A debt owed to a person not engaged in business would remain simply a debt. This distinction — although doubtless containing hidden difficulties until it is authoritatively determined whether debts owed to professionals such as doctors and lawyers are owed to a "business" — accords well with the express reference to "the ordinary course of business" in the old Assignment of Book Debts Act's definition, and to the 19th century English bankruptcy cases which characterized as "book debts" all debts "in some way connected with the trade of the bankrupt" whether or not actually booked. Nevertheless, the preferable course would appear to be to amend the new Act.

Assignments of book debts owed by corporations engaged in a trade or business in Ontario are not affected by any of the foregoing if they are contained in a bond or a trust deed securing bonds of that or any other corporation. Since registration is provided for such assignments in the Corporation Securities Registration Act they are exempted from the provisions of the Act by s. 3(1)(*c*).

Notes and Questions:

1 UCC 9-102 (which corresponds to PPSA s. 2) provides in subsection (3) that "[t]he application of this Article to a security interest in a secured obligation is not affected by the fact that the obligation is itself secured by a transaction or interest to which this Article does not apply." The subsection is illustrated in Comment 4 as follows:

> The owner of Blackacre borrows $10,000 from his neighbor, and secures his note by a mortgage on Blackacre. This Article is not applicable to the creation of the real estate mortgage. Nor is it applicable to a sale of the note by the mortgagee, even though the mortgage continues to secure the note. However, when the mortgagee pledges the note to secure his own obligation to X, this Article applies to the security interest thus created, which is a security interest in an instrument even though the

instrument is secured by a real estate mortgage. This Article leaves to other law the question of the effect on rights under the mortgage of delivery or non-delivery of the mortgage or of recording or non-recording of an assignment of the mortgagee's interest.

In the absence of a provision modelled on UCC 9-102(3), does the result differ under the PPSA?

2   With respect to the application of the PPSA "to every assignment of book debts not intended as security" (s. 2(*b*)), consider the following questions:
  a)   Does the Act apply to an absolute sale of "chattel paper" (as defined in s. 1(*c*)) insofar as the monetary obligation embodied therein qualifies as a "book debt"? Compare to UCC 9-102(1)(*b*).
  b)   Does the Act apply to an assignment of book debts for the purpose of collection only? To "a transfer of a contract right to an assignee who is also to do the performance under the contract"? *Cf.* UCC 9-104(*f*).

3   The larger scope of the Sask. PPSA is discussed at the conclusion of chapter 21(A) *infra*.

C. EXEMPTIONS FROM THE COVERAGE OF THE PPSA — s. 3

For constitutional reasons the PPSA does not apply to transactions governed by federal statutes like the Bank Act, SC 1980, c. 40 (Part I) or the Canada Shipping Act, RSC 1970, c. S-9. In general, for federal security laws, see J. Ziegel and I. Feltham, "Federal Law and a Uniform Act on Security in Personal Property" (1966) 9 Can. Bar J 30.

Section 3 excludes the following transactions from the coverage of the Act:

(a) liens given by statute or rule of law;

(b) transfer of an interest or claim in or under an insurance policy or contract of annuity (but this does not include insurance monies claimed as proceeds under PPSA s. 27);

(c) a mortgage, charge or assignment "whose registration is provided for in the Corporation Securities Registration Act" (RSO 1970, c. 88);

(d) transactions under The Pawnbrokers Act (RSO 1970, c. 341). These are transactions involving the delivery of an article for pawn to a "pawnbroker", defined in s. 1(*b*) of The Pawnbrokers Act as "a person who carries on the business of taking by way of pawn or pledge any article for the repayment of money lent thereon".

The exclusion of a transaction from the coverage of the PPSA leaves open the question of a priority contest between a security interest governed by the PPSA and an interest excluded therefrom (*cf.* PPSA, s. 32). See chapter 22(F) *infra*.

Note that an absolute sale of goods not accompanied by an immediate delivery is governed by (and registrable under) The Bills of Sale Act, RSO 1970, c. 44, as well as SGA s. 25(1). Also keep in mind PPSA s. 3(2), as to the preservation of sellers' and buyers' rights under ss. 20(2), 39, 40, 41 and 43 of the SGA (RSO 1970, c. 421).

Wage assignment was held to come within the scope of the Act in *Re Beaton* (1978) 91 DLR (3d) 755, 21 OR (2d) 812 (SC in Bkcy); aff'd on this point (1980) 101 DLR (3d) 338,

352 (Ont. CA). The Saskatchewan Law Reform Commission (SLRC) recommended the exclusion of wage assignments from the coverage of the PPSA (now enshrined in s. 4(*c*) of the Saskatchewan Act) and provided the following explanation (*Proposals for a Saskatchewan Personal Property Security Act* (1977) p. 11):

> The most significant consequences flowing from a decision not to exclude from the scope of the Act certain types of transactions is that the perfection and priority systems of the Act will apply to them. Before selecting the list of transactions excluded from the Act, the Commission sought answers to the following questions in connection with each type of transaction: Does the lack of registration (or other form of perfection) give rise to the likelihood that some third party will be deceived and suffer loss? If so, are the social and commercial advantages which flow from requiring registration of the transaction outweighed by the costs and inconveniences involved? The exclusions contained in sections ... 4(*c*) ... involve transactions which, in the opinion of the Commission, need not be regulated through the Act.

Do you agree with this reasoning? Can it be reconciled with the Commission's retention of the PPSA for all other types of consumer collateral?

The following is a discussion of the exemptions enumerated in s. 3(1)(*a*) and (*c*).

1. SECTION 3(1)(A): A LIEN GIVEN BY STATUTE OR RULE OF LAW

F. CATZMAN et al.
Personal Property Security Law in Ontario
(1976), p. 25

The exclusion from coverage by the Act of every lien given by statute or law includes possessory liens given by statute, Crown liens and liens given by common law.

Statutes granting possessory liens include The Mechanics' Lien Act (RSO 1970, c. 267, s. 48), The Warehousemen's Lien Act (RSO 1970, c. 488, s. 2), The Innkeepers Act (RSO 1970, c. 223, ss. 2 and 3), The Woodmen's Lien for Wages Act (RSO 1970, c. 504, s. 5), and The Mining Act (RSO 1970, c. 274, s. 641).

Statutes granting Crown liens include The Corporations Tax Act (RSO 1970, c. 91, s. 94), The Retail Sale Tax Act (RSO 1970, c. 415, s. 18(2)), The Crown Timber Act (RSO 1970, c. 102, s. 19), The Mining Tax Act (1972 (Ont.), c. 140, s. 18), and The Highway Traffic Act (RSO 1970, c. 202, s. 154(6)).

Some examples of liens given by common law include those of solicitors, bankers, carriers, auctioneers and wharfingers.

UCC 9-104(i) explicitly excludes "any right of set-off". Is such a provision necessary? Consider the following materials:

RE BERMAN
(1980) 105 DLR (3d) 380, 8 BLR 134 (Ont. CA)

HOULDEN J.A. (orally): This is an appeal from an order of Steele J. which directed the appellant, Astra Trust Company, to pay the proceeds of a mortgage retirement savings plan to the respondent, the trustee in bankruptcy of Dr. Barry Berman. The facts are simple and not in dispute.

In February 1977, Dr. Berman obtained a loan of $5,500 from Astra. He invested the moneys in a mortgage retirement savings plan which was registered under s. 146 of the Income Tax Act, 1970-71-72 (Can.), c. 63. Astra was the trustee of the plan. To secure Astra for the loan, Dr. Berman executed a letter of direction which authorized Astra to first apply the proceeds of any redemption of the plan against the indebtedness of Dr. Berman. Astra did not register a financing statement pursuant to The Personal Property Security Act, RSO 1970, c. 344. On August 15, 1978, Dr. Berman made an assignment in bankruptcy.

The trustee in bankruptcy applied to Steele J. for an order declaring that the trustee was entitled to the proceeds of the redemption of the plan. Steele J. granted the order on the ground that The Personal Property Security Act applied to the transaction, and Astra not having complied with that Act, the trustee was entitled to the proceeds. With respect, we think that the learned Judge erred in finding that The Personal Property Security Act applied to the facts of this case.

In our opinion, the law that applies to this situation is correctly stated in the *Restatement of the Law of Trusts* (2nd ed.), s. 250, at p. 632:

> If the beneficiary incurs a liability to the trustee individually and agrees that the trustee may discharge the liability out of the trust estate, the trustee is entitled to a charge on the interest of the beneficiary in the trust estate, and may deduct the amount of the liability from or set it off against what it would otherwise be his duty under the trust to pay to the beneficiary.

See also *Scott on Trusts* (3rd ed.), s. 250, pp. 2175-76. The right of Dr. Berman to redeem the plan and to receive the proceeds of the redemption, which right has vested in his trustee in bankruptcy, gave Dr. Berman a beneficial interest in the trust that was created when the plan was set up. Astra did not, therefore, have to rely upon the letter of direction. It had a charge on the proceeds of the Registered Retirement Savings Plan for the money that it had advanced to Dr. Berman. As the Restatement points out, the agreement that the trustee may discharge the liability out of the trust estate need not be expressed in words: the trustee has the right to discharge the liability out of the trust estate. The Personal Property Security Act has, therefore, no application to this case.

In the recent decision of *Re Papdopoulos*, 5 BLR 277, [1979] 2 WWR 203, 29 CBR (NS) 295, 93 DLR (3d) 621 [reversed (*sub nom. McMahon* v. *Can. Permanent Trust Co.*) 8 BLR 143 (BC CA)] Anderson J. of the British Columbia Supreme Court arrived at a similar result in an almost identical fact situation. The reasoning of Anderson J. is, however, somewhat different from the reasoning of this Court.

The appeal will be allowed, the judgment below set aside, and in its place there will be a declaration that the appellant is entitled to deduct from the proceeds of the Registered Retirement Savings Plan, the moneys owing to it; the balance, if any, shall be remitted to the trustee in bankruptcy.

Appeal allowed.

Note: The decision of the court below is reported in 24 OR (2d) 79. For a thorough discussion, see J. Ziegel, ''The Quickening Pace of Jurisprudence Under the Ontario Personal Property Security Act'' (1980) 4 Can. Bus. LJ 54, 69-74.

A similar fact situation arose in *Re Papdopoulos* (1979) 93 DLR (3d) 621 (BC SC). Anderson J. held that the right of the trustee in bankruptcy to redeem the value of the RRSP plan was subject to the rights of the trustee under the plan to deduct any moneys remaining unpaid on the loan previously made by him in his capacity as lender to the bankrupt. Anderson J. based the lender's priority on his right to set off a mutual debt, viz. the indebtedness arising from the loan, against the RRSP account. He further reasoned that the relationship between the lender and the bankrupt debtor was not a true trust, or alternatively that the bankrupt was the only person with a beneficial interest in the plan and that the different capacities occupied by the parties at the time of bankruptcy did not preclude the plan's trustee from claiming the right of set-off.

The Court of Appeal reversed (*sub nom. McMahon* v. *Canada Permanent Trust Company* (1979) 8 BLR 143, 147 (BC CA)). It held that ''the RRSP was set up and was a trust'' which had not been terminated or altered on the bankruptcy. It then rejected the trustee-lender's power to set off and further purported to distinguish *Re Berman.* The following is an excerpt from the decision of the B.C. Court of Appeal. Is it persuasive? If the trustee-lender is not entitled to a trustee's charge or to a debtor's right of set-off, does he hold a security interest in the RRSP account?

McMAHON v. CANADA PERMANENT TRUST COMPANY
[1980] 2 WWR 438, (1979) 8 BLR 143, 148 (BC CA)

[Having decided that the trust relationship had survived the bankruptcy, the court continued:]

BULL J.A.: Next, consideration must be given to the right of the respondent to set off against the funds so held by it in trust, and demanded by the appellant, against the earlier personal loans made by it to the bankrupt. The law on set-off is clear although difficulties do sometimes arise in its application in different sets of circumstances. That the ordinary rules respecting set-off are applicable in bankruptcy matters is provided in the Bankruptcy Act in s. 75, and has not been questioned. The basic rule is that set-off (in effect the combination of accounts) is only available short of agreement, express or implied, when the debts or accounts are mutual, between the same parties in the same right. It is not necessary that debts which are mutual must be of the same nature. See Houlden and Morawetz, *Bankruptcy Law of Canada* (1960), at pp. 160 et seq. ''Mutual debts'' are debts or claims due from one to another which are ascertainable and which are in the same right. A person in his individual capacity is not in the same right as he is when acting as trustee for another. Hence, it is trite law that, subject to certain limited exceptions, an amount owed by a person in his capacity as trustee holding property, credits, or funds for another or others cannot combine them with, or set them off against, a personal debt owed to him in his personal capacity by the beneficiary or beneficiaries of the trust: see *Garnett* v. *M'Kewan (P.O.)* (1872) LR 8, Ex. 10, [1868-73] All ER Rep. 686. In such a case there is no mutuality as one account is held in a fiduciary capacity and the other in a personal capacity. The same situation arises where there is not a trust in the strict sense of the word, but one account is set up or exists for a "special purpose" which could be held to deprive it of "mutuality" with another account held with a different or no special purpose. With respect to this concept, the following words of Lord Simon of Glaisdale in *Nat. Westminster Bank Ltd.* v. *Halesowen Presswork & Assemblies Ltd.* [1972] AC 785 at 808 [1972] 1 All ER 641, [1972] 1 Lloyd's Rep. 101, [1972] 2 WLR 455 at 466 (HL) are illuminating:

> I would prefer to say that money is paid for a special (or specific) purpose so as to exclude mutuality of dealing within section 31 if the money is paid in such circumstances that it would be a misappropriation to use it for any other purpose than that for which it is paid.

It is pointed out that s. 31 referred to in the passage was of the English Bankruptcy Act, 1914 (U.K.), c. 59 and provided for set-off when there were "mutual credits, mutual debts or other mutual dealings", the equivalent of s. 75 of our Bankruptcy Act.

The respondent has relied strongly on a line of old, but still accepted, authorities to support what I have referred to above as exceptions. Those cases were, inter alia: *Bankes* v. *Jarvis* [1903] 1 KB 549, [1900-3] All ER Rep. 656; *Jones* v. *Mossop* (1844), 3 Hare 568, 67 ER 506; *Cochrane* v. *Green* (1860) 9 CB (NS) 448, 142 ER 176; and *Bailey* v. *Finch* (1871) LR 7 QB 34. In each of the cases a trust or a "special purpose" was involved and it was held set-off was available with respect to another account. Particular stress was put on *Bailey* v. *Finch, supra,* wherein a bank was held entitled to set off a debt due it by an individual against a credit it held for that individual as an executor of an estate. The ratio of the decision in *Finch* and, in my view, in the other cases cited, was that a Court will, in equity, permit set-off where "mutuality" and the same interests in the debts were in reality and fact found to exist although superficially that might not appear to be the case.

In my view those authorities are inapplicable here as this is a completely different and reversed situation. Here we have the strange position of the claimant for set-off for its own financial benefit and advantage endeavouring to establish that the trust fund it holds and deals with as trustee is to be considered a mutual debt with and in the same right as a personal debt due it. In my view that cannot be.

I think that the respondent's obligations under the RRSP were clearly that of a trustee. Further, when the appellant demanded, as he was entitled to do, the funds constituting the trust property thus limiting the scope and extent of the trust, the respondent nevertheless remained a trustee of that trust property with a trust obligation to carry out the trust as so limited. It was bound to perform its duties qua trustee including the turn over of the trust property (i.e., the fund) to the appellant, and until it actually did so it had a trust to perform. The delivery or payment of the funds to the appellant would be the carrying out of a trust duty and not a payment of debt. I add that, in my view, the respondent's dealing with trust property in any other way (including the asserted right to set off the trust funds against its own debt due from the bankrupt) would probably be considered a conversion of trust assets, or, perhaps, an unauthorized preference.

I think it advisable to mention a recent decision of the Ontario Court of Appeal in *Re Berman*, delivered October 17, 1979 [now reported at 8 BLR 134] which was referred to by both appellant and respondent. The facts are very similar to those here. There, the bankrupt, before his bankruptcy, borrowed from a trust company the required amount of his contribution to a RRSP, at the time giving a direction to the company to first apply the proceeds of any redemption on that loan. After bankruptcy the trustee in bankruptcy requested redemption and the trust company claimed set-off. The only apparent difference in the facts of the two cases was the important one of the express direction given to the trust company by the bankrupt. No direction of that nature was given in the case at Bar. Houlden J.A., speaking for the Court, held that the trust company was entitled to set off the amounts. He made it perfectly clear that his judgment was based on the specific law set out in two United States texts, namely in *Restatement of the Law of Trusts* (2nd ed.), s. 250 at p. 632 (which he set out in his judgment in extenso) and *Scott on Trusts*, (3rd ed.), s. 250, pp. 2175-76. The passage set out in the judgment deals only with a situation where there is an agreement that the trustee discharge the liability to it out of the trust estate and, accordingly, is entitled to set-off. The second citation deals only with (a) the conclusion that a trustee cannot deduct from, or have a charge on, trust property for a personal claim against a beneficiary and must be confined to his suit for debt being in no better position than any other creditor; and (b) the right of the trustee to set-off where that remedy is provided by an agreement or understanding, express or implied. Then, strangely, in my respectful view, the learned Judge said that the trust company did not need to rely on the direction given but, nevertheless, he allowed the set-off. I can only conclude he reached that opinion on the basis of the above citations dealing with an agreement or understanding for a set-off. In my view his reference to the letter of direction must have been either inadvertent or merely a reference to the actual "directions" to pay as opposed to an agreement found to exist that the trust company could exercise a right to repay itself through set-off. Accordingly, as there was no such direction or arrangement, express or implied, in this case to give the respondent the right to set-off, in my view the Ontario decision is of no help to either party here.

Appeal allowed.

2. Section 3(1)(c): Mortgage, Charge or Assignment whose Registration is Provided for in the Corporation Securities Registration Act (CSRA)

The following is an excerpt from a paper prepared by Martin Fingerhut of the Ontario Bar on "Registration of Corporation Charges in Ontario". The author assumes that the charge under consideration is contained in a "debenture". He then goes on to consider where it should be registered.

MARTIN FINGERHUT
Registration of Corporation Charges in Ontario

(a) *Registration under the CSRA*

If the debenture contains a charge on chattels located in Ontario or on book debts owing by a corporation carrying on business in Ontario, then the debenture must be registered under the CSRA in order to avoid the invalidating provisions of that statute. The relevant provision of the CSRA is section 2(1) which reads as follows:

> Every mortgage and every charge, whether specific or floating, of chattels in Ontario created by a corporation, and every assignment of book debts, whether by way of specific or floating charge, made by a corporation engaged in a trade or business in Ontario and contained,
>
> (a)   in a trust deed or other instrument to secure bonds, debentures or debenture stock of the corporation or of any other corporation; or
>
> (b)   in any bonds, debentures or debenture stock of the corporation as well as in the trust deed or other instrument securing the same, or in a trust deed or other instrument securing the bonds, debentures or debenture stock of any other corporation; or
>
> (c)   in any bonds, debentures or debenture stock or any series of bonds or debentures of the corporation not secured by a separate instrument,
>
> is void as against creditors of the mortgagor or assignor, and as against subsequent purchasers or mortgagees from or under the mortgagor or assignor, in good faith, for valuable consideration and without notice, unless it is duly registered . . .

(b) *Registration under the PPSA*

A debenture may charge collateral in addition to chattels and book debts (as defined in the CSRA). For example, it may contain a charge on shares, goodwill, industrial property such as patents and trade marks, or on choses in action other than book debts. In the absence of any judicial decision on point, it would appear prudent for a debenture charging any such property to be registered under the PPSA as well as under the CSRA. This conclusion results from a consideration of section 3(1)(c) of the PPSA. . . .

Registration of Security Agreements

• • •

It is trite to say that the term "debenture" has not received a definitive interpretation from the courts. In a decision which determined that a particular document was a debenture rather than an ordinary promissory note, Lindley, J. said:

> Now, what the correct meaning of "debenture" is I do not know. I do not find anywhere any precise definition of it. . . . You may have a debenture which is nothing more than an acknowledgement of indebtedness. . . . Upon the whole I am

CSRA - coporate Securities Registration Act.

of opinion that this instrument is a debenture and not a promissory-note, although I quite agree that it would be a promissory-note if it were nothing else.

It is not the purpose of this paper to review the numerous cases which have attempted to determine whether a particular document constituted a "debenture". [Suffice it] to say that a document which provides for or acknowledges indebtedness might well, on the existing authorities, be construed to be a debenture. See *Re Provincial Refining Company Ltd.* (1978) 30 CBR (NS) 113 (Nfld. CA).

The non-academic nature of this issue has [strikingly] been brought to the attention of the legal profession by two recent Ontario cases, *Turf Care Products Ltd.* v. *Crawford's Mowers and Marine Ltd.* (1978) 23 OR (2d) 292 (Ont. HC) and *Re Turf World Irrigation Limited* (1979) 30 CBR (NS) 280.

In *Turf Care*, the Bank of Montreal's standard security agreement was reviewed. It was held that a *prima facie* case had been established that the security agreement was required to be registered under the CSRA, and the court enjoined the Bank from proceeding under the agreement against certain chattel collateral secured thereunder. In *Turf World*, the general security agreement of Canadian Imperial Bank of Commerce came under judicial scrutiny. The agreement was held to be properly registered under the PPSA alone.

Unfortunately, the judgments in *Turf Care* and *Turf World* did not thoroughly analyze the issues at hand. The case authority dealing with the interpretation of a "debenture" was not considered nor was the legislative history of the relevant provisions of the CSRA and the PPSA. *Turf World* distinguished the *Turf Care* decision largely on the basis of the intention of the parties to the CIBC General Security Agreement not to create a document that was registerable under the CSRA, a basis which offers little guidance to solving problems of a similar nature in the future. However, an analysis of the debenture cases and the *Turf Care* and *Turf World* decisions indicates that a document having the following characteristics should be registerable under the PPSA only:

(1) The document should not acknowledge or require payment of a specified sum. For example, it might secure payment of all indebtedness from time to time owing from the debtor to the secured party.
(2) The document should not employ the charging language normally found in a debenture or chattel mortgage (i.e., bargain, sell, mortgage, charge, pledge and set over as and by way of a first and specific fixed charge, etc.) but should merely provide for a charge and security interest on the collateral.
(3) One or more references to The Personal Property Security Act would be useful.

Notes:

1 The draft Bill to amend the PPSA (*supra*) proposed to repeal the CSRA and to integrate the registration of documents registrable thereunder into the framework of the PPSA registration system. See further, chapter 21(C) *infra*.
2 The following issues affecting floating charges, whether or not created by an instrument governed by the CSRA, are discussed below: time of attachment under

the Anglo-Canadian floating charge (chapter 21(B)); priority of a floating charge given by a non-corporate debtor and thus governed by the PPSA (chapter 22(A)); and priority between a charge registrable under the CSRA and a PPSA interest (chapter 22(F)). See also chapter 24 (enforcement of security interests by receivers and receiver managers appointed pursuant to the terms governing default in a debenture).

Chapter 21

Security Interests:
Creation, Attachment, Perfection

Central to the scope of the PPSA is a transaction "that in substance creates a security interest": PPSA s. 2(a). The essence of a "security interest" is "an interest in [collateral] that secures payment or performance of an obligation . . .": PPSA. s.1(y). Whether or not a particular agreement creates or provides for a "security interest" (so as to be a "security agreement" under PPSA s. 1(x)) is not always an easy question to determine. What counts is the intention of the parties: PPSA s. 2(a).

The present chapter deals with the following topics:

A. The creation of a security interest by a security agreement and determination of the nature of the agreement. The discussion focuses on the distinction between a "true lease" and "a lease intended as security" (*cf.* PPSA s. 2(a)(ii)). The latter is actually not a lease at all but rather a "security agreement".

B. Attachment and perfection of a security interest — the general rules, the particular issue of the time of attachment in connection with the English floating charge, and the specific provisions relating to farm products and consumer goods financing.

C. Registration of a financing statement as a method of perfecting a security interest: the registration system and the effect of errors and omissions.

A. CREATING A SECURITY INTEREST BY A SECURITY AGREEMENT — TRUE LEASES AND LEASES INTENDED AS SECURITY

Cross-reference — chapter 2(A), *supra.*

Income Tax Interpretation Bulletin IT-233 provides that a transaction will be considered a sale as opposed to a lease where "the lessee has the right during or immediately at the expiration of the lease to acquire the property at a price which at the inception of the lease is substantially less than the probable fair market value of the property at the time of the permitted acquisition." Is the following case consistent with this approach?

In the Matter of WHEATLAND ELECTRIC PRODUCTS CO.
(1964) 237 F. Supp. 820 (DC WD Pa.)

MILLER D.J.: Now before the Court is Burroughs Corporation's Petition for Review of Order filed by the Referee in Bankruptcy on July 22, 1964. Said Order accompanied by Findings of Fact and Conclusion of Law, refused Burroughs' Petition for Reclamation filed May 20, 1964.

Burroughs Corporation, on December 27, 1960, had leased to Wheatland Electric Products Company a Burroughs Style No. F-1503 machine for a term of one year and to continue on a month to month basis until terminated. In that lease, the list price of the machine was established at $8,025.00 and the monthly rental was set at $241.00. The lease contained a purchase option provision, granting Wheatland the right to purchase the machine at the list price at any time during the term of the lease or within thirty days after its termination and further providing that 75% of the rentals paid prior to the purchase date would be applied to the list price up to but not exceeding 75% of that price. On May 16, 1962, a new lease for the same equipment was entered into for one year at a monthly rental of $197.50. Also executed at that time was a purchase option rider, granting Wheatland the option to buy the equipment at the list price. That option was to be exercised within thirty-six months of the commencement of the original lease or to terminate automatically if not exercised. The termination date of said option was December 27, 1963. By the terms of the option rider, 75% of the rentals paid prior to its exercise were to be credited if exercised within one year of the original lease and 70% of the rentals were to be applied to the purchase price up to but not exceeding 75% of that price if exercised after one year from the date of the original lease.

On May 16, 1963, the parties executed a lease extension rider, continuing the lease for one year at a monthly rental of $224.00. No purchase option provision was included in that extension rider. The purchase option rider executed on May 16, 1962, terminated on December 27, 1963, when Wheatland failed to exercise it.

Wheatland filed a Petition for Arrangement under Chapter XI of the Bankruptcy Act on February 5, 1964. The Trustee appointed in these proceedings paid the monthly rental due in March 1964. Thereafter Wheatland was in default on its rental payments and Burroughs filed a Petition for Reclamation. That Petition was refused by the Referee in Bankruptcy on the ground that the lease, being a security agreement under the terms of the Uniform Commercial Code, 12A P.S. §1-201(37), had not been filed as required by the Code, 12A P.S. §9-302, and was therefore invalid against the Trustee.

The question presented by the Petition for Review is whether the lease was intended as security and is to be determined by the facts of the case. In determining the intent of the parties, we may look only to the language of the lease itself, which provided that "there are no understandings, agreements, representations or warranties, express or implied, not specified herein, respecting this lease or the equipment or service hereinabove described." (12A P.S. §2-202)

The Code provides that "the inclusion of an option to purchase does not of itself make the lease one intended for security." It further provides that "an agreement that upon compliance with the terms of the lease the lessee shall become or has the option to become the owner of the property for no additional consideration or for a nominal consideration does make the lease one intended for security." (12A P.S. §1-201(37))

This language of the Code describes what was formerly known in Pennsylvania as a bailment lease, a security device by which one desiring to purchase an article of personal property, but not wishing to pay for it immediately, could secure possession of it with the right to use and enjoy it as long as the rental was paid and with the further right to become the owner, upon completing the installment payments, by the payment of an additional nominal sum. *General Motors Acceptance Corp.* v. *Hartman*, 114 Pa. Super. 544, 174 A. 795 (1934).

The Courts, in referring to the term "nominal consideration", frequently use it interchangeably with the sum of $1.00 or some other small amount. *Valicenti* v. *Central Motors, Inc.*, 115 Pa. Super. 74, 174 A. 799 (1934); *Commercial Banking Corporation* v. *Philadelphia Transportation Company*, 162 Pa. Super. 153, 56 A. 2d 344 (1948).

In the instant case, the additional amount which Wheatland was to pay to secure ownership of the machinery should it choose to exercise the option was a minimum of 25% of the list price, or $2,006.25. That amount is not a nominal consideration for the right to become the owner of the equipment, but represents a substantial proportion of the purchase price. In the case of *In re Royer's Bakery, Inc.*, 56 Berks County Law Journal 48 (1963), the Referee held that an agreement was intended as security when it provided that 80% of the rental payments previously made could be applied to the purchase price. But that provision differed from the instant one in that the credit could be applied up to but not exceeding the list price, so that upon compliance with the terms the lessee could become the owner without paying any additional consideration.

With regard to a lease intended as security, the law recognizes that the ultimate intent of the agreement is a sale, to take effect and become operative only upon compliance with the provisions of the lease. Here considerably more than completion of the rental payments provided for in the lease was required to give Wheatland ownership of the machinery. A further indication that this lease was not intended for security by the parties is the fact that in May 1963, when the lease was extended, the purchase option rider was not likewise extended, although the option would terminate if not exercised, before the end of the term of the extended lease. On February 5, 1964, when Wheatland filed its petition for arrangement, the only agreement in effect between it and Burroughs was the lease, the purchase option rider having expired on December 27, 1963, because Wheatland failed to exercise it.

Because we find that the leasing agreement between Burroughs and Wheatland was not one intended for security within the terms of the Uniform Commercial Code, Burroughs was not required to file a financing statement to perfect its interest and to maintain its right to reclamation. For this reason, the Order of the Referee in Bankruptcy filed July 22, 1964, will be reversed and the case remanded to the Referee for proceedings consistent with this Opinion.

Notes and Questions:

1   The last clause of UCC 1-201(37), relied on by the court in *Wheatland*, reads as follows:

> Whether a lease is intended as security is to be determined by the facts of each case; however, (a) the inclusion of an option to purchase does not by itself make the lease one intended for security, and (b) an agreement that upon compliance with the terms of the lease the lessee shall become or has the option to become the owner of the property for no additional consideration or for a nominal consideration does make the lease one intended for security.

Was the clause properly construed in *Wheatland*? Is the clause good law in Ontario?

2   In *In re Royer's Bakery, Inc.* (1963) 1 UCC Rep. Serv. 342 (DC ED Pa.), the court stated at p. 345-46:

> [W]henever it can be found that a lease agreement concerning personal property contains provisions the effect of which are to create in the lessee an equity or pecuniary interest in the leased property the parties are deemed as a matter of law to have intended the lease as security. . . .

Do you agree? Suppose a piece of equipment whose list price is $100,000 is leased out for 10 years. The lease gives the lessee the option to purchase the lease at any time during or at the end of the leasing period by paying the list price ($100,000) less 80% of the aggregate rental payments previously paid. Is the lease intended as security? It has indeed been stated that "[t]he flaw in *Royer's Bakery* is obviously the breadth of its language, for certainly there could be many cases in which the *bona-fide* lessee would be establishing some substantial equity or pecuniary interest. One such case is *In the Matter of Wheatland Elec. Prods. Co.* . . . .": R. Uskevich, "Secured Transactions: Leases As Security: Some Problems of Identification" (1966-67) 8 Bost. Indus. Comm. L. Rev. 764-67. Do you agree with this criticism?

3   The court in *Re Alpha Creamery Co. Inc.* (1967) 4 UCC Rep. Ser. 794, 798 (DC WD Mich.) stated as follows: "Where the terms of the lease and option to purchase are such that the only sensible course for the lessee at the end of the lease term is to exercise the option and become the owner of the goods, the lease was intended to create a security interest." Is this a workable test?

4   Did the court in *Wheatland* properly consider the absence of an option to purchase in the written contract? In *In the Matter of the Atlanta Times, Inc.* (1966) 259 F. Supp. 820 (ND Ga.), where the written lease agreement contained an entire agreement

clause and no option to purchase, the court cited the parol evidence rule and refused to admit evidence designed to prove an oral option to purchase. This aspect of *Atlanta* was criticized as follows:

> The Code provides that the intention of the parties is determinative of the creation of a security interest, regardless of the form of the transaction. By giving effect to the entire agreement clause the court limits the evidence which can be considered in determining the true intention . . . and at the same time places the emphasis on its form.

(Uskevich, *op. cit.* 769.) Do you agree? Is the criticism relevant to the *Wheatland* decision?

5   As in the case of a lease, whether a given consignment is a "true consignment" or a "consignment intended as security" depends on the parties' intention. The question arose in *Re Stephanian's Persian Carpets Ltd.* (1979) 31 CBR (NS) 196 (Ont. SC in Bkcy) where Ferron, Registrar stated (at 198): "Under the Personal Property Security Act it is only those consignment agreements which are intended as security to which the Act applies. Discovering the intention of a party or parties is always a difficult and perplexing task. Intention must be gathered from facts and events which antedate the transaction. The onus is on the applicant trustee to show that the intention between the bankrupt and the respondent was to create security."

On appeal, Saunders J. ((1980) 34 CBR (NS) 35, 42) stated that "if the arrangement served no other function than to protect the consignor against creditors, it might be considered to be within [the Ont. PPSA]". Do you agree? Recall PPSA s. 1(*y*). In another case, Saunders J. held that "[t]he absence of an agency relationship does not necessarily mean that the agreement is not one of consignment". See *Re Toyerama Ltd.* (1980) 34 CBR (NS) 153, 157 (Ont. SC in Bkcy). Do you agree? In the absence of agency, what would be the relationship between the consignor and a buyer from the consignee? Will the buyer from the consignee be protected under The Factors Act, RSO 1970, c. 156? What does "agency relationship" mean in this context? See the discussion, *supra*, in chapter 2(C).

In determining the intention of the parties, the better view is that where "the consignee is absolutely liable for the price of the 'consigned' goods, with no right to return the goods unsold, then the consignor's reserved claim to the goods should be treated as a security interest . . .": P. Winship, "The 'True' Consignment Under the Uniform Commercial Code and Related Peccadilloes" (1975) 29 SWLJ 825, 848. Is this view consistent with PPSA s. 1(*y*)?

6   A lessor faced with uncertainty as to whether the lease will be held to be a security agreement, "should be permitted to make provisions for precautionary filing without the risk that such provisions would in and of themselves . . . convert the lease into a secured transaction": *Rollins Communications, Inc.* v. *Georgia Institute of Real Estate, Inc.* (1976) 20 UCC Rep. Ser. 1027, 1029-1030 (Ga. App.). This view also holds true for consignors. Nevertheless, the applicability of the PPSA (including the enforcement provisions discussed in chapter 24, *infra*) depends on whether the "lease" or "consignment" is in fact a security agreement. See e.g. *FMA Financial Corp.* v. *Pro-Printers* (1979) 25 UCC Rep. Ser. 950 (Utah SC).

In the following extract, the Saskatchewan Law Reform Commission argues for an extension of the scope of the PPSA.

SASKATCHEWAN LAW REFORM COMMISSION
Proposals for a Saskatchewan Personal Property Security Act
(1977) pp. 7-8

2. In addition, the section brings within the registration and priority provisions of the Act four types of commercial transactions which in technical terms are not security agreements: non-security assignments of chattel paper; non-security assignments of accounts; consignment agreements, and leases of goods for a term of more than one year.

Commercial financing which involves assignment of chattel paper or accounts is carried out in such a way as to make it difficult and commercially unnecessary to draw distinctions between security assignments and sales.

3. True consignments and leases have one feature in common with security agreements. They create a potential for deception of innocent third parties who deal with the lessee or consignor, as the case may be, in the belief that no one else has a claim to the property involved.

Any modern personal property security legislation must embody a system designed to protect innocent third parties who might otherwise suffer loss as a result of dealing with a person who has given a security interest in his property. The Commission has concluded that a system which avoids deception in cases where security transactions are involved can be employed with equal effectiveness in cases where certain types of non-security agreements create the same type of deception. It is totally unrealistic to attempt to bring within the scope of the Act every kind of transaction in which deception results from a separation of interest and appearance of interest. However, it is realistic to include in the registration and perfection system of the Act certain types of transactions which, because of their commercial importance, are likely to continue to produce significant disruption if left out. The Commission has concluded that long-term leases and certain types of true consignment agreements fall within this category. Note, however, that the *inter partes* sections of the Act (Part V) do not apply to these non-security transactions (see section 55).

Not all consignments and chattel leases are subject to the Act. Consignment agreements between private citizens and mercantile agents are excluded (see definition of "consignment agreement", section 2(5)). While there is potential for deception in all leases, it is commercially impractical to require all leases to be registered. The volume of short-term leases such as car rentals would be overwhelming, and the costs of registering every such transaction would be prohibitive. Where long-term leases are involved, these problems are not of such dimension as to cause concern.

Any definition distinguishing long-term leases which fall within the Act from short-term leases which do not, to a large extent must be arbitrary. The Commission has concluded that leases of a term of one year or less should be excluded from the Act unless they are security leases.

The definition of "lease for a term of more than one year" (section 2(20)) is designed to prevent avoidance through the use of leases with indefinite terms, short-term leases with renewal clauses or leases under which the lessee in fact remains in possession for a period in excess of one year. The definition excludes leases of "notorious goods". See section 2(23). Deception is not a problem with respect to leases of certain types of goods such as telephones, and other types of communications equipment. The kinds falling into this category will be listed in regulations so that necessary changes can be made from time to time.

The inclusion of long-term leases within the scope of the Act does not eliminate the necessity to distinguish between true leases and security leases. All security leases are subject to the Act regardless of their term. The Act does not provide guidelines to be used in distinguishing true leases from security leases.

Note: The Sask. PPSA follows these recommendations and provides in s. 2(*nn*) that security interest "is deemed to include (i) an interest arising from an assignment of accounts or transfer of chattel paper; (ii) the interest of a person who delivers goods to another person under a consignment; and (iii) the interest of a lessor under a lease for a term of more than one year." Under s. 2(*g*),

> "consignment" means an agreement under which goods are delivered to a person, who in the ordinary course of his business deals in goods of that description, for sale, resale or lease, by a person who:
> (i) in the ordinary course of his business deals in goods of that description; and
> (ii) reserves a proprietary interest in the goods after they have been delivered;
>
> but does not include an agreement under which goods are delivered to a person for sale or lease if the person is generally known in the area in which he carries on business to be selling or leasing goods of others;

Does this include the interest of a manufacturer who delivers goods to a sub-contractor for packing (or for any other purpose in the production process) and then instructs him to ship the goods to the manufacturer's designated buyers? *Cf. In re Medomak Canning Co.* (1977) 25 UCC Rep. Ser. 437 (Bkcy Ct. D. Me.).

"Lease for a term of more than one year" is extensively defined in s. 1(*y*).

B. ATTACHMENT AND PERFECTION OF A SECURITY INTEREST

In principle, "a security agreement is effective according to its terms between the parties to it and against third parties" (PPSA s. 9). Nonetheless, specific rules exist as to the "attachment", "enforceability" and "perfection" of a security interest.

1. Attachment and Enforceability

a) Introductory Note

Attachment is the term used to denote when, as between the secured party and the debtor, the secured party has acquired rights in the collateral. In effect, it determines when the security interest has been created. The PPSA is permissive and imposes few restrictions on the creation of security interests in personal property.

JACOB S. ZIEGEL
"The Draft Ontario Personal Property Security Act"
(1966) 44 Can. B. Rev. 104, 114

All that is necessary in order to create an effective security interest between the parties is that (a) the parties intend it to attach; (b) value is given; and (c) the debtor has rights in the collateral [s. 12]. In addition, if the secured party wishes to be in a position to enforce a security interest against a third party the agreement must be in writing and signed by the debtor, unless the collateral is already in his possession. Subject to these simple requirements, the security agreement is effective according to its terms between the parties to it and against third parties. In particular it may cover after-acquired property and it may secure future advances or other value, whether or not the advances or other value are given pursuant to commitment. Such clauses are common in inventory financing and other agreements involving the extension of a line of credit, and their express recognition is much to be welcomed.

b) The Elements of Attachment (s. 12(1))

The following is a discussion of the elements of attachment required under s. 12(1).

i) Time of attachment turns first on the intention of the parties (s. 12(1)(a)). This element raises some difficulty in connection with the English floating charge and will be discussed below in this context.

ii) "Value" (required by s. 12(1)(b)) is defined in s. 1(z). "The Catzman Committee was of the opinion that a giving of security in satisfaction of an antecedent debt or a binding commitment to extend credit are encompassed in, and are no more than examples of, the consideration sufficient to support a simple contract . . .": F. Catzman *et al, Personal Property Security Law in Ontario* (1976) p. 62. Do you agree?

iii) In its simplest sense, the requirement that "the debtor has rights in the collateral" (s. 12(1)(c)) is merely an aspect of the *nemo dat* rule: absent rights in the collateral, the debtor cannot give a "security interest" therein. Is there a conflict between s. 12(1)(c) and the definition of debtor in s. 1(g)? The requirement of s. 12(1)(c) plays a crucial role in establishing the time of attachment. See the particular rules of s. 12(2) in connection with crops, fish, minerals and timber as well as the rules of s. 13 in connection with after-acquired property, together with the qualified exceptions as to crops and consumer goods. Do you see the rationale of s. 14? See the concluding note to section (B) *infra*. The owner of the collateral undoubtedly has "rights in the collateral" for the purposes of s. 12(1)(c). When his rights are acquired by purchase, consider the provisions of ss. 17-19 of the Sale of Goods Act dealing with the passage of property. Mere possession (such as that of a lessee or any other bailee) will not qualify as "rights in the collateral". See Law Reform Commission of British Columbia *Report on Debtor-Creditor Relationships (Project No. 2): Part 5 — Personal Property Security* (1975) pp. 39-44. However, a possessor with power to cut off the owner's rights (see e.g. s. 2(1) of the Factors Act, RSO 1970, c. 156) has been held to have "rights in the collateral": *Nasco Equipment Co.* v. *Mason* (1976) 229 SE 2d 278 (NC SC). *Query*: what rights (if any) which fall short of ownership or power to give ownership (and are not mere possessory rights) are "rights in the collateral" for the purpose of s. 12(1)(c)? For "rights in the collateral" by estoppel against a third party owner and the effectiveness of these rights against the owner's own creditors, see *Avco Delta Corp. Canada Ltd.* v. *U.S.* (1972) 459 F. 2d 436 (7th Cir.), accord *In the Matter of Pubs Inc. of Champaign* (1980) 618 F. 2d 432 (7th Cir.)

Problem: Since January 1973, D has been in possession of drilling equipment owned by O. In January 1974 an agreement in principle was reached orally between D and O as to the purchase of the equipment by D. A memorandum of understanding was signed in February 1974. A detailed conditional sale contract was signed in April 1974 and became effective in May 1974. Under the contract O reserved title to the equipment until fully paid. When did O's security interest attach? Will you change your answer if the April 1974 contract purported to apply retroactively from January 1973?

Note on Time of Attachment under the Anglo-Canadian Floating Charge:

The following are the two "judicial definitions [of the Anglo-Canadian floating charge] most often quoted by the commentators, and by judges", according to F. Catzman *et al.*, *Personal Property Security Law in Ontario* (1976) p. 63:

(1) Lord Macnaghten in *Governments Stock & Other Securities Investment Co.* v. *Manila Ry. Co.* [1897] AC 81, 86:

> A floating security is an equitable charge on the assets for the time being of a going concern. It attaches to the subject charged in the varying condition in which it happens to be from time to time. It is of the essence of such a charge that it remains dormant until the undertaking charged ceases to be a going concern, or until the person in whose favour the charge is created intervenes. His right to intervene may of course be suspended by agreement. But if there is no agreement for suspension, he may exercise his right whenever he pleases after default.

(2) Buckley, L. J. in *Evans* v. *Rival Granite Quarries, Ltd.* [1910] 2 KB 979, 999 (CA):

> A floating security is not a future security; it is a present security, which presently affects all the assets of the company expressed to be included in it. On the other hand, it is not a specific security; the holder cannot affirm that the assets are specifically mortgaged to him. The assets are mortgaged in such a way that the

> mortgagor can deal with them without the concurrence of the mortgagee. A floating security is not a specific mortgage of the assets, plus a licence to the mortgagor to dispose of them in the course of his business, but is a floating mortgage applying to every item comprised in the security, but not specifically affecting any item until some event occurs or some act on the part of the mortgagee is done which causes it to crystallize into a fixed security. . . . This crystallization may be brought about in various ways. A receiver may be appointed, or the company may go into liquidation and a liquidator be appointed, or any event may happen which is defined as bringing to an end the licence to the company to carry on business; . . .

What is the time of attachment of the security interest under a floating charge? Is it the time of crystallization? At the time when the debtor has rights in a particular asset? If the latter, will the security interest still be subject to the debtor's right to dispose of the collateral in the course of his business? *Cf.* chapter 22(G), *infra*.

The presumption of Sask. PPSA s. 12(1) is that a security interest attaches as soon as value is given, the debtor has rights in the collateral, and the security agreement becomes enforceable. However, when "the parties intend it to attach at a later time . . . it attaches in accordance with [their] intentions". Applying these provisions, what will be the time of attachment under a floating charge?

Note that the Anglo-Canadian floating charge is not known in American law and that what is referred to as a "floating charge" in American legal literature is a *specific* lien on shifting assets. The PPSA, s. 2(*a*)(i), specifically includes the English style floating charge, but does not clarify its status under the Act. Earlier versions of the Sask. PPSA and the Model Act contained a number of specific rules relating to floating charges, but these were subsequently deleted.

The draft Bill to amend the Ontario PPSA proposed to add the following subsection (1a) to s. 12:

> Unless otherwise agreed, a security interest in the nature of a floating charge shall be deemed to attach to each item or part of the collateral upon the later of the execution of the security agreement and the time at which the debtor acquires rights in the item or part of the collateral.

For further discussion of the floating charge and the PPSA see A. Abel, "Has Article 9 Scuttled the Floating Charge?" in J. Ziegel and W. Foster (eds.) *Aspects of Comparative Commercial Law* (1969) p. 410.

c) Enforceability of a Security Interest (s. 10)

"Attachment" (governed by s. 12) should be distinguished from "enforceability" which is dealt with in s. 10. Enforceability "by or against a third party" requires under s. 10 either possession of the collateral by the secured party or a written security agreement signed by the debtor containing "a description of the collateral". Section 10 does not affect the validity of a security agreement: *Rogerson Lumber Co. Ltd.* v. *Four Seasons Chalet Ltd.* (1979) 1 PPSAC 29 (Ont. HC). Also, "So long as the agreement is signed before proceedings are taken to enforce it, . . . the requirements of s. 10(*b*) are satisfied": *id.* (1981) 29 OR (2d) 193 (CA) *per* Houlden J.A.

Section 10 fails to specify who is a "third party". Does the term encompass the secured party's assignee? A transferee of the debtor's interest in the collateral? A competing secured party? A judgment creditor of the debtor? Anderson J. held in *Re Mercantile Steel Products Ltd.* (1978) 20 OR (2d) 237, 239 (Ont. SC in Bkcy) that "the trustee under a proposal is not a third party within the meaning of s. 10 . . . [Rather he] stands in the shoes of the [bankrupt-debtor] and can assert no higher rights against [the secured party] than could [the debtor]". Do you agree?

With respect to the "description" requirement of s. 10(*b*), note the following from Ziegel, "The Quickening Pace of Jurisprudence . . ." (1980) 4 Can. Bus. LJ 54, 92-93:

> The section requires the debtor to have signed a security agreement that contains a "description" of the collateral. "Description" is not defined nor does s. 10 itself indicate what will be deemed a sufficient description. The pre-PPSA registration Acts usually required "such sufficient and full description of the goods and chattels that the same may be thereby readily and easily known and distinguished". Will the courts imply a similar requirement under s. 10 or will any description, however broad and unhelpful, be deemed sufficient? UCC 9-110 provides that, for the purposes of Article 9, any description of personal property or real estate is sufficient, whether or not it is specific, if it reasonably identifies what is described. The accompanying Comment explains that this test is designed to do the job assigned to a description while rejecting the fastidious and overly exacting demands of earlier chattel mortgage jurisprudence. Until such time as s. 10 is amended, one must hope the Ontario courts will follow the same intermediate route even in the absence of a UCC 9-110 type guide-line.

Under the draft Bill to amend the PPSA, the description under s. 10 must be "sufficient to enable [the collateral] to be identified".

2. PERFECTION

Once attached, the security interest affects the rights of certain third parties who have competing interests in the collateral. Perfection, however, is the process by which an attached security interest acquires greater effectiveness as against third parties: "the term 'perfected' is used to describe a security interest in personal property which cannot be defeated in insolvency proceedings or in general by creditors": Comment to UCC 9-301. It is "the greatest bundle of rights . . . which it is possible for a party to obtain under the law of secured transactions", according to O. Spivack, *Secured Transactions* (1962) at p. 33. A security interest can be perfected by the secured party either *taking possession* of the collateral (s. 24) or *registering* a financing statement in the prescribed public office describing the security interest (s. 25). In some cases the Act also provides for "temporary perfection" of a security interest. See e.g. s. 26. Registration and possession are conceived as alternative vehicles for giving notice of the security interest to third parties. Note that the two methods are not available for all types of collateral. For example, intangible property cannot be physically possessed, but can be the subject of a security interest perfected by registration. Sections 24, 25 and 26 govern the methods of perfection for various types of collateral. As to continuity of perfection, see s. 23(1), and for the position of an assignee of a perfected security interest, see s. 23(2).

The types of collateral as to which a security interest can be perfected by possession are enumerated in s. 24. The types of collateral admitting or requiring perfection by registration are set forth in s. 25(1). Registration does not perfect a security interest in instruments and securities. Possession does not perfect a security interest in intangibles (other than letters of credit and advices of credit) or in non-negotiable documents of title. As to temporary perfection without either possession or registration, see s. 26. Section 26(1) deals with the case where new value is given under a written security agreement signed by the debtor and covering instruments, securities and negotiable documents of title. Section 26(2) provides for the case where a negotiable document of title, or goods held by a bailee where there is no such document, are used by the debtor to facilitate interim dealings. Temporary perfection under s. 26 lasts for 10 days.

The draft Bill to amend the PPSA proposed substituting present s. 25(1) for the following:

> Subject to section 21, registration perfects a security interest in any collateral.

Note that "perfection" contemplates "attachment" *and* the fulfillment of "all steps required for perfection" (s. 21). But, confusingly, "the Act uses 'perfection' in a double sense: (a) when a security interest has attached and the procedural requirements for giving notice of the interest have been met [s. 21]; and (b) to indicate compliance with the procedural requirements *simpliciter* [e.g., ss. 25, 47(1)]". See "Commentary — PPSA Registration Problems" (1978-79) 3 Can. Bus. LJ 222, 234.

Note on Perfection by Possession:

For about 200 years, at least from *Twyne's Case* (1601) 3 Co. Rep. 80b, 86 ER 809 onwards, there was intense hostility to non-possessory security devices. During this period, except in connection with vendor credit arrangements, the safest way to take an effective security interest in personal property was by pledge, namely the transfer of possession of the collateral by the debtor to the creditor.

Prior to 1676, English judges "knew no such animal as mortgage of goods". See E. Durfee, *Cases on Security* (1951) p. 486. The emergence of the chattel mortgage and its gradual evolution into an effective non-possessory security device is described by Professor Durfee (*op. cit.* pp. 489-90) as follows:

> [T]he chattel mortgage gained a foothold in practice while no one was looking. At least there's nothing in the record to suggest that this innovation was challenged at the threshold, nothing in the nature of an argument that pledge was the only chattel security recognized by English law. On the other hand the newcomer was, almost from the start, subjected to attacks of a more limited character. In *Bucknal* v. *Roiston*, Prec. in Ch. 285 (1709), it was argued "that Brewer's keeping possession of the goods after the sale [bill of sale for security] made it fraudulent and void as to creditors, who by this means were induced to think him a man of substance, and to give him credit as such; that the difference has always been taken between such a sale or pledge of goods and a mortgage of lands, for though the mortgagor does keep the possession of lands, that is not fraudulent as to purchasers, who may by inspecting the deeds discover the title; but as to goods, if there be no change of the possession, there is no alteration made of the property, but such sale is fraudulent and void."

The mortgage was sustained, but the terse report makes the decision appear to be a narrow ruling on the facts, and so an implication that chattel mortgages are, as the quoted argument assumed, subject to the same rules of fraud that govern absolute sales. What these rules are, in detail, and how they work, at the grass-roots level, has been an unending subject of debate.

Further litigation merely underscored the points that were implicit in the Bucknal case. It was settled that the same rule of fraud applies to sale and mortgage, and settled that retention of possession does not in either case make the transaction void *per se* but only constitutes evidence of fraud. But what is needed to rebut this evidence? To this question no definitive answer was given, but it was always possible to argue, with show of authority, that all was well if "continuance in possession was in terms provided for." *Martindale* v. *Booth*, 3 B. & Ad. 498 (1832). Looks like a loophole big enough for any normal mortgage? Yet English lawyers continued to fight over the mortgage cases.

After Parliament had intervened, requiring registration of chattel mortgages, Lord Blackburn summed up the earlier cases thus. "If a man came forward suddenly, when there was an execution, for instance, issued against the person in possession of the goods, and said, at an antecedent time I had a security upon these goods, and I left them in the possession of the debtor all that time, the not having taken possession was evidence that the thing was a sham; it was not conclusive; it was not a matter of law, but it was evidence that the thing was a sham. Upon that two evils arose, and very important ones they were. In the first place it often happened that there was really a sham put up to endeavor to defeat a man, and there was a great quantity of perjury, of fighting and expense, before it was proved to be a sham. That was a great evil. The other was that there were real honest transactions which were asserted to be shams when they were not, and in those cases there was apt to be much perjury and great expense before it was decided." *Cookson* v. *Swire*, 9 App. Cas. 653, 665 (1884). . . .

[In the U.S.] courts split on this question of fraud. Some accepted the English view that retention of possession is only evidence of fraud. . . . Other courts held retention of possession was fraud *per se*, but saved hard cases by exceptions variously phrased, e.g. "where, from the very nature of the transaction, possession either could not be delivered at all, or, at least, without defeating fair and honest objects." *Clow* v. *Woods*, 5 S. & R. 275, 281 (Pa., 1819). Then, beginning at least as early as the New York Revised Statutes, 1829, many states defined this type of fraud by explicit legislation, again with wide variations. For present purposes it's enough to say of this whole body of law (decisions and statutes) that it stated verbally simple rules none of which enabled a lawyer to give a positive opinion to the prospective lender except so far as concerned his status if he immediately took possession of the goods. There's no need to look closer at these rules because, so far as concerns the chattel mortgage, they have been almost completely superseded by recording acts.

It was 19th century industrialization which led to the introduction of statutory registration (or recording) systems for security interests. With these statutes, possession ceased altogether to be an exclusive means of giving notice to third parties. See Barron and O'Brien, *Chattel Mortgages and Bills of Sale* (1914) p. 500 (dealing with registration under the Bills of Sale and Chattel Mortgage Act, RSO 1897, c. 148):

> The object in view in requiring registration is that all persons interested in, or desiring to acquire any interest in the mortgaged or sold property can procure

information regarding that property. Possession of the mortgaged property by the bargainor or mortgagor after the sale or mortgage being considered evidence of fraud, it became necessary, in order to protect creditors, purchasers, and mortgagees in good faith, and all persons interested in, or desiring to acquire any interest in the mortgaged or sold property, that some rule should be adopted by which the mortgagor or bargainor might overcome this presumption, and be permitted to retain the property and carry on his business; and by which creditors and others having business with him might be notified of his financial position, and of the incumbrances upon his property; it being, in many cases, a great hardship upon a debtor to be compelled to deliver possession of the very property by which he not only obtains his livelihood, but which is the very means for satisfying the debt for which the property is security. Registration and the consequent publicity given the transaction prevents the inference of fraud above mentioned: *Belanger* v. *Menard*, 27 OR 209; *Cookson* v. *Swire*, 9 App. Cas. 653.

Perfection by possession is nevertheless still a common and highly effective means of perfecting a security interest in chattel paper, instruments, securities and negotiable documents of title. At the same time, perfection by possession has become significantly less important for goods. With the exception of the field warehousing device (discussed below), the pledging of goods for commercial purposes has disappeared almost completely. Also pawnbroking (i.e., the pledging of consumer goods) has suffered substantial decline. It is in any event excluded from the coverage of the PPSA (s. 3(*d*); see chapter 20(C) *supra*.

As to the concept of possession, "it has been frozen law . . . that the possession which perfects a pledge is that of the pledgee himself or of some third party who is independent of the pledgor. There has been some nibbling away at the edges of this clear-cut concept in the case of goods which are unusually difficult to move; occassionally cases . . . held that a 'symbolic' or 'constructive' delivery of possession is enough, such as handing over to the pledgee the key to enclosed premises, segregating the goods and conspicuously marking them as the pledgee's property . . .": Gilmore, *Security Interests in Personal Property* vol. 1 (1965) p. 440. "Possession" thus contemplates control and notice given thereby to third parties.

According to s. 24, possession perfects a security interest only during the "actual holding as collateral". In *In re Chapman* (1968) 5 UCC Rep. 649 (Ref. Bkcy WD Mich.) it was argued that perfection by "the secured party's taking possession of the collateral", as required by UCC 9-305, had not taken place because the secured party had taken possession of the collateral only for examination and copying. The court rejected the argument and held that how possession is obtained by the secured party is immaterial for the purpose of perfecting a security interest. Is this consistent with the language of s. 24? The court also held that possession by one secured party enures for the benefit of another secured party even though the former has not formally attorned to the latter. Is this consistent with the exclusiveness or notoriety of possession? With the language of s. 24? See also *In the Matter of Copeland* (1976) 531 F. 2d 1195, 1204 (3d Cir.), holding that possession by an escrow agent perfects a security interest: "possession of the collateral must [not] be by an individual under the sole dominion and control of the secured party".

Perfection by possession is sometimes used in the U.S. in connection with an inventory type of financing referred to as "field warehousing". Part of the debtor's business premises is cordoned off into a locked area under the exclusive control of an agent of the secured party and appropriate notices are posted around the area. The agent issues warehouse receipts (a type of "document of title" as defined in s. 1(*i*)) to the secured creditor for goods supplied to the debtor and placed in the area (called a "field warehouse"). The secured party advances money to the debtor against the warehouse receipts. Since the secured party holds the warehouse receipts the debtor cannot deal with the goods without his consent. Besides providing a method of perfection, field warehousing thus also provides an effective means of protecting the inventory financer against unauthorized dealings with the collateral. Field warehousing is known but not widespread in Canada. For early examples see *Banque Nationale* v. *Royer* (1910) 20 Que. KB 341 and *In re Wedlock Ltd.* [1926] 2 DLR 263 (PEI) discussing whether possession by an employee, or shareholder and officer, of the debtor to whom part of the premises were leased is not the debtor's possession for the purposes of s. 86 of the old Bank Act, now s. 186 of SC 1980, c. 40, Part I. As to field warehousing in general, see D.M. Friedman, "Field Warehousing" (1942) 42 Colum. L. Rev. 991. See also *Bostian* v. *Park National Bank of Kansas City* (1955) 226 F. 2d 753 (8th Cir.) and in particular its discussion as to whether access to the field warehouse by the debtor destroys the exclusiveness of the secured party's possession and the perfection of his security interest.

For critical views on possession as a means of perfecting a security interest and its declining importance even in perfecting security interests in securities, see P.F. Coogan, "Article 9 — An Agenda for the Next Decade" (1978) 87 Yale LJ 1012, and D.M. Phillips, "Flawed Perfection: From Possession to Filing Under Article 9" (1979) 59 BUL Rev. 1 and 209.

The rights and duties of a secured party in possession are governed by s. 19.

Note on Special Provisions Relating to Financing Farm Products and Consumer Goods:

Unlike the UCC, the PPSA does not classify "farm products" as a separate type of collateral. However, in dealing with attachment (and hence perfection) of a security interest in farm products, attention should be paid to ss. 12(2) and 13(2)(*a*). See also s. 10(*b*) with respect to enforceability and the priority rule of s. 34(1). Compare the latter with the priority given to a purchase-money security interest, discussed in chapter 22(B), *infra*.

As to the financing of consumer goods, it should be noted that, like the UCC, the PPSA is essentially not a consumer protection statute. Nor does it govern the sales aspect of a secured transaction: s. 17. Under s. 68, in the case of a conflict between the provisions of the Ontario Consumer Protection Act (CPA) and those of the PPSA, the CPA provisions prevail. This is the reverse of the general conflict rule of s. 68.

In considering the effect of the CPA on the PPSA read s. 31(1) and (2) of the CPA in conjunction with ss. 9-10 of the PPSA. Note the following consumer protection provisions contained in the PPSA and their relationship with the CPA:

(1) Section 13(2)(*b*) seriously limiting the effect of an after-acquired property clause with respect to consumer goods, and

(2) Section 14 setting a limit to the coverage of a purchase money security interest (defined in section 1(*s*)) with respect to consumer goods.

Both sections should be read in conjunction with section 34 of the Ontario CPA. Does the latter provision produce the same result?

Other consumer protection provisions in the PPSA are s. 16 dealing with waiver of defence clauses (to be compared with s. 42a of the Ontario CPA; see chapter 16(C), *supra*); s. 60(1), limiting the creditor's right to retain a collateral which is consumer goods in satisfaction of the debt (to be compared with s. 35 of the CPA); and s. 62(2)(*b*), setting statutory damages for violation of the disposition provisions of Part V where the collateral is consumer goods. Sections 60(1) and 62(2)(*b*) are discussed in chapter 24, *infra*. Sections 16, 60(1) and 62(2)(*b*) are not concerned with attachment and perfection. They are mentioned here to complete the round-up of consumer protection provisions in the PPSA.

In drafting the PPSA, the basic position of the Catzman committee was that consumer protection should be outside the scope of the Act. The few provisions that were included were borrowed from the Code and resulted from the absence of consumer protection statute in Ontario at the time of the committee's work. With the enactment of the Ontario CPA, the consumer protection provisions of the Ont. PPSA have arguably become superfluous. They have been deleted from the Sask. PPSA as well as the revised MUPPSA.

Problem: The X Furniture Company operates a retail furniture store in Toronto. During the period from 1977 to 1980, Mrs. Williams purchased a number of household items from X Furniture, for which payment was to be made in installments. The terms of each purchase were contained in a standard printed form contract which set forth the value of the purchased item and purported to lease the item to Mrs. Williams for a stipulated monthly rental payment. The contract further provided, in substance, that title would remain in X Furniture until the total of all the monthly payments made equalled the stated value of the item, at which time Mrs. Williams could take title. In the event of default in the payment of any monthly installment, X Furniture could repossess the item.

The printed form contract further provided that "sums due under all outstanding contracts constitute one account. When each periodical installment payment falls due, its amount shall be applied pro rata to all contracts then outstanding."

On April 17, 1980, Mrs. Williams bought from X Furniture a stereo set with a stated value of $814 on the same terms as the other items. At the time of this transaction her account showed a balance of $164 owing from her prior transactions. (The total of all the purchases made over the years in question came to $1,950.) She defaulted shortly thereafter.

Does X Furniture have a valid security interest in all items purchased since 1972? Has it attached? Is it enforceable?

C. REGISTRATION REQUIREMENTS

1. The Financing Statement and the Registration System

One of the methods of perfecting a security interest in prescribed types of collateral is by registration: ss. 25, 47(1), and 53(1)(*a*).

F. CATZMAN et al.
Personal Property Security Law in Ontario
(1976) pp. 170-75

Description of the Personal Property Security Registration System

Under s. 41 of the Act, a central office has been established in Toronto with branch offices throughout the province. The land registry offices have been designated as branch offices of the registration system for the county, provisional county, judicial district or provincial judicial district.

A registrar of personal property has been appointed pursuant to s. 42(1) and branch registrars have been appointed. The registrar's function is to supervise the operation of the personal property security registration system.

The registration system which became the personal property security registration system was originally set up in 1971 under the former chattel security laws. At that time the system operated as an adjunct to the former registration systems to facilitate its development for use under The Personal Property Security Act. Section 65 indicates that all the unexpired filings under The Assignment of Book Debts Act, The Bills of Sale and Chattel Mortgages Act and The Conditional Sales Act are deemed to be registered under The Personal Property Security Act. This permitted the system to be fully operational the day the Act was proclaimed in force as the computer contained records of all former registrations. The transition provisions also eliminated the necessity of re-registering filings carried out under the old chattel security laws.

Registering under the Personal Property Security Act

... It is intended here to give an overview of the operation of the registration system. The system is designed to be a notice filing system. The essence of notice filing is that it gives notice of the existence of a security agreement or of an intention to finance inventory. Additional information concerning the secured transaction must be obtained by consulting the security agreement held by either the secured party or the debtor. The document to be used in the system is called a financing statement. The financing statement is a skeletal outline of the bare essentials of the security agreement. The regulations require that the financing statement contain the names and addresses of all natural persons or artificial bodies who create a security interest and in some cases names of persons who do not create a security interest. The financing statement must also contain the name, address and signature of the secured party as well as a classification of the collateral being used as a security interest.

In order to register under the Act the registrant will have to complete a financing statement in accordance with the regulations. The registrant will have the option of going to any one of the forty-eight branch offices to submit the financing statement for registration or of mailing it to the central location. The registration will be effective from the time that a registration number is assigned to the financing statement. If the statement is taken to a branch registry office the registration number will be assigned at the branch registry office. If the financing statement is mailed to the central registry office the number will be assigned to the statement at the time the information is processed for recording in the central computer files of the personal property security registration system.

Financing statements which are registered at branch offices will not be immediately recorded in the computer files. At the close of the branch office's business hours all the financing statements registered during that day will be delivered by courier service to Toronto. The central office will then place the information from the financing statements in the computer files overnight. By the next day all the financing statements submitted to branch offices will be entered on the computer file. At least in the early years of the registration system, this time lag will be present when filing is done through a branch office.

The alternative method of registering will be to mail in the financing statement to the central office in Toronto.

Searching under the Personal Property Security Act

Only information which has been submitted by a registrant on a financing statement is recorded in the computer file. The regulations require that certain names be recorded on the financing statement. If a natural person creates a security interest, the name is recorded on the line of the statement designated as the individual debtor line. If an artificial body creates a security interest, the name is recorded on the line of the statement designated as the business debtor line.

All the information contained on a financing statement is recorded in the computer exactly as the registrant recorded it on the statement. Information is indexed for storage under the person's name, and to do this two indices are used.

If the individual debtor line of the financing statement has been completed then the information on the statement is indexed under the natural person's name and placed in the individual debtor index. If the business debtor line of the financing statement has been completed then the information on the statement is indexed under the artificial body's name and placed in the business debtor index. It is because of this indexing process that the regulations are drafted requiring different lines on the financing statement to be completed, depending on which kind of person's name is to be recorded.

The information is indexed in the two indices because enquiries will be made in a particular name. There are three methods of initiating an inquiry. If a deposit account has been established with the Ministry of Consumer and Commercial Relations an inquiry may be made by using the inquirer's office telephone. An inquiry may be made at any branch registry office. The branch registry office will initiate the inquiry by telephone. As an alternative to either of these modes of inquiry an inquiry may be mailed to the central office.

The inquiry will reach the central office either by telephone or by mail. At the central office in Toronto there are a number of telephone operators sitting in front of cathode-ray tube devices (CRT devices). These devices are essentially television sets to which a keyboard similar to a typewriter keyboard is attached.

The inquirer will advise the operator whether the individual debtor index, the business debtor index, or both indices are to be searched. The inquirer will then inform the operator of the name against which the search is to be made. The operator will punch the appropriate information into the keyboard and the computer will search the proper index.

The key to an accurate and complete inquiry will be the skill the inquirer uses in selecting the name to be inquired upon. The information which is stored in the computer is indexed and stored exactly as it was recorded on the registered financing statement. The computer executes a search by attempting to match exactly the inquiry name with the debtor names indexed in the designated file. Therefore, a thorough knowledge of the regulation's requirements for completing the debtor name lines of the financing statement will improve the inquirer's skill at choosing a name to be searched.

If an inquiry is to be made of the individual debtor index there are two types of inquiry. A non-specific search of the file or a specific search of the file may be made. To initiate a non-specific search all that is required is a natural person's first given name and surname. The inquirer must use the first given name as that is the requirement of the regulations. It does not matter that the person is never known by his first name.

If the inquired upon name is a common one there may be a number of matches made by the computer. In that case, the inquirer may wish to make a specific search of the file. To initiate a specific search the initial of the second given name, and date of birth of the natural person must be used as well as the first given name and surname. This type of search should result in a match with names of a single natural person.

A non-specific search will result in obtaining maximum information from the system. Assume the registrant of a statement had completed the individual debtor line using the initial of the person's third given name. The registration may not be valid as a result of the noncompliance with the regulations. Nevertheless, the inquirer may want to discover the existence of the secured transaction. If a specific search of the file were carried out using the correct information under the regulations, i.e., the initial of the second given name, no match would occur in the computer search. There is no match because the inquired upon name is not exactly identical with the indexed name in the individual debtor file. A non-specific search will avoid a registrant's error in the initial or date of birth from preventing a match.

An inquiry of the business debtor index will require an even more thorough understanding of the regulations in order to choose the inquiry name. For example, if an inquiry is to be made on a partnership name the regulations contain three different rules for recording the partnership name. There are a number of other variations of this same multiple rule requirement.

Once the operator keypunches the appropriate information into the computer the results will appear on the CRT device within seconds. If an exact match is made then all of the information recorded under the matched debtor name will be available to the inquirer.

There are three forms of response to an inquiry. If the inquiry was initiated by telephone the operator at the central office will read the information to the inquirer. If the inquirer desires he may request an uncertified printout of the result of the inquiry. The inquirer is also entitled under s. 44(1) to request a certificate certifying the results of the inquiry. These latter two responses are the only responses available to a mailed-in inquiry. Only when a certificate is requested will the inquirer be able to make a claim against the assurance fund established under s. 45. . . .

It will be recalled that if a financing statement is registered at a branch registration office there is a time lapse before the registration is recorded in the computer's files. The inquirer must be careful to take account of this time lapse when searches are carried out. Whether the inquirer need take account of the time lapse will depend on the inquirer's reasons for making the inquiry and his use of the inquiry information.

Notes and Questions:

1   A description of the collateral is not required to be included in the financing statement beyond the classification of the collateral as "consumer goods, inventory, equipment, book debts [etc.]". See s. 3(1)(a)(iii) of the PPSA Regulations (O. Reg. 879/75). There are two exceptions concerning motor vehicles:

a)   the fact that "a motor vehicle is or is not included in the collateral" must be specifically mentioned (s. 3(1)(a)((iv)), and

b)   a motor vehicle classified as consumer goods must "be described . . . and the description may include the body style and shall include the last two digits of the model year . . ., the maker, or where there is no maker, the name of the manufacturer and the serial number which may include the model number" (s. 3(2)).

Otherwise, additional description is optional. Where the collateral is classified as consumer goods the financing statement must set out the principal amount and date of maturity (s. 3(1)(a)(v) and (vi) of the Regulations). Additional information required to be set out in every financing statement is the name and address of the secured party (s. 3(1)(a)(ii)) as well as of the debtor (s. 14 incorporated by reference into s. 3(1)(a)(i)). The financing statement must bear "the authorized signature of the secured party" (s. 3(1)(vii)). With respect to the comparable Code requirement, compare *Benedict* v. *Lebowitz* (1965) 346 F. 2d 120 (2d Cir.) (secured party's failure to sign excused) with *In re Carlstrom* (1966) 3 UCC Rep. 766 (U.S. DC D. Me.) (signature is indispensable).

2   Caution filing is governed by s. 4 of the PPSA Regulations. Financing statements must be designated as caution filings where the collateral was brought to Ontario subject either to a security interest in another jurisdiction or to the seller's civil law right (under Quebec law) to revendicate or to resume possession.

3   Could a financing statement serve as a "security agreement" for the purpose of s. 10(*b*)? Consider the requirements of s. 10 of the Act and s. 3 of the regulations and *cf. American Card Co. Inc.* v. *H.M.H. Co.* (1963) 196 A. 2d 150 (SC RI).

4   Note that relevant information not contained in the financing statement can be obtained from the secured party only by the debtor, by a person having an interest in the collateral, or by an execution creditor. See s. 20.

5   The time and effect of registration are governed by ss. 47 and 53. A filed financing statement is effective for a period of 3 years: s. 53(1). Renewal of registration is governed by s. 52. For the provisions on the registration of a financing change statement, see ss. 48-53 and s. 54a. A financing change statement *may* be registered on the assignment of the secured party's interest (s. 48), the amendment of the security agreement or the financing statement (s. 50), a subordination agreement (s. 51), the renewal of registration before its expiration (s. 52), and the discharge of a security interest (s. 54a). It *must* be registered on a transfer of the collateral, or on the debtor's change of name (s. 49). What about a change in the use of the collateral? See *In re Morton* (1972) 9 UCC Rep. 1147 (Me. Bkcy), and *In re Barnes* (1972) 11 UCC Rep. 670 (Me. Bkcy), holding that a financing statement classifying the collateral according to its use at the time of attachment remains effective notwithstanding subsequent change of use. To what extent are these decisions relevant in the Canadian context?

6   The draft Bill to amend the PPSA provided for the repeal of the CSRA and the registration of charges registrable thereunder under the PPSA. See chapter 20, *supra.* The Bill permitted the registration of a financing statement for a perpetual period, and contained special provisions with respect to the application of ss. 20(1) (duty to give information) and 45 (the assurance fund) to trustees under trust indentures. A perpetual registration would have been dischargeable by the registration of a financing change statement or a court order.

2. Errors and Omissions (ss. 4 and 47(s))

RE OVENS
(1979) 103 DLR (3d) 352, 26 OR (2d) 468 (Ont. CA)

HOULDEN J.A.: Henry, J., sitting as Judge in Bankruptcy, made an order declaring that the security interest of the appellant, Bank of Montreal, was not perfected at the date of bankruptcy and accordingly was subordinate to the interest of the respondent, the trustee in bankruptcy of Hazel Ivy Ovens, also known as Hazel Ivy Quick. The sole issue in this appeal is whether Henry, J., was right in holding that the appellant's security interest was not perfected at the date of bankruptcy.

The determination of this issue turns on the interpretation of certain provisions of the Personal Property Security Act, RSO 1970, c. 344, as amended, and O. Reg. 879/75. In interpreting the Act and the Regulation, we have kept in mind that the Personal Property Security Act has introduced an entirely new system in Ontario for transactions intended to create security interests and that one of the principal reasons for enacting the new legislation was to do away with the formalistic traps and pitfalls that plagued the former legislation. We have endeavoured, therefore, to give the Act a large and liberal interpretation, not a narrow and legalistic one. However, the powers of the Court are not unlimited; they are confined and restricted by the wording of the legislation. And if the legislation does not permit the Court to give a remedy, we are unable to grant relief even though, on equitable grounds, we would like to do so.

The facts are not in dispute. Prior to bankruptcy, the debtor operated a truck leasing business under the trade name of "Silver Creek Leasing". The name was registered in accordance with s. 8 [am. 1973, c. 7, s. 6] of the Partnerships Registration Act, RSO 1970, c. 340, as amended.

In July, 1977, the appellant made a loan of $10,000 to the debtor and received a chattel mortgage on two trucks as security. Within the 30-day period stipulated by s. 47(3) [rep. & sub. 1973, c. 102, s. 9] of the Personal Property Security Act, the appellant registered a financing statement. On the line in the statement designated for individual debtor, nothing was filled in; on the line for business debtor, the name "Silver Creek Leasing" appeared.

By s. 47(1) [rep. & sub. *ibid.*] of the Personal Property Security Act, in order to perfect a security interest by registration, a financing statement in the prescribed form must be registered. An unperfected security interest is subordinate to the interest of a trustee in bankruptcy: see s. 22(1)(*a*)(iii) of the Act. The form of a financing statement is prescribed by s. 14 of O. Reg. 879/75.

Section 14 distinguishes between security interests created by natural persons and those created by artificial bodies. The definition of an "artificial body" is set out in s. 1(*a*) of the Regulation; it does not include a person carrying on business under a registered trade name. The security interest in this case was, therefore, created by a natural person.

Where a natural person creates a security interest, s-ss. 14(1), (3) and (4) of O. Reg. 879/75 are the relevant subsections. They provide:

> **14.**(1) Where a natural person creates a security interest, the name of the natural person shall be set out in the financing statement to show the first given name, followed by the initial of the second given name, if any, followed by the surname.
>
> • • •
>
> (3) Where a person identifies himself or itself to the public by a name or style other than his or its own name, as the case may be, the name may be set out in the financing statement on a line designated for business debtor.
>
> (4) Where the name of a person is required to be set out on a financing statement under subsection 1 or 2, the name shall be set out for

(*a*)   a natural person, on a line designated for individual debtor; or
(*b*)   an artificial body, on a line designated for business debtor.

Mr. Nordheimer strongly contended that, by virtue of s. 14(3), it was sufficient for the financing statement to show only the registered trade name under which the debtor carried on business. This same contention was advanced to Henry, J., and rejected by him. Henry, J., was of the opinion that s. 14(3) was only permissive and did not displace the mandatory requirements of s. 14(1). We agree with this interpretation of s. 14(3). Subsection (3), unlike s-ss. (1), (2) and (4) of s. 14, uses the permissive "may" not the mandatory "shall". Hence, if a financing statement is given by an individual carrying on business under a registered trade name, it must set out the name of that person. It may, also, if the creditor wishes, set out the trade name on the line designated for business debtor, but this is permissive not mandatory.

It is common ground that no one was misled by the failure to set out the debtor's name in the financing statement. This being so, has the Court the power to excuse the error in the financing statement?

The Personal Property Security Act contains two curative sections: s. 4 and s. 47(5) [rep. & sub. *ibid.*].

· · ·

Catzman, *Personal Property Security Law* (1976), at p. 191, discusses the relationship between the two curative sections and makes the following comments:

> S. 4 of the Act appears to also provide curative relief. S. 4 is a general section having broader curative provisions than s. 47(5). For example, s. 4 provides curative relief for any document, not just for financing statements or financing change statements. It provides relief from errors in completing the document and also from errors in executing the document. It would therefore appear that in relation to financing statements or financing change statements which are only one type of document used under the Act, the only applicable curative section is s. 47(5). That subsection is more restrictive and specific and, therefore excludes the general and wider s. 4.

This accords with the usual rule of statutory construction that is applicable in these circumstances: see *Craies on Statute Law*, 7th ed. (1971), at p. 222.

Section 4 deals with errors that invalidate documents, s. 47(5) with errors that invalidate registration. We agree with Catzman that s. 47(5) having specifically provided for errors that invalidate registration has excluded the operation of s. 4. Section 47(5) is, therefore, the only applicable curative section for this case.

Section 47(5) provides for two kinds of errors: clerical errors, and errors in an immaterial or non-essential part of a financing statement. In *Re Robert Sist Development Corp. Ltd.* (1977) 17 OR (2d) 305 at p. 306, 80 DLR (3d) 445 at p. 447, 25 CBR (NS) 167, Henry, J., dealt with the meaning of "clerical error" and adopted the definition given in Jowett's *Dictionary of English Law* that a "clerical error" is "an error in a document which can only be explained by considering it to be a slip or mistake of the party preparing or copying it". We believe that this furnishes an adequate definition of "clerical error". The failure to set out the debtor's name in the financing statement is clearly not that kind of error.

Nor do we believe that it is an error in an immaterial or non-essential part of a financing statement. Section 44 [am. 1973, c. 102, s. 8; 1977, c. 23, s. 1(1)] of the Personal Property Security Act provides for the maintenance of two separate *indices* of names, one containing the names of individual debtors; the other, the names of business debtors: see Catzman, *op. cit.*, p. 187. When a search is made under the Personal Property Security Act, a searcher has to decide which index to search. In this case, since the debtor was a natural person, a searcher should have searched the individual debtor index. The failure to set out the debtor's name in the financing statement is, therefore, not an error in an immaterial or non-essential part of a financing statement.

Mr. Nordheimer frankly conceded that, if we found that s. 14 of O. Reg. 879/75 required the debtor's name to be set out in the financing statement, the failure to set out the name was not a clerical error or an error in an immaterial or non-essential part of a financing statement. However, he contended that the failure to set out the name was an "omission" within the meaning of s. 4 of the Act. It is our view, as we have stated above, that s. 4 cannot be resorted to in this case; we, therefore, need express no opinion on the meaning of "omission" in s. 4.

Appeal dismissed.

Note: *Re Ovens* was followed in *In the matter of the bankruptcy of 360081 Ontario Ltd* (1980) (Ont. SC in Bkcy). In this case the secured party registered a financing statement under s. 47(1) under circumstances where he was required to register a financing change statement under s. 49(1). The security interest was held to be unperfected. Neither s. 47(5) nor s. 4 could cure this defect. According to Hollingworth J., "This [error] is more than an error invalidating documents or registration [so as to be subject to the curative provisions of ss. 4 and 47(5)], it is a fundamental error for which there is no valid reason. . . ." For further discussion of these provisions see Comment (1978-79) 3 Can. Bus LJ 106.

Notes on Errors in Financing Statement and Detrimental Reliance:

1   *Errors of a Clerical Nature or in an Immaterial or Non-Essential Part of a Financing Statement (s. 47(5)).* The financing statement in *Re Lawrence* (1980) 26 OR 3 (Ont. SC in Bkcy) purported to cover a motor vehicle. As "in the preparation of the financing statement a typing error was made by the omission of . . . two digits" (*id.* at 5) the serial number of the vehicle was incorrectly stated in the financing statement. Following *Re Robert Sist Development Corporation Ltd.*, Mr. Justice Henry stated (at 5):

> A clerical error is to be identified, not by its location in the financing statement but by its character as a slip or mistake in preparing or copying a document. The Court must determine its character as best it can from the documents and other material before it, and in most cases will no doubt have to do so by inference. I have no hesitation in the case before me in characterizing the error in the serial number as a clerical error within the meaning of s. 47(5). It adds nothing to call it a "fundamental" error.

He then concluded (at 7):

> [A] clerical error does not defeat the security interest, even though it be in a material part of the financing statement, so long as some person has not been misled. It is not sufficient to show that the error is likely to be misleading. . . .

Cf. Re McMullen and Avco Financial Services Canada Ltd. (1980) 98 DLR (3d) 560 (Ont. HC). Here the financing statement erroneously omitted two digits from the serial number of the vehicle (the collateral). A purchaser of the vehicle was misled as he had searched under the correct serial number (see s. 44(1)). Finding that the document was not misleading, Mr. Justice Holland nevertheless held that s. 47(5) cannot cure an error ``that has misled''.

2 *Other Kinds of Error in a Financing Statement.* In *Re Alduco Mechanical Contractors Ltd.; Re Metric Air Systems (Ontario) Ltd.* (1979) 32 CBR (NS) 48 (Ont. SC in Bkcy) the error was not ``of a clerical nature or in an immaterial or non-essential part''. Mr. Justice Anderson followed *Re Ovens* but expressed regret (at 54) that s. 47(5) should have been enacted ``and thereby reduced the beneficent operation of s. 4''. Do you agree? *Cf.* ``Comment — Detrimental Reliance and the PPSA'' (1979-80) 4 Can. Bus. LJ 249, 251-54.

Chapter 22

Perfection, Third Parties and Priorities

This chapter deals with (a) the subordination of an unperfected security interest to the interests of third parties who are not secured parties, (b) priorities among competing security interests, and (c) priority contests between security interests governed by the PPSA and interests governed by other laws.

The PPSA adopts a functional approach to the determination of priority conflicts between competing security interests and to conflicts between a security interest and non-security interests of a third party. The PPSA has abandoned the common law approach which substantially turned on the form of the transaction creating the security interest (e.g., chattel mortgage, conditional sale, or equitable charge) and on the nature of the title in the hands of a particular claimant (e.g., "legal", "equitable", or statutory).

"Perfection of Interest" is the title of Part III of the PPSA (ss. 21-40).

A. SUBORDINATION OF UNPERFECTED SECURITY INTEREST: s. 22(1) and (2)

1. General

Subject to the purchase money security interest exception (provided for in s. 22(3) and discussed in section B *infra*), an unperfected security interest is subordinate to the interest of:

a) one who is entitled to a priority under the PPSA or any other Act (s. 22(1)(*a*)(i));

b) one who assumes control of the collateral through legal process "without knowledge of the security interest and before it is perfected" (s. 22(1)(*a*)(ii));

c) one who represents the creditors of the debtor as an assignee for the benefit of creditors, trustee in bankruptcy or receiver (s. 22(1)(*a*)(iii)) from "the date from which his status has effect . . . without regard to [his] personal knowledge . . . if any represented creditor was, on the relevant date, without knowledge of the unperfected security interest" (s. 22(2)); and

d) one who is a transferee for value (and not a secured party) who without knowledge of the security interest before perfection took possession of the collateral other than in the course of business of the transferor (s. 22(1)(*b*)). Where the collateral is an intangible, the possession and transfer not in the ordinary course of business requirements are waived.

2. ENTITLEMENT TO PRIORITY "UNDER THIS OR ANY OTHER ACT" (s. 22(1)(a)(i))

The provision recognizes priorities created by the PPSA (e.g. s. 35 discussed in section C *infra*) as well as by other statutes. The "other Act" must assign priority to the competing interest. The creation of a lien or security interest under such an Act is neither sufficient nor required for the purposes of s. 22(1)(*a*)(i). What about a statute assigning priority to another interest over a *perfected* security interest? Or a statute creating an interest in personal property but not providing for its priority? *Cf.* section F *infra*.

3. ONE WHO "ASSUMES CONTROL OF THE COLLATERAL THROUGH LEGAL PROCESS" (s. 22(1)(a)(ii))

This clause covers a judgment creditor insofar as he "assumes control" as required by the provision. According to Catzman et al., "[t]he phrase 'legal process' is not to receive a technical interpretation but has the meaning of 'lawful warrant or authority' and specifically means any formal writing issued under authority of law by an official having the authority to issue it as a means of enforcing a judicial order or judgment. It does not include a distress for rent . . . but . . . it does include process of chancery origin, such as a writ of sequestration and an order of attachment under such statutes as the Absconding Debtors Act": F. Catzman *et al., Personal Property Security Law in Ontario* (1976) p. 113. See also *Rogerson Lumber Company Ltd.* v. *Four Seasons Chalet Ltd.* (1981) 29 OR (2d) 193 (CA), *per* Arnup J.A.:

> "By legal process" does not mean "by lawful means". It means "by a process available through the operation of law", such as "by seizure under a writ" of execution. By way of illustration, a landlord's distress carried out by his bailiff would not come within the term "legal process" in s. 22(1)(*a*)(ii).

In the context of goods, the "assume control" requirement probably means physical possession. In the case of intangibles it means whatever is needed in contemplation of law to give control. (In the case of book debt, is notice to the account debtor adequate?) Section 10(1) of the Execution Act, RSO 1970, c. 152 provides that,

> . . . a writ of execution binds the goods . . . from the time of the delivery thereof to the sheriff for execution, but . . . no writ of execution against the goods prejudices the title to such goods acquired by a person in good faith and for valuable consideration.
> . . .

What about a security interest in goods, perfected or unperfected, taken (either in good faith and for value or with notice of the unexecuted writ) between delivery of a writ of execution to the sheriff and the seizure of the goods? Consider PPSA ss. 9, 22(1)(a)(i) and 68.

4. Creditors' Representative (ss. 22(1)(a)(iii), 22(2))

Generally speaking, bankruptcy rules and rules governing assignments for the benefit of creditors are designed to distribute a debtor's assets equitably among his creditors in satisfaction of their debts. Catzman *et al.* (*id.* p. 114):

> Creditors' Representatives
> Trustees in bankruptcy and assignees for the benefit of creditors are persons whose powers derive from The Bankruptcy Act, or statutes like The Assignments and Preferences Act. "Receiver" is a generic term. Status as a receiver does not depend on what the person is called. It depends on his having the attributes characteristic of a receiver in chancery, to wit, he must be an officer judicially appointed and responsible to the Court, with the object of preserving property pending litigation to decide the rights of the parties, but a person such as a liquidator under The Winding-Up Act, or The Corporations Act, who is of that kind is a receiver in the present context, although not so styled. Conversely one without judicial warrant for his appointment though called a receiver is not.

With regard to the trustee in bankruptcy's position, note the following:

a) Section 22(1)(a)(iii) speaks of the subordination of an unperfected security interest to "the interest of . . . [the] trustee in bankruptcy". What is the trustee's interest in the collateral? *Cf. Re Beaton* (1979) 101 DLR (3d) 338 (Ont. CA). According to Professor Ziegel ("The Quickening Pace of Jurisprudence . . ." (1980) 4 Can. Bus. LJ 54, 68-69), the difficulty is that,

> PPSA, s. 22 does not of its own confer on the trustee any interest in the bankrupt's property. That interest is derived from the Bankruptcy Act. Section 47 of the Bankruptcy Act entitles the trustee to step into the bankrupt's shoes and, speaking generally, to claim only the property to which the bankrupt was entitled. If . . . the bankrupt has assigned a part of his wages, to that extent it is no longer a part of his property. That being the case, the trustee has no "interest" to which the unperfected security interest must be subordinated.
> . . . The difficulty could be met in several ways. One is to argue that a debtor always retains an interest in collateral — his equity of redemption — although it may have only slight commercial value. However, it may be objected that it is nonsensical to speak of a security interest being subordinated to the debtor's equity of redemption since the two are as inseparable as the proverbial "horse and carriage". The better argument is that s. 22 must be read as meaning that the unperfected security interest shall be subordinated to the interest which the trustee *would have had* had the security interest not been created. A third possible argument is that the interest referred to in s. 22 is not restricted to an interest in the particular collateral and that it is sufficient if the trustee has a general interest in the bankrupt's estate. Whichever of the foregoing constructions is preferred, it is obvious that the s. 22 interest is an elastic concept which should not be analyzed with Aristotelian exactness.

For case law dealing with the trustee's position as a creditors' representative and his duty (authorized by s. 50(6) of the Bankruptcy Act, RSC 1970 c. B-3) to exercise creditors' remedies, see L. Houlden, Q.C., (1962) 3 CBR (NS) 111.

b) Rights of a creditors' representative "are referable to the date from which his status has effect" (s. 22(2)). Under s. 50(4) of the Bankruptcy Act, RSC 1970, c. B-3, "[t]he bankruptcy shall be deemed to have relation back to and to commence at the time of the filing of the petition on which a receiving order is made or of the filing of an assignment with the official receiver". The effect of this section on PPSA s. 22(2) was held to be that "the date from which the status of the trustee has effect is the date of filing of the petition": *Re Hillstead Ltd.* (1979) 103 DLR 347, 349 (Ont. SC in Bkcy). In this case, registration of a financing statement after the filing of the petition in bankruptcy but before the receiving order came too late to save the security interest from subordination to the trustee in bankruptcy.

c) The position of a trustee under a proposal made under the Bankruptcy Act was considered in *Re Mercantile Steel Products Ltd.* (1978) 20 OR (2d) 237 (Ont. SC in Bkcy). Anderson J. concluded (at 239) that such a trustee "does not represent the creditors of the debtor in any of the capacities outlined in sub.-cl. (iii) of cl. (a) of s-s. (1) of s. 22. The trustee represents the creditors only to the extent necessary to assure performance of the proposal, and not in any broad general sense". Anderson J. did not overlook the provisions of s. 46(1) of the Bankruptcy Act under which "[a]ll the provisions of [the] Act . . . apply *mutatis mutandis* to proposals." He added at 240:

> My conclusions have been arrived at on the wording of the Act and on the relevant provisions of the Bankruptcy Act. I am fortified in my conclusions, however, by consideration of the ultimate purpose and effect of a proposal, and the bearing which that has on the attack made on the position of a secured creditor. The purpose sought by a proposal is continuation of the business carried by the debtor. While the proposal must present benefits for creditors it is fundamentally a mechanism for the advantage of the debtor making it. That being the case, it would be anomalous if the debtor could improve its position through objections put forward by the trustee concerning security, of a nature such that they could not have been successfully asserted by the debtor directly. If the proposal succeeds, the ordinary creditors will have received what they contracted to accept and there is no reason why it should be augmented by an amount realized at the expense of a secured creditor. If this proposal does not succeed, bankruptcy will ensue and the trustee in bankruptcy can assert all the rights created by the Act.

Do you agree?

5. TRANSFEREE FOR VALUE (S. 22(1)(*b*))

To be discussed in section G, *infra*.

6. WITHOUT KNOWLEDGE AND BEFORE PERFECTION (SS. 22(1)(*a*)(ii), 22(1)(*b*), AND 22(2))

An unperfected security interest is subordinate to the interest of a transferee for value (s. 22(1)(*b*)) only to the extent that he assumed his position "without knowledge of the security interest and before it is perfected". By the same token, rights of a creditors' representative under s. 22(1)(a)(iii) "arise without regard to the personal knowledge of the representative if any represented creditor was, on the . . . date [from which the representative's status has effect], without knowledge of the unperfected security interest" (s. 22(2)).

Notes and Questions:

1   "Knowledge" is not defined in the PPSA; *cf.* s. 1(*p*). Consider the following provisions of UCC 1-201:

(25) A person has "notice" of a fact when
(a)   he has actual knowledge of it; or
(b)   he has received a notice or notification of it; or
(c)   from all the facts and circumstances known to him at the time in question he has reason to know that it exists.
A person "knows" or has "knowledge" of a fact when he has actual knowledge of it. "Discover" or "learn" or a word or phrase of similar import refers to knowledge rather than to reason to know. The time and circumstances under which a notice or notification may cease to be effective are not determined by this Act.

(26) A person "notifies" or "gives" a notice or notification to another by taking such steps as may be reasonably required to inform the other in ordinary course whether or not such other actually comes to know of it. A person "receives" a notice or notification when
(a)   it comes to his attention; or
(b)   it is duly delivered at the place of business through which the contract was made or at any other place held out by him as the place for receipt of such communications.

(27) Notice, knowledge or a notice or notification received by an organization is effective for a particular transaction from the time when it is brought to the attention of the individual conducting that transaction, and in any event from the time when it would have been brought to his attention if the organization had exercised due diligence. An organization exercises due diligence if it maintains reasonable routines for communicating significant information to the person conducting the transaction and there is reasonable compliance with the routines. Due diligence does not require an individual acting for the organization to communicate information unless such communication is part of his regular duties or unless he has reason to know of the transaction and that the transaction would be materially affected by the information.

2   What is the effect of "before it is perfected" in ss. 22(1)(a)(ii) and 22(1)(b)? According to Catzman *et al.* pp. 113-14, these words "appear redundant [in s. 22(1)(a)(ii)] since the entire section is applicable only as against unperfected security interests, unless these words were inserted to make it abundantly clear that full assumption of control and not merely steps leading to it must have antedated the perfection of the security interest sought to be subordinated".

3   For the purpose of s. 22, what is the "knowledge" that is required to save the security interest from subordination: knowledge of attachment? Of the terms of

the security agreement? Of the specific security interest? According to Catzman *et al.* p. 116, "[t]he knowledge contemplated [in s. 22(1)(*b*)] is knowledge of the existence of the security interest. The secured party need not establish knowledge of its terms and details. However, it is knowledge of 'the' security interest, not of 'a' security interest, and a transferee knowing of a specific security interest at the time value is given can yet claim subordination of others which were unknown; his position is more doubtful where he knows generally that unperfected security interests exist and refrains from informing himself further". Compare *Bloom* v. *Hilty* (1967) 234 A. 2d 860, 862, n.2. (Pa. SC) where the court opined: "§9-301 speaks of 'knowledge of *the* security interest' (emphasis added). Despite the use of 'the' rather than 'a', in order to be subject to the unperfected security interest, the buyer need not know who the holder of the interest is, simply that it exists. The word 'the' is merely used to refer back to the 'unperfected security interest' in the first line of subsection (1)." Does this analysis apply to s. 22?

4   Consider the following questions on the construction of s. 22:

   a)   At what time must a person who assumes control of the collateral, a creditor's representative, or a transferee for value, be "without knowledge"? What about a fact that had been known but was forgotten at the crucial time?

   b)   Does the personal knowledge of a creditor's representative defeat his priority? What effect has knowledge of one represented creditor? Knowledge of all of them?

5   What is the rationale of the "without knowledge" requirement in s. 22? The requirement has been criticized in connection with UCC 9-301 on the following grounds:

> Consider also a situation where the holder of a judgment, before levying execution, searches the local filing records to determine the status of his debtor's property. He chances to discover a lien of record which had been misfiled. By virtue of this discovery, he destroys any valuable right of execution he might otherwise have had.

(C. Felsenfeld, "Knowledge As a Factor in Determining Priorities under the Uniform Commercial Code" (1967) 42 NYU L Rev. 246, 255-56).

Problem: Bank lent money to Dealer under a written security agreement containing an after-acquired property clause. A financing statement was duly registered. Dealer's judgment creditor assumed control through legal process of Dealer's stock in trade, promissory notes payable to his order, and conditional sale contracts executed by Dealer's buyers. Is Bank entitled to priority against Dealer's judgment creditor? See sections 24 and 25(1). Would you recommend the adoption of a provision modelled on s. 25 of the Sask. PPSA (and suggested for adoption in Ontario), under which registration of a financing statement perfects a security interest in any type of collateral? *Cf.* s. 31 of the Ont. PPSA.

Note: Acknowledging that "the jurisprudence as to the priority position of the floating charge against certain competing interests is not completely unequivocal", Catzman *et* *al.* summarize the common law position as to the priority of the Anglo-Canadian floating charge over other competing interests as follows (p. 64):

> 1. It will have priority over competing security interests if the agreement contains a restriction against creating any prior mortgages or charges; but not necessarily against a mortgagee for value without notice; however, the mortgagee would have to prove value given without notice.
> 2. It will have priority over an execution creditor before sale of the collateral under execution; but not necessarily after sale under the execution.
> 3. It will have priority over garnishee orders.
> 4. It will have priority over an interim receiver in bankruptcy.

Will the Anglo-Canadian floating charge have the same priority under s. 22 of the PPSA? Recall the note on the time of attachment under the floating charge, chapter 21(B), *supra*. Note that is only the priority of a floating charge under a document not registrable under the CSRA which is governed by the PPSA; *cf.* chapter 20(C), *supra* (registration of corporation charges in Ontario) *supra* and chapter 22(F), *infra* (priority between CSRA and PPSA interests).

B. THE PURCHASE-MONEY SECURITY INTEREST AND ITS PRIORITY

Purchase-money security interest (hereafter PMSI) is defined in s. 1(*s*). The Act confers a special priority on PMSIs as follows:

1) Under s. 22(3), a PMSI has priority over an interest set out in s. 22(1)(*a*)(ii) or (iii) as well as, notwithstanding s. 22(1)(*b*), over a transfer not in the ordinary course of business occurring between attachment and registration of the competing security interest, provided the PMSI "is registered before or within ten days after the debtor's possession of the collateral commences". An "unperfected security interest" under s. 22(1) is thus given a ten days' grace period for registration. The reason for this exception is that conditional sellers were historically given a short period to register their security interests and that it is often not practicable for a seller to register before releasing the goods to the buyer.

2) Under s. 34(3), a similar priority is given a PMSI in collateral other than inventory over "any other security interest in the same collateral". The PMSI prevails if it "was perfected at the time the debtor obtained possession of the collateral or within ten days thereafter".

3) Section 34(2) provides for the priority of a PMSI in inventory "over any other security interest in the same collateral", provided the PMSI "was perfected at the time the debtor receives possession of the collateral" (no ten days' grace period exists) and notification is given to competing secured parties as prescribed in s. 34(2)(*b*) and (*c*). The notification requirement is explained by the Comment to UCC 9-312 (1972 text) as follows:

> The reason for the additional requirement of notification is that typically the arrangement between an inventory secured party and his debtor will require the secured party to make periodic advances against incoming inventory or periodic releases of old inventory as new inventory is received. A fraudulent debtor may

apply to the secured party for advances even though he has already given a security interest in the inventory to another secured party. The notification requirement protects the inventory financer in such a situation: if he has received notification, he will presumably not make an advance; if he has not received notification (or if the other interest does not qualify as a purchase money interest), any advance he may make will have priority. Since an arrangement for periodic advances against incoming property is unusual outside the inventory field, no notification requirement is included in [the] subsection . . . [corresponding to PPSA s. 34(3)].

A PMSI in inventory lost priority because of a failure to comply with the notification requirement in *Thomson* v. *O.M. Scott Credit Corporation* (1962) 1 UCC Rep. 555 (Pa. CP). Notification by telephone was held sufficient compliance with the requirement in *GAC Credit Corp.* v. *Small Business Administration* (1971) 8 UCC Rep. 952 (U.S. DC WD Mo.).

It is not always clear when the debtor received or obtained possession of the collateral for the purposes of ss. 22(3), 34(2)(*a*) and 34(3). The difficulty arises where delivery of the goods to the debtor precedes the security agreement. Does "debtor" in these provisions refer to the time of the obligation (*cf.* s. 1(*g*)), or does it merely identify the individual in possession who ultimately becomes indebted? See in general M. Zeitlin, "Purchase Money Security Interest Priority Under the Uniform Commercial Code: When Does Section 9-312(4)'s Grace Period Begin to Run?" (1975) 48 Temple LQ 1025. Is the problem analogous to the issue of when a debtor acquires rights in collateral under s. 12(1)(*c*)?

While a PMSI can be created in intangibles, the special priority rules are hardly appropriate for such types of collateral. Note also the policy arguments suggested by Ziegel, "The Quickening Pace of Jurisprudence . . ." (1980) 4 Can. Bus. LJ 54, 73:

Does PPSA, s. 22(3) in fact apply to a purchase-money security interest in an intangible? The rationale of the Code's counterpart, UCC 9-301(2), is obvious enough. It is directed to retail instalment sales and such like where the buyer is anxious to obtain immediate possession of the goods and it is not practicable, or perhaps possible, for the seller to file a financing statement before releasing the goods. The draftsmen therefore continued the policy of the old Conditional Sales Acts in allowing the seller a short grace period. The Official Comment to UCC 9-301 does not indicate that the draftsmen contemplated the subsection applying to a PMSI in an intangible and no reasons of policy would appear to justify extending the section's language to such cases. It would, however, be desirable to clarify subsec. (3) to restrict its scope expressly to a purchase-money security interest in goods or other tangibles. The alternative would be to delete any reference to the debtor's possession of the collateral and to allow a 10-day grace period from the time the debtor acquires an interest in the collateral. The date of execution of the security agreement would be a less acceptable alternative because in retail transactions a buyer frequently signs a purchase order for goods in which the seller retains a security interest before the goods are delivered to him, and sometimes even before the goods have been manufactured.

Under the Sask. PPSA the grace period for registering a PMSI is 15 days. The priority is also conferred on a PMSI holder in intangibles, in which case the grace period runs from attachment. See ss. 21 and 34(1).

C. PRIORITIES AMONG COMPETING SECURITY INTERESTS: THE BASIC RULES

The general rules for determining the priority of conflicting security interests in the same collateral are set out in s. 35. Unless a special provision applies (as, for example, with respect to the PMSI priority under s. 34), priority is to be determined by three basic rules:

(a) *Rule of First to Register.* If the competing security interests have all been perfected by registration, then the order of registration determines the order of priority (s. 35(1)(*a*)). The time of attachment or perfection of the interest is not relevant.

(b) *Rule of First to Perfect.* If not all of the competing security interests have been perfected by registration, then priority is determined by the order of perfection (s. 35(1)(*b*)). Examples where not all interests have been perfected by registration include the situations where one interest has been perfected by registration and the other by the secured party taking possession of the collateral, and where one interest is perfected and the other is not.

(c) *Rule of First to Attach.* If none of the competing security interests has been perfected, they rank according to the order of attachment (s. 35(1)(*c*)).

A few priority provisions (ss. 30(2) and (3), 34(1), and 37(2)) depend on "knowledge" or "notice". Will registration give the required "knowledge" or "notice"? Consider s. 53(1)(*a*)(i). What is the effect of "knowledge" or "notice" under s. 35(1)?

Problem:

January 1   C advances $50,000 to X against the security of machinery but does not register a financing statement or take possession of the collateral.

January 7   B advances $25,000 to X secured by the same machinery. B takes possession of the machinery.

January 8   C registers a financing statement with respect to his rights in the collateral.

When did each security interest attach? When was it perfected? Between C and B, who prevails in the priority contest as to the machinery? Would B's knowledge on January 7 of C's interest affect your answer? Would your answer be different if B had registered a financing statement on January 7, and had not taken possession of the machinery?

The After Acquired Property Clause and Priority

The equitable interest of a mortgagee in future assets of the mortgagor, created under an after acquired property clause and arising on the acquisition of the property by the mortgagor, was first recognized by the House of Lords in the leading case of *Holroyd* v. *Marshall* (1862) 10 HLC 191, 11 ER 999. Noting the fact that a deed conveying non-existent property is void at law, Lord Westbury stated (at 211):

. . . if a vendor or mortgagor agrees to sell or mortgage property, . . . of which he is not possessed at the time, and he receives the consideration for the contract, and

> afterwards becomes possessed of the property answering the description . . . , there is no doubt that a court of Equity would compel him to perform the contract, and that the contract would, in equity, transfer the beneficial interest to the mortgagee . . . on the property being acquired.

In this case, the mortgagee's interest under the after acquired property clause was held to defeat a judgment creditor who purported to assume control of the property without knowledge of the mortgage.

Holroyd v. Marshall was seriously limited in Joseph v. Lyons (1884) 15 QBD 280. In the latter case, the party who contested the after acquired property clause in the mortgage was a pawnbroker to whom the after acquired property had been pledged by the mortgagor to secure advances. The pawnbroker won as he "had the legal title" and "had no notice of the equitable title" under the after acquired property clause (id. at 286). Because of his legal title a subsequent grantee without notice was thus held to be in a better position than that of a judgment creditor without notice so as to prevail over the equitable interest under the after acquired property clause in the mortgage.

It is noteworthy that the mortgagee in Joseph v. Lyons registered his interest under legislation requiring the registration of bills of sale, but this did not help him. The court emphasized the lack of actual knowledge by the pawnbroker and refused to extend the doctrine of constructive notice. It stated that "a pawnbroker . . . was not bound to search the register of bills . . . as to goods pledged with him in the course of his business" (supra at 286). The doctrine in Joseph v. Lyons has also been followed in Canada, with the notable exception of the decision of the Saskatchewan Court of Appeal in Kozak v. Ford Motor Credit Co. [1971] 3 WWR 1. See e.g. Snyder's Ltd. v. Furniture Finance Corp. Ltd. (1930) 66 OLR 79 (Ont. CA); Re Royal Bank of Canada and Revelstoke Companies Ltd. (1979) 94 DLR (3d) 692 (Alta. SC), and GMAC v. Hubbard, supra, chapter 10.

Section 13 of the PPSA recognizes the validity of a security interest in after acquired property. What is the effect of s. 35(1) or s. 22 on the priority given to such an interest? How would Holroyd v. Marshall and Joseph v. Lyons be decided under the PPSA? Would you find the result under the PPSA more satisfactory?

Problems: The following are priority contests governed by ss. 22, 34, and 35. Consider each problem with particular reference to the relevant subsection.

1   On day 1, Vendor sells and delivers to Debtor a car under a conditional sale contract. Judgment Creditor of Debtor assumes control of the car through legal process on day 7. Vendor registers a financing statement on day 9. As between Vendor and Judgment Creditor, who has priority to the car?

2   C extends credit to Debtor on day 1. B sells and delivers a car to Debtor under a conditional sale contract on day 7. B registers a financing statement on day 27. On day 35 Debtor becomes bankrupt. Who has priority to the car?

3   On day 1, C lends money to Debtor under a security agreement which covers after acquired property. On day 13, Debtor buys and takes delivery of a car under a conditional sale contract with B. Who has priority to the car under the following alternative assumptions:
a)   Neither C nor B registered a financing statement.

b) C registered a financing statement on day 1. B registered a financing statement on day 20.

c) C registered a financing statement on day 15. B registered a financing statement on day 27.

d) On day 1, C took possession of Debtor's existing goods as collateral for his loan. He did not register a financing statement. B registered a financing statement on day 20. Would it matter if B registered on day 27?

4   On day 1, Debtor obtained possession from C of a tractor and has since then used it in his business. On day 35 Debtor borrowed money from B under a security agreement covering all existing and after acquired goods. B promptly registered a financing statement. On day 47 Debtor signed a conditional sales agreement under which he bought the tractor from C. C promptly filed a financing statement. As between C and B, who has priority to the tractor? Does your answer depend on the nature of Debtor's possession in the tractor between day 1 and day 47? Make the following alternative assumptions as to the nature of Debtor's possession until day 47:

a) Debtor's possession was for testing the tractor without any obligation.

b) Debtor's possession was under a true lease.

c) Debtor's possession was on the understanding that a conditional sales agreement would be signed by him.

d) Debtor's possession was on the understanding that some kind of a contract would follow.

e) No evidence as to the nature of Debtor's possession is presented to the court dealing with the matter.

CAIN v. COUNTRY CLUB DELICATESSEN OF SAYBROOK INC.
(1964) 203 A. 2d 441 (Conn. Sup. Ct.)

PASTORE, Judge: This is a motion of the receiver for a determination of priorities and an order of distribution with relation to The First Hartford Fund, Inc., and General Electric Credit Corporation, secured creditors of the defendant, Country Club Delicatessen of Saybrook, Inc.

On order of court, the assets of defendant corporation were sold December, 1963, free and clear of liens and encumbrances, in accordance with the consent of the parties, and the entire proceeds of the sale were ordered held by the receiver in substitution for said property, subject however to such valid and enforceable security interests, liens and encumbrances as might exist against the property, to the extent and in such priority as might be determined by this court.

The claim of The First Hartford Fund, Inc., is for a principal sum of $35,000 plus interest, costs and attorneys' fees. The claim of General Electric Credit Corporation is for $23,835.90 plus interest and attorneys' fees. The remaining fund in the hands of the receiver is about $24,400, representing the net proceeds from the sale of all the assets of the defendant corporation after payment of certain other claims superior to those of the present claimants.

For convenience said parties may be referred to in this opinion as First Hartford and General Electric, respectively.

Defendant corporation opened its restaurant business in Old Saybrook on July 26, 1962. At that time it was fully equipped. Its assets included property subsequently purchased from Hewitt Engineering, Inc., referred to herein as Hewitt. On August 16, 1962, defendant corporation borrowed $35,000 from First Hartford, giving a promissory note secured by a chattel-mortgage type of security agreement covering a security interest in "All goods, personal property, equipment, machinery, fixtures, inventory, leasehold rights, including, but not limited to, the property described below, including all after acquired property of like kind," and then follows an enumeration of specific items, as set forth in schedule A thereof.

The day previously, viz., August 15, 1962, First Hartford had filed a financing statement with the secretary of state, Uniform Commercial Code division, showing the defendant as debtor and First Hartford as the secured party. This financial statement had the same description as to property as did the security agreement mentioned above, and also contained a provision covering after-acquired property, and a description of the real estate and other data relating to requirements as to fixtures, in the event any of the property were fixtures. Also on August 15, 1962, First Hartford executed another financing statement, being a duplicate of the one filed in the office of the secretary of state and filed it with the town clerk of the town of Old Saybrook. The description of the property was the same as in the financing statement filed with the secretary of state. Both these financing statements were executed by the defendant corporation.

On August 30, 1962, defendant corporation and Hewitt Engineering, Inc., executed a conditional sale contract covering property sold by Hewitt to defendant as described in schedule A, attached thereto. Some of this property is expressly mentioned in the financing statement and security agreement of the defendant with First Hartford, above mentioned. On August 30, 1962, a financing statement was filed with the town clerk of the town of Old Saybrook showing Hewitt Engineering, Inc., as the secured party and General Electric as assignee of Hewitt, and defendant corporation as debtor. The description of the types or items of property covered by it read: "Complete restaurant and delicatessen including kitchen equipment and display equipment."

No financing statement of either Hewitt Engineering, Inc., or General Electric was on file with either the secretary of state, Uniform Commercial Code division, or the town clerk of Old Saybrook against defendant corporation up to the time on August 15, 1962, when First Hartford first filed its financing statements respectively in both of said offices. Also, no financing statement of said Hewitt or General Electric was on file with the secretary of state up to September 23, 1962, when the instant proceeding was started.

Some of the property specifically mentioned in the conditional sale contract of Hewitt, assigned to General Electric, appears also in the description of the property covered by the financing statement and security agreement of First Hartford. On trial it was stipulated by these parties that substantially if not all of the items of property described in schedule A of the conditional sale contract of

Hewitt were delivered by Hewitt to the defendant corporation [on] or before July 26, 1962, and that if any of these items were not delivered on or before July 26, 1962, all of them were delivered to the defendant corporation "before August 19, 1962." It appeared also from testimony that all property of defendant corporation, including that concerned with the goods sold by Hewitt, was to be removed from the premises upon termination of the lease between defendant corporation and the owner of the land involved.

The position of First Hartford is that it was first to file, that it filed with the secretary of state so as to cover itself with respect to personal property, that it filed with the town clerk of Old Saybrook so as to cover itself as to fixtures (if any be involved), and that General Electric, by failing to file with the secretary of state, does not have priority as to the personal property, and by filing when it did with said town clerk, acquired no rights superior to those of First Hartford in any fixtures, if any there were.

The claim of General Electric is that the evidence shows that as of August 15, 1962, when the financing statement of First Hartford was filed, and as of August 16, 1962, when its security agreement was made, the debtor defendant corporation had only possession of the property subsequently brought from Hewitt, the assignor of General Electric; that there is no evidence showing that as of those dates and within the meaning of General Statutes §42a-9-204(1) either a "security interest" had been created or the defendant corporation had acquired any "rights" in the property which defendant debtor bought from Hewitt, rights which defendant attempted as of that time to give to First Hartford.[1] The proper place for filing in order to perfect a security interest in goods which at the time the security interest attaches "are or are to become fixtures" is in the office where a mortgage on the real estate concerned would be filed or recorded; and in all other cases, in the office of the secretary of state. §42a-9-401(1). Thus, the recording or filing with respect to fixtures would be in the town clerk's office of the town where the affected real estate was located, and as to personal property, the filing would be in the office of the secretary of state.

Under §42a-9-204(1), a debtor must have "rights in the collateral" before a security interest may be created. The code does not clearly establish the meaning of this phrase, as for instance whether such rights arise when the debtor enters into a contract to buy goods, or only when he has an interest in the goods when identified with a contract under the Uniform Commercial Code, article 2, "Sales" (§§42a-2-101—42a-2-725).

In the instant case, while it is shown that the personal property bought August 30, 1962, from Hewitt, called here the Hewitt goods for convenience, was in the possession of the defendant debtor by July 26, 1962, and at least before August 19, 1962, and that the conditional sale contract between defendant and Hewitt was executed August 30, 1962, there is no showing as to the circumstances or arrangement whereby the defendant had this possession. No legal authority has come, or been brought, to the notice of this court that such mere possession

---

[1] [UCC] 9-204 . . . (1) A security interest cannot attach until there is agreement . . . that it attach and value is given and the debtor has rights in the collateral. . . .

may constitute such "rights in the collateral." An inference that defendant was an unconditional owner of the Hewitt goods on August 15, 1962, would be speculation. Also, there is no evidence showing a sale to defendant corporation in July, 1962, of the Hewitt goods by Hewitt, or that the possession by defendant of them before August 30, 1962, was in conjunction with said conditional sale contract. It is clear that as of the date, August 15, 1962, when First Hartford filed its financing statements, the conditions of §42a-9-204(1) had not been met by Hewitt so as to create a security interest in its favor and so constitute the Hewitt goods "collateral" (§42a-9-105[1][c] in which the defendant debtor could have any "rights."[2]

The claim of First Hartford that the Hewitt goods came under the coverage of its financing statement as of August 15, 1962, by virtue of §§42a-9-312(5)(a) and (b) is not sustained. Those provisions deal with the "priorities among conflicting security interests in the same collateral." As of August 15 or 16, 1962, there was not yet any security interest existing respecting Hewitt, and the Hewitt goods had not yet become "collateral." Since there was no security interest favoring Hewitt in the Hewitt goods until August 30, 1962, when the conditional sale contract was executed between the defendant debtor and Hewitt, it follows that as of August 15 or 16, 1962, there was no security interest in the Hewitt goods to conflict with any other respecting them. Under such circumstances, §42a-9-312(5)(a) and (b), urged by First Hartford, would have no occasion to apply. To adopt the construction of this section urged by First Hartford could result in goods, such as equipment, becoming subject to the security interest of First Hartford although the debtor's possession were only that of a mere bailee, apart from any purchase or contract to buy. This is not determinative of the question of the priority of First Hartford in the Hewitt goods, however.

The financing statements filed by First Hartford on August 15, 1962, with both the secretary of state and the town clerk of Old Saybrook each had an after-acquired property clause in it expressly including in the description of the property covered "all after acquired property of like kind" to the type described and specifically mentioned therein. The description expressly includes certain specific items of the Hewitt goods, and where otherwise, the description of the types of property covered is sufficiently broad to cover any other of the Hewitt goods. A similar clause is also contained in the security agreement between First Hartford and defendant corporation. For the purposes of article 9 of the Uniform Commercial Code, any description of personal property or real estate is sufficient whether or not it is specific if it reasonably identifies what is described. §42a-9-110.

The question arises as to the effect of this after-acquired property clause, in relation to the conditional sale contract of Hewitt and the defendant corporation, in respect of the Hewitt goods as of August 30, 1962. Under §42a-9-204(3), after-acquired property of the kind described in the conditional sale contract of Hewitt can become subject to the security agreement of First Hartford. See Conn. Gen.

---

[2] "Sec. 42a-9-105. Definitions and index of definitions. (1) . . . (c) 'collateral' means the property subject to a security interest, and includes accounts, contract rights and chattel paper which have been sold; . . ."

Stat. Ann. §42a-9-204(3), comment 2. A conditional sale contract comes within the scope and policy of article 9 of the Uniform Commercial Code as to secured transactions. §42a-9-102(1), (2). The retention or reservation of title by a seller of goods notwithstanding delivery to the buyer is limited in effect to a reservation of a "security interest." §42a-1-201(37). Also, the delivery of the Hewitt goods under the conditional sale contract with retention of title in Hewitt does not, in and of itself, affect the rights of First Hartford §42a-9-202.

The conditional sale contract of August 30, 1962, between defendant corporation and Hewitt created a security interest in favor of Hewitt which attached to the property thereby sold. §42a-9-204(1). To perfect this security interest, a financing statement was required to be filed (§42a-9-302[1]), which, as to goods which at the time the security attached were or were to become fixtures, would be filed in the office where a mortgage on the real estate would be filed, and in all other cases would be filed in the office of the secretary of state. §42a-9-401(1).

Hewitt failed to file in the office of the secretary of state; its financing statement was filed only in the office of the town clerk. It described the property covered as the "Complete restaurant and delicatessen including kitchen and display equipment." To the extent that this purports to include that portion of the personal property of the defendant debtor not including the Hewitt goods, it is plain that, Hewitt not having filed at all with the secretary of state and First Hartford having done so August 15, 1962, and perfected its security interest on August 16, 1962, First Hartford has priority over General Electric as to this portion of the personal property of the debtor within the coverage of the security agreement of First Hartford. §§42a-9-301(1)(a), 42a-9-312(5)(a). Included in this priority of First Hartford are such non-Hewitt goods as might be fixtures as of August 16, 1962, as to which First Hartford filed with the town clerk on August 16, 1962, and Hewitt and General Electric not until August 30, 1962, assuming, without deciding, that Hewitt had a security interest in such non-Hewitt goods.

A more fundamental reason for the priority of First Hartford in this non-Hewitt goods portion of the defendant corporation's collateral subject to First Hartford's security agreement, whether fixtures or otherwise, is that neither Hewitt nor General Electric has been shown to have a security interest in that portion of the defendant's property. While the financing statement of Hewitt attempts to be all embracing, there is no security agreement of Hewitt and defendant creating a security interest in that non-Hewitt portion of defendant's property. Without a security agreement (§§42a-1-201[3], 42a-9-105[1][h]), a security interest cannot attach. §42a-9-204(1). Any conflicting security interest would thus relate to such portion of the defendant corporation's property as involved the goods sold by Hewitt to defendant.

The priorities as to the Hewitt goods remain to be considered. In this regard it is convenient to consider it in two aspects, viz., one in regard to such goods as were not fixtures at the time the security interest attached, and the other in regard to such goods as might be fixtures at that time. In respect of the goods as were not fixtures at the time, there is a priority in favor of First Hartford because of its prior filing with the secretary of state under the circumstances in evidence, and the failure to do so by Hewitt, as previously explained regarding the non-Hewitt goods.

The question of the priority of such of the Hewitt goods as at the time the security interest of Hewitt may have attached were fixtures is next considered. Parenthetically, it is noted that when the court acquiesced in hearing this matter on the last day of the session, after usual adjournment hours, upon the reported stipulation of certain facts as of record appear, the court had the impression that General Electric had abandoned its earlier proposal to offer evidence as to claimed fixtures. The subsequent correspondence of its counsel, in essence deploring the lack of opportunity to offer such evidence, has been not without surprise, because, as the court had made clear, although the presentation of such evidence would have required a postponement of the matter, on account of the crowded short calendar docket on the last day of the spring session, General Electric would not have been deprived of an opportunity duly to present the same at a future session of the court. It is noted also that in neither of the two briefs submitted to the court has General Electric discussed its claims as to fixtures. Nevertheless, to avoid any injustice and further delay, the court is assuming to consider this aspect of the matter.

The question when and whether personal property becomes fixtures is determined by the law of the state other than the Uniform Commercial Code. §42a-9-313(1). The conditional sale contract of Hewitt, assignor of General Electric, provided in part as follows: "The equipment shall remain personal property regardless of any affixation to the realty and title thereto shall not pass to buyer until the . . . balance has been fully paid in cash." The parties to the contract were competent to make such an agreement, which was binding as between them, even though any such equipment were to be permanently affixed to the realty. *Hartlin* v. *Cody*, 144 Conn. 499, 506, 134 A. 2d 245. From the fact that the balance was never fully paid, it follows that as of the time the security interest of Hewitt was created and attached to the Hewitt goods as of August 30, 1962, any of such goods as might be affixed to the realty were still personal property. In this respect, the rights of General Electric, as assignee of Hewitt, are no greater than those of Hewitt. On August 30, 1962, the "rights in the collateral" which defendant debtor had (§42a-9-204[1]) with respect to any such fixtures were as personal property. When on that date, therefore, the rights of the defendant in the Hewitt collateral and said collateral came under the coverage of the after-acquired property clause of the First Hartford security agreement, the Hewitt goods were still personal property. On this basis, the failure of Hewitt and General Electric to file with the secretary of state makes their security interest subordinate to that of First Hartford, whose prior filing gives First Hartford priority over that of General Electric. §§42a-9-301(1)(a), 42a-9-312(5)(a). Moreover, there is nothing to indicate that General Electric has any interest in the pertinent real estate which would subordinate the First Hartford security interest to the benefit of General Electric. Cf. §42a-9-313.

In *National Cash Register Co.* v. *Firestone & Co.*, 346 Mass. 255, 191 NE 2d 471 (1963), considered a case of first impression, the security interest of the defendant lender had priority over that of the plaintiff, which thereafter delivered a cash register to the debtor under a conditional sale agreement and did not perfect its interest before or within ten days of delivery, where the security agreement of defendant covered all contents of the debtor's business and the cash register came within the coverage of an after-acquired property clause.

In accordance with the foregoing, it is hereby found and adjudged that the secured claim of The First Hartford Fund, Inc., in its full amount has priority over the secured claim of General Electric Credit Corporation and is entitled to payment in priority to said General Electric Credit Corporation.

The court makes no order of payment of the claim of The First Hartford Fund, Inc., at this time and leaves any such action to the future consideration of this court, pending the filing of such reports, accountings and motions as may be required for a determination and approval by the court of administration expenses, fees and any other deductions which may be required in the matter.

Order accordingly.

Notes and Questions:

1 How would the case have been decided under the PPSA? Take into account ss. 47 and 53(1)(*a*). Assume that filing with the secretary of state in Connecticut has the same effect as registration under PPSA s. 47, and that filing with the town clerk is notice under PPSA s. 54(1).

2 Assume further that both filings by First Hartford occurred on August 16, 1962 rather than on August 15, 1962. How would this affect your answer?

3 What rights did General Electric acquire by the filing relating to Hewitt's conditional sale contract? See PPSA s. 23(2). Did it have any claim with respect to goods not sold under the conditional sale contract?

4 Did the court satisfactorily dispose of the "rights in the collateral" issue? Was the debtor's possession of Hewitt's goods up to August 30 "only that of a mere bailee"?

5 What should (or could) have been done by Hewitt or General Electric to prevail in this priority contest?

NATIONAL TRAILER CONVOY OF CANADA LTD. v. BANK OF MONTREAL
(1980) 10 BLR 196 (Ont. HC)

SAUNDERS J.: This action involves the competing claims to a chattel by the plaintiff, National Trailer Convoy of Canada Limited ("National") under a conditional sales agreement and by the defendant, Bank of Montreal (the "bank") under a chattel mortgage.

National is engaged across Canada in the business of hauling mobile homes, modular homes, recreational vehicles and industrial camps. It does this by means of tractor-trailers owned by National and driven by employees or by vehicles owned by their drivers, each of whom has an agreement with National and is referred to by National as a "contract driver". National prefers to use contract drivers in conducting its business rather than owning its own vehicles and having them driven by employees.

In many cases National procures the vehicle, sells it to the driver by way of a conditional sales agreement and enters into an agreement with the driver whereby in effect the driver makes the vehicle and himself available to National for a specified period on specified terms. The latter agreement is referred to by National as a truckman's agreement.

In March 1978 National purchased and paid for a new tractor which it thereafter referred to as unit GG06789 (the "unit"). As was its practice, National made certain additions to the unit to adapt it for the use for which it was intended and then negotiated the sale of it to William E. Tanton ("Tanton") on the basis that he would become a contract driver.

On April 19, 1978 Tanton and National executed a document which both parties agree may be referred to as a conditional sales agreement (Ex. 6) and on the same day Tanton and National executed a truckman's agreement (Ex. 7). Under the conditional sales agreement the purchase price of $13,953.69 was to be paid for by a down payment of $3,000 and by equal monthly instalments of $369.78 each, commencing May 20, 1978, with the balance of $9,104.79 becoming due and payable on October 20, 1978. It was expressed in the agreement that the title, ownership and right of property in the unit would not pass until the entire purchase price and other specified charges had been paid in full. Tanton paid the down payment of $3,000 on April 19, the necessary licences were obtained and he went to work with the unit on the following day.

Tanton did not have the funds to provide the down payment. He arranged to borrow them from the bank. The arrangement was made with Derek Pass ("Pass") who was the manager of the bank at its Byron branch, Boler Road, London, Ontario. Pass had dealt with Tanton previously in connection with two former businesses and one proposed business that was dropped before it started. As at April 19, 1978 Tanton owed the bank approximately $3,000. Tanton was anxious to be able to provide the down payment for the National vehicle on April 19th and he and Pass met at the bank premises before the commencement of banking hours on that day to complete the arrangement. It was agreed that the Tanton indebtedness would be reconstituted at approximately $6,000 which would comprise the existing indebtedness plus the down payment for the National vehicle. It was further agreed that in addition to the assignment of two life insurance policies which the bank then held as security Tanton would execute a chattel mortgage of the unit in favour of the bank.

Pass knew that Tanton planned to become a contract driver for National, that Tanton was providing only a down payment and that the balance of the purchase price of the vehicle would be financed. In his examination for discovery Pass said that as far as he knew the financing was to be done by conditional sales agreement but he was not as specific as that in his evidence at the trial. He admitted he knew that Tanton was obtaining financing for the balance of the purchase price but he said that he did not know the source of the financing or its terms. He did understand that the bank would only have a second charge on the unit and he noted that understanding in the records of the bank.

On April 19th Tanton executed a loan application, a promissory note and a chattel mortgage, together with other documents requested by the bank. The description of the unit was not furnished at the time the documents were signed but Tanton, or someone on his behalf, furnished the information later that day. The chattel mortgage was completed some time later by the bank employees, possibly several days later.

It is not clear whether National knew in April 1978 that Tanton was borrowing the down payment from the bank. Mr. Hamilton, the president of National, was not sure that he knew about the bank loan at that time but conceded it was possible that he might have known. National did not know on April 19th and did not find out until some time later, that Tanton had given the bank a chattel mortgage on the unit.

The bank registered its interest under the chattel mortgage on April 27th, 1978 under The Personal Property Security Act, RSO 1970, c. 344 (("PPSA") and National registered its interest under the conditional sales agreement on May 17th, 1978. It is not disputed that the form of registration in each case was in compliance with the requirements of the PPSA.

Tanton defaulted on his obligation to the bank and in October 1978 the bank instructed a bailiff to seize the unit which was done on November 17, 1978. National commenced this action on December 6th for conversion and damages. The bank gave notice to National under s. 58 of the PPSA on or about December 11th. National did not redeem the unit or contact the bank with respect to the notice. The unit was sold by the bailiff in late February or early March of the following year for $4,830.

The essence of National's claim is that on the date of the seizure it had a better right to the unit than did the bank. The rights of competing parties to personal property have been a source of difficulty and confusion to generations of lawyers. Until recently, legislation had not alleviated the difficulty and in contrast to the relative certainty in ascertaining rights and priorities with respect to real property it was difficult, if not sometimes impossible, to express the rights of different parties to a specific item of personal property.

If the case at Bar had had to be decided before the enactment of the PPSA the interest of National would have been considered in light of The Conditional Sales Act, RSO 1970, c. 76 and the interest of the bank in light of The Bills of Sale and Chattel Mortgages Act, RSO 1970, c. 45. The PPSA deals with both conditional sales and chattel mortgages and with most other interests in personal property. It provides for, among other things, the rights and priority of parties with respect to the same property.

The case at Bar concerns two transactions, the sale by National to Tanton and the loan by the bank to Tanton. In my opinion the PPSA applies to both transactions. Section 2(a) of the PPSA provides:

• • •

There is no dispute that both the conditional sale agreement of National and the chattel mortgage of the bank in substance create a security interest within the meaning of s. 1(y) of the PPSA.

Counsel for National submitted that s. 3(1)(a) might apply to exclude the National conditional sales agreement from the PPSA on the ground that National had a lien by a "rule of law". I have difficulty following his argument on this point. It seems to me that the only lien that National has arises by contract and not by rule of law and furthermore that the PPSA in s. 2(*a*) specifically provides for the applicability of the legislation to conditional sale agreements. It may be that there are legal issues that should be considered in this case in addition to the application of the provisions of the PPSA but such issues do not, in my opinion, take the transaction outside of the PPSA by reason of s. 3(1)(*a*).

• • •

Counsel for the bank contended that the chattel mortgage of the bank created a "purchase-money security interest" within the meaning of the PPSA. Counsel for National did not urge such a contention on behalf of National, for reasons which will appear later, but could have made such a submission.

Section 1(*s*) of the PPSA defines purchase-money security interest. . . .

• • •

The National conditional sale agreement is clearly a security interest described in sub-clause (i). The chattel mortgage was taken by the bank, who gave $3,000 that enabled Tanton to acquire rights in the unit and the evidence is that such $3,000 was applied to acquire such rights. Sub-clause (ii) would therefore, in my opinion, apply to the security interest of the bank. The difficulty is that the chattel mortgage was also taken to secure an indebtedness that was not a purchase-money indebtedness.

Whether or not the interest of a party may be characterized as a purchase-money security interest is significant because of s. 34(3). . . .

• • •

The National conditional sale agreement does not have the benefit of s. 34(3) because it is agreed that the National security interest was not perfected until May 17th, 1978, which was more than 10 days after Tanton had obtained possession of the unit. As to the requirements of perfection of a security interest in goods under a conditional sale or a chattel mortgage, reference should be made to ss. 21 and 25(1) of the PPSA.

• • •

Subject to the argument that a security interest may not be severed, it would appear that the bank is entitled to priority over any other security interest to the extent of $3,000.

This leads to a consideration of s. 35(1) of the PPSA. . . .

• • •

It was not argued that any other provision of the PPSA was applicable to the issue of priority other than s. 34(3) previously referred to. Both security interests were perfected by registration and as the interest of the bank was registered first that interest has priority over the interest of National. It is therefore unnecessary to consider further or make a finding as to whether the interest of the bank is in whole or in part a purchase-money security interest.

That is not the end of the matter. Counsel for National contends that notwithstanding the provisions of the PPSA consideration must be given to (1) that legal title at all times was in National and that Tanton had no title to mortgage to the bank and no interest at all in the unit at the time he executed the chattel mortgage, and (2) that the bank had notice of a security interest of National at the time it took the chattel mortgage.

When Tanton entered into the conditional sale agreement with National he acquired a property interest in the unit even though at that time he did not acquire legal title. If he fulfilled the conditions imposed on him by the agreement he was entitled to the transfer of legal title. In my opinion he was capable of mortgaging the interest that he acquired on April 19, 1978 in the unit to the bank by way of chattel mortgage and the entering into the chattel mortgage had that effect, notwithstanding that the language of the chattel mortgage contemplated that he was the owner and was mortgaging as such. At the time he actually executed the chattel mortgage he had no interest in the unit. It is not uncommon, however, for security agreements to be entered into prior to a debtor acquiring an interest in the collateral. The subsequent acquisition by a debtor of an interest feeds the security of the secured party.

In the case at Bar the security interest of the bank, created by the chattel mortgage, attached no later than the date when the mortgage was fully completed, which was some time prior to April 27, 1978, as the conditions for attachment set out in s. 12(1) of the PPSA had then been fulfilled. Such interest was perfected by registration on April 27, 1978.

It is made clear in s. 2(a) of the PPSA that the statute applies to a transaction that in substance creates a security interest "without regard to the person who has title". National under its conditional sale agreement and the bank under its chattel mortgage each had a security interest within the meaning of the PPSA. By reason of s. 35(1) the security interest of the bank has priority over the security interest of National and title is not relevant in determining that priority. The bank, therefore, subject to the argument on notice, has a prior interest over National in the unit enforceable in accordance with the terms of the PPSA.

National submits that at the time the bank took the chattel mortgage the bank had notice of the security interest of National. In my opinion the evidence does not go that far. The bank believed and advanced funds in the belief that it only had a second charge on the unit. It did not know who held the first charge or the nature of it. At some later date the bank learned that National had a security interest which had been registered after the registration of the security interest of the bank. After the bank had caused the seizure to be made it first learned that the interest of National was by way of a conditional sale agreement and was prepared to instruct the bailiff to release the unit from seizure. After further consideration the bank changed its position and asserted priority. I find that at the time of the taking of its chattel mortgage the bank had notice of another security interest in the unit but did not have notice of the name of the secured party or that the security interest was in the form of a conditional sale agreement.

It was argued that the knowledge of the bank has the effect of rendering the PPSA inapplicable. As I understand the argument the purpose of the PPSA is to provide a means by which a third party interested in collateral could acquire knowledge of other interests. If the third party already has such knowledge then it is said the PPSA is redundant and the respective rights of the parties should be determined on the basis of long standing equitable principles. With respect I cannot accept this argument. A reading of the PPSA shows that the Legislature intended to provide a code whereby secured interests in personal property could be determined and enforced.

Notice other than is provided in the statute is not an element in determining priority as it was an element in certain of the statutes which were replaced by the PPSA and as it remains an element, for example, in The Registry Act, RSO 1970, c. 409 and The Mining Act, RSO 1970, c. 174. I conclude the omission of any reference to notice or knowledge on the part of the Legislature was deliberate, and that it was intended that priority as between competing security interests was to be determined in accordance with the statute.

Counsel for National was concerned that the bank had made little if any inquiry as to other interests before taking the chattel mortgage. He expressed the view that a lender could take security on no inquiry at all and be able to assert priority over other interests. He felt there was a danger of abuse and that security interests with priority under the PPSA might be invalid while subordinate interests might be valid. Again I have some difficulty following this argument. A party asserting rights under the PPSA must have an enforceable interest in the collateral. If he has no such interests then he has no rights to enforce. Counsel was also concerned that the effect of the legislation was to reward the swift regardless of the equities which might exist. That may be true. It may be that the Legislature was prepared to accept the possibility of some unfairness as a price for certainty. The rules are the same for all and it should be noted that National, if it had registered within the time limit set out in s. 34(3), would have had the benefit of that provision. However, as the bank was asserting that it had a similar benefit an interesting question would have had to have been decided if National had registered in time. Fortunately it is not a question that needs to be decided in these proceedings. It follows that the action of the plaintiff must fail.

Action dismissed.

Notes and Questions:

1   It is not uncommon for a buyer of goods under a conditional sale agreement to borrow the funds providing the down payment and give the lender a security interest in the goods. Each security interest, the seller's and the lender's, is a "purchase money security interest" under s. 1(s) which, if timely filed, is entitled to s. 22(3) or 34(3) priority. Which of the competing PMSIs prevails? A priority contest between two PMSIs whose respective holders had complied with the requirements of s. 34(3) was resolved in *Re Polano and Bank of Nova Scotia* (1979) 23 OR (2d) 324, 95 DLR (3d) 510 (Dist. Ct.) under s. 35 by applying the first-to-register rule. Do you agree with this approach? Does a prorating solution appear more satisfactory? Or should a seller, holder of a s. 1(s)(i) PMSI, always rank prior to a lender-holder of a s. 1(s)(ii) PMSI? See J. Ziegel, "The Quickening Pace of Jurisprudence Under The Ontario Personal Property Security Act" (1979-80) 4 Can. Bus. LJ 54, 76-77. See also *Framingham U.A.W. Credit Union* v. *Dick Russell Pontiac Inc.* (1969) 7 UCC Rep. 252 (Mass. App.), where the court concluded that the seller prevails over the lender

because the seller would be unwilling to part with his security interest unless granted priority. What is the best solution as a matter of statutory construction or policy?

2   Under s. 2(1) of the Mercantile Law Amendment Act, RSO 1970, c. 272, a "surety for the debt or duty of another . . . [who] pays the debt or performs the duty is entitled to have assigned to him . . . every judgment, specialty or other security that is held by the creditor in respect of the debt or duty . . .". Under s. 2(2) the surety "is entitled to stand in the place of the creditor". The section, which is a statutory enunciation of the equitable doctrine of subrogation, was recently applied in *Re Windham Sales Ltd.* (1979) 26 OR (2d) 246, 102 DLR (3d) 459 (SC in Bkcy). In this case, a guarantor who discharged the guaranteed debt was held to succeed automatically to the status of the creditor's security interest securing the debt insofar as registration or perfection is concerned without the need for any formal transfer of the security interest. Was the case correctly decided? For the proper relationship between the doctrine of subrogation and the PPSA priority scheme see B. Geva, "Bonded Construction Contracts: What Are a Surety's Rights to Withheld Funds" (1980) 3 Corp. L. Rev. 50, 57-58.

3   Should s. 35 be read as containing an implied "good faith" limitation? The possibility (in connection with UCC 9-312(5)) is raised by Professor Gilmore, in *Security Interests in Personal Property* vol. II (1965) pp. 895-902 but has not found favour. But *cf. Thompson* v. *United States* (1969) 408 F. 2d 1075, 1084 (8th Cir.) where the court found "extreme bad faith on the part" of a secured party that constituted "more than 'actual knowledge' ". Note however that under UCC 1-203, "[e]very contract or duty within [the UCC] imposes an obligation of good faith in its performance or enforcement." ("Good faith" is defined in UCC 1-201(19) as meaning "honesty in fact in the conduct or transactiion concerned".) There is no corresponding provision in the PPSA. Should PPSA s. 35 be read as containing an implied "without knowledge" limitation? This question is considered in the following case.

THE ROBERT SIMPSON COMPANY LTD. v. SHADLOCK AND DUGGAN
(1981) 31 OR (2d) 612 (Ont. SC)

GRAY J.: The issue is whether priority as between competing security interests in the same collateral security is determined under The Personal Property Security Act by whoever perfects or registers first or whether actual notice may defeat a claim to priority based on prior registration or prior perfection.

It was agreed that if priority is determined only by registration or perfection, the Plaintiff has no claim in law but if the doctrine of actual notice prevails, the Defendant cannot succeed on an application to strike out the Plaintiff's Statement of Claim. Between February 18th, 1976 and June 24th, 1976, pursuant to eleven Conditional Sale Contracts, the Plaintiff sold to the debtor certain chattels for installation at a motel property. On or about June 4th, 1976 an employee of the Plaintiff put the Defendants on notice of the Plaintiff's security interest.

On June 14th, 1976 the debtor mortgaged the motel to the Defendants and also on the same date by Chattel Mortgage mortgaged the Chattels and equipment in the motel, including the Plaintiff's Chattels, to the Defendants. The Defendants' Chattel Mortgage was registered under The Personal Property Security Act on June 17th, 1976, but the Plaintiff did not register its Conditional Sales Contracts under that Act until February 7th, 1978.

The relevant sections of The Personal Property Security Act are [ss. 1(k), 1(y), 12(1), 21, 22(1)(a), 25(1), 25(2), 35(1), and 36(3)]

• • •

The submission made by Counsel for the Defendants in summary form was that the only section of The Personal Property Security Act which applied was Section 35 and this section has provided for a test of priorities with the result that the so-called doctrine of actual notice cannot prevail. It was further argued that the Plaintiff had a purchase-money security interest, that Section 21 defines when a security interest is perfected and that Section 25 covers the question of perfection by registration.

The thrust of this argument was that if no other provision of The Personal Property Security Act is applicable the provisions of Section 35 apply since both security interests were registered with the result that priority would be determined by Section 35(1)(a) by the order of registration if the security interests have been perfected by registration.

The submission made by Counsel for the Plaintiff was that the legislation did not specifically abolish the doctrine of actual notice. My attention was directed to Section 22(1)(a) wherein it is clear that an unperfected security interest is subordinate to the interest of a person who is entitled to a priority under The Personal Property Security Act or any other Act. To decide who is entitled to priority it is necessary to peruse Section 35(1). It was said that subsections (a) and (b) had no application because under (a) both security interests were registered and under (b) both were perfected. In other words Section 35(1)(a) and (b) are of no assistance in resolving the issue in this application because here the contest is between one perfected and one unperfected security interest. The question really involves whether the Defendants are entitled to a priority under Section 22(1) of The Personal Poperty Security Act. The conclusion I was invited to reach was that the only purpose of requiring registration was to give notice to third parties and that if in fact a third party has acquired knowledge of the security interest then the underlying requirement has been met.

I reserved judgment on this application because the legislation is relatively new and the academic writers have indicated that there are conflicting policy arguments with an unresolved problem.

It was said that there is an omission in Section 35(1) which could easily have been rectified by the legislative draftsman so that the case at bar could have been covered. It was also said, with some force, that the doctrine of actual notice is deeply rooted in our law and that one of the well known rules of statutory interpretation is that the provisions of the common law cannot be changed without an express statutory provision to that effect.

I have considered the following cases:

Re Jung and Montgomery [1955] 5 DLR 287.

Pitcher v. *Shoebottom* [1971] 1 OR 106.
Re Dominion Stores Ltd. and United Trust Co. (1973) 42 DLR (3d) 523.
United Trust Company v. *Dominion Stores* [1977] 2 SCR 915.

These cases generally stand for the proposition in cases involving The Land Titles Act, RSO 1970, c. 234 as amended that "the doctrine of actual notice as to all contractual relations and particularly the law of real property has been firmly based in law since the beginning of equity. Such a cardinal principle of property law cannot be considered abrogated unless the legislative enactment is in the clearest and most unequivocal of terms". This latter phrase was used by Spence J. in delivering the majority decision in the Supreme Court of Canada in *United Trust Company* v. *Dominion Stores (supra).*

I have come to the conclusion that this application should succeed. The provisions of The Personal Property Security Act to some extent flow from the earlier provisions of the U.S. Uniform Commercial Code. Although the language is different it is interesting to compare Section 9 - 312 of the UCC with Section 35 of The Personal Property Security Act. The language is similar and notice makes no difference [*Bloom* v. *Hilty* (1967) 234 A 2d 860].

In my view nothing in Section 35 says anything about lack of knowledge being a prerequisite for its operation.

In an action in The County Court of the Judicial District of Ottawa-Carleton between *The Bank of Nova Scotia Plaintiff and Dilauri Chevrolet Oldsmobile Ltd. and Craig Edward Schwartz, Defendants,* the plaintiff bank with prior registration succeeded even though it had notice. Judge E.E. Smith made the following statement:

> It is argued that as between the two claimants in this case, the Bank of Nova Scotia and Dilauri Chevrolet Oldsmobile Ltd., a subsequent registration by the Bank ought not to be allowed to prevail where there was actual notice. It is conceded that Dilauri's failure to comply with the Act was innocent and in no way misled the Bank.
>
> If I were to accede to the argument, it seems to me that I would be reading into this rather comprehensive piece of legislation something which was (deliberately — the concept of actual notice being well known to the drafters) omitted and in the process thwarting many of the obvious purposes of the legislation.

In the present case I adopt that reasoning and that language.

I would also adopt the language of Lord Cozens-Hardy M.R. in *Re Monolithic Building Company; Tacon* v. *The Company* [1915] 1 Ch. 643 at page 556-66 [who,] quoting James L.J. in an earlier case, said:

> I think it would be dangerous to engraft an equitable exception upon a modern Act of Parliament.

and at page 666:

> Both parties stood on their legal rights — neither of them was misleading the other. It is not consistent with the policy of the Legislature to import fine equitable distinctions into these cases, and I am therefore of opinion that the argument founded on the knowledge of the judgment creditor cannot prevail.

I have likewise reviewed Sections 36 and 37 and have concluded that the special priority rules thereunder have no connection with this application. The Plaintiff's submission depends on looking to see a fixed time for registration but there is nothing in The Personal Property Security Act that fixes the time when the Court looks to see if there has been registration. This is a new statute which should be dealt with upon its own merits rather than some considerations which might apply to The Land Titles Act. Sections 22 and 36(3) contemplate knowledge but it is my view that this appears in The Personal Property Security Act for two situations and I draw the inference that the actual notice principal doesn't therefore apply elsewhere in the Act.

Prof. R.H. McLaren in his textbook *Secured Transactions in Personal Property in Canada* Vol. 1, 1979 page 6 — 2 states the general or residual rule [of] Section 35 thus: "The general rule of priority is built around the key concepts of attachment and perfection. No other statute has ever attempted to state even a single priority rule let alone one of such general application as s. 35. If no special priority rule governs then the rules of subs. (1) are used to resolve competing claims in the same collateral. ... The three rules of s. 35 disregard the pre-Act law and its reverence for legal title to the collateral and application of the equitable principle of good faith and notice."

I adopt the foregoing and am reinforced in my view by the judgment of Laskin, C.J. in *United Trust* v. *Dominion Stores (supra)* albeit a dissenting judgment.

Judgment for defendant.

D. SECURITY FOR FUTURE ADVANCES

G.L. BLACKBURN
"Mortgages to Secure Future Advances"
(1956) 21 Mo. L. Rev. 209, 213-15

• • •

Mortgages to secure future advances generally fall into one of four broad categories of form. In the first type the instrument makes no mention of future advances but rather takes the form of a mortgage absolute on its face which states a definite sum which is secured thereby. Actually only a portion of this stated amount is lent to the mortgagor, and, by oral agreement or a written collateral agreement, the parties manifest their intentions with reference to future advances.

In the second category, the instrument is drafted so as to expressly provide for the making of future advances. This type distinguishes itself, however, in that the mortgagee, by the terms of the agreement, contractually binds himself to make these subsequent advances. This form is generally referred to as a mortgage to secure "obligatory future advances."

In the third type, the mortgage will also provide expressly for the making of future advances, but the making of these advancements is strictly within the discretion of the mortgagee. Such a device is termed a mortgage to secure "optional future advances," but currently is becoming more familiarly known as an "open end" mortgage. Instruments purporting to secure optional advances are generally drawn either as "limited" or "unlimited." The unlimited type makes no mention of the total amount or limit which may ultimately be advanced and secured. The limited form is drafted with a provision providing a maximum amount of advances to be made and secured; or it may be limited as to the time during which such advances shall be made as well as limited in amount. Furthermore, where a mortgage on its face states it is to secure future advances or loans up to a stated maximum, it is valid only up to that amount, but it may be made a continuing security so that when advances have been made up to the limited amount and these are partially or totally repaid, the mortgage will continue as security for further loans within the prescribed limits.

The fourth and final classification of future advances is, in a sense, both optional and limited, but here the limitation is one of purpose wherein it is provided that the mortgagee may, at his own option, and without the consent of the mortgagor, make such advances or expenditures as are necessary to protect his interest or preserve the value of the security. Provisions for the payment of taxes, insurance, repairs, and prior liens are typical.

P.F. COOGAN
"The New UCC Article 9"
(1972-73) 86 Harv. L. Rev. 477, 505-07

The term "future advances" is not self-defining — future to what extent? Does the term include all advances subsequent to the date of the original filing? Subsequent to the date of the security agreement? Or is it only subsequent to the date upon which a full-fledged security interest attached and was perfected?

• • •

The [1962] Article 9 [as well as the Ont. PPSA] does not clearly distinguish between future advances made at the option of the secured party and those made pursuant to the secured party's commitment. A future advance made pursuant to an honest-to-goodness commitment should be treated the same as an actual advance: the secured party had parted with value by incurring an obligation that must be honored even it if proves inconvenient to do so. Lenders sometimes commit themselves to make certain future advances without regard to what the debtor's credit standing will be at the time the advance is actually made. More likely, the lender and debtor agree that the lender's obligation to make any further advance is subject to a set of carefully thought-out conditions aimed at assuring the lender that the debtor's credit position will support the advance when it is actually made and at assuring the debtor that credit will ordinarily be available to him.

The distinction between advances under commitment and optional advances no doubt must arise out of the nature of the conditions which will and will not excuse the lender's performance. Clearly, a lender's commitment to make a future advance which excuses performance if he dislikes the way the debtor has parted his hair on the day the latter asks for the advance is not a real commitment. It is quite a different matter, however, if the lender's commitment to make an advance is excused only if the debtor's balance sheet, audited by an independent accountant, shows that the debtor's net current asset-debt ratio has fallen below an agreed-upon, reasonable standard.

The revised Code attempts with apparent success to distinguish between a real and a phony commitment in new paragraph 9-105(1)(k):

> An advance is made "pursuant to commitment" if the secured party has bound himself to make it, whether or not a subsequent event of default or other event not within his control has relieved or may relieve him from his obligation.

Note especially the last clause. Suppose a building construction lender is excused under a security agreement from making further advances if any part of his debtor's assets are subjected to a lien obtained by legal or equitable proceedings involving a claim of $50,000 or more, and a creditor with such a claim levies. The lender, after surveying both his own position as a substantial creditor of the debtor and the probable strength of the lien creditor's claim, decides that he, as an existing creditor, and the debtor will both be worse off if he elects to take advantage of his "out." He consequently makes the advance to complete the building. Under proposed 9-105(1)(k) the lender's advance is entitled to the advantages of one made pursuant to a commitment, notwithstanding the out of which he did not take advantage.

The following case describes the priority of future advances at common law.

WEST v. WILLIAMS
[1899] 1 Ch. 132 (CA)

LINDLEY M.R.: A first mortgagee, whose mortgage is taken to cover what is then due to him, and also further advances, cannot claim the benefit of his security for further advances in priority to a second mortgagee of whose mortgage he had notice before the further advances were made. This rule was ultimately established in the well-known case of *Hopkinson* v. *Rolt* 9 HLC 514, 11 ER 829. In that case the first mortgagee had not agreed to make further advances. We have to consider whether the same rule applies when he has agreed to do so. Kekewich J. has held that it does not. This point is of great general importance, and I have carefully considered it, and have come to a conclusion different from that of the learned judge. *Hopkinson* v. *Rolt* 9 HLC 514 was commented upon and explained by the House of Lords in *Bradford Banking Co.* v. *Briggs* 12 App. Cas. 29 and in *Union Bank of Scotland* v. *National Bank of Scotland* 12 App. Cas. 53. These three cases show very clearly that the principle which underlies the rule established in *Hopkinson* v. *Rolt* is simply this, that an owner of property, dealing honestly with it, cannot confer upon another a greater interest in that property than he himself has. The rule rests on no technicality of English law; it is based on the plainest good sense, and it is as much the law of Scotland as the law of England. When a man mortgages his property he is still free to deal with his equity of redemption in it, or, in other words, with the property itself subject to the mortgage. If he creates a second mortgage he cannot afterwards honestly suppress it, and create another mortgage subject only to the first. Nor can any one who knows of the second mortgage obtain from the mortgagor a greater right to override it than the mortgagor himself has. On the other hand, the first mortgagee has no right to restrain the mortgagor from borrowing money from some one else, and from giving him a second mortgage, subject to the first. Even if the first mortgagee has agreed to make further advances on the property mortgaged to him, the mortgagor is under no obligation to take further advances from him and from no one else, and if the mortgagor chooses to borrow money from someone else, and to give him a second mortgage, the mortgagor thereby releases the first mortgagee from his obligation to make further advances. Whatever prevents the mortgagor from giving to the first mortgagee the agreed security for his further advances releases the first mortgagee from his obligation to make them. A plea of exoneration and discharge before breach would be a good defence at law to an action by the mortgagor against the first mortgagee for not making further advances. If, notwithstanding his release, the first mortgagee makes further advances, with notice of a second mortgage, he is in no better position than any one else who does the like.

Notes and Questions:

1   The notice of the intervening interest which defeats the first mortgagee's priority in respect of the future advances is "notice which gives him real and actual knowledge, and so affects his conscience". Protection is given to the first mortgagee "until he is made aware of a change, not by the hypothetical operation of an instrument registered subsequent to his, but by a reasonable communication of the fact by the one who comes in under the subsequent instrument". See *Pierce* v. *Canada Permanent Loan and Savings Company* (1894) 25 OR 671, 676 (Ch. D.). This was not the universal pre-Code rule in the U.S. For a discussion of the pre-Code rules governing priorities of future advances and the effect of actual or constructive notice of an intervening interest, see Blackburn, *op. cit.* at 218. These pre-Code rules differed in the States from one jurisdiction to another.

2   In *West* v. *Williams, supra*, the intervening interest between the first mortgage and subsequent advances was that of a second mortgagee. The same rules apply also where the intervening interest consists of a judicial lien. See *Falconbridge on Mortgages* (4th ed., 1977) p. 163.

3   The PPSA allows the security agreement to secure future advances (s. 15). The need for the UCC's corresponding provision (9-204(3) in the 1972 text) is explained by the pre-Code's "vaguely articulated prejudice against future advance agreements". See Comment 5 of UCC 9-204 (1972 Official Text). According to Professor Ziegel, the Canadian pre-PPSA position towards future advances was "very much more favourable". He summarizes the statutory position as follows:

It is not clear to what extent "future advance" clauses which do not involve firm commitments on the part of the mortgagee are valid under the existing [chattel mortgage] Acts. Some Acts, like British Columbia's, do not deal explicitly with such clauses; those which follow the Revised Uniform Act require the writing to set forth "the terms or substance" of the agreement in respect of the advances; whereas the Ontario Act limits future advances to those which are to be repaid not later than a year from the making of the agreement. Furthermore, the supporting affidavit must state, *inter alia*, "the extent and amount of the advances intended to be made". It would seem, therefore, that, under this Act at least, the agreement must involve firm commitments to make the advances. Possibly, however, this fatal handicap could be overcome by the use of a debenture, since debentures are governed in Ontario, as in the other provinces, by other provisions which, *semble*, are not subject to the same limitations.

(J.S. Ziegel, "The Legal Problems of Wholesale Financing of Durable Goods in Canada" (1963) 41 Can. Bar Rev. 54, 62, 64-5.)

4   Has the PPSA changed the common law priority scheme as outlined in *West* v. *Williams, supra*? There are no specific provisions in the Ontario Act dealing with the priority of future advances. Their position is thus determined according to the general rules of ss. 22 and 35. However, the application of these provisions to future advances is not straightforward. Consider the following: where a lender makes successive advances against the same collateral, when does his security interest attach? Does he have one security interest securing a floating debt, or does he have several security interests in the collateral, each of which secures a particular advance? These questions are relevant in determining priorities under s. 22 and s. 35(1)(*b*) and (*c*). (Why not under s. 35(1)(*a*)?)

Are ss. 9, 12, 21, 33, or any combination thereof, helpful? See the analysis in Gilmore, *Security Interests in Personal Property*, vol. 2 (1965) pp. 933 *et seq.*, citing also at p. 936 n.3 the opposite view of Mr. Coogan. Professor Gilmore, who argues for one security interest which attaches at the time value is first given, is not disturbed by the adverse effect of his view on an intervening judgment creditor who assumes control of the collateral through legal process between the time of the security agreement and the making of an optional future advance. Professor Gilmore's view is that where a future advance is made after the assumption of control through legal process by the judgment creditor, ". . . the debtor's assets have not been depleted: the . . . advance balances the diminution of his equity in the machinery [subject to the security interest]. The [judgment creditor] will . . . receive less from the sale of the machinery than he would have received before [the advance was made], but his chance of collecting his claim from the debtor's remaining assets (which now include the . . . advance) is as good as ever; presumably it is better than ever since the debtor now has a new supply of working capital": *id.* at p. 939. Do you agree?

Problem: On September 1 the debtor gives S a non-possessory security interest in specified machinery owned by him pursuant to a security agreement containing a future advance clause (i.e., a term under which the collateral also secures future advances). The security agreement does not contain any commitment as to the giving of future advances. S registers a financing statement and advances $5,000. On September 15 the debtor borrows $1,000 from C and signs a security agreement covering the same machinery. A financing statement is duly registered. On September 25, S advances $500 to the debtor. The debtor defaults on September 30 without making any repayment. The machinery is worth $6,000. Consider the following questions:

a) How much will be collected by S? By C? What could C have done to protect himself? See ss. 39 and 51.
b) Suppose C is not an intervening lender but either a buyer of the collateral or a judgment creditor assuming control thereof through legal process on September 15. How will this affect your answer to (a)?
c) Suppose C does not register a financing statement but perfects his security interest by possession. Will this affect your answer to (a)?
d) Suppose the September 25 advance was made by S pursuant to a commitment given by him to the debtor in the September 1 security agreement. Will this affect any of your previous answers?

COIN-O-MATIC SERVICE CO. v. RHODE ISLAND HOSPITAL TRUST CO.
(1966) 3 UCC Rep. Ser. 1112 (RI Superior Ct.)

LICHT J.: This matter is before the court on an agreed statement of facts. The following is a summary of the facts which will help place the case in proper perspective.

On July 11, 1963, Munroe Doroff purchased a motor vehicle from Warwick Motors, Inc. on a time payment basis (Exhibit "A"). The security agreement representing the purchase was assigned to the Rhode Island Hospital Trust Company. The security agreement did not have any provision for after-acquired property or future advances. It described the collateral as one Chevrolet Station Wagon Greenbrier 1963. The financing statement filed July 16, 1963 contained a reference to the same Chevrolet Greenbrier Station Wagon (Exhibit "B").

On October 2, 1964 Doroff became indebted to Coin-O-Matic Service Company in the sum of $5,600.00 represented by a promissory note and secured by a security agreement (Exhibits "C" and "D"). A financing agreement was filed October 23, 1964 (Exhibit "E"). On November 13, 1964, Doroff owed the Hospital Trust Company $302.77 on the security agreement of July 11, 1963 and on that date Rhode Island Hospital Trust Company loaned Doroff the sum of $1,000.00 from which sum he paid to Rhode Island Hospital Trust Company $302.77 in full satisfaction of his July 11, 1963 obligation. Rhode Island Hospital Trust Company thereupon cancelled the old agreement. Doroff executed a new promissory note secured by a security agreement (Exhibit "F"). A new financing statement was filed on November 17, 1964 (Exhibit "G"). On December 7, 1964 Doroff went into bankruptcy. It was stipulated that the value of the motor vehicle at the time it came into Rhode Island Hospital Trust Company's possession was $1,200.00. It was further stipulated that the automobile was used in Doroff's business and there is no question that the automobile was part of the collateral given to Coin-O-Matic Service Company, the plaintiff.

At oral argument defendant stated that it raised no question as to the validity of the financing statement of plaintiff filed October 23, 1964. The technical problem alluded to and which was waived, relates to Exhibit "E". An examination of that exhibit discloses that instead of putting the last name first in the left hand corner of the exhibit, the first name was put first. There is no suggestion that any person was misled or that anything turns upon that fact.

A question arose as to whether the defendant would be entitled to a credit of $302.77 even assuming that the plaintiff prevailed on his claim. In order to avoid a consideration of this issue, which is collateral to the main issue involved herein, the parties stipulated that if the plaintiff recovers he shall recover only the sum of $1,000.00 notwithstanding the agreed statement that the motor vehicle at the time it came into the possession of the defendant had a value of $1,200.00.

This leaves for consideration the sole issue, namely, whether the plaintiff is entitled to a priority with respect to the chattel in question or whether the defendant is entitled to a priority based upon its original financing statement.

The defendant contends that its original financing statement was sufficient not only to protect the original conditional sales agreement but the subsequent agreement despite the fact that there intervened a security agreement between Doroff and Coin-O-Matic and a filed financing statement in connection therewith.

The issues raised require a consideration of the Uniform Commercial Code. There is no dispute that the word "equipment" used in the security agreement between Doroff and Coin-O-Matic was within Section 6A-9-109(2).

Section 6A-9-312 provides in part:

> (5) In all cases not governed by other rules stated in this section (including cases of purchase money security interests which do not qualify for the special priorities set forth in subsections (3) and (4) of this section), priority between conflicting security interests in the same collateral shall be determined as follows:
>
> (a) in the order of filing if both are perfected by filing, regardless of which security interest attached first under § 6A-9-204(1) and whether it attached before or after filing;

The defendant relies wholly upon what it considers the compelling literal meaning of the language of the section. That is to say, that having entered into a security transaction which covered the 1963 Chevrolet Greenbrier Station Wagon and having filed a financing statement it comes ahead of the plaintiff who had a security interest in the same collateral but whose filing of a financing statement was subsequent in time to the original filing and ahead of defendant's second filing. Obviously with respect to the original transaction there is no dispute that the prior filing of the financial statement would govern. But the defendant carries its argument a step further and contends that the original financing statement is an umbrella which gives the defendant a priority with respect to its second security transaction notwithstanding that the plaintiff's security interest was established in point of time prior to defendant's second security transaction.

The defendant contends that as long as there is a financing statement on file the whole world is given notice that the debtor is obligated; that there is a security interest in the particular collateral and that the debtor may at any time after the original transaction become further indebted and enter into an additional security agreement with respect to the collateral. In support of this position the defendant cites a colloquy between Peter Coogan, a member of the Permanent Editorial Board of the Uniform Commercial Code, and a member of the bar at a panel discussion conducted under the auspices of the American Bar Association in August of 1963. The following is the colloquy which is of such interest that the court in order to place the matter in its proper perspective sets it forth as follows:

> Mr. Kripke: Before you go on, let us take a hard case. Let us suppose you had this original mortgage for a dollar and then you have another intervening contractual chattel mortgage, and Sydney has no future advance clause but takes a third mortgage instrument for the half million dollars on the same property and there has already been an intervening filing with respect to it. Now where does Sydney rank?
>
> Mr. Coogan: Let's see if I follow you —
>
> Mr. Kripke: You have an original chattel mortgage for a dollar, perfected by a notice which says "industrial equipment." You have an intervening chattel mortgage for another lender on the same equipment for a hundred thousand dollars, let us say. Then Sydney takes a third piece of paper, a chattel mortgage on the same piece of equipment — one never in the original contemplation of the parties. Where do their parties rank?
>
> Mr. Coogan: Sydney comes ahead of everybody. This is an illustration of the first-to-file rule. Where two security interests have both been perfected through filing, and no specific priority rule applies the priorities date from the time of the filing.
>
> Mr. Kripke: You mean the original notice determines priorities as of its date even for a transaction that was not contemplated at the time?
>
> Mr. Coogan: That is correct.
>
> Mr. Kripke: It would cover an advance which was not even covered by a future advance clause?
>
> Mr. Coogan: That is correct. (19 Bus Law 20, 52 (1963))

It will be observed as already noted that the original conditional sales agreement between Doroff and Warwick Motors, Inc. which was assigned to the defendant has no provision for future advances.

Section 6A-9-204, subsection (5) provides:

> Obligations covered by a security agreement may include future advances or other value whether or not the advances or value are given pursuant to commitment.

Defendant contends that this provision merely permits a lender to include a provision for future advances in the original security agreement and that when this is so provided it obviates the necessity of executing subsequent security agreements with respect to the collateral in question but that it does not in any way affect the priority with respect to future advances as long as the financing statement covering the collateral in question is prior in time and additional security agreements are obtained with each new loan. This is, according to the defendant, the thrust of Mr. Coogan's remarks to which reference has already been made. If this is so, it places a lender in an unusually strong position vis-a-vis the debtor and any subsequent lenders. In fact, it gives the lender a throttle hold on the debtor. For example, a debtor borrows $25,000.00 from a lender to be paid over a three-year period without any right of anticipation. The security is the equipment of the debtor. No provision is made for future advances. The financing statement is filed. The debtor reduces the obligation to $12,500.00 and now seeks to borrow an additional $5,000.00. The original lender is not interested in making a second loan. The debtor is in no position to pay off the loan without borrowing from another lender. The original lender does not desire to liquidate the obligation except in strict accordance with the agreement. Under the theory advanced by the defendant the original debtor cannot borrow from the second lender because no second lender can safely advance the money as long as there is a possibility that a future advance by the original lender would have priority in the collateral over the second lender. The interpretation contended for by the defendant does not appear to this court to be necessary for the protection of lenders nor does it seem necessary for facilitating commercial transactions. Defendant's counsel does not deny that this is so but contends that it makes no difference because Section 6A-9-312(5)(a) gives the original lender such protection. Counsel for the defendant concedes a difference in a case in which the lender is paid off, the balance on the original transaction is reduced to zero and in which the financing statement is not terminated by a termination agreement as provided in Section 6A-9-404 but it distinguishes the instant case from such a situation. The termination statement section provides in part as follows:

> Termination Statement.—(1) Whenever there is no outstanding secured obligations and no commitment to make advances, incur obligations or otherwise give value, the secured party must on written demand by the debtor send the debtor a statement that he no longer claims a security interest under the financing statement, which shall be identified by file number. . . .

It seems, however, that the defendant, notwithstanding his recognition of a difference in the illustration put forth should nevertheless take the position that as long as the financing statement is not terminated the lender is protected even when the original balance is liquidated, provided that additional funds are loaned and a new security agreement is entered into between the original lender and debtor. In such a case the original lender would come ahead of an intervening security transaction in which a financing statement had been filed for the same collateral. But why should the law be so interpreted to produce such a result? In all of these cases a lender can protect himself against the situation involved herein by providing in the original security agreement for future advances. In other words, the conclusion urged upon this court by the defendant is not required in the interest of facilitating commercial transactions particularly in the light of the fact that the Code provides for future advances in Section 6A-9-204(5). Comment 8, under this section, is as follows:

> 8. Under subsection (5) collateral may secure future as well as present advances when the security agreement so provides. At common law and under chattel mortgage statutes there seems to have been a vaguely articulated prejudice against future

advance agreements comparable to the prejudice against after-acquired property interests. Although only a very few jurisdictions went to the length of invalidating interests claimed by virtue of future advances, judicial limitations severely restricted the usefulness of such arrangements. A common limitation was that an interest claimed in collateral existing at the time the security transaction was entered into for advances made thereafter was good only to the extent that the original security agreement specified the amount of such later advances and even the times at which they should be made. In line with the policy of this Article (Chapter) toward after-acquired property interests this subsection validates the future advance interest, provided only that the obligation be covered by the security agreement. This is a special case of the more general provision of subsection (3).

And Example 4 under 6A-9-312 is as follows:

Example 4. On February 1 A makes an advance against machinery in the debtor's possession and files his financing statement. On March 1 B makes an advance against the same machinery and files his financing statement. On April 1 A makes a further advance, under the original security agreement, against the same machinery (which is covered by the original financing statement and thus perfected when made). A has priority over B both as to the February 1 and as to the April 1 advance and it makes no difference whether or not A knows of B's intervening advance when he makes his second advance.

The case falls under subsection (5)(a), since both interests are perfected by filing. A wins, as to the April 1 advance, because he first filed even though B's interest attached, and indeed was perfected, first. Section 9-204(5) and the Comment thereto should be consulted for the validation of future advances. Section 9-313 provides for cases involving fixtures.

It will be observed that under this example the advance is made pursuant to the original security agreement, meaning thereby that the original security agreement contains a future advance provision. The author directs attention to § 9-313 in order to protect a lender in the case of future advances.

This is a case of first impression. No case has been cited to this court but counsel informed the court that there is no decided case involving the precise issue presented herein.

But Hart and Willier, Forms and Procedures under UCC, has the following interesting comment:

91A.08 Description of the Collateral
Secured transactions between the same secured party and debtor probably will follow one of several general procedures:
(1) A single transaction; subsequent transactions are not originally contemplated and, if entered into, each would be separate and distinct.
(2) A continuing series of transactions, each by a separate security agreement with its own collateral.
(3) A secured transaction under one blanket security agreement covering a broad category of present and after-acquired collateral which may or may not contemplate future advances by the secured party or acts of the debtor identifying, segregating, substituting or transferring the collateral from time to time.
In the first situation, a new filing will be required for each transaction . . ."

The provisions of the Code with respect to notice is, in the judgment of this court, helpful in the matter of interpreting § 9-312(5).

Section 9-402 provides for the financing statement and the filing.

Section 9-208 provides that a debtor may request information from the lender as to the amount due on the obligation and the collateral covered by the security agreement. If the secured party, without reasonable excuse, fails to comply with the request he is liable for any loss caused to the debtor thereby and if the debtor has properly included in his request a good faith statement of the obligation or a list of the collateral or both, the secured party may claim a security interest only as shown in the statement against persons misled by his failure to comply.

If the Code gives the lender an interest in the collateral for future advances even though no provision is made for such future advances, then the information secured by the debtor and given to a subsequent lender is of little value because the second creditor surely could not rely upon the information. If the defendant's interpretation of the Code is correct, there seems to be hardly any substantive reason why the original lender should be bound to comply with the borrower's request for information concerning a correct statement of the outstanding balance and the collateral covered under the security agreement.

It should be observed that the defendant and the original debtor believed that the original conditional sales transaction was a single transaction and did not provide for future advances by virtue of the original financing statement. This is clear from an examination of the agreed statement and the exhibits attached thereto. When, on November 15th, Doroff's balance with the Hospital Trust was $302.77 on the security agreement of July 11, 1963, and when, on that date, the defendant loaned Doroff $1,000.00 which paid off the original balance and the old agreement was cancelled, Doroff executed a new promissory note secured by new security agreement and a new financing statement was filed with the Secretary of State on November 17, 1964.

It would seem to this court that without a consideration of the meaning of § 9-312(5) this case might properly be decided on what the parties themselves did and what the parties themselves intended. Insofar as Doroff and the Rhode Island Hospital Trust Company were concerned these parties intended an entirely new transaction when the additional loan was made and they considered the original transaction as terminated. They did not intend to affect an intervening creditor. Certainly Doroff, although he subsequently went into bankruptcy, might well have not agreed to a new transaction if such new transaction was to have the effect of cutting out the intervening creditor. What these parties intended was a completely separate transaction and the claim now that the defendant is entitled to the protection of the original financing statement comes, in the judgment of this court, as an after-thought.

It is the considered judgment of the court after a careful consideration of the agreed statement of facts and the applicable provisions of the Commercial Code that particularly in this case the defendant is not entitled to rely upon the original financing statement in order to bring its subsequent loan ahead of that of the intervening creditor. This is said not because of the application of the principles of estoppel or waiver but because the parties surely are not prohibited under the Code from treating their transactions as separate and unrelated transactions. See 6A-1-102(2) and 6A-1-201(3).

Section 6A-9-312(5) deals with priority between conflicting security interests in the same collateral and gives a priority in the order of the filing but that obviously does not relate to separate and distinct security transactions. Moreover, a careful examination of 6A-9-312 and the other applicable provisions of the Code lead to the conclusion that the reasonable interpretation of 6A-9-312 is that a security agreement which does not provide for future advances is a single transaction and in the case of subsequent security agreements there is required a new financing statement. That is to say, a single financing statement in connection with a security agreement when no provision is made for future advances is not an umbrella for future advances based upon new security agreements, notwithstanding the fact that involved is the same collateral.

For the foregoing reasons decision is entered for the plaintiff in the sum of $1,000.00 plus interest and costs and the Clerk is directed to enter judgment forthwith and to give notice thereof to the parties pursuant to the Rules of Civil Procedure and Rules of Practice of the Superior Court.

Judgment for plaintiff.

Notes and Questions:

1   Was *Coin-O-Matic* a "future advances" case? Is a "future advance" distinguishable from a "future transaction"? *Coin-O-Matic* was not followed in *In re Rivet* (1969) 299 F. Supp. 374 (UC Dist. Ct. ED Mich. ND). See also *Household Finance Corp.* v. *Bank Commissioner of Maryland* (1967) 235 A. 2d 732 (MCA); *In re Glawe* (1969) 6 UCC Rep. 876 (U.S. Dist. Ct. ED Wis.); and *In re Merriman* (1967) 4 UCC Rep. 234 (Dist. Ct. SD Ohio). The revised Article 9 (1972 Version) provides in 9-312(7): "If future advances are made while a security interest is perfected by filing or the taking of possession, the security interest has the same priority for the purpose of subsection (5) with respect to future advances as it does to the first advance. . . ." (Subsection (5) corresponds to PPSA s. 35(1)). It has been said that "[b]y new subsection (7) the draftsmen have made explicit what was implicit to all reasonable men under the old 9-312(5), namely, that future advances made while the security interest is perfected by filing or by the taking of the possession relate back to the original date of filing or taking of possession": J. White and R. Summers, *Handbook of the Law Under the Uniform Commercial Code* (1972) p. 913. (See also the 2nd edition (1980) p. 1042). For a devastating critique of *Coin-O-Matic* see also P.F. Coogan, "The New UCC Article 9" (1973) 86 Harv. L. Rev. 477, 509.

Note that the revised Article 9 (1972 Text) further provides in §9-301(4) that,

> (4) A person who becomes a lien creditor while a security interest is perfected takes subject to the security interest only to the extent that it secures advances made before he becomes a lien creditor or within 45 days thereafter or made without knowledge of the lien or pursuant to a commitment entered into without knowledge of the lien.

A "lien creditor" is the Code equivalent to a person whose interest is governed by subclauses (ii) and (iii) of PPSA s. 22(1)(a). UCC 9-307(3) provides that a buyer not in the ordinary course of business "takes free of a security interest to the extent that it secures future advances made after the secured party acquires knowledge of the purchase, or more than 45 days after the purchase, whichever first occurs . . ."

Would *Coin-O-Matic* and the problem preceding it be decided otherwise under the provisions of the revised Article 9?

2   It has been observed that:

> The wording of s. 15 is similar to but not identical with the corresponding section of Art. 9-204(5) of the USUCC. The variation in wording between the Ontario version and that of the 1962 USUCC was designed to require a specific reference to future advances in the security agreement if they were contemplated in the transaction. It was felt that this would avoid the possibility of a secured party holding a security interest to secure a specific debt attempting at a later date to claim a subsequent unsecured obligation due by the debtor constituted a future advance and as such should be secured by the security interest created with respect to the specific debt.

(Catzman *et al., Personal Property Security Law in Ontario* (1976) pp. 75-6). Is this observation relevant to the applicability of *Coin-O-Matic* under the PPSA? Is the applicability of *Coin-O-Matic* under the PPSA affected by the fact that, unlike under the UCC, no signature of the debtor on the financing statement is required under the PPSA?

3   The Sask. PPSA contains the following "future advances" provisions:

> **2.**(r) "future advance" means the payment of money, the provision of credit or the giving of value by the secured party pursuant to the terms of a security agreement, whether or not the secured party is obligated to pay the money, advance the credit or give the value, and includes all advances and expenditures made by the secured party for the protection, maintenance, preservation or repair of the collateral;

> **14.**(1) A security interest may secure future advances whether or not the advances are given pursuant to an obligation in the security agreement.
>
> (2) No obligation to make future advances is binding on a secured party if the collateral has been seized, attached or charged . . . and the secured party receives notice of this fact.

> **20.**(2) A perfected security interest is subordinate to the rights of persons mentioned in clauses (1)(b) to (d), except to the extent that the security interest secures:
>
> (a) advances made before the interests of such persons arise;
> (b) advances made before the secured party receives notice of the interest of such persons;
> (c) reasonable costs incurred and expenses made by the secured party for the protection, maintenance, preservation or repair of the collateral.

> **35.**(4) If future advances are made while a security interest is perfected, the security interest has the same priority for the purposes of this section with respect to future advances as it has with respect to the first advance.

("persons mentioned in clauses 1(*b*) to (*d*)" within the meaning of s. 20(2) *supra* correspond to those mentioned in Ont. PPSA s. 22(1)(*a*)(ii) and (iii)). What is the difference between these provisions and the Ont. PPSA? Between them and the provisions in revised Article 9 (see *supra*, note 1)? Which represents the better policy?

4   The draft Bill to amend the Ontario PPSA proposed the following revisions:

    9.   Section 22 of the said Act is amended by adding thereto the following subsection:

        (4) A perfected security interest is subordinate to an interest of a person set out in subclause ii or iii of clause *a* of subsection 1 except to the extent that the security interest secures advances made,

        (*a*)   before the interest of such person arises;

        (*b*)   before the secured party receives notification of the interest of such person; or

        (*c*)   pursuant to a commitment entered into by the secured party before he receives notification of the assumption of control.

    13.   Section 35 of the said Act is amended by adding thereto the following subsection:

        (3) For the purposes of this section, where future advances are made while a security interest is perfected, the security interest has the same priority with respect to future advances as it has with respect to the first advance.

What changes in the priority scheme are introduced by the draft bill?

E.   REGISTRATION PROBLEMS AND PRIORITY

Problems:

1   In *In Re Smith and Bank of Montreal* (1978) 19 OR (2d) 157 (Ont. Co. Ct.), the Bank of Montreal made an *ex parte* application for leave to make a late registration pursuant to PPSA s. 63(1):

Judge Borins refused the application but without prejudice to the bank's opportunity to make another application if it was supported by further and better materials. His reasons were that the bank's affidavit completely failed to meet the requirement of s. 63(1) that the judge must be satisfied "that no interest of any other person will be prejudiced by such extension". The bank's affidavit merely deposed that failure to register the chattel mortgage arose from a typing error made on the financing statement.

Was the case correctly decided?

2   In *In Re Brill Shirt Ltd.* (1979) 28 CBR (NS) 317 (OSC in Bkcy):

The security agreement was dated July 4, 1977, but the secured party's affidavit asserted that the agreement was not in fact signed by the debtor until on or about August 25, 1977. The evidence was that the secured party delivered the contract to the debtor for the debtor's execution on or about July 4, 1977, and that after repeated telephone calls the secured party was finally advised on or about August 25, 1977, that the contract had been signed by the debtor and could be picked up from its office. The financing statement was registered on September 2, 1977.

What should be the result? See s. 47(3).

3　*Re Pelee Motor Inn Ltd.* (1978) 83 DLR (3d) 757, 18 OR (2d) 700 (Ont. SC in Bkcy) concerned the relationship between ss. 47(3) and 22(3):

> A conditional sale agreement was signed by the bankrupt and the T. Eaton Company on December 21, 1976. A financing statement was filed on January 25, 1977. Shipment of the goods sold under the conditional sale agreement commenced on January 26, 1977. The effective date of bankruptcy was September 15, 1977.

How would you decide the case? *Cf.* ss. 34(2)(*a*); 34(3).

4　*West Bay Sales Ltd.* v. *Hitachi Sales Corp. of Canada Ltd.* (1979) 28 CBR (NS) 244 (Ont. SC in Bkcy) concerned the relationship between ss. 47(2) and 48(2):

> West Bay was the purchaser for resale of inventory obtained by it from Hitachi. These shipments were aparently governed by a general wholesale conditional sale agreement as well as individual agreements applicable to each shipment. Financeamerica Private Brands Limited (Financeamerica) acted as Hitachi's financing arm in these transactions and the benefit of *each* wholesale conditional sale agreement was assigned to Financeamerica as security for a continuing informal financing arrangement between them. On April 1, 1976, Financeamerica registered a financing statement showing itself as the secured party and West Bay as the debtor. Thereafter numerous shipments were made to West Bay by Hitachi under corresponding standard wholesale conditional sale agreements, each of which was assigned to Financeamerica. The latter registered no further financing statement.

Was Financeamerica obliged to file a separate financing statement in respect of each assignment?

5　In *Rogerson Lumber Co. Ltd.* v. *Four Seasons Chalet Ltd.* (1979) 1 PPSAC 29 (Ont. HCJ); aff'd (1981) 29 OR (2d) 193 (C.A.), lumber was delivered to the debtor between August 16, 1976, and September 9, 1976, pursuant to an oral conditional sales contract. The agreement was reduced to writing which was signed on September 8, 1976. Financing statement was registered on September 27, 1976. What was the effect of the registration?

RE JOHNSON
(1979) 98 DLR (3d) 187, 23 OR (2d) 717 (Ont. SC Bkcy)

STEELE J.: This is an appeal from the order of the Registrar wherein the Registrar dismissed an appeal brought by Rowe International of Canada Limited from the disallowance of its claim to certain property pursuant to s. 59 of the Bankruptcy Act, RSC 1970, c. B-3.

Rowe International of Canada Limited (hereinafter referred to as "Rowe") sold to Johnson certain goods under a security agreement within the meaning of the Personal Property Security Act, RSO 1970, c. 344. Rowe did not register the security agreement within the appropriate time period set out in the Act. Registration was effected on April 5, 1978. On June 16, 1978, Johnson made an assignment in bankruptcy. On July 31, 1978, Rowe obtained an order from a County Court Judge, under the provisions of s. 63 [am. 1973, c. 102, s. 12] of the Act, which order extended the time for registration of the security agreement on a *nunc pro tunc* basis to April 5, 1978. In other words, the order extended the time for registration to the actual date upon which registration had been made. The Registrar held that the provisions of s. 22(1)(*a*)(iii) of the Act created rights in favour of the trustee and that the order validating the registration could not detract from them.

On this appeal, it was argued that the effect of the County Court Judge's order, being *nunc pro tunc*, validated the registration prior to the date of bankruptcy and, therefore, at the time of bankruptcy, there was a perfected security interest in the goods in favour of Rowe. In his reasons the Registrar expressed certain views with respect to the effect of a *nunc pro tunc* order. I do not necessarily agree with those reasons. Neither do I wish to comment on the authority of a Judge to make an order *nunc pro tunc* under the provisions of s. 63 of the Act. For the purpose of this appeal I will assume that there is such authority.

I was referred to the decision of Macdonnell, J.A., in *Re Dainty Confections Ltd.* [1936] OWN 625 at p. 630, [1937] 1 DLR 249 at p. 257, 18 CBR 67, as follows:

> It is said that the defendant, in obtaining the order in question here, is improving his relative position among creditors after the intervention of bankruptcy, which is contrary to the scheme of The Bankruptcy Act: *Re General Fire Proofing Company of Canada, Limited* [1936] OR 510, at page 524. Distinction must be made, however, between the taking of some step that one has chosen not to take or has neglected to take and the mere curing of a technical defect in some step already taken. To allow such a defect as here to be rectified, in accordance with a statute passed expressly for the purpose, is not so much an improvement of the creditor's relative position as an assertion of what was his proper position at the date of the bankruptcy.
>
> Both from the point of view of natural justice and from that of technical application of the law there appears to be no reason why the mortgage in question should not be held to be a valid security for the defendant as against the trustee. Therefore, the appeal should be allowed; the defendant is entitled to his costs here and below from the trustee, which may recoup itself out of the estate.

It was urged upon me that this authority was binding and that I should follow it. I have reviewed the provisions of the Bills of Sale and Chattel Mortgages Act, RSO 1927, c. 164, as amended, applicable to that case, and compared them with the provisions of the Personal Property Security Act. There was no similar provision in the Bills of Sale and Chattel Mortages Act comparable to s. 22 of the Personal Property Security Act and, therefore, I am of the opinion that the decision in *Re Dainty Confections Ltd.* is not applicable to cases under the new Act. In the *Dainty Confections Ltd.* case it was stated that if the Legislature wished to protect trustees in bankruptcy it should say so. I believe that the Legislature has now said so.

I am of the opinion that s. 22 of the Act provides that an unperfected security interest is subordinate to the interest of a trustee in bankruptcy. By virtue of s-s.

(2) of s. 22 the rights of the trustee in bankruptcy with respect to the property that is subject to the security interest are effective on the date of the bankruptcy. These are clear and unambiguous words. In the present case it is clear that on the date of the bankruptcy the security interest was unperfected, and therefore the rights of the trustee are paramount to that of the holder of the security interest.

Section 63 of the Act gives wide powers to a Judge to make orders extending the time for registration, but the section is of general application and is not specific, whereas s. 22 is specific. I am of the opinion that s. 22 prevails over the general s. 63 and that the rights of the trustee in bankruptcy are determined as of the date of the bankruptcy and that no order made under s. 63 after the date of the bankruptcy can interfere with those rights.

Appeal dismissed.

Notes and Questions:

1 Was Steele J. justified in reserving his opinion with respect to whether a judge may make a *nunc pro tunc* order under s. 63?

2 As to the practical implications of the decision, it has been observed that ("The Quickening Pace of Jurisprudence . . ." (1979-80) 4 Can. Bus. LJ 54, 89):

> Steele, J.'s decision will come as an unpleasant surprise to many secured parties. Apparently, because of the delays encountered in some counties in obtaining a late filing order, the practice has developed of registering the financing statement in anticipation of the order being made, and being made retroactive to the date of actual filing. On a literal reading of s. 22, Steele, J., no doubt reached the right conclusion. The purported registration on April 5th was ineffectual in contemplation of law and before it was validated, assuming it could be validated, the trustee's interest had intervened. It may be argued, however, that the trustee and the creditors represented by him were not prejudiced since there *was* a financing statement of record that would have alerted them of the secured party's claim. In the absence of statutory clarification both positions can be argued persuasively. What *Re Johnson* proves once again is the hardship to secured parties of requiring them to obtain a formal order before they can make a late registration and the need to revise PPSA, s. 47(3) to permit registration at any time.

3 The draft Bill to amend the PPSA eliminates the time limits with respect to registration for the purpose of perfection. It is only with respect to consumer goods that "the financing statement . . . shall not be registered before the execution of the security agreement" (proposed new s. 47(2)). The draft bill also repeals s. 63(1). A proposed s. 58a would also provide that "the secured party who fails to register . . . a financing statement within the thirty-day period would be allowed as of right [without a court order] to register the financing statement after the thirty-day period but, as a consequence, would be required to share the proceeds of a disposition of the collateral with an unsecured creditor who advanced credit to the debtor after the thirty-day period and before registration" (letter of September 24, 1980, from the Ontario Minister of Consumer and Commercial Relations to all interested parties, accompanying the distribution of the draft bill). Would you recommend the adoption of these proposed amendments?

RE TRIAD FINANCIAL SERVICES AND THALER METAL INDUSTRIES LTD.
(1980) 98 DLR 555, 24 OR (2d) 423 (Ont. HC); aff'd 106 DLR (3d) 706, 27 OR (2d) 506 (CA)

SOUTHEY J.: This was an application to determine the priorities as between the parties to the proceeds of the sale of a piece of industrial machinery (the "machine") on which the applicant held a conditional sale agreement.

The machine was covered by a conditional sale agreement, dated July 14, 1975, between Gilbert C. Storey Machinery Limited, as vendor, and Thaler Metal Industries Ltd., as purchaser, securing an unpaid balance and finance charges in the total amount of $21,377.50. The conditional sale agreement was assigned to the applicant, Triad, and was duly registered under the Conditional Sales Act, RSO 1970, c. 76, on July 31, 1975. A financing statement was also registered on July 31, 1975, under the Personal Property Security Act, RSO 1970, c. 344, although most of the provisions of that statute had not come into force at that time.

Section 5 of the Conditional Sales Act, which was in force at the date of registration, provided that the conditional sale agreement would cease to be valid as against creditors of Thaler at the expiration of three years from the day of such registration, unless, within 30 days next preceding the date of such expiration, a renewal statement had been registered.

The main provisions of the Personal Property Security Act came into force on April 1, 1976, and the Conditional Sales Act was repealed on the same day [*Ont. Gaz.*, February 21, 1976]. The conditional sale agreement gave the applicant a security interest within the meaning of the new statute, and s. 65 [rep. & sub. 1973, c. 102, s. 13] of the Personal Property Security Act applied thereto.

[Section 65(1) is omitted.]

It is common ground that the unexpired portion of the filing or registration period arising out of the initial registration of the conditional sale agreement terminated on July 31, 1978.

By a debenture dated December 21, 1977, Thaler mortgaged all its equipment, including the machine, to the respondent bank. That debenture was filed under the Personal Property Security Act on December 23, 1977, and under the Corporation Securities Registration Act, RSO 1970, c. 88, on December 23, 1977. Thaler also entered into a general security agreement with the respondent bank on January 11, 1978, under which it charged in favour of and granted a security interest to the bank in all its property, including the machine. The general security agreement was filed under the Personal Property Security Act on January 13, 1978.

Section 52 [rep. & sub. *ibid.*, s. 9] of the Personal Property Security Act provides that where a security interest has been perfected by registration, the registration may be renewed before the expiration of the registration period, or, after the expiration of the registration period, by the registration of a financing statement. Triad failed to renew its registration of the security interest in the machine before July 31, 1978, the date of expiration of the original registration period, but did renew it by filing a financing statement under s. 52(*b*) of the Personal Property Security Act on September 19, 1978.

Meanwhile on August 1, 1978, and September 6, 1978, the bank advanced to Thaler a total of $10,000.

By notice dated November 2, 1978, purportedly given pursuant to s. 58(5) [rep. & sub. *ibid.*, s. 10] of the Personal Property Security Act, the bank gave notice to Thaler and to the applicant that it intended to dispose of the collateral secured by the general security agreement and the debenture, including the machine, unless such security was redeemed within 15 days by payment of $64,500 plus interest and expenses. On December 13, 1978, the applicant obtained an interim *ex parte* injunction restraining the bank from selling or disposing of the machine. That injunction was dissolved on consent as part of an interim settlement between the parties, under which the machine was sold, and $10,200, part of the proceeds of $15,425, was paid to the solicitor for the applicant to be held until the final determination of this application.

The question to be decided is whether the bank has priority under its security agreements in respect of the sums totalling $10,000 advanced between the time the registration of the applicant's conditional sale agreement expired on July 31, 1978, and the registration by the applicant on September 19, 1978, of a financing statement renewing the initial registration.

The following are the relevant provisions of the Personal Property Security Act dealing with renewals:

[Sections 52 and 53(1)(c) are omitted.]

The bulk of the indebtedness of Thaler to the bank resulted from advances made by the bank before August 1, 1978, or after September 19, 1978, at which times the applicant, it is conceded by the bank, had prior security under the conditional sale agreement and registrations relating thereto. The bank made no inquiries of Triad regarding the balance owing under the conditional sale agreement before making any advances to Thaler, and the main submission on behalf of the applicant is that the bank was not prejudiced by the late renewal, because it had made no such inquiries. I think the implication is that the bank was at all material times indifferent as to how much was owing by Thaler to the applicant on the conditional sale agreement, and therefore could not have been prejudiced by the late renewal.

It is also common ground that the bank would have found no record of the conditional sale agreement, if it had made a search of registrations under the Personal Property Security Act during the period August 1 to September 18, 1978. At the end of the day on July 31, 1978, the computer used in the administration of the Personal Property Security Act would have expunged from its record the registration of the financing statement pertaining to the conditional sale agreement. There is no suggestion by the bank, however, that it made such a search during that period.

The effect of s. 65(1) of the Personal Property Security Act, quoted above, was to continue the registration period under the statute until July 31, 1978. Under s. 53, the financing statement constituted notice of the security interest of Triad under the conditional sale agreement to all persons claiming any interest in the machine, and it constituted perfection of the security interest, but only until July

31, 1978. The bank also had a perfected security interest in the machine on July 31, 1978, under its debenture and general security agreement.

On August 1, 1978, the security interest of the applicant under the conditional sale agreement became unperfected, and remained unperfected until September 18, 1978. The bank's security interest in the machine, however, remained perfected during that period, with the result under s. 22 of the Act, that the applicant's security interest was subordinate to that of the bank during that period. While the applicant's interest was thus subordinated, the bank advanced the further $10,000 and became secured for that additional amount.

When the applicant registered a financial statement on September 19, 1978, under s. 52(b), renewing the registration of the security interest under the conditional sale agreement, the effect of the initial registration was extended during the period of three years following registration on September 19, 1978. It may be, as counsel for the applicant contended, that this resulted in an unbroken period of perfection. It certainly restored the applicant's security interest to a position of priority over the bank's security interest in respect of any indebtedness arising before August 1st, because the bank's rights in respect of that portion of the indebtedness were not due to an act or thing done by the bank during the period August 1 to September 19, 1978. But the bank's priority rights as to the $10,000 were acquired by the acts of the bank in advancing further money to Thaler during the period in which the applicant's security interest was unperfected. The subordination of the bank's security rights in respect of the $10,000 by the registration of the financing statement on September 19, 1978, would obviously prejudice those rights. That being so, the effect of s. 53(1)(c) is that the registration of such financing statement is presumed not to have occurred in considering whether the bank obtained such priority rights. If the Court presumes that such registration did not occur, the result, in my judgment, is that the applicant's security interest remains subordinate to that of the bank to the extent of the $10,000.

There is nothing in the Act to suggest that priorities are dependent upon conscious reliance upon the register. It is immaterial to the existence of its priority rights that the bank may not have known it was acquiring them, at the time the advances of $10,000 were made. The fallacy in the applicant's main submission, in my view, is that it is factually incorrect to say that the bank would not be prejudiced by losing its priority rights, simply because it may have been unaware at the time of the advances that it had acquired such rights.

I can see no merit in the two minor points raised by the applicant. It makes no difference, in my view, whether the receiver who took possession of the machine and arranged for its sale was acting as agent for Thaler or for the bank. In either case, the receiver was acting as a stakeholder and was obliged to distribute any proceeds in accordance with the priorities determined by law. There is no reason why the notice to be given under s. 58(5) of the Personal Property Security Act cannot be signed on behalf of the secured party by the solicitor for the secured party. In fact, there does not appear to be any requirement that the notice be signed.

Nor do I think there is any merit in the objection raised by counsel for the respondent to the form of the financing statements registered by the applicant. It is unnecessary for me to deal with the point, however, as the respondent bank did not challenge the priority of the applicant's security interest in the machine for all indebtedness other than the $10,000.

There will be an order declaring the security interest of the applicant in the machine to be subordinate to the security interest of the respondent bank therein to the extent of $10,000 advanced by the bank on August 1, 1978, and September 6, 1978, with interest.

Order accordingly.

Notes and Questions:

1   Does s. 53(1)(c) mean that the deemed period of registration is extended retroactively to the date of expiration of the original registration? Note that the provision has no counterpart in the Code.

2   Did Triad's late renewal prejudice the bank's rights by virtue of "an act or thing done by" the bank in the interim? Consider the following excerpt from "The Quickening Pace of Jurisprudence . . ." (1979-80) 4 Can. Bus. LJ 54, 86-87:

> Section 22(1)(a)(i) provides that an unperfected security interest is subordinate to the interest of a person "who is entitled to a priority under this or any other Act". Section 35 was the applicable priority rule in the present case and, since both Triad and the bank had perfected their security interests by registration, the priority between them would be determined by the order of registration. PPSA, s. 35(1)(a) makes no reference to the dates when advances are made and they have no relevance in determining the parties' priorities. That being so, how could it be said that Triad's late renewal prejudiced the bank's rights by virtue of "*an act or thing done by*" the bank during the period when Triad's security interest was unperfected? The bank's rights were prejudiced but not by virtue of its advances. They were prejudiced because the retroactive perfection would deprive it of the priority it acquired upon lapse of the original registration and the operation of PPSA, s. 35(1)(a). However, this type of prejudice is not covered by the language of PPSA, s. 53(1)(c).
>
> Nevertheless, one can sympathize with the perhaps unintended gloss placed upon the statutory language by Southey, J. If the collateral had been sold to a buyer or seized by a creditor during the unperfected period, their rights would no doubt have been protected because they arose out of "an act or thing done by" them (the purchase in the one case and the seizure in the other); it seems anomalous that the bank's position should be less favourable because its priority had been acquired by reason of a thing or act — the filing of its financing statement — that occurred before the period of unperfection.

3   How should s. 53(1)(c) be amended? Would you recommend the test of s. 63 ("no interest" of any other person ought to be prejudiced)? "The alternative would be to restructure PPSA, s. 53(1)(c), so that a competing security interest would only be protected to the extent of any advances made or other value given during the period of unperfection": *id.* at 87. Is this a sound solution?

4   The basic policy behind s. 53(1)(c) is of doubtful value. According to Professor Ziegel at 87-88:

Not only does [s. 53(1)(c)] create serious problems of draftsmanship but it also creates circular priorities as may be seen from the following example. On June 1st, SP1 and SP2 each has a security interest in the same collateral which has been perfected by filing. SP1 has filed first and therefore enjoys priority. SP1's registration lapses on July 1st for failure to file a renewal statement. During the period of unperfection SP3, a new financer, files a financing statement and makes an advance. On September 1st, SP1 files a renewal statement. On October 1st, SP2 makes a further advance to the debtor. None of the security interests is a purchase-money security interest.

Discuss the priorities among the competing parties.

5   What was the basis of the bank's rights in *Triad*? The security agreement? The debenture? Consider also the following comment:

> Apparently the question was not raised whether they could coexist satisfactorily, whether the later instrument superseded the earlier, or whether at some point the bank was put to its election. The bank served a sale notice under PPSA, s. 58(5) so presumably it had elected to exercise its rights under the general security agreement. But did this also prove that the advances on August 1st and September 6th were made under the general security agreement? If they were not, the notice of sale would not help the bank nor, for the reasons given earlier, would PPSA, s. 22(1)(a)(i).

6   For more on the effect of a lapsed registration, see L.J. Lysaght and R.L. Simmonds, "The Lapsed Registration Problem Under the Ontario Personal Property Security Act" (1979-80), 4 Can. Bus. LJ 442. The authors support the position of the 1972 Code, which provides in UCC 9-403(2) that on the lapse of registration the security interest also becomes unperfected as against competing interests created before the lapse. For the position of the draft Bill to amend the Ontario PPSA, see s. 17 of the draft Bill reenacting ss. 52 and 53 of the Act. Existing s. 53(1)(c) would be repealed. Proposed s. 52a would provide as follows:

> 52a.(1) Where a security interest has been perfected by registration for a three-year period, the registration may be renewed before the expiration of the registration period by the registration of a financing change statement in the prescribed form.
>
> (2) Where a security interest has been perfected by registration for a three-year period and the registration has expired, the security interest may thereafter be perfected by the registration of a financing statement in the prescribed form.

As to a competing security interest created before lapse of registration, does proposed s. 52a(2) have the same effect as UCC 9-403(2)?

F.   RELATIVE PRIORITIES OF PPSA AND NON-PPSA SECURITY INTERESTS

1.   REGULATION UNDER FEDERAL LAWS

Some federal statutes authorize the taking of security but leave the determination of its form and all other matters to provincial law. Others purport to regulate all aspects of the secured transaction. For a detailed classification accompanied by enumeration of statutes, see J. Ziegel and I. Feltham, "Federal Law and a Uniform Act on Security in Personal Property" (1966) 9 Can. Bar J. 30. The most important of the latter type of provision is s. 178 of the Bank Act, Part I of Banks and Banking Law Revision Act, SC 1980, c. 40 (previously s. 88 of the Bank Act, RSC 1970, c. B-1), which deals with loans to (a) merchants dealing with agricultural products, products of the forest, of the mine, or of the sea; (b) manufacturers; (c) farmers; and (d) fishermen. For example, the provision enables a bank to lend money to a manufacturer "on the security of goods, wares and merchandise manufactured or produced by him or procured for such manufacture or production". The security under s. 178 is created by the delivery to the bank of a document giving the security. Where "the person giving security is the owner . . .", the document vests in the bank in respect of the property the same rights and powers as if the bank has acquired a warehouse receipt of bill of lading in which such property was described" (s. 178(2)).

The Bank Act does not regulate the relative priorities between a s. 178 interest and security interests created under provincial law. An exception is s. 179(1) (previously s. 89(1)) providing that an unpaid vendor's lien has priority over the bank unless the bank acquired its interest without knowledge of the lien. *Query:* whether " 'lien' . . . includes a conditional sale agreement or other consensual purchase-money security interest, and to what extent a bank is deemed to have notice of a registered 'lien' ": (1980) 4 Can. Bus. LJ 54, 63. See also s. 178(4)(*a*) (previously s. 88(4)(*a*)), which provides that unless the prescribed notice is registered "in the appropriate agency not more than three years immediately before the security was given", a s. 178 interest is "void as against creditors of the person giving the security and as against subsequent purchasers or mortgagees in good faith of the property covered by the security".

Rogerson Lumber Co. Ltd. v. *Four Seasons Chalet Ltd.* (1979) 1 PPSAC 29 (Ont. HC); aff'd (1981) 29 OR (2d) 193 (CA) was concerned with a contest between a conditional seller of lumber who registered a PPSA financing statement more than 10 days after delivery of the lumber and a bank holding a s. 88 security interest given (and properly registered) prior to the conditional sale agreement. O'Leary J. held in favour of the conditional seller (at 33-4):

> Because of the agreement between [the conditional seller] and [the debtor], benefi-cial ownership in the lumber had not . . . passed to [the debtor]. Since beneficial ownership rested in [the conditional seller], [the debtor] did not, and could not, give security to the bank in regard to that particular lumber. [The debtor] was never the beneficial owner of the lumber in question and did not therefore assign any interest in the lumber to the bank, and the bank had no right to seize it.

Do you agree with this analysis? Do PPSA ss. 9, 22(1)(*a*)(i) and (ii) throw any light on the issue? What would be the effect of a timely PPSA registration? Is either PPSA s. 68 or the doctrine of "federal paramountcy" relevant?

A majority of the Ontario Court of Appeal affirmed the trial judge's decision. Arnup J.A., while avoiding the issue of whether a conditional purchaser is an "owner" within the meaning of s. 88 of the Bank Act, stated that "[i]f a conditional purchaser has paid nothing on account of the purchase price — which is the fact here — then the dollar value of the purchaser's interest is nil." The conditional purchaser could thus give nothing to the bank. "No provision of the PPSA subordinates the interest of [the conditional seller] to that of the bank." In his concurring opinion, Houlden J.A. added that "vendor" in (old) s. 89(1) of the Bank Act (presently s. 179(1)) does not include a conditional seller. He gave no reasons for this conclusion.

Wilson J.A. dissented. She could not "accept that prior to payment [the conditional purchaser] had no rights in the lumber. . . . [I]f this were so, . . . it would be unrealistic to describe [the conditional seller] as the holder of a 'security interest' under the PPSA. [He] would simply be an absolute owner of the lumber." She then concluded that "[t]he Bank . . . has priority by virtue of the Bank Act and nothing in the PPSA can take that away."

2. Registration Under CSRA — RSO 1970, c. 88

As previously noted (chapter 20(C)), the PPSA does not apply "to a mortgage, charge or assignment whose registration is provided for in the Corporation Securities Registration Act": PPSA s. 3(1)(c). Such mortgage, charge or assignment, unless registered under the CSRA, is "void as against creditors of the mortgagor or assignor, and as against subsequent purchasers or mortgagees from or under the mortgagor or assignor, in good faith, for valuable consideration and without notice": CSRA s. 2(1). Potential priority contests between a PPSA interest and a CSRA interest are illustrated by the following examples:

(b) On day 1, S sells goods to B on a conditional sale basis but fails to perfect his security interest under the PPSA. On day 10, B gives a corporate debenture to C secured by a fixed and floating charge. The debenture is properly registered. Does C have priority over S's unperfected security interest? PPSA, s. 22(1)(a)(i) provides that an unperfected security interest is subordinated to the interest of a person "(i) who is entitled to a priority under this or any other Act". The PPSA does not confer priority on the corporate debenture. Nor does the CSRA establish the order of priorities. The CSRA only deals with the effect of an *unregistered* corporate security. Consequently the unperfected seller's security interest will prevail over the interest of the subsequent debenture, a result that offends the clear policy of the PPSA. Nevertheless, it could only be avoided by much pounding and twisting of the language of ss. 3(1)(c) and 22(1)(a) of the Act.

(c) On August 1st, Corporation A grants a secured debenture to B. The debenture includes after-acquired property. On September 10th, A grants C a PPSA security interest on A's existing and future inventory. Both security interests are properly perfected under their respective Acts. On October 1st, A acquires some new inventory. Which of the two, B or C, has priority with respect to the new inventory? B is only deemed to have an equitable interest which can be cut off by the *bona fide* purchaser of the legal interest. Assume C was unaware of B's prior charge or that a doctrine of constructive notice does not apply to registrations under the CSRA. The question nevertheless remains whether C is "a purchaser" of the legal interest in the inventory. The PPSA does not distinguish between legal and equitable interests in collateral. The Act creates a statutory form of security interest which is governed by its own priority rules. Will it be characterized as a legal interest in order to cut off B's prior charge or will a court apply the pre-PPSA rules of characterization? The most sensible solution would be for a court to say that a registration system impliedly repeals the distinction between equitable and legal interests for purposes of priority, but existing precedents foreclose this simple route.

3.   Lien Given By Statute or Rule of Law

In general, ``a lien given by statute or rule of law'' is not governed by the PPSA (s. 3(1)(a)). Statutory or common law liens may, however, be relevant in priority contests (cf. s. 22(1)(a)(i)).

(a) Apart from s. 22(1)(a)(i), the only provision in the PPSA which governs a priority contest between a security interest and a statutory or common law lien is s. 32, giving priority over a perfected security interest in goods to a possessory lien for materials and services furnished in the ordinary course of business. The opinion of F. Catzman et al., *Personal Property Security Law in Ontario* (1976) p. 153 is that:

> Such lien has priority over a perfected security interest, irrespective of the date of perfection, unless the lien is created by statute and the statute excludes such priority. At least this is the logical intention of the section, but in the course of revision by the Ontario Law Reform Commission it acquired a rather confused wording.

Can you see why? Read s. 32 and compare its language to UCC 9-310.

The lien for material and services (artisan's or mechanic's lien) is of common law origin. Its priority is frequently explained on the ground that the work enhances or preserves the value of the collateral or on the ground that the work was done with the express or implied consent of the secured creditor. See further R.M. Goode and J.S. Ziegel, *Hire-Purchase and Conditional Sale* (1965) pp. 180-83. At common law such lien is possessory; with some exceptions it exists only so long as the claimant is in continuous possession of the goods. Furthermore, the lien does not confer upon the claimant the right to sell the chattel and apply the proceeds in satisfaction of the debt.

The Mechanics' Lien Act, RSO 1970, c. 267 provides in s. 48(1) that every person

> who has bestowed money, skill or materials upon any chattel or thing in the alteration or improvement of its properties or for the purpose of imparting an additional value to it, so as thereby to be entitled to a lien upon the chattel has while the lien exists . . . the right . . . to sell by auction the chattel . . . [and apply the proceed to the debt] . . .

Is such a lien entitled to priority over a perfected security interest? Is the answer affected by the common law origin of the lien? By its possible inclusion in the terms of the contract between the repairman and the owner of the chattel? Cf. *Jones v. Davidson*, (1981) 31 OR (2d) 494 (HC). In *Royal A. Vaillancourt Co. Ltd. v. Trans Canada Credit Corp. Ltd.* [1963] 1 OR 411 (Ont. CA) the court stated (at 414):

> The existence of . . . a right to lien in favour of the artisan is recognized by s. 48 of the Mechanics' Lien Act. . . . This section, although it does not attempt to create or confer a lien on personal property, does give to the lienholder, in addition to any other remedy to which he may be entitled, the right of selling, upon compliance with the conditions set out in the section, the personal property to which the lien attaches.

(b) Another lien of common law origin is the landlord's lien for unpaid rent on the goods of the tenant located on his premises. This lien is enforced by the landlord's right to distrain on the goods. It is excluded in Ontario from residential tenancies under s. 86 of the Landlord and Tenant Act, RSO 1970, c. 236. Section 31(2) of the Landlord and Tenant Act provides:

> A landlord shall not distrain for rent on the goods and chattels of any person except the tenant or person who is liable for the rent, although the same are found on the premises; but this restriction does not apply in favour of a person claiming title under an execution against the tenant, or in favour of a person whose title is derived by purchase, gift, transfer, or assignment from the tenant, whether absolute or in trust, or by way of mortgage, or otherwise, nor to the interest of the tenant in any goods or chattels on the premises in the possession of the tenant under a contract for purchase, or by which he may or is to become the owner thereof upon performance of any condition. . . .

Does the landlord's priority under this provision depend on the security interest being unperfected? Cf. *J.R. Auto Brokers Ltd.* v. *Hillcrest Auto Lease Ltd.* [1968] 2 OR 532 (Ont. HC) (a pre-PPSA case). Has the provision survived the enactment of the PPSA? Consider PPSA ss. 2(a)(i), 34(2)(3), and 68. Is a priority contest between a secured party and a landlord governed by PPSA s. 9? Section 22(1)(a)(i)? How could a secured party avoid a contest with his debtor's landlord?

Cf. *Universal C.I.T. Credit Corp.* v. *Congressional Motors, Inc.* (1967) 228 A. 2d 463 (Md. CA). The case held that a statute excluding goods subject to a conditional sale or PMSI chattel mortgage from the Landlord's right of distress was not repealed by UCC 10-102(1) explicitly repealing statutes inconsistent with the Code. The court stated (at 470) that

> the flat and unqualified exclusion of landlord's liens from the application of [Article 9] left the law on such liens as it was. The exclusion was not limited to ruling landlord's liens out as a code security interest or to freeing them from procedural requirements. . . . [I]t provided in effect that no part, including rules as to priorities, of [Article 9] controlled or governed them. This left their status and priority vis-a-vis those of security interests to the existing law.

"The priority in favor of the landlord's lien decreed by that case was explicitly removed by a subsequent . . . statute": V. Countryman and A. Kaufman, *Commercial Law: Cases and Materials* (1971) p. 257.

(c) There are many more statutory liens (see e.g. chapter 20 (C) *supra*). Some provisions confer priority upon a lienor either by creating a trust or giving him a first charge on assets. Many of these liens are government liens. Two such provisions, one in favour of an employee and the other in favour of the Ontario government, are discussed below. The discussion is followed by a case demonstrating the importance of the "trust" or "charge" language in such a provision.

(i) Section 15 of the Employment Standards Act, 1974, SO 1974, c. 112 (as amended SO 1978, c. 2, s. 77) provides as follows:

> Every employer shall be deemed to hold vacation pay accruing due to an employee in trust for the employee whether or not the amount therefor has in fact been kept separate and apart by the employer and the vacation pay becomes a lien and charge upon the assets of the employer that in the ordinary course of business would be entered in books of account whether so entered or not.

The validity in bankruptcy of a claim under the predecessor of this section was recognized in *Re Dairy Maid Chocolates Ltd.* [1973] 1 OR 603, 31 DLR (3d) 699 (SC in Bkcy). The court held "that the trust is enforceable only in respect of *assets of the employer* that were in existence at the date of the termination of the employment . . . [and] that the charge is created on the assets of the employer in the hands of the employer . . ." (*id.* at 702, emphasis in the original). Will a PPSA security interest be subordinate to the trust and charge provided for by this provision? Are PPSA ss. 9, 22(1)(a)(i) or 68 of any help? What about s. 12(1)(c)? *Cf. Canadian Imperial Bank of Commerce* v. *Brooker Trade Bindery Ltd.* (1975) 20 CBR (NS) 280, 282 (Ont. SC Taxing Office) where the lien prevailed over a secured debenture holder because the "trust fund was . . . in existence prior to the execution of the debenture . . .". The report does not disclose whether the debenture had been registered (in any event, recall PPSA s. 3(1)(a)). *Cf.* also *Re Campeau Corp. and Provincial Bank of Canada* (1975) 7 OR (2d) 73, 20 CBR (NS) 99 (HCJ) dealing with another provision of the Employment Standards Act, presently s. 14, providing that "wages shall have priority to the claims or rights . . . of all preferred ordinary or general creditors of the employer. . . ."

(ii) Section 18 of the Retail Sales Tax Act, RSO 1970, c. 415 (as amended SO 1975, c. 9, s. 7; SO 1977, c. 13, s. 6; SO 1979, c. 27, s. 6) provides as follows:

> **18.**(1) Every vendor who collects any tax under this Act shall be deemed to hold it in trust for Her Majesty in right of Ontario and is responsible for the payment over of it.
>
> (2) Where, by the order of a court or otherwise, any property of a vendor is lawfully taken from his control or possession for the purpose of . . . sale by a secured creditor . . . an amount equal to the amount of tax that was collected by the vendor and that by subsection 1 is deemed to be held in trust for Her Majesty in right of Ontario, shall, to the extent of the amount of tax that was collected by the vendor in the year immediately preceding the date when the vendor lost control or possession of his property and was not remitted to the Treasurer as required by subsection 1, be deemed to be separate from, and to form no part of, the estate or property in liquidation, whether or not that amount has in fact been kept separate and apart from the vendor's own property and in trust in accordance with subsection 1 and the amount deemed by this subsection to be separate from, and to form no part of the estate or property in liquidation, shall be paid out of cash and the proceeds of the realization of the vendor's property and the said claim shall be paid in priority to all other claims except those described by subsection 4 to be claims to which this subsection is not applicable.
>
> . . .
>
> (4) Subsection 2 does not apply to claims made against the specific property of a vendor under fixed charges, mortgages and assignments where the specific property is identified by description in the agreements pursuant to which the security was given and does not apply to claims made against accounts receivable of the vendor that were assigned or mortgaged for value under a general assignment of book debts or security agreement registered under The Personal Property Security Act where the assignee or mortgagee has given notice to the vendor's debtor of his assignment or interest and legal entitlement to the debts in question and has directed the vendor's debtor to pay the debt to it or where the assignee or mortgagee is in actual

receipt of the proceeds of the debts prior to the date when the vendor lost control or possession of his property.

(5) The amount deemed by subsection 2 to be separate from, and to form no part, of the estate or property in liquidation shall be paid in priority to claims against all property of the vendor acquired after the date when the vendor gave a fixed charge, mortgage or assignment of specific property and which property by the terms of the fixed charge, mortgage or assignment is to be included in the said security once acquired by the vendor and claims against all property of the vendor secured under a floating instrument purporting to charge the property of the vendor in existence at the date when the security instrument was given as well as property of the vendor acquired after that date.

As between a PPSA security interest and the Crown, who prevails?

RHYNO v. FIREMAN'S FUND INSURANCE CO. OF CANADA
(1980) 110 DLR 362 (NS SC)

HALLETT J.: The issue to be determined in this Chambers application is the priority as between the Canadian Imperial Bank of Commerce (the Bank), an equitable assignee of the future proceeds of a lawsuit brought by the plaintiff against the defendant, and the Provincial Tax Commission (the Commission), which made a statutory demand under s. 27(1) of the Health Services Tax Act, RSNS 1967, c. 126, as amended, upon the defendant subsequent in time to the assignment to the Bank but before the Bank gave notice of its assignment to the defendant. . . .

Critical to the determination of the issue is the interpretation of s. 27 of the Health Services Tax Act which I quote as follows:

27.(1) Where the Commissioner has knowledge that any person is or is about to become indebted to a taxpayer or collector who has not paid or remitted the tax payable under this Act, he may demand of that person that the money otherwise payable by him to the taxpayer or collector be in whole or in part paid to the Minister on account of the taxpayer's or collector's liability under this Act.

(2) The receipt of the Commissioner for money so paid shall constitute a good and sufficient discharge of the liability of such person to the taxpayer or collector to the extent of the amount referred to in the receipt.

(3) Any person discharging any liability to a taxpayer or collector after receipt of a demand under this Section shall be personally liable to Her Majesty in the right of the Province to the extent of the liability discharged, as between him and the taxpayer or collector, or to the extent of the liability of the taxpayer or collector for the taxes due and payable under this Act or that have been collected on behalf of Her Majesty in the right of the Province, but not remitted, including interest and penalties whichever is the lesser amount.

The answer to the issue turns on whether the Commission, pursuant to s. 27 of the Health Services Tax Act, had an equitable interest in the fund. In my opinion, there is nothing in the wording of s. 27 that can be interpreted as creating for the Commission an equitable interest in the fund in the defendant's hands. The Legislature empowered the Commissioner to make a demand on a person indebted or about to become indebted to the defaulting taxpayer that money otherwise payable to the taxpayer (in this case the plaintiff) be paid to the Minister on account of the taxpayer's liability under the Health Services Tax Act.

If the taxpayer's creditor pays the Minister pursuant to the demand, the Commissioner may give receipt for the money so paid, which shall discharge the creditor's liability to the taxpayer. . . .

The demand referred to in s. 27 of the Health Services Tax Act is nothing more than that, a demand to pay; certain consequences flow from the compliance or non-compliance by the taxpayer's debtor but the words do nothing more. The words used in s. 27 do not create an equitable interest as there is no proprietary right in the indebtedness created in the traditional sense; a proprietary right to the fund is essential to obtaining an equitable interest. It is reasonable to infer that had the Legislature intended to give the Commission a proprietary right to such a fund, appropriate language would have been used. To hold that the words used in s. 27 create an equitable interest, is to read into the words a meaning that is neither expressed nor implied. The words used in s. 27 simply do not import an attachment, an encumbrance, or a transfer of or a charge against the fund in the hands of the taxpayer's debtor.

As a consequence, I find that s. 27 of the Health Services Tax Act does not create in favour of the Commission an equitable interest in the fund in the defendant's hands. The plaintiff had assigned the future proceeds of the lawsuit to the Bank prior to the demand by the Commission. Therefore, the Bank, pursuant to the assignment made on January 19, 1978, is entitled to an equitable interest in the fund in the hands of the defendant and therefore entitled to the fund . . .

4. SECURITY INTERESTS IN FIXTURES

a) Defifinition of a Fixture under the PPSA

PPSA s. 36 uses "fixtures" to mean property which, on the one hand, is so closely associated with real estate that it is normally owned and conveyed with the real estate, and which, on the other hand, is so akin to personal property that it may be owned separately if there is an agreement or public notice to that effect. Thus, for the purposes of PPSA s. 36, fixtures constitute an intermediate category between straight personal property and straight real estate.

For a chattel to become a fixture within the meaning of PPSA s. 36, there must be some substantial affixation, ordinarily more substantial than a simple electric cord or a garden hose connection, together with the retention of its identity as a separate and severable chattel. Goods which are incorporated into a structure so as to lose their identity (e.g., bricks and mortar) and which consequently cannot be reclaimed as against the owner of the realty are not fixtures. They are rather part of the real estate. At the same time, goods do not become part of the real estate merely because their removal would cause economic loss to the holder of the interest in the land; cf. s. 36(4). In general on the definition of a fixture (for the purposes of Article 9), see P.F. Coogan, "Security Interests in Fixtures Under the Uniform Commercial Code" (1962) 75 Harv. L. Rev. 1319.

As for the meaning of fixtures in Canadian common law, which is not the same as for the purposes of PPSA s. 36, see *Falconbridge On Mortgages* (4th ed., 1977) §2.4.

Could parties to a conditional sale contract agree that "[t]he equipment [subject-matter of the sale] shall remain personal property regardless of any affixation to the realty and title thereto shall not pass to buyer until the . . . balance has been fully paid in cash"? An affirmative answer was given in *Cain* v. *Country Club Delicatessen of Saybrook Inc.* (1964) 203 A. 2d 441, 446 (Conn. SC) (reproduced in Section (C) *supra*): "The parties to the contract were competent to make such an agreement which was binding as between them, even though any such equipment were to be permanently affixed to the realty." Could such an agreement bind or benefit a third party (such as a competing secured party relying on an after-acquired property clause in his security agreement as was First Hartford in *Cain*, or a mortgagee of the land)?

b) The Priority Scheme

R.M. GOODE AND J.S. ZIEGEL
Hire Purchase and Conditional Sale: A Comparative Survey
(1965) p. 173

The general rule of the common law is that . . . if the . . . buyer under a conditional sale agreement affixes the goods to land in such a way that they become fixtures, the owner's or seller's right to remove the goods may be defeated by the claims of prior or subsequent mortgagees or purchasers of the land to which the goods are affixed, or by the owner or landlord of the premises at the time of affixation. It is true that the general rule is subject to a number of exceptions of varying importance which may mitigate its harshness in particular cases, but the operation of these exceptions is necessarily haphazard and still exposes the secured creditor of the goods to greater risks than he is willing or ought to be expected to incur.

Fortunately the conflicting claims of the several parties are not difficult to reconcile. There is no reason why an existing owner or mortgagee of land shoulld be enriched at the instalment seller's expense by the addition of goods for which he neither bargained nor paid, and his claims should therefore be subordinated to those of the seller. Subsequent purchasers and mortgagees of the land, however, are in a different position. They may be misled by the presence of the fixtures on the premises and should be in a position to ascertain simply whether or not they arersubject to a conditional sale or hire-purchase agreement. To require them to search in the ordinary registries for incumbrances against chattels would be unduly burdensome. The correct solution lies therefore in obliging the owner or seller to register his security interest in the goods in the Land Registry Office in which the land to which the goods are liable to be affixed is itself registered. In this way prospective purchasers and mortgagees of real estate interests will be given all the notice for which they may reasonably ask.

Legislation along these lines was introduced in Canada[27] . . . from an early

---

[27] See Stat. Ont. 1897 (60 Vict. c. 14), s. 80; . . . Most of the other provinces adopted similar legislation over the next 20 years, and it was these provisions which provided the precedent for the Uniform Conditional Sales Act, s. 12.

date onwards . . . [t]he object of [this] legislation . . . appears to be to reverse the common law rule with regard to fixtures, at least in part. . . . The Canadian Revised Uniform Conditional Sales Act provides that ". . . where possession of goods is delivered to the buyer and the goods are affixed to land, they remain subject to the rights of the seller as fully as they were before being affixed." To come within this provision, however, the seller must comply with certain conditions, and in any event "building materials" and other fixtures which cannot be removed without "substantial" injury to the premises are excluded from it. The condition which must be satisfied is that a copy of the conditional sale agreement, together with a description of the land to which the goods are to be affixed, is filed in the land registry office in which the land is registered as well as in the registry where the conditional sale agreement would normally require to be registered. The Act also provides that before the seller may take any steps to remove the goods from the premises he must notify every person with an interest in the land of his intention to do so, and such persons thereupon have a right to retain the goods upon paying off the balance due to the seller.

The provisions in the [1962] Uniform Commercial Code are similar to the Canadian ones, but differ from them in one important respect. UCC 9-313(5) provides that a secured party may remove his collateral from the real estate whether or not the removal causes any material injury to the land, but that he must reimburse any owner or incumbrancer of the real estate who is not the debtor for the cost of repair of any physical injury done to the real estate. Moreover, such persons may refuse permission to remove the fixture until the secured party gives adequate security for the performance of this obligation. However, they are not entitled to be compensated for any diminution in value of the real estate caused by the absence of the goods or by any necessity for replacing them. This seems a more satisfactory way of dealing with the question of injury to the land than is to be found in the Canadian statutes.

Note: The 1962 Code provisions differ from the pre-PPSA Canadian provisions in another respect. While the latter reverse the common law fixtures rules only with respect to conditional sellers, the former deal with secured parties in general. They thus reverse the common law fixtures rules also with respect to chattel mortgages.

The Ontario PPSA fixture priority scheme is modelled on the 1962 Code provisions. It does not take into account the extensive 1972 Code revisions, discussed by P.F. Coogan in "The New UCC Article 9" (1973) 86 Harv. L. Rev. 477, 483. The following is a summary of the fixtures treatment under the Ontario Act:

A security interest in goods remains effective notwithstanding that the goods have become a fixture. Note, however, the special land description requirements in s. 10(*b*) as a condition of the enforceability of a security interest in fixtures "by or against a third party". What practical problems could this raise?

Priority contests between an interest in goods which are fixtures and an interest in the real property are governed by s. 36. Section 36(1) deals with a security interest which attaches to goods before they become fixtures (pre-affixation interest). Section 36(2) governs security interests attaching after affixation (post-affixation interests). The priority given under s. 36(1) and (2) is defeated under s. 36(3) by the described subsequent parties "without actual notice of the security interest". Note the effect of filing a PPSA s. 54 notice. Is it different from perfection by registration? Do you need to register a PPSA financing statement in order to protect your interest in a fixture against a competing real property interest? Against a competing interest under an after-acquired property clause in another PPSA security agreement?

In dealing with the meaning of "subsequent" in s. 36(3), note the observation of Coogan with respect to the corresponding UCC section. His view is that "it would seem best to read 'subsequent' as subsequent to attachment and affixation": *id.* at 1328 and n. 18. Also s. 36(3)(c) should not be read to give priority to "a prior encumbrance of record on the real property" as against a post-affixation interest with respect to advances made *after* "actual notice of the security interest". *Cf. id.* at 1329 and n. 21. In other words, "made or contracted for" in s. 36(3)(c) does not refer to an option or to two stages in the life of the same advance. Rather, the expression refers to two separate situations. "Made" refers to an advance not made pursuant to prior commitment. "Contracted for" refers to an advance contracted for unconditionally. What subordinates the competing security interest is then the conceptual change of position of the person making the advance (whether by making the advance of unconditionally contracting to make it as the case may be) "without actual notice of the security interest".

Under this interpretation of s. 36(3)(c), what is the position of a realty mortgage lender with respect to a building in course of construction where the advances under the loan agreement are geared to progress on the building? Will he be deemed to have contracted to make the advances or must he search in the land registry office before making each advance? Should the PPSA require the holder of the fixture interest to give such lender personal notice of his intention to finance the builder in the same way that a subsequent inventory financer is required to give personal notice to a prior inventory financer under s. 34(2)(b)?

In addition to his land mortgage, would you advise a construction financer to take a PPSA security interest in after-acquired property? Will it give him better protection with respect to goods subsequently affixed to the construction?

The right of a secured party who has priority under s. 36 to remove the collateral is provided for in s. 36(4). Note the duty to compensate the real property interest holder in respect of any physical injury to the land. Under s. 36(5) a subordinate owner of the realty may retain the collateral upon paying off the secured party.

Problems:

1 Smith operates a car washing service on a piece of land owned by him. The land is mortgaged to the Mortgage Company, which duly registered its mortgage. In order to become more competitive, Smith contracted with Manufacturers Inc. for the installation of new equipment. To finance the purchase Smith obtained a loan from the Toronto Bank and signed a security agreement giving the bank a security interest in the new machines. The security agreement was signed two days prior to the complete installation of the new equipment. The Bank registered three days after the equipment had been installed. Manufacturers Inc. received full payment from Smith on the same day. One day after the completion of the installation, a

judgment creditor of Smith levied execution on Smith's new equipment. On the same day, Smith borrowed $15,000 from Nuh Realtors, which immediately registered a real estate mortgage against Smith's land. On Smith's default, who has priority as to the new equipment?

2   The following were the facts of *Montreal Trust Co.* v. *Goldaire Rentals Ltd.* (1967) 1 OR 40, 59 DLR (2d) 338 (as summarized by H.J. Glasbeek (1968) 46 Can. B. Rev. 105), a pre-PPSA decision of the Ontario High Court:

>   (i) Goldaire Rentals Ltd. (the defendant) wished to erect an office building in London, Ontario. Accordingly the defendant first entered into a contract with Otis Elevator Company Limited whereby the latter undertook to supply an elevator for the building. Otis was to retain property in its elevator until all purchase and erection monies had been paid by instalments. This contract was not registered.
>
>   (ii) To finance the undertaking, Goldaire obtain a mortgage from Montreal Trust Co. which was registered promptly. Money was lent then and there and further advances were to be made periodically. Some such advances were made. Then,
>
>   (iii) Otis began to install the elevator. Otis had earlier specified the size of the elevator shaft so that one of its standard models could be inserted easily. This type of construction also permitted removal of the elevator with a minimum of damage to the building. The contract was still not registered.
>
>   (iv) After this installation had begun, the mortgagee made further advances, until finally the full amount promised had been lent. Only then did Otis register its conditional sale contract.
>
>   (v) Goldaire defaulted, causing the mortgagee to foreclose. A default judgment was followed by a sale of the premises, and the question before the court was the deceptively simple one of deciding on the order of priority of distribution of the various monies owed to the mortgagee and the conditional seller.

How would the case be decided under the PPSA?

Note: Security interests in accessions, as defined in s. 1(*a*), and commingled goods are governed by ss. 37 and 38 of the PPSA. The scheme of s. 37 is modelled on s. 36.

G. TRANSFER OF COLLATERAL AND CREATION OF PROCEEDS

1. INTRODUCTION: THE COMMERCIAL SETTING AND THE LEGAL FRAMEWORK

a) The Setting: Sale of Inventory or Other Goods

A sale of goods subject to a prior security interest gives rise to two principal issues. One is the effectiveness of the security interest against the buyer. The second is the right of the secured party to claim the proceeds arising from the sale of his collateral.

Determination of these issues requires a preliminary discussion as to the commercial setting. There is a difference between goods held by the debtor for sale ("inventory" under s. 1(*n*)) and goods acquired by the debtor for his use (whether "consumer goods" under s. 1(*e*) or "equipment" under s. 1(*j*)). In the latter case (non-inventory goods), where the secured party does not authorize sale of the collateral by his debtor, much can be said in support of the continuing existence of the security interest if the security interest has been properly perfected. This would be consistent with the general common law principle, *nemo dat quod non habet*.

As for inventory financing, where the secured party does contemplate sale of the collateral and payment from the proceeds thereof, and where a buyer in the ordinary course of business is not expected to check filings in public offices, sale of the collateral should defeat the security interest. Is this always true? Before answering this and other questions, consider the following description of the categories of inventory financing.

HOMER KRIPKE
"Financial Assistance Through Commercial and Sales Finance Companies, Factors and Field Warehousing"
(1959) 14 Bus. Law 902, 904-05

Inventories are so diverse that no simple classification of the financing thereof will be adequate, but one can discuss briefly three important categories:

First is the financing of large individual units held by a distributor or dealer for sale. This category includes the inventories of dealers in automobiles, refrigerators, and other consumer appliances, farm equipment and construction equipment.* For this type of inventory a pattern of financing has been developed, the legal mechanism of which is usually the trust receipt** or similar legal structure where available under local state law. The financing contemplates that each unit will be paid for by the dealer immediately after it is sold, or in any event within say, three months. Financing practices have developed under which a dealer can borrow as much as 100% of his cost, including freight, and frequently in aggregate amounts equalling or exceeding his net worth. The fact that the security position of the lender is no good against a bona fide purchaser, and that it is expected that there will be such a bona fide purchaser of the inventory, means that the lien position may rapidly be jeopardized. This form of financing therefore embodies considerable legal and practical risks from the point of view of the lender. It is usually handled by banks or sales finance companies in connection with the financing of instalment receivables, discussed below.

Second, for the financing of inventory consisting of work in process, materials and supplies of manufacturers, in such fields as metal fabricating, textiles, etc., there has been developed the factor's lien. This is a non-possessory form of lien representing a continuous claim on a changing aggregate of inventory. Usually, no attempt is made to account for individual items of inventory. While

---

*   As such financing enables the dealer to display the inventory on the floor of his business, it has come to be known as ``floor planning'', or ``floor plan financing''.

** The instrument more commonly used in Canada is the conditional sale contract. Under its terms, the dealer (debtor) ``is usually authorized to sell the goods in the ordinary course of business (with or without the [financer's] prior approval). He undertakes, however, to hold the proceeds of any sale on trust for the [financer]'': J.S. Ziegel, ``The Legal Problems of Wholesale Financing of Durable Goods in Canada'' (1963) 41 Can. Bar Rev. 54, 60.

the factor's lien is available more broadly its principal use has been by the "old line factors" and commercial receivables companies, described below, in connection with their financing of open account receivables.

Both of the above forms of inventory financing are based on non-possessory liens. The borrower holds the goods and can sell them. If he sells them to a bona fide purchaser, the collateral is lost. Where the statutory mechanisms for these non-possessory form of financing are unavailable, or where the creditor is unwilling to assume the inherent credit risks involved in a non-possessory lien, a third form of inventory financing, based on possession, has been developed. It is not feasible for a financial institution directly to take a pledge of raw materials or work in process and store them in the bank vaults, for obvious reasons of space and because the arrangement would defeat the purpose of the financing. For similar reasons such kinds of inventory could not be stored in regular public warehouses, with the warehouse receipts pledged to the lender. Therefore, the warehouse comes to the borrower. Specialized institutions known as field warehouse companies, who are public warehousemen, make arrangements by which they lease a portion of the space in the borrower's premises and set up a warehouse thereon. They issue warehouse receipts to the borrower for the inventory therein contained, and the borrower pledges the warehouse receipts to a lender.* Flexible arrangements can be made by which the necessary inventory is temporarily released from the warehouse while fabricating processes are performed thereon.

b) The Legal Framework: An Overview

The debtor's right to transfer his own rights in the collateral is provided for in s. 33. This power does not prejudice the secured party's rights "under the security agreement or otherwise": *id.* In other words, s. 33 neither diminishes the effect of a contractual provision declaring a transfer to be a default nor does it otehwise affect the security interest. See e.g. *Poydan Inc.* v. *Agia Kiriaki Inc.* (1974) 15 UCC Rep. 739 (NJ SC).

On the transfer of the collateral, the security interest "extends to the proceeds": s. 27(1)(*b*). "Proceeds" are defined in s. 1(*r*). To perfect his interest in the proceeds, does the secured party have to register a new financing statement? Can he perfect by taking possession? See s. 27(2).

Following the transfer, whether the security interest continues in the collateral itself initially depends on whether the transaction was authorized or not. Where the transaction was "expressly or impliedly" authorized by the secured party, the security interest in the collateral is extinguished on the transfer. (What about apparent authority?) Otherwise, the security interest "continues as to the collateral": s.27(1)(*a*).

An "authorized" transfer within the meaning of s. 27(1)(*a*) contemplates a situation where the secured party, typically an inventory financer, authorizes the sale free of his security interest, and looks only to the proceeds for payment. An authorized transfer under s. 27(1)(*a*) thus differs from the transfer "with consent" under s. 49(1), which

---

*   For further material on field warehousing and its use in Canada as a security device, see Note on Perfection by Possession, *supra*, chapter 21(B).

contemplates the *retention* of the security interest by the secured party, typically a security interest in consumer goods or equipment.*

There are two exceptions to the general rule in s. 27(1)(a). First, under s. 22(1)(b), where the security interest is unperfected, a transferee for value and without knowledge takes the collateral free of the security interest. Delivery is required in the case of tangible collateral. Second, under s. 30(1), a purchaser from a seller in the ordinary course of business defeats a security interest given by the seller even with full knowledge of it. The latter exception is discussed below in more detail.

2. UNAUTHORIZED SALE OF GOODS — THE ORDINARY COURSE BUYER EXCEPTION

Under s. 30(1), "a purchaser of goods from a seller who sells the goods in the ordinary course of business takes them free from any security interest therein given by the seller. . . ." Such a provision

> . . . was first adopted in Ontario in an amending Act of 1892, which provided that "an agreement for the sale or transfer of merchandise of any kind to a trader or other person for the purpose of resale by him in the ordinary course of business" . . ., "though signed and filed, shall not affect purchasers from the trader or person aforesaid in the usual course of business". No other province or territory had any comparable provisions when the first Uniform Conditional Sales Act was being drafted and section 4 of the uniform Act was, therefore, inspired by the Ontario model, though its actual wording closely followed section 9 of the American Act. Section 4 read as follows:

>> If the goods are delivered to a trader or other person and the seller expressly or impliedly consents that the buyer may resell them in the ordinary course of business, and such trader or other person resells the goods in the ordinary course of his business, the property in the goods shall pass to the purchaser notwithstanding the other provisions of this Act.

> There have been only minor changes in the section since then. Section 8 of the 1955 Revised Uniform Act now reads:

>> Where a seller of goods expressly or impliedly consents that the buyer may sell them in the ordinary course of business and the buyer so sells the goods, the property in the goods passes to the purchaser from the buyer notwithstanding the other provisions of this Act.

((1963) 41 Can. Bar Rev. 54, 83).

To enjoy the protection of s. 8 of the Revised Uniform Act, *supra,* had the purchaser to be a "bona fide" purchaser and one "without notice"? Notwithstanding "the absence of these familiar landmarks" in the language of s. 8, Professor Ziegel suggested an affirmative answer (*id.* at 90):

> In the first place, the doctrine of "good faith" is much too deeply imbedded in the common law, the law merchant, and equity to be upset by a side wind, and evidence

---

*   Note, however, the registration requirements of s. 49(1). Does s. 49(1) create an absolute temporary perfection during the first 15 days, or does it only provide for a conditional grace period? Note also the different language of s. 49(2) dealing with registration of a financing change statement so as to continue perfection following a transfer which is neither authorized nor with consent. In dealing with the continuation of perfection in a transferred collateral, see also ss. 49(3) and 53(1)(d).

of a much clearer character than the mere omission of these words ought to be required of a legislative intent to repeal so basic a test. Secondly, the trader's section enacts a form of statutory estoppel. It says to the buyer, "You may assume that the dealer owns the goods in his stock, or at any rate that he is authorized to sell them". But it is only a presumption. Once the buyer knows the real facts he is no longer deceived by appearances and therefore has no need of the statutory protection. The same result may be reached by a literal interpretation of the words of the Acts. The seller, it will be recalled, must "expressly or impliedly consent" to the goods being resold. The onus is on the purchaser to prove the consent. Suppose he knows there is no consent. How, then, can he bring himself within the statute?

Unlike the UCC and Sask. PPSA s. 30(1), the Ontario PPSA does not seem to require that the ordinary course purchaser be in good faith. Does Professor Ziegel's analysis support a reading of a good faith requirement into Ont. PPSA s. 30(1)?

Once the purchaser qualifies as an ordinary course purchaser under Ont. PPSA s. 30(1), he takes the goods free only from any security interest given by *his* particular seller. Accordingly, in *National Shawmut of Boston* v. *Jones* (1967) 236 A. 2d 484 (NH SC) — where Dealer 1 sold a car to Consumer 1 under a conditional sale contract, and Consumer 1 sold the car without Dealer's authority to Dealer 2 — Consumer 2, who was an ordinary course buyer from Dealer 2, took the car subject to the perfected security interest of Dealer 1.

Sask. PPSA s. 30(2) extends the concept of s. 30(1) in the following circumstances:

> (2) A buyer or lessee of goods bought or leased primarily for personal, family, household or farming uses takes free of a perfected security interest in the goods if:
> (*a*) he gives new value for his interest;
> (*b*) he bought or leased the goods without notice of the security interest; and
> (*c*) he receives delivery of the goods.
>
> (3) Subsection (2) does not apply to a security interest in:
> (*a*) a motor vehicle as defined in the regulations;
> (*b*) fixtures; or
> (*c*) goods whose purchase price exceeds $500 or, in the case of a lease, whose retail market value exceeds $500.

Would s. 30(2) have assisted Consumer 2 in *Jones's* case, above?

Must an ordinary course purchase be from a seller in possession of the goods? A narrower aspect of this question is whether s. 30(1) protects the buyer where the secured party perfected his security interest by possession rather than by registration. Consider the case of a manufacturer who sells goods to a wholesaler subject to a security interest securing the latter's indebtedness. The goods remain in the manufacturer's possession. The security agreement gives the wholesaler a limited authority to resell the goods free from the manufacturer's security interest. The goods are to be delivered by the manufacturer directly to the wholesaler's buyers according to the wholesaler's instructions. Suppose the wholesaler makes an unauthorized sale. The manufacturer either refuses to deliver the goods or, unaware of the wholesaler's breach, complies with the latter's instructions and delivers the goods to the buyer. Will the buyer enjoy the protection of s. 30(1)? Dealing with a similar situation, *Tanboro Fabrics Corp.* v. *Deering Milliken Inc.* (1975) 369 NYS 2d 146 (1st Dept.); aff'd (1976) 385

NYS 2d 260, allowed the buyer's conversion action against the secured party. The court held that a buyer of goods may be a buyer in the ordinary course of business, even though he knows that the goods are not in his debtor's possession, and are held in the secured party's possession under a contract which does not authorize the seller to sell the goods without the secured party's consent. The decision is criticized by Professor Kripke in (1978) 33 Bus. Law 153, 155:

> The difference between a possessory security interest perfected by virtue of the possession and a non-possessory security interest perfected by filing is more than a difference between alternate methods of perfecting the security interest . . . The fact of possession in the secured party . . . means that the secured party has taken the goods out of the hands of the debtor . . . and thus has made it impossible for the debtor to take any advantage from his apparent ownership of the goods as evidenced by possession. . . .

Should PPSA s. 30(1) be read in conjunction with s. 2(1) of the Factors Act, RSO 1970, c. 156? *Cf.* Kripke, *id.*

The elements and the effect of an ordinary course purchase are examined in the two cases which follow.

FAIRLINE BOATS LTD. v. LEGER
Nov. 10, 1980 (Ont. SC)

LINDEN J. (orally): This is an action in which the plaintiff, a boat manufacturer, seeks possession of a 22-foot cabin cruiser from the defendant boating dealer who claims to have purchased it "in the ordinary course of business" from a third person, Blair, who was the original purchaser of the boat.

The plaintiff contends that the Personal Property Security Act provisions were complied with and that the defendant purchased the boat from Blair subject to the interests of the plaintiff, notice of which was duly registered, and that Leger must therefore return it. The Fairline Holiday 22-foot silvergray cabin cruiser which is the subject of this litigation was built by the plaintiff in the Spring of 1979 and sold to Blair Mower Marine and Cycle for $24,379.99, including many accessories. A conditional sales contract dated July 5th, 1979, was entered into and this contract was assigned to FinanceAmerica Private Brands Limited, which is a financing organization that deals in such matters.

The purchaser, Blair, had earlier entered into a Security Agreement dated December 7th, 1978, with FinanceAmerica, which covered all Fairline boats located at Blair's place of business, 6595 Drummond Road in Niagara Falls, Ontario. A financing statement was registered pursuant to the Personal Property Security Act against the inventory of Blair Mower and against Blair personally on December 13th, 1978, and this was amended slightly on December 18th, 1978, in a document registered on that day. In the Fall of 1979 Blair Mower went into default on its obligation to FinanceAmerica. FinanceAmerica, in a letter dated September 26th, 1979, recommended to Fairline that they repossess the cabin cruiser. This was done immediately by Fairline, who took the boat away from Blair and placed it at Dawson's Marina at Keswick, Ontario, on September 8th,

1979, in the hope that it could be sold by Mr. Dawson for a 10 percent commission during a sale of boats that was taking place there at that time.

John Blair somehow retrieved the cabin cruiser from Dawson's Marina in early October and purported to sell it to the defendant, Leger. The boat was placed on Leger's business premises in St. Charles, Ontario, near Sudbury. When this was discovered by FinanceAmerica, they attended, along with an officer of Fairline, at Leger's place of business and tried to repossess the boat. Leger refused to deliver it up, insisting that he had legally purchased it from Blair for $15,000.00 and that he was entitled to keep it.

Following this, an assignment agreement was entered into on October 16th, 1979, whereby FinanceAmerica assigned its rights under the Conditional Sales Agreement back to Fairline in return for payment in full of the amount owing, $25,494.01, which was the full price of the boat including interest charges until that date. This action was commenced on October 26th, 1979, by Fairline to retrieve the cabin cruiser, or in the alternative, for damages, but counsel has elected to seek the return of the boat rather than any damage award.

Although the defendant made some technical arguments in relation to the validity of the security under the Personal Property Security Act, I find that there were no irregularities such as to render invalid the claim of the plaintiff. I also find that the security was perfected in accordance with the Personal Property Security Act, and that the interest of FinanceAmerica was properly transferred to the plaintiff to enable it to bring this action.

The key issue in the case then is whether the sale to Leger by Blair was one which was "in the ordinary course of business" so as to come within section [30] sub-section 1 of the Personal Property Security Act, ... If the sale was in the ordinary course of business, then Leger received clear title, even though the security interest was registered. If it was not in the ordinary course of business, then Leger took subject to the interest of the plaintiff, since the registration of the document took place on December 13th, 1978, and December 18th, 1978, long before the date of this sale to Leger on October 3rd, 1979, or such other date in that period as the sale actually took place upon.

The objective of this section, as I understand it, is to permit commerce to proceed expeditiously without the need for purchasers of goods to check into the titles of sellers in the ordinary course of their business. Purchasers are allowed by our law to rely on sellers using the proceeds of sales to repay any liens on the property sold. In these days inventory is almost invariably financed, and as a result is almost invariably subject to liens of one kind or another. To require searches and other measures to protect lenders in every transaction would stultify commercial dealings, and so the Legislature exempts buyers in the ordinary course of business from these onerous provisions, even where they know that a lien is in existence. The risk is placed on lenders of an occasional dishonest dealer who may sell some of his goods in the ordinary course of business and then fail to repay the debt because "he is in a much better position than the buyer to weigh the risks." ... Some protection is given to security holders by denying reliance on this section to those who do not buy in the ordinary course of business.

What then is a sale "in the ordinary course of business"? Mr. Fred Catzman *et al.* in the book, *Personal Property Security Law in Ontario* (1976) explains that this language was taken from the older predecessor legislation and from the jurisprudence based thereon which used such language as "ordinary" or "regular" or "usual" course of business. Catzman *et al.* suggest at page 144:

> The person who conduct claims to come under the description must be engaged in carrying on a business. That business must involve as subject of traffic things of the class in which the item dealt falls, and the basis of dealing must be on the normal terms of dealing with that class of item in that type of business. The general commercial practice, rather than the dealer's particular operating method is the criteria. ... The market for goods is the public at large buying for a variety of purposes, non-business as well as business, and the buyer should not be called on to show more than what he bought in the same way as the seller's customers generally.

The authorities on the new Act are non-existent, and even the older authorities are slim indeed, but cases decided before the new Personal Property Security Act have held that there is an implied authority to sell encumbered goods as long as it is in the ordinary course of business. (See McRuer, C.J.H.C. in *Insurance and Discount Corp.* v. *Motorville Car Sales* [1953] OR 16 [aff'd [1953] OWN 828].) If sales are made in fraudulent circumstances in order to abscond with the proceeds, a Court may hold that this is not within the implied authority of the seller. (*Ibid.*) Similarly if a car dealer sells five cars to another car dealer for the express purpose of raising money to lessen the financial pressure that he was under at the time, this was held not to be a sale in the ordinary course of business and a search must be made by the buyer to protect himself. (See *MacDonald* v. *Canadian Acceptance Corporation* [1955] OR 874 (CA).) The Court felt that

> a few such sales for such purpose would be materially to impair the mortgage security, if not destroy it altogether. A license calculated to bring about such a devastating result is not to be imported into the instrument in derogation of the terms creating the security.

(See Aylesworth J.A. at page 882.)
So too, when a car is sold without delivery of a transfer of the ownership permit at the time, or shortly thereafter, this has been held not to be a sale in the ordinary course of business. (See *Rider* v. *Bank of Montreal* [1965] 1 OR 69.)

On the other hand cases have held that the pledging of goods by a factor can be in the ordinary course of business. (*Peoples' Credit Jewellers Ltd.* v. *Melvin* [1933] OWN 76.) Furthermore, a sale of a car by one used car dealer to another can also be a sale in the ordinary course of business. (See *Lipman* v. *Traders Finance* [1951] OWN 838.) This may be so even if the purchase is after hours and is also for a substantial quantity sold to another dealer with whom the seller had previous dealings. (See also *Pacific Motor Auctions Pty. Ltd.* v. *Motor Credits (Hire Finance) Ltd.* [1965] 2 All ER 106 (PC), 29 cars sold, but under a different statutory regime.)

Thus in deciding whether a transaction is one that is in the ordinary course of business, the Courts must consider all of the circumstances of the sale. Whether it was a sale in the ordinary course of business is a question of fact. (See the Ziegel article, *supra*, at page 86.) The usual, or regular type of transaction that people in the seller's business engage in must be evaluated. If the transaction is one that is not normally entered into by people in the seller's business, then it is not in the ordinary course of business. If those in the seller's business ordinarily do enter into such agreements, then, even though it may not be the most common type of contract, it may still be one in the ordinary course of business.

One factor that must be examined is where the agreement is made. If it is at the business premises of the seller it is more likely to be in the ordinary course of business. If it is away from the business premises of the seller, in suspicious circumstances for example, a Court may hold that it is not in the ordinary course of business.

The parties to the sale may also be significant, although certainly not controlling. If the buyer is an ordinary, everyday consumer, the likelihood of his being involved in a sale in the ordinary course of business is greater. If the buyer is not an ordinary consumer, but a dealer or financial institution, then the Court may take this out of the ordinary course of business, but not necessarily so because dealers and other[s] too may, in proper circumstances, receive the benefit of the provision.

The quantity of the goods sold must also be considered, although this too is not definitive. If there is only one or a few articles sold in the ordinary way, the Court is more likely to hold this to be a sale in the ordinary course of business. On the other hand, if a large quantity of items are sold, many more than are sold in the ordinary course of business, and perhaps forming a substantial proportion of the stock of the seller, then the Court is less likely to consider it to be in the ordinary course of business.

The price charged for the goods must also be examined; thus if the price charged is in the range of the usual market price, Courts are more likely to consider the sale in the ordinary course of business, whereas if the price is unduly low, the Courts may hold that this is not a transaction in the ordinary course of business.

There are other circumstances and factors in each sale that may also be viewed by the Court in determining whether, on all of the facts of the case, the sale in question is in the ordinary course of business. . . .

On the facts as I have found them, was this sale one made in the ordinary course of business? Looking at all the circumstances, I find that it was not. I find that it was part of the ordinary business of boat dealers to sell boats to other dealers. Even though some do not, others undoubtedly do. It makes business sense, especially in remote areas, to do so and I find that this is ordinarily done by boat dealers in various parts of Ontario. Thus the fact that Leger was another boat dealer would not by itself preclude him from relying on the protection of section 30, subsection 1. The benefit of this section is not for ordinary consumers only, but can also be relied upon in proper circumstances by other dealers, as the decided cases demonstrate.

I find also that the place where this sale was made was not the seller's usual place of business. This is not necessarily fatal to the buyer's interest. If it had been made at the boat show in Toronto, or anywhere else that business is ordinarily done by boat dealers, this would certainly have been acceptable. However this sale was concluded, I find, either in Keswick or St. Charles, or somewhere in between, or perhaps even at the restaurant near Keswick, as Proulx indicated Leger told him on their initial meeting. None of these places are places where a seller of boats would ordinarily do business and would therefore raise suspicions which would militate against [the sale] being classified as "in the ordinary course of business".

As for quantity, there was only one boat sold, so that there is nothing out of the ordinary about the quantity of the goods sold in this case.

As for the price of the boat and the trailer, I find that it was an unusually low price. It is true that Leger had agreed to purchase a similar boat for $16,000, but the Blair boat had many more options on it, which Leger well knew, and, consequently, it was worth considerably more than the one Leger had bought, which he also well knew, being a Fairline dealer himself.

While the 28 hours use and the few scratches may have lowered the value of the boat to a degree, it would not have lowered it by nearly over $9,000 below the actual sale price of $24,379, to take the $15,000 figure as the sale price. This is even more significant, when the price is something less than $15,000, which I find.

I also find that this was not a used boat at the time of this sale to Leger, but was still a new boat and was consequently worth more.

Another circumstance of this case, which must be considered, is that Blair was in serious financial difficulty, having had the boat in question repossessed, and other stock as well. While he might not have told Leger about all of the details of his financial problems, he must have told him that he would give Leger a good deal because he was in some financial difficulty. Otherwise, why would he sell a boat worth $24,000 for only $15,000, or less as I have found was actually the case, and why else would Leger deal with him? Merely to save $1,000, that is to buy a similar boat that he had agreed to buy for $16,000 for $1,000 less, would not make the transaction worthwhile to Leger, given all of the risks and inconvenience involved in it. He must have known that the boat was worth considerably more than the $15,000 he says he was planning to pay, and that he would be getting it for considerably less than its market value. For such a deal, a gamble may have been worth it, but not merely to save $1,000 or so. Thus I find that even the $15,000 figure was an unreasonably low price in the circumstances, but I also find that the actual price paid was closer to $10,000, and that was clearly below the price that someone dealing in the ordinary course of business would expect to pay for such a boat.

Thus, considering all the circumstances here of the parties, the price paid, the place of the sale, the quantity sold, and all of the other circumstances of this sale, I find that it was not one that could be said to have been in the ordinary course of business.

The defendant, therefore, cannot rely on section [30], subsection 1, and the plaintiff is entitled to the return of its 22-foot Holiday cabin cruiser forthwith.

Judgment for plaintiff.

O.M. SCOTT CREDIT CORP. v. APEX INC.
(1964) 198 A. 2d 673 (RI SC)

ROBERTS Justice: This action of replevin was heard by a justice of the superior court who thereafter gave decision to the plaintiff for possession, for damages in the amount of $126.20, and for costs. From this decision the defendant is prosecuting a bill of exceptions to this court.

The plaintiff, a financing corporation, is affiliated with O.M. Scott & Sons Company, a manufacturer of garden supplies, hereinafter referred to as Scott. Scott distributes its products through authorized dealers who are restricted expressly to the sale thereof to the ultimate consumers. Mass. Hardware & Supply Co., Inc., hereinafter referred to as Massachusetts Hardware, is such an authorized distributor of the Scott products, and it is not disputed that the Scott products in its possession were held pursuant to a trust receipt which provided, inter alia, that the dealer "agrees to hold said products in trust for the sole purpose of making sales to consumers, functioning as a retailer and not as a wholesaler." The defendant, Apex Incorporated, hereinafter referred to as Apex, conducts a discount house and for the purpose of purchasing merchandise therefor also operates the Old Colony Distributing Company, hereinafter referred to as Old Colony.

It appears from the evidence that in January 1961 Jack Rabinowitz, employed by defendant in a managerial capacity, engaged in a discussion with Bernard J. Moran, an employee of Massachusetts Hardware, concerning defendant's difficulty in the procurement of merchandise not ordinarily available to it. In March 1961 Rabinowitz and Moran discussed specifically a sale to Old Colony of three hundred bags of a fertilizer manufactured by Scott. There is some conflict in the evidence concerning the substance of these discussions and particularly whether Moran knew that the sale of fertilizer to Old Colony was in fact a sale to defendant. Rabinowitz testified that Moran knew that defendant was purchasing the fertilizer, while Moran specifically denied having any such knowledge. The trial justice resolved the conflict in the evidence by giving greater credence to the testimony of Moran.

The trial justice summarized the evidence and made findings of fact as follows: "Rabinowitz frankly testified that Moran told him that Massachusetts Hardware could not sell to Apex and accordingly Rabinowitz suggested that the sale be made to Old Colony Distributing Company, a subsidiary of Apex, with the indication some of it would go to a large user, perhaps a golf course, and that later Moran agreed to sell 300 bags in that manner. It thus appears that Rabinowitz knew that a sale to Apex would be contrary to the authority and intention of the seller and if with that knowledge he used a subterfuge to bring it about he could not be found to have acted in good faith. If it is thus clear that Moran made it known he could not sell to Apex it seems most likely, and is found by the Court, that he told Rabinowitz why, namely the restriction upon Massachusetts Hardware to sell only at retail and not to discount houses, together with the information as to the bags bearing serial numbers which would show their origin, which, once disclosed to Scott, would result in loss to Massachusetts Hardware of a valuable line. On these facts the Court must find that the buyer was not acting in good faith as that term has significance at this point."

The trial justice, in our opinion, properly concluded that the sale here under consideration was not in the circumstances attempted in good faith. It is well settled that where litigants submit a case, on the facts as well as on the law, to a trial justice sitting without a jury, his findings of fact are entitled to great weight and will not be set aside unless clearly wrong. *Gettler v. Caffier*, 92 RI 19, 165 A. 2d 730. After closely scrutinizing the transcript and considering the state of the evidence therein, we cannot say that the trial justice was clearly wrong in concluding that defendant did not act in good faith in this transaction.

We turn then to the questions of law raised by the parties. This is a situation, as we understand it, in which plaintiff had perfected a security interest in the merchandise by virtue of its recordation of its trust receipt under the pertinent provisions of chap. 106, art. 9, of the Uniform Commercial Code as enacted in the Commonwealth of Massachusetts, hereinafter referred to as the code.

It is not disputed that on May 6, 1961, the date upon which the fertilizer was replevied, Massachusetts Hardware had not paid plaintiff the purchase price thereof. The plaintiff, in asserting a right to possession of the merchandise superior to that of defendant, contends that the security interest it had perfected continued in the collateral notwithstanding the sale thereof to defendant and in support thereof relies upon the pertinent provisions of §9-306(2) of the code. That section provides in part as follows: "Except where this Article otherwise provides, a security interest continues in collateral notwithstanding sale, . . . by the debtor unless his action was authorized by the secured party in the security agreement or otherwise. . . ."

Basically, plaintiff's contention, as we understand it, is that the instant transaction has been brought within the provisions of the code and, therefore, the sale of the merchandise to defendant did not vitiate the security interest it had perfected in the collateral. In arguing the applicability of the provisions of art. 9 of the code to the instant transaction, it directs attention, first, to the general provisions of §9-102(1)(a) and the specific provisions of §9-102(2) which provide: This Article applies to security interests created by contract including pledge, . . . trust receipt. . . .

One of defendant's two basic contentions appears to posit the applicability of the provisions of art. 9 of the code to the instant transaction, and defendant argues therefrom that the trial justice erred in finding that it did not take the merchandise free from the security interest of plaintiff that is continued in effect in the collateral after a sale by the provisions of §9-306(2). In so arguing defendant contends that it was a purchaser in the ordinary course of business as defined in §1-201-(9) of the code. The provisions of §9-307(1) except such a purchaser in the ordinary course of business from the security interest, but, as we have already noted, the trial justice found that defendant did not purchase the merchandise in the ordinary course of business as contemplated in §9-307(1) and defined in §1-201(9), and we conclude that the trial justice did not err in making such finding.

The defendant's other contention is that art. 9 of the code has no application to the instant transaction, it being one to which the provisions of §1 of chap. 104 of the Annotated Laws of Massachusetts, hereinafter called the Factor's Act, exclusively apply and that, therefore, the trial justice erred in finding that art. 9 of the code amended the Factor's Act so as to bring this transaction within the purview of the relevant provisions of the code. This is to argue, as we understand it, that the legislature, in enacting art. 9 of the code intending to protect the security interests of the owners of merchandise in the possession of agents for sale, did not intend thereby to vitiate the protection given the purchaser in good faith of goods held in the possession of an agent with power to sell, which obviously was the purpose of the legislature in enacting the Factor's Act. In short, defendant, conceding that plaintiff had perfected a security interest in the goods pursuant to art. 9 of the code, argues that it took the goods free of that security interest because it had acquired them pursuant to a bona fide contract of sale within the contemplation of the Factor's Act. The pertinent provisions of that act read: "A factor or other agent intrusted with the possession of merchandise or of a bill of lading consigning merchandise to him with authority to sell the same shall be deemed the true owner of such merchandise, so far as to give validity to any bona fide contract of sale made by him."

Were we to concede that the enactment of the code did not diminish the protection given purchasers of merchandise under the Factor's Act, we would be unable to agree that defendant had acquired the merchandise pursuant to a bona fide contract for the sale thereof within the meaning of that act. We are unable to perceive that the good faith involved in a purchase in the ordinary course of business differs in any respect from the good faith involved in the contract of sale contemplated in the Factor's Act. To the contrary, we are of the opinion that the transaction here was such that it lacked good faith within the purview of either the code or the Factor's Act.

The trial justice in his decision directed attention to the code provisions holding that a buyer in the ordinary course of business is one who buys "in good faith and without knowledge that the sale to him is in violation of" the security rights of a third party. We agree that in such circumstance a buyer takes the goods free of security interest even though he knows there is a security interest therein. It is only when in addition thereto he knows that the sale violates some term of the security agreement not waived by the secured party, either in express terms or by conduct, that he takes subject to the security interest. It is our opinion that the trial justice has correctly disclosed the nature of the good faith contemplated by the provisions of the code relating to purchases in the ordinary course of business.

We do not perceive that this view as to what constitutes good faith in the context of the code is in any manner inconsistent with that which would constitute a bona fide contract of sale as contemplated in the Factor's Act. We are persuaded that such a bona fide contract of sale thereunder may exist even though the purchaser knew of the security interest in the goods when he does not know that the sale thereof to him in some manner violated that security interest or the terms thereof. In *Associates Discount Corp.* v. *C.E. Fay Co.*, 307 Mass. 577, 30 NE 2d 876, 132 ALR 519, the court considered the requirement of the

Factor's Act concerning the meaning of the phrase "bona fide contract of sale" as used therein and concluded that the act would not accomplish its purpose of protecting a purchaser of goods held by an agent if the mere knowledge of the agency imposed a burden upon him of ascertaining whether the sale was in violation of his authority.

The court in that case took the view that a transaction would be considered a bona fide contract of sale within the Factor's Act even though the buyer was aware that the possessor of the merchandise held for sale held it under some agency agreement. The court said 307 Mass. at page 583, 30 NE 2d at page 880: "Bad faith is not to be presumed. Notice to the defendant of circumstances that, if investigated, might have disclosed want of authority to exchange or barter the automobile, was not inconsistent with good faith or with a 'bona fide contract.' The statutory test is good faith, and not reason to believe in the existence of authority nor want of notice under principles of equity."

The facts as found by the trial justice establish that defendant not only knew that Massachusetts Hardware was in possession of the merchandise under a security agreement but knew also that the sale negotiated and executed with respect to the goods was contrary to the terms thereof and violative of plaintiff's security interest as so established. In these circumstances the transaction could not be found to constitute a bon fide contract of sale within the meaning of the Factor's Act, and, that being so, it would avail defendant nothing were this court to undertake to pass upon the question of whether the legislature of the Commonwealth of Massachusetts, in enacting the provisions of the code, intended thereby to repeal or amend the pertinent provisions of that act.

It is then our opinion that the trial justice did not err in holding that the defendant took the merchandise subject to the security interest of the plaintiff, it not having established that it was a buyer thereof in the ordinary course of business. Neither do we perceive that any prejudicial error, at least, inhered in his ruling that the Factor's Act was not controlling on the issues before him, the state of the evidence being such as to preclude any finding that the transaction constituted a bona fide contract of sale contemplated in that act. Because we so conclude, we are of the opinion that the defendant took the merchandise in the instant transaction subject to the security interest of the plaintiff and that, therefore, the plaintiff had a right to possession of the goods superior to that of the defendant and that replevin lies for the recovery thereof.

All of the defendant's exceptions are overruled, and the case is remitted to the superior court for entry of judgment on the decision.

Notes and Questions:

1   "Buyer in the ordinary course of business" is defined in UCC 1-201(9) as "a person who in good faith and without knowledge that the sale to him is in violation of the ownership rights or security interest of a third party in the goods buys in ordinary course from a person in the business of selling goods of that kind . . .". "Good faith" is defined in 1-201(19) as "honesty in fact . . .". Could the definition in 1-201(9) be adopted for PPSA s. 30(1) purposes? Cf. s. 2 of the Factors Act, RSO 1970, c. 156.

2   What was the basis of plaintiff Scott's right to replevin? Was there a breach of contract by Mass. Hardware? Was there "default"? *Cf.* s. 1(*h*) and *Sterling Acceptance Co.* v. *Grimes* (1961) 168 A. 2d 600 (Pa. Sup. Ct.), where the sale below a particular price was specified in the security agreement as "default".

3   Could plaintiff Scott prevail against a bona fide buyer from Apex?

3.   EXTENSION OF THE SECURITY INTEREST TO THE PROCEEDS

Traceable assets "derived directly or indirectly from any dealing with collateral or proceeds" are proceeds. They include indemnification or compensation "for collateral destroyed or damaged" (s. 1(*r*)). Under s. 27(1), "a security interest in collateral that is dealt with so as to give rise to proceeds . . . (*b*) extends to the proceeds". Note the provision as to perfection in s. 27(2). Is the PMSI priority carried into the proceeds of the original collateral? Consider s. 34(2) and (3) and compare with UCC 9-312(3) and (4). See also Gilmore, "The Purchase Money Priority" (1963) 76 Harv. L. Rev. 1333, 1383.

Note that "there is no perfected security interest in proceeds that are not identifiable or traceable": s. 27(2). "The Act [thus] discards the U.S. UCC's elaboration of distinctions between cash and non-cash proceeds and a variety of rules depending on those and other factors and substitutes the Hallet test [named after *Re Hallet's Estate* (1880) 13 Ch. D. 696] as a rule of general application": Catzman *et al.*, *Personal Property Security Law in Ontario* (1976) p. 133. Does this mean that a bona fide purchaser of the proceeds who would in equity take them free from a tracing claim is also able to defeat a perfected security interest in them?

Section 29 deals with the shifting of the security interest from the proceeds back to the original collateral where the latter is returned or repossessed by the original debtor. Under s. 29(1) the security interest "reattaches [to the original collateral] to the extent that the secured indebtedness remains unpaid". See the treatment of the priority problems, discussed *infra*, under s. 29(2).

Problems:

1   A dealer's inventory of new tractors is subject to a bank's security interest. The dealer sells a buyer a new tractor under a conditional sale contract and properly registers a financing statement. The buyer's down payment consists of a trade-in, cash and a cheque. The dealer puts the cash in the drawer and deposits the cheque in a bank account. What are the rights of the bank?

2   Following the sequence of events in Problem 1, the buyer obtains a loan from a finance company which takes a security interest in the new tractor. As a condition precedent to the loan, the finance company requires the buyer to insure the tractor against property damage and to designate the finance company as the beneficiary under the insurance policy. If the tractor is involved in an accident, who is entitled to the insurance money?

3   Suppose the old tractor traded in for the new tractor in Problem 1 was subject to two security interests created prior to the trade-in. One of the security interests

was a PMSI whose registration complied with s. 34. The other, also properly registered, was under a security agreement giving the secured party a security interest in all the debtor's after acquired property. Discuss the priorities to the new and old tractors.

RE KRYZANOWSKI
(1979) 97 DLR (3d) 744, 24 OR (2d) 18 (Ont. SC in Bkcy)

STEELE J.: This is an application by the trustee in bankruptcy of John Hans Kryzanowski, hereinafter referred to as "Kryzanowski", for an order that certain security agreements do not represent perfected security interests in $102,000 deposited in a bank, and that the claims of International Harvester Credit Corporation of Canada Limited are subordinate to the interests of the trustee of the bankrupt.

Several items of farm equipment were purchased by Kryzanowski under the terms of conditional sales contracts which provided that title remain in the vendor until payment in full was made. The contracts were assigned to International and were properly registered under the Personal Property Security Act, RSO 1970, c. 344. Payments under the contracts had been kept up by Kryzanowski, but it became apparent that he would not be able to make the payments due on April 1, 1978. I find that arrangements were made between International and Kryzanowski through International's agent, Vincent, that the equipment would be sold at public auction from Kryzanowski's farm on March 31, 1978, and that the proceeds of the sale would be deposited into a bank account in the joint names of Vincent and Kryzanowski. Cheques on such account were to be signed by both Vincent and Kryzanowski. Out of the proceeds the auctioneer, retail sales tax and a repair account of Vincent's company were to be paid. I find that the agreement provided that the remaining proceeds were to be used to pay International in full with the balance, if any, to go to Kryzanowski. Unfortunately, not all the farm equipment was sold at auction and there was not sufficient funds realized to pay International in full. If International has a valid claim on the proceeds, then all money in the bank account belongs to International.

The auction sale took place on March 31, 1978, after notice to the public of the sale in Kryzanowski's name and, after both Kryzanowski and Vincent had signed the auctioneer's agreement as vendors. I find that Vincent acted as the cashier for the sale proceeds and received such proceeds. I find that the banking arrangements had been made prior to the sale and that on March 31, 1978, after the sale, the proceeds were deposited in the night depository of the bank. At the same time, Kryzanowski and Vincent signed and delivered cheques in payment of the accounts of the retail sales tax, the auctioneer and Vincent's company. I find that at the same time they also signed a blank cheque in favour of International which was delivered to and held by Vincent who was the agent for International. The amount was left blank because it was not known what amount should be inserted because of the intention to close out the account and of the uncertainty of the exact amount that would be remaining in the account.

I find that International had not repossessed the farm equipment under the terms of the sales contracts at the time of the auction sale. My reason for this finding is that no payment was in arrears or would be in arrears until the day after the sale, and no notice of repossession had been given or was given until April 4, 1978. I find that International merely consented to the sale upon the agreed terms. The bankruptcy of Kryzanowski took place on April 7, 1978.

The question to be determined is whether the security interest of International became unperfected with respect to the proceeds of the sale and, if so, whether the agreement between International and Kryzanowski created a trust in accordance with which the proceeds were to be held for International. There are no written documents specifically creating a trust. The bank documents do not refer to a trust account, but only to a joint account which required the signatures of both persons on cheques. The evidence of Vincent is that the agreement with Kryzanowski was to establish a trust. No evidence was given by Kryzanowski. The evidence of the finance manager of International was that at no time were the proceeds of the sale to go into the possession of Kryzanowski until International and the other named persons had been paid. In effect, the finance manager's evidence was that it was a condition of the consent to the sale that the proceeds would be held in trust.

It is clear that International gave consent to the sale of the equipment. Therefore, s. 27 [am. 1973, c. 102, s. 6] of the Personal Property Security Act does not protect the interest in the proceeds thereof even though such proceeds are identifiable.

If there was no trust and there was no perfected security interest, then International's claim would be subordinate to the trustee under s. 22(1)(a)(iii) of the Act. However, in this case I am of the opinion that the Act does not detract from International's rights otherwise acquired. The proceeds of the sale represented by the money in the bank were held by Kryzanowski and Vincent in trust for International. International held valid security on the farm equipment. Why would it give up such security unless it had been agreed that the proceeds thereof would be held for it? I quote from Judson, J., in *Flintoft* v. *Royal Bank of Canada*, [1964] SCR 631 at p. 635, 47 DLR (2d) 141 at p. 145 *sub nom. Re Canadian Western Millwork Ltd.*, 7 CBR (NS) 78, as follows:

> Why would any lender who lends for the purpose of enabling another to acquire and manufacture goods, permit the sale of goods on which he holds security except on terms that the borrower must bring in the proceeds of the sale of those goods?

The present case is stronger than that referred to by Judson, J., because I find that there was an express agreement to the effect that the proceeds would be delivered to International. The trustee in bankruptcy has no higher rights than the bankrupt and, therefore, is subject to the trust created by this agreement.

An order will issue to the effect that International has no perfected security interest in the money in the bank account, but that such money is held in trust for International and it is entitled to the entire beneficial interest therein.

Costs to the respondent, International, payable out of the assets of the estate.

Question: Was the case correctly decided?

BORDEN (U.K.) LTD. v. SCOTTISH TIMBER PRODUCTS LTD.
[1979] 3 WLR 672 (CA)

BRIDGE L.J.: This is an appeal from a judgment of Judge Rubin, sitting as a judge of the Chancery Division, given on November 15, 1978, on the trial of certain preliminary issues of law pursuant to an order of Master Cholmondeley Clarke made on July 6, 1978. We have heard arguments on the essential points of the appeal at some length; that is no criticism whatever of counsel, as the arguments have been extremely helpful, but, in my judgment, the points that we have to decide are, in the end, really rather short ones and I hope it will not be thought that I am in any way being discourteous to counsel if I endeavour to deal with them shortly in this judgment.

For the purpose of the preliminary issues of law which were ordered to be tried, certain facts were agreed between the parties; so far as material to the only points remaining for decision by this court, the agreed facts can be very shortly stated.

The plaintiff company, Borden (U.K.) Ltd., are the manufacturers of a product called urea-formaldehyde chipboard resin. Over a period of some four years up to September 1977, they were the main, but not the exclusive, suppliers of that product to the defendant company, Scottish Timber Products Ltd., for use by the defendants in the manufacture of chipboard. The defendants had a storage capacity for the resin which they needed, which was only sufficient at most to keep them supplied for two days' production in their factory. Accordingly, when their factory was working in the ordinary way it was inevitable that the resin supply would be used in the manufacture within two days of delivery. This circumstance was well known to the plaintiffs and it is really essential to the main issue arising in this appeal that one should infer from those circumstances that the contract clearly permitted the use of the resin in the manufacturing process before it had been paid for, the resin being sold on credit terms.

In the course of the manufacturing process the resin was mixed with certain hardeners and wax emulsion, to form something which is referred to as a "glue mix"; this process of mixture was essentially irreversible in the sense that, once mixed, the resin as such could no longer be recovered. The glue mix was then blended with various grades of wood chippings and finally pressed together to form the end product, the chipboard.

On September 16, 1977, a receiver and manager of the defendant company's undertaking was appointed by debenture holders; the receiver is the second defendant in the proceedings. The defendant company has subsequently gone into compulsory liquidation pursuant to an order made on June 25, 1979, and is now continuing to defend this action by leave of the Official Receiver as provisional liquidator.

The plaintiffs claim that as at September 16, 1977, when the receiver was appointed, the sum of £318,321.27 net was due to them from the defendants for resin supplied since June 1, 1977. They further claim that since February 14, 1977, all sales of resin to the defendants have been made pursuant to an express contractual condition in the following terms:

(2) *Risk and Property.* Goods supplied by the company shall be at the purchaser's risk immediately on delivery to the purchaser or into custody on the purchaser's behalf (whichever is the sooner) and the purchaser should therefore be insured accordingly. Property in goods supplied hereunder will pass to the customer when: (a) the goods the subject of this contract; and (b) all other goods the subject of any other contract between the company and the customer which, at the time of payment of the full price of the goods sold under this contract, have been delivered to the customer but not paid for in full, have been paid for in full.

There is an issue on the pleadings as to whether that was indeed an effective term of the contract between the parties.

It is further pleaded by the plaintiffs in their statement of claim, reading only so much as is relevant to the issues which we now have to decide:

In the premises . . . any chipboard . . . manufactured or fabricated with any of the said resin" — that is, the plaintiffs' resin —" . . . is charged to the [extent that it consists of any of the said resin] with payment to the plaintiff of £318,321.27. Further or alternatively, all moneys and other property representing the . . . chipboard . . . or any of the proceeds of sale or other disposal thereof are charged to the extent that they represent the said resin with the payment to the plaintiff of £318,321.27.

In the relief claimed in the statement of claim appropriate declarations are claimed, pursuant to those pleaded rights.

Master Cholmondeley Clarke's order required the decision of the following points of law, namely:

(a) Whether upon the facts pleaded in the amended statement of claim the condition pleaded in paragraph 5 thereof — that is the alleged condition 2 of the contract — has the result in law: . . . (ii) that any chipboard . . . is charged to the [extent that it consists of any of the said resin] with the payment to the plaintiff of £318,321.27; and/or (iii) that all moneys and other property representing any of the said . . . chipboard . . . or any of the proceeds of sale or other disposal thereof are charged to the extent that they represent the said resin with the payment to the plaintiff of £318,321.27. (b) Whether any charge resulting from such condition was and is void by reason of section 95 of the Companies Act 1948. . . .

I should say that there was a further plea included in the plaintiffs' statement of claim to be entitled to the ownership, in part, of the chipboard. That also was the subject of one of the questions of law raised as a preliminary issue; that was decided by the judge against the plaintiffs and no cross-appeal was raised with regard to that, so we may take it that it is not in dispute that the title to the manufactured chipboard is the title of the defendants.

The judge answered questions (a)(ii) and (iii) affirmatively, in favour of the plaintiffs, and question (b) negatively, also in favour of the plaintiffs. The material part of his order is:

This court doth declare that the plaintiffs are entitled to trace any of their resin supplied after February 14, 1977, the title to which had not passed to the defendants, Scottish Timber Products Ltd., under clause 2 of the plaintiffs' standard conditions in the pleadings mentioned into any chipboard manufactured from such resin or into the proceeds of sale of such chipboard but so that the plaintiffs cannot recover a sum in excess of the contract price of such resin. And this court doth declare that the exercise of such a tracing remedy is not a charge created by the company to which section 95 of the Companies Act 1948 has any application.

It is common ground, I think, that that form of order, which purports to declare finally the rights of the parties, would in any event require some modification, since what the judge was called upon to do was to decide preliminary issues of law upon certain assumptions of fact which had not yet been proved; but nothing turns upon that.

The essence of the judge's reasoning in arriving at the conclusion that the plaintiffs were entitled to a tracing remedy, which was the first issue for consideration, is stated in a few sentences of the judgment. The judge said:

> It seemed to me clear from an early stage in the argument that the defendants received resin which remained the property of the plaintiffs as a bailee for the plaintiffs and accordingly a fiduciary relationship was created. . . . the defendants argued that the tracing remedy does not extend where there is a use in manufacture to the manufactured product and its proceeds of sale. In my judgment unless the fiduciary relationship was brought to an end by the use in manufacture, or it is possible to imply a further term into the contract that the defendants would be entitled to deal with the chipboard on its own account, there is no reason why the tracing remedy should not extend both to the chipboard and its proceeds of sale.

In my judgment, the first question which arises for our decision is whether there was a fiduciary relationship here between the defendants and the plaintiffs in the nature of the relationship of bailee and bailor. As I have already said, it is common ground that the defendants were at liberty to use the resin which had not been paid for in the manufacture of chipboard, so that before the resin was paid for, the result was that it ceased to exist as such. Is that consistent with the relationship of the parties being that of bailor and bailee?

The judge, in deciding that question, did not, I think, have the advantage, as we have had, of being referred to the decision of the Privy Council in *South Australian Insurance Co.* v. *Randell* (1869) LR 3 PC 101, where Sir Joseph Napier, giving the advice of the Board, said, at pp. 108-109:

> A bailment on trust implies, that there is reserved to the bailor the right to claim a redelivery of the property deposited in bailment. . . . The law seems to be concisely and accurately stated by Sir William Jones in the passages cited by Mr. Mellish from his treatise on *Bailments,* 3rd ed., pp. 64 and 102. Wherever there is a delivery of property on a contract for an equivalent in money or some other valuable commodity, and not for the return of his identical subject matter in its original or an altered form, this is a transfer of property for value — it is a sale and not a bailment. Chancellor Kent in his *Commentaries,* 11th ed., vol. 2, p. 781, where he refers to the case of *Seymour* v. *Brown,* 19 Johns. Rep. 44, of which he disapproved in common with Story J., adopts the test, whether the identical subject matter was to be restored either as it stood or in an altered form; or whether a different thing was to be given for it as an equivalent; for in the latter case it was a sale, and not a bailment. This is the true and settled doctrine according to his opinion.

I can well appreciate that in the present circumstances, if the defendants repudiated the contract, or became insolvent, before the resin had been paid for, they might then have become a bailee of any resin which at that time remained unused. But so long as the business transacted between these parties continued in the ordinary way and resin was delivered for use in the manufacturing process at a time before it could have been paid for, in circumstances in which the plaintiffs clearly had no right to call for its return or to object to its use in the manufacture of chipboard, and where it was never intended that the resin should be recovered, either in its original or in its altered form or at all, it seems to me quite impossible to say that this was a contract of bailment. The contract was essentially one of sale and purchase, subject only to the reservation of title clause, whatever its effect may have been.

Now what was the effect of that clause? Looked at in principle, and independently of authority, I find it difficult to see how the clause was apt to create any fiduciary relationship. I am much attracted by the view which was canvassed in argument that the effect of condition 2 was such that the beneficial interest in the resin passed to the defendants, who were to be entirely free to use it for their own purposes in the manufacture of chipboard, and that all that was retained by the plaintiffs was the bare legal title to the resin so long as the resin existed, held as security for the unpaid price of that resin and of any other resin which the plaintiffs had supplied. But I am quite content to assume that this is wrong and to suppose that up to the moment when the resin was used in manufacture it was held by the defendants in trust for the plaintiffs in the same sense in which a bailee or a factor or an agent holds goods in trust for his bailor or his principal. If that was the position, then there is no doubt that as soon as the resin was used in the manufacturing process it ceased to exist as resin, and accordingly the title to the resin simply disappeared. So much is accepted by Mr. Mowbray for the plaintiffs.

The contract contains no express stipulation conferring on the plaintiffs any rights over the chipboard and Mr. Mowbray has repeatedly disclaimed any intention to argue for an implied term in the contract that any rights over the chipboard should be conferred on them. He, nevertheless, argues that the tracing remedy arises from the mixture of the plaintiffs' resin with the defendants' other materials in the manufacture of chipboard, so that an appropriate proportion of the chipboard now represents the plaintiffs' security for moneys due to them as the unpaid price of all the resin delivered. In my judgment, the crux of the whole case is whether this argument can be sustained.

It is conceded that there is no previous authority which establishes that the tracing remedy can be exercised where there has been an admixture of the goods of A with the goods of B in such a way that they both lose their identity and result in the production of goods of an entirely different kind; but it is urged that the availability of such a remedy is supported by the application by analogy of principles derived from the decided cases.

The main authority relied on by the judge in reaching his conclusion, and by Mr. Mowbray in his argument for the plaintiffs, is the decision of this court in *Aluminium Industrie Vaassen B.V.* v. *Romalpa Aluminium Ltd.* [1976] 1 WLR 676. The plaintiffs in that case sold aluminium foil to the defendants. The defendants went into liquidation, owing the plaintiffs over £122,000 and the receiver certified that

£35,152 was held in an account in his name with the defendants' bankers, representing the proceeds of sale of aluminium foil supplied to the plaintiffs, which the defendants had sold to third parties. The plaintiffs, who had a reservation of title clause in their conditions of sale, claimed to be entitled to trace the aluminium foil into the proceeds of sale, and that claim was upheld by Mocatta J. at first instance and by this court on appeal. The particular condition of the contract which applied is set out in the judgment of Mocatta J., at p. 679:

> "The ownership of the material to be delivered by A.I.V." (that is the plaintiffs) "will only be transferred to purchaser when he has met all that is owing to A.I.V., no matter on what grounds. . . . Until the date of payment, purchaser, if A.I.V. so desires, is required to store this material in such a way that it is clearly the property of A.I.V. A.I.V. and purchaser agree that, if purchaser should make (a) new object(s) from the material, mix this material with (an)other object(s) or if this material in any way whatsoever becomes a constituent of (an)other object(s) A.I.V. will be given the ownership of this (these) new object(s) as surety of the full payment of what purchaser owes A.I.V. To this end A.I.V. and purchaser now agree that the ownership of the article(s) in question, whether finished or not, are to be transferred to A.I.V. and that this transfer of ownership will be considered to have taken place through and at the moment of the single operation or event by which the material is converted into (a) new object(s), or is mixed with or becomes a constituent of (an)other object(s). Until the moment of full payment of what purchaser owes A.I.V. purchaser shall keep the object(s) in question for A.I.V. in his capacity of fiduciary owner and, if required, shall store this (these) object(s) in such a way that it (they) can be recognised as such. Nevertheless, purchaser will be entitled to sell these objects to a third party within the framework of the normal carrying on of his business and to deliver them on condition that — if A.I.V. so requires — purchaser, as long as he has not fully discharged his debt to A.I.V. shall hand over to A.I.V. the claims he has against his buyer emanating from this transaction."

The condition is expressed in very curious language because it is a translation from the Dutch, which was the original language of the contract. Mocatta J. held that that clause showed an intention to create a fiduciary relationship between the parties and that the plaintiffs were entitled to follow the proceeds of the sub-sales; he reached that conclusion in the application of the principles of the decision in *In re Hallett's Estate* (1880) 13 Ch. D. 696.

In the Court of Appeal the essence of the reasoning of their Lordships can be collected from some quite short passages, first, from the leading judgment of Roskill L.J. where he says [1976] 1 WLR 676, 689-690:

> Now, the crucial facts to my mind are two: first, that the defendants were selling goods which the plaintiffs owned at all material times; and secondly, that clause 13 as a whole is obviously designed to protect the plaintiffs, in the event of later insolvency, against the consequences of having parted with possession of, though not with legal title to, these goods before payment was received, 75 days' credit being allowed. When, therefore, one is considering what, if any, additional implication has to be made to the undoubted implied power of sale in the first part of clause 13, one must ask what, if any, additional implication is necessary to make effective the obvious purpose of giving the requisite security to the plaintiffs? One is, I think, entitled to look at the second part of clause 13 to answer this; for it would be strange

if the first part were to afford no relevant security when the second part is (as I think) elaborately drawn to give such security in relation to manufactured or mixed goods.

I see no difficulty in the contractual concept that, as between the defendants and their sub-purchasers, the defendants sold as principals, but that, as between themselves and the plaintiffs, those goods which they were selling as principals within their implied authority from the plaintiffs were the plaintiffs' goods which they were selling as agents for the plaintiffs to whom they remained fully accountable. If an agent lawfully sells his principal's goods, he stands in a fiduciary relationship to his principal and remains accountable to his principal for those goods and their proceeds. A bailee is in like position in relation to his bailor's goods. What, then, is there here to relieve the defendants from their obligation to account to the plaintiffs for those goods of the plaintiffs which they lawfully sell to sub-purchasers?

Then, Roskill L.J., a little later, said, at p. 690:

It seems to me clear . . . that to give effect to what I regard as the obvious purpose of clause 13 one must imply into the first part of the clause not only the power to sell but also the obligation to account in accordance with the normal fiduciary relationship of principal and agent, bailor and bailee. Accordingly, like the judge I find no difficulty in holding that the principles in *Hallett's* case, 13 Ch. D. 696 are of immediate application, and I think that the plaintiffs are entitled to trace these proceeds of sale and to recover them, as Mocatta J. has held by his judgment.

Goff L.J. said, at p. 691:

In my judgment the second part of the case comes down to a short question of construction. It is common ground that a power of sale during the period that any money remains owing to the plaintiffs must be implied; but the question is upon what terms.

Then, at the end of his judgment, Goff L.J. said, at p. 693:

In short, my conclusion is that the power of sale to be implied where none has been expressed must be so qualified as not to defeat the intention clearly shown by clause 13 as a whole, including the latter part, which only emphasises this. It follows that there was, as Roskill L.J. says, a sufficient fiduciary relationship between the parties, and this is indeed expressly contemplated in the reference to a fiduciary owner in the second part of clause 13. The implied power must, therefore, in my judgment be a power to sell, not for the defendants' own account, but for the account of the plaintiffs unless and until all moneys owing be paid.

Megaw L.J., still more succinctly, said, at p. 694:

The power of sale to be implied in the first part of clause 13, where none has been expressed, must be such as not to defeat the intention shown by clause 13. It is not a power to sell for the defendants' own account, but it is a power to sell for the account of the plaintiffs.

It seems to me that there are certain very clear distinctions between that case and this. First, it was conceded throughout in that case that the defendants were bailees of the aluminium foil for the plaintiffs; secondly, on the facts on which the decision turns there had been no admixture of the foil with any other material; if there had been, it would have been covered by the express terms of the second part of condition 13, but all that was in issue was a claim to trace the foil into the proceeds of sale of the foil. Thirdly, the case turned on the construction of the particular clause and on what was to be implied in the first part of the clause as to the terms on which the defendants were entitled to sell aluminium foil. Here, by contrast, first, as I have said, in my judgment there clearly was no bailment of the resin; secondly, there was an admixture of the goods of the plaintiffs with other materials of the defendants, producing a wholly new substance. Thirdly, we are not here concerned with any sale of the resin; it is not suggested by either party that the terms of sale here contemplated that the defendants should be at liberty to sell the resin as such; all that was contemplated was that they should be at liberty to use it in their own process of manufacture.

But to my mind the most important distinction is that the essence of the decision in *Romalpa* was that on the facts found or admitted Romalpa were selling the plaintiffs' material, the aluminium foil, as agents for the plaintiffs. It seems to me quite impossible to say here that in using the plaintiffs' resin in their own manufacturing process to manufacture their own chipboard, the defendants could possibly be described as acting in any sense as agents for the plaintiffs. I do not in any way question the correctness of the decision in *Romalpa*, but for my own part I really do not find that it throws any significant light on the questions which we have to decide.

The only argument derived from the consideration of *Romalpa* which is worthy of attention is that it is said here, as it was said in *Romalpa*, that the intention of the clause under consideration must have been to give the plaintiffs an effective security as unpaid purchaser for the purchase price of any resin, and their security would not be effective unless the tracing remedy claimed on behalf of the plaintiffs is an effective remedy. For my part, I am wholly unimpressed by that argument. I accept that in stipulating for condition 2 in their conditions of sale, it was a pious hope on the part of the plaintiffs that they were creating for themselves an effective security for the payment of any unpaid purchase price due to them at any time; but the mere fact that they hoped that that would be so and intended that it should be so, is quite insufficient to carry the day if the language they used in relation to the agreed facts and the legal relationship which they created, whatever it may have been, is insufficient to make their intention an effective one.

I come to what, to my mind, is really the heart of the matter: Can the tracing remedy here claimed be supported in the application, by analogy, of the well-known principles of tracing expounded so clearly in the judgment of Sir George Jessel M.R. in *In re Hallett's Estate*, 13 Ch. D. 696, 708-711? He says:

> The modern doctrine of equity as regards property disposed of by persons in a fiduciary position is a very clear and well-established doctrine. You can, if the sale was rightful, take the proceeds of the sale, if you can identify them. If the sale was wrongful, you can still take the proceeds of the sale, in a sense adopting the sale for the purpose of taking the proceeds, if you can identify them. There is no distinction, therefore, between a rightful and a wrongful disposition of the property, so far as regards the right of the beneficial owner to follow the proceeds. But it very often happens that you cannot identify the proceeds. The proceeds may have been inves-

ted together with money belonging to the person in a fiduciary position, in a purchase. He may have bought land with it, for instance, or he may have bought chattels with it. Now, what is the position of the beneficial owner as regards such purchase? I will, first of all, take his position when the purchase is clearly made with what I will call, for shortness, the trust money, although it is not confined, as I will show presently, to express trusts. In that case, according to the now well-established doctrine of equity, the beneficial owner has a right to elect either to take the property purchased, or to hold it as a security for the amount of the trust money laid out in the purchase; or, as we generally express it, he is entitled at his election either to take the property, or to have a charge on the property for the amount of the trust money. But in the second case, where a trustee has mixed the money with his own, there is this distinction, that the *cestui que* trust, or beneficial owner, can no longer elect to take the property, because it is no longer bought with the trust-money simply and purely, but with a mixed fund. He is, however, still entitled to a charge on the property purchased, for the amount of the trust-money laid out in the purchase; and that charge is quite independent of the fact of the amount laid out by the trustee. The moment you get a substantial portion of it furnished by the trustee, using the word "trustee" in the sense I have mentioned, as including all persons in a fiduciary relation, the right to the charge follows. That is the modern doctrine of equity. Has it ever been suggested, until very recently, that there is any distinction between an express trustee, or an agent, or a bailee, or a collector of rents, or anybody else in a fiduciary position? I have never heard, until quite recently, such a distinction suggested. It cannot, as far as I am aware (and since this court sat last to hear this case, I have taken the trouble to look for authority), be found in any reported case even suggested, except in the recent decision of Fry J., to which I shall draw attention presently. It can have no foundation in principle, because the beneficial ownership is the same, wherever the legal ownership may be. If you have goods bargained and sold to a man upon trust to sell and hand over the net proceeds to another, that other is the beneficial owner; but if instead of being bargained and sold, so as to vest the legal ownership in the trustee, they are deposited with him to sell as agent, so that the legal ownership remains in the beneficial owner, can it be supposed, in a Court of Equity, that the rights of the beneficial owner are different, he being entire beneficial owner in both cases? I say on principle it is impossible to imagine there can be any difference. In practice we know there is no difference, because the moment you get into a Court of Equity, where a principal can sue an agent as well as a *cestui que* trust can sue a trustee, no such distinction was ever suggested, as far as I am aware. Therefore, the moment you establish the fiduciary relation, the modern rules of equity, as regards following trust money, apply. . . .

Now that being the established doctrine of equity on this point, I will take the case of the pure bailee. If the bailee sells the goods bailed, the bailor can in equity follow the proceeds, and can follow the proceeds wherever they can be distinguished, either being actually kept separate, or being mixed up with other moneys. I have only to advert to one other point, and that is this — supposing, instead of being invested in the purchase of land or goods, the moneys were simply mixed with other moneys of the trustee, using the term again in its full sense as including every person in a fiduciary relation, does it make any difference according to the modern doctrine of equity? I say none. It would be very remarkable if it were to do so. Supposing the trust money was 1,000 sovereigns, and the trustee put them into a bag, and by mistake, or accident, or otherwise, dropped a sovereign of his own into the bag. Could anybody suppose that a judge in equity would find any difficulty in saying that the *cestui que* trust has a right to take 1,000 sovereigns out of that bag? I do not like to call it a charge of 1,000 sovereigns on the 1,001 sovereigns, but that is the effect of it. I have no doubt of it. It would make no difference if, instead of one sovereign, it was another 1,000 sovereigns; but if instead of putting it into his bag, or after putting it into his bag, he carries the bag to his bankers, what then? According to law, the bankers are his debtors for the total amount; but if you lend the trust money to a third person, you can follow it.

What are the salient features of the doctrine that Sir George Jessel M.R. there expounds? First, it will be observed that in all cases the party entitled to trace is referred to as the beneficial owner of the property, be it money or goods, which the "trustee," in the broad sense in which Sir George Jessel M.R. uses that word, including all fiduciary relationships, has disposed of. In the instant case, even if I assume that so long as the resin remained resin the beneficial ownership of the resin remained in the plaintiffs, I do not see how the concept of the beneficial ownership remaining in the plaintiffs after use in manufacture can here possibly be reconciled with the liberty which the plaintiffs gave to the defendants to use that resin in the manufacturing process for the defendants' benefit, producing their own chipboard and in the process destroying the very existence of the resin.

Secondly, the doctrine expounded by Sir George Jessel M.R. contemplates the tracing of goods into money and money into goods. In the latter case it matters not that the moneys represent a mixed fund of which a part only is impressed with the relevant trust. The *cestui que* trust has a charge on the mixed fund or the property into which it has passed for the amount of the trust moneys. It is at the heart of Mr. Mowbray's argument to submit that the same applies to a mixture of goods with goods, relying in particular on Sir George Jessel M.R.'s illustration of the mixed bag of sovereigns. Now I can well see the force of that argument if the goods mixed are all of a homogenous character. Supposing I deposit a ton of my corn with a corn factor as bailee, who does not store it separately but mixes it with corn of his own. This, I apprehend, would leave unaffected my rights as bailor, including the right to trace. But a mixture of heterogeneous goods in a manufacturing process wherein the original goods lose their character and what emerges is a wholly new product, is in my judgment something entirely different.

Some extreme examples were canvassed in argument. Suppose cattle cake is sold to a farmer, or fuel to a steel manufacturer, in each case with a reservation of title clause, but on terms which permit the farmer to feed the cattle cake to his herd and the steelmaker to fuel his furnaces, before paying the purchase price. Mr. Mowbray concedes that in these cases the seller cannot trace into the cattle or the steel. He says that the difference is that the goods have been consumed. But once this concession is made, I find it impossible to draw an intelligible line of distinction in principle which would give the plaintiffs a right to trace the resin into the chipboard in the instant case. What has happened in the manufacturing process is much more akin to the process of consumption than to any simple process of admixture of goods. To put the point in another way, if the contribution that the resin has made to the chipboard gives rise to a tracing remedy, I find it difficult to see any good reason why, in the steelmaking example, the essential contribution made by the fuel to the steel manufacturing process should not do likewise.

These are the principal considerations which have led me to the conclusion that the plaintiffs are not entitled to the tracing remedy which they claim. But I am fortified in that conclusion by the further consideration that if the remedy were available in such cases, a most intractable problem could, and in many cases would, arise in quantifying the proportion of the value of the manufactured product which the tracer could claim as properly attributable to his ingredient. In the instant case, a breakdown of the actual costings of chipboard over a period of seven months to July 29, 1977, has been agreed, attributing 17 per cent of the total cost to the cost of resin, subject to a reservation with respect to wastage and over-usage. But one can well see that in many cases where the cost of materials and labour involved in a particular production process were constantly fluctuating, it might be quite impossible to assign a proportion of the total cost properly attributable to one particular ingredient with any certainty at all.

The lesson to be learned from these conclusions is a simple one. If a seller of goods to a manufacturer, who knows that his goods are to be used in the manufacturing process before they are paid for, wishes to reserve to himself an effective security for the payment of the price, he cannot rely on a simple reservation of title clause such as that relied upon by the plaintiffs. If he wishes to acquire rights over the finished product, he can only do so by express contractual stipulation. We have seen an elaborate, and presumably effective, example of such a stipulation in *Aluminium Industrie Vaassen B.V.* v. *Romalpa Aluminium Ltd.* [1976] 1 WLR 676. An attempt to acquire rights over the finished products by a stipulation which proved ineffective for want of registration under section 95 of the Companies Act 1948 is to be seen in the decision of Slade J. in *In re Bond Worth Ltd.* [1979] 3 WLR 629 to which in the course of argument we were helpfully rreferred.

For the reasons that I have attempted to explain, I would allow this appeal and set aside the judge's order. I would answer questions (a)(ii) and (iii) set out in Master Cholmondeley Clarke's order in the negative; in the light of those answers, in my judgment, question (b), as to the effect of section 95, does not arise, and I would express no opinion about it.

Appeal allowed.

[Concurring judgments were delivered by Buckley and Templeman L. JJ.]

Note: How would the case have been decided in Ontario under the OPPSA? Does s. 38 throw any light on the answer? The U.K. has no registration requirements for conditional sale or hire-purchase agreements and, prior to the decision in the *Romalpa* case discussed in Bridge L.J.'s judgment *supra*, it was not customary for inventory to be sold in the U.K. subject to conditional sale terms with a proceeds clause. The implications of *Romalpa* are explored in a wider setting by Prof. Goode in "The Right to Trace and its Impact in Commercial Transactions" (1976) 92 LQ Rev. 360 and 528 (Pts. I & II).

H. CONFLICT OF LAWS PROVISIONS (ss. 5-8)

See in general Baxter, "Secured Transactions and Conflict of Laws" (1978) 3 Can. Bus. LJ 57.

Problem: Jones sold Smith a car under a conditional sale contract in Manitoba. The security interest was properly perfected under Manitoba law. Smith moved to Ontario. What is the status of Jones's interest in Ontario? On the resale of the car by Smith to Bob, what are Bob's rights? In answering the question assume alternatively that the resale to Bob took place:
- a) twelve days after Smith had moved to Ontario;
- b) twenty days after Smith had moved to Ontario; or
- c) seventy-five days after Smith had moved to Ontario.

Is your answer affected by Bob's knowledge of Jones's security interest? By Jones's knowledge of Smith's moving to Ontario? How could Jones protect himself? What would be the effect of registration by Jones in Ontario:
- (a) eleven days;
- (b) seventeen days; or
- (c) seventy-three days

after Smith had moved to Ontario?

Memorandum prepared for the benefit of the MUPPSA Committee (June 1979)

INTRODUCTION

Sections 5 to 8 of the Model Act and the corresponding provisions in the other Canadian Acts, enacted or proposed, deal with choice of law questions arising out of chattel security transactions involving, or deemed to involve, more than one jurisdiction. The Code provisions in UCC 9-103 were substantially revised in 1972. The Ontario and Model Act provisions are substantially based on the 1966 Code provisions, though both sets of provisions depart from the Code provisions in several important respects and neither is simply a copy of the other.
. . .

All the Canadian conflict of laws provisions, with the exception of Saskatchewan's, are limited to "ordinary" goods, mobile goods, goods brought from Quebec, and intangibles. Excluded therefore are documents of title, instruments and securities. . . .

What Questions Should be Decided By The choice Law Rules?

The Model and Ontario provisions only cover the "validity" and the "perfection" of the security interest. Excluded therefore are such important questions as "the proper law" of the security agreement, the law governing priorities between competing security interests perfected in different jurisdictions, and the law governing the enforcement of the security interest. I will briefly consider these questions in turn.

(i) The Proper Law of the Security Agreement

It is well established conflicts doctrine that a secured transaction involves two distinct elements, viz. the creation of a right *in rem* which, in the case of goods, is normally governed by the *lex situs*, and the personal rights and obligations of the parties which, like any other contract, is governed by the proper law of the contract. *Cf. C.A.C.* v. *Matte* (1957) 9 DLR (2d) 304 (Sask. CA); *Traders Finance Corp.* v. *Casselman* (1960) 22 DLR 177 (SCC), and the discussion in 45 Can. Bar Rev. 284 at 313 *et seq.* (The distinction is not as simple or as neat in practice as it looks on paper, but this complication may be ignored for present purposes.) . . .

(ii) Priorities

Although not stated in priority terms, the normal conflict of law rule appears to be that where collateral subject to a valid security interest under the law of A is taken into state B and there sold or pledged to T, the law of B will determine whether T has obtained a good title of pledge. The Article 9 provisions, and their counterparts in Canada, appear to proceed on the same assumption. For example, Model Act 30(1) protects the buyer in ordinary course regardless of the law under which the inventory security interest was perfected or re-perfected.

(iii) Enforcement of the Security Interest

There is a wide difference of opinion among writers and in the meagre case law with respect to the law or laws governing the secured party's enforcement rights, first, against the collateral and, secondly, against the debtor himself with respect to his personal obligations. The proper law of the contract, the *lex situs* at the time of the creation of the security interest, and the *lex situs* at the time of the debtor's default or default proceedings each have their supporters and critics. See the discussion in (1967) 54 CBR, especially at 328 *et seq.* Once again the question will only arise, as it may well arise in the case of consumer transactions, where there is a material difference between the several possible laws. There is nothing in Article 9 or the Canadian Acts that throws direct light on the applicable law, although it could be argued there is an assumption that the *lex situs* at the time of the enforcement proceedings will apply, at least with respect to the secured party's *in rem* rights and buyer's rights of redemption. Given the paucity of Canadian case law and the difficulty of framing satisfactory rules, I recommend no change in the Model Act on this point.

(iv) Should the Conflict Provisions Continue to Govern the "Validity" of a Security Agreement?

"Validity" was deleted from the 1972 provisions on the ground that since all states, with the exception of Louisiana, had adopted the Code it was no longer a relevant issue. Another objection was that the references to "validity" in 9-103 were not consistent. We are not in the same fortunate position as the Americans and may not be for some time. Subject to two caveats, I see no harm therefore in retaining the reference to "validity" in our Act provided it is done consistently. The caveats involve the danger that a court may interpret "validity" to refer to the validity of the security agreement *as well as* the validity of the security interest. This should not happen because all the Canadian Acts refer only to the validity of the security interest — not the validity of the agreement itself — but if I am too optimistic then we should reconsider our position. We may also have to reconsider our position if we find that marrying law governing the validity of a security interest with the law governing its perfection is too difficult or inconvenient.

The Basic Lex Situs Rule

Sections 6 to 8 of the Model Act apply the *lex situs* rule to determine the validity and perfection of a security interest in goods brought into the PPSA province from another jurisdiction but fail to state the applicable choice of law rule in other circumstances, e.g., where the goods are located throughout in the same jurisdiction or where the collateral is taken from a PPSA province to a non-PPSA jurisdiction.

The interpretation of s. 7(1) of the Ont. PPSA is discussed in the case below.

TRANS CANADA CREDIT CORP. LTD. v. BACHAND
(1980) 30 OR (2d) 405, 117 DLR (3d) 153 (CA)

[The following fact summary is from (1980) 4 Can. Bus. LJ 54, 81-2:]

> On February 26, 1976, Lounsbury Motor Company of Newcastle, New Brunswick, sold a motor vehicle on conditional sale terms to one John Mahoney. The agreement was assigned to Trans Canada Credit Corporation (Trans Canada) and registered in New Brunswick. On May 20, 1976, Trans Canada learned that the vehicle was located in Alberta and registered the agreement in that province. On August 13, 1976, the vehicle was registered by John Mahoney in Ontario. On August 20, 1976, the registration permit for the vehicle was transferred to Town & Country Auto Centre, a division of H & J Auto Centre, pursuant to a sale apparently arranged through a friend of Mahoney's. H & J Auto Centre resold the vehicle to the plaintiff [Bachand] on September 3, 1976. Trans Canada registered a financing statement in Ontario on October 27, 1976. On December 13, 1976, bailiffs, acting on Trans Canada's instructions, seized the vehicle while it was in the plaintiff's possession. The plaintiff sued Trans Canada in conversion. . . .

MACKINNON A.C.J.O., delivering the judgment of the court, stated the facts and continued: The learned trial judge held that the 60 day period for perfecting the security interest had lapsed on October 20, 1976 and that the filing of the financing statement on the 27th day of October, 1976 was "inoperative and null and void." He awarded judgment against the defendant Trans Canada Credit Corporation Limited . . .

Counsel for the appellant [Trans Canada] submitted that s. 7 by its terms applied to the security interest held by the appellant and that it was perfected by the statute for the 60 day period. Accepting for the purposes of this appeal that s. 7 does apply here, the motor vehicle was registered on August 13, 1976 in Ontario and transferred from John Mahoney to H & J Auto Centre Limited on August 20, 1976. Whether the 60 day period commenced running under s. 7(1) on August 13th, 1976, or on August 20th, 1976 as the trial judge appeared to conclude, the respondent plaintiff purchased the car on September 3rd, which was well within the 60 day period.

The appellant took the position that the perfection mentioned in s. 7(1) is absolute and although the holder of the security interest does nothing thereafter, if an innocent purchaser buys the goods during that 60 day period, the transaction is liable to be vitiated at any time thereafter; if he still has possession of the goods innocently purchased they can be seized, or, in any event, he will be liable for their money value if he has disposed of them. The appellant draws some comfort in this regard from a decision of the New Jersey Supreme Court in *First National Bank of Bay Shore* v. *Stamper* (1966) 3 UCC Rep. Serv. 949, 225 A. 2d 162 (NJ Sup. Ct.). I can only say that I am not persuaded by the reasoning in that case and note that it is subject to some editorial criticism in the report.

The appellant was given 60 days within which to locate the property covered by its security interest and perfect that interest in Ontario. If he perfects it within the 60 day period it continues to be perfected after the expiration of that period. But, if he fails to perfect it within the 60 day period but perfects it thereafter then under s. 7(3) "such perfection takes effect from the time of its perfection in Ontario." It clearly does not relate back to the day when the collateral is brought into Ontario. To hold that the 60 day perfection is absolute without need for any subsequent action by the security holder could lead to obvious injustice to innocent parties. They would never be secure. I prefer the reasoning of Professor McLaren in his book on *Secured Transactions in Personal Property in Canada*, Vol. 1, p. 7-10 where he says:

> The better view is that the claimants should be able to take advantage of the subsequent lapse. Section 7(1) extends protection to extra provincial security interests. However, the protection is not absolute without action from the secured party in reperfecting his interest. If this step is done, the claimants will be subordinated even though their interest may have arisen prior to the reperfecting act. One can tolerate this result in the interests of provincial comity. However, when the extra provincial secured party never protects his interest by reperfecting in Ontario thus leaving our hypothetical claimants unable to ever discover the security interest there is no reason why that interest should be protected by the Ontario Act over claimants from Ontario. Indeed the secured party would not get such a protection in his own province for failing to perfect. Therefore, the claimants should not be said to have knowledge so as to be subordinated under s. 22 when the automatically perfected extra provincial interest lapses for want of action by the secured party....

In the result, I would dismiss the appeal. . . .

Appeal dismissed.

Notes and Questions:

1   Is the decision consistent with the language of s. 7(1)? Compare s. 7(1) with ss. 22(3) and 34(2) and (3) (10 days grace period for PMSI registration) on one hand, and with

s. 26 (temporary perfection) on the other hand. Should the court have also considered s. 53(1)(c)? *Cf.* the discussion on lapse of registration *supra*, chapter 22(E). Do you find the trial judge's reasoning more convincing? It is criticized in Ziegel, (1979-80) 4 Can. Bus. LJ 54, 81-84.

2   The "editorial criticism" on the N.J. decision referred to by Mackinnon A.C.J.O., is based on Comment 7 to UCC 9-103 (1962 version). See 3 UCC Rep. Ser. 950. According to this Comment, if the secured party does not perfect his security interest in the new state within the statutory period after the property is brought into that state, "his interest, although originally perfected in the state where it attached, is subject to defeat . . . by those persons who take priority over an unperfected security interest [see the section corresponding to PPSA s. 22]. Under [the provision corresponding to PPSA s. 35] the holder of a perfected conflicting security interest is such a person even though during the four month period the conflicting interest was junior. Compare the situation arising under [the provision dealing with what happens] when a filing lapses." Does the Comment (indirectly relied on by Mackinnon A.C.J.O.) correctly describe the position under the PPSA?

3   The draft Bill to amend the PPSA proposed to amend s. 7(3) by striking out "due to the expiration of the sixty-day period" and inserting in lieu thereof "under subsection 2". Section 8 was to be amended by striking out "within thirty days from the date" and inserting in lieu thereof "after". The effect of late registration under ss. 7-8 was to be governed by the general rule as to late registration under the draft Bill (provided for by a proposed s. 58a) described in note 3 following *Johnson* in chapter 22(E) *supra*.

IN RE MILLER
(1974) 14 UCC Rep. 1042 (U.S. DC D. Ore.)

HENRY L. HESS, JR., Bankruptcy Judge: This matter involves a determination of the priorities of the security interests of two creditors and of the rights of the trustee in a 1972 Ford tractor, loader and backhoe. The court has heretofore entered findings of fact. Only the legal issues raised by these findings remain in dispute.

The facts which are material to the issues are briefly as follows.

The defendant, Kenneth C. Miller, was adjudged a bankrupt upon a petition filed by him on October 25, 1973. Prior to April 1, 1973, at a time when the bankrupt was a resident of California, he granted a security interest in the equipment to the defendant, Ford Motor Credit Company (Ford). Ford perfected its security interest in the equipment by filing a financing statement with the Secretary of State of California. On April 1, 1973, the bankrupt removed his residence to Hillsboro, Oregon. On April 15, 1973, he transported the equipment to Hillsboro, Washington County, Oregon. On April 24, 1973, the bankruptcy granted a security interest in the Ford tractor, loader and backhoe to the defendant, Peerless Pacific Company (Peerless). On April 30, 1973, Peerless filed financing statements with the Secretary of State of Oregon and the proper recording officer of Washington County, Oregon.

At the time of the granting of the security interest to Peerless, it had knowledge that Ford claimed a security interest in the equipment.

Between April 15, 1973, and October 17, 1973, the equipment was continuously located in the State of Oregon. On or about October 17, 1973, the bankrupt removed the equipment to the State of California and notified Ford on or about October 18, 1973, that he had done so. On or about November 15, 1973, Miller removed his residence to the State of California.

On December 10, 1973, Peerless filed a financing statement with the Secretary of State of California evidencing its security interest in the 1972 Ford tractor, loader and backhoe.

At no time material herein did Ford file a financing statement in the State of Oregon nor did it file any continuation statement or financing statement, other than the original financing statement, with the Secretary of State of California.

From the above, it is apparent that the equipment had not been in the State of Oregon for a period of four months at the time that Peerless, with knowledge of the security interest of Ford, took its security interest and filed its financing statements in Oregon. Also, it is apparent that the equipment had remained in Oregon for a period of more than four months before it was returned to California and that Ford had at no time filed a financing statement in the State of Oregon.

It is clear that had the property not been returned to the State of California prior to the petition in bankruptcy, the trustee would have taken title to the 1972 Ford tractor, loader and backhoe, subject only to the security interest of Peerless. Section 70c Bankruptcy Act, 11 USC §110, ORS 79.1030(3). The fact that Peerless had knowledge of the existence of the claim of a security interest by Ford would not change the result because the Uniform Commercial Code renders knowledge immaterial. ORS 79.3120(5) makes no mention of the matter of knowledge in the determination of priorities. The official comment to the last referred to section makes it clear that priority is a "race of diligence" in which knowledge is irrelevant. See also In re Smith (Minn 1971) 326 F Supp 1311 [9 UCC Rep 519].

The question then remains whether return of the equipment to California after it had been in Oregon for a period of over four months changed the priorities between the parties. The trustee and Peerless argue that after the four months had expired from the time the equipment was brought to Oregon, the security interest of Ford lapsed and that return of the equipment to California did not have the effect of reviving the security interest of Ford as of the date of the original filing by Ford. Ford contends that its security interest was perfected in California, that the law of California is controlling and that its security interest in California remained unaffected by the fact that the property was for a period of over four months located in Oregon.

Counsel have not furnished to the court any cases directly in point. The California statutes adopting the UCC are identical to the Oregon statutes so far as they are relevant to the question here involved.

ORS 79.1030(3) provides:

> If personal property other than that governed by subsections (1) and (2) of this section is already subject to a security interest when it is brought into this state, the

> validity of the security interest in this state is to be determined by the law (including the conflict of laws rules) of the jurisdiction where the property was when the security interest attached. . . . If the security interest was already perfected under the law of the jurisdiction where the property was when the security interest attached and before being brought into this state, the security interest continues perfected in this state for four months and also thereafter if within the four-month period it is perfected in this state. The security interest may also be perfected in this state after the expiration of the four-month period; in such case perfection dates from the time of perfection in this state. If the security interest was not perfected under the law of the jurisdiction where the property was when the security interest attached and before being brought into this state, it may be perfected in this state; in such case perfection dates from the time of perfection in this state.

When the equipment was brought to Oregon it was subject to the perfected security interest of Ford. It remained subject to Ford's perfected interest for four months. At the end of that period of time, Ford's perfection lapsed, leaving Peerless with the only perfected security interest encumbering the equipment.

> The four month period is long enough for a secured party to discover in most cases that the collateral has been removed and to file in this state; thereafter, if he has not done so, his interest, although originally perfected in the state where it attached, is subject to defeat here by those persons who take priority over an unperfected security interest (see Section 9-301). Under Section 9-312(5) the holder of a perfected conflicting security interest is such a person even though during the four month period the conflicting interest was junior. Compare the situation arising under Section 9-403(2) when a filing lapses. Official Comment to Subsection 3 of ORS 79.1030.

When the equipment was returned to California, California became "this state" and Oregon "the jurisdiction where the property was". Thus, paraphrasing the California UCC, if personal property is already subject to a security interest when it is brought into California, the validity of the security interest in California is to be determined by the law of Oregon. If the security interest was already perfected in Oregon and before being brought into California, the security interest continues perfected in California for four months and also thereafter if within the four-month period it is perfected in California.

In Oregon, the equipment was subject only to the security interest of Peerless. When it was returned to California, it was returned subject to the security interest of Peerless. Ford did not have a perfected security interest in "the jurisdiction where the property was" (Oregon); Peerless did. Consequently, the equipment reached California (this state) subject to "the security interest . . . already perfected under the law of the jurisdiction where the property was when the security interest attached . . ." and just as obviously the equipment arrived in California *not* subject to a security interest unperfected in Oregon.

The Code contemplates that a gap in perfection must be remedied exactly as required by the Code. If it is, the perfection is termed "continuous", and "relates back" to the original perfection date; if it is not remedied as required by the Code, there is a "gap" or a "lapse" and a subsequent perfection does not "relate back" but dates from the later date of perfection and is subject to intervening perfected security interests.

The Official Comment to ORS 79.1030(3) points out "In case of delay beyond the four month period, there is no 'relation back'." The same comment also suggests that the reader "compare the situation arising under Section 9-403(2) when a *filing lapses*" (Emphasis added).

Official Comment Number 3 to ORS 79.4030 is:

Under the fourth sentence of Subsection (2) the security interest becomes *unperfected* when filing *lapses*. Thereafter, the interest of the secured party is subject to defeat by those persons who take priority over an unperfected security interest (see Section 9-301), and under Section 9-312(5) the holder of a perfected conflicting security interest is such a person even though before lapse the conflicting interest was junior. *Compare the situation arising under Section 9-103(3) when a perfected security interest under the law of another jurisdiction is not perfected in this state within four months after the property is brought into this state.* (Emphasis added.)

ORS 79.3030(2) states:

If a security interest is originally perfected in any way permitted under ORS 79.1010 to 79.5070 and is subsequently perfected in some other way under ORS 79.1010 to 79.5070, without an intermediate period when it was unperfected, the security interest shall be deemed to be perfected continuously for the purposes of ORS 79.1010 to 79.5070.

The Official Comment to ORS 79.3030 is:

2. The following example will illustrate the operation of subsection (2) of ORS 79.3030: A bank which has issued a letter of credit honors drafts drawn under the credit and receives possession of the negotiable bill of lading covering the goods shipped. Under subsection (2) of ORS 79.3040 and ORS 79.3050 the bank now has a perfected security interest in the document and the goods. The bank releases the bill of lading to the debtor for the purpose of procuring the goods from the carrier and selling them. Under subsection (5) of ORS 79.3040 the bank continues to have a perfected security interest in the document and goods for 21 days. The bank files before the expiration of the 21-day period. Its security interest now continues perfected for as long as the filing is good. The goods are sold by the debtor. The bank continues to have a security interest in the proceeds of sale to the extent stated in subsection (3) of ORS 79.3060.

If the successive stages of the bank's security interests succeed each other without an intervening gap, the security interest is "continuously perfected" and the date of perfection is when the interest first became perfected (i.e., in the example given, when the bank received possession of the bill of lading against honor of the drafts). If, however, there is a gap between stages — for example, if the bank does not file until after the expiration of the 21-day period specified in subsection (5) of ORS 79.3040, the collateral still being in the debtor's possession — then, the chain being broken, the perfection is no longer continuous. *The date of perfection would now be the date of filing (after expiration of the 21-day period); the bank's interest might now become subject to attack under section 60 of the Federal Bankruptcy Act and would be subject to any interests arising during the gap period which under ORS 79.3010 take priority over an unperfected security interest.*

The rule of subsection (2) of ORS 79.3030 would also apply to the case of collateral brought to this state subject to a security interest which became perfected in another state or jurisdiction. See subsection (3) of ORS 79.1030. (Emphasis added.)

The comment cited above points out that once the gap occurs, subsequent perfection dates from the date of the subsequent perfection, and that the original perfection *is not revived*. The comment specifically applies the rule to ORS 79.1030(3). Consequently, when Ford permitted a gap in perfection to exist in Oregon, Ford's first filing lapsed, and there is no revival.

A major purpose of the UCC was to create uniformity in the creation and perfection of security interests and the priorities to be given to creditors holding security interests in the various states. Under the above view of the UCC, a prospective lender may check the filing records of the state in which the property is located and if he knows that the property has been located in that state for a period of over four months, he can be assured that if he perfects a security interest there it will take priority over any security interest perfected in any other state whether or not prior in time. He is not required to search the filing records of any other state to which the property might later be removed. If the property is later removed, he can maintain his priority by perfecting in the second state within four months. Were the view argued by Ford adopted, a prospective lender could not be assured of priority over security interests earlier perfected in other states to which the property might later be removed without a search of the filing records of all such states. Ford could have maintained its priority status after the property was removed to Oregon by merely filing financing statements in Oregon within four months. This imposes less of a burden than that which would be imposed upon a later lender in another state under Ford's theory.

The court therefore concludes that the title of the trustee to the 1972 Ford tractor, loader and backhoe is subject to the security interest of Peerless but is unencumbered by the security interest of Ford.

Counsel for the trustee may submit an appropriate order.

Subsequent to the entry in the above matter of the opinion of the court dated March 7, 1974, the defendant, Ford Motor Credit Company, filed a motion for reconsideration in which it requested the court to reconsider its opinion. The motion was accompanied by a Memorandum of Points and Authorities in response to which the defendant, Peerless Pacific Company, has also filed a Memorandum. The Trustee has informed the court that he concurs with the position taken by Peerless.

The opinion of March 7, 1974, was based principally upon the provisions of UCC §9-103(3). Ford raises two principal contentions. First, that this case is controlled by UCC §9-103(2). Second, if the cases is controlled by UCC §9-103(3) the 1972 amendments proposed by the American Law Institute and the National Conference of Commissioners on Uniform State Laws indicate that the provisions of UCC §9-103(3) in effect in Oregon and California during the times herein relevant, did not provide a lapse in the security interest of Ford in California despite the fact that the collateral and the place of business of the debtor had been in Oregon for a period of more than four months before the collateral was again returned to California.

UCC §9-103(2) provides in the case of goods normally used in more than one jurisdiction that the law of the state in which the chief place of business is located governs the validity and perfection of a security interest and the effect of proper filing with regard to such goods. This section, however, makes no mention of the situation in which a security interest is perfected in the state of the chief place of business of the debtor but the debtor then moves his place of business and the collateral to another state and the holder of the security interest fails to perfect in the second state within four months.

The Draftsmen's Comments to UCC §9-103 prior to the proposed amendments of 1972 state:

> If we bear in mind that one of the principal questions involved is where certain financing statements shall be filed, two things become clear. *First*: since the purpose of filing is to allow subsequent creditors of the *debtor-assignor* to determine the true status of his affairs, the place chosen must be one which such creditors would normally associate with the assignor; thus, the place of business of the assignee and the places of business or residences of the various account debtors must be rejected. *Second*: since the validity of the assignment against third parties may depend on the filing of a financing statement in the proper place, it is vital that the place chosen be one which can be determined with the least possible risk of error.
>
> • • •
>
> 3.   Another class of collateral for which a special rule is stated (subsection (2)) is mobile goods which are normally moved for use from one jurisdiction to another. Such goods are generally classified as equipment; occasionally they may be classified as inventory, for example, autos owned by a car rental agency. Under many present chattel mortgage and conditional sales acts the mortgagee or conditional vendor must file in each filing district in which such mobile equipment is used — which is possible although onerous in some cases, but not even possible in the case, for example, of non-scheduled trucking operations. Subsection (2) provides that a security interest in such equipment or an inventory subject to this Article when the debtor's chief place of business is in this state. "Chief place of business" does not mean the place of incorporation; it means the place from which in fact the debtor manages the main part of his business operations. That is the place where persons dealing with the debtor would normally look for credit information, and is the appropriate place for filing . . .
>
> Similarly, if the chief place of business of the debtor is moved to "this state" after a security interest has been perfected in another jurisdiction, the secured party should file in this state, since Section 9-401(3) is inapplicable.
>
> • • •
>
> In case of delay beyond the four-month period, there is no "relation back"; and this is also true where, in this state, the security interest is perfected for the first time.

The Draftsmen's Comments are a part of the legislative history and are a persuasive indication of legislative intent. The case of *General Electric Credit Corp. v. R.A. Heintz Constr. Co.*, 302 F. Supp 958 [6 UCC Rep 1137] (D. Or 1969) cited by Ford is not applicable. The conclusions of this court in the present case would be the same under either UCC §9-103(2) or UCC §9-103(3).

Ford's second contention is that the proposed 1972 amendments to UCC §9-103 indicate that the law prior to the adoption of such amendments made no provision for a lapse of perfection when there has been a removal of the property or the chief place of business of the debtor to another state for a period of more than four months without perfection during this period in the second state. To the contrary, the proposed amendments do not appear to be a change in the law but rather a clarification of the law. There is nothing in the comments to the 1972 amendments indicating any change was intended.

While the UCC is not a national law and some minor modifications have been made by states which have adopted it, the UCC was not intended as a device for each state to give special privileges or rights to creditors located in that state. One of its underlying purposes and policies is to make uniform the law among the various jurisdictions. UCC §1-102(2)(c). Without question, the code was designed to bring the body of commercial law into the contemporary world of business.

Ford argues that uncertainty will exist for a lender if a dishonest debtor fails to notify him of a change in location of the collateral or the debtor's place of business. Ford, however, recognizes that if the rule contended by it were followed, a lender would have uncertainty as to his priority if the collateral were later removed to another state in which there had been an earlier perfected security interest. Honesty of a debtor is not a relevant factor when recording statutes are involved. Recording statutes are adopted in order that a purchaser or lender need not rely upon the honesty of the seller or borrower. The UCC has determined that there is less of a burden imposed on one who takes a security interest in property to impose upon him the burden of keeping track of the collateral and the debtor than would be the burden upon a later prospective purchaser or lender to check the filing records in fifty states.

Ford contends that under UCC §9-103(3) removal of the collateral from California to Oregon for a period of more than four months without perfection by it in Oregon may cause a lapse of Ford's security interest in Oregon but not in California. Ford contends that the lapse of a security interest in the state in which the security interest was first perfected is the five year period provided for the filing of a continuation statement under UCC §9-403(2). If this were true, then Ford could permit the property to be removed from California to any number of other states, fail to perfect in such other states, and so long as the debtor returned the collateral to California or Ford itself took possession and returned it to California within five years of perfection of its security interest in California, it could then defeat any security interest of any other creditor in any other state which was perfected within the five year period. A rule requiring reperfection in another state within four months from the time collateral or the place of business of the debtor is moved to another state requires some diligence on the part of the holder of a security interest to preserve his priority status. On the other hand, if as urged by Ford, there were no lapse for a period of five years in the state where the property or principal place of business was located at the time the security interest was perfected, all later lenders or purchasers would have to be concerned with searching the records of all states in which the property may have been located within the preceding five years.

While, in connection with the four month rule, it is true that UCC §9-103(3) speaks only of property "brought into this state" and does not speak of property taken out of "this state", it would seem implicit that each state adopting the UCC sought the uniformity provided in UCC §1-102(2)(c). It is presumed that by providing when property subject to a perfected security interest comes into "this state" the security interest will be recognized in "this state" for only four months unless the prior security interest is perfected in "this state", it was also intended by those adopting the UCC that property leaving "this state" would be subject to the same rule requiring perfection in the second state within four months.

Ford argues that the UCC does not attempt to provide uniformity of law between the states adopting it but simply that the situs of property would determine the law of which state should apply in a given situation. But, when two states have adopted the same provisions of the UCC, as in the present case, then the law is the same in both states and it makes no difference whether the law of one or the other is applied.

For the above reasons, the Motion for Reconsideration filed by Ford is denied.

Notes:

1 Recall *G.M.A.C.* v. *Hubbard* (1978) 87 DLR (3d) 39 (NB CA) (*supra*, chapter 10 (B)) where the goods subject to a conditional sale agreement were improperly re-moved by the buyer from Ontario into N.B. and there sold by him before re-registration by the creditor. It was held that registration of a conditional sale agreement does not constitute constructive notice for the purposes of SGA s. 25, and that the extra-provincial security interest had been overridden by the subse-quent dealing in N.B.

2 As for "intangibles or . . . goods of a type that are normally used in more than one jurisdiction, if such goods are classified as equipment or . . . inventory by reason of their being leased by the debtor to others", the validity and perfection of a security interest, and the possibility and effect of proper registration, are governed by the law, "including the conflict of laws rules", of the jurisdiction in which the debtor's chief place of business is located. See PPSA s. 5.

3 The conflict of laws provisions were extensively revised in the 1972 Code. For a detailed analysis, see P. Coogan, "The New UCC Article 9" (1973) 86 Harv. LR 477, 529-58. For a discussion of the extent of the adoption of these revisions in the Model Uniform and Sask. Acts, see J. Ziegel and R.C.C. Cuming, "The Renewal of Personal Property Law in Canada" (1981) 31 Univ. Tor. LJ.

Chapter 23
Security Interests in Intangibles and Specialties

A. INTRODUCTION

Intangibles and specialties consist of "chattel paper", "document of title", "instrument[s]", "intangible[s]", and "securities" (respectively defined in s. 1(c), (i), (l), (m) and (w). "Book debts" (s. 2(b)) and "letters of credit and advices of credit" (s. 24(e)) are included in the above definitions but for some purposes are referred to separately in the PPSA. *Cf.* the classification of collateral chart, *supra*, chapter 20(B).

In dealing with security interests in copyrights, patents and trademarks, federal law should also be considered. Federal provisions governing security interests in these intangibles "establish their own schemes for the perfection of security interests but, by implication, leave all other questions to be decided by provincial law . . .": J. Ziegel and I. Feltham, "Federal Law and a Uniform Act on Security in Personal Property" (1966) 9 Can. BJ 30, 32. Such "provisions are needed and should be retained. The Acts deal . . . with questions of ownership and require the federal authorities to maintain records of ownership. It seems convenient, therefore, that security interests in such collateral should also be recorded in the same register. The same approach is adopted [in] UCC §9-302(3)(a) . . .": *id.* at 35. See Copyright Act, RSC 1970, c. C-30, s. 40; Patent Act, RSC 1970, c. P-4, ss. 52-53 and Trade Marks Act, RSC 1970, c. T-4, ss. 26(1), and 65(c). Note however that "[t]he Copyright Act . . . and the Patent Act . . . require respectively the registration of every assignment of a patent or any grant of an interest in a copyright. 'Assignment' and 'interest', however, are not defined, and it is not clear whether they include an assignment by way of security or the grant of a security interest. The regulations made under the Trade Marks Act contain a similar requirement, but fail to state what is the sanction in the case of non-compliance": Ziegel and Feltham, *id.* at 33-4.

The materials which follow in this chapter focus on security interests in connection with contract rights financing.

B. BOOK DEBTS (ACCOUNTS RECEIVABLE) AND CHATTEL PAPER

The PPSA applies to "an assignment . . . intended as security" (s. 2(*a*)(ii)) as well as to "every assignment of book debts not intended as security" except an assignment for the general benefit of creditors (s. 2(*b*)). It enumerates chattel paper ("one or more than one writing that expresses both a monetary obligation and a security interest in specific goods", s. 1(*c*)) as one of the types of collateral in which a security interest is perfected by possession (24(*a*)) as well as by registration (25(1)(*a*)). Security interests in intangibles (including "choses in action", s. 1(*m*)) are perfected by registration (25(1)(*c*)).

1. FINANCING ARRANGEMENTS

P. SHUCHMAN,
"Profit on Default: An Archival Study of Automobile Repossession and Repair"
(1969) 22 Stan. L. Rev. 20, 25

With occasional variants, there are five categories of dealer-financer agreements for disposition of the dealer's paper: (1) nonrecourse; (2) full recourse; (3) full repurchase; (4) limited repurchase; and (5) optional repurchase. First, a dealer may sell, assign, or dispose of his paper without recourse; the dealer then has no legal obligation to the financer in the event of the consumer's default. Second, the dealer may dispose of his paper with full recourse: He agrees to repurchase the chattel paper for the balance due in the event of default. The burden is thus on the dealer to repossess the vehicle, resell it, and if need be, proceed against the consumer for a deficiency judgment. Or, the dealer may ignore the collateral and simply institute suit against the consumer for the balance due plus the vigorish allowed under state statutes. Third, the dealer may enter into a full-repurchase agreement. In this case the financer usually repossesses the car, delivers it to the dealer, and then assigns all his rights in the chattel paper to the dealer who pays the financer the balance due on the retail installment contract. Fourth, the dealer may negotiate a limited-repurchase agreement. The agreement is similar to the full-repurchase agreement, except that the dealer obligates himself for the balance due on the retail installment contract only up to a specified maximum. Fifth, under an optional-repurchase agreement, the financer may, and in some instances must, repossess the car. The dealer then buys the car from the financer either at a price fixed in advance, or for the balance due on the chattel paper, which will be the maximum fixed price. The financer or the dealer will then proceed against the consumer.

NORTON v. NATIONAL BANK OF COMMERCE OF PINE BLUFF
(1966) 398 SW 2d 538 (Ark. SC)

GEORGE ROSE SMITH J.: This case presents a number of questions of first impression under the Uniform Commercial Code.

On September 4, 1963, the appellant Norton, an automobile dealer, sold a 1957 Oldsmobile sedan to Billy Goldsmith, who executed a promissory note and a conditional sales contract for the unpaid purchase price. On the same day Norton in turn sold the note and contract to the appellee bank. Norton endorsed the note and executed a written assignment of the contract, with a provision that if Goldsmith should default in his obligation Norton would repurchase the contract for the amount due thereon (with costs and expenses).

Goldsmith defaulted after having made only two monthly payments. On January 9 the bank repossessed the car, notifying Goldsmith by letter that it had done so. On January 24, without notice either to Goldsmith or to Norton, the bank sold the car to one of its customers, by private sale, for $75.00. This left an unpaid balance of $227.88 on the debt. The bank demanded that sum from Norton, who refused to pay.

The bank sued Norton only. According to the undisputed evidence it had been the bank's uniform custom in the past to give Norton and other dealers an opportunity to repurchase such contracts. Norton had never failed to repurchase when asked to do so. The manager of the bank's personal loan department was unable to explain why in this instance the bank for the first time proceeded against the car without notice to the dealer. There is evidence that a 1957 Oldsmobile would sell for from $25.00 to $125.00. It is admitted that an automobile dealer is in a better position than a bank to obtain full value in the sale of a used car.

The circuit court, sitting without a jury, found that the bank had obtained a fair price for the car and entered judgment against Norton for the balance due on the debt. Norton contends that the bank should have given him notice of the proposed sale, so that he might protect himself by repurchasing the commercial paper and reselling the car himself. He insists that the bank's failure to give him notice discharged his entire liability.

We requested *amicus curiae* briefs from Joe C. Barrett and from Harry E. Meek, for which we are grateful. Mr. Barrett states that the Permanent Editorial Board of the Uniform Commercial Code makes its services available to appellate courts when the interpretation of the Code is in issue. Members of the Permanent Board assisted Mr. Barrett in the preparation of his brief.

The two *amicus* briefs discuss the provisions of the Code in greater detail than counsel for the litigants have done. Both *amici* are of the view that Norton was not entitled to notice that a private sale was contemplated, for the reason that Norton was not a "debtor" within the pertinent section of the Code. Ark.Stat.Ann. §85-9-504(3) (Add. 1961). They seem, however, to reach the same result that would follow if Norton had been entitled to notice. That is, they concede that the bank acted improperly, that it should have given Norton an opportunity to repurchase the contract, and that it is liable to Norton for any damages he suffered as a result of the bank's misconduct. (One of the *amici* would award Norton, in addition to his actual damages, the finance charge and penalty set out in §85-9-507 [1] of the Code. The other would award the finance charge plus penalty when the actual damages cannot be fixed with reasonable certainty.)

It is our conclusion that Norton *was* a debtor within the terms of the statute and was therefore entitled to notice that a private sale was impending. The statute requires notice to a "debtor," with certain exceptions. Section 85-9-504(3). We dismiss two possible exceptions to the requirement of notice before reaching the main issue.

First, the Code dispenses with notice when the collateral to be sold "is of a type customarily sold on a recognized market." Section 85-9-504(3). We cannot approve the bank's contention that a used car falls in this category. Obviously the Code dispenses with notice in this situation only because the debtor would not be prejudiced by the want of notice. Thus a "recognized market" might well be a stock market or a commodity market, where sales involve many items so similar that individual differences are nonexistent or immaterial, where haggling and competitive bidding are not primary factors in each sale, and where the prices paid in actual sales of comparable property are currently available by quotation. We agree with the view taken in Pennsylvania, that there is no recognized market for used cars. Alliance Discount Corp. v. Shaw, 195 Pa. Super. 601, 171 A. 2d 543 (1961). What one 1957 Oldsmobile sells for does not fix the amount a different one may be expected to bring.

Secondly, "except in the case of consumer goods" Norton, if he was a person having a security interest known to the bank, would have been entitled to notice of the proposed sale. Section 85-9-504(3). For the moment it is enough to say that all four briefs expressly or tacitly assume that the Oldsmobile was "consumer goods," because Goldsmith bought it as a pleasure vehicle. Hence Norton may not have been entitled to notice under this section of the Code.

We come to the main question: Was Norton a "debtor" to whom notice should have been given? The controlling definition appears in §85-9-105(d): " 'Debtor' means the person who owes payment *or other performance* [our italics] of the obligation secured, whether or not he owns or has rights in the collateral, and includes the seller of accounts, contract rights or chattel paper. Where the debtor and the owner of the collateral are not the same person, the term 'debtor' . . . may include both where the context so requires. . . ."

Norton had promised to repurchase the contract for the amount due. He was a person who owed "other performance" of the obligation. In our judgment the following illustration in Paragraph 4 of the official Comment to §85-9-105 is conclusive of Norton's status as a debtor:

> 4. A dealer sells a tractor to a farmer on conditional sales contract. The conditional sales contract is a 'security agreement', the farmer is the 'debtor', the dealer is the 'secured party' and the tractor is the type of 'collateral' defined in Section 9-109 as 'equipment'. But now the dealer transfers the contract to his bank, either by outright sale [the situation now before us] or to secure a loan. Since the conditional sales contract is a security agreement relating to specific equipment the conditional sales contract is now the type of collateral called 'chattel paper'. In this transaction between the dealer and his bank, the bank is the 'secured party', the dealer is the 'debtor', and the farmer is the 'account debtor'.

For the benefit of those who do not have ready access to the briefs on file in this case, and to the end that the *amici* may know why we do not fully agree with their position, we think it best to explain the arguments presented upon the question of whether Norton was a debtor. As the discussion submitted by Mr. Barrett and the Permanent Editorial Board is more detailed than that in any other brief we will direct our remarks to it.

Mr. Barrett and the Board draw a distinction between the note and contract ("chattel paper") on the one hand and the Oldsmobile on the other. It is their position that Goldsmith alone was the debtor with respect to the Oldsmobile; so Norton was not entitled to notice that it was to be sold. Norton, however, was the debtor with respect to the chattel paper and would have been entitled to notice if the bank had decided to sell that paper.

The distinction urged by the Barrett-Board brief is not, in our opinion, clearly spelled out by the Code, whatever the intention of its draftsmen may have been. In many situations, including the one at bar, it might lead to injustice.

We attach significance to the fact that Mr. Barrett and the Board refer to the initial transaction between Norton and the bank as a "financing" of Norton by the bank. Yet that transaction was not a financing in the same sense that it would have been if Norton had pledged the Goldsmith chattel paper to secure Norton's own note to the bank. In that event if the bank decided to sell the Goldsmith paper to a third person and apply the proceeds to Norton's note, there would be a good reason for giving Norton notice of the proposed sale: to enable him to protect himself against a sale for an inadequate price.

But Norton was not "financed" by the bank in the sense of having a direct personal obligation to pay money in any event. He sold the Goldsmith chattel paper outright, assuming only a secondary liability if Goldsmith should default. In that situation if the bank should decide to sell the chattel paper to a third person, the terms of sale would be of no especial interest to Norton, for his secondary liability to the new holder would remain the same. Norton, however, was directly affected by the sale of the Oldsmobile; the amount obtained in that sale fixed his pecuniary liability. In simple fairness he should have had notice — a requirement entailing no real inconvenience or hardship to the bank.

In resting our decision on the matter of notice we do not imply that we necessarily agree with counsel's view that the Oldsmobile was "consumer goods" merely because Goldsmith bought it as a pleasure vehicle. No doubt the car was within the definition of consumer goods as far as Goldsmith himself was concerned. Section 85-9-109. But, under §85-9-504(3), whether or not Norton, as a person having a pre-existing security interest in the car, was entitled to notice of sale might depend upon whether the car was consumer goods. Yet, as far as Norton was concerned in the matter of notice, it was completely immaterial that Goldsmith had originally bought the car for pleasure rather than for business. A principle should not be extended beyond its underlying reason. We reserve judgment upon this aspect of the case.

The bank also contends that Norton waived his right to notice of the sale by signing a printed assignment of the conditional sales contract (prepared by the bank) which recited that Norton waived all notices to which he might otherwise have been entitled. Under §85-9-501(3) the attempted waiver was ineffective.

Finally, what is Norton's measure of damages? We do not agree with his contention that the bank's failure to give him notice of the intended sale completely discharged his obligation. For the most part the Code follows the theory formerly applicable to mortgages, by which the debtor was entitled to any surplus realized upon foreclosure and was liable for any deficiency. Section 85-9-504(2). The Code also provides that if the secured party has disposed of the collateral in a manner not in accordance with the Code "any person entitled to notification . . . has a right to recover from the secured party any loss caused by a failure to comply" with the provisions of the Code. Section 85-9-507(1).

Upon the issue of Norton's damages simple considerations of fair play cast the burden of proof upon the bank. It was the bank which wrongfully disposed of the car without notice to the debtors. Thus it was the bank's action that made it at least difficult, if not impossible, for Norton to prove the extent of his loss with reasonable certainty. A chattel such as a car may well be a thousand miles away before the debtor learns of its sale without notice. It would be manifestly unfair for the creditor to derive an advantage from its own misconduct. We think the just solution is to indulge the presumption in the first instance that the collateral was worth at least the amount of the debt, thereby shifting to the creditor the burden of proving the amount that should reasonably have been obtained through a sale conducted according to law. The extent to which the penalty set out in §85-9-507(1) may be applicable in the case at bar is an issue that may depend upon the further development of the proof.

Since the case was not tried upon the principles of law that we deem to be controlling the judgment must be reversed and the cause remanded for a new trial.

Notes and Questions:

1   How many PPSA transactions were involved in Norton? What is the terminology used by the Act to describe Norton, Goldsmith and the Bank? What was each party's obligation and to whom did it run? What collateral was taken in each transaction? See: ss. 1(b), (c), (d), (g), (k), (v) and (x). Consider the following illustration of chattel paper financing given in the Comment to UCC 9-105:

> A dealer sells a tractor to a farmer on conditional sales contract. The conditional sales contract is a "security agreement", the farmer is the "debtor", the dealer is the "secured party" and the tractor is the type of "collateral" defined . . . as "equipment". But now the dealer transfers the contract to his bank, either by outright sale or to secure a loan. Since the conditional sales contract is a security agreement relating to specific equipment the conditional sales contract is now the type of collateral called "chattel paper". In this transaction between the dealer and his bank, the bank is the "secured party", the dealer is the "debtor", and the farmer is the "account debtor".

2   The notice of intention to sell is required to be sent pursuant to PPSA s. 58(5) "to any person who has a security interest in the collateral". Unlike UCC 9-504(3), PPSA s. 58(5) does not provide for a "consumer goods" exception. Would Norton be entitled to notice under s. 58(5)?

3   Into which of Shuchman's five categories of dealer-financer agreements does the

Norton-Bank agreement fall? Suppose that Norton, instead of selling the Goldsmith contract to the bank, had pledged it to secure a bank loan to him. What difference would it have made to the outcome? Is the distinction crucial to the issue of Norton's owing "other performance" of Goldsmith's obligation? Would it make any difference if, in the pledge situation, Goldsmith had sent his installment payments directly to the bank?

4 Do you agree with the position of the Permanent Editorial Board as a matter of statutory interpretation? As a matter of policy?

5 A major difference between a non-recourse and a recourse arrangement is explained in Comment 2 to UCC 9-502 as follows:

> In one form of accounts receivable financing, which is found in the "factoring" arrangements which are common in the textile industry, the assignee assumes the credit risk — that is, he buys the account under an agreement which does not provide for recourse or charge-back against the assignor in the event the account proves uncollectible. Under such an arrangement, neither the debtor nor his creditors have any legitimate concern with the disposition which the assignee makes of the accounts. Under another form of accounts receivable financing, however, the assignee does not assume the credit risk and retains a right of full or limited recourse or charge-back for uncollectible accounts. In such a case both debtor and creditors have a right that the assignee not dump the accounts, if the result will be to increase a possible deficiency claim or to reduce a possible surplus.

Is the Comment relevant to the determination of the issue dealt with in *Norton*?

6 The determination whether a particular assignment of book debts constitutes an outright sale or a transfer for security is left to the courts. The presence of recourse in a sale agreement will not, without more, automatically convert an outright sale into a transfer for security: see Comment 4 to UCC 9-502. In *Major's Furniture Mart, Inc.* v. *Castle Credit Corp. Inc.* (1979) 602 F. 2d 538 (3d Cir.) "the allocation of risks [between an assignor and an assignee under an assignment of book debts with recourse] heavily favor[ed] [the assignor's] claim to be considered as an assignor with an interest in the collectibility of its accounts." The court characterized the arrangement as a transfer for security where "Major's debt was secured by a transfer of [its] customer accounts to Castle". It observed that the assignor's "guarantees of quality [namely as to his performance of the underlying contracts as well as to the creditworthiness of the account debtors] alone, or even guarantees of collectibility alone, might be consistent with true sale, but [here the assignee] attempted to shift all risks to [the assignor], and incur none of the risks or obligations of ownership". Do you nonetheless agree with the court's conclusion? What was "Major's debt . . . to Castle"?

In any event, what turns on the characterization of the assignment as an outright sale or assignment for security? Is it the applicability of the PPSA? See ss. 1(*y*) and 2(*b*). Is it the assignee's right to proceed directly against the account debtor? Consider s. 56(1). Is it the assignee's right to retain any surplus collected by him from the account debtor which exceeds the assignor's liability to him? Compare the language of UCC 9-502(2) with PPSA s. 56(2). Does the latter inevitably produce a different result? *Cf.* F. Catzman *et al.*, *Personal Property Security Law in Ontario* (1926) p. 226: "Of course, in the case of [an outright sale of accounts] the 'debtor' is only liable for a deficiency if the assignment so provides." Do you agree?

2. THE PRIORITY SCHEME

a) Introduction

Medieval common law did not recognize the transfer of choses in action. Their assignability was first recognized by Courts of Equity. A statutory form of assignment was introduced in England in s. 25(6) of the Judicature Act 1873, substantially reproduced in s. 54(1) of the Ontario Conveyancing and Law of Property Act, RSO 1970, c. 85 (see chapter 14(A)(2) *supra*).

The pre-PPSA priority rules as to competing interests in choses in action developed in equity. The rules were not affected at all by the introduction of a statutory form of assignment: "The statute has not altered the law in substance. It is merely machinery." See Cheshire and Fifoot, *Law of Contract* (9th ed., 1976) p. 500. Under these rules, priority between two bona fide competing assignees of a chose in action is determined by the order in which notice of the assignment is given to the debtor. This is the rule in *Dearle* v. *Hall* (1828) 3 Russ. 1, 38 ER 475. Where the notices are simultaneous, where no notice has been given to the debtor, or where the first to give notice does it with knowledge of a prior assignment, priority is determined by the chronological order of the assignments. These rules apply to an assignment of future book debts as well as present book debts (*Tailby* v. *Official Receiver* (1888) 13 App. Cas. 523 (H.L.)), and have also been held to apply to assignments governed by the Assignment of Book Debts legislation. See *Snyder's Ltd.* v. *Furniture Finance Corp. Ltd.* (1930) 66 OLR 79, [1931] 1 DLR 398 (CA) and *Re Royal Bank of Canada and Revelstoke Companies Ltd.* (1979) 94 DLR (3d) 692 (Alta. SC).

The above rules only determine priority under pre-PPSA law between competing assignees. Priority between an assignee and a lienor (judgment creditor, trustee in bankruptcy) is determined in favour of an assignee who has either an absolute assignment or a floating charge which crystallized prior to the intervention of the lienor's interest: *Evans* v. *Rival Granite Quarries Ltd.* [1910] 2 KB 979 (CA); *Great Lake Petroleum Co.* v. *Border Cities Oil Ltd.* [1934] 2 DLR 743 (Ont. CA).

Under the PPSA, the general rules of priorities (ss. 22, 35) apply to accounts receivable. Note, however, that where the account is evidenced by a negotiable instrument the rights of a holder in due course are explicitly preserved (s. 31(1)(*a*) and (2)). Note also the specific provisions with respect to chattel paper (s. 30(2), discussed below) and non-negotiable instruments (s. 30(3)).

b) Registration by an Assignee

PPSA 23(2) provides that an assignee of a security interest succeeds to the position of the assignor "so far as . . . perfection is concerned". Stated otherwise, no registration is required to continue the perfected status of the assignor's security interest. Comment 7 to UCC 9-302 illustrates the operation and limitation of the corresponding Code provisions:

> Buyer buys goods from Seller who retains a security interest in them which he perfects. Seller assigns the perfected security interest to X. The security interest, in X's hands and without further steps on his part, continues perfected against *Buyer's* transferees and creditors. If, however, the assignment from Seller to X was itself intended for security [or was an assignment of book debts not intended as security], X must take whatever steps may be required for perfection in order to be protected against *Seller's* transferees and creditors.

Where a secured party has assigned a security interest perfected by registration, "a financing change statement . . . may be registered,": PPSA s. 48(1). The effect of such a financing change statement is not to give the assignee a perfected security interest in the assignor's contract right. Nor, as explained above, is registration required for the purpose of continuing the perfected status of the assignor's security interest in the assignee's hands. Registration of a financing change statement is rather designed to make the assignee "the secured party of record"; s. 48(3). This effect is explained in the Comment to UCC 9-405:

> A secured party who has assigned his interest might wish to have the fact noted of record, so that inquiries concerning the transaction would be addressed not to him but to the assignee. [*Cf.* PPSA s. 20]. After a secured party has assigned his rights of record, the assignee becomes the "secured party of record" and may file a continuation statement . . . a termination statement . . . or a statement of release. . . .

Where a secured party has assigned an unperfected security interest, "a financing statement . . . may be registered in which the assignee is shown as the secured party": s. 48(2). Where the collateral securing the indebtedness under the assigned contract is "goods to be held for sale or lease", may the secured party's assignee take advantage of s. 47(2) and register a financing statement before a security agreement is signed? An affirmative answer was given in *West Bay Sales Ltd.* v. *Hitachi Sales Corp. of Canada Ltd.* (1979) 28 CBR (NS) 244 (Ont. SC in Bkcy). For a summary of the facts, see Chapter 22(E), problem 4. In that case,

> [it was] apparently argued, first, that no financing statement can be registered until there has been an assignment of a subsisting security interest and, secondly, where there are successive assignments, that each must be the subject of a separate registration. Henry, J., was repelled by the practical implications of this strict reading of s. 48(2) and he made short shrift of it. He saw no justification for distinguishing between the position of the assignor and the assignee and he was satisfied "on a true appreciation of the intent of the Legislature" that the assignee was entitled to take advantage of s. 47(2). The alternative, he thought, would lead to "redundant, uniformative and costly" multiple filings.

((1979) 3 Can. Bus. LJ 222, 233).

What is the effect of assignee's registration under s. 48(2)? Does it perfect a security interest in the goods securing the indebtedness to the assignor? Does it perfect a security interest in the assignor's contract right towards the account debtor? *Cf.* s. 48(3). The difference between the security interest in the chattel paper and the security interest in the underlying goods is demonstrated by the following problem, case and notes:

Problem: A dealer sold an electric appliance to a buyer under a conditional sale agreement. A financing statement was duly registered. The conditional sale agreement was assigned to a finance company which neither registered nor took possession of it.

Who is the winner in any of the following priority contests:

a) A judgment creditor of the buyer or the finance company, with the respect to the appliance;

b) A judgment creditor of the dealer or the finance company with respect to the conditional sale agreement;

c) A judgment creditor of the dealer or the buyer with respect to the appliance;

d) A judgment creditor of the dealer or the finance company with respect to the appliance?

GENERAL ELECTRIC CREDIT CORP. v. BANKERS COMMERCIAL CORP.
(1968) 429 S.W. 2d 60 (Ark. SC)

GEORGE ROSE SMITH Justice: This is primarily a dispute between two finance companies about their security interests in a dragline that was sold on credit by Southland Tractors, Inc., to the appellee J. T. Arnold, III. Both security agreements held by the rival finance companies are defective, that of Bankers Commercial Corporation not having met the filing requirements of the Uniform Commercial Code and that of General Electric Credit Corporation being a forgery. This is an appeal by GECC from a judgment holding that Bankers alone has a valid security interest in the dragline. Arnold, the debtor, cross appeals upon another issue.

On April 13, 1966, Southland sold the dragline to Arnold for $33,850.04. The contract of sale was in the form of a three-year lease which recited that Arnold had paid $5,000 as advance rental and would pay the remainder in 36 equal monthly installments. Arnold was given the option of purchasing the dragline at any time during the term of the lease by paying the $33,850.04, less the total amount of rents already paid. Under the Code such a lease is treated as a security agreement. Ark. Stat. Ann. §85-1-201(37) (Add. 1961).

On the same day Southland (*a*) duly filed a financing statement showing itself as the creditor and Arnold as the debtor and (*b*) assigned the lease contract to Bankers for a cash consideration of more than $24,000.00. Bankers did not file anything to show its security interest; so Southland continued as the creditor of record.

About three months later Southland informed Arnold that it had arranged to refinance the debt with General Electric Credit Corporation. The identity of the creditor made no difference to Arnold, who readily signed another financing statement showing GECC as the creditor. Southland then forged Arnold's signature to a three-year lease, similar to the one held by Bankers, and assigned it to GECC. In that transaction GECC, whose manager realized that Southland was having financial troubles, paid Southland $4,107.06 in cash and credited delinquent Southland accounts with $20,091.94. GECC's manager had talked with Arnold by telephone to be sure that he had the dragline and that he understood the gross amount due and the size of the monthly payments. Neither Southland nor Arnold mentioned the outstanding contract with Bankers; so GECC's manager (who had checked the financing statement of record) did not realize that Bankers had a security interest in the dragline. At GECC's request Southland terminated the earlier financing statement, as authorized by the Code. Section 85-9-404. Southland soon went into bankruptcy.

Arnold assumed that the debt had been refinanced, but he soon received demands for payment from both Bankers and GECC. Since that time Arnold has consistently taken the position that he will make his payments when he learns which creditor is entitled to the money.

This action to replevy the dragline was brought by GECC against Arnold. Bankers intervened to assert its claim. The trial court, sitting without a jury, upheld Bankers' security interest, permitted it to accelerate the maturity of its entire claim, and ordered the property sold as in a foreclosure suit. The order of sale was superseded by GECC pending the appeal.

Upon the main dispute the trial court's decision was right. Bankers holds a valid security agreement, admittedly signed by Arnold. Bankers' failure to file any notice of its creditorship might have allowed later valid claims to take priority, but as between the two of them Bankers has an enforceable cause of action against Arnold.

By contrast, the only genuine instrument held by GECC is its financing statement. A financing statement, standing alone, does not create a security interest in the debtor's property. It merely serves notice that the named creditor may have a security interest. Section 85-9-402, Comment 2; Meek, "Secured Transactions Under the Uniform Commercial Code," 18 Ark. L. Rev. 30, 40 (1964). Of course the forged lease assigned by Southland to GECC had no effect upon Arnold's interest in the dragline. *Hall* v. *Mitchell*, 175 Ark. 641, 1 S.W. 2d 59 (1927).

Counsel for GECC insists that Bankers and Arnold have estopped themselves from contesting the GECC claim: Bankers by its failure to perfect its security interest and Arnold by his failure to mention the Bankers contract during his conversation with GECC's manager. We need not speculate whether such an estoppel would run counter to the Code requirement that security agreements be in writing. Section 85-9-203. If Bankers was at fault in failing to file notice, GECC was also at fault in accepting the lease from an assignor of doubtful solvency without verifying Arnold's signature. Arnold's good faith was attested by his own testimony. The issues of estoppel narrow down to disputed questions of fact, upon which there is ample substantial evidence to support the circuit court's judgment.

On cross appeal Arnold is entitled to relief. Both GECC and Bankers sought to accelerate the maturity of their total claims, but their failure to reserve that power in the contracts precluded them from exercising it. *Farnsworth* v. *Hoover*, 66 Ark. 367, 50 S.W. 865 (1899). At best Bankers may be entitled to damages resulting from Arnold's failure to make his payments when due — the measure of such damages presumably being interest at the legal rate and certainly not being the rents to accrue during the remaining life of the lease.

Affirmed on direct appeal; reversed on cross appeal and remanded for further proceedings.

Notes and Questions:

1   Do you agree with the decision? In particular consider the following questions: Was the dispute "between two finance companies about their security interests in the dragline"? Was Bankers' security interest in the lease unperfected? Is it true to say that GECC had no security interest in the dragline?

2   Does a perfected security interest in a true lease (as distinguished from the lease dealt with above in the *GECC* case) constitute a perfected security interest in the lessor's reversionary interest in the leased goods? Into what class of collateral does a lease fall? Note that under UCC 9-105(1)(*b*) "a writing . . . which evidences both a monetary obligation and . . . a lease of specific goods" falls within the definition of "chattel paper". *Cf.* PPSA s. 1(*c*). Is the definition relevant in determining the status of the security interest in the lessor's reversionary right in the leased goods? *Cf. In the Matter of Leasing Consultants Inc.* (1973) 486 F. 2d 367 (2nd Cir.). Here a bank took an assignment of "a continuing security interest in . . . lease(s) and the property leased" as collateral security for advances and loans. The bank filed a financing statement in New York, where the lessor-borrower had its principal place of business (*cf.* PPSA s. 5), but not in New Jersey, where the leased equipment was situated. The financing statement described the collateral as "leases . . . including all related equipment described therein." Stating that "the leased property itself is 'goods'," the court concluded that "the future reversionary interest is likewise an interest in goods", and that "to perfect a security interest in the reversionary interest in the equipment it was necessary to file a financing statement in New Jersey where the equipment was located." Do you agree? Is "the [lessor's] future reversionary interest [in the leased goods]" necessarily "an interest in goods"? *Cf.* PPSA s. 1(*m*) and recall the discussion on collateral classification in Chapter 20(B) *supra*.

c)   Competing Interests in Chattel Paper (s. 30(2))

A purchaser for value of chattel paper "who takes possession of it in the ordinary course of his business" prevails over a previous security interest perfected by registration if he did not know of it (s. 30(2)(*a*)). What precaution should be taken by a chattel paper financer who perfects his interest by registration?

When a security interest attaches to the chattel paper as "proceeds of inventory under section 27", the purchaser for value of chattel paper "who takes possession of it in the ordinary course of his business" prevails regardless of "the extent of his knowledge" (s. 30(2)(*b*)). Can the inventory financer who claims the chattel paper as proceeds defeat the interest of the financer who advances new value against the chattel paper as original collateral? Will s. 30(2)(*b*) defeat an inventory financer who in making the loan placed substantial reliance on the chattel paper resulting from the sale? Compare the language of PPSA s. 30(2)(*b*) to the "merely as proceeds" language of corresponding UCC 9-308. For the rationale and an historical perspective on the chattel paper financer priority under s. 30(2)(*b*), see G. Gilmore, *Security Interests in Personal Property* vol. II (1965) §27.1 (p. 718).

Note that the PPSA, like Article 9, does not confer a s. 30(2)(*b*) priority to a financer of intangible book debts. Arguably, a priority contest between an inventory financer and a financer who takes security interest in the intangible book debts generated by the sale of the inventory is to be determined by the ordinary priority rules, i.e., s. 35(1)(*a*)). Is the PMSI priority of s. 34(2) carried over to the book debts as proceeds of the inventory?

The priority of the chattel paper financer under s. 30(2)(*b*) is carried over by s. 29(3)(*b*) and (*c*) into priorities over returned or repossessed goods. The general rule of s. 29(1) is that a security interest in goods which are the subject of a sale reattaches if the goods are returned to, or repossessed by, the seller or his assignee. It can reattach as a perfected security interest: s. 29(2). A security interest which reattaches under s. 29(1) prevails over the security interest of a transferee of an intangible resulting from the original sale: s. 29(3)(*a*) and (*c*). It is defeated however by a chattel paper financer with priority under s. 30(2)(*b*). See s. 29(3)(*b*). For more on the complex priority problems in connection with returned goods, see inter alia *Osborn* v. *First National Bank of Holdenville* (1970) 472 P. 2d 440 (Okla. SC); *National Savings & Finance Corp.* v. *First National Bank and Trust Co.* (1973) 12 UCC Rep. 753 (Okla. CA); *Bank of Beulah* v. *Chase* (1975) 17 UCC Rep. 259 (ND SC); and R. Lord, "Rights of Secured Creditors in Returned and Repossessed Goods under the Uniform Commercial Code: A Study of Section 9-306(5)" (1976-77) 15 Duquesne L. Rev. 165.

Section 29 primarily applies to inventory. Consider the case of goods sold by a dealer. Suppose his stock in trade is subject to an inventory financer's security interest. A buyer from the dealer usually takes the goods free from this security interest. See ss. 27(1)(*a*) and 30, and the discussion in Chapter 22(G) *supra*. Where the sale from the dealer is on credit, the intangible or chattel paper resulting from the sale can be assigned by the dealer to a financer other than the inventory financer. If subsequent to their sale these goods are either returned to the dealer because of the buyer's dissatisfaction with them or repossessed by the dealer on the buyer's default, the original inventory financer's security interest reattaches: s. 29(1). The relative priorities of the inventory financer and the transferee of the intangible or chattel paper are then determined according to s. 29(3).

Problems:

1   On day 1 Bank made advances against chattel paper in Dealer's hands and properly registered a financing statement. On day 2, Finance Company advanced money against the same chattel paper and took possession thereof. As between Bank and Finance Company, who prevails? Would you change your answer if (a) Finance Company registered a financing statement with respect to the chattel paper instead of taking possession of it? Or if (b) Finance Company took possession but the chattel paper had been stamped by Bank with a notice indicating its security interest? Is s. 53(1)(*a*) relevant in determining any of these questions?

2   Bank made advances to Dealer under a security agreement providing for a security interest in Dealer's inventory and its proceeds. A financing statement was duly registered. Sale of the appliances forming the inventory resulted in chattel paper and intangibles against which Finance Company made advances and properly registered a financing statement. As between Bank and Finance Company, who prevails with respect to the chattel paper? The intangibles? The appliances when repossessed by the seller on the buyers' default?

3   Bank has a security interest in Dealer's car inventory. Dealer sold a car to B-1 under a conditional sale contract. Finance company 1 advanced money against the contract and took a security interest in it. On B-1's default Dealer repossessed the car and resold it to B-2 under a conditional sale contract which was taken as collateral for new value by Finance Company 2. Who has priority in the car? In the chattel paper resulting from the sale to B-2? Does your answer depend on whether the car is in the hands of B-2 or in Dealer's hands on its lawful repossession from B-2? Assume that following B-2's default each security interest was duly perfected. Would reperfection assist any party?

4   Manufacturer sold a car to Dealer under a conditional sale contract which was taken as collateral for new value by Bank. Dealer sold the car to Consumer under a conditional sale contract which was taken as collateral for new value by Finance Company. On Consumer's default and repossession of the car by Dealer or Finance Company, who prevails as to the car? Assume that each security interest was duly perfected.

3. ASSIGNEE'S RIGHTS UNDER THE PPSA (s. 40)

a) General

The assignee-account debtor relationship is governed by s. 40. Following pre-PPSA law, the section provides for the assignee's subjection to all the account debtor's defences arising from the contract (s. 40(1)(a)) as well as to other claims or defences in so far as they "accrued before . . . notice of the assignment" (s. 40(1)(b)). The rule is generally subject to any contrary agreement governed by s. 16. Section 40 further provides for the account debtor's right to pay the assignor until notified of the assignment (s. 40(2)). Note that the account debtor's equities against the assignee can be asserted only defensively. What is the assignee's position in relation to the assignor's remedies under the assigned contract? For a comprehensive discussion of the effect of the assignment on the assignor-account debtor's ongoing contractual relationship, see Gilmore, *Security Interest in Personal Property* vol. 2 (1965) Ch. 41 (p. 1077).

Unlike corresponding UCC 9-318, PPSA s. 40 does not provide that a contractual provision between the assignor and the account debtor which purports to prohibit assignment is ineffective. The Ontario Law Reform Commission observed that "the creditor's right to deal freely with rights to payment is more important than the account debtor's administrative convenience" and favoured the enactment of a provision in the PPSA outlawing "no assignment" clauses: OLRC Sales Report (1979) vol. I, 123. Such a provision appears in Sask. PPSA s. 40(6).

Does s. 40 apply to an assignee of part of the claim against the account debtor? The provision itself is silent. According to Professor Gilmore, "there is no modern authority which suggests that the rights of a 'partial' assignee are in any way inferior to, or different from, the rights of a total assignee": Gilmore, *op. cit.*, vol. II, p. 1081; see also vol. I, §7.5.

b) Notice to the Account Debtor of the Assignment

Under pre-PPSA law notice to the debtor determined the priority between competing bona fide assignees (the rule in *Dearle* v. *Hall* (1828) 3 Russ. 1, 38 ER 475). *Snyder's Ltd.* v. *Furniture Finance Corp. Ltd.* (1930) 66 OLR 79 held that this rule was not affected by the registration requirements of the Assignment of Book Debts Act. See also *Re Royal Bank of Canada and Revelstoke Companies Ltd.* (1979) 94 DLR (3d) 692 (Alta. SC).

Notice to the account debtor is not essential to gain priority under the PPSA. Absence of notification was held not to be a deceptive practice under the B.C. Trade Practices Act in *Director of Trade Practices* v. *Household Finance Corp. of Canada* [1977] 3 WWR 390 (BC CA).

The use of notification and non-notification financing is described by Comment 1 to UCC 9-308 as follows:

> Arrangements where the chattel paper is delivered to the secured party who then makes collections, as well as arrangements where the debtor, whether or not he is left in possession of the paper, makes the collections, are both widely used, and are known respectively as notification (or "direct collection") and non-notification (or "indirect collection") arrangements. In the automobile field, for example, when a car is sold to a consumer buyer under an installment purchase agreement and the resulting chattel paper is assigned, the assignee usually takes possession, the obligor is notified of the assignment and is directed to make payments to the assignee. In the furniture field, for an example on the other hand, the chattel paper may be left in the dealer's hands or delivered to the assignee; in either case the obligor may not be notified, and payments are made to the dealer-assignor who receives them under a duty to remit to his assignee.

Note however that "upon default . . . a secured party is entitled (a) to notify any account debtor or any obligor . . . to make payment to him whether or not the assignor was theretofore making collections. . . ." (s. 56(1)).

Notice to the account debtor is relevant in cutting off the availability of defences arising outside the assigned contract (s. 40(1)(*b*) but *cf.* s. 40(1)(*a*): the availability of defences arising from the terms of the assigned contract is not affected by notice to the account debtor. Of course, until notice, the account debtor pays the assignor (s. 40(2)).

Under the English common law, following notice of the assignment to the account debtor, the original parties were precluded from modifying the underlying contract: *Brice* v. *Bannister* (1878) 3 QBD 569. This position was never fully adopted in the U.S. and was ultimately rejected by UCC 9-318(2) under which, before completing the performance, "notwithstanding notification of the assignment, any modification of or substitution for the contract made in good faith and in accordance with reasonable commercial standards is effective against an assignee". No corresponding provision appears in the Ont. PPSA. In considering the common law position, note the powerful dissent of Brett L.J. in *Brice* v. *Bannister*, at 579-80 *supra*, who could not bring himself to agree that "business transactions are to be hampered by any doctrine which will prevent a man from doing what he otherwise might do, merely because something has happened between other parties". He also lamented that if the original parties could not modify the contract, "it seems . . . to denote a state of slavery in business that ought not to be suffered . . .". His final conclusion was that by virtue of the effective modification of the contract "there never was any money due to the assignor . . ." that could be claimed by the assignee.

The omission from the PPSA of a provision modelled on UCC 9-318(2) was noted with regret by the OLRC in its *Report on the Sale of Goods*. The Commission noted that the provision was adopted in the MUPPSA and has been recommended for adoption in B.C. and Saskatchewan (it has been enacted since then in Sask. PPSA s. 40(2)). The Commission found it "to be a very useful provision" and recommended its adoption in Ontario: *id.* p. 125.

4. FUNDS WITHHELD UNDER BONDED CONSTRUCTION CONTRACTS AND THE PPSA

Funds withheld under a bonded construction contract can be the subject of a dispute between the surety of the construction company and a bank financing the project. Neither the UCC nor the PPSA deals directly with the issue. It is reasonable to suppose that the same principles of law govern the issue under both statutes. The following is a description of the commercial setting and a summary of the determination of the dispute under Article 9 of the Code:

> In a typical fact situation, a construction contract between an owner of land (owner) and a construction company (contractor) provides for payment to the latter by installments made as they are earned with the advance of the work on the land (and, therefore, called "progress payments"). The contract may also provide for the owner's right to hold back, until the satisfactory completion of the project, a certain percentage of the money earned by the contractor under each installment (called "retained percentages" or "retainages"). The owner obtains from a surety company (surety) a performance or payment bond which secures to the owner the completion of the project at the agreed construction price. The bond is issued on the application of the contractor, who undertakes to reimburse the surety to the extent that the expenditure incurred by the surety in the completion of the project exceeds the construction price. The contractor also obtains a line of credit from a bank (bank). Both the surety and the bank take from the contractor assignments of money to become due under the construction contract. The bank secures, thereby, its advances under the line of credit and the surety its right to reimbursement. On the contractor's default and the fulfillment of the surety's undertaking, the bank and the surety compete over earned but unpaid progress payments as well as over the "retainages" (collectively called "withheld funds"). Each claims priority on the basis of its respective rights under the contractor's assignment to it. The surety relies also on the equitable doctrine of subrogation. Under this doctrine, one who, pursuant to a binding obligation, either pays another's debt or otherwise fulfills another's duties is entitled "to assert the right of that other against third persons" as well as "to all the rights of the person he paid to enforce his right to be reimbursed."
>
> • • •

[The leading post-Code authority is *National Shawmut Bank of Boston* v. *New Amsterdam Casualty Co.* (1969) 411 F. 2d 843 (U.S. CCA 1).]

In upholding the surety's priority on the basis of subrogation, the *National Shawmut* court explained that

> the surety in cases like this undertakes duties which entitles it to step into three sets of shoes. When, on default of the contractor, it pays all the bills of the job to date and completes the job, it stands in the shoes of the contractor insofar as there are receivables due it; in the shoes of laborers and material men who have been paid by the surety who may have had liens and not least, in the shoes of the . . . [owner] for whom the job was completed.

• • •

Neither the subrogation to the contractor "which on default has forfeited its rights" nor the subrogation to the laborers' and material men's "peculiarly equitable claim" explains the priority of the surety over the [assignee bank] on completion of the job. Rather, this priority is explained in *National Shawmut* by the fact that "upon default, the surety which is obligated to complete the work steps into the shoes of the [owner] . . . and is subrogated . . . to [his] right to apply to the cost of completion the . . . [withheld funds]."

(B. Geva, "Bonded Construction Contracts: What Are a Surety's Rights to Withheld Funds?" (1980) 3 Corp. L. Rev. 50, 50-4.)

Do you agree with the analysis of the *National Shawmut* court? It was argued in *Re Jason Construction Ltd.* (1972) 16 CBR (NS) 297, 308 (Alta. SC in Bkcy), aff'd 17 CBR (NS) 158, [1972] 6 WWR 203 (CA), that "it is difficult to suppose that [the surety] could be entitled to assume and exercise at the same time both the rights of the building contractor to payment and the right of the owner to withhold payment." Is this a valid criticism of the *National Shawmut* reasoning? See Geva, *id.* at 60. The result of *National Shawmut* is supported there (at 62) by the extinction of the assignee-bank's right prior to the assertion of the owner's claim by the surety:

> The defeat [of the assignee-bank] is explained, in other words, by the principle that an assignee of a chose in action takes title to it "subject to the equities existing between the assignor and debtor" including "the terms and conditions of the contract under which the indebtedness arose." . . .
>
> Having been destroyed by . . . the contractor's default, the assignee-bank's right to the withheld funds is not revived on the eventual completion of the project by the surety. . . .

Chapter 24
Enforcement of Security Interests

The enforcement of a security interest is dealt with in Part V of the PPSA. The provisions govern four stages: (a) debtor's default, (b) taking possession of the collateral by the secured party, (c) retention or disposition of the collateral by the secured party or its redemption by the debtor, and (d) post-disposition situation (viz. the debtor's right to any surplus or the creditor's right to claim for any deficiency).

The following materials deal with the Part V provisions in conjunction with other applicable sources of law. They focus on the creditor's right to take possession, the creditor's duty to sell the collateral in a commercially reasonable manner and his right to claim a deficiency, the debtor's rights to reinstate on payment, the enforcement of a security interest in bankruptcy, and the analogous question of the lessor's rights on the lessee's default.

1. INTRODUCTION

a) Part V of the PPSA and Its Relationship with Consumer Protection Legislation

Consistent with the general approach of the PPSA, the remedies are basically the same, irrespective of the type of transaction by which the security interest was created. Also, all of the remedies are available to the secured party cumulatively (s. 55(1)).

Part V becomes operative upon default by the debtor (s. 55). Default is defined as "the failure to pay or otherwise perform the obligation secured when due or the occurrence of any event whereupon under the terms of the security agreement the security becomes enforceable" (s. (1)(h)). Thus, subject to the standard of manifest unreasonableness, the parties are free to determine what constitutes default (s 55(5)).

Moreover, the secured party is permitted to include in the security agreement an acceleration clause, whereby on default in payment of any part of the obligation secured, the entire amount becomes immediately due. Note, however, that if he has included a right to accelerate the maturity of the entire obligation whenever he deems himself insecure, such a right is exercisable "only if he in good faith believes that the prospect of payment or performance is impaired" (s. 18). Does this mean that a secured party can accelerate the maturity if he believes unreasonably, albeit honestly, that a default is imminent? Also, who has the onus of proof? Under UCC 1-208 (which corresponds to PPSA s. 18), "[t]he burden of establishing lack of good faith is on the party against whom the power has been exercised." Does this reflect sound policy?

The secured party is not required under the PPSA to notify the debtor when there has been a default. Similarly, there is no provision giving the debtor a right to cure a default. Compare this position with the Ontario position in mortgages of real property where the debtor is entitled to remedy a default at any time before final judgment has been granted against him (Mortgages Act, RSO 1970, c. 279, s. 22). Is there any justification for this difference?

Upon default, one option open to the secured party is to obtain a judgment on the debt. Such a judgment does not preclude the secured party from also relying on his security (s. 55(7)). Of course, double recovery is not permitted.

Alternatively, the secured party can enforce his security interest directly. Unless there is a contrary provision in the security agreement, he has the "right to take possession of the collateral by any method permitted by law" (s. 57(a)). Once the collateral is in his possession, the secured party generally has the choice of disposing of it (s. 58) or retaining it in satisfaction of the indebtedness (s. 60(2)). It is not altogether clear, however, whether the secured party has the right to collect a deficiency remaining after the security has been disposed of. Unlike the Uniform Commercial Code, the PPSA does not specifically deal with this problem. Apart from a provision in the security agreement, is there any legal basis for claiming a right to a deficiency?

Part V places various limitations on the exercise of the secured party's remedies. The right to retain the collateral in satisfaction of the indebtedness, for instance, is denied where the collateral is consumer goods and the debtor has already paid at least 60 per cent of the obligation secured and has not signed, after default, a statement renouncing or modifying his rights under Part V (s. 60(1)). Moreover, a party proposing to retain the collateral must notify the debtor and any other secured party who has registered according to the Act or of whom the secured party has actual notice (s. 60(2)). The parties entitled to notice may object to the retention of the collateral and force its sale (s. 60(3)).

With respect to the resale of the collateral, s. 58(5) requires the secured party to give advance notice of his intention to sell. In general, Part V is flexible as to the types of dispositions permitted. The "collateral may be disposed of in whole or in part . . . by public sale, private sale, lease or otherwise . . . at any time or place and on any terms so long as every aspect of the disposition is commercially reasonable" (s. 58(3)). The problem is in determining the standards of commercial reasonableness and, in particular, the extent to which the price received is, or ought to be, relevant in determining reasonableness. Note that the parties can to a certain degree provide for the applicable standards in the security agreement (s. 55(5)). Section 58(9) provides that even if the secured party fails to comply with the relevant requirements, a purchaser is protected from the claims of the debtor or other secured parties provided he purchases for value and in good faith. U.S. courts are divided as to the effect of the secured party's deviation from the notice and reasonableness requirements (ss. 58(3), (5)) on his claim for a deficiency. (See section (4) *infra*.)

The debtor's remedies for the secured party's failure to comply with Part V are set forth in s. 62. Note the statutory damages provided for consumer goods in s. 62(2)(*b*). Although there is no right to remedy a default in the Ontario Act, the debtor is entitled to redeem the collateral by tendering full performance of his obligations after the secured party has taken possession but before he has disposed of the collateral (s. 61). What is meant by "fulfillment of all the obligations secured" in s. 61? Does it include all of the principal and all of the precomputed interest?

Under s. 63 of the Sask. PPSA, "a judge or court may . . . (*c*) relieve any party from compliance with the requirement of [Part V] . . . , (*d*) stay the enforcement of rights provided in [Part V] . . . [or] (*e*) make any order necessary to ensure protection of the interests of any person in the collateral." The power to relieve parties from the requirements of Part V or to stay enforcement of rights thereunder can be exercised under this s. 63 only within the safeguards of "just and reasonable" conditions. The draft Bill to amend the Ontario PPSA would adopt a similar provision. Does it reflect a sound policy?

Two specific provisions only apply to consumer goods: s. 60(1) limiting the right to retain the collateral in satisfaction of the debt, and s. 62(2)(*b*) imposing statutory damages for violations of the disposition provisions of Part V. In general "[w]here there is a conflict between a provision of [the PPSA] and a provision of The Consumer Protection Act", the latter prevails; s. 68. See also Sask. PPSA s. 69(2) giving priority in general to "a provision of any Act for the protection of consumers". Therefore, in dealing with consumer default, any applicable consumer protection legislation must be considered in conjunction with Part V.

b) Enforcement of the Security Interests by Receivers and Receiver Managers and Part V of the PPSA

J.S. ZIEGEL AND R.C.C. CUMING
"The Modernization of Canadian Personal Property Security Law"
(1981) 31 Univ. Tor. LJ 249, 270-71

Another important feature of the corporate indenture in Canada is that it usually provides for the appointment of a receiver and receiver-manager in the event of default or other event entitling the secured party to enforce the security interest. Even where there are no such provisions the secured party can always apply to a court for the appointment of a receiver. How consistent are the Part V provisions with the roles of receivers and receiver-managers? It seems safe to say that the draftsmen of Article 9 did not have them in mind in drafting the enforcement provisions nor did the Catzman Committee in adapting them to Ontario requirements.

The 1970 Model Act was not much more helpful. Section 55(2a) provided that

> Nothing in this Act shall preclude the parties ... from agreeing that the secured party may appoint a receiver or to prevent a court from appointing a receiver and determining his rights and duties.

This left it dangerously unclear whether, and to what extent, a receiver was governed by Part V. The Saskatchewan drafters rightly noted that receivership law is scattered over a variety of Acts, that there is no comprehensive law governing a receiver's rights and duties and, most importantly, that the court has no inherent jurisdiction to police his conduct and to give him instructions where he has been appointed by the secured party. The Saskatchewan drafters concluded that, except as otherwise provided, Part V should apply to receivers and receiver-managers, however appointed, and the Saskatchewan Act so provides [ss. 56(1), (3) and (4)]. It also specifically empowers the court to give them directions, thus tracking comparable provisions in the Canadian Business Corporations Act and the prospective and much delayed revised Federal Bankruptcy Act.

However, the Saskatchewan Act also recognizes that some Part V provisions are inappropriate to receivers and receiver-managers. These provisions are therefore excluded by Section 56(4). Note in particular the wholesale exemption from compliance with Part V requirements where the receiver-manager is acting "in the course of carrying on the business of the debtor" [s. 56(4)(a)]. Even where he is not carrying on the debtor's business, Section 59(7) requires him or a receiver, where either of them intends to dispose of collateral, to give a much less detailed notice of intention to sell than is normally required of the secured party under Section 59(6).

Note: The draft Bill to amend the Ontario PPSA proposed the following amendments with respect to receivers and receiver managers:

20. Section 55 of the said Act is amended by adding thereto the following subsections:

(8) Nothing in this Act prevents,
(a)   the parties to a security agreement from agreeing that the secured party may appoint a receiver or receiver-manager and, except as provided by this Act, determining his rights and duties by agreement; or
(b)   a judge of the Supreme Court from appointing a receiver or receiver-manager and determining his rights and duties by order.

(9) Unless a judge of the Supreme Court orders otherwise, a receiver or receiver-manager is bound by the provisions of this Act.

(10) For the purposes of this Part and section 19, where a receiver or receiver-manager has been appointed by the secured party or the court, "secured party" includes the receiver or receiver-manager.

21. Section 58 of the said Act, as amended by the Statutes of Ontario, 1973, chapter 102, section 10, is further amended by adding thereto the following subsection:
(6a) Unless the collateral is consumer goods, the trustee under a trust indenture, a receiver or a receiver-manager shall be deemed to have complied

with subsection 5 if, before disposing of the collateral, he serves a notice in writing containing a statement of his intention to dispose of the collateral on the debtor, where the debtor is an individual, and to any other person who has a security interest in the collateral that is perfected by registration and to any other person who is known by the secured party to have a security interest in the collateral and the notice shall be served in accordance with subsection 6.

"Trust indenture" was defined in s. 1 as:

> any security agreement by the terms of which a body corporate, with or without share capital and wherever or however incorporated,
> (i)   issues or guarantees debt obligations or provides for the issue or guarantee of debt obligations, and
> (ii) appoints a person as trustee for the holders of the debt obligations so issued, guaranteed or provided for.

The secured party's right, on the debtor's default, to apply to the court for the appointment of a receiver under s. 19 of the Judicature Act, RSO 1970, c. 228 was upheld in *Cantamar Holdings* v. *Tru-View Aluminum Products* (1979) 23 OR (2d) 572 (HCJ) where Callaghan J. accepted the submission that "s. 55(3) of the [PPSA] preserves . . . [the remedy] under s. 19 of the Judicature Act". He ruled (at 573) that the PPSA "in no way impairs the jurisdiction of this Court under s. 19 [of the Judicature Act] to appoint a receiver. Section 19 is fundamental to the jurisdiction of the High Court of this Province and unless it is specifically the subject-matter of limiting legislation, . . . [no] one can, by implication, diminish the jurisdiction conferred upon the High Court by s. 19". In the light of this decision, are the positions in the draft Bill necessary?

2.   THE RIGHT TO TAKE POSSESSION

The right "to take possession of the collateral by any method permitted by law" is explicitly provided for by s. 57(*a*). It exists "unless otherwise agreed" (*id.*). Does the provision authorize a creditor to use physical force against the debtor, to break into the debtor's home, to break into the debtor's office, or to take the collateral from the debtor's parkway or garage? *Cf.* UCC 9-503; and Mikolajczyk, "Breach of Peace and Section 9-503 of the Uniform Commercial Code — A Modern Definition for an Ancient Restriction" (1978) 82 Dick. L. Rev. 351.

The following is a pre-PPSA decision. How would it have been decided under the PPSA? Note also s. 35 of the Ontario CPA.

REGINA v. DOUCETTE
(1960) 25 DLR (2d) 380, [1960] OR 403 (Ont. CA)

SCHROEDER J.A. (fo the court): The Attorney-General appeals against the judgment of His Honour Judge Weaver pronounced in the County Court Judges' Criminal Court of the County of York, whereby he acquitted the three respondents upon an indictment preferred against them, wherein it was charged that on or about November 6, 1959, at the Municipality of Metropolitan Toronto in the County of York, they did commit an assault on one John Chappell thereby causing him bodily harm. . . .

The respondents were duly licensed as bailiffs by the Municipality of Metropolitan Toronto after having received a certificate of qualification in accordance with the provisions of the Bailiffs Act, RSO 1950, c. 30. Under the terms of such licence they were entitled to engage in the business or calling of bailiffs but they were not clothed with any official status as peace officers or as duly authorized officers of any Court. Persons so licensed are frequently engaged by merchants or finance companies to repossess merchandise sold under the terms of conditional sales agreements and when thus engaged they are acting in a private and unofficial capacity as the authorized agents of the vendor of the goods in question or of his assignee.

The facts giving rise to the indictment laid against the respondents arose out of a seizure made by them on the afternoon of November 6, 1959, at or about the hour of 4.30 p.m. at the apartment of one John Chappell contained in a building known and described for municipal purposes as No. 2110 Dundas St. West. Chappell occupied a small second storey apartment at that address with his wife and five young children. The respondents had driven to the premises in a station wagon for the purpose of repossessing a television set which had been purchased by Chappell under the terms of a conditional sales contract. The purchaser, Chappell, stated in evidence that the vendor had accepted an old television set in part payment of the purchase-price and that he had paid approximately $15 in cash. A copy of the contract which has been filed does not indicate that any allowance was made for a used television set, but it is not disputed that at the time of the seizure the payments due under the agreement were in arrear.

Only Doucette and McNutt entered the premises in the first instance. The front door leading to the ground floor hall was opened to them by Chappell's 11-year-old son who called to his father to advise him that some men wished to see him. The visitors did not wait for an invitation to enter Chappell's apartment but immediately proceeded to ascend the stairs. Chappell's evidence is that there was a small gate stretched across the hall entrance to his apartment and placed at the head of the stairs. He stated that the two respondents, while still standing on the stairway, advised him of the purposes of their visit; that they had not at that time passed the gate to enter the upstairs hallway. He then advised them that he would not permit them to take the television set until a policeman could be summoned. He stated that one of the two men then unfastened the gate and pushed him back across the upstairs hall into the living room where the television set was kept. There is a conflict in the evidence upon this point, both Doucette and McNutt having testified that they had not observed the gate referred to; that they did not see Chappell until they entered the living room of the apartment; and that when they announced their intention of repossessing the television set, Chappell stated plainly and emphatically that he objected to their doing so, and when no favourable reaction occurred he attempted to push Doucette out of the room. It is not disputed that Chappell at that time requested his wife to go out to telephone the police and at the same time ordered these two men, Doucette and McNutt, to leave his premises and to remain downstairs until the arrival of the police. They, however, refused to comply with this request and persisted in remaining in the apartment. A fight then occurred between Chappell and Doucette in which McNutt endeavoured to intervene. At this point the third respondent, Dongen, a sturdy man about 6 ft. in height and weighing 240 lbs. entered the room, unbidden by anyone, and his mere presence apparently sufficed to terminate the fighting. One thing that emerges clearly from the evidence is the fact that Chappell had made it abundantly clear that he protested against the presence of these men on his premises; that he objected to the removal of the television set of which he was at the time in peaceable possession under a claim of right, and that he made it very plain that if they attempted to remove it before the arrival of the police he would resist their efforts. In all the circumstances Chappell's suggestion that they desist from carrying out the seizure until the police were called, emanating from a man who had serious doubts as to his legal rights in this affair, was not unreasonable. Notwithstanding this one of the three accused men scoffingly declared that they would be gone before the police arrived. Then, while Chappell was leaning on the television set, Doucette disconnected the electric plug and Dongen seized the instrument and carried it towards the stairs, followed by Doucette and McNutt. The latter acting as a rear guard, walked backwards with his fists raised in order to hold off Chappell, who was apparently following the trio in a threatening manner. McNutt then pushed forward past Doucette who was on the upper steps, and assisted Dongen in carrying the television set down the remaining steps. Doucette who was then last in line, believing that Chappell was about to strike him, directed a hard blow at Chappell's mouth which felled him to the floor. The three bailiffs left the premises carrying the television set with them before the police could arrive on the scene.

The learned trial Judge made no express findings of fact and disposed of the case in these few words:

> With respect to the charge of assault in the second indictment, I am satisfied there that the complainant was the author of his own misfortune and that also will be dismissed.

It is not easy to discern precisely what the learned Judge meant by these words. If he meant that Chappell, by his conduct, had given provocation to the respondents, provocation would certainly not constitute a defence to a charge of assault, although it would be something which ought to be considered in mitigation of the offence, and would have a bearing on the sentence or penalty to be imposed. If, on the other hand, he took the view that the respondents had made out a case of legitimate self-defence, his conclusion was based upon a misapprehension as to what constitutes in law a defence of justification for assault. I cannot think that the learned trial Judge gave proper consideration to the legal rights and obligations of the respondents in attempting to carry out their object and to the corresponding rights and obligations of the complainant, Chappell. Since there appears to be a popular misconception in the minds of many people, particularly in the minds of persons engaged in the business or calling of licensed bailiffs as to the extent of their rights and privileges, it may serve a useful purpose to review the law bearing upon the issues directly involved in this case.

It should be made clear at the outset that the recaption or resumption of possession of goods by the act of the owner through an agent or bailiff acting under his written authority, is not a lawful execution of any process against lands or goods, or is not the making of a lawful distress or seizure within the meaning of s. 110(c) of the Cr. Code which is directed against resistance to or wilful obstruction of any person engaged in the performance of such acts. This is placed beyond question by the decision of the Court of Appeal in *R.* v. *Shand* (1904) 8 Can. CC 45, 7 OLR 190.

The limitations upon the right of an owner to repossess his goods without process of law are stated clearly and succinctly in 3 *Blackstone's Commentaries* at pp. 4-5, from which I quote:

> Recaption or *reprisal* is another species of remedy by the mere act of the party injured. This happens when any one hath deprived another of his property in goods or chattels personal. . . . in which case the owner of the goods . . . may lawfully claim and retake them wherever he happens to find them, so it be not in a riotous manner, or attended with a breach of the peace. The reason for this is obvious; since it may frequently happen that the owner may have this only opportunity of doing himself justice: his goods may be afterwards conveyed away or destroyed; . . . if he had no speedier remedy than the ordinary process of law. If therefore he can so contrive it as to gain possession of his property again without force or terror, the law favors and will justify his proceeding. But as the public peace is a superior consideration to any one man's private property; and as, if individuals were once allowed to use private force as a remedy for private injuries, all social justice must cease, the strong would give law to the weak, and every man would revert to a state of nature; for these reasons it is provided that this natural right of recaption shall never be exerted where such exertion must occasion strife and bodily contention, or endanger the peace of society.

This passage in Blackstone was commented upon and applied by Parke, B., in *Patrick* v. *Colerick*, (1838) 3 M & W 483, 150 ER 1235. See also *Davis* v. *Whitridge* (1847) 2 Strobhart (South Carolina Law) 232.

It is very clear that whatever rights the vendor or his assignee or their authorized agent might have had under the terms of the conditional sales contract (the purchase-money being in arrear and unpaid) to enter upon Chappell's premises to resume possession of the goods in question, it would be illegal for them to take such possession by force. *Traders Bank of Canada* v. *G. & J. Brown Mfg. Co.* (1889) 18 OR 430, cited by counsel for the respondents is authority for this proposition. In *Re Nu-Way Meat Market Ltd. & Grobstein & Commercial Acceptance Corp.* (1940) 22 CBR 46, 46 Rev. de Jur. 418, it was held that the liquidator might claim possession of a truck sold to a debtor under suspensive conditions of property, where the vendor had taken possession of it by force and deceit since the winding-up, and had neglected to furnish the liquidator with the detailed account of what was still owed by the debtor; whatever the terms of the deed, no one had the right to take the law into one's own hands.

Reference may also be made on this point to *Devoe* v. *Long* [1951] 1 DLR 203 at pp. 225-6, 26 MPR 357, a judgment of the Appeal Division of the Supreme Court of New Brunswick.

The right to resort to self-help was again discountenanced in *Nilan* v. *McAndless* (1912) 8 DLR 169, where at p. 171, Macdonald, J., stated:

> He was not justified, however, in taking the law in his own hands when he found that he could not get peaceable possession. His proper course was to obtain possession by legal means.

There must be reasonable limits imposed upon the right of self-help assumed and asserted by private individuals in order to preserve peace and tranquility and to avoid the evil consequences which are bound to flow from insistence upon a right to use private force. Under s. 39 of the Cr. Code, the peaceable possessor of movable property under a claim of right is protected from criminal responsibility (although not from civil responsibility) for resisting its taking even by the person legally entitled.

The principle which must govern in cases of this kind was stated in clear and unmistakable terms by Osler, J.A., in *R.* v. *Shand*, 8 Can. CC at pp. 52-3, 7 OLR at pp. 196-7, from which I quote the following excerpt:

> The law is the same where goods are improperly detained by one in defiance of his agreement to yield them up to the owner with or without demand. If the owner can acquire possession peaceably he may do so. If he attempts to take it forcibly and in a riotous manner as was done in the case before us, he becomes himself a breaker of the law, as much so as one who attempts to take possession of real property by a forcible entry, contrary to 5 Rich. II., stat. 1, ch. 8, even when it has been agreed that he was to re-enter; *Edwick* v. *Hawkes* (1881) 18 Ch. D. 199; and see *Beddall* v. *Maitland* (1881) 17 Ch. D. 174. If resistance is offered or possession refused he should have recourse to his action, and the code, sec. 144, would then have its full force in making unlawful any resistance to seizure made in due course of law. That is what is meant by a lawful seizure. It was never intended to enlarge the civil rights or powers of individuals, or to convert a breach of contract or resistance to private force into a criminal offence.

In *Edwick* v. *Hawkes*, cited by Osler, J.A., in *R.* v. *Shand, supra*, Fry, J., stated [18 Ch. D. at p. 212]:

> I have made those observations because, in my judgment, it is important that there should be no misunderstanding as to the position of persons who have a right of entry on land. Their right is to enter in a peaceable and easy manner, and if they cannot do so they must resort to the Courts. In no other way can the peace and quiet of this country be maintained, and in no other way can the relation of landlord and tenant be prevented from resulting in such acts of violence and disturbance as I regret to say have occurred in the present case.

In the same case it was held that a clause in a lease, authorizing the lessor to eject the lessee forcibly for breach of covenant, or at the end of the term of a lease was void as being a licence to commit an act forbidden by law.

It follows logically that if a person enters premises lawfully in the first instance for the purpose of resuming possession of his movable property and subsequently abuses his authority, he becomes in law a trespasser. It is rather singular that three bailiffs had to descend upon the complainant to repossess a chattel which could be borne by one man, unless it was their purpose to make a display of might, against which the complainant's lone opposition, whether right or wrong, could scarely be expected to prevail. That these men abused their authority after gaining entrance to the premises is too plain for discussion. Once it was made clear to them, as indeed it was, that they would not be suffered to remove the television set without resistance, they grossly exceeded and abused their rights when they persisted in carrying out their project of abducting the television receiver, using force for the purpose if necessary. They thus became trespassers even if their original entry was lawful, a point which, on the evidence, is itself not free from doubt.

The learned Deputy Attorney-General contends that by force of the provisions of s. 38(2) of the Cr. Code alone, quite apart from the actual physical force applied by the respondents to the person of the complainant, they must be held to have committed an assault without justification or provocation. Section 38(2) reads:

> (2) Where a person who is in peaceable possession of movable property lays hands upon it, a trespasser who persists in attempting to keep it or take it from him or from any one lawfully assisting him shall be deemed to commit an assault without justification or provocation.

Also by s. 38(1) the person in peaceable possession of such property is justified in preventing a trespasser from taking it if he does not strike him or cause him bodily harm.

In my view of the facts, the conduct of the respondents towards the complainant Chappell while exercising their purported right to repossess the television set in question by force is in itself sufficient to support a charge of common assault against them. I agree, however, that if it were necessary for the Crown to rely upon the provisions of s. 38(2) of the Cr. Code, those provisions might successfully be invoked against the respondents.

I would allow the appeal, set aside the judgment of acquittal, and direct that a verdict of guilty of common assault be entered against the respondents. I would impose a fine of $50 upon the respondent Doucette, a fine of $25 upon the respondent Dongen, and a fine of $25 upon the respondent McNutt.

Appeal allowed.

Notes and Questions:

1   The creditor's right to repossess consumer goods is limited by s. 35 of the Ontario CPA. No offence is created by breaching the provision: *R. v. I.A.C. Ltd.* [1970] 2 OR 407 (Prov. Ct.); but see s. 48. The provision is not well drafted. Consider the following: does it apply to default otherwise than "default in payment"? To the right to repossess where not based on a contractual provision? See: D. Cheifetz, "Repossession Notwithstanding the Ontario Consumer Protection Act" (1978) 26 Chitty's LJ 333.

2   PPSA s. 57 also deals with two specific aspects of the secured party's right to take possession viz. rendering equipment unusable without removal thereof (s. 57(*b*)), and disposition of the collateral on the debtor's premises (s. 57(*c*)). Collection rights

of a secured party are governed by s. 56 (For the latter provision, *cf.* notes 5-6 following *Norton, supra,* chapter 23(B).

3　Under UCC 9-503 (permitting the secured party to take possession of the collateral without judicial process "if this can be done without breach of the peace"), "the great majority of courts find unauthorized entries into the debtor's residence to be breaches of the peace, and may find entry into his place of business or garage to be such a breach. As one moves away from the residential threshold to the yard, the driveway, and finally the public street, however, the debtor's argument becomes progressively more tenuous . . . [At the same time] [i]f the debtor voluntarily and contemporaneously consents to a repossession it cannot be a breach of the peace" (J. White and R. Summers, *Handbook of the Law Under the Uniform Commercial Code* (2nd ed., 1980) pp. 1096-97).

4　The self-help remedy of taking possession without prior notice and hearing, provided for by UCC 9-503, has been the subject of constitutional challenge under the Due Process Clause of the Fourteenth Amendment of the U.S. Constitution. In its relevant part the Amendment provides that no "State [shall] deprive any person of life, liberty, or property, without due process of law". It has been argued that by providing for a self-help remedy of taking possession, the state deprives a person of property without due process of law.

　　The argument relies on the decisions of the U.S. Supreme Court in *Sniadach* v. *Family Finance Corp. of Bayview* (1969) 395 US 337; *Fuentes v. Shevin, Attorney General of Florida* (1972) 407 US 67; *Mitchell* v. *W.T. Grant Co.* (1974) 416 U.S. 600, and *North Georgia Fishing Inc.* v. *Di-Chem Inc.* (1975) 419 U.S. 601. In these cases the Supreme Court insisted on judicial scrutiny over the exercise of creditors' remedies. However, all of them were concerned with prejudgment "judicial seizures" of property, i.e., the seizure of property under some order from a judge or court clerk. No such order is involved in exercising a 9-503 repossession. This distinction has been drawn in numerous decisions of federal Courts of Appeal and state Supreme Courts and they thus upheld the constitutionality of 9-503. For a compilation of cases see W. Davenport and D. Murray, *Secured Transactions* (1978) p. 264 n. 18.

　　The reasoning of the cases upholding a 9-503 repossession is consistent with the recent decision of the U.S. Supreme Court in *Flagg Bros. Inc.* v. *Brooks* (1978) 436 U.S. 149. Dealing with another self-help remedy (the warehouseman's lien under UCC 7-210(2)), Justice Rehnquist (speaking for the majority) stated (at 157) that ". . . total absence of overt official involvement plainly distinguishes this case from earlier [U.S. Supreme Court] decisions imposing procedural restrictions on creditors' remedies". The state's mere acquiescence in a self-help remedy is not tantamount to sufficient "state action" so as to invoke the constitutional protection under the Due Process Clause of the Fourteenth Amendment.

3. Retention or Disposition of the Collateral

Subject to the debtor's right of redemption in s. 61, the secured party who has taken possession may either retain the collateral or dispose of it. As to disposition "on the debtor's premises" see s. 57(c). Retention of the collateral in satisfaction of the debt is governed by s. 60. It cannot be exercised where "the collateral is consumer goods and the debtor has paid at least 60 per cent of the indebtedness": s. 60(1). Note however the possibility of "renouncing or modifying . . . rights" provided for by s. 60(1).

The secured party's right to dispose of collateral upon default is governed by s. 58. His right to delay the disposition "for such period of time as is commercially reasonable" is provided for by s. 58(4). Section 58(5) and (6) imposes on the secured party a duty to give notice to the debtor (and other secured creditors) of the prospective disposition. Such a duty is dispensed with where "the collateral is perishable or . . . the secured party believes on reasonable grounds that the collateral will decline speedily in value". For the opinion that "warrants and securities are properly viewed as collateral which, in the words of section 58(5), may decline speedily in value", see *Jones* v. *Davidson* (1981) 31 OR (2d) 494 (HC), *per* Parker A.C.J.H. Compare s. 58 notice provisions with the notice requirement under s. 60(2) on retention of the collateral) and consider the definition of "notify" in s. 1(p).

Disposition "may be by public sale, private sale, lease or otherwise". The Act does not define the meaning of any of these terms. Every aspect of the disposition must be "commercially reasonable" (s. 58(3)). Where a "public sale" is held, the collateral may be sold to the secured party himself: s. 58(7). Transfers which are "not a disposition of the collateral" are dealt with in s. 58(10).

Application of the proceeds realized by the disposition is governed by s. 58(1). The effect of a valid disposition is to discharge the security interest (s. 58(8)). Bona fide purchasers are protected even if the disposition has been conducted "otherwise than in accordance with this section" (s. 58(9)). Is the standard provided for in s. 59(9)(a) the same as that provided for in s. 58(9)(b)? According to Professor Gilmore, "[i]t may be hoped that the courts will pay no attention to [the different language] . . . There is a certain danger in the suggestion that purchasers at private sales must meet a higher standard than purchasers at public sales": Grant Gilmore, *Security Interests in Personal Property* Vol. II (1965) p. 1249.

As for the debtor's remedies where "the disposition of the collateral has been made otherwise than in accordance with this Part", see s. 62(2).

The following is a pre-PPSA case dealing with the secured party's duty to the debtor in disposing of the collateral. Is it good law under the PPSA? *Cf.* s. 58(3) and further consider the material discussed in the following section dealing with the creditor's right to deficiency.

BAY MOTORS CO. LTD. v. TRADERS FINANCE CORP. LTD.
(1959) 19 DLR (2d) 331 (NB SC AD)

RITCHIE J.A. (for the court): This appeal is from a judgment dismissing an action instituted in the Queen's Bench Division by the plaintiff appellant in respect of a sale, made by the defendant under a chattel mortgage, which is alleged to have been negligent, reckless, improvident and "in breach of duty".

The plaintiff is an automobile dealer in the City of Saint John. On October 16, 1956, as security for payment of the sum of $3,547 then owing to the defendant, it executed in favour of the latter, a finance company, a chattel mortgage of two automobiles. One was a new 1956 model Jaguar which the plaintiff had recently purchased for resale at the wholesale price of $3,985. The retail price at which the plaintiff had been endeavouring to sell the car approximated $5,100 including taxes. Following the giving of the mortgage, the Jaguar was used freely, one of the drivers being a school age son of the president of the plaintiff company.

On October 28, 1957, a representative of the defendant made a verbal demand for payment of the sum of $1,902.45, the amount remaining owing on the mortgage. The representative understood the plaintiff's president, on whom the demand was made, to say he had put into the Jaguar all the money he was going to put into it and that if the defendant wanted the car it would have to take legal action. The defendant accordingly issued a writ and, a few days later, replevied the vehicle. The Jaguar was stored in Saint John on the premises of Earl Thomas, who does business under the style of "Thomas Motors". At that time the speedometer mileage exceeded 11,000 miles.

The defendant offered the car to two automobile dealers at the amount owing on it but they were not interested. Enquiries were received from six prospective purchasers in the retail market but they made no offers. Finally written bids were invited from three car dealers, Thomas Motors, Ellis Sales and Service, and Laurie Auto Parts. Their bids were $2,127.50, $1,975.00 and $1,900 respectively. The car was sold to Thomas Motors for $2,127.50, being the highest offer.

The grounds of appeal set out in the plaintiff's factum are interspersed with argument. However, as we read the submissions, the chief contention of the plaintiff is that, in order to protect its interests and secure a proper price, the defendant should have sold the car in the retail, rather than in the wholesale, market.

The only proof submitted by the plaintiff with respect to the value of the car when replevied is contained in the testimony of its president and secretary-treasurer who gave its worth as between $4,000 and $4,500. In view of the restricted market for this type of car, an English make, the fact [that] the nearest dealer for the supply of parts is in Montreal, the fact that the plaintiff had for more than a year been endeavouring to sell it without success and the further fact that, having been run for upwards of 11,000 miles, it was a used car, we find it impossible to accept such an estimate as a fair and reasonable valuation.

Earl Thomas, the purchaser, testified he had sold the Jaguar for $2,000 plus a 1954 Kaiser car; that, while the stated price on the sale was $4,500, this did not mean the Kaiser was worth $2,500; that the 1954 Kaiser had been sold for $300 plus a 1952 Kaiser car trade-in; that the 1952 Kaiser had been sold for $300 cash; that the gross profit on the three sales was $472.50; and that approximately $100 had been expended for necessary repairs on the Jaguar.

The gross amount of money received by Mr. Thomas through the various transactions was the $2,000 difference on the original sale plus the $600 realized from the sales of the two trade-ins, a total of $2,600. If the $100 cost of repairs is deducted the amount of cash received is reduced to $2,500 and the overall profit further but no evidence was offered in this connection.

The learned trial Judge found the defendant had acted *bona fide*; that it had taken reasonable steps to obtain a proper price in realizing on its security; and that there was no evidence to support the plaintiff's grounds of complaint. He, accordingly, dismissed the action.

The provisions in the chattel mortgage respecting a sale thereunder are:

> The mortgagor covenants with the mortgagee that in the event of default by the mortgagor in complying with the terms hereof . . . the mortgagee may thereupon take immediate possession of the said chattel . . .; and upon and from and after taking possession of the said chattel as aforesaid, it shall and may be lawful for the mortgagee, and it is hereby authorized and empowered to sell the said chattel or any part thereof at public auction or private sale with or without notice to the mortgagor and upon such terms and in such manner as the mortgagee may determine and the proceeds of any such sale less all expenses incurred by the mortgagee in taking, repairing and selling the said chattel together with a selling commission of Ten per centum (10%) of the sale price including a reasonable solicitor's fee shall be appro-priated to the payment of the balance owing hereunder and the surplus remaining over shall be paid to the mortgagor and in case of a deficiency the mortgagor shall be liable therefore. . . . It is agreed that the mortgagee maay at any such sale, and in its absolute discretion accept as payment on account of the purchase money any other motor vehicle or chattel and may repair the same and make alterations and additions thereto, it being agreed that the mortgagor shall not be entitled to credit upon the principal sum and interest hereby secured until such motor vehicle or chattel shall have been resold by the mortgagee, at which time credit shall be given for the monies received for such motor vehicle or chattel after deducting therefrom all expenses in connection with the possession thereof, its storage and repair, the cost of all repairs, accessories or attachments thereto, advertising, commission and discount in respect of the sale by the mortgagee of any security given by the purchaser thereof.

In the absence of special circumstances, the exercise of a power [of] sale under a chattel mortgage is subject to the general principles stated by Lord Moulton in *McHugh* v. *Union Bank* 10 DLR 562 at p. 570, [1913] AC 299 at pp. 311-12: "It is well-settled law that it is the duty of a mortgagee, when realizing the mortgaged property by sale, to behave, in conducting such realization, as a reasonable man would behave, in the realization of his own property, so that the mortgagor may receive credit for the fair value of the property sold. But such a doctrine recognizes as a necessary corollary the right of the mortgagee to treat the reasonable expenses of such realization as a deduction from the amount realized; and, indeed, unless this is done, the sale-price does not truly represent the value of the property sold, because it is a sum which the owner could not have obtained for it without paying the necessary costs of realization."

Also applicable is *Kennedy* v. *De Trafford* [1897] AC 180, 66 LJ Ch. 413 in which Lord Herschell at p. 415 of the Law Journal volume, says: "I am myself disposed to think that if a mortgagee in exercising his power of sale exercises it in good faith, without any intention of dealing unfairly by his mortgagor, it would be very difficult indeed if not impossible to establish that he had been guilty of any breach of duty towards the mortgagor."

And at p. 419 the following passage is found in the speech of Lord Mac-naghten: "If a mortgagee selling under a power of sale in his mortgage takes pains to comply with the provisions of that power and acts in good faith, his conduct in regard to the sale cannot be impeached."

Two years prior to *McHugh* v. *Union Bank*, Duff J., as he then was in *B.C. Land & Investment Agency* v. *Ishitaka* (1911) 45 SCR 302 said at pp. 316-7:

> It is to be observed that the duty of a mortgagee in exercising a power of sale (as touching the measures to be taken to secure a good price for the property sold) has in recent years been stated by a very high authority, (*Kennedy* v. *De Trafford* [1897] AC 180) Lord Herschell, at page 185; Lord Macnaghten at page 192; *Nutt* v. *Easton* [1899] 1 Ch. 873, *per* Cozens-Hardy J., at pages 877 and 878. The sum of the matter appears to be this. He is bound to observe the limits of the power and he is bound to act in good faith, that is to say, he is bound to exercise the power fairly for the purpose for which it was given. If the mortgagee proceeds in a manner which is calculated to injure the interests of the mortgagor and if his course of action is incapable of justification as one which in the circumstances an honest mortgagee might reasonably consider to be required for the protection of his own interests; if he sacrifice the mortgagor's interest "fraudulently, wilfully or recklessly," then, as Lord Herschell says, it would be difficult to understand how he could be held to be acting in good faith. But that is a vastly different thing from saying that he is under a duty to the mortgagor to take, (regardless of his own interests as mortgagee,) all the measures a prudent man might be expected to take in selling his own property. The obligation of a trustee, when acting within the limits of the power, would be no higher. *Learoyd* v. *Whiteley* 12 App. Cas. 727, at page 733, and it is clear that in exercising his power the mortgagee does not act as trustee.

Halsbury's Laws of England, vol. 23, 2nd ed., pp. 435-6, states the dominant principles as follows:

> A mortgagee is not a trustee for the mortgagor as regards the exercise of the power of sale. He has his own interest to consider as well as that of the mortgagor, and provided that he keeps within the terms of the power, exercises the power *bona fide* for the purpose of realising the security, and takes reasonable precautions to secure a proper price, the Court will not interfere nor will it inquire whether he was actuated by any further motive. A mortgagee is entitled to sell at a price just sufficient to cover the amount due to him, provided the amount is fixed with due regard to the value of the property; and, if the sale is *bona fide,* and he charges himself with the whole of the purchase-money, he can sell on the terms that a substantial part, or even the whole, shall remain on mortgage.
>
> If the mortgagor seeks relief promptly, a sale will be set aside if there is fraud, or if the price is so low as to be in itself evidence of fraud; but not on the ground of undervalue alone; though if the mortgagee does not sell with proper precautions, he will be charged in taking the accounts with any loss thereby resulting.

Kennedy v. *De Trafford* (*supra*) [is] among the authorities cited for the principles thus expressed.

In the evidence of the local manager of the defendant company, there are some passages which, standing alone, suggest he lacks a proper understanding of the duty, in exercising a power of sale, owed to the mortgagor by a mortgagee, to act *bona fide* for the purpose of realizing and securing a proper price. He appears to labour under the misapprehensions his company is entitled to refrain from offering a mortgaged security for sale in the retail market because by so doing it would prejudice its relations with the retail dealers with whom it does business; that if it is not looking to the mortgagor for a deficiency it can sell for whatever price it wishes; and that the interest of the defendant alone need be considered.

Regardless of such lack of appreciation by the defendant's manager of the true position of a mortgagee realizing on his security, there is no evidence adduced by the plaintiff to show that, after reasonable advertising, the defendant might have sold the then used Jaguar to a retail buyer for a greater net price than was realized. Had there been such evidence it is possible we might have reached a different conclusion. Further there is no evidence to support the contention of plaintiff's counsel in respect to bad faith in the sale. The Jaguar is a hard to move car and "an orphan" in the Saint John area. The amount of $2,127.50 appeals to us as a satisfactory price in the second hand car market for a used Jaguar that had logged 11,000 miles. In our view, there is no ground for disturbing the findings of the learned trial Judge.

Appeal dismissed.

Note: With respect to dealers' practices in selling repossessed cars at wholesale prices, see Shuchman, "Profit on Default: An Archival Study of Automobile Repossession and Resale" (1969-70) 22 Stan. L. Rev. 20; and E.B. Corenswet, "I Can Get It for You Wholesale; The Lingering Problem of Automobile Deficiency Judgments" (1974-75) 27 Stan. L. Rev. 1081.

It has however been argued that typically a dealer who has repossessed a default-ing debtor's car, "has enough cars, what he needs is customers". Accordingly,

> If he is forced to resell the car in a retail market, he has lost a sale; he would otherwise have sold two cars and made two profits instead of one. It is important to remember in this context that the secured party must account to the debtor for any surplus resulting from the sale

(M. Miller, "Article Nine Deficiency Sales: The Windfall Factor" (1976-77) 7 Memphis St. UL Rev. 475, 485).

4.   THE RIGHT TO CLAIM A DEFICIENCY

Sawyer v. *Pringle* (1891) 18 OAR 218, a leading case, denied the conditional seller's right to claim any deficiency after repossession and resale on the theory that the contract was an executory agreement for a future sale subject to performance by the buyer of his obligations under the agreement. Resale was held to amount to rescission of the agreement, thus discharging the buyer from any further prior obligations. The rationale of the case was inapplicable to chattel mortgages and was not uniformly applied even with regard to conditional sale contracts. See *Delta Acceptance Corp. Ltd.* v. *Redman* (1966) 55 DLR (2d) 481, [1966] 2 OR 37 (CA), *per* Laskin J.A. (as he then was) (dissenting). It could in any event be circumvented by the seller inserting a clause in the agreement securing his right to a deficiency.

The secured party's right to claim a deficiency is not spelled out in the PPSA; *cf.* UCC 9-504(2). Is this fatal or is the right implied in the concept of a security interest?

In the context of the UCC, the secured party's deficiency right has revolved around the effect of not reselling the repossessed collateral in a "commercially reasonable" manner (UCC 9-504(3), PPSA s. 58(3)). U.S. courts are divided as to the meaning of "commercially reasonable" in this section as well as on the effect of non-compliance with this requirement on the secured creditor's deficiency right.

With respect to the meaning of "commercially reasonable", the dividing line is between those courts which emphasize the *price* realized from the sale (*cf.* UCC 9-507(2)) and those which focus on the *procedures* employed for the sale. But even those of the latter school of thought agree that a wide discrepancy between the sale price and the value of the collateral signals a need for close scrutiny. See *In the Matter of Zsa Zsa Ltd.* (1972) 352 F. Supp. 665 (US DC SD NY), and consider the following extract from *Atlas Construction Co.* v. *Dravo-Doyle Co.* (1965) 3 UCC Rep. Ser. 124, 130-131 (Pa. CP) *per* McKenna J.:

> Plaintiff produced memoranda from defendant's files which stated that the resale took place on March 3, 1962, and not, as defendant contended, on the 15th of that month. For the purposes of the motion for judgment n.o.v., we must assume that the sale took place on the earlier date. This being the case, the letter of February 23rd constituted eight (8) days notice. This was sufficient time within which plaintiff could act to protect its interest in the crane.
>
> Plaintiff also relies upon Section 9-504(3) of the Code and contends that considering all aspects of the disposition to Campbell, the jury could find that it was not carried out in a commercially reasonable manner. Emphasis is placed upon the fact that the resale price of $19,500.00 was substantially lower than the price of between $25,000.00 and $28,000.00 which Mr. Marapese was willing to pay for the crane. From this, it is argued that the resale price was unreasonably low.
>
> In support of this contention, plaintiff introduced a publication known as the Green Guide Handbook, a loose-leaf book containing lists of average prices for new and used construction equipment, and published by the Equipment Guidebook Company (T 30). This book revealed that as of February, 1962, the average sale price for a 1959 Model 375 American Truck Crane was $23,200.00, plus $2,110.00 for booms and equipment, a total value of $25,310.00 (T 95-98).
>
> The average prices listed in this book are competent evidence of value. Plaintiff's President stated (T 30) that the Green Guide is the recognized authority for market values. Charles Hollingsworth, the President of Dravo-Doyle, testified that his company keeps a copy of this book (T 90), and one of its salesmen admitted that he uses it on occasion as an indicator of equipment values (T 131).
>
> In *Family Finance Corp.* v. *Scott*, 24 D & C 2d 587 [1 UCC Rep. 647] (1961), Judge Van der Voort of this court held that since the resale price of a repossessed automobile was substantially lower than its "Blue Book" value, a question was presented whether the sale upon repossession was commercially reasonable. The Green Book for construction equipment is comparable to the Blue Book for automobiles, and should be equally probative of market values.
>
> It is true that Section 9-507(2) of the Code provides that:
>
>> The fact that a better price could have been obtained by a sale at a different method than that selected by the secured party is not of itself sufficient to establish that the sale was not made in a commercially reasonable manner.
>
> In the present case, however, there are factors in addition to the inadequate price, from which the jury could conclude that Dravo-Doyle's disposition of the

crane was not commercially reasonable. George Hickson is a salesman for Dravo-Doyle, in charge of the promotion and sale of cranes (T 112). Hickson testified at the hearing that although his territory covered parts of Pennsylvania, Ohio, Maryland and West Virginia, he made no effort to contact a purchaser for the crane other than Campbell (T 140).

From the fact that the price received by Dravo-Doyle was substantially lower than the value of the equipment, as evidenced by Marapese's testimony and the Green Guide quotation, and from the fact that Dravo-Doyle contacted only one purchaser, the jury could conclude that defendant failed to take adequate steps to ensure that a fair price was received. Therefore the jury was justified in concluding that the sale was not "commercially reasonable."

The motion for judgment non obstante veredicto must be refused.

Note: With respect to the effect of non-compliance with the "commercially reasonable" requirements, five approaches have been taken (see: Braun, "Deficiency Actions, Non-compliance and Article 9" (1975) 19 St. Louis ULJ 488, 500-06):

1) Non-compliance is no bar to deficiency claim.
2) Non-compliance precludes deficiency claim.
3) Non-compliance diminishes deficiency by actual loss.
4) Non-compliance creates a rebuttable presumption that the amount generated by the resale was equal to the amount of the debt. Unless the presumption is rebutted deficiency claim is precluded.
5) Compliance is a condition precedent to deficiency claim.

VIC HANSEN & SONS INC. v. CROWLEY
(1973) 203 NW 2d 728, 730-733 (SC WIS.)

CONNOR T. HANSSEN Justice: August 15, 1970, defendants purchased from the plaintiff a used 1965 Oldsmobile automobile. The original contract called for the payment of a total time price of $2,253.52, comprised of the cash price of $1595, subject to a down-payment credit of $18.51, plus additions for sales' tax and credit health and accident insurance of $157.22, and a time-price differential of $519.81. The annual percentage rate on the contract was 26.58.

Immediately following the sale the vehicle developed mechanical problems and defendants had to return the vehicle several times for repairs. August 24, 1970, after meeting but one partial installment, the defendants refused to make additional payments and surrendered the vehicle to the plaintiff. September 16, 1970, defendants returned the properly executed title to the vehicle to plaintiff, whereupon the plaintiff had the title to the vehicle re-entered into its name. After making a demand for payment and receiving none, plaintiff sent notice to the defendants on October 1, or October 2, 1970, that after October 15, 1970, the vehicle would be sold at a private sale. The vehicle was "purchased" at the private sale by the plaintiff. The "sale" took place by means of an inter-office exchange of papers, wherein defendants were credited with $700 upon plaintiff's ledger. Defendants' account was further credited with the principal payment of $90 and rebates for prepaid insurance and prepaid interest of $523.89; leaving a net balance of $939.63, upon which the plaintiff brought suit in county court to reduce to judgment.

The action was tried before the court. Following trial, the trial court determined that the "sale" of the vehicle on October 15, 1970, was not in accordance with the law, and that the plaintiff had failed to establish the amount to which it was entitled to a deficiency judgment. Judgment was accordingly entered October 29, 1971, dismissing plaintiff's complaint.

The dispositive issue raised on this appeal is whether, under the Uniform Commercial Code (UCC) as adopted in Wisconsin, defendants are liable to plaintiff for any deficiency arising out of their default on their contract for the sale of the automobile. The controversy centers around plaintiff's "sale" of the automobile following defendants' default and the subsequent repossession of the car by plaintiff.

Section 409.504, Stats., in part, provides:

> (1) A secured party after default may sell, lease or otherwise dispose of any or all of the collateral in its then condition or following any commercially reasonable preparation or processing. . . .
>
> (2) . . . .
>
> (3) Disposition of the collateral may be by public or private proceedings and may be made by way of one or more contracts. Sale or other disposition may be as a unit or in parcels and at any time and place and on any terms but every aspect of the disposition including the method, manner, time, place and terms must be commercially reasonable. Unless collateral is perishable or threatens to decline speedily in value or is of a type customarily sold on a recognized market, reasonable notification of the time and place of any public sale or reasonable notification of the time after which any private sale or other intended disposition is to be made shall be sent by the secured party to the debtor, and except in the case of consumer goods to any other person who has a security interest in the collateral and who has duly filed a financing statement indexed in the name of the debtor in this state or who is known by the secured party to have a security interest in the collateral. The secured party may buy at any public sale and if the collateral is of a type customarily sold in a recognized market or is of a type which is the subject of widely distributed standard price quotations he may buy at private sale.

The record indicates that the plaintiff "sold" the automobile to itself through an inter-office exchange of papers. There is no evidence of any bids sought or given, or any attempt to ascertain the value of the automobile other than from those within plaintiff's business organization. It is undisputed that it was a private sale. Much of counsel's arguments and discussion are concerned with the commercial reasonableness of this "sale" and the price obtained. The question of whether the plaintiff could purchase the automobile at his own private sale, regardless of whether or not the sale was conducted in a commercially reasonable manner, is not presented on this appeal.

The trial court held that the sale of the automobile was not "commercially reasonable" as required by sec. 409.504(3), Stats., in that while the defendants were indebted as to the "retail value" of the automobile, plaintiff unilaterally assigned a "wholesale value" upon sale. It was the opinion of the trial court that the application of different standards of valuation results in a sale that is not "commercially reasonable," and that the plaintiff failed to submit sufficient evidence to establish the amount of the deficiency, if any, to which it was entitled.

Section 409.504(3), Stats., requires that ". . . every aspect of the disposition including the method, manner, time, place and terms must be commercially reasonable." Section 401.203 provides further that: "Every contract or duty within this code imposes an obligation of good faith in its performance or enforcement."

Prior to the enactment of the Uniform Commercial Code in Wisconsin, this court held that the secured party owed a duty to the debtor to use all fair and reasonable means in obtaining the best price for the property on sale. *Schwemer* v. *Citizens' Loan & Investment Co.* (1937) 225 Wis. 46, 52, 272 NW 673; *Kellogg* v. *Malick* (1905), 125 Wis. 239, 252, 253, 103 NW 1116. This duty was not abandoned upon the enactment of the Code. The purpose of the Uniform Commercial Code is the protection of both the creditor and the debtor. Each party to the transaction has certain duties. The duty of the secured party in this instance was to obtain the best possible price it could obtain for the collateral for the benefit of the debtor. The secured party does not have to use "extraordinary means" to accomplish this result. Ordinarily, proof that the price obtained was the fair market value thereof would be sufficient.

Although defendants pled as an affirmative defense the allegation that the "sale" and price obtained were not commercially reasonable, there is some conflict as to who has the burden of proof thereto.

One line of authority holds that the secured party must establish that every aspect of the sale was commercially reasonable. *First National Bank of Bellevue* v. *Rose* (1972) 188 Neb. 362, 196 NW 2d 507; 10 UCC Rep. 903, 905; *In re Bro Cliff, Inc.* (1971) United States District Court, WD Mich., 8 UCC Rep. 1144, 1149; *Universal C. I. T. Credit Co.* v. *Rone* (1970) 248 Ark. 665, 453 SW 2d 37, 7 UCC Rep. 847.

Other authorities have held that a secured party makes out a case for a deficiency judgment by proving the debt and security agreement and that a credit of a stated amount has been allowed as the result of the sale of the collateral, and that the burden shifts to the debtor to show why the creditor should not recover the deficiency. *Fryer & Willis Drilling Co.* v. *Oilwell, Division of United States Steel Corp.* (Tex. Civ. App. 1971), 472 SW 2d 857, 9 UCC Rep. 1135; *Ekman* v. *Mountain Motors, Inc.* (1961) Wyo., 364 P. 2d 998, 1001.

It is our opinion that those jurisdictions which hold that the secured party must establish that every aspect of the sale was commercially reasonable enunciate a rule that more appropriately recognizes the tenor of the Code. This will henceforth be the rule in this state in those instances where the property is sold at "private sale." The secured party has the duty under the Code to proceed in good faith and in a commercially reasonable manner. It follows that he who has the duty should also have the burden of proof.

Upon trial it was necessary for the plaintiff to establish that every aspect of the sale was commercially reasonable, including the adequacy of the price for which the collateral was sold.

The evidence submitted on the sufficiency of the sale is scant. When the vehicle was first traded to the plaintiff, prior to sale to the defendants, it was appraised at $800 and, with minor repairs amounting to $107.70, was thereafter resold to the defendants for a cash value of $1595. Approximately 60 days later, after its return, the car was sold back into inventory at an appraised "wholesale" value of $700. The original appraisal of $800 was also designated as "wholesale." Plaintiff's witnesses testified that the $700 was a "fair value," and close to what other dealers would have paid for it. The record is barren on the subject of the retail value of the car on October 15, 1970, the time of the private sale to the plaintiff. The vehicle resold for $995 in February, 1971, after having had repairs made in the amount of $210.12.

There is no evidence as to what the fair market value of the vehicle was upon deficiency sale; nor did plaintiff establish that the $700 was in fact the wholesale price, or what effect the repairs of the vehicle had upon the value of the automobile itself. There is some evidence of abuse to the vehicle but no evidence as to its effect upon the value. All that was submitted were self-serving assertions that the vehicle was worth $800 to $700 wholesale, and $1595 to $995 retail.

The plaintiff has not sufficiently established that $700 was a commercially reasonable price. There is no requirement or prohibition that the secured party sell at "wholesale" or "retail." All that is required is the best possible price under the circumstances.

Plaintiff argues that the price for which the collateral sells at the deficiency sale is evidence of what the fair market value was. While this argument may have some weight where the collateral is sold at a public sale or auction, such is not the case at private sales. Because of the inherent nature of the private sale, the defendants-debtors do not carry this burden of proof. In addition, plaintiff's witnesses testified at trial that the $700 was the "wholesale" value. This court, in *Boehck Construction Equip. Corp.* v. *O'Brien* (1966) 29 Wis. 2d 649, 651, 139 NW 2d 650, 651, stated:

> . . . The wholesale price and the retail sales price are not trustworthy indicators since they obviously reflect prices which, by definition, are either favorable to the original seller or buyer. . . .

Plaintiff's office manager testified that plaintiff took used automobiles in at wholesale to sell at retail and make money. Such a practice has no place in a private sale of debtor's collateral in that the plaintiff, as secured party, owes the duty to the defendants to use reasonable efforts to obtain the best price to protect the debtors' interests. The secured party should not "make money" from the sale of the debtors' collateral.

In *Cities Service Oil Co.* v. *Ferris, supra,* the court held that sale of the collateral at wholesale to the only bidder was not commercially reasonable where there was evidence the collateral was worth substantially more and the secured party was in the business of distributing products of that type through retail outlets and could have received a larger amount for the collateral through the retail outlets. The instant case presents a somewhat similar situation.

Plaintiff's contentions that sec. 409.507(2), Stats., provides otherwise, are not persuasive. Section 409.507(2) in part, provides:

If the secured party either sells the collateral in the usual manner in any recognized market therefor or if he sells at the price current in such market at the time of his sale or if he has otherwise sold in conformity with reasonable commercial practices among dealers in the type of property sold he has sold in a commercially reasonable manner. . . .

The proof submitted would not support a finding that plaintiff sold the automobile in the "usual manner in any recognized market" or at the "price current in such market," or as to "reasonable commercial practices" among dealers in used automobiles. The trial court properly decided that as a matter of law the plaintiff's private sale of defendants' collateral was commercially unreasonable.

The trial court also held that plaintiff failed to show the amount that should reasonably have been obtained through a sale conducted according to law. Upon an examination of the record, it cannot be said that this finding is contrary to the great weight and clear preponderance of the evidence. Therefore, plaintiff in the instant case is precluded from obtaining any deficiency judgment, and it becomes unnecessary for this court to now decide what right, if any, the plaintiff might have because of its failure to comply with the Code.

Judgment dismissing the
plaintiff's complaint affirmed.

Note: Whether the right to deficiency, even on compliance with the "commercially reasonable" requirement, should exist at all, has been a hotly debated issue in Canada and the U.S.: see e.g. British Columbia Law Reform Commission, *Working Paper No. 4, Deficiency Claims and Repossession* (May 1971); and P. Shuchman, "Profit or Default: An Archival Study of Automobile Repossession and Resale" (1969-70) 22 Stan LR 20. Arguments against the right to deficiency are the potential for abuses, the unfortunate position of the debtor who has to pay for goods he no longer enjoys, and the ability of the business community to internalize losses as well as to screen debtors.

The anti-deficiency lobby has won many adherents. As early as 1929 Alberta adopted a "seize or sue" provision (presently embodied in the Conditional Sales Act, RSA 1970, c. 61, s. 19) requiring a conditional seller to elect between seizure in full satisfaction or legal action for the balance due. Such a provision has been adopted in British Columbia, Manitoba, Quebec, Newfoundland and the Northwest Territories. In British Columbia, the "seize or sue" principle is also applied to a secured lender (not only a PMSI holder): Bills of Sale Act, SBC 1961, c. 6, s. 22A (enacted 1973, c. 7, s. 4). In Saskatchewan, subject to a few enumerated exceptions, a secured seller is only allowed to repossess the goods (i.e., he cannot elect to sue): see the Limitation of Civil Rights Act, RSS 1978, c. L-16, s. 18, given full effect under Sask. PPSA s. 69(1)). See, in general: R.C.C. Cuming, "Consumer Credit Law" in Fridman (ed.) *Studies in Canadian Business Law* (1971) pp. 87, 148; R.C.C. Cuming, "Changes in British Columbia Chattel Security Law — Has the Evergreen Playground Become a Debtor's Haven?" (1973) 8 UBCL Rev. 61; R.C.C. Cuming and A. Zysblat, "Changes in British Columbia Chattel Security Law; Some Further Reflections" (1974) 9 UBC L. Rev. 341; and R.C.C. Cuming, "Consumer Credit Law in Selected Countries: Canada" in R.M. Goode (ed.) *Consumer Credit* (1978) pp. 186, 207.

The (American) Uniform Consumer Credit Code (1974) contains a seize or sue provision (5.103(3)) with respect to consumer goods whose purchase price does not exceed $1,750.

The constitutionality of the British Columbia "seize or sue" provision was upheld in *C.I.B.C.* v. *Materi* (1975) 50 DLR (3d) 400 (BC SC). Since the legislation does not affect the rights of a holder in due course, and its "object . . . [was] to restrict a mortgagee to one remedy in connection with the indebtedness", the court held the legislation "*intra vires* as regards to the parties to this transaction": *id.* at 413, 414. The decision has been criticized by Professor Buglass on the ground that: "It is difficult to see how such a provision is not in relation to the obligations contained in a negotiable instrument and therefore *ultra vires*"; Buglass, "Consumer Notes: Recent Judicial and Legislative Developments in Canada in Ziegel (ed.) *Papers and Comments delivered at The Eighth Annual Workshop on Commercial and Consumer Law (1978)* (1980) pp. 39, 58.

The British Columbia "seize or sue" provision was recently construed in *Toronto Dominion Bank* v. *Maxine's Restaurant Ltd.* (1980) 105 DLR (3d) 639 (BC SC). The court held that while bringing an action on the debt precludes the creditor from repossessing the goods, it does not prevent enforcement of a land mortgage also securing the debt. Is this consistent with the policy of the legislation?

5. The Right to Reinstate

PERESLUKA v. G.M.A.C. OF CANADA LTD.
(1966) 56 DLR (2d) 717 (Man. QB)

HALL J.: Plaintiff sued for an order that upon payment by him to defendant of five instalments of $100.56 under a conditional sales contract for the purchase of a 1965 Pontiac Sedan automobile, defendant deliver up possession of the automobile in the same condition it was at the time of seizure. Also sought were general damages for unlawful seizure, or, alternatively, for failure to return the automobile upon tender having been made of the instalment payments from time to time due.

Plaintiff purchased and received delivery of the automobile from Winnipeg Motor Products Ltd. on September 10, 1965, pursuant to the conditional sales contract, ex. 7. He made a down payment in money or its equivalent of $1,600 towards a total cash sale delivery price of $4,395, leaving an unpaid cash price balance of $2,795. To this balance was added $198 for collision insurance coverage, leaving a principal unpaid balance of $2,993. To this amount was added $627.16 finance charges for 36½ months, leaving a time deferred balance of $3,620.16 which was to be financed by the defendant, to whom ex. 7 was assigned. This balance was to be paid in 36 monthly instalments of $100.56 each, the first of which was to be paid on October 25, 1965.

Plaintiff did not make the first payment on its due date as he was saving money for his wedding in early November and thought in view of past experience that defendant would allow 30 days before taking any steps. At the time of making the contract he gave his address as Tyndall, Manitoba, the home of his parents. Shortly thereafter he moved to 810 Bannatyne Avenue, Winnipeg.

Defendant sent a notice to the Tyndall address which was never received by plaintiff or returned to defendant. Representatives of defendant had difficulty locating plaintiff but finally succeeded in seizing the automobile without warrant on November 17, 1965, at the rear of 810 Bannatyne Avenue. Seizure was effected without actual notice to plaintiff when he left the vehicle with its motor running and returned to his residence for cigarettes. After discovering what had happened he telephoned defendant and offered to pay the overdue instalment but was told his business was no longer wanted.

The matter was referred to plaintiff's solicitor who made repeated attempts to restore possession of the automobile by tendering instalment payments as they became due, including the cost of seizure. Defendant, through its solicitor, refused settlement except on payment of the accelerated balance in accordance with cl. 4 of the contract. On December 15, 1965, he wrote plaintiff's solicitor acknowledging two cheques totalling $203.47, but returning them with these remarks:

> In addition to the amounts proposed in settlement, you should have included the sum of $5.00 required by the contract and solicitor's costs and of course, the balance of purchase price in accordance with the acceleration clause in the contract. I understand that the courts cannot relieve against acceleration without a clear statutory authority. It will be interesting to settle this point in relation to conditional sales in Manitoba.

Defendant invoked the acceleration clause on the back of ex. 7, which reads in part:

> In the event Purchaser defaults on any payment due under this contract or fails to comply with any condition of this contract or a proceeding in bankruptcy, receivership or insolvency be instituted against the Purchaser or his property, or in the event either that the Purchaser fails for any reason to comply with Clause 9(a) of the following or that said required automobile insurance is cancelled by the insurer prior to expiration thereof, the unpaid balance, together with any other amount for which the Purchaser shall have become obligated hereunder, shall be immediately due and payable forthwith. Further, upon such default or event, Seller or any officer of the law may take immediate possession of said property without demand (possession after default being unlawful), including any equipment or accessories thereto; and for this purpose Seller may enter upon the premises where said property may be and remove same. Such repossession shall not affect Seller's right, hereby confirmed, to retain all payments made prior thereto by the Purchaser hereunder ...

If invoked plaintiff would lose his down payment of $1,600 and forfeit finance charges of $627.16, having had the car from September 10, 1965, to November 17, 1965.

The question arises as to whether plaintiff is entitled to possession of the automobile upon payment of the aggregate of the instalments due plus the cost of seizure. In my opinion he is so entitled in accordance with the right of redemption afforded by s. 3 of the Lien Notes Act, RSM 1954, c. 144. It is clear to me that the conditional sales contract, ex. 7, is a receipt note within the meaning of that statute. The Act does not define "receipt note", but a reading of the provisions makes reasonably clear that it includes conditional sale agreements. Section 3 reads:

> 3.(1) Where the bailor retakes possession of the chattel for breach of condition in any such receipt note, hire receipt, or order for chattels, he shall retain them for twenty days in the same condition as they are at the time he retakes possession; and the bailee or his successor in interest may redeem them within that period on payment of the amount then in arrear together with interest, if any is payable, and the actual costs and expenses of taking and keeping possession.
>
> (2) This section does not apply to a lien note or conditional sale agreement given or made in respect of the sale of an implement to which The Farm Implement Act applies.

It will be noted that s-s. (2) excepts the application of s-s. (1) to a "lien note or conditional sale agreement given or made in respect of the sale of an implement to which The Farm Implements Act applies". By necessary implication s. 3(1) would apply to all other lien notes or conditional sale agreements.

In *Canadian Law of Conditional Sales*, 3rd ed., by John A. Barron, the author says [p. 222], in reference to the Lien Notes Act, RSM 1913, c. 115:

> A Receipt Note as [sic] an acknowledgment in writing of having received the chattels mentioned therein, upon the terms therein set forth, and is a bilateral contract which each is under obligation to perform — one to sell and the other to buy. It describes the chattels and states the price, and the terms and time of payment, and that when the condition is fully performed the bailee will become the owner.
>
> It is not necessary that the word "receipt" or "received" should appear at all. An instrument which represents that the bailee has received goods for which he holds himself accountable to the bailor is an accountable receipt, although the word "received" does not appear on it.
>
> The receipt note contains an undertaking by the bailee that he will make the payments in the manner and at the times prescribed, and that, in default, the bailor may resume possession. It is not a sale of the goods, but an executory sale thereof, to become a sale, when the bailee does his part; but the important, and necessary, feature in the bailment is, that the possession of the chattel passes to the bailee, but not the ownership, and the receipt must state this. The parties may modify the receipt, as they may agree, and it will still be within the statute.

The omnibus part of the conditional sales contract, ex. 7, reads in part:

CONDITIONAL SALE CONTRACT

The undersigned Seller hereby sells and the undersigned Purchaser . . . purchases and agrees to pay for, subject to the terms and conditions set forth below AND UPON THE REVERSE SIDE HEREOF, WHICH ARE INCORPORATED HEREIN AS PART OF THIS CONTRACT, the following property, delivery and acceptance of which is hereby acknowledged by the Purchaser in good condition and as ordered.

Having regard to the provisions of the statute and the terms of the conditional sales contract, including the reference from Barron, it may be concluded that such a contract is a receipt note within the meaning of the Act and that plaintiff is entitled to the right of redemption afforded by s. 3 thereof.

The further question arises as to whether the amount "then in arrear" means the amount due by the passage of time or the amount payable because of the acceleration clause. In my opinion the acceleration provision cannot operate so as to destroy the right of redemption afforded by s. 3. In such event the bailor-bailee relationship would be at an end and upon payment of the accelerated balance the plaintiff would become the owner in possession which would be inconsistent with a right of redemption restoring the respective parties to their positions under the contract.

In the case of *B.C. Independent Undertakers* v. *Maritime Motor Car Co.* 35 DLR 551, 24 BCR 305, [1917] 3 WWR 22, the majority decision of the Court of Appeal of British Columbia held that the words "the full amount then in arrear" in s. 32 of the Sale of Goods Act, RSBC 1911, c. 203, (similar to s. 3 of the Lien Notes Act) meant the accelerated amount payable under an acceleration clause after seizure in default. The remaining member of the Court held the other way. It seems to me that the case is distinguished on the word "full" as used in the B.C. statute, but regardless of that point I decline to follow the majority decision which is not binding on me. So to do would not be in keeping with contemporary credit sale practices. The right of redemption would in most cases be rendered meaningless. Invoking a clause in the nature of a penalty as regards a redemption provision is repugnant and unacceptable.

In summary, it is my opinion that the conditional sales contract is a receipt note within the meaning of the Lien Notes Act and the words "then in arrear", as they appear in s. 3, mean the amount due by the passage of time and not the amount payable because of the acceleration clause. It follows that the plaintiff was denied the right of redemption afforded by the statute.

The plaintiff was a painter and decorator regularly employed as such. He required the automobile to go to and from whatever work his employer had at various locations. He also used it after hours to go to painting jobs he was doing on his own. Without it he had to find other transportation to and from regular work and could not do extra work nor drive his wife to her job at a nursing home; as a result she quit her job.

In my opinion plaintiff is entitled to nominal damages and a reasonable sum to compensate him for the loss he sustained by not having the automobile for use in his business. While an exact amount has not been proven, I feel justified in assessing $300 for nominal and real damages.

In this case I was quite unimpressed, and so expressed myself at the trial, that defendant should lead evidence to establish that plaintiff was a bad risk so as to justify its demand for the full balance. I said then, and I repeat now, that defendant having accepted plaintiff as a risk, the reason or justification for invoking the acceleration clause was irrelevant.

For these reasons plaintiff is entitled to an order that upon payment by him of $505.19 to defendant, which represents instalments past due and costs of seizure, defendant deliver up possession of the automobile in the same condition as at the time of seizure and pay plaintiff $300 damages. Plaintiff is entitled to his costs, including fiat for discovery. In view of my decision on the Lien Notes Act it is unnecessary for me to consider the other issues that have been raised.

Judgment for plaintiff.

Note: See *contra*: *Delta Acceptance Corp. Ltd.* v. *Novits* (1968) 67 DLR (2d) 208 (Ont. Co. Ct.) where the court held that the amount "then in arrear" in s. 9(1) of the Ontario Conditional Sales Act referred to the accelerated balance. What is the position under s. 61 of the Ontario PPSA? Consider also s. 58(1)(*b*) and (*e*). As to the desirability of the right to reinstate, see R.M. Goode and J.S. Ziegel, *Hire-Purchase and Conditional Sale* (1965) p. 119 n. 17.

Section 61 of the MUPPSA allows a right of reinstatement free of any acceleration clause if the collateral includes consumer goods and, unless a court otherwise orders, the right may only be exercised once during the term of this agreement. In any other case, other than where the security agreement involves a trust indenture, the right may only be exercised pursuant to an order of the court. The exercise of the reinstatement right is restricted under the Sask. PPSA to twice a year (s. 62(2)). Note also that under the Sask. PPSA the creditor's notice of intention to dispose of a repossessed collateral must contain a statement of the debtor's right to reinstate: s. 59(6)(*f*).

6.   THE RIGHT TO REBATE ON PREPAYMENT

The debtor's right to a rebate on prepayment was recognized in Ontario in *Delta Acceptance Corp. Ltd.* v. *Redman* (1966) 55 DLR (2d) 481, [1966] 2 OR 37 (CA) where "all members of the Court agree[d] . . . that, notwithstanding the terms of the conditional sale contract which provided for accelerated payment of all charges upon default, no amounts for unearned finance charges may be recovered" (*id.* at 485, *per* McGillivray J.A.). "Whether this passage correctly sets out the views of all members of the Court in that case, or whether in some way the statement is to be regarded as *obiter*, is now academic, because later in the same year the legislature passed the Consumer Protection Act, 1966 . . .": *Industrial Acceptance Corp. Ltd.* v. *Keeler Ford Sales Ltd.* (1971) 18 DLR (3d) 257, 264, [1971] 2 OR 465 (CA) *per* Arnup J.A. What is the position apart from such a statutory provision? Can the creditor's claim to unearned interest be treated as an unenforceable penalty or does it depend on whether or not the interest is precomputed and becomes part of the principal debt? See *The Protector Endowment Loan and Annuity Co.* v. *Grice* (1880) 5 QBD 592, CA, and cf. *Warner* v. *Caruana* (1974) 2 NSWLR 301.

The borrower's entitlement on prepayment "to a proportionate credit in respect of the cost of borrowing" side by side with the lender's entitlement "to a proportionate part of the cost of lending" is now regulated in s. 40 of the Ontario CPA and implemented in s. 17 of the Ontario Regulations.

The "Rule of 78" is used almost universally in determining rebates of unearned finance charges. The following brief explanation of the operation of the rule is taken from *Bone* v. *Hibernia Bank* (1974) 493 F. 2d 135, 137 (CCA 9):

> The Rule of 78's is also known as the sum-of-the-digits and direct ratio methods. Under the Rule, when a loan is to be repaid in monthly installments, each month of the loan's term is assigned a digit, with the first month's digit equalling the total number of months in the agreed period of the loan. The second month is then assigned a digit one less than that of the first, the third month again one less, and so on, until the digit assigned to the last month equals (1) one. For a twelve month loan, the sum of the digits (12 + 11 + 10 . . . +1) of this arithmetic progression is 78. This

number then serves as the denominator in a fractional equation, with the numerator being the sum of the digits for those months expired at the time of the obligation's prepayment. For example, assuming a twelve month loan obligation, if the entire loan were prepaid at the end of the first month, $^{12}/_{78}$ of the total finance charge would be retained by the creditor. This represents a greater proportion of the finance charge than in any other month because the borrower has had the use of the entire amount of the loan for that month. At the end of the second month, $^{11}/_{78}$ of the finance charge would be retained since the borrower has had the use of $^{11}/_{12}$, or most of the loan proceeds for that month. If the borrower prepaid the entire obligation at this time, $^{23}/_{78}$ of the finance charge would be considered to have been earned and therefore would be retained by the creditor. At the end of six months, the creditor would be entitled to $^{57}/_{78}$ of the total finance charge, and the consumer in turn to $^{21}/_{78}$ charge. . . .

The results obtained by the Rule of 78's method closely approximate those of the "actuarial" method in which the rebate bears a more direct relationship to the amount of money received and the time for which it is used, and in which "true" interest yields are produced. Because the actuarial method requires the use of actuarial tables and more difficult computations, however, the more easily computed Rule of 78's method is widely used by banks and financing institutions as an acceptable substitute for the actuarial method. . . .

For further explanation on the operation of the Rule of 78 and a comparison between its accuracy and that of the "actuarial method", see J.H. Hunt, "The Rule of 78: Hidden Penalty for Prepayment in Consumer Credit Transactions" (1975) 55 Bus. UL Rev. 331. The author's conclusion (at 365) is that the Rule of 78 is "approximate technique when compared with the traditional method of computing interest on a debt, now called the actuarial method." In particular, "[t]he accuracy of the Rule of 78 diminishes rapidly as the interest rate on the debt increases, the term of the debt increases, or particularly as both rate and term increase. The approximate nature of the Rule of 78 imposes an implicit penalty for prepayment . . . [which] can be large . . .".

7. BANKRUPTCY AND ENFORCEMENT OF A SECURITY INTEREST

The debtor's bankruptcy almost invariably amounts to a "default" within the meaning of PPSA s. 1(*h*). However, this does not end the story since, apart from any possible attack by the trustee against the security on the grounds of lack of perfection, the secured creditor's rights are also affected by bankruptcy law. The following is a summary of the secured creditor's rights under the current Bankruptcy Act, RSC 1970, c. B-3, as amended, and its proposed revision in Bill C-12 (introduced in the House of Commons on April 16, 1980).

J.B. COLBURN
"The Position of Retail and Wholesale Financers as Secured Creditors under the Proposed Bankruptcy Act"
(1979-80) 4 Can. Bus. LJ 348, 350-51; 366-68

II. The Current Act
Under the current Act a secured creditor may act virtually independently of

any proposal (arrangement) accepted by other creditors or of any bankruptcy trustee. It has been said that this freedom of action presents a "formidable obstacle" to the proponent of a proposal as the trustee must obtain the co-operation of any secured creditor whose collateral is crucial to the operation of the proposal. In addition, a secured creditor is under no obligation to file a proof of claim in a bankruptcy as a secured or unsecured creditor unless it suits his purposes or unless demanded by the trustee. The trustee's sole rights are to:

(a) inspect the collateral;
(b) redeem the security by paying out the secured creditor's debt and taking title to the collateral;
(c) demand that the secured creditor value its security and provide particulars of its security interest within 30 days; or
(d) force a public sale of the collateral where the trustee has demanded the security be valued in (b) above.

On the other hand, the secured creditor may, where the trustee has not re-deemed, proceed either to realize upon its security and file a proof of claim as an unsecured creditor for any deficiency, or surrender its security and claim for the whole debt due as an unsecured creditor. If the collateral is in the possession of the bankrupt or his trustee, negotiations will normally take place for the volun-tary release by the trustee of the collateral failing which the secured creditor (assuming his security is not invalid) may force a release of the collateral within 15 days by making a s. 59 filing with the trustee.

Practically speaking the trustee is rarely in a position to redeem due either to a shortage of funds or to minimal equity making redemption uneconomical. His options generally are restricted to challenging the security agreement by taking proceedings to set the security aside as invalid. As a result of these limitations, secured creditors may exercise their rights under their security agreements unaffected by the bankruptcy and subject only to requirements of provincial law (including the trustee's right to receive particulars of the sale), the common law obligation to realize *bona fide* and in a reasonable manner, and the trustee's right to be paid any surplus.

• • •

VII. Summary [of the Bill]

From [the preceding] review of the provisions of the Bill it will be obvious that the credit grantor will carefully have to monitor his collateral and in an arrangement/bankruptcy situation will no longer be able to afford to stand aloof. Specific attention should be paid to the following:

(1) In both consumer debtor and commercial arrangements or bankruptcies the secured creditor will be obligated to realize or deal with the collateral honestly, in good faith and in a timely and commercially reasonable manner; to report any conservatory measures taken in respect to the collateral; and to report the results of the realization to the trustee/administrator and remit any surplus.

(2) Positive action will have to be taken to avoid being subjected to a consumer arrangement within the required 25-day time period;

(3) A proof of security interest will have to be filed within 25 days of the trustee's request, failing which the security interest will be deemed to have been renounced. Failure to file will also disentitle a secured creditor to a dividend on the unsecured portion of his claim;

(4) A secured creditor will not be permitted to claim a deficiency after realizing his security if he does not participate in an arrangement;

(5) The trustee/administrator is obligated to provide the secured creditor with information about the collateral and to deliver it up to the secured creditor on request;

(6) All creditors supplying inventory to a commercial account should take advantage of the inventory security provisions of the PPSA so that they may at least have the protection of being a secured creditor. The ease of creating such a security arrangement and the ability to file a single financing statement to cover a series of inventory transactions makes this a highly recommended step even for small suppliers;

(7) Any blanket inventory security agreement or retail finance security agreement should include a provision prohibiting the debtor from transferring the collateral in order to prevent the exercise by the trustee/administrator of his right to transfer the estate's equity in the collateral;

(8) Careful analysis will have to be made of the impact of the various stays and the degree to which they can be ignored;

(9) The PPSA should be carefully examined to make certain that all technical requirements have been complied with, non-compliance with which could expose the security agreement to attack;

(10) The increase in the number of consumer arrangements and bankruptcies and in the number of commercial proposals will require much greater familiarity with the provisions of the Bill as well as continuous monitoring of the administration of bankrupt estates by credit departments; and

(11) In some cases, a credit department will be able to make creative use of the commercial arangement sections to rescue an important customer and perhaps reduce losses as a result.

8. LESSOR'S RIGHTS UPON LESSEE'S DEFAULT

Lessee's default in a true financing lease is not governed by the PPSA. Is the lessee entitled to a notice of default? To a notice of repossession? Is he entitled to cure? Is the lessor's claim to future rent analogous to the secured party's right to deficiency? See in general: J. Varcoe, "Finance Leasing — An Analysis of the Lessor's Rights Upon Default by the Lessee" (1975-76) 1 Can. Bus. LJ 117.

Consider also the desirability of applying PPSA rules in the context of the case that follows:

CANADIAN ACCEPTANCE CORP. LTD. v. REGENT PARK BUTCHER SHOP LTD.
(1969) 3 DLR (3d) 304 (Man. CA)

DICKSON J.A.: The amount at stake in this appeal is small but the issue raised is important to finance companies and to those doing business with them. Briefly expressed it is this: A finance company leases equipment to "A" for a fixed term at a monthly rental. "A" defaults in payment of the rental. The company seizes the equipment and sells it. Can the company then recover from "A" the instalments of rent falling due during the unexpired term of the lease pursuant to a clause contained in the lease purporting to give it that right? In our opinion, for the reasons which follow, it cannot. It can retain the rental payments received prior to seizure. It can retain the proceeds of sale. It can recover, with interest, payments overdue at time of seizure. But that is all.

Plaintiff, which we will call the finance company, sued Regent Park Butcher Shop Ltd., which we will call hirer, as lessee, and Mrs. Joyce Gauthier, as guarantor. The hirer did not defend. Mrs. Gauthier filed a short statement of defence denying liability on the ground that she signed the agreement as signing officer of the hirer and not in her personal capacity. The hirer and Mrs. Gauthier did not appear at the trial before Thompson, Co. Ct. J., nor in the appeal by the finance company to this Court.

It appears from the evidence led on behalf of the finance company before Thompson, Co. Ct. J., that on or about August 19, 1965, H.W. Turner, vice-president of J.G. Turner Ltd., installed a cash register on the premises of the hirer. Turner had a supply of blank forms which he called "C.A.C. Lease Contracts". He filled one out. Mrs. Gauthier signed it on behalf of the hirer. She also signed a personal guarantee. The same day the lease was sent by Turner to the finance company for acceptance, and was accepted by it on September 29, 1965.

The lease was for a term of five years and called for three advance rental payments of $18 each, then 57 rental payments of $18 each, totalling in all $1,080. The lease stated that the total cost of the cash register was $800.

Frank Scarcello, Winnipeg branch manager of the finance company, testified that it received a total of $72 under the lease. The lease went into default, the equipment was taken back by the finance company on February 22, 1966, and sold by it on March 15, 1966, for $520. The finance company sued defendants for $488, being the total rental of $1,080, less rent paid of $72, and less $520 realized on sale.

Thompson, Co. Ct. J., held that the clause under which action was brought was a penalty clause, and that the finance company was entitled only to actual damages suffered as proved in evidence. He held the finance company entitled to recover:

(a)	the value of the goods plus	$800.00
(b)	interest at a reasonable rate up to the time of termination of the lease — he allowed interest at 8% for a period of six months on $800	32.00
	totalling	$832.00

The learned Judge then reduced this amount by

(c)	the rental payments made	$ 72.00
	and	
(d)	the amount realized on sale	520.00
		$592.00

Judgment was given for the resultant figure of $240, plus costs. The finance company appeals.

The lease describes the lessor as "C.A.C. Leasing Company, a Division of Canadian Acceptance Corporation Limited". The hirer's full name and address are given. The full name and address of the supplier, J.G. Turner, Ltd., are given.

In the lease the hirer agrees to pay the "rentals as set forth above plus applicable provincial sales tax if calculated as a percentage of monthly rental payments and not included in TOTAL COST of equipment".

Paragraph 4 provides in part that

> Lessor, not being the manufacturer of the leased equipment, nor manufacturer's agent, makes no warranty or representation, either express or implied, as to the fitness, design or condition of, or as to the quality or capacity of the material, equipment or workmanship in the leased equipment.

Then there is agreement on the part of the hirer, (a) to pay all shipping charges and expenses incurred in connection with shipment of the leased equipment by the seller (*sic*) to the hirer; (b) to pay all charges and expenses in connection with the operation of the leased equipment; (c) to comply with all governmental laws, ordinances, regulations, requirements and rules with respect to the use, maintenance and operation of the leased equipment; (d) to maintain insurance protecting the finance company's interest, and (e) to make all repairs and replacements required to be made to maintain the leased equipment in good condition, reasonable wear and tear excepted.

Paragraph 8 provides that title to the leased equipment shall at all times remain in the finance company and upon the expiration or termination of the lease the hirer will deliver the leased equipment to the finance company.

Paragraph 15 provides that the hirer shall have no option to purchase or otherwise acquire title or ownership of any of the leased equipment.

Paragraph 18 provides that the lease is irrevocable for the full term and aggregate rentals shall not abate by reason of the hirer's right to possession and/ or the taking of possession by the finance company or for any other reason, and delinquent instalments of rent shall bear interest at 12% per annum.

The paragraph, however, with which we are principally concerned is para. 13. This paragraph reads:

> DEFAULT. There shall be deemed to be a breach of this lease (a) if Lessee shall default in the payment of any rent hereunder and such default shall continue for a period of 10 days, (b) if Lessee shall default in the performance of any of the other covenants herein and such default shall continue uncured for 15 days after written notice thereof to Lessee by Lessor, or (c) if Lessee ceases doing business as a going concern, or if a petition is filed by or against Lessee under the Bankruptcy Act or a

proposal arrangement, or reorganization under the Bankruptcy Act, Winding-Up Act, or Companies' Creditors Arrangement Act is requested by Lessee, or if Lessee attempts to remove or sell or transfer or encumber or sublet or part with possession of the leased equipment or any part thereof. In the event of a breach of this lease, as herein defined: (a) the leased equipment shall upon Lessor's demand forthwith be delivered to Lessor at Lessee's expense at such place as Lessor shall designate and Lessor and/or its agents may, without notice or liability or legal process, enter into any premises of or under control or jurisdiction of Lessee or any agent of Lessee where the leased equipment may be or by Lessor is believed to be, and repossess all or any part of the leased equipment, disconnecting and separating all thereof from any other property and using all force necessary or permitted by applicable law so to do, Lessee hereby expressly waiving all further rights to possession of the leased equipment and all claims for injuries suffered through or loss caused by such repossession, and (b) all sums due and to become due hereunder shall, at Lessor's option, become payable forthwith, and the Lessor, in addition to being entitled to take possession of the leased equipment as hereinbefore described, also shall be entitled to recover immediately as and for damages for the breach of this lease and not as a penalty, an amount equal to the difference between the aggregate rent reserved hereunder for the unexpired term of the lease (hereinafter called "Remaining Rentals") and the then aggregate rental value of all leased equipment for the unexpired term of the lease (hereinafter called "Unexpired Rental Value of Leased Equipment"), provided, however, that if any statute governing the proceeding in which such damages are to be proved, specifies the amount of such claim, Lessor shall be entitled to prove as and for damages for the breach an amount equal to that allowed under such statute. The provisions of this paragraph shall be without prejudice to any rights given to the Lessor by such statute to prove for any amounts allowed thereby. Lessor, upon any breach of this lease may sell the leased equipment or may re-lease such equipment for a term and a rental which may be equal to, greater than or less than the rental and term herein provided, and any proceeds of such sale received within sixty days after Lessor receives possession of the leased equipment or any rental payments received under a new lease made within such sixty days for the period prior to the expiration of this lease, less Lessor's expenses of taking possession, storage, reconditioning and sale or re-leasing, shall be deemed and considered for the purposes of this paragraph as being the Unexpired Rental Value of Leased Equipment. If the Unexpired Rental Value of Leased Equipment exceeds the Remaining Rentals, Lessor shall be entitled to the excess. The provisions of this paragraph shall be without prejudice to Lessor's right to recover or prove in full damages for unpaid rent that accrued prior to the breach of the lease. In the event of a breach of this lease, Lessor, at its option, may enforce by appropriate legal proceedings, specific performance of the applicable covenants of this lease as well as any other remedy herein provided. Should any legal proceedings be instituted by Lessor to recover any moneys due or to become due hereunder and/or for possession of any or all of the leased equipment, Lessee shall pay a reasonable sum as attorney's fees.

From the small print of the paragraph one can extract two features worthy of emphasis: (i) if the hirer defaults in the payment of rent or in the performance of any other covenant, and such default continues for the stated number of days, the finance company is to be entitled to recover, as damages and not as a penalty, the aggregate rent for the unexpired term of the lease less any proceeds of sale received within 60 days after the finance company retakes possession or any rental payments received under a new lease made within such 60 days for the period prior to the expiration of the lease. The finance company seeks thereby to ensure that it will receive, upon default of the hirer, an amount which, together with rental payments made prior to default and the net proceeds of sale or re-leasing, will equal $1,080. If the sale or re-leasing is delayed beyond 60 days the hirer does not get credit for any amount received by the finance company on such sale or re-lease. (ii) If net proceeds of sale or re-lease, when added to the amount of the rental payments made prior to default, exceed $1,080, the surplus goes to the finance company, not to the hirer.

LIQUIDATED DAMAGES OR PENALTY

Does the sum agreed to be recoverable on default constitute liquidated damages, in which event it is recoverable, or a penalty, in which event it is not? The essence of liquidated damages is a genuine covenanted pre-estimate of damage: Lord Dunedin in *Dunlop Pneumatic Tyre Co., Ltd.* v. *New Garage & Motor Co., Ltd.* [1915] AC 79 at p. 86, following *Clydebank Engineering & Shipbuilding Co.* v. *Don Jose Ramos Yzquierdo y Castaneda* [1905] AC 6.

In *Canadian General Electric Co.* v. *Canadian Rubber Co.* (1915) 27 DLR 294 at p. 295, 52 SCR 349 at p. 351, Sir Charles Fitzpatrick, C.J., said:

> A penalty is the payment of a stipulated sum on breach of the contract, irrespective of the damage sustained. The essence of liquidated damages is a genuine covenanted pre-estimate of damage.

The fact that the parties may have used the expression "penalty" or "liquidated damages" does not conclude the matter: As Lord Dunedin said in the *Dunlop Pneumatic Tyre* case, at p. 86:

> 1. Though the parties to a contract who use the words "penalty" or "liquidated damages" may prima facie be supposed to mean what they say, yet the expression used is not conclusive.

Lord Dunedin suggested several tests which might prove helpful, or even conclusive, in the task of construction, including [p. 87]:

> 1. It will be held to be a penalty if the breach consists only in not paying a sum of money, and the sum stipulated is a sum greater than the sum which ought to be paid (*Kemble* v. *Farren* 6 Bing. 141).
>
> 2. There is a presumption (but no more) that it is penalty when "a single lump sum is made payable by way of compensation, on the occurrence of one or more or all of several events, some of which may occasion serious and others but trifling damage" (Lord Watson in *Lord Elphinstone* v. *Monkland Iron and Coal Co.* 11 App. Cas. 332).

The aggregate rent reserved under the lease is $1,080. If rent were paid in accordance with the terms of the lease the $1,080 would be paid in instalments over a period of five years. The lease, however, requires that the full $1,080 be paid on default, whenever that may occur. Clearly if default occurs the finance company would receive the full $1,080 (from rental payments made plus the amount received on sale or re-lease, plus the stipulated sum recoverable under para. 13) without having to wait five years and without the loss of interest which such waiting would entail. The damage sustained by the finance company from the hirer's default must vary in amount according to date of default. Yet the sum recoverable under para. 13 is a flat amount payable to the finance company without regard to the date of default. The sum cannot, therefore, be regarded as a genuine pre-estimate of damage.

We do not suggest that all acceleration clauses are in the nature of a penalty and unenforceable. On the contrary, in a mortgage given to secure the due payment by instalments of a sum due, a provision making the total sum due enforceable on any default is not to be considered a penalty: *Wallingford* v. *Mutual Society* (1880) 5 App. Cas. 685. The same holds true with respect to instalments of purchase price payable under a sale agreement. Here, however, we are not dealing with a mortgage nor with a sale agreement. We are dealing with a lease, and in our opinion a provision accelerating the due date of rental payments on default is as foreign to a lease of chattels as to a lease of land.

A further reason for concluding that the sum to be paid under para. 13 is a penalty is that it is payable not only upon breach of the covenant to pay rent, but also upon breach of any one of a number of other covenants, some of a trifling nature.

Guidance in determining whether a stipulated sum is a penalty can be obtained from practical application of the provision sought to be enforced. In the present case, if para. 13 is implemented, the hirer would be required to pay $560 ($72 rental paid plus $488 claimed) for six months' use of a cash register costing $800 new and worth $520 on sale.

In *Bridge* v. *Campbell Discount Co., Ltd.* [1962] 1 All ER 385, a landmark case, the House of Lords held to be a penalty *in terrorem* a provision entitling a finance company, upon breach of the agreement, to take possession of the object hired and to forfeit instalments already paid and to require the hirer to pay "by way of agreed compensation for depreciation of the vehicle such further sum as may be necessary to make the rentals paid and payable hereunder equal to two-thirds of the hire-purchase price". The Court held that such a payment was not a genuine pre-estimate either of depreciation of the vehicle or of loss, but simply a provision designed to secure to the finance company a financial return of not less than two-thirds of the hire-purchase price if the agreement were terminated for any cause. Lord Radcliffe, speaking of this provision, said at p. 395:

> Since the obligation under cl. 9(b) may mature at any time from the beginning to the end of the hiring, a week after the beginning or a week before the end, it seems to me impossible to take a single formula for measuring the damage as any true pre-estimate.

For the reasons outlined, we are satisfied that the sum stipulated in para. 13 of the lease is a penalty, and we so hold.

EFFECT OF HOLDING THE STIPULATED
SUM TO BE A PENALTY

Having concluded that the sum stipulated in para. 13 is a penalty and not recoverable, the next question must be — What amount, if any, is recoverable?

And here it is well to recall the legal form which the transaction took. It can be roughly termed a lease of chattels. Such a transaction is a class of bailment. In 2 Hals., 3rd ed., p. 122, it is said:

> This class of bailment (*locatio conductio rei*) is a contract by which the hirer obtains a right to use the chattel hired, in return for the payment of the price of the hiring to the owner. The proprietary interest in the chattel is not changed, but remains in the owner.

And at p. 125:

> The hirer must pay the rent agreed upon for the use of the chattel hired. . . . If, however, the rent is payable by instalments and the owner retakes possession in pursuance of an agreement enabling him to do so on the failure of the hirer to pay the instalments as they fall due, *he may recover arrears of rent* due at the time when he resumed possession.

(Italicizing mine.)

Canadian jurisprudence on the subject under consideration is not uniform. In *Acme Neon Signs* v. *Testart and Douglas* [1952] OWN 601, an action for balance of rental falling due under a lease of an electric sign, following default and repossession, Ferguson, J., held that the parties, by the agreement, pre-estimated the damage as the "balance of the rental herein provided for" and that this was a genuine pre-estimate and not a penalty. The Court of Appeal varied the judgment. The Court held the clause in the agreement making the moneys to fall due under the agreement due and payable forthwith was not effective because of the plaintiff's failure to give notice declaring the payments due. Therefore the Court proceeded to determine plaintiff's damages. Delivering the judgment of the Court, Pickup, C.J.O., said, [1953] OWN 79 at p. 80:

> Plainly, it would be wrong to allow the plaintiff as damages presently payable the total aggregate amount of the moneys which would have become due over a period of years under the contract, if the contract had been carried out. We do not think that even the present value of those payments constitutes the true amount of damages because there are other factors that require to be considered.

The Court reduced the damages of $2,479.50 awarded by Ferguson, J., to $1,800.

In 1961 two Ontario cases were decided which appear to be in direct conflict. The first is *Re Emil's Furniture & Appliances Ltd.* (1961) 2 CBR (NS) 225n, in which Smily, J., did not allow a claim advanced by the lessor of a neon sign, upon the bankruptcy of the lessee, for rental for the unexpired term of the contract. He awarded an amount equal to such rental less an allowance for maintenance, an allowance for recovery of a lump sum by way of damage in lieu of rental over a period of years, and an allowance for salvage, if any. The report gives the date of judgment as April 25, 1966, obviously an error because the report is contained in a volume published in 1961. The second case is *Neon Products of Canada Ltd.* v. *Smith*, decided by Wilson, J., in April, 1961, but not reported until 1966 (8 CBR (NS) 68), in which the learned Judge allowed the lessor the full amount of the payments due under a sign leasing contract. The Judge declined to adopt the principle applied in *Cooden Engineering Co. Ltd.* v. *Stanford* [1953] 1 QB 86 at p. 97, [1952] 2 All ER 915, and in *Landum Trust Ltd.* v. *Hurrell,* [1955] 1 All ER 839 at p. 841. Wilson, J., based his judgment on the opinion of Ferguson, J., in *Testart* to which we have referred, which was varied by the Court of Appeal of Ontario, and upon the decision in *Re Durnford* v. *Elk Shoes Ltd.* (1916) 11 OWN 59, in which there was a claim for repairs and for items of depreciation but not for rental payments. The report on *Neon Products of Canada Ltd.* v. *Smith, supra,* bears the footnote: "Affirmed on 11th October 1961 by the Court of Appeal for Ontario."

The next case we would mention is *Charterhouse Leasing Corp. Ltd.* v. *Sanmac Holdings Ltd.* (1966) 58 DLR (2d) 656, 57 WWR 615. In that case, Kirby, J., of the Alberta Supreme Court considered a clause in a lease of laundry and dry-cleaning equipment which provided that upon default being made by the hirer the lessor might resume possession of the equipment and that determination of the hiring agreement would not affect the lessor's claim to be paid the whole balance of rent outstanding under the lease. The learned Judge, relying upon several of the English cases cited in this judgment, held that the clause in question was a penalty clause and not enforceable. He held that the plaintiff was entitled to judgment for the actual damages sustained by reason of the default of the defendant, being only the rent unpaid as of the date of determination of the lease.

Finally, *R.C.A. Victor Co. Ltd.* v. *Pelletier* (1968) 68 DLR (2d) 13, a decision of the New Brunswick Supreme Court, Appeal Division, concerning a lease of television sets. The trial Judge refused plaintiff's claim for liquidated damages of $24,709, under a clause permitting plaintiff to recover on defendant's default, the rent reserved for the unexpired portion of the term, discounted at the rate of 4% per annum to present worth. Bridges, C.J.N.B., for the Appeal Division, said, p. 17:

> The learned trial Judge in refusing the claim of the plaintiff for liquidated damages of $24,709, held that it was not a genuine pre-estimate of the loss. . . . I think the learned trial Judge was entirely correct in his view.

Bridges, C.J.N.B., without referring to authorities, assessed plaintiff's damages at the amount of instalments of rental payable after commencement of the action less the value of the sets repossessed and the cost of servicing the sets from the commencement of the action to the due date of the last rental instalment.

There being no uniform pattern emerging from the Canadian decisions we feel free to approach the matter afresh according to our best judgment. It is our considered opinion that the rationale of the series of cases beginning with *Bridge* v. *Campbell Discount Co., Ltd.* [1962] 1 All ER 385, provides the proper approach and we propose to apply it. In one of the cases of that series, *Financings, Ltd.* v. *Baldock* [1963] 1 All ER 443, Lord Denning, M.R., said at p. 445:

> It seems to me that, when an agreement of hiring is terminated by virtue of a power contained in it and the owner retakes the vehicle, he can recover damages for any breach up to the date of termination, but not for any breach thereafter, for the simple reason that there are no breaches thereafter. I see no difference in this respect between the letting of a vehicle on hire and the letting of land on a lease. If a lessor,

under a proviso for re-entry, re-enters on the ground of non-payment of rent or of disrepair, he gets the arrears of rent up to date of re-entry and damages for want of repair at that date, but he does not get damages for loss of rent thereafter or for breaches of repair thereafter. In this and many hire-purchase agreements, the owners have sought to avoid that general principle by inserting a "minimum payment" clause such as we see in cl. (11)(a) here, which provides that, should the hiring be terminated, whether by the owner or the hirer, the hirer has got to pay at least two-thirds of the total hiring cost. By a series of cases starting with the decision of the Court of Appeal in *Cooden Engineering Co., Ltd.,* v. *Stanford,* and culminating in the decision of the House of Lords in *Bridge* v. *Campbell Discount Co., Ltd.,* such a clause has now been held to be a penalty clause. The owners by such a clause are really seeking, on an early termination of the hiring, to recover damages for loss of future rentals, when they have not lost any. They have no right to future rentals after they have terminated the agreement and got the vehicle back.

And at p. 446:

In applying this principle, I asked counsel for the plaintiffs: What were the breaches by the hirer up to the termination of the hiring? He could only point to the simple failure to pay the two instalments of rent. In these circumstances, the only moneys which the plaintiffs can recover are those two instalments which are in arrear and unpaid with the interest thereon. If the plaintiff could prove damages for breach of contract to repair, they could recover them, but no more. . . .

If, however, there is no repudiation, but simply, as here, a failure to pay one or two instalments (the failure not going to the root of the contract and only giving a right to terminate by virtue of an express stipulation in the contract), the owners can recover only the instalments in arrear, with interest, and nothing else; for there was no other breach in existence at the termination of the hiring.

Financings, Ltd. v. *Baldock* was applied in *Brady et al* v. *St. Margaret's Trust, Ltd.* [1963] 2 All ER 275, and in *Anglo-Auto Finance Co., Ltd.* v. *James* [1963] 3 All ER 566. In *United Dominions Trust (Commercial), Ltd.* v. *Ennis* [1967] 2 All ER 345 at p. 348, Lord Denning, M.R., denied the finance company the right to recover even the one instalment in arrear prior to termination because the company had not sued for that instalment and more than six years had elapsed since it fell due.

With respect, we are of the opinion that Lord Denning, M.R., correctly expressed the modern law in the *Baldock* case. If a landlord re-enters land for non-payment of rent he may bring an action for arrears of rent on the express or implied covenant to pay rent but he cannot recover rent falling due after the date of re-entry. No authority has been given us to show why the position of a lessor of a chattel should be stronger than that of a lessor of land.

If in the instant case one asks the question asked by Lord Denning, M.R., in *Baldock*, namely, "What were the breaches by the hirer up to the termination of the hiring?", the answer can only be, "The failure to pay several instalments of rent". In our opinion the finance company can recover those instalments with interest and nothing more. We do not overlook that in the *Bridge* case and those which followed it, including *Baldock*, the contract before the Court was one of hire-purchase, whereas the contract we have to consider is a simple lease giving the lessee neither an option to purchase nor a right to terminate upon terms prior to the expiry of the term. These distinctions do not, in our view, render inapplicable the legal principle enunciated in the cases to which we have referred. If anything that principle applies a *fortiori* in the present case which is not complicated by either a purchase option feature giving an aura of purchase and sale, or by the question which has vexed the English Courts, namely, did the hirer exercise his option to terminate or did the finance company terminate the contract for the hirer's breach?

When the hirer failed to pay the rent as it became due, the finance company had alternative courses. It could sue for the rental payments in arrears, and later, from time to time as they fell due and were unpaid, sue for any further arrears. It could thereby recover the full rent reserved under the lease. Or it could seize and sell the leased chattel and also claim for rental payments due and unpaid to the time of seizure. Having chosen to invoke the remedy of seizure and sale it cannot thereafter recover an amount equivalent to the rent falling due during the unexpired term of the lease. Nor can it recover such amount less an allowance for the fact that it would recover such deferred rent in one sum and earlier than anticipated.

Thompson, Co. Ct. J., assessed damages as if the action were for the price of goods the property of which had passed, or an action for damages for breach of a contract to buy and pay for goods. With respect, in so doing he fell into error. There is no evidence of the amount paid by the finance company to J.G. Turner Ltd. for the cash register. In any event the value of the leased chattel is irrelevant. It has no more significance than the value of the leased land in the case of a defaulting lessee of real estate. The proper measure of damages is overdue instalments plus interest.

The record does not state specifically the number of instalments of rent overdue at the time the finance company took back the cash register, but the number is ascertainable. The lease provides that the first rent payment shall cover the advance rentals and shall be payable on receipt of the finance company's written acceptance. That acceptance is dated September 29, 1965. The first rent payment, amounting to $54, was, therefore, due on September 29, 1965. The lease further provides that the second rent payment shall become due on the last business day of the month in which delivery of the equipment is made by the supplier and accepted by the lessee; provided that if such actual delivery and acceptance occurs on or after the 16th day of any month, the payment shall become due on the last business day of the following month. Delivery and acceptance of the equipment was on or about August 19, 1965. Therefore the second instalment of rent, amounting to $18, fell due on September 30, 1965. A like amount fell due on the last days of each of the months of October, November, and December, 1965, and January, 1966. The equipment was taken back in February, 1966. Prior to February, 1966, rent totalling $144 fell due, of which $72 was paid, leaving a balance of $72. Plaintiff will have judgment for that amount plus interest at 12% from the date each overdue instalment fell due until August 1, 1968, the date of judgment in the County Court. Plaintiff will have its costs in the County Court.

Appeal dismissed; judgment for plaintiff varied.

Note: Lord Denning's judgment in the *Baldock* case, which is the foundation of Mr. Justice Dickson's judgment in *Regent Park Butcher*, is based on the premise that the lessee has not been guilty of a repudiatory breach. Where the lessee is deemed to have repudiated the contract, damages are calculated on the same basis as in the case of a wrongful refusal by a buyer to accept the goods. See *Interoffice Telephones Ltd.* v. *R. Freeman & Co. Ltd.* [1957] 3 All ER 479 (CA) and *Robophone Facilities, Ltd.* v. *Blank* [1966] 3 All ER 128 (CA).

Note that Lord Denning's reference to the landlord and tenant rule, that a lessor cannot at common law recover damages for breach of contract once the lease has been terminated, no longer represents the Canadian position: see *Highway Properties Ltd.* v. *Kelly, Douglas & Co. Ltd.* (1971) 17 DLR (3d) 710 (SCC). In any event the rule never applied to a lease of *chattels: Interoffice Telephones Ltd., supra.*

Regent Park Butcher Shop Ltd. was followed in *Neonoex International Ltd.* v. *Wassill and Pollock* [1974] 1 WWR 587 (Sask. DC); *L.E. Powell & Co. Ltd.* v. *CNR Co. and Nova Scotia Building Supplies Ltd.* (1975) 13 NSR (2d) 713 (NS SC AD); and in *Unilease Inc.* v. *York Steel Construction Ltd.* (1978) 3 BLR 68 (Ont. CA). The case was distinguished in *Direct Leasing Ltd.* v. *Chu, Allan and Gray* (1977) 1 BCLR 166 (BC SC) and was not followed in *Security Leasing Co. Ltd.* v. *Balkan Restaurant Ltd.* [1976] 5 WWR 590 (BC Co. Ct.).

Chapter 25
Consumer Credit Law

A. INTRODUCTION

For Canadian consumer credit law, see in general; R.C.C. Cuming, "Consumer Credit Law" in G. H. L. Fridman (ed.), *Studies in Canadian Business Law* (1971) 87; J. Ziegel, "Recent Developments in Canadian Consumer Credit Law" (1973) 36 Mod. L. Rev. 479; and R.C.C. Cuming, "Consumer Credit in Selected Countries: Canada" R. M. Goode (ed.) *Consumer Credit* (1978) 186. See also The Canadian Welfare Council, *Consumer Credit and the Lower Income Family* (1970), and Law Reform Commission of Saskatchewan *Tentative Proposals for a Consumer Credit Act* (Aug. 1980 and May 1981).

The materials in this chapter focus on issues relating to the price of credit and the disclosure of credit charges.

R.C.C. CUMING
"Consumer Credit in Selected Countries: Canada"
in R.M. Goode (ed.) *Consumer Credit* (1978) pp. 186-96

1. A PERSPECTIVE OF CONSUMER CREDIT IN CANADA

By all economic, social or political measurements, it is clear that consumer credit occupies a very important role in Canadian society; and there is every indication that its importance will increase rather than diminish in the future. At the end of 1976 the outstanding balances of Canadian consumer credit grantors totalled 27,677 millions of dollars, an increase of 16 per cent over 1975 and an increase of 291 per cent over 1965. For the year 1976, the amount of consumer credit outstanding as a proportion of personal expenditures on consumer goods and services (the measurement often used in analysing the importance of consumer credit) was 25 per cent. For the year 1960, the proportion was 16.3 per cent, and at the end of 1969 it was 23.3 per cent.

Consumer credit in one form or another is accepted almost universally by

Canadians as an integral part of their way of life and a factor which contributes to the high standard of living enjoyed by most of them. For consumers, credit permits the acquisition of goods with high unit cost or the acquisition of larger quantities of low unit cost goods and services, all with the advantage of deferred payment of the price. It provides a source of assistance in times of financial stress; and, for some, it imposes a money management régime or budgeting system. For producers, distributors and retailers, instalment financing has proved to be an important factor in the marketing of great quantities of goods and services.

Significant legislative or administrative constraints on the use or increased availability of consumer credit are politically unpopular and are rarely undertaken, even at times when they could be employed as an effective tool in the management of the national economy. Canadian federal and provincial legislative measures affecting consumer credit marketing practices have had only peripheral effect; but they were never designed to do otherwise. Canadian legislators of every political persuasion have accepted the conclusion that the basic marketing system for consumer credit is sound and that legislative measures should be designed to improve it rather than to restructure or replace it.

2. CREDIT GRANTING INSTITUTIONS

[Professor Cuming enumerates the chartered banks, credit unions and caisses populaires, consumer loan companies, and sales finance companies, together with department stores, insurance companies, trust companies and public utilities, as credit granting institutions in Canada.]

3. CREDIT ARRANGEMENT AND LEGAL DEVICES

(1) Lender credit, vendor credit and credit card transactions

• • •

While the distinction between loan credit and sales credit has always been a central feature of the Canadian consumer credit market and the law relating to it, approximately 85 per cent of consumer credit advanced in Canada in 1976 was in the form of direct loans. Sales credit, the bulk of which is advanced by department stores and sales finance companies, has lost much of its appeal to Canadians, primarily because of its high cost.

Basically, a lender credit transaction is one in which the lender, usually a chartered bank, credit union, consumer loan company or trust company, advances a specific amount of money in return for the borrower's promise that the amount plus a predetermined credit charge will be repaid in a lump sum or, more frequently, by periodic payments over a period of time. Vendor credit transactions are of two kinds: single transaction instalment sales, and revolving multi-purchase arrangements. A single transaction instalment sale is one in which the buyer gets immediate performance by the seller, but is given the contractual right to defer payment. Except in cases where the purchase price is small and the time for payment is short, the sales contract is sold and assigned to a sales finance company or chartered bank. The buyer is notified of the assignment and usually deals directly with the assignee when making the instalment payments.* Under

---

* For further details on this aspect see Chapter 20(B) *supra*. [Eds.]

a revolving multi-purchase arrangement operated by the major department stores, the customer signs a master credit agreement under which goods or services can be purchased on credit from time to time without the necessity to enter into an instalment repayment contract for each purchase. The buyer is given the option to pay the full amount owing or a specified portion of it at the end of the billing period. As long as the buyer makes the payments as required, he is entitled to purchase further items and to have the purchase price of them added to the balance owing by him.

Credit card transactions, other than direct loans made by an issuing bank to card holders and purchases made from airlines, oil companies or other vendors who issue limited use cards, do not fall neatly into either of the traditional categories of lender credit or vendor credit.* Under the two existing major credit card systems in Canada, cards are issued free of charge by a particular bank to selected customers who are given a line of credit with maximum credit limits. The cards are accepted in lieu of cash by participating retailers for the purchase of consumer goods or services. The issuing bank purchases at a discount the accounts from the retailers. The card holders are billed by the bank, and are given the right to pay the total balance owing or a specified portion of it.

Credit card systems are being used extensively by credit consumers to provide short-term financing. However, at present these systems are not structurally designed to accommodate financing of high-cost durable goods since they do not provide for security interest in the goods purchased and they require relatively short repayment periods.

(2) Legal devices and collection remedies

The underlying legal structure through which loan credit is marketed involves a simple contract between the lender and borrower providing for repayment of specified amounts. Frequently a promissory note is used in order to facilitate collection in the event of default or to give to the obligation greater currency in the event that the lender assigns its accounts to secure its own borrowing.

In most consumer loans, some form of security is demanded. If the loan is being used to purchase goods with high unit value, the borrower is required to execute a chattel mortgage covering the goods purchased. It is not uncommon for consumer lenders to require the borrower to execute a "blanket" chattel mortgage under which he offers as security for the loan all of his present and after-acquired chattel property. Consumer loan companies have recently adopted a practice of taking real property mortgages to secure consumer debt. In most cases these mortgages will be subordinate securities since few borrowers who deal with consumer loan companies have unencumbered ownership rights in their homes. Other forms of security for consumer loans include pledges of negotiable securities, third party guarantees, assignments of insurance equities and, where permitted by law, wage assignments.

Sales credit used in connection with the purchase of consumer goods with a high unit value usually involves the use of a conditional sales contract. Under

---

* For further details on credit card transactions see Chapter 16(D) *supra*. [Eds.]

this form of contract, legal title and a right to resume possession upon the buyer's default are given to the seller. The buyer becomes the full owner of the goods when he has made all payments as provided in the contract. When sales financing is to be provided from a third party source, the contract or chattel paper is assigned to the financer. In some cases, the buyer is required to sign a promissory note designating the seller as payee. This note is "negotiated" to the financer along with the contract.

Credit purchases made under the revolving credit plans of the large department stores follow a somewhat different pattern. The master agreement covering all purchases made under these schemes provides for the retention of title by the seller until the full purchase price of each item is paid. However, since the monthly payment made by a buyer is a single sum determined by reference to the total balance owing at the end of the billing period, it is common for the agreement to contain special terms under which the point in time at which ownership in each item vests in the buyer is determinable.

CONSUMER CREDIT: OUTSTANDING BALANCES OF SELECTED HOLDERS*

Millions of dollars									
End of period	Not seasonally adjusted								
	Chartered bank ordinary personal loans	Sales finance and consumer loan companies	Life insurance company policy loans	Quebec savings banks (unsecured personal loans)	Depart-ment stores	Trust and mortgage loan companies	Total of fore-going	Credit unions and caisses populaires	Total
	B100	B101	B102	B103	B104	B105	B106	B107	B108
1969	4,157	3,046	660	24	705	—	8,592	1,401	9,993
1970	4,663	2,851	759	22	720	—	9,015	1,493	10,508
1971	5,777	2,366	784	25	754	—	9,706	1,690	11,396
1972	7,144	2,646	813	30	823	46	11,502	2,000	13,502
1973	8,878	2,912	884	36	961	82	13,753	2,420	16,173
1974	10,817	3,118	1,066	44	1,126	145	16,315	2,762	19,077
1975	13,149	3,054	1,149	58	1,232	199	18,843	3,243	22,085
1976	16,114	3,014	1,232	72	1,314	287	22,032	3,884	25,916
1977	18,634	2,937	1,291	87	1,381	368	24,697	4,512	29,209
1978	21,575	3,073	1,373	104	1,519	650	28,294	5,490	33,779
1979	25,081	3,072	1,569	142	1,632	981	32,477	6,218	38,695
June 1980	26,608	3,043	1,736	158	1,375	1,256	34,177	6,413	40,590

* This table is based on the Bank of Canada Review, Dec. 1980. [Eds.]

In the event of default in payment by a consumer borrower, a secured credit grantor is permitted under law to realise on his security, subject, however, to restrictions which vary widely from jurisdiction to jurisdiction. If the security is inadequate or no security has been taken, the credit grantor must look to the judgment enforcement system available to all creditors. He must first obtain a court judgment confirming the debt. He can then employ standard judgment enforcement measures such as execution against goods, execution against lands and attachment of wages and other money owing to the debtor. There are significant differences among the laws of the various provinces and territories of Canada with respect to the use of these collection measures.

4. ABUSES AND CONTROL TECHNIQUES

[The regulation of disclosure in credit contracts, objectionable terms in credit agreements, improvident or destructive collection measures, credit insurance, credit cards, and credit reporting, fall into this category.]

B. DISTRIBUTION OF LEGISLATIVE POWER IN RELATION TO CONSUMER CREDIT

See in general L.J. Romero, *Federal-Provincial Relations in the Field of Consumer Protection* (Consumer Research Council of Canada, 1976).

JACOB S. ZIEGEL,
"The Legal Regulation of Consumer Credit"
in J. Ziegel and R. Olley (eds.) *Consumer Credit in Canada* (1966) p. 70

[A] few words about the constitutional allocation of powers in Canada between the provinces and the federal government so far as they relate to consumer credit . . .

The federal government derives its jurisdiction in this area from five specific heads of power enumerated in Section 91 of the British North America Act. These are the power to legislate with respect to banks and banking (s. 91(15)), bills of exchange and promissory notes (s. 91(18)), interest (s. 91(19)), bankruptcy and insolvency (s. 91(21)), the criminal law (s. 91(27)). In addition the federal government may make laws for the "peace, order and good government" of the Dominion, which includes a residuary power over matters not specifically assigned to the provinces. The first of these powers, however, is only exerciseable in time of war and other national emergencies and the second apparently only has a limited reach. Specifically, so far as consumer credit is concerned, it has been, or may be, used to justify the federal power to incorporate small loan and sales finance companies and thus to regulate the activities of these agencies. . . .

The provinces derive their powers principally from the right to adopt laws concerning property and civil rights (s. 92(13)) and in relation to matters of a merely local or private nature (s. 92(16)) and, to a much lesser extent, from the right to incorporate companies for provincial purposes (s. 92(11)).

HARVIN PITCH
"Consumer Credit Reform: The Case for a Renewed Federal Initiative"
(1972) 5 Ott. LR 324, 333-39

IX. CONSTITUTIONAL JURISDICTION

Federal jurisdiction in the field of consumer credit rests on the interest power and criminal law power and the power to regulate trade and commerce.

A. *The Interest Power*

The interest power represents the *main* head of jurisdiction to justify federal consumer credit legislation. Superficially, it would appear that a jurisdiction over interest would entitle the federal government to enact legislation regulating the interest rate and requiring the disclosure of the interest. However, there is considerable argument as to whether the federal government, under the interest power, can regulate all the cost components of a consumer credit transaction and, even if such is the case, whether under that power, it can regulate *all types* of consumer credit transactions.

(1) *Regulating All the Cost Components of a Consumer Credit Transaction: Defining "Interest"*

Whether the federal government can, in the exercise of its jurisdiction over interest, encompass all the costs of a loan depends in part upon how the term interest is defined.

Until recently, judicial pronouncements had defined the constitutional term "interest" in broad terms equating it, in effect, with all the costs of a loan. Thus, for example, Mr. Justice Rand in a leading case defined interest as, "in general terms, the return or consideration or compensation for the use or retention by one person of a sum of money, belonging to, in a colloquial sense, or owed to, another." In 1963, however, the Supreme Court in upholding the constitutional validity of the Ontario Unconscionable Transactions Relief Act provided a more limited definition of interest, "[i]nterest accrues *de die in diem* even if payable only at intervals, and is, therefore, apportionable in point of time between persons entitled in succession to the principal."

The Court distinguished various components of the cost of the loan (the term employed in the Unconscionable Transactions Relief Act) and especially interest and bonuses.

In his testimony before the Joint Committee of the Senate and House of Commons on Consumer Credit, K. R. MacGregor, the former Superintendent of Insurance (responsible for the administration of the Small Loans Act), adopted an interpretation of the case which has since become popularized by provincial ministers in charge of consumer protection bureaus. Basically, he argued that the Court had defined the interest power as something less than the entire cost of the loan; in particular the Court held that the term interest did not include other costs such as bonuses. Therefore, he argued that the federal government exercising jurisdiction under the interest power was limited to regulating that portion of the loan restrictively defined as interest. It can be readily observed that, in order to defeat the purpose of such federal legislation, a lender need only classify the components of the cost of the loan in terms other than interest.

It is questionable as to whether the definition of interest is involved in the ratio decidendi of the case. The Court merely held that on the basis of the property and civil rights power, the Unconscionable Transactions Relief Act was a valid exercise of provincial jurisdiction. Furthermore, even if one adopts this narrow interpretation of the scope of the term interest (constitutionally), the conclusion arrived at above need not be valid. If a federal statute based on the interest power will be circumvented because lenders will classify their costs as bonuses rather than interest, then the federal government can legislate, incidentally, to cover these other areas. As Professor Jacob Ziegel pointed out in his November 10, 1964 testimony to the Joint Committee: "... the federal government has admitted jurisdiction over the so called interest element in loans — whatever the term 'interest' means in this context — it has also incidental jurisdiction to cover other charges so as to prevent evasion of the regulation of the interest element."

(2) *Can the Legislation, Based on the Interest Power, Be Extended to All Consumer Credit Transactions? The Time-Price Doctrine*

It has been suggested by Professor Ziegel, in his testimony that the federal government may not be able to legislate with respect to credit sales (vendor credit) because of the existence of the time-price doctrine.

In the United States and England the courts have developed the time-price doctrine to exempt from the operation of the usury statutes, conditional sale contracts and other forms of credit sales. The rationale for this exemption is, briefly, that in the credit sale situation, there exists two types of prices: a cash price and a time-price. The latter price is not considered to be a loan and therefore is not subject to usury legislation but is defined as the consideration paid for a time sale. Constitutionally the significance of this doctrine is that if a credit sale is a sale rather than a loan, the finance charge is considered not interest on a loan but a time-price. Therefore, under the interest power, the federal authority over interest would not extend to the regulation of credit sales transactions.

The time-price doctrine is an economic absurdity. The time-price in all cases is simply the result of adding the finance charge to the cash price. The reason for the development of the time-price doctrine was to avoid the operation of the usury statutes which were designed to protect the necessitous borrower. At the time when the time-price doctrine was established credit purchases were considered luxury-buying practices and from that perspective little warranted the same protection afforded by the usury statute. More important, the prevailing usury statutes in the United States and the Moneylenders Act in England prescribed unreasonably low rates. Had these statutes applied to the budding sales finance industry in the early period of the twentieth century, it would have resulted in its immediate demise. The time-price doctrine was the court's method of resolving the problem.

Would the time-price doctrine prevail in our courts? The doctrine was never dealt with in our courts and if dealt with, would not face a usury statute spelling out unreasonable interest rate prohibitions.

While it is true that the time-price doctrine continues to prevail in the United States and in England, there has been some judicial refusal to continue recognizing the doctrine. In Nebraska and Arkansas, the courts have rejected the time-price doctrine. In England, the Crowther Committee has recommended the abolition of the time-price doctrine. It is therefore suggested that in light of these current trends, and in the absence of a restrictive usury statute, a Canadian court might be willing to reject the time-price doctrine and with this rejection, the only impediment facing the federal regulation of credit sales would be removed.

B. *The Criminal Power*

At one time, courts attempted to take a restrictive attitude towards the criminal law power, limiting federal criminal power to matters inherently criminal. Thus, in *Re Reciprocal Insurance Legislation* [1924] 1 DLR 789 the Privy Council declared the Federal Insurance Act unconstitutional and rejected attempts to classify such regulatory legislation as criminal legislation.

However, modern definitions, established by Lord Atkin and Mr. Justice Rand, give some hope that the consumer credit field can be regulated under the criminal law power. Lord Atkin was prepared to accede to any federal jurisdiction based on the criminal law power as long as the legislation was enforced by a penal sanction and did not represent a colourable attempt to invade provincial jurisdiction.

The definition offered by Mr. Justice Rand offers some guidance: "Is the prohibition then enacted with a view to a public purpose which can support it as being in relation to criminal law? Public peace, order, security, health, morality: these are the ordinary though not exclusive ends served by that law . . ." Under this definition, the courts have upheld the misleading labeling provisions and "adultering" provisions, of the Food and Drug Act, the conspiracy provisions of the combines legislation, the resale price maintenance provisions of the combines legislation and the Criminal Code provisions dealing with securities fraud.

Federal disclosure legislation could be justified on the basis of criminal law on grounds analogous to the securities fraud legislation provisions in the Criminal Code and the basic criminal prohibitions against fraud in general contained therein. Certainly a misleading credit advertising provision could be so justified. The federal statute under consideration would go further by imposing the obligation to disclose certain specific information in a loan contract especially the percentage rate. An argument can be made that the consumer is indeed misled *unless* he is told the annual percentage rate in a credit transaction and to mislead by such an omission would be criminal fraud. On this basis, consumer credit disclosure provisions could be justified as a valid exercise of the criminal law power.

Could the criminal law power be employed to justify the imposition of statutory finance charge rates? In one sense this legislation, especially if combined with licensing provisions, is designed to regulate trade and prices rather than prohibit an activity which is considered a public evil. However, in another sense, such an imposition of interest ceilings is a form of a usury statute and, as has been pointed out, for centuries usury was considered a crime and a social evil.

This would be the distinguishing feature which might uphold the legislation. It should be mentioned that one drawback to the legislation being based on the criminal law jurisdiction is that the legislation could not license lenders. This type of enforcement provision would probably place the legislation in constitutional jeopardy.

C. *Trade and Commerce*

The federal government's jurisdiction in relation to consumer credit could be justified under the trade and commerce power. The trade and commerce power, at one time, was interpreted narrowly so that federal legislation based upon it could not regulate specific contracts and trades under the guise of legislation aimed at inter-provincial trade and commerce.

The development of the modern trend in considering the operation of trade and commerce gives some hope that this clause could be used to justify consumer credit legislation. The cases establishing this modern trend have indicated a willingness on the part of the Supreme Court to examine a transaction to determine whether it has a valid inter-provincial aspect. In the event that the transaction meets this test, then the fact that the legislation affects purely inter-provincial matters will not prove constitutionally fatal to the scheme. One writer has suggested that in light of these modern developments, the combines legislation could now be sustained under the trade and commerce power.

Is the regulation of consumer credit a regulation of inter-provincial trade and commerce? Unfortunately, the insurance cases dealing with the federal regulation of the insurance industry indicate that the courts would be likely to consider consumer credit legislation as the regulation of a particular trade and interference with contracts (property and civil rights). However, there are some aspects of the consumer credit field which are inter-provincial in nature. Consumer credit in Canada can be seen as the economic flow of capital across provincial boundaries from the capital sources in the east to the various provincial distribution centres. Unfortunately, notwithstanding this inter-provincial nature of consumer credit, what is in fact regulated is the end product of the transaction, that is, the federal loan on sale.

Notes and Questions:

1   What is the relationship between federal and provincial jurisdictions in the consumer credit area? Can they overlap? Recall the "double aspect doctrine" and the doctrine of "federal paramountcy", both discussed by P. Hogg, *Constitutional Law of Canada* (1977) pp. 84, 102. Under the former, "subjects which in one aspect and for one purpose fall within s. 92 [of the BNA Act], may in another aspect and for another purpose fall within s. 91": *Hodge* v. *The Queen* (1883) 9 App. Cas. 117, 130 (PC). Under the latter, "where there are inconsistent (or conflicting) federal and provincial laws, it is the federal law which prevails": Hogg, *supra* at 102.

2   The 1963 case giving a narrow definition to "interest" discussed in Mr. Pitch's article is *A.-G. Ont.* v. *Barfried Enterprises Ltd.* [1963] SCR 570. This aspect of *Barfried* has

since then been qualified in *Tomell Investments Ltd.* v. *East Marstock Lands Ltd.* (1977) 77 DLR (3d) 145 (SCC). In the latter case, the majority of the Supreme Court (*per* Mr. Justice Pigeon) agreed that interest meant day-to-day accrual, but held that legislation in relation to additional charges is "a valid exercise of ancillary power" of Parliament in relation to interest: *id.* at 154. The minority (*per* Laskin C.J.C.) saw no need to rely upon the doctrine of ancillary powers and classified legislation governing "fines" and "penalties" imposed by lenders as "an assertion of the interest power *simpliciter*": *id.* at 147. See in general MacKenzie, "What is Interest? *Tomell Investments Ltd.* v. *East Marstock Lands Ltd.*" (1979) 25 McGill LJ 121.

3   In *Re Hanson and Harbour Tax Services Ltd. (No. 2)* (1978) 87 DLR (3d) 96, 99 (BC SC) the court held that the "broad definition" of interest as used by "students of economics", namely " 'the cost of money' or . . . the reward which a person receives for doing without his money . . . is not applicable to constitutional issues relating to 'interest' ". The court went on to state that "[t]he powers of the Provinces to enact social legislation in the consumer field should not . . . be limited by giving a wide interpretation without regard to the object sought to be achieved". Do you agree? Doesn't the court's reasoning confuse the tests of "validity" and "consistency"?

4   As to the scope of the federal criminal power in relation to consumer credit, note the recent case *Krassman* v. *The Queen* (1980) 102 DLR (3d) 262 (FC TD). The court held that the federal Tax Discounting Act, 1977-78 (Can.), c. 25, making it an offence for a "discounter" to acquire the right to a refund of tax from the person entitled to the refund, for less than 85 per cent of the refund (s. 3(1)), was a valid federal legislation under the criminal power of Parliament under BNA Act s. 91(27). "This legislation," the court explained, "is, in pith and substance, an exercise of the criminal law power. Parliament has determined that tax refund discounting is an economic practice that should, by criminal sanction, be strictly controlled. The legislation is . . . properly within federal competence": *id.* at 266.

5   A broad exercise of federal jurisdiction was embodied in the ill-fated Bill C-16, the Borrowers and Depositors Bill, which was introduced in the House of Commons in 1976. The bill applied to all credit transactions, not only to loans. It purported to unify the requirements for disclosure of finance charges, to protect debtors from unwarranted charges and prepayment penalties, and to combat loansharking by establishing a "criminal rate" of finance charge which cannot legally be exceeded. For an extensive discussion, see Panel Discussion, "Bill C-16, The Borrowers and Depositors Protection Act: Retrospect and Prospect" in J. Ziegel (ed.) *Proceedings of the Seventh Annual Workshop on Commercial and Consumer Law* (1979), pp. 87-110.

C. INTEREST REGULATION: POLICIES AND OVERVIEW OF THE CANADIAN EXPERIENCE

1. POLICIES

D. CAYNE AND M.J. TREBILCOCK
"Market Considerations in the Formulation of Consumer Protection Policy"
(1973) UTLJ 396, 411

A. INTEREST RATE CEILINGS: THE RATIONALE OF RATE REGULATION

The imposition of interest rate ceilings tends to occupy a central place in the dogma of those who believe that rules prescriptive of a merchant's business policies or practices can protect low-income consumers against problems in the market place. The FTC study recommended regulation of finance charges to "help low-income as well as other consumers make more rational buying decisions." Professor Ziegel in his brief to the Canadian Senate Committee on Poverty recommended comprehensive rate ceilings in consumer credit transactions on the grounds that "a ceiling serves a double function: it protects the unsophisticated and vulnerable borrower against exploitation and it encourages the lender to adopt more prudent credit standards." The history of usury regulation also, of course, reflects a ready and long-standing disposition in many jurisdictions to regulate interest rates. However, the incoherent pattern of rate regulation in consumer credit transactions that now obtains in many jurisdictions should be enough to raise one's suspicions that clear rationales for rate regulation cannot be as easily identified or sustained as many of its proponents seem to assume. . . .

The predilection which has persisted both historically and among contemporary consumer commentators towards imposing rate ceilings on money-lending transactions has to be regarded as aberrant from an economic perspective because it violates traditional free-market economic norms which are inconsistent with price control, of which rate ceilings are, of course, an example. Price control has generally only been accorded a "consumer protection" role in monopoly situations; otherwise, more recently, it has been used for macroeconomic ends as a means of controlling inflation. But taking a consumer protection perspective, and pursuing our present assumption of a competitive market, the central question in relation to rate ceilings becomes the policy objectives, whether economic or social, which this form of price control can achieve. . . . Can a ceiling, in Professor Ziegel's terms, protect "the unsophisticated and vulnerable borrower against exploitation and [encourage] the lender to adopt more prudent credit standards"? We think not. Ceilings set above market rates are mere surplusage and those which prove to be uneconomic will in most cases be equally irrelevant because of the difficulty of regulating the vendor-credit market. In the unlikely event that such difficulties can be overcome, an inordinately low ceiling will merely initiate exclusionary or degenerative processes. Although minor redistributive effects may result, the mass of consumers will not find themselves in the position of procuring credit on more advantageous terms.

That result can only be achieved where competitive input is added to a structurally unsound market. Rearticulating the assumption that workable competition prevails, however, the significant policy conclusion is that the most effective small loans law is the one which least interferes with the free flow of market forces. It is competition, not legislation, which protects the low-income consumer's market position.

Notes and Questions:

1   The terminology used by Professors Cayne and Trebilcock in their conclusion (*id.*) requires some explanation. In their language, "a rule might be *redistributive* in the sense that it will reduce and allocate to the consumer excess profits previously earned by the merchant. . . . An *exclusionary* rule is one which, by imposing additional costs or constraints upon the merchant, causes him to respond with increases in price, with reductions in quality, or by withdrawing from the market. . . . Exclusionary rules may be labelled *degenerative* where, because of the nature of the commodity to which the rule applies, violators remain mostly unsanctioned. Illegal markets will respond to meet needs which the policy makers have left unsatisfied, thereby leaving the consumer in a weaker position than would otherwise have been the case had normal market processes been left to operate". See *id.* at 407, 408, emphasis in the original.

2   Report of the National Commission on Consumer Finance, Consumer Credit in the United States (1972) at p. 95:

> Although the Biblical tenets against taking *any* return for the use of credit have largely been rejected in today's society, other reasons have been advanced to justify placing upper limits on rates charged for the use of credit-rate ceilings. These reasons include:
> 1.   To redress unequal bargaining power.
> 2.   To avoid overburdening consumers with excessive debts.
> 3.   To administer credit grantors as public utilities.
> 4.   To assure that consumers pay fair rates for credit.

3   Support for low ceilings is based on the rate of default among high risk debtors. It is argued that "[l]ow ceilings can be justified as an attempt to promote equality by preserving the basic dignity of the debtor and the debtor family . . . by seeking to avoid catastrophes that would destroy stability, self-esteem and family life." Thus, "protecting high risk debtors from the psychic harm associated with default — suggests that a moderately low ceiling applied to all forms of consumer credit provides a significant improvement in the distribution of benefits within society": G.J. Wallace, "The Uses of Usury: Low Rate Ceilings Re-examined" (1976) 56 Bos. UL Rev. 451, 479, 495. It is further argued that low ceilings prevent borrowing resulting in a future income level which is below the consumption floor as to impose harmful externalities upon the non-impoverished members of society. Avio, "An Economic Justification of Statutory Interest Rate Ceilings" (1973) 13 Q. Rev. Ec. and Bus. 3: 61-64. But see Durkin, "More on Economic Rationale for Statutory Interest Rate Ceilings" (1974) 14 Q. Rev. Ec. and Bus. 3: 95. For further criticism of the

application of the free market approach to the regulation of the price of consumer credit, see Comment, ``An Alternative to the UCCC: Publicly Subsidized Consumer Loans'' (1973) 4 *Golden Gate L. Rev.* 239.

4   Note that the cost of credit consists of (a) the cost of forbearance, (b) the cost of risk of non-payment, and (c) expenses associated with the granting of the loan. Is this relevant for the purpose of setting a rate ceiling? With respect to the creditor's expenses, see the following exposition by Waters, in J. Ziegel (ed.) *Proceedings of the Seventh Annual Workshop on Commercial and Consumer Law* (1979) 102-03:

HOW DO LOAN COSTS IMPACT UPON RATE CEILINGS?

When the matter of costs is considered, certain elementary economic principles must be recognized. First, the costs of *initiating* a loan are essentially unrelated to the size of the loan. For any size of loan, an interview must be conducted; a contract must be completed. (The investigation undertaken of the would-be borrower's financial circumstances may be more intensive for larger loans.)

Second, loan initiation costs are independent of the length of time for which the loan is made. Thus, the costs of initiating a loan which is to run one month are little different from the costs of initiating one which is to run for one year. All of this suggests that the smaller the loan and the shorter its term, the greater initiation costs will be as an annualized percentage of the loan principal. For example, initiation costs of $10 are equivalent to 120 per cent per annum of a loan of $100 made for one month. They are equivalent to one per cent per annum of a loan of $1,000 made for one year.

The foregoing indicates that initiation costs can cause almost any rate ceiling to become operative and inhibiting for loans involving small amounts or short periods of time. What would be the sensible response of any "legitimate" lender to operative ceilings? Three possibilities readily come to mind:
(1)   Forego business involving small amounts or short lending periods;
(2)   Increase the requirement with respect to the minimum amount borrowed, so that the initiation costs can be spread over a larger amount;
(3)   Make the loan at the ceiling rate, and thereby recover only a fraction of costs, and hope that this "generous act" will result in a "repeat" business for larger amounts. In effect, treat the unrecovered costs as marketing expenditures to be recovered (hopefully) out of future loans.

What if the loan is not made by a "licensed" lender? There appear to be two possibilities:

The first possibility is that the borrower will seek out an unlicensed lender. Such a lender probably has the same cost structure (not as formal though) as a licensed one. Consequently, this lender will have to charge at least the same rate as the licensed one, if it is to be a profitable loan. I say "at least" because the unlicensed lender must also charge something to recover those costs related to the fact that he is operating illegally. In any event, the consequences of the rate ceiling for the would-be borrower will certainly be more bother and most likely higher costs!

The second possibility is for the would-be borrower to do without. In such a case, *society* has decided *for him* that he is better off without the loan than with it. This hardly seems to be the point, however, at which society's concern with his economic decisions should become so heightened.

5   The regulation of finance charges in the vendor-credit market raises distinct problems. They are discussed by Professors Cayne and Trebilcock (*id.* at 412) as follows:

In the case of vendor credit, serious problems arise in trying to regulate interest charges without regulating the cash price. These problems are particularly acute in the low-income market where most sales are likely to be on credit and a merchant need not be concerned to keep his cash price competitive in order to attract cash buyers. For example, the FTC study found that low-income market retailers used instalment credit in 93 per cent of their sales compared to 25 per cent for general market retailers. Here, if a ceiling on interest charges is set below the figure at which it is profitable for a merchant to extend credit, the obvious answer is to bury a portion of the credit charge in an inflated cash price. . . .

Presumably in an attempt to meet this difficulty, Caplovitz suggests the enactment of laws regulating prices, on the grounds that low-income area merchants would then "be unable to offer the 'easy credit' plans they now do." While this conclusion my be well founded, depending, of course, upon the price levels which the regulators deem appropriate, it does not follow that low-income area merchants will deal with their customers on more palatable (and less profitable) terms. On the contrary, existing evidence points to consequences fundamentally different from this. Profit margins are already such that, if one accepts the conclusions of the FTC study, altruism of this kind is unlikely to be forthcoming. Instead the merchant might either go out of business in that area, entirely excluding from the market consumers whom he could only have dealt with at prices not prohibited; alternatively he or other suppliers will be prepared to continue selling the goods to these consumers at the old price, illegally, on the black market. In short, regulation of prices would have only an exclusionary or degenerative effect on the low-income market.

Even in the more affluent vendor credit market, rate ceilings are unlikely to achieve any greater purpose. Here, as elsewhere, the market will establish the operative rate in the event that the prescribed ceiling exceeds the level necessary to ensure an adequate return on capital. Indeed, there exists a substantial body of supportive evidence indicating that, in such circumstances, rate ceilings are superfluous. Where, on the other hand, legislation forces ceilings below economic rates, the credit seller, like the low-income area merchant, will as far as possible try to build part of his credit charge into the cash price of the goods, which has the objectionable consequences of subverting the purpose of the rate ceiling and forcing cash buyers to subsidize credit buyers. Hence rate ceilings governing vendor credit would not appear to be viable policy instruments in either low or high income markets. Even where price controls are annexed in order to render them enforceable, they can only produce consequences essentially exclusionary or degenerative in nature. As we shall see, this fundamental difficulty undermines rules which govern lender credit transactions as well.

2. THE CANADIAN EXPERIENCE — AN OVERVIEW

Prior to the enactment of Bill C-44 in 1980 (discussed in section D(3) *infra*), no general usury law existed in Canada. The following extract reviews the position up to 1970:

R.C.C. CUMING
"Consumer Credit Law"
in Fridman (ed.) *Studies in Canadian Business Law*
(1971) p. 87, 89-92, 97-100

[The] division of legislative power has coincided with and has perpetuated the legal categorization of consumer credit marketing into lender credit and vendor credit: lending money and selling goods and services on the deferred payment basis. The conclusion that the charge made by a seller for the privilege of paying the purchase price of goods or services over a period of time is not interest has meant that, apart from its specific jurisdiction over banks and banking and negotiable instruments, the Federal Parliament's primary jurisdiction in this area is confined to credit granting which involves money lending in the narrow sense. This leaves to the provincial legislatures jurisdiction over by far the greatest portion of the consumer credit industry under the category of property and civil rights.

Apart from pre-Confederation legislation in the provinces of Upper and Lower Canada and later in the united province of Canada, all of which was repealed in 1858, the first legislative attempt to regulate credit charges on a nation-wide basis was embodied in the Money-Lenders Act, 1906. However, little change from the regulation-free period between 1858 and 1906 was brought about by the Money-Lenders Act:

> The Money-Lenders Act was conceived in good intentions but over the years proved to be quite ineffective. Its main defect lay in the fact that interest was not defined and could not be held to include ancillary expenses, especially in view of the conflicting references to 12 percent for interest alone in section 6 and 12 percent for both interest and expenses in section 7. Other reasons for its ineffectiveness were that no licencing or supervision of money lenders was required, no one was charged with the responsibility of enforcing its terms, and borrowers were reluctant to incur the publicity and expense of taking remedial action themselves.
>
> The result was that even though the Interest Act had been on the statute books in one form or another since before Confederation and the Money-Lenders Act since 1906, the business of money lending in Canada was for all practical purposes unregulated during the first quarter, or more, of the present century.

The Money-Lenders Act remained law until 1956 when it was repealed.

Interest charges made by chartered banks were set by statute until 1967 when the long standing "six percent" interest ceiling was removed entirely. As was the case with ceilings set by the Money-Lenders Act, the Bank Act ceiling was illusory because of the lack of any definition of the term "interest". In any event, ceilings on bank interest charges were never intended to apply to consumer loan transactions since they were set at a time when Canadian chartered banks were not actively participating in the consumer loan business. During the years prior to the repeal of s. 91 when bank loans began to be a significant factor in the consumer credit market, consumer lending was made economically feasible for banks by the use of a discount method of calculating interest charges, a practice specifically permitted by the Act, and by requiring borrowers to pay extra service charges, a practice not prohibited by the Act.

Apart from the very limited disclosure provisions in the Interest Act, cost of credit disclosure was largely ignored until the recent amendments to the Bank Act were enacted.

By far the most significant step taken by the Federal Parliament to regulate those aspects of the consumer credit industry falling within its jurisdiction came with the enactment of the Small Loans Act in 1939. During the ten-year period immediately prior to 1939, federal legislative involvement in the consumer credit field came in the form of regulatory provisions, primarily credit and expense charge ceilings contained in the special acts of Parliament creating consumer loan companies. The special rate ceilings set in the various acts were replaced in 1934 by a uniform ceiling contained in amendments to the Loan Companies Act which applied to a few Dominion letters patent companies engaged in the small loans business in addition to the special act companies. However, very little by way of uniformity resulted:

> The situation in the early thirties, therefore, was that Dominion companies were limited in their charges whereas other lenders were not. Moreover, the chattel mortgage fee (permitted by some of the special acts and standardized by the Loan Companies Act) was authorized only for disbursements actually made and one of the three Dominion small loans companies was operating mainly in the Province of Quebec where lending under security of a chattel mortgage was impractical since the Civil Code of that province required physical possession of the chattels to be taken by the creditor in order that the pledge be effective. This company . . . supplemented its revenues by requiring borrowers to insure their lives to the extent of their loans through the agency of the company, the premiums and commissions being established at relatively high levels. Further questions arose concerning the propriety of charging chattel mortgage fees to borrowers again when loans were refinanced, and there were complications involving refunds when loans were refinanced or prepaid by reason of the fact that all charges were deducted in advance. The entire situation continued to be unsatisfactory from almost every point of view.

Between 1934 and 1938, considerable pressure for revised uniform legislation built up both inside and outside Parliament. In 1938, the Banking and Commerce Committee of the House of Commons, after holding hearings and studying the issues involved, produced a draft bill which was enacted the next year as the Small Loans Act, 1939.

The original form and content of the Small Loans Act was significantly influenced by the Uniform Small Loans Law proposed by the Russell Sage Foundation in 1916 and enacted widely throughout the United States between 1917 and 1932. The Canadian Small Loans Act was designed to regulate certain lending practices of the small loans company and of "any person other than a chartered bank who carries on the business of money lending or advertises himself, or holds himself out in any way, as carrying on that business including provincially incorporated lenders other than credit unions. Its most important features are that it establishes, for loans of $1,500 or less, uniform, all-inclusive credit charge ceilings which must be calculated on the retiring balance, it regulates delinquency charges and gives prepayment rights without penalty, and it requires licencing of lenders making credit charges in excess of 12 percent per annum (virtually all consumer loan companies) and annual inspection of their records by the Superintendent of Insurance.

[As for provincial legislation:]

The first widely-accepted measure of this period was the adoption of unconscionable transactions relief legislation by all provinces except Ontario between 1962 and 1967. The basic concept of these acts, while not a new one, became popular after the Supreme Court of Canada ruled those aspects of the legislation affecting credit charges *intra vires* of provincial legislatures. The object of this legislation is to give wide powers to the courts to open certain types of credit transactions and to set aside or to rewrite any provisions contained in them so as to prevent usury and harsh and unconscionable results. . . .

Every province has enacted legislation providing for the incorporation and operating procedures of credit unions or caisses populaires. While some of these acts regulate interest charges, their primary object is to protect members by insuring that each credit union is operated on an honest and competent basis.

D. INTEREST REGULATION: SPECIFIC LEGISLATION

1. Unconscionable Loan Transactions Legislation

Provincial legislation empowers courts to give remedies in the case of unconscionable loan transactions. Ontario passed the Unconscionable Transactions Relief Act (UTRA) in 1960.

The constitutionality of such legislation was upheld by the majority of the Supreme Court in *The Attorney General for Ontario* v. *Barfried Enterprises Ltd.* [1963] SCR 570. According to a later decision, the principal holding of *Barfried* was that "the federal jurisdiction over interest [under the BNA Act s. 91(19)] does not exclude all provincial jurisdiction [in relation to property and civil rights under BNA Act s. 92(13)] over contracts involving the payment of interest so as to invalidate provincial laws authorizing the Courts to grant relief from such contracts, when they are adjudged to be harsh and unconscionable": *Tomell Investment Ltd.* v. *East Marstock Lands Ltd.* (1977) 77 DLR (3d) 145, 152-153 (SCC).

Under the Ontario UTRA, where the "cost of loan" (broadly defined) is "excessive" and "the transaction is harsh and unconscionable" the court may relieve the debtor from the obligation to pay any excessive sum, order repayment of any such amount already paid, and set aside or revise the loan contract. Most other provinces have similar provisions either in specific statutes or in their general Consumer Protection Acts.

MOREHOUSE v. INCOME INVESTMENTS LTD.
(1965) 53 DLR (2d) 106, [1966] 1 OR 229 (Ont. Co. Ct.)

SWEET Co. Ct. J.: This is an application for relief under the Unconscionable Transactions Relief Act, RSO 1960, c. 410. It arises out of a mortgage of 728 Ashley

Ave., Burlington. The applicants resided there. It is dated January 7, 1958. The applicants are named the mortgagors and the respondent, Helen Forbes, is named as mortgagee. It was registered January 8, 1959, as No. 92132. The mortgage is stated to be for the principal sum of $4,050. According to its wording, and subject to provisions for acceleration of payment and prepayment, it is payable as follows:

> The sum of Forty Dollars ($40.00) shall become due and payable on the 16th day of February, 1959 and continuing monthly thereafter until the 16th day of January, 1964 when the balance of the said principal sum shall become due and payable. The aforesaid monthly payments of $40.00 are to be applied FIRSTLY on account of interest at the rate of seven per cent (7%) per annum and SECONDLY in reduction of principal. Interest is to be calculated half-yearly on the 16th days of July and January in each year.

The mortgage was assigned by Helen Forbes to the respondent, Income Investments Limited, by an instrument bearing the same date as the mortgage. The Deputy Registrar's certificate indicates that its registration was on January 8, 1958, as No. 92133. It seems that "1958" was inadvertently inserted and that it was registered on January 8, 1959, immediately following the registration of the mortgage.

Helen Forbes was a secretary in the office of the solicitor of Income Investments Ltd. I find that Helen Forbes never had any personal interest in the transaction, that all the money advanced was money of Income Investments Ltd., that she never occupied any position other than as trustee for Income Investments Ltd., that the mechanics of the handling of the matter, which included her participation, was an expedient for some purpose of Income Investments Ltd., that she was merely the instrument for the accomplishment of that purpose and, that according to the actual substance of the matter, Income Investments Ltd. should be treated and dealt with in exactly the same manner as if it had been named as mortgagee in the mortgage. Indeed, as I understand the position taken at the trial by its counsel, it was conceded on behalf of Income Investments Ltd. that it should, for these proceedings, be treated as though it had been named as mortgagee in the mortgage. In any event and regardless of that, I find that Income Investments Ltd. is a creditor within the meaning of s. 2 of the Unconscionable Transactions Relief Act.

Although the mortgage indicates that the principal was $4,050, the total amount received by the mortgagors was $2,370.80. They received it on January 13, 1959. Included in the sum of $4,050 was a bonus of $1,550. Income Investments Ltd. also charged and retained a so-called "commission" of $75. Presumably, the balance of $54.20 was retained by the solicitor of Income Investments Ltd., for fees and disbursements.

Mrs. Morehouse contacted Income Investments Ltd. by telephone to obtain a second mortgage on the property. On January 2, 1959, Mr. Bernard Greenbaum, the president of Income Investments Ltd. inspected the property. While there, he had Mr. and Mrs. Morehouse sign a document. Imprinted on it are the words "Income Investments Limited" and below them "Authorization to Arrange". Included in it is: "in consideration of Income Investments Limited agreeing to endeavour to arrange on the Security known as Lt. #86, P1 616, Twp of Nelson, County of Halton Value $15,000 and owned by me/us and registered in the Land Register Office at Milton in the name of As Above & Wife, hereby authorize Income Investments Limited my/our exclusive agent to arrange a Second Mortgage on the terms hereinafter set out". It indicates that the amount is to be $2,500.00 with a bonus of $1,550.00 bearing interest at the rate of not more than 7% per annum. It also includes the following: "I/We hereby agree to pay Income Investments Limited a commission of $75 and to pay all legal expenses in connection with the arranging of this mortgage." Also included is: "This application and authorization shall be Exclusive and Irrevocable for a period of 30 days."

The matter of revision of security or of its terms is something not lightly to be approached. Questions as to whether or not or when or how a transaction should be altered may be of major importance. Enforced alteration of a contract presents serious problems. Great caution is required when dealing with a consideration agreed to be paid by a borrower for the use of a lender's money. In my view, the intent and purpose of the legislation is only to correct situations where, in some way, unfair advantage has been taken of the borrower and then only to the extent that there is clear and unequivocable authorization in the legislation for the revision. However, when that situation does exist, revision is, in my opinion, mandatory. Parts of s. 2 of the Unconscionable Transactions Relief Act are:

> **2.** Where, in respect of money lent, the court finds that, having regard to the risk and to all the circumstances, the cost of the loan is excessive and that the transaction is harsh and unconscionable, the court may,
>
> (*a*) re-open the transaction and take an account between the creditor and the debtor; . . .
>
> (*c*) order the creditor to repay any such excess if the same has been paid or allowed on account by the debtor;
>
> (*d*) set aside either wholly or in part or revise or alter any security given or agreement made in respect of the money lent, and, if the creditor has parted with the security, order him to indemnify the debtor.

The "cost of the loan" is defined in s. 1 of the Act as follows:

> **1.**(*a*) "cost of the loan" means the whole cost to the debtor of money lent and includes interest, discount, subscription, premium, dues, bonus, commission, brokerage fees and charges, but not actual lawful and necessary disbursements made to a registrar of deeds, a master or local master of titles, a clerk of a county or district court, a sheriff or a treasurer of a municipality.

In the same section "creditor" is defined as follows:

> (*c*) "creditor" includes the person advancing money lent and the assignee of any claim arising or security given in respect of money lent.

In that section "money lent" is also defined, its meaning in the Act being:

> (*e*) "money lent" includes money advanced on account of any person in any transaction that, whatever its form may be, is substantially one of money-lending or securing the repayment of money so advanced and includes and has always included a mortgage within the meaning of The Mortgage Act.

I do not think that an attempt should be made to set out here firm and unelastic definitions of what constitutes unfair advantage or as to what is "harsh and unconscionable". The minds of many are often facile in the devious and agile in ingenuity for its accomplishment. It would, I think, be futile, perhaps even dangerous, to attempt to establish total safeguards in the hope that they would be effective against all selfishness and chicanery. Invention often adds new oppression to the old.

Furthermore, the cost of a loan in a transaction between some men and under some circumstances might be fair and reasonable but the same cost in transactions between other men and under other circumstances might be harsh and unconscionable. Then, too, what might be an excessive cost at one time might be a reasonable cost at another. Each case must be decided upon its own facts and against its own background.

However, without in any way attempting to limit them, there are certain factors which should be considered.

One of such factors is whether there was on the part of the lender honesty, fair dealing, frankness and full disclosure in terms intelligible to the borrower.

Associated with that is the footing upon which the parties were negotiating. Of importance in this area are such matters as the relationship of the parties to each other, whether there was a fiduciary relationship, their respective experience and whether there was urgency for the borrower of which undue advantage was taken by the lender.

A factor, and a very important one, is the risk involved. Relevant to this would be the security, if any, given for the loan, the ability of the borrower to pay and his attitude towards his obligations.

Another matter for consideration would be whether or not the cost of the loan was reasonably consistent with the prevailing market in the area for the same general type of loan involving a similar risk.

Still another factor is whether the documentation securing the lender's position is fair and reasonable under the circumstances or whether it contains provisions which might work serious hardship against the borrower quite unnecessary for adequate protection of the lender.

The words "harsh and unconscionable" appeared years ago in the Money-Lenders Act of England [1900 (U.K.), c. 51]. They have received judicial interpretation with relation to that legislation. Furthermore, cases dealing with that legislation indicate that the relief available under it went beyond that previously available in respect of what were sometimes referred as hard bargains.

Though the relevant wording of that Act is not the same as s. 2 of the Unconscionable Transactions Relief Act, the interpretation placed by authorities in England upon the words "harsh and unconscionable" in the Act passed in England has, I think, relevance here.

In *Re A Debtor, Ex p. The Debtor* [1903] 1 KB 705 at pp. 708-9, Collins, M.R., referring to the Money-Lenders Act, 1900 said:

> Now the words of s. 1 are these: "there is evidence which satisfies the Court that the interest charged in respect of the sum actually lent is excessive, or that the amounts charged for expenses . . . or any other charges, are excessive, and that, in either case,

the transaction is harsh and unconscionable, or is otherwise such that a Court of Equity would give relief, the Court may reopen the transaction ... and relieve the person sued from payment of any sum in excess of the sum adjudged by the Court to be fairly due in respect of such principal, interest, and charges as the Court, having regard to the risk and all the circumstances, may adjudge to be reasonable"; and the latter words afford some indication of what the Legislature regarded as "excessive interest." Ridley J. held on the construction of these words that the Legislature must be taken to have limited the relief which a Court of Equity would have given before the Act. I cannot agree with that construction. In my opinion the relief which may be given under the Act cannot be thus limited. Upon the natural grammatical construction of the words, I think the words "harsh and unconscionable" are distinct from and independent of the words which follow. Relief may be given if the bargain is harsh and unconscionable by reason of excessive interest or other excessive charges.

The following is an extract from the report of *Poncione* v. *Higgins* (1904) 21 TLR 11 [at p. 12]:

Lord Justice Vaughan Williams said that with regard to the Money Lenders Act, 1900, the intention of the Legislature was to deal with cases of persons in financial distress coming to money-lenders to borrow money in order to get out of their financial distress which was often urgent and pressing, and not to deal with the case of persons who were in a position to make their own bargain on terms of equality with the moneylender. The Legislature threw upon the moneylender who chose to advance money to persons in a position of financial distress the obligation not to take advantage of their distress or of their incapacity to negotiate.

The following is from the report of the judgment of Romer, L.J., in that case [p. 12]:

In his Lordship's opinion it would be mischievous to formulate what conduct on the part of a moneylender was "harsh and unconscionable" within the words of the Act. He would content himself with saying that the Judge should in every case consider the various circumstances under which the loan had been effected and the terms of the loan, such as the rate of interest, the security, and so forth.

The following is an extract from the judgment of Cozens-Hardy, L.J., in *Poncione* v. *Higgins* [p. 12]:

It was possible that the interest might be deemed excessive, and yet the transaction might not be deemed harsh and unconscionable. And it was possible that the interest might be deemed so extravagantly excessive as alone to satisfy the Court that the transaction was harsh and unconscionable. It was obviously not possible to lay down a fixed general rule as to rate of interest. The circumstances of each case must be considered, including the necessities of the borrower, his pecuniary position, the presence or absence of security, the relation in which the money lender stood to the borrower, and the total remuneration derived by the money lender from the whole transaction.

The words "harsh and unconscionable" were considered in *Samuel et al.* v. *Newbold* [1906] AC 461. In that case Lord Loreburn, L.C., said at p. 467:

The section means exactly what it says, namely, that if there is evidence which satisfies the Court that the transaction is harsh and unconscionable, using those words in a plain and not in any way technical sense, the Court may re-open it, provided, of course, that the case meets the other condition required. A transaction may fall within this description in many ways. It may do so because of the borrower's extreme necessity and helplessness, or because of the relation in which he stands to the lender, or because of his situation in other ways. These are only illustrations, and, as in the case of fraud, it is neither practicable nor expedient to attempt any exhaustive definition. What the Court has to do in such circumstances is, if satisfied that the interest or charges are excessive, to see whether in truth and fact and according to its sense of justice the transaction was harsh and unconscionable. We are asked to say that an excessive rate of interest could not be of itself evidence that it was so. I do not accept that view. Excess of interest or charges may of itself be such evidence, and particularly if it be unexplained. If no justification be established, the presumption hardens into a certainty. It seems to me that the policy of this Act was to enable the Court to prevent oppression, leaving it in the discretion of the Court to weigh each case upon its own merits and to look behind a class of contracts which peculiarly lend themselves to an abuse of power.

Further, Lord Atkinson said [p. 477]:

I am quite unable to accede to the argument so much pressed upon your Lordships that interest however excessive cannot amount to prima facie evidence that advantage was taken, or a market made, of the borrower's necessity or weakness, or that an unconscionable use was made of the power over him which the lender was in a position to exercise so as to entitle the borrower to relief under the statute, or that the transaction was not reasonably consistent with any course of fair dealing.

It will, of course, be always competent for the lender to shew that, despite the excessive rate of interest, the transaction was in fact fair and reasonable; but to permit a lender to succeed in retaining the benefit of a bargain securing to him gains apparently so inordinate as those attempted to be secured by the lender in this case, without giving satisfactory proof of the character I have mentioned, would, in my opinion, altogether defeat the object of this remedial legislation.

Re Scott & Manor Inv. Ltd. [1961] OWN 210, is a case dealing with an application under the Unconscionable Transactions Relief Act. The following is an extract from the judgment of Timmins, Co. Ct. J. [p. 212]:

On the cases, and having regard to s. 2 of the statute, it is clear that each of these lending transactions stands on its own feet. Excessive interest itself may be sufficient to render the bargain harsh and unconscionable — so as to entitle the borrower to relief. What would be considered harsh, unreasonable and oppressive having regard to the risk, circumstances, rate of interest, and over-all cost of loan to a small man, may be reasonable and entirely proper under the circumstances of the case, to a man of business engaged in a business venture who has to pay for it to get the money.

A fair test in these cases, having regard to the authorities, would seem to be, could the loan have been procured for less?

The document which the president of Income Investments Ltd. had Mr. and Mrs. Morehouse sign on January 2, 1959, makes it clear that there was to be a bonus of $1,550. However, I find that in an important respect, the document is quite inconsistent with the intention of the responsible officers of Income Investments Ltd. According to its wording, Income Investments Ltd. was to be the exclusive agent of Mr. and Mrs. Morehouse to arrange a second mortgage. Income Investments Ltd. was to have a commission of $75. Income Investments Ltd. did not perform the duties of agent for Mr. and Mrs. Morehouse. It is clear that the president of Income Investments Ltd. never intended that that corporation would perform such duties. I find that he always intended that if a loan were made, the corporation would lend its own money and then try to sell the mortgage for its own benefit and profit. If the corporation were the agent of the applicants, as the document indicates they were to be, then, of course, Mr. and Mrs. Morehouse would be entitled to all the benefits of the fiduciary relationship. Certainly, the agent would not be entitled to a secret profit on the transaction.

There was no evidence adduced that at the time the applicants were informed the loan would be made Income Investments Ltd. had already arranged to sell the mortgage at a profit. On the other hand, and by a document dated January 14, 1959, one Edward H. Moore agreed to purchase this mortgage for $3,000 and an acceptance by Income Investments Ltd. bears the same date. January 14, 1959, is one day after Mr. and Mrs. Morehouse received the $2,370.80 in connection with the mortgage.

I find that under the circumstances the $75 retained by Income Investments Ltd. as "commission" is part of the cost of the loan within the meaning of s. 1 of the Unconscionable Transactions Relief Act.

Accordingly, without taking into consideration the solicitor's charges, the cost of the loan was $1,625 and the advance by Income Investments Ltd. was $2,425.

In connection with the claim of Income Investments Ltd., as to the effective rate of interest, three computations were produced. They all are based on the advance being $2,500 instead of $2,425. In my opinion, they all also contain other basic inaccuracies.

The general approach in one of those computations is that indicated in a circular communication dated June 1, 1963, from the Superintendent of Insurance. It purports to indicate the "average minimum interest cost per yr." Whatever value it may have as a rough calculation, it is not, in my opinion, the correct actuarial approach and neither are the other two computations submitted by Income Investments Ltd.

To express the actual average annual cost of the loan in terms of percentages, regard should be had to the amount of the advance outstanding from time to time and the bonus should be discounted and related to the reducing unpaid balances of the advance.

Although only $2,425 was advanced by Income Investments Ltd., the mortgage provides for interest at 7% per annum computed half-yearly on $4,050. This interest would be payable in the first instance at 7% per annum calculated half-yearly not only on the money advanced but also on $1,625 not advanced.

The monthly payments of $40 would be more than sufficient to pay that interest so that part of the monthly payments would go to the reduction of principal. Each month, then, the mortgagee would get back part of its advance. Because the principal sum is reduced the amount of money payable for interest *per se* would reduce but the interest rate on the diminishing unpaid balance of the advance would increase as that balance decreased. The $1,625 included in the principal sum does not decrease and the mortgagors continue to pay interest on the full sum of $1,625 not advanced even though the mortgagee has outstanding less of the money it advanced.

The bonus and "commission" totalling $1,625 must also be brought into the computation. According to the wording of the mortgage, the mortgagors are to pay that amount even though they did not receive it. The present value of money payable in the future is less than the amount so payable in the future. Thus to determine how the sum of $1,625 affects the annual rate, appropriately discounted amounts should be related to each of the 60 gale days provided for in the mortgage and those discounted amounts applied respectively only to the amount of the advance still to be outstanding and unpaid on each such gale day.

The total cost stated in percentages per year would be the percentage figure developed from the 7% per annum (the interest *per se* as distinguished from bonus and "commission") computed as above plus the percentage figure developed from the bonus and "commission" treated as above.

I think that Mr. and Mrs. Morehouse would have difficulty in determining the actual rate of percentage they were being charged. Mr. Morehouse went to grade eight in school. Mrs. Morehouse was a registered nursing assistant.

It has been, in effect, urged on behalf of Income Investments Ltd. that there were other sources of funds available to the applicant and that they had no need, out of necessity, to borrow from Income Investments Ltd. The evidence does indicate that there may have been other sources available to them.

One of the reasons given for their borrowing from Income Investments Ltd. was to obtain funds for Mr. Morehouse to visit his ailing father. It was also said that they needed money to pay bills.

Neither Mr. nor Mrs. Morehouse are very young, but the years do not seem to have brought them wisdom in financing. They have a considerable history of borrowing. I think that at the time they gave the mortgage it was a matter of them needing money, anxious to get it to satisfy their immediate needs, influenced by not having to pay more than $40 monthly for the time being, and the day of final reckoning apparently five years away.

It appears that Income Investments Ltd. carried on a sizeable mortgage business and that primarily its business was the acquiring of mortgages either by original lending or by purchase and then selling them. It would be expected that to operate such a business the operator would be astute, have adequate knowledge of the value of securities offered and understand the implications associated with the lending on, buying and selling of mortgages including rates of interest and the actual yield, however arising.

I do not think that Mr. and Mrs. Morehouse were any match for Mr. Greenbaum, the president of Income Investments Ltd. To put them on anything like an equal footing with the lender, the borrowers would need help and advice but, so far as the evidence discloses, they had none. The only solicitor who appears to have entered into the transaction was the one acting for Income Investments Ltd., whose fee the borrowers seem to have paid.

It has also been urged that the lender's risk was great, so great that it justified the cost of the loan.

Pursuant to s. 2 of the Unconscionable Transactions Relief Act, regard is to be had "to the risk and to all the circumstances". It would seem to me that by the singling out of the one factor "risk" and including all other factors in the omnibus wording "all the circumstances" there is legislative emphasis on risk. Although risk is not the only important factor to be considered in determining whether or not the cost of a loan is excessive and the transaction harsh and unconscionable, risk is, indeed, a very important factor.

Within reasonable limits, and subject to other conditions or circumstances which might exist, the risk would be expected justifiably to affect the yield to the lender.

The mortgage in question was taken subject to a mortgage to the London Life Insurance Company under which there was owing $10,519.33 subject to a tax credit of $13.92. That mortgage bore interest at 5½% per annum. It provided for monthly payments of $66.62 including principal and interest, together with a monthly tax payment of $24.38. The date of maturity was February 22, 1982. It was not in arrears.

The applicants had purchased the premises in 1957 at the price of $13,600. Between the time of purchase and the time of the giving of the mortgage in question, they had storms and screens put on at a cost of $570, had pavement laid at a cost of $225, and landscaping had been done by Mr. Morehouse.

Mr. Arthur Kent Craig, who was in the real estate business in Burlington in 1959, placed a valuation on the property as of 1959 of approximately $14,700. Other than Mr. Greenbaum saying that he felt the house was worth in the neighbourhood of $13,000 to $14,000, that was the only thing in the nature of appraisal given in evidence. I think that Mr. Craig was competent to make the valuation. I consider his evidence preferable to that of Mr. Greenbaum.

Although Mr. Greenbaum said he felt the house was worth in the neighbourhood of $13,000 to $14,000, Income Investments Ltd. required that the fire insurance on the house be increased from $11,500 to $14,500. If the insurable value of that house was $14,500 and the value of the land was added, the total would, of course, have been in excess of Mr. Craig's valuation.

I find that the property at the time of the placing of the mortgage had a value in the neighbourhood of $14,700.

The terms of payment of the first mortgage were an advantage to the second mortgagee. They were realistic for an owner and presented no problem of early payment or refinancing. The monthly tax payments required under the first mortgage would tend to prevent arrears of taxes. The monthly payments under both mortgages would permit close control and reduction of principal.

Both Mr. and Mrs. Morehouse worked. Mr. Morehouse's gross income was apparently in the neighbourhood of $85 per week. Mrs. Morehouse appears to have been earning $235 per month.

The Morehouses were chronic borrowers and often in debt. This might add to the risk. On the other hand, I would not think it unusual for second mortgage dealers to lend to this classification of borrower. I would think that if there were not many of such people the market for the second mortgage lender would be lessened.

It appears that they met their relatively considerable obligations at least fairly well.

Mr. Ritchie, assistant manager of the Hamilton Employees Credit Union, gave evidence to the effect that Mrs. Morehouse's credit was good.

Counsel for the respondents submitted that the applicants were in a hurry to obtain the loan and that that hurry prevented adequate investigation. As I understand it, it was claimed that this affected the risk on the ground that the lender would not have had sufficient knowledge of the borrowers' credit rating.

If the applicants were desirous of obtaining money quickly, as I think they were, the inclusion in the form which Mr. Greenbaum had them sign on January 2, 1959, of a provision that the "application and authorization shall be Exclusive and Irrevocable for a period of 30 days" would not appear to have been helpful to them in that regard.

If urgency or emergency on the part of the borrower is taken advantage of by the lender, that is a circumstance to be taken into consideration.

If Mr. Greenbaum had any real qualms about the company advancing the money, I do not think his action at the time indicated it. I think that one of the reasons he had Mr. and Mrs. Morehouse sign the so-called "authorization to arrange" so quickly was because he was fearful that without it they would borrow elsewhere.

The sale of the mortgage by Income Investments Ltd. so soon after the advance under it does not indicate undue risk. Reference has already been made to the offer dated January 14, 1959, by Mr. Moore to purchase the mortgage for $3,000. The mortgage was assigned to Edward H. Moore by instrument dated January 22, 1959, and registered on that day.

The loan involved significant risk but having regard to the second mortgage field generally, the risk, considering all the relevant elements, was not inordinate. That risk would justify a yield to the lender substantially in excess of a reasonable rate for a good first mortgage but not more than a yield reasonably consistent with the prevailing rate generally available in the area on a competitive basis for second mortgage loans involving similar risks.

Evidence regarding appropriate cost of the loan was given by Mr. Marvin Farewell and Mr. Albert Miller Greenaway. I consider the evidence of Mr. Farewell to be preferable to that of Mr. Greenaway.

Produced on behalf of Income Investments Ltd. in connection with the yield was a memorandum purporting to set out particulars in respect of a number of mortgages purchased by that company, which purports to indicate yields to the purchaser. The lowest of these purported yields is 17.39% and the highest 60%. I do not consider that this has significant, if any, probative value. The circumstances surrounding the various transactions and the motivation of the vendors may not be indicated by the bare statistical data in the memorandum. Each item would require consideration based on the respective circumstances and against its own background. If the transactions listed are justified, they may be justified because of conditions respectively and exclusively applicable to them. If they are not justified, repetition does not make them so.

In any event, purchasing mortgages and lending on mortgages are quite different kinds of transactions. Persons who have mortgages for sale often are in an entirely different category than persons wishing to borrow on mortgages. The reasons for selling a mortgage often are quite different than reasons for borrowing money. This is pointed up by this case. Mr. and Mrs. Morehouse were borrowers on a mortgage, in respect of which the advance by Income Investments Ltd. was $2,425. Income Investments Ltd. sold that mortgage in less than a month for $3,000.

The mortgage contains a provision to the effect that if the mortgagors make default as to any of the covenants or provisos contained in the mortgage, the principal thereby secured shall at the option of the mortgagee forthwith become due and payable. It also provides that should default be made by the mortgagors in the observance or performance of any of the covenants, provisos, agreements or conditions contained in any mortgage to which it is subject, the moneys secured by it would forthwith become payable.

Accordingly, if default occurred in respect of even the first of the monthly payments, the mortgagors would, according to the wording of the mortgage, be obliged to pay for the use of $2,425 for the short time which would have elapsed, the sum of $1,625 as well as any accrued interest on $4,050 which might be payable. In the event of default under the first mortgage, the whole of the principal of the mortgage in issue would be payable.

Of course, a lender is entitled to adequate protection, but protection is one thing and harshness is another.

I find that having regard to the risk and to all the circumstances the cost of the loan was excessive and that the transaction was harsh and unconscionable within the meaning of the Unconscionable Transactions Relief Act.

Order accordingly.

Notes and Questions:

1 Does the Ontario Business Practices Act make the UTRA redundant? Do the statutes overlap?

2 What is the position of a third party who purchases an agreement subject to the UTRA? Does he take it subject to the borrower's equities or is he immune from them? The provincial Acts are divided on the issue, though the majority favour the third party. For the Ontario position, see UTRA s. 5. What is the meaning of a "*bona fide* assignee or holder for value without notice"?

3 Repayment of the loan in full, and discharge of the mortgage securing the debt, is not a bar to relief under the Unconscionable Transactions Relief Act, RSN 1970, c. 382. "Debtor" in the Act does not require the applicant to be a debtor at the time of the action: *Churchill* v. *Le Barron Mortgages Ltd.* (1978) 86 DLR (3d) 538 (Nfld.

Dist. Ct.). Thus, "the fact that the plaintiff repays the loan does not prevent him from bringing the action and asking the Court for relief on the basis that the cost of the loan was excessive and that the transaction was harsh and unconscionable": *id.* at 541.

4   In *Unrau* v. *Modern Finance Ltd.* (1970) 74 WWR 662 (BC CA), the borrower sought relief on the basis of an excessive rate of interest and bonus. He was able to provide evidence as to the availability of a substantially cheaper source of financing at the time of the loan but was nonetheless unable to convince the majority of the court. Considering "the absence of pressure or coercion or haste" the majority of the court concluded that "the transaction should not be described as harsh and unconscionable . . ." (*id.* at 673).

In *All-Canadian Peoples Finance Ltd.* v. *Marcjan* (1970) 10 DLR (3d) 352 (BC SC), defendant real estate agent accepted terms of a mortgage that included substantial bonus provisions that brought the effective yield on the mortgage up from 60 per cent to 74 per cent. In the court's view, having entered the transaction with "his eyes open", the defendant could not be heard to complain. He subsequently sold one of the three properties involved, thereby binding himself to obtain a discharge of the existing mortgage affecting that property. Knowing of his situation, All-Canadian Peoples extracted a further bonus which brought the effective yield to over 100 per cent. This rate, in itself, would apparently not have been found harsh and unconscionable, but the fact that Marcjan, described as a wheeler-dealer, was in no position to refuse the new terms persuaded the B.C. court to intervene. The court allowed the plaintiff the principal plus interest at a rate of 1.5 per cent per month.

Other cases have found similar rates of interest and discounts to be fair in the circumstances. See *Adams* v. *Fahrngruber* (1976) 62 DLR (3d) 256 (OHC), and *Brechin* v. *Gary Holdings Ltd.* (1975) 54 DLR (3d) 631 (BC CA).

Professor I. Davis discusses numerous cases under the Unconscionable Transactions Relief Act in "Comments: Unconscionable Contracts — Some Recent Cases" (1972) 50 Can. B. Rev. 296, 303-04 and concludes as follows:

> It might be argued that these cases are not of much assistance to the practitioner in providing advice to his client, but this is only partially correct. Clearly the courts will consider in each action certain matters exemplified in the illustrations provided. In most jurisdictions a high interest rate alone will not necessarily be decisive, much will depend on the profit gained by the lender which may equally well be achieved by a low interest rate and a large bonus.

> There is no doubt that quite apart from any consumer protection legislation an onus has been placed on any lender to ensure that his client fully understands the terms and effect of the transaction. Where this has been done there is a reluctance of the courts to intervene except in completely improvident agreements. Providing this knowledge exists, the inequality of the parties assumes less importance. However, the grantor has rather unfairly been placed under one disadvantage in that he must try and ascertain the necessity of the borrower for the funds; the greater the need, the greater the likelihood of relief.

> One consideration that is always relevant is whether or not the benefit received by the applicant could have been obtained elsewhere, either for less, or at all.

Evidence on this point seems to have been led by at least one of the parties in each of the transactions outlined above. The only situation where this may not be material is where the borrower has knowingly made no effort to search for other terms. Generally speaking, expert evidence on the condition of the relevant money market is advisable in most litigation and essential to some positions.

In summary one can say that the legislation has extended the jurisdiction of the courts to grant the equitable relief they have been doing for years. Many of the same considerations will still be applicable. To advise on any given situation, counsel must take a broad view since a fundamentally fair contract will be upheld, an unfair one relieved against. At the same time an ill-advised agreement, made freely with full knowledge and understanding between parties of equivalent knowledge, is in no worse a position since the passage of the Unconscionable Transactions Acts than it was before.

2. TAX REFUND DISCOUNTING LEGISLATION

EDWARD BELOBABA
"Regulating the Income Tax Discounter; A Study in Arbitrary Government"
(1979) 1 Canadian Taxation 21-23

The Perception of The Tax Discounter as "Social Vulture." The stagflation of the seventies brought with it a new phenomenon in consumer financial services — cash discounting of income tax refunds. Almost overnight tax discounters, with their "Get instant cash for your tax refund" sales pitch, appeared in the inner-city rooming-house areas of large Canadian cities. The operation of the typical tax discounting outlet was straightforward: the discounter calculated the taxpayer's expected tax refund and then negotiated the appropriate "cash advance" in return for the taxpayer's assignment of the expected refund. Revenue Canada was then directed to mail the refund to the tax discounter. Although in form a mere assignment for value, in substance the nature of the tax discounting transaction was undoubtedly that of a loan. The tax discounter was in effect a short-term moneylender. The expected tax refund was treated initially as collateral for a loan and ultimately (via the assignment) as the means for its repayment.

By the mid-seventies, some 65 tax discounting facilities were operating in low-overhead storefronts in the large urban centres. British Columbia, Alberta and Ontario had attracted most of the tax discounting business. The greatest concentration understandably was in Toronto, where 30 tax discounting outlets were in operation by the spring of 1977.

The size of the tax discounting market was not insignificant. In 1977 alone, some 24,000 Canadian discounted $10 million worth of tax rebates. The average size of the expected refund was $414. The average rate of discount was approximately 40 per cent. Thus, a $400 refund netted a $240 cash advance. Given, on average, a three-month "turn-around" period on the assigned refunds, the 40 or 50 per cent discount rate when expressed as an annual interest charge approached 200 and 300 per cent and sometimes more.

Who would possibly agree to a 200 to 400 per cent annual interest charge? Obviously, anyone who needed cash immediately and lacked the necessary collateral to secure consumer financing at the more traditional outlets. The profile of the typical customer was predictable: he was a single male, between the ages of 18 and 30, seasonally or temporarily employed, a transient. His annual income was under $4,000. His only real collateral was his income tax rebate.

To no one's surprise, the operation of the tax discounter attracted the attention of first the media and then the legislators. The tax discounter was seen by many to be a "social vulture . . . preying on the poor, the unemployed and those that can least look after themselves." Both the print and the electronic media called on government to "do something about it."

The Provinces Respond. Because the tax discounting "problem" was seen mainly as a problem of consumer protection and more particularly truth-in-lending, provincial legislators had no constitutional qualms about intervening. At a minimum, the provinces could impose precise disclosure requirements so that the true costs of borrowing were made clear to the customer. This approach was followed in Nova Scotia and Alberta. So long as a tax discounter made full and complete disclosure of all charges, annual interest rates, etc., these provinces were satisfied. No attempt was made to regulate the actual rate of discount. Perhaps the concern was a constitutional one — a regulation of the rate of discount might be characterized as legislation in relation to "interest," a matter traditionally within the exclusive jurisdiction of the federal government.

The province of British Columbia was less reticent. At first it tried to deal with tax discounting as a potentially unfair or unconscionable consumer trade practice. The courts, however, complicated matters by refusing to find unconscionability in the absence of specific evidence as to the particular circumstances of the transaction, the credit worthiness of the particular customer, and the various risks involved in tax discounting generally. The B.C. legislature responded by enacting a more specific regulation of the tax discounter. In March, 1977, the Consumer Protection Act was amended to require not only disclosure, but also an 85 per cent minimum "hand-back." By setting 15 per cent as the maximum allowable discount rate, B.C. hoped to remove the more usurious aspects of tax rebate discounting while preserving its over-all commercial viability.

The approach taken in Manitoba, Saskatchewan and Ontario was even more severe. The Minimum "hand-back" requirement was set at 95 per cent. The fact that a 5 per cent maximum discount rate would virtually drive discounters out of business was not an inadvertent consequence. The 95 per cent hand-back requirement was intentionally designed to do just that.

The Controversy Continues. The passage of provincial legislation did little to stem the growing tide of controversy and criticism. In Alberta and Nova Scotia, of course, the tax discounter continued to operate, virtually unimpeded by the minimal requirements of fair disclosure. In B.C. the enterprising discounters discovered an obvious loophole in the 85 per cent hand-back requirement: by burying their interest charges in a higher service fee (which was not subject to any maxima) a de facto discount rate in excess of the provincial ceiling was easily maintainable. And in Ontario it seemed that the new legislation was making no discernible impact on the nature and extent of the tax discounters' operations.

Meanwhile, investigative journalists were documenting incidents of 600 per cent, 800 per cent and even 1200 per cent interest charges when calculated on a per annum basis. Editorial writers and television commentators began to urge federal intervention to regulate if not prohibit this "modern-day form of loan-sharking."

The federal government, however, had already examined the tax discounting question and had decided to deal with the matter in its proposed Borrowers and Depositors Protection Act. Under the proposed B.D.P.A., the tax discounter would not be obliged to adhere to any maximum discount rate (short of the "criminal" or "loan-sharking" rate that would be stipulated by regulation) so long as the rate charged was not "unwarranted."

This approach differed fundamentally from that of the provinces. Unlike B.C., Saskatchewan, Manitoba and Ontario, the federal government did not propose any specific regulation of the discount rate. It was thought that the B.D.P.A.'s repeal of the Small Loans Act, and with it the rate ceilings on small consumer loans, would encourage the more traditional consumer lenders to service this market. Combined with a full-disclosure requirement and a precise stipulation of a "criminal rate," the "unwarranted credit rate charge" was seen as a meaningful and workable consumer protection measure. This theory, however, was never put to the test. The comprehensive nature of the reforms proposed in the B.D.P.A. managed to attract the criticism of both consumer groups and finance industry lobbies. The B.D.P.A. never got past first reading and was quickly shelved. The demand however for some federal legislative response to the "tax discounting problem" did not subside. If anything the shelving of the B.D.P.A. and the possibility of a protracted period of re-examination and revision strengthened the position of those who were now actively advocating ad hoc regulations of the tax discounter. Their pleas did not fall on deaf ears.

Parliament Enacts the Tax Rebate Discounting Act. On April 17, 1978, in a record twenty-three and one-half minutes, Parliament gave second and third readings to Bill C-46: "An Act Relating to the Discounting of Over-payments of Tax Under the Income Tax Act." The Honourable Warren Allmand, Minister of Consumer and Corporate Affairs, had no difficulty persuading his colleagues in the House of Commons that Bill C-46 was the necessary legislative response to a "distasteful practice" that had been "directed particularly against the poor, the uninformed and the unemployed." Accepting the view that the tax discounters were nothing more than "social vultures who preyed on the poor, the unemployed and those that could least look after themselves," and that the practice of tax discounting "has no place in contemporary Canadian society," the House of Commons gave speedy passage to Bill C-46.

The Tax Rebate Discounting Act did two things. It set out an explicit and rigorous full disclosure requirement, but more importantly it imposed an 85 per cent minimum hand-back requirement. The 15 per cent discount that could be retained by the discounter was expressly defined to include all fees and charges, as well as interest. The decision to regulate the discount rate rather than prohibit the practice altogether was explained by the Honourable Warren Allmand as follows:

> We decided to allow discounting within this limit rather than banning it altogether because we feel there is a legitimate place for certain discounting under the limits described . . . we did not want to create a black market in discounting. We merely limited the discounting to 15 per cent. We do not think this will drive discounters out of business. It will restrict them to what is probably a reasonable profit rather than an unconscionable profit.

This "explanation" should have prompted several questions in the House. Could the Minister substantiate his claims that a 15 per cent maximum discount rate would not be prohibitive? Could the Minister advise the House of any evidence that he had obtained from the tax discounters to support his opinion that "legitimate" tax discounters would still find a 15 per cent rate ceiling commercially viable? Would the Minister reassure the House that in the event that his information was inaccurate or inadequate and the legislation would in fact drive the discounters out of business, there would be alternative proposal(s) forthcoming to deal with the low income consumer's need for short-term credit? Would a rigorous economic impact analysis expose the Tax Rebate Discounting Act as a shortsighted, retrogressive, middle-class, legislative placebo that would hurt the very group it was ostensibly designed to protect?

These questions were never asked. An attempt was made by one M.P. to suggest that Bill C-46 would simply "cut off that source of funds for the poor taxpayers who are most in need" and thus encourage a "black market." Allmand responded by reiterating his earlier point that a 15 per cent discount rate "still provides a pretty good rate of interest and a pretty good income." The data? The evidence? Allmand wasn't pressed. The important questions were never asked. The Bill was sent across to the Senate.

The Hearings before the Senate Banking, Trade and Commerce Committee. Here perhaps was the greatest of the many ironies surrounding Bill C-46. The only rigorous examination of the many implications of Bill C-46 was the examination undertaken by a sub-committee of the much maligned Upper House. The Senate Banking, Trade and Commerce Committee grilled the Consumer Affairs and Revenue Canada witnesses, asked pointed questions, demanded the evidence which prompted the federal departure from the "unwarranted credit rate" concept to specific rate regulation, queried the justification for a below market rate ceiling, and sensibly concluded that "the logical starting point to produce a fair and effective regulation of the business of tax discounters is to start where the problem starts, namely in the income tax office of the Department of National Revenue . . . a means should be found whereby the clearing and paying of tax refunds may be proceeded with expeditiously so as to reduce or eliminate recourse to tax discounters . . ."

The analytical challenge, however, was short-lived. Conceding that it was "sympathetic to the objectives of the bill," the Committee decided that Bill C-46 would be reported without amendments. The Senate, in turn, gave its approval and the Tax Rebate Discounting Act became law. Middle-class consumer groups and media commentators applauded the quick action of Parliament. The Government had indeed "done something about it." Unfortunately, no one knew quite what.

Notes and Questions:

1 Professor Belobaba went on to argue that a "legislative analysis of the federal Tax Rebate Discounting Act is in many ways a study in the disintegration of both policy and process". He criticized the Minister of Consumer and Corporate Affairs for not undertaking an economic impact assessment. His observation (at 24) was that:

> The evidence was quite formidable that even a straight 15 per cent maximum discount rate would close down many if not all of the tax discounting operations. The Tax Rebate Discounting Act, however, went even further. Section 3(2) of the Act expressly defined the maximum to include all fees and charges, including any service or preparation fee. If indeed the Minister preferred a non-prohibitory response to the tax discounting "problem," this preference was lost sight of either in the Department or perhaps at Cabinet. The section 3(2) inclusion of all fees and charges would effectively prohibit all legitimate tax discounters and thus encourage recourse to an illegitimate or black market lender — the very consequence that Bill C-46 set out to avoid.

Professor Hasson, in "In Defence of Simple Solutions for Simple Problems — A Reply" (1979) 1 Canadian Taxation 25, responded by indicating his "skepticism as to what an economic impact assessment would yield" and concluded (at 26):

> I have serious doubts about the Tax Rebate Discounting Act. In the first place, it legitimizes a business which ought not to exist and which exists solely because the government cannot be bothered to set up a more accurate system for deducting taxes. Second, I fear that the Tax Rebate Discounting Act will be evaded (as it was in British Columbia for more than a year) or avoided by its practitioners. These are my concerns about the Tax Rebate Discounting Act. Sadly, Professor Belobaba's article does not attempt to address these concerns.

Note that a spokesman for the industry claimed that a 30 per cent discount rate was the minimum necessary to break even. Can you see why? What is the risk of non-payment faced by tax discounters?

2 For a list of provincial tax refund discounting statutes, which "is not necessarily complete", see *Krassman* v. *The Queen* (1980) 102 DLR (3d) 262, 266-267 (FC TD). The list consists of Alberta, British Columbia, Manitoba, Nova Scotia, Ontario and Saskatchewan. Alberta and Nova Scotia merely prescribe certain informational requirements. The others limit the discount to between 5 and 15 per cent. The constitutional validity of the British Columbia provision was upheld in *Re Hanson and Harbour Tax Services Ltd. (No. 2)* (1978) 87 DLR (3d) 96 (BC SC). The provision (limiting the discount) was regarded (at 98-99) as "not [being] legislation in relation to interest but legislation relating to a specific contract made between a vendor and purchaser . . . [which] for the protection of the public, fixed a minimum price payable by the purchaser, thereby fixing the maximum profit available to [him]". The provision was regarded as an integral part of a consumer protection statute, reflecting the doctrine of unconscionability, and dealing with price and profit. As for the room left for federal power, "the fact that some of the Provinces have concurrently legislated in respect of tax refund discounting neither detracts from nor enhances the right of the federal power, in its criminal aspect, to enter the field": *Krassman* v. *The Queen, supra* at 267. Which provision prevails in the case

of ''inconsistency''? Is a provincial statute limiting the discount to 5 per cent ''inconsistent'' with the federal statute prescribing a 15 per cent limit? *Cf.* in general P. Hogg, *Constitutional Law of Canada* pp. 103 *et seq.* As for the constitutionality of the federal statute, see section (B) note 3 *supra*.

3. BILL C-44: REPEAL OF THE SMALL LOANS ACT AND ENACTMENT OF NEW CRIMINAL USURY PROVISION

Bill C-44, ''An Act to amend the Small Loans Act and to provide for its repeal and to amend the Criminal Code'', was given second and third readings by the House of Commons on July 22, 1980, only one day after its first reading. The Senate gave third reading on December 17, 1980 and the Bill received the Royal assent on the same day. See SC 1980, c. 43.

According to Professor Ziegel, ''The Bill deals with questions of major social, economic, and legal importance which warranted careful examination.'' However, it ''was not debated and its adoption had the unanimous support of all three political parties. Any public discussion of the merits of the Bill was effectively forestalled by the haste with which it was rushed through the House''. The following is Professor Ziegel's analysis of the Bill.

JACOB S. ZIEGEL
''Bill C-44: Repeal of the Small Loan Act and Enactment of a New Usury Law''
(1981) 59 Can. Bar. Rev. 188 *et seq.*

Bill C-44 has two objectives. First, subject to some transitional provisions, it repeals the Small Loans Act* on a day to be determined by proclamation. Secondly, it adds a new section 305.1 to the Criminal Code which will make it an offence for a person to enter into an agreement or arrangement to receive interest at a criminal rate, the ''criminal rate'' being fixed at an effective annual interest rate exceeding sixty per cent. These two components of the Bill will be discussed in turn. . . .

1. *Repeal of the Small Loans Act.*

The Small Loans Act was first adopted in 1939. Since then more than forty years have elapsed and it is widely agreed that the Act is in need of extensive overhaul. In the eyes of its critics — not necessarily the same critics — it suffers from three major weaknesses. First, its graduated rate ceilings have become totally unrealistic in the light of the rapidly escalating cost of money. Secondly, the Act only applies to loans up to $1,500.00 and therefore invites easy evasion of its provisions. A more fundamental attack comes from a third group of critics who argue that rate ceilings are counterproductive and an economic absurdity. They are either too high and therefore serve no exclusionary purpose or they are too low, in which case they exclude borrowers from access to legitimate lenders

---

* However, important parts of the Small Loans Act were repealed immediately upon proclamation of Bill C-44, viz. ss. 3-5 of the Small Loans Act dealing with licensing requirements and imposing rate ceilings. See Bill C-44, s. 1. [Eds.]

and drive them into the arms of loan sharks. This school of thought essentially favours an unrestricted rate structure in which the market determines how much borrowers have to pay for their loans.

The first two criticisms could easily have been met by a revised Small Loans Act, and recommendations to this effect were already made by the Porter Commission in 1964 and by subsequent bodies that studied the question. Even consumer loan companies, which initially favoured complete abolition of rate regulation, would have been willing to accept a revised rate structure as a second best solution. Since Bill C-44 does not follow this route, it would be logical to conclude that the government shared the de-regulator's philosophy. This is probably an oversimplification of the various motives that influenced the authorities. Bill C-44 does not contain an official explanation of its rationales. It is an open secret however that the credit unions have long been unhappy with the low rate ceilings and sought relief from this obstacle in their operations. From the perfunctory remarks during the first reading of the Bill, it is a fair inference that the members of Parliament were responding to this pressure and not to any profound convictions about the virtues of a wholly de-regulated interest market.

The perfectly legitimate concerns of the credit unions could have been met by revising the step rates upwards. They did not require the total repeal of the Small Loans Act. Other alternatives were also available. For example, credit unions could have been excluded from the Act on the grounds that being member controlled and subject to fairly stringent provincial regulation there was no need for an additional layer of regulation. Another possibility would have been to follow the British precedents and to replace the ceiling on rates with an unconscionability test while retaining the licensing provisions for otherwise unlicensed lenders and introducing additional monitoring devices. It is lamentable that these alternatives were not even raised, much less debated, during the lightning passage of the Bill. . . .

Equally distressing is the fact that in sounding the death knell to the Small Loans Act the House of Commons ignored over a hundred years of Canadian experience. Prior to the 1850s the Provinces, like the United Kingdom, operated under a general usury ceiling. The law was repealed, in the case of Upper Canada, in 1858, and, subject to some important exceptions, lenders were thereafter free to charge what the market would bear. This laissez-faire policy was restated in the first federal Interest Act and is still found in the present Act. However, early complaints began to emerge from farmers and others about unfair lending practices and this led to the adoption of the disclosure requiremens in the present Interest Act.

An equally strong reaction manifested itself against the alleged depredations of "loan sharks" who were exploiting impecunious wage earners. This led to the adoption *inter alia* of the federal Money-Lenders Act of 1906, pawnbroker's legislation at both the provincial and federal levels, and, later, of the Unconscionable Transactions Relief Acts. The Money-Lenders Act did not work well and there ensued a prolonged, if not overly celerious, search for a better substitute. The substitute was found in the Small Loans Act of 1939. The Act was adopted after detailed hearings before a committee of the House of Commons. It was based on the sixth draft of the American Uniform Small Loan Law. The Uniform Law has exercised much influence in the United States and its principles apparently continue to obtain in the interest legislation of many of the American states.

It may fairly be argued that the small loans legislation was spawned in an era of highly restricted consumer credit markets, in which there was a need to encourage the entry of legitimate lenders, and that the situation has altered radically. There is no longer a shortage of lenders (to continue this reasoning) anxious to cultivate the consumer market. The reverse is true. The credit market has become highly competitive. There is an embarrassment of riches.

It is no doubt true that the consumer credit market today is much more competitive than it was before the war. It is not true however that low income consumers, financially illiterate consumers, and consumers who have overcommitted themselves no longer need protection. They are "rationed" consumers. They may not be eligible for low cost credit or have exhausted their sources of supply. They are the ones that may be susceptible to exploitation or may only be able to obtain credit at rates that may compound their economic and social difficulties. The earlier interest rate legislation reflected these concerns and, to the extent that such legislation survives, continues to reflect it. The repeal of the Small Loans Act does not resolve these difficulties, any more than did the adoption of section 2 of the Interest Act in 1873. It will create a new vacuum which will have to be filled by the provinces or by new federal band-aids. In fact, the evidence is already at hand. As recently as 1978 Parliament adopted the Tax Rebate Discounting Act in order to combat the allegedly unconscionable practices of tax rebate discounters. Bill C-44 does not repeal this Act and it is specifically excluded from the new criminal usury provisions. Bill C-16, the ill-fated Borrowers and Depositors Protection Bill introduced by the government in 1976, at least envisaged alternative policing measures to the repeal of the small loans ceilings; Bill C-44 simply walks away from the problem.

2. *The New Criminal Usury Provision.*

It is still more difficult to reconcile the concept of a free market in interest rates with the new criminal usury provision. A similar provision already appeared in Bill C-16. The old and the new provisions were and are designed to combat loansharking. Loansharking is said to be rampant in Montreal and other major Canadian cities and the usury provision was apparently requested by the Montreal police to assist them in their fight against the underworld.

Loansharking is not a term of art. Implicit in the proposed new section 305.1 of the Criminal Code is the assumption that any rate exceeding sixty per cent is extortionate and indelibly stamped with a criminal intent, including presumably the willingness to use violent collection methods to ensure repayment of the loan. These assumptions are demonstrably unsound. Assume an employee requests a loan of $10 from another employee and promises to repay $11 a week later. The one dollar charge if interpreted as interest, corresponds to an annual interest rate of approximately 520 per cent, which sounds extortionate. In fact it is not because the time spent by the fellow employee in making and collecting the loan would alone be worth a dollar. In any event it is economically unsound to stigmatize any cost of credit as extortionate if the borrower was a free agent and not coerced into borrowing the money. To take another example, now somewhat dated American studies show that an effective annual interest rate of 91.36 per cent would be necessary to enable a consumer loan company to lend $100 repayable over a year with an eleven per cent return on equity after covering its total estimated costs. These figures were available to the Department of Consumer and Corporate Affairs and appear to have influenced the government in accepting a sixty per cent cut off point in section 305.1.

One is led to ask therefore why Bill C-44 should repeal the Small Loans Act on the one hand and in effect proscribe loans with a high built-in cost on the other. Was it because high cost loans were regarded as inherently objectionable, or was it because the draftsmen thought it a necessary price to fight loansharking?

One could accept the trade-offs if one was convinced that the impact on legitimate transactions will be marginal, that there are no practical alternatives to a criminal usury ceiling, and that the legislation will achieve its purposes. The available evidence falls far short of answering any of these questions satisfactorily.

In considering the potential impact of the Bill on lenders and other creditors it is important to note that the Bill is not confined to consumer transactions, since section 305.1 applies to all types of agreement and arrangement involving the advancement of credit, whether for commercial or consumer purposes. It also applies to corporate borrowers. It is surely not correct to assume that the aggregate costs of a "legitimate" commercial loan, if converted to an interest rate according to the statutory definitions, will never exceed the magical sixty per cent figure. One can visualize a variety of familiar commercial transactions where the forbidden boundary may be crossed. The danger to creditors will arise not from the fear of criminal prosecution, which may be slight because of the provision in section 305.1(7) that no prosecution shall be commenced under the section without the consent of the provincial Attorney General. Rather the danger lies in the probability that the debtor will plead violation of the section as a common law defence in a civil action by the creditor to collect his debt.

Section 305.1 also raises a significant number of technical points, and these must be briefly noted.

(a) *"Credit Advanced"*. The section applies to all arrangements and agreements under which credit is advanced at a criminal rate. "Credit advanced" is defined in section 305.1(2) as:

> "credit advanced" means the aggregate of the money and the monetary value of any goods, services or benefits actually advanced or to be advanced under an agreement or arrangement minus the aggregate of any required deposit balance and any fee, fine, penalty, commission and other similar charge or expense directly or indirectly incurred under the original or any collateral agreement or arrangement;

"Credit advanced" is a new term in Canadian interest lexicography and, so far as I am aware, appears to have no exact counterpart in extant Canadian legislation. If

I interpret the definition correctly it applies to vendor's credit, whether relative to a sale of goods or services, as well as to conventional loans, secured or unsecured. In view of the definition of "interest" in Bill C-44, it also clearly applies to land mortgage transactions. It is not so clear whether "credit advanced" includes a credit sale of land (as distinct from sale of goods or services on credit). This will depend on how wide a meaning a court is willing to ascribe to "goods, services *or benefits*". "Credit advanced" presumably also covers all forms of revolving lines of credit, credit card transactions, and arguably, public utility transactions in which the consumer is exposed to a "penalty" for late payment.

(b) *"Criminal Rate"*. This term is defined in the Bill as:

> "criminal rate" means an effective annual rate of interest calculated in accordance with generally accepted actuarial practices and principles that exceeds sixty per cent on the credit advanced under an agreement or arrangement;

An apparent ambiguity here is that the definition fails to indicate how the statutory interest formula is to be applied to open-ended credit and credit card transaction type accounts. If it is to be computed from the date each itemized transaction occurs to the actual date of payment then this may create difficulties for creditors who do not calculate charges on a daily balance basis.

(c) *"Interest"*. This term is defined comprehensively as:

> "interest" means the aggregate of all charges and expenses, whether in the form of a fee, fine, penalty commission or other similar charge or expense or in any other form, paid or payable for the advancing of credit under an agreement or arrangement, by or on behalf of the person to whom the credit is or is to be advanced, irrespective of the person to whom any such charges and expenses are or are to be paid or payable, but does not include any repayment of credit advanced or any insurance charge, official fee, overdraft charge, required deposit balance or, in the case of a mortgage transaction, any amount required to be paid on account of property taxes;

This definition, as much as "credit advanced", is bound to provoke much anxious debate, even after allowing for the clarifying definitions of "insurance charge", "official fee", "overdraft charge" and "required deposit balance". The definition clearly rejects the narrow definition of interest adopted by the Supreme Court of Canada in *A. G. Ontario* v. *Barfried Enterprises* in favour of the economist's cost of loan concept previously popularized in the Small Loans Act and other modern consumer oriented legislation. This may push a creditor with fixed charges across the threshhold into the criminal rate territory since only the enumerated items, and not fixed charges as such, appear to be excluded from the all embracing definition of credit. . . .

Note: Prior to Bill C-44, the repeal of the Small Loans Act was proposed by Bill C-16, referred to in the extract above as "the ill-fated Borrowers and Depositors Protection Bill" (and briefly discussed in Section B note 5, *supra*). Bill C-16 provided for a "criminal interest rate" to be set by regulations. Penalties for demanding or collecting a credit rate exceeding the criminal rate ranged from $1,000 to $10,000 or two years imprisonment on summary conviction, or fines at the court's discretion and five years imprisonment for conviction by indictment. The bill also proposed to give borrowers (including buyers on credit) the right to apply to a court for a declaration that a credit charge which is not necessarily "criminal" is nonetheless "unwarranted". The burden would be on the creditor to prove that the charge is warranted. On finding an unwarranted rate, the court could reopen the transaction, relieve the borrower's obligation, order repayment to him, or set aside the agreement. In addition, Bill C-16 proposed to impose strict disclosure requirements in credit advertisements and provided for generous rights of prepayment without penalty.

E. DISCLOSURE OF CREDIT CHARGES

1. INTRODUCTION

R.C.C. CUMING
"Consumer Credit Law"
in G.H.L. Fridman (ed.) *Studies in Canadian Business Law* (1971) p. 87, 114-17

Mandatory, uniform, meaningful disclosure of credit charges has been the primary objective of consumer advocates during the last decade. While the disclosure controversy in Canada between consumer groups and the credit granting industry has not approached in size and intensity that occuring contemporaneously in the United States, nevertheless, a great deal of public discussion of the issue preceded and accompanied the widespread enactment of disclosure legislation in Canadian jurisdictions.

Prior to the enactment of statutory cost of credit disclosure requirements, to the extent it existed at all, disclosure of the cost of borrowing came in various forms, primarily because different types of consumer lenders used different methods of calculating credit charges. For example, credit unions, insurance companies and some chartered banks calculated and disclosed credit charges as an effective annual rate on the retiring balance. Small loans companies, required by statute to calculate charges on loans up to $1,500 on the basis of a graduated monthly rate on declining balances, disclosed charges on the same basis on which they were calculated without stating a composite rate. On loans over $1,500, they used add-on, discount or percent per month methods of calculating and disclosing charges. Department stores operating variable credit plans disclosed as a dollar charge on outstanding balances at the end of the month or on an average outstanding balance during the month. Some chartered banks and sales finance companies used the discount method of calculating and disclosing charges, while other sales finance companies used the add-on method. However, no attempt was made to inform credit consumers of the significance of the use of these methods of calculating, leaving them with the impression that they were paying interest on a declining balance basis. Many finance companies disclosed charges as so many dollars per year for each $100 of the original debt.

Confusion was compounded by the fact that there was very little standardization with respect to the components used in the calculation or disclosure of a credit charge. Frequently extra charges are made by credit grantors. Some are mandatory "service charges", while some represent the actual or inflated cost of mandatory or optional benefits provided to the borrower, such as insurance, or to the credit grantor such as registration fees for chattel security agreements. When pre-contract disclosure or rate advertising occurred, it was seldom that these charges were included in the rate quotation.

To most Canadian consumer advocates, disclosure means making explicit the total cost of borrowing stated as an effective annual rate, and, where meaningful, both percentage rate and dollars and cents cost. While seldom attempting to justify the diversity of methods used, the credit granting industry takes the position that percentage rate disclosure is infeasible and potentially misleading. Its alternative, and particularly that of the sales finance segment of the industry, is dollars and cents disclosure.

The primary *raison d'être* of disclosure is to give to that segment of the credit-consuming public which has the economic power to choose alternatives the necessary information to use in making the choice. Viewed in this light, it is apparent that disclosure benefits the "middle and upper class" credit consumer and is in no sense a panacea for the multitude of problems faced by marginal credit consumers. It is generally accepted that disclosure of credit costs to a potential credit consumer has three functions. First, it allows him to determine whether the advantage gained by entering into a transaction justifies the cost of credit. Secondly, if a uniform method of disclosure is required, he can determine which of the alternative sources of credit offered to him is the most economical. Thirdly, if disclosure is available in such a way as to permit comparison of the cost of credit with the return paid to him on his savings or investments, he can determine whether or not it would be better to rely on his own resources rather than to finance the transaction through other sources. The first and third functions are usually lumped together under the heading "comparison functions", while the second is referred to as the "shopping function". Dollar disclosure is likely the best method for fulfilling the first function. Any type of percentage rate disclosure permits fulfilment of the second. Dollar disclosure cannot be used when comparing the cost of credit from various sources when different repayment periods are involved. However, because an effective annual rate is used to calculate returns on bank, trust company and credit union deposit accounts and savings certificates, and on government and corporate bonds, fulfillment of the third function depends on disclosure by this method. Accordingly, if effective annual rate disclosure is economically feasible for all or the great bulk of consumer credit transactions, disclosure in that form and in actual dollar cost seem the most acceptable approach. While the credit industry in its rearguard action against the enactment of disclosure legislation stressed the problems, some real and some imaginary, of using effective annual rate disclosure, it met with little success. All disclosure acts in Canada adopt the combination of dollar and effective annual rate disclosure or modifications of it. All provincial acts permit credit consumers to discover the credit terms of their contract before being contractually bound.

[For a Canadian panel discussion on truth in lending during the height of the controversy, see J. S. Ziegel and R. E. Olley (eds.), *Consumer Credit in Canada* (1966), ch. I.]

2. Disclosure of the Cost of Borrowing and the Annual Percentage Rate Under Provincial Legislation

a) Disclosure of the "Cost of Borrowing" (Dollar Disclosure)

Apart from the charge for the use of the credit-grantor's money, consumer credit agreements frequently contain other charges that are payable by the consumer. Some of these charges reflect the credit grantor's disbursements. For example, a registration fee for a PPSA financing statement will not yield any additional profit to the credit grantor.

This aspect of the disclosure problem polarizes two interest groups. Consumer advocates argue that it is the cost to the consumer that should be considered. Credit grantors respond that charges which do not constitute part of the "interest" should not be included in the "cost of borrowing" disclosure requirement.

Much of the debate has focussed on charges for credit insurance. There are two basic types of credit insurance. Credit life insurance insures the creditor against loss if the debtor dies. Credit accident and health insurance insures the creditor against loss if the debtor is disabled and cannot make payments. Both assure the debtor that the debt will be paid and that dependents will be freed of the obligation. While the beneficiary under a credit insurance policy, whether life insurance or accident and health insurance, is the credit-grantor, charges for credit insurance are borne by the consumer-debtor. It has been a common practice for credit-grantors to offer credit insurance and even to insist that it should be obtained by consumers through them. Must charges for credit insurance be disclosed as part of the "cost of borrowing"? In general on credit insurance issues, see Brown, "Credit Insurance: Abuse and Reform" (1969) 10 BC Ind. and Com. L. Rev. 439.

Disclosure of the cost of borrowing in the case of credit other than variable credit is governed by s. 36 of the Ont. CPA (to be read in conjunction with the definitions under s. 1). The sanction for violating s. 36 is provided for in s. 39:

> A borrower is not liable to pay a lender as the cost of borrowing any sum in excess of the sum shown in the statement required by section 36 or 37 . . .

Note that a s. 36 statement is one of the items required to be disclosed to a buyer under s. 31(1) dealing with the form of an executory contract. An executory contract which is not made in accordance with s. 31(1) "is not binding on the buyer": s. 31(2). But see *J. Schofield Manuel Ltd.* v. *Rose* (1975) 9 OR (2d) 404 (Co. Ct.), *supra*, chapter 3(A). Compare the sanctions provided by ss. 31(2) and 39 with s. 130 of the U.S. Consumer Credit Protection Act under which any disclosure violation entails a civil liability which "in the case of an individual action [is] twice the amount of any finance charge . . . [but] not . . . less than $100 nor greater than $1,000".

Questions on Ont. CPA:

1   Does the "cost of borrowing" concept in the Ontario CPA focus on the cost to the borrower or the profit to the lender?

2   Does the "cost of borrowing" include a bonus given by a borrower?

3   Does "cost of borrowing" include charges payable in conjunction with vendor credit arrangements?

Problems:

1   Friendly Finance Co. approved a car loan to John Consumer. After selecting the Dealer and notifying Friendly Finance Co. of Dealer's name, John Consumer obtained from the company a cheque payable to the Dealer in the sum of the loan as previously approved. For the purposes of Ont. CPA. s. 36, was the loan "actually received in cash" by John Consumer?

2   Two lenders offer the same amount of credit on the same interest and other instalment terms. Both make their loans conditional on the borrower's obtaining insurance, e.g., credit life or accident insurance to protect the lender from the borrower's death or disability, or property insurance to protect the secured lender against the destruction of the collateral. One requires the borrower to purchase the insurance from him. The other gives the borrower the option of obtaining the insurance elsewhere. Whose "cost of borrowing" and "annual rate" is lower?

Note: For the disclosure of cost of borrowing under the federal Bank Act, see s. 202 of the Bank Act, SC 1980, c. 40, Part I, and Regs.

b) Disclosure of the Annual Percentage Rate

Notes: Under the Ontario CPA ss. 36 and 37 the creditor must indicate the cost of borrowing as an annual percentage rate. Section 38 provides that the latter "shall be applied in the manner prescribed by the regulations":

1   Under s. 14(2) of the regulations, apart from variable credit accounts,

> the annual percentage rate shall be deemed to have been charged not in advance on the principal sum from time to time outstanding, so long as the payments required to be made by the borrower are made as they become due and such payments are applied first to the reduction of the accrued cost of borrowing.

2   Slight deviations ("tolerances") from the actual percentage rate calculated under the regulations are permitted under s. 15.

3   For the comparative disclosure provisions in the U.S. Consumer Credit Protection Act, see §§103, 106, 107.

4   In February 1981, by an amendment to the regulations under the CPA (see O. Reg. 102/81), credit unions and *caisses populaires* were exempted from the disclosure requirements in s. 36 of the CPA. The amendment was apparently inspired by credit union concerns that s. 36 did not allow them to use variable rates for loans in a fixed amount. They deemed it important to have this facility because of the volatility of interest rates in an inflation heated economy. Granting the legitimacy of their concern, was total exemption an appropriate response?

3. DISCLOSURE BY A LENDER EXTENDING VARIABLE CREDIT

In the case of variable credit, disclosure has to be made before the granting of the credit (Ont. CPA, s. 37(2)(a) as well as periodically (Ont. CPA s. 37(2)(b); "period" should be between 4 and 5 weeks; s. 37(1)).

For a lengthy discussion from a U.S. perspective, see Landers, "Open-end Credit Disclosure Requirements under the Truth in Lending Act" (1979) 52 So. Cal. L. Rev. 1005.

a) Pre-Credit Extension Disclosure

CONSUMERS' ASSOCIATION OF CANADA (TORONTO)
The Billing Practices Study
(Ottawa: Consumer Research Council Canada, 1975) pp. 3-4

The protective provisions regarding disclosure that are available in some provinces, notably Manitoba and Quebec, but not in Ontario, require that the following be stated:

a. the penalty for not making payment on due date
b. the annual and monthly percentage rate
c. the number and timing of billing dates
d. the method of computing minimum payment on varying amounts
e. whether or not service charges are added to the principal, i.e. compounded

• • •

In Ontario there is no requirement that the consumer be given a copy of the master agreement with all disclosure items on it. Consequently it is unclear when diclosures must be made. Invariably the only document the Ontario consumer signs is the application for the credit card, so that he has little chance to read and understand the terms of the agreement he is entering into.

The use of the wording, "before agreeing to extend variable credit, etc., make the required disclosures" (sect. 37(2) of the Consumer Protection Act) has led to considerable confusion. Most credit card applications stipulate that the signing or use of the credit card finalizes the credit contract. It seems, therefore, the application itself does not constitute an offer in law, but is, if this is the correct analysis, a mere invitation to treat. It is the sending of the credit card, after credit checks have been made on the applicant, that constitutes the offer which the consumer may then accept or reject. Thus the card issuer can argue that as he has not yet agreed to extend any credit, he need not disclose at the time of the application. This argument is based on the premise that since the terms of credit are not covered in the application there is no contract until essential terms are agreed; hence there is no agreement until the consumer accepts the credit card. This interpretation, however, seems to contradict the aims of the Act; so it may be maintained that the application is an offer, which is accepted by performance on the part of the creditor of his first obligation, namely issuance of the credit card. Hence the issuer may be in breach of sect. 37(2) if the application does not disclose the required information.

A further point in favour of rejecting the issuers' arguments is that Sect. 41 of the Act provides that no lender shall represent either orally or in writing or by radio or television broadcast his charge for credit or cause such charge to be so represented unless the representation includes the full cost of borrowing and is expressed in the manner required by sect. 36 or 37. The title of the section is "Advertising the Cost of Borrowing."

Furthermore, it could be asked whether the partial information contained in the application is a representation of the cost. It would be extremely difficult to deny this (or that it is written or that the lender is advertising his credit arrangement with it.) Thus, if the application contains any reference to credit charges at all, sect. 37 must be complied with. If this is so the lender would be better off saying nothing at all. If he makes no reference to charges, sect. 41 does not apply and he can stand on his argument under sect. 37(2).

The intent of the Act is to ensure that people are informed of what they are agreeing to. If the terms of agreement are not disclosed on the application it is usually stated that the use of the card shall be deemed to be evidence of the fact that the customer has received and read the cardholder agreement and is bound by it. In effect, the consumer is put in a position where he will be legally bound without necessarily having been informed, and this could not have been the intent of the Act.

If the terms of the agreement are not explained at the time the consumer signs, it is likely they will not be read at all. For when the credit card eventually arrives it will probably be detached and the explanatory letter thrown away. To give adequate protection, therefore, the Act should state unambiguously that full disclosure must be made on the application form.

b) Periodical Disclosure in Ontario

CONSUMERS' ASSOCIATION OF CANADA
op. cit., pp. 6-7

1.   The statement must be sent out at intervals of not less than four and not greater than five weeks. Thus, the interest period in variable credit is between four and five weeks.

2.   The statement must show:

     a.   the outstanding balance at the beginning of the period;
     b.   the date and amount of each new extension of credit and the identity of the goods and services for which it was extended. Thus, goods must be

identified in the statement. There is some question as to whether descriptive billing is sufficient for this.

   c.   all the payments made by the consumer during the period, their dates, and "occasion" thereof. ("Occasion" is not defined);

   d.   the cost of borrowing, in dollars and cents, for the period;

   e.   the outstanding balance at the end of the period;

   f.   the percentage rate that is being applied;

   g.   the minimum charge if any;

   h.   a schedule of amounts, in dollars and cents, with the varying service charges due on each.

3.   Ontario also stipulates that the percentage rate must produce the service charge if it was applied to the previous balance.

There are two criticisms to make about Ontario's Act. There should be a required disclosure of the interest free period. If one can pay in full within a certain time and avoid service charges, this information should be contained somewhere on the statement. No doubt the regulation about the percentage rate is intended to be favourable to the customer. It ensures that if the previous balance method is employed the actual rate applied to his account is disclosed to him. Without this provision, the credit grantor could say his rate is 10%, but in reality it will be much greater.

     However, there should be some rider attached (as in the Quebec statute) specifying that calculation of the charge could be made on the adjusted balance even if disclosure is on the previous balance. Alternatively there could be provision for disclosure of the rate on the adjusted balance if that is the method employed.

c) Disclosure of the Cost of Borrowing

Section 37(2)(a) of the Ontario CPA requires the lender, inter alia, to disclose "the cost of borrowing in respect of the *unpaid balances from time to time*" (emphasis added). The meaning of the italicized phrase as discussed in the following case.

ZACHARY v. R.H. MACY & CO. INC.
(1972) 340 NYS 2d 908 (NY CA)

SCILEPPI J.: There are four different methods of periodically calculating finance charges on revolving charge accounts. The method used by the retailer in computing charges is set forth in full, first in the credit agreement and then at the end of each billing cycle as part of the customer's monthly statement. Invariably provision is made for minimum payments at monthly intervals.

1. The Previous Balance Method.

     Under this method, the balance is computed at the end of a monthly billing cycle on the basis of all debits and credits through that date (closing balance). Finance charges are deferred until the end of the next billing cycle. If payment is made in full during this deferral period, no finance charge is imposed. Should the customer not elect to pay in full, the finance charge is computed on the former balance, which — because of the deferral — is both the closing balance of the prior month (hence the phrase previous balance) and the opening balance for the current month. The balance is not reduced to reflect partial payments or purchases during the month in which such payments and purchases are made. These are carried over in the closing balance for that month (prior billing cycle) or the "previous balance" upon which finance charges are computed in the next month (current billing cycle).

Finance charges are thus computed on the basis of the balance outstanding at the close of a monthly billing cycle, modified by all purchases and payments as of that point in time. Since the finance charge is deferred for one monthly billing cycle the customer has between 30 and 59 days, depending on the date of purchase, to avoid a finance charge.

In short, the procedure is simply one of deferred billing, but with a "kick": current account activity, except current credits which fully discharged the amount due and owing when the balance is struck (the close of the prior billing cycle), is disregarded. Finance charges, also deferred during the current billing cycle, are then assessed at the beginning of the subsequent billing cycle retroactive to the date when the account's previous balance was struck and for that amount. Though there seems little in logic to commend its use, the practice makes sound business sense: the consumer enjoys one monthly billing cycle plus, depending on the date of purchase, to avoid a finance charge and without the worry of further inflating that charge by current purchases, while the retailer, where the amount owing has not fully been discharged, is free to disregard current payments — his *quid pro quo* for exempting current purchases — and compute his finance charge on the basis of the account's previous balance. By relating these charges back, the retailer concentrates his assessments, sometimes recouping losses he might sustain by the apparently liberal deferral provisions. In other words, the deferral feature is not only the system's attraction; it explains its over-all success.

2. The Adjusted Balance Method.

The finance charge is computed on the basis of the balance at the end of the current billing cycle, with credit for any payment made and merchandise returned during the current cycle, but without additional debits for current purchases. Finance charges computed on the adjusted balance are lower in the aggregate than those computed under other methods.

3. The Closing Balance Method (Ending Balance).

Finance charges are characteristically computed on the closing balance in the account as of the end of the current billing cycle. Allowance is made for all payments and other credits during the cycle, but also the closing balance includes a charge on all purchases made during the current cycle even though they were never billed before.

4. The Average Daily Balance Method.

The finance charge is computed upon an amount which is the sum of the amount of the actual daily balances each day during the billing cycle divided by the number of days in the billing cycle. Payments are credited on the date of receipt; and early payments or payments in excess of minimum payment due result in smaller finance charges.

[The court concluded at 922 that the phrase "outstanding indebtedness from month to month" denoting the basis of computing the finance charges under a N.Y. statute "merely requires that finance charges be computed at consistent monthly intervals on the customer's outstanding indebtedness at that time". The previous balance method was held to satisfy this requirement. What about the other three methods?]

Notes and Questions:

1   At the beginning of a billing cycle the balance of Cardholder shows a $100 debt. Cardholder pays $50 on account at the end of 20 days in the 30-day cycle. The annual percentage rate of the cost of borrowing is 18 per cent. What balance will be the basis for computing the cost of borrowing in the monthly billing statement under each of the methods described in *Zachary*? What will be the monthly payment? When is it payable?

2   At the beginning of another billing cycle the balance of Cardholder again shows a $100 debt. Cardholder pays $80 on account at the end of 3 days in the 30-day cycle. He makes a purchase worth $90 at the end of 28 days in the cycle. The annual percentage rate of the cost of borrowing is the same. Consider the same questions as in 1.

3   The Consumers' Association of Canada, *The Billing Practices Study* (1975) 26 describes as follows the methods used by credit-card issuers in Canada to calculate credit charges:

> Master Charge uses the average daily balance method of computing interest. According to the company this method is not only the most equitable to the consumer, but is the fairest for both parties. Some Chargex operations, as well as Shell (gasoline) and Kresges, use the adjusted balance method.* All other companies, except the utilities, use the previous balance method; those using it agreed that the adjusted balance method would decrease revenues and interest charges might have to be raised. Some retailers do adjust the balance, however, if a payment exceeds 50% of the amount owing. (This is required by law in Quebec.)
>
> Several credit card officials were cautious about implementation of the average daily balance method. It seems that this method calls for rather complex calculations that would need computers if any substantial number of accounts are to be handled. Although all companies in this survey use computerized billing it was the opinion of some that if legislation required adoption of the daily average method, smaller companies that do not use computers would necessarily be forced out of credit operations.
>
> In general, the service charge or penalty imposed by the utilities is a flat charge applied only once. But utilities have, of course, the added ability to enforce payment through threat of cutting off service.

---

* All Chargex (now Visa) operations now use the average daily balance method. [Eds.]

4   Whatever period is prescribed in the contract, the actual length of the interest-free period depends on a creditor's billing practices as well as on the crediting of payments by him. The Canadian position is described in the *Billing Practices Study* (*id.* at 26-7) as follows:

All the credit card programs surveyed offer the customer an interest free period, usually 25 to 30 days. This is a provision with many built-in ambiguities. Does this period start from date of purchase, from the billing date on a statement or on the day a statement is received? If payment is made by mail, must time be allowed for postal delivery? Must time also be allotted for the credit grantor's accounting department to process the payment? Just how much time does a customer really have to pay a bill and avoid incurring interest charges? This question was an attempt to obtain a more precise definition of interest-free periods.

Summary

Most companies indicated that once a payment is received at the computer centre, it will normally take less than 24 hours and no more than 48 hours for payment to be posted to an account and therefore to appear on the next statement. Eaton's and the Bay pointed out that the new "280" registers being installed in many of their stores eliminate much of the former time delays. These registers are connected to the data processing centre and a payment is posted immediately it is paid.

Delays in posting payments to an account occur when payments are made at a branch of a store or a bank on the due date. It will often take several days after a payment is made until it can be transferred to the data centre and posted to an account. In these cases a customer might find that interest is computed on the balance of his account even though he has made a payment. Canadian Tire, however, allows a grace period and no interest is charged unless a payment is not received by the next billing cycle. This policy was instituted because of the slow mail service to Canadian Tire's data processing centre in Welland, Ontario. Eaton's says it posts payments on the transaction date rather than on the processing date and adjustments are made on next month's statement if necessary.* Kresges on the other hand must receive a payment by the due date at its data centre if a payment is to be, in fact, received; otherwise interest will be computed.

It was agreed that the length of time between billing date and date of receipt by the consumer does reduce the interest free period. Many companies indicated that statements are mailed between two and four days after the billing. Allowing for mailing time of two or three days, a customer's interest free period is shortened by at least six to eight days. Only Master Charge said it mails out statements on the billing date or no more than one day later.**

Companies using country club billing take longer to mail out statements, possibly not until seven or eight days after the billing date. This is attributed entirely to the additional processing of receipts required in country club billing.

---

* At least some banks do the same. The practice is known as "value adding". [Eds.]
** The bulk of Visa bank statements are also mailed out on the billing date. [Eds.]

F. DEBTORS IN DISTRESS — LOW-INCOME AND OVERCOMMITTED DEBTORS

R.C.C. CUMING
"Consumer Credit in Selected Countries: Canada"
in R. M. Goode (ed.), *Consumer Credit* (1978) p. 186, 212-16.

(1) The low-income debtor

While Canadian legislators, particularly those at the provincial level, have demonstrated over the years a sincere willingness to search for legislative solutions to many of the problems faced by Canadian credit consumers, there remains one problem which continues largely unsolved. This is the problem of the low-income debtor.

For a portion of the Canadian population, consumer credit is an integral part of a chaotic and brutal social and economic environment. Consumer credit provides temporary relief during the frequent economic crises faced by many low-income Canadians. However, too often, this relief is obtained at very high cost. Even if the relatively high credit charges which these people must pay and the sharp practices to which they are subjected are ignored, there remains the destructive effect which the misuse of consumer credit can have on many of them. While there have been no scientifically controlled studies of the effect of harsh collection measures on the poor in Canada, there is convincing evidence to indicate that the enforcement of credit obligations plays a significant role in loss of employment, family breakdown and personality disorders.

Simplistic solutions such as government guaranteed loans or blanket prohibition of collection measures have been proposed, but have received little general support. Marginal gains are being made in some areas through extended counselling facilities, and poor people's credit unions. However, there is one approach which has received too little attention. This involves the use of the same system which has been so effective in the middle-income segment of the consumer credit market: the banking system.

The Canadian banking system is ideally suited to play a major role in providing needed credit and credit counselling to low-income Canadians. The chartered banks have branches throughout the country, including areas in which large concentrations of low-income Canadians are found. They have developed expertise in consumer credit marketing which could be employed in the service of low-income Canadians. They have the ability to make credit available to poor people for provident purposes, at rates which do not escalate the repayment obligations of low-income borrowers.

The chartered banks have had for years and continue to have a preferred position in the economic structure of Canada. If Canadians are to be subjected to the disadvantages of a highly-concentrated banking system they should be entitled to expect that the strengths of that system be used to deal with a major social problem, the solutions to which are not otherwise available. The same demands can be made of credit unions in areas of Canada where strong centralised credit union movements exist.

• • •

(4) The role of bankruptcy law

Canadian federal legislators have been much slower, or more reluctant, than their counterparts in the United States to recognise that bankruptcy law is an important aspect of any legal structure designed to regulate the consumer credit market. It was not until 1966 that federal bankruptcy law could be viewed as having anything but theoretical significance for over-committed credit consumers. While technically a consumer had the right to seek relief through bankruptcy law, in practice he was barred from doing so unless he could acquire sufficient funds to pay the charges of a private trustee.

At the urging of provincial legislators, the Federal Parliament enacted in 1966 amendments to the Bankruptcy Act under which an over-committed debtor can get an order barring his unsecured creditors from pursuing collection remedies in return for an undertaking on his part to pay a set portion of his income to an administrator. The amounts paid by the debtor are distributed *pro rata* to his creditors. This system is, of course, not a substitute for regular bankruptcy, nor is it available to all Canadians. It provides no relief to the debtor who is unable to pay his debts in full over a short period of time. No discharge of debts is permitted.

A far more significant step was taken by the Federal Government in 1972 when the decision was made to provide at small cost public trustees who would manage low-income consumer bankruptcies. For the first time in Canadian history, all Canadians were given the opportunity to get relief which until then had been available only to insolvent business enterprises or to persons who could obtain further credit.

It is clear, however, that the Federal Government has not accepted the view that a discharge should be easily obtained by an over-committed consumer. Government officials view with undisguised horror the volume of consumer bankruptcies in the United States, and tenaciously adhere to the belief that sound economics and moral precepts dictate that consumers not be given the opportunity to escape debt obligations without significant sacrifice. The position of the federal government in this regard was embodied in proposed legislation presented to Parliament in 1965, but not enacted at that time. It is likely that very similar proposals will be enacted in 1978.

Under the federal proposals an over-committed consumer debtor would have available three possible courses, depending upon his circumstances: straight bankruptcy, an arrangement by way of extension or an arrangement by way of composition. An arrangement by way of extension is a rough equivalent of the pro-rating scheme embodied in the existing Act. No discharge is permitted since full payment of the debtor's obligations is contemplated. An arrangement by way of composition is a hybrid of straight bankruptcy and extension. An insolvent debtor who enters this scheme is required to make payments to his creditors for a three or four year period at the end of which he obtains discharge from his debts. No debtor can be required to choose an arrangement by way of extension or composition rather than straight bankruptcy, but he is given incentives to do so. The primary incentive is that the debtor need not surrender property exempt from seizure under execution if he chooses an arrangement. If, however, he chooses straight bankruptcy, or is forced into straight bankruptcy because his lack of adequate income renders him ineligible for an arrangement or because his creditors have rejected his proposal for a composition, he must surrender all property in excess of a total value of $3,000. In effect, he would lose the right which he has under existing law to retain his provincial exemptions and at the same time obtain a discharge of his debts.

This feature of the federal proposals has induced a great deal of opposition from provincial legislators and consumer advocates living in provinces where exemptions are liberal. Most take the position that, in effect, low-income consumers who have modest equities in their homes will be denied bankruptcy relief since they are unlikely to surrender their homes in order to get discharged from their debts. The public policy basis for the federal proposals is very simple: it is not just and equitable that a bankrupt debtor should be able to withhold from his creditors property of any substantial value. It remains to be seen whether or not the Canadian Parliament will adopt the commercial puritanisms represented by this policy.

Note: For further discussions of the problems of consumer bankruptcies and over-indebtedness, see Canadian Welfare Council, *Consumer Credit and the Lower Income Family* (1970); Claude Masse, Ejan Mackaay, and Jean Hérard, *Vivre ou Exister?*, Étude de l'efficacité sociale des programmes juridiques d'aide aux débiteurs surendettés (Univ. de Montréal, 1974); and J. Ziegel, ``Consumer Bankruptcies'' (1972) 20 Chitty's LJ 325. Current statistics on consumer bankruptcies and Part X proceedings will be found in *Insolvency Bulletin* published by the Office of the Superintendent of Bankruptcy, Dept. of Cons. and Corp. Affairs, Ottawa. Consumer bankruptcies have grown rapidly in Canada in recent years and there were 21,025 such bankruptcies in 1980.

APPENDIX

Forms of Agreement and Conditions of Sale*

1. Westinghouse Canada Inc., General Conditions of Sale (Domestic Contracts).

2. Westinghouse Canada Inc., General Conditions of Sale (Export Contracts).

3. Standard Form of Motor Vehicle Sales Agreement for use in Ontario — sponsored by The Automobile Dealers Association of Ontario.

4. Canadian Imperial Bank of Commerce, Chattel Mortgage Agreement.

5. John Deere Limited, Purchaser's Statement — Industrial.

6. John Deere Limited, Security Agreement — Inventory: Consumer Products.

7. Canadian Imperial Bank of Commerce, General Assignment of Accounts.

8. Canadian Imperial Bank of Commerce, Pledge Agreement.

9. Canadian Imperial Bank of Commerce, Conditional Sale Agreement.

---

* Several of the forms have had to be reduced in size to accommodate them to the size of the casebook pages.

Form 1

GENERAL CONDITIONS OF SALE

Westinghouse Canada Inc.

1. WARRANTY

Where the product sold by the Company is also manufactured by the Company, the Company warrants the product supplied hereunder to be of the kind designated or specified. Unless otherwise expressly agreed in writing, the Company shall repair or replace any defective part or parts, f.o.b. the Company's plant or warehouse, which prove to be defective under normal and proper use within one year from the date of shipment provided that the Purchaser gives the Company immediate written notice of any such defect or defects. On expiration of the Warranty period, any liability of the Company shall terminate.

Where the product sold by the Company is not also manufactured by the Company, it is the product of a reputable manufacturer sold under that manufacturer's brand or trade name and the Company warrants that it will fulfill the same warranty obligations as it receives from the manufacturer.

The applicable Warranty expressed in this paragraph constitutes the only Warranty of the Company and no other warranty or condition, statutory or otherwise, shall be implied.

2. TITLE

The title to the product or any part thereof shall pass from the Company as soon as all payments due have been fully made in cash, except as otherwise expressly stipulated herein. The said product shall be and remain personal property, notwithstanding its mode of attachment to realty or other property. If default is made in any of the payments herein, the Company may retain any partial payments which have been made, as liquidated damages, and the Company shall be entitled to the immediate possession of the product and shall be free to enter the premises where the product may be located and remove it as the Company's property, without prejudice to the Company's right to recover any further expenses or damages the Company may suffer by reason of such non-payment. Notwithstanding the terms hereof, risk will pass to the purchaser at point of delivery.

3. FORCE MAJEURE

The Company shall not be responsible or liable for any loss, damage, detention or delay caused by war, invasion, insurrection, riot, the order of any civil or military authority, or by fire, flood, weather or other acts of the elements, breakdown, lockouts, strikes or labour disputes, the failure of the Company's suppliers to meet their contractual obligations, or, without limitation of the foregoing, any other cause beyond the reasonable control of the Company and the receiving of the product by the Purchaser shall constitute a waiver of all claims for loss or damage due to delay.

4. PATENTS

The Company agrees that it will at its own expense defend all actions or proceedings instituted against the Purchaser and pay any award of damages assessed against the Purchaser in such actions or proceedings, insofar as the same are based on any claim that the said product or any part thereof constitutes an infringement of any claim of a Canadian patent, other than a claim covering a process or a product thereof, provided the Purchaser gives the Company immediate notice in writing of the institution of the actions or proceedings and permits the Company through its Counsel to defend the same and gives the Company all needed information, assistance and authority to enable the Company so to do. In case such product is in such action held to constitute infringement, and its use is enjoined, the Company, within a reasonable time, will either secure for the Purchaser the right to continue using said product by suspension of the injunction, by procuring for the Purchaser a license or otherwise, or will at its own expense, replace such product with non-infringing product or modify it so that it becomes non-infringing or remove the said enjoined product and refund the sums paid therefor.

5. PRICES, TAXES AND PAYMENTS

The prices quoted are based on Government taxes, or regulations in force at the date of this proposal, and such prices are subject to increase or decrease in accordance with any changes in taxes made prior to delivery of the product. All payments shall be in Canadian dollars. In case partial shipments are made at different times, pro-rata payments shall be made therefor. If shipments of the product herein specified, or any material part thereof, are delayed from any cause for which the Purchaser is directly or indirectly responsible, the date of completion of the product by the Company shall be regarded as the date of shipment in determining when payments for said product are to be made, and the Company shall be entitled to receive reasonable compensation for storing the completed product which shall be held at Purchaser's risk. The Purchaser agrees that should any of the payments not be made to the Company when due under the terms of this proposal, then a service charge on such overdue payments shall be billed by the Company and paid by the Purchaser until the price including service charges, has been fully paid in cash, but this shall not be construed as obligating the Company to grant any extension of time in the terms of payment. The minimum billing on any order shall be $25.00.

6. DELIVERY

Unless otherwise expressly agreed in writing, delivery of the product will be made f.o.b. the Company's plant or warehouse. Delivery dates herein specified are subject to prior sale of manufacturing and engineering space and to the receipt of all information necessary to allow maintenance of the Company's engineering and manufacturing schedules.

7. LIMITATION OF LIABILITY

Notwithstanding any other provision in this contract or any applicable statutory provisions, neither the Company nor the Purchaser shall be liable to the other for special or consequential damages or damages for loss of use arising directly or indirectly from any breach of this contract, fundamental or otherwise or from any tortious acts or omissions of their respective employees or agents and in no event shall the liability of the Company exceed the unit price of the defective product or of the product subject to late delivery.

8. DEFINITION

The term "Company" shall be deemed to include Westinghouse Canada Inc. or its associate or subsidiary companies as the case may be.

9. AGREEMENT

This proposal, providing it is accepted within 30 days (or such time as may otherwise be expressly agreed), shall constitute the entire agreement between the parties and there are no other agreements or understandings, either written or oral, to conflict with, alter or enlarge this agreement unless agreed to in writing between the parties subsequent to the date of acceptance of the proposal. Acceptance is subject to approval of the Purchaser's credit by the Company. Notwithstanding such acceptance and/or approval, if in the Company's judgment the Purchaser's financial condition does not at any time warrant the continuation of production or shipment on the original terms, the Company reserves the right to request payment in advance.

Purchaser Reference .... Company Reference .... Page ....

FORM 1124-2   REV. 5-80

Form 2

Westinghouse Canada Inc.

GENERAL CONDITIONS OF SALE

1. WARRANTY

Where the product sold by Westinghouse Canada Inc. (the Company) is also manufactured by the Company, the Company warrants the product supplied hereunder to be of the kind designated or specified. Unless otherwise expressly agreed in writing, the Company shall repair or replace any defective part or parts, Ex Works, with freight prepaid and allowed as for the original equipment, which parts prove to be defective under normal and proper use within 12 months of normal operation or 18 months from the date of shipment from the plant (whichever is earlier) provided that the Purchaser gives the Company immediate written notice of any such defect or defects. The above warranty does not apply to products which have a life under normal use of less than the 12 month period referred to above. On expiration of the Warranty period, any liability of the Company shall terminate.

Where the product sold by the Company is not also manufactured by the Company, it is the product of a reputable manufacturer sold under that manufacturer's brand or trade name and the Company warrants that it will fulfill the same warranty obligations as it receives from the manufacturer.

The applicable Warranty expressed in this paragraph constitutes the only Warranty of the Company and no other warranty or condition, statutory or otherwise, shall be implied.

2. DELIVERY AND TITLE

A. Delivery dates refer to the estimated dates by which the products will be ready for shipment at the Company's plant or the plants of its suppliers. These dates are based on the prompt receipt by the Company of the Purchaser's order together with all supporting documentation and information required for manufacturing to commence and to continue without interruption. Such supporting documentation and information required along with the Purchaser's order includes the letter of credit, payment deposit and the engineering data necessary to proceed with the order.

Delivery dates are subject to prior sale of engineering and manufacturing space and will be confirmed on acceptance of the Purchaser's contract.

B. When the product or any part thereof is ready for delivery and the contemplated shipment is deferred either at the request of the Purchaser, or due to any other circumstance beyond the control of the Company, the Company may, unless other agreement is made with the Purchaser, ship such product or parts by moving them to storage for the Purchaser's account and risk, with all charges and expenses thereby incurred for the account of the Purchaser. Such shipment shall constitute delivery of the product and thereby qualify for any payments due on shipment or delivery.

C. Risk of loss shall pass to the Purchaser upon delivery Ex Works of the Company or its supplier including delivery into storage as covered in 2B. However, title shall not pass until due payment of the price and storage charges have been received by the Company.

3. FORCE MAJEURE

The Company shall not be liable for loss or damage due to delay in manufacture or delivery resulting from any cause beyond the Company's reasonable control or due to compliance with any regulations, orders, acts, instructions or priority requests of any Federal, Provincial or Municipal Government, or any department or agency thereof or any civil or military authority, or due to acts of God, acts or omissions of the Purchaser, fires, floods, weather, strikes, lockouts, factory shutdowns or alterations, faulty castings or forgings, embargoes, wars, riots, delays or shortages in transportation or inability to obtain labour, manufacturing facilities or material from the Company's usual sources and any delay

resulting from any such cause shall extend delivery dates to the extent caused thereby. The Purchaser's receiving of the product shall constitute a waiver of any claims for delay.

4. EXPORT AND IMPORT LICENCES

If an export permit is required, the Company, as agent for the Purchaser will, upon receipt from the Purchaser of all necessary information, submit an application to the appropriate government authorities. The Purchaser shall be responsible for any required import licence. The obligation of the Purchaser to pay for the product shall not be waived by the delay or failure to secure or renew any required export or import licence or by the cancellation thereof.

5. PRICES, PACKING, TESTS AND TAXES

A. All prices are on the quotation quantities and, unless otherwise specified, are in Canadian funds Ex Works of the Company or its supplier.

B. Charges for packing as normally supplied by the Company for the method of shipment specified, are included in the price. Any additional charges for special packing will be for the account of the Purchaser.

C. Tests required by the Purchaser other than those normally performed by the Company in accordance with industry practices, will be for the Purchaser's account.

D. The payment of all present and future taxes, duties, corporate income taxes, tariffs, fees and other charges, including, but not limited to, excise, import, purchase, sales, use, turnover, added value, consular, gross receipts, gross wages and similar assessments imposed by the Purchaser's government (or the government of any country through which the product must pass en route to the country of destination) or any subdivision thereof or any taxing authority or any agencies therein with respect to this order or the subject matter thereof, shall be the obligation of the Purchaser. Any such items paid by the Company shall be added to the price and the Purchaser shall reimburse the Company for the amount of such taxes, duties, tariffs, fees and other charges and expenses incidental thereto upon presentation of an invoice therefor. Any taxes or other charges imposed by the Government of Canada or its authorized agencies in connection with the manufacture of the goods will be for the account of the Company.

6. TERMS OF PAYMENT

Unless otherwise stated in writing, payment shall be made by an irrevocable Letter of Credit, in Canadian funds, in a form acceptable to the Company and confirmed by a Canadian chartered bank. The Letter of Credit shall be established by the Purchaser in the Company's favour at the time of issue of his order and shall remain in effect until all payments due under the terms of the order, including but not limited to escalation payments, as accepted are completed. The Letter of Credit shall make provision for sea and/or air shipment, transhipment, pro rata payments for partial shipment and other payment terms as contained in the accepted order. All costs incidental to the establishment of the Letter of Credit and the confirming of the same shall be for the Purchaser's account. If the products are stored as detailed in Paragraph 2, (Delivery and Title), payment shall be due upon completion of manufacture and certification of completion issued by the Company. If any of the payments are not made to the Company when due under the terms of the agreement, then a service charge on such overdue payments shall be billed by the Company at the rate then in effect and paid by the Purchaser until the price including service charges has been fully paid but this shall not be construed as obligating the Company to grant any extension of time in the terms of payment.

(Continued on reverse side)

Purchaser Reference ....   Company Reference ....   Page ....

Form 1748-CA Rev. 5-80

Form 3

	DAY	MONTH	YEAR
CONDITIONS ON BACK FORM PART OF THIS CONTRACT			

(NAME OF DEALER)

PURCHASER				ADDRESS			APT.NO.
CITY		PROV.	POSTAL CODE	RES. PHONE	OCCUPATION		
EMPLOYER				ADDRESS		BUS. PHONE	

If new vehicle is sold herein the prices shown in this section are the manufacturers suggested retail prices of basic vehicle and optional extras.

I/WE HEREBY OFFER TO PURCHASE FROM THE ABOVE DEALER, THE FOLLOWING VEHICLE ON THE TERMS AND CONDITIONS HEREIN SET FORTH, INCLUDING THE CONDITIONS ON THE BACK HEREOF.

	NEW USED DEMO	YEAR	MAKE	MODEL NAME	MODEL NO.	COLOUR
	TRIM	TOP	SERIAL NO.		LIC. NO.	STOCK NO.

OPT.	OPTIONAL EQUIP.	LIST PRICE
	BASIC VEHICLE	

IF DEMONSTRATOR WARRANTY TIME IS MEASURED FROM   19   ODOMETER READING   KM ☐ / MI ☐   PURCHASER'S INITIAL

| A REPLACEMENT MOTOR VEHICLE PERMIT TRANSFER CANNOT BE OBTAINED WITHOUT A SAFETY STANDARDS CERTIFICATE PURSUANT TO THE HIGHWAY TRAFFIC ACT. | THE VEHICLE HEREIN WILL BE DELIVERED WITH AN "UNFIT VEHICLE PERMIT" AND THE PURCHASER IS RESPONSIBLE FOR REMOVING THE VEHICLE AND FOR TRANSFERRING THE UNFIT MOTOR VEHICLE PERMIT AT HIS OWN COST. ☐ | THE VEHICLE HEREIN WILL BE DELIVERED AT THE PRICE HEREIN STATED WITH A SAFETY STANDARDS CERTIFICATE ☐   NO. _____ | WARRANTY | YES ☐ NO ☐ |

TRADE-IN DESCRIPTION & LIEN DISCLOSURE

TERMS OF SETTLEMENT

YEAR	MAKE	MODEL		TOTAL SALE PRICE	
LICENSE NO.	YR. OF ISSUE	ENGINE NO.		TRADE-IN ALLOWANCE	
SERIAL NO.		ODOMETER READING KM ☐ MI ☐		NET DIFFERENCE	
WAS VEHICLE PREVIOUSLY USED AS A TAXICAB?	☐ YES ☐ NO		SALES TAX	
WAS VEHICLE PREVIOUSLY USED AS A POLICE CRUISER?	☐ YES ☐ NO		LICENSE FEE	
NET AMOUNT OF LIEN OWED TO			GASOLINE	
LAST REGISTERED OWNER			RUST INHIBITOR TYPE........	
ADDRESS	OWNER'S SIGNATURE		PAYOUT LIEN ON TRADE-IN	

CUSTOMER INFORMATION

NAME OF INSURANCE COMPANY		**BALANCE DUE**	
POLICY NO.	EXPIRY DATE	DEPOSIT CASH ☐ CHEQUE ☐	
NAME OF AGENT	TELEPHONE NO.	**PAYABLE ON DELIVERY**	
DRIVER'S LICENSE NO.	EXPIRY DATE	BALANCE FINANCED SUBJECT TO APPROVAL	
REMARKS		LIFE/DISABILITY INS. (IF REQUESTED)	
		COLLISION INS. (IF REQUIRED)	
		REGISTRATION FEE (IF NECESSARY)	
		NET AMOUNT TO BE FINANCED	

TOTAL MANUFACTURER'S SUGGESTED RETAIL PRICE	$

CONDITIONS OF SALE

COST OF BORROWING   %

1. ODOMETER READING: The dealer does not warrant or guarantee the odometer reading of any used motor vehicle sold herein and makes only such disclosure as is required under the Motor Vehicle Dealers Act and Regulations thereunder.

| FREIGHT | | TOTAL BALANCE DUE | $ |
| PRE-DELIVERY EXPENSE | | AMOUNT OF PAYMENTS | NO. OF PAYMENTS |

2. ACKNOWLEDGEMENT OF CONDITIONS: The purchaser acknowledges having read the conditions printed on the reverse side hereof and   (continued on back ➞)

TOTAL	$	PAYMENTS START ON

CREDIT APPROVAL

| DISCOUNT (IF APPLICABLE) | |

THIS ORDER IS NOT BINDING UNLESS ACCEPTED BY AN AUTHORIZED OFFICIAL OF THE DEALER.

ANY FINANCE INFORMATION PROVIDED IS IN ACCORDANCE WITH THE CONSUMER PROTECTION ACT R.S.O.

| TOTAL SALE PRICE | $ |

The vendor warrants that the pollution control equipment on the vehicle sold is intact and operative.
The said purchase to be for the price as hereinafter set forth and shall include the transfer to you of my used vehicle if any, as described above, which said used vehicle I warrant to be free of all encumbrances, except as herein disclosed.
The undersigned purchaser warrants all information supplied herein to be true and that the pollution control equipment on the vehicle traded in is intact and operative.

VENDOR'S ACCEPTANCE	DEALER REG. NO.	REGISTRATION NO.
DATE		
	ACCEPTOR'S REG. NO.	SALESMAN'S NAME (PLEASE PRINT)
NAME OF OFFICIAL (PLEASE PRINT)	PURCHASER'S SIGNATURE VOID	
SIGNATURE	TITLE	SALESMAN'S SIGNATURE
	CO-SIGNER (IF ANY)	

VCA-201-5(1/81)

▼ (INFORMATION BELOW THIS LINE IS NOT PART OF THE CONTRACT) ▼

CONDITIONS (Continued)

agrees that the same are hereby incorporated by reference and shall constitute part of this agreement as fully as if printed on the face of the agreement and above the Purchaser's signature.

WARRANTIES

3.   There are no warranties or representations by the dealer with respect to the motor vehicle described herein or affecting the rights of the parties, other than those set out in any applicable legislation and in the case of a new motor vehicle, provided in the new car warranty given by the manufacturer and/or the dealer. No other warranty agreement or representation made hereto, nor any modification hereof, shall be binding upon the dealer or his assigns unless endorsed hereon in writing.

TITLE

4.   The title and right of property in the said motor vehicle shall not pass to the purchaser until the entire purchase price is paid in full and the purchaser agrees to pay to the dealer upon delivery of the said motor vehicle, in addition to the applicable amounts set out on the reverse hereof, amounts equal to all increases in federal and provincial taxes payable in respect of the vehicle or this transaction due to the imposition of new taxes or increases in applicable tax rates, between the date hereof and delivery of the vehicle to the purchaser. In the event that a financing contract cannot be arranged by reason of any default or misrepresentation by the purchaser, then the entire purchase price shall forthwith become due and payable.

DEFAULT IN PAYMENT

5.   In the event that the Purchaser shall make default in any payment due hereunder then the entire purchase price shall forthwith become due and payable and subject to the provisions of The Conditional Sales Act and The Consumer Protection Act the dealer or his assigns shall have the right to repossess and resell the motor vehicle by private sale or by public auction, without notice to the purchaser and to that end shall have the right to make whatever repairs are deemed necessary. Such a repossession and resale shall not affect the dealer's right to retain all payments made theretofore as liquidated damages and not as a penalty.

CANCELLATION OF AGREEMENT

6.   It is mutually understood and agreed that in the event of this agreement being cancelled by mutual consent, the dealer shall forthwith return the deposit, if any, and any used motor vehicle which has been taken in exchange as part payment of purchase price sold by the dealer prior to such cancellation, shall be accounted for by the dealer at the trade-in allowance as shown on the face of the agreement.

DELIVERY BY DEALER

7.   It is mutually understood and agreed that where the motor vehicle herein described, is a new motor vehicle, and the dealer is unable to make delivery within three months of the date of the contract, the dealer shall forthwith notify the purchaser on expiration of the three month period and,
   (i)   The agreement may be extended within 5 days of notification by mutual consent to be evidenced in writing or,
   (ii) The 5 day period referred in sub(i) has expired or on express notification by either party, the agreement may be cancelled and the dealer shall forthwith return the deposit if any, and the motor vehicle given as a trade, to the purchaser and such return shall operate as a full release of all claims. Where the motor vehicle given as a trade has been sold by the dealer, the purchaser, on cancellation shall be entitled to recover only the amount set out on the agreement as a trade-in allowance.

ACCEPTANCE BY PURCHASER

8.   It is mutually understood and agreed that where the purchaser fails to accept delivery of the motor vehicle within seven days of the date of mailing of a notice from the dealer of the availability of the vehicle for delivery the agreement may be cancelled by the dealer and all moneys paid as a deposit, including any motor vehicle taken in exchange, may be retained by the dealer as liquidated damages and not as a penalty. The said notice is to be sent by prepaid registered mail addressed to the Purchaser's last known address.

TRADE-IN VEHICLE

9.   It is mutually understood and agreed that any motor vehicle given in exchange or as part payment towards the purchase price of the motor vehicle sold herein shall be equipped and in the same condition, reasonable wear and tear only excepted, at the time of delivery for acceptance of the said motor vehicle as it was at the date hereon and any repairs prior to delivery but after the date hereon shall be the sole responsibility of the purchaser.

LIENS ON PURCHASED VEHICLE

10. The purchaser shall not hereafter cause or permit any charge, lien or encumbrance whether possessory or otherwise, to exist against the said motor vehicle until the purchase price has been paid in full.

INSURANCE

11. It is expressly agreed that the dealer is not responsible and in no way guarantees the provision of insurance coverage of any kind for the said motor vehicle, but may, if so requested, assist the purchaser in obtaining insurance coverage for the said motor vehicle.

MANUFACTURER'S SUGGESTED RETAIL PRICE

12. In the event that an increase in the manufacturer's suggested retail price occurs after this agreement is signed, the increase shall be added to the original purchase price. In the event that the purchaser refuses to pay the increased purchase price the dealer shall elect either to waive the increase or to cancel this agreement and return the deposit.

Form 4

(For use in all Provinces except Alberta, Quebec and British Columbia)   BL 36-76

CANADIAN IMPERIAL BANK OF COMMERCE — CHATTEL MORTGAGE

THIS INDENTURE made the   day of   , 19   between

Insert full name of mortgagor if given under trade style or if by individual(s) use first given name followed by second given name, if any, then surname (last name).

| (Full names) | Date of Birth | | | Sex |
| | Day | Month | Year | M/F |

ADDRESS: Street number and name, apt. no. if any, OR lot, concession and township   City, Town or Village (and rural route if any)   Prov./State

(herein called "the Mortgagor") and CANADIAN IMPERIAL BANK OF COMMERCE,

...., (herein called "the Mortgagee").
                                                    Address of Personal Loan Department

Whereas the Mortgagor is indebted to the Mortgagee by reason of a loan for which the Mortgagee holds a Note made by the Mortgagor in favour of the Mortgagee, a copy of which appears in Schedule A hereto;

And Whereas it was a term of the said loan that the Mortgagor would execute and deliver this Mortgage as collateral security for the due payment of such indebtedness;

Insert Proceeds Amount of loan in Figures. **Witnesseth** that in consideration of the premises and the sum of $ (receipt whereof is hereby acknowledged) the Mortgagor doth hereby grant, bargain, sell and assign unto the Mortgagee the following goods and chattels (herein called "the Property"):

Cross out if not applicable and have initialled.

New or Used	Model No.	Manufacturer and Description of Goods	Serial No.	Motor No. (If Motor Vehicle)	License No. (If Motor Vehicle)

Cross out if not applicable and have initialled.

and all household goods and chattels which are now or may hereafter be located in, upon or about the following premises namely
.... or any other premises to which the Mortgagor may remove the same or any part thereof and, without limiting the generality of the foregoing, the following:

To Have and to Hold the same unto the Mortgagee to and for its sole and only use forever.

Insert the Gross Amount of the Note in Figures **Provided** that if the Mortgagor shall pay unto the Mortgagee in lawful money of Canada the full sum of .... Dollars in accordance with the provisions for payment contained in Schedule A hereto and any other moneys hereby secured, then these presents shall be void;

The Mortgagor doth put the Mortgagee in full possession of the Property by delivering to it this indenture in the name of all the Property at the sealing and delivery hereof.

The Mortgagor hereby covenants with the Mortgagee:

1.   THAT except as disclosed by Mortgagor's application for said loan he exclusively possesses and owns the Property free and clear of all encumbrances and will warrant and defend the Property against the Mortgagor and against all and every other person or persons whomsoever;

2.   THAT the Mortgagor will pay to the Mortgagee all moneys hereby secured as and when the same shall become due and payable and will observe and perform all covenants, terms and provisions contained in this Mortgage;

3.   THAT the Mortgagee may pay off in whole or in part any lien, encumbrance, contract, debt, charge or encumbrance claimed, whether validly or not, in respect of the Property or any part thereof and may pay any amount which in its sole discretion it may consider requisite to secure possession of the Property with or without litigation or to compromise and settle any litigation in respect of the Property or the possession thereof; and all amounts so paid by the Mortgagee together with all expenses of the Mortgagee in connection with any such payment shall be secured hereby and shall forthwith be due and payable by the Mortgagor to the Mortgagee;

4.   THAT the Mortgagor will not sell, pledge, encumber, dispose of or part with possession of the Property or any part thereof without the written consent of the Mortgagee and shall keep the same free and clear of all taxes, assessments, claims, liens and encumbrances and shall promptly notify the Mortgagee of any loss of or damage to the said Property;

5.   THAT the Mortgagor will keep the Property insured in accordance with the reasonable requirements of the Mortgagee and that the proceeds of any insurance will be paid by the Mortgagor to the Mortgagee; and upon default the Mortgagee may effect the insurance and charge it to the Mortgagor;

6.   THAT should the Mortgagor fail to repay when due any sum hereby secured or fail to observe or perform any covenant, term or provision hereof, or should the Mortgagor become bankrupt or insolvent or should any proceedings be taken by or against the Mortgagor under any Act now or hereafter in force for bankrupt or insolvent debtors, or should the Mortgagor without the consent of the Mortgagee sell or dispose of or encumber or in any way part with possession of the Property or any part thereof or attempt to do any of the foregoing, or should the Mortgagee at any time during the currency of these presents feel unsafe or insecure or deem the Property or any part thereof in danger of being sold or removed (of each of which contingencies the Mortgagee shall be the sole judge) then and in any and every such case the Mortgagee may enter into and upon the lands and premises wheresoever and whatsoever where the Property or any part thereof may be and take possession of the same. In the event that the Property is so repossessed and is not thereafter redeemed in the manner and within the period, if any, prescribed by law, the Mortgagee may sell all or part of the Property at any time and from time to time by public auction or by private sale, and either for cash or credit or part cash and part credit as to the Mortgagee may seem best, and out of the proceeds of such sale to pay and reimburse itself for all moneys secured and all such reasonable expenses of retaking, holding, repairing, processing, preparing for disposition and disposing of the Property, including reasonable solicitor's costs and legal expenses, as may have been incurred by the Mortgagee in the protection and taking possession of the Property or in consequence of the Mortgagor's action or default, and in the event of a sale on credit or for part cash and part credit the Mortgagee shall not be accountable for or charged with any moneys until actually received in cash. PROVIDED nevertheless that it shall not be incumbent upon the Mortgagee to sell or dispose of the Property or any part thereof, but in case of any such action, default, neglect or failure by the Mortgagor as aforesaid or upon the occurrence of any of the events aforesaid, or of any default by the Mortgagor hereunder, the Mortgagee may, subject to any applicable law, peaceably take, hold, use, occupy, possess and enjoy the Property or any part thereof without the let, molestation, eviction, hindrance or interruption of the Mortgagor or any other person whomsoever;

7.   THAT any provision of this Indenture prohibited by the law of any province shall, as to that province, be ineffective to the extent of such prohibition without invalidating the remaining provisions hereof;

8.   THAT in the event of the Mortgagee taking possession of the Property or any part thereof, the Mortgagee may maintain the same upon the premises on which the same may then be situated and for such purpose shall be entitled to the free use and enjoyment of all necessary buildings, premises and accommodation, and the Mortgagor covenants and agrees to provide the same without cost or expense to the Mortgagee.

AND IT IS AGREED:

(a) THAT each part of the Property whether severable or not, shall stand charged with the whole of the moneys hereby secured and that no person shall have any right to require that the said moneys shall be apportioned;

(b) THAT the Mortgagee may from time to time discharge any part or parts of the Property for such consideration as it may think proper, or without consideration if it sees fit, and no such discharge shall diminish or prejudice the security as against the Property remaining undischarged or against any person whomsoever;

(c) THAT the said loan and any other indebtedness hereunder shall be secured hereby notwithstanding any new transactions between the parties by way of further loans, discounts or advances or the deposit or withdrawal of moneys by the Mortgagor or the crediting or debiting of amounts in any account of the Mortgagor;

(d) THAT this Mortgage shall not operate by way of merger of any indebtedness of the Mortgagor to the Mortgagee or any contract by which the same may now or at any time hereafter be represented or evidenced, and that no judgment recovered by the Mortgagee shall operate by way of merger of this Mortgage or in any way affect the security hereby created.

This Indenture shall extend to, bind and enure to the benefit of the respective heirs, executors, administrators, successors and assigns of the parties hereto, and where there is more than one Mortgagor or there is a female party the provisions hereof shall be read with all grammatical changes thereby rendered necessary; and where there is more than one Mortgagor the covenants shall be deemed to be joint and several.

In Witness Whereof the Mortgagor has hereunto set his hand and seal, on the day, month and year first set forth above.
SIGNED, SEALED AND DELIVERED

.... VOID .... VOID ....(SEAL)

.... VOID ....(SEAL)

SCHEDULE A
COMMERCE BANKPLAN NOTE

CANADIAN IMPERIAL BANK OF COMMERCE

.... 19....
(Place and date)

FOR VALUE RECEIVED I promise to pay to Canadian Imperial Bank of Commerce at

....
(Insert address of P. L. Dept.)

Information to be inserted to be copied from note.

the sum of $..................... (being the total of my Bankplan Loan and the Cost of Borrowing thereof) in monthly instalments as follows: the sum of $................. on .... 19.... and the sum of $.................. on the same day of each month thereafter to and including.............................. 19....; and upon default in payment of any instalment upon the due date thereof all remaining instalments (less the portion of the Cost of Borrowing included in such remaining instalments) shall forthwith become due and payable without notice. All amounts in arrear under this Note shall bear interest at the rate of............% per annum until paid.

AND I HEREBY AGREE with Canadian Imperial Bank of Commerce (herein called "the Bank") as follows:

1.   During the currency of my Bankplan Loan I will not obtain any loan elsewhere without first informing the Bank.
2.   The Bank may make application (to which I hereby expressly consent) to The Canada Life Assurance Company for insurance on my life, such insurance to be owned by and payable to the Bank and to be effective as and from the date hereof and on such terms and conditions as may be agreed between the Bank and such insurer, but the amount thereof shall not exceed the amount first mentioned above.
3.   The principal amount of my Bankplan Loan is $..................... and the Cost of Borrowing in relation thereto is

Information to be inserted to be copied from note.

$..................... which, expressed as a nominal annual percentage rate is............% per annum.
4.   Each payment hereunder shall be applied first in payment of the Cost of Borrowing accrued to the due date of such payment, secondly in payment of interest as aforesaid on any amount in arrear and thereafter in reduction of my Bankplan Loan.
5.   All statements of fact contained in the form of application for my Bankplan Loan are true and complete and were made for the purpose of obtaining such Loan, and such application includes the express representation that I am not being sued, that no judgment is outstanding against me and that I am not indebted to any other lender except as shown in the said application.

AFFIDAVIT OF BONA FIDES — FOR USE IN ATLANTIC PROVINCES, MANITOBA AND SASKATCHEWAN

CANADA: I,..of the.............
Province of..........   of.......................................in the Province
                        of.....................................make oath and say:
TO WIT:

1.   That I am an employee of Canadian Imperial Bank of Commerce, a Corporation, the Mortgagee in the accompanying Bill of Sale by way of Mortgage named, and I am aware of all the circumstances connected with the said Bill of Sale by way of Mortgage, and have a personal knowledge of all the facts herein deposed to.
2.   That the amount set forth in the said Bill of Sale by way of Mortgage as being the consideration therefor is a present advance being made by the said Mortgagee to the Mortgagor therein named.
3.   That the said Bill of Sale by way of Mortgage was executed in good faith and for the purpose of securing to the said Mortgagee the payment of such amount and not for the mere purpose of protecting the goods and chattels therein mentioned against the creditors of the said Mortgagor or for the purpose of preventing such creditors from recovering any claims which they have against the said Mortgagor.

SWORN before me at the........... of........... }
in the Province of................................... }
this............day of.............A.D. 19....... }

....
A Commissioner, etc.

AFFIDAVIT OF EXECUTION

(a) Insert name of County or Judicial District if there be such.

CANADA: I,.....................................of the....................
Province of.........   of.............................. in the....................
(a)   of .... ,
TO WIT: make oath and say: (occupation)
             That I was personally present and did see the within Bill of Sale by way of Mortgage duly signed, sealed and

(b) Insert name(s) of Mortgagor(s) and "One of", "two of", etc., as case may be.

executed by (b)...
the parties thereto, and that the name "..............................." set and subscribed
as a witness to the execution thereof is in my handwriting, and that the same was executed at the....................
of....................in the....................of....................on the....................
day of................A.D. 19....

(c) The Official style of the person before whom the affidavit is sworn should be inserted here.

SWORN before me at the..................... }
of (a).................................. }
in the Province of......................... }
this............day of............A.D. 19.... }

....
(c) A Commissioner, etc.

I hereby acknowledge receipt of a copy of this Chattel Mortgage following its execution this...............................

day of........................, 19.....

VOID
....

....

Form 5

PURCHASER'S STATEMENT

INDUSTRIAL

APPLICANT'S NAME

TELEPHONE NO   (BUSINESS)   (HOME)

STREET ADDRESS	TOWN	COUNTY	PROV

DATE OF BIRTH DAY	MO	YR.	AGE	MARRIED ☐ SINGLE ☐	NO. OF DEPEN-DENTS	YEARS AT ABOVE ADDRESS	IS YOUR GENERAL HEALTH GOOD?	INDIVIDUAL ☐ PARTNERSHIP ☐ CORPORATION ☐	ARE YOU ACTIVE IN THE BUSINESS?	HOW MANY YEARS IN PRESENT BUSINESS?

IS EQUIPMENT BEING PUR-CHASED FOR YOUR OWN USE?	EQUIPMENT WILL BE USED FOR ☐ EXCAVATING ☐ LOGGING ☐ BULLDOZING ☐ OTHER	AMOUNT OF COMMITMENTS ON LEASED EQUIPMENT $	NET INCOME LAST YEAR $	EST THIS YEAR $

ASSETS

(Statement as of _____ 19____)

LIABILITIES

ASSETS	$	LIABILITIES	$
Tractors, Machinery & Equipment:		Accounts Payable-Unsecured_____	
		Owe Banks-Loans & Mortgages:	
		NAME SECURED BY	
_____ Autos _____ Trucks_____			
Cash_____			
Stocks & Bonds_____		Real Estate Mortgages other than to banks:	
Notes & Accounts Receivable_____		Name_____	
Real Estate owned_____		Name_____	
Other:_____		Owe on Machinery & Equipment, Autos & Trucks:	
TOTAL ASSETS	$	**TOTAL LIABILITIES**	$

BUSINESS CREDIT REFER-ENCES	(Name and Address)
	(Name and Address)

BANK WITH _____ AT _____ ACC'T. NO. _____

FOR THE PURPOSE OF OBTAINING CREDIT FROM YOU, I(WE) AFFIRM THAT THE INFORMATION CONTAINED IN THE ABOVE STATEMENT ACCURATELY DESCRIBES MY(OUR) AFFAIRS AS OF THIS DATE. IN CONNECTION WITH THIS APPLICATION FOR CREDIT, I(WE) HEREBY CONSENT THAT JOHN DEERE LIMITED (1) CONDUCT AND/OR CAUSE TO BE CONDUCTED PERSONAL, MEDICAL AND/OR CREDIT INVESTIGATIONS, AND (2) MAKE USE OF REPORTS CONTAINING THE RESULTS OF SUCH INVESTIGATIONS IN DETERMINING WHETHER CREDIT WILL BE MADE AVAILABLE OR NOT.

DATE _____

Signed _____   Signed _____

———— DO NOT WRITE BELOW ———— THIS SECTION TO BE COMPLETED BY DEALER ————

Have you sold or leased to this customer before ?	YES ☐	No ☐	Did references report favorable payment of accounts ?	YES ☐	No ☐
Has he paid you promptly ?	YES ☐	No ☐	To the best of your knowledge is the general health	YES ☐	No ☐
Have you checked references given you by customer ?	YES ☐	No ☐	of this customer good ?		
Has customer previously financed with JDFP ?	YES ☐	No ☐			

If yes, DATE _____

DEALERSHIP NAME _____   By _____

NOTE: DETACH FROM SET BEFORE COMPLETING

END-USER CERTIFICATE UNDER THE LOGGING ITEM (411A)

IN CONSIDERATION OF BEING PERMITTED TO ENJOY THE CONDITIONAL AND PREFERRED CUSTOMS TREATMENT AFFORDED BY TARIFF ITEM 411A

I/WE _____ OF _____
        NAME OF END-USER   ADDRESS OF END-USER

HEREBY UNDERTAKE TO EMPLOY THE _____
                          NAME OF ARTICLE AND SERIAL NUMBER

IMPORTED BY ME/US OR. PURCHASED FROM _____
                                  NAME OF SELLER

OF _____ _____ 19 ____
        ADDRESS OF SELLER   DATE OF PURCHASE

STRICTLY IN ACCORDANCE WITH THE REQUIREMENTS OF THE ITEM. VIZ.. EXCLUSIVELY IN THE OPERATION OF LOGGING. SUCH OPERATION TO INCLUDE THE REMOVAL OF THE LOG FROM STUMP TO SKIDWAY LOG DUMP OR COMMON OR OTHER CARRIER. I/WE FULLY APPRECIATE AND UNDERSTAND THAT SHOULD I/WE USE THE EQUIPMENT OTHER THAN EXCLUSIVELY AS OUTLINED ABOVE. EVEN FOR A TEMPORARY OR LIMITED PERIOD. THE GOODS CEASE TO QUALIFY FOR CONTINUED TREATMENT UNDER TARIFF ITEM 411A. AND IF SUCH DIVERSION TAKES PLACE. I/WE UNDERTAKE TO AMEND THE COVERING CUSTOMS ENTRY OR TO NOTIFY THE ABOVE-MENTIONED VENDOR IN WRITING IMMEDIATELY IN ORDER THAT HE MAY ARRANGE FOR AN APPROPRIATE AMENDING ENTRY ACCOUNTING FOR THE ADDITIONAL CUSTOMS DUTY AND/OR EXCISE TAX PAYABLE. I/WE AGREE TO REPAY SAID ADDITIONAL CUSTOMS DUTY AND/OR EXCISE TAX TO THE VENDOR IMMEDIATELY UPON RECEIPT OF ADVICE OF AMOUNT PAID OR TO BE PAID BY THE VENDOR. FULL STATEMENT AS TO THE PURCHASE OR PURPOSES FOR WHICH THE ABOVE NAMED ARTICLE IS TO BE USED.

_____ 19 ____
PLACE AND DATE

VOID

SIGNATURE OF END-USER

Security Agreement/1.

SECURITY AGREEMENT - INVENTORY   CONSUMER PRODUCTS

John Deere Limited, P.O. Box 1000, Grimsby, Ontario (the "Company"), as secured party, and the undersigned Dealer, as debtor, hereby agree as follows:

1. INDEBTEDNESS SECURED

The Dealer agrees to pay to the Company, as and when due, all indebtedness which is now owed by the Dealer to the Company and all additional indebtedness hereafter incurred by the Dealer to the Company for or incident to the purchase of Goods (as defined in the John Deere Authorized Consumer Products Dealer Agreement in effect from time to time), as well as all other indebtedness which may at any time be owing by the Dealer to the Company, whether pursuant to Authorized Dealer Agreements, the Company's Dealer Terms Schedules, the Finance and Leasing Agreements, or otherwise, and whether evidenced by notes, lien notes, open accounts, or otherwise, all of which indebtedness is collectively referred to herein as "indebtedness". The John Deere Authorized Consumer Products Dealer Agreement, its supplementary Dealer Terms Schedule, the Finance and Leasing Agreements, and this Security Agreement, as subsequently amended or replaced, are sometimes hereinafter collectively referred to as the "Dealer agreements".

2. COLLATERAL

The collateral to be subject to the security interests created and provided for under this Security Agreement includes the following:

(a) The Dealer's entire stock of Goods (as defined in the John Deere Authorized Consumer Products Dealer Agreement in effect from time to time), including without limiting the generality of the foregoing, the following:

(i) complete machines,
(ii) accessories,
(iii) certain items of the John Deere Merchandise ("JDM") line, and
(iv) service, repair or replacement parts for (i), (ii) and (iii),

all of which were supplied to the Dealer by the Company and which form part of the Dealer's inventory;

(b) That portion of the Dealer's equipment inventory financed or floor planned by the Company, including without limitation:

(i) used equipment sold by the Company to the Dealer which are subject to Floor Plan Lien Notes,
(ii) used equipment sold by the Company to the Dealer which are subject to Machine Re-purchase Lien Notes, and
(iii) new or used equipment owned by the Dealer and financed by the Company under floor plan or installment lien notes, chattel mortgages or other forms of security agreement,

all of which form part of the Dealer's inventory of equipment;

all of the foregoing being collectively referred to in this Security Agreement as "collateral". Any reference to Dealer's inventory shall include all of the Dealer's presently existing inventory of collateral and that which the Dealer shall hereafter acquire, and includes collateral located either at the Dealer's place(s) of business or at any other location used or maintained by the Dealer for the storage of collateral and whether in transit, or on lease, rental or demonstration.

3. GRANT OF SECURITY INTEREST

As security for the payment of the indebtedness, the Dealer hereby grants to the Company:

(a) a security interest in any unpaid-for item of collateral and the Company reserves title to any such collateral provided by it; and

(b) a security interest in each paid-for item of collateral, both of the foregoing being collectively referred to in this Security Agreement as the "security interest" and each item of collateral shall remain as security for the Dealer's entire indebtedness until the unpaid balance of such indebtedness is paid in full. The security interest shall extend to (i) the collateral presently in the Dealer's possession, (ii) all collateral subsequently acquired as additions or replacements, (iii) all proceeds (as defined in The Personal Property Security Act) of the sale or lease of such collateral, including proceeds of proceeds, as well as all proceeds now in the Dealer's possession, and (iv) all returned or repossessed collateral.

4. ATTACHMENT

The security interest created and provided for in Section 3 above shall attach upon execution of this Security Agreement in respect to all items of collateral in which the Dealer has rights at that moment, and shall attach to all rights of the Dealer acquired hereafter, immediately upon such acquisition.

5. SALE OF COLLATERAL BY DEALER

The Dealer may sell any item of the collateral to retail purchasers or may lease such items in the ordinary course of business, but (i) shall do so in accordance with the terms of the Dealer agreements and (ii) shall not otherwise use or dispose of any items of the collateral or allow any lien, charge or encumbrance to be created or remain on the collateral without the prior written permission of the Company. The Company's security interest shall continue in any leased item of collateral subject to the rights of the Lessee.

6. USE OF PROCEEDS

The Dealer may use, commingle or dispose of proceeds of collateral, other than trade-ins, in the normal operation of his business or by way of distributions of earnings and profits to the owners of the business, but any such use, commingling or disposition shall not affect the Company's security interest in any such proceeds which at any time remain in the Dealer's possession, or the Company's right to require notes or accounts in the Dealer's possession to be turned over to the Company as provided in Section 13 hereof. The liberty provided for herein to use or dispose of proceeds of collateral does not include the right or power to pledge or encumber such proceeds to secure a debt or other obligation of the Dealer, and any attempted pledge of such proceeds or the creation or continuance of any such encumbrance without the written permission of the Company constitutes a default hereunder.

7. DEFAULT

General

The following shall constitute events of default by the Dealer:

(a) (i) The Dealer's authority to sell Goods pursuant to a John Deere Authorized Consumer Products Dealer Agreement is cancelled; (ii) The Dealer defaults in the payment or performance of any obligation to the Company, in particular his obligations and duties under the Dealer agreements and this Security Agreement; (iii) The Dealer fails, upon request, to turn over proceeds or provide information; (iv) The Dealer, in violation of Section 5 or 6 hereof, sells or disposes of any part of the collateral without first obtaining the written consent of the Company or sells or disposes of proceeds, including trade-ins, or allows any lien or encumbrance to be created or remain on the collateral; (v) The Dealer or any member of the Dealer's firm if a partnership becomes insolvent, has a Receiver or Receiver Manager appointed for any part of Dealer's assets, makes an assignment for the benefit of creditors, institutes or has instituted against him proceedings under any bankruptcy or insolvency law, or the Dealer has his stock in trade or any part thereof levied upon or attached; (vi) The happening of one or more of the events specified in Section 3 of the John Deere Authorized Consumer Products Dealer Agreement in effect between the Dealer and the Company; (vii) The Dealer fails to tender promptly any collateral which he becomes obligated to resell to the Company under the John Deere Authorized Consumer Products Dealer Agreement in effect between the Dealer and the Company; (viii) The falsification of records or reports.

Unsafe Debt or Security

(b) If in the Company's opinion the debt or security is unsafe or insecure.

Security Agreement/3.

8. RIGHTS ON DEFAULT

If default occurs or continues, the Company may:

Acceleration and Suit

(a) Declare immediately due and payable all indebtedness owing by the Dealer to the Company including the indebtedness secured hereby and collect the same together with reasonable expenses including court costs, lawyer's fees and all other legal expenses;

Restrict Shipments

(b) Discontinue or withhold the delivery of collateral to the Dealer, or make further deliveries only on a cash or C.O.D. basis;

Repossess

(c) Take possession of any or all collateral by any method permitted by law;

Acceleration of Installments

(d) Discontinue deferral of any unpaid portion of the purchase price of collateral after the collateral has been removed from the Dealer's place of business, personally used by the Dealer or settled for by a retail customer.

Notice of (a) or (b) shall be given to the Dealer in such manner and at such time as the Company may see fit. No notice of any other action taken or to be taken by the Company hereunder shall be necessary except where required by provincial law, such notice being hereby expressly waived by the Dealer.

9. REPOSSESSION OF COLLATERAL

If the Company elects to take possession of any collateral, it shall have the right, to the full extent allowed by law, to enter any premises occupied by or under the control of the Dealer for that purpose. The Dealer shall, when requested to do so by the Company, gather at his principal place of business any items of collateral which are not already located there and will place any such collateral in transportable condition. If the Dealer is unable to gather the collateral he will disclose the location of the collateral on the Company's request. After taking possession, the Company may at its election take any one of the following actions or a combination of (a) and (b), or of (b) and (c);

Sale

(a) Dispose of all or any part of such collateral at one or more public and/or private sales or by lease or deferred payment in the manner prescribed by law.

Return

(b) Return to the Dealer any part of the collateral when the Company, in its sole discretion, determines:
(i) There is sufficient other collateral available to satisfy the Dealer's indebtedness and costs, or
(ii) Those parts of the collateral are not of sufficient value, because of obsolescence, wear and tear or any other reason which the Company deems sufficient, to justify the trouble and expense of attempting to dispose of them.

Full Satisfaction

(c) Propose to accept all or a part of the collateral and other collateral held by it in full satisfaction of the Dealer's indebtedness as provided by law. The Company shall not be bound by its proposal to so elect unless and until it has sent the notice(s) required by law and the time for interested persons to require disposition has passed.

10. APPLICATION OF PROCEEDS

The proceeds of sale of collateral pursuant to Section 9(a) hereof shall be applied: first, in the satisfaction of all expenses reasonably incurred by the Company, including without limitation the reasonable expenses of retaking, holding, repairing, processing, preparing for disposition and disposing of the collateral and all reasonable court costs, lawyer's fees and other legal expenses; second, to the satisfaction of the Dealer's indebtedness as required by law; and third, to the satisfaction of any subordinate security interest where the notices required by law have been received by the Company before disposition of the proceeds. If after such application there is (i) a surplus, the Company will pay such surplus over as provided by law, and (ii) if there is a deficiency, the Dealer shall be liable for it and shall pay it forthwith provided that provincial law permits the collection of such a deficiency.

11. PROCEDURES FOR DISPOSITION

Without suggesting that other procedures may not also be commercially reasonable, or that any of the following procedures are mandatory in any particular case, it is agreed that the following are all commercially reasonable methods of disposing of collateral repossessed hereunder should the Company decide to follow one or more of them as to all or a part of the collateral:

New Equipment

(a) Sale of complete machines and attachments by units or in one or more parcels by private sale to another dealer or dealers at current dealer price, together with increased value, if any, negotiated with the buying dealer resulting from the fact that freight from the factory has been paid. (This procedure will be reasonable only if the collateral is equivalent to new unused machines of current production.)

Used or Depreciated Goods

(b) Sale of collateral (including parts) by units or in one or more parcels at private sale at the best price submitted in sealed bids taken from three or more dealers, provided that in the Company's judgement such best bid represents a reasonable price. (This procedure is in conformity with reasonable industry practices in disposing of complete inventories of goods, or of items coming into the possession of manufacturers or distributors which are not saleable as new unused machines of current production.)

Parts

(c) Sale of current parts and attachments in good condition for which there is a ready market to dealers through the Company's regular parts distribution facilities at regular prices and terms. The Company may commingle such parts with its regular inventory of parts and account for the sale of the parts repossessed hereunder on the assumption that the first parts sold after such commingling are those repossessed. The Company's expenses of reinventorying and merchandising returned and repossessed parts (exclusive of costs incurred in listing, tagging, packing, and loading them at the Dealer's place of business and of transportation expenses from the Dealer's place of business to the Company's parts distribution facility) are considerably in excess of 15% of their invoice price, and it is agreed that a 15% charge for such services may be made without further itemization or analysis of such expenses.

Public Sale

(d) Public sale at auction of all collateral or any portion thereof not disposed of by some other method. Either the publication once of the time and place of such sale and of the property to be sold at least five days prior thereto in a newspaper circulating in the geographical area where the sale is to be held, or the posting of such notice in at least three public places in such geographical area at least five days prior to the sale, constitutes sufficient notice thereof.

12. PROTECTION OF GOODS

Storage

The Dealer shall:

(a) Unless a different storage location is approved by the Company in writing, properly store all collateral in his possession at his regular place of business and protect the same from injury or damage of any kind.

Insurance

(b) Where insurance is not provided by the Company pursuant to the Dealer agreements, continuously keep all collateral insured with all risk type coverage satisfactory to the Company and with insurers satisfactory to the Company, in an amount equal to one hundred per cent (100%) of the invoice price thereof. Such insurance may be issued in the name of the Dealer who may retain possession of the policies, but each policy shall contain, (i) a clause naming the Company as an additional insured, (ii) a clause stipulating that loss is to be payable to the Company and the Dealer as their interests may appear, (iii) a cross liability clause containing the insurance coverage for the benefit of the Company not-withstanding any default or breach of condition by the Dealer, and (iv) a clause providing for at least ten (10) days prior written notice to the Company of any cancellation or termination of the policy or any part of the coverage thereof, all in form reasonably satisfactory to the Company. The Dealer shall immediately furnish the Company with the name of the insurer and the number, amount, effective date and expiration date of each policy issued; and upon request of the Company shall furnish it with copies of each such policy or certificate of insurance issued by the insurer.

(c) Where insurance is provided by the Company, the Dealer hereby assigns the

Security Agreement/5.

proceeds of such insurance to the Company to the extent of any loss or damage done to unpaid-for collateral.

Taxes

(d) Pay when due all taxes, license fees and charges of any kind whatsoever that may be assessed or charged on or against any of the collateral, or the sale or use thereof, at any time on or after the date of delivery of the collateral to the Dealer.

Liens and Encumbrances

(e) Keep all collateral free and clear of all liens and encumbrances however arising, except with the written permission of the Company.

Payment by Company

If the Dealer fails to insure or to pay said taxes and charges or allows any lien or encumbrance to attach to the collateral, the Company, without obligation to do so, may obtain such insurance, pay such taxes, and charges, or discharge such lien, and the Dealer shall reimburse the Company promptly for all money so paid out together with interest at 14% per annum, or the highest contract rate permitted by law if less than 14%. The amounts so paid by the Company shall be deemed conclusive as to the amounts properly payable, and such amounts shall be secured hereunder as part of the indebtedness.

13. DELIVERY OF PROCEEDS

The Dealer will at any time upon request deliver to the Company all proceeds of collateral which are in his possession in the form of customers' notes, together with appropriate endorsement thereof to the Company, and will provide the Company with information concerning proceeds in the form of customers' accounts sufficient to enable the Company to collect such accounts directly, and the Company may collect such accounts.

14. CASH PROCEEDS

In the event of insolvency proceedings instituted by or against the Dealer, the Company's security interest hereunder in proceeds shall, in addition to identifiable non-cash proceeds and identifiable cash proceeds in the form of money or cheques not deposited in a bank account, include all cash and bank accounts of the Dealer up to an amount not greater than the amount of cash proceeds received by the Dealer within ten days before the institution of the insolvency proceedings, and commingled or deposited in a bank account prior to the insolvency proceedings, less the amount of cash proceeds received by the Dealer and paid over to the Company during the ten-day period.

15. COLLECTION OF NOTES AND ACCOUNTS

The provisions of this Section 15 and all references in this Agreement to "notes and accounts" shall apply to any proceeds in the form of notes of which the Company has taken possession and accounts which the Company desires to collect directly, but not including notes or other evidences of indebtedness accepted by the Company for credit under any finance plan in effect between the parties.

At any time and regardless of whether the Dealer is in default, the Company is authorized to reduce open accounts to notes, renew or extend the time of payment of any note or account or any securities securing the same, any such renewal to be in its own or the Dealer's name as the Company may elect, take, waive, release or exchange any security therefor, make such compromise settlements thereof as it deems advisable, and take such steps for the enforcement, collection, securing, renewing, extending, or compromising of any note or account or any part thereof, or any security therefor, as it deems advisable. Any proceeds realized from the collection or enforcement of said notes and accounts or any security therefor shall be applied on the indebtedness of the Dealer. The Company may return said notes and accounts to the Dealer at any time. After any default by the Dealer the Company may sell the whole or any part of said notes and accounts at one or more public or private sales, applying the proceeds in the manner prescribed by Section 10.

16. ACTS NOT A WAIVER

The acceptance of a note or notes and renewals thereof for the whole or any part of the Dealer's indebtedness, or the institution of legal action or the recovery of a judgement for the whole or a part of such indebtedness or on any note given therefor, shall not be deemed a waiver of any part of the security interest granted hereby.

17. INVALIDITY OF PROVISION

The invalidity or unenforceability of any one or more of the provisions of this Agreement shall in no way affect the validity or enforceability of any of the other provisions hereof, and any provision hereof which is prohibited under the laws of any province shall be ineffective in such province to the extent of such prohibition only and shall not invalidate or in any wise affect the other provisions hereof.

18. RIGHTS CUMULATIVE

The rights of the Company hereunder are in addition to those available to it under any applicable legislation and are cumulative and not alternative; the exercise of any one right is not an election or waiver of the power to exercise any other right. Waiver of any default hereunder is not a waiver of any prior or subsequent default.

19. METHOD OF GIVING NOTICE

Without limitations on any other method of giving notice, any notice required hereunder shall be deemed sufficient and complete by mailing the same by prepaid registered or certified post addressed to the other party at the address specified in this Agreement or such other address as may be designated in writing and shall be deemed to have been received on the third day after such mailing.

20. AMENDMENT OF AGREEMENT

This Agreement may not be altered or amended, or have any of its specific provisions waived, unless such alteration, amendment or waiver is in writing and is executed by the Dealer and an officer of the Company.

21. EFFECT OF TERMINATION

Any termination of this Agreement shall in no way affect the security interest(s), rights and remedies of the Company or the Dealer, or the indebtedness which existed prior to the effective date of the termination.

22. SUCCESSORS

This Agreement shall enure to the benefit of the heirs, executors, administrators, successors and assigns of the Company and the Dealer.

23. ASSIGNMENT

The Agreement may be assigned by the Company at any time and may be further assigned by any such assignee, without in either case the consent of the Dealer. Dealer agrees not to assert against any assignee as a defence, counter claim, set-off or otherwise any claim which Dealer has now or hereinafter acquires against the Company.

24. APPLICABLE LAW

Unless the context of this Agreement otherwise requires, all references to the "Company" may be treated as references to the "Secured Party", and all references to the "Dealer" may be treated as references to the "Debtor". This Agreement shall be governed by the law of the province in which the Dealer resides.

25. CONTINUOUS APPLICATION OF AGREEMENT

Dealer agrees that this Agreement shall become effective immediately on its execution by the Dealer and shall continue in effect until (i) replaced by a new Security Agreement, or (ii) terminated by the Dealer and the Company, notwithstanding that a new John Deere Authorized Consumer Products Dealer Agreement may be entered into from time to time.

26. DEALER AGREEMENT(S)

Dealer has been appointed, or concurrently with the execution of this Security Agreement is being appointed as an authorized John Deere dealer under the terms of a John Deere Authorized Consumer Products Dealer Agreement between the Dealer and the Company covering the sale of Goods by the Dealer and pursuant to which the Dealer has been (or will be) granted the benefit of the Company's Finance Plans, Floor Plans, and/or other deferred payment terms as provided for in the Dealer agreements as amended and replaced from time to time.

Security Agreement/7.

Dealer's Place of Business_____

_____

_____
Dealer (Firm Name)

____Corporation
____Partnership   By _____
____Proprietorship

Title _____

Date _____

Signatures   _____
of other
Partner(s)   _____

_____

JOHN DEERE LIMITED

By _____

Title _____

Date _____

Form 7

To be completed for registration in Alberta

Initials of ASSIGNOR(S)	Social Insurance Number

GENERAL ASSIGNMENT OF ACCOUNTS, ETC.

. . . .
(Branch Designation)

FOR VALUABLE CONSIDERATION the undersigned (1)

(1) Insert full name of assignor

. . . .
(Name)

of . . . .
(Street number and name, apt. no. OR lot, concession and Township)   (City, Town or Village and rural route)   (Prov./Territory)

hereby assign(s) and transfer(s) all debts, accounts, claims, moneys and choses in action which now are or which may at any time hereafter be due or owing to or owned by the undersigned, and also all securities, bills, notes and other documents now held or owned or which may be hereafter taken, held or owned by the undersigned or anyone on behalf of the undersigned in respect of the said debts, accounts, claims, moneys and choses in action or any part thereof, and also all books and papers recording, evidencing or relating to said debts, accounts, claims, moneys and choses in action or any part thereof (all of the foregoing being herein called the "assigned premises") to CANADIAN IMPERIAL BANK OF COMMERCE (herein called the "Bank") as a general and continuing collateral security for payment of all existing and future indebtedness and liability of the undersigned to the Bank wheresoever and howsoever incurred and any ultimate unpaid balance thereof, and as a first and prior claim upon the assigned premises.

2. The Bank may collect, realize, sell or otherwise deal with the assigned premises or any part thereof in such manner, upon such terms and conditions and at such time or times as may seem to it advisable and without notice to the undersigned (except as otherwise required by any applicable law), and may charge on its own behalf and pay to others reasonable sums for expenses incurred and for services rendered (expressly including legal advices and services) in or in connection with collecting, realizing, selling or obtaining payment of the assigned premises and may add the amount of such sums to the indebtedness of the undersigned.

3. The Bank shall not be liable or accountable for any failure to collect, realize, sell or obtain payment of the assigned premises or any part thereof and shall not be bound to institute proceedings for the purpose of collecting, realizing or obtaining payment of the same or for the purpose of preserving any rights of the Bank, the undersigned or any other person, firm or corporation in respect of the same.

4. The Bank may grant extensions of time and other indulgences, take and give up securities, accept compositions, grant releases and discharges and otherwise deal with the undersigned, debtors of the undersigned, sureties and others and with the assigned premises and other securities as the Bank may see fit without prejudice to the liability of the undersigned or the Bank's right to hold and realize this security.

5. All moneys collected or received by the undersigned in respect of the assigned premises shall be received as trustee for the Bank and shall be forthwith paid over to the Bank.

6. All moneys collected or received by the Bank in respect of the assigned premises (whether by virtue of paragraph 5 hereof or otherwise howsoever) may be applied on account of such parts of the indebtedness and liability of the undersigned as to the Bank seems best or in the discretion of the Bank may be released to the undersigned, all without prejudice to the Bank's claims upon the undersigned.

7. The undersigned shall from time to time forthwith on request furnish to the Bank in writing all information requested relating to the assigned premises and the Bank shall be entitled from time to time to inspect the aforesaid securities, bills, notes, books, papers and other documents or take temporary custody thereof and for such purposes the Bank shall have access to all premises occupied by the undersigned.

8. The undersigned shall from time to time forthwith on the Bank's request do, make and execute all such financing statements, further assignments, documents, acts, matters and things as may be required by the Bank or with respect to the assigned premises or any part thereof or as may be required to give effect to these presents, and the undersigned hereby constitutes and appoints the Manager or acting Manager for the time being of the above mentioned branch of the Bank the true and lawful attorney of the undersigned irrevocable with full power of substitution to do, make and execute all such statements, assignments, documents, acts, matters or things with the right to use the name of the undersigned whenever and wherever it may be deemed necessary or expedient.

9. The provisions hereof shall enure to the benefit of the successors and assigns of the Bank and shall be binding upon the respective heirs, executors, administrators, successors and assigns of the undersigned.

WITNESS the hand and seal of the undersigned this . . . . day of . . . . 19 . . .

Witness:

⟨ SEAL ⟩

(To be completed for registration in Ontario)

If an individual(s), first given name, initial of second given name, if any, then surname.

FULL NAME AND ADDRESS OF ASSIGNOR(S)	If given by individual(s) record		
	Initials of ASSIGNOR(S)	Date of Birth Day, Month, Year	Sex M/F

Form 8

Form 1076-79

PLEDGE AGREEMENT

Description of Debenture

Principal Amount: _____

Date: _____

(delete inapplicable clause) Interest Rate:
(a) Nominal annual rate of _____%
(b) A variable nominal annual rate _____ percentage points above the Minimum Lending Rate of Canadian Imperial Bank of Commerce from time to time.

The undersigned hereby assigns, deposits with and pledges to CANADIAN IMPERIAL BANK OF COMMERCE (the "Bank") the debenture created by the undersigned and described above (the "Debenture") to be held by the Bank as a general and continuing collateral security for the payment of all present and future indebtedness and liability of the undersigned to the Bank however incurred and any ultimate unpaid balance thereof (the "Indebtedness").

In the event of any default in payment of any part of the Indebtedness or in the performance of any other obligation of the undersigned to the Bank, the Bank may at any time during the continuance of any such default realize upon the Debenture by sale, transfer or delivery, or exercise and enforce all rights and remedies of a holder of the Debenture as if the Bank were absolute owner thereof, without notice to or control by the undersigned, and any such remedy may be exercised separately or in combination and shall be in addition to and not in substitution for any other rights of the Bank however created; provided that the Bank shall not be bound to exercise any such right or remedy.

The proceeds of the Debenture may be applied by the Bank on account of such part of the Indebtedness as it chooses without prejudice to the Bank's claim upon the undersigned for any deficiency.

The Bank may grant extensions of time or other indulgences, take and give up securities, accept compositions, grant releases and discharges and otherwise deal with the undersigned and with other parties, sureties or securities as the Bank may see fit without prejudice to the liability of the undersigned or the Bank's rights in respect of the Debenture.

Payment to the Bank of interest for any period in respect of the Indebtedness shall be deemed payment in satisfaction of the interest payment for the same period under the Debenture.

The Debenture shall not operate by way of merger of any of the Indebtedness and no judgment recovered by the Bank shall operate by way of merger of or in any way affect the security of the Debenture which is in addition to and not in substitution for any other security now or hereafter held by the Bank.

The provisions hereof shall be binding upon and shall enure to the benefit of the undersigned and the Bank and their respective successors and assigns.

In witness whereof the undersigned has duly executed this instrument the day of _____ , 19 _____ .

_____
(Company name)

VOID
_____
(Signature and title)

c/s

_____
(Signature and title)

Form 9

CONDITIONAL SALE AGREEMENT

CANADIAN IMPERIAL
BANK OF COMMERCE

ORIGINAL

ORIGINAL SIGNATURE REQUIRED ON
FIRST FOUR COPIES

DATE _____ 19 ____

	DATE OF BIRTH			SEX
	DAY	MONTH	YEAR	M/F

FULL NAME OF BUYER

ADDRESS: Street number and name, apt. no. if any, OR lot, concession and township | City, Town or Village (and rural route if any) | Prov./Terr.

	DATE OF BIRTH			SEX
	DAY	MONTH	YEAR	M/F

FULL NAME OF CO-BUYER(S)

ADDRESS: Street number and name, apt. no. if any, OR lot, concession and township | City, Town or Village (and rural route if any) | Prov./Terr.

FULL NAME OF SELLER

ADDRESS: Street number and name, apt. no. if any, OR lot, concession and township | City, Town or Village (and rural route if any) | Prov./Terr.

NAME OF BUYER (IF MORE THAN ONE) DESIGNATED FOR INSURANCE UNDER PARAGRAPH NINE (9) OF THE TERMS AND CONDITIONS HEREOF

Insert full name of Buyer(s); if not an individual, full business or corporate name

Buyer hereby purchases from Seller, on the terms and conditions herein set forth, the property described below complete with all attachments and accessories (herein called the "property"), delivery and acceptance of which in good condition and as ordered is hereby acknowledged by Buyer.

MANUFACTURER AND DESCRIPTION OF PROPERTY (INCLUDING MAKE & BODY STYLE)	NEW OR USED AND YEAR	MODEL NO.	SERIAL NO.	NO. CYL.	MOTOR NO. (IF MOTOR VEHICLE)	LICENCE NO. (IF MOTOR VEHICLE)	PRICE

CHECK ACCESSORIES AND INSERT COST	RADIO	AUTO-TRANS.	POWER STEERING	POWER BRAKES	POWER SEATS	POWER WINDOWS	AIR CONDIT.	OTHER (ITEMIZE)	
$	$	$	$	$	$	$	$		$ $ $

Itemize all services for which separate charge is made, e.g. delivery, installation and inspection

1. BASIC CASH PRICE	(a) PROPERTY		$	
	(b) SERVICES		$	
			$	
		TOTAL	$	$
2. PLUS PROVINCIAL SALES TAX				$
3. RETAIL CASH PRICE (1 + 2)				$
4. OFFICIAL FILING OR REGISTRATION FEES PAYABLE BY SELLER AT BUYER'S REQUEST				$
5. INSURANCE PREMIUM PAYABLE BY SELLER AT BUYER'S REQUEST INSURING FOR ACCIDENTAL PHYSICAL DAMAGE TO THE PROPERTY. (CHECK INSURANCE COVERAGE INCLUDED) COVERAGE APPLICABLE TO PROPERTY Term _____ months. Effective date _____ 19 ____				$

$ _____ Deductible Collision □ Comprehensive □ Fire and Theft

NO BODILY INJURY OR PROPERTY DAMAGE LIABILITY INSURANCE INCLUDED

6. TOTAL CASH PRICE (3 + 4 + 5)		$
7. A. GROSS TRADE-IN ALLOWANCE	$	
B. AMOUNT PAYABLE TO ____ BY SELLER AT BUYER'S REQUEST FOR ____		
	$	
C. NET CREDIT FOR TRADE-IN (A-B)	$	
D. CASH DOWN PAYMENT	$	
E. TOTAL DOWN PAYMENT (C + D)	$	$
8. BALANCE OF TOTAL CASH PRICE (6-7E)		$
9. COST OF BORROWING-ANNUAL PERCENTAGE RATE OF ____ % OF BALANCE OF TOTAL CASH PRICE		$
10. TOTAL AMOUNT PAYABLE (HEREIN CALLED THE "UNPAID BALANCE") (8 + 9)		$
11. OFFICIAL FEES PLUS INSURANCE PREMIUMS (4 + 5)		$
12. RETAIL CASH PRICE LESS TOTAL DOWN PAYMENT (3-7E)		$
13. COST OF BORROWING PLUS TOTAL CASH PRICE (9 + 6)		$

Insert particulars of obligation paid.

COMPLETE IN P.E.I. & N.S. ONLY
COMPLETE IN ALTA., N.B.C., P.E.I. & NFLD. ONLY
COMPLETE IN MAN. ONLY

The Unpaid Balance shall be paid by Buyer to Canadian Imperial Bank of Commerce,*
as follows: $ _____ on the ____ day of _____ , 19 ____ and _____ equal consecutive payments of
$ _____ each on the ____ day of each month commencing on the ____ day of _____ , 19 ____ .
and ending on the ____ day of _____ , 19 ____ , totalling $ _____ ; with interest after maturity
on each instalment at the rate of ____ % per annum and upon default in any such payment, all remaining instalments shall forthwith become due and payable without notice.
PAYMENT OF THE UNPAID BALANCE MAY ALSO BE ACCELERATED UNDER THE TERMS AND CONDITIONS ON THE REVERSE HEREOF WHICH CONSTITUTE PART OF THIS AGREEMENT.
BUYER ACKNOWLEDGES RECEIPT OF A COMPLETE EXECUTED COPY OF THIS AGREEMENT.

DATED this ____ day of _____ , 19 ____ .

WITNESS: _____

_____
SIGNATURE OF BUYER

_____
SIGNATURE OF CO-BUYER (IF ANY)

Seller hereby agrees to the foregoing and assigns the within contract to Canadian Imperial Bank of Commerce upon the terms and conditions of the Assignment and Transfer set forth on the reverse hereof and Buyer acknowledges and accepts such Assignment and Transfer and undertakes to make payment to the Bank at _____ * .

DATED the ____ day of _____ , 19 ____ .

VOID

VOID

Signature of Buyer

Signature of Seller

By _____

Signature of Co-Buyer if any

* FILL IN COMPLETE ADDRESS

TERMS AND CONDITIONS

The following terms and conditions form part of the Agreement set forth on the face hereof:

1. The title to and ownership of the property shall not pass to Buyer on delivery thereof but shall remain in Seller at Buyer's risk until the Unpaid Balance together with interest and all other amounts payable by Buyer hereunder is paid in full.

2. Destruction of or damage to the property shall not release Buyer from liability hereunder and Buyer will keep the property insured in favour of Seller against such risks as Seller may require for an amount sufficient to secure the interest of Seller therein. If Buyer fails to keep the property insured, Seller may so insure (but shall be under no obligation to do so) and charge the amount of the premium to Buyer who shall pay the same forthwith.

3. Buyer shall keep the property free of all liens, charges and encumbrances and if any such lien, charge or encumbrance is created, Seller may pay off the same and any amount so paid with all costs and expenses shall be paid forthwith by Buyer.

4. No notice, demand or mise-en-demure shall be required to put Buyer in default under this agreement and if Seller shall grant or tolerate any extension or delay for the payment or performance of any obligations of Buyer, no such extension, delay or tolerance shall be deemed an acquiescence by Seller in such default, or a waiver of any of Seller's rights or recourse under this agreement.

5. Buyer shall keep the property in good repair.

6. If Buyer makes default in payment or fails to perform any obligation hereunder of if Seller deems itself insecure (of which Seller shall be sole judge) or if Seller has reasonable cause to believe that its security is in jeopardy or if any proceeding in bankruptcy, receivership or winding up be taken by or against Buyer or if Buyer fails to insure the property and Seller does not place such insurance forthwith or if the Buyer parts with possession of the property or removes the same for more than 20 days from the county or district within which Buyer resides at the time the property is delivered to Buyer hereunder or uses the property for hire without the written consent of Seller, the amount of the Unpaid Balance and all other amounts then outstanding hereunder shall immediately become due and payable and Seller may enter upon any premises where the property may be and repossess and remove the same without legal process; provided that if the rights of the parties hereunder with respect to the property are subject to the laws of the Province of Manitoba, Buyer may so remove the property within the Province of Manitoba or may charge his interest in the property if Buyer shall have given to Seller by delivery or registered mail at the address specified on the reverse hereof at least ten (10) days' prior written notice of his intention to do so, specifying the place within Manitoba to which the property is to be removed and the person in whose favour any such charge is to be created.

7. In the event that the property is repossessed under paragraph 6 hereof and is not thereafter redeemed in the manner and within the period prescribed by law, or within 30 days, whichever is greater, all or part of the property may from time to time be sold at public or private sale at the option of Seller, and after deducting the costs and expenses of sale, of taking and keeping possession and of repair and legal fees, the net proceeds of sale shall be applied on the amount then owing by Buyer and any surplus shall be paid to Buyer and any deficiency shall be forthwith paid by Buyer.

8. This agreement and all rights of Seller including the right to repossess the property may be assigned and transferred to Canadian Imperial Bank of Commerce (herein called the "Bank") and such assignment (and any further assignments) shall not be subject to any equities as between Buyer and Seller unless otherwise required by law.

9. Buyer consents to life insurance being arranged under a Group Life Insurance Policy with The Canada Life Assurance Company, such insurance to be owned and paid for by and payable to the Bank, be effective as of the date of assignment of this contract to the Bank, and be subject to such terms and conditions as may be agreed upon between the Bank and said insurer, but the amount of insurance shall not exceed the amount of the Unpaid Balance. The name of Buyer (if more than one) whose life is to be insured is specifically designated on the face hereof. Such insurance shall terminate upon such terms and conditions as may be agreed upon between the Bank and said insurer. If the insurance becomes payable prior to such termination, the Unpaid Balance and all other amounts then outstanding hereunder shall be repaid to the extent possible from the insurance proceeds. Failure of the Bank to obtain or keep in force any or sufficient insurance for any reason shall not limit or lessen the liability of Buyer hereunder.

10. If the rights of the parties hereunder with respect to the property are subject to the laws of the Province of Saskatchewan, Buyer (if a body corporate) agrees that The Limitation of Civil Rights Act of Saskatchewan shall not apply to this contract or to any security for the payment of money made or created by or pursuant thereto or any agreement or instrument renewing or extending or collateral to this contract and any of the benefits of the said Act are hereby specifically waived.

11. Buyer expressly waives the benefit of every statute or law which prevents or restricts Seller from recovering a deficiency from Buyer after resale by Seller following repossession of the property, and without limiting the generality of the foregoing, if the rights of the parties hereunder with respect to the property are subject to the laws of the Province of Alberta, Buyer expressly waives the benefit of Section 19 of The Conditional Sales Act of Alberta.

12. Any term or condition or part thereof of this agreement which is prohibited or unenforceable by the law of any province shall, as to that province, be ineffective to the extent of such prohibition or unenforceability without invalidating the remaining terms and conditions of this agreement.

13. There are no representations, conditions, warranties, guarantees or collateral agreements, express or implied, statutory or otherwise, in respect of the property or this agreement, other than as set out herein, and without limiting the generality of the foregoing, if the rights of the parties hereunder with respect to the property are subject to the laws of the Province of Ontario, the implied conditions, warranties and guarantees contained in Section 13, 14, 15 and 16 of The Sale of Goods Act of Ontario are expressly excluded from this agreement.

14. This agreement shall enure to the benefit of and shall bind the respective heirs, executors, administrators, successors and assigns of Buyer and Seller.

15. In the event that this agreement is signed by more than one buyer then "Buyer" wherever it appears in this agreement shall be read and construed as "Buyers" with all grammatical changes thereby rendered necessary, and the liability of such persons under this agreement shall be joint and several.

ASSIGNMENT AND TRANSFER

FOR VALUE RECEIVED Seller hereby assigns and transfers to Canadian Imperial Bank of Commerce,

•

(herein called the "Bank") the within contract, all rights, claims and moneys payable thereunder, all right, title and interest in and to the property therein described and the benefits of insurance upon the same and warrants that the contract is genuine and is not subject to rescission and that the property has been delivered to and accepted by Buyer, in default of which the agreement set out below in the paragraph entitled With Recourse shall apply.

Seller's liability hereunder shall not be affected by any extension, indulgence, compromise, security, variation of the contract or release of Buyer or other interested person whether by operation of law or otherwise. This assignment is supplemented by the agreement set out below in the paragraph initialled by Seller and these provisions shall apply to and bind the heirs, executors, administrators, successors and assigns of Seller and shall enure to the benefit of and be enforceable by the Bank, its successors and assigns.

Initial applicable paragraph:

☐ WITHOUT RECOURSE: Save as to the warranties set forth above, this assignment is without recourse to the Seller.

☐ WITH RECOURSE: Seller unconditionally agrees to repurchase the within contract forthwith upon demand, for the Unpaid Balance and all other amounts outstanding under the contract at the date of demand whether or not the contract shall then be in default.

☐ REPURCHASE: If within 90 days after any default which is not cured the property described in the within contract is repossessed by the Bank and delivered to Seller, Seller shall forthwith pay to the Bank the Unpaid Balance and all other amounts then outstanding under the contract regardless of the condition of the property, and Seller also agrees to repurchase the property for such amount after expiration of the said 90 day period provided the Bank institutes legal action to repossess the property within such period and the property is delivered to Seller within 30 days after the Bank has obtained legally indisputable possession thereof.

☐ LIMITED REPURCHASE: The above paragraph entitled Repurchase shall apply provided that the obligation of Seller thereunder shall terminate upon payment by Buyer to the Bank of the first _____ monthly instalments within 15 days of their respective due dates.

☐ OPTIONAL PURCHASE: If the Bank repossesses the property described in the within contract Seller shall have the option after demand by the Bank either to pay the Bank $ _____ or to buy the property in its then condition and location from the Bank for the Unpaid Balance and all other amounts then outstanding under the contract.

*fill in complete address

INDEX